T'es branché? 3

Second Edition

Annotated Teacher's Edition

Author

Jacqueline King Donnelly

Contributing Writers

Sébastien DeClerk
Henry Menninger

EMC Publishing®

ST. PAUL, MINNESOTA

Publisher: Alex Vargas
Senior Editor: Nathalie Gaillot
Senior Associate Editor: Nicki Stevenson
Assistant Editor: May Vang
World Language Production Editor: Emily Tope
Cover and Text Designer: Leslie Anderson
Production Specialists: Tammy Norstrem, Ryan Hamner
Reviewer: Emily Wentworth

ISBN 978-1-53383-190-3

875 Montreal Way
St. Paul, MN 55102
Email: educate@emcp.com
Website: www.emcp.com

Printed in the United States of America

27 26 25 24 23 22 21 20 19 18 1 2 3 4 5 6 7 8 9 10

Meet the Textbook Authors

Toni Theisen is a National Board Certified Teacher of French at Loveland High School in Loveland, Colorado, and the Thompson School District World Language Curriculum Representative. She holds an M.A. in Foreign Language Teaching and an M.A. in Education of Diverse Learners. She is also a Google Certified Teacher. She has received Teacher of the Year and Excellence in Teaching Awards and has worked closely with ACTFL, including as president.

A passionate and active world language advocate, Theisen has presented numerous workshops, keynotes, and webinars for national, regional, and state conferences and institutes. Also an author, she has written several middle and high school French language series and many articles on multiple intelligences, differentiated instruction, and technology for the 21st-century learner. Theisen presented "Activating Communication" as part of the first ACTFL Webinar Series and also presented at the 2011 LARC (National Language Acquisition Resource Center) STARTALK Institute at San Diego State University.

Theisen led the effort in 2009 to revise the Colorado World Languages Academic Standards and co-chaired the revision committee of the National Board for Professional Teacher Standards for WLOE (World Languages Other than English) in 2009. Most recently she chaired the ACTFL 21st-Century Skills Map committee in collaboration with the Partnership for 21st-Century Learning.

Thiesen's many additional honors include the ACTFL Nelson Brooks Award for the Teaching of Culture, the Colorado Governor's Award for Excellence in Teaching, the SWCOLT Excellence in Teaching Award, and the Genevieve Overman Memorial Service Award from the Colorado Congress of Foreign Language Teachers.

Jacques Pécheur is a French author at CLE International in Paris. He is best known as the chief editor of the French review ***Le français dans le monde***. He has worked as director of the Cultural Center of Palermo and Sicily, and as cultural ambassador to the French embassy in Switzerland. As head of the Mission to the General Delegation for the Languages of France (DGLF), Pécheur has conducted numerous missions to promote multilingualism, the French language, and **la Francophonie** in the world. He also worked for the French Ministry of Foreign Affairs, the European Council, the European Union, and the Intergovernmental Agency of **la Francophonie** (AIF), where he was entrusted with conducting and managing conferences and training workshops in more than 50 countries.

Pécheur's numerous involvements in political, cultural, and language-related occupations have led him to gain expertise in language policies and the language marketplace. As someone who has developed many strategies to promote the learning of French, Pécheur has been a spokesman in numerous conferences related to language learning and has published many articles. His 20 years of experience in ***Le francais dans le monde***, as well as his many publications on French civilization, cinema, and contemporary literature, have shaped his proactive approach to the editorial world.

Honorary member of the AATF, Pécheur is recognized in the United States by the Cultural Services of the French Embassy in the United States (SCAC), the Alliance Française, and many American universities.

Contents

Scope and Sequence

Level 1, Units 1–10

	Unité 1	Unité 2	Unité 3	Unité 4	Unité 5
Essential Question	In what ways is learning another language beneficial?	What do activities and pastimes reveal about a culture?	How does education shape individuals and societies?	What activities do friends in other countries do together?	What is the nature of relationships in other cultures?
Vocabulary: ***Vocabulaire actif***	**Leçon A** ▪ greetings ▪ nationalities **Leçon B** ▪ respond to **Ça va?** ▪ say good-bye **Leçon C** ▪ locations ▪ introducing your parents	**Leçon A** ▪ pastimes ▪ Olympic sports ▪ weather ▪ food **Leçon B** ▪ likes and dislikes ▪ indoor activities **Leçon C** ▪ sports ▪ pastimes ▪ music ▪ numbers 0–20	**Leçon A** ▪ classroom objects ▪ numbers 20–100 **Leçon B** ▪ classroom subjects ▪ adjectives ▪ time expressions **Leçon C** ▪ places in school ▪ places in the city	**Leçon A** ▪ soccer ▪ soccer clothes ▪ the **métro** **Leçon B** ▪ food and drink ▪ numbers 100–1,000 **Leçon C** ▪ movie genres ▪ early, on time, and late ▪ actors and filmmakers	**Leçon A** ▪ family members ▪ physical descriptions ▪ numbers 1,000–1,000,000 **Leçon B** ▪ months of the year ▪ birthdays ▪ descriptions of character **Leçon C** ▪ French-speaking African countries and nationalities ▪ professions
Functions: ***Pour la conversation***	**Leçon A** ▪ introduce oneself ▪ introduce someone else ▪ respond to an introduction ▪ ask someone's name **Leçon B** ▪ ask how someone is ▪ say how I am doing **Leçon C** ▪ extend an invitation ▪ accept an invitation ▪ refuse an invitation	**Leçon A** ▪ ask what someone likes to do ▪ say what I like to do ▪ say what I don't like to do **Leçon B** ▪ ask how much someone likes to do something ▪ say how much I enjoy doing things **Leçon C** ▪ state my preferences ▪ ask what someone prefers ▪ agree and disagree ▪ ask for someone's phone number	**Leçon A** ▪ say what I need ▪ ask what someone else needs ▪ ask what something costs ▪ state what something costs **Leçon B** ▪ describe a class ▪ ask for a description of someone ▪ describe someone **Leçon C** ▪ ask where someone is going ▪ ask when someone is going somewhere ▪ ask why someone cannot do something ▪ establish a place and time to meet	**Leçon A** ▪ give a reason ▪ set a time and place to meet ▪ suggest a different time **Leçon B** ▪ understand what the server will ask ▪ order food ▪ ask for the bill **Leçon C** ▪ make a prediction ▪ respond to a prediction	**Leçon A** ▪ ask for a description ▪ point out resemblances **Leçon B** ▪ ask someone's age ▪ tell my age ▪ tell what gift I am giving ▪ plan a party with others **Leçon C** ▪ find out someone's profession ▪ ask where someone comes from ▪ tell where I come from
Culture: ***Points de départ***	**Leçon A** ▪ greetings ▪ popular first names ▪ **La Francophonie:** Immigrants in France; Francophones in North America **Leçon B** ▪ back to school ▪ ways to say good-bye ▪ **La Francophonie:** Europe; North Africa **Leçon C** ▪ French teens ▪ **La Francophonie:** Sub-Saharan Africa; Caribbean and South America	**Leçon A** ▪ eSports ▪ Olympics ▪ Paris ▪ **La Francophonie: Tour de France**; hockey in Canada **Leçon B** ▪ Lyon ▪ **La Francophonie:** mancala in Africa **Leçon C** ▪ count on fingers ▪ Amadou and Mariam ▪ Singer Corneille ▪ **Fête de la musique** ▪ **La Francophonie:** kora in Africa	**Leçon A** ▪ **Carrefour** ▪ school supplies ▪ the euro and the eurozone ▪ online formation **Leçon B** ▪ 24-hour clock ▪ classes and exams, the **lycée**, the **bac** ▪ **La Francophonie:** French Polynesia; naming schools **Leçon C** ▪ **la cantine** and school meals ▪ **lycées hôteliers** ▪ **Fête de la musique** ▪ English words of French origin ▪ **La Francophonie:** education in Mali	**Leçon A** ▪ soccer in France ▪ soccer clubs ▪ famous soccer players **Leçon B** ▪ cafés and **bistrots** ▪ Paris cafés and art ▪ new fast food chains in France **Leçon C** ▪ French cinema ▪ French comedies ▪ ***Qu'est-ce qu'on a fait au Bon Dieu?*** comedy	**Leçon A** ▪ the metric system ▪ **la Francophonie:** Martinique **Leçon B** ▪ birthdays and saints' days ▪ **La FNAC** ▪ **La Francophonie:** birthday celebrations in francophone Africa and the Middle East **Leçon C** ▪ **La Francophonie:** Sub-Saharan francophone Africa; African women writers
Structure: ***Structure de la langue***		**Leçon A** ▪ subject pronouns ▪ **tu** versus **vous** ▪ infinitives ▪ present tense of regular **-er** verbs **Leçon B** ▪ position of adverbs **Leçon C** ▪ gender of nouns and definite articles ▪ the verb **préférer** ▪ negation with **ne... pas**	**Leçon A** ▪ indefinite articles ▪ plurals of articles and nouns ▪ present tense of the irregular verb **avoir** ▪ **avoir besoin de** **Leçon B** ▪ telling time ▪ present tense of the irregular verb **être** ▪ agreement and position of regular adjectives **Leçon C** ▪ present tense of the irregular verb **aller** ▪ **à** + DEFINITE ARTICLES ▪ forming questions with **est-ce que**	**Leçon A** ▪ **aller** + INFINITIVE ▪ forming questions **Leçon B** ▪ present tense of the irregular verb **prendre** ▪ **avoir** expressions: **avoir faim/soif** **Leçon C** ▪ the interrogative adjective **quel** ▪ present tense of the irregular verb **voir**	**Leçon A** ▪ possessive adjectives ▪ indefinite articles in negative sentences **Leçon B** ▪ present tense of regular **-ir** verbs ▪ dates ▪ the expression **avoir... ans** ▪ present tense of the irregular verb **offrir** **Leçon C** ▪ **c'est** versus **il/elle est** ▪ present tense of the irregular verb **venir** ▪ **de** + DEFINITE ARTICLES
End-of-lesson strategies	**Leçon B** ▪ ***Stratégie communicative***: register in speaking and writing **Leçon C** ▪ ***Culture sur place***: assess comfort level with Francophone cultures ▪ ***Le monde visuel***: Impressionistic techniques (Jean Béraud) ▪ ***Lecture thématique***: answer the five "W" questions and decipher words (***Belle du Seigneur***, Albert Cohen)	**Leçon B** ▪ ***Stratégie communicative***: cognates **Leçon C** ▪ ***Culture sur place***: sports viewing habits ▪ ***Le monde visuel***: coloration (Béatrice Boisségur) ▪ ***Lecture thématique***: paraphrasing and finding meaning in repetition (***Penser/classer***, George Perec)	**Leçon B** ▪ ***Stratégie communicative***: combine sentences **Leçon C** ▪ ***Culture sur place***: reflect on learning about French schools and compare them to schools in the United States ▪ ***Le monde visuel***: focal point (Robert Doisneau) ▪ ***Lecture thématique***: point of view and context clues (***Le Petit Nicolas***, René Goscinny)	**Leçon B** ▪ ***Stratégie communicative***: use adjectives and adverbs **Leçon C** ▪ ***Culture sur place***: remakes of French films ▪ ***Le monde visuel***: poster art ▪ ***Lecture thématique***: identify the conflict in a story and recognize false cognates (***LOL***, Anonymous blogger)	**Leçon B** ▪ ***Stratégie communicative***: ask questions to extend a conversation **Leçon C** ▪ ***Culture sur place***: collect anecdotal evidence about a Francophone family ▪ ***Le monde visuel***: composition (Alfred Wolf) ▪ ***Lecture thématique***: theme and monitoring comprehension (***L'enfant multiple***, Andrée Chedid)

	Unité 6	Unité 7	Unité 8	Unité 9	Unité 10
Essential Question	How is shopping different in other countries?	What makes a house a "home"?	How do major world cities tell their stories?	How do people stay healthy and maintain a healthy environment?	How do travel experiences shape our worldview?
Vocabulary: *Vocabulaire actif*	**Leçon A** ▪ articles of clothing ▪ colors **Leçon B** ▪ stores and grocery items ▪ quantities **Leçon C** ▪ fruits and vegetables	**Leçon A** ▪ stories in a building ▪ rooms in a house ▪ furniture in the kitchen and living room **Leçon B** ▪ meals ▪ table setting **Leçon C** ▪ the bedroom and bathroom ▪ computer and other technology	**Leçon A** ▪ weather ▪ seasons ▪ pets **Leçon B** ▪ places in the city ▪ monuments in Paris **Leçon C** ▪ time expressions	**Leçon A** ▪ parts of the body ▪ parts of the face **Leçon B** ▪ body aches ▪ illnesses and other health expressions **Leçon C** ▪ environmental problems ▪ environmental solutions ▪ endangered species	**Leçon A** ▪ Quebec essentials ▪ compass directions **Leçon B** ▪ at the train station ▪ features of the countryside **Leçon C** ▪ European countries ▪ European nationalities ▪ expressions for giving directions
Functions: *Pour la conversation*	**Leçon A** ▪ what to ask the salesperson ▪ what the salesperson says **Leçon B** ▪ sequence my activities **Leçon C** ▪ make a purchase at the market ▪ respond to questions from the vendor	**Leçon A** ▪ give a tour of a house or an apartment ▪ ask where someone lives ▪ agree and disagree **Leçon B** ▪ give directions in the kitchen **Leçon C** ▪ say that I don't understand ▪ talk about computers	**Leçon A** ▪ extend an invitation ▪ accept or refuse an invitation **Leçon B** ▪ excuse oneself ▪ describe actions that took place in the past ▪ sequence past events **Leçon C** ▪ express actions that took place in the past ▪ sequence past events	**Leçon A** ▪ say it is necessary to do, or not do, something **Leçon B** ▪ ask for advice ▪ give advice **Leçon C** ▪ persuade someone ▪ respond to persuasion	**Leçon A** ▪ tell someone where a place is located **Leçon B** ▪ remind someone to do something ▪ wish someone a good trip **Leçon C** ▪ ask for directions ▪ give directions
Culture: *Points de départ*	**Leçon A** ▪ eCommerce ▪ French flea markets ▪ high fashion houses in Paris ▪ **la Francophonie:** clothing in West Africa **Leçon B** ▪ superstores versus small shops ▪ French cheeses ▪ metric measurements **Leçon C** ▪ outdoor markets ▪ slow food movement ▪ **la Francophonie: souks** in North Africa	**Leçon A** ▪ housing in France ▪ bathrooms in France ▪ **la Francophonie:** Algeria; North African dwellings **Leçon B** ▪ Marseille ▪ Provence ▪ regional culinary specialties **Leçon C** ▪ technology and French youth ▪ **la Francophonie:** New Brunswick; the **Grand Dérangement** of the Acadians; singer Natasha St-Pier	**Leçon A** ▪ Paris ▪ Parisian pastries ▪ **la Francophonie:** Haiti and Port-au-Prince **Leçon B** ▪ **Notre-Dame de Paris** ▪ **l'Arc de Triomphe** ▪ **la tour Eiffel** **Leçon C** ▪ **le jardin des Tuileries** ▪ **le métro**	**Leçon A** ▪ social security in France ▪ **"Manger-bouger"** ad campaign ▪ thermalism **Leçon B** ▪ **la Francophonie:** Fighting AIDS in Rwanda; home health-care workers in Rwanda **Leçon C** ▪ **les Verts** in France ▪ Vélib' Paris	**Leçon A** ▪ **la Francophonie:** Quebec; Montreal; **FrancoFolies** festival in Montreal **Leçon B** ▪ departments and regions of France ▪ Loire castles ▪ Tours **Leçon C** ▪ **la Francophonie:** Switzerland; Geneva; **le musée international de la Croix-Rouge**
Structure: *Structure de la langue*	**Leçon A** ▪ present tense of the verb **acheter** ▪ present tense of the irregular verb **vouloir** ▪ demonstrative adjectives **Leçon B** ▪ present tense of regular **-re** verbs ▪ expressions of quantity **Leçon C** ▪ the partitive article ▪ the partitive in negative sentences	**Leçon A** ▪ ordinal numbers **Leçon B** ▪ comparative of adjectives ▪ present tense of the irregular verb **devoir** ▪ present tense of the irregular verb **mettre** **Leçon C** ▪ present tense of the irregular verb **pouvoir**	**Leçon A** ▪ present tense of the irregular verb **faire** ▪ expressions with **avoir**: **avoir froid, avoir chaud, avoir envie de** **Leçon B** ▪ **passé composé** with **avoir** ▪ irregular past participles ▪ position of irregular adjectives **Leçon C** ▪ **passé composé** with **être** ▪ position of adverbs in the **passé composé**	**Leçon A** ▪ present tense of the irregular verb **falloir** **Leçon B** ▪ the imperative **Leçon C** ▪ Verbs + INFINITIVES ▪ **de** + PLURAL ADJECTIVES	**Leçon A** ▪ prepositions before cities, countries, and continents **Leçon B** ▪ negative expressions **Leçon C** ▪ superlative of adjectives
End-of-lesson strategies	**Leçon B** ▪ ***Stratégie communicative***: tell a story through pictures **Leçon C** ▪ ***Culture sur place***: go shopping online ▪ ***Le monde visuel***: post-war black-and-white photography (Sabine Weiss) ▪ ***Lecture thématique***: setting and word families (***Le fils du boulanger***, Maurice Pons)	**Leçon B** ▪ ***Stratégie communicative***: write effective descriptions with adjectives **Leçon C** ▪ ***Culture sur place***: evaluate whether student's home is like or unlike Francophone home ▪ ***Le monde visuel***: Impressionism and Cubism (Paul Cézanne) ▪ ***Lecture thématique***: rhyme scheme and deciphering new grammatical structures (**"Le chat"**, Guillaume Apollinaire)	**Leçon B** ▪ ***Stratégie communicative***: personal narrative **Leçon C** ▪ ***Culture sur place***: identify customs and react to French culture ▪ ***Le monde visuel***: Pointillism (Paul Signac) ▪ ***Lecture thématique***: personification and making inferences (**"Chanson de la Seine"**, Jacques Prévert)	**Leçon B** ▪ ***Stratégie communicative***: "how-to" writing **Leçon C** ▪ ***Culture sur place***: hunting for diabetes education aids in Francophone countries ▪ ***Le monde visuel***: Cubism (Roger de La Fresnaye) ▪ ***Lecture thématique***: characterization, text organization, and making a prediction (***L'homme rompu***, Tahar Ben Jelloun)	**Leçon B** ▪ ***Stratégie communicative***: writing a postcard **Leçon C** ▪ ***Culture sur place***: interviewing a traveler who has visited a Francophone location ▪ ***Le monde visuel***: perspective (Achille Varin) ▪ ***Lecture thématique***: imagery and the progression of stanzas (**"Je me souviens"**, Louis Aragon)

Level 2, Units 1–10

	Unité 1	Unité 2	Unité 3	Unité 4	Unité 5
Essential Question	What do young people do in the summer in other cultures?	What stories are told by the art and architecture of Paris?	How do the routines of people in other cultures differ from mine?	How does the past shape us?	What do you need to know to travel successfully?
Vocabulary: *Vocabulaire actif*	**Leçon A** ▪ holidays in France, Quebec, and the United States **Leçon B** ▪ television programs ▪ television professions **Leçon C** ▪ rides and attractions at amusement parks	**Leçon A** ▪ art terms ▪ types of paintings **Leçon B** ▪ places in the neighborhood **Leçon C** ▪ modes of transportation ▪ Versailles	**Leçon A** ▪ toiletries ▪ daily routine **Leçon B** ▪ household chores ▪ household items **Leçon C** ▪ expressions with reflexive verbs	**Leçon A** ▪ farm animals ▪ farm work **Leçon B** ▪ professions of the past **Leçon C** ▪ university life	**Leçon A** ▪ at the airport **Leçon B** ▪ types of cars ▪ car servicing ▪ parts of cars **Leçon C** ▪ hotel amenities ▪ French breakfast ▪ North American breakfast
Functions: *Pour la conversation*	**Leçon A** ▪ ask someone if they celebrate a particular holiday ▪ ask when something takes place and respond **Leçon B** ▪ ask for an opinion ▪ give an opinion ▪ find out what someone is thinking ▪ agree or disagree **Leçon C** ▪ inquire about future plans ▪ respond	**Leçon A** ▪ describe a painting **Leçon B** ▪ say I'm lost ▪ tell someone not to worry ▪ ask for directions ▪ give directions **Leçon C** ▪ ask about transportation ▪ respond	**Leçon A** ▪ complain ▪ respond to a complaint ▪ express frustration ▪ respond **Leçon B** ▪ make comparisons ▪ respond to comparisons ▪ express injustice **Leçon C** ▪ find out if someone remembers something ▪ recount past events	**Leçon A** ▪ reminisce ▪ describe past events **Leçon B** ▪ say what used to be **Leçon C** ▪ make a suggestion	**Leçon A** ▪ describe a health problem ▪ give instructions **Leçon B** ▪ express that I'm looking forward to something **Leçon C** ▪ ask for a hotel room ▪ ask if something's included in the price ▪ understand what the receptionist asks
Culture: *Points de départ*	**Leçon A** ▪ **la Francophonie:** Quebec City; 400th anniversary of the founding of Quebec; celebrations in Quebec and France ▪ singer Cœur de pirate **Leçon B** ▪ **la Francophonie**: Luxembourg; French and Luxembourg TV channels ▪ Reality shows in France **Leçon C** ▪ French fair **la Fête des Loges** ▪ amusement parks and other attractions in France ▪ **la Francophonie: la Ronde**	**Leçon A** ▪ the **Louvre** ▪ the **musée d'Orsay** ▪ the **Centre Pompidou** **Leçon B** ▪ Paris's newest arrondissements ▪ **le Quartier latin** ▪ Saint-Germain des Prés **Leçon C** ▪ tourist offices ▪ the **RER** ▪ Versailles	**Leçon A** ▪ **la Francophonie:** Cameroon; goals of the community of **la Francophonie** **Leçon B** ▪ **la Francophonie**: Ivory Coast; artists from the Ivory Coast ▪ African immigrants in France today **Leçon C** ▪ **la Francophonie:** Senegal; **Griots**; singer Youssou N'Dour	**Leçon A** ▪ agriculture in France ▪ world ranking of France's agricultural products ▪ French rural life today **Leçon B** ▪ Montmartre ▪ Toulouse-Lautrec **Leçon C** ▪ demonstrations ▪ May 1968 ▪ University of Vincennes-Saint-Denis	**Leçon A** ▪ **Air France** ▪ airports in Paris ▪ Bordeaux **Leçon B** ▪ PSA Group car company ▪ Renault-Nissan car company ▪ learning to drive in France **Leçon C** ▪ hotels, inns, and bed & breakfasts in France ▪ luxury hotels and the movies ▪ AccorHotels chains
Structure: *Structure de la langue*	**Leçon A** ▪ present tense of regular **-er**, **-ir**, and **-re** verbs ▪ negation ▪ possessive adjectives ▪ forming questions ▪ dates **Leçon B** ▪ present tense of the irregular verbs **avoir** and **être** ▪ indefinite articles in negative sentences ▪ demonstrative adjectives ▪ agreement and position of adjectives ▪ comparative of adjectives **Leçon C** ▪ present tense of the irregular verbs **aller** and **faire** ▪ **de** and **à** + DEFINITE ARTICLES ▪ the irregular verb **venir** and **venir de** + INFINITIVE ▪ telling time	**Leçon A** ▪ present tense of the irregular verb **suivre** ▪ **passé composé** with **avoir** ▪ present tense of the irregular verbs **mettre, prendre,** and **voir** **Leçon B** ▪ present tense of the irregular verbs **vouloir, pouvoir, devoir,** and **falloir** ▪ irregular past participles ▪ imperative **Leçon C** ▪ present tense of the irregular verbs **partir** and **sortir** ▪ **passé composé** with **être** ▪ superlative of adjectives	**Leçon A** ▪ present tense of reflexive verbs ▪ irregular plural forms of nouns and adjectives **Leçon B** ▪ present tense of the irregular verb **s'asseoir** ▪ the imperative of reflexive verbs **Leçon C** ▪ **passé composé** of reflexive verbs	**Leçon A** ▪ imperfect tense ▪ present tense of the irregular verb **croire** **Leçon B** ▪ **Il y a** + TIME ▪ **imparfait** and **passé composé** **Leçon C** ▪ **Si on** + IMPERFECT	**Leçon A** ▪ direct object pronouns: **me, te, nous, vous** **Leçon B** ▪ direct object pronouns: **le, la, l', les** ▪ direct object pronouns in the **passé composé** ▪ present tense of the irregular verb **conduire** **Leçon C** ▪ indirect object pronouns: **lui, leur** ▪ indirect object pronouns: **me, te, nous, vous** ▪ present tense of the irregular verb **boire** ▪ the adjective **tout**
End-of-lesson strategies	**Leçon B** ▪ ***Stratégie communicative***: create a TV commercial **Leçon C** ▪ ***Culture sur place***: investigate bilinguism in Canada ▪ ***Le monde visuel***: realism (Jean-Louis Ernest Meissonier) ▪ ***Lecture thématique***: visualization and character name (***Le journal d'Aurélie Laflamme***, India Desjardins)	**Leçon B** ▪ ***Stratégie communicative***: describe art **Leçon C** ▪ ***Culture sur place***: explore **le musée d'Orsay** ▪ ***Le monde visuel***: modern art (Marc Laberge) ▪ ***Lecture thématique***: drama basics and finding evidence in the text (***Art***, Yasmina Reza)	**Leçon B** ▪ ***Stratégie communicative***: tell a story through pictures **Leçon C** ▪ ***Culture sur place***: examine the controversy of **le burkini** in France ▪ ***Le monde visuel***: batik (Anonyme) ▪ ***Lecture thématique***: sensory details and making inferences (***Le ventre de l'Atlantique***, Fatou Diome)	**Leçon B** ▪ ***Stratégie communicative***: write an oral history **Leçon C** ▪ ***Culture sur place***: discover the reasons why people demonstrate ▪ ***Le monde visuel***: Impressionism's use of light (Camille Pissarro) ▪ ***Lecture thématique***: text organization and fact versus opinion (***L'enfant et la rivière***, Henri Bosco)	**Leçon B** ▪ ***Stratégie communicative***: write a dialogue **Leçon C** ▪ ***Culture sur place***: find a hotel that meets your needs ▪ ***Le monde visuel***: Pop art (Ganesh Vadora) ▪ ***Lecture thématique***: motif and cause and effect (***Carnet de routes***, Marie Lopez)

	Unité 6	Unité 7	Unité 8	Unité 9	Unité 10
Essential Question	How do other cultures enrich our lives?	How do smaller communities enrich a country's culture?	What are the benefits of encountering other cultures?	What influences and changes contemporary society?	What opportunities does travel afford us?
Vocabulary: ***Vocabulaire actif***	**Leçon A** ▪ things we read ▪ things we write **Leçon B** ▪ music genres ▪ musical instruments **Leçon C** ▪ accessories and fabrics ▪ jewelry	**Leçon A** ▪ foods and courses **Leçon B** ▪ French regions and their adjectives **Leçon C** ▪ things to eat and drink in a **crêperie** ▪ youth hostels	**Leçon A** ▪ fauna and flora in Guadeloupe ▪ activities in Guadeloupe **Leçon B** ▪ carnival in Martinique ▪ weddings **Leçon C** ▪ seafood ▪ water management	**Leçon A** ▪ features of smartphones ▪ steps for taking a digital photo **Leçon B** ▪ problems in contemporary society ▪ possible solutions **Leçon C** ▪ job sectors ▪ today's professions	**Leçon A** ▪ at the beach **Leçon B** ▪ camping **Leçon C** ▪ continents and bodies of water ▪ adventure tourism
Functions: ***Pour la conversation***	**Leçon A** ▪ say what a book is about ▪ introduce an author or a novel ▪ borrow something **Leçon B** ▪ ask if someone plays a particular instrument ▪ say what instrument I play **Leçon C** ▪ begin and end a letter ▪ thank someone formally	**Leçon A** ▪ compliment the host or hostess ▪ politely refuse more food ▪ offer help ▪ express irony **Leçon B** ▪ ask a friend what's new ▪ find out someone's associations with a place ▪ say I like a suggestion **Leçon C** ▪ understand what the server asks ▪ order food	**Leçon A** ▪ ask what someone prefers ▪ state ambivalence **Leçon B** ▪ make an observation **Leçon C** ▪ say what I'm in charge of ▪ express appreciation	**Leçon A** ▪ ask someone to lend me something ▪ say that I know or do not know how to use something ▪ express what someone was happy about **Leçon B** ▪ hypothesize ▪ propose solutions **Leçon C** ▪ express my future goals ▪ give a reason	**Leçon A** ▪ say I've been wanting to do something for a long time **Leçon B** ▪ say I need something ▪ ask someone to return something as soon as possible **Leçon C** ▪ ask what to bring
Culture: ***Points de départ***	**Leçon A** ▪ **la Francophonie:** Morocco ▪ French language comic books **Leçon B** ▪ **la Francophonie:** Algeria ▪ Raï music ▪ Singer Faudel ▪ North African musical instruments **Leçon C** ▪ **la Francophonie:** Tunisia ▪ how to write a formal letter	**Leçon A** ▪ Alsace ▪ Strasbourg ▪ **la Francophonie:** Kabylie in Algeria **Leçon B** ▪ Normandy ▪ Rouen **Leçon C** ▪ Brittany ▪ Saint-Malo ▪ youth hostels	**Leçon A** ▪ **la Francophonie:** Guadeloupe; **Parc national de la Guadeloupe**; green and blue tourism **Leçon B** ▪ **la Francophonie:** Martinique; carnival in Martinique **Leçon C** ▪ **la Francophonie:** Haiti; Toussaint Louverture	**Leçon A** ▪ French transportation technologies: aviation, space program, rail **Leçon B** ▪ nuclear energy ▪ objectives and problems in French education ▪ unemployed young people **Leçon C** ▪ **la Francophonie:** Belgium; famous Belgians; Brussels ▪ European Union	**Leçon A** ▪ French Riviera ▪ Nice ▪ Chagall and Matisse museums **Leçon B** ▪ Alps ▪ Grenoble ▪ camping in France **Leçon C** ▪ **la Francophonie:** adventure tourism in France and French Guiana
Structure: ***Structure de la langue***	**Leçon A** ▪ present tense of the irregular verb **lire** ▪ present tense of the irregular verb **écrire** **Leçon B** ▪ present tense of the irregular verb **savoir** ▪ present tense of the irregular verb **connaître** **Leçon C** ▪ present tense of the irregular verb **recevoir** ▪ present tense of the irregular verb **ouvrir**	**Leçon A** ▪ the relative pronouns **qui** and **que** ▪ the partitive ▪ the pronoun **en** **Leçon B** ▪ interrogative pronouns **Leçon C** ▪ stress pronouns	**Leçon A** ▪ present tense of the irregular verb **vivre** ▪ pronoun **y** **Leçon B** ▪ double object pronouns **Leçon C** ▪ **depuis** + PRESENT TENSE	**Leçon A** ▪ conditional tense **Leçon B** ▪ conditional tense in sentences with **si** **Leçon C** ▪ future tense	**Leçon A** ▪ adverbs ▪ verbs + INFINITIVES **Leçon B** ▪ present tense of the irregular verb **dormir** ▪ comparative of adverbs **Leçon C** ▪ superlative of adverbs
End-of-lesson strategies	**Leçon B** ▪ ***Stratégie communicative***: Write a character sketch **Leçon C** ▪ ***Culture sur place***: reflect on negotiating a price in North African souks and in North America ▪ ***Le monde visuel***: perspective in modern photography (Peet Simard) ▪ ***Lecture thématique***: images and refrain ("**Mon Pays**", Faudel)	**Leçon B** ▪ ***Stratégie communicative***: combine sentences **Leçon C** ▪ ***Culture sur place***: explore regional identities ▪ ***Le monde visuel***: still lifes (Paul Cézanne) ▪ ***Lecture thématique***: refrain and tone, and anticipating vocabulary ("**Le verger**", Rémy de Gourmont)	**Leçon B** ▪ ***Stratégie communicative***: circumlocution **Leçon C** ▪ ***Culture sur place***: find a good humanitarian organization ▪ ***Le monde visuel***: seascapes (Claude Salez) ▪ ***Lecture thématique***: theme and citing others' works (***Cent poèmes d'Aimé Césaire***, Daniel Maximin)	**Leçon B** ▪ ***Stratégie communicative***: write a proposal **Leçon C** ▪ ***Culture sur place***: investigate what new words in ***Le Petit Larousse*** reveal about contemporary French culture ▪ ***Le monde visuel***: textures of acrylic paints (Daniel Cacouault) ▪ ***Lecture thématique***: dystopias in fiction and social commentary (***Péplum***, Amélie Nothomb)	**Leçon B** ▪ ***Stratégie communicative***: travel writing **Leçon C** ▪ ***Culture sur place***: compare French and American vacation destinations ▪ ***Le monde visuel***: point of view (Delphine D. Garcia) ▪ ***Lecture thématique***: point of view and characterization ("**La plage, c'est chouette**", René Goscinny)

Level 3, Units 1–10

	Unité 1	Unité 2	Unité 3	Unité 4	Unité 5
Essential Question	Comment change-t-on de l'enfance à l'âge adulte?	Qu'y a-t-il d'universel dans les rapports entre les gens?	Comment les communautés francophones conservent-elles leurs traditions?	Qu'est-ce qu'on doit connaître de sa destination pour réussir son voyage?	De quelles compétences ai-je besoin pour voyager?
Vocabulary: *Vocabulaire actif*	**Leçon A** ▪ human emotions ▪ teen destinations **Leçon B** ▪ different types of families ▪ childhood games and activities **Leçon C** ▪ weddings	**Leçon A** ▪ Christmas Eve dinner **Leçon B** ▪ descriptions: shapes, sizes, material, and usage ▪ kitchen utensils **Leçon C** ▪ topics of conversation	**Leçon A** ▪ extended family members ▪ states in the United States **Leçon B** ▪ types of stories ▪ words from a North African children's story **Leçon C** ▪ types of housing	**Leçon A** ▪ sports and activities to do on vacation **Leçon B** ▪ at the ski resort ▪ ski clothing and equipment **Leçon C** ▪ other winter sports ▪ travel planning expressions	**Leçon A** ▪ at the hotel ▪ hotel amenities **Leçon B** ▪ food in **Bourgogne**: meats, dishes, sauces **Leçon C** ▪ movie expressions
Functions: *Pour la conversation*	**Leçon A** ▪ say where I met someone ▪ advise someone ▪ tell someone not to worry ▪ describe how something appears **Leçon B** ▪ say what I discovered ▪ explain how something happened ▪ ask for a suggestion **Leçon C** ▪ say I don't care ▪ express where I'd like to work	**Leçon A** ▪ talk on the phone ▪ invite someone ▪ respond affirmatively to an invitation ▪ say that something works out **Leçon B** ▪ ask for help ▪ respond to a request for help ▪ ask someone to pass me something **Leçon C** ▪ express what I can't keep myself from doing ▪ say someone is right ▪ ask about dinner table topics	**Leçon A** ▪ say where my ancestors came from ▪ say where my ancestors settled **Leçon B** ▪ start a fairy tale **Leçon C** ▪ respond to an introduction ▪ say where I grew up ▪ give a compliment	**Leçon A** ▪ ask someone's opinion ▪ react positively to someone's opinion ▪ react negatively to someone's opinion **Leçon B** ▪ say what I must do ▪ tell someone they'll have an opportunity to do something ▪ say what I was expecting **Leçon C** ▪ say I'm doing something different (from other people) ▪ tell someone to avoid injury	**Leçon A** ▪ find out information about my stay in a hotel **Leçon B** ▪ ask about restaurant specialties ▪ ask what is served with a dish **Leçon C** ▪ say what I'm not in the mood for ▪ relate someone else's opinion ▪ ask for an opinion ▪ express disagreement
Culture: *Points de départ*	**Leçon A** ▪ teen socialization ▪ scouting ▪ poetry slams **Leçon B** ▪ different types of families in France ▪ **La Francophonie:** families and family values in Africa; **Provence-Alpes-Côte d'Azur** **Leçon C** ▪ preparatory schools and prestigious universities ▪ civil and religious marriage ceremonies ▪ **La Francophonie:** marriage ceremony in the Maghreb	**Leçon A** ▪ Christmas Eve holiday ▪ **La Francophonie**: Ramadan; **l'Aïd el-Fitr** **Leçon B** ▪ classic French cooking ▪ **la nouvelle cuisine** **Leçon C** ▪ rules of table etiquette	**Leçon A** ▪ **Alliance française** and its outreach programs ▪ French immigration to Quebec and **île d'Orléans** ▪ French-Canadian immigration to New England **Leçon B** ▪ **La Francophonie:** Tunisia; immigration of **Maghrébins** to France; overview of **contes maghrébins** **Leçon C** ▪ **HLM** and **allocations familiales** ▪ **La Francophonie:** Senegal; African housing	**Leçon A** ▪ **La Francophonie**: **La Réunion**; **La Corse**; Chamonix and other **stations de ski** in France **Leçon B** ▪ **Haute Savoie** traditions and specialties ▪ **classes de neige** ▪ Annecy ▪ **La Francophonie:** aquatic or **bleu** activities in Saint-Martin **Leçon C** ▪ volunteer travel experiences in Francophone countries	**Leçon A** ▪ hotel industry in France ▪ **La Francophonie:** Monaco; Monte Carlo; Rainier family **Leçon B** ▪ Dijon and its region ▪ food specialties in Burgundy region ▪ **La Francophonie:** North African dishes **Leçon C** ▪ **le septième art** ▪ **le Festival de Cannes** ▪ **les César**
Structure: *Structure de la langue*	**Leçon A** ▪ present tense of regular **-er**,**-ir**, and **-re** verbs ▪ present tense of irregular verbs ▪ **depuis** + PRESENT TENSE **Leçon B** ▪ the irregular verb **courir** ▪ **passé composé** with **avoir** ▪ **passé composé** with **être** ▪ imperfect tense ▪ imperfect and **passé composé** **Leçon C** ▪ conditional ▪ conditional with **si** ▪ future tense	**Leçon A** ▪ interrogative pronouns ▪ direct object pronouns **Leçon B** ▪ indirect object pronouns ▪ **c'est** versus **il/elle est** **Leçon C** ▪ relative pronouns **qui**, **que** ▪ relative pronouns **ce qui**, **ce que**	**Leçon A** ▪ pronouns **y**, **en** ▪ double object pronouns **Leçon B** ▪ pronominal verbs **Leçon C** ▪ comparative of adverbs ▪ superlative of adverbs	**Leçon A** ▪ present participle ▪ negation ▪ other negative expressions **Leçon B** ▪ **savoir** versus **connaître** ▪ subjunctive of regular verbs after **il faut que** ▪ subjunctive of irregular verbs **Leçon C** ▪ subjunctive after impersonal expressions	**Leçon A** ▪ subjunctive after expressions of wish, will, desire **Leçon B** ▪ subjunctive after expressions of emotion ▪ subjunctive after expressions of doubt or uncertainty **Leçon C** ▪ interrogative adjective **quel** ▪ interrogative pronoun **lequel** (**duquel**, **auquel**)
End-of-lesson strategies	**Leçon B** ▪ ***Stratégie communicative:*** write a personal narrative **Leçon C** ▪ ***Culture sur place:*** describing adolescent cultures ▪ ***Le monde visuel***: line drawing (Édouard Albert) ▪ ***Lecture thématique***: setting and using context clues (***Les petits enfants du siècle***, Christiane Rochefort)	**Leçon B** ▪ ***Stratégie communicative:*** use circumlocution **Leçon C** ▪ ***Culture sur place:*** identify food preferences ▪ ***Le monde visuel***: landscapes behind portraits (Jules Ernest Renoux) ▪ ***Lecture thématique***: dialogue and conflict (***Deux couverts***, Sacha Guitry)	**Leçon B** ▪ ***Stratégie communicative:*** use transitions in a story **Leçon C** ▪ ***Culture sur place***: needs of new immigrants ▪ ***Le monde visuel***: primitive art (Cécile Delorme) ▪ ***Lecture thématique***: make cultural inferences, gender criticism (***Une si longue lettre***, Mariama Bâ)	**Leçon B** ▪ ***Stratégie communicative***: write a "how-to" piece using the subjunctive **Leçon C** ▪ ***Culture sur place***: volunteer travel experiences ▪ ***Le monde visuel***: classicism (Sébastien Bourdon) ▪ ***Lecture thématique***: structure and meaning, allusions (**"Heureux qui, comme Ulysse, a fait un beau voyage,"** Joachim Du Bellay)	**Leçon B** ▪ ***Stratégie communicative***: helpful expressions **Leçon C** ▪ ***Culture sur place***: planning a trip online ▪ ***Le monde visuel***: bright colors (Georges Rouault) ▪ ***Lecture thématique***: epistolary novel (***La quarantaine***, Jean-Marie Le Clézio)

	Unité 6	Unité 7	Unité 8	Unité 9	Unité 10
Essential Question	Comment s'intégrer à une autre culture?	Comment l'art est-il un reflet de la culture?	Comment le passé influence-t-il le présent?	Quels sont les défis de la vie contemporaine?	Qu'apprend-on de la culture d'un pays en étudiant son économie?
Vocabulary: *Vocabulaire actif*	**Leçon A** ▪ banking terms ▪ university departments **Leçon B** ▪ things to read **Leçon C** ▪ at the post office	**Leçon A** ▪ art descriptions ▪ art movements **Leçon B** ▪ music **Leçon C** ▪ literature	**Leçon A** ▪ French Revolution **Leçon B** ▪ applying and interviewing for a job **Leçon C** ▪ health care terms ▪ debate terms	**Leçon A** ▪ emotions **Leçon B** ▪ physical description: hair, age, ethnicity, clothing **Leçon C** ▪ reactions	**Leçon A** ▪ export products **Leçon B** ▪ types of companies ▪ French and US trade **Leçon C** ▪ professional qualifications ▪ job positions within a company
Functions: *Pour la conversation*	**Leçon A** ▪ open a bank account ▪ get a debit card ▪ make a promise **Leçon B** ▪ ask what a book is about ▪ say I can't decide **Leçon C** ▪ say what I need ▪ specify items	**Leçon A** ▪ say when a painting was painted ▪ describe an artist's approach ▪ describe colors in a painting **Leçon B** ▪ describe an artist's development ▪ say that an artist was successful ▪ describe an artist's ability to connect with his or her audience **Leçon C** ▪ describe how an artist raises themes ▪ describe how a work of art takes a position ▪ describe what an artist worked on ▪ attribute new inventions ▪ describe how an artist fits into a culture	**Leçon A** ▪ express what someone was obligated to do ▪ say what someone makes me do **Leçon B** ▪ indicate quantity ▪ say I did something in vain ▪ tell someone to stop with the flattery **Leçon C** ▪ express my rights ▪ discuss what I can afford ▪ say I want to discuss something further	**Leçon A** ▪ express how someone looked ▪ express what I was unable to do **Leçon B** ▪ say I have realized something ▪ ask if someone noticed something **Leçon C** ▪ ask when someone got the idea to do something ▪ say that I was not expecting something	**Leçon A** ▪ say where an item was made ▪ express what I feared about something **Leçon B** ▪ ask how long someone has been in a certain place ▪ express my desire to get away **Leçon C** ▪ describe adaptability
Culture: *Points de départ*	**Leçon A** ▪ French banks ▪ withdrawing money in Europe **Leçon B** ▪ French reading habits ▪ J. M. G. Le Clézio and Patrick Modiano ▪ **La Francophonie:** Maryse Condé **Leçon C** ▪ French post office and its services	**Leçon A** ▪ impressionism ▪ neo-impressionism ▪ expressionism and fauvism ▪ **La Francophonie:** art in West Africa **Leçon B** ▪ the modern French song and its themes ▪ **La Francophonie:** music in Quebec **Leçon C** ▪ French poets	**Leçon A** ▪ Louis XVI and Marie-Antoinette ▪ **les États généraux** ▪ ***La Déclaration des droits de l'homme et du citoyen*** ▪ **La Francophonie:** Arab Spring in Tunisia **Leçon B** ▪ European Union institutions **Leçon C** ▪ rights of the French citizen under **la sécu:** unemployment, health care, family, disabled protection, retirement	**Leçon A** ▪ French school system ▪ **le bac** and student stress **Leçon B** ▪ different types of French police ▪ crime in France **Leçon C** ▪ Internet and social media	**Leçon A** ▪ French attitude toward globalization ▪ luxury products and LVMH **Leçon B** ▪ France's position in world trade ▪ multinational companies **Leçon C** ▪ evolution of French marketing strategies
Structure: *Structure de la langue*	**Leçon A** ▪ future tense in sentences with **si** ▪ future tense after **quand** **Leçon B** ▪ VERB + **de** + NOUN ▪ relative pronoun **dont** **Leçon C** ▪ demonstrative adjectives ▪ demonstrative pronouns	**Leçon A** ▪ agreement and position of adjectives ▪ comparative of adjectives ▪ superlative of adjectives **Leçon B** ▪ the irregular verb **plaire** **Leçon C** ▪ **pour** + INFINITIVE ▪ subjunctive after **pour que**	**Leçon A** ▪ expressions with **faire** ▪ **faire** + INFINITIVE **Leçon B** ▪ expressions with **avoir** ▪ past infinitive **Leçon C** ▪ expressions with **être** ▪ pluperfect tense	**Leçon A** ▪ past conditional ▪ past conditional with **si** **Leçon B** ▪ possessive adjectives ▪ possessive pronouns **Leçon C** ▪ indefinite adjectives ▪ indefinite pronouns	
End-of-lesson strategies	**Leçon B** ▪ ***Stratégie communicative*:** persuade someone to read a book or see a movie **Leçon C** ▪ ***Culture sur place*:** problem solving **sur place** ▪ ***Le monde visuel*:** cartoon art (Marjane Satrapi) ▪ ***Lecture thématique*:** narrator and narration, direct and indirect reporting (***Persepolis***, Marjane Satrapi)	**Leçon B** ▪ ***Stratégie communicative*:** compare and contrast **Leçon C** ▪ ***Culture sur place*:** compare French and American music ▪ ***Le monde visuel*:** multiple exposure (Walter Limot) ▪ ***Lecture thématique*:** free verse and oxymorons ("**Familiale**," Jacques Prévert)	**Leçon B** ▪ ***Stratégie communicative*:** write a CV **Leçon C** ▪ ***Culture sur place*:** rights issues and challenges the press faces abroad ▪ ***Le monde visuel*:** theatrical photography (Joseph Nicéphore Niépce) ▪ ***Lecture thématique*:** word families and setting (***Le bourgeois gentilhomme***, Molière)	**Leçon B** ▪ ***Stratégie communicative*:** tell a story through pictures **Leçon C** ▪ ***Culture sur place*:** interview a French speaker about challenges of life today ▪ ***Le monde visuel*:** book illustrations (Anonymous) ▪ ***Lecture thématique*:** characterization and **le passé simple** (***Les Misérables***, Victor Hugo)	**Leçon B** ▪ ***Stratégie communicative*:** make a storyboard to sell a product in France **Leçon C** ▪ ***Culture sur place*:** how globalization affects our lives ▪ ***Le monde visuel*:** advertising photography ▪ ***Lecture thématique*:** tone and breaking through the fourth wall (***5,90 €***, Frédéric Beigbeder)

Level 4, Units 1–6

	Unité 1	Unité 2	Unité 3
Vocabulary: *Vocabulaire actif*	**Leçon A** Comment l'enfant et l'adolescent se construisent-ils dans leur environnement familial et communautaire? ▪ les besoins des adolescents ▪ les problèmes des adolescents **Leçon B** Quel rôle la famille et la société jouent-elles dans nos choix amoureux? ▪ l'amour et l'amitié ▪ les rapports ▪ les sentiments **Leçon C** Comment les rapports sociaux évoluent-ils dans la société moderne? ▪ les relations ▪ les groupes	**Leçon A** Comment les cultures marquent-elles le passage de l'enfance à l'adolescence puis à l'âge adulte? ▪ les rites (de passage) et les rituels **Leçon B** Comment le marketing façonne-t-il et/ou reflète-t-il les tendances culturelles des communautés? ▪ les mots de la pub ▪ les effets de la pub ▪ le marketing **Leçon C** En quoi les loisirs et le sport contribuent-ils à la qualité de la vie? ▪ sports ▪ lieux de sport ▪ objets de sport ▪ loisirs	**Leçon A** Comment la langue influence-t-elle l'identité? ▪ langues maternelles ▪ idiome, dialecte, patois, idiotisme, néologisme **Leçon B** Comment est-on enrichi par les produits, les pratiques, les points de vue d'autres cultures? ▪ rapports entre les cultures ▪ une experience personnelle avec le pluriculturalisme **Leçon C** Quel rôle le nationalisme joue-t-il pour les individus et les institutions? ▪ le nationalisme ▪ le patriotisme ▪ des symboles de la France
Functions: *Pour la conversation*	**Leçon A** ▪ *J'aimerais que vous cessiez de...* ▪ *Sans..., je ne sais pas où je serais.* ▪ *Grâce à..., je me suis rendu compte que...* **Leçon B** ▪ *Le plus dur a été...* ▪ *... a été le meilleur moyen de se mettre tous à l'aise.* ▪ *... au cas où...* **Leçon C** ▪ *J'ai grandi à...* ▪ *... m'ont attiré.* ▪ *... a tant de...*	**Leçon A** ▪ *Je serai durant...* ▪ *Il ne manque plus que...* ▪ *Je ne maîtrise pas totalement...* ▪ *Je me suis aperçu que...* ▪ *Je me suis dit...* **Leçon B** ▪ *Imagine-toi que...* ▪ *... depend de...* ▪ *Je lui ai expliqué comment cela s'était passé...* **Leçon C** ▪ *Depuis que je suis petit(e), je pratique...* ▪ *Ça fait 7 ans que je fais de...* ▪ *... permet de...* ▪ *Il m'apporte...*	**Leçon A** ▪ *C'est en... que je me sens à l'aise dans...* ▪ *Ce n'est donc pas... qui me vient à l'aide quand...* ▪ *J'avance dans mon apprentissage de...* **Leçon B** ▪ *J'ai fait pas mal de...* ▪ *J'essaie de faire en sorte que... soient...* **Leçon C** ▪ *C'est pour cela que...* ▪ *Que...!* ▪ *J'ai mis...*
Narratives	**Leçon A** ▪ Une lettre aux adultes ▪ Interview d'un ado ▪ Retrouver le chemin de l'école (LSI) ▪ La pension **Leçon B** ▪ Crise d'une jeune musulmane ▪ D'ici et d'ailleurs ▪ L'amour mixte interdit ▪ Conseils **Leçon C** ▪ Intégrer une Grande école ▪ Mixité sociale à l'école ▪ Logement intergénérationnel ▪ L'Accorderie	**Leçon A** ▪ Une élève passe son bac ▪ Mamans de futurs bacheliers ▪ Passer le test de conduite **Leçon B** ▪ Confronté au marketing ethnique ▪ La publicité dans la vie quotidienne ▪ Conseils: Comment passer au bio **Leçon C** ▪ Opinions des Québécois sur les sports ▪ Le handicap en athlétisme ▪ Aya Cissoko, boxeuse ▪ Hobbies des jeunes	**Leçon A** ▪ Récits de 2 femmes qui n'ont pas perdu leurs langues maternelles ▪ Interview de Rokia Traoré, musicienne malienne **Leçon B** ▪ Témoignage d'un séjour linguistique ▪ Le gipsy raï de Cheb Aïssa ▪ Alex Petit et ses habits métissés **Leçon C** ▪ Discours de Charles de Gaulle à la fin de la guerre ▪ Opinions sur le patriotisme ▪ Récit d'un réfugié en France
Culture	**Leçon A** ▪ Ados sous influence ▪ **La Francophonie:** l'éducation des enfants en france, chez les Peuls ▪ L'internat pourquoi? ▪ **La culture de tous les jours:** Christine se révolte à table **Leçon B** ▪ **La Francophonie:** couples mixtes en France, en Tunisie; amitié entre filles et garcons; SMS et les rapports; amours adolescentes ▪ **La culture de tous les jours:** Julie tchate sur MSN **Leçon C** ▪ éducation en France ▪ formes de sociabilité ▪ changements de formes de sociabilité ▪ société sans contact ▪ **La Francophonie:** l'Accorderie au Québec; logement intergénérationnel ▪ **La culture de tous les jours:** Marie-France prend l'initiative (la Fête des voisins).	**Leçon A** ▪ tout sur le bac ▪ **La Francophonie:** rite de passage dans les pays musulmans; ados en quête de rites ▪ **La culture de tous les jours:** Les rituels de Fatima et Martin **Leçon B** ▪ futur de la publicité ▪ marketing ethnique ▪ quand la pub colle au genre ▪ marketing du lobby des industriels bio ▪ **La culture de tous les jours:** L'instruction de Damien sur la publicité **Leçon C** ▪ **La Francophonie:** jeux d'hiver au Québec; handisport; boxe feminine; loisirs des Français; activités extrascolaires; MJC ▪ **La culture de tous les jours:** Un weekend de bricolage	**Leçon A** ▪ langues maternelles des immigrés ▪ le français dans le monde ▪ le riche passé du français ▪ **La Francophonie:** le français en Afrique ▪ **La culture de tous les jours:** Séjour linguistique **Leçon B** ▪ le programme Erasmus ▪ la world music ▪ L'art des mélanges ▪ la cuisine métissée ▪ **La Francophonie:** diversité culturelle au Canada; le métissage dans la science ▪ **La Culture de tous les jours:** Rendez-vous dans un resto fusion **Leçon C** ▪ la libération de la France ▪ l'asile et l'acquisition de la nationalité française ▪ **La Francophonie:** aide pour les réfugiés au Canada; le sentiment national en France ▪ **La culture de tous les jours:** Le 14 juillet
Structure	**Leçon A** **Révision:** les temps du passé ▪ le participe passé pris comme adjectif **Leçon B** **Révision:** la durée (*il y a*, *depuis*) **Leçon C** **Révision:** changements orthographiques des verbes au présent ▪ *vouloir*, *pouvoir*, *devoir*, *savoir*	**Leçon A** **Révision:** comparaisons d'adjectifs et d'adverbes ▪ l'expression de l'intensité ▪ le pronom explétif *il* **Leçon B** **Révision:** la forme pronominale ▪ le *faire* causatif **Leçon C** ▪ *faire*/*laisser* + INFINITIF ▪ *se faire*/*laisser* + INFINITIF	**Leçon A** **Révision:** l'hypothèse: concordance des temps avec **si** + CONDITIONNEL **Leçon B** **Révision:** la négation ▪ pronoms interrogatifs **Leçon C** **Révision:** le participe présent ▪ le gérondif
Lectures	**Leçon A** ▪ "Cinq ou six années" par Jeanne Cherhal **Leçon B** ▪ "Les enfants qui s'aiment" par Jacques Prévert ▪ *La folle allure* par Christian Bobin **Leçon C** ▪ *Bel ami* par Guy de Maupassant ▪ *La place* par Annie Ernaux	**Leçon A** ▪ *Le gone du Chaâba* par Azouz Begag ▪ Je suis morte et *je n'ai rien appris* par Solenn Colleter **Leçon B** ▪ *5,90 €* par Frédéric Beigbeder ▪ *César Birotteau* par Honoré de Balzac **Leçon C** ▪ "Le fossé" par Samir Barris	**Leçon A** ▪ *Les mots étrangers* par Vassilis Alexakis ▪ *L'hospitalité de la langue* par Edmond Jabès **Leçon B** ▪ "Voyageur" par Bernard Lavilliers **Leçon C** ▪ "C'est du lourd" par Abd al Malik

	Unité 4	Unité 5	Unité 6
Vocabulary: *Vocabulaire actif*	**Leçon A** En l'ère moderne, que signifie lutter pour les droits de l'homme? ▪ l'histoire d'Haïti ▪ les droits de l'homme ▪ l'histoire contemporaine **Leçon B** Peut-on justifier la violence et la guerre, et quelles en sont les alternatives? ▪ crimes et violence ▪ le tempérament ▪ guerre et paix **Leçon C** Que signifie la tolérance à l'égard des autres, et quelles en sont les limites? ▪ le respect et la tolérance ▪ la tolérance et le fanatisme ▪ les idéologies	**Leçon A** Comment les inventions changent-elles notre vision du monde? ▪ les découvertes et les inventions: la démarche, les conséquences et la vie du scientifique **Leçon B** Comment les progrès scientifiques et technologiques affectent-ils notre vie? ▪ l'avenir de la technologie ▪ aspects du progressiste et du rétrograde **Leçon C** Quels débats les progrès scientifiques suscitent-ils dans les sociétés d'aujourd'hui? ▪ métiers et secteurs scientifiques ▪ des espérances aux résultats ▪ éthique de la science	**Leçon A** Comment les canons de la beauté évoluent-ils? ▪ la beauté extérieure ▪ la beauté intérieure ▪ les traits physiques **Leçon B** Comment les expériences personnelles nourrissent-elles l'art? ▪ les genres littéraires **Leçon C** En quoi est-ce que l'architecture reflète et modifie l'environnement culturel? ▪ les métiers et les responsabilités de l'architecte
Functions: *Pour la conversation*	**Leçon A** ▪ *Je ne pouvais pas… autrement* ▪ *… par colère* ▪ *En matière de…, c'est la zone!* **Leçon B** ▪ *… soi-même.* ▪ *… sont très attachés aux…* ▪ *Ce qui me fait sortir de mes gonds, ce sont…* **Leçon C** ▪ *… ne pas s'attaquer aux…* ▪ *De quoi s'agit-il?*	**Leçon A** ▪ *Je suis issu(e) de…* ▪ *Le déclic s'est produit, j'ai…* ▪ *En commençant par…* **Leçon B** ▪ *C'est réservé au… … doté de…* ▪ *Il ne s'agissait pas de…* **Leçon C** ▪ *J'ai fait appel à… …, alors que j'étais…* ▪ *Au contraire…*	**Leçon A** ▪ *… du premier coup* ▪ *C'est à l'autre de…* **Leçon B** ▪ *C'est la formule de…* ▪ *… dès…* ▪ *… qui ont une très bonne facilité à…* **Leçon C** ▪ *… de toutes mes forces.* ▪ *… à sa façon*
Narratives	**Leçon A** ▪ *Indignez-vous* par Stéphane Hessel ▪ Récit d'une jeune femme qui lutte pour le logement pour tous ▪ Lina, blogueuse de la révolution tunisienne **Leçon B** ▪ Témoignage d'un arbitre de foot ▪ La violence à l'école ▪ Témoignage d'un président de Tribunal pour enfants **Leçon C** ▪ Une Manouche parle des roms ▪ Actes anti-chrétiens vus par un Français	**Leçon A** ▪ Jean-Louis Etienne: médecin, explorateur et défenseur de la planète ▪ Jean-Michel Cousteau et sa mission de sauvegarder les océans ▪ Claudie Haigneré, spationaute **Leçon B** ▪ Résidente d'une maison futuriste parle ▪ Témoignage: L'Internet a changé ma vie ▪ Le Concours Lépine à Paris (inventions) **Leçon C** ▪ Témoignage: Mes filles sont nées d'une mère porteuse ▪ Récit d'une fille qui ne connaît pas son père biologique ▪ Ma position sur les OGM	**Leçon A** ▪ Une femme change son attitude envers l'apparence physique ▪ la beauté des mannequins ▪ Une actrice définit l'idéal de beauté **Leçon B** ▪ Témoignage: Où je trouve l'inspiration pour écrire ▪ Amélie Nothomb: De la souffrance à la littérature ▪ Katherine Pancol: Une romancière qui observe **Leçon C** ▪ la maison écolo du futur ▪ critiques sur la tour Eiffel et réponse de G. Eiffel
Culture	**Leçon A** ▪ biographie de Stéphane Hessel ▪ collectif français "Jeudi noir" ▪ le rôle des réseaux sociaux dans la révolution ▪ **La Francophonie:** la lutte sur Internet pour la liberté d'expression au Maghreb ▪ **La culture de tous les jours:** Non au harcèlement! **Leçon B** ▪ Le hooliganisme au stade de foot ▪ **La Francophonie:** la neutralité suisse ▪ **La culture de tous les jours:** l'association "Jeunes violences" **Leçon C** ▪ le racisme contre un Africain ▪ l'Islam et les Français ▪ **La culture de tous les jours:** deux manifestations sur les roms	**Leçon A** ▪ Peugeot fabrique une voiture hybride ▪ L'Équipe Cousteau ▪ le satellite Planck et l'enfance de l'univers ▪ **La culture de tous les jours:** le Minitel (à l'apogée de sa gloire) **Leçon B** ▪ **La Francophonie:** maison du futur en Belgique; les bénéfices d'Internet; débat sur la science et le progrès ▪ **La culture de tous les jours:** le TGV **Leçon C** ▪ l'homme face aux avancées scientifiques et techniques ▪ les OGM ▪ **La culture de tous les jours:** options pour la fin de la vie	**Leçon A** ▪ Souffrir pour être belle: le bronzage ▪ la beauté féminine dans le monde ▪ le regard qui déforme: les handicapés ▪ **La culture de tous les jours:** l'Art nouveau **Leçon B** ▪ l'art dans la vie de l'homme ▪ portrait de Dai Sijie ▪ **La Francophonie:** les arts littéraires en Guadeloupe (Maryse Condé) ▪ **La culture de tous les jours:** une explication de texte **Leçon C** ▪ interview de l'architecte Kazuyo Sejima ▪ histoire de la tour Eiffel ▪ **La Francophonie:** Expo '67 Montréal ▪ **La culture de tous les jours:** Centre Pompidou
Structure	**Leçon A** **Révision:** les pronoms *en* et *y* ▪ les pronoms relatifs simples: *qui, que, dont, où* ▪ constructions relatives introduites par un pronom démonstratif **Leçon B** **Révision:** le subjonctif ▪ subjonctif versus indicatif ▪ subjonctif versus infinitif **Leçon C** **Révision:** le subjonctif et les conjonctions ▪ le subjonctif passé	**Leçon A** ▪ le discours direct ▪ le discours indirect **Leçon B** **Révision:** le futur ▪ le futur antérieur **Leçon C** ▪ le passif et comment l'éviter ▪ *plaire* et *déplaire*	**Leçon A** **Révision:** le passé simple ▪ le passé simple: code oral et code écrit **Leçon B** **Révision:** l'article ▪ omission de l'article **Leçon C** **Révision:** les prépositions ▪ la place des adjectifs
Lectures	**Leçon A** ▪ "Les Vautours" par David Diop ▪ "Hoquet" par Léon-Gontran Damas **Leçon B** ▪ *Voyage au bout de la nuit* par Louis Ferdinand Céline **Leçon C** ▪ *Traité sur la tolérance* par Voltaire	**Leçon A** ▪ "L'homme-songe" par Guillaume Aldebert **Leçon B** ▪ *Ravage* par René Barjavel **Leçon C** ▪ *Troisième humanité* par Bernard Werber ▪ Si la planète pouvait parler: les lecteurs de Werber répondent en ligne	**Leçon A** ▪ "Dolly… on est comme on est" par France D'Amour **Leçon B** ▪ "Page blanche" par Pierralun ▪ *Les Mémoires* de Chateaubriand **Leçon C** ▪ *Germinal* par Émile Zola

Introduction

T'es branché? was designed to give French teachers a program that focuses on the three modes of communication—interpersonal, presentational, and interpretive—thus helping students to become proficient in the five skill areas. Based on detailed surveys involving hundreds of experienced French educators, and written in partnership with CLE International in Paris, this program exposes students to authentic print, audio, and video texts, and responds to teachers' expressed interests and priorities.

Students receive comprehensible input in the **Vocabulaire actif** and **Structure de la langue** sections, which they use in the accompanying activities to develop reading, listening, speaking, and writing skills. Students have opportunities to develop communication skills at the end of each lesson in **À vous la parole**. The **Projets finaux** section provides paired, small group, and cooperative group activities and projects that have clear guidelines and expectations.

Points de départ is a culture-centered section that reinforces language learning through products, practices, and perspectives; the readings are appropriately scaffolded as students progress from early to later units. Students assume a more active role with a hands-on approach to francophone cultures in **Culture sur place**, where they investigate topics of interest to teens and reflect on their "experience." Opportunities for critical thinking can be found throughout the program, such as in comparing francophone cultures to American culture, comparing French grammar to English grammar, and using strategies and analytical tools with the dialogues in **Rencontres culturelles** and the literary readings in **Lecture thématique**.

At the end of each unit, **Système D** fosters the acquisition of 21st-century skills to further language proficiency, as students apply their language skills in connection with communication, business literacy, and social and cross-cultural skills, to name a few. Finally, students reflect on their language experience as they progress through each unit, as each is framed around an essential question.

With the ***T'es branché?*** textbook series, students have opportunities to develop critical thinking and problem-solving skills. They also have the opportunity to prepare for the AP exam throughout each unit as well as with targeted AP practice in the **Bilan cumulatif** in every other unit. An extensive set of components delivered through EMC's Passport® online learning environment enriches the textbook instruction.

T'es branché? provides the tools needed to address the National Standards in the following areas:

ACTFL World-Readiness Standards for Learning Languages

Communication

Communicate Effectively in More than one Language in Order to Function in a Variety of Situations and for Multiple Purposes

Interpersonal Communication (formerly Standard 1.1): Learners interact and negotiate meaning in spoken, signed, or written conversations to share information, reactions, feelings, and opinions.

Interpretive Communication (formerly Standard 1.2): Learners understand, interpret, and analyze what is heard, read, or viewed on a variety of topics.

Presentational Communication (formerly Standard 1.3): Learners present information, concepts, and ideas to inform, explain, persuade, and narrate on a variety of topics using appropriate media and adapting to various audiences of listeners, readers, or viewers.

Cultures

Interact with Cultural Competence and Understanding

Relating Cultural Practices to Perspectives (formerly Standard 2.1): Learners use the language to investigate, explain, and reflect on the relationship between the practices and perspectives of the cultures studied.

Relating Cultural Products to Perspectives (formerly Standard 2.2): Learners use the language to investigate, explain, and reflect on the relationship between the products and perspectives of the cultures studied.

Connections

Connect with Other Disciplines and Acquire Information and Diverse Perspectives in order to Use the Language to Function in Academic and Career-Related Situations

Making Connections (formerly Standard 3.1): Learners build, reinforce, and expand their knowledge of other disciplines while using the language to develop critical thinking and to solve problems creatively.

Acquiring Information and Diverse Perspectives (formerly Standard 3.2): Learners access and evaluate information and diverse perspectives that are available through the language and its cultures.

Comparisons

Develop Insight into the Nature of Language and Culture in order to Interact with Cultural Competence

Language Comparisons (formerly Standard 4.1): Learners use the language to investigate, explain, and reflect on the nature of language through comparisons of the language studied and their own.

Cultural Comparisons (formerly Standard 4.2): Learners use the language to investigate, explain, and reflect on the concept of culture through comparisons of the cultures studied and their own.

Communities

Communicate and Interact with Cultural Competence in order to Participate in Multilingual Communities at Home and Around the World

School and Global Communities (formerly Standard 5.1): Learners use the language both within and beyond the classroom to interact and collaborate in their community and the globalized world.

Lifelong Learning (formerly Standard 5.2): Learners set goals and reflect on their progress in using languages for enjoyment, enrichment, and advancement.

Since a modern challenge in world language instruction is reaching all students—those with varying abilities, backgrounds, interests, and learning styles—the ***T'es branché?*** program has many opportunities beyond the textbook to help meet those needs. The Annotated Teacher's Edition provides suggested activities for different types of learners, from those with special needs to those who would benefit from enrichment. The Workbook contains Basic and Advanced activities so that students can make progress from where they begin and at their own pace. The online Grammar and Vocabulary Practice Games provide immediate feedback, allowing students to find out what they need more practice on well in advance of the test. Online Pre-tests also have immediate feedback, so that students can find out what they need to study more before their assessment experiences. Tailor-made products such as these ensure that each student makes progress and meets their potential as they embrace the French language and francophone culture.

Common Core State Standards

The Common Core State Standards (CCSS) initiative seeks to raise academic standards for students and provide articulation of academic standards between states. The CCSS is designed for courses in English Language Arts, History/Social Studies, Science, and Technical Subjects, each containing four strands: Reading, Writing, Speaking and Listening, and Language. Having CCSS drive curricula will result in new assessment benchmarks for students.

T'es branché? was designed with the CCSS in mind. It emphasizes the purpose behind the communication by labeling activities that provide interpersonal (speaking-listening or writing-reading), interpretive (reading, listening, viewing), and presentational (writing, speaking, representing visually) communication. The goal of the textbooks is to move students from novice, to intermediate, to advanced proficiency levels by the time they complete the ***T'es branché?*** four-level program. Connection activities in ***T'es branché?*** that are specific to history and science allow students to learn about francophone history and scientific contributions made by French speakers. Technology skills are developed, as in the readings of **Points de départ**, where students research online using search words provided, and the **Projets finaux**, which allow for individual, pair, and group work using technology such as the Internet, video, smartphones, and online programs. ***T'es branché?*** uses the CCSS to make sure all students are ready for post-secondary learning, working, and becoming global citizens. A correlation of ***T'es branché?*** to the CCSS is at the end of the Annotated Teacher's Edition front pages.

Bienvenue à *T'es branché?*!

Key Features: Student Textbook

The unit openers provide clear objectives and helpful hints.

Unité 4 Préparatifs de départ

Question centrale ? A

Qu'est-ce qu'on doit connaître de sa destination pour réussir son voyage ?

B

À savoir

Quatre Français sur dix partent en vacances d'hiver.

Citation

« Pour bien aimer un pays il faut le manger, le boire et l'entendre chanter. »

To really like a country, you must eat it, drink it, and hear it sing.

—Michel Déon (1919–2016), écrivain, dramaturge, et académicien français

Conseil pratique

When visiting a French website, make a list of words and expressions you have learned there. Then compare your list with a partner who has visited the same site.

C

Que dit Clémentine de son caractère ? Elle est comment ?

D

Dans quelle ville fête-on ce carnaval ?

Contrat de l'élève

Leçon A I will be able to:

- ask for an opinion and respond appropriately.
- discuss **La Réunion**, **la Corse**, **Chamonix**, **le Mont Blanc**, and **les Alpes**.
- use the present participle and negative expressions.

Leçon B I will be able to:

- say what I must do, tell someone they'll have an opportunity to do something, and say what I was expecting.
- discuss the **Savoie** region of France, **les classes de neige**, **Annecy**, and **Saint-Martin**.
- review **savoir** and **connaître** and use the subjunctive of regular and irregular verbs after **il faut que**.

Leçon C I will be able to:

- say I'm going to do a different activity and tell someone to avoid injury.
- discuss ski resorts in France and volunteer tourism in Francophone countries.
- use the subjunctive after impersonal expressions.

200 deux cents | Unité 4

Unité 4 | deux cent un 201

A Each unit is entered on an **Essential Question** that anchors learning.

B ***À savoir***, ***Citation***, and ***Conseil pratique*** present an interesting fact and quote connected to the unit theme, and a helpful hint for students.

C Each unit features an episode of the video program ***Rendez-vous à Nice !***. Students can scan the QR code to watch the episode.

D A culture question is accompanied by a photo. Students will watch for the answer in one of the culture readings of the unit.

E Learning objectives encourage the students to anticipate the unit content.

Themes such as technology, social media, music, and art motivate students to speak French!

Leçon A

Vocabulaire actif

La peinture et les mouvements d'art A

La peinture

Musée des Beaux-Arts 20 Place des Terreaux, 69001 Lyon

un musée des **beaux-arts** (m.) : musée dans lequel on peut trouver des peintures, des objets d'art, des sculptures, etc.

un atelier: pièce dans laquelle l'artiste travaille

une toile: support sur lequel le peintre **applique** les couleurs

un pinceau: sorte de brosse pour appliquer des couleurs sur la toile

Pour la conversation B

How do I say when a painting was painted?

» *Les Coquelicots* de Monet a été **peint** en 1873.
The Poppies by Monet was painted in 1873.

How do I describe an artist's approach?

» Avec ce tableau, Renoir recherche de plus en plus les effets de **lignes**.
With this painting, Renoir is looking more and more into the effects of lines.

» Avec **cette méthode**, Seurat **s'éloignait des impressionnistes**.
With this method, Seurat distanced himself from the Impressionists.

How do I describe the colors used in a painting?

» L'artiste a utilisé le jaune **pâle**.
The artist used pale yellow.

Et si je voulais dire... ? C

une aquarelle	*watercolor*
un cadre	*frame*
foncé	*dark (color)*
un fusain	*charcoal*
un modèle	*model*
une palette	*palette*
une gravure	*etching / engraving*
graver	*to etch / engrave*
poser	*to pose*

D

1 Une journée au musée des beaux-arts

Interpretive Reading

Lisez le blog d'un étudiant, puis répondez aux questions.

Bon d'accord, je ne suis pas un spécialiste de l'art, mais cette exposition ne m'a pas impressionné ! Tous les tableaux se ressemblent : des couleurs sombres, pas de couleur vive, pas de paysage, pas de nature morte, pas de portrait, juste des lignes. Il est évident que le peintre n'a pas besoin de travailler en plein air pour capturer ses sujets. Un atelier lui suffit ! Pourquoi a-t-il créé ces peintures ? Je ne pourrais pas le dire. J'ai observé les autres visiteurs, et ils semblaient s'intéresser aux œuvres d'art, mais je ne comprends pas pourquoi ! Je préfère l'art qui représente quelque chose. Les nouvelles techniques, les nouvelles méthodes, et les effets de lignes — à quoi ça sert ? J'ai quitté cette exposition pour en voir une autre sur la bande dessinée, un art que je peux comprendre.

Théo

1. Quelle est la réaction du blogueur aux tableaux qui sont exposés ?
2. Préfère-t-il l'art moderne ou l'art qui représente quelque chose ?
3. D'après le blogueur, où travaille le peintre ?
4. Quelle était la réaction des autres visiteurs du musée ?
5. Est-ce que le blogueur a aimé sa visite à l'exposition de peinture ?

2 La peinture française

Interpretive Reading

Complétez les phrases avec un mot ou une expression ci-dessous.

un atelier **une peinture** **au premier plan** **la toile** **en plein air**
un paysage **à l'arrière-plan** **une fête champêtre** **une nature morte** **un pinceau**

1. L'artiste-peintre utilise... pour étaler (*spread*) les couleurs sur la toile.
2. Le peintre met des couleurs vives sur....
3. Quand l'artiste travaille dans son espace personnel pour l'art à l'intérieur, il est dans....
4. Un artiste qui peint dehors (*outside*) travaille....
5. Une œuvre peinte exposée (*exhibited*) dans un musée s'appelle un tableau ou....
6. Les détails ou les personnages qui semblent être à une certaine distance sont... et ceux qui semblent être plus proches sont....
7. Une représentation de fruits, de fleurs, ou d'objets est....
8. Une scène avec une rivière au premier plan et des montagnes à l'arrière-plan est....
9. Une peinture du 18ème siècle représentant une fête dans un jardin ou un parc s'appelle....

A Active ***Vocabulaire*** is highlighted in red text or with a blue label, introduced with an image, and recorded by a native speaker.

B ***Pour la conversation*** elaborates on the vocabulary by teaching students grammar in context.

C ***Et si je voulais dire...?*** introduces additional words and expressions that relate to the active vocabulary.

D Listening comprehension activities are indicated with a headphone icon. The mode of communication practiced in each activity is highlighted in green font.

Additional features such as ***Connexions***, ***Produits***, ***Traditions et pratiques***, or review activities are provided throughout the unit.

Vocabulary and grammar are integrated in context.

Rencontres culturelles

Un hôtel à Monaco

A

Léo et Justin veulent réserver une chambre à Monaco.

Léo : La déscription de l'hôtel et les photos sont plutôt bien, mais c'est un peu cher.
Justin : Mais c'est Monte Carlo ! Moi, je trouve qu'ils sont très imprécis sur les prestations.
Léo : Ah ! Tu es bien américain : toujours le côté pratique.
Justin : Je te laisse la poésie des lieux monégasques et la vue imprenable sur la mer....
Léo : Tu veux qu'on leur téléphone ?
Justin : Oui, je vais le faire avec mon accent américain ! *(Au téléphone, Justin parle au réceptionniste.)* Bonjour, je voudrais que vous me donniez quelques précisions sur les prestations de l'hôtel.... Merci. Au revoir.
Léo : Alors ?
Justin : Ils ont le wifi*, des chaînes câblées, il y a un jacuzzi dans la chambre, et on peut prendre le petit déjeuner dans la chambre sans payer le supplément.
Léo : Parfait ! Réservons !

B

***Je parle bien !**
Le mot **wifi** se prononce comme **oui-fi**.

C

4 Un hôtel à Monaco

Répondez aux questions.

1. Est-ce que le prix d'un hôtel à Monaco est un peu cher ou bon marché ?
2. Sur quoi est-ce que Justin voudrait se renseigner ?
3. Est-ce que Léo est plus pratique que Justin ? Ou est-ce que Justin est plus pratique ?
4. Selon Justin, à quoi Léo s'intéresse ?
5. Que comprennent les prestations de l'hôtel ?

EXTENSION Les prestations désirées

Clément et Laurence aident leurs parents à chercher un bon hôtel pour leurs vacances en famille.

Clément : Bon alors, si tu veux le bain à remous, moi je veux les chaînes câblées et une connexion wifi.
Laurence : Tu ne vas quand même pas passer ton temps en vacances à regarder le sport à la télé !
Clément : Si, pendant que toi et maman serez au centre de remise en forme !
Laurence : Pour la connexion wifi d'accord : pas besoin de passer des heures à attendre un ordinateur libre au centre d'affaires.
Clément : Vérifie quand même qu'il y ait la climatisation dans cet hôtel.
Laurence : À Saint-Pierre et Miquelon, on n'en aura pas besoin !
Clément : Mais, Maman et Papa ont changé d'avis et préfèrent aller à Saint-Louis au Sénégal.

EXTENSION Quelles prestations désirent Laurence et Clément ? Où vont-ils passer leurs vacances ? Avec qui ?

Leçon A | deux cent soixante-neuf 269

Structure de la langue

D

Present Participle

Marie-Alix prend une photo en faisant de l'escalade.

The present participle is a verb form that ends in **–ant**. This ending corresponds to the suffix *–ing* in English. To form the present participle, add **–ant** to the stem of the **nous** form of the verb in the present tense.

Verb	*Nous* Stem	Present Participle
faire	fais-	**faisant**
attendre	attend-	**attendant**
finir	finiss-	**finissant**
aller	all-	**allant**
partir	part-	**partant**

Comparaisons

What is another function of the present participle in English? Is this also possible in French?

The teacher woke the *sleeping* student.
Le prof a réveillé l'élève **qui dormait**.

E

The three verbs indicated below have irregular present participles.

Verb	Present Participle
avoir	**ayant**
être	**étant**
savoir	**sachant**

The preposition **en** usually precedes the present participle. **En** means *while*, *upon*, *in*, or *on* if the two actions in the sentence take place at the same time.

En voyant la neige, mon frère a voulu faire de la luge. — *Upon seeing the snow, my brother wanted to go sledding.*

Nous ne regardons jamais la télé **en mangeant**. — *We never watch TV while eating.*

En means *by* if a cause-and-effect relationship is expressed.

C'est **en écoutant** le prof que tu pourras réussir à ton examen. — *By listening to the teacher, you will be able to pass the test.*

212 deux cent douze | Unité 4

A The ***Dialogue*** demonstrates how to apply the recently presented vocabulary and functions. Filmed on location, it is provided as audio and video for added practice.

B Additional **pronunciation** and **learning strategies** help students with comprehensible input. Additional products and practices are provided to tie the language and culture together.

C An ***Extension*** dialogue is provided as text and audio recording for advanced learners.

D ***Structure de la langue*** explains grammatical concepts clearly and concisely with charts, examples, and illustrations.

E A **Comparaisons** feature prompts students to **reflect** on their language learning and to **make comparisons** with their own.

Up-to-date culture topics expand the language learning.

Points de départ

Pre-AP | Question centrale ? Comment l'art est-il un reflet de la culture? **A**

L'impressionnisme

L'impressionnisme est un mouvement de la seconde moitié du 19ème siècle. Les peintres expriment* dans leurs tableaux les impressions que les objets et la lumière suscitent*. Les impressionnistes aiment peindre en plein air, pas dans un atelier. Quoique différents par leurs styles et leurs perspectives, les peintres associés à ce mouvement sont Édouard Manet, Claude Monet, Pierre-Auguste Renoir, l'Américaine Mary Cassatt, Camille Pissarro, Berthe Morisot, Edgar Degas, l'Anglais Alfred Sisley, Paul Cézanne, Armand Guillaumin, et Frédéric Bazille.

B **Recherche :** impressionnisme france, NOM DE L'ARTISTE + impressionnisme, mouvements artistiques france

exprimient *express* ; **suscitent** *spark*

Produits ***Impression, soleil levant*** (1872) est le tableau de Monet qui a donné le nom « impressionnisme » à ce nouveau mouvement artistique.

Comparaisons

Est-ce que le mouvement impressionniste aux États-Unis est venu avant ou après l'impressionnisme en France? Qui sont les maîtres de l'impressionnisme américain?

Mère et enfant, 1897. Mary Cassatt.

Impression, soleil levant, 1872. Claude Monet.

Près du lac, 1880. Pierre-Auguste Renoir.

Traditions et pratiques

Comme les peintres impressionnistes peignaient en plein air, ils ont représenté de nombreuses régions françaises, dépeignant (*picturing*) ainsi la côte de Normandie, la région de la Seine, Giverny avec ses nénuphars (*water lilies*), la Provence, et les paysages méditerranéens de la Côte d'Azur.

C

Leçon A | trois cent quatre-vingt-cinq 385

La Francophonie

D

Art et traditions

En Afrique de l'Ouest

L'art africain traditionnel est essentiellement composé de produits artisanaux*. L'artisanat correspond à la fabrication d'objets, principalement en bois ou en bronze, tels des masques, statues, armes, ou d'autres objets traditionnels comme des poteries ou encore les vêtements. Ces arts sont considérés des Arts premiers. Ils sont à l'image des thèmes ou scènes de la vie de tous les jours de groupes ethniques particuliers, telles les statues tribales Ashanti du Ghana, ou Bambara du Mali. Il en est de même* pour la fabrication d'instruments de musique : les congas* en bois et peau de chèvre*, les balafons*, les cloches*, reflètent un lien entre l'expression artistique et la nature dans les cultures africaines.

La peinture africaine a toujours été décorative, privilégiant* les bas-reliefs plutôt que les représentations bidimensionnelles* propres aux cultures occidentales*. De l'art traditionnel, dit « naïf », aux formes géométriques simples et aux couleurs primaires, à l'art populaire qui donne de nouvelles formes aux matériaux naturels (fresques, portraits, posters), la peinture africaine contemporaine reflète l'évolution et les contradictions des réalités urbaines. La peinture africaine est à l'origine des grands mouvements occidentaux tels le cubisme (Pablo Picasso), le néo-impressionnisme, et la peinture murale. Il est important de comprendre les liens indissociables entre l'Afrique et l'Occident dans la peinture moderne, car bien souvent, les peintres africains contemporains s'inscrivent dans les mouvements occidentaux de peinture, tel Chéri Samba, peintre congolais, dont l'art figuratif a été exposé à Paris et à New York.

Recherche : l'art africain traditionnel, produits artisanaux africains, peintres africains, chéri samba

produits artisanaux *crafts* ; **Il en est de même** *It is the same* ; **conga** *drum-like instrument* ; **peau de chèvre** *goat skin* ; **balafon** *xylophone-like instrument* ; **cloches** *bells* ; **privilégiant** *favoring* ; **bidimensionnelle** *two-dimensional* ; **occidentales** *Western*

L'art africain est connu pour ses sculptures et objets artisanaux.

Le Nid dans le nid, 1996. Chéri Samba.

Leçon A | trois cent quatre-vingt-sept 387

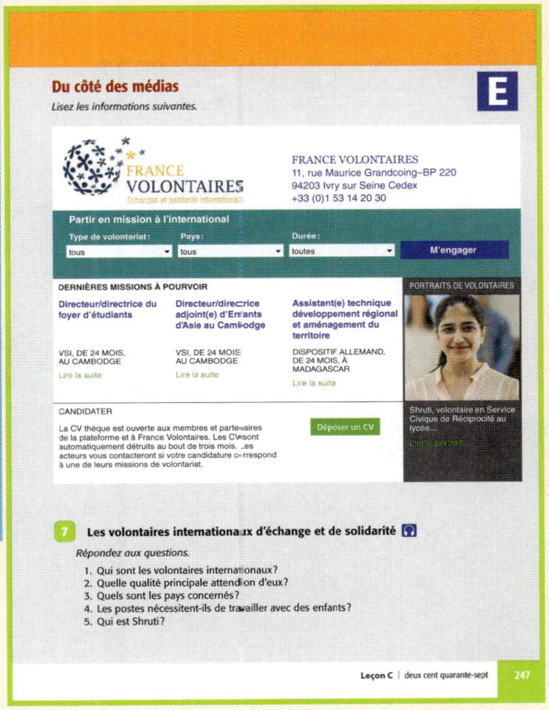

Du côté des médias

E

Lisez les informations suivantes.

FRANCE VOLONTAIRES
Échanges et solidarité internationale

FRANCE VOLONTAIRES
11, rue Maurice Grandcoing–BP 220
94203 Ivry sur Seine Cedex
+33 (0)1 53 14 20 30

Partir en mission à l'international
Type de volontariat : tous | Pays : tous | Durée : toutes | M'engager

DERNIÈRES MISSIONS À POURVOIR

Directeur/directrice du foyer d'étudiants	Directeur/directrice adjoint(e) d'Enfants d'Asie au Cambodge	Assistant(e) technique développement régional et aménagement du territoire
VSI, DE 24 MOIS, AU CAMBODGE	VSI, DE 24 MOIS AU CAMBODGE	DISPOSITIF ALLEMAND, DE 24 MOIS, À MADAGASCAR
Lire la suite	Lire la suite	Lire la suite

PORTRAITS DE VOLONTAIRES

Shruti, volontaire en Service Civique de Réciprocité au lycée...

Lire le portrait

CANDIDATER

La CV thèque est ouverte aux membres et partenaires de la plateforme et à France Volontaires. Les CV sont automatiquement détruits au bout de trois mois. Les acteurs vous contacteront si votre candidature correspond à une de leurs missions de volontariat.

Déposer un CV

7 Les volontaires internationaux d'échange et de solidarité

Répondez aux questions.

1. Qui sont les volontaires internationaux?
2. Quelle qualité principale attend-on d'eux?
3. Quels sont les pays concernés?
4. Les postes nécessitent-ils de travailler avec des enfants?
5. Qui est Shruti?

Leçon C | deux cent quarante-sept 247

A Students are guided by the **Essential Question** to uncover the depth and richness of francophone cultures. They are also prepared as AP learners.

B ***Recherche*** provide blended-learning opportunities and encourage students to research at their own pace using French keywords.

C Culture paragraphs are enhanced with **Products**, **Practices**, or **Perspectives**, which guide AP students to reflect on various aspects of the culture.

D ***La Francophonie*** connects with the francophone world by zooming in on a particular place or country where French is spoken.

E Students read and interpret authentic sources in ***Du côté des médias***.

Going beyond the basics!

Prononciation A

Pauses and Intonation in a Sentence

» Commas indicate pauses at the beginning or in the middle of a sentence. In French, there is typically rising intonation before a comma or an exclamation point (**intonation montante**). There is typically falling intonation before a period (**intonation descendante**).

A L'intonation montante et descendante

Répétez les phrases, en faisant attention à l'intonation.

1. Écoutez, nous, on prend du poisson.
2. À mon avis, ça sera très bien!
3. Bienvenue, Messieurs-Dames, à La Belle Époque!
4. Il n'y a pas grand-chose, sur cette carte!
5. Je n'aime pas le poisson, moi.
6. Ici, c'est un très bon restaurant.

B L'intonation est montante ou descendante?

*Écoutez les phrases. Écrivez **MONT** si vous entendez une intonation montante à la fin de la phrase, ou **DESC** si vous entendez une intonation descendante à la fin de la phrase.*

The Sound /ə/

» Native French speakers tend to cut out certain sounds, especially the pronunciation of the sound /ə/. Generally, the /ə/ is pronounced when it falls between three or more pronounced consonants, but is dropped at the end of a word and between two pronounced consonants.

Pronounced: CC ə C	Unpronounced: C ə C
Il insistera.	Il bougera.

B

» The style in which one speaks greatly affects whether or not the /ə/ is pronounced. The more relaxed the style is, the more often the /ə/ is dropped.

C Prononciation du /ə/ interne

Répétez les phrases suivantes, faisant attention à prononcer le /ə/ lorsqu'il est souligné en caractère gras (bold).

1. Je mets mon portefeuille dans mon vêtement.
2. Nous dînons simplement le dimanche.

D Registre courant, familier, et populaire

Écoutez et répétez les phrases. Notez combien de fois vous entendez le son /ə/ pour chaque style.

	Courant	Familier	Populaire
1.	Maintenant, je vais à la boulangerie.	Maintenant, je vais à la boulangerie.	Maintenant, je vais à la boulangerie.
2.	Je ne veux pas acheter de bottes.	Je ne veux pas acheter de bottes.	Je ne veux pas acheter de bottes.

E Registre courant, familier, ou populaire?

*Écrivez **C** si vous entendez le registre courant, **F** si vous entendez le registre familier, ou **P** si vous entendez le registre populaire.*

Culture sur place C

Question centrale ? Qu'est-ce qu'on doit connaître de sa destination pour réussir son voyage? D

Les voyages volontaires

Introduction et interrogations

Dans la **Leçon C**, on vous a informé sur les voyages volontaires qui attirent les jeunes Français. Votre but est de définir le volontarisme pour vous et vos camarades de classe. Comment est-ce que vous voulez aider les autres? Que signifient les mots «bénévole» et «humanitaire» pour vous?

8 Réfléchir

Pensez à vos préférences et à vos expériences. Qu'est-ce vous aimez (ou aimeriez) faire comme travail bénévole ou humanitaire? Servez-vous des informations suivantes:

- construire ou réparer une maison
- travailler avec des jeunes ou des personnes âgées
- enseigner l'anglais
- préserver l'environnement
- fournir de l'eau propre
- autre chose

Trouvez deux ou trois camarades de classe qui ont les mêmes intérêts que vous. Faites des recherches sur Internet pour identifier une communauté où ce genre de travail ferait le plus grand bien.

9 Préparer

En groupes, imaginez que vous voulez commencer votre projet bénévole ou humanitaire dans un autre pays, mais que vous avez besoin d'un bienfaiteur (benefactor) pour vous donner de l'argent. Préparez une présentation pour ce bienfaiteur. La présentation doit inclure:

- une description de votre projet (où, quand, comment, qui, etc.)
- une description des objectifs de votre projet (pourquoi; résultats attendus)
- une liste de provisions ou de ressources pour le projet
- une liste des bénéficiaires du projet (à qui s'adresse le projet; combien de personnes devraient pouvoir en bénéficier)

10 Faire le point! E

Discutez de ces questions en classe.

1. Quels sont les différents centres d'intérêt de vos camarades de classe vis-à-vis (*regarding*) du travail bénévole ou humanitaire?
2. Si votre classe faisait les projets proposés par chaque groupe, où iriez-vous? Qu'est-ce que vous feriez?
3. Comment est-ce que vous définiriez les mots «volontarisme», «bénévole», et «humanitaire» aujourd'hui?

A A **pronunciation** section appears at the end of each ***Leçon A***, written and recorded by native speakers.

B In this section, stressed letters have been bolded and underlined, and unpronounced letters have been grayed out and underlined, to help students who learn visually.

C ***Culture sur place*** encourages students to investigate and make cultural comparisons through hands-on activities, surveys, interviews, and research.

D Activities encourage students to reflect on culture through the **Essential Question**.

E AP and IB students benefit from activities that build communities, and from interpretive readings presented as charts and graphs that help them organize their thoughts.

Students develop proficiency through communicative activities.

À vous la parole A

B Question centrale ? Comment l'art est-il un reflet de la culture?

Communiquez!

17 J'interprète un poème

Interpretive Reading, Presentational Speaking

Trouvez un poème francophone que vous aimez. Présentez ce poème devant votre classe. Soyez sûr(e) de (d'):

- choisir un poème de huit vers (*lines*) minimum.
- lire le poème plusieurs fois.
- chercher les mots que vous ne comprenez pas.
- écrire une introduction qui présente le titre, le nom du poète, et le sujet ou le thème du poème.
- pratiquer devant un miroir.

Recherche: prévert, baudelaire, rimbaud, apollinaire, hugo

18 En Haïti

Interpretive Writing C

Vous avez appris qu'Haïti a une culture et une histoire très riches en traditions créoles. Voici des idiomes créoles avec leurs traductions littérales. En vous aidant d'Internet, cherchez une meilleure traduction qui explique mieux le sens. Enfin, recherchez une expression équivalente en anglais.

1. **Dwèt ou se pa'w, ou pa kab koupe'l jete**
   Literally: Your fingers are yours. You can't cut them off.
2. **Lave men, siye atè**
   Literally: Wash your hands, [only to] wipe them on the ground.
3. **Wòch nan chodyè goute grès gras a diri**
   Literally: Little rocks that get mixed with rice (during harvest) will taste the richness of grease thanks to the rice.
4. **Lè ti poul fè dan**
   Literally: When cows fly.
5. **Pye, sa'm te manje m'pat ba ou**
   Literally: Feet, what did I eat that I did not share with you?
6. **Pye kout pran devan**
   Literally: Short legs go first.

19 La poésie: Un conte numérique

Presentational Writing

Vous allez écrire un conte numérique (présentation digitale) en vous servant de six mots de vocabulaire de la *Leçon C* (par exemple: **cueillir**, **la vieillesse**, **un corbeau**, **un renard**, **mentir**, **l'aube**, **demeurer**, **le brouillard**, **cacher**). Après l'avoir écrit, choisissez des images et de la musique pour embellir (*to embellish*) votre conte. Finalement, mettez votre conte en ligne avec ceux de vos camarades de classe pour comparer vos contes.

430 quatre cent trente | Unité 7

Stratégie communicative D

Pre-AP

Communiquez!

Write a Comparison-Contrast Essay

Comparer quelque chose c'est montrer les similarités qui existent entre deux choses. Contraster c'est montrer ce qui les différencie. Lorsqu'on écrit une rédaction, on compare et on contraste. C'est très simple, il y a deux manières d'organiser ses idées; vous pouvez comparer et contraster un élément à la fois (point par point) ou tout écrire sur le premier élément et ensuite passer au second (tout d'un bloc).

1. Choisissez deux tableaux, chansons, styles de musique, ou artistes que vous comparerez et opposerez. Préparez un diagramme de Venn dans lequel vous montrerez les similarités et les différences qui existent entre les deux.

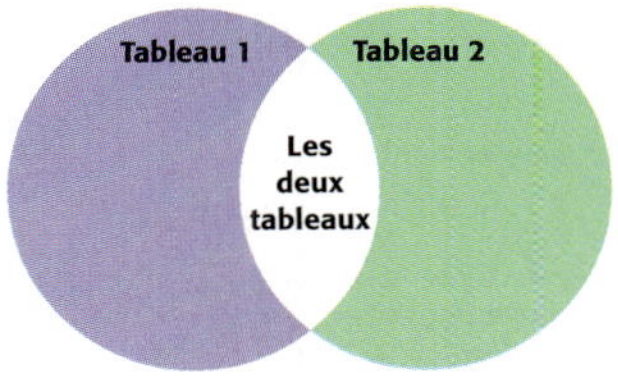

2. Complétez votre organigramme en utilisant les mots ci-dessous pour comparer et contraster:

Similarités	Differences
ressembler à	par contre
tous (toutes) deux	cependant
aussi	mais
également	bien que/qu'
(tout) comme	s'opposer: *Les couleurs s'opposent.*
comparé(e) à	pendant que
tel, telle: *Elle est grande, telle sa mère.*	contrairement à
le même, la même	en comparaison de: *Il est triste, en comparaison de la fille.*

3. Il est également utile d'utiliser le comparatif dans ce type de rédaction.
   Le tableau de Monet est plus sombre que le tableau de Renoir en ce qui concerne l'atmosphère.
   Vous pouvez aussi comparer des noms en utilisant la structure suivante:
   Il y a autant de personnages dans le tableau de Renoir que dans l'autre, mais ceux du tableau de Renoir ont l'air plus heureux.
4. Remettez votre rédaction à un(e) camarade de classe. Il s'assurera que vous avez:
   - suivi le schéma d'organisation.
   - inclu une thèse et un fait sur le sujet.
   - inclu votre point de vue.
   - fait une conclusion.
5. Mettez au propre et publiez en ligne ou partagez votre rédaction avec votre classe.

412 quatre cent douze | Unité 7

A ***À vous la parole*** is a communicative section, signaled by the green *Communiquez!* speech bubble.

B Students reflect on the **Essential Question** as they do a variety of targeted communicative activities.

C Each mode of communication is in green text for easy reference.

D ***Stratégie communicative*** is a communicative section, signaled by the green *Communiquez!* speech bubble. It focuses on one aspect of the language at a time, which students practice and integrate to improve their communication skills.

Students are exposed to literary and informal reading material.

Lecture thématique A

Pre-AP

Heureux qui, comme Ulysse, a fait un beau voyage

Rencontre avec l'auteur

Joachim Du Bellay (1522–1560) était un poète de la Renaissance française qui a fait ses études dans un collège humaniste. Il a écrit son recueil (*collection*) de poèmes *Les regrets* pendant un long séjour en Italie, destination de beaucoup de jeunes Français et artistes qui voulaient voir la grandeur de l'Italie antique et les chefs-d'œuvre de la Renaissance. En 1533, avec Ronsard, il a fondé un groupe de poètes, la Pléiade, dont le but était de définir de nouvelles règles poétiques. Il est mort très jeune, à 37 ans, et on l'a enterré à Notre-Dame de Paris. Son poème le plus célèbre est celui que vous allez lire. Le poète est-il content à Rome ou est-ce qu'il a des regrets?

Pré-lecture

Quel voyage est-ce que vous voudriez faire?

Stratégie de lecture

Structure, Meaning, and Theme. Ce poème est un sonnet en alexandrins avec deux quatrains et deux tercets; un quatrain est une strophe (*stanza*) avec quatre vers, tandis qu'un tercet en a trois. Dans ces quatre strophes, le poète développe un thème. Remplissez l'organigramme en indiquant l'idée centrale de chaque strophe; au centre mettez le thème du poème.

Strophe 1 :
Strophe 2 :
Thème :
Strophe 4 :
Strophe 3 :

Outils de lecture

Allusions. Une allusion est une référence à une personne, un événement, un objet, ou une oeuvre de l'histoire ou de la littérature. Du Bellay se sert de deux allusions classiques. Vous les trouverez dans les deux premiers vers du poème. Recherchez ces deux allusions mythiques. Comment est-ce qu'elles renforcent son idée d'un «beau voyage»?

B

«Heureux qui, comme Ulysse»

Heureux qui, comme Ulysse, a fait un beau voyage,
Ou comme cestuy-là*, qui conquit* la toison*,
Et puis est retourné, plein d'usage et raison,
Vivre entre ses parents le reste de son âge!

Quand reverrai-je, hélas*, de mon petit village
Fumer la cheminée, et en quelle saison
Reverrai-je le clos* de ma pauvre maison,
Qui m'est une province, et beaucoup davantage*?

Plus me plaît le séjour* qu'ont bâti* mes aïeux,
Que des palais Romains le front audacieux,
Plus que le marbre* dur me plaît l'ardoise* fine:

Plus mon Loir gaulois*, que le Tibre* latin,
Plus mon petit Liré, que le mont Palatin,
Et plus que l'air marin* la doulceur* angevine*.

Pendant la lecture
1. Qui a fait un beau voyage?

Pendant la lecture
2. Qui est retourné «plein d'usage et raison»?

Pendant la lecture
3. Quel mot indique le regret?

Pendant la lecture
4. À quoi pense le poète?

Pendant la lecture
5. Quel matériel vient de sa région, le marbre ou l'ardoise?

Pendant la lecture
6. Où sont le Tibre et le mont Palatin?

Pendant la lecture
7. Où est-ce que le poète préfère vivre, à Rome ou dans les pays de la Loire?

cestuy-là celui-là (Ancien français); **conquit** *conquered*; **toison** *Golden Fleece*; **hélas** *alas*; **clos** *property*; **davantage** *more*; **séjour** *dwelling*; **bâti** *built*; **marbre** *marble*; **ardoise** *slate (used on roofs in Loire Valley)*; **gaulois** *gallic, or French*; **Tibre** *Tiber* (fleuve à Rome); **air marin** *sea air*; **doulceur [archaic]** *sweetness*; **angevine** *from/of the Angers area*

Le monde visuel C

Sébastien Bourdon (1616–1671), peintre français, a peint *Ulysse découvre Astyanax caché dans le tombeau d'Hector* dans le style classique. Les peintres de mouvement s'intéressaient aux sujets classiques de la tradition grecque et romaine comme les histoires d'Ulysse, roi d'Ithaque, leader dans la guerre de Troie, et voyageur par excellence pour ses aventures en revenant de la guerre. Les classiques aimaient la proportion, les couleurs vives, et la formalité. Ils peignaient leurs sujets dans les vêtements de leur époque, souvent parmi des urnes et des piliers (*pillers*). La composition de ces tableaux est souvent symétrique. Quelles sont les caractéristiques classiques de ce tableau?

Ulysse découvre Astyanax caché dans le tombeau d'Hector, c. 1654–1656. Sébastien Bourdon. Collection privée.

A ***Lecture thématique*** prepares students to approach a literary text with information about the author, pre-reading activities, and a reading strategy.

B The literary selection is provided as interpretive reading and listening. ***Pendant la lecture*** questions guide students' comprehension.

C ***Le monde visuel*** increases the depth of literacy using art as yet another support of thoughts and statements.

Analyse has students reflect on and analyze words, expressions, or language in general.

Projects, 21st-century skills, and language learning are mutually beneficial

Système D **A**

Pre-AP 21

Question centrale ? Qu'est-ce qu'on doit connaître de sa destination pour réussir son voyage?

Communiquez!

19 Les globe-trotters

B

Connecting to Civic Literacy, Health Literacy, Productivity and Accountability
Interpersonal Speaking, Interpretive Reading, Presentational Writing

Les règles et formalités pour visiter un pays changent selon la nationalité du voyageur et le pays qu'il veut visiter.

1ère Partie: Avec un partenaire, choisissez trois pays francophones de différentes régions du monde. Faites des recherches sur les papiers à obtenir et les règles à suivre pour visiter ces pays depuis les États-Unis. Complétez un diagramme comme celui de dessous: ajoutez les spécifications que vous désirez ou que vous trouverez. Ensuite, visitez le site web de l'Office du Tourisme des États-Unis et comparez ce que les voyageurs venant de chacun de ces pays francophones doivent faire pour visiter les États-Unis.

Pays	Nationalité des voyageurs	Documentation d'entrée	Durée maximum du voyage	Documentation de santé/ vaccins	Activités/ endroits interdits	Autre
Pays 1	américain					
Pays 2	français					
Pays 3	congolais					

Recherche: ambassade de (+ PAYS) aux états-unis; office du tourisme (+ PAYS)

2ème Partie: Avec les informations que vous avez trouvées, jouez les rôles d'un(e) touriste américain(e) dans l'un des pays francophones que vous avez recherchés, et d'un(e) employé(e) de l'ambassade de ce pays. Le ou la touriste posera des questions sur les règles du pays et l'employé(e) pourra se servir des informations dans le diagramme pour lui répondre et faire des recommandations.

3ème Partie: Trouvez un groupe qui a recherché au moins un pays en commun avec vous. Comparez vos informations, puis expliquez comment les règles sont différentes d'un pays à l'autre. Donnez des suggestions pour faire un long voyage dans chaque pays.

20 Voyagez en groupe!

C

Connecting to Collaboration, Flexibility and Adaptability
Interpersonal Speaking, Presentational Writing and Speaking

Votre classe veut organiser un voyage en groupe dans un pays que vous n'avez jamais visité et où chacun(e) pourra faire quelque chose qu'il ou elle n'a jamais fait.

Préparez trois à quatre questions à poser à un minimum de dix personnes, pour découvrir quelles activités vos camarades n'ont jamais faites et voudraient faire. En fonction des résultats de votre sondage, recommandez un pays étranger à visiter, et des activités à faire en groupe. Présentez un itinéraire de voyage à votre classe en expliquant vos choix.

256 deux cent cinquante-six | Unité 4

Finale

Question centrale ? Qu'est-ce qu'on doit connaître de sa destination pour réussir son voyage?

Projets finaux **D**

A Connexions par Internet: la littérature

Un storyboard

Dans cette unité vous avez lu le poème «Heureux qui, comme Ulysse, a fait un beau voyage» de Du Bellay. Cherchez le dessin animé de Ridan et découvrez son interprétation du poème. Ensuite, créez un storyboard où vous dessinez votre propre vidéo du poème qui en montre votre interprétation.

Recherche: ridan heureux qui comme ulysse vidéo

B Communautés en ligne

Le chien du Saint-Bernard

Visitez un club pour les passionnés du chien du Saint-Bernard et trouvez les réponses à ces questions:

- Quelle est la devise du chien du Saint-Bernard?
- Comment est-il physiquement?
- Comment décrit-on son caractère?
- Il est connu pour quels exploits?
- Il a quels problèmes de santé?
- C'est la vedette de quels films?
- Il faut payer combien pour avoir un chien du Saint-Bernard?

Recherche: chien du saint-bernard

C Passez à l'action!

Le WWOOFing: un voyage volontaire

Créez un document qui décrit ce qu'est le WWOOFing. Faites une carte qui montre dans quels pays francophones on peut faire du WWOOFing. Faites une liste de dix projets qui vous intéressent. Avec votre classe, choisissez parmi tous les projets, un projet que vous pourriez sponsoriser. Contactez l'organisation bénévole pour savoir s'ils préféreraient recevoir de l'argent ou du matériel. Organisez une collecte auprès de votre lycée.

D Faisons le point!

Mes progrès

Servez-vous de l'organigramme que votre prof va vous donner. Remplissez-le avec ce que vous avez appris.

Leçon C | deux cent cinquante-sept 257

A ***Système D*** is designed for students to apply unit vocabulary and structures to communicative activities that foster 21st-century skills.

B Activities encourage students to expand their knowledge and contribute to their own learning process.

C For easy reference, red headings indicate the particular 21st-century skills targeted, while green headings indicate the modes of communication being practiced.

D **Final projects** allow students to work in pairs or small or large groups in order to benefit from one another's contributions. Projects may be used as formative assessments.

Evaluating student's progress and performance

Question centrale ? Comment l'art est-il un reflet de la culture?

D Faisons le point! A

Diagramme

Faites un diagramme comme celui de dessous et remplissez-le pour montrer vos connaissances de l'art comme reflet de la culture. Un exemple a été fait pour vous.

Leçon A **Rencontres culturelles:** Les impressionnistes montrent la société de quel siècle? →	Les impressionnistes montrent comment vivaient les gens du 19ème siècle.
Leçon A **Rencontres culturelles:** Pourquoi est-ce que le tableau impressionniste *Impression, soleil levant* était-il révolutionnaire? →	
Leçon A **Points de départ: Le néo-impressionnisme:** Qu'est-ce que les néo-impressionnistes ont ajouté au processus artistique? →	
Leçon A **Points de départ: La Francophonie:** Quels objets les artistes africains fabriquent-ils? →	
Leçon B **Rencontres culturelles:** Quels genres de musique les Français ont-ils apprécié de 1945 jusqu'à aujourd'hui? →	
Leçon B **Points de départ:** Les musiciens contemporains en France s'intéressent à quels genres de musique? →	
Leçon B **Points de départ:** Quel est un genre de musique québécois? →	
Leçon B **Points de départ: Perspectives:** Quel est le rôle et l'influence du chanteur français, selon Georges Brassens? →	

B Pre-AP

Évaluation

A Évaluation de compréhension auditive

*Écoutez Kevin et Annie discuter de leurs intérêts artistiques. Ensuite, indiquez si chaque phrase que vous entendez est vraie (**V**) ou fausse (**F**).*

B Évaluation orale

À tour de rôle, jouez les rôles d'un(e) ado américain(e) et d'un(e) ado français(e). Avant de commencer, l'élève qui joue le rôle de l'ado américain(e) doit écrire des notes sur ce qu'il/elle sait d'un chanteur/d'une chanteuse américain(e) de son choix. L'élève qui joue le rôle de l'ado français(e) doit rechercher un chanteur ou une chanteuse français(e) pour ses notes.

Dans votre conversation, comparez vos artistes en ce qui concerne:

- leurs genres
- les albums ou les chansons qui leur ont valu d'immense succès
- le public qu'ils ont séduit (les ados? les adultes? leurs pays?)
- leurs thèmes

Finalement, choisissez un album de votre artiste à prêter à votre ami(e) et dites pourquoi il faut qu'il/elle l'écoute. Servez-vous des expressions dans Pour la conversation.

C Évaluation culturelle

Vous allez comparer les cultures francophones à votre culture. Vous aurez peut-être besoin de faire des recherches sur la culture américaine.

1. **L'impressionnisme**
   Qui sont les maîtres de l'impressionnisme en France? Comment ces peintres ont-ils transformé la façon de peindre? Quel impressionniste préférez-vous? Pourquoi? Qui sont les impressionnistes de l'école américaine? Lesquels aimez-vous? Pourquoi?
2. **L'art traditionnel**
   Comparez les objets traditionnels fabriqués en Afrique de l'Ouest aux objets fabriqués en Amérique par les Amérindiens.
3. **Les auteurs-compositeurs-interprètes contemporains**
   Qui sont les grands auteurs-compositeurs-interprètes contemporains en France et en Amérique? Comparez-les.

A In every odd-numbered unit, ***Faisons le point!*** asks students to self-evaluate and keep track of their progress. You may direct them to use "I can" statements based on the unit objectives in the **student contract** at the beginning of the unit.

In every even-numbered unit, ***Faisons le point!*** asks students to respond to the **Essential Question** by analyzing various texts in each lesson. The complete graphic organizer may be found in the Copy Masters supplement.

B The **Évaluation** section provides formal assessment opportunities for speaking, listening, reading and writing. These activities may also be used as pre-tests.

Preparation for Pre-AP starting at Level 1!

Vocabulaire de l'Unité 4 A

abandonner to abandon C
s' **attendre (à)** to expect (something) B; **Je m'y attendais** I was expecting that B
avoir: avoir l'occasion (de) to have the opportunity (to) B
aucun(e) any, none, no one A; **aucun de nous ne (+ VERB)** none of us (+ VERB) A
un **bâton de ski** ski pole B
le **bénévolat** volunteer work C
se **casser: se casser le poignet** to break one's wrist C
un **casque de ski** ski goggles B
les **chaussures (f.) de ski** ski boots B
une **classe de neige** ski class B
le **consulat** consulate C
correctement correctly B
de: de toute façon in any case B
différemment differently A
dire: (NOUN +) te dit? How do you feel about (+ NOUN)? A
le **domaine** property C
emporter to take (away) C
en upon, while A; **en skiant** while skiing B; **en y réfléchissant bien** on second thought A; **en y regardant de plus près** on a closer look A
s' **ennuyer** to get bored A
faire: faire du canyonisme to go canyoning A; **faire du deltaplane** to go hang gliding A; **faire de la motoneige** to snowmobile C; **faire de la luge** to go sledding C; **faire de la planche à voile** to wind surf A; **faire de la raquette à neige** to go snowshoeing C; **faire de l'escalade** to rock climb A; **faire du parapente** to go paragliding A; **faire des sauts à ski** to go off ski jumps A; **faire du saut à l'élastique** to bungee jump A; **faire du ski de fond** to cross-country ski A; **faire du ski joering** to skijor C; **faire du ski de piste** to ski downhill C; **faire du ski hors-piste** to backcountry ski C; **faire du snowboard** to snowboard B; **faire du speed riding** to speed ride C; **faire du taxi-ski** to take a ski-taxi ride C; **faire du télémark** to telemark ski C; **faire le coup (à quelqu'un)** to play a trick (on someone) A; **faire sa valise** to pack B; **faire une randonnée équestre** to go on a trail ride A; **faire un séjour** to stay C
se **faire vacciner** to get vaccinated C
un **forfait de ski** ski pass B
se **fouler la cheville** to sprain an ankle C
des **gants (m.)** gloves B
le **hors-piste** off-road skiing C
humide humid A
il: il est essentiel que it's essential that C; **il est indispensable que** it's indispensable that C; **il est important que** it's important that C; **il est surprenant que** it's surprising that C; **il est utile que** it's useful that C; **il se pourrait que** it's possible that C; **il vaut mieux que** it's better that C
une **île** island A
un **moniteur, une monitrice** instructor B
ne: ne (n')... aucun(e) no, none, not any, not one A; **ne (n')... ni... ni** neither... nor A; **ne (n')... que** only A
obtenir to obtain C
l' **office (m.) de tourisme** tourist office C
organisé(e) organized B
un **pantalon (de) ski** ski pants B
le **passé** past C
un **passeport** passport C
persuadé(e) convinced A
une **pièce d'identité** identification (document) C
une **piste (de ski)** (ski) slope B
planifier to plan A
les **préparatifs (m.) de départ** travel preparations C
se **renseigner** to get information C
La **Réunion** Reunion A
sans aucun doute without a doubt A
seulement only A
un **ski** ski A
le **snowboard** snowboarding C
le **sommet** peak A
une **station de ski** ski resort B
sur: sur place on the premises B
un **télésiège** ski lift B
tout(e): tout schuss full throttle A
un **tremplin de saut à ski** ski jump B
tu: tu n'y es pas du tout you don't get it A
une **veste (de) ski** ski jacket B
le **Vietnam** Vietnam C
un **visa** visa C
un **volcan** volcano A

Bilan cumulatif B

Pre-AP

Multiple Choice

I. Interpretive Communication: Print texts

Lisez ce reportage sur les initiatives en France aujourd'hui, puis répondez à la question.

Les jeunes et le bricolage? Certains d'entre eux ont anticipé une opportunité incroyable de créer une petite société qui offrirait des services de réparation, d'entretien et de rénovation dans les condos, HLM, maisons individuelles et maisons mitoyennes. Ils offrent toutes sortes de projets de bricolage—peindre les murs, poser le papier peint, accrocher des peintures, changer la moquette ou installer du parquet en bois.

1. Selon cet article, cette initiative s'est créée parce que....
   A. c'est une affaire familiale de père en fils
   B. le gouvernement encourage les jeunes à être créatifs
   C. le bricolage n'est pas très à la mode avec les jeunes
   D. les jeunes sont des entrepreneurs.

II. Interpretive Communication: Audio texts

Écoutez le dialogue deux fois, puis répondez aux questions en choisissant la lettre de la réponse correcte.

1. Où est-ce que Nora et Bruno vont faire du ski?
   A. dans les Vosges
   B. en Savoie
   C. dans les Pyrénées
   D. en Italie
2. Quand ils ont planifié le voyage, qu'est-ce qu'ils ont décidé de faire avant de partir?
   A. réserver un condo
   B. obtenir des forfaits de ski
   C. acheter des billets de train
   D. A, B, et C
3. Qu'est-ce qui est vrai en ce qui concerne Bruno?
   A. Il sait bien faire du ski alpin.
   B. Il a déjà goûté à la raclette savoyarde.
   C. Il veut faire du taxi-ski et de la luge.
   D. Il n'a ni skis ni bâtons, mais il compte les louer sur place.

Free response

III. Presentational Writing: Persuasive Essay

Vous allez écrire un essai persuasif basé sur une source que vous allez lire d'abord. Votre but est de présenter les différents points de vue soulevés par la source, puis de donner votre propre point de vue. Utilisez des exemples précis de la source pour soutenir votre point de vue.

IV. Interpresonal Speaking: Conversation

Vous allez avoir une conversation avec Marc, un collègue qui enseigne dans la même école que vous. Ensemble, vous allez parler des préparatifs pour la classe de neige de l'hiver prochain. Suivez les indications suivantes.

Marc: Le directeur de l'école m'a demandé de vous aider à planifier la classe de neige. Il faut réserver le séjour bien à l'avance. L'Italie? La Suisse? Qu'en pensez-vous?

Vous: **Parlez des stations que vous connaissez en Savoie et de vos préférences.**

Marc: Vous avez raison. Pas besoin d'aller trop loin pour trouver de la neige. Je vais m'occuper de l'hébergement, des billets de train et des cours de ski.

Vous: **Demandez ce que les élèves doivent emporter dans leurs valises.**

Marc: Nous aurons l'occasion d'en parler lors des réunions avec les parents d'élèves. N'oublions pas l'importance de l'assurance médicale pour tout le monde!

Vous: **Rappelez au collègue que vous avez peur des accidents sur la piste.**

Marc: Rassurez-vous! Les moniteurs vont nous accompagner. Nous ne faisons pas de ski hors-piste! Mais, avez-vous des idées pour des cours?

Vous: **Parlez des activités scolaires et culturelles que vous pouvez ajouter au programme.**

Marc: Ça vous dit de fêter la fin de la semaine avec un repas spécial pour tout le groupe au chalet?

Vous: **Suggérez qu'on prépare des spécialités savoyardes.**

Marc: Nous mettrons des photos sur le blog du voyage. Je ne m'attendais pas à avoir tant à faire pour organiser un tel voyage. Heureusement que vous êtes bien organisé(e)!

A An end-of-unit vocabulary list clarifies active vocabulary words and expressions that students are responsible for learning.

B The ***Bilan cumulatif*** occurs in every other unit. It includes information learned in the previous two units. Students are tested on their skills and knowledge in a format that resembles that of the AP test.

Key Features: Teacher's Edition

In the side margins

Resources — A

- Audio
- Video
- Pre-AP Listening
- eVisual
- Workbook
- Listening Activities
- G & V Practice Games
- Flash Cards
- Communicative Activities
- Quiz
- Pre-test
- Test
- Explore
- Perform
- Share
- Create

Answers — B

D Script

1. Je suis canadienne.
2. Tu es algérien?
3. On est mexicain.
4. Vous êtes vietnamienne?
5. Tu es norvégienne?
6. Nous sommes américains.

1. –; 2. +; 3. +; 4. –; 5. –; 6. +

Expansion — C

Personalized Questions and Answers (PQA)

Engage students by asking them about their personal preferences, likes, and dislikes. Use the vocabulary and poll the class. Keep a running tally of class responses to polls.

Critical Thinking — D

Comparisons

French cinemas generally sell concessions such as ice cream and candy bars. Compare this to concessions found in American cinemas. Discuss favorite food items that students like to eat while watching a movie. Continue the conversation to include movie theater etiquette in both countries. Have students research online ticket prices for a matinee and an evening showing in France and in their area.

Reference Desk — E

To provide an adequate model for the adjective **meilleur**, write **mon meilleur ami** on the board and then a chart with **meilleur**, **meilleure**, **meilleurs**, and **meilleures** to introduce masculine and feminine singular and plural forms.

nouvelle orthographe **un supporteur**

Connections — F

Media

BeIN SPORTS is another leading sports channel. Ask your students to go online to the **Eurosport** TV programs and then to BeIN SPORTS. For each channel, have them review the types of sports being shown, how many programs, and at what time of day and night, and then have them vote for their favorite sport channel of the two.

Recherche: bein sport grille tv, eurosport programme de télé

Game — G

Fais une phrase!

Divide students into two teams. Have them line up facing each other. One student begins by naming a food, beverage, or noun related to items needed for sports. The corresponding partner from the other line responds with an expression appropriate for the item, using **avoir** (**faim/soif/besoin de**). For example, if the first student says, **une eau minérale**, the partner might say, **J'ai soif! Je prends une eau minérale!** When finished, pairs go to the end of the opposite line.

Culture — H

Products: Activity

Survey students about the movies they have seen that take place in French-speaking countries. Explore any French actors and directors who might be familiar to them. What have they learned about French or francophone culture from the movies?

Communication — I

Interpersonal: Paired Practice

To practice **quel**, distribute vocabulary picture cards. Have students ask each other and answer which they prefer when shown two cards from the same category. For example, **Quel acteur préfères-tu?** or **Quelle équipe est-ce que tu préfères?**

French in the Workplace — J

Explain to students that simultaneous interpretation is one manner in which they can make a living using French. To practice this, have students work in pairs with one student reading an activity aloud, sentence by sentence, as the other student, without reading along, listens carefully and interprets aloud what is being said. If this is too difficult, allow students to read and understand the text first, then interpret based on what they hear. You can do this in pairs or groups. Throughout the **unité** and future ones, have students practice this when reading texts and dialogues aloud. Then have students select a commercial, a short film, or a scene from a French movie and provide a recorded overdubbing of the scene in English.

Social Justice — K

Have students research which groups in the francophone world suffer from starvation or hunger. Ask them to share existing solutions that address these problems, as well as suggest new solutions. Finally, discuss whether there are similar problems in their community, and how they can make a difference.

A The **Resources** indicate which ancillary material may be used at various points in the unit. This section is typically found at the top of the page.

B **Answers** to activities, as well as **scripts** for interpretive listening activities, are provided at point of use.

C **Expansion** boxes give ideas for expanding on an activity in the student textbook.

D **Critical Thinking** boxes provide additional opportunities to have students compare, reflect on, or analyze aspects of the culture.

E The **Reference Desk** provides background information on cultural or linguistic information on the student pages. The **nouvelle orthographe** logo points out words that may be spelled differently today.

F **Connections** boxes provide supplemental activities to give to students. As these supplemental activities connect to various disciplines (Math, Science, Language Arts, HIstory, Music, Spanish, Health, etc), they may be used to differentiate learning.

G **Game** boxes provide opportunities for practicing the language in a fun way.

H **Culture** boxes provide additional cultural information or activities related to products or perspectives.

I **Communication** boxes supply additional communicative interpersonal or presentational activities.

J The **French in the Workplace** box is in the ***Système D*** section. It is designed to encourage students to apply their skills in a business setting.

K **Social Justice** activities encourage students to use their language skills to make changes in their community and lives, themes that are tied to the unit themes, such as poverty, racial and social inequalities, or bullying.

At the bottom of the page

Resources

- *Vocabulaire actif*
- eVisual
- Workbook 1–4
- Flash Cards
- Listening Activity 1
- G & V Practice Games

Reference Desk

1. There are many different film **genres: un western, une comédie, un film d'horreur, un film de science-fiction, un film classique, un film d'aventures, un film d'action, un film policier** (*detective*), **un documentaire, un drame, une comédie musicale, un voyage dans le temps** (*time travel*).
2. Useful terms: **le premier rôle** (*leading male actor*), **le premier rôle féminin** (*leading female role*), **le second rôle** (*supporting actor*), **le metteur en scène** (*director*), **une course-poursuite** (*car chase*). **Un navet** (*a turnip*) is a bad film.
3. The word **un synopsis** may also be used in the feminine form, **une synopsis**.

Expansion

Ask students to write a synopsis for the movie *Black Panther*, featured in the vocabulary spread. Or, ask them to write an entire posting for a movie of their choice.

Culture

Products : Information

AlloCiné was launched as a telecommunications company in 1993, but since then, it has switched its primary attention to its website (allocine.com), on which it offers news and information on the latest French cinematic releases, and its phone- and web-based movie ticket sales.

Leçon C — Vocabulaire actif

Le cinéma 1.2, 2.2, 3.1, 5.2

CINÉMA — **LES NOUVEAUTÉS (f.)**

1. Le sens de la fête

Genre (m.): Comédie
Durée (f.): 1h 56min
Réalisateurs (m.): Éric Toledano et Olivier Nakache
Casting (m.): Jean-Pierre Bacri, Gilles Lellouche, Eye Haïdara plus
Date de sortie (f.): le 4 octobre

Le synopsis du film :
Max est traiteur organisateur de réceptions de mariage. Cela fait une trentaine d'années qu'il travaille. Cette fois, il s'agit du mariage de Pierre et Héléna. Préparé comme à son habitude, Max voit pourtant cette soirée tourner en catastrophe. Humour et émotions viendront défier le sens de la fête!

On a tourné le film dans un château.

Les critiques (f.):
Presse (24 critiques)
Internautes (3 avis)

Voir la bande-annonce.

Les horaires (m.) et les salles (f.) de cinéma :
UGD Capitole
134 la Canebière
13001 Marseille
12h15 ; 16h30 ; 20h45

2. Black Panther — le titre
Pays de Production : États-Unis
Film d'action/fantastique américain
Réalisateur : Ryan Coogler
Acteurs : Chadwick Boseman, Michael B. Jordan, Lupita Nyong'o plus — une vedette
Durée : 2h 14min — un long métrage
13h45 (vo, sous-titrée), 17h35 (vf, doublée) — le doublage
la version originale (VO) — les sous-titres (m.) — la version française (VF)

Pour la conversation

How do I say what I'm not in the mood for?
» **Je ne suis pas trop d'humeur pour** une comédie dramatique.
I'm not in the mood for a dramatic comedy.

How do I relate the opinion of others?
» **Il paraît que** c'est très drôle.
It appears it's very funny.

How do I ask about someone's impression?
» Quelles sont **tes impressions** du film ?
What are your impressions of the movie?

How do I express disagreement?
» Je ne **partage** pas ton avis.
I don't share your opinion.

Et si je voulais dire… ?

un cascadeur	*stuntman*
la distribution	*the cast*
un figurant	*extra (actor)*
une représentation	*performance*
applaudir	*to clap*
huer	*to boo*

L'argot des ados

Le Cinéma

le cinoche	le cinéma
un(e) mordu(e) du cinéma	un fan
un nanar/ un navet	un mauvais film
une star	une vedette

1 Une critique 1.2, 2.2, 3.1

Interpretive Reading

Lisez la critique du film suivant, puis répondez aux questions.

Boule & Bill
2013. 2h10. Comédie française en couleurs.
La dernière grande comédie pour ceux qui aiment rire vient de sortir dans les salles. Allez voir ce film tout de suite ! Le casting est très fort. Un long métrage par un réalisateur bien connu qui pourrait devenir un classique. Évitez la bande-annonce, qui en révèle trop sur les personnages et les événements. Si vous voulez voir une comédie, ou tout simplement rire de bon cœur, ne cherchez pas plus loin : *Boule & Bill* est ce qu'il vous faut. C'est un film touchant et drôle à la fois au sujet d'un chien adopté qui a un peu trop d'énergie. Vous partagerez mon avis. Je vous le promets.

1. Quelle est la durée du film ?
2. Quand est-ce qu'il est sorti ?
3. Que pense le critique de ce film ?
4. Qu'est-ce qu'on ne doit pas faire ?
5. Quand est-ce qu'on devrait choisir ce film ?
6. Quel est le synopsis du film ?

Resources

- *Pour la conversation*
- *Et si je voulais dire… ?*

Answers

1

1. 2h10
2. 2013
3. Il pense que le film a un très bon casting et pourrait devenir un classique.
4. On ne doit pas regarder la bande-annonce.
5. On devrait choisir ce film quand on veut rire.
6. Il s'agit d'un chien adopté qui a trop d'énergie.

Reference Desk

1. **Mordu(e)** comes from the verb **mordre** (*to bite*). Someone who loves the movies is "bitten" by them. The expression also applies to other passions.
2. French films have often been the inspiration for American movies, including:
   - **Intouchables**, 2011 (*The Upside*, 2017)
   - **Banlieue 13**, 2004 (*Brick Mansions*, 2014)
   - **LOL (Laughing Out Loud)**, 2008 (*LOL*, 2012)
   - **Le Dîner des Cons**, 1998 (*Dinner for Schmucks*, 2010)
   - **Inside**, 2007 (*Inside*, 2016)
   - **Plein Soleil**, 1960 (*The Talented Mr. Ripley*, 1999)
   - **La Cage aux Folles**, 1978 (*The Birdcage*, 1996)
   - **Trois hommes et un couffin**, 1985 (*Three Men and a Baby*, 1987)

nouvelle orthographe: **paraitre, il parait que**

Critical Thinking

The movie posters and film titles of French adaptations of American movie titles provide interesting topics for discussion. Show students some posters of movies they may recognize and discuss decisions made to appeal to a French audience. Discuss, for example, why "Black Panther" is not literally translated "La Panthère Noire."

Essential Instruction

1. Have students listen to the vocabulary **Le cinéma**. Ask them questions about the text using the vocabulary in the margins.
2. Have the students listen to **Pour la conversation** and the additional vocabulary.
3. Put the vocabulary from *Reference Desk* on the board and ask students to give examples of each genre. Ask students to name their favorite actors and directors, a film with a car chase, and **navets** that they have seen.
4. Expand the discussion to current television shows as well since they have the same elements and students are apt to watch televison more regularly.
5. Have students read **Activité 1**. Ask them questions 1–6.
6. Let students know that "VO" refers to the original language the film was made in, which may or may not have French subtitles (since it is being shown in France), whereas the designation "VF" refers to a film that is dubbed in French over the original foreign (non-French) language dialogue.

Differentiated Learning

Accelerate
Have students go online to research current popular French films. Ask them to determine the percentage of foreign films to French films that are in theaters and to identify the popular American actors in current films.

Recherche : l'officiel des spectacles

Decelerate
Give students time to go online to explore **AlloCiné**. Ask them to list what American television series are playing in France. Have them select one, read five critiques, and then make a list of positive and negative expressions used by viewers. Lower-ability students may enjoy this site, the result being that they read more French out of curiosity.

Special Needs Students

At-Risk Students
Discussing films can be a good hook to get these students involved. Young people enjoy going to movies and watching Netflix. Look for ways to engage them in conversations about topics that interest them.

296

297

The **Essential Instruction** is preparation help for the day's lesson; these tips suggest a logical order of approach.

Differentiated Learning provides tips on how to accelerate, decelerate, adapt, or expand material **Multiple Intelligences** provides tips on how to reach students who learn through linguistic, naturalist, bodily-kinesthetic, musical-rhythmic, verbal-linguistic, visual-spatial, or mathematical intelligences.

Learning Styles

Visual Learners
Have students find or create a Fahrenheit-to-Celsius conversion chart.

Special Needs Students

AD(H)D
Have students choose either **Activité 16** or **17**. Write step-by-step instructions for them. Add a checklist for these students to assess their work.

Learning Styles provides tips on how to reach students who are auditory, visual, or kinesthetic learners.

Special Needs Students provides tips on how to reach students who may have learning, behavioral, or physical challenges.

Program Resources

Teacher Materials

The **Annotated Teacher's Edition** includes margin notes featuring games and activities, cultural information, and teacher suggestions. The **eATE** includes the full Annotated Teacher's Edition plus all program resources:

- **Textbook Audio Program** includes the audio transcripts for the textbook audio as well as access to all recordings for vocabulary, dialogues, narratives, and activities.
- **Dialogue Videos** include the subtitled and non-subtitled versions of the dialogues in the ***Rencontres culturelles*** section.
- **Workbook Teacher's Edition** includes the answers to the student activities that reinforce vocabulary, grammar, and cultural information.
- **Listening Activities and Simulated Conversations Teacher's Edition** includes additional listening comprehension activities as well as the audio files and answer key.
- **eVisuals** are images and scenes, accompanied by audio, to teach and reinforce vocabulary. They are available in flat and interactive formats.
- **Grammar Videos** include fun and engaging explanations of select grammar concepts.
- **Communicative Activities** include information gap activities, postcard activities, and situation card activities.
- **Activities for Mastery** include games and activities that are designed to encourage students to practice the material presented in the program.
- **TPR Storytelling** includes step-by-step instructions for basic and advanced stories.
- **Video Program Teacher's Edition** contains transcripts for Documentaries 1–5 of *Rendez-vous à Nice !* Access to the subtitled and non-subtitled **video files** is also provided, along with student activity sheets and an answer key.
- **Pre-AP Reading** includes additional readings and interpretive activities based on various sources.
- **Integrated Performance Assessments** allows teachers to evaluate students' performance in the three modes of communication in a natural way.
- **Copy Masters** includes graphs and charts to give students to complete certain textbook activities.
- **Quizzes Teacher's Edition** includes end-of-lesson quizzes and an answer key.
- **Tests Teacher's Edition** includes one test per unit to assess speaking, listening, reading, and writing based on unit vocabulary, grammar, and culture. It also includes two proficiency tests, one for mid-year and one for the end of the course.
- **Lesson Plans,** available for 50-minute and 90-minute periods, assist in daily planning and classroom preparation.
- **End-of-Unit Vocabulary lists** are categorized by lesson and are editable to suit teachers' needs.
- **Correlations to the National Standards and Common Core Standards** include complete correlations to activities and readings.
- **Correlations to ACTFL Can-Do Statements** help teachers assess student proficiency, and help students track their learning goals.

ExamVIEW® is a software program that enables teachers to adapt **Tests** and **Quizzes** for differentiation.

Student Materials

The **Textbook** provides the core material to engage and motivate life-long French learners.
The **eBook** includes all textbook activities, many of which are interactive and provide immediate feedback; access to the ***Rencontres culturelles*** dialogue videos, and the ***Rendez-vous à Nice !*** videos (non-subtitled), and all audio for vocabulary, dialogues, narratives, and listening activities.
The **Workbook** provides activities that reinforce vocabulary, grammar, and cultural information.
The **eWorkbook** includes interactive activities with immediate feedback.
Video Activities for *Rendez-vous à Nice !* include student activity sheets linked to the documentaries of ***Rendez-vous à Nice !***
Listening Activities and Simulated Conversations are interactive and provide immediate feedback.
eVisuals are interactive images and scenes accompanied by audio to reinforce vocabulary.
Flash Cards (powered by Quizlet®) are audio recorded vocabulary lists to help students practice and learn vocabulary from each unit.
Grammar and Vocabulary Practice Games are online games for students to practice vocabulary and structure. They are available as basic and advanced.
Pre-AP Listening includes online quizzes that provide AP-style practice for interpretive listening.
Pre-Tests are online quizzes that provide practice for the unit tests.
WebQuests are practical activities that encourage students to use online resources.

Passport®
www.emcpassport.com

Passport®: The learning environment for the French classroom of tomorrow… today!

Passport® "brings it all home" with its unique, "anytime, anywhere" learning platform. In the classroom, at home or on the go, students show what they know while connecting to curriculum, culture, classmates, and communities.

Teachers can…

- assign activities from the eBooks (eBook, eWorkbook, eListening Activities, Video Activities, Tests and Quizzes, and Games to practice vocabulary and structures–available in basic and advanced versions); assign projects based on ACTFL's Integrated Performance Assessment; engage students in cultural enrichment activities (videos, news, and songs); and check oral proficiency through video-based performance tools
- track student progress and grades
- provide individualized video or written feedback
- communicate with classes
- access all program resources
- incorporate blended learning

Students can…

- access materials anytime, anywhere
- complete assignments and practice activities
- work on project-based tasks
- receive immediate feedback
- submit work
- track their progress

Discover

Students connect to core curriculum via their eBooks and other supplemental materials.

Create

Students complete pre-made, IPA-aligned project-based activities that engage students in real-life situations using the three modes of communication—interpretive, interpersonal and presentational.

Explore

Students explore language and culture through virtual tours, news articles, video documentaries, and music.

Share

Students use this video-based tool to post for peers their opinions, ideas, stories, and more.

Perform

Students demonstrate oral proficiency through video assessment tasks.

Planning and Pacing

Teaching Notes and Tips

- The authors recommend that teachers complete most vocabulary and grammar instruction from each unit of the book in order to prepare students to use ***T'es branché?*** 2nd edition Level 4 at the beginning of the following school year.
- It is not necessary to do every exercise on every page. Gauge how easily students grasp a concept and which topics interest them.
- Expose students to vocabulary, grammar, and culture every day.
- Challenge students to speak, read, write, and listen to French every day.
- Provide more or less practice on a specific topic according to the mastery level of your students.
- At the beginning of each daily lesson, review what you did the day before.
- At the end of each daily lesson, review the learning that was accomplished during class.
- Always prepare an activity for students to complete after they have finished a test or quiz.
- Assign small amounts of homework often. (Requiring students to practice independently what they learned in class will help them retain information.)
- Do a warm-up with your students each day by checking homework or reviewing the previous day's activities.

Traditional Schedule (50-minute classes)

10 *T'es branché?* units
× 18 days per unit

---

180 days of instruction

Block Schedule (90-minute classes)

10 *T'es branché?* units
× 9 blocks per unit

---

90 blocks of instruction

Sample Unit Lesson Plan

The following chart illustrates how to pace one unit of ***T'es branché?*** All units contain the same instructional components. Based on Unit 4, this sample lesson plan can be applied to all units.

Traditional Schedule (50 minutes)	Block Schedule (90 minutes)	Page(s)	Unit Content	Practice, Review, and Recycle
Day 1	Block 1	200–201 202–203 206	**Lesson A.** Unit Opener *Vocabulaire actif* and *Pour la conversation* Dialogue: *Rencontres culturelles*	Textbook Activities 1–5 Workbook Activities 1–4
Day 2	Block 2	206–207 212–213 208–210	*Rencontres culturelles* *Structure de la langue* Culture: *Points de départ*	Information Gap Activity Communicative Activities eVisuals Textbook Activities 7–8 Workbook Activity 6 Grammar and Vocabulary Practice Games
Day 3		212–213 211	*Structure de la langue* Culture: *Du côté des médias*	Communicative Activities Textbook Activities 9–12 Workbook Activities 7–9 Grammar and Vocabulary Practice Games
Day 4	Block 3	214–218	*Structure de la langue*	Communicative Activities Textbook Activities 10–14 Workbook Activities 10–12 Grammar and Vocabulary Practice Games
Day 5		200–221	Review of Lesson A	eVisuals Grammar and Vocabulary Practice Games Communicative Activities Online Pre-tests
Day 6	Block 4		Quiz Unit 3 Lesson A	Vocabulary, structure, and culture review
Day 7		222–225 226	**Lesson B.** *Vocabulaire actif* and *Pour la conversation* Dialogue: *Rencontres culturelles*	Textbook Activities 1–7 Workbook Activity 4
Day 8	Block 5	231–232 227–229	*Structure de la langue* Culture: *Points de départ*	eVisuals Grammar and Vocabulary Practice Games Textbook Activity 9 Workbook Activities 6, 10
Day 9	Block 6	233–234 230	*Structure de la langue* Culture: *Du côté des médias*	Communicative Activities Textbook Activities 10, 12–14
Day 10		235–237 239 238	*Structure de la langue* *Stratégie communicative* *À vous la parole*	Communicative Activities Textbook Activities 15–20 Workbook Activity 11
Day 11	Block 7	222–239	Review of Lesson B	eVisuals Grammar and Vocabulary Practice Games Communicative Activities Online Pre-tests
Day 12			Quiz Unit 3 Lesson B	Vocabulary, culture, and structure review
Day 13		240–243 244	**Lesson C.** *Vocabulaire actif* and *Pour la conversation* Dialogue: *Rencontres culturelles*	Textbook Activities 1–4 Workbook Activities 1–3 Grammar and Vocabulary Practice Games
Day 14	Block 8	252	*À vous la parole*	Communicative Activities Textbook Activities 15–17
Day 15		249–250 245–247	*Structure de la langue* Culture: *Points de départ* and *Du côté des médias*	Textbook Activities 11–12 Textbook Activities 6–7 Workbook Activity 5
Day 16		251 253–255	*Structure de la langue* Reading: *Lecture thématique*	Textbook Activities 13–14 Textbook Activity 18
Day 17		248, 256 258 260	Culture: *Culture sur place* and *Système D* Communication: *Évaluation* Review of Lesson C	Textbook Activities 8–10, 19–20 Flash Cards Quiz Lesson C Video: *Rendez-vous à Nice !* eVisuals Grammar and Vocabulary Practice Games Communicative Activities Online Pre-tests
Day 18		260	Test Unit 4	Communicative Activities Vocabulary, structure, and culture review

World Language Learning in the 21st Century

By Toni Theisen

Our world is an ever increasingly diverse, globalized, and complex media-saturated society. Our 21st-century learners need a multi-sensory and multi-layered learning environment that is designed to inspire creativity, synthesis, and collaboration, as well as to provide opportunities to analyze, reflect, and evaluate. So what are the critical skills and multiple literacies that our students will need in order to participate successfully in the global community of today's world? How do we engage them in meaningful contexts that are relevant and challenging? How do we provide project-based learning opportunities that help students reach higher levels of proficiency? How do we help students set personal learning goals and become self-directed learners? How do we personalize learning?

Quite often, 21st-century skills are equated with technology. True, technology is a part of the skills learners will need to master, but this concept is much broader. ACTFL, collaborating with the Partnership for 21st-Century Skills, created the 21st-Century Skills Map for Pre-K–16 to address these questions. The map, outlined below, helps teachers plan and guide instruction, while giving concrete examples to administrators and policymakers across the country. (Examples of activities in the Novice, Intermediate, and Advanced ranges can be found at www.actfl.org.)

Here are the 12 skills statements from the ACTFL World Languages 21st-Century Skills Map and their four interdisciplinary themes:

1. **Communication**
   Students as effective communicators use languages to engage in meaningful conversation; to understand and interpret spoken language and written text; and to present information, concepts, and ideas.
2. **Collaboration**
   Students as collaborators use their native and acquired languages to learn from and work cooperatively across cultures with global team members, sharing responsibility and making necessary compromises while working toward a common goal.
3. **Critical Thinking and Problem Solving**
   Students as inquirers frame, analyze, and synthesize information as well as negotiate meaning across language and culture in order to explore problems and issues from their own and different perspectives.
4. **Creativity and Innovation**
   Students as creators and innovators respond to new and diverse perspectives as they use language in imaginative and original ways to make useful contributions.
5. **Information Literacy**
   Students as informed global citizens access, manage, and effectively use culturally authentic sources in ethical and legal ways.
6. **Media Literacy**
   Students as active global citizens evaluate authentic sources to understand how media reflect and influence language and culture.
7. **Technology Literacy**
   Students as productive global citizens use appropriate technologies when interpreting messages; interacting with others; and producing written, oral, and visual messages.
8. **Flexibility and Adaptability**
   Students as flexible and adaptable language learners are open-minded, are willing to take risks, and accept the ambiguity of language while balancing diverse global perspectives.
9. **Initiative and Self-Direction**
   Students as lifelong learners are motivated to set their own goals and reflect on their progress as they grow and improve their linguistic and cultural competence.

10. **Social and Cross-Cultural Skills**
Students as adept language learners understand diverse cultural perspectives and use appropriate socio-linguistic skills in order to function in diverse cultural and linguistic contexts.

11. **Productivity and Accountability**
Students as productive and accountable learners take responsibility for their own learning by actively working to increase their language proficiency and cultural knowledge.

12. **Leadership and Responsibility**
Students as responsible leaders leverage their linguistic and cross-cultural skills to inspire others to be fair, accepting, open, and understanding within and beyond the local community.

Interdisciplinary Themes

Global Awareness

Language education and cultural understanding are at the heart of developing global awareness for students. In order to understand and address global issues, it is important to understand the perspectives on the world that speakers of other languages bring to the table. By learning other languages, students develop respect and openness to those whose culture, religion, and views on the world may be different. Language students are able to interact with students from the target language in order to discuss and reach solutions regarding global issues.

Financial, Economic, Business, and Entrepreneurial Literacy

Students in language classes learn about the financial and economic issues from the target language culture and are able to compare and contrast with those of the United States. According to the Committee for Economic Development (CED), "cultural competence and foreign language skills can prove invaluable when working on global business teams or negotiating with overseas clients." Those who are able to communicate with others in their native language will naturally feel more empowered to negotiate with those around the world as they engage in entrepreneurial activities.

Civic Literacy

Language learners become aware of the judicial, legislative, and government functions of the target-language country or countries and are able to compare and contrast those with equivalent functions in the United States. Because they can communicate in the target language, they are able to engage in discussions with other students to participate in activities in which they discuss civic life in their respective countries.

Health Literacy

Language learners are engaged in a value-added activity as they can address global health and environmental issues in the target language and understand materials that were written for native speakers of that language. They have access to information because they can understand the language and can thus engage in global discussions on health, environmental, and public safety issues as they prepare for careers in these fields.

By focusing on these essential skills, the interdisciplinary themes, and the integration of technology in a meaningful, relevant, standards-based curriculum, teachers can empower students to participate actively in the global community.

Sources:
ACTFL World Languages 21st-Century Skills Map
Partnership for 21st-Century Skills

21st-Century Skills Section: *Système D !*

In IT language, **un système D** refers to **un système d'exploitation** (*operating system*), otherwise known as OS or OIS. The OS is that which permits all elements of a computer system to work together and to provide the user with the ability to utilize the material.

Most of all, **le système D** is a common French expression which means "the ability to figure things out without any particular help or support, instead using one's own capacity to reason, think logically, induce, or infer." In this expression, the letter **d** refers to **la débrouillardise** (*figuring things out on one's own*). The expression **Débrouille-toi !** simply means "to use **le système D**."

Système D is a new section in ***T'es branché ?*** 2nd edition. It appears at the end of every unit, and is designed for students to apply unit vocabulary and structures to communicative activities that foster 21st-century skills. These activities demonstrate how 21st-century skills are cultivated in the language classroom and how these skills and the language learning process are mutually beneficial.

In this section, each activity is clearly connected to the 21st-century skills it calls upon and to the mode of communication to which it applies.

Oral Proficiency in the 21st Century

By Toni Theisen

At the center of the national standards are the three modes of communication. The interpersonal and the presentational modes are focused on both oral and written communication. In the interpersonal mode, learners engage in conversation, provide and obtain information, express feeling and emotion, and exchange opinions. This mode occurs in two-way, spontaneous exchanges that involve negotiation of meaning and is unrehearsed. Activities and strategies include debates, discussions, phone or video calls, asking for and giving directions, and making plans.

In the presentational mode, learners present information, concepts, and ideas to an audience of listeners or readers on a variety of topics. It is one-way and planned, and it can be rehearsed. There is no feedback from another person. Presentational activities include creating videos, blogs, and advertisements; telling a story; delivering a speech; creating a public service announcement; or presenting a skit or play.

With ***T'es branché ?***, students gain practice in the three modes of communication in vocabulary and structure activities, as well as in the **À vous la parole**, **Système D**, and **Projets finaux** sections. Rubrics for spoken and written communication can be found at EMCL. A student contract on the Unit Opener page makes it clear to students what material they will be responsible for learning and helps them take ownership of this content from the beginning. Students reflect on what they can do and what they can learn to do better in **Faisons le point !** at the end of each unit. The final projects are designed to showcase student learning and to make students feel successful, engaged, and purpose-driven in their French language learning experiences with ***T'es branché ?***.

A New Emphasis on Teaching Culture: Explore and Investigate *sur place*

By Pamela M. Wesely

Foreign language teachers have examined and debated the issue of teaching culture in the foreign language classroom for many years. One of the ways that ***T'es branché ?*** attempts to respond to this debate is through the presentation of **Culture sur place** sections in every unit. They are designed to engage students differently with francophone culture(s) by promoting a spirit of inquiry and treating the students as social actors, not as passive recipients of culture. The idea of developing intercultural competence in the language classroom rather than relying solely on teaching *about* the target culture(s) is not a new one, but it is one that has rarely been incorporated into a textbook.

The format of these sections varies throughout the text, but generally one of six different styles of activity is used for each one.

- **Submersion**: Students are encouraged to feel that they are "on location" in a francophone culture—observing, asking questions, finding answers, drawing conclusions, and finding different perspectives and viewpoints. They report on their findings to the class.
- **Poll**: Students conduct a survey of their fellow students that parallels a survey of French or francophone people. The students can then draw conclusions from a comparison of the results, focusing on current characteristics and realities in francophone cultures, as well as on the diversity of their own lives.
- **Advocacy**: Students write a plan for taking action, making their voices heard, or serving as advocates for a specific population in the face of human rights abuses, current events issues, or other topics of discussion.

- **Reaction**: Via self-assessment, students examine potential areas of discomfort with French or francophone cultures and identify what they might need to do to gain more comfort in, or become more habituated to, the practices of these cultures.
- **Comparison**: Students take two explicitly different but related phenomena (encompassing products, practices, and perspectives) in their own culture and in the target culture(s) and examine why those two phenomena might be different.
- **Contact**: Students investigate the reality of one individual from a French-speaking culture through an interview conducted in written form or face-to-face.

  "Culture" in **Culture sur place** is thus not intended as something to be learned, but rather something to be explored, questioned, and examined. Students will be able to use their 21st-century skills in applying themselves to get through the steps of these activities that are meaningful, structured, and open to student self-expression.

Teaching Grammar to Enhance Communication

"I took French for three years and I can't say anything." Perhaps you know someone with such an experience with language instruction. The drill-and-practice instruction of yesteryear relied on mechanical, repetitive exercises that were not linked to meaningful expression. Today's teachers still want their students to learn grammatical concepts incrementally so that their language production doesn't fossilize. They also want their students' oral and written expression to be comprehensible to native speakers, acceptable in different social contexts, and accurate. To reach these goals, today's teachers often provide activities that allow for structured input (learning the grammar rules and examining models), structured output (practicing the grammar point in communicative exercises), and communicative output (doing a communicative task that uses the grammar point).

Structured Input

In ***T'es branché?***, grammar points are presented concisely with the use of charts and examples. Students can use these pages as reference when they want to try to expand on their expression; they don't have to learn everything at once. For example, they may learn quickly how to use the **passé composé** in declarative sentences, but can refer back to the grammar presentation later in order to see how to form a question using inversion in the **passé composé** for an interview or survey. Many of the examples used in the grammar presentation come from the first **Rencontres culturelles** dialogue that students can hear and see as many times as they wish on their mobile devices.

Structured Output

T'es branché? begins with mechanical activities, and then builds to activities that are more creative, meaningful, and open-ended. A mechanical activity might ask students to insert the right preposition before the names of cities, countries, and continents they learned about in the culture readings. A creative activity might have them use the adverbs **bien**, **un peu**, **beaucoup** with the verb **aimer** to report on critics' reviews of new French films. A meaningful and more open-ended activity might include interviewing their partner about their lifestyle habits for the week and then writing sentences using **toujours**, **souvent**, **ne (n')… pas souvent** or **ne (n')… jamais** to describe those weekly activities. For example: **Zach ne mange jamais de légumes frais.**

Communicative Output

In the **À vous la parole** section, students put their knowledge of grammar to use in interpretive, presentational and interpersonal communication activities. For example, they might use **il faut** in a conversation at the doctor's office, use possessive adjectives to describe a photo of their family, or use a website to tell what vacation they chose (**choisir**, regular **-ir** verb).

Communicative Competence

Students build communicative competence by using ***T'es branché?*** in part because they learn grammar from a logical grammatical syllabus that builds on and recycles grammar points. Some teachers like to provide an immersion experience, having their students build structural knowledge naturally. For these teachers we have the TPR Storytelling manual, which is correlated to the textbook. Students will pick up on the grammar topics in the original story and soon be able to tell their own variation, using accurate and comprehensible grammar.

Meeting the Needs of the 21st-Century Reader

"Qui que vous soyez qui voulez cultiver, vivifier, édifier, attendrir, apaiser, mettez des livres partout."
Whoever wishes to cultivate, enliven, edify, soften, pacify, put books everywhere.
—Victor Hugo

Research on reading reveals that successful readers read extensively, integrate information in the text with pre-existing knowledge, have a reading style that adapts to the text, are motivated, read for a purpose, and rely on different skills to comprehend a text. The readings in ***T'es branché?*** were designed to provide contextual reading activities that hone all of these skills and guide the reader to greater comprehension. These readings are always accompanied with supports to make every French student a successful reader.

Successful Readers Read Extensively

In ***T'es branché?***, students read the dialogues (the Extension dialogue in **Rencontres culturelles** is for students who want to go farther and faster), which incorporate the vocabulary, functions, structure, and culture of the lesson. In each lesson, there is a comprehensible-input paragraph so that students can build understanding of the new vocabulary before using it. A piece of realia, such as a transportation schedule, calendar, movie schedule, map, or tourism website, appears in the section **Du côté des médias**. Beginning in Unit 6 of Level 1, students read the culture readings in French also. Their unit learning culminates in a literary selection, linked to the theme of the unit; pre-reading questions, strategies, guided reading questions, and post-reading questions give students ideas and themes with which to tackle literary selections with confidence.

Successful Readers Integrate Information in the Text with Pre-Existing Knowledge and Adapt to the Text

In the culture section, students are asked to connect to what they know about culture in the United States and Canada with **Comparaisons** questions, which become their starting point for comparisons with francophone cultures. The **Perspectives** questions ask students to consider the point of view of a French speaker in excerpts from songs, poems, blogs, etc. In the literary selection, students are asked a pre-reading question to connect the theme of the selection to their own experience. The repeated supports in these sections help students to adapt to the text, whether it is experiential (**Rencontres culturelles**), factual (**Points de départ**), opinion-based (**Perspectives**), informational (**Du côté des médias**), or literary (**Lecture thématique**).

Successful Readers Are Motivated and Read for a Purpose

For whatever reason students are learning French (a love of languages, to test out of French at the post-secondary level, to travel to French-speaking countries, to have an interesting career, etc.), the texts in ***T'es branché?*** underline their reasons for study, thus motivating them toward their goal. Students also read with a purpose: for enjoyment (the serial cartoon **Les copains d'abord** in Levels 1 and 2), for information (culture section), to confirm prior knowledge (dialogues and culture section), to evaluate ideas (literary selection), and to grapple with other points of view (**Perspectives**). Students who want to learn more about a certain culture topic will benefit from the search words that connect them to texts online. These are found after each culture paragraph and in activities that require students to do additional research.

Successful Students Rely on Different Skills to Comprehend a Text

Although woven throughout the various reading activities of each unit, specific strategies that can help students read more quickly and effectively receive greater focus in **Lecture thématique** and in the ancillary manual of the same name. These strategies include previewing, predicting, skimming and scanning, monitoring comprehension, using text organization, tackling difficult vocabulary, visualizing, writing things down (with the help of charts and graphic organizers), guessing from context, and paraphrasing.

Since research has shown that reading is the skill that endures the longest, French students who study with ***T'es branché?*** will be on their way to becoming lifelong readers of French: successfully reading literary selections; reading nonfiction; and reading Internet, reference, and visual materials.

Immersion Lessons in the Non-Immersion Classroom

Connecting to Literature and Art

"The subject matter class is a language class if it is made comprehensible to the language student."
— Stephen Krashen

Research has shown that immersion experiences provide the best experience for language acquisition outside of interaction with a native community. The sections of ***T'es branché?*** that easily lend themselves to immersion experiences are the **Lecture thématique** and **Le monde visuel**, both in Lesson C. Students can build a literary and artistic vocabulary, which will result in an appreciation and understanding of literature and art.

La littérature

Begin the reading lesson by asking students to read the **Rencontre avec l'auteur**. Identify the time period of the writer by making a timeline on the wall and placing the names of the authors, as you encounter them, where they belong, along with a flag identifying their nationality. Have students identify the question at the end of the paragraph that they should be able to answer after reading the selection; you may want them to write it in their notebook and jot down ideas as they come to them while they read. Have students share responses to the **Pré-lecture** question as a class, unless you consider the question personal and want students to write a response in their notebook. Although the strategy is presented in English, you can give directions on how to complete it in French. Since interaction is the key to a good immersion experience, have students compare their graphic organizers in pairs or small groups. Put useful expressions on the board to help students share information. For example, **J'ai mis...**, **Pourquoi n'as-tu pas considéré...?**, **J'ai une autre idée**, etc.

You may want to begin the selection by playing the audio recording. Point out that there will be words students won't know, but these words are glossed below the selection. Wherever possible, a French synonym is given. Ask students to answer the **Pendant la lecture** questions after listening to the recording, or pause the recording where there is a question in order to monitor their comprehension. Then have students share their responses to the **Post-lecture** question in pairs or small groups, and ask for volunteers to share once you reassemble as a class. Finally, students do the **Activités d'expansion**. Encourage students to publish their writings on the Internet and put some in their portfolio so they can see how they improve at analyzing literature over time.

L'art

To familiarize your students with keys to understanding art as presented in **Le monde visuel**, you may want to have students keep a notebook in which they define the art terms they encounter with each new painting. Provide them with some words and expressions to answer the question(s) at the end of each paragraph. Have students work in pairs to answer the question(s).

Since not all art movements are covered in ***T'es branché?***, you might begin with an overview of the major art movements, so that students understand the basic characteristics of each movement. The chart that follows provides simple phrases you can use to distinguish these movements. Bring in art books and pass around paintings by the artists mentioned so students understand which artists are associated with each movement and the evolution of French art. Students should learn these types of paintings: **une nature morte**, **un portrait**, **un autoportrait**, **un paysage**, **une scène**. Post some examples in class and do a station activity in which students identify the type of painting and the movement to which it belongs.

Overview of Art Movements

Mouvement	Dates approximatives	Caractéristiques	Peintres
Renaissance	1492–1600	Inspirée par la Renaissance italienne Conception nouvelle du portait Débuts du paysage, par exemple, dans *La Joconde*	Léonard de Vinci Fouquet Clouet Dubreuil (Ambroise) Dubois
Classicisme	1575–1700	Sujets nobles de l'antiquité, de la mythologie, de la Bible La symétrie dans la composition	Poussin Charles Le Brun
Baroque	1625–1700	Histoires venant des légendes, de la mythologie, de la Bible Couleurs chaudes et vives Sentiments visibles sur les visages L'asymétrie dans la composition Impression du mouvement	Chardin Fragonard Lebrun Lorrain Poussin
Rococo	1730–1789	Compositions frivoles et légères Scènes pastorales et aristocrates	Boucher Watteau
Néo-classicisme	1760–1830	Inspiré par la Rome antique Style plus simple que celui du rococo Allégories, mythologie comme sujets	David Gérard Gros
Romantisme	1775–1850	Rejet du classicisme (trop rigide) Désir de montrer l'idéal, les sentiments, l'exotique, les fantaisies du peintre	Delacroix Gros Géricault
Réalisme	1830–1890	Scènes de la vie courante Observation Stylisation Coloration sombre	Corot Courbet Daumier Millet Fantin-Latour
Impressionnisme	1850–1900	Rejet de l'art académique Note les impressions fugitives avec une touche rapide Taches de couleurs juxtaposées composent une image à distance	Monet Renoir Pissarro Sisley Morisot Bazille Manet
Cubisme	1907–1914	Sujets décomposés Formes géométriques	Picasso, Gris Braque

Differentiated Instruction and *T'es branché?*

Differentiated instruction occurs when teachers design learning to meet individual student needs. It differentiates between **content** (the material the student needs to learn); **process** (practice that allows the student to learn the material); **products** (projects that get the student to rehearse, apply, and extend his or her learning); and, according to Carol Ann Tomlinson, fosters a positive **learning environment** (the way the classroom functions and feels).

Tailoring activities to different ability levels in your classroom can be time-consuming, so having a program like ***T'es branché?*** that is designed to meet differing ability levels and learning styles means you won't have to develop many materials on your own. Below are a few examples from ***T'es branché?*** for each aspect of differentiated instruction.

Content

1. **Use reading materials for different ability levels.**

   T'es branché? has a basic dialogue and a more advanced dialogue in each lesson; the advanced dialogue is called *Extension*. If a literary selection in **Lecture thématique** is too easy or hard for a student, pick an alternative for him or her in the **Lecture thématique** manual. Ideas for differentiated learning appear in the Annotated Teacher's Edition wraparound notes.

2. **Present materials visually and auditorily.**

   For the visual learner, ***T'es branché?*** includes many activities based on a visual illustration, piece of realia, or graphic. Take advantage of the eVisuals and electronic flash cards for learning vocabulary, for example. Students are encouraged to fill out graphic organizers throughout ***T'es branché?*** to help them conceptualize and form ideas. ***T'es branché?*** has seven listening activities in every odd-numbered unit and eight in even-numbered units; also, the first dialogue in the **Rencontres culturelles** section is available as a video and an audio file. These listening activities will help students who are primarily aural learners.

3. **Use materials that result in analysis and evaluation.**

   While some students may find their comfort area in knowledge, comprehension, and application, ***T'es branché?*** allows for analysis and evaluation as students progress and move forward to reach their potential.

Process

1. **Provide opportunities for students to work in pairs and groups.**

   Students learning with ***T'es branché?*** receive many opportunities to work cooperatively in pairs and groups.

2. **Adapt instruction to appeal to multiple intelligences and other learning styles.**

   Different learning styles are built into the activities of ***T'es branché?***; suggestions for implementation appear in the Annotated Teacher's Edition wraparound notes.

3. **Provide differentiated testing.**

   With ***T'es branché?***, students can be tested with a slower-paced test, an at-standard test, or an advanced test.

Products

1. **Provide opportunities for communication.**

   With the ***T'es branché?*** program, students learn to enact dialogues (interpersonal communication); write memos, e-mails, postcards, blogs, etc. (presentational communication); and make presentations based on online research (interpretive and presentational communication).

2. **Provide challenging and engaging tasks.**

   The activities in ***T'es branché?*** move from those that are more mechanical to those that are meaningful, open-ended, and creative. Students practice recalling, check their comprehension, apply what they have learned, analyze, synthesize, and evaluate using ***T'es branché?***

3. **Provide a variety of final projects based on learning styles.**

   Students have the opportunity to develop three types of final projects in ***T'es branché?***: **Connexions par Internet**, **Communautés en ligne**, and **Passez à l'action!** In the first activity, students do cross-disciplinary research in French using presentational communication. In the second activity, they reach out to or learn about a francophone community online, which results in interpersonal or presentational communication. The third activity may have them designing the house of the future, researching French links to the Olympics, or donating books to Africa, often as a group activity.

Learning Environment

People passing by your classroom will see a lot of activity when you teach with ***T'es branché?***, but it is a good idea to include days for working quietly without distraction, to keep all your students comfortable. Qualitative assignments in ***T'es branché?*** mean that students dig deeper and go beyond comprehension questions; learning revolves around an essential question that ties each unit together and that allows for reflection on learning in **Faisons le point!** The technology that accompanies ***T'es branché?*** means that your students can be engaged every day with video, audio, interactive eVisuals, and electronic flash cards—using a variety of electronic devices. They can have fun while they learn at their own pace because you have planned and organized instruction that accommodates their learning styles.

Blended Learning in the Second Language Environment

What Is Blended Learning?

Blended learning occurs when teachers combine face-to-face learning with online learning. With self-paced e-learning, students experience differentiated learning. In a blended learning environment, activities that may have previously taken place during classroom time are moved online. In one model, students might meet in the traditional classroom only a few times per week and do the rest of their learning online.

What does Passport® provide?

EMC's Passport® supports student-directed and project-based learning, interpersonal communication, and performance tasks. Within this digital environment, students **discover** the content of ***T'es branché?*** anytime, anywhere, through eBooks, listening activities, and other supplemental materials; **create** meaningful, project-based tasks centered in IPA-aligned modules; **explore** linguistic and cultural horizons through virtual tours, video documentaries, and current news articles and songs; **share** opinions, ideas, and perspectives through short video posts; and **perform** to demonstrate their cultural knowledge and oral proficiency through video tasks.

What Kind of Blended Learning Experience Can I Create for My Students with *T'es branché?*

Today's students are digitally literate, interactive, experiential, social, and possessed of strong visual-spatial skills. They look for fast response times and are adept at multitasking. ***T'es branché?*** is motivated by the belief that to be successful, teachers need to communicate in the language and style of today's students. To achieve this goal, we have created materials that coordinate with a blended-learning approach that allows for three types of learning:

Face-to-Face Learning	**Self-Paced Learning**	**Online Collaborative Learning**

Face-to-Face Learning

Classroom learning with ***T'es branché?*** centers on the three modes of communication: interpersonal, presentational, and interpretive, or a combination of these. Activities move from mechanical to meaningful to creative and open-ended as students progress with concepts and information. Assessment is geared to the level of the student with three possibilities for testing: tests for the advanced learner, tests for the at-standard learner, and tests for the slower-paced learner.

Self-Paced Learning

In today's student-centered classroom, students need to be able to learn at their own pace. To learn vocabulary, ***T'es branché?*** allows for students to learn words and expressions at their own pace with digital flash cards and eVisuals, some of which are interactive. In the culture section, called **Points de départ**, students can find out more online about any covered topic by using search words that are provided under each informational paragraph. Students can learn each unit's content at their own pace with the interactive textbook; for example, they can listen to and watch the dialogues as many times as they need to. Students can see if they have learned the vocabulary and structure content by playing the *Grammar and Vocabulary Practice Games*, which allow for immediate feedback. Immediate feedback is also provided in the online pre-tests so that students can see what they need to go back and review before each Unit Test. These are a just few of the features of ***T'es branché?*** available on Passport®, EMC's online learning environment.

Online Collaborative Learning

Students work collaboratively using ***T'es branché?*** in the **À vous la parole**, **Culture sur place**, **Système D**, and **Projets finaux** sections. Fun and worthwhile activities in which they can participate online include interviewing or surveying francophone teens, communicating with francophone communities, exchanging videos with other French or francophone classes, participating in a service project with other French speakers, posting and commenting on movie reviews, sharing and describing personal photos, and planning a class trip to a French-speaking location.

The blended learning approach of ***T'es branché?*** provides a technology-rich learning environment that responds to the needs and expectations of students and teachers of the 21st century and extends the second-language environment beyond the classroom. ***T'es branché?***, in conjunction with EMCL, speaks the multimedia language of students today. **On est branché!**

Pre-AP French Language and Culture

The new AP French Language and Culture exam is centered around themes, incorporates overarching essential questions, and focuses on the three modes of communication (interpersonal, presentational, and interpretive). It also relies on authentic print, audio, and video materials, and requires students to comprehend cultural perspectives and make comparisons between cultures. These are some of the ways in which ***T'es branché?*** prepares students for the eventual AP French language exam:

- Units are organized thematically—for example, "**Les rapports personnels**," "**Les arts francophones**," and "**La culture des affaires**."
- All units have a **Question centrale**, or essential question around which students frame their learning. For example: **Qu'y a-t-il d'universel dans les rapports entre les gens? Qu'apprend-on de la culture d'un pays en étudiant son économie?**
- The culture readings (**Points de départ**) take students to French-speaking locations. The **Produits** boxes introduce key cultural products in French-speaking countries. The **Perspectives** questions get students to read excerpts from songs, poems, blogs, etc., and to think about cultural perspectives in **la Francophonie**. The **Traditions et pratiques** boxes prompt students to approach cultural information through practices. In this section, students also make comparisons with the cultures they know in the culture section.
- The **Stratégie communicative** sections provide clear and effective strategies (such as how to use appropriate register, how to notice cognates to infer meaning in a text, how to write descriptively, how to use interrogative words to continue a conversation, or how to write a postcard) to help students use the three modes of communication in meaningful, creative activities that use critical thinking skills.
- The **Lecture thématique** sections present authentic texts from the French-speaking world (novels, poetry, dialogues, blogs, etc.) that students use critical thinking skills to read and appreciate. There are also readings in French in the culture section and authentic texts in **Du côté des médias**.

- **Système D** presents students with real-life situations that require them to use interpretive, analytical, and problem-solving skills, and to research and reflect on outcomes and perspectives, in order to present a meaningful response or presentation.
- Finally, the **Bilan cumulatif**, at the end of every other unit, provides a practice test experience in listening, reading, writing, composition, and speaking.
- The online Pre-AP Listening resource allows students to listen to audio that is followed by multiple-choice questions, as on the AP French exam. However, since this is Pre-AP, students who are unable to answer the questions with audio alone are prompted to "watch" the video to help them understand before trying the questions again.

Students who use ***T'es branché?*** will learn to use French in real-life settings (Communities), demonstrate an understanding of francophone cultures (Culture), incorporate interdisciplinary learning (Connections), make comparisons between their cultures and languages and those of the French-speaking world (Comparisons), all while communicating in French (Communication).

T'es branché? and the International Baccalaureate

The International Baccalaureate (IB) program is recognized in many schools in more than 146 countries, with more than 1,700 schools participating in the United States. It seeks to develop global citizens with a strong sense of cultural awareness who recognize and develop universal human values. The program stimulates curiosity and inquiry as students learn and acquire knowledge across different disciplines in a quest toward lifelong learning.

With ***T'es branché?***, students are exposed to **la Francophonie** in culture readings, activities, projects, and literature selections, so they gradually become global citizens who can embrace the cultures of places where French is spoken. They interact with francophone students in **À vous la parole** and **Projets finaux** activities and projects. **Culture sur place** asks students to interact directly with francophone culture as participants. Students see universal human values at work in the **Lecture thématique** selections and **Points de départ** sections, and they build relationships by working collaboratively with others in pair and group activities. Pushing the boundaries of their knowledge in cross-disciplinary activities, they connect to math, literature, meteorology, art, science, technology, and many other subject areas.

Each unit of ***T'es branché?*** is organized around a **Question centrale**—a backdrop against which all the content of the unit is set. At the end of the unit, students are asked to recapture and reflect on what they have learned and to self-assess in **Faisons le point!**

As students learn with ***T'es branché?***, they begin to acquire important IB characteristics, becoming:

- **knowledgeable** about French language and culture (students learn and reflect on many aspects of the French language (registers, idioms, etc.), and are exposed to various cultural information through the French and francophone world in **Points de départ**)
- **inquiring** about many subject areas (students have opportunities to make connections with other disciplines throughout the unit, especially in **Projets finaux**)
- **reflective** about human values, social issues, and their own learning process (**Rencontres culturelles** presents students with conversations varying from day-to-day concerns to social issues and human values; students reflect on their learning in **Faisons le point!**)
- **open-minded** about other cultures, their values, and different points of view (in **Culture sur place**, students experience French culture by investigating and reflecting on various points of view)
- **caring** about their classmates and francophone students with whom they collaborate (students are encouraged to build communities as they collaborate with partners on various projects in **Projets finaux**)
- **communicative** as they interact orally and write memos, web pages, formal and informal letters, journal articles, reports on surveys they have taken, brochures, and critiques of books and films (in **À vous la parole** and **Système D**, students use the three modes of communication to present information or interact with peers)

With ***T'es branché?*** as a tool, IB students become great communicators who practice interpersonal, presentational, and interpretive language skills in activities and projects that are engaging, challenging, and open ended.

La nouvelle orthographe

T'es branché? and *la nouvelle orthographe*

by Henry Menninger

Une Grenoüille vid un Bœuf,
Qui lui sembla de belle taille.
Elle qui n'estoit pas grosse en
tout comme un œuf…

(from the original *Fables* by La Fontaine, 17th century)

Une grenouille vit un bœuf,
Qui lui sembla de belle taille.
Elle qui n'était pas grosse en
tout comme un œuf…

(the same text, using modern French spelling)

Those of us who can read and understand La Fontaine and Molière today owe a debt of gratitude to three centuries of French spelling reforms. The accumulation of orthographic inconsistencies over the years has required that the written language be "tidied up" and standardized from time to time. With the publication of the third edition of its ***Dictionnaire*** in 1740, the **Académie française** undertook its first major successful spelling reform, adjusting nearly a third of French words by adding accent marks and removing superfluous double consonants. Several decades later saw the simplification of words of Greek origin: ***alchymie***, for example, became **alchimie**. And in 1835, the letter **t** was officially reinstated in plural words such as ***enfans*** and ***contens***, while **ai** replaced **oi** in ***j'avois***, ***il étoit***, etc.

In 1990, the **Académie française**—along with the official language-regulating bodies of other francophone countries (such as in Belgium, Switzerland, and Quebec)—unanimously approved new spelling recommendations by the **Conseil supérieur de la langue française**, the French government's advisory board on matters pertaining to the French language. Insofar as only 5 percent of French words are affected by these **rectifications orthographiques**, their scope is far more limited than that of major spelling reforms of centuries past.

So why *these* changes, and why now? The written forms of a language should always be at the service of human communication, not the reverse. Though it affects only one word per page on average (usually involving an accent mark), **la nouvelle orthographe** (also known as **l'orthographe recommandée**) aims to bring more consistency and uniformity to French spelling conventions, thereby refining comprehensibility. It eliminates anomalies that are no longer justifiable, while standardizing the spelling of certain words and word families whose irregularities have long caused hesitation, uncertainty, and frustration among native and non-native users alike. The new spellings have already been incorporated into dictionaries (e.g., Larousse, Le Robert, Hachette), verb conjugation guides (e.g., Bescherelle), and other widely available reference materials from major publishers (e.g., ***Le bon usage*** by Maurice Grevisse and André Goosse). The French-language versions of applications by Apple and Microsoft, including their spell-checking features, now comply with these new spelling rules. Teachers in Belgium have been notified to give priority in their instruction to the updated spellings. Switzerland was the first francophone country to make an official statement about **la nouvelle orthographe** to its nationwide body of teachers. And France's Ministry of Education has urged elementary school educators to teach their students **la nouvelle orthographe** and has declared that for instruction in French at all levels, "**l'orthographe révisée est la référence**." To that end, publishers of school textbooks in France are now required to apply the updated spellings.

Though the new spellings are recommended, it is important to note that *traditional and revised spellings are both still considered correct*. While a number of the updated forms have already implanted themselves into everyday usage (**weekend**, **médias**, **cafétéria**, **évènement**, **sandwichs**, **spaghettis**), most of the **rectifications** will require time to percolate through the culture before they gain widespread traction. (As an example, one still encounters the written form ***grand'mère*** on occasion, though the official spelling of this word has been **grand-mère** for nearly a century!) This slow progression is to be expected, as older generations typically take more time to change their writing habits. Just as the updates brought to American English orthography by lexicographer Noah Webster in the 18th century took time to alter such entrenched forms as *colour*, *centre*, *defence*, and *traveller* in the United States, so will these latest French spelling updates be gradual to take hold

In ***T'es branché?***, new spellings are indicated in the Annotated Teacher's Edition on the pages where affected words are included in the active vocabulary, or other sections. The relevant updated spellings are indicated by this symbol, and the teacher may decide if he or she wants to present the words to the students.

Rectifications orthographiques: les grandes lignes

RÈGLES	ORTHOGRAPHE TRADITIONNELLE	NOUVELLE ORTHOGRAPHE
With select exceptions, the circumflex accent is no longer used on the letters **i** and **u**.	**abîme**, **boîte**, **connaître**, **il apparaît**, **coûter**, **brûler**, **une huître**, **s'il vous plaît**, etc.	**abime**, **boite**, **connaitre**, **il apparait**, **couter**, **bruler**, **une huitre**, **s'il vous plait**, etc.
The grave accent replaces the acute accent in certain words to align their spelling with standard pronunciation.	**un événement**, **crémerie**, **réglementaire**, **elle protégerait**, etc.	**un évènement**, **crèmerie**, **règlementaire**, **elle protègerait**, etc.
The hyphen is eliminated from instances of onomatopoeia and elements of certain compound nouns, which are now fused together.	**coin-coin**, **hi-han**, **entre-temps**, **une auto-école**, **le week-end**, **un porte-monnaie**, etc.	**coincoin**, **hihan**, **entretemps**, **une autoécole**, **le weekend**, **un portemonnaie**, etc.
The dieresis is displaced (or added) to the letter **u** to signal its pronunciation where appropriate.	**aigue**, **ambiguë**, **ambiguïté**, **arguer**, **gageure**, **rongeure**	**aigüe**, **ambigüe**, **ambigüité**, **argüer**, **gageüre**, **rongeüre**
Conjugated forms of verbs ending in **-eler** and **-eter** (with the exceptions of **appeler**, **jeter**, and their compounds) eliminate the double consonant, replacing it with a single consonant and a grave accent before a syllable containing mute **e**; the same goes for nominal derivatives of these words ending in **-ment**.	**étiqueter → *j'étiquette*** **niveler → *elle nivelle, nivellement,*** **renouveler → *elle renouvelle, le renouvellement***, etc.	**j'étiquète** (like **j'achète**) **elle nivèle** (like **elle pèle**), **le nivèlement, elle renouvèle, le renouvèlement**, etc.
Elements of compound numerals, both cardinal and ordinal, are now systematically joined by hyphens.	**vingt et un mille cinq cent quatre-vingt-un** (21 581) **sept centième** (700e)	**vingt-et-un-mille-cinq-cent-quatre-vingt-un** (21 581) **sept-centième** (700e)
Compound nouns joined with hyphens (or fused together) add **s** or **x** always and only in their plural form.	**un essuie-mains**, **des essuie-mains** **un coupe-ongles**, **des coupe-ongles** **un hors-jeu**, **des hors-jeu** **un sans-papier**, **des sans-papier** **un abat-jour**, **des abat-jour**	**un essuie-main**, **des essuie-mains** **un coupe-ongle**, **des coupe-ongles** **un hors-jeu**, **des hors-jeux** **un sans-papier**, **des sans-papiers** **un abat-jour**, **des abat-jours**
Loan words from other languages now bear accent marks that reflect their standard pronunciation in French, and form their plural according to standard French rules for pluralization.	**la cafeteria**, **le diesel**, **un media**, **un revolver** **les gentlemen**, **les sandwiches**, **les spaghetti**, etc.	**la cafétéria**, **le diésel**, **un média**, **un révolver** **les gentlemans**, **les sandwichs**, **les spaghettis**, etc.
The past participle of **laisser**, like that of **faire**, is now invariable when followed by an infinitive.	**les élèves qu'on a laissés partir** **Elle s'est laissée gronder**.	**les élèves qu'on a laissé partir** **Elle s'est laissé gronder**.
Miscellaneous residual anomalies have been rectified.	**s'asseoir** **un oignon**, **un nénuphar**, **un relais** the past participles **absous/absoute** and **dissous/dissoute**, etc.	**s'assoir** (now aligned with the spelling of **voir** and **choir**) **un ognon** (like **pognon** and **rognon**), **un nénufar**, **un relai** (like **balai**) the past participles **absout(e)** and **dissout(e)**, etc.
Except in the names of trees and plants (**groseillier**, **vanillier**, etc.), the ending **-illier** is now replaced by **-iller** in words where the **i** following the **ll** is unpronounced.	**un joaillier**, **un marguillier**, **une serpillière**, etc.	**un joailler**, **un marguiller**, **une serpillère**, etc.

T'es branché ? 3

Second Edition

Author

Toni Theisen

With the collaboration of

Jacques Pécheur

Contributing Writers

Stephen R. Adamson
Rogers, AR

Caroline Busse
Pasadena, CA

Nathalie E. Gaillot
Lyon, France

Jennifer Kilmore
West Memphis, AR

Lynne I. Lipkind
West Hartford, CT

Diana I. Moen
St. Paul, MN

Annie-Claude Motron
Paris, France

Virginie Pied
Salt Lake City, UT

Nicki Stevenson
Glasgow, Scotland

Emily Wentworth
Branford, CT

Pamela M. Wesely
Iowa City, IA

EMC Publishing®

ST. PAUL, MINNESOTA

Senior Editor: Nathalie Gaillot
Senior Associate Editor: Nicki Stevenson
Assistant Editor: May Vang
World Language Production Editor: Emily Tope
Cover and Text Designer: Leslie Anderson

Illustrators: TSI Graphics
Production Specialists: Tammy Norstrem, Ryan Hamner, Sara Schmidt Boldon, and Jaana Bykonich
Reviewers: Sébastien DeClerk, Emily Wentworth, Henry Menninger

Credits: Photo Credits, Art Credits, and Realia Credits follow the Index.

ISBN 978-1-53382-166-9

875 Montreal Way
St. Paul, MN 55102

Email: educate@emcp.com

Website: www.emcp.com

Printed in the United States of America

27 26 25 24 23 22 21 20 19 18 1 2 3 4 5 6 7 8 9 10

To the Student

Pensez-vous à votre avenir?

Ms. Brown used her knowledge of French to become a conference interpreter for the UN Development Program.

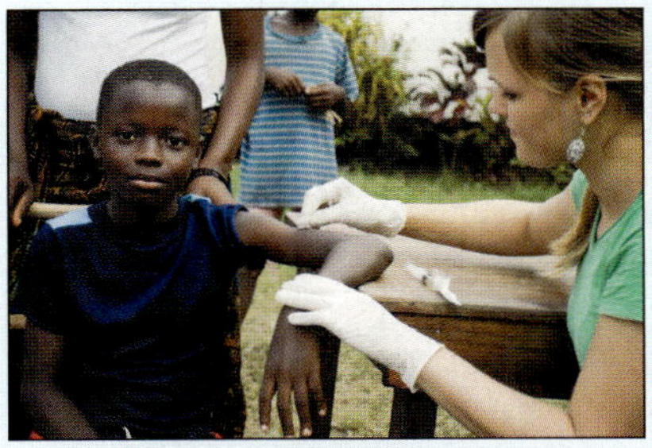

Médecins sans Frontières recruits medical professionals who speak French to help African countries such as the Ivory Coast.

A career using French may be in your future. Combining your French skills with training in a profession of your choice may open doors when entering the workforce. With a degree in law, medicine, or political science you could work as a lawyer in international law or as a paralegal, be a doctor or nurse working for **Médecins Sans Frontières**, or work for a Non-Governmental Organization (NGO) in a francophone country. You might choose to teach English in a francophone country, or apply for a Fulbright Teacher Exchange in a francophone location. French speakers are in high demand for all Peace Corps assignment sectors right now including: environment, agriculture, health, business, education, and community/youth development. There are also jobs in the foreign service, a branch of the government that offers diplomatic services overseas in embassies and consulates.

Universities such as Thunderbird in Arizona prepare students for jobs in business and French. You could work for an American company with a presence in France like 3M, Bank of America, or Hewlett-Packard, or for a French company with a presence in the United States such as Air France (air travel), Accor (hotels), or L'Oréal (cosmetics). According to Bloomberg Rankings, French is the second most useful language in the world for business, after English. You might want to apply for **un stage**, or apprenticeship, at a company while in college or right after you've earned your degree. You might consider working as an insurance agent, banker, financial services provider, public relations specialist, or marketing director using your French.

If you're interested in communications, there are jobs as reporters, production assistants, news anchors, book editors, translators, or editors and proofreaders. The areas of hospitality and recreation offer jobs such as tour guides, sales coordinators, and museum tour guides. Whatever job you're interested in pursuing, think about positioning yourself in a company, agency, or NGO with your bilingual skills.

This year you will learn about French history, more francophone travel destinations, French companies and luxury products, famous French singer-songwriters, and much more! **Bonne continuation** as you continue your learning about French language and francophone cultures!

Recherche: careers in french, thunderbird, state department, careerinsider/vault, concordia language villages, gale's public relations career directory

Contents

Unité 3
La Francophonie 136

Unité 4
Préparatifs de départ 200

Unité 5
Comment se renseigner en voyage 264

Unité 6
On se débrouille en France 320

Unité 7
Les arts francophones 376

Unité 8
La France d'hier et d'aujourd'hui 440

Unité 9
Récits de la vie contemporaine 504

Unité 10
La culture des affaires 568

Francophonie World Map

Topographic Map of France

Administrative Map of France

Regions and Departments

Map of Paris

CLICHY
LEVALLOIS-
PERRET
Arche de la Défense
Avenue Charles de Gaulle
NEUILLY-SUR-SEINE
Bd Bessières
Av. de Clichy
Av. de St-Ouen
Boulevard Berthier
Bvd
Malesherbes
17e
Bd. G. St. Cyr
Bd des Batignolles
Gare Saint-
Lazare
Bd Malesherbes
Av. de la
Grande Armée
Pl. Charles
de Gaulle
Arc de Triomphe
Bd
Haussmann
8e
Av. Foch
Avenue des Champs-Elysées
Place de la
Concorde
R. Royale
Bd Lannes
Av. Victor Hugo
Av. Kléber
Bois de
Boulogne
16e
Tour
Eiffel
Av. Bosquet
la Seine
Champ
de Mars
Invalides
7e
Bvd St-
Bvd Raspail
Bd Suchet
Statue de la liberté
la Seine
Bvd
de Grenelle
Bd. Garibaldi
Av. Émile Zola
Bd
Pasteur
Bd du Montp
Bd
Exelmans
Avenue de Versailles
Rue de la Convention
15e
Rue de Vaugirard
Gare
Montparnasse
Av. du Maine
Bvd
Victor
R. de Vouillé
Bd
Lefèbvre
Rue
Boulevard
Brune
BOULOGNE-
BILLANCOURT
ISSY-LES-
MOULINEAUX
VANVES
MALAKOFF
MONTROUGE
0
1 Mile
0
1 Kilometer

Aéroport Roissy-Charles de Gaulle
ST-OUEN
AUBERVILLIERS
PANTIN
LE PRÉ-ST-GERVAIS
LES LILAS
BAGNOLET
MONTREUIL
VINCENNES
ST-MANDÉ
CHARENTON-LE-PONT
IVRY-SUR-SEINE
Boulevard Ney
Bd MacDonald
Bd Ornano
Bd Barbès
18e
Sacré-Cœur
Bd de la Chapelle
Bvd de Rochechouart
Gare du Nord
Gare de l'Est
9e
10e
Parc de La Villette
Canal St-Martin
Rue de Flandre
Avenue Jean Jaurès
Bd Sérurier
19e
Parc des Buttes-Chaumont
Bd de la Villette
Rue Lafayette
Rue de Belleville
Bd Montmartre
Bd Poissonnière
Bd de Magenta
Paris
2e
1er
Palais Royal
Place de la République
Rue du Faubourg du Temple
Bd de Belleville
Av de la République
20e
Av Gambetta
R. Belgrand
Bd Mortier
Bd Davout
Centre Pompidou
3e
11e
Boulevard Voltaire
Cimetière du Père-Lachaise
Bd de Ménilmontant
Bd de Charonne
Musée du Louvre
Bd de Sébastopol
Pont-Neuf
Rue de Rivoli
Rue des Francs-Bourgeois
4e
Place Dauphine
Place des Vosges
Place de la Bastille
Notre-Dame
Opéra Bastille
Rue du Faubourg St Antoine
Place de la Nation
Cours de Vincennes
6e
Panthéon
5e
Bd Saint Michel
Bd Diderot
Avenue Daumesnil
12e
Bd Raspail
Bd de Port Royal
Palais de Bercy
Bd de Reuilly
Quai de Bercy
Bd Arago
Av. des Gobelins
Bd de l'Hôpital
Bd Auriol
Bd Blanqui
13e
Bois de Vincennes
Rue de Tolbiac
Av. d'Italie
Bd Masséna
Bd Kellermann
Boulevard Jourdan
d'Alésia
la Seine
Marne

Le monde francophone

Des musiciens sénégalais

Ville de Sidi Bou Saïd, en Tunisie

Le canal du Luxembourg

Déjeuner à Marseille

Un souk à Marrakech

Le port de Labadie, à Haïti

La Saint-Jean, à Montréal

Au Carnaval de la Martinique

Reference Desk

1. Each unit opener spread will have a **Citation**, or quote, designed to connect students to the theme of the unit. The quotation on p. 1, how time reveals secrets, brings opportunities to life, and confirms good counsel, is closely linked to the overriding question of the unit: How do people change as they progress through different stages of life?
2. Each unit opener spread also has a **Conseil pratique** to provide students with a helpful hint to develop proficiency in French.
3. The photo on the opening page spread is intended to highlight a topic from the unit; here, it is teens who are enjoying their youth. The teen years are the focus of **Leçon A**, childhood is the focus of **Leçon B**, and early adulthood is the focus of **Leçon C**.
4. **À savoir** provides a fact or statistic about unit content.

Unité

1 Les moments de la vie

Essential Instruction

1. Ask your students to make a list of ideas that they have about childhood in France, youth culture, preparing for college in France, and French weddings. Have students create a Venn diagram in which they compare and contrast these life events in France with their own experiences.
2. Use their perceptions as the basis of a class discussion, including questions they have.
3. Ask students which grammar topics they have already seen (all but **courir**).
4. Go over the student contract with the class.

Question centrale ?

Comment change-t-on de l'enfance à l'âge adulte ?

À savoir

En France, approximativement un quart de la population a moins de 20 ans.

Citation

« Le temps découvre les secrets ; le temps fait naître les occasions ; le temps confirme les bons conseils. »

Time unveils secrets; time brings opportunities to life; time confirms good counsel.

—Jacques-Bénigne Bossuet, écrivain et homme d'Église français du 17ème siècle

Conseil pratique

To quickly get your French skills back, listen to French (songs, news, podcasts, etc.) while doing everyday activities like cooking, walking, or cleaning.

Quel est le loisir favori de Laurent?

Cette femme se prépare à quelle cérémonie?

Contrat de l'élève

Leçon A I will be able to:

- say where I met someone, advise someone, tell someone not to worry, and say how something appears.
- talk about French young people, scouting associations, and slam poetry.
- review the present tense of regular and irregular verbs and **depuis** + PRESENT TENSE.

Leçon B I will be able to:

- say what I discovered, explain how something happened, and ask for a suggestion.
- talk about childhood, the composition of French and African families, and the **département Provence-Alpes-Côte d'Azur**.
- use the verb **courir** and review the **passé composé** and the **imparfait**.

Leçon C I will be able to:

- say I don't care and express where I'd like to work.
- talk about higher education and elite universities, and weddings in France and North Africa.
- review the conditional, including sentences with **si**; review the future, including sentences with **quand**.

Answers

Possible choices for the video question:
A. la cuisine
B. le bricolage
C. la peinture
D. la danse
Correct answer: C

The answer to the culture question is: **le mariage**. The answer can be found in **Points de départ**, **Leçon C**.

Reference Desk

1. The **Question centrale** is designed to help frame students' learning around an essential question for the entire unit. Students will summarize their ideas about the question in the **Faisons le point!** section in **Leçon C**.
2. The **Contrat de l'élève** shows students the core content of the unit that they must master: the functions, culture topics, and structure topics.
3. In each unit opener there will be two culture questions (for example, this unit's question is about identifying the village in the photo). This question will be answered in one of the cultural readings, and the students should be encouraged to search for the correct response.

Differentiated Learning

Accelerate

Ask students to write a paragraph about their summer using the **passé compose** and **imparfait**, which are reviewed in **Leçon B**.

Decelerate

Ask students guided questions about their summer using the **passé composé** and **imparfait**. You may need to give them cues to initiate proper responses, or as a hint tell them they should listen to the verb form and tense in each question.

Resources

Vocabulaire actif

eVisual

Workbook 1–4

Flash Cards

Listening Activity 1

G & V Practice Games

Reference Desk

1. Lesson vocabulary is presented with photos or illustrations. Vocabulary practice activities follow the vocabulary presentation.
2. Young Americans enjoy many extracurricular activities organized by their schools. French students, by contrast, enjoy activities outside of school, such as art and photography classes, or music, theater, and dance. For student athletes, parents in France depend on local clubs to which they pay fees; the sports complex may offer basketball and tennis courts, a pool, and/or soccer fields, depending on the community assets.
3. **La soirée** is a more formal word for *party*.

nouvelle orthographe **le cinéclub**

Critical Thinking

Comparisons

Two of the lexical items on this page make this a good time to review with students that idiomatic expressions cannot be translated word for word. To express how someone looks, French speakers use **avoir l'air de**, meaning "to seem to be" as in **Il a l'air d'être fâché**. (*He seems to be angry* is more natural in English than *He has an air of being angry*.) The same would be true of the key phrase **Je fréquente**, which could be translated into English as "I often go" rather than "I frequent."

Leçon A — Vocabulaire actif

Quand je sors.... 1.2, 5.1

J'ai l'air de (d')....

détester quelque chose

être fâché(e)

être affolé(e)

réfléchir

Je fréquente....

le ciné-club

la discothèque

le festival

l'association (f.) de scoutisme (m.)

l'aquaparc (m.)

le skatepark

le tournoi de slam (m.)

la soirée

le complexe sportif

le cours particulier (en ligne)

Essential Instruction

1. Ask students which sentence is definitive and which is a conjecture: **Il est fâché** and **Il a l'air d'être fâché**.
2. Ask students to suggest other examples using adjectives that they have learned such as **content**, **triste**, and **pauvre**. Vary the subject forms of **avoir** for more practice.
3. Ask students where they met their **meilleur(e) ami(e)** to elicit the response **Je l'ai rencontré(e)....** For the remaining expressions in **Pour la conversation**, model the expressions or ask students to help you create scenarios such as **Tu vas sortir avec Jean? Tu ferais bien de l'inviter à la maison. Tu ne le connais pas bien? Oui, mais ce n'est pas la peine de t'inquiéter. Tu as l'air de bien l'aimer. Oui, il est super sympa!**
4. You may want to put students in pairs to do **Activité 1**.

Pour la conversation

1.2

How do I say where I met someone?

» Je l'ai rencontré(e) au ciné-club.
I met him/her at the film club.

How do I advise someone?

» **Tu ferais bien de** l'inviter à la maison.
You would do well to invite him/her to the house.

How do I tell someone not to worry?

» **Ce n'est pas la peine de t'inquiéter.**
It's not worth worrying about.

How do I describe how something seems?

» Tu as l'air de bien l'aimer.
It looks like you really like him/her.

Et si je voulais dire... ?

l'auto-école (f.)/ l'école (f.) de conduite	*driving school*
la bibliothèque	*library*
la fête foraine	*(fun)fair*
la salle de jeux vidéo	*video arcade*
la patinoire	*ice rink*
Tu as l'air crevé(e).	*You look exhausted.*
Ça n'a pas l'air d'aller.	*You don't seem so well.*
Ils ont l'air de bien s'entendre.	*They look like they get along well.*
Tu as l'air d'être déprimé(e).	*You look down (literally depressed).*

1 Vendredi soir 1.2

Interpretive Reading

Certains élèves du lycée Victor Hugo ne sont pas restés à la maison ce soir. Lisez le paragraphe ci-dessous. Puis, répondez à la question.

Pierre a bien réfléchi, puis il a choisi d'aller au tournoi de slam avec Saloua. Marie-Alix a décidé de ne pas jouer au foot au complexe sportif. Maxime a fêté l'anniversaire de Chantal à une soirée. Julien est allé retrouver ses copains au skatepark. Julianne voulait voir un film de François Truffaut, elle est donc allée au ciné-club avec son copain. Abdou et Annie se sont rencontrés à la discothèque. Chloé et son frère ont suivi un cours particulier en ligne.

Qui a passé la soirée seul(e) ?

Differentiated Learning

Adapt
You may wish to ask some comprehension questions before assigning the critical thinking question below the paragraph.

Learning Styles

Visual Learners
Students may benefit from creating vocabulary lists, which illustrate the terms that they are learning. Encourage artistic students to create charts, posters, and flash cards for your classroom if you yourself are not artistically inclined.

Multiple Intelligences

Artistic
To check for comprehension of **Activité 1**, have students draw a comic strip of the passage and include a caption taken directly from the text.

Resources

Pour la conversation
Et si je voulais dire... ?
Activity 1

Answers

1
Marie-Alix

Reference Desk

1. **Pour la conversation** showcases the functions for the lesson. Encourage students to learn and practice these functions.
2. **Activité 1** is an example of a comprehensible input paragraph. It is designed so that students read the new vocabulary words in context before using them orally and in written activities.
3. The vocabulary in **Et si je voulais dire... ?** is not included in the end-of-textbook glossary and is intended for students who want to learn more or move at a faster pace in learning French.

nouvelle orthographe **l'autoécole**

Expansion

PQA (Personal Questions and Answers)

Introduce new vocabulary by circling personal questions that engage students in conversations about their own lives. Integrate answers in the questions so that students are not intimidated into speaking, but rather find pleasure in it. For example:
"Christine, tu as l'air d'être fatiguée. Classe, Christine a l'air d'être fatiguée ou elle a l'air d'avoir de l'énergie?" (Class responds.) **"Elle a l'air d'avoir de l'énergie?"** (Class responds.) **"Elle a l'air d'être fatiguée?"** (Class responds.) **"Elle a l'air d'être fatiguée ou elle a l'air d'être complètement crevée?"** (Class responds.) **"Christine, tu as l'air d'être crevée; tu es crevée?"**

Answers

2

1. Martine a l'air de réfléchir.
2. Simon a l'air de détester les haricots verts.
3. Alex et Claire ont l'air d'être tristes.
4. Éric et Sébastien ont l'air d'être affolés.
5. Les garçons ont l'air de s'amuser.

Expansion

After completing **Activité 2**, put students in pairs. Challenge each pair to expand on the activity by adding **parce que** or **quand** to provide additional examples of how to use **avoir l'air de**. Example: **Martine a l'air triste parce qu'elle a eu 10/20 sur son contrôle de maths**.

2 Avoir l'air de.... 1.2, 1.3, 5.1

Interpretive Viewing, Presentational Speaking or Writing

*Regardez les illustrations, puis utilisez **avoir l'air de (d')** et choisissez une expression ci-dessous. Faites attention à l'accord des adjectifs.*

être triste **détester (quelque chose)** **s'amuser**
être affolé **réfléchir** **être content**

MODÈLE

les ados
Les ados ont l'air **d'être contents**.

1. Martine

2. Simon

3. Alex et Claire

4. Éric et Sébastien

5. les garçons

Connexions 1.2, 3.1

Théâtre

You have joined the drama club at a French **lycée**. You are part of the creative team that gets to decide which play or musical the school will perform this year! With a partner, put together a proposal showing the choice of play/musical and a list of characters or actors you will need. Include musicians, stage hands, and props. Present it to another group.

Essential Instruction

1. Review the conjugation of the verb **avoir** before assigning **Activité 2**. You can do this as a relay race or a game.
2. Have students write the answers to **Activité 2** on the board.
3. Do a quick review of direct object pronouns before **Activité 3**. You can do this by cutting up sentences and having students put them in the proper order. Remember to point out the change in the past participle with the use of a direct object pronoun.
4. Check answers to **Activité 4** as a class.
5. You may choose to do the **Questions personnelles** as a teacher/student exchange or put students in pairs.

3 Je l'ai rencontré(e).... 1.1, 1.3, 5.1

Presentational or Interpersonal Speaking or Writing

Dites où chaque ado a rencontré son ou sa meilleur(e) ami(e). Choisissez un endroit dans la banque de mots. Suivez le modèle.

le tournoi de slam **la discothèque** **l'association de scoutisme** **le complexe sportif**
l'aquaparc **le festival de musique** **le skatepark** **la soirée de Yasmine**

MODÈLE Jérémy aime les activités avec d'autres ados. Où a-t-il rencontré Amadou?
Il l'a rencontré à l'association de scoutisme.

Maylis aime les concerts en plein air. Où a-t-elle rencontré Camille?
Elle l'a rencontrée au festival de musique.

1. Amina aime la poésie. Où a-t-elle rencontré Florence?
2. Sophie aime danser. Où a-t-elle rencontré Julien?
3. Karim aime s'amuser dans l'eau. Où a-t-il rencontré Théo?
4. Sarah aime faire du sport et regarder des matchs de basket. Où a-t-elle rencontré Marianne?
5. Marco aime faire du skate. Où a-t-il rencontré Antoine?
6. Jun-Lin aime faire la fête. Où a-t-elle rencontré Fatima?

4 Où sont-ils allés? 1.2

Interpretive Listening

Écrivez les numéros 1–8 sur votre papier. Écrivez la lettre qui correspond au lieu auquel chaque conversation se réfère.

A. la discothèque
B. le complexe sportif
C. la soirée
D. le festival de musique
E. le cours particulier
F. le skatepark
G. l'association de scoutisme
H. le ciné-club

5 Questions personnelles 1.1, 5.1

Interpersonal Speaking

Répondez aux questions suivantes avec un partenaire.

1. Qu'est-ce que tu fais quand un(e) ami(e) a l'air triste?
2. Quels genres de films est-ce que tu détestes?
3. Est-ce que tu réfléchis bien avant de prendre une décision?
4. Où as-tu rencontré tes meilleur(e)s ami(e)s?
5. Y a-t-il un complexe sportif sympa dans ta ville ou ta région? Quels sports peut-on y pratiquer?

Resources

Activities 4–5

Answers

3
1. Elle l'a rencontrée au tournoi de slam.
2. Elle l'a rencontré à la discothèque.
3. Il l'a rencontré à l'aquaparc.
4. Elle l'a rencontrée au complexe sportif.
5. Il l'a rencontré au skatepark.
6. Elle l'a rencontrée à la soirée de Yasmine.

4 Script
1. –Quels chanteurs étaient là?
–Rachid Taha et Faudel.
2. –Tu as l'air fâché. Qu'est-ce qu'il y a?
–Je devais voir Karim. On allait danser, mais il n'est pas venu.
3. –Tu as l'air de détester ta classe d'allemand!
–Oui, je suis nul! Mais M. Morel va m'aider samedi après-midi.
4. –Tu as l'air content. Qu'est-ce que tu as fait ce weekend?
–J'ai fait du camping avec d'autres ados. C'était super!
5. –Tu veux faire du footing?
–Oui, je veux bien.
6. –Si on faisait du skate?
–D'accord. Je suis libre à 14h00.
7. –Qui était chez Chloé?
–J'ai rencontré une fille super belle et sympa. Tu vas l'aimer.
8. –Tu veux voir le drame de Scorsese?
–Oui, si tu veux. Ça a l'air intéressant!

1. D; 2. A; 3. E; 4. G; 5. B; 6. F; 7. C; 8. H

5 Answers will vary.

Reference Desk

Point out that **avoir l'air de** is followed by an infinitive (as shown in **Activité 2**), but that **avoir l'air** can be followed by an adjective.

Expansion

Use **Activité 5** to create a class survey. Assign one question to different groups and tell them to alter the question into a multiple choice question. Have them ask their question to the entire class and report the results.

Differentiated Learning

Adapt

There are many different ways to organize your classroom to maximize productive interaction among students. Some activities are designed to work well in pairs, others in groups of three and four. You can randomly group students by organizing a deck of playing cards according to the number of students in your class. The four students who draw the same number will be working together. Or you might want to organize groups intentionally by pairing mixed-ability students together.

Special Needs Students

Auditory Impairment

To help students who have trouble listening to French audio, make sure they understand the directions for **Activité 4**. You may also want to allow them to have their books open to the vocabulary presentation.

Resources

Dialogue
Activity 6

Dialogue Video

WB Workbook 5–6

Answers

6

1. Élodie; 2. Léo; 3. Léo; 4. Élodie; 5. Élodie; 6. Élodie

Analyse
Answers will vary.

Reference Desk

1. In **Rencontres culturelles**, students can watch the dialogue, which has been filmed, or just listen to the audio.
2. **Mot-clé** is a new feature in Level 3 that highlights the etymology of key words so that students make the connection between Latin and French and learn that languages are constantly evolving. Note that the term **les bandes** may refer to gangs as well, so the distinction is made in the context.
3. Point out some lexical items in the dialogue. The past participle **connu** comes from **connaître**. Ask students to find direct objects that precede verbs: **l'aimer**, **te regarde**, **te sourit**, **tu le trouves**, etc. The infinitive for **vous ne vous quittez plus** is **se quitter**.
4. The expression **au courant** is also used in English.
5. Have students make a list of reasons why Leo thinks that Karim likes Elodie. Example: "**Il la regarde.**"
6. The word **bande** may also refer to a *gang* in journalistic writings.

Critical Thinking

Comparisons

Point out to students the verb **trouver** has two meanings, just like *to find* in English. **Trouver** means *to find something that is missing or lost*. It also means *to find*, as in to have an opinion: **Je trouve que le chocolat est délicieux**. Ask them which verbs would be synonymous with this sense (**penser, croire**).

Rencontres culturelles

Comment tu le trouves ? 1.2, 5.1

Élodie montre à Léo des photos de ses amis sur son portable.

Élodie : On fait une super bande… je n'avais jamais connu ça avant.
Léo : Et lui ? Tu as l'air de bien l'aimer.
Élodie : Pourquoi tu dis ça ?
Léo : Comme ça… il te regarde, il te sourit… ça s'appelle de la complicité….
Élodie : Comment tu le trouves ?
Léo : Karim ? C'est le frère d'un copain, je l'aime bien : il réussit à ses examens ; il adore le cinéma…. Tu le connais depuis quand ?
Élodie : Je l'ai rencontré au ciné-club : ce soir-là, on n'était absolument pas d'accord sur le film….
Léo : Et maintenant il te fait de beaux sourires ; il t'attend après les cours ; et vous ne vous quittez plus… tu ferais bien de l'inviter à la maison….
Élodie : Mais que va dire Maman ?
Léo : Ce n'est pas la peine de t'inquiéter, elle est déjà au courant !

6 Comment tu le trouves ? 1.2, 5.1

Identifiez la personne décrite.

1. Cette personne a l'air de bien aimer Karim.
2. Cette personne connaît le frère de Karim.
3. Cette personne sait qu'Élodie aime bien Karim.
4. Cette personne a rencontré Karim au ciné-club.
5. Cette personne passe beaucoup de temps avec Karim.
6. Cette personne a une super bande.

Mot-clé

Bande. (provençal 15ème siècle, banda : *la troupe, la compagnie des gens*). Une bande se définit comme un groupe de personnes ayant des activités et des intérêts en commun. Par exemple : Je vais toujours au ciné avec la même bande de copains.

Analyse

What does Léo insinuate about his sister? What reasoning does he adopt to come to that conclusion? Present your ideas in a logical order, using textual clues.

Essential Instruction

1. Before watching the video, ask students to look at the photos. What might Élodie and Léo be looking at? Have the students scan the dialogue for cognates like **complicité** and to use context clues to guess other words they may not know. Ask them to predict what they think the video is about. Watch the video together so students can confirm if their predictions were correct.
2. To make sure students understand the dialogue, do **Activité 6** as a class.
3. The **Extension** is a dialogue for advanced students who enjoy being challenged; a critical-thinking question always follows this dialogue. The words in **Extension** dialogues are not in the end-of-unit or end-of-book vocabulary list.

EXTENSION **Le profil d'une lycéenne** 1.2, 5.1

Un journaliste interviewe une lycéenne pour faire un profil de l'ado typique.

Journaliste : Tu as beaucoup de copains et copines au lycée ?

Julie : On est toute une bande : on se retrouve tout le temps à la fin des cours, pour sortir, pour aller prendre un verre au café, on organise des soirées....

Journaliste : Ton petit ami fait partie du groupe ?

Julie : Ben, oui.

Journaliste : Mais ce n'est pas gênant de ne pas avoir de temps à toi ?

Julie : Au contraire ! On a tous notre profil sur Facebook ; comme ça on sait toujours ce que tout le monde fait. Même les copains des copains !

Journaliste : Alors, tu es toujours connectée avec tes amis ?

Julie : Notre génération est toujours connectée !

EXTENSION Qu'est-ce que le reporter apprend de la vie des lycéens ?

1.2, 2.1

Traditions et pratiques

Le concept de « dating » n'existe pas en France. Lorsqu'on aime bien quelqu'un, on passe du temps avec cette personne mais il n'y a pas de règles officielles. On sort au café, en boîte (en discothèque), en ville, ou avec une bande de copains. Si une relation romantique se développe, alors on devient « petits amis ». Si un garçon aime la même fille qu'un autre garçon aime, il peut toujours sortir au café avec elle jusqu'à ce qu'elle décide d'avoir un petit ami.

Produits

Le **réseau social** Facebook est le plus populaire dans le monde. En France, les plus importantes des FanPages sont consacrées au foot (PSG–Paris St-Germain), et à la haute couture (Vuitton et Chanel).

1.2, 2.2

Connexions

Médias et marketing 1.2, 3.2

Vous voulez ouvrir un lieu de rencontres pour jeunes à Paris. Faites une publicité pour décrire le local et attirer votre clientèle. Sur quel réseau social voudriez-vous la publier ?

Differentiated Learning

Accelerate

Have advanced students interview a peer in the class, asking the same questions as **le journaliste** in the **Extension** dialogue. Have the pairs present their dialogues to the rest of the class.

Decelerate

As you read the dialogue aloud, ask your students to sub-vocalize the words as you speak. (They will mouth the words without speaking.) In doing so, they will register the correct pronunciation without the stress of reading aloud. Ask them after each line of the interview what words or expressions they do not understand.

Learning Styles

Auditory Learners

After listening to the main dialogue, ask these students to share what they understand. Only then ask students to look at the text in their books. If they have a hard time understanding, encourage them to close their eyes and focus on the audio input. Explain that closing their eyes restricts visual input to their brain.

Resources

Extension

Answers

EXTENSION

Il apprend que les lycéens aujourd'hui sont très connectés par les réseaux sociaux comme Facebook.

Reference Desk

1. The **Extension** dialogue is for advanced students who wish to challenge themselves. The dialogue is followed by one critical-thinking question.
2. **Ben** is the shortened form of **bien** used as a filler in the conversation the way we might say "well."
3. This would be a good time to review the forms of **tout**. Ask students to find examples of these forms in the dialogue.
4. Recently, the use of Facebook by French teens is on the decline, due in part to the growing popularity of Twitter and Instagram. Despite that, Facebook predicts that its number of users in France will continue to grow as more adults log on to the social network.

Culture

Practices: Information

Level 3 is a good time to start discussing language patterns. The French love to truncate words. For example, **un ado** is short for **un adolescent**; **un dico, un dictionnaire**; **un appart, un appartement**; and **un ordi, un ordinateur**. Ask the students reading the **Extension** dialogue to make a list to share with the class. Encourage students to add to this list throughout the year as they discover more truncated vocabulary.

Resources

Points de départ
WB Workbook 7
Explore

Answers

Comparaisons
Answers will vary.

Reference Desk

1. **Points de départ** is the name of the culture section. Note that the **Question centrale** reappears here. Beside the paragraphs about francophone practices, there are **Produits** boxes and **Comparaisons** questions that allow students to connect French and francophone cultures with their own.
2. Students are not expected to memorize, nor will they be tested on, the glossed vocabulary.
3. If you have access to Passport, find a video or a news article related to **les loisirs** and show it to your students.
4. In contrast to scouting in the United States, scouting in France is based on a model of young leadership, in which older scouts (17–21 years old) lead the troop. Adult leadership exists only at the highest administrative levels and adults do not generally participate in outings.

Culture

Products: Information

For your students who are **branché**, here are some terms they would find on a French social media page. Ask students if they can figure out the equivalents in English for the following: **mentions j'aime** (*likes*), **actualiser une photo de profil** (*update a profile picture*), **historique personnel** (*personal information*), **Exprimez-vous?** (*What's on your mind?*), **mot de passe** (*password*), **mises à jour** (*updates*), and **signaler comme indésirable** (*unfriend*).

Points de départ

Pre-AP

Question centrale ? Comment change-t-on de l'enfance à l'âge adulte?

Modes de vie des adolescents 1.2, 2.1, 2.2, 5.1

Les jeunes pratiquent des sports individuels (judo, natation, sports de neige, badminton, squash, roller, skate, tennis) ou collectifs (football, basket, volley-ball, handball). Ils ont des loisirs audiovisuels partagés (séries TV, cinéma, jeux vidéo). À cela il faut ajouter les smartphones, l'usage d'Internet, les modes d'échanges instantanés (tweets, textos) et surtout les réseaux sociaux (Facebook, Twitter, Instagram, Snapchat) qui participent au développement de communautés virtuelles de goût, d'intérêt ou de pratiques sociales.

Les groupes de jeunes se rassemblent autour de la mode, de la musique, du sport, et des jeux. Ils partagent les mêmes styles d'habillement*, lisent les mêmes mangas, se reconnaissent dans les mêmes héros de séries télé, écoutent le même style de musiques ou encore soutiennent* les mêmes sportifs. Les jeunes ont surtout un goût commun pour la fête dans laquelle la musique occupe une place importante : c'est un moment pour mieux « délirer* ».

Recherche : jeunes et réseaux sociaux, mode de vie des jeunes français

Pascal passe deux heures par jour sur Internet.

habillement vêtements ; **soutiennent** *support* ; **délirer** *to have a blast*

1.2, 2.2

Produits

Les jeunes français aiment se servir des **blogs** pour parler de leurs vies et leurs intérêts, comme Kek, la Blogothèque, ou Et voilà le travail. Il y a plus de blogueurs en France que dans n'importe quel autre pays européen.

1.2, 4.2

Comparaisons

Comparez les modes de vie des jeunes français avec les vôtres.

Le scoutisme* 1.2, 2.2, 3.2, 5.1

Le scoutisme est très populaire en France auprès des* jeunes de 6 à 21 ans. Plus de 80 000 jeunes Français y participent. Ils font des activités en plein air comme des courses*, des relais et des jeux ; ils apprennent des choses pratiques comme monter* une tente ou faire un feu de bois et survivre dans la nature. La fédération du Scoutisme Français (SF) est l'organisation la plus reconnue, mais il existe de nombreuses associations de scoutisme qui reconnaissent différentes religions et méthodes éducatives. À l'origine, les associations scoutes étaient majoritairement catholiques, mais aujourd'hui il existe des associations telles que les Éclaireuses et Éclaireurs de France (EEDF, association laïque*), ou les Scouts Musulmans de France (SMF).

Recherche : scouts de france, uniforme des scouts

Scouts de France

scoutisme *scouting* ; **auprès des** *with* ; **courses** *races* ; **monter** *set up* ; **laïque** *secular*

Essential Instruction

1. Introduce the reading by having students list their own interests. After completing the reading, students compare the interests of French students with their own by making two columns on a piece of paper. The first column will be a numbered list of interests of French teens mentioned in the **Points de départ**. Across from each item is the corresponding interest of American youth, according to what American students have experienced. To add to the list, encourage students to find a teen blog online and follow it for a few days. At the end of the week ask students to share what they have learned.
2. Have students look at the website of a French scouting organization, then have them share what they learned with the class.

Slam poésie 1.2, 2.1, 2.2, 4.2, 5.1

Le Slam est un tournoi de poésie importé des États-Unis. Populaires en France depuis les années 2000, ces compétitions sont considérées comme un sport, et ont pour but de favoriser l'expression orale, afin de donner la parole à tous sans discrimination. On peut apprendre le slam dans des ateliers* de nombreuses villes de France ou prendre part à* des compétitions ou tournois. La Fédération Française de Slam Poésie organise une fois par an le Grand Slam National, un concours* qui regroupe des slameurs et slameuses de tous les pays du monde. Les champions du Slam prennent souvent des noms reflétant* la nature de leurs thèmes ou idées : Grand Corps Malade, Abd al Malik, Oncle Sam, Souleymane Diamanka, ou Nevché.

Soirée slam dans un club local

Recherche : tournoi de slam (+ VILLE), grand corps malade, souleymane diamanka, oncle sam

---

ateliers *workshops* ; **prendre part à** participer à ; **concours** *competition* ; **reflétant** *that reflect*

À DISCUTER

Avez-vous participé à un tournoi de slam ? Pensez-vous que ce moyen de communication soit efficace pour s'exprimer ? Pourquoi ou pourquoi pas ?

Traditions et pratiques 1.2, 2.1

La poésie est une grande part de la littérature française. Elle remonte au Moyen Âge, sous forme orale, où les troubadours allaient chanter pour divertir (amuser) les rois et les nobles. Lyrique, classique, engagée, chanson populaire, ou slam, la poésie se sert de la forme de la langue française pour favoriser un message.

Perspectives 1.2, 2.1

Le slam, c'est la création, l'improvisation qui encourage la liberté d'expression. On prend la plume au lieu de prendre les armes !
—Fabio

Que veut dire ce blogueur ? Êtes-vous d'accord avec lui ?

L'argot des ados

faire la teuf	faire la fête
J'hallucine !	Je n'y crois pas !
Ça déchire !	C'est formidable ! ; c'est génial !
un gadjo	un garçon qu'on ne connaît pas (mot emprunté au gitan)
T'es relou.	Tu es lourd (embêtant, énervant).
Il est grave.	Il est bizarre.
Elle badtrippe.	Elle s'inquiète.

Answers

Perspectives

Il veut dire que le slam permet de se battre avec les mots plutôt qu'avec des armes ou de l'agressivité.; Answers will vary.

À DISCUTER

Answers will vary.

Reference Desk

L'argot des ados is a new feature in Level 3 that highlights slang words.

Culture

Practices: Information

For generations, young French people have spoken a unique sub-language called **le verlan**. It is, in its simplest form, inverted French and similar to what students may know as "pig latin." The very name is a good illustration. **L'envers** means *the reverse*. Take the two syllables and reverse them with a slight spelling change and you have **verlan**. Ask your students if they can guess what the following words mean: **ripa** (**Paris**), **remps** (**parents**), **tromé** (**métro**), **blèmpro** (**problème**). For more information, use the search words **verlan** and **dictionnaire de la zone**.

Expansion

Have students watch some French slam poetry online (that you have vetted). Choose videos that are subtitled and, if possible, provide the script.

Communication

Interpersonal: Paired Practice

Have each student write a problem on a slip of paper. Put the slips in a bowl or hat and ask half the students to take one. Move the desks so that the class is in two circles facing each other. Students in the inner circle will read their "problem" to the opposing partner, for example: **Je voudrais organiser une soirée, mais je n'ai pas d'argent.** The student opposite presents a solution using **Tu ferais bien de (demander à tes amis d'apporter de la nourriture).**

Differentiated Learning

Decelerate

1. While reading **Modes de vie des adolescents**, have the stronger students ask comprehension questions to aid students in their comprehension of the text.
2. Have students participate in a lexical scavenger hunt in which pairs have to search for clues that you have prepared in English. For example, "Find the sentence that states that French young people share an enjoyment of parties and music." (**"Les jeunes ont surtout un goût commun pour la fête dans laquelle la musique occupe une place importante."**)

Special Needs Students

Reading Difficulties

For students who have trouble reading longer texts in French and grasping the concept of the main ideas, create a structured outline for them to complete.

Answers

7. All activities will vary.

8.

1. Il rend plus facile les rencontres entre les gens qui prennent le métro.
2. Il s'agit de rencontres amoureuses.
3. On peut habiter dans de nombreuses villes principales de France, comme à Paris, Lyon et Lille, mais aussi à Montréal et à Bruxelles.
4. Il a perdu son numéro de téléphone.
5. Elle a eu lieu mardi soir.

Reference Desk

1. Review with students what they learned about **le métro** in previous levels. It is composed of 16 routes, mostly underground, transporting more than 4.2 million people per day. It is 133 miles long, composed of 302 stations with 62 transfer stations. The lines are indicated by color and number. The directions are listed by the last station on the line called **un terminus**. The Paris metro operates from 5:30 A.M. to 12:15 A.M. on weekdays and until 2:15 A.M. on weekends. It was ranked the best in the world by the Institute for Development and Transportation Policy (IDTP) for its 100% accessibility to people living in Paris, though it is criticized for poor handicap accessibility. It is the second largest subway system in Europe (after Moscow).
2. The **RER** is a commuter train system that runs through Paris, servicing a more limited number of stations. There are five lines indicated by colors: A (red), B (blue), C (yellow), D (green), and E (pink). Travelers can take the **RER** to locations further afield such as Charles de Gaulle airport as well as to Eurodisney, among other destinations. For more information, search **RATP** and **RER**. Naturally, people using public transportation notice fellow passengers, which leads many to attempt to find those who caught their attention.
3. The "**Croisé dans le Métro**" site is a great resource with much of the language being comprehensible and coming in short spurts that students are accustomed to reading.

7 Activités culturelles 1.2, 1.3, 2.1, 3.2, 5.1

Faites les activités suivantes.

1. Recherchez des clubs où les ados français peuvent pratiquer les sports mentionnés à la page 8.
2. Cherchez un sondage sur la fréquence et l'usage des smartphones et des réseaux sociaux des jeunes français. Donnez le même sondage à dix personnes de votre entourage et comparez les résultats.

Recherche : sondage sur l'usage du numérique en france

3. Faites une recherche sur Internet d'une compétition de slam. Identifiez un texte approprié qui vous plaît et que vous trouvez assez compréhensible. Partagez-le avec votre classe.
4. Cherchez une association de scoutisme en France, et présentez-la à la classe : décrivez les activités proposées, les heures et périodes de ces activités, et la popularité de l'association.
5. Écrivez un slam avec un partenaire dans lequel vous utilisez deux ou trois expressions argotiques. Présentez-le à la classe.

Du côté des médias 1.2

Lisez le texte, puis faites les activités ci-dessous.

Croisé dans le Métro

Croisé dans le métro favorise les rencontres dans les transports

Paris — Publier une annonce à Paris

Coup de foudre
RER A Noisy-le-Grand
Bonjour, On s'est rencontré dans la ligne D. lire la suite

Lyon — Publier une annonce à Lyon

Femme au chapeau vert
M T1 Bellecour
Tu m'as donné ton numéro de téléphone mais je l'ai perdu ! lire la suite

On s'est souri
M T1 Gare de Vénissieux
Samedi matin, à 8h25, tu es monté dans le métro avec ton imper vert et tes beaux cheveux courts ! lire la suite

Homme loyal
M T1 Bellecour
Je recherche une femme qui a pris le métro mardi soir. Je regardais mon portable quand… lire la suite

Paris, Lyon, Lille, Toulouse, Rennes, Marseille, Montréal, Bruxelles….

8 Le courrier du cœur de « Croisé dans le métro » 1.2, 2.2, 3.2

Répondez aux questions.

1. Quel est le but de ce site ?
2. Quelles sortes de rencontres sont publiées ?
3. Dans quelles villes faut-il habiter pour pouvoir publier une annonce ?
4. Qu'est-il arrivé à l'homme qui cherche la dame au chapeau vert ?
5. Quand a eu lieu la rencontre de l'homme loyal ?

Essential Instruction

1. You may wish to allow students to work in pairs to complete the **Activités culturelles**.
2. Before reviewing the conjugation forms, have students explain to one another what a conjugation is (how a verb changes as determined by the subject, or who is doing the action). Have them compare this with what a tense is (when a verb, or action, takes place).
3. Before reviewing the formation of regular verbs, have students see if they can do the Game activity in yellow. Students who are ready can proceed to **Activités 9–11** while you review with the rest of the class.

Révision: Present Tense of Regular Verbs Ending in *-er*, *-ir*, and *-re* 1.2

On recycle!

Do you remember the endings to regular verbs in the present tense? See if you can match the endings below to the correct pattern for regular verbs.

1. **-s**, **-s**, **-**, **-ons**, **-ez**, **-ent** — A. regular **-er** verbs
2. **-e**, **-es**, **-e**, **-ons**, **-ez**, **-ent** — B. regular **-ir** verbs
3. **-is**, **-is**, **-it**, **-issons**, **-issez**, **-issent** — C. regular **-re** verbs

If you got one or more wrong, read the summary below.

To form the present tense of a regular **-er** verb, add the ending **-e**, **-es**, **-e**, **-ons**, **-ez**, or **-ent** to the stem of the verb, depending on the subject pronoun.

trouver			
je	trouve	nous	trouv**ons**
tu	trouv**es**	vous	trouv**ez**
il/elle/on	trouve	ils/elles	trouv**ent**

Usage Tip

Remember that **-ger** verbs (**manger**, **voyager**) are slightly changed in the **nous** form in that the ***e*** is retained. For example: **nous mangeons**.

Comment tu **trouves** le garçon? — *What do you think of the boy?*
Je le **trouve** génial! — *I think he is fantastic!*

To form the present tense of a regular **-ir** verb, add the ending **-is**, **-is**, **-it**, **-issons**, **-issez**, or **-issent** to the stem of the verb, depending on the subject pronoun.

réussir			
je	réuss**is**	nous	réuss**issons**
tu	réuss**is**	vous	réuss**issez**
il/elle/on	réuss**it**	ils/elles	réuss**issent**

Réussissez-vous à vos contrôles? — *Are you passing your tests?*
Oui, nous y **réussissons**. — *Yes, we are passing them.*

Connexions 1.2, 3.1

STEM

Create a conjugation table, using a multiplication table as a model. Replace the first column with subject pronouns, and the first row with **-er**, **-ir**, and **-re**. If using a spreadsheet, consider creating a formula to automate conjugations. Then test your partner on French verb conjugations, the same way you would test them on math.

	-er	-ir	-re
je	e	is	s
tu	es	is	s
il/elle/on	e	it	–
nous	ons	issons	ons
vous	ez	issez	ez
ils/elles	ent	issent	ent

	-er	-ir	-re
je	chante	finis	entends
tu	chantes	finis	entends
il/elle/on	chante	finit	entend
nous	chantons	finissons	entendons
vous	chantez	finissez	entendez
ils/elles	chantent	finissent	entendent

Resources

WB Workbook 8–11
LA Listening Activity 2
G & V Practice Games

Answers

On recycle!

1. C
2. A
3. B

Reference Desk

1. **Structure de la langue** is the grammar section of the textbook. Here students review grammar topics from Levels 1–2, learn new grammar, and practice each grammar concept, whether new or reviewed. There is more practice for new grammar topics than for review topics.
2. Students originally learned regular verbs in Level 1: **-er** verbs, **Unité 2**; **-ir** verbs, **Unité 5**; **-re** verbs, **Unité 6**. All three types of regular verbs were reviewed in Level 2, **Unité 1**.

Game

Dice Conjugation

In a group of four students, distribute one die to a pair of students opposite another pair with a die, so that two pairs compete against each other. Explain that each number corresponds to a subject pronoun you write on the board: 1 is for **je**, 2 for **tu**, etc. Call out a verb. Students take turns rolling the die and conjugating the regular verbs according to the subject pronoun. Have a sample verb from each conjugation on the board so that students can correct their work. Circulate to see what pronunciation errors you hear and point out a few tips to remember when the class reconvenes.
Note: You may create or purchase pre-printed oversized "dice," as well as dice whose sides you can cover with sticky notes for your own terms or vocab. Students and teachers may make their own sets of large "dice" for the class that can be re-used for different topics.

Differentiated Learning

Decelerate

Have students scan the entire reading and circle all the words they do not know. Then have them look at the context of each word individually and see what they can understand. Have them work to decode the full message with an advanced learner.

Multiple Intelligences

Musical-Rhythmic/Bodily-Kinesthetic

Have students clap or tap out verbs as they conjugate them. They will "feel" the syllables change in the **nous** and **vous** forms as they tap the beat.

Answers

Comparaisons

Yes, those verbs are regular in English; they are all conjugated the same, with only one *s* added at the end of the third-person singular *he* or *she*. Point out that very few verbs (*to be* and *to have*) are irregular in the present tense in English.

9

Leïla et Karim arrivent au parc.
Amadou joue de la guitare.
Mathis et moi mangeons des sandwichs.
Philippe aide Océane.
Léa apporte des boissons.
Julie et Claire jouent au foot.
Salim et toi préparez des hamburgers.

Reference Desk

Activité 9 reviews regular -**er** verbs, **Activités 10–11** all three regular types of verbs.

To form the present tense of a regular **-re** verb, add the ending **-s**, **-s**, **-**, **-ons**, **-ez**, or **-ent** to the stem of the verb, depending on the subject pronoun.

Comparaisons 4.1

Are *to find*, *to succeed*, and *to wait for* regular verbs in the present tense in English?

attendre			
j'	attend**s**	nous	attend**ons**
tu	attend**s**	vous	attend**ez**
il/elle/on	attend	ils/elles	attend**ent**

Qui **attends**-tu? — *Who(m) are you waiting for?*
J'**attends** mon copain. — *I'm waiting for my friend.*

9 Un après-midi au parc 1.2, 1.3, 5.1

Interpretive Viewing, Presentational Speaking or Writing

Dites ce que ces jeunes font au parc. Utilisez une des expressions ci-dessous.

apporter des boissons **jouer de la guitare** **arriver au parc** **manger des sandwichs** **aider (quelqu'un)** **jouer au foot** **préparer des hamburgers**

Essential Instruction

1. Reintroduce regular **-er**, **-ir**, and **-re** verbs as bargain verbs by telling students that with these patterns they can conjugate hundreds of verbs! Brainstorm with them the verbs from these conjugations that they learned in Levels 1 and 2. Review the meanings of the verbs in **Activité 10** and **Activité 11**.
2. Have the students conjugate a sample verb of each type side by side in their notebook. What forms do these verbs have in common? Point out that different types of verbs are used in each activity.
3. Do **Activité 9** as a class, **10** in small groups, and **11** individually or in pairs.

10 La rentrée 1.3, 2.1, 5.1

Presentational Writing

Complétez chaque phrase pour indiquer ce que Marine et sa sœur font pour se préparer pour la rentrée.

1. Marine... une nouvelle jupe dans son magasin préféré. (chercher)
2. Elle... une belle jupe grise qui... 25€. (choisir, coûter)
3. Elle... un pull à sa meilleure amie Amélie pour le premier jour de classe. (emprunter)
4. Le jour de la rentrée, Marine et sa sœur... des sandwichs parce qu'elles n'aiment pas ce qu'il y a à la cantine. (préparer)
5. Il est 7h45 quand elles... de nettoyer la cuisine. (finir)
6. Marine... son sac à dos avec ses cahiers, son dictionnaire anglais-français, et sa trousse. (remplir)
7. Marine... sa sœur au collège. (accompagner)
8. Elle... que sa sœur.... (remarquer, grandir)
9. Marine... à sa sœur de bien étudier. (conseiller)
10. Ensuite, Marine... Amélie devant le lycée. (attendre)

11 Qu'est-ce qu'on fait pendant les vacances? 1.3, 5.1

Presentational Speaking or Writing

Choisissez un élément de chaque colonne (A, B, et C), puis formez des phrases logiques. Attention à la conjugaison des verbes en ***-er***, ***-ir***, *et* ***-re***.

A	B	C
mes copains et moi	écouter un concert de jazz	au parc
tu	finir ses devoirs	à la discothèque
je	dessiner sa famille	au festival de musique
Marco	attendre tes amis	à la soirée
ton cousin et toi	danser la salsa	au cours particulier
les ados	regarder un documentaire	au ciné-club de la ville
Sophie et Ahmed	nourrir les chevaux	à la ferme

Answers

10

1. cherche
2. choisit, coûte
3. emprunte
4. préparent
5. finissent
6. remplit
7. accompagne
8. remarque, grandit
9. conseille
10. attend

11 Possible answers:

Mes copains et moi dessinons nos familles au cours particulier.
Tu attends tes amis à la soirée.
J'écoute un concert de jazz au festival de musique.
Marco finit ses devoirs au parc.
Ton cousin et toi dansez la salsa à la discothèque.
Les ados regardent un documentaire au ciné-club de la ville.
Sophie et Ahmed nourrissent les chevaux à la ferme.

Expansion

1. To anchor the pronunciation of regular present-tense verbs in the three conjugations, ask the students to put their index finger to their mouth as if to say "shhh" each time you say a conjugation that has a silent ending. Through this physical action, they will internalize which forms have pronounced endings and which do not.
2. Select students to put the sentences on the board for correction after they have completed **Activité 11**. Then have the students do the exercise orally, ideally without consulting their written work. Challenge each student in the class to write a sentence on the board without repeating one that has already been written.

Multiple Intelligences

Intrapersonal

Students who like to work on their own can find extra practice on wonderful interactive verb web sites that provide activities online.

Recherche: conjuguemos French, verbs-online, funtrivia

Resources

WB Workbook 12–13

G & V Practice Games

Answers

On recycle!

1. C
2. A
3. D
4. B

TPR

Have students, as a class, come up with four distinct gestures for each verb: **aller**, **avoir**, **être**, and **faire**. As you read complete sentences out loud using a variety of conjugations, students should gesture the verb they hear. Have them do this first with their books open, then with their books closed. At first, gesture the verbs with students. Later on, let them gesture on their own and check for comprehension. Afterwards, students may come up with complete sentences of their own and read them aloud to partners.

Game

Relai de conjugaison

Sit the students in straight rows of 4–6, facing the board. Place a conjugation chart on the back seat of each row. Assign one or two subject pronouns at each desk. Shout out a verb. Students conjugate their assigned verbs and then pass the chart forward. When the chart gets to the front of the row, only the student in the front seat can make corrections before writing all the answers on the board. The first row with a correct conjugation on the board wins the round. Next, the student in the front seat moves to the back and students move forward one chair. Shout out a different verb for round 2.

Révision: Present Tense of Irregular Verbs 1.2

On recycle!

See if you can figure out the meanings of the verbs below. If you have any trouble, read the grammar summary that follows.

1. **ils ont**	A. you do, you make
2. **vous faites**	B. you are
3. **ils vont**	C. they have
4. **tu es**	D. they are going

Many French verbs are considered irregular because they do not follow a regular pattern. Here are the present-tense forms of the "building block" irregular verbs **aller**, **avoir**, **être**, and **faire**.

	aller	**avoir**	**être**	**faire**
je	**vais**	**ai**	**suis**	**fais**
tu	**vas**	**as**	**es**	**fais**
il/elle/on	**va**	**a**	**est**	**fait**
nous	**allons**	**avons**	**sommes**	**faisons**
vous	**allez**	**avez**	**êtes**	**faites**
ils/elles	**vont**	**ont**	**sont**	**font**

Vous **allez** au ciné-club? — *Are you going to the film club?*
Non, nous n'**avons** pas envie d'y aller. — *No, we don't feel like going (there).*

Où **êtes**-vous? — *Where are you?*
Je **suis** au skatepark et Djamel **est** au cinéma. — *I am at the skate park and Djamel is at the movies.*

On the next page you will find the **je** form of the other irregular verbs that you have already learned. An example sentence is included containing one of the other forms of the verb. Do you remember what these verbs mean? To review them, turn to the Grammar Summary at the back of the book.

1.2, 2.2

Produits

Les **ciné-clubs** ont été créés au début du 20ème siècle à Paris, pour les amateurs de cinéma. Ce sont des salles de projection de films. Dépopularisés par les salles de cinéma modernes, les ciné-clubs sont toujours fréquentés par ceux qui aiment les films indépendants ou bilingues, ou les documentaires. Ces clubs organisent aussi des rencontres locales ou des activités éducatives.

Essential Instruction

1. Explain to the students that **aller**, **avoir**, **être**, and **faire** are four high-frequency verbs in French that are the basis for many idiomatic expressions, so they need to be mastered.
2. Allow students who already know these verbs to use them to write a creative story.
3. Give students who need additional practice with these verbs the assignment of writing an original sentence for each one in the list on p. 15, using a pronoun other than **je**.

Verb	Present Tense	Example
s'asseoir	je **m'assieds**	Élodie **s'assied** sur la chaise devant moi.
boire	je **bois**	Que **buvez**-vous au café ?
conduire	je **conduis**	Ils **conduisent** mal leur voiture !
connaître	je **connais**	Nous ne **connaissons** pas la nouvelle élève.
croire	je **crois**	Elle **croit** qu'elle peut réussir !
devenir	je **deviens**	Un œuf **devient** un oiseau.
devoir	je **dois**	Elles **doivent** travailler pour gagner de l'argent.
dire	je **dis**	Le prof me **dit** de faire mes devoirs.
dormir	je **dors**	Tu **dors** tard le weekend !
écrire	j'**écris**	Elle **écrit** une composition.
falloir	il **faut**	Il **faut** étudier pour le contrôle.
lire	je **lis**	Quel livre est-ce que tu **lis** ?
mettre	je **mets**	Il **met** une veste quand il fait froid.
offrir	j'**offre**	Qu'**offrez**-vous à vos parents pour Noël ?
ouvrir	j'**ouvre**	N'**ouvrez** pas la porte ! Il fait trop froid !
partir	je **pars**	L'autobus **part** à huit heures.
pouvoir	je **peux**	Nous **pouvons** aller à l'aquaparc.
prendre	je **prends**	Tu **prends** des notes ?
recevoir	je **reçois**	Qu'est-ce qu'il **reçoit** pour son anniversaire ?
revenir	je **reviens**	Quand **revenez**-vous de votre voyage ?
savoir	je **sais**	On **sait** qui est le président des États-Unis.
sortir	je **sors**	Nous **sortons** au ciné avec nos copains.
suivre	je **suis**	Quel cours **suivent**-elles à 10h00 ?
venir	je **viens**	D'où **viens**-tu ?
vivre	je **vis**	Nous **vivons** à Nice dans un joli appartement.
voir	je **vois**	La plage est déserte, on ne **voit** personne.
vouloir	je **veux**	Raoul **veut** devenir infirmier.

12 Un weekend chargé 1.3, 2.1, 5.1

Presentational Speaking or Writing

Dites où on est et ce qu'on fait ce weekend.

MODÈLE

les ados (faire une randonnée à pied)

Les ados sont dans la forêt. Ils font une randonnée à pied.

1. tu (faire du sport)

2. Luc et moi (faire du camping)

3. je (faire des hamburgers)

4. Alima (faire la vaisselle)

5. Les Castinot (faire une excursion)

6. vous (faire du shopping)

Answers

12

1. Tu es au complexe sportif. Tu fais du sport.
2. Luc et moi sommes à la campagne. Nous faisons du camping.
3. Je suis à la maison. Je fais des hamburgers.
4. Alima est à la maison. Elle fait la vaisselle.
5. Les Castinot sont à la montagne. Ils font une excursion.
6. Vous êtes en ville. Vous faites du shopping.

Reference Desk

Of the irregular verbs in the chart, these verbs were introduced in Level 1: **aller**, **avoir**, **devenir**, **devoir**, **être**, **faire**, **falloir**, **mettre**, **offrir**, **pouvoir**, **prendre**, **revenir**, **venir**, **voir**, **vouloir**. The remaining verbs were introduced in Level 2.

TPR

As this is a daunting list of infinitives for the average student to learn, break down the list into groups of six and work on only those verbs. Ask the students to invent with you a gesture which illustrates the meaning of each verb for the first six. Here are a few suggestions:

Je m'assieds (Pretend you are sitting down.); **Je bois** (Put your thumb to your mouth.); **Je conduis** (Turn the wheel of a car.); **Je connais** (Shake hands.); **Je crois** (Put your hands in a prayer position.); **Je deviens** (Pretend you are a dancer.) Write a pronoun on the board, for example, **nous**. Then say **nous nous asseyons** and have students do the corresponding gesture.

Differentiated Learning

Accelerate

Ask students to write cloze activities that you will distribute to those who need more practice. Make sure students provide an answer key on a separate piece of paper.

Decelerate

Prepare bell-ringers for students to do at the beginning of class for a few days. Inform them that each day they will need to learn all the forms of 2–3 verbs, and tell them which ones you are testing each day.

Learning Styles

Kinesthetic/Visual Learners

For **Activité 12**, ask these students to draw other locations on the board to use for additional practice. Ask the class for expressions to use to continue the textbook activity.

Resources

Activity 14

Answers

13

1. Ma famille et moi avons envie de manger des pâtes. Nous allons au restaurant.
2. Mon meilleur ami a envie d'acheter des billets de concert. Il va à la FNAC.
3. Tu as envie de faire du cheval. Tu vas à la ferme.
4. Mon oncle a envie d'acheter une voiture. Il va à la banque.
5. J'ai envie de faire la cuisine. Je vais au supermarché.
6. Nathan et toi avez envie de faire un tour de grande roue. Vous allez au parc d'attractions.
7. Jean et Clara ont envie de voir un film. Ils vont au ciné-club.
8. Awa a envie de danser. Elle va à la discothèque.

14 Script

1. –Tu as envie d'aller à la discothèque ce soir?
   –Désolée, mais je ne peux pas. Il y a un contrôle de maths demain.
2. –Vous suivez un cours d'anglais?
   –Oui, nous sommes en train de lire Huckleberry Finn.
3. –Tu veux aller en ville avec moi?
   –Si on peut jouer au basket au complexe sportif.
4. –Je conduis ou tu conduis au festival?
   –Je ne peux pas conduire. Je n'ai pas de permis de conduire.
5. –Vous écrivez une rédaction sur la pièce de Molière?
   –Oui, il faut la rendre lundi, et je viens d'écrire le premier paragraphe.
6. –Chéri, tu mets le couvert pour moi?
   –Non, maman, je ne peux pas. Je lis ma leçon d'histoire.
7. –Vous venez à la soirée de Guillaume vendredi soir?
   –Non, nous ne connaissons pas ses amis.
8. –Vous faites vos devoirs de français?
   –Non, nous recevons nos amis.

1. oui; 2. oui; 3. non; 4. non; 5. oui; 6. oui; 7. non; 8. non

15

3. Tu vas…?; 4. Tu fais…?; 5. Tu conduis…?; 6. Tu veux…?; 7. Tu peux…?; 8. Tu connais…?; 9. Tu écris…?; 10. Tu lis…?; 11. Tu suis…?; 12. Tu dors…?; 13. Tu offres…?; 14. Tu sais…?; 15. Tu vis…?

Partner answers will vary.

13 On a envie de.... 1.3, 2.1, 5.1

Presentational Speaking or Writing

Selon ce qu'on a envie de faire, dites où on va.

MODÈLE Julien (lire *Cahiers du cinéma*)
Julien a envie de lire *Cahiers du cinéma*. Il va au kiosque à journaux.

à la FNAC **au parc d'attractions** **au restaurant** **au supermarché**
à la ferme **à la banque** **au kiosque à journaux** **à la discothèque** **au ciné-club**

1. ma famille et moi (manger des pâtes)
2. mon meilleur ami (acheter des billets de concert)
3. tu (faire du cheval)
4. mon oncle (acheter une voiture)
5. je (faire la cuisine)
6. Nathan et toi (faire un tour de grande roue)
7. Jean et Clara (voir un film)
8. Awa (danser)

14 On étudie ou pas? 1.2

Interpretive Listening

*Écrivez les numéros 1–8 sur votre papier. Écoutez les dialogues et décidez si la personne étudie. Si oui, écrivez **oui**. Si non, écrivez **non**.*

15 Trouvez quelqu'un qui.... 1.1, 1.3, 5.1

Presentational Writing, Interpersonal Speaking

Préparez des questions à poser à vos camarades de classe. Chaque personne qui répond affirmativement doit signer votre grille.

Questions	Prénom	Signature
1. Tu as un chat ou un chien?		
2. Tu dois faire la vaisselle après le dîner?		

1. avoir un chat ou un chien
2. devoir faire la vaisselle après le dîner
3. aller souvent au skatepark
4. faire du jogging tous les jours
5. conduire une décapotable
6. vouloir devenir homme ou femme d'affaires
7. pouvoir sortir avec tes amis pendant la semaine
8. connaître un homme ou une femme politique
9. écrire des poèmes ou des chansons
10. lire des blogs chaque jour
11. suivre un cours d'art
12. dormir jusqu'à midi le samedi matin
13. offrir des cartes pour la Saint-Valentin
14. savoir faire de la plongée sous-marine
15. vivre à la campagne

Essential Instruction

1. Review the meaning of **avoir envie** before doing **Activité 13**. Ask students what they feel like doing or what things they feel like having. Complete **Activité 13** as a class or in small groups. Ask for synonyms for **a envie de** (**voudrait, aimerait**). Remind students of the concept of an infinitive construction and point out that **avoir envie de** is an example of an infinitive construction. They will not need to conjugate the second verb because **avoir** in **avoir envie de** is already conjugated. Point out other common infinitive constructions such as the **futur proche**, which students will encounter in **Activité 16**.
2. Read the listening script before having students do **Activité 14** in case you need to review some words.
3. Allow 20 minutes for students to do **Activité 15**.
4. After doing **Activité 16**, you may want students to create a French social media page similar to Zach's using the review verbs and new lesson vocabulary.

16 Le réseau social de Zach 1.2, 1.3, 2.1, 5.1

Interpretive Reading, Presentational Writing

Zach passe l'année en France avec une famille française. Aidez-le à finir sa page de réseau social.

Mon réseau social Recherche

- Fil d'actualités
- Messages (3)
- Événements (11)
- Photos
- Amis

Exprimez-vous

Zach Martin
Afficher mon profil

Me voici à Marseille chez les Simenon. Je (1. être) un vrai membre de la famille. Je (2. mettre) le couvert et (3. faire) la vaisselle tous les soirs. Les Simenon (4. recevoir) beaucoup d'amis qui viennent le weekend. M. Simenon (5. travailler) pour la ville et il (6. connaître) le maire. À leurs soirées, il (7. falloir) parler français.

Au lycée je (8. suivre) un cours d'informatique super ! Ça va m'aider parce que je (9. vouloir) devenir graphiste.

Avec mes copains, on (10. aller) au café après les cours où on (11. boire) un coca et (12. prendre) un goûter. Mon meilleur ami, David, (13. savoir) parler trois langues — le français, l'anglais, et l'italien. Nous (14. aller) souvent au ciné-club et aux concerts de rap. Nous (15. vouloir) commencer un groupe de rock, mais nous (16. avoir) besoin d'un guitariste. Moi, je (17. jouer) de la batterie et David (18. chanter).

Les Simenon et moi, nous (19. partir) vendredi soir pour Nice. En général, nous (20. pouvoir) nager dans la mer parce qu'ils (21. avoir) une villa près de la plage. Nous (22. revenir) dimanche soir. Je (23. croire) que je vais conduire un peu, c'est sûr !

Qu'est-ce que vous (24. voir) au cinéma ? Qu'est-ce que vous (25. lire) ? Vous (26. venir) me voir en France ?

Zach

samedi 10 septembre

Answers

16

1. suis; 2. mets; 3. fais; 4. reçoivent; 5. travaille; 6. connaît; 7. faut; 8. suis; 9. veux; 10. va; 11. boit; 12. prend; 13. sait; 14. allons; 15. voulons; 16. avons; 17. joue; 18. chante; 19. partons; 20. pouvons; 21. ont; 22. revenons; 23. crois; 24. voyez; 25. lisez; 26. venez

Reference Desk

Some highlights to help your students understand the passage **Mon réseau social**:

1. **Le réseau social** means social media.
2. In French, one does not add an **s** to the family name: *I am going to the Simenons'*; the definite article **les** indicates more than one person: **Je vais chez les Simenon.**
3. A synonym for **mettre le couvert** is **mettre la table. Un couvert** is a place setting.
4. **Le weekend** in this reading means *on weekends*.

Game

Debate

Divide the class into two groups: one group is the positives, the other the negatives. Further divide each group into subsections, assigning each section an Internet-related topic (for example, "online dating," "school work and research," and "social media"). Have each subgroup "face off" in a debate, giving pros and cons of the Internet in regards to their particular topic. Instruct students to speculate what their opponents may say and prepare rebuttals accordingly. You may play the role of the mediator to make sure the debate remains productive and fair.

Differentiated Learning

Accelerate

Ask students to prepare a written or oral summary of what they learned about their classmates after completing **Activité 15**.

Decelerate

To prepare for **Activité 15**, which requires the mastery of many irregular verbs, have students prepare by writing down the **tu** form and the **je** form of each infinitive so that they may be successful in interviewing their classmates and responding.

Resources

- Activity 17
- WB Workbook 14
- G & V Practice Games

Answers

On recycle!
1. A
2. B

17
1. Depuis quand
2. Depuis combien de temps
3. depuis quand
4. Depuis quand
5. depuis quand
6. depuis combien de temps
7. depuis quand
8. Depuis combien de temps

Reference Desk

1. Students learned **depuis** + PRESENT TENSE in **Leçon C** of **Unité 8** in the Level 2 textbook.
2. To illustrate that **depuis** expresses an action that started in the past and is still continuing, you might want to dramatize the concept. Write a series of commands on pieces of paper and put them in a hat (**danse**, **conduis**, **dors**, **bois**). Ask for student volunteers to do the activity until you say **Arrête!** Then ask the class to answer your questions in writing. For example: **Depuis combien de temps Annie danse-t-elle?** (**Quinze secondes**).
3. All review activities are labeled with **Révision**.

Critical Thinking

Comparaison

Ask students which two English expressions are equivalent to the French expressions with **depuis**: **Depuis quand?** and **Depuis combien de temps?** (*since when, for how long*)

Révision: Depuis + PRESENT TENSE 1.1, 1.2

On recycle!
See if you can select the correct question for each answer below.

1. Nous sommes en cours depuis hier. A. **Depuis quand...?**
2. J'étudie le français depuis trois ans. B. **Depuis combien de temps...?**

If you could not match the questions and answers correctly, read the grammar review below to review how to use **depuis**.

Depuis quand (*Since when*) followed by a verb in the present tense is used to ask about an action that began in the past and is still going on in the present. To answer this question in a complete sentence, use a present-tense verb form, **depuis**, and an expression of time.

Depuis quand est-ce que Léo travaille à l'association de scoutisme?	*Since when has Leo been working at the scouting association?*
Il y **travaille depuis mars**.	*He has been working there since March.*

Depuis combien de temps (*For how long*) followed by a verb in the present tense is used to ask how long an action has been going on. To answer this question in a complete sentence, use a present-tense verb form, **depuis**, and an expression of time.

Depuis combien de temps êtes-vous au complexe sportif?	*How long have you been at the sports center?*
Nous y **sommes depuis deux heures**.	*We have been here for two hours.*

17 Complétez! 1.1, 1.2

Interpretive Reading, Interpersonal Speaking or Writing

*Complétez chaque dialogue avec **depuis quand** ou **depuis combien de temps**, selon les réponses.*

MODÈLES **Depuis quand** regardes-tu le match?
Je le regarde depuis 14h00.

Depuis combien de temps vit-il en France?
Il y vit depuis cinq ans.

1. ... est-ce qu'elle travaille à la ferme?
   Elle y travaille depuis le 10 juin.
2. Désolé! ... m'attends-tu?
   Je t'attends depuis dix minutes.
3. Vous vivez à Lyon...?
   Nous y vivons depuis l'année 2010.
4. ... est-ce que tu écris cette composition?
   Je l'écris depuis ce matin.
5. Tu lis les bandes dessinées d'*Astérix*...?
   Je lis *Astérix* depuis l'âge de sept ans.
6. Vous cherchez une nouvelle voiture...?
   J'en cherche une depuis un mois.
7. Tu es fâché...?
   Depuis ce matin.
8. ... suis-tu ce cours particulier?
   Depuis six mois.

Essential Instruction

1. Remind students that the present tense, in French, is the equivalent of the English simple present (*I do*) and progressive present (*I am doing*). However, after **depuis**, the present in French takes the equivalent of the present perfect in English (*I have been doing*). You may simply tell students that instead of saying, "I have been studying for four hours," French people say, "I study for four hours." Have them translate the sentences in **Activité 17** into English, as if they were funny French actors: "Since when does she work at the farm?" "Oh, she works at the farm since June 10."; "How long do you wait for me?" "No biggie, I wait for you for 10 minutes."; and so on. To make sure they will not speak like that in English class, tell them to use a thick French accent.
2. You may want to have students respond to only **Depuis quand...?** questions, and then only **Depuis combien de temps...?** questions by using question circling, prior to doing **Activité 17**.
3. You may want to divide the class into three groups and have each group complete one of the activities in **À vous la parole**.

Communiquez!

18 Vivement les vacances! 1.1, 5.1, 5.2

Interpersonal Speaking

C'est presque la fin de l'année scolaire. Avec votre partenaire, vous planifiez vos vacances et discutez où vous voulez aller cet été. Choisissez des endroits (à la campagne, au bord de la mer, etc.) et faites des suggestions sur ce qu'on peut y faire.

MODÈLE **A: Je voudrais passer les vacances à la campagne.**
B: Tu peux choisir un programme à l'association de scoutisme, comme faire du camping dans le sud de la France, faire des randonnées dans la forêt, ou explorer la faune.

19 Ma vie d'ado 1.3, 2.1, 3.2, 4.2, 5.1, 5.2

Interpretive Viewing, Presentational Writing

Vous voulez partager votre vie et votre perspective d'adolescent qui habite aux États-Unis avec des jeunes Français. Vous avez décidé de créer un blog pour un site d'ados francophones. Décrivez ce que vous aimez, où vous allez, ce que vous faites et ce que vous pensez. Pour vous inspirer, lisez des blogs français, puis comparez votre vie à celles des jeunes Français que vous avez rencontrés en ligne. Faites une présentation de votre blog à la classe.

20 Un sondage 1.1, 1.2, 1.3, 2.1, 3.2, 4.2, 5.1, 5.2

Interpersonal Speaking, Presentational Writing

Avec un partenaire, choisissez un thème et créez une liste de dix questions que vous aimeriez poser à des étudiants français ou francophones pour connaître leurs habitudes et leurs préférences. Ensuite, posez vos questions dans un forum ou à travers un appel vidéo, selon les directives de votre professeur. Vous devrez faire une synthèse de votre échange pour la classe.

Produits 1.1, 2.2

Il existe de nombreux sites internet populaires en France. Le service **Lycos France** favorise les communications tels réseaux sociaux, blogs, vidéo, jeux, chats, recherches et autres. **L'Internaute** est un magazine d'informations (actualité, loisirs, culture, finance, métier, sport, voyages, auto, etc.) **ClicNet FLE** produit des ressources littéraires et culturelles pour les enseignants et étudiants de français langue étrangère.

Resources

CA Communicative Activities

Share

Answers

18 Discussions will vary.
19 Presentations will vary.
20 Surveys will vary.

Reference Desk

1. In **À vous la parole**, students will engage in interpersonal, presentational, or interpretive communication to build their proficiency.
2. **Activité 18** is ideal for students who like to work with a partner whereas **Activités 19** and **20** would appeal to students who like to work on their own. Their choice of project will give you an insight into your students' working style.
3. For **Activité 20**, you may use a language exchange website such as *Speaky*, *How do you do*, *The Mixxer*, or *Conversation Exchange*.
4. If you have access to Passport, create a question for your students to share their response to a communicative activity.

Differentiated Learning

Adapt

In your class, it is likely that there are students who are very advanced users of technology. Not all will be your high-ability students; often they will be your low-ability language students who are gifted computer users. Enlist their aid in structuring and executing technology-based projects. This will give them a sense of satisfaction and pride that they can make a valuable contribution to the class.

Multiple Intelligences

Intrapersonal

Your tech-savvy students may want to do **Activité 19** or **20**. They can report on blog posts, thus encouraging the other students to take a look; the blog could be an ongoing class project spearheaded by these students.

Resources

Prononciation
Pre-test
Leçon Quiz

Reference Desk

In this section, stressed letters have been bolded and underlined (for example, **e**, **s**, **l**, or **t**). Unpronounced letters have been grayed out and underlined (for example, e, s, l, or t).

Answers

E Script

1. douze boutiques
2. Vous bougez.
3. Tu veux?
4. des boucles d'oreille
5. Ça coûte cher.
6. Je peux.

1. u
2. u
3. ø
4. u
5. u
6. ø

Prononciation

Accentuation in Phrases 1.1, 1.2

» Only the last word or syllable in a phrase is accentuated. This is called **accent tonique**. The rest of the words in the group are not accentuated.

A Le mariage

Répétez les noms suivants relatifs au mariage. Accentuez uniquement la syllabe en caractère gras (bold).

1. la bague de fian**çaill**es
2. une demoiselle d'ho**nneur**
3. un garçon d'ho**nneur**
4. le gâteau de ma**riag**e
5. la lune de **miel**
6. le voyage de **noc**es

B Les objets technologiques

Répétez les noms à gauche ; faites attention à les accentuer correctement. Les caractères gras indiquent les syllabes qu'il faut accentuer. Ensuite, répétez en ajoutant (adding) le deuxième mot. N'accentuez que les syllabes en caractères gras !

1. un mi**cro** … ordinateur (un micro-ordina**teur**)
2. un télé**phon**e … portable (un téléphone por**tabl**e)
3. une impri**mant**e … laser (une imprimante la**ser**)

The Vowels /y/ - /u/ - /ø/ - /o/

» These four vowels are pronounced with the mouth closed and the lips pursed. Place your tongue as far forward as possible for /y/ (**vue**), far back for /u/ (**vous**), and in the middle for /ø/ (**peu**) and /o/ (**pot**).

C Quelle vue !

Répétez les phrases suivantes, en faisant attention aux sons /y/ et /o/.

1. Quelle vue des roses !
2. Quelle vue des eaux !
3. Quelle vue des autos !
4. Quelle vue des beaux bureaux !

D Deux euros ou douze euros ?

*Répétez les phrases suivantes, en faisant attention au son /ø/ comme dans **deux**, et au son /u/ comme dans **douze**.*

1. Tu as dit deux euros ou douze euros ?
2. Qu'est-ce que tu veux, deux euros ou douze euros ?
3. Excusez-moi, ça coûte deux euros ou douze euros ?

E Distinguez !

*Écrivez /ø/ si vous entendez le son /ø/ de **deux**, ou /u/ si vous entendez le son /u/ de **douze**.*

Essential Instruction

1. Introduce the concept of accentuation in phrases, then have students listen and repeat **Activités A** and **B**. Repeat the recordings as necessary.
2. Make a list of words students know that incorporate the sounds of the four vowels. Ask for volunteers to read the words. (Some students may feel overwhelmed to do that in front of others so be selective.) Put the students in paired groups to read each section to each other. Circulate to correct pronunciation errors. Have the class listen to **Activité E** together.
3. Have students write the three types of families in their notebooks, listing names of fictional families they know that belong to each type.
4. When showing the **Vocabulaire actif**, provide supplemental vocabulary expressions for **Les activités enfantines** that reflect the experiences of your students.

Leçon B

Vocabulaire actif

La famille et les activités enfantines 1.2

Les types (m.) de familles

une famille nucléaire

une famille monoparentale

une famille recomposée

Les activités enfantines

jouer à cache-cache

jouer à la marelle/ à la poupée

jouer aux petites voitures/aux billes

collectionner des coquillages/des timbres

courir

sauter à la corde

faire des châteaux de sable

jouer sur son smartphone

faire semblant d'être une princesse/un super-héros

Resources

- *Vocabulaire actif*
- eV eVisual
- WB Workbook 1–3
- FC Flash Cards
- LA Listening Activity 1
- G & V Practice Games

Reference Desk

1. The three types of families are a nuclear family, a single-parent family, and a blended family.
2. Have students offer other **activités enfantines** in which they participated as a child; write all these terms on the board and use them in subsequent in-class activities.

nouvelle orthographe **jouer à cachecache un superhéros**

Differentiated Learning

Adapt
Make a list of TV shows and ask students to identify the types of families in them. This may be preferable to asking students personal questions about their own families.

Decelerate
Make a list of age groups (**2–3 ans**, **4–5 ans**, **6–8 ans**, **9–11 ans**) and ask students to put the illustrated activities in the age group that fits their own experience.

Resources

Pour la conversation
Et si je voulais dire... ?
Activity 1

Answers

1
Martin collectionne des timbres, il fait semblant d'être un super-héros, il fait un château de sable, il joue aux petites voitures, il saute à la corde, puis il joue aux billes.

Reference Desk

In **Activité 3**, **découvrir** is a new verb from the **Rencontres culturelles** dialogue. Tell students it is in the same family as the verbs **ouvrir**, **couvrir**, **souffrir**, and **offrir**. Note that **ouvrir** can serve as a model for **couvrir** and **découvrir**. Students should get used to prefixes. Show the similarity with **prendre**, **apprendre**, and **comprendre**.

Expansion

After students read **Martin s'ennuie?**, ask them some questions. How old do they think Martin is? Why is he bored? What does he do to keep himself busy? Why does he not play with the babysitter? How does he treat the dog? Is he a typical child? Why or why not?

Pour la conversation 1.2

How do I say what I discovered?

» J'ai découvert la vie des supermarchés ici.
I discovered (the experience of) shopping in supermarkets here.

How do I explain how something happened?

» **C'est comme ça que** l'on est arrivé à Nice.
That's how we arrived in Nice.

How do I ask for a suggestion?

» Tu proposes quoi ?
What are you suggesting?

Et si je voulais dire... ?

la famille éloignée	*extended family*
un enfant mixte	*biracial child*
un enfant adopté	*adopted child*
une mère/un père célibataire	*single parent*
un animal en peluche	*stuffed animal*
un jouet à piles	*battery-operated toy*
un jouet mécanique	*wind-up toy*

1 Martin s'ennuie ? 1.2, 1.3

Interpretive Listening

Lisez le paragraphe sur Martin. Ensuite, répondez à la question qui suit.

Martin habite sur la côte Atlantique en France. Il n'a pas de frère ni de sœur. Ses parents sont en ville cet après-midi. Martin n'aime pas sa baby-sitter. Elle ne joue pas avec lui. Elle lui propose d'aller dans sa chambre, mais lui, il n'est pas d'accord. D'abord, il est fâché, puis il a des idées pour passer le temps. Il met des timbres dans son album ; il aime collectionner les timbres des pays différents. Il fait semblant d'être un super-héros dans le jardin, mais il fait peur au chien. Il s'amuse à faire un château de sable avec quatre tours. Ensuite, il joue aux petites voitures. Enfin, il saute à la corde et joue aux billes.

Comment est-ce que Martin passe l'après-midi ?

Essential Instruction

1. To review family vocabulary from Level 1, have students make a family tree of their own, of an imaginary family, a family from the media, or a family from a work of fiction. There are free family tree templates online to make the task simpler.
2. For **Activité 2**, have students pick a family to write a description or story about.

2 Les familles 1.2, 1.3, 5.1

Interpretive Viewing, Presentational Speaking or Writing

Décrivez chaque famille.

MODÈLE  **C'est une famille monoparentale.**

1. 

2. 

3. 

4. 

3 Les découvertes 1.2, 1.3

Interpretive Viewing, Presentational Speaking

Dites ce que vous avez appris à faire quand vous étiez petit(e).

MODÈLE  **J'ai appris à faire des châteaux de sable.**

1. 

2. 

3. 

4. 

5. 

6. 

Answers

2

1. C'est une famille nucléaire.
2. C'est une famille recomposée.
3. C'est une famille nucléaire.
4. C'est une famille monoparentale.

3

1. J'ai appris à collectionner les coquillages.
2. J'ai appris à sauter à la corde.
3. J'ai appris à jouer aux billes.
4. J'ai appris à jouer à la poupée.
5. J'ai appris à collectionner les timbres.
6. J'ai appris à jouer sur mon smartphone.

Expansion

Have students imagine that they are ten years old and are writing a list of gifts they want for their birthday. Have them visit a French toy store's web site for ideas. They have a 100€ budget. They must write the name of the toy, a brief description, and the price.

PQA (Personalized Questions and Answers)

Ask students at what age they discovered certain interests: **les voitures, la télévision, les smartphones, les jeux vidéo**, etc. Ask students to bring (pictures of) toys they liked from their own generation (and also their parents') at different ages, and do a show and tell.

4 Quand Louis et Lola étaient petits 1.2, 1.3

Interpretive Viewing, Presentational Speaking

Dites ce que Louis et Lola faisaient quand ils étaient petits.

MODÈLE

Ils faisaient semblant d'être des super-héros.

1. 

2. 

3. 

4. 

5. 

5 Ce que j'aime faire 1.2, 5.1

Interpretive Listening

*Écrivez les numéros 1–8 sur votre papier. Écoutez la petite Marie parler de sa vie. Écrivez **V** si les phrases sont vraies ou **F** si elles sont fausses.*

1. Marie vient d'une famille monoparentale.
2. Marie n'a pas d'amis.
3. Marie, Karim, et Julie jouent à cache-cache.
4. Marie joue à la poupée chez elle.
5. Marie aime courir avec Karim.
6. Julie adore jouer à la marelle et à la corde à sauter.
7. Karim gagne toujours aux billes.
8. Marie aime jouer aux petites voitures.

Resources

Activity 5

Answers

4

1. Ils jouaient à cache-cache.
2. Ils faisaient des châteaux de sable.
3. Ils jouaient aux petites voitures.
4. Ils jouaient à la marelle.
5. Ils sautaient à la corde.

5 Script

Moi, c'est Marie. Tous les lundis, je vais à l'école. C'est ma maman qui m'emmène. Nous habitons dans un bel appartement, elle et moi. À l'école, j'ai une copine qui s'appelle Julie et un copain Karim. Pendant la récréation, on joue à cache-cache ou on fait semblant d'être des super-héros. Moi, j'aime jouer à la poupée à la maison, mais pas à l'école. Julie adore jouer à la marelle et sauter à la corde. Moi aussi, mais je préfère jouer aux billes parce que je gagne toujours. Karim lui, il préfère faire des courses de petites voitures chez lui. Moi, je n'aime pas ça.

1. V
2. F
3. V
4. V
5. F
6. V
7. F
8. F

Communication

Interpersonal: Paired Practice

Have students, working in pairs, ask each other what they "used to do" when they were children, using the new vocabulary and the imperfect tense.

Essential Instruction

1. Since the imperfect tense will be reviewed in Lesson B on p. 39, only a brief explanation will be necessary to complete **Activité 4**.
2. Have the students suggest other activities that they might have done when they were young.
3. Before playing the recording that goes with **Activité 5**, ask students to read sentences 1–8 so they can prepare for what they are going to hear.
4. Play the recording as many times as it takes so that all students are successful.

6 Chère Mamy 1.2, 1.3, 5.1

Interpretive Reading, Presentational Speaking or Writing

Lisez le mail que Cédric, qui a neuf ans, a écrit à sa grand-mère. Puis, répondez aux questions.

À: Mamy
Cc:
Objet: Halloween

Chère Mamy,

C'est bientôt Halloween. Je vais mettre un costume de Superman. Cécile fait toujours semblant d'être une princesse. Donc, elle va mettre son costume de Cendrillon. Samedi, j'ai joué avec mes copains aux petites voitures. J'ai gagné. Papa a dit que j'avais l'air d'être très content ! Je continue de collectionner les timbres. Tu peux m'apporter des timbres de ton voyage ? Cécile collectionne les coquillages maintenant. Quand est-ce que tu viens nous voir à Nice ?

Bisous,

Cédric

1. C'est bientôt quelle fête ?
2. Cédric et sa sœur vont faire semblant d'être qui ?
3. À quoi est-ce que Cédric a gagné ?
4. Il avait l'air d'être triste ?
5. Qu'est-ce que Cédric voudrait savoir ?
6. Qu'est-ce que sa sœur Cécile collectionne ?

7 Questions personnelles 1.1

Interpersonal Speaking

Répondez aux questions suivantes avec un partenaire.

1. Est-ce que tu fais partie d'une famille nucléaire, monoparentale, ou recomposée ?
2. Est-ce que tu collectionnes quelque chose ? Si oui, quoi ?
3. Que faisais-tu quand tu étais petit(e) ?
4. Quand tu étais petit(e), est-ce que tu faisais semblant d'être une princesse ou un super-héros ?
5. Aimes-tu courir en plein air ?
6. Qu'est-ce que tu as découvert pendant tes dernières vacances ?
7. Tu proposes quoi à tes amis pour le weekend ?

Resources

Activities 6–7

Answers

6

1. Halloween
2. Superman, une princesse (Cendrillon)
3. à une course de petites voitures
4. Non, il avait l'air très content.
5. quand sa grand-mère vient les voir, et si elle peut lui apporter des timbres de son voyage
6. les coquillages

7 Answers will vary.

Reference Desk

1. Although it is an Anglo-Saxon holiday, Halloween is more and more celebrated in France, due to globalization.
2. You may want to vary how you approach the **Questions personnelles**. They are intended to get students to ask each other questions, but you may want to ask students the questions individually using **vous**.

Communication

Interpersonal: Groups

Use **Activité 7** to create a survey for your classroom community. Assign one question per group and have students re-write the questions as a multiple-choice exercise. Each group must make sure that the entire class is surveyed and must create a presentation of their survey results. In their presentation, they should compare the results of their survey to the trends in France that they may have been able to find by doing online research.

Differentiated Learning

Expand

You may want students to create a digital or traditional storybook using clipart, photos from magazines, or personal photos illustrating what they did when they were younger (**quand j'étais petit(e)**). Tell them how many pages with commentary in French you expect. Have the students submit their sentences for correction before putting them in the storybook. They can use online storybook programs or storybook apps.

Decelerate

If students are having a hard time understanding **Activité 5**, provide the script so they can read along after they have heard it a few times.

Resources

Dialogue
Activity 8

Dialogue Video

WB Workbook 4

Answers

8

2, 6, 4, 5, 1, 3

Reference Desk

1. Explain that this dialogue is written in the imperfect tense because Karim is talking about what life was like when he was younger. Ask students what they remember about the **imparfait**.
2. Point out that **se connaissait** is an example of a reflexive thought: Everyone knew "one another." Ask students where they see another such example.
3. The past participle **vécu** comes from **vivre**.
4. Point out the difference between **en fait** (*in fact*) and **au fait** (*by the way*).

nouvelle orthographe **connaitre, reconnaitre, méconnaitre**

Rencontres culturelles

L'enfance de Karim 1.2, 5.1, 5.2

Karim et Léo se promènent à Nice.

Karim : C'était plus possible… un jour ma mère est partie… nous, on a suivi… c'est comme ça que l'on est arrivé à Nice.

Léo : Et tu n'as pas eu de regrets?

Karim : Si, le village où on habitait… tout le monde se connaissait. Il n'y avait qu'une école dans le village ; les commerçants nous appelaient par notre prénom ; on se retrouvait tous au foot, on y jouait le mercredi après-midi…. Et puis on avait une grande maison avec une piscine….

Léo : En fait, tu n'avais jamais vécu en ville?

Karim : Non, jamais ! J'ai découvert la vie des supermarchés ici. Dans l'immeuble, à l'étage où on habitait, personne ne nous parlait au début… et puis le foot aussi, ça a été fini… je n'y ai jamais plus joué. Heureusement, il y a eu le cinéma….

Léo : Et c'est comme ça qu'on s'est connu….

Karim : Au fait, on va voir quoi ce soir?

Léo : Élodie, elle propose quoi?

Mot-clé

Connaître. Le verbe *connaître* vient de l'infinitif latin *cognoscere*. Le latin est la base de plusieurs langues européennes, dites *langues romanes*. *Connaître* est la racine des verbes *reconnaître* (*to recognize*) et *méconnaître* (*to misread, to be unaware of*).

8 L'enfance de Karim 1.2, 1.3

Remettez les phrases en ordre chronologique.

1. Karim a arrêté de jouer au foot.
2. La mère de Karim est arrivée à Nice.
3. Léo a fait la connaissance de Karim au ciné-club.
4. Karim a découvert les supermarchés.
5. Les gens de l'immeuble à Nice n'ont pas parlé à Karim et à sa famille.
6. Karim a déménagé (*moved*) à Nice.

Stratégie

In a diagram, make one column (or circle) to show how life was in Karim's village, and another to show how his life has been in Nice. Find and copy context clues from the dialogue to fill your diagram.

Essential Instruction

1. Discuss the title of the video dialogue, **L'enfance de Karim**, asking what past tenses Karim will be using.
2. Watch the video and ask students to summarize what they understand.
3. Ask the students to read the dialogue and the sentences in **Activité 8** and watch the video a second time.
4. Do **Activité 8** in pairs and write the sentences in the correct order on the board.

EXTENSION **Les enfants vont bien?** 1.2

Au café, deux femmes parlent de leurs nouvelles vies.

Mme Duhamel: Avec Pierre, nous nous sommes arrangés. J'ai les enfants une semaine, et il les prend la semaine suivante, et ainsi de suite. C'est plus simple.

Mme Laforge: Mon ex-mari ne prend les enfants qu'un weekend sur deux. Je lui ai dit que ce n'était pas bon pour les enfants. Ils veulent le voir plus. Mais, non!

Mme Duhamel: Je vois: la règle, c'est la règle. Et les enfants, ils le vivent comment?

Mme Laforge: Pas très bien. Ils ont été très déstabilisés au début. Avec Sandrine, la compagne de Julien, ça se passe moyennement bien. Ils sont très nostalgiques de notre vie d'avant. Toi, tu as de la chance.

Mme Duhamel: Pierre n'a pas de compagne fixe pour le moment, il est très attentif aux enfants et puis il s'entend bien avec Marc. Il passe souvent à la maison.

EXTENSION 1.1, 1.2 Qu'est-ce qui a changé dans les vies de Mme Duhamel, de Mme Laforge, et de leurs enfants?

1.2, 4.2

Comparaisons

Il y a en France plus de 40% de divorces, la plupart intervenant après 15 ans de mariage. Quelles sont les raisons qui peuvent pousser au divorce en France? Comparez avec votre pays.

Analyse

How many parental figures do the children of Mme Duhamel have, compared to those of Mme Laforge? Examine the composition of each new family, and discuss the effect each situation has on the children.

Resources

Extension

Answers

EXTENSION

Mme Duhamel et Mme Laforge ont divorcé de leurs maris.

Comparaisons

Answers may include: les unions libres, le PACS, la longévité de la population, les opportunités professionnelles pour les femmes, les raisons personnelles (manque de communication, problèmes d'argent, infidélité, addictions, etc.)

Analyse

Mme Duhamel's children have three parental figures: Mme Duhamel, her companion Marc, her ex-husband Pierre. Mme Laforge's children have also three parental figures: Mme Laforge, her ex-husband Julien, his companion Sandrine.

Reference Desk

Here are some expressions students may need help understanding: **Nous nous sommes arrangés.** (*We have worked things out.*) **Ainsi de suite.** (*And so on.*) **Ils le vivent comment?** (*How are they taking it?*)

Differentiated Learning

Adapt

Ask students to determine which lines of the main dialogue fit this outline: 1. Change in Karim's life as a child. 2. His old life. 3. His new life. 4. His friendship with Léo and Élodie.

Special Needs Students

At-Risk Students

The **Extension** dialogue relates the difficulty children have adapting to divorce. Look for signs that certain students are struggling with the topic, being sensitive to their personal and individual situations.

Resources

- *Points de départ*
- WB Workbook 5
- Explore

Reference Desk

1. The **loi Taubira** legalized same-sex marriages in France in 2013. Today, they make up approximately 3.5% of marriages in France.
2. Other common family words include **Mamy** (*Grandma*) and **Papy** (*Grandpa*). Children may be called **les gamins** or **les gosses**.
3. If you have access to Passport, find a video or a news article related to **la famille** and show it to your students.

Culture

Practices: Activity

To make a comparison to American culture, draw two columns on the board and write the facts from the paragraph **L'enfance en France** in the left column. Then discuss with students what they think is true about childhood in America, and write those observations down on the right. Point out that anecdotal evidence is not scientific evidence. Gauge whether any students would like to uncover the facts, statistics, and percentages to verify the observations about American culture.

Points de départ

Pre-AP

Question centrale ? Comment change-t-on de l'enfance à l'âge adulte ?

L'enfance en France 1.2, 2.1, 3.1, 5.1

En France, tout est fait pour encourager la natalité* : l'État verse des allocations familiales à partir du second enfant. Les familles bénéficient également de réductions d'impôts* mais aussi dans les transports en commun ou pour des activités culturelles. Elles ont accès aux bourses d'études* pour les enfants si leurs revenus* sont insuffisants. Elles perçoivent* également l'allocation de rentrée scolaire. À partir du deuxième enfant les mères peuvent bénéficier d'un congé parental d'un an, rémunéré. L'État considère qu'élever un enfant est un métier ; aussi, les femmes qui ont élevé trois enfants et qui n'ont pas pu avoir une autre activité professionnelle ont droit à une retraite*.

Les communes ont des crèches* qui accueillent les enfants toute la journée et des halte-garderies* pour des gardes occasionnelles. L'accueil à l'école maternelle à partir de deux ans est aussi une manière de permettre de concilier vie professionnelle et vie familiale.

Recherche : allocations familiales, aides familiales

natalité *childbirth* ; **impôts** *taxes* ; **bourses d'études** *scholarships* ; **revenus** *income* ; **perçoivent** *receive* ; **retraite** *retirement* ; **crèches** *day care centers* ; **halte-garderies** *drop-in day care centers*

Traditions et pratiques 1.2, 2.1

En France, on privilégie l'égalité hommes-femmes. Suite à la naissance d'un bébé, les mères ont droit à un congé maternité et les pères à un congé paternité.

La famille 1.2, 2.1, 3.1, 4.1, 5.1

Les Français restent très attachés à la famille, mais les modèles familiaux ont considérablement évolué. 73% des couples sont mariés, avec environ 240 000 mariages par an. Les femmes se marient en moyenne à 28 ans, et les hommes à 30 ans, souvent après une longue période de cohabitation* et en ayant déjà des enfants. Une autre forme de vie commune concurrence* le mariage : le PACS* (Pacte civil de solidarité). Institué en 1999, le PACS est un contrat légal entre deux personnes qui veulent former un couple ; il accorde des droits et des devoirs*, mais est moins conséquent* que le mariage. Environ 4% des couples sont « pacsés* » aujourd'hui. Enfin, l'union libre, la simple cohabitation, représente 23% du mode de vie des couples ; elle attire surtout les jeunes Français vivant majoritairement dans les grandes villes.

Un mariage sur deux se termine en divorce, et 20% des enfants de moins de 25 ans vivent avec un seul de leurs parents. Les remariages ont donné naissance aux* familles recomposées où cohabitent souvent demi-frères et demi-sœurs.

Restent les célibataires* qui représentent 14% des Français. Une vie solitaire par choix tend à devenir un véritable phénomène de société.

L'argot des ados

La famille

les remps/vieux	les parents
le vieux/le reup	le père
la vieille/la reum	la mère
le frangin/reuf	le frère
la frangine/reusse	la sœur
le tonton	l'oncle
la tatie/tata	la tante
le beauf	le beau-frère
mon zinc	mon cousin

Recherche : mariages et divorces en france, pacs, statistiques sur les familles françaises

cohabitation *state of living together* ; **concurrence** fait compétition à ; **PACS** *civil pact of union between two adults* ; **devoirs** *duties* ; **conséquent** *consequential* ; **pacsés** *legally united by a PACS* ; **donné naissance aux** *given birth to* ; **célibataires** *single people*

Essential Instruction

1. Here are some questions that you could ask to ascertain how much the students understood of **L'enfance en France**: How does the government help parents? What types of early childcare exist in France? When can a mother be granted one year of paid maternity leave?
2. Here are questions to check reading comprehension for the paragraph on **La famille**: How many couples are not married in France? What is a PACS and why was it established? Approximately how many one-parent families exist in France? How many people in France choose to live alone? Is the number growing?
3. After students have read the paragraph on **Les familles en Afrique** (p. 29), help them compare African families with French families or families in their country.

Answers

Comparaisons
Answers will vary.

Perspectives
Elle dit que le mariage est associé à certaines valeurs et craint que ces valeurs ne disparaissent.; Opinions will vary.

Critical Thinking

Analysis
The article **La Francophonie** states **"Mais il faut aussi reconnaître que les valeurs familiales sont différentes selon la situation économique, religieuse, et culturelle des pays…."** Ask your students: **Cette affirmation est-elle pour la France aussi? pour votre pays? Pourquoi?**

Expressions liées à l'enfance

C'est le berceau de son enfance.	C'est là qu'il a grandi.
C'est l'enfance de l'art.	C'est très simple.
C'est un jeu d'enfant.	C'est facile à faire.
Il a replongé dans l'enfance.	Il régresse.

Comparaisons 1.2, 4.2

Quel est le taux de mariage aux États-Unis? de divorce?

Perspectives 1.2, 2.1

Le mariage rassemble des principes que je soutiens (fidélité, entraide); si jamais le mariage disparaissait, bien d'autres valeurs précieuses disparaîtraient aussi. —Linette791

Quelle remarque fait la lectrice au sujet du mariage? Êtes-vous d'accord avec elle?

La Francophonie

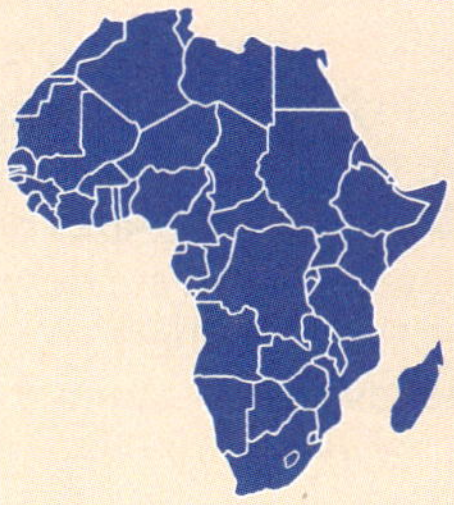

Un jeune couple africain

Sociétés

Les familles en Afrique 1.2, 2.1, 3.1, 4.2

Dans la plupart des pays d'Afrique, la structure familiale est déterminée par des valeurs traditionnelles. Le père a le statut de chef de famille: il lui incombe* de travailler pour faire vivre sa famille. La mère est responsable des tâches* domestiques, et surtout d'élever les enfants et de leur inculquer* les valeurs de leur culture. Toutefois, contrairement à la notion de famille nucléaire occidentale, les familles africaines sont souvent des familles élargies*; souvent, les grands-parents, et quelquefois, les oncles, les tantes, et les cousins vivent sous un même toit. Aussi, la notion de la famille a un sens communautaire où des groupes ethniques, ou même les habitants d'un village, constituent un macrocosme familial solidaire. La polygamie est aussi pratiquée par certaines ethnies et communautés religieuses, plus ou moins acceptée par les jeunes générations.

Mais il faut aussi reconnaître que les valeurs familiales sont différentes selon la situation économique, religieuse, et culturelle des pays et des peuples d'Afrique. Aussi, les plus jeunes générations, hommes ou femmes, ont tendance à privilégier* l'éducation et la réussite économique. Ces générations transforment les valeurs traditionnelles. On peut dire que les familles africaines connaissent aussi le divorce, les familles monoparentales, et les familles recomposées.

il lui incombe *it's up to him*; **tâches** corvées; **inculquer** *to implant*; **élargies** *extended*; **privilégier** *to favor*

Produits 1.2, 2.2

La fécondité est une grande valeur existentielle en Afrique. L'enfant est vu comme un don de Dieu. De grandes festivités et rituels sont organisés lors d'une grossesse et d'une naissance.

Differentiated Learning

Accelerate
Have students write a dialogue in which they use one of the expressions linked to childhood.

Adapt
Divide the class into three groups and assign one of the three readings to each group. Have each group present the content of their culture paragraph.

Special Needs Students

Linguistically Challenged
The culture paragraphs may be difficult for these students. Provide a cloze activity for them that focuses only on the main ideas.

Dyslexia
Give these students a paper that they can refer to when they read, with the key words to understand the main ideas in each paragraph.

Reference Desk

You may want to expose your students to the southern accent of Marseille. The characters of Oncle Jules and Bouzique in the films ***La Gloire de mon père*** and ***Le Château de ma mère***, based on Marcel Pagnol's autobiography, accurately and humorously capture the rolling *r* and accentuated *e* and *a* of the region's dialect.

Connections

Cinema

Since Cannes is the site of the international film festival, assign pairs of students to find interesting film footage to share with the class, going back as far as they can. Some interesting things to look for include: What American films have premiered at Cannes? What films won the **Palme d'Or**? What are some themes of the winning films? How many of the French films were subsidized by the French government?

Culture

Products: Information

1. Marcel Pagnol (1895–1974) was born in Aubagne, near Marseille. Originally a teacher, he resigned to become a playwright and filmmaker. His notable films reflect the life of lower-class French living in the Marseille area, capturing their unique accent and traditions. Films that the students may enjoy are ***Marius, Jean de Florette; Manon des Sources***; ***La Gloire de mon père***; and ***Le Château de ma mère***.
2. The **Festival de Film de Cannes**, which takes place every year in May, draws worldwide attention to the work of international film directors and actors. The coveted **Palme d'Or** is awarded to the director of the winning film. Brad Pitt, Sean Penn, Alec Baldwin, and Bruce Willis are among the many American stars who have climbed the famous red stairs to the **Palais des Festivals**.

Provence-Alpes-Côte d'Azur (la région PACA) 1.2, 2.1, 2.2, 3.2

Saint-Paul de Vence

Comme le dit si bien la chanson, « Il y a le ciel, le soleil, et la mer ». Il y a aussi des paysages immortalisés par les peintres van Gogh et Cézanne, et des villes mythiques telles que Cannes, Nice, et Saint-Tropez. Marseille, la deuxième ville la plus grande de France, est l'un des plus vieux ports d'Europe (fondée en 600 av. J-C). C'est une ville cosmopolite et le symbole du lien de la France avec le monde méditerranéen, maghrébin, africain, ou proche oriental*. La région a été popularisée par des écrivains comme Marcel Pagnol qui en ont fait une légende, par des artistes français et étrangers qui ont associé leur nom à ces lieux (Picasso, Matisse, Colette, F. Scott Fitzgerald, Françoise Sagan, Brigitte Bardot, Alfred Hitchcock, Winston Churchill). Et bien entendu, la Côte d'Azur est aussi l'un des lieux de rendez-vous favoris des vedettes* internationales du cinéma et des célébrités d'aujourd'hui.

Au-delà* de la légende, la région Provence-Alpes-Côte d'Azur est la troisième région la plus dynamique de France : pôle scientifique (Nice) et universitaire (Aix-Marseille) ; industries chimiques et pétrochimiques (Marseille) ; industries du numérique* (Nice) ; industries aéronautiques dans la Vallée du Rhône ; industries du luxe (parfums de Grasse) ; et, agriculture (vignoble, fruits). Il ne faut pas oublier le tourisme avec la mer et les paysages (Alpes de haute Provence, Montagne de la Sainte Victoire, du Lubéron), la beauté des villages (Saint-Paul de Vence, Saint-Tropez), le tourisme de luxe (Cannes, Nice, Antibes), et aussi le tourisme culturel attaché aux villes de festivals notamment l'été (Avignon, Aix en Provence, Orange, Arles, Orange et Antibes).

Recherche : région provence-alpes-côte d'azur, tourisme provence-alpes-côte d'azur

proche oriental *Near East* ; **vedettes** stars ; **Au-delà** *Beyond* ; **numérique** *digital technologies*

1.2, 2.1

Traditions et pratiques

Les habitants de la région PACA ont un accent inimitable qui a été popularisé par le cinéma et des acteurs de légende (Raimu, Fernandel ou Daniel Auteuil).

1.2, 2.2

Mon dico marseillais

- bastonner *battre*
- bomber *courir vite*
- un cacou *un garçon qui se la joue*
- une bombasse *une jolie fille*
- un fada *un fou*
- galéjer *plaisanter*
- se décarcasser *se débrouiller*

Produits

Grasse est une ville située dans l'arrière-pays niçois connue pour sa production de fleurs. Elle est célébrée comme **la capitale des parfums**. Grasse envoie ses parfums partout dans le monde. Au Musée International de la Parfumerie de Grasse, on apprend comment un parfum se fait et on peut aussi y découvrir l'histoire de l'industrie.

Ancienne distillerie de parfum

Essential Instruction

1. Play a trivia game such as Jeopardy with your class, asking questions about PACA and other regions students have studied such as **la Bretagne** and **la Normandie : Quelle ville est connue pour ses fleurs ? PACA est connue pour quels produits agricoles ?**
2. Consider having students work in pairs to do questions 4–5 in the **Activités culturelles**.
3. Have students look at the photos and subheadings in **Du côté des médias** to prepare for the reading.
4. Organize a game of **pétanque**, also known as **boules**, for your class.

9 Activités culturelles 1.2, 1.3, 2.1, 3.1, 3.2, 5.1

Faites les activités suivantes.

1. Retrouvez à quoi correspondent ces chiffres qui concernent la famille française :
   - 240 000
   - 4%
   - 14%
2. Faites des recherches, puis faites un graphique (en barres, ou en secteurs) pour comparer le taux de mariages et de divorces, de familles monoparentales et recomposées, en France et aux États-Unis.
3. Choisissez un pays d'Afrique francophone et cherchez trois ou quatre valeurs liées à la famille. Donnez votre point de vue sur ces valeurs.

Recherches : la famille au/aux/en (+ PAYS)

4. Faites des recherches sur une personne célèbre liée à la région Provence-Alpes-Côte d'Azur, puis présentez-la à la classe.
5. Choisissez une de ces villes : Saint-Tropez, Cannes, ou Saint-Paul de Vence. Recherchez ce qui la rend célèbre. Préparez un album de photos avec une carte et un texte.

Perspectives 1.2, 2.1

Selon le romancier Honoré de Balzac, « La famille sera toujours la base des sociétés ». Êtes-vous d'accord ? Pourquoi, ou pourquoi pas ?

Du côté des médias 1.2, 1.3, 3.1, 5.1

Saint-Paul de Vence

Lisez les informations suivantes sur les visites à faire à Saint-Paul de Vence. Préparez huit questions. Puis, échangez votre liste de questions avec celle de votre partenaire.

Histoire et Patrimoine

À Saint-Paul, chaque pierre raconte quelque chose : la venue de François 1er, les inspections de Vauban, le destin des grandes familles telles les Alziary et les Bernardi qui ont chacune laissé leur empreinte au village. Les façades, les remparts, les maisons et les tours racontent à qui sait les regarder le riche passé du village.

Durée de la visite : 1 heure + entrée au Musée d'Histoire Locale et à la chapelle Folon
Visite en français, anglais, italien, allemand et espagnol

Sur les pas de Marc Chagall

Marc Chagall a vécu à Saint-Paul pendant près de 20 ans. Admirez les mêmes paysages que l'artiste contempla avant de les reproduire sur la toile. Découvrez les liens étroits qui ont uni à Saint-Paul de 1966 à 1985 à travers 3 œuvres reproduites sur lutrins, la mosaïque de l'école et la sépulture de l'artiste.

Durée de la visite : 1 h 30 + entrée au musée Chagall
Visite en français et en anglais

La Pétanque

Sous les platanes de la plus célèbre place en sable dur du monde, l'Office du Tourisme vous propose une initiation au célèbre jeu de boules provençal. Se tenir « pieds tanqués » ? Faire Fanny ? La pétanque n'aura plus de secrets pour vous. Yves Montand pointait, Lino Ventura tirait… et vous ?

Durée du jeu : 1 heure
Animation en français, anglais, allemand et espagnol

À Saint-Paul de Vence avec Jacques Prévert

Pour Jacques Prévert, Saint-Paul était un refuge loin de l'agitation de la capitale. C'est au village qu'il a cultivé son amitié avec Picasso et Verdet, qu'il a exercé ses talents de scénariste, qu'il a écrit ses plus belles pages….

Durée de la visite : 1 heure
Visite en français – sur réservation

Answers

9

1. 240 000 : le nombre de mariages en France par an; 4% : le pourcentage de couples unis par un PACS; 14% : le pourcentage de célibataires en France

2–5. Answers will vary.

Perspectives
Answers will vary.

Du côté des médias
Answers will vary.

Expansion

In **Du côté des médias**, **"Sur les pas de Marc Chagall"**, note the use of the **passé simple** in the following sentence: **"Admirez les paysages que l'artiste contempla avant de les reproduire sur la toile."** You may want to point it out to (advanced) students and ask what other tense they know would be an appropriate replacement. If they are not sure, give them the choice between the **passé composé** and the **imparfait**. Ask them why the **passé composé** makes more sense and have them discuss in groups.

Differentiated Learning

Accelerate
Have students create a travel brochure in French for a city in the PACA region. It could contain photos, statistics, hotel and restaurant suggestions, and a list of things to do. Have students research old, classic travel posters for the region. Also research "La Colombe d'or" restaurant, favored haunt of Montant, Signoret, et al.

Decelerate
Prepare a matching activity for the second paragraph of the reading about the PACA region.

Multiple Intelligences

Naturalist
Have students look for paintings by artists such as Van Gogh and Cézanne who lived in the PACA region. Ask them to label six paintings with what they learned about the natural world in this area: olive trees, vineyards, red soil, bright sunlight, azure seawater, etc.

Resources

- Activity 10
- WB Workbook 6
- G & V Practice Games

Answers

10

1. Aimée court depuis quatre heures et trente minutes.
2. Tu cours depuis quinze minutes.
3. Marion et Théo courent depuis trois heures.
4. M. Dupont court depuis une demi-heure.
5. Chloé et moi, nous courons depuis deux heures et quinze minutes.
6. M. Roger et toi, vous courez depuis une heure et trente minutes.
7. Thomas court depuis une heure et quarante minutes.
8. Je cours depuis deux heures et quinze minutes.

Comparaisons

Je cours is the equivalent of *I run*, *I am running*, and *I do run* in English. Point out to students that these multiple meanings hold true for all present tense verbs in French.

Reference Desk

1. **Parcourir** is conjugated like **courir**. It means *to cover a distance*. **Je peux parcourir le village en une heure.** (*I can get through the village in one hour.*)
2. **Parcourir** also means *to skim*. **J'ai parcouru le livre.** (*I skimmed the book.*) The noun **un parcours** often refers to a course through a museum or a park.

Structure de la langue

Present Tense of the Irregular Verb *courir* 1.2

Alain court le plus vite dans le marathon.

The verb **courir** (*to run*) is irregular.

courir			
je	**cours**	nous	**courons**
tu	**cours**	vous	**courez**
il/elle/on	**court**	ils/elles	**courent**

Est-ce que tu **cours** quand tu es au complexe sportif? — *Do you run when you are at the sports center?*

Non, je ne **cours** jamais là-bas. — *No, I never run there.*

The irregular past participle of **courir** is **couru**. It takes the auxiliary verb **avoir** in the **passé composé**.

J'ai **couru** jusqu'à la maison. — *I ran home.*

10 Le marathon 1.3

Presentational Speaking

*Il est 13h30. Les personnes ci-dessous s'entraînent (*are training*) pour le marathon. Dites depuis combien de temps elles courent aujourd'hui.*

MODÈLE Julien (9h30)
Julien court depuis quatre heures.

1. Aimée (9h00)
2. toi (13h15)
3. Marion et Théo (10h30)
4. M. Dupont (13h00)
5. Chloé et moi (11h15)
6. M. Roger et toi (12h00)
7. Thomas (11h50)
8. moi (11h15)

Jeanne et Thibault aiment courir.

Comparaisons 4.1

What are the three ways to express **je cours** in English?

Essential Instruction

1. Ask students why **courir** is an irregular verb. Compare its endings to those of **finir**. Ask students what other **-ir** verbs are conjugated differently from the **finir** group (for example: **partir**, **sortir**, and **dormir**).
2. The past participle ends in **u**. Is that typical of an **-ir** verb? Point out that **venir** and other verbs with that stem (**revenir, devenir**) also have a past participle ending in **u**: **venu**.
3. Ask the class the questions about the **passé composé** with **avoir** at the top of the next page. Depending on what students remember, move to practice activities or do a thorough review.
4. Ask students to place a piece of paper over the left two columns of the irregular past participles chart. They then take turns reading the sentences aloud and giving the infinitive; a volunteer writes the infinitives and past participles in two columns on the board.

Révision: Passé composé with avoir 1.2

On recycle!

Do you remember how to form the **passé composé** with **avoir**? What follows the conjugated form of **avoir**? Are most verbs in the **passé composé** conjugated with **avoir** or **être**? If you cannot answer these questions, read the summary below.

	SUBJECT +	PRESENT TENSE OF AVOIR +	PAST PARTICIPLE
(-**er** verbs)	**Lise**	**a**	**joué** à cache-cache.
	Lise		*played hide-and-seek.*
(-**ir** verbs)	**Nous**	**avons**	**choisi** des cartes de foot.
	We		*chose soccer trading cards.*
(-**re** verbs)	**Elles**	**ont**	**perdu** leurs poupées.
	They		*lost their dolls.*

The **passé composé** tells what happened in the past. For most verbs, the **passé composé** consists of the appropriate present-tense form of **avoir** and the past participle of the main verb.

Here are the verbs you have already studied that have irregular past participles in the **passé composé** formed with **avoir**. Note the position of negative expressions in the **passé composé** and how to form questions using inversion. Remember that the past participle agrees in number and in gender with a preceding direct object.

Verb	Past Participle	Passé Composé
avoir	**eu**	Elle n'**a** pas **eu** la grippe.
boire	**bu**	**As**-tu **bu** toute la limonade?
conduire	**conduit**	J'**ai conduit** une voiture de sport.
connaître	**connu**	Où les **avez**-vous **connus**?
courir	**couru**	Après l'accident, il n'**a** plus **couru**.
croire	**cru**	La voyante? Nous ne l'**avons** pas **crue**.
devoir	**dû**	Tu **as dû** faire la vaisselle après le dîner.
dire	**dit**	Ils **ont dit** oui.
écrire	**écrit**	Ces lettres? Thomas me les **a écrites**.
être	**été**	Nous **avons été** contents.
faire	**fait**	Tu n'**as** jamais **fait** des châteaux-forts?
falloir	**fallu**	Il n'**a** pas **fallu** partir!
lire	**lu**	**Avez**-vous **lu** le blog d'Alima?
mettre	**mis**	Tes chemises? Mamy les **a mises** dans ta chambre.
offrir	**offert**	Il n'**a** rien **offert** comme cadeau.
ouvrir	**ouvert**	La porte? Richard l'**a ouverte**.
pleuvoir	**plu**	Il n'**a** pas **plu** hier, mais il a neigé.
pouvoir	**pu**	On **a pu** profiter de la neige.
prendre	**pris**	J'**ai pris** le petit déjeuner chez moi.
recevoir	**reçu**	Djamel n'**a** pas **reçu** mes textos.
savoir	**su**	L'**ont**-elles **su**?
suivre	**suivi**	J'**ai suivi** un cours de chimie.
vivre	**vécu**	Nous n'**avons** jamais **vécu** au Canada.
voir	**vu**	Non, je n'**ai vu** personne.
vouloir	**voulu**	Notre bande **a voulu** partir après le film.

Resources

WB Workbook 7–11

G & V Practice Games

Answers

On recycle!

Answers will vary; the past participle; avoir

Reference Desk

The **passé compose** with **avoir** was introduced in Level 1 in **Unité 8** and reviewed in Level 2 in **Unité 2**.

nouvelle orthographe **le diner**

Critical Thinking

Analysis

Have students look at the sentences to deduce language patterns and answer these questions: How are negative sentences formed in the **passé composé**? What are some of the negative expressions? How do you form a question using inversion? Where are direct object pronouns placed? How do you make direct object pronouns agree?

Game

Line-up

Arrange the class into two teams, A and B, facing each other in two lines. Throw a ball to the first student in line A as you conjugate a verb in the present tense: **Il écrit**. The student has to catch the ball and conjugate the verb in the **passé composé**: **Il a écrit**. If the student is successful, he or she may stay in line. If the student misses the verb or the ball, the student must sit down. Do the same thing for the first student in line B. The object of the game is to see which team is left standing the longest. Seated students can get back in the game if a team member doesn't know the answer and gives him or her the ball within five seconds.

Differentiated Learning

Accelerate

Have these students tell a group story in front of the class that uses some of the irregular past participles in the chart.

Decelerate

1. Practice the verbs in the chart by introducing gestures to anchor the meaning for these students. For example, for the verb **prendre**, take a student's textbook and bring it to your desk, saying, "**J'ai pris le livre de Martine.**"
2. Break up the three points of the **passé composé** (negation, inversion, and direct object pronouns) into three separate mini-lessons, and have students identify the sentences in the chart that are examples of each point.

Answers

11

1. Djamel et toi avez étudié la biologie. Vous avez eu 19 et 18 sur 20 au contrôle. Vous avez réussi.
2. Nadia a étudié la physique. Elle a eu 17 sur 20 au contrôle. Elle a réussi.
3. Karim et Rania ont étudié la physique. Ils ont eu 15 et 16 sur 20 au contrôle. Ils ont réussi.
4. Léo et Djamel ont étudié la biologie. Ils ont eu 17 et 19 sur 20 au contrôle. Ils ont réussi.
5. Sandrine et moi avons étudié la chimie. Nous avons eu 11 et 10 sur 20 au contrôle. Nous n'avons pas réussi.
6. Tu as étudié la biologie. Tu as eu 18 sur 20 au contrôle. Tu as réussi.
7. Yasmine a étudié la chimie. Elle a eu 16 sur 20 au contrôle. Elle a réussi.

Comparaisons

The past participles are *received*, *said*, and *drunk*.

Reference Desk

Allow your students to choose whichever Connection activity they prefer.

Expansion

Use the context of **Activité 11** as an opportunity to talk about careers in STEM/STEAM subjects (Science, Technology, Engineering, Art, Math). Have students help you make a list of careers that require courses in those subjects: aeronautics, computer programming, laboratory research, graphic design, game design, space technology, oceanography, marketing, etc.

Culture

Practices: Information

French students are graded on a 20-point scale; they do not receive letter grades. A grade of 16–20 is considered excellent, 14–15 good, 12–13 satisfactory, 10–11 passing, 0–9 failing.

11 Les sciences 1.1, 1.2, 1.3, 5.1

Les élèves suivants ont suivi un cours de sciences. Pour réussir au premier contrôle, il fallait avoir 12 ou plus. Dites quelle matière chaque ado a étudiée, combien de points il ou elle a reçus, et s'il ou elle a réussi.

Élève	Cours	Contrôle
Sandrine	chimie	11
Djamel	biologie	19
Léo	biologie	17
Karim	physique	15
moi	chimie	10
Rania	physique	16
toi	biologie	18
Nadia	physique	17
Yasmine	chimie	16

MODÈLE Sandrine
Sandrine a étudié la chimie. Elle a eu 11 sur 20 au contrôle. Elle n'a pas réussi.

1. Djamel et toi
2. Nadia
3. Karim et Rania
4. Léo et Djamel
5. Sandrine et moi
6. toi
7. Yasmine

Comparaisons 4.1

What is the past participle in each of these sentences?

Djamel *has* not *received* my texts.
They *have said* yes.
Have you *drunk* all the lemon-lime soda?

Connexions 3.1

Sciences

Conduct a demonstration of a scientific law. For example, for Darcy's law (**la loi de Darcy**), you may show the results of pouring water over a solid object, versus pouring water over sand. State what happened in each of your demonstrations, using the **passé composé**.

Connexions 3.1

Histoire

Create a summary for a docufiction about an important moment in history. Describe eight to ten main events, using the **passé composé**. You may create a short film by putting together images and reading your narration.

Essential Instruction

1. Ask students for the past participles of **étudier**, **avoir**, and **réussir** before doing **Activité 11** as a class.
2. If your students are struggling with the **passé composé**, have them write out the answers to **Activité 11**; otherwise have students work with a partner.
3. Remind students that questions using inversion do not take **est-ce que**. After students write out the questions, have them close their notebooks and do **Activité 13** orally.

12 Dans quel ordre? 1.3, 5.1

Presentational Writing

Composez deux phrases grâce aux indices qui vous sont donnés, et mettez-les dans l'ordre. Suivez le modèle.

MODÈLE Jacques (vivre à Lyon, grandir à Marseille)
Jacques a grandi à Marseille.
Puis, il a vécu à Lyon.

1. ma famille et moi (choisir un terrain de camping, pêcher)
2. toi (atterrir en Côte d'Ivoire, décoller de Paris)
3. les Lambert (faire les magasins, finir leurs corvées)
4. je (emprunter une tondeuse, tondre la pelouse)
5. Alex (composter son billet, acheter son billet de train)
6. Luc et toi (mettre le couvert, dîner en famille avec vos grands-parents)

Romain est venu chez Alex. Puis, il l'a aidé à faire ses devoirs.

13 Au parc d'attractions 1.3, 5.1, 5.2

Presentational Writing

Pendant l'été, vos copains sont allés dans un parc d'attractions. Écrivez les questions que vous voulez leur poser. Utilisez le passé composé et l'inversion.

MODÈLE avec qui (tu, faire un tour de montagnes russes)
Avec qui as-tu fait un tour de montagnes russes?

1. pourquoi (Alexandre, faire un tour de grande roue)
2. avec qui (Julie, essayer des jeux d'adresse)
3. pourquoi (Cécile et Eva, avoir une consultation avec la voyante)
4. comment (vous, conduire les autos tamponneuses)
5. que (on, boire au parc d'attractions)
6. quand (vous, devoir partir)

Resources

Activities 12–13

Answers

12

1. Ma famille et moi avons choisi un terrain de camping. Puis, nous avons pêché.
2. Tu as décollé de Paris. Puis, tu as atterri en Côte d'Ivoire.
3. Les Lambert ont fini leurs corvées. Puis, ils ont fait les magasins.
4. J'ai emprunté une tondeuse. Puis, j'ai tondu la pelouse.
5. Alex a acheté son billet de train. Puis, il a composté son billet.
6. Luc et toi avez mis le couvert. Puis, vous avez dîné en famille avec vos grands-parents.

13

1. Pourquoi Alexandre a-t-il fait un tour de grande roue?
2. Avec qui Julie a-t-elle essayé des jeux d'adresse?
3. Pourquoi Cécile et Eva ont-elles eu une consultation avec la voyante?
4. Comment avez-vous conduit les autos tamponneuses?
5. Qu'a-t-on bu au parc d'attractions?
6. Quand avez-vous dû partir?

Reference Desk

Most short, common adverbs come before the past participles, for example, **Julien est vite descendu de l'auto tamponneuse**.

Expansion

For additional practice, have students complete the paragraph below, using the **passé composé**.

Le matin de la rentrée, Aïcha (mettre) un nouvel ensemble. Elle (prendre) une tartine et un jus d'orange. Puis, elle (chercher) ses cahiers et ses livres. Elle (attendre) Chloé devant leur immeuble. Mais elle était en retard. Donc, les filles (courir vite) au lycée. En cours, Aïcha (ne pas pouvoir) prendre des notes. Elle (oublier) d'apporter son stylo. La rentrée (commencer mal)!

Differentiated Learning

Accelerate
After all students have written the questions for **Activité 13**, ask accelerated students to practice speaking in pairs; one student asks the question and the other responds.

Decelerate
Have these students listen to the mini-dialogues presented by the advanced students and treat it as a listening activity. Encourage them to write down what they learned about the experience of each teen (Alexandre, Julie, etc.) at the amusement park.

Learning Styles

Auditory Learners
Have someone in class read aloud the cues for **Activités 12–13** to help these students.

Resources

- WB Workbook 12–13
- LA Listening Activity 2
- G & V Practice Games

Answers

On recycle!

1. C; 2. A; 3. B

Reference Desk

1. The **passé compose** with **avoir** was introduced in Level 1 in **Unité 8** and reviewed in Level 2 in **Unité 2**.
2. A classic way to teach or review **être** verbs is to draw a house with people coming, going, arriving, leaving, going out, coming in, being born, dying, climbing, falling, remaining, entering, returning home, etc. (Your artistic students can provide a drawing for you to use.)
3. MR. and MRS. P. VANDERTRAMP and *The Alamo of* ***être*** are mnemonic devices used to recall all 17 verbs that take **être** in the **passé composé**. Only 13 of those verbs are presented here, as those are the ones students have seen previously introduced in the **Rencontres culturelles** dialogues. The other four are **passer**, **tomber**, **naître**, and **mourir**. Students learn **tomber** and **mourir** in **Unité 8**.
4. Consider writing the mnemonic device on the board every day until students can recall all 16 verbs, if that is your goal, or give an extra credit quiz to get students to remember them all.

Expansion

Have students write two statements about what someone did, each on a separate note card. One sentence should be an activity done at home and the other outside of the home. Collect the cards and mix them up. Then put students in groups of four. Give each group eight note cards. One member of each group reads the sentences, then calls on group members to say if the person stayed home or not. Groups exchange note cards with those of another group when they are done.

Révision: Passé composé with *être* 1.2

On recycle!

Do you remember how to make past tense sentences using the verb **être**? What two parts make up a sentence in the **passé composé**? What is different with past participles used with **être**? See if you can correctly complete the sentences below.

1. Océane est allé__ à Paris.	A. **-s**
2. Lucas et Léo sont parti__ à 13h30.	B. **-es**
3. Martine et Amélie sont rentré__ tôt.	C. **-e**

If you could not answer the questions or do the activity, read the summary below.

Certain verbs form their **passé composé** with the helping verb **être**. Most verbs that use **être** in the **passé composé** *express motion or movement* of the subject from one place to another. Note that the ending of the past participle of the verb agrees in gender and in number with the subject.

Elles **sont arrivées** à huit heures. *They arrived at 8:00.*

Here are the verbs you have already learned that use the helping verb **être**, along with their past participles. In addition to the agreement of the past participles, note the position of negative expressions and how to form questions using inversion.

Verb	Past Participle	Passé Composé
aller	**allé**	Ils ne **sont** jamais **allés** à Cannes.
arriver	**arrivé**	J'y **suis arrivé(e)** il y a deux heures.
descendre	**descendu**	**Est**-elle **descendue** à Nice de Paris?
devenir	**devenu**	Marame **est devenue** médecin.
entrer	**entré**	Nous **sommes entré(e)s** dans la discothèque.
monter	**monté**	Elle **est** déjà **montée** dans sa chambre?
partir	**parti**	Florianne, à quelle heure **es**-tu **partie**?
rentrer	**rentré**	**Êtes**-vous **rentré(e)(s)** avant minuit?
rester	**resté**	Nous n'y **sommes** pas **resté(e)(s)**.
retourner	**retourné**	Anne **est retournée** en France.
revenir	**revenu**	Je ne **suis** plus **revenu(e)**.
sortir	**sorti**	Kate, **es**-tu **sortie** avec tes amis?
venir	**venu**	Éric n'**est** pas **venu** à la soirée.

Essential Instruction

1. Have students answer the questions and do the quiz in the top section. Depending on how well they do, proceed to the practice activities or review thoroughly.
2. Ask students to find examples of inversion and negation in the sample sentences in the yellow box.
3. Do **Activité 14** as a class, having students write down the proper form of the past participle. Make sure students are paying attention to agreement of the past participle.
4. Have students work on **Activité 15** in pairs.

14 Complétez ! 1.2, 1.3, 5.1

Interpretive Reading, Presentational Writing

*Lisez l'histoire de la classe de Mme Merrick qui est allée à Paris. Complétez les phrases avec la forme convenable d'**être** et le participe passé du verbe entre parenthèses.*

1. Le premier jour à Paris, le groupe... tôt parce qu'il y avait beaucoup à voir et à faire à Paris. (partir)
2. Tous les élèves... en haut de la tour Eiffel pour prendre de belles photos de Paris et des monuments. (monter)
3. La prof, Mme Merrick, ... voir une amie française à midi. (aller)
4. Sonia et moi, nous... dans le Louvre pour voir la *Joconde*. (entrer)
5. Benoît... avec nous. (venir)
6. Vers 20h00, Sonia et moi, ... à la recherche d'un bon restaurant pas cher. (sortir)
7. Morgane et toi, vous... à l'hôtel, mais pourquoi? (rester)

15 Samedi ! 1.2, 1.3, 2.2

Interpretive Viewing, Presentational Speaking

Dites où tout le monde est allé samedi. Choisissez une des expressions ci-dessous.

la discothèque	**le festival de musique**	**l'aquaparc**
le complexe sportif	**le tournoi de slam**	**la soirée jazz**

1. les copains et moi

2. toi

3. Sylvaine et Guillaume

4. Malika

5. les ados

6. moi

Answers

14

1. est parti
2. sont montés
3. est allée
4. sommes entré(e)s
5. est venu
6. sommes sorti(e)s
7. êtes resté(e)s

15

1. Les copains et moi sommes allés au tournoi de slam.
2. Tu es allé(e) à la discothèque.
3. Sylvaine et Guillaume sont allés au festival de musique.
4. Malika est allée à l'aquaparc.
5. Les ados sont allés à la soirée jazz.
6. Je suis allé(e) au complexe sportif.

Expansion

Ask each student to write down the names of five cities they would like to visit in the United States. Collect the information, and then make a list of all the cities. Distribute the list to pairs of students. Students take turns asking and expressing if they have been to these cities: **Es-tu allé(e) à Boston?** The partner answers **Oui, j'y suis allé(e)** or **Non, je n'y suis pas allé(e).** When pairs are done, place a map of the United States on the bulletin board. Ask students randomly if they have gone to the cities on the list. Have a kinesthetic learner or a student with AD(H)D place a thumb tack on each city visited by someone in the class. (The pronoun **y** was introduced in **Unité 8** of Level 2.)

Communication

Interpersonal: Paired Practice

To practice the **passé composé** using **avoir** and **être**, have students work in pairs to prepare a dialogue about one day or a trip during summer vacation. Encourage students to write cues in English to help them remember what to say so they can perform them without a script for the class.

Differentiated Learning

Accelerate

Have students tell a story about one of the numbered items in **Activité 15**. The sentence from the activity can be their beginning or ending.

Decelerate

Slow-paced students may benefit from *Grammar and Vocabulary Practice Games* designed for ***T'es branché?***, verb games online, or activities available at stores that sell educational materials.

Special Needs Students

Dyslexia

Conjugation can be challenging for these students. Allow them to use their own charts and notes when doing the activities. Display posters of conjugations for high-frequency verbs in your classroom. Students may benefit from having an oral quiz on the **passé composé** with **avoir** and **être**, rather than a written one.

Resources

Activities 16–17

Answers

16

1. a grandi
2. a joué
3. a arrêté
4. est partie
5. est allée
6. ont quitté
7. a découvert
8. a fait
9. a vu
10. est arrivé
11. sont allés

17

1. Romain est resté souvent à la maison.
2. Audrey a découvert un festival de jazz dans la rue Malherbe.
3. Audrey est allée au zoo voir les gorilles et les pandas.
4. Audrey est partie faire du ski à la montagne.
5. Romain a visité le musée d'histoire.
6. Audrey a couru dans le parc.
7. Audrey est montée dans la grande roue.
8. Romain est allé au ciné-club.

Reference Desk

By now students may have questions about the various French verbs for *leaving*, including **quitter** (used in **Activité 16**), which means *to leave someone or something*. Here are some more to clear up: **partir** (*to leave*), **sortir** (*to go out*), **retourner** (*to return to where you started*), **rentrer** (*to go home or back to where you live*), **s'en aller** (*to go away*). Have students note that **quitter** takes **avoir** as an auxiliary, not **être**.

Communication

Interpersonal: Cooperative Groups

Have students pretend they are in **la cour** at school after summer break talking to their friends. Their task is to find out what everyone in their group did during the summer vacation and ask follow-up questions to make their dialogues as long as possible. It is up to each group if they want to tell true stories, imagined stories, or a combination thereof. The students not presenting have to write down whether the story narrated by each student is completely true or all or partially imagined. Vote on the best "fooler" in class.

16 La vie de Karim 1.2, 1.3, 5.1

Interpretive Reading, Presentational Writing

*Complétez l'histoire de Karim en mettant les verbes au passé composé. Attention à utiliser le bon auxiliaire (**avoir** ou **être**).*

1. Karim… dans un petit village. (grandir)
2. Il y… au football avec des amis. (jouer)
3. Mais à Nice, il…. (arrêter)
4. Un jour la mère de Karim… du village. (partir)
5. Sa mère… à Nice avant les autres membres de sa famille. (aller)
6. Ils… leur maison avec la piscine. (quitter)
7. À Nice, Karim… les supermarchés. (découvrir)
8. D'abord, il… la connaissance de Léo. (faire)
9. Ensuite, il… Élodie au ciné-club. (voir)
10. Ce soir, il… chez Léo et Élodie. (arriver)
11. Lui et ses amis… voir un film. (aller)

17 Les jumeaux 1.3, 5.1

Presentational Speaking

*Audrey aime les activités en plein air et son frère, Romain, préfère les activités à l'intérieur. Dites qui a fait chaque activité pendant les vacances. Attention si le verbe prend **avoir** ou **être**.*

MODÈLES sortir avec des copines
Audrey est sortie avec des copines.

passer des heures à la médiathèque
Romain a passé des heures à la médiathèque.

1. rester souvent à la maison
2. découvrir un festival de jazz dans la rue Malherbe
3. aller au zoo voir les gorilles et les pandas
4. partir faire du ski à la montagne
5. visiter le musée d'histoire
6. courir dans le parc
7. monter dans la grande roue
8. aller au ciné-club

Audrey a vu les ruines gallo-romaines avec son grand-père.

Essential Instruction

1. Model the **passé composé** by explaining what you did yesterday, last weekend, or during vacation. Encourage students to ask you questions about your experience.
2. For students needing more practice, have them say where certain people went, and then say what they did there, for example, **Maxime est allé à l'aéroport. Il a voyagé en Europe**.

Révision: The *imparfait* 1.2

On recycle!

When do you use the **imparfait** rather than the **passé composé**? Can you figure out which verbs in the paragraph below would be in the **imparfait**?

Julie put a novel and sunscreen in her bag and changed into her swimsuit. She got in the car and drove for 15 minutes. It was a sunny day at the beach. Many people were sunbathing. Others swam.

If you need help, read the summary below.

The **imparfait** is another tense used to talk about the past. You use the **imparfait** to describe how people or things were and to describe what used to happen or what people used to do in the past.

Karim **collectionnait** des cartes de football. *Karim collected soccer cards.*

To form the imperfect, add the ending **-ais, -ais, -ait, -ions, -iez,** or **-aient** to the stem of the present-tense **nous** form.

faire **Imperfect stem: *fais-* (from *nous faisons*)**			
je	**faisais**	nous	**faisions**
tu	**faisais**	vous	**faisiez**
il/elle/on	**faisait**	ils/elles	**faisaient**

À quoi **jouais**-tu à l'âge de cinq ans? *What did you play at the age of five?*
Je **faisais** semblant d'être un super-héros. *I pretended to be a superhero.*

The verb **être** has an irregular stem in the imperfect: **ét-**.

Vivianne et son frère jouaient à la poupée quand ils **étaient** petits. *Vivianne and her brother played with dolls when they were young.*

The imperfect is used to describe:

Use	Example	
People or things as they were or used to be	Mon grand-père **était** médecin.	*My grandfather was a doctor.*
Conditions as they were or used to be	Il n'y **avait** pas d'arbres.	*There were no trees.*
Actions that took place repeatedly, regularly, or habitually in the past	Nous **allions** souvent à l'aquaparc.	*We often used to go to the waterpark.*

Differentiated Learning

Decelerate

Pair students and have them make a list of 20 verbs (some with **être** as the auxiliary and some with **avoir**). Put the verb infinitives on slips of paper and place them in a bowl or hat, or face down on the desk. One student chooses a slip of paper, looks at the verb, and acts out the action for the other student. The partner has to say what the student did, using the **passé composé**. If the student guessing needs help, the student who acts out the verb could supply, "**J'ai…**" and the student guessing would have to supply the past participle. Pairs in the class could compete to do the activity fastest and with the most correct statements.

Learning Styles

Kinesthetic Learners

Have the students chant: **ais, ais, ait, ions, iez, aient heh!** You may also search "Etienne A-I-S grammar song" and have your students sing the chorus, to quickly teach them the endings of the imperfect.

Resources

WB Workbook 14–16

G & V Practice Games

Answers

On recycle!

The **imparfait** is used to describe people, things, or conditions as they were or used to be, or habitual, repeated actions. In the English paragraph the last three sentences would be in the imperfect tense: **Il faisait du soleil. Beaucoup de gens bronzaient. D'autres nageaient.**

Reference Desk

1. **The imparfait** was introduced in **Unité 4** of Level 2. If you did not do the Oral History project on p. 213 featured in Level 2 last year, you might consider having students do it during this unit.
2. Point out that the endings **-ais**, **-ait**, and **-aient** all sound alike.
3. Verbs that end in **-cer** have a cedilla under the final **c** when it precedes an **a**; however, the cedilla does not appear in the **nous** and **vous** forms, for example**, ils commençaient** but **nous commencions**.
4. Verbs that end in **-ger** have an **e** after the **g** and before the endings in all forms except for **nous** and **vous**, for example, **il mangeait** but **nous mangions**.
5. Other verbs with spelling changes in the present tense form the imperfect regularly, for example**, je préférais**, **j'achetais**, and **je nettoyais**.
6. Verbs that end in **-ier** have **-ii** in the **nous** and **vous** forms, for example, **vous étudiiez**. These require a longer vowel sound.
7. **Falloir, neiger**, and **pleuvoir** have only an **il** form. In the imperfect they are **il fallait, il neigeait**, and **il pleuvait**.
8. When expressing a past idea, these verbs are generally in the **imparfait**, not the **passé composé**: **adorer**, **aimer**, **avoir**, **connaître**, **être**, **penser**, **pouvoir**, **savoir**, and **vouloir**.

Answers

18

1. Quand Fatouma et Jacques étaient petits, ils jouaient à la poupée.
2. Quand Diane et moi étions petit(e)s, nous faisions des châteaux de sable.
3. Quand Myriam était petite, elle jouait du piano.
4. Quand tu étais petit(e), tu jouais à la marelle.
5. Quand Yanis était petit, il collectionnait les coquillages.
6. Quand j'étais petit(e), j'allais à l'aquaparc.
7. Quand Romy et toi étiez petit(e)s, vous couriez.

Comparaisons

Those examples of past tenses are equivalent to the **passé composé**, because they refer to complete and nonrepetitive actions, as opposed to the **imparfait**.

Communication

Presentational: Cooperative Groups

Ask students to bring in a picture from a magazine or the Internet showing an activity such as a family eating in a restaurant. Collect the images, then put the students in groups. Give each group a picture that elicits a lot of descriptive sentences in the imperfect. For example: **Les Lenoir étaient dans un restaurant. Il y avait le père, la mère, et les deux enfants. Ils mangeaient ensemble. Ils prenaient des pâtes. Le repas était délicieux.** Finally, post all the pictures. A representative from each group reads their story, and the rest of the class matches the description with the right image.

Culture

Products: Activity

Make copies of popular song lyrics, such as ***On savait*** (La Grande Sophie) or ***Le petit pain au chocolat*** (Joe Dassin), and ***La Bicyclette*** (Yves Montand) leaving blanks for all the verbs in the imperfect for students to fill in. Use Prévert's ***Déjeuner du matin*** to practice the **passé composé**.

18 Les activités enfantines 1.2, 1.3

Interpretive Viewing, Presentational Speaking

Dites ce que tout le monde faisait quand ils étaient petits.

MODÈLE

Marame
Quand Marame était petite, elle sautait à la corde.

1. Fatouma et Jacques

2. Diane et moi

3. Myriam

4. toi

5. Yanis

6. moi

7. Romy et toi

Comparaisons 4.1

There are three possible ways in English to express the past.

I *have seen* the movie.
I *saw* the movie.
I *did see* the movie.

In French, would these sentences be equivalent to the **imparfait** or the **passé composé**? Why?

Essential Instruction

1. Reviewing the **passé composé** and the **imparfait** at the beginning of every class, and especially after a weekend, will help keep the forms fresh in students' minds. As a warm-up, ask students what they did yesterday or on the weekend (to encourage use of the **passé composé**). Then, to elicit use of the **imparfait**, ask how the previous day or weekend was, how they felt, and how the weather was.
2. Students might find it helpful to think of the **passé composé** as a photo that freezes an action in the past, and the **imparfait** as a movie that shows continuous and repeated actions. Encourage students to write an opening scene for a movie. Post the stories that are in the **passé composé** on the right wall of the classroom, those that use only the **imparfait** on the left wall of the classroom, and those that use both tenses on the back wall of the classroom.
3. Do **Activité 18** as a class, and ask students to work on **Activité 19** with a partner.

19 Un accident de voiture 1.1, 1.2, 1.3, 5.1, 5.2

Interpretive Viewing, Interpersonal or Presentational Speaking

Un accident de voiture a eu lieu. Le conducteur responsable est parti. Vous êtes le seul témoin (witness). *Téléphonez à la police et répondez à ses questions.*

1. Où étiez-vous quand vous avez vu cet accident?
2. Quelle heure était-il?
3. Est-ce qu'il pleuvait?
4. Il y avait combien de voitures, de conducteurs et de passagers?
5. Les conducteurs sont-ils partis?
6. Comment est arrivé l'accident?
7. Quel âge avait le conducteur?
8. Qu'est-ce qu'il faisait quand l'accident est arrivé?
9. La conductrice a-t-elle eu mal?
10. Son fils a-t-il été blessé (*hurt*)?

Révision: The *imparfait* and the *passé composé* 1.2

On recycle!
If you wrote a sentence that used both the **imparfait** and the **passé composé**, which tense would be used to describe a continuous action? Which one would be used for an action that interrupted the first one? If you do not know, read the summary below.

You have learned two past tenses in French, the **imparfait** and the **passé composé**. These two tenses are not used in the same way.

The **imparfait** describes how people or things were in the past, what happened regularly, or a condition that existed at some time in the past.

En été, Laure et Awa **couraient** au bord de la mer.	*During the summer, Laure and Awa ran on the seashore.*
Moi, je **préférais** rester à la maison.	*Me, I preferred staying home.*

The **passé composé** indicates a single, completed action.

Un jour, nous **sommes allés** à la plage.	*One day, we went to the beach.*
Mamy **a ramassé** des coquillages avec nous.	*Grandma picked up sea shells with us.*

Differentiated Learning

Accelerate
Students who have mastered the **imparfait** might enjoy making a story out of one of the images in **Activité 18**.

Decelerate
As a class, write a short story in English in the past that shows repeated actions and habitual conditions. Using the criteria on p. 41, decide whether each verb should be written in French in the **passé composé** or the **imparfait**. Point out that often, though not always, non-action verbs take the **imparfait** when used in the past.

Resources

WB Workbook 17–18

G & V Practice Games

Answers

19 Possible answers:

1. J'étais devant un magasin/je marchais dans la rue/je conduisais ma moto, etc.
2. Il était 13h15.
3. Non, il faisait beau.
4. Il y avait deux voitures, un camion rouge et blanc conduit par un homme seul, et un monospace vert conduit par une femme et son enfant.
5. Le conducteur du camion est parti, mais la conductrice du monospace est restée.
6. Le camion a heurté le monospace à une intersection.
7. Il avait une trentaine d'années.
8. Je pense qu'il parlait sur son portable.
9. Oui, elle a dû recevoir un choc, elle avait mal à la tête.
10. Non, il n'a pas été blessé.

On recycle!
If you want to describe a continual action, that part of the sentence would be in the imperfect; an action that interrupted that description would be in the **passé composé**.

Reference Desk

There are many online activities to help with the difference between the **imparfait** and the **passé composé**.

Game

Machine à écrire
Divide the class into two teams, then assign at least one letter or accent mark to each student. Start the game by giving one team a subject pronoun and an infinitive in French. This team must quickly spell out loud the correct form of the verb in the imperfect tense. For example, if you say **il/neiger**, students must spell **neigeait**. If done correctly, the team earns a point. Then the other team gets its turn at a word. Whenever a team fails, its rival gets a chance to spell the same word and win another point. If students are having trouble with a verb, write it on the board, erase it, and then put the item back on the list.

Answers

Comparaisons

The first sentence shows an interrupted action because the verb form changes. In French, the **imparfait** would be used to express the English *was/were + ing* form.

20 Possible paragraph:

En 1901, Pablo Picasso était déjà artiste quand il est venu à Paris. Il a fait la connaissance de Georges Braque, en 1907. Les deux artistes ont inventé le Cubisme. Ils décomposaient leurs sujets en formes géométriques. En 1910, Picasso est allé en Provence, où il a travaillé dans un grand atelier. Il était révolté contre le fascisme en Espagne, par conséquent il a fait son chef d'œuvre *Guernica* en 1936. Le tableau est devenu un symbole de la Résistance pendant la Deuxième Guerre mondiale. En 1948, Picasso a commencé à travailler avec la céramique. En 1957, le MoMA à New York a organisé une exposition de son œuvre. Plus de 100 000 visiteurs sont venus admirer....

Reference Desk

Pablo Picasso is the subject of **Activité 20** because he was mentioned in the culture reading about PACA on p. 30. Although born in Spain, he lived much of his life in Paris and southern France.

Game

Quand le professeur est entré....

Tell students you will be going into the hallway for two minutes, and that when you come back, they have to be in the process of doing something. Also, they must observe what everyone else is doing. When you come back in the classroom, ask students what everyone was doing when you entered, and have them respond with a sentence in the **imparfait** and the **passé composé**, for example, **Monique dessinait un cheval au tableau quand vous êtes entré(e) dans la salle de classe**.

To tell a story, use the imperfect to give background information and to describe circumstances in the past. The imperfect answers the question, "How were things?" Use the **passé composé** to express what events took place only once in the past. The **passé composé** answers the question, "What happened?"

Tu **étais** en ville.	*You were in town.*
Un accident de voiture **a eu** lieu.	*A car accident took place.*

The imperfect and the **passé composé** are often used in the same sentence to describe an ongoing action that was interrupted by another action. Use the imperfect to express the background condition or ongoing action and the **passé composé** to describe the completed action.

Vous **aviez** peur pour la conductrice ; donc, vous **avez téléphoné** à la police.	*You were afraid for the driver; therefore, you called the police.*

Comparaisons 4.1

Which sentence shows an interrupted action? How can you tell?

Kyle *was reading* when his mom *came home*.
We *were jumping up* and *raising* our arms when the song *was playing*.

20 La vie de Pablo Picasso 1.2, 1.3, 3.1, 5.1

Interpretive Reading, Presentational Writing

Pablo Picasso était, selon beaucoup de critiques, l'artiste le plus important du 20ème siècle. Utilisez les informations ci-dessous pour écrire un paragraphe sur sa vie.

MODÈLE **En 1901, Pablo Picasso....**

1901 : Pablo Picasso (être déjà artiste) quand il (venir à Paris)
1907 : il (faire la connaissance de Georges Braque) ; les deux artistes (inventer le Cubisme) ; ils (décomposer leurs sujets en formes géométriques)
1910 : Picasso (aller en Provence) où il (travailler dans un grand atelier)
1936 : il (être révolté contre le fascisme en Espagne) ; par conséquent il (faire son chef-d'œuvre *Guernica*) ; le tableau (devenir un symbole de la Résistance) pendant la Deuxième Guerre mondiale
1948 : il (commencer à travailler) avec la céramique
1957 : le MoMA (or Museum of Modern Art) à New York (organiser une exposition de son œuvre) ; plus de 100 000 visiteurs (venir admirer ses tableaux, ses objets d'art, et ses céramiques)

Le Château de Vauvenargues, résidence de Picasso

Essential Instruction

1. Tell students what you did over the weekend, speaking in the two tenses, and using dramatic storytelling to emphasize the verbs. Have students retell your story in the **vous** form using the same exaggeration. Then have them write it in the third person singular form.
2. Pair up advanced students with those who are slow-paced to complete **Activité 20**.
3. Depending on your students' comprehension of the grammar topic, you may want to read the story in **Activité 21** in your own voice at a slow pace before having students listen to the recording. If there are errors, make sure students understand why they made a mistake by showing them the script after they have completed the listening activity.
4. Do **Activité 22** as a class and **Activité 23** as written practice.

21 La journée de Mme Aknouch 1.2

Interpretive Listening

*Écrivez les numéros 1–6 sur votre papier. Écoutez l'histoire. Ensuite, dites si chaque phrase est vraie (**V**) ou fausse (**F**).*

1. Mme Aknouch n'a pas d'enfants.
2. Elle a travaillé aujourd'hui.
3. Elle a fait du footing au complexe sportif.
4. Elle a fait les courses.
5. À l'école sa fille jouait à cache-cache avec ses copains.
6. Amina et sa mère ont pris le métro pour rentrer.

22 La soirée 1.2, 1.3, 5.1

Interpretive Viewing, Presentational Speaking

Dites ce que tout le monde faisait quand l'actrice est arrivée à la soirée. Choisissez une des expressions ci-dessous.

danser **jouer du piano** **discuter du film** **regarder un tableau**
manger des hors-d'œuvres **chanter** **profiter du buffet**

MODÈLE Pierre
Pierre mangeait des hors-d'œuvre quand l'actrice est arrivée.

1. Mlle Duchamp
2. M. et Mme Laforêt
3. Serge et moi
4. M. Dumont
5. toi
6. Mme Declerc
7. Pierre

23 Un super-héros 1.2, 1.3, 5.1

Interpretive Reading, Presentational Writing

Complétez l'histoire suivante en utilisant le passé composé et l'imparfait. Puis devinez le nom du super-héros.

Il y _1_ (avoir) un homme qui _2_ (venir) d'une autre planète. Il _3_ (avoir) les cheveux noirs et il _4_ (être) beau. Un jour, il _5_ (trouver) un travail de reporter dans une grande ville. Il _6_ (porter) toujours des lunettes et un costume quand il _7_ (travailler) au bureau. Quand il y _8_ (avoir) un crime, il _9_ (mettre) vite un costume rouge et bleu. Il _10_ (être) très fort, mais il _11_ (devenir) moins fort à chaque fois qu'il _12_ (être) près d'une pierre (*stone*) verte. Il _13_ (aimer) Loïs Lane. Un jour, Loïs _14_ (tomber) des chutes du Niagara, et il l' _15_ (aider). Elle _16_ (découvrir) son identité. Comme ils _17_ (s'aimer) beaucoup, ils _18_ (se marier).

Resources

Activity 21

Answers

21 Script

Hier Mme Aknouch a quitté la maison à une heure. D'abord, elle est allée au complexe sportif pour courir. Puis elle est allée à la station de métro. Là, elle a pris le métro et elle est descendue au supermarché. Elle a fait les courses avant d'aller chercher sa fille à l'école. Sa fille Amina jouait à la marelle avec une amie. Elle était contente de voir sa maman. Mme Aknouch et sa fille sont rentrées à l'appartement à pied.

1. F
2. F
3. V
4. V
5. F
6. F

22

1. Mlle Duchamp jouait du piano quand l'actrice est arrivée.
2. M. et Mme Laforêt dansaient quand l'actrice est arrivée.
3. Serge et moi discutions du film quand l'actrice est arrivée.
4. M. Dumont chantait quand l'actrice est arrivée.
5. Tu regardais un tableau quand l'actrice est arrivée.
6. Mme Declerc profitait du buffet quand l'actrice est arrivée.
7. Pierre mangeait des hors-d'œuvres quand l'actrice est arrivée.

23

1. avait; 2. venait; 3. avait; 4. était; 5. a trouvé; 6. portait; 7. travaillait; 8. avait; 9. mettait 10. était; 11. devenait; 12. était; 13. aimait; 14. est tombée; 15. a aidée; 16. a découvert; 17. s'aimaient; 18. se sont mariés

Differentiated Learning

Accelerate
Ask these students to write an activity similar to **Activité 23**, a story with verbs in parentheses. Collect them, and then pass them out to students to complete, making sure they don't receive their own story!

Decelerate
Have students determine which tense to use first and then come back to forming each answer according to the subject and the tense they identified.

Resources

CA Communicative Activities

Share

Answers

24 Surveys will vary.
25 Activities will vary.
26 Activities will vary.

Reference Desk

If you have access to Passport, create a question for your students to share their response to a communicative activity.

Expansion

If you are collaborating with another Level 3 class, or a class in a French-speaking culture, you may want students to conduct the poll with those students before making comparisons between their own class and the other class. You might include polling of what activities are generally for boys, and which ones are generally for girls in the French-speaking culture, to speculate on why there may be such differences between the cultures. If you have a website for your class, consider posting the results for **Activité 24**, as well as the projects in **Activités 25–26**.

À vous la parole

Communiquez!

24 Quand j'avais dix ans.... 1.1, 1.3, 5.1, 5.2

Interpersonal and Presentational Speaking

Faites un sondage auprès de vos camarades de classe pour déterminer leurs loisirs préférés quand ils avaient dix ans. Faites une grille comme celle de dessous et écrivez les réponses de dix élèves. Ensuite, partagez vos résultats avec la classe en expliquant quelles étaient les activités les plus populaires.

MODÈLE **A : Qu'est-ce que tu faisais quand tu avais dix ans ?**
B : Je jouais aux jeux vidéo.

Nom	Activité
Abdou	Il jouait aux jeux vidéo.
Manon	Elle jouait à la poupée.

Résumé possible :
À l'âge de dix ans, quatre garçons jouaient aux jeux vidéo. Une fille jouait à la poupée....

25 Une famille francophone 1.2, 1.3, 2.1, 2.2, 3.2, 5.2

Interpretive Viewing, Presentational Writing and Speaking

Faites des recherches sur une famille francophone. Ça peut être la famille de votre correspondant(e), la famille royale belge, la famille Rainier de Monaco, ou une famille en ligne qui partage ses photos ou vidéos. Créez un document pour décrire cette famille (les membres, âges, loisirs, professions, vacances, etc.). Ensuite, présentez cette famille à vos camarades de classe. Enfin, discutez en groupe de ce que vous avez appris sur les familles francophones.

26 À la découverte de Nice 1.2, 1.3, 3.1, 3.2, 5.2

Interpretive Viewing, Presentational Writing

Avec vos camarades de classe, préparez un site web dédié à Nice et au tourisme. Chacun va choisir un rôle et travailler en équipe pour créer une page d'accueil. (1) Sélectionnez des sites pour obtenir de bonnes informations ; (2) trouvez des photos et images pour illustrer votre page ; (3) sélectionnez quatre à six lieux que vous mentionnerez (une plage, un restaurant, un hôtel, un monument, etc.) ; (4) écrivez un paragraphe sur la ville et les environs (critique de restaurant, description d'un lieu, interview avec des passants, etc.) ; (5) Enfin, finalisez votre page.

Essential Instruction

1. Depending on time, you may want to do one, two, or all three of the **À vous la parole** activities offered on this page. Another option is to have students choose the one that most interests them.
2. The sample Personal Narrative may be above your students' ability level, but it gives them something to strive toward.
3. Work with students to help them pick an appropriate topic for their ability level: either a narrative that describes an event (easiest), explores feelings (more difficult), or leads to a personal discovery (most difficult).

Pre-AP

Communiquez!

Personal Narrative 1.2

Interpretive Reading

Un récit personnel est un essai écrit, en général, à la première personne (**je**/**nous**). L'auteur raconte un moment particulier de sa vie, et expose souvent ses sentiments, ses découvertes, ou ses expériences intimes. Lisez le récit ci-dessous et dites si ce récit personnel (1) décrit un événement, (2) explore des sentiments sur quelque chose qui s'est passé, ou (3) mène à une découverte personnelle.

Il y a des événements et des rencontres qui changent toute une vie. Ma vie a changé l'année de mes dix-huit ans. J'étais encore au lycée, en terminale, et j'allais passer mon bac. J'étudiais la langue de Shakespeare depuis maintenant six ans. L'anglais me fascinait. Je regardais tous les films possibles et imaginables anglais et américains en version originale, je lisais le dictionnaire français-anglais, je tenais un journal en anglais où j'écrivais tous les mots que j'apprenais dans mes lectures. Je n'étais pas encore allée en Angleterre ou en Amérique mais j'en rêvais. L'année de mon bac j'ai eu l'opportunité d'aller deux semaines dans une famille d'accueil en Angleterre avec ma classe d'anglais. Ma famille était une famille nucléaire avec six enfants. Le père était professeur de français et de religion et la mère prof d'anglais. Chaque jour nous parlions tous ensemble, parents et enfants, de la langue, de la culture britannique, dans le salon, dans la cuisine, ou à table. J'ai trouvé ces conversations fascinantes. Un jour, le père de ma famille d'accueil m'a invitée à son lycée où il m'a demandé de parler de la France et surtout de répondre aux nombreuses questions de ses élèves et c'est comme ça que j'ai découvert ma vocation pour l'enseignement. Aujourd'hui, je fais le plus beau métier du monde : je suis prof et tous les jours je partage avec les autres ma langue et ma culture, et c'est un grand bonheur.

27 Le passé composé ou l'imparfait? 1.2

Interpretive Reading

*En écrivant un récit, vous devez choisir correctement le temps des verbes. Dans ces phrases écrites par d'autres élèves, conjuguez les verbes en choisissant le bon temps (*tense*).*

1. Je/J'... mon meilleur ami au skatepark. (faire la connaissance de)
2. Après cela, je... mes camarades de classe. (ne plus insulter)
3. Pour mon neuvième anniversaire, ma grand-mère... un gâteau en forme d'un terrain de foot. (me servir)
4. Enfin, je/j'... que j'... plus sportive que mes cousins. (réaliser, être)
5. Alors, j'... que le prof... m'aider. (apprendre, vouloir)

28 Je choisis un thème 1.3, 5.1

Presentational Writing

Pour écrire votre récit personnel, remplissez un organigramme avec des idées. Vous pouvez regarder des photos, faire une liste d'objets personnels importants, ou lire d'autres récits en ligne.

Recherche : souvenirs d'enfance, souvenirs d'adolescence

Resources

Pre-T Pre-test

Q *Leçon* Quiz

Answers

Personal narrative

(3) mène à une découverte personnelle

27

1. ai fait la connaissance de
2. n'ai plus insulté
3. m'a servi
4. ai réalisé, étais
5. ai appris, voulait

28 Paragraphs will vary.

Expansion

This activity demonstrates the importance of pre-writing or brainstorming before undertaking a composition. It may be helpful to write a short class **récit personnel** together to model the process. Find out which of the three types (description of an event, exploration of feelings tied to a personal story, or description of a personal discovery) interests the most students, and write that one as a class. Students will see that the more they prepare in advance and add to their pre-writing outline, the easier it will be for them to effectively complete their writing.

Differentiated Learning

Accelerate

Students may be interested in publishing their **récits** online.

Decelerate

These students may not be able to write their own **récit**. Other options for them include a story in which they provide the correct verb tense and verb forms, a cartoon that they describe by answering questions you have written, or changing personal pronouns to the third person.

Resources

Vocabulaire actif
eV eVisual
WB Workbook 1–3
FC Flash Cards
LA Listening Activity 1
G & V Practice Games

Reference Desk

1. Point out that **le mariage** is a **faux ami** in this context; it means *wedding*.
2. A wedding anniversary is **un anniversaire de mariage**.
3. Students learned several **domaines** and **secteurs** on p. 510 of **Unité 9** in the Level 2 textbook. You may want to review these with the class.
4. Describe to students the two types of French weddings—civil and religious—before they do **Activité 1**.
5. Point out to students that **le gâteau de mariage** may be **une pièce montée** (*a tiered cake*).
6. **JDN** stands for "**Journal du Net**" and is a French online economics publication.

Leçon C Vocabulaire actif

Le mariage et le travail 1.2

Emma se marie avec Théo

la réception

la demoiselle d'honneur

le garçon d'honneur

la bague de fiançailles

les alliances (f.)

le gâteau de mariage

le voyage de noces

Vous voulez travailler….

pour **un cabinet d'avocats**

dans **un laboratoire de recherches**

en plein air

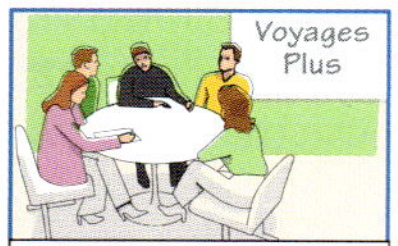

pour **une PME (petite et moyenne entreprise)**

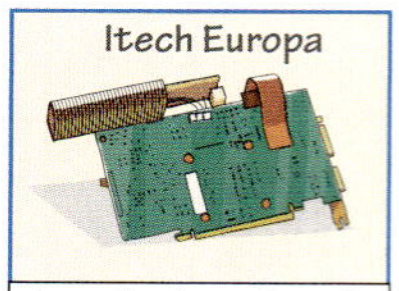

dans le domaine de **la haute technologie**

chez Airbus

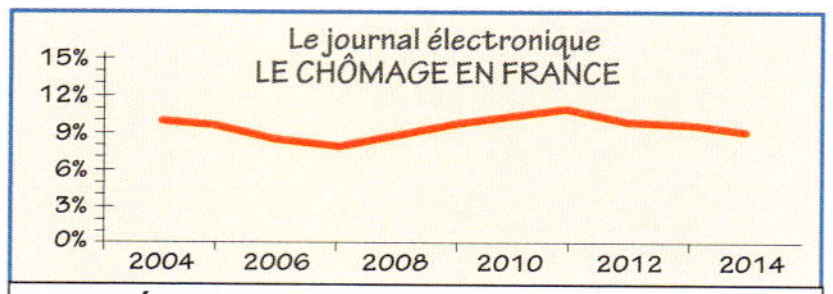

à JDN Économie

Essential Instruction

1. Play the audio for both groups of words.
2. Write a short love story together on the board.
3. Ask students where they would like to work, or conduct a class poll.

Pour la conversation 1.2

How do I say I don't care?

» **Je m'en fiche.**
I don't care.

How do I say where I'd like to work?

» J'aimerais bien travailler dans un laboratoire de recherches.
I'd like to work in a research laboratory.

Et si je voulais dire... ?

la lune de miel	*honeymoon*
la pièce montée	*wedding cake*
le témoin	*witness (to the ceremony)*
le vin d'honneur	*reception*
se fiancer	*to get engaged*
une entreprise	*company*
monter une entreprise	*to set up a company*
un entretien	*job interview*

1 Jean-Pierre et Marie-France vont se marier 1.2, 2.1, 5.1

Interpretive Reading

Lisez l'histoire du mariage de Jean-Pierre et Marie-France. Puis, répondez à la question qui suit.

Jean-Pierre était amoureux de Marie-France. Il lui a demandé de se marier avec lui. Elle a accepté la bague de fiançailles que Jean-Pierre lui a offerte. Ils ont décidé de se marier à la mairie. Ils y sont allés avec la demoiselle d'honneur, la sœur de Marie-France, et le garçon d'honneur, le cousin de Jean-Pierre. Ils ont invité 89 amis et membres de leur famille à la réception, qui a eu lieu dans un restaurant. On a servi les invités du saumon et du steak. Le gâteau de mariage était violet et rose. Le lendemain, Jean-Pierre et Marie-France sont partis en voyage de noces, destination Tahiti !

Est-ce que Jean-Pierre et Marie-France ont respecté les traditions françaises ? Justifiez votre réponse.

2 Une réception de mariage 1.2, 1.3, 2.1

Interpretive Viewing, Presentational Speaking or Writing

Regardez la scène et répondez aux questions.

1. Où sont les personnes ?
2. Qui vient de se marier ?
3. Que porte la mariée ?
4. Elle porte quels bijoux ?
5. Où sont assis la demoiselle d'honneur et le garçon d'honneur ?
6. Que font les invités ?
7. Qu'est-ce qu'ils vont manger à la fin du repas ?

Resources

Pour la conversation
Et si je voulais dire... ?

Answers

1

Ils ont respecté les traditions culturelles (fiançailles, cérémonie civile, réception, voyage de noces), mais ils n'ont pas respecté a tradition de se marier à l'église.

2

1. Elles sont à un repas de mariage.
2. Noémie et Ethan viennent de se marier.
3. La mariée porte une belle robe blanche.
4. Elle porte un collier (en perles), une bague (de fiançailles), et probablement une alliance.
5. Ils sont assis à la table des mariés.
6. Ils attendent de pouvoir manger.
7. Ils vont manger un gâteau de mariage.

Reference Desk

1. Point out that **Je m'en fiche** is familiar French.
2. After students have read the story in **Activité 1** silently, discuss the answer to the critical thinking question as a class.
3. After doing **Activité 2** orally, ask students to write a narrative about the wedding, expanding on the story by saying what happened before and after the action in the illustration. You may want each student to have his or her story peer edited before handing it in to you.

Culture

Practices: Information

In France, a bride and groom must be married at **la mairie** in a civil ceremony. They then have the option of having a church service. **Le vin d'honneur** is the reception immediately following one or both ceremonies; this is described more in detail on p. 51.

Differentiated Learning

Accelerate
Have students use each of the words and expressions in **Et si je voulais dire...?** in original sentences. Then have them research **les pièces montées** and give creative names to the photos of the cakes that they find.

Decelerate
Pair students who are slow-paced, and have them work together, reading the story aloud. They can ask each other questions, motivating each other to reach comprehension.

Resources

Activities 3, 5

Answers

3 Script

1. Le marié met un morceau de gâteau dans la bouche de la mariée.
2. Claudia met une longue robe blanche.
3. Beaucoup d'invités dansent et chantent.
4. Claudia met une alliance au doigt de Philippe.
5. On prend une photo de la demoiselle d'honneur avant la cérémonie.
6. Philippe, dans un smoking noir, attend que le père de Claudia l'accompagne.
7. Le garçon d'honneur donne l'alliance à Philippe.

1. R; 2. E; 3. R; 4. E; 5. E; 6. E; 7. E

4

1. Inès aimerait travailler pour une PME.
2. Maxime aimerait travailler dans un laboratoire de recherches.
3. Mathilde aimerait travailler dans le domaine de la haute technologie.
4. Julien aimerait travailler pour un cabinet d'avocats.
5. Julianne aimerait travailler chez Airbus.
6. Nicolas aimerait travailler à JDN Économie.

5

1. Elle s'appelle Clara.
2. Elle avait le collier de perles de sa grand-mère.
3. Il s'appelle Hervé.
4. Il y en avait presque cent.
5. Le couple est allé à la Guadeloupe.
6. Ils reviennent le 15 septembre parce que Clara commence son travail.

Reference Desk

1. You may want the class to brainstorm vocabulary related to a church ceremony and a reception before they listen to the audio in **Activité 3**.
2. If you are unsure if students know what types of companies **Airbus** and **JDN Économie** are, review with them before completing **Activité 4**. Airbus is a line of airplanes made by a European consortium of countries. **JDN Économie** is an online magazine.
3. **Activité 5** is another comprehensible input paragraph like **Activité 1** on p. 47.

3 Le mariage de Claudia et Philippe 1.2

Interpretive Listening

*Écrivez les numéros 1–7 sur votre papier. Écrivez **E** si la phrase décrit la cérémonie à l'église ou **R** si la phrase décrit la réception.*

4 Où on aimerait travailler 1.2, 1.3, 3.1, 5.1

Interpretive Reading, Presentational Speaking or Writing

Dites où chaque personne aimerait travailler en choisissant une expression de la colonne.

MODÈLE Jacques a besoin d'argent de poche (*pocket money*) et son oncle a une petite entreprise de construction.
Jacques aimerait travailler pour une PME.

1. Inès est secrétaire et cherche un nouveau travail dans une plus petite compagnie.
2. Maxime finit ses études à la faculté des sciences pharmaceutiques.
3. Mathilde a des idées pour créer la nouvelle génération de smartphones.
4. Julien aime le droit.
5. Julianne a de l'expérience comme designer d'avions.
6. Nicolas a étudié le marché international.

une PME
Airbus
un cabinet d'avocats
JDN Économie
un laboratoire de recherches
le domaine de la haute technologie

5 Au téléphone 1.2, 5.1

Interpretive Reading

Lisez la conversation entre Mme Garnier et sa sœur Gabriella, qui habite en Australie, et qui n'a pas pu venir pour le mariage de sa nièce.

Mme Garnier: Je t'envoie des photos. Clara était très belle dans sa robe de mariée.
Gabriella: Tu lui as prêté des bijoux?
Mme Garnier: Le collier de perles de maman et le bracelet de diamants qu'Hervé m'a donné pour notre anniversaire de mariage l'année dernière.
Gabriella: Il y avait combien d'invités à la réception?
Mme Garnier: Presque cent.
Gabriella: Ils sont partis où pour leur voyage de noces, Clara et Lucas?
Mme Garnier: Ils voulaient aller à la Guadeloupe.
Gabriella: Ils reviennent quand?
Mme Garnier: Le 15 septembre. Clara commence à travailler pour un journal en ligne le 17.

1. Comment s'appelle la mariée?
2. Elle avait quels bijoux de sa grand-mère?
3. Comment s'appelle le mari de Mme Garnier?
4. Il y avait combien d'invités à la réception?
5. Où est-ce que le couple est allé en voyage de noces?
6. Pourquoi est-ce que le couple revient le 15 septembre?

Essential Instruction

1. Before doing **Activité 4**, explain that **aimerait** is in the conditional. You may want to review the formation of the conditional.
2. Have students take turns playing the roles of Mme Garnier and Gabriella in **Activité 5**. Then put students in pairs to answer the questions.
3. Have students listen to the dialogue on p. 49 and then answer the questions. Do **Activité 6** as a class.

Élodie va assister à un mariage

1.2

Élodie parle à son cousin, Mathieu, qui va bientôt se marier.

Mathieu : Crois-moi, Élodie ! Le mariage, c'est une vraie entreprise : la réception, la liste des invités, le choix du garçon et de la demoiselle d'honneur. Et mettre d'accord ma mère et ma belle-mère, ça demande beaucoup de diplomatie.

Élodie : Et Sophie ?

Mathieu : Elle s'en fiche ! Il n'y a qu'une chose qui l'intéresse : notre voyage de noces en Italie ! Ombrie et Toscane… je ne te raconte pas le nombre de châteaux et d'églises que nous devrons visiter !

Élodie : Et après ?

Mathieu : Je finis cette année à Centrale et après j'aimerais bien travailler dans un laboratoire de recherches sur les nanotechnologies. J'ai une piste à Grenoble, j'y ai déjà fait un stage… ils sont intéressés.

Élodie : Et si on t'offrait le poste, vous déménageriez ?

Mathieu : Oui, il faudrait aussi que Sophie change de travail ou qu'elle se fasse muter dans la région….

Élodie : Et le bébé ?

Mathieu : On aimerait en avoir un très vite.

Élodie : Eh bien, j'aurai le rôle de ma vie : marraine !

Mot-clé

Noce (du latin *nuptiae, mariage*). Au début du 12ème siècle, *la noce* signifiait l'union spirituelle d'un homme avec le Christ. Au 13ème siècle, *la noce* représentait l'heureuse célébration qui suit un mariage, avec par exemple un festin (gros dîner), de la musique, et une danse.

6 Élodie va assister à un mariage

Répondez aux questions. 1.2

1. Élodie va assister au mariage de qui ?
2. Comment s'appelle la mariée ?
3. Où vont-ils en voyage de noces ?
4. Où Matthieu aimerait-il travailler ?
5. Élodie voudrait être la marraine de qui ?

EXTENSION **Quand on vous dit « mariage », vous pensez à quoi ?** 1.2

Un journaliste interviewe un couple dans une joaillerie où ils achètent leurs alliances.

Journaliste : Quand on vous dit « mariage », vous pensez à quoi ?

Elle : La robe, la bague de fiançailles, les alliances, la cérémonie à l'église… ce qui fait rêver, quoi !

Lui : La réception, le voyage de noces….

Elle : À la joie de ma mère, à mon père la larme à l'œil….

Lui : Mettre d'accord ma mère et ma belle-mère, bonjour l'ambiance ! Si c'était à refaire, je me pacserais… plus vite fait, moins de cérémonial, et donc moins de problèmes….

EXTENSION Comparez l'attitude de la femme et de l'homme vis-à-vis du mariage.

Resources

Dialogue
Activity 6
Extension
Dialogue Video
WB Workbook 4

Answers

6

1. de son cousin
2. Sophie
3. en Italie
4. dans un laboratoire de recherches à Grenoble
5. du premier bébé

EXTENSION

La femme voit les préparatifs du mariage comme un rêve, et l'homme comme beaucoup de responsabilités.

Reference Desk

1. The expression **se faire muter** means *to get oneself transferred*, while **avoir une piste** means *to have an in*. Students will learn the definition *ski slope* for **piste** in **Unité 4**.
2. **L'École centrale** is **une grande école** for business students; it is located in Paris. Graduates of **grandes écoles** often hold important positions in politics, government, business, etc.
3. Students may be interested to look up the uniform of the **École polytechnique**, another **grande école**.
4. While France is often a romantic destination for American couples, the French often go to Italy.

Expansion

Cut up each part in the dialogue and put all the parts of the dialogue in an envelope. Ask students, working in pairs, to put the dialogue in order. Tell them the easiest place to start is with the questions.

Differentiated Learning

Accelerate

Ask your advanced students to find an example of the future and conditional in the main dialogue. Have pairs of these students prepare the **Extension** dialogue and present to the rest of the class from memory. Let the class know ahead of time the general topic of the conversation and then discuss what they did not understand when they heard the dialogue.

Decelerate

Have students find a wedding present for Mathieu and Sophie online, based on what they know about their life together.

Special Needs Students

Auditory Impairment

Allow students to read the dialogue while they are viewing it so that they have a better chance of grasping the main ideas.

Resources

Points de départ
WB Workbook 5
Explore

Answers

Comparaisons
Answers may include Ivy League schools, such as Harvard, Cornell, Princeton, Yale, or other higher institutions of learning, such as Berkeley, M.I.T., Caltech, and the "Seven Sisters" (such as Wellesley, Mt. Holyoke, and Bryn Mawr colleges).

Reference Desk

1. **Les classes préparatoires aux grandes écoles** (**CPGE**) are affiliated with the Ministry of Education, while **les grandes écoles** depend on other ministries such as agriculture, culture, defense, industry, justice, and health.
2. The first **grandes écoles** were created during the 18th century.
3. According to the Ministry of Education, **une grande école** is an "**établissement d'enseignement supérieur qui recrute ses élèves par concours et assure des formations de haut niveau.**"
4. If you have access to Passport, find a video or a news article related to **l'université** or **le mariage** and show it to your students.

Expansion

Have students research famous, contemporary French public figures and which schools they attended.

Points de départ

Pre-AP

Question centrale ? Comment change-t-on de l'enfance à l'âge adulte?

L'enseignement supérieur en France 1.2, 2.1, 5.1

L'enseignement supérieur français est un système qui comprend les grandes écoles*, les universités, et des écoles spécialisées privées*. Tout étudiant ayant obtenu son bac peut s'inscrire à l'université. Cependant, l'accès aux grandes écoles se fait de manière très sélective sur concours*. Les écoles supérieures privées possèdent chacune leurs propres* conditions d'entrée : concours, dossier*, obtention préalable* d'une licence* ou d'un master universitaire.

Les classes préparatoires* préparent aux concours. Ces classes proposent deux années d'un enseignement général intensif, soit* à dominante littéraire, soit à dominante mathématique et scientifique.

Tous les grands secteurs d'activités ont leur grande école : l'administration a l'ENA (École nationale d'administration) ; les finances ont HEC (École des hautes études commerciales) ; les sciences, l'École polytechnique ; l'éducation, les Écoles normales supérieures (ENS) ; la justice, l'École nationale de la magistrature ; l'armée, l'École spéciale militaire de Saint-Cyr. Toutes ces écoles supérieures ne dépendent pas du Ministère* de l'éducation mais sont rattachées à des ministères différents.

Recherche : classes préparatoires aux grandes écoles, ena, hec, école polytechnique, écoles normales supérieures, école spéciale militaire

grandes écoles *elite schools* ; **privées** *private* ; **concours** *competitive exam* ; **propres** *own* ; **dossier** *selection on merit* ; **préalable** *prerequisite* ; **licence** *B.A.* ; **préparatoires** *preparatory* ; **soit… soit** *either… or* ; **Ministère** *Department*

L'École des Beaux-Arts à Paris prépare des carrières dans la création photo, le design, ou le graphisme.

Comparaisons 1.2, 4.2

Quelles universités américaines ressemblent aux grandes écoles ?

Mon dico grandes écoles 1.2

Hypokhâgne *première année de classe préparatoire (du grec hypo qui veut dire « en-dessous »)*
Khâgne *deuxième année de lettres supérieures*
Taupins *surnom donné à ceux qui vivent enfermés dans les bibliothèques, au milieu des livres*
X *désigne à la fois les élèves et l'École polytechnique elle-même*

Mot-clé 1.2

Étudiant (apparaît en 1260). Il est en concurrence avec *escolier* (aujourd'hui *écolier*) jusqu'à la fin du 17ème. *Étudiante* n'apparaît dans son sens actuel qu'à la fin du 19ème siècle ; auparavant, elle désignait la petite amie de l'étudiant.

Connexions 1.2, 3.1

Arts
À quelles carrières les grandes écoles, comme l'École normale supérieure ou l'École des Beaux-Arts, préparent-elles les étudiants ? Quelles grandes écoles vous attirent, et pourquoi ? Discutez en groupe.

Recherche : grandes écoles en france

Produits 1.2, 2.2

Les **grandes écoles** ont été créées afin de disposer d'une élite qui aide l'État dans tous les grands domaines d'intervention : armée, industrie et techniques (mines), environnement (eaux et forêts), administration centrale, ponts et chaussées (aménagement du territoire) agriculture, ports et arsenaux, science vétérinaire, etc. C'est Louis XIV qui a créé la première grande école.

Essential Instruction

1. Review with students what they already know about higher education in France.
2. Have students look at the websites of the **grandes écoles** in the first culture reading.
3. Compare weddings in France and North Africa. Find an interesting video of each online.

   Recherche : mariage maroc vidéo

4. After students have read the culture paragraphs, ask which wedding ceremony they would want.

Le mariage : fête civile et fête religieuse

1.2, 2.1, 5.1

Aujourd'hui, en France, 240 000 couples se marient et 170 000 se pacsent chaque année. Le mariage est une cérémonie qui doit d'abord être civile, selon la loi française. Ensuite, les mariés peuvent décider d'avoir une cérémonie religieuse ou non.

La cérémonie civile se passe à la mairie devant un officier d'État civil qui enregistre l'échange de consentement entre le futur époux et la future épouse. Si c'est l'unique cérémonie, on y échange les anneaux qui symbolisent l'union et l'autorité civile remet aux époux le livret de famille* qu'ils signent et qu'ils doivent conserver*. Les naissances des enfants et les décès* seront par la suite inscrits dans le livret de famille. Dans un pays majoritairement catholique, la cérémonie religieuse a lieu à l'église. Elle peut donner lieu à une simple bénédiction ou à une messe. Les jeunes mariés cherchent aujourd'hui à personnaliser la cérémonie : décoration florale de l'église, choix des textes, et surtout choix des chants et des musiques.

La cérémonie du mariage est généralement suivie d'une réception. En soirée, un repas de mariage est servi aux invités. Le repas, assis ou sous forme de buffet, peut comprendre : une entrée, un poisson, une viande, un plat d'accompagnement, du fromage, et des desserts, dont notamment* le gâteau de mariage. On y boit aussi des vins excellents et du champagne. Le dîner est souvent suivi d'une animation musicale qui permet de danser. C'est le moment où les mariés reçoivent des cadeaux généralement choisis sur une liste de mariage.

Recherche : mairie mariage civil (+ NOM DE LA VILLE), cérémonie de mariage vidéo

Traditions et pratiques

1.2, 2.1

Les anniversaires de mariage célèbrent les noces d'argent (25 ans), d'or (50 ans), de diamant (60 ans) et de platine (70 ans).

livret de famille *family record book* ; **conserver** *to keep* ; **décès** *deaths* ; **notamment** *notably*

La Francophonie

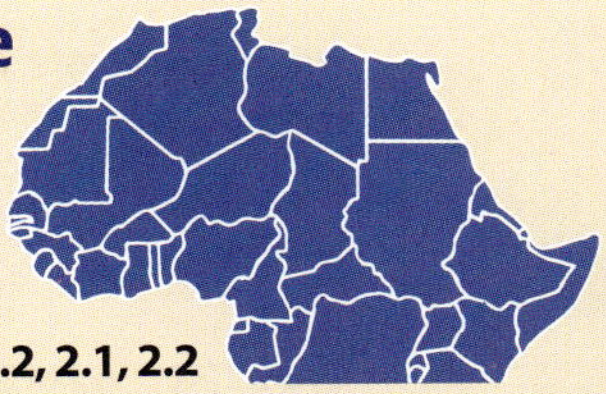

Culture

Les mariages au Maghreb

1.2, 2.1, 2.2

En Afrique du nord, le mariage est une cérémonie culturelle et religieuse, qui comporte* plusieurs rituels. La cérémonie du henné* est une façon de préparer une jeune femme musulmane à sa vie de femme mariée, et aux responsabilités qu'elle comporte. Cette fête se déroule* sept jours avant le mariage, chez les parents de la future mariée, en soirée et uniquement entre femmes. On teint le corps de la future mariée de henné, dans le but de lui porter chance dans son mariage.

La future mariée teintée de henné

comporte *entails* ; **henné** *henna* ; **se déroule** *takes place*

Reference Desk

Here is some additional vocabulary to use when discussing weddings in France: **l'unique cérémonie** (*the only ceremony*); **le repas assis** (*a sit-down meal as opposed to a buffet*); **suivi de** (*followed by*); and **en soirée** (*in the evening*).

Connections

Graphic Arts

Ask students to create a wedding invitation and draw from their imagination a wedding ceremony at a city hall in France, or a reception; or ask them to make a travel poster for a francophone location aimed at honeymoon couples.

Differentiated Learning

Adapt

Ask questions that elicit the main ideas from the culture readings, for example, What do students need to provide when applying to **une grande école**? Which wedding ceremony is required, the one at the church or city hall?

Special Needs Students

Reading Difficulties

Provide an outline of the readings or a cloze exercise that focuses on the main ideas of the culture sections.

Answers

7

1. l'ENA : à Strasbourg; HEC : à Paris; l'École polytechnique : à Paris; les Écoles normales supérieures (ENS) : à Paris, à Cachan, à Rennes, à Lyon; l'École spéciale militaire de Saint-Cyr : à Guer
2. l'armée : l'École spéciale militaire de Saint-Cyr; le commerce : HEC; les sciences et techniques : l'École polytechnique; l'éducation : les Écoles normales supérieures (ENS); l'administration : l'ENA
3. Answers will vary.
4. Answers will vary.

À DISCUTER

Answers will vary.

Comparaisons
Answers will vary.

Perspectives
Elle voudrait reconnaître les traditions des deux cultures qui forment son identité ; une robe blanche pour la France traditionnelle et une robe algérienne pour célébrer ses origines.

Communication

Interpersonal: Paired Practice

Have pairs of students prepare dialogues during different stages of a relationship: first date, a particular anniversary, engagement, wedding preparations, the photographer taking pictures, reception, honeymoon, birth of first child, and 25th wedding anniversary. Have each pair present their dialogue, and ask the rest of the class to identify where each pair is in their relationship.

7 Activités culturelles 1.2, 1.3, 3.1, 3.2, 5.1

Faites les activités suivantes.

1. Faites des recherches et indiquez où se trouvent les grandes écoles mentionnées dans la lecture.
2. Quelle grande école choisir pour faire carrière dans les secteurs suivants ?
   - l'armée
   - le commerce
   - les sciences et techniques
   - l'éducation
   - l'administration
3. Faites une liste de choses à planifier pour une fête de mariage religieuse.
4. Composez un menu de dîner de mariage en vous aidant d'Internet. Choisissez :
   - une entrée
   - un poisson
   - une viande
   - un plateau de fromages
   - des desserts

À DISCUTER

Comment est-ce que le mariage représente un rite de passage ?

Produits

Le gâteau de mariage est traditionnellement une pièce montée (*tiered cake*) faite de choux à la crème (*cream puffs*).

Comparaisons 4.2

Savez-vous comment se déroulent les cérémonies de mariage musulmanes aux États-Unis ? Comparez-les aux cérémonies musulmanes en France.

Perspectives

Moi, je vais mettre ma robe blanche pour la mairie, puis une robe algérienne traditionnelle type caftan pendant la cérémonie religieuse.
—Tagada

Pourquoi cette jeune femme va-t-elle porter deux robes différentes pour se marier ?

Une jeune mariée marocaine

Essential Instruction

1. The first and second culture activities would appeal to lower-ability students because they can easily find the answers in the readings. The third and fourth options would be more appropriate for higher-ability students.
2. Put a student who has worked on each activity in a group to share what he or she has learned.
3. Meet as a class to discuss together.
4. Have students read the wedding invitation; then answer the questions in **Activité 8** as a class.

Du côté des médias 1.2

Lisez le faire-part de mariage ci-dessous.

Mme Brochant et M. et Mme Lacroix
sont très heureux
de vous annoncer le mariage de leurs enfants :

Tania et Sébastien

qui, après 5 ans de réflexion, se décident enfin !

Ils vous attendent avec impatience
le samedi 13 juin 2020 pour fêter cet événement.

Célébration à 15h30
Mairie de Fontenay aux Roses
75 rue Boucicaut
92260 Fontenay aux Roses

Réception à partir de 18 heures
Restaurant la Forestière
1 avenue du Président Kennedy
78100 Saint-Germain en Laye

RSVP Tania Brochant et Sébastien Lacroix
9 rue Victor Hugo
92260 Fontenay aux Roses
Tel : 01 53 50 60 82
valoubroch@orange.fr

8 Le faire-part de mariage de Tania et Sébastien 1.2, 1.3, 5.1

Répondez aux questions.

1. Comment s'appelle la future mariée? le futur mari?
2. Où est-ce que le couple va se marier?
3. Dans quelle ville a lieu la réception?
4. Quelle est la date du mariage?

Resources

Du côté des médias
Activity 8

Answers

8

1. Tania Brochant; Sébastien Lacroix
2. à la mairie de Fontenay aux Roses
3. à Saint-Germain en Laye
4. le samedi 13 juin 2020

Culture

Practices: Activity

In the United States, traditional wedding invitations list the parents of the bride as hosts. Who is listed on the wedding invitation in the textbook? What kind of a wedding is it going to be: religious, civil, or both? (civil, **la mairie**, without a mention of a church) What element of humor renders the invitation less formal? (… **se décident enfin !**) How do you know that the young couple is not traditional? (The bride is keeping her name.) What does **à partir de 18 heures** mean? (from six o'clock on)

Differentiated Learning

Accelerate

Have students write their own wedding invitation, perhaps for a famous couple from history or current events.

Decelerate

Ask these students to find three French wedding invitations online and explain to the class how they are different from the example provided in the textbook.

Special Needs Students

Dyslexia

Students often benefit from reading aloud or following along as they listen to others read. Either read the wedding announcement aloud or pair students with one partner reading aloud. Allow students to answer one or two questions about the text to increase their confidence.

Answers

All activities will vary.

Reference Desk

1. The **Culture sur place** section is intended to provide active cultural experiences for students through investigation and developing relationships with Francophones. This spirit of inquiry will help francophone culture come alive for students.
2. A reproducible blackline master of the chart is available in the Copy Masters supplement.

Culture sur place

Question centrale ? Comment change-t-on de l'enfance à l'âge adulte?

La culture ado

Introduction et interrogations

Est-ce que la culture est surtout une idée nationale (la culture française)? Y a-t-il aussi une culture des enfants, une culture des adolescents? Dans cette **Culture sur place**, vous allez examiner la culture des ados.

9 Réfléchir 1.2, 1.3, 2.1, 3.2, 5.1

*Recopiez cet organigramme sur une feuille de papier. Dans la première colonne, écrivez ce que vous savez déjà des adolescents en France. Ces connaissances (*knowledge*) peuvent venir de vos expériences personnelles ainsi que de ce programme. Dans la deuxième colonne, écrivez ce que vous voulez savoir des ados français, sous forme de questions. N'écrivez rien dans la troisième colonne pour l'instant.*

MODÈLE

Ce que je SAIS	Ce que je VOUDRAIS SAVOIR	Ce que J'AI APPRIS
Les jeunes Français aiment beaucoup les blogs.	Est-ce qu'ils voyagent souvent à l'étranger?	

10 Rechercher

*Même s'il faut se souvenir que les blogs ne représentent qu'un point de vue, rechercher les intérêts des adolescents dans un autre pays francophone est facile aujourd'hui grâce à (*thanks to*) ces ressources en ligne.*

1. Accédez à une liste de blogs d'ados (jeunes âgés de 16 à 20 ans) francophones. Par exemple, vous pouvez voir des profils sur Skyrock.
2. Identifiez trois blogs intéressants.
3. Sur chaque blog, examinez les photos, les liens, et les détails de la vie de l'auteur. Écrivez ce que vous apprenez de ces ados français sur votre organigramme dans la troisième colonne.

11 Faire l'inventaire ! 1.2, 1.3, 2.1, 3.1, 4.2, 5.1

Avec votre partenaire ou avec toute la classe, répondez à ces questions.

1. Qu'est-ce que vous avez en commun avec les ados dont vous avez lu les blogs? Qu'est-ce que vous n'avez pas en commun? (Vous pouvez faire un diagramme Venn.)
2. Y avait-il beaucoup de différences parmi les trois blogs que vous avez lus? beaucoup de similarités? Citez des exemples.
3. Est-ce que l'on peut identifier une culture à laquelle tous les ados français appartiennent? Pourquoi, ou pourquoi pas?
4. Vous pensez qu'il y a une «culture des adolescents» qui traverse les frontières nationales? Quels sont les aspects de cette culture, si elle existe?

Essential Instruction

1. Before assigning **Activité 9**, have students review previous chapters for information about adolescents in France. Filling in the first column together as a class will get students started on this personal graphic organizer.
2. Give students time to read some French blogs (that you have vetted) outside of class before doing **Activité 10**.
3. Conduct a debriefing of the pairs or class as a whole to make sure all students benefit from the points of view of others.
4. Point out the difference between the stem for the imperfect and the conditional.

Révision: The Conditional 1.2

On recycle!

Do you remember how to say "I would like a ticket"? What mood is that? Does a sentence like this describe reality? How are verbs in this mood formed? How do you get the stem? If you cannot answer these questions, read the summary below.

The **conditionnel** is used to tell what people *would* do or what *would* happen.

Caro **aimerait** travailler dans un laboratoire de recherches.	*Caro would like to work in a research laboratory.*

To form the conditional of regular **-er** and **-ir** verbs, add to the infinitive the endings of the imperfect tense: **-ais, -ais, -ait, -ions, -iez, -aient**. For regular **-re** verbs, drop the final **e** from the infinitive before adding the imperfect endings.

Vendriez-vous votre bague de fiançailles?	*Would you sell your engagement ring?*
Je **choisirais** Paris pour mon voyage de noces.	*I would choose Paris for my honeymoon.*

Some irregular French verbs have an irregular stem in the conditional, but their endings are regular.

Infinitive	Irregular Stem	Conditional	Examples
aller	**ir-**	**j'irais**	Tu **irais** à Saint-Paul-de-Vence?
s'asseoir	**assiér-**	je **m'assiérais**	Papa **s'assiérait** dans son fauteuil.
avoir	**aur-**	**j'aurais**	Nous **aurions** une décapotable.
courir	**courr-**	je **courrais**	Marc **courrait**-il dans le marathon?
devoir	**devr-**	je **devrais**	Vous **devriez** étudier pour l'interro.
être	**ser-**	je **serais**	**Serais**-tu un comptable?
faire	**fer-**	je **ferais**	Ils ne **feraient** pas du ski alpin.
falloir	**faudr-**	il **faudrait**	Il **faudrait** faire le ménage.
pleuvoir	**pleuvr-**	il **pleuvrait**	Il **pleuvrait** avant notre arrivée.
pouvoir	**pourr-**	je **pourrais**	On **pourrait** faire une soupe?
recevoir	**recevr-**	je **recevrais**	Les Cheval **recevrait** l'Italienne.
savoir	**saur-**	je **saurais**	Tu **saurais** les solutions.
venir	**viendr-**	je **viendrais**	**Viendrais**-tu au concert avec moi?
voir	**verr-**	je **verrais**	Marie **verrait** toute l'Europe.
vouloir	**voudr-**	je **voudrais**	Nous **voudrions** nous habiller bien.

Resources

WB Workbook 6–8

G & V Practice Games

Answers

On recycle!

The French sentence would be **Je voudrais un billet**. It is an example of the conditional, which doesn't describe reality, but rather what *might* happen. To form the conditional, add the ending **-ais**, **-ais**, **-ait**, **-ions**, **-iez**, or **-aient** to the infinitives for regular verbs. Students might grasp how to form the present conditional more easily if you give them this little formula: **conditionnel** = future base + **imparfait** endings.

Reference Desk

1. As a memory aid, students might like to think of "Mr. W. (Would) Conditional" since the conditional is translated by the word "would" in English.
2. Here is a list of some other irregular verbs in the conditional: **j'achèterais**, **je m'appellerais**, **je deviendrais**, **j'emmènerais**, **je me lèverais**, **je nettoierais**, **je reviendrais**.
3. In the conditional, **devoir** means *should* or *ought* and **pouvoir** means *could*.
4. The conditional was introduced in the Level 2 textbook on p. 490 of **Unité 9**.

nouvelle orthographe **s'assoir**

Expansion

Make a set of note cards with the name of one verb tense (**P** for present, **PC** for **passé composé**, **I** for **imparfait**, **F** for **futur**, or **C** for **conditionnel**) on each card. Give a card to each student. Then read short stories that contain examples of each tense. As you read the texts, have students hold up their card for the entire class to see each time they hear the verb tense on their card. At the beginning, it is a good idea to pause for a few seconds after each verb.

Differentiated Learning

Decelerate

Have students listen to other students' points of view first if they are reluctant to share their own opinions in **Activité 11**. Be sure to include these students in the discussion at some point.

Accelerate

Have students complete a set of sentences for one verb using each of the verb tenses reviewed so far in this unit.

Special Needs Students

Linguistically Challenged

Give these students a worksheet that asks them to break down the formation of regular and irregular verbs in the conditional by listing their parts before using them:
Verb and subject: **avoir**; **elles**
Stem: **aur-**
Sentence: **À Nice elles auraient besoin d'un maillot de bain**.
The sentence needs to prove the student understands the meaning of the verb.

Answers

12 Possible answers:

1. Noah pourrait acheter un pantalon pour homme et un pull beige.
2. Khaled et moi pourrions acheter deux pantalons, deux polos, et deux pulls.
3. Laure et Milo pourraient acheter une cravate en soie et un pull beige.
4. Tu pourrais acheter une robe rouge, un collier en diamant, un pantalon gris, une jupe rose, et une chemise blanche.
5. Vous pourriez acheter un pantalon gris, une paire de chaussettes noires, un polo blanc, une chemise blanche, et des boucles d'oreilles en perles.
6. Quentin pourrait acheter un polo de toutes les couleurs, un pull beige, dix paires de chaussettes noires, deux colliers en diamant, et une jupe bleue.

Comparaisons
The first sentence would not be in the conditional because it expresses a past idea; it would be expressed using the **imparfait** in French.

Critical Thinking

Comparisons

Ask your students what these expressions mean in English: **j'aimerais**, **j'irais**, and **je serais**. Then ask them to explain what they use in English to express *I would (do something)* to indicate what would happen. They should say that, in English, *would* is used before a verb.

Communication

Presentational: Cooperative Groups

Put students in small groups. Then write a hypothetical question on the board, for example: **Si vous gagniez à la loterie, qu'est-ce que vous feriez? Si un astéroïde venait frapper la terre et que vous n'aviez qu'une heure à vivre, que feriez-vous?** The first student asks the person on his or her left the question, changing to the pronoun **tu**. He or she gives two or three responses, asks the next student in the circle, and so on. Finally, each student presents what someone in the group would do, changing the pronoun again, this time to **il** or **elle**.

As in English, the conditional is often used to make suggestions or to make a request more polite.

À ta place, j'**irais** à la réception avec le garçon d'honneur.	*If I were you, I would go with the best man to the reception.*
Tu **devrais** lui téléphoner. Tu **voudrais** le faire maintenant?	*You should call him. Would you like to do it now?*

12 Un nouveau poste 1.2, 1.3, 2.2, 5.1

Interpretive Viewing, Presentational Speaking or Writing

Les personnes ci-dessous cherchent un nouvel emploi. Que pourraient-elles acheter pour aller à leur entretien avec l'argent qu'elles ont?

MODÈLE Jeanne : 165€
Jeanne pourrait acheter une jupe bleue et une chemise blanche.

1. Noah : 274€
2. Khaled et moi : 432€
3. Laure et Milo : 143€
4. toi : 511€
5. vous : 312€
6. Quentin : 616€

Comparaisons 4.1

Which sentence would not be in the conditional in French?

When I was a child, I *would go* to my grandma's after school.

Jeremy *would like* to order now.

Essential Instruction

1. Place pairs of expressions in the imperfect and conditional side-by-side on the board, for example, **Chloé gagnait, Chloé gagnerait**. If students have difficulty, prepare a worksheet and ask them to circle the expressions in the conditional. You may find that students also need this practice with the conditional and the future.
2. Put students in groups to do **Activité 12**, and in pairs to do **Activité 13**.
3. Now that students have had practice with the conditional, do **Activité 14** as a class.
4. Point out that, in English, the construction *used to* is often replaced with the helping verb *would*. This may explain the similarities in the French formation of the **imparfait** and **conditionnel**.

13 Le mariage 1.1, 5.1, 5.2

Interpersonal Speaking

Posez des questions à votre partenaire au sujet de son mariage idéal. Puis, changez de rôles.

MODÈLE à quel âge (se marier)
A : À quel âge est-ce que tu te marierais ?
B : Je me marierais à 28 ans.

1. combien de personnes (inviter)
2. que (porter)
3. qui (choisir comme demoiselle d'honneur ou garçon d'honneur)
4. que (offrir comme alliance)
5. où (avoir lieu la réception)
6. où (aller pour ton voyage de noces)

14 Les conseils 1.1, 5.1, 5.2

Interpersonal Speaking

Vos amis ont beaucoup de problèmes. Donnez-leur des conseils en accord avec la situation de chacun. Utilisez le conditionnel dans vos réponses.

MODÈLE J'ai perdu le portable de mon frère.
À ta place, je lui achèterais un nouveau portable.

1. J'ai eu 7 sur 20 à mon contrôle d'anglais.
2. Je suis toujours en retard pour mon premier cours.
3. J'ai très faim et soif.
4. J'ai besoin d'argent pour aller au concert.
5. Je me dispute avec mes parents parce que j'oublie de faire mes corvées.
6. Je suis fâché(e) quand je fais le plein parce que l'essence coûte cher.
7. Je vais faire du camping, et je n'ai pas de sac de couchage.
8. C'est l'anniversaire de Colette le 4 octobre, et je ne sais pas ce que je peux lui offrir.

On recycle !
En petit groupe, discutez de ce que vous feriez pour résoudre (*solve*) les problèmes économiques, écologiques, ou sociaux de votre société.

le chômage ▪ faire un don ▪ arrêter la pollution ▪ créer des emplois ▪ le terrorisme ▪ les sans-abri ▪ user de dipomatie ▪ trouver un remède contre ▪ la pauvreté ▪ intervenir ▪ la guerre ▪ enseigner la tolérance

Resources

Activities 13–14

Answers

13
1. Combien de personnes est-ce que tu inviterais ?
2. Qu'est-ce que tu porterais ?
3. Qui choisirais-tu comme demoiselle d'honneur ou garçon d'honneur ?
4. Qu'offrirais-tu comme alliance, une alliance en argent ou en or ?
5. Où aurait lieu la réception ?
6. Où irais-tu pour ton voyage de noces ?

Partner answers will vary.

14 Possible answers:
1. À ta place, je suivrais des cours particuliers.
2. À ta place, je mettrais un réveil dans ta chambre, sur ton smartphone, ou sur ton ipod.
3. À ta place, je prendrais un goûter.
4. À ta place, je passerais à la banque.
5. À ta place, j'essayerais de faire mes corvées tout de suite en rentrant de l'école.
6. À ta place, je prendrais les transports en commun plus souvent.
7. À ta place, j'en emprunterais un.
8. À ta place, j'irais au centre commercial pour voir plusieurs magasins.

TPR

Pair the following high-frequency conditional expressions with a gesture: **Je devrais** (Wag your finger); **Je pourrais** (Show your muscles); **J'aimerais** (Tap your heart twice). Then say several sentences that use these verbs and ask the class to show you the appropriate gesture.

Expansion

For **Activité 13**, ask students to extend the activity to asking questions about their partner's career, the city they plan to live in, the number of children they'd have, whether they'd have a cat or dog, etc. Or, have them extend the conversation by having Speaker A give a different response, **"À ta place, je me marierais à 32 ans. Je pense que 28 est trop jeune."**

Differentiated Learning

Accelerate
Have students write a dialogue that uses the conditional; for example, it could be about a student who wins **un billet d'avion gratuit** and is planning his or her trip.

Decelerate
Slow-paced students can contribute to an extension of **Activité 14** by thinking up other scenarios for their partner to comment on.

Multiple Intelligences

Intrapersonal
Give students, working in pairs, a problem situation to solve together, for example, **"Tu n'as pas eu une invitation pour le prom."** Students come up with original solutions, for example, **"Je ferais une publicité sur Internet pour trouver quelqu'un pour m'accompagner."** Students share their problems and solutions with the class. Ask for other solutions from the rest of the class.

Resources

Activity 15
WB Workbook 9
G & V Practice Games

Answers

On recycle!
In the *if* clause the imperfect tense is used; it is followed by the conditional mood. However, the order of clauses is interchangeable.

Comparaison
The first sentence (*Tell me if/whether you are coming tonight*), because it presents two alternatives rather than a condition.

15
1. Si je dormais, je ne serais pas fatigué(e).
2. Si elle allait à Versailles, elle connaîtrait la vie des rois et reines français.
3. Si tu rangeais tes vêtements, tu la trouverais.
4. S'ils faisaient le plein, ils pourraient conduire.
5. Si nous suivions des leçons de guitare, nous pourrions jouer la musique rock et former un groupe.
6. S'ils préparaient une choucroute garnie, ils pourraient manger.
7. Si je suivais un cours particulier, je pourrais faire ce problème de maths.

Game

Funny Sentences
Divide the class into two teams. One half of the class will write **si** clauses on note cards, for example, **Si j'avais beaucoup de temps**.... The other half of the class writes result clauses on note cards, for example **je danserais le tango**. Gather all the cards and put them in two piles. Ask for volunteers to take a card from each pile and read the sentence aloud. Many of the sentences will be nonsensical.

Révision: The Conditional in Sentences with *si* 1.2

On recycle!
"If I were president, I would build homes for the homeless and working poor." What tense is used in the first clause in the French equivalent? What verb form is used in the second clause?

If you do not remember, read the summary below.

Use the conditional along with **si** and the imperfect tense to tell what would happen if something else happened or *if* some condition contrary to reality were met.

si + IMPERFECT	CONDITIONAL

S'il ne **pleuvait** pas, tu **pourrais** nager. — *If it wasn't raining, you could go swimming.*

Nous **aurions** plus d'argent si nous **étions** avocats. — *We would have more money if we were lawyers.*

The clause with **si** and the imperfect can either begin or end the sentence; when it comes first, it is marked by a comma.

Comparaison 1.2, 4.2

The word **si** can also mean *whether*. In which sentence does **si** have the sense of *whether*, and why?

Dis-moi si tu viens ce soir.
Éric viendra à la soirée si nous l'invitons.

15 Des changements 1.1, 5.2

Interpersonal Speaking

Dites comment la vie des personnes suivantes serait différente si elles faisaient les changements indiqués.

MODÈLE Tu n'es pas en forme. (faire des promenades au parc)
Si tu faisais des promenades au parc, tu serais en forme.

1. Je suis fatigué(e). (dormir)
2. Virginie ne connaît pas la vie des rois et reines français. (aller à Versailles)
3. Tu ne peux pas trouver ta tablette dans ta chambre. (ranger tes vêtements)
4. Mohammed et Lucie ne peuvent plus conduire. (faire le plein)
5. Marina et moi, nous ne pouvons pas former un groupe de rock. (suivre des leçons de guitare)
6. Les ados ont faim. (préparer une choucroute garnie)
7. Je ne sais pas faire ce problème de maths. (suivre un cours particulier)

Essential Instruction

1. Have students try to answer the questions in the top section. Tell them to read the grammar summary if they have trouble remembering.
2. Project some **si** clauses on the board and see if students can match them to conditional choices on the right.
3. Ask students to write some personal conditional statements that use **si**, or ask a personal question addressing another student.
4. After doing **Activité 16**, see if students can extend the activity with other cues.
5. Review the near future before reviewing the future tense.

16 Que feriez-vous? 1.1, 5.2

Interpersonal Speaking

Que feriez-vous dans les situations suivantes? À tour de rôle, posez des questions à votre partenaire.

MODÈLE gagner à la loterie
A: Si tu gagnais à la loterie, que ferais-tu?
B: Si je gagnais à la loterie, j'achèterais une voiture de sport.

1. faire du scoutisme
2. voir un accident de voiture
3. perdre ton smartphone
4. faire la connaissance de ton acteur ou ton actrice préféré(e)
5. recevoir un billet d'avion gratuit
6. visiter un parc d'attractions
7. faire les courses au marché

Que feriez-vous si la boulangerie était fermée?

Révision: Future Tense; Future Tense after *quand* 1.2

The future tense consists of only one word. To form the future tense, use the same stem as that of the conditional (the infinitive for **-er** and **-ir** verbs or the infinitive minus the **-e** for **-re** verbs). The future endings are **-ai**, **-as**, **-a**, **-ons**, **-ez**, and **-ont**.

assister			
j'	**assisterai**	nous	**assisterons**
tu	**assisteras**	vous	**assisterez**
il/elle/on	**assistera**	ils/elles	**assisteront**

Vous **assisterez** au mariage de Manon? — *Will you attend Manon's wedding?*
Non, nous **voyagerons** au Maroc. — *No, we'll be traveling to Morocco.*

As with the conditional, some irregular French verbs have an irregular stem in the future, but their endings are regular. Note that for all verbs, the future stem ends in **-r**.

C'est elle qui **fera** un stage à JDN Économie? — *Is she the one who will do an internship at JDN Économie?*

Resources

WB Workbook 10–13
LA Listening Activity 2
G & V Practice Games

Answers

16

1. Si tu faisais du scoutisme, que ferais-tu?
2. Si tu voyais un accident de voiture, que ferais-tu?
3. Si tu perdais ton smartphone, que ferais-tu?
4. Si tu faisais la connaissance de ton acteur ou ton actrice préféré(e), que ferais-tu?
5. Si tu recevais un billet d'avion gratuit, où irais-tu?
6. Si tu visitais un parc d'attractions, que ferais-tu?
7. Si tu faisais les courses au marché, qu'achèterais-tu?

Partner answers will vary.

Reference Desk

1. **Aller** + INFINITIVE is generally used to express events that will occur in the immediate future, while **le futur** is used for events that will take place in the more distant future, for example, **dans dix ans, pendant les grandes vacances**, etc.
2. Many verbs with spelling changes in the present keep them in the future: **j'achèterai, j'emmènerai, je nettoierai**, etc.

Critical Thinking

Analysis

Ask students why the conditional and the future tense appear in the same lesson. What do they have in common? (Both share the same stem.) Then ask them how many sounds are in the future endings (only four). Finally, write the conjugation of a verb in the future. Circle the endings and ask what irregular verb the endings resemble (**avoir**).

Differentiated Learning

Accelerate

Ask students to change a list of near future statements to the future tense. Then have them write six sentences of their own in the near future and work with slow-paced students who may need help putting them in the future tense.

Decelerate

Point out to students who are having trouble with the future that the future endings resemble the present tense of the verb **avoir**. If they continue to struggle, allow them to master one future form (**aller** + INFINITIF or the future) before moving on to the second. Explain to them that the two forms are virtually interchangeable and that they may only need to be able to recognize the form they have a harder time producing.

Multiple Intelligences

Visual-Spatial

Have students make an album that illustrates what they would do if they won the lottery, using images from the Internet or drawing their own illustrations.

Resources

Activity 18

Answers

17

1. Jérémy n'assistera pas au mariage, mais il ira à la réception.
2. J'assisterai au mariage et j'irai à la réception.
3. Paul et Zohra assisteront au mariage et iront à la réception.
4. Jérémy et toi n'assisterez pas au mariage, mais vous irez à la réception.
5. Nadine n'assistera pas au mariage, et elle n'ira pas à la réception.
6. Zohra et moi assisterons au mariage et irons à la réception.
7. Tu n'assisteras pas au mariage, mais tu iras à la réception.

18 Script

1. J'aimerais bien travailler dans un laboratoire de recherches.
2. Si tu étais un garçon, tu serais le garçon d'honneur à mon mariage.
3. Nous irons en Italie après la cérémonie.
4. Amélie aura beaucoup d'invités à sa réception.
5. Nous préférerions aller à Nice qu'à Cannes.
6. Tu achèteras un cadeau pour le couple?
7. Si son fiancé avait de l'argent, il lui achèterait une bague avec un gros diamant.
8. Ils prendront le train quand ils iront en voyage de noces.

1. C; 2. C; 3. F; 4. F; 5. C; 6. F; 7. C; 8. F

Comparaisons

The future tense in English is a compound tense (*You will succeed in college.*), whereas the future tense in French is expressed in one word. In the example sentence, the *when* clause is in the present in English (unlike in French), even though the second clause is in the future tense.

Reference Desk

"**Quand Futur Futur**" is a mnemonic device to help students remember that **quand** and **lorsque** clauses are in the future in a future sentence.

Another use of the future tense is to tell what will happen *when* something else happens in the future. Here is the order of tenses in these sentences with **quand**:

Quand Anne **dira** oui, Salim **se mariera** avec elle. — *When Anne says yes, Salim will marry her.*

first clause	second clause
quand + FUTURE	FUTURE
lorsque (*when*) + FUTURE	FUTURE
aussitôt que (*as soon as*) + FUTURE	FUTURE
dès que (*as soon as*) + FUTURE	FUTURE

Lorsque Salim **achètera** sa bague de fiançailles, Anne **cherchera** sa robe de mariée. — *When Salim buys the engagement ring, Anne will look for a wedding dress.*

Aussitôt que Salim **sera** ingénieur, il **travaillera** chez Airbus. — *As soon as Salim is an engineer, he'll work for Airbus.*

Dès que Salim et Anne **se marieront**, ils **déménageront** à Toulouse. — *As soon as Salim and Anne marry, they will move to Toulouse.*

17 Le mariage d'Anne et Salim 1.1, 1.2

Interpretive Viewing, Presentational Speaking

Voici la liste des invités au mariage de Salim et Anne à Saint-Paul de Vence. La deuxième liste indique qui ira à la réception. Dites qui assistera au mariage et à la réception.

MODÈLE **Hervé assistera au mariage, mais il n'ira pas à la réception.**

1. Jérémy
2. moi
3. Paul et Zohra
4. Jérémy et toi
5. Nadine
6. Zohra et moi
7. toi

Le mariage		La réception	
Zohra	✔	Zohra	✔
toi		toi	✔
Nadine		Nadine	
Paul	✔	Paul	✔
Hervé	✔	Hervé	
moi	✔	moi	✔
Jérémy		Jérémy	✔

18 Le conditionnel ou le futur? 1.2

Interpretive Listening

Écrivez les numéros 1–8 sur votre papier. Écoutez les phrases suivantes. Écrivez **C** *si la phrase est au conditionnel et* **F** *si la phrase est au futur.*

Comparaisons

In what way is the future tense in English different from the future tense in French? What tense is used in each clause of the sentence below?

When I'm in Paris, I will visit the Louvre.

4.1

Essential Instruction

1. Do **Activité 17** together as a class.
2. Have students ask you questions about your future. When a question is too personal, you may say, "**Question suivante?**"
3. Before doing **Activité 18**, review with students what the endings of the conditional and future sound like so that they can be successful. It will be helpful to remind students that although the first person singular future and conditional seem to sound the same, the other endings are easier to distinguish. The conditional has a predominant long "a" sound.
4. Students can work in pairs to complete **Activités 19–20**.

19 Nos avenirs 1.1, 5.1, 5.2

Interpersonal Speaking

Que ferez-vous quand vous aurez 25 ans? À tour de rôle, posez des questions à votre partenaire.

MODÈLE que (faire le weekend)

A: Quand tu auras 25 ans, qu'est-ce que tu feras le weekend?

B: Quand j'aurai 25 ans, j'irai au complexe sportif pour faire du sport.

1. où (habiter: dans un appartement ou une maison)
2. dans quelle ville (habiter)
3. où (travailler)
4. que (faire comme loisir)
5. où (aller pendant les vacances)

20 Qu'est-ce que tu feras demain? 1.1, 5.1, 5.2

Interpersonal Speaking

À tour de rôle, posez des questions à votre partenaire.

MODÈLE se lever

A: Dès que tu te lèveras, qu'est-ce que tu feras?

B: Dès que je me lèverai, je m'habillerai.

1. prendre ton petit déjeuner
2. arriver au lycée
3. entrer dans la cantine
4. quitter l'école
5. rentrer chez toi
6. dîner
7. faire tes devoirs

Resources

Activity 19

Answers

19

1. Quand tu auras 25 ans, où habiteras-tu, dans un appartement ou dans une maison?
2. Quand tu auras 25 ans, dans quelle ville habiteras-tu?
3. Quand tu auras 25 ans, où travailleras-tu?
4. Quand tu auras 25 ans, que feras-tu comme loisir?
5. Quand tu auras 25 ans, où iras-tu pendant les vacances?

Partner answers will vary.

20

1. Dès que tu prendras ton petit-déjeuner, qu'est-ce que tu feras?
2. Dès que tu arriveras au lycée, qu'est-ce que tu feras?
3. Dès que tu entreras dans la cantine, qu'est-ce que tu feras?
4. Dès que tu quitteras l'école, qu'est-ce que tu feras?
5. Dès que tu rentreras chez toi, qu'est-ce que tu feras?
6. Dès que tu dîneras, qu'est-ce que tu feras?
7. Dès que tu feras tes devoirs, qu'est-ce que tu feras?

Partner answers will vary.

Communication

Interpersonal: Paired Practice

Ask students to prepare a dialogue in which they discuss with a classmate what things they are going to do during the next **grandes vacances**. Once students have presented their dialogues, ask them to write eight statements about what they remember of their classmates' plans.

Presentational: Cooperative Groups

Have students work in small groups to prepare a time capsule (**une capsule témoin**) that shows teens in 2090 what life was like for teens in the U.S. in 2012. They should include several objects with a description for each in the future tense.

Special Needs Students

Social Anxiety

Approach individually and discretely the students who have anxiety issues to see if they have any questions about **Activité 17**. Some may prefer to respond to taped questions at home rather than speak in class.

AD(H)D

Help these students do **Activités 19–20** by dividing the tasks into parts. Review the formation of the future for each of the verbs and help them add relevant vocabulary to complete the sentences. Work with the students one sentence at a time rather than asking them to complete the exercise on their own.

Speech Impairment

Pair students with patient partners who understand that they should not finish sentences for students who have speech difficulties.

Resources

CA Communicative Activities

Share

Answers

21 Answers will vary.

22 Possible answers:

Alec va probablement travailler dans un laboratoire de recherches médicales.
Angèle va probablement travailler à JDN économie.
Saloua va probablement travailler en plein air dans le domaine de la haute technologie.

Reference Desk

1. If students enjoy **Activité 22**, ask them to find **une petite annonce** online for a job they think they would enjoy now or in the future.
2. Tell students that colleges in France have now a graduate studies course called **L.M.D. (Licence, Master, Doctorat)**, copied from the British and American system. This is so it can improve mobility between European and international students.
3. If you have access to Passport, create a question for your students to share their response to a communicative activity.

Culture

Practices: Information

Often in the United States the bride and groom prepare a special choreographed first dance. In France, a video program of the couple from infancy to wedding day is often shown.

Communiquez!

21 Les mariages français et américains 1.1, 1.2, 1.3, 2.1, 3.2, 5.1, 5.2

Interpersonal Speaking, Interpretive Viewing, Presentational Writing

Avez-vous déjà assisté à un mariage américain? Si non, trouvez une vidéo d'un mariage américain sur Internet. Ensuite, regardez une vidéo d'un mariage français en ligne. Expliquez ce qui se passe sur la vidéo du mariage français à votre partenaire. Puis, remplissez un diagramme Venn comme celui de droite.

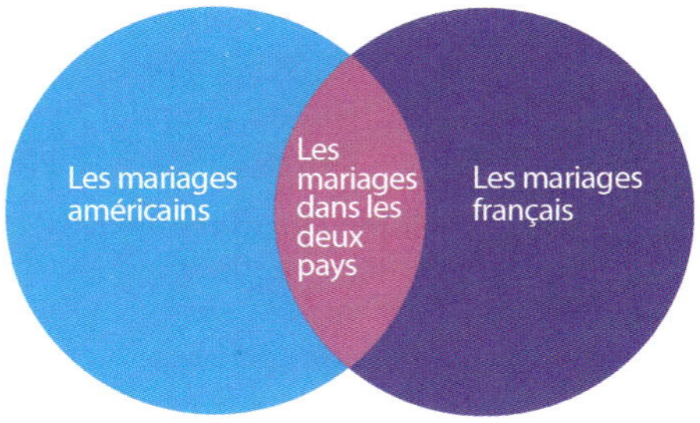

Recherche: cérémonie de mariage (dailymotion, vimeo, youtube)

22 Où est-ce qu'ils vont travailler? 1.2, 1.3, 5.1

Interpretive Reading, Presentational Speaking or Writing

Lisez les profils des jeunes gens suivants. Ensuite, dites où chacun d'entre eux va probablement travailler.

Alec

Salut! Je m'appelle Alec et j'ai 26 ans. Je suis en deuxième année d'études de pharmacologie à l'université Clermont Auvergne (UCA). J'ai fait des études de biologie à l'université pendant 3 ans avant de commencer mon master. Je devrais obtenir mon diplôme à la fin de l'année.

Angèle

Bonjour à tous! Moi, c'est Angèle. J'ai 23 ans. J'ai passé mon bac ES (économiquue et social), puis j'ai commencé une formation DUT GEA (gestion des entreprises et des administrations) à l'université. Je ne voulais pas vraiment travailler dans une entreprise, alors j'ai commencé une licence à l'école de commerce à Toulouse. Dans deux ans, je veux rejoindre le Journal du Net Économie, car je connais des personnes qui y travaillent.

Saloua

Salut les potes! Je m'appelle Saloua, et j'ai 21 ans. Je viens de commencer une formation technique en électricité à CFORPRO. Je ne veux pas joindre une entreprise et travailler dans un bureau. Je voudrais faire des études sur le terrain, c'est-à-dire à l'extérieur, comme installer des panneaux solaires.

Essential Instruction

1. Information to include in **Activité 21** is what the bridal party and guests are wearing, how the tables are decorated, what kind of music is selected, what food is served, and of particular interest what kind of "animation" has been prepared.
2. Have students write **une petite annonce** for their ideal job.
3. Read the author biography. In **Rencontre avec l'auteur** there is always a critical thinking question to refer back to.
4. Have students share their personal experiences when they respond to the **Pré-lecture** question.
5. The graphic organizer is available in the Copy Masters supplement. You may want to go over the answers after listening to recorded audio.

Pre-AP

Les petits enfants du siècle

Rencontre avec l'auteur 1.2, 2.1, 3.1, 5.1

Christiane Rochefort (1917–1998) a publié son premier roman à succès à l'âge de 41 ans, *Le repos du guerrier* (1958), qui est devenu un film. C'est en 1961 que *Les petits enfants du siècle* a été publié. Ce roman raconte la vie d'une petite fille, Josyane, qui grandit (*grows up*) dans la banlieue de Paris dans les années d'après-guerre (*post-war years*). Souvent poétique, son écriture (*writing*) traite de (*deals with*) l'exploitation des enfants et des femmes. Rochefort a reçu deux prix littéraires prestigieux. De quelle façon *Les petits enfants du siècle* est-il une étude psychologique d'une enfant maltraitée (*mistreated*)?

Pré-lecture

À quel âge avez-vous commencé à faire des corvées à la maison pour aider vos parents?

Stratégie de lecture 1.3, 3.2

Setting. Dans la fiction, le cadre spatio-temporel regroupe tous les détails qui déterminent le lieu et l'époque où se situe l'action. Mais il y a aussi le milieu (*setting*) social, politique, moral, et psychologique que les personnages (*characters*) traversent. Alors que vous lisez le texte, recherchez tous les éléments qui déterminent le milieu dans lequel (*in which*) le personnage de Josyane évolue (*evolves*), et remplissez l'organigramme ci-dessous.

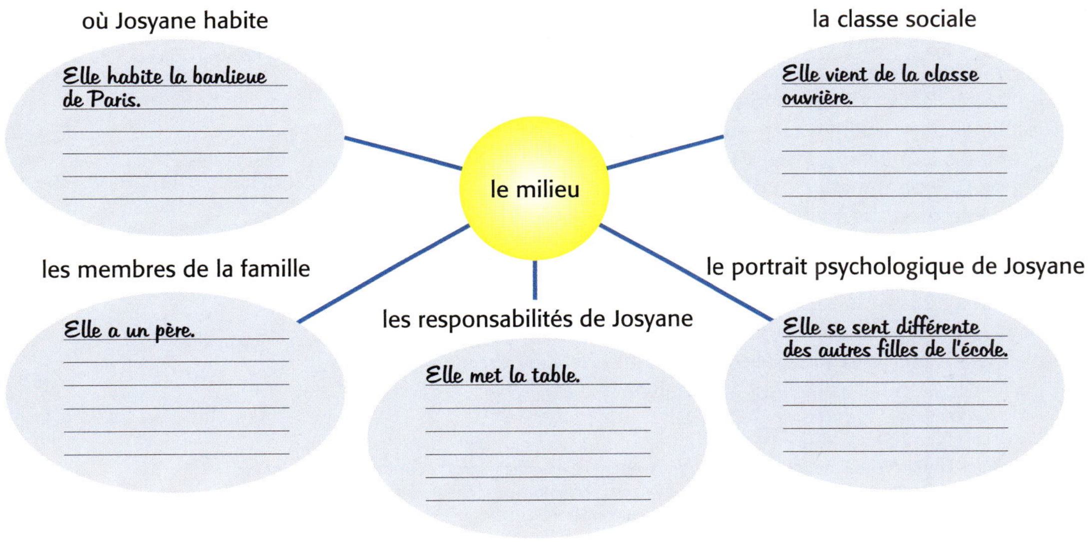

Resources

Rencontre avec l'auteur

Answers

Pré-lecture
Answers will vary.

Stratégie de lecture
où Josyane habite: Elle habite dans un appartement avec trois chambres, dans une cité. Il y a une salle de bains, une cuisine-salle de séjour. Ils ont une machine à laver.
la classe sociale: Son père et sa mère travaillent dans une usine.
les membres de la famille: son frère Patrick, ses frères jumeaux, sa mère
les responsabilités de Josyane: Elle s'habille. Elle met le couvert. Elle va à l'école. Elle prépare le petit déjeuner pour ses frères, elle les emmène à l'école et les ramène à la maison. Elle fait les courses. Elle fait la vaisselle. Elle fait ses devoirs.
le portrait psychologique de Josyane: Sa mère est malade, alors elle a beaucoup de responsabilités pour aider à s'occuper de ses frères.

Reference Desk

1. Students make a connection to literature in this section. Each reading section contains a strategy, a pre-reading question, during-reading questions, and a post-reading question.
2. In the **Rencontre avec l'auteur**, students discover a brief biography of the writer.
3. In the **Stratégie**, students learn a literary term that they will apply to the selection.
4. Christiane Rochefort challenged the rosy picture of economic development and social progress **d'après-guerre** by illustrating the negative aspects of France's rapid modernization in *Les petits enfants du siècle* (1961). Considered **un roman réaliste**, it won **le Prix Populiste** in 1962. Rochefort's first novel, ***Le repos du guerrier***, caused a scandal with its realistic use of language. She also wrote ***Les stances à Sophie*** (1963) and ***Une rose pour Morrison*** (1966).

Differentiated Learning

Accelerate
Students with high-level reading skills should be able to read the excerpt and complete the **Stratégie de lecture** independently. After they have filled it in, check their work for completeness and accuracy.

Decelerate
Play the recording of the reading to lower-ability students, and stop several times to verify global comprehension. Sample questions could be: What is this passage about? Who is telling the story? Who were the members of her family and what were they like? What jobs did she have to do? What did she like to do? Point out information they can insert in their **organigramme**.

Multiple Intelligences

Intrapersonal
Students might best understand the broad sense of setting by analyzing a popular TV show and focusing on the social, political, moral, and psychological conditions as they define one main character. Have each student read a description to group members, who then try to guess the name of the show.

Resources

Les petits enfants du siècle

Answers

Pendant la lecture

1. Ils lui ont dit qu'elle ne faisait pas les choses comme il faut.
2. Il y a quatre enfants.
3. Elle l'aimait parce qu'elle pouvait manger et elle n'avait pas besoin de travailler.

Reference Desk

1. The **Outils de lecture** provides another tool to help students understand the selection. Give them some examples of how to read using context clues to decode new vocabulary.
2. The tense in the clause "... **quand je la connus**" is the **passé simple**. You may point this tense out to students as a literary tense, and mention its usage is similar to that of the **passé composé**.

Expansion

You may want your students to write the answers to the **Pendant la lecture** questions, designed to help them determine the main points of the story.

Outils de lecture 1.1, 1.2

Reading in Context. Vous allez sans doute trouver des mots et expressions que vous ne connaissez pas quand vous lisez en français. C'est une bonne idée de les analyser en contexte, c'est-à-dire (*that is to say*), de trouver le sens (*meaning*) des autres mots d'une phrase et de considérer la progression des idées. Comme ça, vous pouvez mieux deviner (*guess*) le sens des nouveaux mots. Essayez de lire cet extrait (*selection*) sans utiliser le glossaire du dessous.

Les petits enfants du siècle

C'était un dimanche au début de l'hiver. Mes parents... étaient heureux, mais ils avaient besoin d'argent. Les allocations familiales* arriveraient donc au bon moment.

Je naquis*... le 2 août. C'était ma date correcte, mais je faisais rater les vacances à mes parents, en les retenant* à Paris tout le mois d'août, alors que l'usine, où travaillait mon père, était fermée. Je ne faisais pas les choses comme il faut.

J'étais pourtant* en avance pour mon âge : Patrick avait à peine* pris ma place dans mon berceau* que je me montrais capable, en m'accrochant* aux meubles, de quitter la pièce dès qu'il se mettait à pleurer. Au fond je peux bien dire que c'est Patrick qui m'a appris à marcher.

Quand les jumeaux* firent leur arrivée* à la maison, je m'habillais déjà toute seule et je savais poser sur la table les couverts et le pain, en me mettant sur la pointe des pieds.

—Et dépêche-toi de grandir*, disait ma mère, pour que tu puisses m'aider un peu.

Elle était déjà malade quand je la connus. Elle ne pouvait pas aller à l'usine plus d'une semaine de service, aller acheter le pain, pousser les jumeaux dans leur double landau*, le long des blocs, pour qu'ils prennent l'air, et surveiller* Patrick, qui était en avance lui aussi, malheureusement. Il n'avait même pas trois ans quand il mit un petit chat dans la machine à laver. Cette fois-là, quand même, papa lui donna une bonne gifle* : on n'avait même pas fini de payer la machine.

Je commençais à aller à l'école. Le matin je préparais le déjeuner pour les garçons, je les emmenais à la maternelle, et j'allais à l'école. À midi, on restait à la cantine. J'aimais la cantine, on s'assoit* et les assiettes arrivent toutes remplies. C'est toujours bon ce qu'il y a dans des assiettes qui arrivent toutes remplies. Les autres filles en général n'aimaient pas la cantine, elles trouvaient que c'était mauvais. Je me demande ce qu'elles avaient à la maison.

Pendant la lecture
1. Qu'est-ce que les parents de Josyane ont dit à leur fille ?

Pendant la lecture
2. Il y a combien d'enfants dans cette famille ?

Analyse
How do you feel about Josyane's memories? What emotions are evoked when you learn about the responsibilities she took on? Does this environment have positive or negative repercussions on a young child? Use context clues to justify your answer.

Pendant la lecture
3. Pourquoi est-ce que Josyane aimait la cantine de l'école ?

---

allocations familiales *welfare* ; **naquis** *was born* ; **retenant** *holding them back* ; **pourtant** *though* ; **à peine** *barely/hardly* ; **berceau** *cradle* ; **m'accrochant** *holding on* ; **jumeaux** *twins* ; **firent leur arrivée** *made their appearance* ; **grandir** *grow up* ; **landau** *baby stroller* ; **surveiller** *look after* ; **gifle** *slap* ; **s'assoit** s'assied

Essential Instruction

1. Ask the students to read the passage for comprehension, using context clues to figure out new vocabulary.
2. Play the recording of the selection, pausing to answer the **Pendant la lecture** questions.
3. All students should complete the first activity in **Activités d'expansion**, which is always based on the **organigramme** they filled out as they read.

(Suite en fin)

Le soir, je ramenais* les garçons et je les laissais* dans la cour, à jouer avec les autres. Je montais prendre les sous* et je redescendais aux commissions*. Maman faisait le dîner, papa rentrait et ouvrait la télé, maman et moi nous faisions la vaisselle, et ils allaient se coucher. Moi, je restais dans la cuisine, à faire mes devoirs.

Maintenant, notre appartement était bien. Avant, on habitait dans le treizième*, une sale* chambre avec l'eau sur le palier*. Quand le quartier avait été démoli, on nous avait mis ici, dans cette Cité. On avait reçu le nombre de pièces auquel nous avions droit selon le nombre d'enfants. Les parents avaient une chambre, les garçons une autre. Moi, je couchais avec les bébés dans la troisième. On avait une salle de bains, où on avait mis la machine à laver, et une cuisine-salle de séjour, où on mangeait. C'est sur la table de la cuisine que je faisais mes devoirs. C'était mon bon moment: quel bonheur* quand ils étaient tous couchés, et que je me retrouvais seule dans la nuit et le silence! Le jour, je n'entendais pas le bruit*, je ne faisais pas attention; mais le soir j'entendais le silence. Le silence commençait à dix heures: les fenêtres s'éteignaient*, les radios se taisaient*, les bruits, les voix*, et, à dix heures et demie, c'était fini. Plus rien. Le désert. J'étais seule, en paix*. Je me suis mise à aimer mes devoirs peu à peu. J'aurais bien passé ma vie à ne faire que des choses qui ne servaient à rien.

Pendant la lecture
4. Quels services est-ce que Josyane rendait à sa mère?

Pendant la lecture
5. Comment était le vieil appartement de Josyane? Combien de pièces y avait-il dans le nouvel appartement?

Pendant la lecture
6. Que représentaient les devoirs, le soir, pour Josyane?

Pendant la lecture
7. Quelle est l'opinion de Josyane à propos des devoirs?

ramenais *walked back*; **laissait** *would leave*; **sous** l'argent; **commissions** *errands*; **treizième** *thirteenth district of Paris*; **sale** *dirty*; **palier** *landing*; **bonheur** *happiness*; **bruit** *noise*; **s'éteignaient** *turned off*; **se taisaient** *would turn quiet*; **les voix** *voices*; **en paix** *at peace*

Post-lecture

D'où vient l'attitude de Josyane envers elle-même?

Le monde visuel

Immeuble, rue Croulebarbe, Paris, c. 1957. Albert Édouard. Musée national d'art moderne, Centre Georges Pompidou. Don de Famille Albert en 2009.

23 Activités d'expansion 1.2, 1.3, 5.1, 5.2

Faites les activités suivantes.

1. Utilisez les informations de votre organigramme pour écrire un paragraphe qui décrit le milieu du roman *Les petits enfants du siècle* et ce qu'il révèle de Josyane.
2. Mettez les événements du roman en ordre chronologique. Écrivez « 1 » pour la première phrase, « 2 » pour la deuxième phrase, etc.
3. Vous êtes la concierge (*superintendent*) de l'immeuble où habite Josyane. Vous vous inquiétez parce qu'elle a trop de responsabilités pour son âge. Écrivez une lettre à l'assistante sociale qui s'occupe de l'immeuble.

Resources

Pre-T Pre-test
Q *Leçon* Quiz

Answers

Pendant la lecture

4. Elle allait chercher les enfants à l'école et allait faire les courses.
5. Son vieil appartement était très sale et ils avaient une chambre. Dans le nouvel appartement, il y avait quatre pièces (trois chambres et une cuisine-salle de séjour).
6. Les devoirs représentaient la tranquillité, une rupture des corvées de la journée.
7. Ils ne servent à rien mais elle aime la paix qu'ils lui donnent.

Post-lecture

Possible answer: Elle vient de son expérience.

23

1. Paragraphs will vary.
2. 1. Josyane est née.; 2. Elle s'occupe de son petit frère Patrick.; 3. Les jumeaux sont nés.; 4. La mère de Josyane est malade.; 5. Josyane aide sa mère avec les bébés.; 6. Josyane va à l'école.; 7. La famille de Josyane change d'appartement.
3. Letters will vary.

Reference Desk

Le monde visuel is intended to connect students to art. Share with students this paragraph: L'architecte français Édouard Albert (1910–1968) est connu pour ses bâtiments (*buildings*) en acier (*steel*) et en aluminium. Le dessin d'un architecte est une interprétation visuelle et spatiale de ses idées. Pour représenter cet immeuble parisien, Albert se sert des lignes pour rendre une idée concrète, facile à visualiser pour les clients et les amateurs d'art. Le tracé en ligne est un style d'art en deux dimensions, montrant les contours et les ombres (*shading*). Ici qu'est-ce qui a des lignes ou des bords (*edges*) visibles? Ce dessin est « de l'art » en terme de beauté ou de fonction?

Differentiated Learning

Accelerate

Point out that **Je naquis** uses **le passé simple**, a literary tense. Make a list of sentences using regular and irregular verbs in **le passé simple** and ask students to put them in **le passé composé**.

Decelerate

These students may need to work with a partner to complete **Activité 1** in the **Activités d'expansion**. If it's something they are incapable of doing, even with help, have them turn in answers to the **Pendant la lecture** questions.

Multiple Intelligences

Offer the students a choice of activities in **Activité 23**, based on their learning style. **Activité 1** might appeal most to the Intrapersonal learners. **Activité 2** might intrigue the Logical-Mathematical learners, while **Activité 3** might engage the Interpersonal learners the most. Offer the Visual-Spatial learners the option of finding artwork that portrays Josyane's world.

Recherche: bridgeman art library

Reference Desk

This section is designed for students to apply unit vocabulary and structures to communicative activities that foster 21st-century skills. These activities demonstrate how 21st-century skills are cultivated in the classroom and how these skills and the language learning process are mutually beneficial.

French in the Workplace

Statement of Interest for Employment

To work in France, students will need to express their abilities, education, and desires in French in a letter to a potential employer. Have students prepare a brief statement to a potential French-speaking employer in which they express their interest in the field, and their skills and relevant educational and work background. They should use the present to speak to what they are able to do (**je peux**, **je sais**, **je suis capable de**), the past to provide their studies and work experience (**j'ai fait des études de**, **j'ai travaillé dans**), and the conditional to say what they could do (**j'aimerais**, **je pourrais**) or to ask questions (**Pourriez-vous…?**)

Social Justice

In France, the **Pacte Civil de Solidarité (PACS)** offers unmarried couples a legal status carrying some, but not all, of the benefits of marriage. The **PACS** is defined as "**un contrat entre deux personnes majeures, de sexe différent ou de même sexe, pour organiser leur vie commune.**" In groups, have students research the specifics of the PACS law as opposed to a marriage contract, and compare both with similar laws or legal statuses in their own state/country. What are their personal views on **PACS** and civil unions versus marriage? Students can organize, compare and contrast their findings visually, and report to the class.

Système D

Pre-AP | 21 | Question centrale ? Comment change-t-on de l'enfance à l'âge adulte ?

Communiquez!

24 Mes intérêts 1.2, 1.3, 2.1, 2.2, 3.1, 5.2

Connecting to Information Literacy, Media Literacy, and Technology Literacy
Interpretive Viewing, Presentational Speaking

Aujourd'hui c'est facile de faire des recherches et de communiquer avec d'autres personnes autour du monde qui partagent les mêmes intérêts que nous. Réfléchissez à vos passions et vos intérêts comme, par exemple, le cinéma, les jeux vidéo, les livres, la musique, ou le sport. Trouvez une personne (ou un groupe) connectée à ce sujet (un blog, un site web, une personne ou un groupe à suivre, etc.). Essayez de trouver des sources des pays différents, puis compilez ces informations pour les présenter à votre classe. Considérez ces questions:

- Qu'est-ce que vous avez en commun avec ce groupe?
- Quelles sont des différences culturelles qui sont évidentes entre vous?
- Qu'est-ce que vous voulez découvrir ou continuer à examiner dans ce groupe?

25 Je suis un enfant du monde 1.2, 1.3, 2.2, 5.2

Connecting to Leadership and Responsibility, Global Awareness
Interpretive Viewing, Presentational Speaking

Vous voulez être volontaire pour un groupe international qui travaille avec les enfants dans des pays francophones. Pour vous préparer à votre voyage, vous voulez vous renseigner sur ce qui intéresse les enfants. Recherchez des activités, des jeux, et chansons enfantines d'un pays et apprenez deux ou trois choses qui vous permettront d'avoir un impact positif sur ces enfants. Préparez-vous aussi à partager et à expliquer vos activités préférées de manière simple et concise. Présentez les activités ou les jeux que vous avez découverts à un groupe de camarades de classe de façon didactique.

26 Un mariage international 1.1, 1.2, 2.2, 3.2, 5.2

Connecting to Collaboration, Creativity and Innovation, and Social and Cross-Cultural Skills
Interpersonal Speaking, Interpretive Viewing, Presentational Writing

Vous planifiez le mariage de deux personnes. Chaque personne vient d'un pays francophone différent et souhaite que la cérémonie et la réception soient une réflexion des coutumes de mariage de son pays. En groupe, jouez les rôles du coordinateur (ou de la coordinatrice) des événements, et d'autres membres du personnel de service, comme le chef, le serveur/la serveuse, ou le décorateur/la décoratrice, sans oublier le couple. Chacun doit faire des recherches pour déterminer les coutumes et les traditions à intégrer pendant la cérémonie et la réception, puis préparer des suggestions à présenter à la première réunion du personnel. (Par exemple: le gâteau, les invitations, la musique, la location, etc.). Lors de cette réunion, qui se fera devant la classe, chacun échangera ses idées et ses opinions, posera des questions, afin de prendre des décisions. Enfin, le groupe présentera le projet de mariage en intégrant toutes les décisions prises sur un document.

Essential Instruction

Read through the **Projets finaux** and brainstorm with students the various tasks related to each project. If you only have time for students to do one activity, let them pick the one that appeals to them the most. Provide a detailed rubric so students know in advance how they will be graded.

Finale

Projets finaux

A Connexions par Internet : la sociologie 1.2, 1.3, 3.1, 3.2

Traditions de vie

Écrivez une petite composition sur la famille, l'enfance, ou le mariage dans un pays francophone. Commencez par faire des recherches sur votre sujet en ligne. Commencez votre composition en donnant une définition de la sociologie et faites une phrase d'introduction. Puis, parlez tout d'abord des traditions. Ensuite, notez les changements dans les familles, l'enfance, ou le mariage dans la société contemporaine. À quelles influences est-ce que vous attribuez ces changements ? Terminez par une conclusion qui soutient votre point de vue.

B Communautés en ligne 1.2, 1.3, 3.2, 5.1, 5.1

Étudier à l'étranger pour perfectionner votre français

Vous voulez devenir un citoyen du monde, alors vous avez pris la décision d'étudier à l'étranger pour perfectionner votre français. Si vous voulez faire un programme d'échange pendant que vous êtes au lycée, cherchez un programme comme AFS ou un autre programme d'immersion. Si vous préférez participer à un tel programme à l'université, cherchez le *Junior Year Abroad Program* d'une université. Ensuite, écrivez 6–10 questions pour un(e) élève ou étudiant(e) qui est revenu(e) après un séjour à l'étranger via le programme que vous avez choisi. Vous pouvez trouver cette personne en ligne ou écrire un mail au programme qui vous mettra en contact avec quelqu'un. Finalement, discutez de ce que vous avez appris en petits groupes.

C Passez à l'action ! 1.2, 1.3, 3.2, 5.1

Un tournoi de slam chez nous

Votre communauté a décidé d'organiser un tournoi de slam en français parce que les écoles de votre ville ont montré un fort intérêt dans la langue et la culture françaises. Vos camarades de classe et vous-même avez été recrutés pour organiser cet événement.

En groupe, faites des recherches pour trouver des slameurs et slameuses francophones que vous aimeriez inviter à cette occasion. Vous devrez :

- envoyer une invitation par mail à deux slameurs
- faire de la publicité dans votre ville (des affiches à coller ou à mettre dans des petites annonces sur Internet)
- prendre des photos, interviewer des jeunes slameurs et expliquer leurs opinions sur l'importance du slam (dans un article ou sur vidéo)
- créer une page web pour inviter tous les francophiles de la région

Resources

Create

Answers

Projects will vary.

Reference Desk

1. **Connexions par Internet** connects students to an educational subject matter such as sociology, architecture, literature, math, art, career planning, or music.
2. **Communautés en ligne** is intended to help students build online francophone communities.
3. **Passez à l'action !** is an activity for the whole class, often suggesting roles and tasks for students.
4. Teachers have suggested that "**Romeo kiff Juliette**" by **Grand Corps Malade** is an appropriate video. Depending on the maturity level of your class, you may want to suggest a specific song from each artist.

Expansion

Activité A: You may want to model a paragraph about family, childhood, or marriage in France, then encourage students to research a different francophone country or region.
Activité B: Share your **formation en français** experiences abroad with the class.
Activité C: Make sure each student has a role; you may want to create groups for each bulleted task.

Differentiated Learning

Accelerate
Allow students, working in a group, to devise their own final project based on unit content.

Decelerate
Have students revisit the **Contrat de l'élève** and self-assess how well they know the unit content.

Resources

Create

Answers

D

Leçon A: Extension: Elle est toujours connectée au réseau social Facebook.
Leçon A: Points de départ: Ils partagent des intérêts sportifs, audiovisuels et culturels.
Leçon A: Points de départ: Elles sont de plus en plus hétérogènes.
Leçon A: L'argot des ados: Answers will vary.
Leçon A: Du côté des médias: Ils peuvent passer des petites annonces dans des sites comme « Croisé dans le métro ».
Leçon B: Rencontres culturelles: Il a arrêté de jouer au foot. En ville, il y a plus d'habitants et on ne se connaît pas les uns les autres comme à la campagne.
Leçon B: Extension: Elles ont divorcé et partagent la garde de leurs enfants.
Leçon B: Points de départ: Il y a aujourd'hui un grand nombre de divorces et plus de couples non mariés.
Leçon B: La Francophonie: Les jeunes africains, comme les jeunes européens, poussent leurs pays à se moderniser.
Leçon B: Du côté des médias: Ils veulent préserver la culture et les arts locaux.
Leçon C: Rencontres culturelles: Mathieu va se marier. Élodie a hâte d'avoir un neveu.
Leçon B: Rencontres culturelles: Ils se pacseraient pour avoir moins de problèmes.
Leçon C: Points de départ: Ils doivent passer un concours sélectif et remettre un dossier.
Leçon C: Points de départ: Il y a deux cérémonies: une civile à la mairie, et une religieuse.
Leçon C: La Francophonie: Elles se mettent du hénné sur le corps.
Leçon C: Lecture thématique: Josyane est plus tranquille, elle apprécie le calme pour faire ses devoirs.

Reference Desk

1. The **Faisons le point!** section asks students to respond to the essential question by analyzing various texts in each lesson. The graphic organizer for **Activité D** may be expanded by using the complete chart in the Copy Masters supplement.
2. If you have access to Passport, assign your students an IPA task related to the unit.

D Faisons le point! 1.2, 1.3, 2.1, 2.2, 3.1, 3.2, 4.1, 4.2, 5.1

Diagramme

Faites un diagramme comme celui de dessous et remplissez-le pour montrer vos connaissances concernant la question suivante: Comment change-t-on de l'enfance à l'âge adulte? Un exemple a été fait pour vous.

Leçon A **Rencontres culturelles: Comment tu le trouves?** Qu'est-ce qui est nouveau dans la vie d'Élodie? →	Élodie fait partie d'une bande de copains et elle a un nouveau petit ami.
Leçon A **Extension: Le profil d'une lycéenne** Comment est-ce que Julie communique avec ses amis? →	
Leçon A **Points de départ: Modes de vie des adolescents** Qu'est-ce que les jeunes Français ont en commun? →	
Leçon A **Points de départ: Le scoutisme** Comment ont évolué les associations de scoutisme? →	
Leçon A **Du côté des médias** Comment est-ce que les jeunes Français se rencontrent? →	
Leçon B **Rencontres culturelles: L'enfance de Karim** Qu'est-ce que Karim a arrêté de faire quand il a déménagé à Nice? Qu'est-ce qui était nouveau pour lui à Nice? →	
Leçon B **Extension: Les enfants vont bien?** Qu'est-ce qui est nouveau dans les vies de Mme Duhamel et Mme Laforge? →	
Leçon B **Points de départ: La famille** Pourquoi les Français se pacseraient-ils? →	
Leçon C **Points de départ: L'enseignement supérieur en France** Que doivent faire les jeunes Francais s'ils veulent s'inscrire à une grande école? →	

Essential Instruction

A graphic organizer is available in the Copy Masters supplement for **Faisons le point!** Ask students to include the page number where they can find the information as they review the Unit and to evaluate what they remember.

1. Have students read through the answers in **Activité A** before listening to the questions. Replay the audio as needed. Some students, especially those with auditory difficulties, will benefit from seeing the script.
2. For **Activité B**, ask students to brainstorm vocabulary, functions, and structures they need to know to complete the dialogue. Then assign partners to create the dialogue. Select several pairs to present.

Pre-AP

Évaluation

A Évaluation de compréhension auditive 1.2

Écrivez les numéros 1–7 sur votre papier. Ensuite, écoutez l'histoire, et écrivez la lettre qui correspond à l'endroit où les personnes feront les activités suivantes pendant les vacances.

1. Caroline	A. le ciné-club
2. Serge	B. le skatepark
3. Amélie et Amadou	C. le festival de musique
4. Jacques	D. la discothèque
5. Martine	E. le complexe sportif
6. Yasmine et Julien	F. le cours particulier
7. Chloé	G. l'association de scoutisme

B Évaluation orale 1.1, 1.2, 1.3, 5.1, 5.2

Avec un partenaire, jouez les rôles de deux ados qui sont à l'association de scoutisme.

Vous voulez savoir si votre copain/copine a fait la connaissance d'un(e) nouvel(le) ami(e).	
	Dites que c'est vrai.
Demandez son prénom.	
	Dites comment votre nouvel(le) ami(e) s'appelle.
Demandez où votre copain/copine a rencontré cette personne.	
	Dites où vous avez rencontré votre nouvel(le) ami(e).
Demandez comment il/elle est.	
	Décrivez votre ami(e). Dites ce que vous avez découvert de lui/d'elle. (Peut-être qu'il/elle aime quelque chose que vous aimez aussi.)
Dites que ce serait bien de le/la présenter à votre bande de copains.	
	Dites que vous proposez d'organiser une soirée pour le/la présenter à vos copains.
Dites que vous aimeriez le/la connaître.	
	Demandez ce que votre copain/copine aimerait faire ce soir.
Proposez une activité pour ce soir.	
	Acceptez ou refusez.

Resources

- Activity A
- LA Listening Activity *Synthèse*
- Pre-AP Listening *Unité 1*
- Perform

Answers

A Script

Les ados du lycée Lafontaine ont beaucoup de projets pour les vacances. Caroline s'intéresse aux activités en plein air avec d'autres ados. Serge passera beaucoup de temps à faire du skate. Amélie et Amadou verront tous les drames de Truffaut parce qu'ils adorent le cinéma français. Jacques aimerait assister aux FrancoFolies à La Rochelle. Martine n'a pas réussi en anglais ; donc, elle étudiera avec le prof anglais. Yasmine courra et Julien jouera au foot. Chloé dansera tous les vendredis et samedis soirs.

1.G; 2. B; 3. A; 4. C; 5. F; 6. E; 7. D

B Conversations will vary.

Reference Desk

1. **Évaluation** quizzes students on the following skills: listening, speaking, culture, writing, and visual (reading) comprehension. It lets each student know what he or she needs to practice more or review thoroughly before the unit test.
2. **Évaluation de compréhension auditive** is based on scripts that usually combine unit vocabulary and grammar.
3. **Évaluation orale** provides paired speaking practice. Sometimes you may want to vary it by playing one of the roles yourself and choosing different partners before putting students in pairs.
4. If you have access to Passport, assign a task to evaluate your students' oral proficiency.

Differentiated Learning

Accelerate
Have students do **Activité E** or **F** in addition to **A–D**.

Special Needs Students

Auditory Impairment
Allow students with hearing difficulties to listen to **Activité A** several times. You may also want to read the questions which will give them ample time to process the information.

Multiple Intelligences

Intrapersonal
Ask students to share with the class or a small group how their view of francophone life has changed or expanded after studying **Unité 1**.

Answers

All activities will vary.

Reference Desk

1. **Évaluation culturelle** asks students to make comparisons between francophone and American cultures.
2. **Évaluation écrite** is intended to build writing proficiency.
3. **Évaluation visuelle** is designed for visual learners who do best with a visual prompt.
4. **Évaluation compréhensive** is designed for those students who have a desire to be creative with unit content. Sometimes it works to pair an artist with a good writer to complete this activity. These students could do this activity in place of **Activité D**.

Game

Définitions

Put students in two teams. Read a definition for one of the unit's new vocabulary words. A designated player from each team races to the board to write the word. Whoever writes the word correctly earns a point for his or her team. Here are some definitions to get you started: 1. **une bague de mariage** (**une alliance**); 2. **un parc où on joue dans l'eau** (**un aquaparc**); 3. **un groupe de copains** (**une bande**); 4. **un enfant qui a moins d'un an** (**un bébé**); 5. **l'endroit où les avocats travaillent** (**le cabinet d'avocats**); 6. **un groupe qui se rencontre pour voir des films** (**un ciné-club**); 7. **un endroit où on fait toutes sortes de sports** (**un complexe sportif**); 8. **aller très vite à pied** (**courir**); 9. **s'installer dans une nouvelle maison** (**déménager**); 10. **la jeune femme qui aide son amie pendant sa cérémonie de mariage** (**la demoiselle d'honneur**)

C Évaluation culturelle 1.2, 3.2, 4.2

Vous allez comparez les cultures francophones à votre culture aux États-Unis. Vous aurez peut-être besoin de faire des recherches sur la culture américaine.

1. **Les modes de vie des adolescents**
   Comparez les modes de vie des adolescents francophones et américains. Quelles sont les similarités et les différences entre les deux groupes? Est-ce qu'il y a une « culture ado » qui rassemble (*gathers*) ces deux groupes?
2. **Les associations de scoutisme**
   Avez-vous fait du scoutisme? Où? À quelles activités avez-vous participé et qu'avez-vous appris à faire? Faites des recherches sur le scoutisme en France et comparez votre expérience à celle des Français.
3. **Les familles**
   Faites un sondage auprès de vos camarade de classe pour savoir dans quel type de famille (nucléaire, monoparentale...) vos amis vivent. Comparez les pourcentages à ceux des familles françaises.
4. **Classes préparatoires et grandes écoles**
   Si un ado voulait travailler pour la Banque de France un jour, qu'est-ce que vous lui conseilleriez? Si vous vouliez vous inscrire à UCLA ou Duke, qu'est-ce que vous devriez faire?
5. **Le mariage**
   Quels genres de cérémonies de mariage existent en France? Laquelle est la plus populaire en France? Et aux États-Unis? Comparez aussi les réceptions de mariage en France et aux États-Unis.

D Évaluation écrite 1.3, 2.1, 5.1

Écrivez un faire-part de mariage pour un couple français à Nice. N'oubliez pas d'inclure (include)*:*

- le nom du couple et de leurs parents
- la date et l'endroit de la cérémonie et de la réception
- l'adresse de l'église et du restaurant où la réception aura lieu
- l'adresse où on envoie son RSVP

E Évaluation visuelle 1.3, 2.1, 3.1, 5.1

Écrivez un paragraphe qui décrit le mariage d'Albert et Claudette. Décrivez ce que vous voyez à la cérémonie et imaginez ce qui se passera après, pendant la réception. Dites depuis combien de temps Albert connaît Claudette et où ils travaillent. Parlez de leurs rêves pour l'avenir (future)*.*

F Évaluation compréhensive 1.3, 5.1

Créez une histoire avec six illustrations: dessinez une famille en vacances sur la Côte d'Azur. Montrez les activités de cette famille. Vous devrez décider quelle sorte de famille c'est. Les enfants ont moins de dix ans et aiment les jeux d'enfants.

Essential Instruction

1. You may want to organize the class in five small groups to complete **Activité C**, then have each group present their comparisons to the class.
2. All students should complete **Activité D** since they will complete a proficiency writing section on the unit test; assign **Activités E–F** to those students who need a visual cue or who are creative.

Learning Styles

Auditory Learners

Students may benefit from saying and spelling the vocabulary words out loud. Pair similar-ability-level students and have them work together to review the vocabulary in this way.

Vocabulaire de l'Unité 1

absolument absolutely *A*
les **alliances (f.)** wedding rings *C*
l' **aquaparc (m.)** water park *A*
assister (à) to attend *C*
l' **association (f.) de scoutisme (m.)** scouting association *A*
aussitôt que as soon as *C*
la **bague: bague de fiançailles** engagement ring *C*
une **bande** group of friends *A*
le **bébé** baby *C*
un **cabinet d'avocats** law firm *C*
le **ciné-club** film club *A*
collectionner to collect *B*
comme: c'est comme ça que.... that's how.... *B*
le **complexe sportif** sports center *A*
la **complicité** complicity *A*
un **coquillage** seashell *B*
courir to run *B*
le **cours particulier** private class *A*
déménager to move *C*
la **demoiselle d'honneur** bridesmaid *C*
détester to detest *A*
la **discothèque** nightclub *A*
l' **enfance (f.)** childhood *B*
enfantin(e) childish *B*
une **entreprise** business, company *C*
être: être affolé(e) to be panicked *A*; **être fâché(e)** to be angry *A*
une **famille: famille monoparentale** single-parent family *B*; **famille nucléaire** nuclear family *B*; **famille recomposée** blended family *B*
faire: faire semblant (de) to pretend (to) *B*; **Tu ferais bien de....** You would do well to.... *A*
se **faire: se faire muter** to get transferred *C*
le **festival** festival *A*
s'en **fiche: Je m'en fiche.** I don't care. *C*; **Elle s'en fiche.** She doesn't care. *C*
le **garçon: garçon d'honneur** best man *C*
la **haute technologie** high tech *C*
s' **inquiéter** to worry *A*
intéressé(e) interested *C*
jouer: jouer à cache-cache to play hide-and-seek *B*; **jouer à la marelle** to play hopscotch *B*; **jouer à la poupée** to play with dolls *B*; **jouer aux billes** to play marbles *B*; **jouer aux petites voitures** to play with toy cars *B*
un **laboratoire de recherches** research laboratory *C*
lorsque when *C*
une **marraine** godmother *C*
mettre: mettre d'accord to get people to agree *C*
les **nanotechnologies (f.)** nanotechnology *C*
la **peine: ce n'est pas la peine** it's not worth it *A*
une **piste** lead *C*
une **PME (petite et moyenne entreprise)** small business *C*
un **poste** job position *C*
une **princesse** princess *B*
se **quitter** to leave each other/one another *A*
la **réception** reception *C*
un **regret** regret *B*
le **sable** sand *B*
sauter to jump *B*; **sauter à la corde** to jump rope *B*
le **skatepark** skateboard park *A*
la **soirée** evening out *A*
sourire to smile *A*
un **sourire** smile *A*
un **super-héros, une super-héroïne** superhero, superheroine *B*
un **timbre** stamp *B*
le **voyage de noces** honeymoon *C*

Resources

FC Flash Cards
Rendez-vous à Nice ! Documentaire 1
T *Unité 1* Test

Reference Desk

1. Remind the students that the **Leçon** where each vocabulary word can be found is indicated in red.
2. A quick Jeopardy! board can be put together using Post-It notes with the points on one side and the questions hidden on the back.

nouvelle orthographe **le cinéclub, jouer à cachecache, un superhéro, une superhéroïne**

Game

Jeopardy!

Create categories of questions: vocabulary, culture, grammar, speaking in French (perhaps answering questions), potpourri. Place the questions on your board so that the easiest one in each category comes first and the most difficult one comes last; give each question a point value that is visible to students (10–50). Divide the class into two teams. The first player picks a category and a point value. The team with the highest number of points, once all the questions have been asked, is the winner.

Reference Desk

1. When a **jour férié** falls on a Friday or Monday, the French have a three-day weekend. This is called "**faire le pont**." An extended weekend is also called **un weekend prolongé**.
2. The photo on the unit opener shows the center of Paris, the 7th **arrondissement** (where the Eiffel Tower is located), at Christmas time.

Unité

2 Les rapports personnels

Essential Instruction

1. After the students read the quotation, have them discuss if it's true that we become aware of ourselves solely in interacting with others. Some students may raise the point that you can learn a lot about yourself by taking part in group activities *and* doing things alone.
2. Review the **Question centrale** and have students ponder their personal experiences and explore whether they correspond to experiences of people of all cultures.

Question centrale

Qu'y a-t-il d'universel dans les rapports entre les gens?

À savoir

Quand les Français ont un weekend prolongé grâce à un jour férié, ils disent: « On fait le pont. »

Citation

« C'est dans le rapport à autrui que l'on prend conscience de soi. . . . »

It's in our relationships with others that we become aware of ourselves.

—Michel Houellebecq (1956–), écrivain européen

Conseil pratique

Read articles about French politics, media, fashion, sports, or the economy, and share with a partner interested in the same topics.

Quel est cet établissement?

Pour quelle fête sert-on ce plat?

Contrat de l'élève

Leçon A I will be able to:

- talk on the phone, invite someone, respond affirmatively to an invitation, and say that something works out.
- talk about holidays in France and North Africa.
- review interrogative pronouns and direct object pronouns.

Leçon B I will be able to:

- ask for help, respond to a request for help, and ask someone to pass me something.
- talk about French cuisine and eating habits.
- review indirect object pronouns and **c'est** versus **il/elle est**.

Leçon C I will be able to:

- express what I can't keep myself from doing, say someone is right, and ask what someone is talking about.
- talk about dining etiquette in France.
- use the relative pronouns **qui/que** and **ce qui/ce que**.

Answers

Possible choices for the video question:
A. une maison
B. un hôtel-restaurant
C. un musée
D. une ancienne prison
Correct Answer: B

The answer to the culture question is: **l'Aïd el-Fitr**. The answer can be found in **Points de départ**, **Leçon A**.

Reference Desk

With the **Question centrale**, students are asked to examine their relationships and compare them to those in the francophone world.

Differentiated Learning

Accelerate

Ask students who are seeking more of a challenge to conduct the review of the **Contrat de l'élève** with the rest of the class.

Decelerate

Review the **Contrat de l'élève** with students. Reassure them that in addition to learning these new concepts, they will be doing a thorough review of the basics that they learned in Level 1. Encourage them to believe that this year they are capable of achieving their greatest success yet. Show them a language acquisition curve and note that there is a moment when language begins to "click." That moment often occurs in the third or fourth year of language study.

Resources

- *Vocabulaire actif*
- eV eVisual
- WB Workbook 1–3
- FC Flash Cards
- LA Listening Activity 1
- G & V Practice Games

Reference Desk

1. Traditionally, **le réveillon** was the meal served after midnight mass on Christmas Eve and New Year's Eve. Now in France masses are said at 10:00 P.M. (**la messe anticipée**), so the meal is served earlier in the evening.
2. Traditional dishes will vary by region. For example, in Alsace-Lorraine, **vin chaud** (hot wine), **Mannëlle** (a man-shaped pastry often dipped in hot chocolate), and **oie à la choucroute** (goose on sauerkraut) make up traditional holiday fare. In Provence, thirteen traditional meals representing Christ and his twelve apostles are consumed on Christmas Eve: black nougat, white nougat, figs, dates, mandarins, walnuts or hazelnuts, quince paste or marzipan, green grapes, green melon, **calissons** (a candied fruit and almond cookie), **pompa** (a cake of olive oil), almonds, and raisins.
3. Even the French take shortcuts when it comes to cooking and entertaining. Do a search using the word **Picard**, which is a popular chain store in France that largely sells frozen products. See if you can locate some frozen herbs, sauces, main courses, and desserts.
4. **La bûche de Noël**, like the yule log, harkens back to the persecution of Christians in Ancient Rome, when they were permitted to meet on Christmas for the time that it took to burn one log.

nouvelle orthographe **des huitres, une buche de Noël**

Leçon A Vocabulaire actif

Le réveillon de Noël 1.2, 5.1

Le menu

L'apéritif (m.)

des brochettes (f.) apéritives

du jambon serrano

Les hors-d'œuvre (m.)

des huîtres (f.)

du foie gras

du saumon fumé

Les plats principaux

de la dinde aux marrons

des côtes (f.) de chevreuil

un magret de canard

Les desserts (m.)

des mandarines (f.)

une bûche de Noël

des truffes (f.) au chocolat

Essential Instruction

1. Have the students guess what each dish is by looking at the photos on the page, or larger, more vivid photos of these foods online.
2. Ask students what traditional American dishes would correspond to each category (appetizer, first course, main course, and dessert) in their home.
3. Review with students the order of courses.
4. The activities in the Lombard home on Christmas are in chronological order.

Noël chez les Lombard

Les Lombard **accueillent** leurs invités.

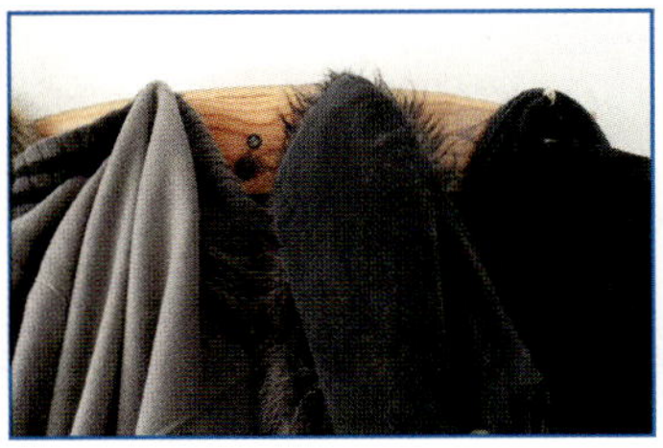

M. Lombard range leurs manteaux.

Il les emmène au salon.

Chloé **embête** son frère dans la cuisine.

Mme Lombard sert le repas.

Les Lombard mettent les cadeaux pour leurs enfants sous **le sapin de Noël**.

Pour la conversation

1.1, 1.2

What do I say when I phone someone?

» **Je ne te dérange pas?**
I'm not bothering you?

How do I invite someone?

» Vous aimeriez passer la soirée du réveillon avec nous?
Would you like to come spend Christmas Eve with us?

How do I respond affirmatively to an invitation?

» Pourquoi pas? On n'a rien de **prévu**.
Why not? We don't have anything planned.

How do I say a proposal works for me?

» **Ça tombe bien.**
That works out well.

Et si je voulais dire...?

un plateau de fruits de mer	*seafood platter*
un homard	*lobster*
une langouste	*rock lobster*
une fougasse	*lattice-shaped bread popular in Provence*
une brioche	*slightly sweet bread*

Resources

Pour la conversation
Et si je voulais dire...?

Reference Desk

1. Useful expressions for phoning in French include **Oui?** (*Hello?*); **Je ne vous dérange pas?** (*I'm not bothering you, am I?*); **Rappelle-moi.** (*Call me back.*); **Je t'envoie un texto/SMS.** (*I'm sending you a text.*)
2. Students learned **ranger** (*to put things away*) in Level 2, **Unité 3**. **Ranger la cuisine** means *to clean the kitchen*. **Ranger les placards** means *to straighten up the closets*, whereas **ranger les manteaux** has the sense of *to put the coats where they belong*.
3. **Une bête** means *a beast*, but it can also mean an *insect* or *bug*. Hence, *to bug someone* is **embêter quelqu'un. Ma bête noire** is the thing that you dread or hate.
4. **Servir** is an irregular -**ir** verb that is conjugated like **partir**.

Communication

Interpersonal: Paired Practice

Put students in pairs to have a phone conversation about Christmas. Student A calls Student B and invites him or her to **le réveillon**, explaining what will be served at dinner for all courses except dessert. Student B accepts the invitation and offers to bring dessert. Invite some students to present their dialogue in front of the class.

Culture

Products: Information

Have students listen to the following songs: "**Une lettre au père Nöel**" (sung by Patrick Bruel), "**Le père Noël c't'un Québécois**" (sung by Joseph or a more recent artist), or "**Mon beau sapin**" (performed by Algerian-Quebecois band Labess). Ask students to describe the cultural differences in each song.

Recherche: une lettre au père nöel patrick bruel

Differentiated Learning

Accelerate

Have the accelerated students research photos of the foods in **Et se je voulais dire...?** Have them select a recipe and make a shopping list of all the items they will need to preparre their dish.

Kinesthetic Learners

Have students cut the sentences of **Activité 2** into strips and place then in order.

Resources

Activity 1

Answers

1

1. Ils ont servi des brochettes apéritives, des huîtres, une salade verte, du canard, des mandarines, et une bûche.
2. Léa a accueilli ses grands-parents, rangé leurs manteaux, et elle leur a servi l'apéritif.
3. Elle était très occupée à l'université.
4. Oui, ils ont passé la fête en famille, avec les grands-parents.
5. Ils ont mis des cadeaux sous le sapin.
6. Elle va ouvrir ses cadeaux demain matin.

2 Correct order: 4, 7, 2, 5, 3, 6, 1

Reference Desk

1. Point out that the subject line of the e-mail literally means *Christmas—you are missing to me*, or more idiomatically, *Christmas, I miss you*.
2. Generally speaking, Christmas in France is spent with family and New Year's Eve is spent with friends (and family).

1 Absente à Noël 1.2, 5.1

Interpretive Reading

Lisez le mail de Léa à sa grande sœur, qui n'habite plus à la maison. Puis répondez aux questions suivantes.

À: Élodie@orange.fr
Cc:
Objet: Noël – tu me manques!

Salut, Élodie!

Je sais que tu as beaucoup à faire à l'université à New York. C'est dommage que tu n'aies pas été là pour Noël. Maman et Papa ont préparé un bon repas pour le réveillon de Noël — des brochettes apéritives, des huîtres, une salade verte, du canard. Et comme dessert il y avait des mandarines et une bûche, bien sûr! Pour une fois je ne les ai pas embêtés pendant qu'ils préparaient tout. En fait, je les ai aidés. J'avais beaucoup de responsabilités. J'ai accueilli papi et mamie, j'ai rangé leurs manteaux, je les ai emmenés au salon, et je leur ai servi l'apéritif. Heureusement, ils ont mis des cadeaux pour moi sous le sapin de Noël! Je vais les ouvrir demain matin. Et toi, tu as bien mangé chez ton ami? Téléphone-nous bientôt!

Je t'embrasse,
Léa

1. Qu'est-ce que les parents de Léa ont servi pour le réveillon de Noël?
2. Comment Léa a-t-elle aidé ses parents?
3. Pourquoi est-ce qu'Élodie n'est pas venue?
4. Est-ce que la famille de Léa a passé la fête en famille?
5. Qu'est-ce que les invités ont fait?
6. Quand est-ce que Léa va ouvrir ses cadeaux?

2 Le réveillon de Noël 1.2, 3.1

Interpretive Reading

Mettez les événements pour le réveillon de Noël en ordre chronologique.

1. Après le repas, les grands-parents mettent les cadeaux sous le sapin de Noël.
2. M. Gaillot range les manteaux des invités.
3. La belle-mère de Mme Gaillot l'aide dans la cuisine.
4. M. Gaillot invite ses parents et son oncle.
5. M. et Mme Gaillot emmènent leurs invités au salon.
6. Tout le monde s'assied à table et Mme Gaillot sert le repas.
7. Les Gaillot les accueillent à la porte le soir du réveillon.

Essential Instruction

1. After reading the e-mail, have students respond as Léa's big sister Élodie who no longer lives at home. In the e-mail, they could describe the American Christmas meal Élodie enjoyed in her friend's home in New York, or any other traditions or activities she took part in.
2. Have students work in pairs to do **Activités 2** and **3**.
3. Do **Activité 4** as a class.

3 Invitations 1.1, 5.1, 5.2

Interpersonal Speaking

À tour de rôle, invitez votre partenaire qui va dire s'il ou elle a quelque chose de prévu ou pas.

MODÈLE m'accompagner au ciné-club jeudi soir
A : Tu voudrais m'accompagner au ciné-club jeudi soir ?
B : Oui, je n'ai rien de prévu.
ou
Non, désolé(e), j'ai quelque chose de prévu.

1. venir à l'aquaparc cet été
2. faire du foot au complexe sportif mercredi après-midi
3. faire du scoutisme mardi soir
4. voir un festival de musique le 14 décembre
5. aller en discothèque samedi soir
6. m'accompagner à la soirée de Léo le 31 décembre

4 À table ! 1.2, 5.1

Interpretive Viewing, Presentational Speaking

Dites ce que M. Lapouze a servi comme....

1. apéritif
2. hors-d'œuvre
3. plat principal
4. dessert

Comparaisons 1.1, 4.2

En France, les enfants mettent des chaussons (*slippers*) près du sapin ; au matin de Noël, ils les retrouvent remplis de bonbons ou autres friandises. Quelle tradition similaire existe-t-il dans votre pays ?

Connexions 1.2, 3.1

Restauration

Imaginez que vous êtes en France et qu'on vous demande de partager vos recettes de Noël préférées de votre pays, afin de les publier dans un magazine en ligne. Choisissez une entrée, un plat principal, ou un dessert. Donnez les ingrédients et les mesures en utilisant le système métrique !

Answers

3

1. Tu voudrais venir à l'aquaparc cet été ?
2. Tu voudrais faire du foot au complexe sportif mercredi après-midi ?
3. Tu voudrais faire du scoutisme mardi soir ?
4. Tu voudrais voir un festival de musique le 14 décembre ?
5. Tu voudrais aller en discothèque samedi soir ?
6. Tu voudrais m'accompagner à la soirée de Léo le 31 décembre ?

Partner answers will vary.

4

1. des brochettes apéritives
2. du foie gras et des huîtres
3. de la dinde aux marrons
4. une bûche de Noël et des mandarines

Comparaisons

Possible answer: Aux États-Unis, les enfants mettent des *stockings* au mur, qu'on remplit de petits cadeaux.

Expansion

Students can expand **Activité 3** by using the following expressions: To accept: **Volontiers ! C'est une très bonne idée ! Pourquoi pas ? Oui, ça me dit ! Ça tombe bien !** To decline: **Malheureusement, je ne peux pas. Dommage. Je regrette.**

Special Needs Students

AD(H)D/Dyslexia/Linguistically Challenged

Allow students who have difficulty with concentration, reading, or language to write out their lines phonetically on note cards to help them better memorize target language.

Multiple Intelligences

Visual-Spatial

Ask these students to make **le menu** for the meal in **Activité 4**. Pass out the menu to the class before undertaking the exercise. Have students who still struggle with speaking write out the dialogue for the Communication activity before saying it aloud. When they have practiced both roles a few times, have them try without their notes.

Resources

Activity 5

Answers

5 Script

Le soir du réveillon de Noël, M. et Mme Kétif accueillent leurs invités à 19h20. M. Kétif range leurs manteaux. Les enfants, Saloua et Ahmed, emmènent les invités au salon. Mme Kétif leur sert des brochettes. Avant le dîner, les invités offrent des cadeaux aux enfants. Mme Kétif sert la dinde aux marrons dans la salle à manger. À table, Ahmed embête sa soeur. Dans le salon, on mange la bûche de Noël et des mandarines. Avant de se coucher, les enfants mettent leurs chaussures devant le sapin de Noël. Le lendemain Ahmed et Saloua ont beaucoup de cadeaux à ouvrir.

1. Quelle est la date?
2. Qui arrive chez les Kétif?
3. Qui range leurs manteaux?
4. Où est-ce que Mme Kétif sert des brochettes?
5. Qu'est-ce qu'on mange avec la bûche de Noël?
6. Qui a beaucoup de cadeaux le lendemain?

1. le 24 décembre
2. les invités
3. M. Kétif
4. au salon
5. des mandarines
6. les enfants/Ahmed et Saloua

6 Answers will vary.

5 Un réveillon traditionnel! 1.2, 5.1

Interpretive Listening

Écrivez les numéros 1–6 sur votre papier. Écoutez la description du réveillon de Noël chez les Kétif. Ensuite, écrivez un mot ou une expression pour répondre aux questions que vous entendez.

6 Questions personnelles 1.1, 4.2, 5.1

Interpersonal Speaking

Répondez aux questions avec un partenaire.

1. Quand est-ce qu'on sert la dinde chez toi?
2. As-tu déjà mangé du canard? des côtes de chevreuil? des mandarines? des huîtres?
3. Qu'est-ce que tu mets sur les brochettes?
4. Qu'est-ce que tu fais pour accueillir tes amis quand ils te rendent visite?
5. Quels cadeaux est-ce que tu vas offrir à ta famille cette année?
6. Est-ce que tu as quelque chose de prévu pour samedi soir?

Une assiette d'huîtres

Traditions et pratiques 1.2, 2.1

À l'occasion de Noël, certains Français mettent des décorations lumineuses devant leurs habitations, mais ce sont surtout les communes qui décorent les rues et les avenues piétonnes de guirlandes et de lumières, pour donner une ambiance festive.

Essential Instruction

1. Listen to the first description in **Activité 5** together as a class. Model an appropriate answer because students are not used to writing open-ended answers to listening questions.
2. After students have completed **Activité 6** in pairs, call on students at random to answer questions 1–6.
3. Play the video of the dialogue for the class. After finding out where the gaps in their comprehension are, read the dialogues aloud, selecting three students for the roles.
4. Ask students the questions in **Activité 7**.

Rencontres culturelles

Une invitation 1.1, 1.2, 2.1, 5.1

Les parents d'Élodie et de Léo prennent un café au salon et discutent à propos du réveillon de Noël.

Mère : Bon, tu es d'accord, mais qui est-ce qu'on invite pour le réveillon ?
Père : Appelle les Martin… je suis sûr qu'ils n'ont rien de prévu.
Mère : C'est un peu tard, non ? On est quand même à cinq jours du réveillon.
Père : Écoute, tu leur dis qu'on improvise quelque chose….
Mère : Et s'ils disent qu'ils ont déjà accepté une invitation ?
Père : Eh bien, on passera le réveillon en famille… vas-y, appelle, je te dis !

(La mère d'Élodie et de Léo téléphone à Amélie Martin.)

Mère : Allô ? Amélie, je ne te dérange pas ? C'est pour le réveillon de Noël, vous faites quelque chose ?
Amélie : Non….
Mère : Vous aimeriez venir passer la soirée du réveillon avec nous ?
Amélie : Pourquoi pas ? On n'a rien de prévu… mais vous, vous n'avez rien accepté de votre côté ?
Mère : Non… puisque je vous invite… on avait envie d'une soirée un peu tranquille, en petit comité.
Amélie : Ça tombe bien, alors ! C'est moi qui fais les toasts. J'insiste !
Mère : C'est gentil. Au 24, alors !

Stratégie

Faites une liste des problèmes soulevés par la mère, et des solutions suggérées par le père.

7 Une invitation 1.2, 1.3

Répondez aux questions.

1. Pourquoi est-ce que la mère d'Élodie et de Léo téléphone à Amélie ?
2. Qui a l'idée de téléphoner aux Martin ?
3. Si les Martin n'acceptent pas l'invitation, que va-t-il se passer ?
4. La mère d'Élodie et de Léo prévoit (*foresees*) quelle sorte de soirée ?
5. Qu'est-ce que Mme Martin offre de préparer ?
6. La soirée, c'est pour fêter quelle fête ?

Resources

- Dialogue
  Activity 7
- Dialogue Video
- WB Workbook 4

Answers

7
1. pour l'inviter pour le réveillon de Noël
2. le père d'Élodie
3. La famille d'Élodie passera le réveillon en famille.
4. une petite soirée tranquille
5. les toasts
6. le réveillon de Noël

Reference Desk

Help students understand words and expressions they haven't seen before. See if they can figure out the meaning by using the context before giving them the answers:
- **À propos de** is used with **discuter**; it can also be used with **parler**.
- **Ils n'ont rien de prévu** means *They have nothing planned.*
- **On est quand même à cinq jours du réveillon** means *But **le réveillon** is only five days away.* Ask students to give additional examples of the **à** + TIME/DISTANCE formula.
- **Puisque** means *since*. However, in the sentence **Puisque je vous invite…** it can be translated as *That's why we are inviting you.*
- **En petit comité** means *in a small group.*
- **Au 24 alors !** means *We'll see you on the 24th!*
- **Les toasts** is another expression for **les brochettes**.

Differentiated Learning

Accelerate

Have accelerated students make a cloze activity based on the new vocabulary in the dialogue. They can then trade cloze activities with peers and attempt to complete them.

Decelerate

Allow these students to see the questions for **Activité 5** before listening to the dialogue. Do **Activité 6** as an all class discussion in which you circle questions (yes/no, either/or, information) and ask students to respond to questions about one another. **"Bob, est-ce qu'on sert de la dinde chez toi à Thanksgiving?" "Classe, quand est-ce qu'on sert de la dinde chez Bob?"**

Special Needs Students

Social Anxiety

If you have students perform or read the dialogue aloud, they may appreciate reading one of the roles in the dialogue with you privately since performing in front of a group might be too stressful for them.

Resources

Extension

Answers

EXTENSION

Elle se plaint que ses invités sont difficiles, parce qu'ils ont tous des restrictions alimentaires différentes.; Oui.

Analyse

Possible answer: M. Laurent doit choisir entre imprimer les invitations ou les envoyer par Internet. Il choisit l'Internet car c'est plus économique. Mme Laurent doit choisir le menu; elle ne prend pas de décision car ses invités sont trop difficiles.

Reference Desk

1. **La Saint Sylvestre** (New Year's Eve) is also known as **le Réveillon du Nouvel An**. It is often celebrated publicly with friends. Municipalities will organize large concerts and firework displays. As in the United States, people will often make resolutions (**des résolutions**) on this occasion. Another tradition has party guests list the best and the worst of the previous year as well as their hopes for the upcoming year.
2. French people of Jewish tradition celebrate **Roch Hachana** instead of **le Nouvel An**. It honors the day when God created the earth, and is typically celebrated in September, beginning a ten-day celebration of peace, culminated by the **Yom Kippour** celebration, which recalls the forgiveness of God towards those of his people who had worshipped a golden calf.
3. Muslims celebrate the New Year also in September with **Raas Assana**, the beginning of **Muharram**, the first month of the Islamic calendar. The new year commemorates the exile of the prophet Muhammad (**Mahomet**) to Medina in 622 to form a common Muslim faith. French Muslims share festive meals and may exchange gifts.

EXTENSION **Une autre fête : Le réveillon de la Saint-Sylvestre** 1.1, 1.2, 5.1

Le 27 décembre, M. et Mme Laurent parlent d'une fête qui s'approche.

M. Laurent : Tiens regarde, j'ai préparé un carton d'invitations pour le réveillon.
Mme Laurent : Très joli… tu le tires sur papier ou tu l'envoies aux Roland par Internet ?
M. Laurent : Par Internet, chérie… Comme dit ton fils : « Pensez à économiser la planète. » Et qu'est-ce que tu vas servir ?
Mme Laurent : Tu sais, les Roland sont difficiles : pas trop gras pour lui, pas de viande pour elle, pas trop de sucre pour les deux…
M. Laurent : À ce rythme-là, ce n'est pas un menu de réveillon qu'il faut préparer mais leur proposer le menu minceur de leur cure de thermalisme.

EXTENSION De quoi est-ce que la mère se plaint ? Pourquoi ? Son mari est-il du même avis ?

Traditions et pratiques 1.2, 2.1

La Saint-Sylvestre est l'occasion de faire du bruit, pour, selon la tradition chrétienne, faire fuir les mauvais esprits. De nombreux Parisiens se réunissent sur l'avenue des Champs-Élysées pour faire la fête.

Analyse 1.1, 1.2, 5.1

À quels dilemmes font face M. et Mme Laurent ? Quelle décision chacun a-t-il prise et pourquoi ?

Produits 1.2, 2.2

Les Français juifs fêtent **Roch Hachana**, qui est le commencement de l'année du calendrier hébraïque, en septembre ou octobre. On sonne une corne (*horn*) pour appeler à la repentance et l'introspection de soi. On mange aussi des plats festifs.

Produits 1.2, 2.2

En France, **le Nouvel An bouddhiste** est célébré en février. Il commence une période de quinze jours de festivités, d'offrandes et de prières pour la paix dans le monde.

Essential Instruction

1. Have students read the first culture reading to themselves. Then ask them the comprehension questions.
2. Ask students to design **une bûche de Noël** and vote on the top three.
3. Brainstorm the different types of holidays that your students celebrate at home. Discuss the cultural similarities and differences among the different celebrations in the USA and those in France and/or francophone countries.

Points de départ

Pre-AP | Question centrale ? Qu'y a-t-il d'universel dans les rapports entre les gens?

Le réveillon de Noël 1.2, 2.1, 3.2, 4.2

Le réveillon est un vrai moment de fête.

La coutume* du réveillon de Noël du 24 décembre très importante en France, est aussi observée dans de nombreuses villes et régions francophones, comme en Belgique, au Québec, à La Nouvelle Orléans et à Toronto.

La soirée se passe* généralement en famille, contrairement au réveillon du Nouvel An (nuit de la Saint-Sylvestre), qui réunit plutôt les amis. Le soir du réveillon de Noël, on dîne en famille ; puis, le jour de Noël, toute la famille (grands-parents, oncles, tantes, etc.) se réunit pour le déjeuner. Le repas du réveillon est un vrai festin*. On mange souvent des pintxos* basques*, des brochettes et tapas variés, à la crème d'olives, à la mozza-tomates séchées, au chèvre et à la charcuterie basque, suivis de saumon fumé ou de dinde aux marrons. En dessert, le gâteau traditionnel est la bûche de Noël.

La France étant un pays de tradition catholique, il existe la tradition des Treize desserts (en référence à Jésus et aux douze apôtres). Certaines familles assistent à la messe de minuit. À minuit on se souhaite un « joyeux Noël ». Les enfants mettent leurs chaussons* sous le sapin de Noël avant d'aller se coucher. Selon leur âge, ils pensent que le père Noël y déposera des cadeaux, qu'ils trouveront à leur réveil*, le 25 décembre.

Recherche : noël en france

la coutume *custom* ; **se passe** *is spent* ; **festin** *feast* ; **pintxos** *snacks of Spanish origin served with toothpicks* ; **basques** *from the Basque region* ; **chaussons** *slippers* ; **à leur réveil** *upon waking*

Produits

La bûche de Noël est un gâteau en forme de bûche (*log*). Traditionnellement, elle est à base de crème au beurre (*butter cream*), mais depuis plusieurs années on peut trouver une version glacée (*iced*). La bûche de Noël existe en plusieurs parfums : vanille, praliné, chocolat, ou café. Le pâtissier la décore avec des Pères Noël, des haches (*axes*), des scies (*saws*), des lutins (*elves*), etc. en sucre. Cette tradition existe dans de nombreux pays francophones comme en France et en Belgique.

1.2, 2.2

Comparaisons

Quelles sont vos traditions familiales pour les fêtes de Noël ?

1.2, 2.2, 4.2

Resources

- *Points de départ*
- WB Workbook 5
- Explore

Answers

Comparaisons
Answers will vary.

Reference Desk

1. There are approximately 465,000 Jews residing in France, many of whom celebrate the eight-day Festival of Lights (*Hannukah*) in December. The date is dictated by the Hebrew calendar. There is a series of rituals that are performed during the celebration; some are family-based, and others are celebrated communally. Many families exchange small gifts each night. Fried foods are eaten to remember the importance of oil during the festival of Hanukkah. Here are some terms to share with the class: **juif/juive** (*Jewish*); **le Sabbat** (*Sabbath*); **la Ménorah** (*Menorah*); **la prière** (*prayer*); **kasher** (*kosher*); **une bougie** (*candle*); **une galette aux pommes de terre** (*latke*); **une toupie** (*dreidel*, or *spinning top*).
2. Because Jesus is considered a prophet in Islam, some Muslims celebrate his birth. Many Muslims in France have adopted the commercial aspects of Christmas: gifts, Christmas trees, and **le Père Noël**.
3. If you have access to Passport, find an engaging video or a news article related to **Noël** and show it to your students.

Differentiated Learning

Accelerate
Ask students to write a culture reading, similar to **"Le réveillon de Noël,"** about **une fête** that their family celebrates.

Learning Styles

Kinesthetic Learners
Students who love to cook might like to make a **bûche de Noël** for the class. (Remember to check for students who have allergies.) Consider having students collaborate on ideas for decorating the frosting.

Multiple Intelligences

Musical-Rhythmic
On the day before winter break, ask other classrooms if your students may swing by and sing a carol or two in French. Collaborate with other language teachers to have students teach one another a festive or holiday carol in each language that your school offers.

Answers

8 Activities will vary.

Reference Desk

Islam is the second most practiced religion in France, after Roman Catholicism. With 8.5 million Muslims, France has the largest Islamic population in Western Europe. This is in large part due to immigration from former French colonies (primarily Algeria) in the 1960s and 1970s. Most Muslims in France are born into the religion.

La Francophonie

Festivités

Les fêtes au Maghreb 1.2, 2.1, 2.2, 3.2, 4.2

Les dattes et le thé commencent le repas de la fête de l'Aïd.

À la fin du mois sacré du Ramadan, on fête la rupture (la *id al-fltr* en arabe, «fête de la rupture») du jeûne*. C'est la fête de l'Aïd, un jour de fraternité, de pardon* et de réconciliation. Elle s'accompagne de tout un cérémonial : il y a le don* de rupture du jeûne (la *Zakat el-Fitr*), la prière, le repas avec les dattes, la présentation des vœux* à la famille et aux amis.

Au Maghreb, c'est la tradition de préparer des gâteaux aux amandes ou à la pistache. Les enfants et les maris aident les femmes en amenant les immenses plateaux* remplis de pâtes dans les boulangeries de quartier qui louent leurs fours. L'acte le plus important de la fête est le don aux pauvres de la communauté. Les enfants reçoivent de l'argent et des cadeaux.

En France, où l'on compte entre 8 et 9 millions (environ 1/8ème de la population française) de Musulmans, cette fête a pris une dimension nationale. Dans les grandes villes (Paris, Lyon, Lille, Marseille), elle donne lieu à de grands rassemblements*. La Mairie de Paris ouvre l'Hôtel de Ville de Paris aux Musulmans et à tous ceux et celles qui veulent partager cette fête. La fête de l'Aïd a *aussi* pris une dimension citoyenne : c'est une occasion de lutter contre l'islamophobie.

Recherche : ramadan, aïd el-fitr

Mot-clé

Fête (du latin *festa*, 1050). Le mot renvoie à un contexte religieux, puis une rupture avec la vie quotidienne, et une commémoration (14ème). Au 20ème siècle, il désigne toute occasion de débauche surtout dans l'expression **faire la fête**.

jeûne *fasting* ; **pardon** *forgiveness* ; **don** cadeau ; **vœux** *wishes* ; **plateaux** *trays* ; **rassemblements** *gatherings*

8 Activités culturelles 1.3, 3.2, 4.2

Faites les activités suivantes.

1. Comparez les plats servis pour le réveillon de Noël en France et le jour de Noël en Amérique. Servez-vous d'un organigramme Venn.
2. Faites un dessin qui montre la tradition du jour de Noël pour les enfants en France et dans votre pays.
3. Trouvez la date de l'Aïd el-Fitr cette année.
4. Consultez Internet pour voir comment l'Aïd el-Fitr est célébrée en France cette année.
5. Trouvez en ligne une recette de couscous ou de gâteau d'Aïd el-Fitr. Cochez les ingrédients que vous avez à la maison et faites une liste des ingrédients qu'il vous faut acheter pour servir 12 personnes.

1.2, 2.1

Traditions et pratiques

Sur l'île de la Réunion, la télévision diffuse en direct la prière de l'Aïd.

Produits

Le réveillon prend une saveur différente aux Antilles avec le punch, les accras, **le boudin créole** de Noël, et le jambon de Noël. Au Québec, **les barres Nanaïmo**, des gâteaux secs aux fruits, constituent le dessert principal.

1.2, 2.2, 4.2

Essential Instruction

1. Ask a student to point out on a world map where **le Maghreb** is located.
2. Read **Les fêtes au Maghreb** with your students.
3. Discuss the importance of Islam in France. Have students brainstorm what they already know about **le Maghreb** and Islam.
4. Assign one or more of the **Activités culturelles**. You may want to assign one activity per group, combining 3 and 4 into one activity.
5. Discuss the **Perspectives** on p. 83.
6. Put students in pairs to read the realia and complete **Activité 9**.

Perspectives

« Avant d'aller faire la prière rituelle à la mosquée, nous distribuons la *Zakat el-Fitr*, l'aumône donnée aux pauvres par acte de générosité et de compassion. Ce don purificateur permet aux personnes pauvres de ne pas avoir faim et représente une libération de la mendicité (*begging*) en ce jour sacré. » Selon ce Musulman, quel est le but de la *Zakat el-Fitr* ? 1.2, 2.1, 3.2, 4.2

Du côté des médias 1.2, 2.1, 3.2, 4.2

Lisez l'introduction et la liste des jours fériés en France.

La France compte 11 jours fériés qui correspondent à des fêtes civiles ou religieuses. Il y a des jours fériés fixes et des jours fériés mobiles. Le 1er mai, c'est la fête du travail, elle donne l'obligation à tous de ne pas travailler tout en étant payé. En mars et en avril, on fête le Lundi de Pâques ; entre mai et juin on fête le Jeudi de l'Ascension (40 jours après Pâques), puis le Lundi de Pentecôte (50 jours après Pâques). Le Vendredi Saint est un jour férié supplémentaire dans les départements de la Moselle, du Bas et du Haut-Rhin et en Guadeloupe, Martinique et Polynésie française.

France	2018	2019	2020
Nouvel An	1 jan	1 jan	1 jan
Lundi de Pâques	2 avril	22 avril	13 avril
Fête du Travail	1 mai	1 mai	1 mai
Fête de la Victoire (Guerre 1939–1945)	8 mai	8 mai	8 mai
Jeudi de l'Ascension	10 mai	30 mai	21 mai
Lundi de Pentecôte	21 mai	10 juin	1 juin
Fête Nationale	14 juillet	14 juillet	14 juillet
Fête de l'Assomption	15 août	15 août	15 août
Toussaint	1 nov	1 nov	1 nov
Armistice (Guerre 1914–1918)	11 nov	11 nov	11 nov
Fête de Noël	25 déc	25 déc	25 déc

9 Les jours fériés en France 1.2, 1.3, 2.1, 3.2, 4.2

Faites les activités suivantes.

1. Comptez les fêtes civiles.
2. Comptez les fêtes religieuses.
3. Comptez les jours fériés fixes.
4. Choisissez un jour férié et faites des recherches sur Internet ; puis, faites une présentation en classe.

Answers

9

1. 5
2. 6
3. 8
4. Answers will vary.

Perspectives

Son but est de reduire le taux de pauvreté.

Critical Thinking

Comparisons

Point out to students that **jours fériés** are official holidays recognized by the state. Have them compare the holidays in France with those in the United States. Also have them identify the ten federal holidays in the U.S. (New Year's Day, MLK Day, Presidents' Day, Memorial Day, Independence Day, Labor Day, Columbus Day, Veterans Day, Thanksgiving, and Christmas). How do they differ? French people are very focused on the month of May because there are more holidays than in other months. It is unofficially called **le mois à trous** (*the month of holes*). If a holiday falls on a Monday, they will have a three-day weekend. Ask the students to look at this year's calendar. Is this a good year for French holidays in May? Which holiday schedule would they prefer?

Expansion

Have your students visit the website for **Éducation nationale**. They will choose a school zone and examine the school holiday schedule. Have them put each vacation date on a calendar for this academic year. Then ask them to add the holidays as seen on p. 83. Ask them to determine how many days a year French students do *not* attend class out of the total number of school days.

Learning Styles

Mathematical/Logical

Ask students to compare the French work year to the work year in the United States. Have them consider official holidays, hours worked per week, and paid holidays. They could then compare productivity levels between the two countries and present a hypothesis on the relationship between work, vacation, and productivity.

Resources

WB Workbook 6–8

LA Listing Activity 2

G & V Practice Games

Answers

On recycle!

1. **Qui** a invité des amis à dîner?
2. **Qu'est-ce qu'**il y a sur la table?
3. **Qui est-ce qu'**elle a invité?
4. **Avec qui** Amélie **a-t-elle** fait la cuisine?/**Avec qui est-ce qu'**Amélie a fait la cuisine?
5. **De quoi se sont-elles** servies?/**De quoi est-ce qu'**elles se sont servies?

Structure de la langue

Révision: Interrogative Pronouns 1.2

On recycle!

See if you can write a question for each answer below, using an interrogative pronoun (**qui**, **qui est-ce que**, **qu'est-ce qui**, **qu'est-ce que**, **que**, **quoi**):

1. Amélie est la personne qui a invité des amis à dîner.
2. Il y a un bouquet sur la table.
3. Elle a invité M. et Mme Dumont.
4. Amélie a fait la cuisine avec sa fille.
5. Elles se sont servies des recettes de la mère d'Amélie.

If you were unable to come up with some of the questions, read the grammar summary below to review.

Interrogative pronouns are used to ask for information. The pronoun you use depends on whether you are referring to a person or a thing and on whether the pronoun is the subject, direct object, or object of a preposition.

	Subject	Direct Object	Object of Preposition
People	**qui** **qui est-ce qui**	**qui** (+ INVERSION) **qui est-ce que**	(à, avec, de, par) **qui**
Things	**qu'est-ce qui**	**que** (+ INVERSION) **qu'est-ce que**	(à, avec, de, par) **quoi**

Use **qui**, **qui est-ce *qui***, or **qu'est-ce *qui*** as the subject of the verb.

Qui mange les huîtres?	*Who is eating the oysters?*
Qui est-ce *qui* mange les huîtres?	*Who is eating the oysters?*
Qu'est-ce *qui* est sous le sapin de Noël?	*What's under the Christmas tree?*

Use **qui**, **qui est-ce *que***, **que**, or **qu'est-ce *que*** as the direct object of the verb.

Qui invites-tu?	*Who(m) are you inviting?*
Qui est-ce *que* tu invites?	*Who(m) are you inviting?*
Qu'achètent-ils?	*What are they buying?*
Qu'est-ce *qu'* ils achètent?	*What are they buying?*

Use **qui** or **quoi** as the object of a preposition.

À qui est-ce que tu téléphones?	*Who(m) are you calling?*
De quoi as-tu envie comme cadeaux?	*What do you want for presents?*

Essential Instruction

1. For your logical-sequential thinkers this chart is self-explanatory. **Qui** and **que**, interrogative pronouns, are used to refer to people and things. Other students will learn better from the examples.
2. For students of different learning styles, try using manipulatives by creating different characters (actors/singers/politicians/athletes) who you can fashion from lollypop sticks and cut out head shots. You can model some questions such as: **Qui va épouser ______? Qui est-ce qui va épouser ______? Qu'est-ce qui se passe aujourd'hui? Qui invitent-ils au mariage? Qui est-ce qu'ils n'invitent pas? Que reçoivent-ils comme cadeaux? Qu'est-ce qu'ils reçoivent comme cadeaux? Avec qui ______ va-t-il passer son voyage de noces? Avec quoi ______ coupe le gâteau?** Students can be creative by pairing together bizarre or unlikely characters and asking their peers amusing questions using key interrogative pronouns.

10 Ramadan 1.2, 2.2, 3.2, 5.2

Interpretive Reading

Complétez la phrase avec l'expression interrogative convenable.

1. ... fête le Ramadan? Les Musulmans fêtent le Ramadan.
2. ... est-ce qu'on fête le Ramadan? On fête le Ramadan pendant le mois qui suit la nouvelle lune.
3. ... les enfants reçoivent? Ils reçoivent des cadeaux et de l'argent.
4. ... les Musulmans aident pendant le Ramadan? Ils aident les gens pauvres.
5. ... on prépare à la fin du Ramadan? On prépare de délicieux gâteaux à la fin du Ramadan.
6. ... il y a dans les gâteaux? Il y a souvent des amandes.
7. ... prépare les gâteaux? Les mères préparent tous les gâteaux, mais les autres membres de la famille les aident.
8. ... est-ce qu'on parle le jour de l'Aïd el-Fitr? On parle du délicieux repas.

11 Le réveillon de Noël chez les Lagarde 1.1, 2.1, 3.2, 4.2, 5.2

Interpersonal Speaking

Votre ami vous a envoyé des photos du réveillon sur son smartphone. Utilisez une des expressions interrogatives ci-dessous pour poser des questions. Votre partenaire va jouer le rôle de votre ami et vous répondre.

qu'est-ce qui qui de quoi qu'est-ce que à qui qui est-ce que

MODÈLE

accueillir les invités
Qui accueille les invités?

1. ranger les manteaux

2. emmener les grands-parents au salon

3. embêter le chef

4. être sur la table

5. servir

6. téléphoner

7. parler

Answers

10

1. Qui (est-ce qui)
2. Quand
3. Qu'est-ce que
4. Qui est-ce que
5. Qu'est-ce qu'
6. Qu'est-ce qu'
7. Qui (est-ce qui)
8. De quoi

11

1. Qui range les manteaux?
2. Qui emmène les grands-parents au salon?
3. Qui embête le chef?
4. Qu'est-ce qui est sur la table?
5. Qui sert? Qu'est-ce qu'on sert?
6. Qui téléphone?
7. Qui parle?

Multiple Intelligences

Intrapersonal
Ask these students to write questions that use the interrogative pronouns. Collect the questions and distribute them to the other students, who will write a paragraph that answers all the questions. If students are uncomfortable talking about their own lives, they can imagine that the questions address a celebrity or historical figure of their choice.

Interpersonal/Artistic
Have students create a **tableau vivant** of the scenes in **Activité 11** (or scenes of their own) and send pictures to one another to engage in a texting conversation.

Resources

- Activity 12
- WB Workbook 9–10
- G & V Practice Games

Answers

12 Script

1. Cette année je vais manger des huîtres en hors-d'œuvre.
2. Mon frère va mettre les huîtres dans des assiettes.
3. Mes parents vont offrir des cadeaux à leurs enfants.
4. Je vais préparer les brochettes apéritives.
5. Ma mère va avoir besoin de marrons pour la dinde.
6. Nous allons inviter mes grands-parents.
7. Je vais préparer la bûche pour toute la famille.
8. Nous allons accueillir notre famille.

1. A
2. A
3. B
4. B
5. A
6. B
7. A
8. A

On recycle!
Direct object pronouns are placed in front of the verb of which they are the object. In the **passé composé**, the past participle agrees with the preceding direct object (here, **la limonade**), so an **-e** has to be added to show that the word is feminine.

Reference Desk

1. In the Level 2 textbook, students learned the direct object pronouns **me**, **te**, **nous**, and **vous** first (**Unité 5, Leçon A**), followed by **le**, **la**, **l'**, and **les** (**Unité 5, Leçon B**, where the concept of direct object pronouns in the **passé composé** was also first introduced).
2. You may want to go over the **On recycle!** questions together as a class, as students often require reinforcement with the concept of direct object pronouns.

12 Qui et quoi à Noël? 1.2, 2.1, 2.2

Interpretive Listening

Écoutez les réponses suivantes. Ensuite, choisissez la question correspondante.

1. A. Qu'est-ce que tu vas manger en hors-d'œuvre?
   B. Qui est-ce que tu vas manger en hors-d'œuvre?
2. A. Que va-t-il mettre dans les assiettes?
   B. Qui va-t-il mettre dans les assiettes?
3. A. Qu'est-ce qui va offrir des cadeaux?
   B. Qui est-ce qui va offrir des cadeaux?
4. A. De quoi vas-tu préparer?
   B. Que vas-tu préparer?
5. A. De quoi ta mère va-t-elle avoir besoin?
   B. Qu'est-ce que ta mère va servir?
6. A. Qu'est-ce qui va être invité?
   B. Qui est-ce qu'on va inviter?
7. A. Pour qui vas-tu préparer la bûche de Noël?
   B. De qui vas-tu parler?
8. A. Qui va accueillir ta famille?
   B. Que va accueillir ta famille?

Révision: Direct Object Pronouns: *me, te, le, la, nous, vous, les* 1.2

On recycle!
Do you remember where to place direct object pronouns in a sentence? Why is there an **-e** on the past participle in the exchange below?

—Marie, tu as bu la limonade?
—Oui, je l'ai bue.

If you were unable to answer the questions above, read the grammar summary to review direct object pronouns.

Direct object pronouns answer the question "who" or "what" and replace direct objects. **Le**, **la**, and **les** may refer to either people or things; **me**, **te**, **nous**, and **vous** refer only to people.

	Masculine	Feminine	Before a Vowel Sound
Singular	me te le	me te la	m' t' l'
Plural	nous vous les	nous vous les	nous vous les

Le sapin? Non, je ne l'ai pas touché!

Essential Instruction

1. After students listen to each recorded statement using interrogative pronouns, pause the recording and choose the correct answer as a class. Explain why the other choice is wrong.
2. To review direct object pronouns, write some questions on the board and ask for volunteers to say which pronoun is needed in the response. Then discuss placement of the pronouns in the present tense, near future, and **passé composé**.
3. Complete **Activité 13**, calling on students at random. If they have difficulty, use classroom objects as manipulatives to practice the direct object pronouns **le**, **la**, **l'**, and **les**.

These direct object pronouns come right before the verb of which they are the object. The sentence may be affirmative, interrogative, negative, or have an infinitive.

Désolé ! Vous **m**'attendez ?	*I'm sorry! Are you waiting for me?*
Non, nous ne **t**'attendons pas, mais Camille t'attend.	*No, we aren't waiting for you, but Camille is.*
Les cadeaux ? Où **les** mets-tu ?	*The presents? Where are you putting them?*
Je vais **les** mettre sous le sapin de Noël.	*I'm going to put them under the Christmas tree.*

In the **passé composé**, the past participle agrees in number and in gender with the preceding direct object pronoun.

Les huîtres ? Tu **les** as achet**ées** ?	*The oysters? Did you buy them?*
Non, mais le foie gras, je **l**'ai acheté.	*No, but the goose liver pâté, I bought that.*

13 Sandrine met le couvert pour la fête 1.3

Presentational Writing

*Sandrine met la table pour le réveillon de Noël. Utilisez les pronoms d'objet direct et les expressions **à gauche de**, **à droite de**, **entre**, **sur**, **au-dessus de**, etc. pour dire où elle met chaque chose.*

MODÈLE les assiettes
Elle les met entre les fourchettes et les couteaux.

1. la nappe
2. les fourchettes
3. les cuillères
4. le verre de Diane
5. le couteau d'Éric
6. les serviettes
7. le poivre
8. la tasse de Diane
9. le bol d'Éric

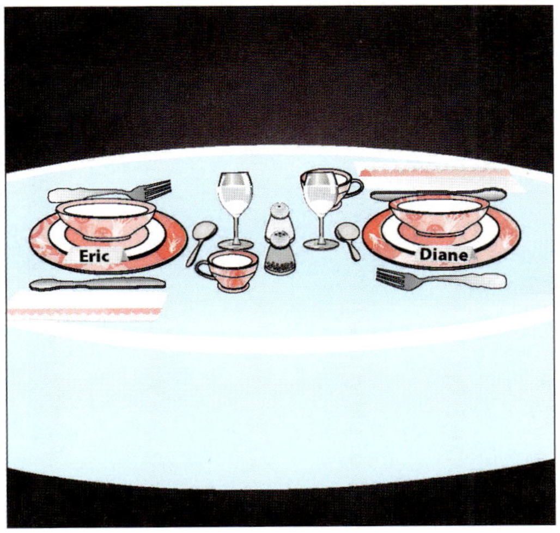

Answers

13 Possible answers:
1. Elle la met sur la table.
2. Elle les met à gauche des assiettes.
3. Elle les met au-dessus des assiettes.
4. Elle le met au-dessus de la petite cuillère.
5. Elle le met à droite de l'assiette.
6. Elle les met à droite des couteaux.
7. Elle le met sur la table.
8. Elle la met à droite du verre.
9. Elle le met sur l'assiette.

Reference Desk

1. In infinitive constructions, the direct object pronoun goes before the second verb, the infinitive.
2. Ask students how you might tell if **l'** is referring to a masculine or feminine subject. By adding an **e** on **vu**, we can see that: **Je l'ai vue**. *I saw her.*

Culture

Practices: Information

In some families, forks and spoons are inverted when placed on the table to show the monogram on the silver. Bread is placed on the tablecloth, not on a bread plate. With the exception of certain provinces, such as Normandy and Vendée, butter is not served with bread. There is a small object, which varies in size and shape, called a **porte-couteau**, upon which the knife rests between courses. Students may need reminding that the fork goes on the left (*fork* has four letters and so does the word left), and the knife and spoon go on the right (*knife* and *spoon* have five letters and so does the word *right*). A glass designated for water is a **un verre à eau**. A glass of water is a **verre d'eau**. (See p. 112 for more information on table setting.)

Learning Styles

Artistic Learners
Have students draw and label a table setting, then write a description.

Kinesthetic Learners
Bring in plastic cutlery, paper plates and napkins, and plastic cups, and have students ask and tell one another where to put the objects for a place setting. **"Où est-ce que je mets la fourchette ?" "Mets-la à gauche de l'assiette."**

Answers

14

1. Tu m'attends après les cours?
2. Tu comprends bien la chimie?
3. Tu as vu la prof en ville vendredi soir?
4. Tu as mis la table hier soir?
5. Tu appelles ton ami(e) le soir?
6. Tu sais les noms de tous les États américains?
7. Tu vas acheter des tennis ce weekend?
8. Tu nous invites à ta soirée?
9. Tu écoutes toujours ta mère?

Partner answers will vary.

15

1. Yasmine l'a appelée à neuf heures moins cinq.
2. Bruno et toi, vous l'avez appelée à huit heures trente-deux et à midi.
3. Yasmine l'a appelé à dix-sept heures trente.
4. Manon l'a appelée à sept heures.
5. Nous l'avons appelée à neuf heures et à neuf heures huit.
6. Yasmine les a appelés à neuf heures moins cinq et à onze heures onze.
7. Je l'ai appelée à neuf heures.
8. Bruno l'a appelée à midi.

Reference Desk

Before students complete **Activité 15**, make sure they understand the *X* indicates Yasmine called that person and the *T* indicates who made a call to her.

14 On joue au morpion 1.1, 5.2

Interpersonal Speaking

Faites une grille comme celle de droite. À tour de rôle, posez des questions à votre partenaire. Il ou elle va répondre avec une phrase qui emploie un pronom complément d'objet direct. Essayez de gagner le jeu.

Attention au temps des verbes!

MODÈLE **A: Tu m'attends après les cours?**
B: Non, je ne t'attends pas.

m'attendre après les cours	bien comprendre la chimie	voir la prof en ville vendredi soir
mettre la table hier soir	appeler ton ami(e) le soir	savoir les noms de tous les États américains
aller acheter des tennis ce weekend	nous inviter à ta soirée	écouter toujours ta mère

15 Oui? 1.1

Interpersonal Speaking

Dites qui Yasmine a appelé (X) et qui l'a appelée (T), et à quelle heure.

MODÈLE Noah
Noah l'a appelée à neuf heures huit.

1. Simone
2. Bruno et toi
3. Thomas
4. Manon
5. Noah et moi
6. Khaled et Simone
7. moi
8. Bruno

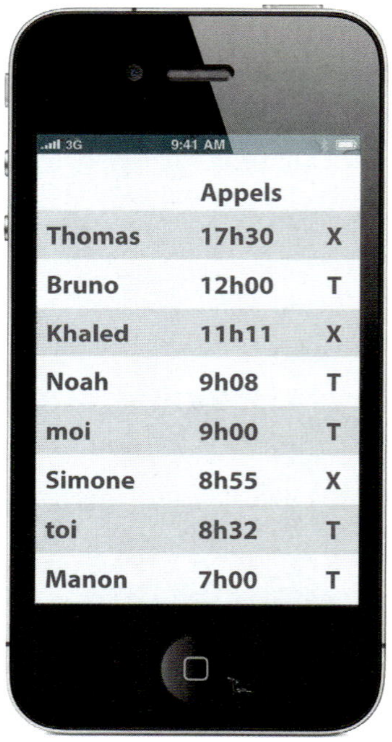

Essential Instruction

1. Play a quick game of Tic-Tac-Toe on the board to review the rules. Pair up students and have them take turns asking questions. The other student responds with a sentence that uses a direct object pronoun.
2. Do **Activité 15** as a class to ensure students understand the symbols on the phone.
3. You may want students to select an activity of their choice. Students who can follow instructions online may like to do **Activité 16**. **Activité 17** may be fun for students who really enjoy culture. Students with strong interpersonal skills may enjoy **Activité 18** the most.

À vous la parole

Question centrale ? Qu'y a-t-il d'universel dans les rapports entre les gens?

Communiquez!

16 Une carte de vœux 1.3, 2.2, 5.2

Presentational Writing

Envoyez une carte de vœux par Internet à un(e) ami(e) ou parent francophone, à l'occasion d'une fête qui approche. Écrivez un message. Envoyez la carte en suivant les instructions du site web choisi.

Recherche : dromadaire, cybercartes, cartes de vœux virtuelles, jolies cartes

17 Festivités 1.2, 1.3, 2.2, 3.2, 5.1

Interpretive Listening, Presentational Speaking

Organisez une petite fête en classe. Invitez vos camarades et transformez la salle de classe en « maison ». Rangez les manteaux de vos invités, emmenez-les au salon, servez-leur des apéritifs et passez un agréable quart d'heure à parler français avec eux. Préparez des sujets de conversations.

18 Repas de Noël 1.3, 2.2, 5.2

Presentational Writing

Imaginez que vous allez préparer un repas de Noël pour votre famille d'accueil française. Honorez leurs traditions en choisissant quelques plats français et un ou deux plats ou accompagnements de votre culture que vous mangez chez vous traditionnellement à Noël. Pensez aux hors-d'œuvre, aux plats principaux et aux desserts. N'oubliez pas les boissons ! Vous pouvez faire des recherches sur Internet pour vous aider. Présentez votre menu à la classe. Bon appétit !

Recherche : menu de noël, recettes de noël

19 Venez à la fête ! 1.1, 1.3, 2.1, 5.2

Interpersonal Speaking

Avec un partenaire, jouez les rôles d'un hôte ou d'une hôtesse qui reçoit des amis chez eux pour célébrer la Saint-Sylvestre. Donnez des détails sur la fête (ce que les invités doivent apporter, le thème de la soirée, etc.).

Resources

CA Communicative Activities

Share

Answers

16 Cards will vary.

17 Activities will vary.

18 Menus will vary.

19 Role-plays will vary.

Reference Desk

If you have access to Passport, create a question for your students to share their response to a communicative activity.

Communication

Interpersonal: Paired Practice

Write student names on the board, for example: (1) **la prof d'histoire** (2) **Johnny** (3) **moi** (4) **Lachante et Meshe**. Students ask their partner if they saw these people over the weekend: **Est-ce que tu as vu Johnny au match de foot samedi?** The other student responds: **Non, je ne l'ai pas vu.** Finally, have each pair take turns writing down their dialogues to check for correct agreement in the **passé composé**.

Expansion

Arrange students into groups, have them form circles, and then have them prepare a suitcase to travel to Africa. One student chooses an object (clothing item, toiletry, etc.) that starts with the letter A. The second player must repeat the object, and add another that starts with the letter B, and so on, repeating each time the previous objects When a student cannot repeat all previous objects, he or she is eliminated. The winner is the student who can repeat the most words.

Differentiated Learning

Accelerate

Challenge students to make up their own tic-tac-toe game to encourage them to further practice direct object pronouns.

Decelerate

Before students do **Activité 14**, tell them there will be one question in the near future, two in the **passé composé**, and six to eight in the present.

Learning Styles

Kinesthetic Learners

Draw stick figure cartoons on the board and caption them with direct object pronouns. "**Marc cherche Marie. Il la voit et l'invite au café. Il achète des fleurs et il les donne à Marie.**" Recycle the exercise (at a later date) by writing the captions in the past and near future as well and return to them when you review indirect object pronouns. Students can also make stick figures with popsicle sticks and paper "heads" and role-play by matching the sticks to the phrases on the board or identifying the actions out loud.

Resources

Prononciation
Pre-test
Leçon Quiz

Answers

D Script

1. aujourd'hui
2. Louis IX
3. Suis-moi !
4. Tu aimes les kiwis ?
5. le 14 juillet
6. Depuis quand ?

1. /ɥ/
2. /w/
3. /ɥ/
4. /w/
5. /ɥ/
6. /ɥ/

Reference Desk

1. The symbols used to express sounds come from the International Phonetic Alphabet.
2. In this section, stressed letters have been bolded and underlined (for example, **e**, **s**, **l**, or **t**). Unpronounced letters have been grayed out and underlined (for example, e, s, l, or t).

Expansion

To practice the loss of accentuation in a response after a question, have students give an answer to these questions: (1) **Tu pourrais me donner un coup de main ? (Te donner un coup de main ? Avec plaisir !)** (2) **Tu pourrais me passer le chinois ? (Te passer le chinois ? Avec plaisir !)** (3) **Tu pourrais ouvrir cette boîte ? (Ouvrir cette boîte ? Avec plaisir !)**

Prononciation

Accentuation within a Sentence 1.1

» Within a group of words, only the last word is accentuated, with the last vowel slightly longer than the others. This is called the "tonic accent" or **accent tonique**.

MODÈLES Je suis fatigu**é**.
Je suis fatigu**é** d'attendre mon am**i**.

A Une invitation pour le réveillon

Répétez les phrases en faisant attention aux voyelles accentuées.

1. Voilà l'invita**tion** que je pro**pos**e. (2 exemples)
2. Comme tu **voi**s, c'est tout **simpl**e. (2 exemples)
3. On va l'envo**yer** par Inter**net**. (2 exemples)
4. Je peux en faire une **autr**e pour le me**nu**, si tu **veu**x. (3 exemples)
5. Pas du **tou**t, la même serait très **bien**, à mon a**vi**s. (3 exemples)

B Des dialogues dans la cuisine

Vous allez entendre les dialogues suivants deux fois. La deuxième fois, vous entendrez uniquement la question. Répondez.

1. Tu pour**rai**s me donner un coup de **main** ? — Te donner un coup de **main** ? Avec plai**sir** !
2. Tu pour**rai**s me passer le poi**vr**e ? — Te passer le poiv**r**e ? Avec plai**sir** !
3. Tu pour**rai**s ouvrir cette **boît**e ? — Ouvrir cette **boît**e ? Avec plai**sir** !

The Semi-Consonants /ɥ/ et /w/

» The sound /w/ appears in the word **oui**. The sound /ɥ/ appears in the word **nuit**.

C Louis, demande-lui !

Répétez les phrases en faisant attention aux sons /w/ (oui) dans la première phrase et /ɥ/ (nuit) dans la deuxième phrase.

1. Louis et Louise sont ici ? Ah oui !
2. Lui, il a fui dans la nuit.

D Écoutons les sons /ɥ/ et /w/

Écrivez /w/ si vous entendez un son comme dans ***oui****, et /ɥ/ si vous entendez un son comme dans* ***nuit****.*

Essential Instruction

1. Have students create more examples like the first model, **"Je suis fatigué."** Circulate, correcting any models with errors and discussing with students where they have made a mistake.
2. Model the first sentence in **Activité B** with a student volunteer, and then put students in pairs to practice all three sentences.
3. Replay the audio for **Activité D** as often as is needed.
4. Use manipulatives to introduce the vocabulary on p. 91.

Leçon B Vocabulaire actif

Les dimensions (f.) et les formes (f.) 1.2

Les formes

C'est un machin....

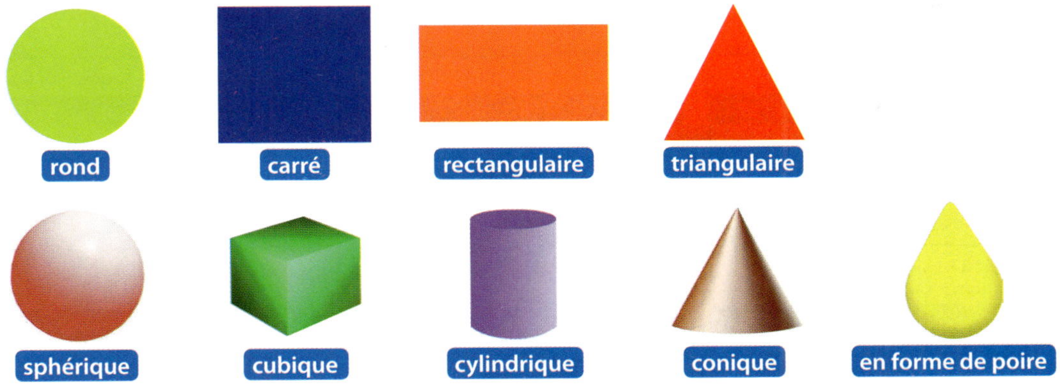

Les dimensions

C'est...

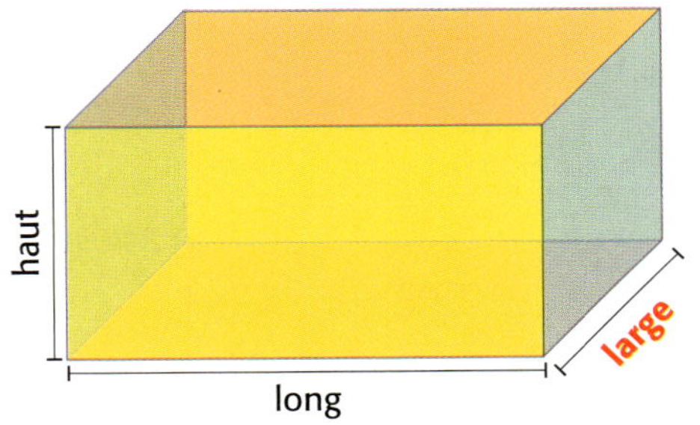

Les matières (f.)

C'est....

en plastique

en métal

en bois

en tissu

Resources

- *Vocabulaire actif*
- eV eVisual
- WB Workbook 1–4
- FC Flash Cards
- LA Listening Activities 1–2
- G & V Practice Games

Reference Desk

1. A synonym for **un machin** is **un truc** or **une chose**.
2. You may want to ask students to make a list in French of all the objects they can think of that have each shape. Collect the lists and then ask the class **la forme** of several objects from the list.
3. Encourage students to have fun writing a short dialogue in which they exaggerate the height, length, or width of an object or animal—for example, a fish they caught, a snake they saw, a birdhouse they built, or a sandwich they made.
4. Point out that **large** is a false cognate, or **faux ami**, because it means *wide*, not *large*.

Learning Styles

Kinesthetic Learners

While doing **Activité A**, have students tap or clap the syllables, with the last syllable tapped more emphatically as they say the words.

Artistic Learners

Have students play Pictionary with the shapes. One student draws the shape and the others shout out the name in French. The first team to correctly draw and identify each shape wins.

Special Needs Students

Auditory Impairment

Before listening to **Activité D** as a class, eliminate extraneous noise by closing the door to help hearing-impaired students concentrate and focus on the recorded activity. If possible, supply these students with earphones.

Resources

Pour la conversation

Et si je voulais dire... ?

Reference Desk

1. The kitchen items students need to know are illustrated.
2. The verbs to use with these utensils are boxed.
3. Additional kitchen verbs include **faire cuire** *(to cook)*; **faire chauffer** *(to heat)*; **faire griller** *(to grill)*; **faire bouillir** *(to boil)*; **racler une carotte** *(to peel a carrot)*; **peler une pomme** *(to peel an apple)*; **verser** *(to pour)*; and **ajouter** *(to add)*.
4. **Un coup** in **Pour la conversation** is used idiomatically in many French expressions. Here are a few to share with students: **avoir un coup de chance** *(to have a bit of luck)*; **avoir un coup de pompe** *(to feel tired suddenly)*; **boire un coup** *(to have a drink)*; **donner un coup de pied** *(to kick)*; **être dans le coup** *(to be in on it)*; **jeter un coup d'œil** *(to glance)*; **sur un coup de tête** *(to do something impulsively)*; **un coup de foudre** *(love at first sight* [literally *lightning strike*]); **un coup de téléphone** *(a phone call)*.
5. Point out the irregular pronunciation of **la poêle**, which is pronounced like the word **poil**.

Communication

Interpersonal: Paired Practice

To use the **Pour la conversation** vocabulary, put students in pairs to prepare a dialogue. Student A asks for help with something. Student B accepts; refuses (giving a reason); or hesitates (asking for more information). Together, the pair determines a time and place to meet if Student B ultimately accepts.

Lexique des ustensiles (m.) de cuisine

la casserole

Ça sert à chauffer la soupe.

le chinois

Ça sert à **filtrer les herbes** (f.).

la cuillère en bois

Ça sert à **remuer** la sauce.

la cuillère à mesurer

Ça sert à **mesurer** les petites quantités.

le mixeur

Ça sert à **mélanger** les ingrédients.

la passoire

Ça sert à filtrer l'eau.

la poêle

Ça sert à **cuire** les steaks.

la spatule

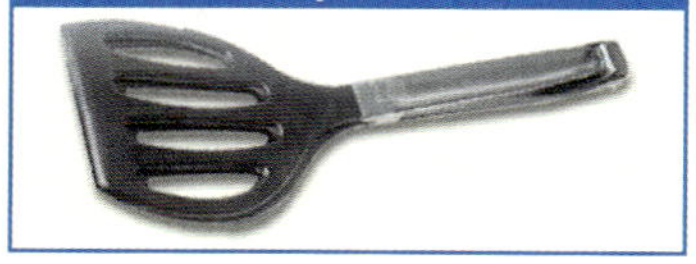

Ça sert à **racler** la sauce.

le verre mesureur

Ça sert à mesurer les grandes quantités.

Pour la conversation 1.2

How do I ask for help?

» Tu pourrais me donner **un coup de main**?
Could you give me a hand?

How do I accept a request for help?

» Avec plaisir.
With pleasure.

How do I respond negatively?

» **Je crains que non.**
I'm afraid not.

How do I hesitate in responding to a request for help?

» **Ça dépend.**
That depends.

How do I ask someone to pass me something?

» Tu peux me passer la passoire?
Can you pass me the colander?

Et si je voulais dire... ?

un autocuiseur	*pressure cooker*
un moule	*baking pan*
un rouleau à pâtisserie	*rolling pin*
griller	*to grill*
refroidir	*to chill*
rôtir	*to roast*

Essential Instruction

1. Have the students listen to the audio recording of the new vocabulary words and expressions, while you hold up each item that you have brought from home.
2. Put all kitchen objects on a table. Have students stand around the table. Ask them to pass the utensils to you: **Ariane, tu peux me passer une cuillère à mesurer?** Alternatively, have students close their eyes while you remove an item from the table. Then ask the class, "**Qu'est-ce qui manque?**"
3. Have students read **Activité 1** silently at their desks.
4. Students can work on **Activité 2** in pairs.

1 On fait un gâteau 1.2, 2.1, 5.2

Interpretive Reading

Pour son club de scouts, Amélie doit trouver les objets suivants dans la cuisine. Faites une liste des ustensiles. Puis, devinez ce qu'elle va préparer.

Trouvez d'abord six fruits rouges dans votre frigo. Coupez-les. Faites fondre (*melt*) cinq grammes de beurre dans *un machin rond qui sert à chauffer*. Ajoutez les fruits. Faites cuire pendant dix minutes en remuant de temps en temps avec *un objet long en bois*. Pour faire la pâte (*crust*), mettez 300 grammes de farine (*flour*) dans *un machin conique en métal*; avec *un machin en forme d'une grande tasse*, ajoutez 50 grammes de sucre. Ajoutez 150 grammes de beurre. Mettez la vanille dans *un objet qui sert à mesurer les petites quantités* et ajoutez. Vous aurez besoin d'*un objet rond et large en plastique* pour verser les fruits une fois rincés. Mettez les fruits sur la pâte. Faites cuire au four à 180°C pendant 35 minutes.

2 Donnez-moi.... 1.3

Presentational Speaking or Writing

Demandez l'objet illustré.

MODÈLE  **Donnez-moi le machin cubique en plastique!**

1. 

2. 

3. 

4. 

5. 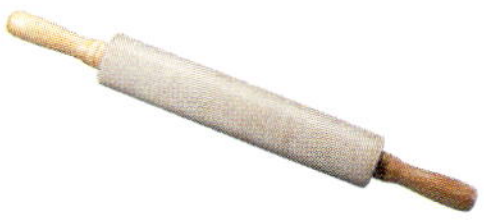

6. 

7. 

Differentiated Learning

Accelerate

Ask students to find and label images that show their understanding of the **Et si je voulais dire...?** vocabulary words.

Expand

Ask students to think of other objects with these shapes and bring them into class the next day. For additional practice, students can do **Activité 2** again, but using the new objects, such as ones in the classroom or in school in general.

Learning Styles

Auditory/Kinesthetic Learners

Allow students to come up to the front of the class and select the kitchen objects that you name. You might ask them also to use gestures to show their understanding of the verbs in the box on the vocabulary presentation page, for example, "**Faites chauffer la soupe.**"

Resources

Activity 1

Answers

1

Ustensiles: une poêle, une cuillère en bois, un chinois, un verre mesureur, une cuillère à mesurer, une passoire; Elle va préparer une tarte.

2

1. Donnez-moi le machin rectangulaire en plastique!
2. Donnez-moi le machin cylindrique en bois!
3. Donnez-moi le machin carré en papier!
4. Donnez-moi le machin conique en plastique!
5. Donnez-moi le machin long et rond en bois!
6. Donnez-moi le machin cubique en plastique!
7. Donnez-moi le machin sphérique en plastique!

Expansion

1. Show a picture of Julia Child's famous kitchen wall rack of pots, pans, and utensils. Have students identify the items of her **batterie de cuisine**.
2. Show clips from the film *Julie & Julia* when the Cordon Bleu teacher chef does demonstrations (chopping carrots), when Julie and fellow students whip cream in copper bowls, or when Julia and Simka go shopping in a cooking supply store. Discuss the items and gestures.

TPR

1. Once the students have understood the text for **Activité 1** and found the answers, read the text aloud slowly as they act out the steps of cooking the pie.
2. Play some clips from the animated movie *Ratatouille* (with sound muted) that show Rémy manipulating the cooking gestures of Linguini. Have students express the cooking gestures/steps in French. Many scenes from this movie can be used to practice cooking terms, utensil vocabulary, and gestures.

Answers

3 Possible answers:

1. Passe-moi l'objet en soie.
2. Passe-moi l'objet en bois.
3. Passe-moi l'objet en plastique.
4. Passe-moi l'objet en laine.
5. Passe-moi l'objet en plastique et en coton.
6. Passe-moi l'objet en métal.

4

1. C'est une poêle. Ça sert à cuire les steaks.
2. C'est une casserole. Ça sert à chauffer la sauce.
3. C'est une passoire. Ça sert à rincer les légumes.
4. C'est une spatule. Ça sert à racler la sauce.
5. C'est un verre mesureur. Ça sert à mesurer les liquides.
6. C'est un mixeur. Ça sert à mélanger les ingrédients.

Reference Desk

Students learned **en velours**, **en coton**, **en soie**, and **en laine** in **Unité 6C** on p. 339 of the Level 2 textbook, and table vocabulary (**le verre**, **la tasse**, etc.) on p. 353 of the Level 1 textbook. You may want to review these vocabulary words with students before they complete **Activité 3**.

Games

À l'aveuglette

Put a kitchen object or another object students know the name for in a pillowcase. Ask for a student volunteer who will reach in and feel for the object. He/she will describe it first, then identify it. For example, "**C'est conique, petit, et en métal. C'est un chinois.**" Repeat until you have reviewed all the kitchen utensils introduced in this lesson.

Bingo

Find 30 images of common items that students can describe with the vocabulary they have learned. Create sets of four bingo cards using only 25 of the 30 images each time, making sure each card shows the images in a different order, and not all showing the exact same images. Make sure there is a free space on the cards.

3 Passez-moi l'objet.... 1.3, 5.2

Presentational Speaking or Writing

Demandez qu'on vous passe l'objet en décrivant de quoi il est fait.

bois velours métal coton plastique soie laine

MODÈLE  **Passe-moi l'objet en velours.**

1. 
2. 
3. 
4. 
5. 
6. 

4 Ça sert à quoi? 1.1, 1.2

Interpretive Reading and Viewing, Presentational Speaking

Identifiez l'ustensile et dites à quoi ça sert.

mélanger les ingrédients chauffer la sauce cuire les steaks mesurer les liquides remuer les ingrédients rincer les légumes racler la sauce

MODÈLE  **C'est une cuillère en bois. Ça sert à remuer les ingrédients.**

1. 
2. 
3. 
4. 
5. 
6. 

On recycle!

Do you remember the vocabulary for describing a table setting? Draw an image, or find one that you like. Exchange your image with a partner; each of you will describe the other's image. You may comment on whether or not you like your partner's setting, giving details.

Essential Instruction

1. Do **Activité 3** as a class; bring other objects from home for students to describe. Call on students at random as this activity is quite easy.
2. Ask for student volunteers to show and explain the use of each item in **Activité 4**. If you have brought these objects to class, have the student hold the object while responding in front of the class.
3. Have students listen to the audio recording to complete **Activité 5**. You may want to ask students to shout out the correct answer.
4. If you prefer, call on students to answer the questions in **Activité 6** rather than having student pairs communicate. If students are still acquiring the vocabulary, have them write out some of the answers before asking them to answer aloud.

5 À quoi ça sert? 1.2

Interpretive Listening

Écrivez les numéros 1–6 sur votre papier. Écoutez les descriptions suivantes. Ensuite, choisissez l'objet qui correspond à la définition.

A. le chinois
B. le mixeur
C. la spatule
D. la passoire
E. la casserole
F. le verre mesureur

6 Questions personnelles 1.1, 5.1

Répondez aux questions avec un partenaire.

1. De quels ustensiles est-ce que tu te sers pour préparer ton plat préféré? C'est quoi?
2. Quand tu fais la cuisine, est-ce que tu te sers d'un verre mesureur ou est-ce que tu préfères deviner combien d'ingrédients il faut ajouter (*add*)?
3. En quoi est ton verre mesureur—en plastique ou en verre?
4. À qui est-ce que tu donnes un coup de main dans la cuisine en général?
5. En quelles matières préfères-tu les couverts (assiettes, verres, fourchettes et couteaux) et pourquoi? Et les casseroles?

Quels ustensiles de cuisine y a-t-il dans la cuisine de Patrick et son père?

1.2, 2.1

Perspectives

Moi, je ne me sers plus de casseroles en aluminium, car au bout d'un certain temps ce métal peut se diffuser et être toxique pour la santé.
—Gégé

Pourquoi le métal des ustensiles de cuisine est-il important pour cette femme? Qu'en pensez-vous? En quels métaux sont faites vos poêles et vos casseroles?

Resources

Activity 5

Answers

5 Script

1. C'est un machin en métal ou plastique. Ça sert à passer l'eau des spaghetti.
2. C'est un ustensile souvent en métal. Ça sert à filtrer les herbes.
3. C'est un machin souvent en verre. Ça sert à mesurer le sucre.
4. C'est un ustensile en bois et plastique. Ça sert à racler toute la sauce.
5. C'est une petite machine en métal et verre. Ça sert à mélanger les ingrédients.
6. C'est un machin en métal. Ça sert à faire chauffer la soupe.

1. D
2. A
3. F
4. C
5. B
6. E

6 Answers will vary.

Perspectives

Elle se préoccupe de la toxicité de certains métaux dans les ustensiles de cuisine.; Opinions will vary.

Reference Desk

Other metals for cookware may include **l'acier** (*steel*), **le cuivre** (*copper*), and **le fer** (*iron*).

Culture

Products: Information

Kitchens in traditional French homes built before the start of this century will generally be smaller and less thoroughly equipped than kitchens in the United States, due mostly to the fact that homes are generally smaller in France and that more space is given to entertainment and living areas. Most of these homes will have formal dining rooms. The open floor plan that combines the kitchen with a den, living room, or dining room, separating them only by a counter, has grown in popularity in French architecture and is referred to as a "**cuisine américaine**."

Differentiated Learning

Expand

Divide the class into three groups. Have students in Group A search online for the menus of the top restaurants in Paris. They will select a restaurant, and choose three **entrées**, three **plats principaux**, and three **desserts**, which they will transfer to a menu that they have decorated. Students in Group B will search online for menus of the top **brasseries** in Paris. They will select a restaurant and choose three **entrées**, three **plats principaux**, and three **desserts**, which they will transfer to a menu that they have decorated. Students in Group C will visit the websites of the three top pastry stores in Paris. On poster board, they will make an advertisement for a shop of their choosing, labeling selected photos of pastries. Have groups display their final products.

Recherche: pierre hermé, café lenôtre, gérard mulot

Resources

- Dialogue
  - Activity 7
  - Extension
- Dialogue Video
- WB Workbook 5

Answers

7

1. le père de Léo
2. le père de Léo
3. Léo
4. le père de Léo
5. la mère de Léo

EXTENSION

Il a besoin d'un ouvre-boîte. La cuisine n'est pas moderne.

Reference Desk

1. Ask students to scan the dialogue to find the French equivalents of these words and expressions: (1) That smells good; (2) ruin the sauce; (3) I'm going then...; (4) Can you give me a hand?; (5) Here (it is); (6) Nothing's ever where it should be; (7) I put it there to help you proceed.
2. Vocabulary expressions that students may not know in the **Extension** dialogue include: **une molette** (*cutting wheel*); **mord(re)** (*cuts into, to cut into*); **un ouvre-boîte** (*can opener*); **le Moyen Âge** (*Middle Ages*).

nouvelle orthographe: **le diner, ces boites, un ouvre-boite**

Culture

Products: Information

Have students work in pairs to figure out what each proverb means: **Trop de cuisiniers gâtent la sauce./Il faut manger pour vivre, et non pas vivre pour manger./Après grand banquet petit pain./L'appétit vient en mangeant.**

Rencontres culturelles

On fait la cuisine 1.2, 5.2

Le père d'Élodie et de Léo prépare le dîner avec l'aide de son fils.

Léo : Hum... ça sent bon ici !
Père : Bon ben, pas touche... tu vas me faire rater la sauce.
Léo : Ah bon, eh bien, je m'en vais alors....
Père : Non, non, reste là... tu pourrais me donner un coup de main ?
Léo : Mais avec plaisir.
Père : Tu peux me passer la passoire ?
Léo : Tiens !
Père : Non, ce n'est pas ça.
Léo : C'est quoi alors ?
Père : Tu sais bien, elle est ronde et conique, un peu plus étroite que celle-là, en métal et haute* comme ça. Ça sert à filtrer les herbes.
Léo : Il n'y a rien qui ressemble à ça....
Père : Mais si. Tu vois bien ce que je veux dire.... Oh, ça s'appelle comment déjà ?

(La mère de Léo entre dans la cuisine.)

Mère : Un chinois ! Il est devant toi... posé sur la casserole dans laquelle tu vas verser la sauce.
Père : Toujours la même chose : rien n'est jamais à sa place.
Mère : Moi qui l'avais posé là pour t'avancer....

***Je parle bien !**

In French, the letter *h* is usually not pronounced. The word **haute** is pronounced somewhat like the English word *oat*.

7 On fait la cuisine 1.2

Identifiez la personne.

1. Cette personne fait la cuisine.
2. Cette personne a besoin d'un chinois.
3. Cette personne a du mal à trouver un ustensile.
4. Cette personne décrit l'ustensile.
5. Cette personne a voulu avancer la préparation du repas.

EXTENSION **Leïla rend un service à son frère** 1.2

Leïla et son frère Khaled sont dans la kitchenette.

Khaled : Tu pourrais me donner un coup de main ? Il faut juste que tu ouvres ces boîtes.
Leïla : Oui, comment ?
Khaled : Avec un... j'oublie le nom. C'est un machin en métal, avec deux poignées recouvertes de plastique blanc, une petite molette avec des dents qui mord le métal.
Leïla : Il faut acheter un ouvre-boîte électrique pour Maman pour Noël. C'est le Moyen Âge ici !

EXTENSION De quoi est-ce que Khaled a besoin ? Comment est la cuisine de sa mère ? 1.1, 1.2

Essential Instruction

1. Do the first activity in **Reference Desk** with the class.
2. Show the filmed dialogue.
3. Check comprehension by doing **Activité 7**.
4. Have students read the culture reading silently, and then ask easy comprehension questions.
5. Guide students to interpret the graphs on pp. 97–98 and summarize the main point of each in one sentence. The graph for **La cuisine française** reveals that the French spent much less time eating in 2018 than they did in 1990, and that lunch has seen the most dramatic decrease in the time. The graph for **Jambon-beurre** reveals that the cost of a ham baguette sandwich in smaller, less expensive towns has caught up to the cost in larger, more expensive towns. Ask students what this might indicate (a homogenization of the French economy).

Points de départ

Pre-AP | Question centrale ? Qu'y a-t-il d'universel dans les rapports entre les gens?

La cuisine française 1.2, 2.1, 3.2

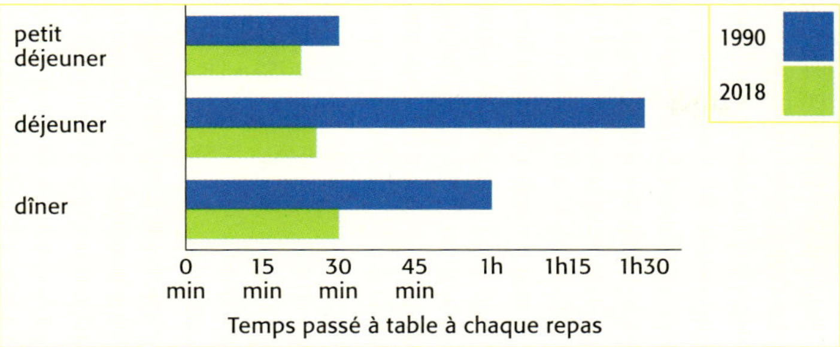

Cuisine au wok

Aujourd'hui les Français consacrent* moins de temps et d'argent pour se nourrir. Les femmes préparent le plus souvent les repas, mais les hommes participent de plus en plus. Traditionnellement les Français prenaient trois repas par jour: le petit déjeuner, le déjeuner et le dîner, mais la pratique du grignotage* et du nomadisme (on mange où l'on se trouve: restaurant d'entreprise, lieu de restauration rapide type McDo ou multiples sandwicheries) modifie considérablement ce rituel. Les composants* des repas restent les mêmes: la viande, le poisson, la volaille, le fromage, les yaourts, les fruits, et le pain. La cuisine a beaucoup changé: on ne cuisine plus, on assemble avec des sauces et des assaisonnements souvent pré-cuisinés, pour une cuisine rapide, mais aussi diététique* (légumes cuits à la vapeur*, salades composées sucrées–salées, salades de fruits au lieu des desserts traditionnels).

Se développe également la cuisine du plat unique, avec une influence italienne (la pizza), espagnole (la paella), maghrébine (couscous) ou asiatique (cuisine au wok).

Ce qui domine dans la pratique gastronomique des Français, c'est une grande liberté: on mélange les ingrédients d'origines différentes, on détourne* les techniques de cuisson venues d'ailleurs, on associe des genres culinaires variés. La cuisine est devenue ludique*, mais c'est aussi une pratique multiculturelle qui traduit un esprit d'accueil et d'ouverture.

Recherche: recettes de cuisine, plats diététiques, cuisine française

consacrent *spend*; **grignotage** *snacking*; **composants** *components*; **diététique** *healthy*; **à la vapeur** *steamed*; **détourne** *tweak*; **ludique** *playful*

Perspectives

1.2, 2.1

Chez nous, on prend le repas du soir entre 19h30 et 20h30.
—Raikou4

Selon vous, est-ce que cette personne dîne tôt ou tard? Comparez avec votre famille et vos amis.

Mot-clé

Cuisine vient du bas-latin: *cocina*, 1155. Dès son origine, il a le sens du lieu où l'on cuisine et l'art de cuisiner. Il désigne surtout un espace spécifique dans les milieux nobles et bourgeois; il est inconnu du monde paysan et ouvrier jusqu'à la fin du 19ème siècle.

Comparaisons

1.2, 4.2

Dans votre famille, est-ce que vos repas sont plus souvent assemblés, ou est-ce que vous prenez le temps de cuisiner? Qu'est-ce que vous mangez qui n'est pas considéré «américain»?

Resources

Points de départ
WB Workbook 6
Explore

Answers

Comparaisons
Answers will vary.

Reference Desk

1. The eating habits of the French have changed radically in the last twenty years. McDonald's, called **McDo**, has 1,200 restaurants in France. It is interesting to note that the French McDonald's is considered more healthy and offers different choices than that of the American McDonald's.
2. The supermarket chain **Carrefour** sells fresh and frozen food, paper goods, clothing, makeup, in short, everything you would find in an American big box store chain, similar to Target in the United States. Most supermarkets are not open on Sunday, with a few exceptions such as the three Sundays preceding Christmas.
3. Outside markets are very popular on the weekends. However, despite changes to traditional shopping imposed by households with two working partners short on time, every day you still hear "**Il faut aller chercher du pain chez le boulanger.**"
4. If you have access to Passport, find a video or a news article related to **la cuisine** and show it to your students.

Communication

Interpersonal: Paired Practice

Ask students to find out from their parents or guardians the percentage of the household budget that is spent on food and the time taken by the cook in the family to prepare meals during the week. The next day, ask students to interview ten classmates to share and compare information collected. Have them tabulate the results and make a graph to show comparable U.S. results to the French graphs.

Answers

8 Activities will vary.

Perspectives
Possible answer: La cuisine doit avoir une personnalité, une intelligence propre.; Opinions will vary.

Reference Desk

1. The AP French Language and Culture Test asks students to write an essay interpreting a graphic image, an audio recording, and a written text. You may want to use the graphics on this page to work with students on how to change graphic text into words and to theorize on what the data reveals about cultural and economic trends.
2. Other food expressions include **C'est la cerise sur le gâteau! (Il ne manquait plus que ça!)** and **On ne fait pas d'omelette sans casser des œufs. (On ne passe pas à l'action sans faire des dégâts.)**

Culture

Information

Le Cordon Bleu, a cooking school opened in Paris in 1895, has since grown into the largest and most prestigious culinary school in the world, with 35 campuses in 20 countries and more than 20,000 graduates of more than 100 nationalities every year. Students of the Cordon Bleu can earn their "**grand diplôme du Cordon Bleu**," an internationally recognized culinary certificate, in a little less than a year. The school also offers bachelors and masters degree programs.

Critical Thinking

Comparisons

Have students compare and contrast a French fast food restaurant with an American equivalent. Some ideas: **Flunch**, **Pizza del Arte**, **Brioche Dorée**, **Planétalis**, **Pomme de Pain**, **Restaumarché**.

Produits

L'indétrônable* «jambon-beurre»

La France est le seul pays au monde où le sandwich tient tête* au hamburger : le «jambon-beurre baguette» représente 51% des ventes en 2018. Ce sandwich est un marché de plus de 8 milliards* d'euros, il fait toutefois, depuis 2016, face à de plus en plus de concurrence avec notamment* le hamburger, le panini, et le bagel. À côté, les Français ont consommé 819 millions de pizzas et 310 millions de kebabs.

OÙ ACHETER SON JAMBON-BEURRE?

ÉVOLUTION DE L'INDICE JAMBON-BEURRE

SELON LA TAILLE DES AGGLOMÉRATIONS

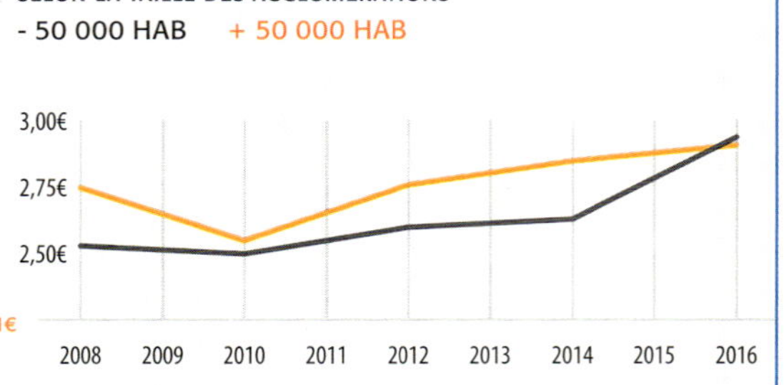

Recherche: le sandwich jambon-beurre, sandwichs préférés des français

indétrônable *undefeated*; **tient tête** fait compétition; **milliards** *billions*; **notamment** *notably*

1.2, 2.2

8 Activités culturelles 1.3, 2.1,2.2, 3.2

Faites les activités suivantes.

1. Dans un paragraphe, interprétez les graphiques aux pages 97 et 98. Donnez votre opinion.
2. Voici ce qui caractérise aujourd'hui la cuisine française ; illustrez chaque phrase par un exemple de repas.
   - On ne cuisine plus, on assemble.
   - On pratique le grignotage.
   - On fait une cuisine rapide.
   - On fait une cuisine avec un plat unique.
   - On mélange les ingrédients d'origines différentes.
3. Cherchez différentes présentations du sandwich jambon-beurre chez divers marchands français.

Recherche: recette jambon-beurre (paris/mcdo/brioche dorée), les meilleurs jambon-beurre

4. Écrivez un dialogue qui emploie plusieurs expressions du dico gastronomique ; le dialogue doit avoir un sens logique.

1.2, 2.1

Perspectives

La cuisine, comme la vie, doit avoir de l'allure.
—Pierre Gagnaire

À votre avis, que veut dire ce chef français ? Quelle est votre opinion ?

Mon dico gastronomique

Il a mangé du lion. *Il a une énergie incroyable.*
Il s'est mis à table. *Il a avoué.*
Je ne suis pas dans mon assiette. *Je ne me sens pas bien.*
Ne me raconte pas de salades. *Dis la vérité/Sois franc(he).*

Essential Instruction

1. Ask students to read silently the text in the **Produits** box about **Le Jambon-Beurre**.
2. Discuss the two graphs, interpreting the data and inviting the students to identify what the data might reflect about broader trends in France.
3. Have students choose a cultural activity to do in **Activité 8** based on their interest.
4. Divide the class into three groups. Each one is responsible for presenting one of the main paragraphs in the **Du côté des médias** reading.
5. For a bit of fun, show a clip from *Julie and Julia* where Julia Child attempts to learn French cooking at the Cordon Bleu cooking school in Paris.

Recherche: meryl streep, new julie & julia clip, cooking class

6. Do **Activité 9** together as a class.

Du côté des médias 1.2

Lisez l'article du site du Cordon Bleu à Paris.

Le Cordon Bleu est fier de vous annoncer la sortie en France du film *Julie et Julia* inspiré de l'ouvrage du même nom.

Le livre, qui était à l'origine un blog, retrace l'histoire de Julie Powell, secrétaire trentenaire, qui décide de prendre une année sabbatique pour réaliser en 365 jours les 524 recettes du livre *Mastering the Art of French Cooking* de la célèbre chef américaine Julia Child, diplômée de l'école Le Cordon Bleu Paris en 1951.

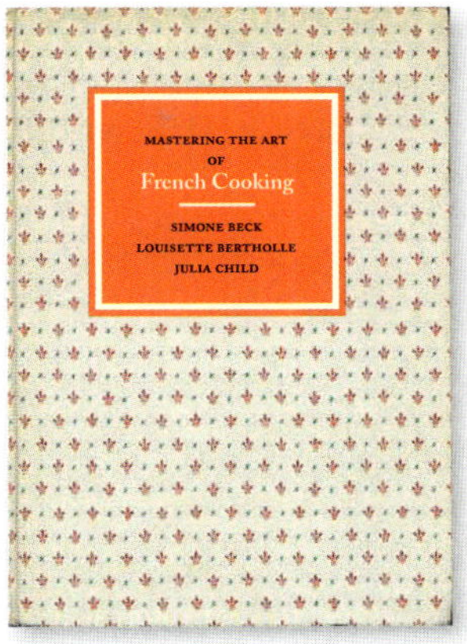

Julia Child a été l'une des premières femmes à mettre en valeur les techniques culinaires françaises enseignées à l'école Le Cordon Bleu Paris auprès du grand public américain à travers des émissions de télévision et de nombreux ouvrages. Julia Child a reçu la Légion d'Honneur en 2000 et la Médaille Présidentielle de la Liberté en 2003. Le projet de Julie Powell présente Julia Child comme un modèle à suivre pour les nouvelles générations de chefs et d'amateurs culinaires enthousiastes.

Devant le succès rencontré par le livre *Julie et Julia*, Columbia Pictures a produit le film avec en tête d'affiche, Meryl Streep dans le rôle de Julia Child, Amy Adams dans le rôle de Julie Powell et Stanley Tucci dans le rôle de Paul Child. Le succès du film aux États-Unis a permis au livre de Julia Child, *Mastering the Art of French Cooking,* de devenir un best-seller près de 50 ans après sa parution originale.

Produits

1.2, 2.2

De nombreux films autour de la cuisine ont eu du succès en France et dans le monde :
- *Le Sens de la fête* (2017, France), avec Jean-Pierre Bacri et Benjamin Lavernhe
- *The Lunchbox* (2013, Inde), avec Irrfan Khan et Nimrat Kaur
- *Ratatouille* (2007, États-Unis), animation, avec Patton Oswalt et Ian Holm
- *La Graine et le mulet* (2007, France), avec Habib Boufares et Hafsia Herzi
- *Super Size Me* (2004, États-Unis), avec Morgan Spurlock et Daryl Isaacs
- *Le Chocolat* (2000, Grande-Bretagne), avec Juliette Binoche et Alfred Molina
- *L'Aile ou la cuisse* (1976, France), avec Louis de Funès et Coluche

9 Le Cordon Bleu présente *Julie et Julia* 1.2, 1.3, 5.1

*Indiquez si chaque phrase est vraie (**V**) ou fausse (**F**). Corrigez les phrases fausses.*

1. *Julie et Julia* est d'abord un blog, puis un livre, finalement un film.
2. Le but de Julie est de préparer 250 recettes du livre de Julia Child.
3. Julia Child est connue seulement pour les recettes de ses livres.
4. Amy Adams joue le rôle de Julia Child dans le film.
5. *Mastering the Art of French Cooking* est redevenu un best-seller après la sortie du film.

Answers

9

1. V; 2. F; 524 recettes; 3. F; Julia Child est connue pour ses émissions de télévision et pour avoir été pionnière dans la présentation de la cuisine française aux États-Unis.; 4. F; Meryl Streep joue le rôle de Julia Child.; 5. V

Reference Desk

Julia Child's TV show **"The French Chef,"** along with her two-volume opus *Mastering the Art of French Cooking*, are credited with changing the way Americans relate to food. During her heyday, 96 US stations aired her TV show. She was awarded the prestigious Peabody Award in 1964 and an Emmy in 1966; in the 1970s and 1980s she made frequent appearances on *Good Morning America*. However, not everyone was a fan of Julia Child. Critics complained that she did not wash her hands enough and put too much fat in her dishes. Nevertheless, she launched or aided many a chef's career (including that of Jacques Pépin) and set the stage for a plethora of TV cooking shows to come. Julia Child would have turned 100 in 2012. Her original entire kitchen from her home in Cambridge, Mass., where her TV show was filmed, is now located at the Smithsonian in Washington, D.C.

Culture

Products: Activity

Students who like to cook can make several French dishes from Julia Child's recipes, such as French baguette or onion soup, for all to taste. (Remember to check for allergies.) It took almost a year "and 284 pounds of flour" for Julia Child to develop the master bread recipe made with American ingredients. These recipes are available online.

Differentiated Learning

Decelerate

Show an excerpt from the movie *Julie & Julia*, or a segment of Julia Child's TV show to help these students understand the realia reading.

Learning Styles

Auditory Learners

Students may like to participate in a French chef cooking contest. Film these students demonstrating a recipe for a French dish, and have their classmates devise the criteria for judging and then vote on the best "show."

Expansion

In groups or pairs, have students research other movies about food and gastronomy, as presented in the **Produits**. Ask each students to prepare a short synopsis, and present the movie to their group.

Resources

- Activity 10
- Workbook 7–9
- G & V Practice Games

Answers

On recycle!
Indirect object pronouns mean *to me*, *to you*, *to her*, *to him*, *to us*, and *to them*. Like direct object pronouns, indirect object pronouns are placed before the verb of which they are the object. Some verbs that take indirect object pronouns include **donner**, **parler**, **montrer**, **téléphoner**, and **ressembler à**.

10
1. Elle lui téléphone pour lui demander si elle est libre pour le réveillon de Noël.
2. Il propose de leur dire de venir chez eux.
3. Elle lui offre de faire les toasts.
4. Léo lui donne un coup de main.
5. Oui, elle lui montre où il se trouve.
6. Il lui répond que rien n'est jamais à sa place

Reference Desk

While **lui** means *to him* or *to her*, and **leur** means *to them*, in a sentence like **Je lui fais un gâteau** it means *for him* or *to her*. Indirect object pronouns are often used with verbs of communication, such as **proposer à**, **lire à**, **écrire à**, **téléphoner à**, **dire à**, and **parler à**. In English, the preposition *for* or *to* is often not used with indirect objects but is still understood: **Je lui ai écrit un message** (*I wrote her a message* or *I wrote a message to her*).

Structure de la langue

Révision: Indirect Object Pronouns: *me, te, lui, nous, vous, leur* 1.2

On recycle!
Do you remember how indirect object pronouns differ from direct object pronouns? Where are they placed in sentences? What are some verbs that take indirect object pronouns?

If you cannot answer the questions above, read the grammar summary below to review.

	Masculine or Feminine	Before a Vowel Sound
Singular	me	m'
	te	t'
	lui	lui
Plural	nous	nous
	vous	vous
	leur	leur

Indirect object pronouns come right before the verb of which they are the object.

Tu peux **lui** donner un coup de main? — *Can you give him/her a hand?*
Non, je ne **lui** donnerai pas un coup de main. — *No, I won't give him/her a hand.*
Leur offre-t-il un cadeau? — *Is he giving them a gift?*
Oui, il **leur** offre des machins en bois. — *Yes, he is giving them some things made of wood.*

Unlike direct objects, indirect objects do not agree in number and gender with the past participle in the **passé composé**.

Laure et Lise? Tu **leur** as téléphoné? — *Laure and Lise? Did you phone them?*
Lise, oui. Je **lui** ai téléphoné. — *Lise, yes. I phoned her.*

10 Invitation et préparatifs 1.2, 1.3

Interpretive Reading, Presentational Speaking or Writing

*Répondez aux questions sur les deux premiers dialogues en utilisant **lui** ou **leur**.*

1. Pourquoi est-ce que la mère d'Élodie et de Léo téléphone à Amélie Martin?
2. Qu'est-ce que le père propose de dire aux Martin?
3. Qu'est-ce qu'Amélie offre à son amie?
4. Qui donne un coup de main à son père dans la cuisine?
5. Est-ce que la mère montre à son mari où se trouve le chinois?
6. Que répond le père à la mère?

Essential Instruction

1. Before the students write out their answers for **Activité 10**, ask them to find the expressions beginning with **à** or **aux** which will be replaced by **lui** or **leur**. You may want them to write a paragraph using the answers to the questions. Remind students to add a title to their paragraph.
2. Review the kitchen utensils using the eVisuals.
3. You may want students to do **Activité 11** orally first, and then in writing.
4. On the board, draw a picture of a stick figure offering flowers to another stick figure. Write the following three sentences on the board and ask students to translate them:

Il donne les fleurs à la fille.
Il les donne à la fille.
Il lui donne les fleurs.

Then do a similar drawing, give the three sentences in English and have students translate into French.

11 Les cadeaux de mariage 1.3

Presentational Speaking or Writing

L'année dernière beaucoup d'amis et de couples qu'Isabelle connaît se sont mariés. Voici la liste des cadeaux qu'elle leur a offerts. Dites ce qu'elle a offert à chaque personne ou couple.

MODÈLE  Sabrina et Édouard
Isabelle leur a offert une passoire et un chinois.

1.  Olivier
2. 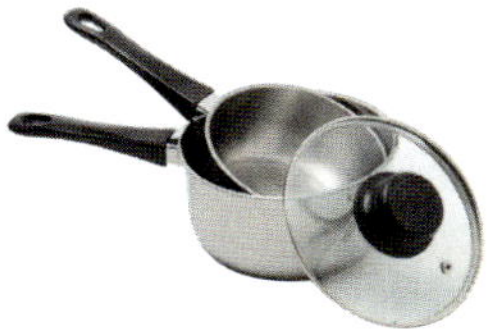 Fred et Julie
3.  Bruno et toi
4. 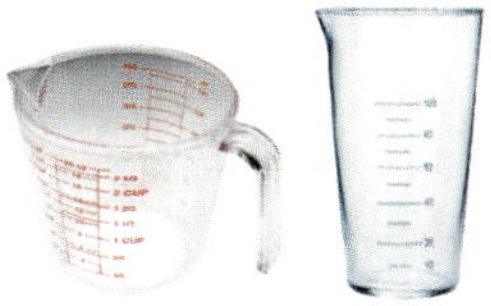 Assia
5.  Djamel et Leïla
6.  Mamadou et Lamina
7.  Éric et moi
8.  toi
9.  Chloé
10.  moi
11.  Jamila et Théo
12.  Abdel-Cader

Answers

11

1. Isabelle lui a offert un bol.
2. Isabelle leur a offert des casseroles.
3. Isabelle nous a offert des cuillères en bois.
4. Isabelle lui a offert des verres mesureurs.
5. Isabelle leur a offert des poêles.
6. Isabelle leur a offert des tasses.
7. Isabelle nous a offert des serviettes.
8. Isabelle t'a offert un mixeur.
9. Isabelle lui a offert des cuillères, des fourchettes, et des couteaux.
10. Isabelle m'a offert des assiettes.
11. Isabelle leur a offert une spatule.
12. Isabelle lui a offert des verres.

Reference Desk

As in the United States, French couples register wedding gifts they would like to receive by creating **une liste de mariage**, but this is a relatively new phenomenon. You may want students to do the culture activity below.

Culture

Products: Activity

Have students imagine they and their friends are 28 years old and couples are starting to marry. Have them find appropriate wedding gifts for five friends and make a list of what they would buy and what each gift would cost.

Recherche: fête du mariage, galeries lafayette, le catalogue cadeau, printemps maison, printemps chambre, printemps salon, printemps cuisine

Differentiated Learning

Expand

Have students extend their responses in **Activité 11** with **parce que**, giving a reason why the gift will be appreciated. Example: **Isabelle leur a offert une passoire et un chinois parce qu'ils adorent faire des pâtes.**

Accelerate

Ask these students to do **Activité 11** in the present tense. Remind students that **offrir** is conjugated similarly to **-er** verbs.

Resources

WB Workbook 10–11

G & V Practice Games

Answers

12

1. lui
2. leur
3. vous
4. te
5. m'
6. nous

On recycle!

C'est takes both a proper or modified noun. **Il/Elle est** is followed by an adjective or stress pronoun: **C'est ma cousine. Elle est intéressante et vraiment sympa. Comme c'est curieux!**

Reference Desk

In the activity **Les fêtes**, the first two sentences follow the pattern from the previous exercises. The students will look for **à** + PERSON and replace it with **lui** or **leur**. For the rest of the sentences, the students have to search for the clues that indicate the pronoun replacement. **Tu *nous* montres…** leads to **Je *vous* montre…**, for example. Before asking the students to complete this activity, do a few sample replacements of pronouns other than **lui** and **leur** to ensure their success.

Expansion

PQA (Personalized Questions and Answers)

Students will best understand when to use **c'est** or **il/elle** est based on repetition. They will begin to "hear" which is right. Engage the students in conversations about one another. **« Tu connais ce garçon ? » (« Oui, c'est Thomas. C'est un ami. ») « Il est gentil ? » (« Oui, il est très gentil. »)**

12 Les fêtes 1.2

Interpretive Reading

Complétez chaque dialogue avec un pronom objet indirect.

1. –Qu'est-ce que tu vas offrir à ta mère pour la fête des Mères?
   –Je vais… offrir un foulard en soie.
2. –Vous allez remercier vos grands-parents pour vos cadeaux de Noël?
   –Nous… avons déjà écrit.
3. –Tu nous montres tes photos de Noël?
   –Non, je ne… montre pas mes photos de Noël.
4. –C'est mon anniversaire dimanche.
   –Je… dis « bon anniversaire » alors.
5. –Qu'est-ce que ton père t'a envoyé de Québec pour ta fête?
   –Il… a envoyé un album québécois et un blouson en cuir.
6. –Vous allez… téléphoner pour nous dire quand aura lieu votre soirée?
   –Je peux vous dire maintenant même que c'est le 14 février.

Révision: C'est versus *il/elle est* 1.2

On recycle!

Would the sentences below be completed with **c'est**, **il est**, or **elle est**?

Voici Nathalie.
__________ ma cousine.
__________ intéressante et vraiment sympa.
Tu la connais? Comme __________ curieux!

If you cannot do the activity above, read the grammar summary below to review.

Both **c'est** and **il/elle est** can mean *it is* as well as *he/she is*. The expression that you use depends on what follows the verb **être**.

C'est Kenji Tanaka.
C'est un ado.
Il est japonais.
C'est un élève diligent?
Oui, c'est lui!

Essential Instruction

1. Complete **Activité 12** as a class.
2. The rule is very straightforward for **c'est** vs. **il/elle est**; still, students have difficulty internalizing it. To practice the concept, do a chain exercise. Put students in small groups. In each group, the first student introduces a teen: **C'est Marie. Elle est grande et sympa.** Marie will respond, **C'est moi?** The first person will respond, **Oui, c'est toi.** Then Marie will introduce a student using the same pattern, but different adjectives, until everyone in the group has had a turn. This activity also works as a whole-class activity.
3. Play the audio recording for **Activité 13** and discuss any errors students may make.
4. Students can do **Activité 14** in pairs.

C'est….

+ PROPER NOUN	**C'est** Christiane Rochefort?	*Is it Christiane Rochefort?*
+ MODIFIED NOUN	**C'est** un écrivain français.	*She's a French writer.*
+ STRESS PRONOUN	Oui, **c'est** elle.	*Yes, it is she.*
+ ADJECTIVE REFERRING TO PREVIOUS IDEA	Et son roman, **ce n'est pas** difficile.	*And her novel, it isn't difficult.*

Il/Elle est….

+ ADJECTIVE	**Il n'est pas** bon marché.	*It isn't cheap.*
+ PROFESSION	**Elle est** metteur en scène.	*She is a director.*
+ NATIONALITY	**Il est** sénégalais.	*He is Senegalese.*
+ RELIGION	**Il est** catholique.	*He is Catholic.*
+ PREVIOUSLY MENTIONED PERSON OR THING	Où est le magasin? **Il est** là-bas.	*Where is the store? It is over there.*

13 C'est qui? 1.2

Interpretive Listening

Écrivez les numéros 1–6 sur votre papier. Écoutez les descriptions. Puis, choisissez la personne décrite.

A. Natalie Portman
B. Marie NDiaye
C. Dany Boon
D. Mark Zuckerberg
E. Maître Gims
F. Natasha St-Pier

14 Des personnages historiques célèbres 1.2

Interpretive Reading

*Choisissez **C'**, **Il**, ou **Elle** pour compléter les descriptions de ces personnages historiques francophones. Puis, devinez à qui correspond chaque description en choisissant un nom ci-dessous.*

Mariama Bâ **Napoléon Bonaparte** **Toussaint Louverture**
Gustave Eiffel **Marie-Antoinette** **Jeanne d'Arc**

1. … est un chef militaire. … est haïtien. … est très important pour la révolution et l'abolition de l'esclavage.
2. … est un ingénieur français. … est le créateur de la tour Eiffel. … est aussi connu pour avoir construit la statue de la liberté.
3. … est une femme écrivain sénégalaise. … est elle qui a écrit *Une si longue lettre*. … est aussi militante.
4. … est militaire. … est le premier empereur de la France. … est puissant pendant le 19ème siècle.
5. … est une jeune femme courageuse. … est elle qui a combattu contre les Anglais pendant la guerre de Cent ans. … est morte brûlée à Rouen.
6. … est une reine de l'histoire de France. … était une belle femme riche… est morte pendant la Révolution française.

Resources

Activity 13

Answers

13 Script

1. C'est un programmeur informatique américain. Il est riche. C'est le co-fondateur de Facebook.
2. C'est un Français. Il est drôle. Il a joué un rôle important dans le film *Bienvenue chez les Ch'tis*.
3. C'est une bonne actrice. C'est une Américaine. Elle a joué le rôle de Jacqueline Kennedy dans *Jackie*.
4. C'est un chanteur français. Il fait du rap. Il est très populaire.
5. Elle est canadienne. C'est une chanteuse. Elle est originaire du Nouveau-Brunswick.
6. Elle est d'origine sénégalaise. C'est une écrivaine d'origine française. Elle écrit des romans et des pièces de théâtre.

1. D
2. C
3. A
4. E
5. F
6. B

14

1. C'; Il; Il; C'est Toussaint Louverture.
2. C'; C'; Il; C'est Gustave Eiffel.
3. C'; C'; Elle; C'est Mariama Bâ.
4. Il; C'; Il; C'est Napoléon Bonaparte.
5. C'; C'; Elle; C'est Jeanne d'Arc.
6. C'; C'; Elle; C'est Marie-Antoinette.

Communication

Interpersonal: Cooperative Groups

Have each student write a description of a celebrity on a note card. Collect the note cards and distribute several to each group. Each student in the group reads a description and the other students try to guess his or her identity.

Differentiated Learning

Accelerate

Have students prepare an original dialogue that uses indirect object pronouns and present it with their partner to the class.

Decelerate

Write all the answers that will be used in **Activité 12** on the board for these students, but out of order.

Learning Styles

Auditory Learners

Read the answers to **Activité 14** aloud.

Resources

CA Communicative Activities

Share

Answers

All activities will vary.

Reference Desk

1. For **Activité 16**, you may want to explain to students the difference between **gourmet** (*distinguished*) and **gourmand(e)** (*gluttonous*).
2. If you have access to Passport, create a question for your students to share their response to a communicative activity.

Expansion

Before putting students in partners to do **Activité 15**, ask them to brainstorm vocabulary that they have learned for the following categories: **cuisine**, **école**, **maison**, **camping**, and **voyage**. Write the vocabulary on the board for students to refer to as they create their **devinettes**. Give a word bank of possible answers to students who are struggling.

À vous la parole

Question centrale ? Qu'y a-t-il d'universel dans les rapports entre les gens?

Communiquez!

15 Devinettes 1.1, 5.2

Interpersonal Speaking

Pensez à cinq objets communs (de cuisine, dans votre chambre, ou que vous avez chez vous) et écrivez le nom de ces objets sur un morceau de papier adhésif (genre *Post-it*). Votre partenaire fera de même. Choisissez, par exemple, quelque chose qu'on a typiquement dans la cuisine, à l'école, ou dans votre chambre. Mélangez les bouts de papier. À tour de rôle, prenez un bout de papier (sans le regarder) et mettez-le sur votre front. Posez des questions fermées (oui ou non) à votre partenaire pour deviner de quel mot il s'agit. Vous avez deux minutes pour trouver la réponse et marquer un point. La personne qui a marqué le plus de points remporte la partie!

MODÈLE
A: Est-ce qu'on me trouve dans la cuisine?
B: Oui.
A: Est-ce que je suis un objet en métal?
B: Oui.
A: Est-ce que je sers à faire cuire les steaks? Je suis une poêle?
B: Oui. Tu marques un point.

16 J'enrichis mon vocabulaire 1.2, 1.3, 4.1

Interpretive Reading, Presentational Writing

Il y a beaucoup d'expressions culinaires françaises dans le dictionnaire anglais. Faites huit phrases en anglais avec des mots de la liste ci-dessous. Montrez que vous comprenez bien le sens du mot ou de l'expression.

Pas acceptable: I ordered *à la carte*.
Acceptable: I paid more ordering *à la carte*—first, a plate of snails for 12 euros, and then a spinach soufflé that cost 15 euros.

à la carte	**entremets**
à votre santé	**gourmand(e)**
charcuterie (*food, not place*)	**gourmet**
connoisseur	**au gratin**
cordon bleu	**haute cuisine**
crème de la crème	**chef**
hors-d'œuvre	**maître d'hôtel**
	RSVP

17 Chef de cuisine 1.3, 2.2, 3.1, 5.1

Presentational Writing and Speaking

D'abord, trouvez une recette simple en ligne. Ça peut être une recette française, martiniquaise, maghrébine, etc. Vous allez filmer votre préparation comme pour une émission de cuisine. Montrez les ingrédients à vos spectateurs, puis chaque étape de la préparation. Montrez votre vidéo à la classe. Apportez votre plat en classe pour vos camarades de classe.

Recherche: recettes marocaines/bretonnes/belges/etc.

Essential Instruction

1. Have the entire class do **Activité 15** in pairs.
2. Ask students to choose either **Activité 16** or **17**.
3. Give an example of circumlocution in English before students read the paragraph in **Stratégie communicative**.
4. Have students complete **Activités 18** and **19** in pairs.

Pre-AP

Communiquez!

Using Circumlocution 1.2

Vous voulez dire quelque chose en français mais vous ne connaissez pas le mot exact. La meilleure solution est de définir le mot en faisant des phrases avec des mots que vous connaissez déjà. Cette technique s'appelle la circonlocution ; elle vient de deux mots latins et signifie « parler autour ». Il est important de pratiquer la circonlocution lorsque nous apprenons une langue étrangère. Elle vous permet d'enrichir vos conversations en français. Voici un petit truc très utile pour parler d'un object dont vous ne connaissez pas le nom ; identifiez sa forme, en quoi il est fait, et quand et où il est utilisé. Par exemple : **S'il vous plaît, je cherche un objet conique en métal pour la cuisine qui sert à filtrer les herbes. (un chinois)**

18 Vous pouvez m'aider? 1.3, 5.1

Imaginez que vous venez de vous installer en France. Vous avez besoin de beaucoup de choses pour votre nouvel appartement. Le problème c'est que vous ne connaissez pas le nom de tous ces objets. Essayez de décrire les objets ci-dessous selon le modèle. Utilisez le vocabulaire de la Leçon B.

MODÈLE  (un porte-stylos)
C'est un objet cylindrique en métal. Ça sert à ranger les stylos.

1. (un vase)

2. (une louche)

3. (un entonnoir)

4. (une boîte à mouchoirs)

5. (un grille-pain)

6. (un couvercle)

19 Devinez ! 1.1, 2.1, 5.1, 5.2

*Utilisez des gestes (**Il est haut/long/large comme ça**) pour commencer un jeu avec votre partenaire. Votre partenaire doit identifier l'objet que vous décrivez. S'il ou elle ne peut pas le deviner tout de suite, donnez plus de détails, par exemple, **On l'utilise à l'école**. Vous pouvez également préciser sa forme et en quoi il est fait. Voici quelques suggestions :*

une trousse | **une calculatrice** | **un sac à dos** | **une raquette de tennis** | **un gant de toilette**

MODÈLE **C'est un objet rond ou carré que l'on porte au bras gauche en général. Il indique l'heure. Il permet de ne pas être en retard. (une montre)**

Answers

18 Possible answers:

1. C'est un objet haut en verre. Ça sert à porter des fleurs.
2. C'est un objet long en métal. Ça sert à servir la soupe.
3. C'est un objet cylindrique en métal. Ça sert à filtrer le lait.
4. C'est un objet rectangulaire en bois. Ça sert à garder des mouchoirs en papier.
5. C'est un objet rectangulaire en plastique. Ça sert à préparer des toasts.
6. C'est un objet rond en métal. Ça sert à couvrir les casseroles.

19 Answers will vary.

Reference Desk

1. Here is some useful vocabulary for students to learn/review before completing **Activité 18**: **un récipient** (*container*); **un appareil** (*appliance*); **un ustensile** (*utensil*); **en tissu** (*made of fabric*). You may want students to add the location (**dans le salon, garage**) where the object is generally used.
2. Challenge each student to think of additional objects to describe to expand **Activité 18**.

Game

L'objet mystérieux

Tape a secret vocabulary word on the back of each student. Students will walk around the room asking questions about the secret word, trying to guess what it is. **L'objet est grand ou petit? Il est rond? On s'en sert dans la cuisine?**

Differentiated Learning

Adapt

Write out descriptions of different objects, and have students identify them in writing. They may need to use their French-English dictionary.

Special Needs Students

Linguistically Challenged/Behavior Problems/ Speech Impairment

Students would benefit from working in a group with you to complete **Activité 19**.

Resources

- *Vocabulaire actif*
- eV eVisual
- WB Workbook 1–4
- FC Flash Cards
- LA Listening Activities 1–2
- G & V Practice Games

Reference Desk

1. Put the following terms on the board: **le socialisme**, **l'entraîneur**, **réaliser**, **champion**, **la candidature**. Ask students what expressions these new words are related to, whether they're nouns or verbs, and to guess what they might mean. For students interested in increasing their vocabulary, one strategy is to learn other words related to a new vocabulary word.
2. Explain why **réaliser** in this context is a **faux ami**.
3. Amine is a French singer who was born in Morocco but grew up in Paris. He helped to develop the music genre **Raï&B** (*Raï'n'B*).

nouvelle orthographe **s'entrainer**

Communication

Interpersonal: Paired Practice

To practice the expressions in **L'art de la conversation** and **Pour la conversation,** have students work in pairs to prepare a dialogue about topics discussed at their dinner table. Ask students to expand and include many points of view from the various family members.

Culture

Perspectives: Information

High fashion in France has a world-wide reputation, and it was the French who coined the term **haute couture**. Unlike **prêt-à-porter** retail stores, the fashion houses where this luxurious apparel is created must adhere to strict rules; their work must be done by hand, and they must not exceed a certain number of employees.

Leçon C — Vocabulaire actif

L'art de la conversation 1.1, 1.2, 5.1

la politique

C'est bientôt **les élections** (f.) **présidentielles**. Les Français vont **voter** pour **le candidat** de quel **parti politique** cette année?

les médias (m.)

On **passe** le nouveau **hit** d'Amine à la radio. Ce **blogueur** suit les manifestations à Paris.

la mode

Pour **le prêt-à-porter** femme, on remarquera **la longueur** des jupes cette saison. **Le look tradi** sera **à la page**.

le sport

Sylvain **s'est entraîné** au **club** pour **le championnat d'athlétisme** (m.). Il a gagné **une médaille**.

le cinéma

On passe une comédie **dramatique** au Gaumont. **Réalisé** par Noémie Lvovsky, le film *Camille redouble* a reçu deux **récompenses** (f.).

l'économie (f.)

À cause de l'endettement (m.) des pays, **le PNB** de l'Europe **a baissé**. **La hausse** du **taux d'inflation réduit la valeur** des **revenus** (m.).

Essential Instruction

1. Introduce the new vocabulary with the eVisuals for this lesson.
2. Tell students they will listen to news on the radio. Play the recording twice with textbooks closed. The third time, play the recording, stopping at specific points to ask students to identify what is being discussed.
3. Have students listen again, this time with their books open. Make sure students understand each bolded word.
4. Have students listen to the three expressions in **Pour la conversation** with their books open. Ask them to respond to the last question.
5. You might have pairs of students read each mini-dialogue in **Activité 1**, and then ask the class to identify the **thème**.

Pour la conversation

1.1, 5.2

How do I express I can't stop myself from doing something?

» **Je ne peux pas m'empêcher de** penser aux gens qui souffrent dans le monde.
I can't help but think about the people who are suffering in the world.

How do I say that someone is right?

» Élodie a raison.
Elodie is right.

How do I ask about dinner table topics?

» Et à votre table, vous parlez de quoi?
And at your dinner table, what do you talk about?

Et si je voulais dire...?

le scrutin, le bulletin	*ballot*
un électeur, une électrice	*voter*
le dirigeant	*leader*
un programme électoral	*political platform*
une crise économique	*economic crisis*
un défilé de mode	*fashion show*
une station de radio	*radio station*

Traditions et pratiques

1.2, 2.1

Les Français aiment beaucoup discuter de politique. Ils n'ont pas peur d'avoir des opinions opposées à celles des gens avec qui ils parlent. Ils présenteront souvent des points de vue différents pour faire avancer une discussion.

1 Thèmes de conversation

1.2

Interpretive Reading

Indiquez le thème des conversations suivantes.

la politique **l'économie** **la mode** **le sport** **le cinéma** **les médias**

1. –C'est une co-production franco-canadienne.
   –De vrais serveurs jouent les rôles principaux, pas des vedettes.
2. –Tu as remarqué la longueur des manteaux cette saison?
   –Oui, ça me fait penser aux années 1950.
3. –Tu suis les manifestations à Paris?
   –Oui, je lis le blog d'un blogueur qui y participe.
4. –Tes parents soutiennent les partis centristes?
   –Oui, ils ont tendance à soutenir le centre-droit.
5. –L'endettement change notre mode de vivre.
   –Le gouvernement va augmenter les impôts (*taxes*), c'est sûr!
6. –Il a gagné ses deux courses (*races*) au championnat de France indoor.
   –Il se prépare pour ça depuis des mois.

En politique européenne, on se réunit au Parlement de l'Union européenne à Strasbourg pour prendre de nouvelles mesures.

Resources

Pour la conversation
Et si je voulais dire...?

Answers

1

1. le cinéma
2. la mode
3. les médias
4. la politique
5. l'économie
6. le sport

Reference Desk

Here is some useful supplemental vocabulary about politics: **une campagne électorale** (*political campaign*); **un challenger** (*challenger*); **un mouvement populaire** (*grassroots movement*); **le/la perdant(e)** (*the loser*); **une urne** (*ballot box*).

Critical Thinking

Comparisons

The French are known for their skills in **la polémique**, or argument, practicing it even at the dinner table. Ask students if their families get into heated discussions at the dinner table. What topics are the most controversial?

Game

Dinner Topics

Divide the class into two teams. The first player of the first team picks a card; the cards contain the six topics, or themes, from p. 106. The player has 20 seconds to state a sentence that pertains to the topic. If it is accepted by the teacher, the player earns a point for his or her team.

Differentiated Learning

Accelerate

Have students learn the **Et si je voulais dire...?** and supplemental vocabulary from **Reference Desk** to create a radio or television broadcast.

Learning Styles

Visual Learners

Have students create a campaign poster for a real or imaginary political candidate.

Multiple Intelligences

Visual-Spatial

Divide the class into six teams, with each one tasked to find clips online about one of the six topics/themes: politics, the media, fashion, sport, cinema, and the economy in France. Students could choose their team's topic by picking slips from a hat. Have them play the clips for the class. While they watch, students write down a theme for each one. You may want to award points for those students who can grasp some of the details in the clips.

Answers

2

1. inflation
2. endettement
3. candidat
4. voter
5. PNB
6. revenu
7. look
8. prêt-à-porter
9. passe
10. médailles
11. sortie

3

1. Il a des questions sur l'économie.
2. Ils sont endettés.
3. Ce qu'est le PNB.
4. Ils participent aux discussions en classe.
5. si elle peut lui proposer des livres, magazines ou blogs

Reference Desk

1. **Le PNB (produit national brut)** is equivalent to the GNP (gross national product). It refers to the total value of a nation's economic activity.
2. **BCBG** refers to **bon chic**, **bon genre**. In addition to being a clothing brand, it is the French term for the preppy look.

2 Complétez ! 1.2

Interpretive Reading

Complétez les phrases en choisissant un mot ou une expression ci-dessous.

endettement **PNB** **médailles** **revenu** **voter** **look**
prêt-à-porter **passe** **sortie** **candidat** **inflation**

1. L'... diminue la valeur du dollar ou de l'euro.
2. Quand une personne doit (*owes*) beaucoup d'argent à une banque ou quand un pays doit de l'argent à un ou plusieurs autres pays, ça s'appelle l'....
3. Pour les élections présidentielles américaines, il y a généralement un... républicain et un autre démocrate.
4. À l'âge de 18 ans, on peut....
5. La valeur de toute l'activité économique d'un pays s'appelle le....
6. L'argent qu'on gagne (*earn*) quand on travaille s'appelle le....
7. Connais-tu quelqu'un qui a un... BCBG?
8. Dans les défilés de mode (*fashion shows*), les mannequins portent des vêtements haute couture et non de....
9. On... le nouveau hit d'Adele à la radio.
10. Aux Jeux olympiques, Shaun White a gagné deux... d'or.
11. J'attends la... du deuxième film *Tintin*, basé sur la BD belge.

3 La politique et l'économie 1.2

Interpretive Reading

Lisez la lettre que Gabriel a écrite à sa tante à propos de son cours d'économie, puis répondez aux questions.

Salut Tata!

J'espère que tu pourras m'aider avec mes difficultés au lycée en ce moment parce que tu es forte en politique et en économie. Comment peut-on savoir si l'endettement dans les pays occidentaux en ce moment va causer une crise? Moi, je ne comprends même pas ce qu'est le PNB, ou comment les revenus d'un pays changent la situation globale. Je veux vraiment dire à mon prof: « De quoi parlez-vous, exactement? » Mais certains de mes camarades entrent dans la discussion, alors je me sens vraiment bête. Quels livres ou magazines ou blogs me proposes-tu? Je voudrais mieux comprendre la politique et l'économie, et je dois le faire vite!

Grosses bises à tous,
Gabriel

1. Pourquoi est-ce que Gabriel écrit à sa tante?
2. Qu'est-ce qui se passe dans les pays occidentaux (*Western*) en ce moment?
3. Qu'est-ce que Gabriel ne comprend pas?
4. Que font les autres élèves?
5. Qu'est-ce que Gabriel demande à sa tante?

Essential Instruction

1. Do **Activités 2** and **3** as a class. Ask students to read the letter silently at their desks.
2. For **Activité 4** have students work in pairs. When finished, each person shares one thing in small groups that he or she can and cannot help doing.
3. After listening to **Activité 5**, make sure students understand any incorrect answers.
4. Have students complete **Activité 6** as written homework for a change. The next day, give them a few minutes to review their answers before asking for volunteers to answer the questions orally without looking at their homework.

4 Je ne peux pas m'empêcher de.... 1.3

Presentational Speaking

Dites si vous pouvez ou si vous ne pouvez pas vous empêcher de faire les choses suivantes.

MODÈLE manger de la glace
Je peux m'empêcher de manger de la glace.
ou
Je ne peux pas m'empêcher de manger de la glace.

1. manger du chocolat
2. faire du shopping
3. jouer aux jeux vidéo
4. surfer sur Internet
5. envoyer des textos
6. prendre de la pizza
7. regarder des films
8. téléphoner à mes copains

Ma sœur ne peut pas s'empêcher de rater la dinde !

5 De quoi parle-t-on ? 1.2

Interpretive Listening

Écrivez les numéros 1–6 sur votre papier. Écoutez les histoires et les descriptions. Ensuite, choisissez la catégorie à laquelle chacune correspond.

A. le cinéma
B. la mode
C. la politique
D. l'économie
E. les médias
F. le sport

6 Questions personnelles 1.1

Interpersonal Speaking

Répondez aux questions suivantes avec un partenaire.

1. Chez toi, on parle de quoi à table ? Est-ce qu'il y a certains sujets que tu évites ?
2. Est-ce que tu suis la politique intérieure ? Et la politique internationale ? À ton avis, est-ce que les hommes et femmes politiques ont souvent raison ?
3. On passe souvent les chansons de tes musiciens préférés à la radio ?
4. As-tu déjà gagné une médaille ? Dans quel sport ?
5. Es-tu un blogueur ou une blogueuse ? Si oui, quels sont tes thèmes ?
6. Quels films est-ce qu'on passe au cinéma ce weekend ?

Resources

Activities 5–6

Answers

4 Answers will vary.

5 **Script**

1. C'est bientôt les élections pour la ville ! Allez voter pour cette femme politique. Vous la connaissez depuis longtemps. Elle est intelligente et prête à vous servir. C'est le candidat du parti socialiste.
2. Un nouvel athlète africain a couru aux Jeux olympiques et a gagné une médaille. Est-ce l'homme le plus rapide du monde ? On verra demain.
3. Cette semaine, c'est la sortie d'un bon film réalisé par un jeune metteur en scène. On va le passer dans un cinéma près de chez vous.
4. À cause de l'endettement, le PNB de l'Italie a baissé. Ce n'est pas une question d'inflation. Les revenus du pays déclinent face à l'endettement public.
5. On va parler des blogueurs célèbres. Qui est-ce que vous suivez ? Contactez-nous !
6. La collection du prêt-à-porter automne/hiver vient de sortir. À cause de la longueur des jupes, on dirait un look années 1960.

1. C
2. F
3. A
4. D
5. E
6. B

6 Answers will vary.

Expansion

To extend **Activité 4**, ask each student to write two new cues. Project the new cues for the pairs to see and use.

Differentiated Learning

Accelerate
Have students listen to a **France Info** broadcast and make a list of the general topics discussed.

Decelerate
Allow slower-paced students to read the scripts as they listen to **Activité 5**.

Learning Styles

Visual-Spatial
After doing **Activité 5**, pair the students up and give one student the script. Have the student re-jumble the questions and read them aloud to their partner who must identify the answer.

Resources

Dialogue
Activity 7

Dialogue Video

WB Workbook 5

Answers

7

1. Léo et Élodie
2. Ce n'est pas correct devant les invités.
3. Léo et Élodie
4. Ils étaient aussi idéalistes.
5. le sport et le cinéma

Reference Desk

1. **La politique… ne fait jamais grève** means that politics never goes on strike.
2. Ask students to give you the verb for **le réveillon**. (**réveillonner**)
3. The forms of **souffrir** in the present tense are: **souffre**, **souffres**, **souffre**, **souffrons**, **souffrez**, **souffrent**. It follows the pattern of **offrir** and **ouvrir**.
4. **Tuer** is a regular -**er** verb.
5. **Envahi** is the past participle of **envahir** (*to invade*).
6. The expression **en guerre** means *at war*.
7. Ask students the name of Tolstoy's opus. (***La guerre et la paix***)

nouvelle orthographe **les sans-abris**

Rencontres culturelles

On ne parle pas politique à table!

1.2, 3.1, 5.1

Le soir du réveillon de Noël, Léo, Élodie, leurs parents, et les Martin sont à table.

Mère : J'ai déjà dit : on ne parle pas politique à table le jour du réveillon quand même ! Pensez à nos invités….

Léo : Mais la politique, Maman, elle, ne fait jamais grève.

Élodie : Et pendant que nous réveillonnons, moi, je ne peux pas m'empêcher de penser aux gens qui souffrent dans le monde.

Léo : Élodie a raison. Les dictatures tuent, des territoires sont envahis, même les démocraties emprisonnent et usurpent les droits des hommes.

Élodie : Ce qui me donne le plus de soucis, ce sont les sans-abri….

Léo : N'oublie pas les prisonniers politiques et les nations en guerre.

Mère : Oh là là ! Oui, c'est vrai que tout le monde n'a pas la chance de se retrouver autour d'un bon repas comme nous, dans la paix. Qu'en penses-tu, mon chéri ?

Père : Ah, nos enfants ont récupéré notre idéalisme de jeunesse ! Il faut les encourager !

(Il s'adresse aux Martin.)

Et à votre table, vous parlez de quoi ?

M. Martin : Plutôt du sport ou du cinéma, mais pas si passionnément !

7 On ne parle pas politique à table!

1.3

Répondez aux questions.

1. Qui veut parler politique à table ?
2. Pourquoi est-ce que la mère de Léo et d'Élodie ne veut pas qu'on parle politique à table ?
3. Qui parle le plus passionnément ?
4. Comment étaient les parents d'Élodie et de Léo quand ils étaient jeunes ?
5. Quels sont les sujets de conversation chez les Martin ?

Stratégie

Faites une liste des problèmes politiques qui touchent Élodie et Léo.

Essential Instruction

1. After playing the dialogue audio and showing the video, have student volunteers read the main dialogue aloud.
2. Ask the class the questions in **Activité 7**.
3. Have three advanced students enact the scene in the **Extension** dialogue for the rest of the class. Students should be able to understand the general topic of conversation. Ask an advanced student to answer the **Extension** question.

EXTENSION **Les médias** 1.1, 1.2, 2.2, 3.1

Les Gagnon sont à table pour le dîner.

Papa : Qu'est-ce qu'on entend, c'est la radio ou ton lecteur MP3 ?
David : C'est une émission qui passe à la radio, sur mon lecteur MP3.
Papa : Ah, la radio à diffusion numérique ! On peut dire au revoir aux émissions de qualité !
David : Mais qu'est-ce que tu dis ? Au contraire, la qualité de la réception est inouïe, on peut l'écouter à toute heure, où qu'on se trouve !
Papa : Tout dépend, la diffusion sur même fréquence empêche l'accès aux petites radios indépendantes. Donc, comme je l'ai dit, la fin des meilleures stations de radio !
Maman : En tout cas, numérique ou non, mangez au lieu de discuter. Ça refroidit !

EXTENSION Selon le père de David, quels sont les inconvénients de la diffusion numérique ? 1.1, 1.2, 2.2, 3.1

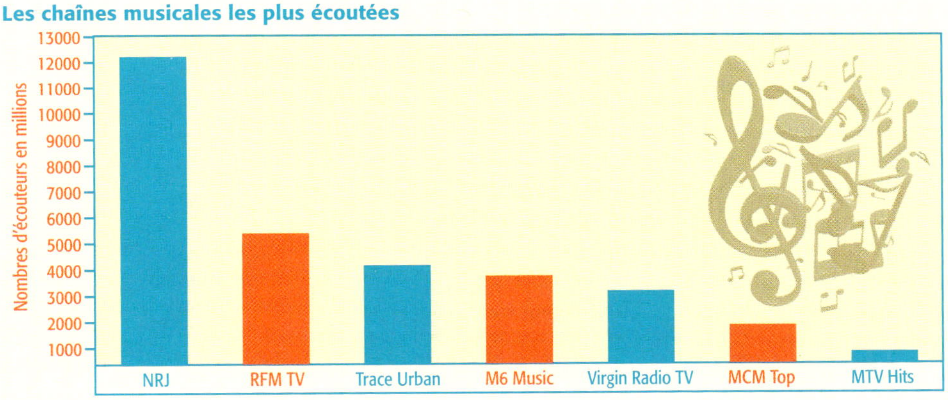

Learning Styles

Logical/Mathematical
Have students explain to the class how radio waves work and why David's dad is concerned about the accessibility of radio frequencies for smaller stations.

Resources

Extension

Answers

EXTENSION

Elle ne donne pas accès aux meilleures stations.

Reference Desk

Here are some vocabulary words from the **Extension** conversation that students might not know: **la diffusion numérique** (*digital broadcasting*); **inouï(e)** (*incredible, unheard of*); **Ça refroidit !** (*It's getting cold!*).

nouvelle orthographe **le diner, les chaines**

Resources

- *Points de départ*
- WB Workbook 6–7
- Explore

Answers

Comparaisons
Answers will vary.

Reference Desk

1. Some differences between table manners in France and in the United States include the following: In France, both hands remain visible on the table, and guests are not to leave the table during a meal; in the United States, one hand is frequently placed on your lap, and politics and religion are generally not discussed.
2. If you have access to Passport, find a news article related to **les bonnes manières** and show it to your students.

TPR

Ask a student to make an example of a table place setting for one person at either a simple family meal or an elegant dinner. Repeat this process with other students.

Expansion

Have students share the table manners they were taught. Students may especially like to hear this from their classmates from other cultures.

Points de départ

Pre-AP

Question centrale ? Qu'y a-t-il d'universel dans les rapports entre les gens?

Manières de table 1.2, 2.1, 3.1

Quand vous êtes invité(e) à 20h30, vous pouvez arriver dans la demi-heure qui suit l'heure d'invitation. Si vous apportez un petit cadeau, ça peut être des fleurs, du vin, ou des chocolats. Si vous êtes l'hôte ou l'hôtesse et que vous recevez ces cadeaux, les fleurs doivent être mises dans un vase, le vin offert aux invités, et les chocolats proposés au moment du café. Si vous recevez un livre ou un autre cadeau, vous devez l'ouvrir et le laisser visible.

Un beau couvert donne de l'appétit.

On commence toujours à servir par le couvert le plus éloigné*. Dans la tradition française, la lame* du couteau regarde toujours vers l'intérieur. Les couverts qui ne sont pas plats se placent les dents vers le haut pour les fourchettes, et côté bombé* pour les cuillères.

La France produit beaucoup de vin pour consommation à l'intérieur et à l'extérieur du pays. Le vin fait partie des repas au quotidien et en particulier lorsqu'il y a des invités. Chaque vin est alors choisi avec attention pour accompagner chaque plat. Il existe plus de 40 verres à vin différents suivant les vins et leur origine.

Recherche : manières de table, chocolatier paris, fleuriste paris

éloigné *far away* ; **lame** *blade* ; **bombé** *rounded*

La conversation 1.2, 2.1, 3.1

Le devoir des hôtes est de mettre à l'aise* leurs invités. C'est l'hôte ou l'hôtesse qui crée l'ambiance, et qui choisit les sujets de conversation. Les Français adorent le débat*, mais il y a des sujets dont on ne parle pas, comme l'argent et la sexualité. La politique peut enflammer* la soirée, et elle n'est pas toujours soulevée*. La conversation sur le dernier film qu'on a vu, le dernier livre qu'on a lu, la musique qu'on écoute, la série télé qu'on regarde, le sport qu'on pratique ou dont on est fan, les réseaux sociaux qu'on fréquente, ou les voyages qu'on a faits est toujours appréciée. Elle permet d'opposer les jugements. Toute conversation est un affrontement*, un exercice d'intelligence. La France est le pays qui a inventé la polémique*. Il faut savoir aussi que tout ça est un jeu.

Recherche : manières de table conversations

mettre à l'aise *make (guests) comfortable* ; **le débat** *debate* ; **enflammer** *to fuel* ; **soulevée** *raised* ; **affrontement** *clash* ; **polémique** *controversy*

Mot-clé

Manière de l'ancien adjectif français *manier* (1119), *que l'on fait fonctionner à la main* (1140), mais aussi *habile* (1155) et *bien dressé* (d'un faucon, vers 1175). Aujourd'hui, il désigne principalement la façon d'être, d'agir, et de se comporter. On l'utilise couramment sous la forme plurielle (les bonnes et mauvaises manières, 1662) pour désigner un comportement en société.

Comparaisons

1.2, 2.1, 4.2

Quels sont vos sujets de conversation à table quand vous avez des invités ? Sont-ils différents de vos sujets de conversation quotidiens ? Y a-t-il des sujets dont les Américains évitent de parler pendant les repas ?

Essential Instruction

1. After students read **Manières de table**, have them make a list of points to remember regarding being a guest at a French home.
2. Ask students what to do in this situation: **Vous êtes invité(e) chez une famille française. Qu'est-ce que vous offrez ?**
3. After they read the **Produits** box, students can research the Paris wine tasting of 1976 (the Judgment of Paris).
4. Call on individual students to read the situations in **Activité 8**. Divide the class into pairs and have each set of pairs draw a number (1–4). This represents the activity they will complete. Pairs can exchange numbers if they wish. One pair in each group presents their project.

Produits

On produit du **vin** en France depuis l'ère de la Grèce antique. La France est le premier producteur mondial de vin, produisant 20 pourcent du vin de la planète, et on l'appelle souvent « le pays du vin ». Il y a plus de 3 400 vins en France.

1.2, 2.2

Traditions et pratiques

En famille, les gens font ce qu'ils veulent, mais invité à un repas, tout Français bien éduqué doit suivre les règles des bonnes manières suivantes :

- mettre sa serviette sur ses genoux
- se servir de tous les aliments proposés, même si on ne les aime pas (exceptions : si on a prévenu l'hôte d'allergies)
- ne jamais commencer de manger avant que tout le monde ne soit servi, y compris l'hôte et hôtesse

1.2, 2.1, 4.2

8 Activités culturelles 1.3, 2.2, 4.2

Faites les activités suivantes.

1. Vous voulez impressionner votre hôte parisien avec un bon cadeau. Cherchez en ligne ce que vous pourriez apporter, et faite une liste des diverses possibilités ; pour chacune, indiquez le pour et le contre (y compris le prix). Puis, faites votre choix et expliquez votre raisonnement à votre partenaire.

Recherche : cadeaux d'hôtesse

2. Le père de votre correspondant français vous a invité(e) à dîner. Décrivez le repas.
3. Faites une liste de sujets que vous pouvez soulever au dîner avec un collègue de travail.
4. Faites la liste des manières de table américaines et comparez-les aux manières françaises avec un organigramme venn.

Dire « merci » avec des fleurs.

Une boîte de chocolats est toujours un bon cadeau à offrir à ses hôtes.

À DISCUTER

Avec vos copains, vous parlez de quels sujets à table ?

Mon dico des manières

employer la manière forte *agir agressivement*
faire une bonne manière *faire un geste amical*
Tu fais des manières. *Tu es difficile.*
Il a l'art et la manière. *Il sait faire les choses.*
Il est sans manière. *Il est naturel.*
À chacun sa manière. To each his own (way).

Answers

8 Activities will vary.

À DISCUTER

Answers will vary.

Culture

Products: Information

French wines are highly regarded throughout the world. They are, however, in fierce competition with Spanish, Australian, Chilean, Argentine, and Californian wines.

Reference Desk

1. Flower bouquets are less expensive and flower shops more common in France than in the United States.
2. Do your students know that not all flowers are created equal in France? White lilies and chrysanthemums are reserved for funerals, red roses for lovers, and yellow flowers have the connotation of infidelity. Be careful when offering these flowers to your hostess. Advise students to ask the **fleuriste** for suggestions.

Communication

Interpersonal: Cooperative Groups

Designate a table in the classroom as a dining room table. Have groups of students prepare a short dialogue that highlights one of these concepts from the culture reading: French punctuality, offering the host a gift, serving the main dish, place settings, how a host puts guests at ease, a common or risqué topic of conversation. The rest of the class tries to figure out what culture point is being shown.

Differentiated Learning

Decelerate

Students may be interested in presenting a dialogue that shows what topics teens talk about when they dine together in different places (for example, **au fast-food, à la cantine du lycée, à la maison**).

Answers

Du côté des médias
Answers will vary.

Expansion

Have students design a T-shirt with a motto that depicts one of their values.

Du côté des médias 1.2, 1.3, 3.1

Lisez la page d'accueil du site Judo Club Sorguais. Faites quatre phrases pour montrer votre compréhension des valeurs mentionnées.

Code moral du judo

Le Judo véhicule des valeurs fondamentales qui s'imbriquent les unes dans les autres pour édifier une formation morale.

Le respect de ce code est la condition première, la base de la pratique du Judo.

友情
L'amitié
C'est le plus pur des sentiments humains.

勇気
Le courage
C'est faire ce qui est juste.

名誉
L'honneur
C'est être fidèle à la parole donnée.

謙虚
La modestie
C'est parler de soi-même sans orgueil.

敬尊
Le respect
Sans respect aucune confiance ne peut naître.

自制
Le contrôle de soi
C'est savoir se taire lorsque monte la colère.

礼儀
La politesse
C'est le respect d'autrui.

誠
La sincérité
C'est s'exprimer sans déguiser sa pensée.

Essential Instruction

1. Have students who play sports share their values or the values of their team or coach.
2. Ask them to prioritize the values from the realia on a list of one to eight, one being the most important value in their lives to eight being the least.
3. Have students complete **Activité 9**. If they have difficulty connecting with family members who do not live with them, encourage them to interview a teacher or the parent of a friend.
4. Consider doing **Activité 10** as a class if finding a Francophone proves difficult. Local universities, churches, or community centers may have names of people who may volunteer to be interviewed. If a guest cannot visit the class, consider an interview via an Internet video service.

Question centrale ? Qu'y a-t-il d'universel dans les rapports entre les gens?

Les préférences culinaires

Introduction et interrogations

Dans cette unité, utilisez vos connaissances personnelles en matière de cuisine.

9 Réfléchir 1.1, 2.1, 2.2, 3.2, 4.2, 5.1

Répondez par écrit aux questions suivantes.

1. Quel est votre repas préféré?
2. Quel est le repas préféré des adultes avec qui vous habitez (vos parents ou vos gardiens)? Y a-t-il des différences entre vos préférences, vos goûts, et les leurs?
3. Parlez avec deux membres de votre famille qui n'habitent pas avec vous: quelqu'un de votre âge (comme un cousin) et quelqu'un de plus âgé (comme un grand-parent). Qu'est-ce qu'ils préfèrent manger?

Formulez plusieurs hypothèses pour expliquer pourquoi il y a des différences et des ressemblances entre les gens en ce concerne la cuisine.

10 Rechercher 1.1, 1.3, 2.1, 2.2, 3.2, 4.2, 5.1, 5.2

Interviewez une personne francophone, individuellement ou en groupe, en personne ou sur Internet. Le sujet de votre interview concerne les repas et les générations.

1. Faites une liste de questions que vous voudriez poser à cette personne, puis posez-les-lui.
2. Présentez oralement un résumé de votre interview. Comparez les réponses de la personne que vous avez interviewée avec vos opinions à vous.

11 Faire l'inventaire! 1.1, 1.2, 5.2

Discutez des questions suivantes en classe.

1. Est-ce qu'il y avait des thèmes similaires à travers les différentes présentations? Lesquels?
2. Est-ce que les opinions recueillies lors des interviews individuelles correspondent à ce que vous avez appris dans cette unité? Est-ce que certaines opinions vous ont surpris(e) et pourquoi (pas)?
3. Est-il possible de faire des généralités pour comprendre une culture? Pourquoi, ou pourquoi pas?
4. En groupes, analysez les résultats de vos interview, puis, si possible, faites une liste de généralités que vous pensez pouvoir faire sur une culture francophone particulière. Ensuite, faites une liste qui correspond aux goûts individuels de chacun.

Answers

All activities will vary.

Expansion

Link the information gleaned from these activities to the AP preparation chart on p. 97, which shows the change in time spent on each meal since 1990. How have the eating habits of people changed over the last two or three generations? What are the causes and consequences of these changes? As an answer to the latter question, students might point out that more and more households have two working parents due to decreased or stagnant income(s) and/or to an increase in single-parent households (in turn due to a rise in women's rights and, consequently, divorce). Possible consequences include an increase in unbalanced diets and the rise of fast food and related health problems (obesity, diabetes, heart disease). Ask students to reflect upon how all these various elements are interrelated. For advanced students preparing for the AP test, consider assigning individual students a 5-paragraph essay about this inter-relativity, or having the class collaborate as a whole to write a sample essay.

Differentiated Learning

Expand

Before assigning **Culture sur place**, review the vocabulary for breakfast, lunch, snack, and dinner to prepare students to answer the questions in **Activité 9**. For **Activité 10,** if the students have no access to a native French speaker, they might ask their questions on a French blog. In **Activité 11,** students are asked to decide if it is more valuable to generalize about a culture or to experience it firsthand. This discussion aligns closely with the **Question centrale** running throughout the unit: whether there is a universal thread that links us all together.

Resources

WB Workbook 8–9

G & V Practice Games

Answers

12

1. qui; 2. qui; 3. que; 4. que; 5. que; 6. qui; 7. qu'; 8. qui; 9. qui; 10. que

Reference Desk

1. Students learned the relative pronouns **qui** and **que** in Level 2, **Unité 7**, p. 379.
2. **Qui** never takes an apostrophe.
3. Students should understand that if something is relative it means that it depends on a context for its meaning. This instruction is true for **qui** and **que** since, as relative pronouns, what they mean depends on their direct antecedent. Students should look to the dependent clause for clues. If there is no subject in the dependent clause, **qui** must be used. If there is a subject, **que** is the choice: **L'homme *qui* parle**.... **L'homme *que* je connais**....

Expansion

PQA

Students will best internalize **qui** and **que** by hearing them used repeatedly and realizing which one sounds right. Engage them in conversations about themselves: **Qui est cette fille? C'est Alice. C'est la fille avec qui Marianne joue au foot. C'est une étudiante que je trouve très sérieuse, mais qui est aussi très sympathique.**

Communication

Interpersonal: Cooperative Groups

Put students into small groups and have each group write sentences about their teachers. The rest of the class tries to identify the teacher. For example, **C'est la prof qui conduit une BMW. Le sport que ce prof préfère est le rugby.**

Structure de la langue

Révision: The Relative Pronouns *qui* and *que* 1.1, 1.2

The relative pronouns **qui** and **que** connect two clauses in a complex sentence. The pronouns **qui** and **que** introduce a dependent clause that describes a preceding person or thing, called the antecedent.

Qui is used as the subject of the dependent clause. The verb that follows **qui** agrees with the antecedent.

J'ai voté pour Emmanuel Macron, **qui** était le meilleur candidat, à mon avis.	*I voted for Emmanuel Macron, who was the best candidate, in my opinion.*
Le parti politique des Verts, **qui** veut protéger l'environnement, manifeste à Paris.	*The Green political party, which wants to protect the environment, is demonstrating in Paris.*

Que is used as the direct object of the dependent clause.

L'athlète **que** j'admire le plus a gagné une médaille aux Jeux olympiques.	*The athlete whom I admire the most won a medal in the Olympics.*
Le championnat **qu'**on regarde est aussi à la télé.	*The championship that we are watching is also on TV.*

When the dependent clause is in the **passé composé**, the past participle of the verb agrees in gender and in number with the antecedent of **que**.

Les robes **qu'**on a vu**es** à Paris étaient longues.	*The dresses we saw in Paris were long.*

12 Dans les médias 1.2

Interpretive Reading

*Choisissez **qui** ou **que** pour compléter les phrases suivantes.*

Le président de la compagnie, qui est parti le mois dernier, s'est installé à New York.

1. Les élections présidentielles, ... ont eu lieu cette année, ont coûté cher.
2. Le candidat... était socialiste a gagné.
3. Le problème... je vois pour l'Europe, c'est l'endettement.
4. Le PNB de la Chine, ... tout le monde regarde, n'a pas baissé.
5. Le look tradi... les mannequins portent cette année est dans tous les magazines de mode.
6. L'athlète... s'est entraîné le plus a gagné le championnat d'athlétisme.
7. La médaille... il a gagné est dans sa chambre.
8. On passe une nouvelle comédie... est une co-production franco-américaine.
9. Le blogueur, ... aime bien l'actrice Eva Green, dit qu'elle joue très bien dans ce rôle.
10. La marque de vêtements... je porte est à la mode.

Essential Instruction

1. Have students do **Activité 12** before starting the lesson, to gauge the level of instruction needed to review this concept.
2. Have students review all the possible English equivalents for **qui** and **que** (who, whom, which, that).
3. Ask the students to read each sentence in **Activité 12**, inserting **qui** or **que**. Correct the sentences, explaining in each case why the pronoun was appropriate.
4. Before completing **Activité 13**, do some practice sentence combinations that resemble those they will hear. Put these sentences on the board and discuss why **qui** or **que** is the correct choice. After students have completed **Activité 13**, give them the sentences to combine with the appropriate pronoun.
5. Point out the example of **ce qui** in the dialogue on p. 110, and write on the board: **Ce que j'apprécie, c'est que vous posez des questions.** Then review the model examples on p. 117.

13 Qui ou que? Là est la question! 1.2

Interpretive Listening

*Écrivez les numéros 1–8 sur votre papier. Écoutez les deux phrases. Puis, écrivez le pronom relatif **qui** ou **que** que vous utiliseriez pour créer une seule phrase au lieu de deux.*

The Relative Pronouns *ce qui* and *ce que* 1.1, 1.2

You just reviewed that the relative pronouns **qui** and **que** always have a definite antecedent. But if the antecedent is not specific or if it is unknown, use **ce qui** or **ce que**.

Ce qui (*what*) is used as the subject of the dependent clause.

Ce qui est un problème, c'est l'endettement.	*What is a problem is the debt.*
Le candidat sait **ce qui** est important.	*The candidate knows what is important.*

Ce que (*what*) is used as the direct object of the dependent clause.

Ce que nous voulons, c'est un nouveau look.	*What we want is a new look.*
Ce qu'on remarquera cette année, c'est la longueur des jupes.	*What we'll notice this year is the length of skirts.*

Comparaisons 4.1

How would you express these linking words in English?

Montre-moi **ce que** tu as dessiné.
Le gouvernement ne réduit pas son endettement, **ce qui** sera un problème.

Resources

- Activity 13
- WB Workbook 10–11
- G & V Practice Games

Answers

13 Script

1. Je préfère le réveillon de Noël. Le réveillon de Noël a lieu le 24 décembre.
2. Le candidat fait partie de la droite. J'aime ce candidat.
3. L'équipe de foot a gagné. Elle vient de Nantes.
4. J'ai l'ustensile. Il filtre les herbes.
5. L'athlète s'appelle Zinédine Zidane. Les Français le préfèrent.
6. Elle porte un look à la mode. C'est des années 1960.
7. Ils choisissent le candidat socialiste. C'est le meilleur homme politique.
8. J'ai vu le film *Le fabuleux destin d'Amélie Poulain*. C'est un bon film.

1. qui
2. que
3. qui
4. qui
5. que
6. qui
7. qui
8. qui

Comparaisons

Ce que is best translated as *what*, and **ce qui** as *which*:

Show me *what* you drew.

The government is not reducing its debt, *which* will be a problem.

Differentiated Learning

Accelerate

Ask students to give the French equivalents of these sentences: (1) Here is what I bought. (2) Tell me what you learned at school today. (3) I don't know what they are discussing. (4) We don't know that verb, which is a problem. (5) To know French table manners is what I want.

Special Needs Students

AD(H)D/Dyslexia/Linguistically Challenged

For many students, a grammatical explanation will not lead to comprehension. Understanding that **ce qui** and **ce que** mean *what* in English will help. Give them ample opportunities to practice oral and written examples. Giving students short but frequent quizzes will ensure that they are learning.

Answers

14

1. Ce que
2. Ce qu'
3. ce que
4. Ce qu'
5. ce qui
6. Ce que
7. Ce que
8. Ce que
9. ce qui
10. Ce qui

15

1. Ce qui est le plus important pour Max, c'est le problème de l'inflation. Ce qu'il trouve le moins important, c'est le problème de l'endettement.
2. Ce qui est le plus important pour Claire, c'est le problème de l'inflation. Ce qu'elle trouve le moins important, c'est le problème du chômage
3. Ce qui est le plus important pour Nicole, c'est le problème du chômage. Ce qu'elle trouve le moins important, c'est le problème de la pollution.
4. Ce qui est le plus important pour Thomas, c'est le problème de l'endettement. Ce qu'il trouve le moins important, c'est le problème de l'inflation.
5. Ce qui est le plus important pour Abdel, c'est le problème de la pollution. Ce qu'il trouve le moins important, c'est le problème de l'endettement.
6. Ce qui est le plus important pour Anne, c'est le problème du chômage. Ce qu'elle trouve le moins important, c'est le problème de la pollution.

Reference Desk

Students may need to be reminded that in sentence 5 of **Activité 14**, **se passer** means *to happen*. **Se** is not the subject, but rather is part of the pronominal verb.

Expansion

Have students compare themselves and their classmates to the people named in **Acitivité 15**. Have them prepare mini-dialogues similar to the one in the illustration: "**Ce que je ne comprends pas, c'est ton intérêt/désinterêt de…!**"

14 Le réveillon d'Élodie et Léo 1.2

Interpretive Reading

*Complétez les phrases suivantes avec **ce qui** ou **ce que**.*

1. … la mère d'Élodie et Léo connaît bien, ce sont les manières à table.
2. … elle dit à ses enfants est direct: « On ne parle pas politique à table. »
3. Elle n'aime pas… ses enfants disent devant les Martin.
4. … Élodie n'aime pas, c'est voir les sans-abri.
5. Léo n'aime pas… se passe dans beaucoup de pays.
6. … les enfants cherchent, ce sont des solutions aux problèmes contemporains.
7. … le père pense, c'est que ses enfants ont hérité de son idéalisme et celui (*that*) de sa femme quand ils étaient jeunes.
8. … les Martin aiment, c'est la passion de la discussion.
9. Les enfants parlent de politique, … n'est pas poli, dit leur mère.
10. … amuse leur père, c'est l'idéalisme de ses enfants.

15 La politique 1.2, 1.3

Interpretive Viewing, Presentational Speaking or Writing

Dites ce qui est le plus important pour chaque personne et ce qui est le moins important selon les informations données dans la grille. Le plus grand chiffre indique le problème le plus important pour la personne.

	l'endettement	la pollution	le chômage	l'inflation
Noah	4	2	1	3
Anne	2	1	4	3
Nicole	3	1	4	2
Max	1	3	2	4
Thomas	4	2	3	1
Abdel	1	4	2	3
Claire	2	3	1	4

MODÈLE Noah
Ce qui est le plus important pour Noah, c'est le problème de l'endettement. Ce qu'il trouve le moins important, c'est le problème du chômage.

1. Max
2. Claire
3. Nicole
4. Thomas
5. Abdel
6. Anne

Essential Instruction

1. Do **Activité 14** as a class.
2. Ask students to add their names to the chart in **Activité 15** saying, **Ce qui est le plus important pour moi, c'est**…, and **Ce que je trouve le moins important, c'est… parce que**…. Students can work in pairs. They may also wish to change the topics according to their interests or concerns.
3. Before starting the game in **Activité 16** you might want to do a comprehensive review of the lesson vocabulary. **Activité 16** can serve as a good review for the **Leçon** Quiz.
4. For **Activité 17** consider having interested groups video tape their presentations.
5. Have all students complete **Activité 18** as written homework.

Communiquez!

16 Juste une minute! 1.1, 3.2, 5.2

Interpersonal Speaking

Formez deux équipes et choisissez un thème (ou c'est votre prof qui le choisit). À tour de rôle, vous allez devoir parler pendant une minute sur ce sujet sans hésitation ni répétition de mots ou d'expressions de vocabulaire. Si vous hésitez ou faites une répétition, un élève de l'autre équipe vous arrêtera. Si l'élève a raison, c'est à lui ou à elle de continuer à parler. La personne qui parle à la fin de la minute marque un point. Vous pouvez continuer avec un autre thème jusqu'à ce qu'une équipe gagne.

Thèmes possibles:

l'art
le cinéma
les émissions de télévision
l'environnement
les stars (francophones)
les médias (livres, musique, blogs)
les réseaux sociaux
le sport
la technologie
la mode

17 De quoi parlez-vous? 1.3, 3.2, 5.2

Presentational Writing

Pour vous préparer à jouer à ce jeu, faites une liste des mots de vocabulaires utiles pour chaque thème indiqué de l'activité **Juste une minute**. Puis, formez deux équipes. Le premier joueur de l'Équipe 1 et le premier joueur de l'Équipe 2 vont au tableau. Quand le prof propose un thème, les joueurs ont une minute pour écrire tous les mots et expressions de vocabulaire qu'ils savent sur ce thème. Le joueur avec la liste la plus longue gagne un point pour son équipe.

18 Mon dîner chez... 1.1, 1.2, 1.3, 2.1, 2.2, 5.1

Interpretive Listening, Interpersonal and Presentational Speaking

En petits groupes, vous allez faire de l'improvisation théâtrale. Deux personnes vont jouer les rôles suivants dans la situation suivante: vous êtes allé(e) dîner (choisissez chez qui) hier soir, et votre ami(e) vous pose des questions. Pendant que vous posez et répondez aux questions, les autres membres du groupe devront jouer (*act out*) la scène devant la classe. Ils peuvent jouer sérieusement, ou de façon comique.

MODÈLE
A: **Est-ce que tu as apporté un cadeau à l'hôtesse?**
B: **Oui, je lui ai offert des fleurs.**
(sur la scène)
C: **Madame, voici des fleurs pour vous.**
D: **Merci beaucoup, elles sont très belles!** (*Puts them in a vase.*)
ou
Merci, mais j'ai des allergies. (*Throws them in the garbage.*)

Resources

CA Communicative Activities
Share

Answers

16 Team games (winners) will vary.
17 Team games (winners) will vary.
18 Diary entries will vary.

Reference Desk

If you have access to Passport, create a question for your students to share their response to a communicative activity. Encourage students to utilize Passport (Explore) to further enhance and practice the key vocabulary and grammar for this section.

Connections

Sports

You may want to consider dedicating a full class period (or several within a week) to do all three of these activities as a "**journée (ou semaine) Jeux olympiques.**" Award medals or other tokens to winning teams and individuals. Students can sign up for any or all of the three events, **Activités 16**, **17**, and **18**.

Extension

Have students prepare **Activité 18** for a school performance and invite other French classes to attend.

Differentiated Learning

Expand

In **Activité 18** the journal entry might be all about the **faux pas** the guest made at the dinner party, or the gift chosen for the host.

Learning Styles

Auditory Learners

Have students do **Activité 15** among themselves and report the results to the class.

Resources

Rencontre avec l'auteur

Answers

Rencontre avec l'auteur
Il veut fêter les résultats du bac de son fils.

Pré-lecture
Answers will vary.

Stratégie de lecture
2. Les mauvais résultats scolaires du fils
3. Les différentes attentes entre le père et le fils pour l'avenir scolaire du fils
4. Les difficultés qu'a le père à imposer son autorité à son fils

Reference Desk

Sacha Guitry was born in Saint Petersburg, Russia, in 1885. His father, Lucien Guitry, was a well-known actor. In fact, Sacha started performing on stage at the age of 5. He knew he was going to be an artist so he did not take his studies seriously. In the 1920s, Guitry wrote 124 plays (some written in fewer than three days), more than 30 books, and he later fell in love with film, directing 33 movies. During the occupation by the Nazis, he was accused of accepting favors from the enemy. He wrote a tribute to Maréchal Pétain entitled *1929–1942: From Joan of Arc to Philippe Pétain*. After the war, because of his suspected collaboration, he was imprisoned for two months and absolved in 1947. His career, however, never recovered from this accusation. Guitry was married five times and is known for his witty and caustic remarks on love and marriage. He died in 1957 in Paris and is buried in the Montparnasse Cemetery. Advanced students may find Guitry's short story "**La mort du comte d'Astrac**" enjoyable and comprehensible.

Deux couverts

Rencontre avec l'auteur 1.2

Sacha Guitry (1885–1957) est un homme de théâtre et de cinéma. Il a écrit 124 pièces de théâtre qui sont encore souvent jouées en France. Son style est basé sur le dialogue et il crée des mondes avec un langage original. Ses pièces sont souvent centrées sur les problèmes quotidiens. Dans *Deux couverts*, une comédie en un acte, un père voudrait dîner avec son fils. Qu'est-ce qu'il veut fêter?

Pré-lecture

Préférez-vous dîner en famille ou avec vos amis?

Stratégie de lecture 1.1, 1.2, 1.3, 4.2

Generational Conflict. Dans un texte littéraire, un conflit, ou une crise, est une lutte entre deux forces opposées. Un type de conflit est la lutte entre deux personnages de générations différentes — par exemple, une mère et une fille, ou un grand-père et son petit-fils. Lisez l'extrait (*excerpt*) de la pièce de théâtre et trouvez dans le dialogue les conflits qui existent entre le père et son fils. Un exemple a été fait pour vous.

Fils	Père	Description du conflit
1. « J'ai été avec des camarades.... »	« Et tu n'as pas pensé à moi... tu ne t'es pas souvenu que j'attendais ici le résultat. »	La perte de temps que le fils a occasionnée à son père, et son impolitesse
2. « En géographie, il m'a demandé quels étaient les principaux fleuves de l'Australie!!! Comment veux-tu savoir ça! »	« À plusieurs reprises, cet hiver, mon petit, je t'ai proposé de t'appliquer davantage.... »	
3. « Oui... je ne connais rien de plus bête que ce truc-là! »	« Oui, seulement, moi, je ne m'en fiche pas du baccalauréat! »	
4. « ...et tu crois que je vais rester de seize à vingt-trois ans sans profiter de la vie? ... »	« Tu me laisseras le soin, je te prie, de diriger ton instruction et ton éducation jusqu'à ta majorité. »	

Essential Instruction

1. Have students listen to **Rencontre avec l'auteur** to learn about Sacha Guitry, and have them follow along in their books. Ask them pertinent questions such as: How many plays did he write? What was a theme running through many of his works?
2. As students each answer the **Pré-lecture** question, tally the results in two columns on the board: **en famille** and **avec des amis**. Encourage students to give a reason.
3. Present the **Stratégie de lecture** to students so that as they read the play they can look for these examples of intergenerational conflict.
4. Read and discuss the definition of irony in **Outils**. Ask for examples of dramatic irony found in *Romeo and Juliet* or a French movie you have shown in class.
5. Read through the **Pendant la lecture** questions before reading or listening. If students get a question wrong, make sure they understand the relevant passage before moving on.

Outils de lecture 1.2

Irony. L'ironie fait la différence entre l'apparence et la réalité. L'ironie dramatique révèle une information dont le lecteur ou les spectateurs sont conscients, mais pas les personnages. À la fin de la pièce, pourquoi est-ce ironique quand le père dit « … tu vas voir que je ne dîne pas seul ! D'ailleurs… regarde… deux couverts… » ? Quel personnage ignore que Pelletier va dîner seul ?

Deux couverts

Le Valet : Monsieur, Marie voudrait savoir pour quelle heure est le dîner.
Pelletier : Je me le demande ! … Sept heures ! … Est-il possible de faire attendre ainsi des enfants… et des parents ! … Que voulez-vous, nous dînerons sitôt que monsieur Jacques sera là ! …
Le Valet : C'est à cause des perdreaux*…
(*On sonne*)
Pelletier : Elle peut les mettre ! … Allez ouvrir… enfin ! … C'est toi ? …
(*Jacques entre.*)
Jacques : Oui, Papa !
Pelletier : Eh ! Bien ?
Jacques : Recalé* !
Pelletier : Oh ! … Embrasse-moi tout de même !
(*Jacques embrasse son père.*)
Pelletier : Mon pauvre petit ! … Oh ! … Et… quand l'as-tu su ?
Jacques : Que j'étais recalé ?
Pelletier : Oui…
Jacques : À… cinq heures et demie.
Pelletier : À cinq heures et demie ?
Jacques : Oui, Papa…
Pelletier : Oh ! Ce n'est pas possible !
Jacques : Mais si, Papa, pourquoi ?
Pelletier : Oh ! … Tu sais l'heure qu'il est ?
Jacques : Oui, il doit être six heures…
Pelletier : Non, mon petit, non… il est sept heures cinq ! … Et j'attends depuis quatre heures !
Jacques : Je te demande pardon, Papa.
Pelletier : D'où viens-tu ?
Jacques : Je… j'ai été… heu…
Pelletier : Où as-tu été ?
Jacques : J'ai été avec des camarades…
Pelletier : Oui, mais, où… où as-tu été ?
Jacques : Nous avons été prendre quelque chose….

Pendant la lecture
1. Qui est-ce que le père attend ?

Pendant la lecture
2. Jacques a-t-il réussi au bac ?

Pendant la lecture
3. Le père attend depuis quand ?

Pendant la lecture
4. Jacques a-t-il déjà mangé ? Avec qui ?

perdreaux *partridges* ; **Recalé** *Held back in school*

Resources

Deux couverts

Answers

Outils de lecture
Jacques

Pendant de lecture
1. Le père attend son fils.
2. Non, il n'a pas réussi au bac.
3. Le père attend depuis quatre heures.
4. Oui, il a mangé un snack avec son ami.

Reference Desk

Consider these strategies for reading the play: (1) Divide the play into sections and include both choral and individual readings. (2) Read stage directions and **Pendant la lecture** questions before reading, and encourage students to predict what will happen next. (3) Ask students to visualize the characters and contemplate the setting. (4) Provide a focus or final question to contemplate while reading. This acts both as a learning and comprehension check.

Differentiated Learning

Accelerate
Have these students work together to explain how Guitry's play is about **les problèmes quotidiens**. They can present their findings to the rest of the class.

Decelerate
Divide the reading into small sections. Have students act out each section, and ask them questions to test basic understanding. Who are the characters? Why was the father waiting? Where was the son? When the students demonstrate basic understanding, they can answer the questions in the margins. Ask them to find the lines that justify their answers. Continue reading the play in segments (short segments). Encourage students to find evidence in the text for their answers.

Answers

Pendant la lecture

5. Son attitude était mauvaise. Il dit que les questions étaient stupides.
6. Il lui a conseillé de travailler diligemment.
7. Non.

(Suite)

Pelletier: Vous avez été prendre quelque chose!!! C'est superbe! Et tu n'as pas pensé à moi... tu ne t'es pas souvenu que j'attendais ici le résultat....

Jacques: Si, Papa... mais le temps a passé si vite!

Pelletier: Je ne trouve pas! (*Un temps.*) Assieds-toi, ne reste pas debout*. Et, pourquoi as-tu été recalé?

Jacques: Ils m'ont posé des questions stupides!

Pelletier: Ça m'étonne*! Peut-être t'ont-elles semblées stupides parce que tu les ignorais! Quelles sont les questions auxquelles tu as mal répondu?

Jacques: D'abord, il m'a posé en histoire une question que je n'avais jamais étudiée....

Pelletier: À qui la faute*?

Jacques: Alors, comme je n'ai pas su répondre... il a fait le malin*, et il m'a demandé sur un ton vexant si je savais au moins quel avait été le héros de la bataille d'Arc....

Pelletier: Et tu as répondu?

Jacques: J'ai répondu en rigolant: Jeanne d'Arc!

Pelletier: Oui, eh bien, je trouve la réponse plus stupide que la question! En géographie?

Jacques: En géographie, il m'a demandé quels étaient les principaux fleuves de l'Australie!!! Comment veux-tu savoir ça!

Pelletier: En l'apprenant*! Je ne vois pas d'autre moyen! À plusieurs reprises, cet hiver, mon petit, je t'ai proposé de t'appliquer davantage... tu ne me semblais pas au point... mais, chaque fois que je t'en ai fait l'observation, tu m'as juré* que tout « allait très bien... » et ma foi, tu avais fini par me donner ta confiance! ... Enfin, c'est fait, c'est fait! Je ne m'exagère pas la gravité de cette aventure, bien sûr... ce n'est pas un désastre, mais c'est un avertissement*, et je te conseille de donner un bon coup de collier* cet été afin d'être prêt, afin d'être complètement prêt en octobre prochain. C'est bien en octobre, n'est-ce pas, que tu repasses*?

Jacques: Oui, on peut se représenter en octobre.

Pelletier: Comment, on peut? Qu'est-ce que ça veut dire?

Jacques: Heu... ben....

Pelletier: Parle....

Jacques: Ben, ça veut dire que j'aimerais autant ne pas repasser....

Pelletier: Qu'est-ce que tu dis?

Pendant la lecture
5. Quelle était l'attitude du fils quand on l'a interrogé?

Pendant la lecture
6. Quel conseil le père a-t-il donné au fils?

Pendant la lecture
7. Le fils veut-il repasser le bac?

debout *standing*; **Ça m'étonne** *I'm astonished*; **faute** *fault*; **faire le malin** *to act smart*; **En l'apprenant** *By learning it*; **as juré** *swore*; **avertissement** *warning*; **bon coup de collier** *good effort*; **repasses** passes un examen pour la deuxième fois

Essential Instruction

1. Play the recording in its entirety and ask basic comprehension questions.
2. Play the recording again, stopping at intervals to furnish supplementary vocabulary, and ask and answer questions.
3. Allow your high-ability students to work in small groups to answer the **Pendant la lecture** questions.
4. Work with your lower-ability students to help them understand the reading. See footnote p. 123.

Answers

Pendant la lecture

8. Selon Jacques, seuls les idiots ont réussi au bac.
9. On a recalé Mareuil parce qu'il ne savait pas la réponse à une question d'histoire.

Analyse

Possible answer: Selon le père, l'intelligence est mesurée par la performance à l'école, tandis que, selon le fils, c'est la créativité qui importe.

Expansion

Have students point out another example of irony: Mareuil's genius (he invented an airplane) is not recognized by the school system (he failed to answer a social studies question).

(Suite)

Jacques :	Oui, quoi… j'aimerais mieux en rester là. Moi, je m'en fiche du baccalauréat !
Pelletier :	Ah ! Oui ?
Jacques :	Oui… je ne connais rien de plus bête que ce truc-là !
Pelletier :	Allons donc ?
Jacques :	Ah ! La, la !
Pelletier :	Oui, seulement, moi, je ne m'en fiche pas du baccalauréat !
Jacques :	Ça, c'est autre chose !
Pelletier :	Oui, et c'est même une chose qui a son importance ! Mais tout de même, je ne serais pas fâché de savoir pourquoi tu te fiches du baccalauréat !
Jacques :	Oh ! C'est bien simple… je me suis aperçu* aujourd'hui que tous les idiots avaient été reçus !
Pelletier :	Vraiment ?
Jacques :	Oui !
Pelletier :	Et les élèves intelligents ont tous été refusés ?
Jacques :	Oui !
Pelletier :	Exemple : toi !
Jacques :	Oui.
Pelletier :	C'est admirable !
Jacques :	Moi, je les connais, Papa, les camarades de ma classe ! Il y en a deux, tiens… Rondel et Debacker, ils ont eu le maximum de points… eh ! Bien, je n'ai jamais rencontré deux types plus bêtes ! Il n'y a pas moyen de causer* avec eux cinq minutes !
Pelletier :	Mais, mon enfant, la vie ne se passe pas en conversations ! Tu as d'étranges idées sur l'intelligence…. Les deux camarades dont tu parles n'ont peut-être pas ton toupet*, ton bagout* et ton exubérance… ce sont sans doute des enfants réfléchis et sérieux….
Jacques :	Ils sont abrutis*, tout simplement ! Quand on pense qu'ils ont refusé Mareuil !
Pelletier :	Mareuil ? Qui est Mareuil ?
Jacques :	Mareuil, tu sais bien, que je t'ai amené un matin, à déjeuner….
Pelletier :	Oui, oui, parfaitement. C'est ce jeune homme qui a inventé un aéroplane.
Jacques :	C'est ça ! Eh ! Bien, ils l'ont recalé parce qu'il ne savait pas qui avait succédé à Pépin-le-Bref ! Je me demande un peu à quoi ça peut servir de savoir qui a succédé à Pépin-le-Bref, pour un type qui veut être aviateur ! Veux-tu que je te dise, Papa… je suis sûr que Mareuil a du génie* !

Pendant la lecture
8. Selon Jacques, qui a réussi au bac ?

Analyse
Expliquez les différentes conceptions qu'ont le fils et le père de l'intelligence.

Pendant la lecture
9. Pourquoi a-t-on recalé Mareuil ?

je me suis aperçu j'ai réalisé ; **causer** parler ; **toupet** *nerve* ; **bagout** *way with words* ; **abrutis** *dazed, dumb* ; **génie** *genius*

Differentiated Learning

Accelerate/Decelerate

Have students create a list of clues in the scene that indicate the story takes place sometime in the past.

Learning Styles

Auditory Learners

Have these students work in pairs to read the play to each other. This will imprint the sound of the words in their mind.

Special Needs Students

Dyslexia/AD(H)D

Make copies of the play to distribute to these students so that they can underline, highlight, and write comments and translations to help them break down this long excerpt into smaller parts.

Answers

Pendant la lecture

10. Il a seize ans.
11. parce que sans le bac, le fils n'aura pas un bon métier

Critical Thinking

Comparisons

Ask students to read the poem "**Le cancre**" by Jacques Prévert and compare the attitude of Jacques to the student in the poem.

Culture

Products: Comparison

Have students compare educational and civil obligations of this time and culture to their own: **le bac** to get a job, and, in this case, three years of mandatory military service. Point out to students that jobs for government agencies, such as postal worker or teacher, are desirable, primarily for their stability and generous pension.

(Suite)

Pelletier : Je n'ai jamais dit le contraire ! … D'ailleurs, il ne s'agit pas de ton ami Mareuil en ce moment, il s'agit uniquement de toi ! … Il est possible que ton camarade ait du génie… mais, sans vouloir te désobliger*, comme jusqu'à présent, toi, tu ne me sembles avoir de dispositions géniales pour aucune branche, tu me laisseras le soin*, je te prie, de diriger ton instruction et ton éducation jusqu'à ta majorité.

Jacques : Ah ! Non !

Pelletier : Comment « Ah ! Non ! » ? Est-ce que tu perds la tête ? … Je ne discute pas avec toi, en ce moment… je te renseigne simplement !

Jacques : Je peux tout de même te répondre !

Pelletier : Parle-moi autrement, je te prie ! Vas-y… réponds… je t'écoute !

Jacques : J'ai seize ans, n'est-ce pas… or à vingt ans, il faudra que je fasse mon service militaire… et tu crois que je vais rester de seize à vingt-trois ans sans profiter de la vie ?

Pelletier : Ne crie pas, c'est inutile ! Je n'ai pas l'intention de t'empêcher de profiter de la vie !

Jacques : Est-ce qu'on peut profiter de la vie, quand on travaille !

Pelletier : Oh ! Oui, petit malheureux !

Jacques : Mon intention est d'interrompre dès aujourd'hui mes études !

Pelletier : Ton intention !!!

Jacques : Oui !

Pelletier : Oui, eh bien, ma volonté à moi est que tu les termines comme je l'entendrai !

Jacques : Mais, Papa, laisse-moi t'expliquer…

Pelletier : Non, assez ! À moi, de parler maintenant ! J'ai vu le fond de ta pensée, et tu m'as fait connaître ton intention ! Tu n'as rien à m'expliquer. Tu vas maintenant connaître ma pensée et ma décision ! Si tu dois avoir un jour du génie, mon enfant, ton baccalauréat n'en empêchera pas l'éclosion*… mais si toute ta vie tu dois rester un cancre*, tu auras du moins la possibilité d'entrer aux Postes et Télégraphes, étant bachelier ! (*Temps.*) Si par malheur, tu refusais d'obéir, je me séparerais de toi ! (*Un temps.*) Ainsi, j'ai passé quinze années de ma vie à me priver de bien des choses pour te donner une éducation aussi forte que ma tendresse, et voilà le fruit de mes peines ! Est-ce que tu te rends compte de ce que j'ai fait pour toi ?

Connexions Théâtre 1.2, 3.1

Imaginez que vous êtes metteur en scène. Trouvez des adverbes pour indiquer à chaque acteur de la scène comment lire les répliques (*cues*). Proposez aussi des gestes. Échangez votre script avec celui de votre partenaire.

Pendant la lecture

10. Quel âge a le fils ?

Stratégie

Faites une liste de toutes les choses sur lesquelles le papa et le fils ne sont pas d'accord.

Pendant la lecture

11. Pourquoi le père veut-il que son fils repasse son bac ?

désobliger *to offend* ; **soin** *care* ; **n'en empêchera pas l'éclosion** *won't prevent the birth (of your genius)* ; **cancre** *dunce (educ.)*

Essential Instruction

1. Have the students find pieces of evidence in the text that illustrate the conflict the father has in disciplining his son.
2. Ask students to make a list of the ways in which the son manipulates, threatens, alarms, and/or confuses the father.
3. Ask students to point out the classic ways the son justifies himself. Have they ever said the same things? "The test was stupid." "None of my friends did well." Discuss with students whether or not Guitry drew an accurate portrayal of a teenage boy. Ask students to agree with the son or the father's point of view, and then invite them to consider the opposing perspective.

(Suite et fin)

Jacques : Oui, quoi… tu as….

Pelletier : Oh ! Non, ne me dis pas que j'ai fait ce qu'ont fait les autres pères.

Jacques : Tu t'es privé ?

Pelletier : Oui… mais tu ne t'en es jamais aperçu ! Nous ne sommes pas si riches que tu crois ! Nous ne sommes pas riches. Tu es très élégant… tu t'habilles très bien… moi, c'est tout fait ! Je ne me plains pas… je l'ai voulu… et je ne le regrette pas encore…. Ah ! Mon petit bonhomme, tu ne t'es rendu compte de rien ! Ta mère est morte deux ans après ta naissance… il y a quatorze ans de cela, comprends-tu ?

Jacques : Quoi ?

Pelletier : Quoi ? J'avais trente-six ans, mon petit, et j'en ai cinquante, à présent ! J'étais jeune… je ne le suis plus ! J'ai vieilli* pour toi… je me suis consacré* entièrement* à toi ! Écoute bien… deux fois j'ai dû me remarier… la première fois, tu étais trop petit… la seconde fois, tu étais trop grand… Penses-y de temps en temps !

(Un temps.)

Jacques : *(regarde la pendule et se lève.)* Au revoir, Papa….

Pelletier : Quoi ?

Jacques : Au revoir, Papa !

Pelletier : Où vas-tu ?

Jacques : Je dîne chez Mareuil… et il est sept heures et demie….

Pelletier : Ah ! Tu dînes chez Mareuil….

Jacques : Oui, Papa… ça t'ennuie* ?

Pelletier : Du tout, mon enfant, du tout… c'est tout naturel… ça doit être sûrement naturel !

Jacques : Et toi ?

Pelletier : Moi ? Oh ! Mon petit, ça se trouve bien… je ne dîne pas seul !

Jacques : Ah !

Pelletier : Oui… regarde toi-même ! *(Il ouvre la porte de la salle à manger.)* Tu vois ! Tu peux lire le menu… tu vas voir que je ne dîne pas seul ! D'ailleurs… regarde… deux couverts !

Jacques : *(vexé.)* Au revoir, Papa… à demain….

Pelletier : À demain, mon petit…. *(Jacques embrasse son père et sort.)* Et il me fait la tête ! *(Et après avoir pensé qu'il pourrait peut-être téléphoner à Madame Blandin—et, après y avoir renoncé, Pelletier entre dans la salle à manger, en disant :)* Émile, vous pouvez servir !

Analyse

Pourquoi le père et le fils ont-ils une perspective différente de l'enfance de Jacques ? Le père a-t-il, selon vous, fait de réels sacrifices pour son fils ? Expliquez en vous servant du texte, puis donnez votre opinion personnelle.

Pendant la lecture

12. Qu'est-ce que le père a fait pour son fils ?

Pendant la lecture

13. Pourquoi le père ment-il ?

J'ai vieilli *I've gotten old* ; **je me suis consacré** j'ai sacrifié ; **entièrement** complètement ; **ça t'ennuies** *do you mind*

Answers

Pendant la lecture

12. Il a tout sacrifié pour son fils.
13. Il ment parce ce qu'il ne veut pas que son fils se sente coupable

Analyse

Answers will vary.

Differentiated Learning

Accelerate

Have students find instances in the script where the father is trying to make the son feel guilty. According to the father, why didn't he remarry? What is the irony in the father's words **"et je ne le regrette pas encore"** when referring to his son?

Resources

Pre-T Pre-test

Q *Leçon* Quiz

Answers

Post-lecture

Possible answers: Pelletier est un bon père parce qu'il fait des sacrifices pour son fils. Pelletier est un mauvais père parce qu'il n'est pas assez autoritaire envers son fils. Jacques est un mauvais fils car il laisse son père qui a tout sacrifié pour lui dîner seul.

Le monde visuel

Le style de l'arrière-plan est un peu impressionniste. Le sujet frappe l'œil car il est peint avec des touches plus nettes et mieux définies que le paysage de l'arrière-plan, ce qui crée un contraste.

19 Activities will vary.

Communication

Presentational: Cooperative Groups

Arrange students into two heterogeneous groups, the prosecution and the defense. The groups will work cooperatively to write arguments for both sides to determine if Pelletier was a good father or not. A representative from each side will play the role of his or her side's lawyer, and the remaining students will be in the jury box. Encourage your students to embellish the story with details and use lots of drama.

Expansion

Have student compare the painting to another of the same subject by the same painter: *Portrait of Marcel in a Sailor Suit.*

Post-lecture 1.3

Pelletier est-il un bon ou mauvais père? Pourquoi? Et son fils, est-il un bon ou mauvais fils? Pourquoi?

Le monde visuel 1.2

Dans ce tableau, Jules Ernest Renoux (1863–1932) a peint un petit garçon de manière réaliste, sur un arrière-plan de style différent. L'interprétation artistique des paysages d'arrière-plan en peinture a changé à travers l'histoire de l'art. Au 16ème siècle, on peut voir derrière la *Joconde*, de Léonard de Vinci, un arrière-plan qui annonce la peinture de paysage. Au 18ème siècle, Claude Lorrain a essayé de peindre ses paysages d'arrière-plan de manière plus réaliste que les peintres de son époque. Mais au 19ème siècle, les peintres voulaient plutôt montrer des impressions de paysage. Dans quel style est peint le paysage à l'arrière-plan de ce portrait? Qu'est-ce qui frappe l'œil en premier, le sujet ou le paysage? Selon vous, pourquoi une telle juxtaposition du portrait réaliste et d'un paysage de style différent?

Portrait de Marcel Renoux vers 13 ou 14 ans, c. 1912. Jules Ernest Renoux. Collection privée.

19 Activités d'expansion 1.3, 5.2

Complétez les activités suivantes.

1. Écrivez un paragraphe dans lequel vous expliquez les conflits entre le père et son fils dans cette pièce. Servez-vous des informations de votre grille.
2. Jouez le rôle du père et écrivez une lettre que vous allez glisser (*slip*) sous la porte de la chambre de votre fils, et dans laquelle vous expliquez ce que vous voulez pour lui et pourquoi.
3. Imaginez que le père et le fils dînent ensemble et discutent de l'avenir du fils. Écrivez un dialogue pour cette scène entre le père et le fils.
4. Écrivez un texte dans lequel vous expliquez pourquoi vous préférez les paysages ou les portraits en peinture. Expliquez aussi si vous préférez un style réaliste ou plus abstrait.

Produits 1.2, 2.2

Jules Ernest Renoux (1863–1932) était un peintre français très actif pendant la période impressionniste. Comme les Impressionnistes, il préférait peindre en plein air (bien qu'il était timide et choisissait des lieux discrets pour peindre). Par contre, il préférait se concentrer sur les portraits, souvent plus détaillés et réalistes que les œuvres de ses contemporains.

Essential Instruction

1. Students interested in art should always try to answer the questions in **Le monde visuel**. Emphasize that you are not looking for a specific answer to the **Post-lecture** questions.
2. Assign the first task in **Activité 19** as written homework. Have students refer to the **Stratégie de lecture** on p. 120.
3. Offer a choice of the other two activities in **Activité 19**.
4. Challenge your drama students to act out a section of ***Deux couverts***.

Pre-AP 21

Question centrale ? Qu'y a-t-il d'universel dans les rapports entre les gens?

Communiquez!

20 Soyez chef! 1.1, 1.2, 1.3, 3.1, 4.1, 5.2

Connecting to Creativity and Innovation, Collaboration

Interpersonal Speaking, Interpretive Reading, Presentational Writing and Speaking

Les cuisiniers modernes aiment se servir de plats traditionnels et les modifier quelque peu pour y ajouter « leur propre goût ». Travaillez avec un partenaire pour créer deux ou trois nouvelles recettes pour une fête francophone, religieuse ou non. Cherchez des recettes traditionnelles, puis, modifiez-les pour y ajouter votre propre touche, un goût légèrement différent et unique. Avec un partenaire, réfléchissez sur les ingrédients et les méthodes de préparation de chaque recette pour décider de ce que vous pourriez changer, ajouter, ou retirer. Prenez des notes pour expliquer comment vous avez modifié les recettes ; ensuite présentez les nouvelles recettes dans un blog, une vidéo, un site web, ou en classe.

21 Un dîner politique 1.1, 1.2, 1.3, 3.2, 5.2

Connecting to Leadership and Responsibility, Social and Cross-Cultural Skills

Interpersonal Speaking, Interpretive Reading, Presentational Writing

Vous faites un stage à un bureau politique de votre région. Votre supérieur(e) (*manager*) a organisé un dîner chez lui/elle auquel sont invités des hommes et des femmes politiques de pays francophones et leurs conjoints. Pour ce dîner, il est très important pour votre supérieur(e) de connaître la culture des pays des invités, afin de pouvoir avoir une petite conversation avec eux. Votre supérieur(e) vous demande donc de préparer une liste de sujets de conversation appropriés, et aussi de sujets qu'il vaut mieux éviter (*avoid*). Faites des recherches sur trois pays francophones de votre choix et préparez une liste de bons et de mauvais sujets de conversation. Vous pouvez ajouter des manières de table, ou d'accueil. Avec un partenaire qui va jouer le rôle de votre supérieur(e) pratiquez des mini-conversations. Ensuite, démontrez une conversation polie et une conversation impolie à la classe.

22 Un diner désastreux 1.1, 1.2, 1.3, 3.2, 5.2

Connecting to Social and Cross-Cultural Skills, Productivity and Accountability

Interpersonal Speaking, Interpretive Viewing, Presentational Speaking

Imaginez que chacun de vos camarades de classe est un personnage politique d'un pays particulier (président, premier ministre, ministre de l'intérieur, etc.), francophone ou non. Le président Emmanuel Macron vous a tous invités à une soirée internationale au palais de l'Élysée. Malheureusement, tout le monde fait des erreurs sociales ! Choisissez le personnage politique (personnage réel) dont vous allez jouer le rôle, puis écrivez votre nom, votre poste, et le pays que vous représentez, sur une étiquette que vous collerez sur vous. Faites une petite liste de choses à faire et à ne pas faire dans votre pays, et attachez-la sur vous aussi. À la soirée, tout le monde circule et fait la conversation. Regardez les listes attachées sur votre partenaire et commencez à parler de chaque sujet interdit. Les partenaires doivent être très dramatiques quand ils réagissent et expliquent les erreurs faites.

Differentiated Learning

Accelerate

Students may welcome the challenge inherent in working on **Activité A**.

Decelerate

Have students write a paragraph about the ideal father before answering the **Post-lecture** question. They should use adjectives and give examples. Review some adjectives with them before they write.

Learning Styles

Artistic

Invite your artistic students to draw or paint a portrait in the style of Renoux, with realistic, detailed attention to the figure and more abstractions in the background. Ask them what they think of these artistic decisions.

Reference Desk

This section is designed for students to apply unit vocabulary and structures to communicative activities that foster 21st-century skills. These activities demonstrate how 21st-century skills are cultivated in the language classroom and how these skills and the language learning process are mutually beneficial.

French in the Workplace

Translating graphs into words

Interpreting data is an important aspect of the economic and political worlds. Have students look back at the graphs on pp. 97 and 98 and discuss with a partner what each graph reveals about the eating habits of the French and the cost of **la baguette jambon-beurre**, respectively. They should then extrapolate the data and explain what each graph suggests about French societal trends (a shorter lunch, for example, may indicate that more people are working today than in 1990, or that fewer mothers are staying home to prepare large midday meals). When they have finished interpreting the two graphs, ask them to find another graph online regarding a topic that interests them. Have them prepare a presentation for the class in which they explain the graph's data and extrapolate a broader societal trend.

Social Justice

While culture plays an important part in one's relationship with food, **la faim** is a phenomenon that transcends cultures. Have students research which groups in the francophone world suffer from starvation or hunger. Have them look at several countries or regions, or focus on one. Then ask students to share existing solutions that address these problems, as well as suggest new solutions. Finally, discuss whether there are similar problems in their community, and how they can make a difference.

Resources

Create

Answers

All activities will vary.

Reference Desk

If you have access to Passport, assign your students an IPA task related to the unit.

Finale

Projets finaux

A Connexions par Internet : l'éducation civique 1.2, 1.3, 3.1, 3.2

Les partis politiques

Allez faire des recherches en ligne sur un sujet politique qui vous intéresse.

1. Préparez une liste de quatre partis politiques en France. Pour chacun, dites les idéaux qu'ils représentent (ce pourquoi ils sont pour, et ce pourquoi ils sont contre).
2. Écrivez une petite biographie d'un homme ou d'une femme politique. Référez-vous aux suggestions ci-dessous.

Recherche : charles de gaulle, georges pompidou, simone veille, françois mitterand, jacques chirac, nicolas sarkozy, françois hollande, christine lagarde, emmanuel macron, sibeth ndiaye, marine le pen

B Communautés en ligne 1.3, 3.1, 3.2, 4.2, 5.1

Dans les médias

Faites un profil du paysage médiatique des États-Unis. Vous pouvez parler des best-sellers, des émissions de télé et des films populaires, ou des blogueurs célèbres. Préparez des commentaires qui montrent votre compréhension des médias actuels et ce que vous pensez de ces médias. Ensuite, envoyez votre document à une classe francophone, une autre classe de français aux États-Unis, ou postez votre document en ligne. Demandez à vos lecteurs de préparer un document semblable avec leurs réactions sur les médias là où ils habitent. Finalement, comparez les deux documents.

C Passez à l'action ! 1.3, 2.2, 3.1, 3.2, 4.2, 5.1

Un livre de recettes

Avec votre classe, préparez un livre de recettes de pays ou régions francophones. Chaque groupe choisit le pays ou la région qui l'intéresse le plus, et cherche des recettes de provinces françaises, ou des recettes maghrébines, québécoises, belges, ou antillaises. Cherchez ces recettes en ligne, puis, écrivez une version simplifiée et avec les mesures converties en *cups* et en *ounces*.

Le cari créole se prépare avec de la viande ou du poisson, des lentilles, du thym, du curcuma, du gingembre, et des oignons.

Essential Instruction

1. For the **Projets finaux**, have students choose **A** or **B**. **Activité C** offers an opportunity for all students. Consider the different jobs students can fill: researchers, photographers, graphic designers, typists, editors, and taste testers!
2. **Activité D** is designed to help students become independent learners. They should fill in the grid as they review **Leçons A**, **B**, and **C**. They can consider this assignment a way of personally assessing what they know and what they need to study before the Unit Test.
3. Have students write you a letter outlining what they would like you to help them with before the final assessment. This may be a non-threatening way for them to ask you for help. Allow them to do this in English.

D Faisons le point! 1.3

Mes progrès

Remplissez les organigrammes pour montrer ce que vous avez appris dans cette unité.

Je comprends	Je ne comprends pas encore	Mes connexions

What did I do well to learn and use the content of this unit?	How can I apply what I have learned this year?
How can I effectively communicate to others what I have learned?	What was the most important concept I learned in this unit?

Answers

Answers will vary.

Reference Desk

The **Faisons le Point!** section asks students to self-evaluate and keep track of their progress. When students complete the activity, direct them to use "I can" statements based on the unit objectives in the **Contrat de l'élève**. The graphic organizer for **Activité D** can be found in the Copy Masters supplement.

Special Needs Students

Linguistically Challenged

These students may lack confidence due to their language skills. Let them share their experiences and knowledge in **Activité C** about life in the United States by allowing them to prepare a response ahead of time.

Resources

- Activity A
- LA Listening Activity *Synthèse*
- Pre-AP Listening *Unité 2*
- Perform

Answers

A Script

Chez moi, on fête le Nouvel An avec les amis et la famille. En général, on loue une salle des fêtes que l'on décore. On achète des vêtements et des jouets de fêtes. Ma cousine est toujours à la dernière mode et papa porte le même smoking tous les ans. Maman et ma tante font les courses et c'est Jean-François, mon cousin qui est chef, qui prépare la cuisine. Bien sûr, on l'aide tous un peu ! Au menu, il y a toujours des huîtres, du foie gras, une dinde, et des pâtisseries. C'est moi qui accueille tout le monde et je range les manteaux. C'est une grande soirée avec un DJ et on écoute tous les hits de l'année. On mange bien, on discute politique et cinéma, on danse jusqu'à minuit quand on boit un verre de champagne.

1. Laure parle du réveillon de Noël.
2. On porte des vêtements spéciaux pour cette fête.
3. La mère et la tante de Laure font la cuisine.
4. Laure accueille tout le monde.
5. On écoute tous les hits de l'année et on danse jusqu'à minuit.
6. On invite juste des amis.

1. F; 2. V; 3. F; 4. V; 5. V; 6. F

B Conversations will vary.

C Activities will vary.

Reference Desk

If you have access to Passport, assign a task to evaluate your students' oral proficiency.

Communication

Interpersonal: Paired Practice

For **Activité B** have students use their mobile phones as props. Ask them to embellish the conversation using any expressions that they have learned to create an interesting, realistic conversation. You may want to time the dialogues and reward pairs with the longest or most accurate dialogues.

Pre-AP

Évaluation

A Évaluation de compréhension auditive 1.1, 1.2

*Écrivez les numéros 1–6 sur votre papier. Écoutez Laure parler d'une fête dans sa famille. Puis, écrivez **V** si la phrase est vraie et **F** si la phrase est fausse.*

B Évaluation orale 1.1, 2.1, 4.2, 5.2

Téléphonez à votre partenaire. Demandez si vous le/la dérangez et s'il ou elle peut vous donner un coup de main dans la cuisine pour préparer la soirée du Nouvel An que vous organisez. Votre partenaire va vous dire ce qu'il ou elle est en train de faire, et s'il ou elle peut venir. Utilisez quelques expressions de la section Pour la conversation.

C Évaluation culturelle 3.1, 3.2, 4.1, 4.2,5.1

Vous allez comparer les cultures francophones à la culture américaine.

1. **Les grandes fêtes**
   Comment est-ce que les Français passent le réveillon de Noël ? Qu'est-ce qu'ils mangent, selon leurs traditions culturelles ou religieuses ? Qui est-ce qu'ils invitent ? Qu'est-ce qui se passe le lendemain pour les enfants ? Dites comment les Américains fêtent Noël. Si vous et votre famille fêtez Noël, vous pouvez parler de vos expériences personnelles. Si vous ne célébrez pas Noël mais une autre fête (Ramadan, Hanoukka, Kwanza, etc.), expliquez ce que vous faites.
2. **La cuisine française**
   Expliquez comment la cuisine française a changé. Comment est-ce que les Français préparent leurs repas maintenant ? Quelles influences internationales est-ce qu'on remarque dans la cuisine française ? Comment est-ce que la cuisine américaine ressemble à la cuisine française ? Où est-ce qu'on peut apprendre l'art de la cuisine française traditionnelle en France et chez vous ?
3. **Les expressions gastronomiques**
   Si un Français ou une Française vous dit, « Je ne suis pas dans mon assiette » et « Ne me raconte pas de salades », qu'est-ce qu'il ou elle veut dire ? Faites une liste d'expressions gastronomiques en anglais, par exemple, « bringing home the bacon » et « You're just buttering me up ».
4. **Les bonnes manières à table**
   Comparez les bonnes manières à table en France avec celles (*the ones*) que vos parents vous ont apprises.
5. **Le vin**
   Quel pays est le premier producteur mondial de vin ? Est-ce que l'on produit du vin dans votre région ? Combien de vins différents produit-on aux États-Unis ? Quel est le rang (*ranking*) des vins américains ?
6. **L'art de la conversation à table**
   De quoi est-ce qu'on évite de parler à table en France ? Et chez vous ?

Essential Instruction

1. In the **Évaluation**, students should all do **Activités A** and **B** to help prepare them for the Listening and Speaking portions of the Unit Test.
2. For **Activité C**, have groups draw a number from a hat to select an activity. All students with the same number work together, and then present their work to the class.
3. Let the high-ability, self-directed learners proceed at their own pace while completing **Activités D, E**, and **F**. When they finish, check their work. Have them collaborate to make a jeopardy game with categories and questions for the class to review unit content.
4. By responding to the questions in **Activité E**, students will have drafted a paragraph. You may want to allow time for peer-editing.
5. Storyboard templates are available online to help with **Activité F**.

D **Évaluation écrite** 1.3, 2.1, 4.1, 4.2

Vous êtes un(e) journaliste américain(e) à Paris. Un collègue français vous a invité(e) chez ses parents pour le réveillon de Noël. Écrivez un article dans lequel vous parlez :

- de ce que vous avez offert à votre hôte
- de ce qu'on vous a servi
- des bonnes manières à table que vous avez observées (En France, on....)
- des sujets de conversation

E **Évaluation visuelle** 1.3, 2.1, 4.2

Écrivez un paragraphe en français sur la fête illustrée ci-dessous en répondant aux questions.

1. De quelle fête s'agit-il?
2. Quelle est la date?
3. Qu'est-ce qui s'est passé ce soir-là chez les Roussin? Imaginez!
4. Qu'est-ce qu'on va mettre dans les chaussons qui sont sous le sapin de Noël?
5. Qu'est-ce que les enfants vont ouvrir demain matin?

F **Évaluation compréhensive** 1.3, 2.1

Créez une histoire avec six illustrations et des dialogues en bulles, comme dans une bande dessinée. Dessinez une famille et leurs invités à table. Présentez un conflit.

Answers

D Articles will vary.
E Paragraphs will vary.
F Stories will vary.

Reference Desk

1. For **Activité D** have students review vocabulary for possible menus in **Leçon A** pp. 74–75, 81–82, and **Leçon B** p. 97.
2. For ideas regarding manners and gifts for the host, see **Leçon C** p. 112, and for conversation topics see **Leçon C** pp. 106–107, 110–111, and 119.

Communication

Interpersonal: Cooperative Groups

Put students in six heterogeneous groups. A student from each group will draw a card with a number from one to six. That number is the activity that they are assigned to complete. Write the number down for your records. The student groups are to compare French and American cultures by doing one of the six activities. Encourage students to share the responsibility for the end product and to build on each member's strengths to complete the activity.

Differentiated Learning

Accelerate/Decelerate

By grouping students heterogeneously, it is anticipated that the lower-ability students will benefit from working with stronger language students and feel free to ask questions they might not feel comfortable asking you. Have students do **B** before listening to **A**, as they may inadvertently use some of the vocabulary they will need to recognize in **A**.

Expand

To review vocabulary, give students small white boards. Ask a question about the vocabulary: **Comment s'appelle le grand repas avant Noël? Quel est l'équivalent français du *GNP*?** Put a time limit on how long they have to answer, and then ask them to turn their boards around/hold them up. Write the word or expression on the board for reinforcement. A student could also lead the activity.

Resources

FC Flash Cards

Rendez-vous à Nice ! Documentaire 1

T *Unité 2* Test

Reference Desk

1. Remind students that the **Leçon** where each vocabulary word can be found is indicated in red.
2. Have students find the vocabulary words that are related to these words: **long**, **la dette**, **la prison**, **la tranquillité**, **l'univers**, **le vote**, **la passion**, **un champion**, **un drame**, **l'idéal**, **national**.

nouvelle orthographe **une buche, s'entrainer, les huitres**

Game

Panique !

This review game offers lots of flexibility. Use it here for reviewing vocabulary with a focus on antonyms. Divide the class into two teams. Choose one helper from each side. The helpers will count points for the opposite side. Prepare a list of antonyms from the unit vocabulary: **hausser/baisser, froidir/chauffer, blasé/dramatique,** etc. Call out a word; all students must write its antonym. Call time. Helpers circulate and count the number of correct responses. Spelling counts! Teams receive one point for every correct response. The team with the most points wins.

Vocabulaire de l'Unité 2

à: à cause de because of *C*; **à la page** in fashion *C*; **à propos de** about *A*; **à sa place** in its place *B*; **à table** at the (dinner) table *C*
accueillir to welcome *A*
s' adresser (à) to address (someone) *C*
un apéritif drink and food offered before the meal *A*
l' athlétisme (m.) track and field *C*
autour de around *C*
avoir: avoir la chance (de) to have the opportunity (to) *C*
baisser to decrease *C*
un blogueur, une blogueuse blogger *C*
des brochettes (f.) apéritives skewered appetizers *A*
une bûche de Noël yule log *A*
ça: ça tombe bien that works out well *A*; **Ça dépend.** It depends. *B*; **Ça sert à....** It's used for.... *B*
le candidat candidate *C*
le championnat championship *C*
chauffer to heat (up) *B*
un chinois conical strainer *B*
le club club *C*
conique conical *B*
un côté: de votre côté as for you *A*
des côtes (f.) de chevreuil venison chops *A*
un coup de main (helping) hand *B*
craindre: Je crains que non. I'm afraid not. *B*
cubique cubical *B*
une cuillère à mesurer measuring spoon *B*
cuire to cook *B*
cylindrique cylindrical *B*
les démocraties (f.) democracies *C*
déranger: Je ne te dérange pas? I'm not bothering you? *A*
les dictatures (f.) dictatorships *C*
la dimension dimension *B*
la dinde aux marrons turkey with chestnuts *A*
dramatique dramatic *C*
les droits (m.) de l'homme human rights *C*
l' économie (f.) economy *C*
les élections (f.) présidentielles presidential elections *C*
embêter to annoy *A*
emprisonner to imprison *C*
en: en bois wooden *B*; **en guerre** at war *C*; **en métal** made of metal *B*; **en petit comité** with a few friends *A*; **en tissu** made of fabric *B*; **je m'en vais** I'm going (away) *B*
encourager to encourage *C*
l' endettement (m.) debt *C*
s' entraîner to practice (sports) *C*
envahi(e) invaded *C*
étroit(e) narrow *B*
faire: faire grève to go on strike *C*
filtrer to filter *B*
le foie gras goose liver pâté *A*
la forme shape *B*; **en forme de (poire)** (pear)-shaped *B*
la hausse increase *C*
les herbes (f.) herbs *B*
le hit (musical) hit *[inform.]* *C*
un hors-d'œuvre appetizer *A*
des huîtres (f.) oysters *A*
l' idéalisme (m.) idealism *C*
improviser to improvise *A*
une invitation invitation *A*
le jambon serrano prosciutto *A*
la jeunesse youth *C*
large wide *B*
la longueur length *C*
le look tradi traditional look *C*
le machin thing *B*
un magret de canard duck breast *A*
des mandarines (f.) mandarin oranges *A*
une matière material *B*
une médaille medal *C*
les médias (m.) media *C*
mélanger to mix *B*
mesurer to measure *B*
un mixeur blender *B*
la mode fashion *C*
les nations (f.) nations *C*
la paix peace *C*
un parti (politique) (political) party *C*
passer: passer à la radio to play on the radio *C*; **on passe...** ... is playing (at the movies) *B*
passionnément passionately *C*
une passoire colander *B*
personnel, personnelle personal *A*
le PNB (produit national brut) GNP (gross national product) *C*
la politique politics *C*
posé(e) set down *B*
poser to put down *B*
pour: pour t'avancer to help you *B*
pouvoir: Je (ne) peux (pas) m'empêcher de.... I can('t) stop myself from.... *C*
le prêt-à-porter ready-to-wear *C*
prévu(e) planned *A*
un prisonnier, une prisonnière prisoner *C*
puisque since (because) *A*
quand: quand même after all *A*; regardless *C*
que whom *C*
racler to scrape, to scrub *B*
les rapports (m.) relationships *A*
rater to mess up *B*
réalisé(e) (par) directed (by) *C*
une récompense award *C*
rectangulaire rectangular *B*
récupérer to recapture *C*
réduire to reduce *C*
remuer to stir, to toss *B*
le réveillon de Noël Christmas Eve celebration *A*
réveillonner to celebrate Christmas/New Year's Eve *C*
le revenu income *C*
rond round *B*
le sapin de Noël Christmas tree *A*
la sauce sauce *B*
le saumon: saumon fumé smoked salmon *A*
si so *C*
une spatule spatula *B*
sphérique spherical *B*
le souci worry *C*
souffrir to suffer *C*
le taux d'inflation inflation rate *C*
des territoires (m.) territories *C*
un toast canapé *A*
tranquille calm, quiet *A*
triangulaire triangular *B*
des truffes (f.) truffles *A*
tuer to kill *C*
universel, universelle universal *A*
les ustensiles (m.) utensils *B*
usurper to usurp *C*
la valeur worth *C*
un verre mesureur measuring cup *B*
verser to pour *B*
voter to vote *C*

Bilan cumulatif

Pre-AP

Multiple Choice

I. Interpretive Reading: Print texts **1.2, 4.2**

Lisez ce reportage sur les activités des familles d'aujourd'hui, puis répondez à la question.

Une association de scoutisme près de chez vous

Dans la société actuelle où les familles sont si occupées entre le travail, l'école, et la vie à la maison, et où les jeunes passent beaucoup de temps devant un écran, il est bon de savoir qu'il y a des endroits où les enfants et les ados peuvent faire des activités manuelles ou physiques en communauté et loin de leurs smartphones et ordinateurs. En France, les associations de scoutismes sont indépendantes et liées sur le plan européen et international. Populaires dans toutes les régions de France et d'outre-mer, elles proposent une variété d'activités sportives et de loisirs qui rendent les ados heureux.

Les activités proposées aux jeunes varient entre sorties (camping, excursions, randonnées), enseignement (comment cuisiner, faire un feu, etc.), et divertissement (danse, théâtre, peinture, jeux).

1. Cette association n'offre pas....
   A. d'activités pour les ados
   B. de cours des finances personnelles pour adultes
   C. d'excursions dans la montagne
   D. de cours de théâtre

II. Interpretive Listening: Audio texts **1.2, 4.2**

Écoutez le dialogue suivant deux fois, puis complétez les phrases.

1. Cette conversation a lieu entre....
   A. deux amies
   B. une femme et sa mère
   C. une Française et sa demoiselle d'honneur
   D. une fiancée américaine et une organisatrice de mariage française
2. L'objectif principal de cette entrevue est de/d'....
   A. aider Victoria à choisir sa demoiselle et son garçon d'honneur
   B. permettre à Victoria de comprendre son futur mari
   C. prendre connaissance des traditions françaises sur le mariage
   D. sélectionner un gâteau de mariage bien français
3. Dans le contexte de l'interview, Victoria aurait tendance à poser une question prochainement sur....
   A. le travail en France
   B. le rôle du garçon d'honneur
   C. la cathédrale de Chartres
   D. des destinations pour un voyage de noces spécial

Resources

Activity II

Answers

I

1. B

II Script

–Bonjour, Victoria et félicitations tout d'abord pour vos fiançailles avec Alexandre. Merci bien de nous avoir contactés pour parler du mariage en France.
–Oui, c'est bien ça. Comme vous le savez déjà peut-être, aux États-Unis, on a toutes sortes de traditions pour le mariage. Mes parents se sont mariés en plein air, mais moi et Alexandre, mon futur mari, nous souhaitons avoir un mariage traditionnel français à la cathédrale de Chartres. Je ne connais que très peu de choses sur les traditions françaises et encore moins sur comment on se marie en France. Vous avez l'air de tout savoir sur le mariage, alors je vous écoute.
–Ce n'est pas la peine de vous inquiéter. Nous sommes là pour vous aider et vous guider. Des invitations à la réception, nous pouvons tout organiser pour vous. Commençons par le domaine de la culture. Tout d'abord en France, il y a la cérémonie civile qui est obligatoire et, si vous le désirez, vous pouvez avoir une cérémonie religieuse. La demoiselle et le garçon d'honneur sont en général les parents ou amis du couple. Le garçon d'honneur, lui, porte l'anneau des futurs mariés. Le gâteau traditionnel est ce que l'on appelle une pièce montée, donc il est grand, beau, et délicieux! Maintenant, que vous en savez un peu plus sur le mariage en France, avez-vous des questions, Victoria?
–Oh, merci. Je me sens vraiment rassurée! Oui, j'ai une question sur ce que vous proposez après le mariage et la réception.

1. D
2. C
3. D

Reference Desk

1. The **Bilan cumulatif** is based on the French Language and Culture AP exam prepared by the College Board. It assesses students' proficiencies in the Interpersonal, Interpretive, and Presentational modes of communication. Students are also asked to demonstrate their understanding of the products, practices, and perspectives of the target cultures.
2. The Print Text section consists of a variety of authentic print materials such as articles and correspondence. A multiple choice question follows the text.
3. The Audio Text is a professional recording, usually a dialogue. Encourage students to preview and skim the questions before listening. They should then answer the multiple choice questions.
4. The E-mail Reply is a free response test section that helps students develop their interpersonal writing skills.
5. The Presentational Writing section asks students to write a persuasive essay.

Free response

III. Interpersonal Writing: E-mail Reply **1.1, 1.3, 5.2**

Vous allez écrire une réponse à un message électronique. Répondez à toutes les questions et donner des détails à propos du sujet du message. Écrivez formellement. N'oubliez pas d'écrire une salutation au début et une formule de politesse (closing) *à la fin de votre message.*

C'est un message électronique du propriétaire de la boutique Espace Cuisine à Montréal. Vous lui avez écrit parce que vous préparez une grande réunion de famille pour célébrer les 90 ans de votre grand-mère. Donc, vous avez besoin d'acheter du matériel de cuisine et de louer des couverts et ustensiles de cuisine.

De : Philippe Bourdon
Objet : Organisation d'une fête et matériel nécessaire

Monsieur ou Madame,

Merci de votre demande de renseignements. Nous sommes en effet spécialistes du matériel de cuisine. Nous vendons toutes les grandes marques de la profession et aux meilleurs prix. Nous louons aussi de la vaisselle et du matériel. Vous pouvez commander chez nous tout ce que vous désirez pour compléter votre batterie de cuisine et faire que votre projet soit un franc grand succès. Mais pour mieux vous conseiller, dites-nous quels outils de préparation et ustensiles vous manquent et si vous envisagez de faire de la pâtisserie. Vous devriez aussi préciser le nombre de couverts, et les plats et boissons que vous comptez servir. Nous sommes prêts à vous aider à bien fêter les 90 ans de votre grand-mère.

Dans l'attente de vous lire, veuillez agréer, chère Madame ou cher Monsieur, l'expression de nos sentiments distingués.

Philippe Bourdon
Espace Cuisine
3640 avenue St-Denis
Montréal

IV. Presentational Writing: Persuasive Essay **1.3, 2.1, 4.2**

Expliquez les manières de table en France et aux États-Unis et dites pourquoi elles sont importantes ou pas importantes dans la vie contemporaine.

Essential Instruction

1. Make copies of Activities III and IV for students, so that they can jot down notes. Students must answer every question posed in the e-mail, but since they are not posed in full questions with an interrogative mark, instruct students to underline and/or number each request made.
2. In the same way, have students underline and/or number all talking points in the Presentational Speaking and Cultural Comparison activities.

V. Presentational Speaking: Cultural Comparison 1.3, 2.1, 2.2, 3.2, 4.2

Vous êtes étudiant(e) américain(e) en France. Pendant la fête de Noël, vous vous trouvez loin de votre propre famille. Alors, votre meilleure amie française vous a invité(e) à passer cette fête chez elle près de Lyon. C'est le 26 décembre et vous venez de passer la fête avec trois générations de sa famille. Vous avez même aidé la famille à préparer le repas du réveillon. Parlez de votre expérience : tout ce que vous avez fait et ce que vous avez mangé, et comparez les traditions françaises avec les traditions de chez vous ou de votre communauté.

Festival des lumières à Lyon

Reference Desk

In the Speaking section of the assessment, students are asked to participate in a conversation or make a cultural comparison using their presentational speaking skills.

Reference Desk

1. In **Unité 3** students will learn to appreciate the heritage of the French language in the world. You may remind students that French is an international language spoken either as an official language or one of the official languages in 29 countries around the world. This unit focuses on Quebec, Tunisia, and Senegal.
2. Habib Bourguiba (1903–2000) is revered as the Father of Tunisia. He led Tunisia's fight for independence from France, which was achieved on March 20, 1956. He served as President of Tunisia from 1957–87. Habib Bourguiba studied law and political science at the Sorbonne before returning to Tunisia to practice law and become politically active. He was a moderate president whose policies earned women the right to vote, banished polygamy, and urged the removal of the veil. His domestic policies strengthened Tunisian industry and tourism. The per capita income and literacy rates rose during his term of office.
3. The photo opener shows a low-income housing building in downtown Dakar, Senegal, and looks like many **HLM (habitation à loyer modéré)** in French cities. After the African independence (1960s), Senegal witnessed a substantial growth of its cities, along with massive urbanization. The government organized an **Office des HLM** to centralize and structure housing for all Senegalese. Today, this establishment has become **la Société Nationale des Habitations à Loyer modéré**, whose mission is to develop strategic housing based on social equity. In this unit, students learn about housing in France and French-speaking African countries.
4. The French language began to spread throughout the world as early as the 16th century, a result of French and Belgian colonialism.

Unité 3 La Francophonie

Essential Instruction

1. Remind students that **la Francophonie** refers to countries throughout the world where French is spoken.
2. Put students in teams to try to name as many francophone countries as they can.
3. Distribute a list of the francophone countries, and have the teams count how many they were able to name and which ones they missed. If possible, use a list that differentiates countries where French is an official language, and those where it is not. Provide students with a blank map of the world and have them place these countries on their maps. They should refer to their maps as needed.
4. Preview with students the **Contrat de l'élève** to give them an overview of the unit.
5. Challenge students to guess the answers to the questions accompanying the photos: **Quelles études fait Clémentine?** and **Comment s'appelle cette habitation au Sénégal?**

Question centrale

Comment les communautés francophones conservent-elles leurs traditions ?

À savoir

Il y a environ 220 millions de personnes qui parlent français dans le monde.

Citation

« La langue française constitue l'appoint à notre patrimoine culturel, enrichit notre pensée, exprime notre action, contribue à forger notre destin intellectuel et à faire de nous des hommes à part entière. »

The French language defines our cultural heritage, enriches our thinking, expresses our action, contributes to the formation of our intellectual destiny so as to set us apart from all of humanity.

—Habib Bourguiba (1903–2000), ancien Chef de l'État tunisien

Conseil pratique

To spice up your writing, use adjectives and transitions such as **au début**, **à la fin**, **avant**, **après**, **pendant que**, and **ensuite**.

Quelles études fait Clémentine ?

Comment s'appelle cette habitation au Sénégal ?

Contrat de l'élève

Leçon A I will be able to:

- say where my ancestors came from and where they settled.
- discuss the goals and services of the **Alliance française**, French immigration to Quebec, and Quebec emigration to New England.
- review the pronouns **y** and **en** and double object pronouns in a sentence.

Leçon B I will be able to:

- start a fairy tale.
- discuss Tunisia, North African immigration to France, and North African stories.
- review reflexive verbs.

Leçon C I will be able to:

- respond to an introduction, say where I grew up, and give a compliment.
- discuss subsidized housing, government payments to families, and talk about Senegal.
- review the comparative and superlative of adverbs.

Answers

Possible choices for the video question:
A. des études littéraires
B. des études de danse
C. des études de claquette
D. des études de droit
Correct Answer: D

The answer to the culture question is: **une case bambara**. The answer can be found in **Points de départ, Leçon C**.

Expansion

1. To set the tone for the appreciation of the French language, have students search the song **"La Langue de chez nous"** by Yves Duteil, which is a tribute to **la langue française**.
2. Discuss the lyrics and sing the song as a class.
3. Put students in groups and have them record their own rendition of the song.

Recherche : la langue de chez nous, yves duteil, paroles

Differentiated Learning

Decelerate

Using the map distributed in class to list francophone countries, ask students to write down the name of each continent where French is spoken. Then have them identify the continent(s) where Quebec, Tunisia, and Senegal are located.

Learning Styles

Visual Learners

Show images of various recognizable places in the world (the Eiffel Tower, the Great Wall of China, Buckingham Palace, the Egyptian Pyramids, Château Frontenac [with Quebec flag flying over it], a Mardi Gras parade in New Orleans, the Coliseum in Rome, etc.). Ask students what city or country each image represents and if it is a francophone country.

Resources

- *Vocabulaire actif*
- eV eVisual
- WB Workbook 1–3
- FC Flash Cards
- LA Listening Activities 1–2
- G & V Practice Games

Reference Desk

1. When names of family members contain the adjective **grand**, this adjective is used figuratively and refers to a length of time, not size. To make it easier for students to remember which generation **grand-oncle** and **grand-tante** refer to, point to their similarity with **grand-père** and **grand-mère**, just like *grandfather* and *grandmother* in English. The word **arrière** is added to the previous generation. To refer to family members from a generation farther back than one's great grandparents, the French use the adjective **arrière** over and over, just like Americans use the adjective *great*. Although *grand* does not agree in gender with **grand-mère**, it agrees in the plurality of **grands-parents**.
2. The singular form of **aïeux** is **aïeul** which is pronounced /ajœl/, a good tongue twister!

Game

Moi aussi !

Student A starts the game selecting a family member: "**J'ai un arrière-grand-père qui s'appelle Paul.**" Student A throws a ball to Student B who quickly must answer, "**Quelle coïncidence ! Moi, j'ai une arrière-grand-mère qui s'appelle Paulette.**" Student B throws the ball to Student C who says, "**J'ai une cousine germaine qui s'appelle Paulette.**" The game continues using any family members that students can think of in masculine and feminine forms. If the game is going too slowly, consider adding a second or third ball or dividing the class into smaller groups. (Use names such as Georges/Georgette, Louis/Louise, and Jules/Julie.)

Leçon A Vocabulaire actif

Ma famille et où elle s'est installée 1.2

La famille éloignée

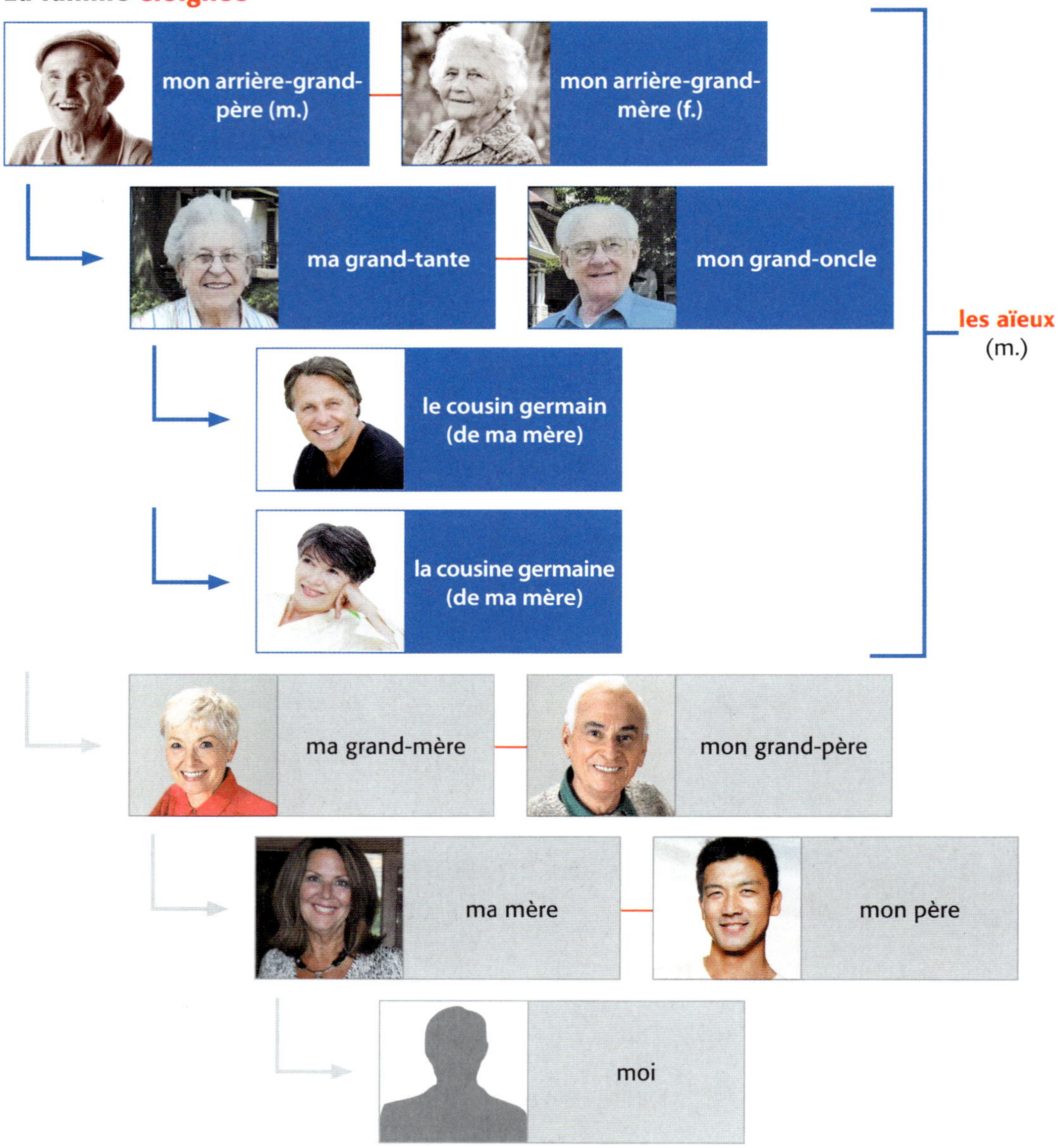

Essential Instruction

1. Bring photos of your family or find photos of famous families online. Present the photos as your family members providing their names, ages, and occupations. Feel free to embellish or add bizarre or comical information.
2. Ask students the names of their relatives.
3. Give students a map of the United States. Have them draw their family tree on the map, labeling the family members as seen in **Ma famille et où elle s'est installée**; they should name as many people as they can, in as many states as they can. Then ask who has a family member in such and such state.
4. Have the students examine the list of states. Ask them why the names of some states are preceded by **dans**, others **en**, and still another by the preposition **à**. See the **Accelerate** note at the bottom of p. 139 for an explanation of which geographical prepositions to use.

Aux États-Unis : Ma famille s'est installée….

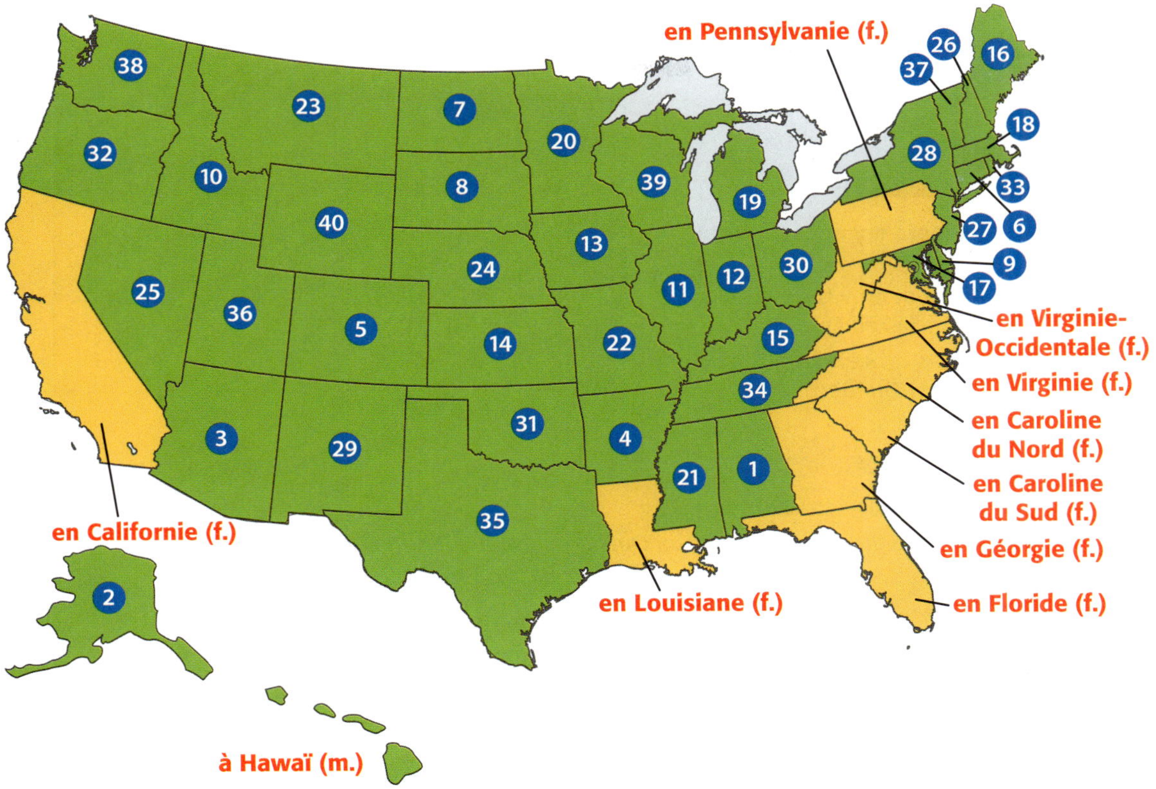

1 dans l'Alabama (m.)
2 dans l'Alaska (m.)
3 dans l'Arizona (m.)
4 dans l'Arkansas (m.)
5 dans le Colorado
6 dans le Connecticut
7 dans le Dakota du Nord
8 dans le Dakota du Sud
9 dans le Delaware
10 dans l'Idaho (m.)
11 dans l'Illinois (m.)
12 dans l'Indiana (m.)
13 dans l'Iowa (m.)
14 dans le Kansas
15 dans le Kentucky
16 dans le Maine
17 dans le Maryland
18 dans le Massachusetts
19 dans le Michigan
20 dans le Minnesota
21 dans le Mississippi
22 dans le Missouri
23 dans le Montana
24 dans le Nebraska
25 dans le Nevada
26 dans le New Hampshire
27 dans le New Jersey
28 dans l'État de New York (m.)
29 dans le Nouveau-Mexique
30 dans l'Ohio (m.)
31 dans l'Oklahoma (m.)
32 dans l'Oregon (m.)
33 dans le Rhode Island
34 dans le Tennessee
35 dans le Texas
36 dans l'Utah (m.)
37 dans le Vermont
38 dans l'État de Washington (m.)
39 dans le Wisconsin
40 dans le Wyoming

Differentiated Learning

Accelerate

Tell students that the preposition **dans le**, when used before masculine states, may be changed to **au** for states beginning with a consonant, and **en** for states beginning with a vowel: **J'habite dans le Nebraska. Nous sommes au Nebraska. Nous sommes dans l'Idaho. Nous allons en Idaho**. Note that because **Hawaï** does not require an article, it is the exception to these patterns, and exclusively uses the preposition **à** in its unaltered form.

Learning Styles

Visual Learners

Students should rewrite the list of states, grouping them in the following columns: **dans**, **dans l'État de**, **en**, and **à**. It will be easier for them to remember which prepositions are used with which states by seeing the list in their minds.

Auditory Learners

Students may learn best by repeating the names of the states and their prepositions three times each.

Reference Desk

1. In Level 1, Unit 10A, p. 523, we introduced the prepositions before cities, countries, and continents as follows:
   to = **à** (**aller à**, **vivre à**, etc.)
   à + NAME OF CITY (**à Dakar**) OR ISLAND (**à Tahiti**)
   au + MASCULINE COUNTRY (**au Canada**)
   en + FEMININE COUNTRY (**en Afrique**)
   aux + PLURALS (**aux États-Unis**)
2. There is a slightly different rule regarding US states. For feminine states, the preposition **en** is used (**la Floride → en Floride**). For masculine states beginning with a vowel, we use **dans l'** or **en** (**l'Ohio → dans l'Ohio/en Ohio**). For masculine states beginning with a consonant, we use **dans le** or **au** (**le Texas → dans le Texas/au Texas**). Here we introduce all masculine states with the preposition **dans le** for simplicity. If a student gets used to saying "**en Alabama**," he or she will not recognize this state as being masculine.
3. You may tell advanced students that the difference between **dans le** versus **au/en** and **dans le** for masculine states has a lot to do with context (with **dans le**, the interlocutor considers the location as being *within* a region, whereas with **au/en**, the interlocutor considers the location as a place on a map).
4. States on the map that are masculine in gender in French have been colored green; states that are feminine in French have been colored gold on the map. Note that these nouns have been "Frenchified."
5. Note that most countries that begin with a vowel are feminine, and use the preposition **en** (**en Italie**). (Exceptions are **l'Iran**, **l'Irak**, **l'Israël**.) But note that masculine country names that begin with a vowel also use **en** (**en Iraq, en Iran, en Afghanistan, en Israël**).
6. Note that French provinces and departments are typically feminine, and thus also use the preposition **en** (**la Bretagne → en Bretagne**; **la Normandie → en Normandie**; **la Seine-et-Oise → en Seine-et-Oise**).

Resources

Pour la conversation
Et si je voulais dire… ?

Answers

1

1. Elle est allée aux États-Unis.
2. Elle habite à Seattle, dans l'État de Washington.
3. Cette personne s'appelle grand-père Félix.
4. C'est la sœur de Félix. Elle s'est installée en Californie.
5. C'est le frère de Romane et de Félix.
6. C'est la fille d'Alexis. Elle habite en Californie.
7. Ils habitent dans le Nevada.
8. Elle n'a pas vu son grand-oncle Raymond. Il habite trop loin.

Reference Desk

Remind students that for question 2 of **Activité 1**, even though the question refers to a male (**le grand-père Félix**), they are to use the feminine pronoun that corresponds to **personne**, the subject of the question.

Culture

Products: Information

You may wish to show scenes from the award-winning movie ***Le bonheur de Pierre***, a comedy about a contemporary immigrant, a French professor from Paris who inherits an inn in Canada. With his wife, he leaves France for a small village in Quebec. Instead of the idyllic life they seek, they find nothing but problems created by the local mayor. In addition to providing the opportunity to use some of the structures from this lesson, it will give the students the chance to hear some Canadian accents and Canadian French.

Recherche : le bonheur de pierre

Connections

Human Geography

Work with social studies teachers to track genealogies and migration movements in the United States throughout different periods.

1.2

Mot-clé

C'est au 16ème siècle qu'est apparue la forme moderne du mot **aïeux**, tiré du latin *avus*, *aviolus*, *aiol*. Ce sont les poètes classiques qui lui ont donné cette belle orthographe, afin de le faire rimer avec *cieux*, *Dieu*, *glorieux*, etc. Aujourd'hui même, ce terme marque le respect et la nostalgie du passé. L'expression *Oh mes aïeux !* exprime l'incrédulité, et insinue que les ancêtres seraient choqués.

Pour la conversation 1.2

How do I say where my ancestors came from and settled?

» Mes aïeux sont arrivés de Bretagne et se sont installés au Québec.

My ancestors arrived from Brittany and settled in Quebec.

Et si je voulais dire… ?

la descendance	*descent, lineage*
le droit de garde	*custody*
la marraine	*godmother*
le parrain	*godfather*
descendre de	*to be descended from*

1 Un long voyage 1.1, 1.2, 5.1

Interpersonal Writing, Interpretive Reading

Lisez le mail de Sandrine à son frère au Québec, puis répondez aux questions.

À: Cédric
Cc:
Objet: Mon long voyage

Salut, Cédric !

Tu vas bien ? Quel voyage pour rendre visite à toute notre famille qui s'est installée aux États-Unis ! J'ai atterri à Seattle, dans l'État de Washington. D'abord on a rendu visite au grand-père Félix qui y habite. Il s'y est installé quand il s'est remarié avec Sandy. Puis, on a pris la route pour aller voir sa sœur, Romane. Il a fallu qu'on traverse l'Oregon car elle est toujours en Californie, avec son autre frère Alexis. La fille d'Alexis, Michèle, habite tout près, mais les enfants de Michèle habitent dans le Nevada. Encore de la route ! Tu te souviens de notre grand-oncle Raymond ? Il habite maintenant dans le Maryland. Trop loin ! Cela faisait beaucoup trop de route, alors je ne l'ai pas vu ! C'est à toi de lui rendre visite quand tu iras à ta conférence à Baltimore.

Bises,
Sandrine

1. Où est-ce que Sandrine est allée pour voir ses aïeux ?
2. Où habite la première personne qu'elle a vue ?
3. Comment s'appelle cette personne ?
4. Qui est Romane ? Où s'est-elle installée ?
5. Qui est Alexis ?
6. Qui est Michèle ? Elle habite dans quel État ?
7. Où habitent les enfants de Michèle ?
8. Qui est-ce que Sandrine n'a pas vu ? Pourquoi ?

Essential Instruction

1. Students will listen to **Pour la conversation** and **Et si je voulais dire… ?** Ask students, "**Savez-vous d'où sont arrivés vos aïeux et où ils se sont installés ?**"
2. Have students read **Un long voyage** to each other, alternating sentences. They will then complete questions 1–8 together.
3. For **Activité 2** students will work in pairs using the family tree to ask the question **Qui est… ?** and respond. **Qui est Rose ? C'est mon arrière-grand-mère**. They will add detail: **C'est mon arrière-grand-mère qui était professeur dans une petite école en Pennsylvanie en 1900.**
4. In pairs, students will complete **Activité 3**.

2 C'est qui? 1.2, 1.3

Interpretive Viewing, Presentational Speaking or Writing

Imaginez que vous êtes Jean-Luc. Identifiez chaque membre de votre famille selon le modèle.

MODÈLE Étienne
C'est mon cousin germain.

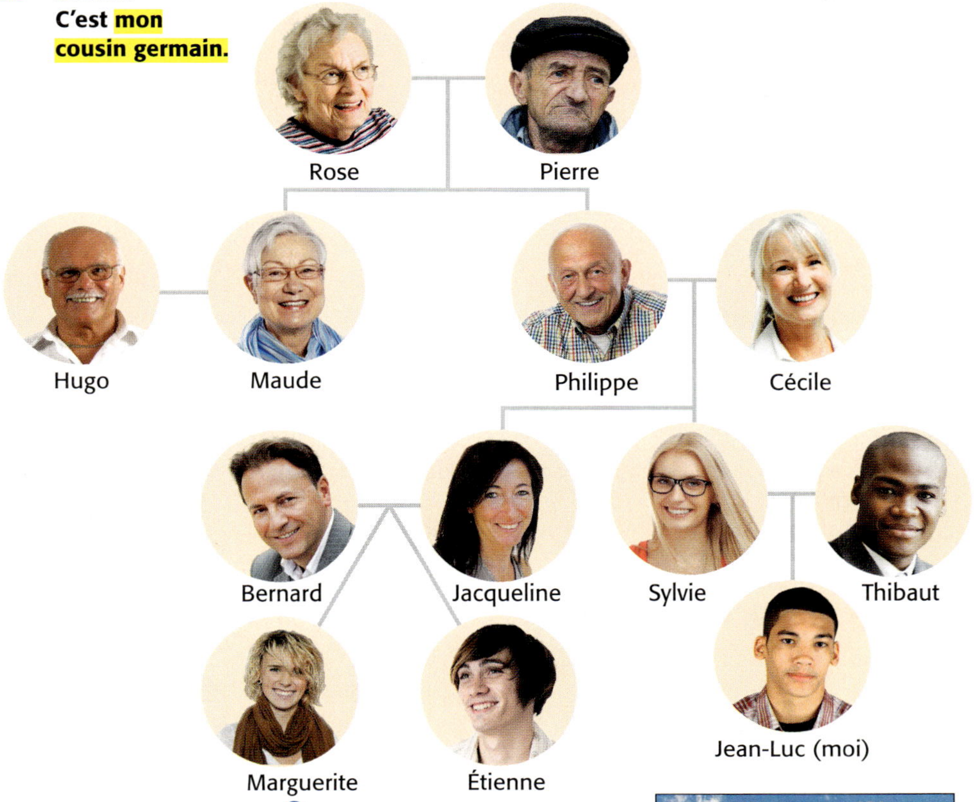

3 Les États américains 1.3, 3.1

Presentational Speaking or Writing

Dites que vous visitez chaque capitale dans son État.

MODÈLE Baton Rouge
Je visite Baton Rouge en Louisiane.

1. Albany
2. Harrisburg
3. Santa Fe
4. Salt Lake City
5. Boston
6. Oklahoma City
7. Atlanta
8. Richmond
9. Austin
10. Raleigh

À Baton Rouge

Resources

Activity 3

Answers

2

Rose: C'est mon arrière-grand-mère.
Pierre: C'est mon arrière-grand-père.
Hugo: C'est mon grand-oncle.
Maude: C'est ma grand-tante.
Philippe: C'est mon grand-père.
Cécile: C'est ma grand-mère.
Bernard : C'est mon oncle.
Jacqueline : C'est ma tante.
Étienne: C'est mon cousin germain.
Marguerite: C'est ma cousine germaine.
Sylvie: C'est ma mère.
Thibault: C'est mon père.

3

1. Je visite Albany dans l'État de New York.
2. Je visite Harrisburg en Pennsylvanie.
3. Je visite Santa Fe dans le Nouveau Mexique.
4. Je visite Salt Lake City dans l'Utah.
5. Je visite Boston, dans le Massachusetts.
6. Je visite Oklahoma City dans l'Oklahoma.
7. Je visite Atlanta en Georgie.
8. Je visite Richmond en Virginie.
9. Je visite Austin dans le Texas.
10. Je visite Raleigh en Caroline du Nord.
11. Je visite Tallahassee en Floride.
12. Je visite Honolulu à Hawaï.
13. Je visite Montpelier dans le Vermont.
14. Je visite St. Paul dans le Minnesota.

Culture

Products: Information

On the theme of family members, ***Tatie Danielle*** is a classic film about a cranky aunt who lives life her way. Students may enjoy watching scenes from this comedy that can be found online.

Recherche: tatie danielle

Differentiated Learning

Accelerate

Have students do **Activité 2** again, replacing the people in the activity with their own family members, and adding their godparents using vocabulary from **Et si je voulais dire... ?**

Decelerate

Before completing **Activité 3**, review the state capitals with students who may not know them, or allow them to use an outside resource. Have them identify the proper preposition (**en** or **dans le**) before doing the exercise.

Learning Styles

Kinesthetic Learners

1. Project Jean-Luc's family on a screen. Two students with fly swatters will go to the screen and try to tap the picture of the chosen family member faster than the other: **C'est la mère de Jean-Luc.**
2. Project the map of the United States. Using the same flyswatter technique, call out a state. Students must tap it and use **dans**, **en**, or **à** with the state. Teacher: **le Tennessee!** Student: **dans le Tennessee.**

Resources

Activity 5

Answers

4

1. Mes grands-parents se sont installés dans le Texas.
2. Ma petite cousine s'est installée dans l'Arizona.
3. Mon cousin s'est installé dans l'Alaska.
4. Mon arrière-grand-mère et sa fille se sont installées dans l'Illinois.
5. Ma tante s'est installée dans le Massachusetts.
6. Mon cousin germain s'est installé dans l'État de Washington.

5 Script

Professeur : Alors, vous avez trouvé des informations en ligne sur vos aïeux ? Annie ?
Annie : Oui, moi, j'ai découvert que mon arrière-grand-mère était québécoise. Elle s'est installée dans le Maine et c'est là qu'elle a rencontré mon arrière-grand-père.
Professeur : Et lui, il était de quelle origine ?
Annie : Il était anglais.
Professeur : Et toi, Roger, qu'as-tu découvert ?
Roger : Eh bien, ma famille vient d'Allemagne. Ils se sont installés dans le Minnesota où ils étaient fermiers.
Professeur : Chase, tu veux nous dire ce que tu as trouvé ?
Chase : Ma grand-tante Mathilde, ses ancêtres viennent d'Acadie et ils ont quitté le Canada et se sont installés en Louisiane.
Professeur : C'est passionnant ! Quelqu'un d'autre ? Oui, Melissa.
Melissa : Moi, mon arrière-grand-père de Moscou habitait en Alaska. C'est là où une partie de ma famille habite.

1. V; 2. F; 3. F; 4. F; 5. V; 6. F

6 Answers will vary.

Communication

Interpersonal: Paired Practice

In pairs, students will ask and answer questions for **Activité 4**. Student A: **"Où s'est installée ta grand-tante ?"** Student B: **"Elle s'est installée dans l'Iowa."** Roles will be reversed so that student B forms the questions and student A responds. Expand the exercise by adding the question **pourquoi ?**

4 Où se sont-ils installés ? 1.3, 3.1

Presentational Speaking or Writing

*Après l'ouragan (*hurricane*) Katrina à La Nouvelle-Orléans, beaucoup de membres de la famille de Joséphine ont déménagé. Jouez le rôle de Joséphine et dites où ils se sont installés.*

MODÈLE ma grand-tante (Iowa)
Ma grand-tante s'est installée dans l'Iowa.

1. mes grands-parents (Texas)
2. ma petite cousine (Arizona)
3. mon cousin (Alaska)
4. mon arrière-grand-mère et sa fille (Illinois)
5. ma tante (Massachusetts)
6. mon cousin germain (l'État de Washington)

Connexions 1.2, 3.1
Géographie

Demandez à votre partenaire :
Où peut-on trouver des vedettes de cinéma ?
Où est-ce que la Déclaration de l'Indépendance a été écrite ?
Où se trouve le centre de commerce et la Bourse ?
Où peut-on trouver des casinos ?
Où est-ce que Thomas Jefferson a vécu ?
Où peut-on trouver des surfeurs ?
Où parle-t-on français ?

5 Qui sont vos aïeux ? 1.2, 5.1

Interpretive Listening

Écrivez les numéros 1–6 sur votre papier. Écoutez la discussion entre le prof d'histoire et ses élèves. Ensuite, indiquez si les phrases sont vraies (V) ou fausses (F).

1. Le professeur a demandé à ses élèves de faire des recherches sur un site généalogique en ligne.
2. L'arrière-grand-mère et l'arrière-grand-père d'Annie se sont rencontrés au Québec.
3. La famille de Roger vient d'Italie.
4. La famille de Roger s'est installée dans le Michigan où ils étaient forgerons.
5. Chase a de la famille en Louisiane.
6. Une partie de la famille de Melissa habite à Hawaï.

6 Questions personnelles 1.1, 5.1

Interpersonal Speaking

Répondez aux questions avec un partenaire.

1. Comment s'appellent votre arrière-grand-père et votre arrière-grand-mère ?
2. Est-ce que vous connaissez ou avez connu votre grand-tante ou grand-oncle ? Où habitent/habitaient-ils ?
3. D'où sont arrivés vos aïeux ? En quelle année ? Comment sont-ils venus ?
4. Avez-vous voyagé dans d'autres États ? Si oui, lesquels ?
5. Quels États voudriez-vous visiter ? Pourquoi ?

Essential Instruction

1. Students will do **Où se sont-ils installés ?** in pairs.
2. Students will listen to **Qui sont vos aïeux ?** answering **vrai** or **faux** to 1–6.
3. For **Activité 6** put students in groups of three and have them ask each question to one another to practice using the vocabulary in context.
4. Students will listen to **Les ancêtres de Justin** and individually answer questions 1–7 on p. 144.
5. Before assigning **Activité 4**, review with students that **s'installer** is a reflexive verb which requires **être** in the **passé composé** and affects the past participle.

Rencontres culturelles

Les ancêtres de Justin

1.2, 2.1, 3.1, 5.1

Léo et son ami américain, Justin, se parlent au cercle de conversation de l'Alliance française de Nice.

Léo : Tes ancêtres sont venus de France ? C'est incroyable ! Tu en es sûr ?

Justin : Absolument. Mon père a fait des recherches généalogiques sur l'histoire de notre famille : il me les a montrées. C'est passionnant.

Léo : Et alors ?

Justin : Eh bien, mes aïeux sont arrivés de Bretagne et se sont installés au Québec sur l'île d'Orléans. Mon ancêtre devait être forgeron. Mais il en a profité pour changer de métier. Il s'est occupé de mécanique. Ils étaient très pauvres. La vie était très difficile.

Léo : Mais ils ne sont pas restés ?

Justin : Plusieurs générations y ont vécu. C'est en 1929 avec la grande crise qu'ils sont venus tenter leur chance aux États-Unis. Ils se sont installés dans le Maine.

Léo : C'était une manière de garder le contact avec la Francophonie.

Justin : Si tu veux ! Pour mon arrière-grand-père, c'était surtout le moyen de trouver du travail ! Mon arrière-grand-père a travaillé sur les bateaux comme pêcheur et mon arrière-grand-mère travaillait dans une conserverie. Après, ça a été mieux....

Léo : Et ton grand-père, il vit toujours dans le Maine ?

Justin : Mon grand-père a compris que le Maine allait devenir très touristique alors, il a ouvert un petit restaurant, puis un hôtel, sur Mount Desert Island ; maintenant ce sont des cousins qui le tiennent.

Léo : Et tout ce temps tu ne m'as rien dit !

Un forgeron

Le Maine

Stratégie

As you listen to the dialogue, trace the migration route of Justin's ancestors. Include dates.

Resources

- Dialogue
- Dialogue Video
- WB Workbook 4

Reference Desk

1. **L'île d'Orléans** is located 3.1 kilometers east of Quebec City in the Saint Lawrence River. It was one of the first outposts of **la Nouvelle-France** settled in the 17th century. In 1535, the explorer Jacques Cartier originally called it **Bacchus** for the grapevines he found there. Later it was named in honor of the **duc d'Orléans**, son of King François I. A large percentage of French Canadians can trace their ancestry to the early settlers who lived on the island. It is often called **le berceau de l'Amérique française**, the birthplace of French America. See pp. 146, 148–149.
2. Many believe the name **Québec** comes from the Algonquin word meaning *narrow passage or strait*.
3. In French, one says **à Québec** to refer to the city of Quebec, but **au Québec** to refer to the province of Quebec. (One must differentiate in the same way between the country and capital city of Luxembourg, Panama, and Kuwait, among others.)
4. The word **forgeron** (*blacksmith*) comes from the verb **forger**, which means *to shape or form a piece of metal*.

Expansion

Put students in groups and ask them the following question: **Comment les photos sur cette page correspondent-elles à la lecture « Les ancêtres de Justin » ?** You may give each group a few minutes of discussion time and then invite them to share their answers with the class.

Differentiated Learning

Accelerate

Students may answer the **Questions personnelles** by pretending that they belong to a well-known American family such as the Kennedys, the Lincolns, or the Obamas.

Special Needs Students

Auditory Impairment

Allow students with auditory impairment to follow the script while the recorded dialogue plays.

Social Anxiety

Be selective and sensitive to students when asking the **Questions personnelles**. It could be that some of them know little of their family or may be unwilling to discuss their family's immigration history. Precede the activity with a discussion of the history and positive impact of migration on the United States.

Resources

Activity 7
Extension

Answers

7 Possible answers:

1. Le père de Justin a fait des recherches généalogiques pour mieux connaître ses ancêtres.
2. Les aïeux de Justin se sont installés au Québec sur l'Île d'Orléans.
3. Justin pense que son ancêtre était forgeron.
4. La grande crise de 1929 a poussé la famille de Justin à venir s'installer aux États-Unis.
5. L'arrière-grand-père de Justin était pêcheur.
6. L'arrière-grand-mère de Justin travaillait dans une conserverie.
7. Le grand-père de Justin vit dans le Maine.

EXTENSION

Il cherche des documents civils de ses ancêtres pour faire l'arbre généalogique de sa famille.

7 Les ancêtres de Justin 1.2, 1.3

Utilisez chacune des expressions suivantes dans une phrase pour montrer votre compréhension du dialogue et du vocabulaire.

MODÈLE l'Alliance française
Justin et Léo sont à l'Alliance française, une organisation associée à la promotion de la langue et la culture françaises.

1. des recherches généalogiques
2. l'Île d'Orléans
3. forgeron
4. la grande crise de 1929
5. pêcheur
6. une conserverie
7. le Maine

EXTENSION Un projet de famille 1.2, 5.2

Alexis interrompt son père qui travaille sur son ordinateur.

Alexis : Mais qu'est-ce que tu cherches là ?
Père : Là, je suis sur le site des archives départementales : on y trouve tous les actes officiels.
Alexis : C'est-à-dire ?
Père : Eh bien, les actes de naissance, les changements de propriété, les changements d'état civil, différents types de contrats….
Alexis : Et avec ces documents, on remonte loin ?
Père : Pour notre famille, je les ai presque tous retrouvés. Je suis remonté jusqu'à la Révolution française.
Alexis : Alors cet arbre généalogique, on le voit quand ?
Père : Bientôt… patience….

EXTENSION Qu'est-ce que le père d'Alexis cherche sur Internet ? Ses recherches l'aident à faire quoi ?

1.2, 5.1

Essential Instruction

1. Have students answer **Activité 7** in pairs. Ask several pairs to give an answer for each question in order to get students used to the repetition of the correct syntax associated with each group of words.
2. Ask students with theatrical inclination to volunteer to read the **Extension** dialogue as a skit.
3. Have the students read **L'Alliance française** individually or in pairs. You may ask them to summarize each paragraph in one sentence in French or English.
4. The following are comprehension questions that can be asked orally, or done in student pairs:
En quelle année l'Alliance française a-t-elle été fondée et par qui ?
Quels sont les objectifs de l'organisme ?
Quel est le plus grand centre de l'Alliance française aux États-Unis ?
Combien d'étudiants participent aux programmes dans le monde entier ?
Quels sont les programmes organisés par l'Alliance française ?

Points de départ

Pre-AP

Question centrale ? Comment les communautés francophones conservent-elles leurs traditions?

L'Alliance française 1.2, 2.1, 2.2, 5.1

Fondée en 1883 sous l'égide* de Paul Cambon, l'Alliance française est une association qui a pour objectif de participer au rayonnement* de la culture française et à l'enseignement de la langue française. Elle compte, parmi ses membres fondateurs, Ferdinand de Lesseps, Louis Pasteur, Jules Verne et Ernest Renan. Ses valeurs sont celles de la philosophie des Lumières : l'humanisme, les droits de l'homme, l'esprit de liberté, et l'importance de la raison pour aborder* les choses et les événements.

L'Alliance française est aujourd'hui une fondation qui a son siège à Paris et dont le président d'honneur est le président de la République française. Elle compte environ 850 implantations réparties dans 136 pays. Elle accueille plus de 500 000 étudiants à travers* le monde. Les Alliances françaises organisent des conférences, des programmes de cinéma, des concerts, et des représentations théâtrales. Elles coopèrent aussi avec de nombreuses associations artistiques locales.

La Fondation des Alliances françaises aux États-Unis est l'une des plus importantes : elle a été créée en 1902 grâce au mécène* et grand ami de la France, James Hazen Hyde. On trouve des Alliances françaises à travers tous les États-Unis, aussi bien sur la côte Est que dans le Wyoming, l'Idaho, le Kansas, le Michigan, ou encore en Floride, Californie et Pennsylvanie. Le French Institute-Alliance française de New York est le centre le plus important.

Recherche : alliance française de nice, alliance française usa

égide protection ; **rayonnement** *influence* ; **aborder** *to approach* ; **à travers** *throughout* ; **mécène** *patron*

Mot-clé

Au début, le mot **alliance** désigne le phénomène religieux et le caractère psychologique du lien par mariage entre deux grandes familles. Ce terme évolue à une union par engagement mutuel et développe un sens juridique et politique au 13ème siècle.

Comparaisons

1.2, 4.2

Quelle est la mission des ambassades américaines à l'étranger ? Donnez des exemples, si possible, pour montrer comment les États-Unis participent au rayonnement de l'anglais et de la culture américaine.

Recherche: voice of america

Produits

1.2, 2.2, 5.1

L'Alliance française offre des examens agréés (*approved*) par la Chambre de Commerce et d'Industrie de Paris (CCIP). Elle délivre aussi les diplômes universellement reconnus du **DELF** et du **DALF**. Donc, si vous vous intéressez à travailler dans les affaires (*business*), pour une compagnie avec une succursale (*branch*) en France, vous pouvez vous inscrire à l'Alliance française pour vous préparer.

Resources

- *Points de départ*
- WB Workbook 5
- Explore

Answers

Comparaisons

Possible answer: Elles aident les Américains expatriés à maintenir un contact avec leur pays d'origine. Elles permettent aux habitants locaux de faire les documents administratifs nécessaires pour voyager aux États-Unis. Elles permettent aux étrangers d'établir un lien avec les États-Unis afin de promouvoir la langue et la culture américaines.

Reference Desk

1. **DELF** stands for **Diplôme d'études en langue française**, and **DALF** for **Diplôme approfondi de langue française**.
2. If you have access to Passport, find a video or news article about **l'Alliance française** and show it to your students.

Game

Qui est-ce ?

Divide the class in two teams. Each team must find the name of one famous French person (scientist, entertainer, philosopher, etc.) that starts with each letter of the alphabet from A–Z. Give students fifteen minutes to find as many people as possible. You may allow them to repeat letters or not.

Connections

Sponsorship

Ask students what kind of events and activities they would plan if they were asked to help run an **Alliance française**.

Differentiated Learning

Accelerate

Ask high-ability students to listen to the **Extension** on p. 144, **Un projet de famille**, and answer the question prior to looking at the script.

Decelerate

Students can visit the **Alliance française** website for the city of Nice and the **French Institute-Alliance française de New York** website. They can compare the two centers in terms of cultural events, classes for adults and children, and diplomas offered.

Multiple Intelligences

Musical-Rhythmic

Ask students to write a song or poem that explains what the **Alliance française** is, who founded it, where the centers are located, and what activities they offer.

Reference Desk

1. The French-Canadian accent varies from the continental French accent, as our American accent is different from the British. You may want to find online and show the video **"Cours de Québécois Saguenéen"** to expose the students to the sound of French spoken in Canada, and to learn a few more French-Canadian expressions as an extension of **Mon dico québécois**.
2. Maine, along with Lousiana, is one of two officially French-English bilingual states.
3. If you have access to Passport, find a video or a news article related to **l'Île d'Orléans/ Quebec** and show it to your students.

Recherche : cours de québécois saguenéen

Expansion

The following are comprehension questions that can be asked orally or done in student pairs:

En quelle année a été fondé le Québec et par qui ?
D'où proviennent les premiers colons venus de France ?
Pourquoi les « filles du Roi » ont-elles émigré ?
Qui était Félix Leclerc ? De quelles nationalités étaient les personnes venues s'installer à l'Île d'Orléans au 20ème siècle ?
Les habitants de quelles régions de la Nouvelle-France sont-ils venus s'installer en Nouvelle-Angleterre ? À quelle époque ?
Dans quelle industrie ont-ils commencé à travailler ?
Dans l'État du Maine, quel est le pourcentage de la population qui parle français actuellement à la maison ?
Comment sait-on que la recherche des ancêtres québécois est importante aujourd'hui ?

La Francophonie

Immigration

L'immigration française : de l'île d'Orléans au Québec 1.2, 2.1, 2.2, 3.1

Après les trois voyages d'exploration de Jacques Cartier dans la région (en 1534, 1535, et 1541), c'est avec Samuel de Champlain que l'aventure coloniale française au Québec se poursuit. Ce dernier* fonde la ville de Québec en 1608 et fait venir les missions religieuses. Mais c'est vers 1630 que commencent les premières grandes migrations. Plus de 1 250 colons* arrivent de Bretagne, de Normandie, d'Anjou, puis 770 filles du Roi* sont envoyées pour agrandir l'empire colonial. Les conflits militaires amènent 1 200 hommes supplémentaires du Dauphiné, de Ligurie, et de Savoie.

L'Île d'Orléans, proche de* Québec, aujourd'hui reliée* par un pont, est le berceau* de peuplement* de la Nouvelle-France. Sainte Famille, le village le plus ancien, a été fondé en 1661. C'est sur cette île qu'est enterré* Félix Leclerc (1914–1988), l'un des plus grands chanteurs québécois et francophones.

Dans les années 1960–1970, les immigrants francophones sont venus principalement d'Haïti et du Viêt-Nam ; aujourd'hui, la majorité des immigrants au Québec viennent de France, de Belgique et du Maghreb (Algérie, Tunisie, Maroc).

Recherche : île d'orléans tourisme, familles souches de l'île d'orléans, île d'orléans région du québec

Mon dico québécois

Qu'est-ce que ça mange ça ? *Qu'est-ce que ça signifie ?*
J'ai ben de la misère avec ça. *Je supporte cela difficilement.*
Ça m'a coûté une beurrée. *Ça m'a coûté cher.*
Ça n'a pas d'allure ton affaire. *Ça n'a pas de sens.*
T'es rendu végétarien maintenant ? *Tu es devenu végétarien ?*

Ce dernier *The latter* ; **colons** *settlers* ; **filles du Roi** *King's Daughters [group of young and single women sent to* la Nouvelle-France *to get married to the settlers and have children]* ; **proche de** *close to* ; **reliée** *connected* ; **berceau** *cradle* ; **peuplement** *populating* ; **enterré** *buried*

La ville de Québec exhibe une présence francophone en Amérique.

Au début de la colonisation, les Québecois habitaient dans la « Nouvelle-France ».

Essential Instruction

1. Distribute a map of **Québec** to your students. Then project the map of North America from **Unité 10** Level 1 (p. 514). Help your students locate **l'Île d'Orléans** and **la Nouvelle-France**.
2. Now ask students to find where **la Nouvelle-Angleterre** is located, and see if they all knew it is a region of the United States, not Canada.
3. You may ask students to brainstorm what other states or regions in the United States have a francophone (linguistic or cultural) heritage.
4. Divide the class in two groups. One group will read **L'immigration française : de l'Île d'Orléans au Québec**, the other **La Nouvelle-Angleterre**, and **Traditions et pratiques**.

Immigration francophone

La Nouvelle-Angleterre   1.2, 2.1, 3.1

On estime* à 900 000 le nombre de Francophones en Nouvelle-Angleterre. Ce sont les descendants des Québécois et des Acadiens qui, sans travail, sont venus s'y installer entre le milieu du 19ème siècle et la Seconde Guerre mondiale. Ils travaillent tout d'abord dans l'industrie textile; leurs descendants sont maintenant journalistes, avocats, commerçants, etc. Il existe aujourd'hui 500 organisations qui s'occupent de la recherche des ancêtres québécois. Dans le Maine, on estime que 5% de la population parle français à la maison.

Recherche: la nouvelle-angleterre guide michelin

estime *estimates*

8 Activités culturelles 1.3, 3.2

Complétez les activités suivantes.

1. Faites des recherches et identifiez les professions de Ferdinand de Lesseps, Louis Pasteur, Jules Verne et Ernest Renan.
2. Faites la carte d'identité de l'Alliance française:
   - Siècle de création
   - Nombre de pays
   - Valeurs
   - Activités
   - Nombre de comités d'implantation
3. Trouvez l'Alliance française la plus proche de chez vous et faites une liste d'activités ou de programmes qui vous intéressent.
4. De quelles régions venaient les premiers colons du Québec? Situez-les sur une carte de France.
5. Faites une liste des noms de famille français des habitants de l'Île d'Orléans et de la Nouvelle-Angleterre.

Traditions et pratiques
1.2, 2.1

Au cours des dernières années, il y a eu un renouvellement de l'intérêt envers (*towards*) la langue française et l'héritage québécois de la part des immigrés de la Nouvelle-Angleterre, et de leurs enfants. Le Ministère de la Culture et des Communications du Québec prend des mesures pour préserver la langue française sur l'Île d'Orléans.

Le parc national de l'Acadie dans le Maine a été découvert par Samuel de Champlain.

1.2, 2.1

Perspectives

Selon moi, les médias sociaux, comme Radio Canada, et Groupe Média TFO, rendent la connexion à l'héritage culturel du monde franco-canadien à portée de main (*within reach*) à tout moment. C'est une pinotte! —TonythaPhony

Comment est-ce que cet Américain avec des ancêtres québécois profite des médias canadiens pour enrichir sa vie aux États-Unis?

Differentiated Learning

Decelerate

Give students a map of North America and have them circle **la Nouvelle-France** and **la Nouvelle-Angleterre** in different colors. Have them write **le Québec** under **la Nouvelle-France**, and ask them to research when the region changed its name. Finally, ask students to make a list of the six American states that make up the region of **la Nouvelle-Angleterre**.

Multiple Intelligences

Naturalist

Students research the canoes, hunting instruments, and animals hunted by the **voyageurs** and **les coureurs des bois**.

Musical-Rhythmic

Students teach two songs of the **voyageurs**, "**Alouette**" and "**À la Claire Fontaine**," to the class.

Visual-Spatial

Students make a chart of the trading posts and routes travelled by the **voyageurs.**

Answers

8

1. Ferdinand de Lesseps: diplomate et entrepreneur; Louis Pasteur: scientifique; Jules Verne: écrivain; Ernest Renan: écrivain et historien
2. siècle de création: 19ème; nombre de pays: 136; valeurs: l'humanisme, les droits de l'homme, la liberté, la raison; activités: conférences, cinéma, concerts, théâtre; nombre de comités: 850
3. Answers will vary.
4. de Bretagne, de Normandie, d'Anjou; au nord-ouest de la France
5. Answers will vary and may include Arrivé, Aubin, Beaudoin, Chrétien, Charpentier, Dufresne, and Fontaine.

Perspectives

Il utilise des ressources en ligne.

Reference Desk

Les voyageurs and **les coureurs des bois** were hearty, daring fur traders in the 17th and 18th centuries, who left Quebec and Montreal and headed westward in search of beaver pelts. They would be gone for months at a time, travelling thousands of miles, paddling ten to twelve hours a day in birch bark canoes (substantially reinforced with spruce and pine gum caulking, hardwood ribs, and cedar planks). These adventurers set up outposts along the waterways of the United States. Many of our cities bear French names due to their presence. These colorful merchants were known for their dress, music, and fo klore.

Communication

Interpersonal: Cooperative Groups

Arrange students into five groups. Each group will draw a card from 1 to 5, corresponding to the numbered activities in **Activités culturelles**. Each group collaborates to complete the activity. Students working on the first activity should expand it to include a brief biography of each person listed. All groups will share their work with the class.

Communication

Presentational: Cooperative Groups

Assign online research to groups of students. Each group chooses a place featured in the brochure and finds more photos and information. Then each group prepares a short presentation for the class as if they were tour guides.

Culture

Products: Information

L'Île d'Orléans is located 5 km east of Quebec City. Situated in the St. Lawrence River (**le [fleuve] Saint-Laurent**), it is, at its longest, 34 km, and at its widest, 8 km. Known as "the Garden of Quebec," it remains a primarily rural place of local agriculture with abundant apple and other fruit orchards, vineyards, "**cidreries**," and vegetable cultivation, and is popular among tourists.

Expansion

Have students use an online map tool to take a virtual tour of any one of the **parcours** suggested by the brochure. Let them select highlights of their tours and present them to members of other groups. They should select their own scenic highlights rather than just images of the restaurants and hotels marked on the map.

Du côté des médias 1.2

Lisez les brochures sur l'île d'Orléans.

à voir!

Espace Félix-Leclerc

Un musée dédié à l'œuvre du poète, chanteur et dramaturge Félix Leclerc. Découvrez une boîte à chansons, une boutique et des sentiers pédestres. Bref, un endroit où il fait bon s'attarder le temps qu'il faut!

Cassis Monna & filles

La famille Monna cultive le cassis… et le bonheur aussi! Plusieurs expériences exceptionnelles et nouveautés sont offertes aux épicuriens sur leur domaine enchanteur: boutique, restaurant-terrasse, visites VIP, crémerie artisanale…

Le Nouveau théâtre de l'Île d'Orléans

Le Nouveau théâtre de l'Île d'Orléans présente la comédie *Un pied dans la bouche* de Claude Montminy dans une mise en scène de Carol Cassistat. Salle climatisée, terrasse avec vue sur le fleuve, stationnement gratuit. Soupers-théâtres disponibles!

Domaine Steinbach Cidrerie

Grâce à leur concept inédit de dégustations, cette cidrerie familiale novatrice a su élaborer d'authentiques produits du terroir. Procurez-vous le panier de pique-nique à déguster sur la terrasse avec vue sur le fleuve.

Essential Instruction

1. Have students work in pairs to read **Du côté des médias**. The students will condense into 1–2 sentences the importance of each of the four tourist sites highlighted in the brochure.
2. Students prioritize which sites they would personally like to visit in descending order and state why.
3. Students continue in pairs to read the tourist brochure **l'Île d'Orléans.** They can do the corresponding activity.
4. As an extension to the fourth activity, have the students find lodgings and restaurants for their visit to the island.

Recherche: mrc île d'orléans, tourisme île d'orleans

9 L'Île d'Orléans 1.3, 3.2, 5.2

Complétez les activités suivantes.

1. Quels types d'attraits sont représentés sur la carte?
2. D'après les icônes, par quels moyens de transport peut-on se déplacer sur l'île?
3. Quel sites décrits pouvez-vous retrouver sur la carte? Que sont-ils et où se situent-ils?
4. Quel site culturel pouvez-vous visiter?
5. Qu'y a-t-il de particulier au Nouveau théâtre de l'Île d'Orléans?

Produits 2.2

The province of Quebec is known for its production of maple syrup. **Une érablière**, also called **une cabane à sucre**, is a place where artisans produce maple syrup. There is one traditional **érablière** left on **Île d'Orléans**. In Quebec, maple syrup is typically eaten with cream and bread, in yogurt, over ice cream, fruit, pancakes, and French toast, and some even use it to sweeten coffee and tea or as a base for broth or gravy.

Au nord de l'Île d'Orléans

Answers

9

1. les hôtels et les restaurants
2. en voiture, en vélo
3. Cassis Monna & filles, et Domaine Steinbach Cidrerie. Le premier est un restaurant-terrasse qui se situe au Nord-Est de l'île à Saint-Pierre, 1225 chemin Royal ; le deuxième est une cidrerie qui se situe à 1865 chemin Royal, à Saint-Pierre également.
4. l'Espace Félix-Leclerc
5. On y joue une comédie théâtrale, et on peut aussi y dîner.

Culture

Practices: Information

Since the passage of Bill 101 in 1977, Quebec remains an officially French-speaking province of Canada. After the passage of that law, it was widely feared that Quebec would secede from Canada. The success of that law, which was widely challenged in Canadian courts and the United Nations, is still debated today. The French-speakers argue for the preservation of a culture and language (many public signs prior to the passage of Bill 101 were exclusively in English), while English-speakers fear isolation and a violation of their freedom of expression. As a result of a United Nations' verdict, Bill 101 was amended from requiring all signs in Quebec to be exclusively in French to all signs being bilingual.

Expansion

Have students debate Bill 101, which requires the use of French in all public signs in Quebec. Have students with intrapersonal learning skills prepare the arguments on paper and pair them with students with interpersonal learning skills who can then take the arguments before the class. (You may choose to debate the original law, which declares French the exclusive language of Quebec, or the amended version, effective in 2018, which requires bilingual signs.)

Differentiated Learning

Accelerate

Students can make a brochure for their state or their hometown using the same format as found on p. 148.

Decelerate

Have students collaborate to make a map of Canada, contrasting with different colors the provinces considered Francophone, Anglophone, and bilingual. They can label key cities in each province. Each group will present their poster or visual to the classroom.

Special Needs Students

AD(H)D

Students with short attention spans may benefit from focusing on one tourist site at a time from the **Du côté des médias** brochure, and listing essential elements described in each paragraph.

Resources

WB Workbook 6–9

G & V Practice Games

Answers

On recycle !

The affirmative answers using the pronouns **y** and **en** are:

1. J'y vais le weekend.
2. Oui, j'en ai.
3. J'aime en manger.
4. Je voudrais y aller.

Reference Desk

1. **Y** replaces prepositional phrases beginning with **à**, **chez**, **dans**, **derrière**, **devant**, **en**, and **sur**. When the noun following **à** is a person, the indirect object pronouns **lui** and **leur** are used.
2. Here are additional verbs followed by **à** + THING: **s'intéresser à**, **s'habituer à**, **résister à**, **obéir à**, **répondre à**, **assister à**.
3. Point out the elision when using the pronoun **y** in negative sentences and with reflexive verbs: **Mme Martin n'y voyage plus avec son mari**. **Je m'y repose souvent**.
4. You may want to review the four uses of **en** with your students.
5. In the **passé composé** there is no preceding direct object agreement: **J'en ai écrit trois**.

Expansion

Throw a ball to a student as you say a sentence in French that requires a pronoun replacement. The student will return the ball to you as he or she restates the sentence with a pronoun. **Paul, tu vas aller au cinéma avec Charles? Oui, je vais y aller avec Charles**. The ball adds an element of surprise since students don't know when it will be their turn.

Communication

Interpersonal: Paired Practice

Partners will ask each other if he or she wants pleasant or unpleasant things, using the pronoun **en**.

Structure de la langue

Révision: The Pronouns *y* and *en* 1.2

On recycle !

Do you remember how to answer the questions below affirmatively, replacing what's underlined with the correct pronoun?

1. Vas-tu au cinéma le weekend ?
2. Tu as des dictionnaires français-anglais ?
3. Tu aimes manger de la pizza ?
4. Voudrais-tu aller en France ?

If you are unable to answer these questions, read the grammar summary below.

The pronouns **y** and **en** are placed before the verb of which they are the object in all sentences, including those that are affirmative, interrogative, negative, or have an infinitive.

À Paris ? Non, nous ne voudrions pas **y** aller. — *To Paris? No, we wouldn't like to go there.*

Des oranges ? Oui, j'**en** ai pris une. — *Oranges? Yes, I had one of them.*

Pronoun	Replaces	Examples	
y	preposition + PLACE	Ta grand-tante était en Arizona ? **Y** est-elle restée ? Elle va **y** déménager.	*Your great-aunt was in Arizona?* *Did she stay there?* *She's going to move there.*
y	certain verbs, such as **penser à**, **réfléchir à** + NAME OF THING	Son idée ? Tu **y** penses ? Oui, j'**y** pense.	*Her idea? Are you thinking about it?* *Yes, I'm thinking about it.*
en	**de** + EXPRESSION	Du vélo ? **En** faites-vous en famille ? Oui, nous **en** faisons ensemble.	*Biking? Do you do it with your family?* *Yes, we do it together.*
en	quantity + NOUN	Tu veux un café ? Oui, j'**en** veux **un**.	*Would you like a coffee?* *Yes, I'd like one.*

In an affirmative command, **y** or **en** follows the verb and is attached to it by a hyphen; an **-s** is also added to the **tu** form of **-er** verbs before the pronoun **y** or **en**. In a negative command, **y** or **en** precedes the verb.

Manges-**en** ! — *Eat some!*

Mais n'**en** mange pas trop ! — *But don't eat too much/many!*

When a specific quantity is implied in a sentence with **en**, that quantity is stated after the verb.

Tu as **des** frères ? — *Do you have (any) brothers?*

Oui, j'**en** ai **quatre**. — *Yes, I have four.*

2.2, 4.1

Produits

Pronouns are often used in expressions of exasperation, such as **J'en ai marre !** (I'm sick of it!), and **Je n'y arrive pas !** (I can't do this!).

Essential Instruction

1. To review the pronoun **y,** refer to p. 437 in Level 2 of ***T'es branché?*** Then give students 10 sentences in which they replace expressions with the pronoun **y**. You may want to recycle the unit's vocabulary on p.139. **Paul habite *en Pennsylvanie*. Paul *y* habite. Paul veut habiter *en Virginie*. Paul veut *y* habiter.**
2. Remind students that **lui** and **leur** are used to replace expressions containing the preposition **à** followed by a person, whereas **y** is used to replace the pronoun **à** plus the name of a place or a thing. **Je parle *à Paul*. Je lui parle. Je vais *à Paris*. J'y vais.**
3. To review the pronoun **en**, refer to p. 384 in Level 2 of ***T'es branché?*** Remind students that **en** replaces places in sentences using a verb followed by the preposition **de**. Give students 10 sentences in which they replace expressions with the pronoun **en**.

10 Tu penses à...? 1.1, 5.2

Interpersonal Speaking

*À tour de rôle, demandez à votre partenaire s'il ou elle pense aux sujets suivants. Répondez affirmativement ou négativement avec **y**. Utilisez aussi les adverbes **toujours**, **souvent**, **de temps en temps**, **rarement**, et **jamais** dans vos réponses.*

MODÈLE les activités que tu faisais quand tu étais petit(e)
A : Tu penses aux activités que tu faisais quand tu étais petit(e) ?
B : Oui, j'y pense de temps en temps.
ou
Non, je n'y pense pas.

1. les cadeaux de Noël que tu vas offrir
2. les questions que tes profs posent en classe
3. l'avenir
4. les informations à la télé
5. les amis que tu invites à ta fête
6. les problèmes de la vie contemporaine
7. les vacances
8. la personne avec qui tu vas vivre ta vie

11 Vous vous en servez ? 1.1, 5.2

Interpersonal Speaking or Writing

*Répondez aux questions pour dire si on se sert des ustensiles suivants dans la cuisine. Utilisez **en**, et soyez logique !*

MODÈLES Vous vous servez d'une cuillère en bois pour remuer la sauce ?
Oui, nous nous en servons pour remuer la sauce.

Marianne se sert d'un bol pour préparer des steaks ?
Non, elle ne s'en sert pas pour préparer des steaks.

1. Vous vous servez d'un chinois pour filtrer les herbes ?
2. Madeleine se sert d'une poêle pour faire un gâteau ?
3. Les sœurs Delattre se servent d'un verre mesureur pour mesurer le lait ?
4. Tu te sers d'une cuillère en bois pour mesurer le sucre ?
5. Jacques et Karim se servent d'un mixeur pour faire des frites ?
6. Je me sers d'une casserole pour faire chauffer la sauce ?
7. Nous nous servons d'une passoire pour rincer les pâtes ?

Answers

10

1. Tu penses aux cadeaux de Noël que tu vas offrir ?
2. Tu penses aux questions que tes profs posent en classe ?
3. Tu penses à l'avenir ?
4. Tu penses aux informations à la télé ?
5. Tu penses aux amis que tu invites à ta fête ?
6. Tu penses aux problèmes de la vie contemporaine ?
7. Tu penses aux vacances ?
8. Tu penses à la personne avec qui tu vas vivre ta vie ?

Partner answers will vary.

11

1. Oui, nous nous en servons pour filtrer les herbes.
2. Non, elle ne s'en sert pas pour faire un gâteau.
3. Oui, elles s'en servent pour mesurer le lait.
4. Non, je ne m'en sers pas pour mesurer le sucre.
5. Non, ils ne s'en servent pas pour faire des frites.
6. Oui, tu t'en sers pour faire chauffer la sauce.
7. Oui, vous vous en servez pour rincer les pâtes.

Reference Desk

In everyday speech, the negative particle **ne** in negative sentences with **y** and **en** may be omitted: **J'y pense pas. T'en as pas ?**

Communication

Interpersonal: Paired Practice

Pair students to do **Activités 10** and **11**. One student holds the book and the other writes. The person with the book reads the question. The person responding can look at the question if necessary in order to answer. For the next item, students will trade roles.

Differentiated Learning

Decelerate

Low-ability students will need to break down the pronoun replacement lesson into smaller steps. They will benefit from a set of sentences featuring only the pronoun **y**. They should underline the words to be replaced, then rewrite the sentences using **y**. Next, they should do a series of sentences with pronoun replacements using **en**, again underlining the words they intend to replace.

Multiple Intelligences

Musical-Rhythmic

To help auditory learners with switching from declarative to negative sentences with object pronouns, encourage them to do **Activité 10** and **Activité 11** by paying attention to the number of syllables it takes to answer a question in the declarative form. Then let them know that sentences in the negative are simply sentences in the declarative form with two more syllables: **J'y pense (2)**, **Je n'y pense pas (4)**, **Nous nous en servons (5)**, **Nous ne nous en servons pas (7)**, etc.

Resources

- Activity 12
- WB Workbook 10–11
- G & V Practice Games

Answers

12 Script

1. Tu es allé dans le Delaware l'été dernier?
2. Est-ce que tu prends souvent de la soupe à l'oignon?
3. Est-ce que vous avez vu vos cousins au Texas?
4. Où ont-ils acheté des fraises?
5. Quand vas-tu en Louisiane?
6. Tes grands-parents ont vécu au Québec?
7. Combien de fois par semaine l'enfant mange-t-il des légumes?
8. Combien de CD Michèle a-t-elle achetés?

1. y; 2. en; 3. y; 4. en; 5. y; 6. y; 7. en; 8. en

On recycle !

These are the affirmative answers to the questions:

1. Je te la montre.
2. Je pourrais t'en prêter un.

Reference Desk

1. To help students remember the order of object pronouns, create one or two sentences they can learn by heart such as **Je donne des bonbons aux enfants. Je leur en donne.**
2. Help students remember that **y** always comes before **en** by stressing that the pair **y en** sounds a bit like the sound a donkey makes in French: "**hi-han**."

12 De petites conversations 1.2

Interpretive Listening

*Écrivez les numéros 1–8 sur votre papier. Écoutez les questions et indiquez si vous répondriez avec **y** ou **en**.*

Révision: Double Object Pronouns 1.1, 1.2

On recycle !

Imagine there is a new French student in your school. Answer her questions affirmatively, replacing what's underlined with two pronouns.

1. Tu <u>me</u> montres <u>la cantine</u>?
2. Pourrais-tu <u>me</u> prêter <u>un stylo</u>?

If you are unable to answer these questions, read the grammar summary below.

When there are two pronouns in one sentence, their order before the verb in a declarative sentence is:

SUBJECT	+	**me** **te** **nous** **vous**	+	**le** **la** **les**	+	**lui** **leur**	+	**y**	+	**en**	+	VERB

These pronouns come right before the verb of which they are the object in sentences that are affirmative, negative, interrogative, or have an infinitive. They also precede the verb in a negative command.

As-tu vu mes cousins germains en ville? Je ne **les y** ai pas vus hier.	*Did you see my first cousins in town?* *I didn't see them there yesterday.*
Les vacances d'été? Je **leur en** ai parlé au téléphone.	*Summer vacation? I talked to them about it on the phone.*
Vous allez inviter vos cousins germains chez vous? Oui, je vais **les y** inviter. Non! Ne **m'en** parle pas!	*Are you going to invite your first cousins to your house?* *Yes, I'm going to invite them there.* *No! Don't talk to me about it!*

Produits

Pour pratiquer les pronoms, cherchez les chansons et les paroles de chansons comme ***Dis-lui oui*** (Bénabar), ***Un homme debout*** (Claude Capéo), ***Ma beauté*** (Maître Gims), ou ***Laissez-moi!*** (Zaz). 1.2, 2.2

Essential Instruction

1. As a bell-ringer activity, do a quick review of **y** and **en** by having students listen to **De petites conversations** answering questions 1–8.
2. Reacquaint students with the position of the pronouns by asking them questions: **Tu aimes le chocolat? Tu l'aimes?; Chris connaît Sara? Il la connaît?; Vous donnez des conseils à tes camarades? Vous leur en donnez?** Students must respond with pronouns.
3. Review pronoun positions in the affirmative and negative commands.
4. In pairs, have students ask and answer the questions in **Logique ou non?**

In an affirmative command, the order of pronouns is:

VERB	+	le la les	+	lui leur	+	moi toi nous vous	+	y	+	en

Je donne l'invitation à ta grand-tante?
Oui, **donne-la-lui**!

Should I give the invitation to your great-aunt?
Yes, give it to her!

Comparaisons 4.1

Many verbs can be transitive and intransitive. A transitive verb takes a direct object; an intransitive verb does not. Are the verbs in the sentences below used transitively or intransitively?

1. Chelsea *is arriving* at 6 P.M.
2. Zach *sees* Chelsea.
3. Zach *writes* Chelsea a text message.

13 Logique ou non? 1.1, 1.2

Interpersonal Speaking or Writing, Interpretive Reading

Si la question est logique, répondez affirmativement. Si non, répondez négativement. Faites attention au temps du verbe. Utilisez des pronoms dans vos réponses. Attention à l'ordre.

MODÈLES Tu lis le conte de fées à ton petit cousin?
Oui, je le lui lis.
ou
Non, je ne le lui lis pas.

1. Est-ce que votre frère ou votre sœur conduit une auto tamponneuse au supermarché?
2. Avez-vous acheté la nouvelle Renault décapotable pour votre mari?
3. Vos camarades de classe vont-ils donner leurs smartphones à leurs parents?
4. Est-ce que vous offrirez des cadeaux à vos parents pour leur anniversaire de mariage?
5. Simon et toi, vous avez parlé au prof de vos devoirs?
6. Votre meilleur ami rend son livre de poche à son voisin?
7. Votre grand-mère va donner des euros à son chien?

Answers

Comparaisons

In sentence 1, *is arriving* is used intransitively. In sentences 2–3, *sees* and *writes* are used transitively because these verbs take direct objects (*Chelsea* and *a text message*).

13

1. Non, il/elle n'y en conduit pas.
2. Non, je ne la lui ai pas achetée.
3. Non, ils ne vont pas les leur donner.
4. Oui, je leur en offrirai.
5. Oui, nous lui en avons parlé.
6. Oui, il le lui rend.
7. Non, elle ne va pas lui en donner.

Expansion

This activity can be done by individual students or in pairs depending on the size of your class.

1. For a pronoun review, prepare by writing a series of sentences in the affirmative, negative, declarative, or imperative. Cut the sentences into the different words. Paper clip the words of the sentence into packets. On one side of the paper, write the direct and indirect objects, prepositions, and places needed to make a meaningful sentence. On the back of those slips of paper, write the appropriate pronoun.
2. Pair students and ask them to clear their desks. Give each pair of students a packet.
3. Have them unscramble the words to make two sentences, the first without pronouns and the second with. Students make a note of their sentence in their notebooks.
4. When students are done, or when you say "**Changez**," students may exchange their packet with another pair of students. At the end of the exercise, ask students to write the sentences on the board.

Differentiated Learning

Accelerate

Tell advanced students that in the negative the particles **ne… pas** always surround the conjugated verb, but the pronouns always precede the verb they refer to. Have them add **ne… pas** in parentheses on the object pronouns charts on pp. 152 and 153.

Learning Styles

Auditory Learners

Students will repeat a series of sentences containing double object pronouns many times to solidify the sound of the pronoun combinations in their memory.

Multiple Intelligences

Visual-Spatial

Students will create a chart with columns for each of the following pronoun types: direct, indirect, **y**, **en**, and stress pronouns. At the top of each column they will indicate what type of noun the pronouns replace (person, thing, place) and write an example for each category.

Artistic

Have students draw stick figure images of sentences that require more than one pronoun. They can trade images with a partner and write captions using the appropriate pronouns in the correct order.

Connections

Music

"**Je te le dis quand même**" by Patrick Bruel, and "**Belle, belle, belle**" by Claude François are popular songs that feature object pronouns.

Recherche: paroles je te le dis quand même, paroles belle belle belle

Resources

CA Communicative Activities

Share

Answers

14 Possible partner answers:

1. Oui, donne-les-lui !
2. Non, ne la lui donne pas !
3. Oui, donne-les-leur !
4. Non, ne le lui donne pas !
5. Oui, donne-le-lui !
6. Non, ne les leur donne pas !
7. Oui, donne-les-leur !
8. Non, ne la lui donne pas !

15 Presentations will vary.

Reference Desk

If you have access to Passport, create a question for your students to share their response to a communicative activity.

Connections

Music

Jean-Jacques Goldman wrote a song, "**Je te donne**," that stayed on the charts in France for months. It is a bilingual English-French song that is easy to sing, and imprints the pronoun word order in students' memory through repetition. Print off copies of the song and leave blanks for some key words in the lyrics. Have students listen to the song and fill in the missing words as they do so. Afterwards discuss the grammar, vocabulary and meaning of the song together.

Recherche : je te donne paroles goldman

Communiquez !

14 Des cadeaux de Noël pour les enfants à l'hôpital 1.1, 5.2

Interpersonal Speaking

Avec votre partenaire, imaginez que vous allez donner des cadeaux à des enfants à l'hôpital pour Noël. Jouez le rôle du Père Noël et de son elfe. L'elfe demande au Père Noël à quel enfant on doit donner chaque cadeau. Le Père Noël doit répondre logiquement.

MODÈLES les cartes de foot au garçon de 8 ans
A : Je donne les cartes de foot au garçon de 8 ans ?
B : Oui, donne-les-lui !

le collier en argent à la fille de 2 ans
A : Je donne le collier en argent à la fille de 2 ans ?
B : Non, ne le lui donne pas !

1. les jeux vidéo au garçon de 15 ans
2. la poupée à la fille de 16 ans
3. les livres de science Jeunesse aux petites filles de 10 ans
4. le petit ours au garçon de 17 ans
5. le ballon de foot au garçon de 12 ans
6. les BD aux garçons de 3 ans
7. les costumes de super-héros aux petits enfants de 6 ans
8. la corde à sauter à la fille de 17 ans

15 L'Alliance française 1.2, 1.3, 2.1, 4.2

Interpretive Reading, Presentational Writing and Speaking

Imaginez que vous êtes le directeur ou la directrice de l'Alliance française de votre ville. Vous devez organiser un camp d'été d'une semaine pour les enfants de 8 à 14 ans. Vous voulez qu'ils s'amusent tout en apprenant le français. Créez un programme d'événements pour la semaine annonçant votre camp aux parents. Indiquez l'horaire, les thèmes et les activités principales du camp. Donnez aussi toutes les informations importantes concernant le camp — les heures, les dates, l'endroit et ce que les enfants devront apporter avec eux pour le camp. Vous pouvez présenter votre programme sous forme de dépliant ou autre brochure. Présentez votre programme à la classe.

Essential Instruction

1. Before beginning **Activité 14** have students brainstorm, with books closed, the kinds of gifts that children and adolescents generally like to receive.
2. Allow students to research a family other than their own for **Activité 16**.
3. **Les familles souches de l'île d'Orléans** is an activity that will require students to do research online.

16 D'où viennent vos aïeux? 1.3, 3.1, 5.2

Presentational Writing

Faites une présentation dans laquelle vous :

- expliquez lesquels de vos ancêtres ont quitté leur pays d'origine et le nom de ce pays
- donnez la date de leur voyage si vous la connaissez
- précisez comment ils ont voyagé (en bateau ? en avion ?)
- expliquez où ils se sont installés
- dites pourquoi ils s'y sont installés

Peut-être qu'il faudra que vous parliez à vos parents ou grands-parents pour vous renseigner sur l'histoire de votre famille. Servez-vous de cartes pour montrer les pays, les États, ou les provinces en question pendant votre présentation.

17 Les familles souches de l'Île d'Orléans 1.2, 1.3, 3.2, 4.2

Interpretive Reading, Presentational Writing

L'Île d'Orléans était la terre d'accueil de 300 familles souches (*founding*) canadiennes qui ont immigré de France pendant le 17ème siècle. Les noms de famille comprennent Pichet, Drouin, Goulet, Noël, Rousseau, Gagnon, Gosselin. Choisissez et complétez l'un des projets suivants :

A. Trouvez les dates de naissance et de mort d'un fondateur de l'Île d'Orléans et écrivez une phrase pour décrire sa vie ; par exemple : **Jean Pichet est né en Bretagne à une date inconnue, et il est mort à X, en 1788, dans la Nouvelle-France.**

B. Trouvez l'arbre généalogique d'une de ces familles et parlez du point de vue d'un membre de la famille qui est toujours vivant ; par exemple : **Mon arrière-grand-père était X. Il est né à Sainte-Famille en 1903 et mort à Québec en 1975.**

C. Imaginez que vous êtes membre d'une famille souche venant d'arriver à l'Île d'Orléans au 17ème siècle. Décrivez votre vie quotidienne, et présentez les membres de votre famille.

Recherche : ancestry canada île d'orléans, arbre généalogique québec + NOM DE FAMILLE, familles souches île d'orléans

Answers

16 Presentations will vary.

17 Research will vary.

Critical Thinking

Analysis

Have students research the meaning of **souche**. What is the literal meaning of the word? (*stump of a tree*) How is it used when referring to genealogy? (It has the sense of "born and raised.") Ask students if they can think of a similar English term that is used when referring to heritage and ancestory. (roots) What social implications does **souche** have in French-speaking regions today? (It creates an "us vs. them" atmosphere of native French vs. foreigners.)

Special Needs Students

Social Anxiety

You may have students who do not know much about their family origins, or who find the questions invasive. You might propose that they research a well-known family.

At-Risk Students

Be attentive to the fact that some students may not have Internet at home. Make sure you provide a time and space for students to do online research at school.

AD(H)D

Giving students with attention difficulties too many topic choices can inhibit their forward momentum. Meet with them individually to help them choose a topic that fits their interests and skills.

Answers

18 Research will vary.

Reference Desk

Canada is one of the countries with the highest number of immigrants and political refugees. The country welcomes approximately 250,000 permanent immigrants each year. It is one of the top destinations of immigrants, with Switzerland, Germany, the United Kingdom, the United States, Japan, and Saudi Arabia.

18 L'immigration au Canada 1.2, 1.3, 3.1, 3.2, 4.2

Interpretive Reading, Presentational Speaking

En groupe, choisissez l'un des trois sujets ci-dessous. Puis, individuellement, allez sur le site réservé à l'immigration du gouvernement canadien. Recherchez les formulaires et guides de demandes d'immigration au Canada aujourd'hui. Cliquez sur « français ». Renseignez-vous sur l'une des trois possibilités suivantes :

A. Visiter le Canada de façon temporaire
B. Immigrer au Canada de façon permanente
C. Parrainer (*sponsor*) une famille

Une fois vos recherches finies, mettez vos informations en commun et présentez vos résultats à la classe.

Recherche : citizenship and immigration canada

Des immigrés maghrébins jouant aux échecs à Toronto

Essential Instruction

1. Explain that each Canadian province has its own particular laws for short and long-term stays.
2. In **Activité 17** have students imagine that they are considering a long-term stay in Canada to study French, and they need to find out what is required for entry into the country.
3. Have students compare the immigration laws in the United States to those of Canada.
4. For the pronunciation exercises on p. 157, play **A**, **B**, **C**, and **D** separately. Replay each section several times to give students practice repeating the intonation.

Prononciation

Rising and Falling Intonation in Commands 1.2

» In commands, the voice descends abruptly on the last syllable. In longer commands, the voice rises in the first group of words and falls abruptly at the end of the sentence.

A Des phrases impératives

Répétez chaque phrase. Faites attention à la descente de la voix à la fin de la phrase.

1. Fais entrer ta grand-tante !
2. Fais entrer ta petite cousine !
3. Fais entrer ton arrière-grand-mère !

B Jacqueline fait du babysitting

Répétez la phrase déclarative, suivie de la phrase à l'impératif. Faites attention à l'intonation.

1. Il faut fermer la porte. N'oubliez pas de fermer la porte !
2. Il faut lui donner son dîner. N'oubliez pas de lui donner son dîner !

Open and Closed Vowels

» In the following pairs, the first vowel is open and the second closed. The sounds can be found in the words underneath. Listen carefully for the distinction in the vowel sounds in the pairs of words.

/ɛ - e/	/o - ɔ/	/ø - œ/
faites – été	mot – mort	heureux – bœuf

C Les aïeux

Répétez les phrases suivantes. Faites attention aux sons des voyelles.

1. Vos aïeux sont français, et les nôtres sont anglais.
   /o/ /ø/ /ɛ/ /e/ /e/ /o/ /ɛ/
2. Notre aïeul est anglais, et le vôtre est japonais !
   /o/ /œ/ /ɛ/ /ɛ/ /e/ /o/ /ɛ/ /ɛ/

D Pendant deux heures

Répondez affirmativement à la question d'après le modèle que vous entendez ; utilisez l'expression « pendant deux heures ».

MODÈLE Tu as travaillé jeudi ?
Oui, j'ai travaillé pendant deux heures.

Resources

Prononciation
Pre-test
Leçon Quiz

Answers

D Script

1. Tu as regardé la télé hier ?
2. Tu as fait du sport la semaine dernière ?
3. Tu as porté un blouson à l'école hier ?
4. Tu as décoré ta chambre avec des tableaux ?

1. Oui, j'ai regardé la télé pendant deux heures.
2. Oui, j'ai joué (au foot) pendant deux heures.
3. Oui, j'ai porté un blouson pendant deux heures.
4. Oui, j'ai décoré ma chambre pendant deux heures.

Reference Desk

In this section, stressed letters have been bolded and underlined (for example, **e**, **s**, **l**, or **t**). Unpronounced letters have been grayed out and underlined (for example, e, s, l, or t).

Differentiated Learning

Decelerate

Students can collaborate to make a poster featuring the English and French lyrics of the national anthem "**O Canada**." They can decorate the borders of the poster with symbols of the entire country such as a maple leaf, **fleur de lys**, hockey stick, the Quebec flag, and pictures of Montreal and Quebec.

Adapt

Before doing **Activité 17**, ask students to think of the reasons why someone might want to emigrate to Canada (work, studies, etc.). Then have students brainstorm what kind of questions a potential immigrant may have to answer on an application to the Canadian government.

Multiple Intelligences

Musical-Rhythmic

Ask these students to present the Canadian national anthem "**Ô Canada**," integrating the words and the music in a slideshow presentation where each page features a line of music and a photo of Canada.

Resources

- *Vocabulaire actif*
- eV eVisual
- WB Workbook 1–3
- FC Flash Cards
- LA Listening Activity 1
- G & V Practice Games

Reference Desk

1. Supplementary vocabulary to write a fairy tale:
   Personnages: **un fantôme**, **une sorcière** (*witch*), **le roi** (*king*), **la reine** (*queen*)
   Actions: **tomber amoureux de** (*to fall in love with*), **jeter un sort** (*to cast a spell*), **se venger de** (*to get revenge for*), **bannir de** (*to banish from*), **tuer** (*to kill*), **se transformer en** (*to transform into*)
   Éléments: **une baguette magique** (*wand*), **du poison**, **le feu** (*fire*)
   Lieux: un chemin, **le château hanté**, **une rivière**, **une chaumière** (*a small rural house*)
   Essentiels: en ce moment-là (*at that time*), **d'abord** (*first of all*), **ensuite** (*then*), **puis** (*then*), **finalement**, **tout d'un coup** (*all of a sudden*)
2. Definition of genres:
   Un conte de fées is a short story that typically features characters such as fairies, elves, trolls, dwarfs, giants, or gnomes who have the ability to use magic or enchantments.
   Une fable is a fictional story, in prose or verse, featuring animals and mythical characters that have human characteristics.
   Une ballade is a poem set to music.

Leçon B Vocabulaire actif

Les contes francophones 1.2

Essential Instruction

1. The picture of the young boy with the book in his hands presents the theme of storytelling: **un conte de fées**, **une fable**, **une histoire vraie**, and **une ballade**.
2. Put the above key terms on the board. Ask students to tell you what stories they heard as children that would be classified under these categories. Write their examples under each heading.
3. Ask students to define each genre. What are the differences among them? Which do they prefer and why?
4. Have students name elements in a fairy tale in English. Give them the equivalent words in French that they will copy in their notebooks.
5. Listen to **Pour la conversation** and **Et si je voulais dire...?**
6. Students will repeat these terms, then add them to their vocabulary list.

Resources

Pour la conversation

Et si je voulais dire... ?

Reference Desk

La gazelle d'or is an Algerian tale by Nora Aceval. You may search for additional francophone tales on TV5Monde.

Expansion

Play excerpts of Walt Disney's ***Blanche-Neige et les sept nains*** for the students. They should understand a lot since they know the story and the articulation is clear.

Recherche : walt disney's snow white and the seven dwarfs french

« La gazelle d'or »

Un sultan algérien a annoncé qu'un prince devra découvrir le secret de sa fille pour pouvoir se marier avec elle.

Un bon prince **rusé** a décidé de **jouer un tour** au sultan pour apprendre le secret. Il s'est caché dans une gazelle en or.

Le prince est sorti de la gazelle. La princesse a cru que c'était **un magicien**. Elle lui a dit son secret.

Le prince a **déjoué** le plan du sultan et a épousé la princesse.

Pour la conversation

1.2

How do I start a fairy tale?

» **Il était une fois** un petit garçon, Fahim.

Once upon a time there was a little boy, Fahim.

Et si je voulais dire... ?

un carrosse	*carriage*
un crapaud	*toad*
un grimoire	*magic book*
un ogre	*ogre*
un pays lointain	*far-away country*
une potion magique	*magic potion*

Culture

Products: Information

Like their counterparts across the Western world, fairy tales in France derive from a rich oral tradition that was first put to writing by the German brothers Grimm and the Danish writer Hans Christian Andersen. The tales, with some variance, remain relatively intact across languages. Here are common titles your students may be able to guess:

« **Cendrillon** » (*Cinderella*)
« **La Belle au bois dormant** » (*Sleeping Beauty*)
« **Blanche-Neige et les sept nains** » (*Snow White and the Seven Dwarves*)
« **Le Petit Chaperon Rouge** » (*Little Red Riding Hood*)
« **Les trois petits cochons** » (*The Three Little Pigs*)
« **La Belle et la bête** » (*Beauty and the Beast*)
« **La petite sirène** » (*The Little Mermaid*)
« **Tom Pouce** » (*Tom Thumb*)

Note that some of the original stories, intended as cautionary tales, often do not have the "happily ever after" endings with which your students may be familiar. The little mermaid, for example, in some versions becomes the foam of the sea when her prince does not fall in love with her. For another example, Cinderella's evil sisters cut their toes off to try and fit them into the crystal slipper.

Differentiated Learning

Accelerate

Have your high-ability students write the fairy tale **"La gazelle d'or"** using the comic strip as a guide.

Decelerate

Have students find the translation in French of the titles of popular fairy tales from their youth. They will present their findings to the class who will guess the titles in English.

Resources

Activity 1

Answers

1

1. Ce n'est pas aussi sérieux qu'elle pensait.
2. Elle lui lisait des histoires.
3. Elle a appris à se méfier des personnes qui pourraient lui jouer un mauvais tour.
4. des magiciens, des fées, et des animaux
5. de lui envoyer ses livres

2

1. C'est une fille qui se méfie du loup.
2. C'est une histoire vraie.
3. C'est une fable.
4. C'est une ballade.
5. C'est un animal rusé.
6. C'est un conte de fées.
7. C'est une pièce de théâtre.
8. C'est une histoire vraie.

Game

Un conte de fées

Divide the students into two teams. Each team will collaborate to choose a fairy tale and organize three scenes from it, which they will act out. The other teams must name the fairy tale (1 point) and describe what is happening in each scene (3 points). One point will be deducted for any English spoken.

Culture

Products: Information

Fairy tales, their purpose, their history, and their literary elements, are part of the national high school French language curriculum in many French-speaking countries, including France and Belgium.

1 Un cours pour la future prof 1.2

Interpretive Reading

Lisez la lettre de Valérie à sa mère, puis répondez aux questions.

Salut Maman!

J'espère que tout va bien pour toi et Papa. On dit qu'il faut se mettre aux choses sérieuses à la fac, mais non! Tu ne vas pas croire ce que nous lisons ce semestre. Tu te souviens de toutes les histoires que tu me lisais quand j'étais petite, où j'ai appris qu'il fallait me méfier des personnes qui me joueraient peut-être un mauvais tour? Maintenant ce sont les textes du cours. On les analyse pour voir s'ils sont toujours d'actualité pour les élèves d'école primaire. Tu savais déjà, tous les soirs qu'on passait ensemble à lire, que ces histoires de magiciens, de fées, d'animaux allaient me servir à la fac? Peux-tu m'envoyer tous mes vieux livres?

Bises,
Valérie

1. Quelle impression a Valérie de la fac?
2. Que faisait la maman de Valérie quand elle était petite?
3. Valérie a appris une leçon quand elle était jeune. Laquelle?
4. Qui étaient les personnages dans les livres de son enfance?
5. Que demande Valérie à sa mère?

2 La lecture 1.2, 3.2

Interpretive Reading

Choisissez la définition ci-dessous qui correspond aux définitions suivantes.

une histoire vraie **une ballade** **une fable** **un conte de fées** **un poème**
une pièce de théâtre **une fille qui se méfie du loup (*wolf*)** **un animal rusé**

MODÈLE « Ce soir, c'est tout le Québec que j'invite chez-nous »
C'est un poème québécois.

1. le Petit Chaperon Rouge
2. *La vie de Marie Curie*
3. « Le lièvre (*hare*) et la tortue (*tortoise*) »
4. « Annabel Lee »
5. le loup dans « Le Petit Chaperon Rouge »
6. « Cendrillon »
7. *Roméo et Juliette*
8. *La vie de Louis XIV*

Essential Instruction

1. Students work in pairs to do **Activité 1**. They alternate reading each sentence aloud from Valerie's letter, and answer the questions.
2. Bring students together to share their answers.
3. Do **La lecture** together, as a class activity. Challenge the students to expand their answers: **« Le Petit Chaperon Rouge » est un conte de fées qui raconte l'histoire d'une petite fille qui se perd dans la forêt et qui rencontre un loup.**

3 Je vous lis.... 1.2, 1.3, 3.1

Interpretive Viewing, Presentational Speaking

Jouez le rôle de la maîtresse d'une école primaire et dites ce que vous lisez aux enfants selon le modèle. Choisissez un mot ou une expression ci-dessous.

poème **conte de fées** **fable** **histoire** **pièce** **histoire vraie** **roman**

MODÈLE 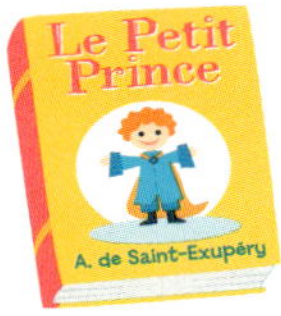

Les enfants, aujourd'hui je vous lis une histoire.

1. 

2. 

3. 

4. 

5. 

6. 

7. 

8. 

9. 

Answers

3

1. Les enfants, aujourd'hui, je vous lis une pièce de théâtre.
2. Les enfants, aujourd'hui, je vous lis un conte de fées.
3. Les enfants, aujourd'hui, je vous lis une histoire vraie.
4. Les enfants, aujourd'hui, je vous lis un conte de fées.
5. Les enfants, aujourd'hui, je vous lis une fable.
6. Les enfants, aujourd'hui, je vous lis une histoire vraie.
7. Les enfants, aujourd'hui, je vous lis un roman.
8. Les enfants, aujourd'hui, je vous lis un conte de fées.
9. Les enfants, aujourd'hui, je vous lis une ballade.

Communication

Interpersonal: Paired Practice

Students will be placed in pairs. They will stand with their books open to this page. One student in the pair will point to a picture of a literary genre and the other, following the formula, will say "**Les enfants, aujourd'hui je vous lis**...." They will alternate who points to a picture and who speaks. At your discretion, you will call "**Changez**" and they will form new partners to continue the exercise. As an alternative, they may change the exercise to say "(STUDENT NAME) **aujourd'hui je te lis**...."

Special Needs Students

Behavior Problems

To some students, telling fairy tales might seem childish and not a serious subject. They need to be reminded that these are excellent ways of self-expression that allow them to express their creativity. Point out that fairy tales are considered a historically and culturally important literary genre and are studied in many universities. Invite students to research some of the more provocative endings to these tales.

Linguistically Challenged/Social Anxiety

Students can be placed with more outgoing or confident students in learning groups. When doing presentational activities, they can be given roles that correspond to their abilities. For example, confident students in a play might assume the lead role, and those who are less comfortable can have minor parts. All should cooperate equally in the writing of the activity, however.

Resources

Activity 4

Answers

4 Script

Il était une fois une très belle princesse. Elle habitait dans un grand château. Tous les matins, la princesse se levait, se lavait, se maquillait, et se brossait les cheveux pour se préparer pour la journée avant de sortir pour faire une longue promenade dans la forêt. Un jour, un magicien a décidé de lui jouer un mauvais tour. Il a changé le chemin de la promenade de la princesse. Mais la princesse était aussi rusée que belle. Elle se méfiait des magiciens et savait qu'un magicien méchant habitait dans la forêt. Donc, elle a mis des cordes jaunes aux arbres pour indiquer le chemin. Comme ça, elle a pu déjouer le tour du magicien et rentrer au château.

1. D; 2. C; 3. A; 4. B; 5. E

5 Answers will vary.

Communication

Interpersonal: Paired Practice
Presentational: Cooperative Groups

In pairs, students interview each other with the **Questions personnelles**. Then, in groups, students share information about literary preferences that they learned about their partner: **Voici Jean. Quand il était petit, ses parents lui lisaient des contes de fées.**

TPR

Invent a story and have students act out the story, or create a **tableau vivant** for each of the scenes. Alternatively, invite artistic or shy students to turn your story into a comic strip. Example:

Il était une fois une princesse qui était petite comme une souris.
Il y avait un ogre qui aimait chasser les princesses. Le prince était un peu myope, alors, il n'a pas vu l'ogre entrer dans sa maison.
L'ogre a enlevé la princesse.
Le roi était inconsolable.
Le prince est allé voir le magicien qui l'a transformé en rat.
Le prince-rat est allé chez l'ogre et a repris la princesse.
Le roi a acheté des lunettes pour le prince.

4 Une princesse rusée 1.2

Interpretive Listening

Écoutez le conte de fées, puis choisissez la lettre de la partie qui complète la phrase.

1. Il était une fois…
2. D'habitude, la princesse…
3. Elle aimait…
4. Le magicien a…
5. Mais il n'a pas réussi parce que…

A. marcher dans la forêt.
B. joué un mauvais tour.
C. se préparait dans la salle de bains avant de faire une promenade.
D. une princesse qui habitait dans un château.
E. la princesse a mis des cordes aux arbres pour se rappeler du chemin.

5 Questions personnelles 1.1, 3.1, 5.2

Interpersonal Speaking

Répondez aux questions avec un partenaire.

1. Quelles sortes d'histoires est-ce que tes parents te lisaient quand tu étais petit(e)?
2. Quel est ton conte de fées préféré? En existe-t-il une version cinématographique? Est-ce que tu préfères lire ou regarder cette histoire?
3. Aimes-tu lire des histoires vraies? Si oui, sur quels sujets ou sur qui?
4. Quelles sortes de textes est-ce que tu dois lire pour tes cours de littérature au lycée?
5. Qui est ton magicien préféré—Merlin, Harry Potter, ou Mickey Mouse dans «Fantasia»?
6. Si tu pouvais jouer un tour, qu'est-ce que tu ferais?

On recycle!

Allez en ligne et trouvez une version française d'un conte de fées que vous aimez bien. Prenez note de tous les verbes que vous voyez à l'imparfait et réfléchissez à la raison pour laquelle ces verbes sont formés de cette façon plutôt qu'au passé composé.

Par exemple, «*il **était** une fois une petite fille qui **s'appelait** Petit Chaperon Rouge et qui **habitait** dans la forêt….*»

Essential Instruction

1. Before the students listen to **Une princesse rusée**, have them skim the choices of answers. This is good training for future language exams where questions give valuable cues to the main idea of the listening or reading passage.
2. The same strategy can be applied to the reading **Un conte maghrébin**. Students should peruse the questions for **Activité 6** before listening to the story.
3. After listening to **Un conte magrébin**, ask questions for general comprehension, including the questions on p. 164. Have students identify typical "little sister remarks" that they find in the dialogue. Examples: **"Je n'ai pas faim."** "**….je vais tout lui dire.**"

Rencontres culturelles

Un conte maghrébin

1.2, 5.2

Karim garde sa petite sœur, Aïcha, qui va bientôt se coucher.

Karim : C'est prêt... tu viens? Tu t'es lavé les mains?
Aïcha : Je n'ai pas faim....
Karim : Ah non, tu ne vas pas commencer! Je t'ai préparé une soupe comme tu l'aimes....
Aïcha : Je n'aime pas la soupe.... Il y a une heure j'ai mangé un yaourt. Et Maman m'a fait un bon goûter....
Karim : D'accord, alors va te coucher tout de suite!
Aïcha : Tu vas te faire disputer par Maman si je ne me brosse pas les dents : je vais tout lui dire.
Karim : Bon ça suffit : tu te brosses les dents et tu vas te coucher.
Aïcha : Qu'est-ce que tu me lis comme histoire?
Karim : Je te raconte « L'élève du magicien ». Tu l'aimes, n'est-ce pas?
Aïcha : Je l'adore.
Karim : Il était une fois un petit garçon, Fahim. C'était un enfant très intelligent. Sa mère l'avait envoyé chez un maître qu'on lui avait conseillé, loin, dans la montagne. Mais pendant que les autres élèves apprenaient, lui devait s'occuper des travaux de la ferme, pour payer ses études. Il passait très peu de temps en classe, mais il arrivait à apprendre si vite que son maître avait commencé à se méfier de lui. Mais Fahim sera plus rusé, et découvrira* même que son maître est un magicien.
Aïcha : Et après?
Karim : La suite demain....
Aïcha : Moi, je la connais. Il apprendra les mêmes choses que le magicien et comme ça il pourra déjouer ses mauvais tours.... Bonne nuit!

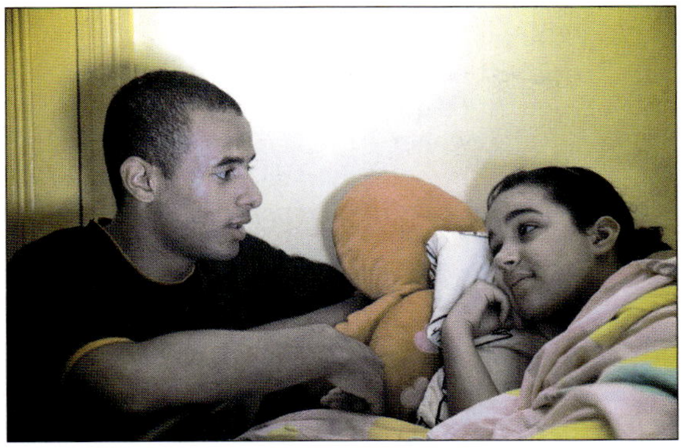

*Je parle bien!

Make sure to pronounce four syllables in the word **découvrira**. The *r* sound is a marker of the future tense, and in this word this sound appears twice in a row: **dé-cou-vri-ra**.

Analyse

Find all the excuses that Aïcha uses to not obey her brother's instructions. Do you believe these constitute valid justifications? Why or why not?

Mot-clé

Le mot **maître** a plus ou moins trois sens : celui d'instructeur (maître d'étudiants), celui de dominateur (maître d'esclaves), et celui de propriétaire (maître de maison). Il reflète en fait les trois facettes de l'autorité : positive si elle est éducative ou protectrice, mais négative si elle est dominatrice.

Resources

- Dialogue
- Dialogue Video
- WB Workbook 4

Answers

Analyse
She is not hungry, she doesn't like soup, she already had yogurt and a snack, and she needs to brush her teeth.; Answers will vary.

Reference Desk

L'élève du Magicien : Un conte du Maghreb is an illustrated fairy tale for children written in 2007 by Nora Aceval, a French author born in Algeria. The hero, Fahim, whose name means "the cunning one," lives with his mother in a poor and rural region of Algeria. Determined to give her son an education, Fahim's mother sends him to a boarding school, where he learns that his schoolmaster is in fact a magician who transforms his students into mules. Eventually, Fahim will learn the importance of knowledge, honesty, and justice.

nouvelle orthographe **un gouter, un maitre**

Learning Styles

Visual Learners
Have students illustrate a storyboard of **Un conte maghrébin** with captions.

Auditory Learners
Students will benefit from having access to the recording so that they can repeatedly hear the French as they are reading it. Listening helps them make the association with the written word.

Kinesthetic Learners
Have students mime the story as the audio is being played.

Accelerate
See if students can figure out the answers to **Activité 4** before listening to the recording; then check their understanding of the audio by asking them to summarize the story in English.

Resources

Activity 6
Extension

Answers

6

1. Karim garde sa petite soeur, Aïcha, qui doit se coucher bientôt.
2. Elle ne veut pas de soupe, même si d'habitude elle l'aime.
3. Elle veut se brosser les dents avant de se coucher ou elle va tout dire à sa maman.
4. Fahim est un petit garçon qui travaille dur à la ferme de son école.
5. Il découvre que son maître est un magicien.
6. Fahim apprend à déjouer les mauvais tours du magicien.

EXTENSION

Possible answer: Ils sont stricts.

Expansion

Have students create a dialogue in pairs or groups of three, where a parent/parents interview a potential babysitter. Students should stress the parental values they are portraying, and the potential babysitter could be an ideal or terrible fit. The dialogue may be realistic or comical.

6 Un conte maghrébin 1.2

Répondez aux questions suivantes.

1. Qu'est-ce que Karim fait?
2. Qu'est-ce qu'Aïcha ne veut pas?
3. Qu'est-ce qu'Aïcha veut faire, avant de se coucher?
4. Qui est Fahim?
5. Qu'est-ce que Fahim découvre de son maître?
6. Qu'est-ce que Fahim apprend à faire contre le magicien?

EXTENSION **Le babysitting** 1.2

Coralie fait du babysitting chez les Darras.

Mme Darras: On ne va pas rentrer très tard, avant minuit.
M. Darras: N'oubliez pas de lui faire réciter ses leçons avant le dîner.
Coralie: Je peux la laisser regarder la télévision un petit moment?
Mme Darras: Non, juste sa leçon de chinois. Le DVD est dans le salon.
Coralie: J'y veillerai.
Mme Darras: Pour le dîner, il faut qu'elle mange un légume, un yaourt, et un fruit.
M. Darras: Il faut qu'elle se brosse les dents avant de se coucher....
Mme Darras: ... et qu'elle se couche à 20h30.
Coralie: Entendu. Bonne soirée!

EXTENSION Comment sont les parents envers leur enfant? 1.3

Cette mère est-elle attentive envers sa fille?

Essential Instruction

1. After listening to **Un conte maghrébin**, students can answer questions 1–6.
2. Play the **Extension** dialogue without having students see the script, and see if they can answer the question. Then play the dialogue again while allowing them to follow the script. Encourage students to give specific examples to illustrate their answer.
3. Read the passage **La Francophonie** to the students, stopping to ask comprehension questions.
4. Have students research **la Tunisie** using the search words provided. They can research where it is located, what kind of government it has, languages spoken, major industries, and what there is to see and do.
5. Students will report their findings using a graphic organizer of their choice.

Pre-AP

Question centrale ? Comment les communautés francophones conservent-elles leurs traditions ?

La Francophonie

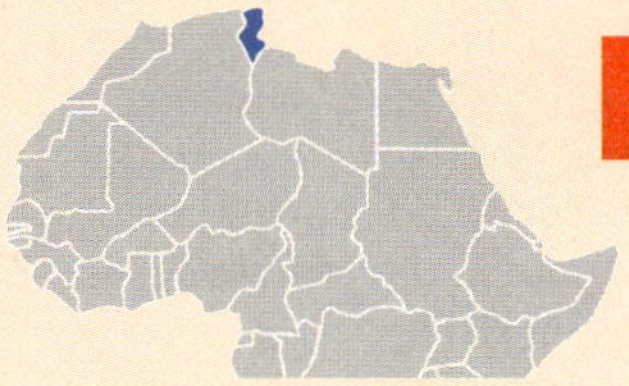

Profil touristique

La Tunisie 1.2, 2.1, 3.1, 4.2

La Tunisie est le plus petit des trois pays du Maghreb. Elle compte aujourd'hui plus de 11 millions d'habitants, et sa capitale est Tunis. La plus grande partie de la population vit sur la côte, à Gabès, Bizerte, Sfax, et Sousse. Le nombre de Tunisiens résidant à l'étranger est estimé à 1,2 millions dont* 85% en Europe.

Protectorat* français à partir de 1883, la Tunisie devient indépendante en 1956. Habib Bourguiba devient le premier Président d'une république qui se caractérise par un pouvoir détenu par* un parti unique, le Néo-Destour. La Tunisie a connu de nombreux épisodes de révolte en 2010, jusqu'à la révolte du Printemps arabe, la fin de la dictature et le retour d'élections libres.

La Tunisie a toujours accordé une place importante à l'éducation ; elle lui consacre 21% de ses ressources. Aujourd'hui, presque 80% de la population est alphabétisée* et 70%, garçons et filles à égalité, est scolarisée*. Plus de 20 000 étudiants fréquentent l'université dont 30% des professeurs sont des femmes.

Recherche : bonjour tunisie, tunisie tourisme, actualités tunisie, gouvernement tunisie

dont *among which* ; **Protectorat** *Protectorate* ; **pouvoir détenu par** *power held by* ; **alphabétisée** *literate* ; **scolarisée** *sent to school*

Des étudiantes discutent de la lecture pour le cours de sciences po.

L'université de Tunis Carthage est l'une des meilleures universités de Tunisie.

Traditions et pratiques

1.2, 2.1

Si l'islam est la religion principale et officielle de la Tunisie, le christianisme et le judaïsme, bien que minoritaires, sont représentés dans ce pays qui se caractérise par sa tolérance et son ouverture aux autres cultures.

Resources

- *Points de départ*
- WB Workbook 5
- Explore

Reference Desk

1. Tunisia measures almost 64,000 square miles in area, approximately the size of the state of Wisconsin. It has an estimated population of 11.4 million. The median age is 30.5. Its name is derived from the capital, Tunis, located in the northeast.
2. Ninety-eight percent of the population of Tunisia is Arab or Berber, and one percent is European, mostly French and Italian. Islam is the state religion although Tunisia has a secular culture which is tolerant of other religions. The language is called **Derja**, which is a blend of Tunisian and Arabic. Many people speak French, but it is not an official language.
3. The climate in the north is rainy and mild in winter, and hot and dry in summer. The south has a desert climate.
4. The Arab Spring revolutions started in December 2010 with the immolation of Mohamed Bouazizi, a young fruit and vegetables merchant.
5. If you have access to Passport, find a video or a news article related to **la Tunisie** and show it to your students.

Differentiated Learning

Accelerate

High-ability students listen to **Le babysitting** and answer the question about the dialogue. They will then compare Coralie's babysitting rules to those they had as children.

Decelerate

Students write in French a list of rules that their parents used to give their babysitter when they were young. If they did not have a babysitter, they should imagine what rules their parents would have given a babysitter.

Learning Styles

Logical/Mathematical

Have students compare the statistics given in **La Tunisie** to other Arab world countries.

Answers

Comparaisons
Answers will vary.

Critical Thinking

Comparisons

1. Ask students to research the five biggest groups of immigrants in the United States. Have them choose one group and research social, economic, political, or racial issues attributed to this particular group.
2. Ask students to compare their research with what they have learned about North African immigrants in France. They should do more in-depth research and may focus on one or two particular issues, for example, immigration status, health care, education, jobs, and voting blocks.
3. In their studies, students should focus on comparing the country's percentage of immigrants to the percentage of business owners, CEOs, doctors and other professions. They may want to compare these numbers to the numbers provided in the text.
4. Students should also research the primary reason for immigration into the United States: family or economic reasons, or refugee status.

L'immigration maghrébine en France 1.2, 2.1, 3.1

On compte aujourd'hui trois générations d'immigrés d'origine maghrébine en France (immigrés, enfants, et petits-enfants). Elles représentent autour de 4,6 millions de personnes soit 8,7% de la population française. Les plus nombreux sont les immigrés d'origine algérienne (2,4 millions), puis marocaine (1,5 millions), et enfin tunisienne (655 000). Aujourd'hui, l'immigration est d'abord une immigration de regroupement familial (50%) et dans une moindre mesure* économique (13%). L'asile* politique représente 16% des demandes ; il est donc plus important que l'immigration sur le plan économique.

Près de 16% des enfants nés en France entre 2006 et 2008 ont au moins un grand-parent maghrébin. 8% des jeunes de moins de 18 ans en France sont d'origine maghrébine. Ils sont surtout concentrés dans la région parisienne où ils représentent 12% de la population. Parmi* les étudiants venant étudier en France, un quart des étudiants étrangers est originaire de la Tunisie, du Maroc, ou de l'Algérie.

Construite en 1926, la mosquée de Paris représente l'importance de la culture maghrébine en France.

Les Maghrébins représentent 10% des entrepreneurs d'Île de France et 5,9% des chefs d'entreprise en France, et 8,5% des médecins. Sur le plan culturel, la communauté maghrébine a donné des artistes de cinéma aujourd'hui très populaires : Kad Merad, Dany Boon, Gad Elmaleh, Jamel Debbouze, Tahar Rahim ou Roschdy Zem. La star des stars pour le Maghreb reste toutefois Zinedine Zidane.

dans une moindre mesure *to a lesser extent* ; **asile** *asylum* ; **parmi** *among*

Produits 1.2, 2.2, 4.2

Il y a beaucoup de **restaurants maghrébins** en France où on sert le couscous et d'autres plats d'Algérie, de Tunisie, et du Maroc. Certaines spécialités de la région sont la pastilla, la chorba, la brick, le tajine, et les gâteaux arabes. Trouvez des photos de ces plats en ligne.

Comparaisons 1.2, 4.2

Y a-t-il des immigrés dans votre communauté ou votre lycée ?

D'où viennent-ils ?

Perspectives 1.2, 2.1

Animées par le bruit et toujours remplies de monde, les rues Château-Rouge et Goutte-d'Or à Paris portent des noms africains : Oran, Tombouctou (Tombouctou), Suez… Le quartier parisien Goutte d'Or ressemble à un véritable souk : attendez-vous au coton ciré des ateliers, des restaurants caribéens, des pâtisseries tunisiennes, des épiceries exotiques indéfinies et des salons de beauté noirs. La culture nord-africaine existe dans d'autres parties de la ville aussi ! Recherchez un de ces quartiers avec un partenaire et comparez vos resultats avec vos camarades de classe !

Mot-clé

Immigrer (1840) est emprunté (*is borrowed*) du latin *immigrare* qui signifie *venir dans*. Il vient de *migrare* qui signifie *changer de résidence*. Les mots **immigré** et **immigration** apparaissent vers 1770.

Essential Instruction

1. Students read **L'immigration maghrébine en France**, noting the statistics for Algerians, Moroccans, and Tunisians.
2. They look at the photo of the mosque in Paris and research the location of other large mosques in France.
3. Students read **Les contes maghrébins** and work in groups to answer **Activités culturelles**.

Littérature

Les contes maghrébins 1.2, 2.2, 3.2, 4.2

Comparaisons

Quelles histoires enfantines vous a-t-on lues quand vous étiez petit(e)? 1.2, 4.2

La nature imaginative et poétique de l'âme* berbère* et arabe a donné naissance à une littérature de contes très variée. On distingue des contes religieux qui attribuent aux saints d'extraordinaires miracles, comme « Lalla Mimouna », histoire d'une femme vertueuse dont la détermination d'apprendre la prière pour connaître Dieu lui donne le pouvoir d'arrêter un navire* et de marcher sur l'eau.

Il y a aussi des contes plaisants* et humoristiques comme le héros comique le plus populaire de l'Orient, Joha, à la fois malin* et naïf. Il joue des tours à ses concitoyens*, leur dit des vérités* pas bonnes à entendre. Joha s'appelle Bechkerker dans l'Aurès algérien, Brozi et Moussa dans le Riff marocain, BenChekran, l'ivrogne, ou Bou Hamar, l'homme à l'âne dans les tribus arabes. Ces anecdotes ont un rôle moralisateur.

Il y a aussi de nombreux contes d'animaux, notamment* en Kabylie : le chacal*, le hérisson*, ou le lièvre* sont des héros familiers pleins de ruse*. Quant aux* contes merveilleux, ils doivent être racontés le soir, selon la tradition, sous peine de devenir* méchant ou d'avoir des enfants méchants. Enfin il existe de nombreux contes dont le récit est proche de celui des contes occidentaux : Le Petit Poucet (*Tom Thumb*) devient Mqidech ou Haddidouan, celui qui lutte* contre l'ogresse (Ghoula en arabe, Teriel en kabyle).

Recherche : contes maghrébins, l'élève du magicien

âme *soul*; **berbère** *Berber*; **navire** *ship*; **plaisants** *nice*; **malin** *clever*; **concitoyens** *fellow citiyens*; **vérités** *truths*; **notamment** *notably*; **chacal** *jackal*; **hérisson** *hedgehog*; **lièvre** *hare*; **ruse** *trick*; **Quant aux** *As for*; **sous peine de devenir** *under the threat of becoming*; **lutte** *fights*

7 Activités culturelles 1.3, 3.1, 3.2, 4.2

Faites les activités suivantes.

1. Choisissez une ville tunisienne : Sousse, Gabès, Sfax, Bizerte, ou Tunis. Faites des recherches sur cette ville et présentez-la à votre classe.
2. Dites à quoi correspondent ces pourcentages sur la Tunisie :
   - 21%
   - 80%
   - 70%
   - 30%
3. Faites un graphique en secteurs (*pie chart*) montrant le nombre d'immigrés en France d'origine algérienne, marocaine, et tunisienne.
4. Trouvez une recette pour un plat tunisien et faites votre liste d'achats.
5. Identifiez ces personnages de contes maghrébins :
   - Lalla Mimouna
   - Joha
   - Mqidech

Le tajine de poulet au citron est un plat principal servi dans les restaurants tunisiens en France.

À DISCUTER 1.3

Qu'est-ce que vous pensez des immigrés qui gardent les traditions de leurs pays d'origine? Est-ce que votre famille observe des traditions d'un pays différent de celui où vous habitez? Quelle est l'origine de ces traditions?

Answers

Comparaisons
Answers will vary.

7

1. Answers will vary.
2. 21%: les ressources de la Tunisie consacrées à l'éducation ; 80%: la population alphabétisée ; 70%: la population qui fait des études ; 30%: les professeurs d'université femmes en Tunisie
3. immigrés d'origine algérienne : 2,4 millions ; d'origine marocaine : 1,5 millions ; d'origine tunisienne : 655 000
4. Answers will vary.
5. Lalla Mimouna : une femme vertueuse ; Joha : un héros comique ; Mqidech : le Petit Poucet

À DISCUTER

Answers will vary.

Critical Thinking

Comparisons

Maghrébin folk heroes are either religious or humorous people, or animals with extraordinary abilities. What would these characters correspond to in American culture? What is the effect of Walt Disney and contemporary television characters on our folklore?

Recherche : lives of saints, walt disney, the simpsons, saturday morning television

Connections

Folklore

There is a direct link between American and African folklore characters, notably Brer Rabbit, who has been linked to African and Cherokee cultures. Have students research popular folk stories in the United States as well as the cultural groups they come from.

Recherche : uncle remus, brer rabbit, american folk tales

Learning Styles

Visual Learners

Students will draw or find pictures of the major characters in Maghrebin folklore.

Multiple Intelligences

Mathematical-Logical

Students who enjoy graphs and charts can work to create a graph that illustrates the statistics found in the reading **L'immigration maghrébine en France** and present their visual to the class.

Musical-Rhythmic

Students research Maghrebin music. They can identify the instruments used and play recordings for the class.

Answers

8 Activities will vary.

Reference Desk

The upheavals of the Arab Spring started in Tunisia in 2010, where the first demonstrations and revolutions led to the resignation of the president. Viewed as a progressive North African country, Tunisia has been an example to other Arab nations aspiring to democratic rights and privileges, such as Egypt, Libya, Bahrain, Yemen, and Syria. Tunisian society seeks better economic opportunities and more progressive rights for women.

Expansion

Have students visit the Cap Fémina website and view the video on that page. They can explore the opportunities and share the experiences of this humanitarian mission/friendly competition as well as get some stunning visuals of Morocco's natural topography. The French featured on the website should be comprehensible to most students.

Du côté des médias 1.2, 4.2

Lisez les informations sur les événements au Maroc pendant l'année.

L'agenda des fêtes au Maroc

> **Tanjazz à Tanger**
Septembre *Fête, festival.* Le grand festival de jazz du Maroc, l'un des grands moments musicaux du Maghreb aussi, avec des artistes venus d'une douzaine de pays.

> **Cap Fémina Aventure au Maroc**
Octobre *Sport.* Ce rallye solidaire en voiture et à pied dans le désert du Grand Sud marocain rassemble plus de 140 participantes de toutes nationalités. Ce rallye de 10 jours prévoit 6 étapes. Les participantes sont équipées d'une boussole et d'un *road-book*. L'objectif est de rallier toutes les étapes, en passant par des points de contrôle.

> **Festival du safran à Taliouine**
Octobre-novembre *Fête, festival.* Ce festival créé en 2007 nous immerge dans les effluves de safran, locomotive économique de la région de Taliouine, avec des visites de safranières et de coopératives.

> **Festival international du film documentaire à Khouribga**
Décembre *Fête, festival.* L'association du festival du film documentaire de Khouribga, à 120 km au sud-est de Casablanca, veut montrer, avec le soutien du Centre cinématographique marocain et d'autres institutions, un Maroc fidèle à ses engagements, «le Maroc des changements et des initiatives».

> **Festival international des nomades à M'hamid El Ghizlane**
Mars *Fête, festival.* Musiques, danses, sports et activités traditionnels, forum de conférences et débats, expositions d'artisanat et produits du terroir...

> **Sultan Marathon des sables à Ouarzazate**
Avril *Sport.* Cette course à pied suit un parcours de 240 km dans les sables du désert. 600 sportifs se lancent dans ce périple exigeant en autosuffisance alimentaire, avec leur équipement sur le dos. Chaque jour, 9 litres d'eau et une tente pour bivouaquer leur sont fournis. À cette époque de l'année, la température dans le Sud marocain dépasse en effet les 40° C!

> **Festival Timitar à Agadir**
Juillet *Fête, festival.* Un rendez-vous authentique de la culture amazigh ou berbère, qui, depuis 2003, met en valeur les musiques et les traditions chansonnières populaires du Maroc et du monde.

Pour plus d'informations www.routard.com

8 Calendrier d'événements 1.3, 2.1, 3.1, 4.1, 5.2

Faites les activités suivantes.

1. Aimeriez-vous participer à l'un des événements sportifs présentés dans l'agenda? Justifiez votre réponse en vous servant de détails précis du texte.
2. Imaginez que vous êtes chargé(e) de préparer la liste des artistes à l'un des festivals musicaux. Quels artistes voudriez-vous inviter? Justifiez votre choix en vous servant des détails du texte.
3. Vous revenez du Maroc où vous avez participé à trois festivals. Le Guide routard.com vous invite à partager votre expérience. Écrivez un paragraphe indiquant les villes que vous avez visitées et ce que vous y avez fait.

Essential Instruction

1. Have students read **Du côté des médias** and rank the events in order of the most to least interesting. Survey the class about their preferences.
2. Have students prepare brief 1–2 minute spoken responses to one of the questions about the **Calendrier d'événements**.
3. As a review of reflexive verbs, students tell you what they do to get ready for school. This will serve as a review of **se lever**, **se laver**, **se brosser les dents**, **se peigner**, **se maquiller**, and **s'habiller**.
4. Ask a student to conjugate one of these verbs on the board as a review.
5. Give examples of reflexive verbs in affirmative and negative sentences as well as affirmative and negative commands.

Structure de la langue

Révision: Pronominal Verbs 1.2

On recycle!

See if you remember the reflexive pronouns by completing the sentences below with the correct pronoun.

1. Alice... prépare pour la journée. — A. te
2. Je... dépêche chaque matin. — B. se
3. Les Duval... amusent au parc d'attractions. — C. s'
4. Tu... brosses les cheveux ou tu... peignes? — D. me

Answer the questions affirmatively.

5. Vous vous levez tôt, Pierre et Jean?
6. T'es-tu brossé les dents avant l'école?
7. Martine et Jacques vont-ils bien s'entendre avec leur nouveau beau-père?

If you have trouble with 1–7 above, be sure to read the grammar summary below to review pronominal verbs.

Pronominal verbs are constructed with a reflexive pronoun (**me**, **te**, **se**, **nous**, **vous**). They often describe reflexive actions, which are actions that the subject performs on or for itself (**se laver**, **s'habiller**, **se maquiller**, etc.). Pronominal verbs may also be idiomatic (**s'inquiéter**, **s'amuser**, **se souvenir**, etc.). In affirmative and negative declarative sentences or questions, the reflexive pronoun comes directly before the verb.

Note the forms of the pronominal verb **se promener** below.

se promener			
je	**me promène**	nous	**nous promenons**
tu	**te promènes**	vous	**vous promenez**
il/elle/on	**se promène**	ils/elles	**se promènent**

Pourquoi est-ce que tu **t'inquiètes**? — *Why are you worrying?*

Je ne **m'inquiète** pas. Je **m'amuse** beaucoup! — *I'm not worrying. I'm having a lot of fun!*

To make a negative sentence, put **ne** in front of the reflexive pronoun and **pas** after the verb.

Nous **ne nous habillons pas** en jean aujourd'hui. — *We aren't wearing jeans today.*

Comparaisons 4.1

How would you translate the following sentences? What is used in place of the reflexive verb in English?

1. Tu **t'es** lavé les mains?
2. Je **me** brosse les dents tous les jours.

Resources

WB Workbook 6–10

LA Listening Activity 2

G & V Practice Games

Answers

On recycle!

The correct reflexive pronouns are:
1. B; 2. D; 3. C; 4. A.

The answer to the questions are:
5. Oui, nous nous levons tôt.
6. Oui, je me suis brossé les dents avant l'école.
7. Oui, ils vont bien s'entendre avec leur nouveau beau-père.

Comparaisons

English sometimes uses personal pronouns instead of a reflexive verb:
1. Did you wash *your* hands?
2. I brush *my* teeth every day.

Reference Desk

1. Pronominal verbs are divided into three categories: reflexive (**se laver**), reciprocal (**se parler**), and idiomatic (**se passer, s'enfuir**).
2. Some verbs may be either reflexive (when the subject performs the action on itself) or non-reflexive (subject performs an action on someone or something else). For example: **Michèle se lave** (reflexive), but **Michèle lave le chien** (non-reflexive).

nouvelle orthographe: Spelling changes and accent modifications are used in all forms of the future and conditional:
je me lèverai, tu te lèveras, elle se lèvera, nous nous lèverons, vous vous lèverez, ils se lèveront; je me lèverais, tu te lèverais, elle se lèverait, nous nous lèverions, vous vous lèveriez, ils se lèveraient; je m'inquièterai, tu t'inquièteras, elle s'inquiètera, nous nous inquièterons, vous vous inquièterez, ils s'inquièteront

je m'inquièterais, tu t'inquièterais, elle sinquièterait, nous nous inquièterions, vous vous linquièteriez, ils s'inquièteraient

Differentiated Learning

Accelerate

Have students make a slideshow presentation entitled "**Ma journée**" featuring photos of themselves performing reflexive verb activities. Provide students a list of reflexive verbs and encourage them to use costumes and props to add interest, and not spare the drama!

Decelerate

Students may benefit from a step-by-step review of reflexive verbs in the affirmative, negative, and affirmative and negative command forms. Allow them to use these review sheets when taking written exams.

Learning Styles

Kinesthetic Learners

Ask students to form an **accent grave** with their right arm, dipping their elbow and pointing fingers up. Then conjugate the verb **se lever** with them. They may practice the **accent aigu** with their left arm at a later time.

Answers

Comparaisons

Ils se parlent can be expressed in English as *They talk to each other*. *Each other* expresses a reciprocal action between two people or things.

Reference Desk

1. In the **passé composé**, reflexive verbs agree with the preceding direct object. Example: **Nous *nous* sommes lavés**.
2. However, when the body part follows the verb, the subject does not agree with the reflexive verb because it is no longer the subject but rather the part of the body that undergoes the action. In the sentence **Nous nous sommes lavé la figure**, only the face got washed, so the second **nous** is demoted to an indirect object.
3. The pronominal verbs **s'asseoir**, **se plaindre**, and **se souvenir** do have irregular past participles: **assis**, **plaint**, and **souvenu**.
4. Help students handle reflexive verbs easily by reminding them to focus on the subject and verb agreement first. Teach them that **se dépêcher** is no different than **aimer**; you need to conjugate the verb in the right tense, then add the reflexive pronoun right before the verb. For example, "**Je suis allé(e)….**" is very similar to "**Je (me) suis dépêché(e).**"

Notice that the form and placement of pronominal verbs change in command forms.

Use	Explanation	Example	
affirmative command	reflexive pronoun after the verb	Laure, **dépêche-toi**!	*Laure, hurry up!*
negative command	reflexive pronoun before the verb	Ne **t'inquiète** pas!	*Don't worry!*

The **passé composé** of pronominal verbs is formed with **être**. Notice the rules for using pronominal verbs in the **passé composé**.

Rule	Example	
reflexive pronoun is placed before **être**	Pourquoi **t'es**-tu **couché**?	*Why did you go to bed?*
past participle agrees in gender and number with the subject	Elle ne **s'est** pas **réveillée** tard ce matin.	*She didn't wake up late this morning.*
no agreement of the past participle if a direct object follows the verb	Elles **se sont brossé** les dents après le dîner.	*They brushed their teeth after dinner.*

Blanche neige ne s'est pas méfiée de la méchante magicienne.

4.1

Comparaisons

Some verbs can be made pronominal in French by adding the reflexive pronoun **se**.

Jacques parle à Océane.
Océane parle à Jacques.
Ils se parlent.

In the second sentence, how is the reciprocal idea expressed in English?

Connexions 1.2, 3.1

Science médico-légale

Avec un partenaire, imaginez qu'on a retrouvé le corps d'un personnage connu. Servez-vous du passé composé et de verbes pronominaux, et de votre imagination, pour expliquer sa mort.

On recycle!

Avec un partenaire, jouez le rôle d'un papa ou d'une maman qui dit à son enfant de se préparer le matin. Utilisez l'impératif. Changez de rôle. Ensuite, écrivez pour raconter ce que vous avez fait, au passé composé.

MODÈLE **Lève-toi! Brosse-toi les dents! Ne te lave pas les cheveux avec du savon! Regarde-toi dans la glace et peigne-toi!**
Aujourd'hui, je me suis levé(e), puis je me suis brossé les dents. Je me suis lavé les cheveux mais pas avec du savon. Après, je me suis regardé(e) dans la glace et je me suis peigné(e).

se réveiller ▪ se lever ▪ se brosser les cheveux/les dents ▪ se laver ▪ se doucher ▪ se dépêcher ▪ se rappeler ▪ se rencontrer ▪ s'habiller ▪ se coucher ▪ se remettre à ▪ se peigner ▪ se regarder ▪ bien/mal s'entendre avec ▪ se reposer

Essential Instruction

1. Have students do **On s'entraîne!**, paying attention to agreement.
2. Review the affirmative and negative imperative of pronominal verbs by having students transform simple sentences into commands.
3. Write sentences with pronominal verbs on the board, and have students transform them in the **imparfait** and **passé composé**.
4. Pair a high and low-ability student together to collaborate on the activity **L'élève du magicien**.
5. Students will complete **Le bal** individually.

9 On s'entraîne ! 1.3, 2.1, 5.2

Presentational Speaking

Dites si les personnes suivantes s'entraînent au stade, au fitness, à la piscine, ou au complexe sportif ; le complexe sportif propose roller, footing, et vélo.

MODÈLE Marcel nage.
Il s'entraîne à la piscine.

1. Marc et moi, nous courons.
2. Sophie et Florence plongent.
3. Jérémy et Saïd font du vélo.
4. Les footballeurs jouent au foot.
5. Mlle Dumont et toi, vous faites de l'aérobic.
6. Tu fais du footing.
7. Je fais du yoga.
8. L'équipe de rugby joue au rugby.
9. Sabine fait du roller.

10 L'élève du magicien 1.2, 3.1, 4.2

Interpretive Reading

Racontez ce conte maghrébin en utilisant les verbes entre parenthèses au présent, au passé composé, à l'imparfait, ou à l'infinitif.

Dans ce conte, il (1. s'agir) d'un petit garçon intelligent qui (2. s'appeler) Fahim. Fahim était un bon élève. Il (3. adorer) faire ses devoirs. Un jour, il (4. se lever) tôt et (5. s'habiller) de son meilleur pantalon et de sa meilleure chemise parce qu'il allait voyager à sa nouvelle école. Il (6. s'inquiéter) parce qu'il n'avait jamais quitté son village. Il (7. se rendre) à sa nouvelle école qui (8. se trouver) loin de son village. Quand il y est arrivé, ses nouveaux camarades de classes (9. se présenter). Ils (10. s'entendre) bien avec Fahim. Mais le maître était strict. Un jour, il a dit à Fahim qu'il devait (11. s'occuper) des travaux de la ferme pour payer ses études. Il (12. ne plus s'amuser) parce qu'il préférait étudier. Un jour, Fahim a réalisé que son maître était magicien. Qu'est-ce qui est arrivé ? Fahim a appris à déjouer les mauvais tours du magicien parce qu'il était plus rusé que lui !

11 Le bal 1.2

Interpretive Listening

Écrivez les numéros 1–5 sur votre papier. Écoutez l'histoire et écrivez une réponse courte à la question que vous entendez.

Special Needs Students

Linguistically Challenged
Before undertaking written activities, students may benefit from doing the first three examples of any exercise one on one with their teacher or an advanced student, so that they feel confident about how to proceed.

Multiple Intelligences

Verbal-Linguistic
Students may enjoy retelling the story of **L'élève du magicien** as a fairy tale beginning with **"Il était une fois…"**

Bodily-Kinesthetic
Students would enjoy acting out scenes from the story as it is narrated.

Resources

Activity 11

Answers

9
1. Nous nous entraînons au stade.
2. Elles s'entraînent à la piscine.
3. Ils s'entraînent au complexe sportif.
4. Ils s'entraînent au stade.
5. Vous vous entraînez au fitness.
6. Tu t'entraînes au complexe sportif.
7. Je m'entraîne au fitness.
8. Elle s'entraîne au stade.
9. Elle s'entraîne au complexe sportif.

10
1. s'agit
2. s'appelle
3. adorait
4. s'est levé
5. s'est habillé
6. s'inquiétait
7. s'est rendu
8. se trouvait
9. se sont présentés
10. s'entendaient
11. s'occuper
12. ne s'amusait plus

11 Script
Jacqueline rêvait de devenir princesse. Un jour, elle a reçu une invitation à un bal au château du prince Jean. Elle s'est habillée d'une très jolie robe rose et le jour du bal, elle s'est levée très tôt. Elle s'est lavée et s'est maquillée. Elle s'est regardée dans la glace. Elle était très belle. Enfin, elle a mis ses petites chaussures en soie. Elle s'est rendue au château du roi et de la reine. Au bal, le prince a tout de suite voulu danser avec Jacqueline et les deux jeunes gens sont tombés amoureux. Jacqueline est rentrée chez elle à minuit et s'est couchée tout de suite. Elle ne s'est même pas brossé les dents. Elle rêvait d'une grande bague de fiançailles.

1. De quoi Jacqueline s'est-elle habillée ?
2. Comment s'est-elle préparée pour le bal ?
3. Où s'est-elle rendue ce soir-là ?
4. Comment s'est-elle amusée ?
5. Avec qui veut-elle se marier ?

1. une jolie robe rose
2. Elle s'est lavée et s'est maquillée.
3. au château
4. Elle a dansé.
5. le prince

Resources

CA Communicative Activities

Share

Answers

12 Presentations will vary.

13 Projects will vary.

14 Research will vary.

Reference Desk

1. If you have access to Passport, create a question for your students to share their response to a communicative activity.
2. **Yves Montand** was a famous French singer and actor born in Italy. **Albert Uderzo**, son of Italian immigrants, is the creator of the French comic book *Astérix*. **Louis de Funès** was a French comedic actor born to Spanish immigrant parents. Cubist painter **Pablo Picasso** was born in Spain and lived a good part of his life in France. **Isabelle Adjani** is a French actress born to a father of Algerian origins and a German mother. Raï singer **Faudel** was born to parents of Algerian origin. **Basile Boli** is a French soccer star born in the Ivory Coast. French author and member of **l'Académie française Amin Maalouf** was born in Lebanon. **Zinedine Zidane** is a French soccer star born in Marseille to parents of Algerian origins. **Jean Reno** is a French actor of Spanish origins born in Casablanca, Morocco. Former president **Nicolas Sarkozy**'s father was a Hungarian immigrant.

Connections

Artistic Interpretation

Have students create publicity slogans and ads for various toiletry items, using the imperative of a reflexive verb: **Brossez-vous les dents avec le dentifrice Flurocaril!** Students may choose to draw a comic of the Interpretive Listening activity to demonstrate their comprehension.

À vous la parole

Question centrale ? Comment les communautés francophones conservent-elles leurs traditions?

Communiquez!

12 Un conte maghrébin à la radio 1.3, 2.2, 3.2, 5.1

Presentational Speaking

En groupe, trouvez un conte maghrébin en ligne. Lisez-le et transformez-le en script pour une émission de radio. Vous aurez besoin d'un narrateur ou d'une narratrice, d'un animateur ou d'une animatrice qui introduit l'émission, et d'acteurs pour jouer les rôles avec leurs voix. Si vous voulez, créez aussi des bruitages (*sound effects*). Enregistrez (*Record*) votre émission pour la classe.

Recherche: contes maghreb, contes et légendes de tunisie/algérie/maroc

13 Les immigrés célèbres en France 1.2, 1.3, 3.2

Interpretive Reading, Presentational Speaking

Dans la liste ci-dessous, vous trouverez les noms des immigrés célèbres ou d'autres célébrités françaises dont les parents étaient immigrés. Recherchez si l'arrivée d'un(e) immigré(e) correspond à une vague (*wave*) d'immigration en France, et expliquez pourquoi la personne que vous recherchez est célèbre.

Yves Montand, Albert Uderzo, Louis de Funès, Pablo Picasso, Isabelle Adjani, Faudel, Basile Boli, Amin Maalouf, Zinedine Zidane, Jean Reno, Nicolas Sarkozy

Recherche: immigrés en France, immigration en France historique

14 La nouvelle Tunisie 1.1, 1.2, 1.3, 3.1, 3.2

Interpretive Reading, Interpersonal and Presentational Speaking

Beaucoup de choses ont changé dans l'histoire de la Tunisie. Faites des recherches sur un des thèmes suivants. Ensuite, faites une présentation en groupe où chaque membre présente un thème différent.

A. la révolution du jasmin ou la révolution de la dignité
B. le président; de 2014–présent (Beji Caid Essebsi)
C. la grève générale
D. la révolte de Sidi Bouzid
E. la caravane de la libération

Essential Instruction

1. Have students come up and pick a card with the number 12, 13, or 14 written on it (the cards will be face down). The number on the card will place them in groups corresponding to the number of the activity in **Communiquez!** that they will work on together.
2. For the activity **Un conte de fées,** students of various learning styles and talents can be grouped together to collaborate on creating a fairy tale. There are various formats to choose from: video, slideshow presentation, large storyboards with captions, to name a few. Use the following search words: **launchpadtoys/toontastic, puppetpals** for online storytelling programs.
3. Students can write an original story using characters from their daily lives, or retell a classic tale. If they want to be more creative they can change the details or ending of a classic story.
4. Time on task can be divided into: brainstorming, rough draft, editing, teacher support, and then creating the story in a format of their choice.

Pre-AP

Communiquez!

Using Transitions in a Story 1.2, 4.1, 5.2

Pour raconter une histoire, il est nécessaire de faire une liste des personnages et des événements principaux. Utilisez des adjectifs, des adverbes, et les pronoms relatifs **qui** et **que** pour ajouter des détails et faire de belles et longues phrases. Pour finir, liez les descriptions et les événements en utilisant des adverbes et des locutions conjonctives. Combien en connaissez-vous dans la liste suivante? Cherchez dans le dictionnaire les mots que vous ne connaissez pas.

d'abord/au début/au commencement	plus tard	en même temps
avant, après	pendant que	ensuite/par la suite
dès que	tandis que	finalement/enfin/à la fin
	pendant ce temps, en attendant	

15 Un conte de fées 1.2, 1.3, 3.1, 3.2, 5.1

Interpretive Reading, Presentational Writing

Vous allez écrire un conte de fées. Choisissez un conte bien connu avec un milieu moderne, ou un conte classique de Charles Perrault tel que «La Belle au bois dormant», «Le Petit Chaperon Rouge», ou encore «Cendrillon». Vous pouvez aussi surfer le net et découvrir des contes pour enfants du Sénégal ou autre pays francophone. Racontez le conte avec vos propres mots, puis donnez-lui une fin différente de l'original.

16 On rédige! 1.1, 5.1

Interpersonal Writing

Maintenant faites lire votre conte à votre partenaire et corrigez le sien *(his or hers)* en suivant les directives ci-dessous:

	Les accords entre les sujets et leurs verbes sont corrects.
	Les adjectifs sont placés au bon endroit.
	Il est clair de qui ont parle.
	Toutes les phrases sont reliées entre elles.
	Chaque mot est écrit correctement.
	Les signes de ponctuation sont bien utilisés.

Pour finir, publiez votre conte en ligne ou préparez un document avec tous les contes de la classe.

Resources

Pre-T Pre-test

Q *Leçon* Quiz

Answers

15 Writings will vary.

16 All boxes should be checked by every student.

Expansion

1. To prepare students for this activity, ask them to think of well-known fairy tales, and summarize them in French in logical main action lines, using, for example: **D'abord**..., **puis**..., **en même temps**, **ensuite**..., and **enfin**....
2. Suggested criteria for the fairy tales:
   –Must be written in the **passé composé** and the **imparfait**.
   –Must be all original work, no computer translation or plagiarism.
   –Will contain the following elements:
   - A struggle between good and evil
   - An honorable and courageous hero or heroine
   - A powerful ogre, monster, or sorcerer/sorceress
   - A negative consequence from not following orders
   - A task to complete
   - A happy or tragic ending

Special Need Students

Linguistically Challenged

Students who have difficulty expressing themselves verbally often have imaginative thoughts but do not easily understand how to express those complex thoughts simply and in a logical manner. Help such students think of storytelling in terms of events that follow each other. Ask them first to list a series of events they would like to use in their stories, then to arrange those events in chronological order by writing simple sentences and adding a transition word in front of each one. They should add details and images last.

Learning Styles

Interpersonal

Students might want to read and/or perform their fairy tales bilingually to a nearby elementary school. A walking field trip for either group (high school to elementary or elementary to high school) is a great way to cultivate interest in French at an early age and may help to build your program.

Resources

- *Vocabulaire actif*
- eV eVisual
- WB Workbook 1–4
- FC Flash Cards
- LA Listening Activity 1
- G & V Practice Games

Reference Desk

1. **Une copropriété** is a condominium where there is a collective ownership and board of directors.
2. If you rent, you are **un(e) locataire**. If you own the property, you are **un(e) propriétaire**.
3. In French Polynesia, a traditional house is called **un faré**.
4. **Mr. Bricolage** and **Bricomart** are home improvement stores. Their websites offer photos of various tools and how-to videos that can serve as listening comprehension exercises.
5. **Maison mitoyenne** refers both to single family homes and row or track.
6. **Une HLM (habitation à loyer modéré)** is rent-controlled housing. Contrary to common perception, the vast majority of **HLM**, which can be either private or state-owned, are individual houses or building with fewer than 20 units. **HLM** is further discussed in the reading on page 180.

Recherche : mr bricolage

Leçon C — Vocabulaire actif

Le logement et le bricolage 1.2, 2.2, 4.2

Le logement

un studio

une villa

une maison mitoyenne

une maison individuelle

une résidence secondaire

une ancienne ferme

Essential Instruction

1. Have students listen to **Le logement**.
2. Ask students "**Où habites-tu ?**" using the new vocabulary.
3. Students will listen to **Nos projets de bricolage**.
4. Explain to students what an **HLM** is and ask if there are any collective housing projects in their community.

Une HLM dans une cité

Nos projets de bricolage

Reference Desk

The term **une cité** refers to a small town, or a group of houses or buildings forming a community (public housing). It is sometimes used as a derogatory term, similar to the American term "hood" or "projects."

TPR

Place a hammer, nail, screw, wax, paintbrush, piece of carpet, and picture frame on a table. Ask students to do novel commands: "Take the paint brush and paint my desk." "Take the wallpaper and put it under the hammer." You may want to use plastic toy tools.

Connections

Music

"**Nettoyage de Printemps**," a song by Gilbert Laffaille, lists all of the repair work the singer did to prepare for his love to move in. The song also features many pronominal verbs and useful daily vocabulary.

Recherche: nettoyage de printemps gilbert lafaille

Expansion

Ask students to imagine how to redo their bedroom. They should make a list of tools and materials needed by visiting the **Mr. Bricolage** or **Bricomart** websites.

Learning Styles

Kinesthetic Learners

This unit is ideal to involve kinesthetic learners in vocabulary presentations. Have students mime do-it-yourself activities as you introduce vocabulary.

Visual Learners

Post a map of your city on the board and ask students to identify the types of housing in different neighborhoods.

Special Needs Students

At-Risk Students

Students with difficult living situations may not be comfortable talking about their housing. Instead of asking them where they live, present short scenarios and ask them where these people might live. For example: **Pierre a 20 ans. Il est célibataire. Il n'a pas beaucoup d'argent. Où habite-t-il?; Oprah veut habiter en France pendant l'été. Quelle habitation va-t-elle choisir?** Or, consider asking students where they would like to live in the future.

Resources

Pour la conversation
Et si je voulais dire… ?

Answers

1

1. Je vous propose une maison individuelle.
2. Je vous propose une résidence secondaire.
3. Je vous propose une ancienne ferme.
4. Je vous propose une maison mitoyenne.
5. Je vous propose une villa.

Reference Desk

State that **Cela a été fait** is a combination of two verb forms. Which ones? Explain that this is a form of the **passé surcomposé**, a hybrid form of the **passé composé** of **être** + PAST PARTICIPLE OF ANOTHER VERB to express the passive voice: "That has been done."

Game

Devinettes

There are many words for a dwelling. Put students in teams and see which team can look up the meaning of the following terms the fastest: **demeure**, **domicile**, **foyer**, **gîte**, **habitation**, **logement**, **cabane**, **cabanon**, **bastide**, **bungalow**, **chalet**, **pavillon**, **bicoque**, **mas**, **masure**, **échoppe**, and **buron**. They must add the appropriate article, **le** or **la**. Then expand the game to include **devinettes**. Students will give definitions for others to identify. **Une maison dans la montagne ? C'est un chalet.**

Expansion

Have students visit a French real estate site and explore rentals and homes for sale in different French regions, including Paris and its suburbs.

Recherche : immobilier france

Pour la conversation

What do I say when I'm introduced to someone?

» **Très heureux.**/Très heureuse.
Pleased to meet you.

How do I say where I grew up?

» J'**ai grandi** dans une HLM qui n'était pas très propre.
I grew up in a subsidized apartment building that wasn't very clean.

How do I give a compliment?

» On dirait que **cela** a été fait par **un professionnel** !
It looks like it was done by a professional!

Mot-clé

À l'origine, le mot **bricolage** avait un sens presque péjoratif (*derogative*). Issu du mot *bricole*, qui est une petite chose sans valeur, le bricolage était l'action de réparer des choses sans valeur. Aujourd'hui, c'est une activité professionnelle ou de loisirs importante si l'on considère la popularité des magasins et émissions de bricolage pour aider les particuliers.

Et si je voulais dire… ?

un agent immobilier	*real estate agent*
un logement	*lodging*
un pavillon	*single-family house*
une résidence	*apartment/condo building*
un terrain à bâtir	*building lot*

1 Agent immobilier 1.2, 4.2, 5.1

Interpretive Reading

Jouez le rôle d'un agent immobilier et suggérez des logements pour les personnes en fonction de leurs préférences ou de leurs besoins. Choisissez un logement parmi ceux les suivants.

studio **maison individuelle** **ancienne ferme** **villa**
résidence secondaire **maison mitoyenne**

MODÈLE J'ai 60 ans, et je ne travaille plus. Je vis seule dans une maison individuelle trop grande pour une personne. Mes revenus sont modestes, mais je n'ai pas besoin d'habiter dans une HLM. Je n'ai pas beaucoup de meubles. J'aimerais vivre en ville.
Je vous propose un studio.

1. Nous avons trois enfants, deux filles et un garçon. Donc, nous avons besoin de trois chambres. Mon mari et moi, nous travaillons en banlieue. Nous prenons la voiture pour aller au travail, nous aimerions avoir un garage.
2. Nous habitons en appartement pendant la semaine, mais ma famille et moi, nous voudrions un deuxième logement à la campagne. Nous aimons nager et faire des randonnées.
3. Il me faut un grand jardin à la campagne pour tous mes animaux. Mon mari et moi, nous aimons beaucoup bricoler.
4. Je préfère ma chambre au premier étage et la cuisine au rez-de-chaussée. Je n'ai pas besoin d'une maison individuelle, c'est trop grand pour moi.
5. Ma famille et moi, nous recherchons une maison au bord de la mer pour les vacances d'été.

Essential Instruction

1. Have the students listen to the vocabulary for **Pour la conversation**.
2. Ask students to think of a sentence that would precede each recorded remark. **« Je vous présente M. Labec. Ah, oui, très heureux/heureuse ! »; « Tu as fait ce travail ? On dirait que cela a été fait par un professionnel. »**
3. Select students to read aloud the sentences in **Agent immobilier**. The class will choose the appropriate housing option. Have students do the activity first by reading along as their partner reads aloud, and then simply by listening.
4. Pair students to do **Nos projets de bricolage**.
5. Change partners to do **À l'agence immobilière**.

2 Nos projets de bricolage 1.2

Interpretive Reading

Complétez les phrases avec un mot ou une expression ci-dessous.

un marteau **peint** **pose le papier peint** **un tournevis**
accroche des tableaux **la moquette** **propre** **nettoyer** **les vis**

1. Des jeunes ont fait des graffiti sur les murs extérieurs de notre maison, alors on les....
2. Pour enfoncer un clou, il faut....
3. Nous voulons enlever... qui est sale dans les chambres et mettre du parquet.
4. On a peint les murs. Maintenant on....
5. Notre fille n'aime pas les murs blancs de sa chambre ; donc, on....
6. Pour réparer les meubles cassés, il nous faut serrer (*tighten*)... avec....
7. Les murs de la cuisine sont sales ; il faut les....
8. Après tout notre travail, notre maison est beaucoup plus....

Les jeunes de la cité ont peint les murs de la ville.

3 À l'agence immobilière 1.1, 1.2, 5.2

Interpersonal Speaking, Interpretive Reading

*Un agent immobilier (*real estate agent*) parle au téléphone avec une cliente qui cherche un logement. Avec votre partenaire, jouez les rôles de l'agent et de la cliente. Si vous êtes la cliente, vous devez choisir la bonne phrase de la liste.*

–Je sais peindre et poser le papier peint.
–C'est encore mieux ! Je peux voir l'appartement aujourd'hui ?
–Ça me conviendrait parfaitement. Je n'ai pas peur de travailler avec mes mains.
–Bonjour, Monsieur ! Je m'appelle Mlle Delacroix. Je vais déménager dans la région, et je cherche un logement.
–Non, pas du tout. J'aime une ambiance vivante, mais pas trop la nuit.
–C'est que... j'ai grandi loin d'ici, et je ne connais personne. J'aimerais connaître mes voisins dans un immeuble en ville, mais pas trop grand.

L'agent : Allô ! Ici M. Rivard. — **La cliente :** (1.)
L'agent : Très heureux. Vous désirez habitez en ville ou à la campagne ? — **La cliente :** (2.)
L'agent : Ah bon. Mais bricoler, vous aimez ça ? — **La cliente :** (3.)
L'agent : Et les passants, ça vous dérange ? — **La cliente :** (4.)
L'agent : J'ai une idée. Il y a un immeuble en ville, pas trop grand, près de la rue commerçante, mais il y a quelques problèmes avec les appartements. On va baisser le prix pour les locataires qui feront les réparations eux-mêmes. Qu'en pensez-vous ? — **La cliente :** (5.)
L'agent : Je ne vous ai pas dit, mais l'immeuble est tout près du métro. — **La cliente :** (6.)
L'agent : Disons à 15h30. Je vous enverrai l'adresse par mail. À bientôt, madame !

Answers

2
1. peint
2. un marteau
3. la moquette
4. accroche des tableaux
5. pose le papier peint
6. les vis, un tournevis
7. nettoyer
8. propre

3
1. Bonjour, Monsieur ! Je m'appelle Mlle Delacroix. Je vais déménager dans la région et je cherche un logement.
2. C'est que... j'ai grandi loin d'ici, et je ne connais personne. J'aimerais connaître mes voisins dans un immeuble en ville, mais pas trop grand.
3. Je sais peindre et poser le papier peint.
4. Non, pas du tout. J'aime une ambiance vivante, mais pas trop la nuit.
5. Ça me conviendrait parfaitement. Je n'ai pas peur de travailler avec mes mains.
6. C'est encore mieux ! Je peux voir l'appartement aujourd'hui ?

Differentiated Learning

Accelerate
Students visit the site of an **agence immobilière** and read descriptions of apartments and houses for sale to use as a template. They will make a facsimile of a listing for the apartment or house they live in, illustrated with photos. Square footage will be converted to square meters.

Decelerate
Students will visit the site of an **agence immobilière** and read descriptions of apartments and houses for sale. They will select three residences that they would like to buy, copy their photo and listing, and record why each kind of residence appeals to them.

Resources

Activity 5

Answers

4

1. Nous pourrions cirer le parquet.
2. Nous pourrions poser un nouveau papier peint.
3. Nous pourrions accrocher des tableaux.
4. Nous pourrions enfoncer des clous dans le bois.
5. Nous pourrions installer une nouvelle moquette.

5 **Script**

1. J'habite dans une HLM en banlieue. J'aime mon logement, mais la HLM n'est pas très propre. Je déteste les graffiti sur les murs de ma cité !
2. Henri vient d'acheter un appartement dans un grand immeuble. Il adore bricoler, peindre les murs, réparer les meubles. Son projet aujourd'hui est le parquet, qui est sale.
3. Les Dumas habitent une nouvelle maison individuelle. M. Dumas n'aime pas bricoler. C'est sa femme, Mme Dumas qui veut décorer les salles, mais pas avec des affiches !
4. Mes grands-parents habitent une ancienne ferme. Ma grand-mère veut que mon grand-père répare un placard dans la cuisine.
5. Aïcha habite une maison mitoyenne très jolie. Mais elle n'aime pas peindre ; elle préfère plus de décoration aux murs.
6. Les Fleury ont une maison individuelle à Tours. Mais ils veulent passer toutes les vacances à la campagne.

1. A; 2. D; 3. B; 4. F; 5. C; 6. E

6 Answers will vary.

Communication

Interpersonal: Paired Practice

Have students prepare their answers to **Questions personnelles**. Each student will then stand and pass from student to student asking and answering questions 1–3 until they have interacted with all of their classmates, time permitting.

Interpersonal: Cooperative Groups

Students will be divided into two or three groups, depending on class size, to participate in a discussion of questions 4 and 5 of **Activité 6**.

4 Les frères Jarreau : réparations et décorations 1.2, 1.3

Interpretive Viewing, Presentational Speaking or Writing

Votre compagnie a reçu des photos de particuliers qui se plaignent de leurs habitations. Dites-leur ce que vous pourriez faire pour les aider.

poser un nouveau papier peint **repeindre le mur** **accrocher des tableaux**
enfoncer des clous dans le bois **installer une moquette** **cirer le parquet**

MODÈLE  **Nous pourrions repeindre le mur.**

1.  2.  3.  4.  5. 

5 Comment réparer ? 1.2

Interpretive Listening

Écrivez les numéros 1–6 sur votre papier. Écoutez les descriptions suivantes. Choisissez la solution à chaque problème de logement.

A. peindre les murs
B. accrocher des tableaux
C. poser de nouveaux papiers peints
D. nettoyer et cirer le parquet
E. acheter une résidence secondaire
F. se servir d'un marteau et enfoncer des clous

6 Questions personnelles 1.1

Interpersonal Speaking

Répondez aux questions avec un partenaire.

1. Où voudrais-tu habiter—dans une villa, une maison mitoyenne, un immeuble, une maison individuelle, ou une ancienne ferme ?
2. Quand tu pars en weekend ou en vacances, où séjournes-tu *(where do you stay)* ?
3. Est-ce que tes parents aiment bricoler ? Si oui, qu'est-ce qu'ils ont fait dans votre maison ? Les as-tu déjà aidés ?
4. Quels problèmes est-ce que tu associes avec les cités ? Pourquoi est-ce que ces difficultés existent ? Si tu pouvais changer quelque chose, que changerais-tu pour éliminer ces problèmes ?
5. Est-ce qu'il y a des graffiti dans ton école ? Quelle solution proposes-tu ?

Essential Instruction

1. Have students do **Les frères Jarreau : réparations et décorations**.
2. Students will listen to **Comment réparer ?** and answer A–F.
3. Pair students to improvise scenes in **Le premier appartement d'Adja**.
4. Do questions 1–3 of **Activité 6** as an all-class discussion and have students work on questions 4 and 5 with a partner.
5. After listening to **Le premier appartement d'Adja**, ask comprehension questions that make students dig into the passage for the answers.
6. Have students work in pairs to answer the questions in **Activité 7**.

Le premier appartement d'Adja

1.2, 2.2, 5.2

Élodie et sa mère rendent visite à une employée de sa mère, Adja, qui est d'origine sénégalaise.

Mère : Élodie, je te présente Adja.
Élodie : Très heureuse.
Mère : Dis, tu aimes ton nouvel appartement ?
Adja : Pour moi c'est un château. Tu sais, j'ai grandi dans un HLM* qui n'était pas très propre.
Mère : Quel travail tu as fait ! Tu as tout fait le plus rapidement possible.
Adja : Le plus difficile, ça a été de poser le papier peint.
Mère : On dirait que cela a été fait par un professionnel ! Tu bricoles mieux que moi. Finalement tu as tout repeint ?
Adja : Oui, vous arrivez juste pour m'aider à poser les tableaux.
Élodie : Justement, nous avons apporté un marteau et des clous pour vous aider.

1.2, 2.1

EXTENSION **Le nouvel appartement de Michèle**

Un peintre entre dans le salon de Michèle.

Peintre : Alors, dites-moi un peu ce que vous voulez faire….
Michèle : Pas de papier peint, de la peinture blanche partout, et vous me faites enlever la moquette. Elle est si sale !
Peintre : Qu'est-ce qu'il y a dessous ?
Michèle : Soulevez, là….
Peintre : Des parquets de Versailles !
Michèle : Tout l'appartement est comme ça ! Alors la moquette, *out* !
Peintre : Mon frère cire les parquets.
Michèle : Ça tombe bien. Vous avez sa carte ?

EXTENSION Pourquoi est-ce que Michèle est contente d'avoir cet appartement ?

1.3, 2.1

1.3, 5.2

7 Le premier appartement d'Adja

Jouez les scènes suivantes avec votre partenaire. Servez-vous du nouveau vocabulaire du dialogue et de votre imagination.

1. Au bureau il y a trois jours, Adja et la mère d'Élodie prennent rendez-vous.
2. À la maison ce matin, la mère d'Élodie suggère que sa fille l'accompagne chez Adja.
3. Après avoir aidé Adja, Élodie et sa mère discutent de leur visite.

***Je parle bien !**

The word HLM is an acronym, pronounced letter by letter. Say **hache-elle-aime**.

Resources

Dialogue
Extension
Dialogue Video
WB Workbook 5

Answers

7 Skits will vary.

EXTENSION

parce que l'appartement a de beaux parquets

Reference Desk

1. The noun **HLM** is acceptable as a masculine or feminine noun. Recent usage favors the feminine form, **une HLM**. Remind students there is no **s** in the plural: **des HLM**.
2. The dialogue showing Adja, a woman of African descent living in subsidized housing, is a fair representation of the fact that there is a high concentration of first- and second-generation immigrants in **HLM** communities in France. You may ask your students to compare this situation with that in the United States, and open a discussion to the class.
3. The word **papier peint** refers to a paper-based material brought from China in the 18th century; it is used to decorate walls. Despite its name, today's wallpaper is not hand-painted; it is printed. **Papier peint** (*wallpaper*) is different from the traditional **tapisserie**, a thicker, cloth-based fabric, which covered walls in the past.

Differentiated Learning

Accelerate
High-ability students will do the **Extension** in pairs and answer the corresponding question.

Decelerate
Low-ability students will work with you to read the **Le premier appartement d'Adja**. This will give you an opportunity to help them in a small group to improve their comprehension and pronunciation.

Resources

Points de départ

WB Workbook 6

Explore

Answers

Comparaisons

Answers will vary.

Reference Desk

1. The French refer to several **HLM** buildings as **un parc HLM**. This designation, which brings to mind the elements of a natural space, is preferred over **une cité**, which too often denotes filth and poverty associated with urban living.
2. In the 1980s, French singer Renault brought attention to the social issues associated with subsidized housing with his song "**Dans mon HLM**." You might show students the song on video, but we recommend not showing the lyrics, which contain some slang and inappropriate expressions. The students will not understand the lyrics if they hear them, but it is best not to draw attention to them in writing and/or teach them. Renault is a very positive figure who has used his fame to deliver social messages.
3. If you have access to Passport, find a video or a news article related to housing and show it to your students.

Points de départ

Pre-AP

Question centrale ? Comment les communautés francophones conservent-elles leurs traditions ?

Les HLM 1.2, 2.1, 2.2, 4.2, 5.1

Créées en 1894, les HLM (habitation à loyer* modéré) sont un système d'immeubles qui offre des appartements à bon marché. La construction des HLM est limitée, et seul un Français sur cinq peut bénéficier de ce type de logement. Ce sont les plus défavorisés*, souvent les immigrés ou les familles nombreuses, qui y habitent. Plus de quatre millions de ménages* habitent dans des HLM. Les étudiants peuvent aussi bénéficier des avantages offerts par les HLM. Autrefois réservés aux banlieues, on construit* depuis 1981 des HLM en centre-ville parmi d'autres immeubles où habite une population différente, afin d'intégrer les résidents à la population du quartier. Près d'un tiers des HLM a été bâti après 1985. Aujourd'hui, les Français font pression sur le gouvernement pour construire davantage de HLM.

En France, une HLM peut avoir jusqu'à 30 étages.

Recherche : logement social, banlieue parisienne

le loyer *rent* ; **défavorisés** *underprivileged* ; **ménages** *households* ; **construit** *builds*

Comparaisons 1.2, 2.2, 4.2

Existe-t-il des logements de type HLM dans votre communauté ? Où sont-ils ? Comment sont-ils ?

Produits 1.2, 2.2, 4.2

Il existe **des HLM** en France, en Suisse, en Algérie, au Sénégal et modiquement au Québec.

Les allocations familiales* 1.2, 2.1, 3.1, 4.2, 5.1

Depuis les années 1940 la France conduit une politique nataliste*. Elle a aujourd'hui l'une des démographies les plus dynamiques d'Europe, avec un taux de renouvellement de génération de 1,9. L'État français subventionne* fortement les gardes d'enfants afin d'aider les familles, notamment* les mères, à allier vie familiale et vie professionnelle. Les allocations familiales font partie de cette politique. Elles sont versées* à partir du deuxième enfant et constituent un revenu* supplémentaire pour les familles. Toutes les familles les touchent quel que soit* leur revenu. De la même manière, les familles bénéficient de réductions d'impôts* qui augmentent avec le nombre d'enfants. Enfin, à partir du troisième enfant, la mère ou le père peut bénéficier d'un congé* parental sans perte de salaire pendant un an.

L'argot des ados

Expressions

Il a un air de famille.	Il ressemble à un membre de la famille.
C'est un bien de famille.	On ne s'en sépare pas.
Ça ne sort pas de la famille.	On ne doit pas en parler.
C'est de famille.	C'est une attitude qui lui vient de ses parents.
Il gère en bon père de famille.	C'est un bon administrateur.
On lave son linge sale en famille.	Il y a des choses qui ne se disent qu'en famille.

Recherche: caf, allocations familiales

allocations familiales *government benefits for families* ; **nataliste** *pro-life* ; **subventionne** *funds* ; **notamment** *particularly* ; **versées** *provided* ; **revenu** *income* ; **quel que soit** *whatever may be* ; **impôts** *taxes* ; **congé** *time off*

Essential Instruction

1. Have students listen to **Les HLM**. You might want to have students repeat certain words after they have heard the recording.
2. Next, ask students to record themselves reading that paragraph and then listen to themselves.
3. Put students in different groups and have them listen to either **Les allocations familiales** or **Le Sénégal**.
4. Each group will need to summarize the text they heard.

La Francophonie

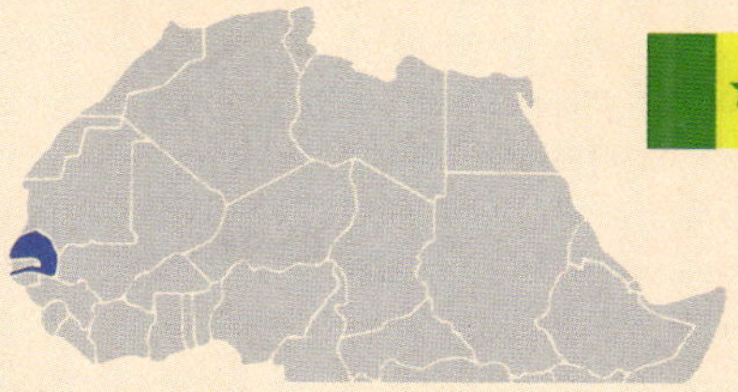

Profil touristique

Le Sénégal 1.2, 2.1, 3.1, 3.2

Le Sénégal est un pays de l'Afrique de l'Ouest. Il doit son nom au fleuve qui le traverse. Les habitants sont les Sénégalais. Il existe six langues nationales différentes dont la plus importante est le wolof ; ce plurilinguisme* explique que le français soit* la langue officielle. Le Sénégal compte 14,5 millions d'habitants, et sa capitale est Dakar ; l'autre grande ville est Saint-Louis, l'ancienne capitale.

Ancienne colonie française, indépendante depuis 1960, le Sénégal est une république semi-présidentielle. Le Sénégal fait partie des pays les plus industrialisés avec la présence de nombreuses compagnies multinationales françaises et américaines. L'économie sénégalaise est dominée par la pêche et le tourisme. L'essor* du tourisme s'explique par le développement de réserves et parcs naturels qui couvrent* 8% du territoire. Le Sénégal compte six parcs nationaux et une trentaine de réserves naturelles. Le Sénégal accorde une grande place à la culture dans son développement. Voici une liste des personnalités qui contribuent au rayonnement* de la culture sénégalaise et de la culture francophone dans le monde.

Écrivains	Léopold Sédar Senghor (poète, président fondateur, père de la Francophonie), Cheikh Hamidou Kane, Boubacar Boris Diop, Birago Diop, Aminata Sow Fall, Mariama Bâ, Fama Diagne Sène, Fatou Diome
Artistes	Ousmane Sow (sculpteur), Babacar Touré (peintre)
Metteurs en scène	Ousmane Sembène, Safi Faye, Djibril Diop Mambéty
Musiciens	Youssou N'Dour, Viviane Ndour, Baaba Maal, Ismael Lô, Omar Pène
Styliste (mode)	Oumou Sy, Collé Ardo Sow

Recherche : tourisme sénégal, gouvernement du sénégal

plurilinguisme *multilingualism* ; **soit** *is* ; **essor** développement ; **couvrent** *cover* ; **rayonnement** *influence*

Produits

1.2, 2.2, 3.1

Le Sénégal, avec l'Île de Gorée, située au large de Dakar, a été l'un des deux grands centres du commerce des esclaves, ce **commerce triangulaire**, par lequel des pays européens ont acheté des esclaves d'Afrique, comme on achète de la marchandise, pour les envoyer aux Caraïbes et en Amérique. Le marché d'esclaves a facilité l'envoi des produits en Europe, bouclant la route triangulaire.

Traditions et pratiques

1.2, 2.1

La tradition orale constitue une grande partie de l'identité Sénégalaise. Birago Diop a fait l'une des premières tentatives de préserver l'oralité (*oral tradition*) des griots traditionnels en publiant *Les Contes d'Amadou Koumba* en 1947.

Recherche: conte-moi

Les réserves naturelles du Sénégal protègent les animaux en voie de disparition.

Connections

Nature

Have students research the endangered species in Senegal. What are they, and why is their existence threatened?

Reference Desk

Senegal's political system consists of both a president (head of state) and a prime minister (head of government).

Special Needs Students

Social Anxiety

Discussing where your students live might be stressful to some if they are living in subsidized housing, commuting between divorced parents, or living with extended family members. If you sense this might be true for some of your students, you could invite the class to answer the question about where they are living by using a fanciful lodging from the options listed in the **Game** on p.176.

Answers

8

1. Drawings will vary.
2. Answers will vary.
3. Situation géographique : Afrique de l'Ouest ; Langues : wolof, français, et 4 autres langues africaines ; Régime politique : république semi-présidentielle ; Capitale : Dakar ; Ressources naturelles : parcs nationaux et réserves naturelles
4. Answers will vary.

Perspectives

dans l'ombre et les arbres ; la religion animiste ; oui, parce qu'il pense que l'âme des morts est dans la nature.

Logement

Le logement traditionnel au Sénégal 1.2, 2.1, 2.2, 3.2

Traditionnellement, les Sénégalais habitent dans des concessions, formées d'un groupe de cases ou de maisons. Le style de ces cases varie quelquefois selon l'ethnie* et surtout selon la situation géographique des peuples. La case bambara est la plus typique non seulement au Sénégal mais dans toute l'Afrique. C'est une habitation circulaire avec un toit en chaume*.

ethnie *ethnic group* ; **chaume** *thatch*

On voit beaucoup de cases bambara dans les villages du Sénégal.

8 Activités culturelles 1.3, 2.1, 3.1, 3.2, 5.1

Complétez les activités suivantes.

1. Faites un dessin de cinq ou six appartements dans une HLM au même étage. Imaginez une famille dans chaque appartement ; écrivez le nom de la famille, son origine, et le prénom et l'âge de chaque membre de la famille.
2. Recherchez combien le gouvernement français donne cette année selon le nombre d'enfants par famille, et déterminez le montant d'allocations familiales que touche une famille avec :
   - deux enfants qui ont 4 et 6 ans
   - quatre enfants qui ont 10, 12, 14, et 17 ans
   - six enfants qui ont 6, 8, 12, 16, 17, et 18 ans
3. Faites la carte d'identité du Sénégal :
   - Situation géographique
   - Régime politique
   - Capitale
   - Langues
   - Économie
   - Ressources naturelles
4. Faites des recherches sur un(e) Sénégalais(e) célèbre et présentez cette personne à la classe.

1.2, 2.1, 3.2, 4.2

Perspectives

Dans son poème « Souffles », le poète sénégalais Birago Diop dit : « Ceux qui sont morts ne sont jamais partis :/Ils sont dans l'Ombre qui s'éclaire/Et dans l'ombre qui s'épaissit./Les Morts ne sont pas sous la Terre :/Ils sont dans l'Arbre qui frémit,/Ils sont dans le Bois qui gémit. . . . » Où vont les morts, selon Diop ? Ses idées appartiennent à quelle religion ? Basé sur ce qu'il croit, est-ce qu'il voudrait sauvegarder l'environnement ? Pourquoi, ou pourquoi pas ?

Habitation dans un village sénégalais

Essential Instruction

1. As a bell-ringer activity, put the following terms on the board and ask students to define them: **une HLM**, **les allocations familiales**, **une famille nombreuse**, **une réduction d'impôts**, **le plurilinguisme**, **Dakar**, **des griots**.
2. Students will work in teams to answer **Activités culturelles** questions 1 and 2. Students will answer questions 3 and 4 from **Activités culturelles** individually.
3. Assign the reading **Visite de l'Île de Gorée** for an in-class activity.
4. Students will collaborate to make a list from the reading of attractions offered to a tourist visiting Senegal.

Du côté des médias 1.2, 2.1, 3.1, 3.2, 4.2, 5.2

Lisez le paragraphe sur l'Île de Gorée.

VISITE DE L'ÎLE DE GORÉE

Senegal
ONLINE

La visite de l'île de Gorée peut se faire en une journée.

En novembre 1975 le patrimoine architectural de Gorée fut inscrit sur l'inventaire des monuments historiques du Sénégal et depuis septembre 1978 il figure sur la liste du patrimoine mondial établie par l'UNESCO.

La **Maison des Esclaves** (fermée le lundi) constitue le passage obligé de quiconque se rend à Gorée pour la première fois. Cependant, le rôle réel de la célèbre maison rose – et plus généralement de l'île – dans le commerce triangulaire (traite atlantique) mérite d'être très sensiblement minoré : le nombre de captifs déportés depuis Gorée ne dépasserait pas 3 500 sur toute la période de la traite vers les Amériques.

Située au centre de l'île, sur la rue du Chevalier de Boufflers, l'imposante **église Saint-Charles-Borromée** est l'un des deux édifices sacrés de Gorée. Elle est dédiée au cardinal italien Charles Borromée.

Gorée possède l'une des plus anciennes mosquées en pierre du pays. Celle-ci a été construite en 1890, au pied du versant ouest du Castel.

Situé sur la pointe nord de l'île, le **Musée historique** – rattaché à l'Institut fondamental d'Afrique noire (IFAN) – occupe l'ancien **Fort d'Estrées**. Il est consacré à l'histoire générale du pays, des origines à l'indépendance, et tout particulièrement à celle de l'île de Gorée.

Aménagé dans l'ancienne demeure d'une riche signare, Victoria Albis, le **Musée de la Femme** a été ouvert en 1994, sous la direction de la femme de lettres Annette Mbaye d'Erneville.

Également lieu de formation et d'animation, le musée rend hommage aux femmes du pays, connues ou non, et rend compte de leur vie quotidienne.

Surplombant l'île sur sa pointe sud, le **Castel** constituait une position stratégique et offre aujourd'hui un large panorama sur Dakar et la prequ'île du Cap-Vert. Face à l'ouest, le **fort Saint-Michel** y fut construit par les Français en 1892. En 1907 on y installa un télémètre permettant de mesurer l'éloignement des navires afin de régler les canons. De l'autre côté un canon permit à la France de Vichy de couler un bateau anglais le 23 septembre 1940.

Au milieu des bougainvillées, une grande maison de la Compagnie des Indes construite au XVIIIème siècle abrite le **Musée de la Mer** ouvert en 1960 par l'IFAN et entièrement restauré en 1995. Il est réputé pour sa collection de 750 espèces de poissons et 700 espèces de mollusques. Les écosystèmes et l'habitat de la région y sont également présentés.

L'**Université des Mutants** fut un centre international de rencontres et de conférences fondé en 1979 à l'initiative du Président Léopold Sédar Senghor et de l'écrivain et philosophe français Roger Garaudy.

voir :

- *Histoire de l'île de Gorée*
- *Horaires et tarifs de la chaloupe de Gorée*
- *La Maison « des Esclaves »*
- *Visite de l'île de Gorée*

9 Guide touristique Sénégal 1.2, 1.3, 3.2, 5.2

Choisissez une des activités suivantes.

1. Faites un collage avec des vues du Sénégal.
2. Dessinez et colorez l'une des scènes décrites dans le paragraphe.

Answers

9 Activities will vary.

Reference Desk

L'Île de Gorée is a small 45-acre island 2 km off the coast of Dakar, of which it is also an **arrondissement**. It is most known for its intact **Maison d'Esclaves**, from which slaves departed for the Americas between 1780 and 1784.

Expansion

1. Ask students to find images and information about **l'île de Gorée** and its relationship to slavery. This would be a good time to remind students why there are francophone countries in Africa, the Caribbean, and northern South America, and how **la Francophonie**, which is now a positive term that focuses on cultural and linguistic diversity, bears the origin of painful roots.
2. Have students use an online map site to take a walking tour of **l'île de Gorée** and the sites mentioned here.

Learning Styles

Visual Learners

Students will collaborate to do **Activité 9**, making a collage of different aspects of Senegal that transmit the essence of the country: its natural resources, industry, music, wildlife, its cities, and villages.

Multiple Intelligences

Naturalist

Students interested in nature will research Senegal's six national parks and thirty nature preserves to answer the question, "What is Senegal committed to doing to preserve the wildlife of its country?"

Mathematical-Logical

What are the current economic challenges facing the people of France and/or Senegal today?

Intrapersonal

In **Perspectives,** the Senegalese poet Birago Diop suggests that our dead are always with us, embedded in nature. Students will read the poem **"Souffles"** and answer the question posed about the poet's commitment to the environment as evidenced in his work.

Answers

All activities will vary.

Expansion

Use the following questions as a springboard for class discussion.

1. **Est-ce que l'organisation que vous avez choisie répond aux besoins que vous considérez importants pour les immigrés ? Pourquoi ou pourquoi pas ?**
2. **Quelles sont les responsabilités des organisations humanitaires envers les immigrés ?**
3. **Quelles sont les responsabilités d'un pays d'accueil envers ses immigrés ? Y a-t-il des limites ?**
4. **En considérant la pyramide, quels besoins n'ont pas été satisfaits ? Comment pourrait-on répondre à ces besoins-là ?**

Culture sur place

Question centrale ? **Comment les communautés francophones conservent-elles leurs traditions ?**

Les besoins des immigrés

Tous les immigrés arrivent d'un pays et s'installent dans un autre pays, mais leurs expériences ne sont pas identiques. Dans cette *Culture sur place*, considérons les besoins des immigrés. De quoi ont-ils besoin ? Quel est le lien entre leurs besoins et leurs expériences ? Qu'est-ce que les organisations humanitaires dans leur pays d'accueil pourraient leur donner ?

10 Réfléchir 1.3, 2.1, 3.2, 4.2, 5.1, 5.2

Nous allons d'abord penser aux besoins des immigrés qui s'installent dans un nouveau pays.

1. Avec un partenaire, faites une liste de ce dont les immigrés pourraient avoir besoin en s'installant dans un nouveau pays. Écrivez en français, et utilisez un dictionnaire si nécessaire.
2. Organisez votre liste dans un organigramme selon les cinq types de besoins :
3. Une fois votre liste finie, partagez-la avec deux autres étudiants ou avec la classe.

La pyramide des besoins d'Abraham Maslow

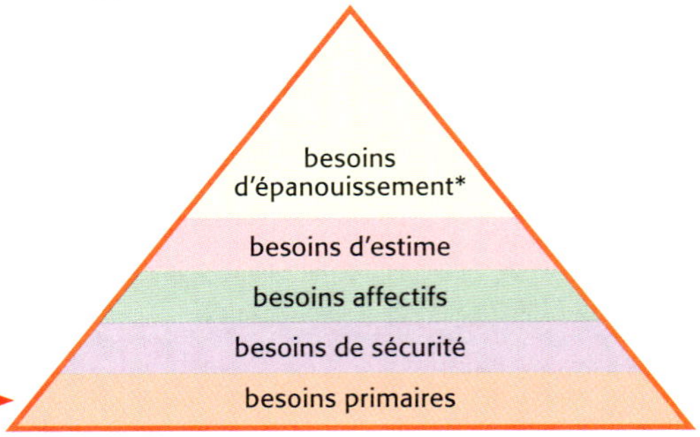

**self-actualization*

11 Rechercher 1.3, 3.1, 3.2, 4.2

Maintenant, avec votre partenaire, recherchez les buts d'une organisation humanitaire dédiée (*dedicated*) aux besoins des immigrés. Choisissez parmi les organisations suivantes :

- Croix-Rouge de Belgique
- Défense des Enfants International
- Mentor-Escale
- Les Amis d'Accompagner
- Caritas International Belgique
- Mouvement Convivial (ou « Convivium »)

Faites des recherches sur l'organisation que vous avez choisie. Cochez dans votre organigramme les aides que les immigrés peuvent recevoir de la part de cette organisation.

Recherche : donorinfo.be, ong belges

Essential Instruction

1. Present **Activité 10**. Explain the mechanics of the exercise, making certain that the students understand how to proceed.
2. Explain the correspondence between **Activités 10** and **11**. Each organization listed has a specific focus. Students will choose or be assigned an organization to research. For example, **Mentor-Escale** is dedicated to offering social and educational education to the exiled averaging 16–17 years old.
3. In their search, students may discover other organizations that they would like to add to the list of support for immigrants.
4. Have students read the **Révision** and take the mini-test to see what they recall.
5. Review **plus**…**que**, **moins**…**que** and **aussi**…**que**, as well as the irregular forms of **bien**, **beaucoup**, and **peu**.

Révision: Comparisons with Adverbs 1.1

On recycle !

Can you tell which sentence uses an adverb, and which one uses an adjective?

1. C'est une voiture rapide.
2. La voiture circule rapidement.

See if you can complete the following sentences in the comparative:

3. Je conduis… que ma sœur. (*bien*)
4. Alain travaille… en classe que moi. (*peu*)
5. Tu joues au foot… que Sylvie. (*beaucoup*)

If you got any wrong in 1–5, be sure to read the grammar summary below to review the comparative of adverbs.

Comparisons using adverbs are formed in the same way that comparisons with adjectives are formed.

plus + ADVERB + **que**	Tu as fini **plus** rapidement **que** moi ! (+)	*You finished faster than I (did)!*
moins + ADVERB + **que**	Adja voyage **moins** souvent **que** sa sœur. (-)	*Adja travels less often than her sister.*
aussi + ADVERB + **que**	Aïcha peint **aussi** rapidement **qu'**un professionnel. (=)	*Aïcha paints as quickly as a professional.*

When making comparisons, some adverbs have irregular forms.

Adverb	Comparative	Example	
bien (*well*)	**mieux** (*better*)	Chantal pose **mieux** le papier peint **qu'**Abdou.	*Chantal puts on wallpaper better than Abdou does.*
beaucoup (*a lot, much*)	**plus** (*more*)	David travaille **plus qu'**Antoine.	*David works more than Antoine.*
peu (*little*)	**moins** (*less*)	Ils nagent **moins que** tes amis.	*They swim less than your friends.*

4.1

Comparisons

Madison makes *good* drawings.
She draws *well*.
The train is very *rapid*.
The train travels *rapidly*.
My singing is *bad*.
I sing *badly*.

It is useful to be able to distinguish between adjectives and adverbs. Which words in the above sentences are adjectives, and which are adverbs?

Marc marche plus rapidement que Valérie.

Resources

WB Workbook 7–9
LA Listening Activity 2
G & V Practice Games

Answers

On recycle !

Sentence 1 uses the adjective **rapide**. In sentence 2 **rapidement** is an adverb. The ending **-ment** is like *-ly* (*actively*, *carefully*) in English. The answers for sentences 3–5 are: 3. **mieux**; 4. **moins**; 5. **plus**.

Comparisons

Adjectives are *good*, *rapid*, and *bad*. Adverbs are *well*, *rapidly*, and *badly*. Remember, adjectives describe nouns, whereas adverbs describe verbs.

Reference Desk

1. To help students form correctly the comparative with adverbs, remind them that just like **ne… pas** always surrounds the verb in a simple sentence unless an adverb is irregular, **plus/aussi/moins… que** always surrounds the adverb in a comparative sentence.
2. For practice, pair students and ask them to form comparative sentences using adverbs about their classmates. For example, **Jack court plus rapidement que Jill**. Caution students not to provide any negative attributes.

Differentiated Learning

Accelerate

Have students compare what they can do now to what they could do when they were seven. They are to write as many comparisons as they can, using regular and irregular adverbs. Award a small token to the student who writes the most comparisons correctly.

Decelerate

Students will need a structured review of adjectives and adverbs. They need to see, side by side, how adjectives and adverbs are formed and used in sentences. Insist on where adjectives are placed, versus adverbs, as placement plays an important role in comparative sentences. Give sample sentences with adjectives and others with adverbs, and then have students figure out where the **plus… que** goes.

Resources

Activity 14

Answers

12

1. La France s'est classée dans la Coupe du Monde plus souvent que les Pays-Bas.
2. L'Uruguay s'est classé dans la Coupe du Monde moins souvent que l'Allemagne.
3. L'Allemagne s'est classé dans la Coupe du Monde plus souvent que la France.
4. La République de Corée s'est classée dans la Coupe du Monde moins souvent que les Pays-Bas.
5. L'Italie s'est classée dans la Coupe du Monde plus souvent que l'Angleterre.
6. La Suède s'est classée dans la Coupe du Monde moins souvent que l'Argentine.
7. Le Brésil s'est classé dans la Coupe du Monde plus souvent que la Turquie.
8. L'Argentine s'est classée dans la Coupe du Monde plus souvent que le Portugal.

13

1. mieux
2. moins mal
3. plus souvent
4. moins sérieusement
5. aussi souvent
6. moins souvent
7. moins
8. plus tard

14 Script

Abdoulaye se couche à 10h00, mais Étienne se couche à minuit. Abdoulaye se couche plus tôt qu'Étienne. Abdoulaye se lève à 7h30, mais Étienne se lève à 8h15. Étienne se lève plus tard qu'Abdoulaye et arrive souvent en retard au lycée. Pendant la semaine, après les cours, Étienne fait du sport. Il va à la bibliothèque une fois par semaine, mais Abdoulaye y va quatre fois par semaine pour étudier et faire ses devoirs. Abdoulaye va plus souvent à la bibliothèque qu'Étienne. Abdoulaye réussit plus aux contrôles qu'Étienne.

Abdoulaye travaille plus sérieusement qu'Étienne.

Reference Desk

The **FIFA (Fédération Internationale de Football Association)** gathers national soccer teams every four years to compete for the World Cup.

12 La coupe du monde de la FIFA 1.2

Interpretive Reading

Voici le classement des pays qui ont gagné une place à la Coupe du Monde de football depuis 1986. Comparez les gagnants.

1ère place : Espagne, Italie, Brésil, France, Brésil, Allemagne, Argentine

2ème place : Pays-Bas, Allemagne, France, Brésil, Italie, Argentine, Allemagne

3ème place : Allemagne, Turquie, Croatie, Suède, Italie, France

4ème place : Uruguay, Portugal, République de Corée, Pays-Bas, Bulgarie, Angleterre, Belgique

MODÈLE l'Espagne/l'Italie
L'Espagne s'est classée dans la Coupe du Monde moins souvent que l'Italie.

1. la France/les Pays-Bas
2. l'Uruguay/l'Allemagne
3. l'Allemagne/la France
4. la République de Corée/les Pays-Bas
5. l'Italie/l'Angleterre
6. la Suède/l'Argentine
7. le Brésil/la Turquie
8. l'Argentine/le Portugal

13 Une enquête pour un Français et une Américaine 1.2, 2.1, 4.2

Interpretive Reading

Tristan habite en France et sa cousine Kelsey habite aux États-Unis. Kelsey a envoyé une enquête à son cousin français pour voir comment il vit. Complétez les phrases avec la forme comparative appropriée. Utilisez l'adverbe indiqué.

	Tristan	Kelsey
1. Quels sports fais-tu bien ?	foot et tennis	basket et softball
2. Combien de fois par semaine vas-tu au café ?	3–4	0–1
3. Combien d'heures étudies-tu chaque soir ?	3	1–1.5
4. Combien de films américains regardes-tu chaque mois ?	2	2
5. Combien de fois par an voyages-tu ?	3	1
6. Combien de corvées fais-tu à la maison ?	1	3
7. À quelle heure arrives-tu au lycée ?	8h00	7h15

1. Tristan joue… au foot que Kelsey. (*bien*)
2. Kelsey joue… au softball que Tristan. (*mal*)
3. Tristan va… au café que Kelsey. (*souvent*)
4. Kelsey étudie… que Tristan. (*sérieusement*)
5. Tristan regarde des films américains… que Kelsey. (*souvent*)
6. Kelsey voyage… que Tristan. (*souvent*)
7. Tristan travaille… à la maison que Kelsey. (*peu*)
8. Tristan arrive au lycée… que Kelsey. (*tard*)

14 Qui est le meilleur élève ? 1.2

Interpretive Listening

Écoutez le paragraphe qui compare Abdoulaye et Étienne. Dites quel élève travaille plus sérieusement, Abdoulaye ou Étienne.

Essential Instruction

1. Ask students to respond orally to the questions for **Activité 12**. Allow them time to write each answer in their notebooks.
2. Pair students to do **Activité 13**.
3. Personalize this activity by asking two of your own students to respond to the same questions. The class will compare these two students using the same format as in the activity.
4. Students will listen to **Qui est le meilleur élève?** to decide if the answer is Abdoulaye or Etienne. Ask students to justify their answer by recalling what they learned about each student.
5. After a review of the superlative of adjectives, use **Activité 15** as the basis for a debate. One half of your class will assume the role of chauvinist Americans and the other chauvinist French. Each side will argue that their country is better than the other in the categories 1–9.

Révision: Superlative of Adverbs 1.2

On recycle!

Can you tell which sentence uses the comparative and which the superlative of adverbs?

1. Mon ami fait du ski nautique plus souvent que toi.
2. Je conduis le plus prudemment dans ma famille.

What grammatically correct sentence can you make with the parts below?

3. le plus/Julien et/en classe/Annick/parlent

If you cannot do 1–3, read the grammar summary below.

The superlative of adverbs is formed in the same way as the superlative of adjectives.

le + **moins/plus** + ADVERB	Mon frère loue une résidence secondaire le plus souvent.	*My brother rents a second home the most often.*

Adverbs that are irregular in the comparative are also irregular in the superlative.

Adverb	Superlative	Example	
bien	le mieux	Qui peint **le mieux**?	*Who paints the best?*
beaucoup	le plus	Daniel nettoie **le plus** dans sa famille.	*Daniel cleans the most in his family.*
peu	le moins	C'est moi qui étudie **le moins** dans la classe.	*I'm the one who studies the least in class.*

15 Les Français ou les Américains? 1.1, 2.1, 4.2, 5.2

Interpersonal Speaking

Après plus de deux années d'études de français, vous connaissez bien la France et les Français. Dites si, selon vous, les Français ou les Américains font les activités suivantes le plus + ADVERBE.

MODÈLE discuter passionnément

Selon moi, les Français discutent le plus passionnément.

ou

Selon moi, les Américains discutent le plus passionnément.

1. protéger l'environnement attentivement (*attentively*)
2. passer les vacances tranquillement (*peacefully*)
3. travailler efficacement
4. parler joliment
5. se saluer (*greet*) affectueusement
6. vivre simplement
7. s'habiller bien
8. voyager souvent
9. dîner tard

Resources

Activity 15

WB Workbook 10–11

Answers

On recycle!

Sentence #1 uses the comparative and sentence #2 the superlative of adverbs. The reordered sentence is: **Julien et Annick parlent le plus en classe.**

15 Subjects of answers will vary.

1. ... protègent l'environnement le plus attentivement.
2. ... passent les vacances le plus tranquillement.
3. ... travaillent le plus efficacement.
4. ... parlent le plus joliment.
5. ... se saluent le plus affectueusement.
6. ... vivent le plus simplement.
7. ... s'habillent le mieux.
8. ... voyagent le plus souvent.
9. ... dînent le plus tard.

Expansion

Show pictures of different means of transportation and ask students to decide which one is **le/la plus/moins rapide, le/la meilleur(e) marché**, or **le/la meilleur(e) ou le/la pire pour l'environnement**. You could choose an elephant, horse, moped, bicycle, car, train, jet, rocket, or car models.

Connections

Automotive

Ask students to bring in a toy car or truck. Each student will pit his or her toy against another student's in a race to see which one goes faster or slower. This exercise can be expanded to ask who has the better car, the faster car, and the slower car so as to juxtapose the comparative and superlative forms of adjectives and adverbs.

Learning Styles

Auditory Learners

Have students clap or tap a particular rhythm as they say the superlative sentences as found in the adverb chart and in corrected activities.

Visual-Spatial

Since students tend to think in images, have them make a poster that illustrates the comparative and superlative regular and irregular adverbs.

Multiple Intelligences

Mathematical-Logical

Have students create a template for the comparative and superlative forms of adjectives and adverbs, with examples. This visual can be posted on the wall for reference.

Resources

CA Communicative Activities

Share

Answers

All activities will vary.

Reference Desk

1. The activities on this page may be used to prepare students for the AP French Language and Culture Exam. The first spoken portion of the exam requires students to complete one part of a dialogue like the one presented here in **Activité 16**. The second AP speaking assessment requires that students compare one aspect of francophone culture with their own culture in a two-minute presentation, as in **Activité 18**.
2. If you have access to Passport, create a question for your students to share their response to a communicative activity.

À vous la parole

Question centrale ? Comment les communautés francophones conservent-elles leurs traditions?

Communiquez!

16 Dans ma résidence HLM 1.1, 4.2, 5.2

Interpersonal Speaking

Deux locataires, qui viennent de s'installer dans la même HLM, parlent de l'état de leurs appartements et de leurs projets pour les rénover (*renovate*). Avec un partenaire, jouez les rôles de ces deux locataires et parlez de ces sujets:

1. votre famille
2. l'étage où se trouve votre appartement
3. l'état de votre appartement (sale? propre?)
4. combien de pièces vous avez
5. la couleur de vos pièces
6. les changements que vous comptez faire (couleurs des murs, papier peint, moquette, etc.)
7. les tableaux que vous voulez poser aux murs

17 Mon logement de rêve 1.3, 2.2, 4.2, 5.2

Presentational Writing

Trouvez une habitation en France où vous voudriez vivre. Imprimez les photos qui sont disponibles. Ensuite, écrivez un paragraphe sur les changements que vous voudriez faire, en parlant des meubles ou appareils électroménagers, tapis ou moquettes, tableaux ou objets d'art, papier peint ou peinture, etc. Si vous préférez, vous pouvez dessiner votre habitation et montrez comment vous l'avez décorée.

Recherche: acheter maison, immobilier france, se loger, green acres france

18 À mon tour! 1.3, 2.2, 4.2, 5.1

Presentational Speaking

Faites des recherches sur les divers logements à Paris. Puis, préparez un discours de deux minutes en français pour comparer les types de logement dans votre communauté à ceux de Paris (prix, prestations, localisation, architecture, population, etc.).

Recherche: logements à pour étudiants à paris (centre-ville)

Essential Instruction

1. To review vocabulary from **Leçon C** and prepare students for **Activité 17**, ask students what kinds of renovations can be expected for an apartment. Write key phrases on a board or project them on a screen.
2. Pair students and have them prepare a script for **Activité 16**. Assign **Activité 16** to be performed as a skit before the class.
3. Assign **Activité 17** as individual homework. You may want to allow students to select between the writing and the speaking activity.
4. Have students work in groups for **Activité 18**. Give or allow students to take on specific roles based on their abilities and skills.
5. Prepare a date ahead of time to showcase art for **Activité 19**. In addition to printing an image, you may ask students to write a paragraph describing the image, mentioning the artist, the art movement, or their reaction and reason for choosing this art. Students with culinary interest might enjoy preparing a typical Senegalese dish.

19 Une nouvelle HLM 1.3, 2.1, 5.1, 5.2

Presentational Speaking

Imaginez que vous êtes architecte et que le gouvernement français vous paie pour dessiner une nouvelle HLM en centre-ville parmi d'autres immeubles qui ne sont pas subventionnés (*subsidized*) par l'État. Faites un dessin. Pensez à ce que vous voulez proposer pour les enfants, les ados, les personnes handicapées, et les personnes âgées de cette HLM. Finalement, présentez votre dessin et répondez aux questions de la classe.

20 Une galerie sénégalaise 1.3, 3.1, 3.2, 5.1

Presentational Writing

Transformez votre salle de classe en une galerie sénégalaise. Imprimez en couleurs des tableaux d'artistes sénégalais. Accrochez aussi des poèmes sénégalais entre les tableaux. Pendant que vous travaillez, écoutez de la musique sénégalaise traditionnelle ou moderne. Vous pouvez inviter les autres classes de langue (espagnol, allemand, chinois...) et aussi de sciences humaines et sociales (*social studies*) à visiter votre galerie.

Sculpture africaine en cuivre

Une peinture sénégalaise sur coton

21 *Ma Maison de Star* 1.3, 3.1, 3.2, 5.2

Presentational Writing and Speaking

Imaginez que les producteurs français de la célèbre émission télévisée *Ma Maison de Star* vous contactent car votre maison a été choisie pour apparaître sur un prochain épisode de leur émission qui sera diffusé en France. Vous êtes tellement content(e) de leur montrer votre maison ! Trouvez un partenaire ; l'un d'entre vous filmera et jouera le rôle de l'intervieweur, tandis que l'autre montrera la maison. Vous pouvez la montrer pièce par pièce et être aussi créatif/créative que vous voulez. Par exemple : voulez-vous montrer le contenu de votre réfrigérateur ? Qu'est-ce qu'il y a dans votre placard à vêtements ? Si vous préférez, vous pouvez créer votre maison de rêve avec des images et filmer en montrant les images. Vous pouvez aussi dessiner un plan détaillé de votre maison, en indiquant les différents aspects et détails. Présentez votre petit film à la classe.

Answers

All activities will vary.

Reference Desk

Ma maison de Star is the equivalent of the American show *Cribs*. For this activity, allow students who may not want to show their actual home, or who may not want to draw a plan, to use a doll house or an area of the school to film their presentation. Also, make sure to provide a camera to those students who may not have access to one.

Special Needs Students

Behavior Problems

Activité 19 is a collaborative exercise for those who like working in a team to transform their classroom into Senegal through its art and music. Students who are easily distracted when there is less structure should not be left without a specific task to perform. Be sure to give them a responsibility in which they can take on a leadership role.

Recherche : spirit of senegal

Social Anxiety

For **Activité 17** and **Activité 18**, students with a difficult housing situation might not want to share their personal experience; however, they might want to contribute their thoughts, feelings, and knowledge to generate a list of concerns associated with subsidized housing in their region or country.

Pre-AP

Une si longue lettre

Rencontre avec l'auteur 1.2, 3.2

Mariama Bâ (1929–1981) est née au Sénégal. Elle est élevée par ses grands-parents maternels à la mort de sa mère dans un univers musulman traditionnel. Après de brillantes études, elle devient institutrice, métier qu'elle exercera pendant 12 ans. Mère de neuf enfants, mariée trois fois, elle décide de se consacrer à la cause des femmes et s'engage dans des associations féministes. Elle lutte pour les droits des femmes et contre la polygamie. En 1979, elle publie *Une si longue lettre* qui devient très vite un grand succès. Il s'agit d'une lettre de confidences à une amie sur sa vie de femme, et sur le comportement de son beau-frère. À partir de la lecture de cet extrait, qu'apprenez-vous de la culture sénégalaise ?

Pré-lecture 1.3

Si vous deviez écrire une lettre de confidences, que souhaiteriez-vous raconter de votre vie et à qui ?

Stratégie de lecture 1.2, 1.3, 2.1, 4.2

Making Cultural Inferences. Lorsque vous lisez un texte, vous en tirez (*draw*) naturellement des conclusions. Cela s'appelle faire des inférences. Quand un texte donne des indications culturelles, comme dans la lecture qui suit sur le Sénégal, vous faites des inférences culturelles. Au cours de la lecture, inscrivez dans la colonne de gauche d'un tableau comme celui de dessous les indices textuels concernant la culture sénégalaise. Dans la colonne de droite, expliquez les renseignements que ces citations fournissent (*furnish*). Un exemple vous est donné.

Textual clue	Cultural inference
C'est « le quarantième jour de la mort de Modou », le mari de la narratrice.	Au Sénégal, on célèbre le quarantième jour après la mort d'un membre de la famille.
« Des initiés ont lu le Coran. »	

Resources

Rencontre avec l'auteur

Answers

Rencontre avec l'auteur
le rituel du deuil (*mourning*)

Pré-lecture
Answers will vary.

Stratégie de lecture
"Des initiés ont lu le Coran." La religion officielle du Sénégal est l'Islam.
"En général, c'est le petit frère qui hérite de l'épouse laissée par son aîné." La tradition du Sénégal est que si un homme marié meurt, son frère épouse la veuve (*widow*).
"Je te préfère à l'autre, trop légère, trop jeune." / "Et tes femmes, Tamsir?" Tamsir, comme l'était Modou, est polygame ; la polygamie est acceptée dans certaines régions du Sénégal.
"J'égrène mon chapelet." La religion officielle du Sénégal est l'Islam.
"l'une de tes épouses fait des travaux de teinture, l'autre vend des fruits, la troisième inlassablement tourne la manivelle de sa machine à coudre." Le Sénégal est un pays peu modernisé et il y a beaucoup de métiers artisanaux.

Reference Desk

According to Muslim traditions, the soul of a dead person remains in the tomb for 40 days, after which it passes on. That day, friends and family gather to pay their respects to the dead, and eat and celebrate the passing on of the soul. The period a wife should mourn her husband is four months and ten days.

Connections

Music and Literature

Jean Ferrat in his song "**La Femme est l'avenir de l'homme**" speaks to the role of women in modern society. Have students outline the images of these women presented in the song vis-à-vis the treatment of Mariama Bâ in Senegalese society. Students may want to use the same chart in **Stratégie de lecture** to analyze the song as well. The song references a short poem by the poet Louis Aragon:

**"L'avenir de l'homme est la femme/
Elle est la couleur de son Âme/
Elle est sa rumeur et son bruit/
Et sans Elle, il n'est qu'un blasphème."**

Essential Instruction

1. To prepare students to read an excerpt from **Une si longue lettre** they will listen to the **Rencontre avec l'auteur** with Mariama Bâ. From what they learn about the author, what can they expect to read?
2. Ask students if they would ever write **une lettre de confidences**. To whom would it be written? Who would be the most understanding, a parent, an adult mentor, or a friend? What are the risks of writing a personal letter? What would be the reason to do so?
3. Students will complete the **Stratégie de lecture** as they read the extract.
4. Asks students to answer the **Pendant la lecture** questions after listening to the recording, or pause where there is a question to monitor their comprehension as you go through. Students can work on the questions in pairs or small groups and then share their findings with the class.

Outils de lecture 1.2, 2.1, 4.2

Gender Criticism. Il existe plusieurs études critiques d'un texte littéraire, par exemple l'analyse des liens (*ties*) entre un récit de la vie personnelle de l'auteur (critique biographique), ou l'analyse des personnages d'un roman selon la psychologie moderne (critique psychologique). La critique de genre s'intéresse à l'identité de l'homme et de la femme en littérature, et à comment ces images reflètent ou rejettent les paramètres sociaux traditionnels qui ont freiné (*put brakes on*) l'égalité entre l'homme et la femme.

Retour au marché, 2005. Cécile Delorme.

Une si longue lettre 1.2, 4.2

J'ai célébré hier, comme il se doit, le quarantième jour de la mort de Modou. Je lui ai pardonné. Que Dieu exauce* les prières* que je formule quotidiennement pour lui. Des initiés ont lu le Coran. Leurs voix ferventes sont montées vers le ciel. Il faut que Dieu t'accueille parmi ses élus, Modou Fall !

Après les actes de piété*, Tamsir est venu s'asseoir dans ma chambre dans le fauteuil bleu où tu te plaisais*. En penchant* sa tête au dehors, il a fait signe à Mawdo ; il a aussi fait signe à l'Imam de la mosquée de son quartier. L'Imam et Mawdo l'ont rejoint. Tamsir parle cette fois. Ressemblance saisissante* entre Modou et Tamsir, mêmes tics de l'inexplicable loi de l'hérédité. Tamsir parle, plein d'assurance ; il invoque (encore) mes années de mariage, puis conclut* : « Après ta "sortie" (du deuil*), je t'épouse. Tu me conviens* comme femme et puis, tu continueras à habiter ici, comme si Modou n'était pas mort. En général, c'est le petit frère qui hérite de l'épouse laissée par son aîné. Ici, c'est le contraire. Tu es ma chance. Je t'épouse. Je te préfère à l'autre, trop légère, trop jeune. J'avais déconseillé ce mariage à Modou. »

Quelle déclaration d'amour pleine de fatuité* dans une maison que le deuil n'a pas encore quitté. Quelle assurance et quel aplomb tranquilles ! Je regarde Tamsir droit dans les yeux. Je regarde Mawdo. Je regarde l'Imam. Je serre* mon châle noir. J'égrène mon chapelet*. Cette fois, je parlerai.

Ma voix connaît trente années de silence, trente années de brimades*. Elle éclate*, violente, tantôt sarcastique*, tantôt méprisante*.

Pendant la lecture
1. Depuis combien de temps Modou est-il mort ?

Pendant la lecture
2. Comment sait-on que la narratrice est pieuse ?

Pendant la lecture
3. Qui est venu s'asseoir dans la chambre de la narratrice ?

Pendant la lecture
4. Que propose Tamsir ?

Pendant la lecture
5. Pourquoi Tamsir ne s'intéresse-t-il pas à l'autre femme de Modou ?

Pendant la lecture
6. Comment est-ce que la narratrice se sent après avoir entendu la proposition de Tamsir ?

exauce *grants* ; **prière** *prayer* ; **piété** *piety* ; **où tu te plaisais** que tu aimais ; **En penchant** *In leaning* ; **saisissante** *striking* ; **conclut** *concludes* ; **le deuil** *mourning* ; **Tu me conviens** *You suit me* ; **fatuité** *self-conceit* ; **serre** *pull closer* ; **J'égrène mon chapelet** *I touch my strings of beads while praying* ; **brimades** *vexations* ; **éclate** *explodes* ; **tantôt sarcastique** *sometimes sarcastic* ; **méprisante** *scornful*

Resources

Une si longue lettre

Answers

Pendant la lecture
1. depuis quarante jours
2. Elle prie beaucoup pour son mari.
3. Tamsir, le frère de Modou, l'Imam, et Mawdo
4. Il voudrait épouser la narratrice.
5. Elle est trop jeune et mince pour lui.
6. Elle se met en colère.

Expansion

Use the images brought by students from **Activité 20**, and ask them to imagine that each painting represents a scene from the novel ***Une si longue lettre*** that the excerpt does not describe. Have them choose a painting and narrate a very short story of what might have happened in the novel. This game can be played before or after the reading.

Differentiated Learning

Accelerate
High-ability students will be able to listen to the passage and pass directly to the **Pendant la lecture** and **Post-lecture** questions. After they have finished this assignment, ask them to make a family tree of Mariama Bâ's family with notes about each person drawn from the story.

Decelerate
Low-ability students will appreciate you working with them, one on one or in a group, to break the passage down into smaller sections, explaining vocabulary and structure and helping them answer the **Pendant la lecture** and **Post-lecture** questions.

Special Needs Students

Auditory Impairment
For students who have difficulty hearing, make arrangements for them to use earphones to listen to the recording, or be placed near the source of the broadcast.

Resources

Q *Leçon* Quiz

Answers

Analyse
Un homme peut hériter de la femme de son ami.; Un homme peut avoir plusieurs femmes.

Pendant la lecture
7. C'est un acte d'amour et de foi, c'est aussi un choix.
8. trois ; des petits travaux

Post-lecture
Possible answer:
La narratrice est une femme d'une cinquantaine d'années, obéissante à la tradition de sa culture. Après la mort de son mari, elle remet en question ses croyances. Ce qui est remarquable dans cette transformation est que la femme change d'opinion après trente ans.

Le monde visuel
Possible answer:
Les couleurs sont vives, les dimensions sont plates, il n'y a pas de reliefs ou même d'ombres.

22 Activities will vary.

Communication

Interpersonal: Cooperative Groups

In groups, students will discuss the picture "**Retour au marché**" from **Le monde visuel** as an example of primitive art, and as a metaphor of the life of women in Senegal. They will need to compare it to other Senegalese art pieces which have been presented in class.

(Suite et fin)

—As-tu jamais eu de l'affection pour ton frère ? Tu veux déjà construire un foyer neuf sur un cadavre chaud. Alors que l'on prie pour Modou, tu penses à de futures noces. Ah ! oui : ton calcul, c'est devancer* tout prétendant* possible, devancer Mawdo, l'ami fidèle qui a plus d'atouts* que toi et qui, également, selon la coutume, peut hériter de la femme. Tu oublies que j'ai un cœur, une raison*, que je ne suis pas un objet que l'on se passe de main en main. Tu ignores ce que se marier signifie pour moi : c'est un acte de foi* et d'amour, un don* total de soi à l'être que l'on a choisi et qui vous a choisi. Et tes femmes, Tamsir ? Ton revenu ne couvre ni leurs besoins ni ceux de tes dizaines d'enfants. Pour te suppléer* dans tes devoirs financiers, l'une de tes épouses fait des travaux de teinture*, l'autre vend des fruits, la troisième inlassablement* tourne la manivelle* de sa machine à coudre*. Toi, tu te prélasses en seigneur vénéré*, obéi au doigt et à l'œil. Je ne serai jamais le complément de ta collection....

Analyse
How many examples of Senegalese culture can you find in the reading? Support your answer with textual clues and references.

Pendant la lecture
7. Pour la narratrice, qu'est-ce que c'est que le mariage ?

Pendant la lecture
8. Combien de femmes Tamsir a-t-il ? Que font-elles pour contribuer aux finances de la maison ?

devancer *to forestall* ; **prétendant** *suitor* ; **atouts** *assets* ; **raison** *mind* ; **foi** *faith* ; **don** cadeau ; **suppléer** *to provide* ; **teinture** *dyeing* ; **inlassablement** sans fatigue ; **manivelle** *crank* ; **machine à coudre** *sewing machine* ; **tu te prélasses en seigneur vénéré** *you lounge around like an honored lord*

Post-lecture 1.2, 1.3

Comment décririez-vous la narratrice ? Que pouvez-vous dire de la femme que la narratrice était dans le passé, et de celle qu'elle est devenue ? Qu'est-ce qui rend cette transformation remarquable ?

Le monde visuel 1.2, 3.1

Cécile Delorme (1946–) est une artiste française qui passe beaucoup de temps en Afrique. Le tableau, à la page 191, montre la vie des femmes, qui marchent à la file (*in single file*) en revenant du marché, presque comme dans un défilé de mode. Le style est naïf, c'est-à-dire pas réaliste en ce qui concerne l'architecture, l'anatomie, et la perspective. L'art naïf est souvent marqué par une simplicité, de petits détails, et une coloration brillante. Quels aspects de l'art naïf sont visibles dans ce tableau ? Soyez précis.

22 Activités d'expansion 1.3, 4.2, 5.2

1. Écrivez un paragraphe pour décrire la vie traditionnelle des femmes au Sénégal. Servez-vous de votre grille.
2. Avec un partenaire, jouez le rôle des protagonistes. Tamsir donne ses raisons pour vouloir se marier, et la narratrice refuse avec ses propres raisons.
3. Imaginez que vous correspondez avec la narratrice. Dans un mail, donnez-lui des conseils.
4. Faites des recherches et comparez le(s) rôle(s) des femmes dans votre culture avec celui (ceux) des femmes sénégalaises.
5. À quel personnage du texte vous identifiez-vous et pourquoi ?

Essential Instruction

1. **Activité 22** challenges students to draw inferences from the reading about Mariama's life to use as a basis to write an essay, dramatic scene, letter, a cultural analysis, or a personal philosophy statement. Give the students a choice of activity, or assign one or more to them. The pre-writing outline should be done in class under your supervision so that they write a thoughtful, well-structured piece of writing.
2. For **les Projets finaux,** ask groups to select **A** or **B** as their final project. Reserve a day in the lab or class for them to work. Have each group present its project to the class.
3. For **C**, form groups with a balance of extroverts and quieter students. Encourage students to film their work in advance, which gives them the opportunity to redo it if they are not pleased with the first try.

Pre-AP 21

Question centrale ? Comment les communautés francophones conservent-elles leurs traditions ?

Communiquez !

23 **Un mail du centre social** 1.1, 2.1, 3.2, 4.2, 5.1, 5.2

Connecting to Communication, Global Awareness, Leadership and Responsibility
Interpersonal Writing

Vous avez fait une demande pour travailler dans un centre social (*community center*) pendant l'été. La directrice vous contacte. Lisez, puis répondez à son mail de façon formelle et avec le plus de détails possible.

De: Madame la directrice
Objet: Votre demande d'emploi au centre social

Cher candidat, chère candidate

Je vous remercie de l'intérêt que vous portez à notre centre social. Nous sommes fiers des services que nous rendons aux habitants de notre commune. Après avoir lu votre demande d'emploi, nous pensons que votre expérience serait utile dans notre service d'accueil et d'aide aux immigrés. Nous vous demandons de répondre aux questions suivantes pour confirmer votre intérêt. Selon vous, de quelle sorte de soutien une famille d'immigrés a-t-elle besoin quand elle arrive dans la communauté, et pourquoi ? Pourquoi pensez-vous être capable d'aider et de renseigner les immigrés qui viennent dans notre centre social ? Le poste que nous vous proposons vous intéresse-t-il toujours ?

En vous remerciant de bien vouloir communiquer vos réponses d'ici la fin de la semaine, et vous prie d'agréer mes salutations distinguées,

Madame la Directrice

24 **Raconte-moi un conte !** 1.2, 1.3, 2.2, 3.1, 5.1

Connecting to Information Literacy, Creativity and Innovation
Interpretive Reading, Presentational Speaking

Les contes sont à l'origine une tradition orale. Parfois, ils expliquent les lois de la nature, par exemple le lever du soleil ou le feu. Trouvez un conte en ligne qui explique un élément de la nature. Racontez l'histoire à la classe en utilisant des accessoires visuels.

25 **Un exposé** 1.1, 1.2, 1.3, 2.2, 3.1, 3.2, 5.2

Connecting to Creativity and Innovation, Collaboration
Interpersonal Speaking, Interpretive Reading, Presentational Speaking and Writing

Pour préparer une exposition de logements autour du monde, La Maison de l'architecture Rhône-Alpes, à Lyon, propose un concours (*competition*) ouvert au public ! En groupe, préparez une illustration ou un modèle en 3D qui représente une habitation idéale, selon vous, dans un pays francophone (un quartier, une habitation, une pièce) et une description (localisation, climat, tradition des habitants, etc.). Présentez à la classe !

French in the Workplace

Teaching English to French speakers

If your students want to live and work in a French-speaking country, one of their most likely professional opportunities may be to teach English to French speakers. Have students look at a grammar concepts taught in this unit, or in preceding units. What are its English equivalents? How would one teach English grammar to a group of French-speaking students? Have them prepare a lesson that includes a reading, writing, speaking, listening, and kinesthetic activity. Then have them give their lesson to a group of classmates. Be sure to use both French and English appropriately, keeping in mind that your audience is a group of early English-language learners!

Social Justice

The highway that encircles Paris is known as **le boulevard périphérique**. Entering or leaving the suburbs is often called "crossing the Périphérique," as if it were a frontier. Suburbs are isolated from the city and from France itself; residents joke that going into Paris requires a visa and a vaccination card. Rarely visited, suburbanites complain that journalists come only to report on car burnings and drug shootings. Compared with American slums, the **banlieues** have relatively decent standards of housing and safety; however, the psychological distance between "**le département 93**" and the Champs-Élysées is greater than that between the Bronx and Times Square. In groups, have students examine the historical, political, cultural, and or ethnic/racial make-up of the HLM in Paris. They may focus on one aspect (immigration, riots/violence, race) or tackle an overview of the elements; contrast and compare with equivalent American housing, such as that in the Bronx; or focus on how Parisian HLM has been portrayed in modern popular culture, art, and/or literature.

Learning Styles

Kinesthetic Learners

For **Activité 22**, consider transforming your class or the school library into a museum (if time and resources allow), and have students share their presentations in front of other classes.

Resources

Create

Answers

All activities will vary.

Reference Desk

If you have access to Passport, assign your students an IPA task related to the unit.

Game

Jeopardy!

Create a *Jeopardy!* board by making a table with six columns across and five rows down. On the far left column write point values. Across the top, choose categories from the chapter: **Vocabulaire**, **Grammaire**, **Francophonie**, **Culture**, etc. Write five questions for each category. Divide students in groups of four or five to play.

Finale

Projets finaux

A Connexions par Internet : l'anthropologie 1.2, 1.3, 3.1, 3.2

Les Berbères

L'anthropologie culturelle est l'étude des variations culturelles entre les hommes et les sociétés humaines grâce à la collecte de données concernant l'impact des processus économiques et politiques mondiaux sur les réalités culturelles locales. Les anthropologues utilisent différentes méthodes : observations, interviews, et enquêtes. Faites des recherches sur les Berbères. Imaginez que vous êtes au Maghreb et que vous étudiez les Berbères. Préparez un sondage pour mieux connaître ces gens. Quelles réponses anticipez-vous après vos recherches ?

Les Berbères sont les descendants des premiers habitants d'Afrique du Nord.

B Communautés en ligne 1.3, 3.1, 3.2, 5.1

L'Alliance française

Trouvez l'Alliance française la plus proche de chez vous et choisissez un cours auquel vous pouvez vous inscrire ou un événement culturel auquel vous voudriez assister. Expliquez à votre partenaire pourquoi ce cours ou cet événement culturel vous intéresse.

C Passez à l'action ! 1.3, 3.1, 3.2, 5.1, 5.2

Un conte de fées

Avec deux ou trois camarades de classe, préparez des scènes pour un conte de fées de Charles Perrault ou un conte maghrébin. Décidez qui va introduire le conte, qui va être le narrateur/la narratrice, qui va jouer les rôles des personnages, qui va préparer le décor, et qui va écrire les invitations.

Essential Instruction

1. Conduct a guided review of the unit using the chart **Faisons le point !**
2. For each entry on the left, have students find the answers in the unit.
3. Lead an expanded discussion of the questions. Assign a class participation point every time a student contributes to the conversation.
4. For **Évaluation de compréhension auditive,** have students write down the answer. Replay each sentence for students who missed the correct answer.
5. Give students a few minutes to prepare before they do the dialogue for **Évaluation orale**. They can flip a coin to see who plays the American and who plays the immigrant. You may also give students a sheet that lists expectations you have regarding their conversation (length, vocabulary control, grammar accuracy, etc.).

D Faisons le point! 1.3, 2.1, 2.2, 3.1, 4.2

Diagramme

Faites un diagramme comme celui-ci et remplissez-le pour montrer vos connaissances concernant la question suivante: Comment les communautés francophones conservent-elles leurs traditions? Un exemple vous est donné.

Leçon A **Unit Opener** Selon Bourguiba, quels sont les avantages du français? →	Le français constitue l'appoint au patrimoine culturel; il enrichit la pensée, exprime l'action, contribue à forger le destin intellectuel….
Leçon A **Rencontres culturelles** Comment le père de Justin se met-il en contact avec la vie de ses ancêtres? →	
Leçon A **Points de départ** Avec quelle organisation les Français assurent-ils le rayonnement de leur langue et culture? →	
Leçon A **Points de départ: Produits** Quelle langue et quel héritage intéressent les gens de la Nouvelle-Angleterre? →	
Leçon A **Points de départ: Perspectives** Comment cet Américain avec un héritage québécois se met-il en contact avec la langue de ses aïeux? →	
Leçon A **Du côté des médias** Quels bâtiments touristiques permettent de conserver l'héritage de l'Île d'Orléans? →	
Leçon B **Rencontres culturelles** Quelle histoire de leurs pays ancestral Karim partage-t-il avec sa soeur? →	
Leçon B **Points de départ: L'immigration maghrébine en France** Qu'est-ce que les immigrés maghrébins apportent en France de leurs pays d'origine? Comment restent-ils en contact avec leur culture? →	
Leçon C **Points de départ: Le Sénégal** Imagine qu'Amadou est un jeune immigré sénégalais en France. Quels musiciens écoute-t-il probablement? →	

Answers

D

Leçon A: Rencontres culturelles: Il fait des recherches sur Internet.
Points de départ: avec l'Alliance française
Produits: la langue française et leurs ancêtres québécois
Perspectives: Il utilisent des ressources en ligne.
Du côté des médias: l'espace Félix Leclerc, le restaurant Cassis Monna & filles, le Nouveau théâtre de l'Île d'Orléans, la cidrerie Domaine Steinbach
Leçon B: Rencontres culturelles: Karim lit *L'élève du magicien* à sa sœur.
Points de départ: Les maghrébins immigrés en France créent des commerces qui permettent aux Français de profiter d'objets artisanaux et de la cuisine du Maghreb.
Leçon C: Points de départ: Il écoute peut-être Youssou N'Dour, Baaba Maal, Viviane Ndour, Ismael Lô, et Omar Pène.

Reference Desk

The **Faisons le point!** section asks students to respond to the essential question by analyzing various texts in each lesson. The graphic organizer for **Activité D** may be expanded by using the complete chart found in the Copy Masters supplement.

Differentiated Learning

Accelerate

For **Passez à l'action!**, students will do the project as indicated, or your more adventurous students may be given random words by the class, approved by the teacher, that they must integrate into their fairy tale.

Decelerate

Meet with low-ability students to describe what is involved in project **A** and **B**. Help students decide what to select, and make a plan of action. They will need to see an example of what the final project should look like. For **C**, find time to help them brainstorm their fairy tale, assign roles, and write the story. The more guidance they receive, the more successful they will become. These fairy tales can be done with the help of online programs.

Recherche: show me, launchpadtoys/toontastic, puppet-pals

Resources

- Activity A
- LA Listening Activity *Synthèse*
- Pre-AP Listening *Unité 3*
- Perform

Answers

A Script

Amina : Qu'est-ce que tu fais ?
Ahmed : Bon, j'écris un conte de fées moderne pour mon cours de français.
Amina : Moderne comment ?
Ahmed : Eh bien, il y a un garçon. Il s'appelle David. Il habite dans une cité HLM. La cité est sale est il y a plein de graffiti sur les murs.
Amina : Et qu'est-ce qui se passe ensuite ?
Ahmed : Eh bien, David a un arrière-grand-père africain qui est magicien. Cet ancêtre a donné un marteau magique au père de David. Tu devines ce que David va faire avec le marteau ?
Amina : Il va enfoncer un clou, bricoler dans sa chambre….
Ahmed : Mais non, utilise ton imagination ! Avec le marteau, David va réparer la cité. Les HLM vont devenir de belles maisons mitoyennes. Chaque locataire aura un beau petit jardin. Tout va être propre ! Plus de graffiti sur les murs, plus de passants méchants. Ce sera le quartier le plus beau de la ville.
Amina : Et comment va-t-il réussir ?
Ahmed : Eh bien, il va frapper trois fois le marteau sur sa porte et dire ce qu'il veut avant d'aller se coucher. Le lendemain, quand il va se réveiller, la cité sera transformée.
Amina : C'est un conte moderne formidable. Bravo, Ahmed !

1. F; 2. F; 3. F; 4. V; 5. F; 6. V; 7. F

B Conversations will vary.

Reference Desk

If you have access to Passport, assign a task to evaluate your student's oral proficiency.

Pre-AP

Évaluation

A Évaluation de compréhension auditive 1.2

Écoutez la conversation entre Amina et Ahmed, qui décrit un conte de fées. Ensuite, indiquez si les phrases sont vraies (V) ou fausses (F).

1. Amina lit un conte contemporain.
2. Le héros du conte s'appelle Jean et habite dans une belle villa.
3. La cité où le héros habite est très propre.
4. L'arrière-grand-père africain du héros est magicien.
5. L'ancêtre a donné un couteau magique au père de David.
6. La cité sera belle et propre.
7. Sa sœur pense que le conte d'Ahmed est bête.

B Évaluation orale 1.1, 5.2

Avec un partenaire, jouez les rôles d'un(e) immigré(e) et d'un(e) Américain(e) qui se sont inscrit(e)s dans un cours de français à l'Alliance française à New York. Dans votre conversation :

- L'Américain(e) se présente et demande de faire sa connaissance.
- L'immigré(e) donne son nom à l'Américain(e).
- L'Américain(e) demande à l'immigré(e) où il ou elle a grandi (pas l'Amérique).
- L'immigré(e) dit dans quel pays il ou elle a grandi.
- L'Américain(e) demande où la famille de l'immigré(e) s'est installée.
- L'immigré(e) répond.
- L'Américain(e) demande si toute la famille de l'immigré(e) est venue en Amérique.
- L'immigré(e) dit lesquels de ses parents sont venus en Amérique et lesquels sont restés dans son pays d'origine.

Essential Instruction

1. Number cards from 1 to 7, enough for every member in the class.
2. Students will draw a card that will indicate which topic they will work on in **Évaluation culturelle**.
3. Organize the students into groups according to their randomly chosen topic.
4. Provide a rubric and a list of vocabulary and structures to include.
5. Have them identify pages in their book and sources online that will help them complete their evaluation. They should include a visual when they present their topic to the class.
6. For **Évaluation écrite** insist that the students take 10–15 minutes to brainstorm and outline their essay before starting to write.
7. Provide a storyboard to each student in which they will draw a cartoon-story, one event for each box. This will be the writing prompt for the **Évaluation compréhensive**.

C Évaluation culturelle 1.3, 2.1, 3.1, 3.2, 4.2, 5.1, 5.2

Vous allez comparer les cultures francophones à votre culture aux États-Unis. Vous aurez peut-être besoin de faire des recherches sur la culture américaine.

1. **L'Alliance française**
   Expliquez ce que l'Alliance française offre en général. S'il y a une Alliance française dans votre région, présentez son programme et dites de quelles activités ou cours vous profiteriez.
2. **L'immigration**
   Faites un résumé des vagues migratoires de la France vers le Québec et du Québec vers les États-Unis. Existe-t-il une présence francophone dans votre région? Si oui, qu'est-ce que vous pouvez remarquer? Quelles traces sont toujours visibles?
3. **La Tunisie**
   Comparez la Tunisie aux autres pays du Maghreb. On y parle quelles langues? C'est une ancienne (*former*) colonie de quel pays? La Tunisie est-elle plus ou moins libérale que le Maroc et l'Algérie? De quelles façons? Et comment compareriez-vous les États-Unis par rapport à ses voisins, le Canada et le Mexique?
4. **Les étudiants maghrébins**
   Des étudiants venant étudier en France, combien sont originaires du Maghreb? D'où viennent les étudiants étrangers qui étudient dans les universités américaines?
5. **Les subventions du gouvernement**
   De quelles aides pouvez-vous bénéficier en France pour le logement et pour élever vos enfants? Quelles aides existent aux États-Unis?
6. **Les contes maghrébins**
   Qu'est-ce qui est universel dans les contes pour enfants que vous connaissez? Quels aspects des contes maghrébins sont uniques?
7. **Le logement traditionnel au Sénégal**
   Comparez le logement traditionnel au Sénégal avec les logements traditionnels aux États-Unis, par exemple, ceux des Amérindiens.

D Évaluation écrite 1.3, 3.1

*Votre famille vient de déménager. Vous avez acheté une maison en ligne et vous trouvez qu'il y a beaucoup de choses à faire. Écrivez à vos grands-parents québécois. Expliquez les problèmes qu'il y a avec la maison et qui fait quoi pour la rénover (*renovate*).*

Cet homme reconstruit les murs de sa maison.

Answers

All activities will vary.

Reference Desk

Any of the **Évaluation** activities can be used as an assessment tool. Include additional visual prompts similar to those in **Activité E**, which are particularly helpful for students with difficulty processing language.

Communication

Interpersonal: Cooperative Groups

Have students in small groups sit in a circle. Each student spends one minute writing down information he or she remembers from the chapter according to a topic you call out. Call time and have the paper passed to the student on the right. The next student reviews and edits what is written, if necessary, and adds more ideas. After ideas have been exhausted, call time and have students review in their groups. Students then verify the information from the book.

Game

Les Frères Parker

Create a template for a game board that you can use for each chapter. Have one die per board and enough game pieces for each student. You will want to have 20–30 spaces. Write questions from the unit on cards, and put the cards face down in a pile in the middle of the board. Students will roll the die, move their game piece the number of spaces corresponding to the die, and answer a question from the pile. Students may refer to their books if necessary.

Special Needs Students

Linguistically Challenged
Students will need more help preparing for their dialogues. Help them be less self-conscious presenting the dialogue to the class by giving them an opportunity to rehearse it with their partner ahead of time.

AD(H)D
Students will need help organizing their review of the **Unité**. Encourage them to use their flash cards to practice vocabulary, review their exercises and activities, and meet with you to answer any outstanding questions.

Answers

E

Ma tante et mes cousins se sont installés en Californie.
Mon oncle s'est installé dans le Missouri.
Mes grands-parents se sont installés en Virginie-Occidentale.
Mes parents et moi, nous nous sommes installés en Floride.

F Answers will vary.

Game

Les prépositions

To review the prepositions associated with American states, and prepare students to complete **Évaluation visuelle**, ask them to stand up on their chairs. Call out a state, for example, *Minnesota*. Point to a student randomly. He or she should state the correct preposition associated with it, in this case, **dans le Minnesota**. If the student is correct, he or she will remain standing. If incorrect, he or she will be asked to sit down. Play the game until there is only one student left, or a certain amount of time has passed. For a variation, you may divide the class in two or three groups, and assign one student to call out names of states.

E **Évaluation visuelle** 1.2, 1.3, 3.1, 4.1

Votre famille vient d'immigrer aux États-Unis. Dites où tous les membres de votre famille se sont installés.

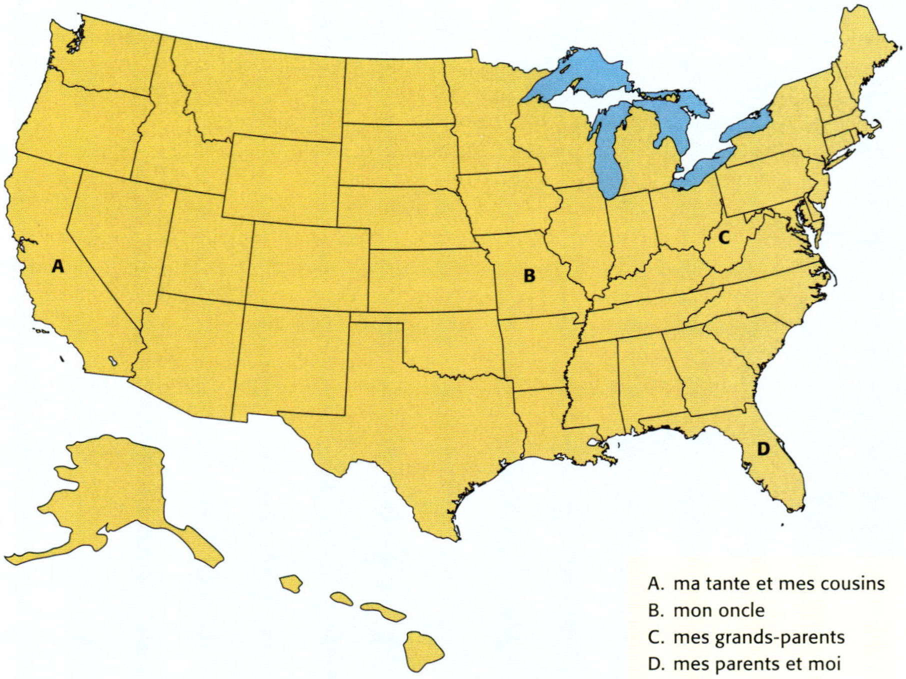

A. ma tante et mes cousins
B. mon oncle
C. mes grands-parents
D. mes parents et moi

F **Évaluation compréhensive** 1.3, 2.2

*Créez une histoire avec six illustrations : dessinez une HLM ou autre résidence et montrez ce qui se passe (*happens*) entre les locataires. Montrez votre histoire à vos camarades de classe ou publiez-la en ligne.*

Essential Instruction

The alphabetical listing of vocabulary words is an excellent reference for students, but it may not be the best way for them to learn. Encourage them to group the words into similar topics to support their learning. Encourage them also to create a sentence, whether orally or in writing, using each vocabulary word correctly.

Vocabulaire de l'Unité 3

accrocher (des tableaux) to hang (paintings) *C*
un **aïeul, une aïeule (les aïeux)** ancestor(s) *A*
un(e) **ancêtre** ancestor *A*
ancien(ne) old *C*
l' **arrière-grand-mère (f.)** great-grandmother *A*
l' **arrière-grand-père (m.)** great-grandfather *A*
une **ballade** ballad *B*
le **bricolage** do-it-yourself repairs *C*
bricoler to do DIY projects *C*
ça: ça suffit that's enough *B*
cela it *C*
un **cercle** circle, group *A*
cirer le parquet to polish hardwood flooring *C*
une **cité** housing community *C*
un **clou** nail *C*
conseiller to recommend *B*
une **conserverie** canning company *A*
un **conte de fées** fairy tale *B*
le **cousin germain, la cousine germaine** first cousin *A*
déjouer to defeat, thwart *B*
éloigné(e) distant, extended *A*
un(e) **employé(e)** employee *C*
enfoncer to push, hammer *C*
être: être d'origine (+ ADJECTIVE) to come from (+ COUNTRY) *C*
une **fable** fable *B*
se **faire: se faire disputer (par)** to get in trouble (with) *B*
finalement in the end *C*
une **fois: Il était une fois....** Once upon a time (there was).... *B*
la **Francophonie** French-speaking world *A*
garder: garder le contact to keep in touch *A*; **garder un enfant** to babysit *B*
une **génération** generation *A*
un **graffiti, des graffiti** graffiti *C*
grand(e): la grande crise Great Depression *A*
grandir to grow up *C*
le **grand-oncle** great uncle *A*
la **grand-tante** great aunt *A*
une **histoire** story *B*
une **HLM (des HLM)** subsidized housing *C*
jouer: jouer un tour to play a trick *B*
juste just *C*
justement fittingly *C*
un(e) **locataire** tenant *C*
le **logement** housing *C*
un(e) **magicien(ne)** magician *B*
une **maison: maison individuelle** single-family house *C*; **maison mitoyenne** row house *C*
un **maître, une maîtresse** tutor; primary school teacher *B*
une **manière** way *A*
un **marteau** hammer *C*
la **mécanique** mechanics *A*
se **méfier (de)** to be wary (of) *B*
même: même que even though *[inform.]* *B*
la **moquette** carpeting *C*
un **mur** wall *C*
un(e) **passant(e)** passerby *C*
un **pêcheur, une pêcheuse** fisherman, fisherwoman *A*
peindre to paint *C*
pendant: pendant que while *B*
poser le papier peint to put up wallpaper *C*
un **professionnel, une professionnelle** professional *C*
propre clean *C*
rapidement quickly *C*
la **recherche: des recherches généalogiques** genealogical research *A*
repeindre to repaint *C*
une **résidence secondaire** second home *C*
rusé(e) cunning *B*
sale dirty *C*
un **studio** studio apartment *C*
la **suite** (the) rest *B*
tenir: tenir un restaurant to own a restaurant *A*
tenter: tenter sa chance to try one's luck *A*
touristique touristy *A*
un **tournevis** screwdriver *C*
très: Très heureux/heureuse. Pleased to meet you. *C*
une **villa** villa *C*
une **vis** screw *C*

Resources

FC Flash Cards
Rendez-vous à Nice ! Documentaire 2
T *Unité 3* Test

Reference Desk

1. There is a high correlation between retaining information and getting enough sleep. We often encourage students to get enough sleep before an exam, but it would serve them well to get enough rest every night to increase their productivity and memory retention. Discuss this issue and other wellness practices with your students.
2. The photo on this page represents the coast of **Rocher Percé** in the Gaspé Peninsula, Quebec.

nouvelle orthographe **des graffitis, un maitre, une maitresse**

Learning Styles

Kinesthetic Learners
Create flash cards with information lines on the topics seen in the unit mentioned in **Évaluation culturelle**, 1–7. Have your kinesthetic learners sort these cards correctly under the appropriate categories. This will help them see what topics they know, and what still needs to be studied.

Auditory Learners
Before preparing the activities, these students should discuss with a partner what each topic is about, what vocabulary words they can associate with it, and what cultural information they remember from their research or in-class participation.

Reference Desk

1. In **Unité 4**, **Préparatifs de départ**, students learn about winter vacations in the Alpine regions of France and in tropical **La Réunion**. We learn that four out of ten French people take off to a destination for winter break, so let's join them!
2. The accompanying quotation tells us that to really love a country we must savor its food, drink, and song. To set the tone, in the opening photos we see the Alps and a celebration of **Carnaval** in Annecy.
3. The photo on this unit opener is of air balloons over a small village in the Swiss Alps.

Unité

4 Préparatifs de départ

Essential Instruction

1. Looking at a map of France, ask students to guess where one would go skiing for winter break.
2. Find in the unit where the opening photo of **Carnaval** was taken. What is the equivalent of **Carnaval** in the United States?
3. Students will review the **Contrat de l'élève** to gain an overview of what they will learn in **Unité 4**.

Question centrale

Qu'est-ce qu'on doit connaître de sa destination pour réussir son voyage ?

À savoir

Quatre Français sur dix partent en vacances d'hiver.

Citation

« Pour bien aimer un pays il faut le manger, le boire et l'entendre chanter. »

To really like a country, you must eat it, drink it, and hear it sing.

—Michel Déon (1919–2016), écrivain, dramaturge, et académicien français

Conseil pratique

When visiting a French website, make a list of words and expressions you have learned there. Then compare your list with a partner who has visited the same site.

Que dit Clémentine de son caractère ? Elle est comment ?

Dans quelle ville fête-on ce carnaval ?

Contrat de l'élève

Leçon A I will be able to:

- ask for an opinion and respond appropriately.
- discuss **La Réunion**, **la Corse**, **Chamonix**, **le Mont Blanc**, and **les Alpes**.
- use the present participle and negative expressions.

Leçon B I will be able to:

- say what I must do, tell someone they'll have an opportunity to do something, and say what I was expecting.
- discuss the **Savoie** region of France, **les classes de neige**, **Annecy**, and **Saint-Martin**.
- review **savoir** and **connaître** and use the subjunctive of regular and irregular verbs after **il faut que**.

Leçon C I will be able to:

- say I'm going to do a different activity and tell someone to avoid injury.
- discuss ski resorts in France and volunteer tourism in Francophone countries.
- use the subjunctive after impersonal expressions.

Answers

Possible choices for the video question:
A. sérieuse et aimable
B. dynamique et souriante
C. sympa et travailleuse
D. énergique et diligente
Correct Answer: B

The answer to the culture question is: **à Annecy**. The answer can be found in **Points de départ**, **Leçon B**.

Reference Desk

1. The charming city of Annecy is a popular year-round tourist destination. It is known as "The Venice of France" because of the Thiou canal running through **la vieille ville**. Visitors can take a cruise on **Le Lac d'Annecy**, rent a paddleboat or canoe, or run, bike, or walk along the lake's paved paths.
2. Annecy is well-known for its annual **Festival international du film d'animation**. It is also one of France's hot spots for paragliding (**le parapente**).

Special Needs Students

AD(H)D

As you begin the unit, check to make sure that students have their notebooks and other items they will need for class. Help them organize their notebooks, designating specific pages for the new vocabulary, structure, and culture of the unit.

Resources

- *Vocabulaire actif*
- eV eVisual
- WB Workbook 1–4
- FC Flash Cards
- LA Listening Activity 1
- G & V Practice Games

Reference Desk

1. Expressions with **faire** were introduced in Level 1, **Unité 8** p. 402 and revisited in Level 2, **Unité 1** p. 46.
2. Ask students if they know the differences among **le parachutisme ascensionnel** (*parachuting/parasailing*), **le deltaplane** (**hang gliding**), and **le parapente** (*paragliding*), which they have seen previously. **Le parachutisme ascensionnel** uses a large round sail that allows a person to free-fly; the sail slows down the flight and the passenger may be towed by a vehicle in the water. **Deltaplane**, on the other hand, uses a smaller, triangular sail, and **parapente** a longer and narrower sail.
3. Ask students the difference between **randonnée équestre** (by horse, also called **faire du cheval**) and **randonnée pédestre** (by foot).

Culture

Winter sports represent a significant cultural and athletic practice in France. There are more than 60 ski resorts with more than 20,000 km (12.5 mi) of ski slopes, nearly all of them located in the Alps and Pyrenees. Schools frequently take extended winter field trips in which students and teachers study together in the mornings and ski together in the afternoons over a period of one week or more. The French school calendar plans a "Ski Week" (**semaine de ski**) in February (**les vacances de février**). During the Easter or Spring one-week vacation (**les vacances de printemps**), the French often practice "**le ski de printemps**."

Leçon A Vocabulaire actif

Les activités en plein air 1.2, 5.1

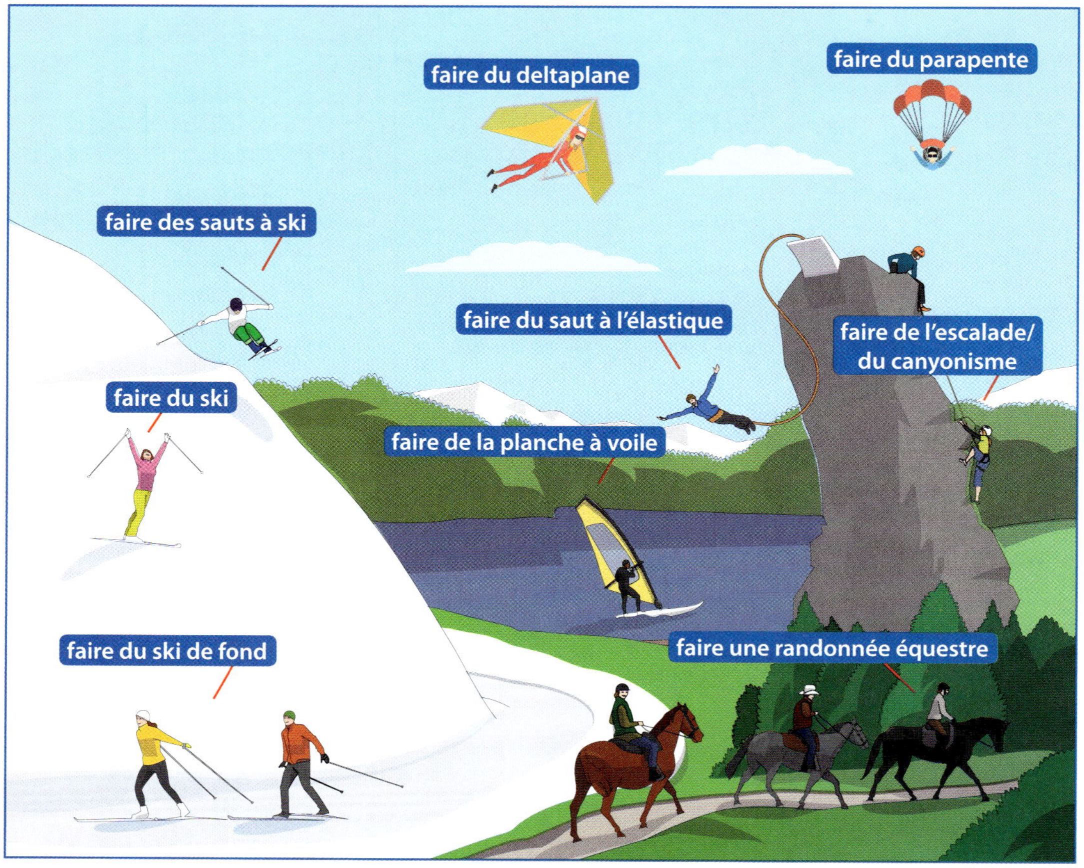

Essential Instruction

1. Have students illustrate the vocabulary in their notebooks for **Les activités en plein air**, **Pour la conversation**, and **Et si je voulais dire…?**
2. Play **Pour la conversation** and **Et si je voulais dire…?** three times before asking the students to repeat. By delaying oral production, students have time to internalize the sounds, thereby reinforcing their French accent and minimizing the interference of their native language.
3. Brainstorm other **faire** expressions used to describe sports in order to jog students' memories. Utilize choral repetition of **faire** in **présent** and **passé composé**.
4. For **Activité 1,** read Florence's letter to the students and ask the comprehension questions 1–5. Students should have their books closed but may take notes on what they hear.
5. Reread the letter, this time with students following in their books. Discuss any questions that pose problems.

Pour la conversation 1.2

How do I ask someone's opinion?

» Chamonix **te dit**?

How do you feel about Chamonix?

How do I react positively to someone's opinion?

» **Sans aucun doute.**

Without a doubt.

» Je suis **persuadé(e)** que….

I'm convinced that….

How do I react negatively to someone's opinion?

» Je vois les choses un peu **différemment**.

I see things a little differently.

Et si je voulais dire… ?

aller à la chasse	*to go hunting*
se balader	*to go walking*
faire du surf	*to surf*
faire du rafting	*to go whitewater rafting*
faire du VTT	*to go mountain biking*
faire du kite surf	*to go kite surfing*

1 Ah, le plein air! 1.2, 5.1

Interpretive Reading

Lisez le mail que Florence envoie à sa copine. Puis, répondez aux questions.

À: Emma
Cc:
Objet: Il faut que tu viennes ici!

Salut, Emma!

Nous (ma tante, mon oncle, ma cousine et moi) sommes à Chamonix, et comme c'est chouette le plein air! Je suis persuadée que les Alpes, c'est le plus bel endroit du monde. Bien sûr que j'ai fait une randonnée équestre et que j'ai fait des sauts à ski, mais j'ai aussi essayé deux activités pour la première fois. On a dit: «Tu aimes l'aventure, n'est-ce pas?» et moi j'ai répondu: «Mais oui! Sans aucun doute.» Hier j'ai fait de l'escalade, et puis ce matin j'ai fait du saut à l'élastique, et ça, c'est la meilleure activité de toutes! Alors, Chamonix te dit pour les prochaines vacances?

Bises,
Florence

1. Avec qui voyage Florence?
2. Quel est le plus joli endroit selon Florence?
3. Quelles activités est-ce que Florence a faites avant d'essayer quelque chose de nouveau?
4. Quelle nouvelle activité est-ce que Florence préfère?
5. Qu'est-ce que Florence propose à Emma?

Resources

Pour la conversation
Et si je voulais dire… ?
Activity 1

Answers

1

1. Elle voyage avec sa tante, son oncle, et sa cousine.
2. les Alpes
3. Elle a fait une randonnée équestre et des sauts à ski.
4. Elle préfère le saut à l'élastique.
5. Elle lui propose d'aller à Chamonix avec elle pour les prochaines vacances.

Expansion

Students work in small groups. Each group receives a set of three to four pictures of people, items, and pastimes based on winter sports and activities with which they are familiar. Instruct students to create a story based on the pictures. Call upon each group to present the story collectively with each successive student repeating the previous sentence(s) before adding the next sentence of the story. If you are teaching during the months (or year) preceding or following the actual Winter Olympics, students may want to link their stories to French athletes who qualified for or participated in the Winter Games.

Differentiated Learning

Accelerate

Students write a response to Florence's letter in which they propose a winter ski vacation for the following year. They must say where they would like to go and what activities they would like to do. Encourage them to elaborate by adding details and reasons for their choices.

Decelerate

Students will research the village of **Chamonix** as a potential winter vacation site. They will write in French the activities they would like to do.

Learning Styles

Kinesthetic Learners

Have students give mini-lessons on how to ski jump, ride a horse, mountain climb, paraglide or hang glide, or bungee jump. They should act like a sports instructor and the class should "practice" with gestures.

Answers

2

1. Fais-tu du parapente?
2. Fais-tu des sauts à ski?
3. Fais-tu de la plongée sous-marine?
4. Fais-tu de l'escalade/du canyonisme?
5. Fais-tu des randonnées équestres?
6. Fais-tu du saut à l'élastique?
7. Fais-tu du ski nautique?
8. Fais-tu du ski de fond?

Partner answers will vary.

Reference Desk

1. Before doing **Activité 2**, provide students with additional review and practice of the **passé composé** of **faire** with negatives. Choral repetition of the negative response will help set the pattern: "**Je n'ai jamais fait de**…" Remind students that the negative expression uses **de** or **d'**.
2. Before having students do the **Connexions** activity, consider reviewing the geographical and cultural characteristics of this region (climate, sports, activities), learned previously in Unit 8 of Level 2.

Communication

Interpersonal: Paired Practice

Pair students to complete **Activité 2**. Students expand their answers by adding an extension using **parque que**, **quand**, **avec**, and/or a place. For example, "**J'ai fait de la planche à voile *quand j'étais dans le Colorado avec mes amis.***" Put these words on the board as a reminder.

TPR

Help students internalize the vocabulary for **Activité 2** by having the class come up with gestures for each of the activities pictured. Then check for comprehension by shouting out commands (**"Faites du parapente!"**) and watching students complete the gesture.

2 Les activités en plein air 1.1, 5.1

Interpersonal Speaking or Writing

À tour de rôle, demandez à votre partenaire s'il ou elle fait l'activité sur la photo. Votre partenaire va répondre en suivant le modèle.

MODÈLE

A: Fais-tu de la planche à voile?
B: J'ai fait de la planche à voile une fois.
ou
Je n'ai jamais fait de planche à voile.
ou
Je fais souvent de la planche à voile.

1. 
2. 
3. 
4. 
5. 
6. 
7. 
8. 

Connexions 1.2, 3.2

Géographie

Pensez à ce que vous avez appris de **la Guadeloupe**, et, avec un partenaire, planifiez trois activités sportives à faire pendant un weekend en Guadeloupe.

Essential Instruction

1. As a bell-ringer activity, create some **devinettes** based on the vocabulary. For example, **C'est une excursion où on monte à cheval**. Put the **devinettes** on cards with answers and let students read them to the class.
2. Review the future forms of **faire**, and then do **Activité 3** with the class as a whole. After each response, ask more questions to keep the students speaking.
3. Have students read questions 1–5 silently before doing **Activité 4**. Replay any statements that the students do not understand.
4. For **Activité 5**, have students write their answers to the questions. When finished writing, everyone circulates to ask and answer questions as if at a "mocktail" party. Students could record the answers of five different classmates, and then report back to the class.

3 Précisez ! 1.3, 3.1

Presentational Speaking

Dites ce que les personnes indiquées feront pendant les vacances selon les indications. Choisissez une expression ci-dessous.

du parapente **du jet ski** **des randonnées équestres**
de la planche à voile **de l'escalade** **des sauts à ski** **du kayak**

MODÈLE Mathis et Cédric passent beaucoup de temps à la plage.
Pendant les vacances, ils feront de la planche à voile.

1. Awa aime passer du temps à la campagne avec son cheval.
2. Marc et moi, nous emmenons nos scooters de mer.
3. Nasser aime faire du ski alpin.
4. Gabrielle et Bruno aiment monter sur des rochers (*rocks*).
5. Abdoulaye aime voler (*fly*) comme un oiseau.
6. Tu aimes ton petit kayak vert.

4 La Réunion, je kiffe ! 1.2

Interpretive Listening

*Écrivez les numéros 1–5 sur votre papier. Écoutez Stéphane décrire sa vie à La Réunion. Écrivez **V** si la phrase que vous lisez est vraie et **F** si elle est fausse.*

1. Stéphane fait des sports d'hiver à La Réunion.
2. Il fait de la planche à voile avec des copains.
3. La randonnée équestre est une activité qu'il fait avec sa classe.
4. Stéphane ne sait pas faire de l'escalade.
5. Stéphane aime faire du saut à l'élastique le weekend.

5 Questions personnelles 1.1, 5.1

Interpersonal Speaking

Répondez aux questions avec un partenaire.

1. Préfères-tu les activités en plein air ou les activités à l'intérieur ?
2. Qu'est-ce que tu aimes faire en été ? en hiver ? en automne ? au printemps ?
3. Un voyage à la montagne te dit ? Pourquoi, ou pourquoi pas ?
4. Quelles activités en plein air as-tu déjà essayées ? Lesquelles est-ce que tu ne voudrais pas essayer ?
5. Comment est-ce que tes choix sont différents de ceux de tes amis ?

Multiple Intelligences

Naturalist
The theme of mountains and an island will appeal to students who are interested in the world and the environment.

Visual-Spatial
Encourage these students to make a poster of a map of France and **La Réunion** with symbols of the winter and summer sports that are offered there.

Special Needs Students

Social Anxiety
There will be some students who, due to their economic situation, will have never been on vacation, let alone been skiing or to an island. Encourage all students to use their imaginations to think about trips or vacations they may want to take in the future.

Resources

Activity 4

Answers

3
1. Pendant les vacances, elle fera des randonnées équestres.
2. Pendant les vacances, nous ferons du jet ski.
3. Pendant les vacances, il fera des sauts à ski.
4. Pendant les vacances, ils feront de l'escalade.
5. Pendant les vacances, il fera du parapente.
6. Pendant les vacances, tu feras du kayak.

4 Script
Mes parents et moi habitons à La Réunion depuis trois mois. Il y a beaucoup de choses à faire ici. Je parle des activités en plein air. Le lundi après les cours, je fais de la planche à voile avec des copains. Le mardi matin, je fais de la randonnée équestre avec mon école. C'est génial, on découvre beaucoup de paysages superbes.
Le mercredi après-midi, je fais de l'escalade et du parapente en descente.
Le weekend, j'aime sauter à l'élastique.
Quelles activités en plein air est-ce que vous aimez faire ?

1. F; 2. V; 3. V; 4. F; 5. V

5 Answers will vary.

Expansion

Students adopt **une station de ski** in France or in Quebec and track the weather conditions on the slopes for **le ski alpin** and **le ski du fond** for one week. They create a graph showing the snowfall in both inches and centimeters, and temperatures in both Fahrenheit and Celsius.

Game

Vive le sport !
Do this fast-paced game to practice vocabulary. Distribute a set of five to six vocabulary flash cards to each student featuring winter sports vocabulary as well as sports that they have learned in the past. At your signal have them play charades, acting out each sport for a partner. Call time after one minute. The partners with the most correct guesses win the game.

Resources

- Dialogue Activity 6
- Dialogue Video
- WB Workbook 5

Answers

6

1. La Réunion
2. Chamonix et La Réunion
3. Chamonix
4. Chamonix et La Réunion
5. La Réunion

Analyse

Élodie and her mother hint about the weather and the geography of **La Réunion** ("**un sommet… plus chaud… plus près de la mer**"), without naming the place. Léo does not figure it out, but his father does, perhaps because he knows his wife well, or he has already traveled there.

Reference Desk

1. **La Réunion** is a French island and department located in the Indian Ocean, east of Madagascar. It has a population of approximately 800,000.
2. **Piton de la Fournaise** (*Peak of the Furnace*) is an active volcano located on the eastern side of **La Réunion**. Residents refer to it as **le Volcan**, and it is currently one of the most active volcanoes in the world, erupting most recently in July 2017.
3. **"Tout schuss,"** an expression used by Léo in the second line of the dialogue, originates from the German word **Schussfahrt**, and means, *going quickly and directly down a slope*.

nouvelle orthographe **une ile**

Critical Thinking

Analysis

What kinds of volcanoes are there? Why are some volcanoes extinct, some dormant, and some active? Are there any volcanoes in the United States? If so, what kind of volcanoes are they?

Rencontres culturelles

Les prochaines vacances

1.2, 2.1

Élodie, Léo, et leurs parents planifient un voyage.

Père : Alors, Léo, Chamonix te dit ?
Léo : Sans aucun doute… ça me tente de passer des vacances tout schuss*….
Mère : Bon, eh bien, nous avec Élodie, on voit les choses un peu différemment….
Élodie : Autrement dit, oui, au sommet, mais pas dans les Alpes.
Mère : On aimerait moins froid, plus humide, et plus chaud.
Élodie : Et plus près de la mer….
Léo : Alors pas Chamonix, mais plutôt les Alpes du Sud : le ski avec vue sur la mer ?
Père : Mais non, tu n'y es pas du tout ! Ce n'est pas ça qu'elles veulent ! Moi, j'ai trouvé : c'est une île avec un volcan et du soleil, n'est-ce pas ?
Mère : En y réfléchissant bien, ça pourrait être ça.
Élodie : Oui, en y regardant de plus près, ça doit être ça.
Léo : Ah, d'accord ! Elles veulent nous faire le coup de La Réunion ! Qu'est-ce qu'on peut y faire ?
Élodie : On peut nager, faire des randonnées équestres, visiter le Piton de la Fournaise… aucun de nous ne s'ennuiera.
Léo : Je suis persuadé qu'on s'amusera. Alors, on part quand ?

Analyse

What hints do Élodie and her mother give to suggest a vacation destination to Léo and his dad? Who understands and who does not? Try to infer why.

***Je parle bien !**

L'expression **tout schuss** vient de l'allemand et rime avec **couscous** ; prononcez **tou-chousse**.

6 Les prochaines vacances

1.2

Identifiez l'endroit dont on parle : Chamonix, La Réunion, ou les deux.

1. Il y a de belles plages.
2. On y voit des montagnes.
3. On peut y faire du ski alpin.
4. Il y fait chaud et du soleil.
5. On peut y faire des randonnées équestres.

Essential Instruction

1. As a bell-ringer, put **au bord de la mer** and **dans les montagnes** on the board. Have students brainstorm activities that can be done in each place.
2. Have students skim the questions in **Activité 6** before listening with books closed. Then have them answer the questions.
3. Explain that **En y réfléchissant** means *(While) thinking it over…* The –**ant** ending is –*ing* in English. **Parlant** = *speaking*, **finissant** = *finishing*. This foreshadows the lesson on p. 212.
4. Before playing **Extension**, ask students to imagine differences of opinion that families might have when planning a vacation.
5. Play **Extension**. Put two columns on the board, **Client** and **Cliente**. Have the students cite from the text the conflicting points of view of the two travelers.

EXTENSION **À l'agence de voyages** 1.2

Dans une agence de voyages, une agente essaie d'aider un jeune couple.

Agente : Reprenons depuis le début. Vous êtes sûr que vous voulez partir ensemble ?
Client : Sans aucun doute !
Agente : Bon, alors, il va falloir vous mettre d'accord.
Client : On est vraiment désolé, mais moi, je préfère la mer, et elle, la montagne.
Agente : Proche ou loin ?
Cliente : Plutôt loin.
Client : Mais pas trop loin....
Agente : Les Antilles vous disent ?
Les clients : Oui !
Agente : Seuls ? Je veux dire... dire... vous deux, ou en groupe ?
Cliente : On pourrait essayer en groupe.
Client : Il me semble que ça serait mieux juste nous deux.
Agente : Ah non, vous n'allez pas recommencer !

EXTENSION 1.3

Pourquoi est-ce que la région proposée par l'agente marche pour le client et la cliente ? Pourquoi est-ce que l'agente est frustrée avec ce couple ?

Resources

Extension

Answers

EXTENSION

Cette région marche parce que le paysage est varié et réunit les préférences de chaque personne. ; Ils continuent à avoir une opinion différente.

Expansion

Your students have just won the lottery and have the option to travel to **La Réunion**, **la Corse**, or **Chamonix** and **le Mont Blanc**. Have students research flights, the route, number of stops, and pricing for each of these destinations, all leaving from their hometown. How many hours would it take to get to each destination? What are the high, low, and shoulder season prices for each destination? What is the difference in price for economy and first class? The purpose of this exercise is for students to make a personal connection with these destinations, and to be aware of how they would have to travel to get there.

Recherche : discount airfare sites

Differentiated Learning

Accelerate

High-ability students continue the dialogue in **Extension** until the **client** and **cliente** have arrived at a compromise or an impasse about their future trip.

Decelerate

Have students write a short summary of the **Extension** conversation in English, explaining each point of view. They can cite liberally from the text but must transform the dialogue from first person to third.

Learning Styles

Kinesthetic

Have students write out the lines from the **Les prochaines vacances** and **Extension** dialogues on separate strips of paper. Then have them shuffle the paper strips, trade with a partner, and put them back in order.

Resources

Points de départ
WB Workbook 6
Explore

Reference Desk

If you have access to Passport, find a video related to **La Réunion** and show it to your students.

Communication

Presentational: Cooperative Groups

Students work in small groups to write two lists of reasons: one for using **un agent de voyage** and one for planning a trip themselves. Have groups write their lists on large pieces of paper and then post these around the room. Once completed, students take a tour of the lists and discuss the most frequently cited reasons for both situations.

Connections

Literature

Have students read Charles Baudelaire's poem "**À une dame créole**," and decide whether its form (especially its rhyme scheme) more closely matches that of a Shakespearian or Petrarchan sonnet. If possible, you may want to invite an English teacher to give a brief presentation on sonnets during your class period(s). Then lead the students in discovering the meaning of the poem, which honors a native woman, and is also a poignant jab at slavery and colonialism. Discuss how the form of the poem affects its meaning.

Alternative: For students advanced in both French and English, ask them to research the Marotic sonnet (and the ***couplet marotique***), and present Baudelaire's poem in contrast with a Shakespearian sonnet of their choice, perhaps one that has a similar theme.

Points de départ

Pre-AP

Question centrale ? **Qu'est-ce qu'on doit connaître de sa destination pour réussir son voyage?**

La Francophonie

Profil touristique

La Réunion 1.2, 2.1, 2.2, 3.1, 3.2, 4.2

L'île de La Réunion est un département français situé dans l'océan Indien à côté de Madagascar et de l'île Maurice. C'est une île volcanique très montagneuse*. Elle abrite* l'un des volcans les plus actifs du monde, le piton de la Fournaise. Avec 850 000 habitants, l'île se caractérise par sa jeunesse. Elle a une population métissée*: elle est composée principalement de descendants d'esclaves venus d'Afrique et d'Inde, amenés* dans l'île pendant la colonisation au 17ème siècle pour cultiver le café et les épices*, de descendants des colons blancs, et aussi d'immigrés venus de Chine. Sa capitale est Saint-Denis.

L'agriculture est importante pour l'économie. À côté de la canne à sucre* et de la vanille se sont développées les cultures maraîchères* et fruitières. Mais c'est le tourisme qui est la première activité économique de l'île.

Les musiciens ont contribué à populariser les deux rythmes réunionnais: le *maloya*, proche du blues, qui est issu* de chants et de danses rituelles d'esclaves noirs, et le *séga*, plutôt danse de salon, qui regroupe des danses et musiques créoles populaires. Au 19ème siècle, le poète français Charles Baudelaire a séjourné* quelque temps à l'île de La Réunion, qui lui a inspiré des poèmes tels que «À une dame créole».

Recherche: île de la réunion voyage, île de la réunion vacances, visite virtuelle réunion

Un champ de canne à sucre et de cocotiers à La Réunion

montagneuse *mountainous*; **abrite** *is home to*; **métissée** d'ethnies mixtes; **amenés** *brought*; **épices** *spices*; **canne à sucre** *sugar cane*; **maraîchères** *of garden produce*; **issu** *comes from*; **séjourné** voyagé

1.2, 2.1

Produits		
	Artistes	Manu Payet, Tonton David, Danyel Waro, Faf Larage
	Hommes politiques	Raymond Barre (Premier ministre)
	Sportifs	Roland Garros, Dimitri Payet, Surya Bobaly, Jackson Richardson
	Écrivains	Leconte de Lisle (poète, 19ème siècle), Axel Gauvin et Michel Houellebecq (romanciers du 20ème et 21ème siècles)

1.2, 4.1

Mon dico réunionnais

Comen i lé? *Comment ça va?*
Siouplé *S'il vous plait.*
Nou sar dansé. *On va danser.*
Mi aim à ou. *Je t'aime.*
la kaz *la maison*

Essential Instruction

1. Have students locate **La Réunion**, **la Corse**, **Chamonix**, and **Le Mont Blanc** using the maps in the front pages of their textbooks.
2. Students read the three selections in **Points de départ**. Using a graphic organizer of their choosing, they note the population, industry, culture, famous people, and additional important details of each location.
3. Ask the students to compare orally the three destinations using the above categories.

La Corse 1.2, 2.1, 2.2, 3.1

La Corse est une île de la mer Méditerranée où l'on parle français et corse. Considérée une région française, elle est composée de deux départements : la Corse-du-Sud et la Haute-Corse. Surnommée « Île de Beauté », on y trouve de belles plages, des vues panoramiques montagneuses*, une bonne cuisine de terroir*, et des espaces naturels grâce à un parc marin international, des réserves naturelles, ainsi que le Parc naturel régional de Corse. Les activités principales de la Corse sont l'agriculture et le tourisme.

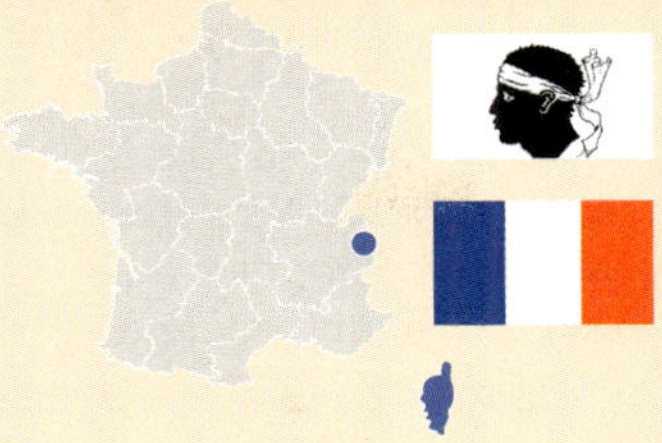

montagneuses *mountainous* ; **terroir** *rural flavor*

1.2, 4.2

Comparaisons

La Corse est détachée géographiquement de la France, mais fait partie du territoire français. Y a-t-il des îles près des États-Unis qui ont une situation similaire ?

Bonifacio, une ville de la Corse, est situé sur des falaises.

Chamonix et le Mont Blanc 1.2, 2.2, 3.1

Chamonix, petite ville de 10 000 habitants, est considéré la commune la plus haute d'Europe. Elle doit ce titre à la présence sur son territoire du sommet le plus haut d'Europe, le Mont Blanc (4 810 m). C'est un atout* touristique considérable car le Mont Blanc est le troisième site naturel le plus visité au monde. Il possède le sentier* de randonnées le plus populaire d'Europe qui fait le tour du Mont Blanc (170 km). C'est aussi de Chamonix que part le téléphérique* de l'aiguille* du Midi qui monte à 3 777 m. La Mer de Glace*, la Vallée Blanche, et le Lac Blanc sont d'autres atouts touristiques à Chamonix.

Chamonix est devenu la capitale des amateurs d'alpinisme et des sportifs de haute montagne. Elle abrite l'École Nationale de Ski et d'Alpinisme spécialisée dans la formation des guides de haute montagne qui ont leur association et leur compagnie à Chamonix. Roger Frison-Roche pour ses récits* littéraires, Gaston Rebuffat pour ses films, et René Desmaison pour ses exploits en sont parmi les plus célèbres des guides.

Recherche : intérêts touristiques à chamonix, chamonix mont blanc, ski chamonix

atout *asset* ; **sentier** chemin ; **téléphérique** *cable car* ; **l'aiguille** le sommet ; **glace** *ice* ; **récits** contes

Answers

Comparaisons

Answers may include Puerto Rico, Hawaii, the US Virgin Islands, Guam, Northern Mariana Islands, and American Samoa.

Reference Desk

1. Corsica, sold to the French in 1768, remains independently minded and fiercely proud of its history and culture, which is often differentiated from that of mainland France. Vestiges of Genoese (Italian) culture remain. Napoléon Bonaparte (born "Buonaparte") was Corsican.
2. The image at the bottom of the page is of two ibex (**des bouquetins**) in the Mont Blanc. Another popular animal in the Alps is **un chamois**. You may show images of those animals to students.

Expansion

Have students research the origins of **le drapeau de la Corse**, and then compare it to **le drapeau de la Sardaigne** (Sardinia). Locate Sardinia on a map. How are the two flags similar yet different? Encourage students to describe in French what they see on each flag.

Multiple Intelligences

Musical-Rhythmic

Encourage students to search for the best rendition of "**Ti fleur fanée**," the unofficial national anthem of **La Réunion**, and samples of **le maloya** and **le séga** to play for the class.

Naturalist

Encourage students interested in nature and the environment to investigate **La Réunion**, **la Corse**, **Chamonix**, and **le Mont Blanc** from the point of view of natural resources, agriculture, or local food specialties that are unique to the regions. They may be especially drawn to **piton de la Fournaise**, since it is one of the most active volcanoes in the world.

Linguistic

Have students investigate the political culture of **La Réunion** to understand how the music became intertwined with political thought.

Answers

7

1. Situation : Département français dans l'océan Indien ; Nombre d'habitants : 850 000 ; Capitale : Saint-Denis ; Économie : l'agriculture, le tourisme
2. Answers will vary.
3. Possible answers: haut, naturel, visité, populaire, touristique, célèbre
4. Maps should include la France, l'Italie, l'Allemagne, l'Autriche, la Suisse, and la Slovénie.
5. la gentiane ou l'edelweiss, le chamois ou la marmotte
6. Answers will vary.

Comparaisons
Answers will vary.

Communication

Presentational: Cooperative Groups

Divide students into small groups. Prepare a list of national and/or regional parks and then transfer the names of the parks to index cards, one per card. Have groups randomly choose a card. Each group researches advice for visitors to that park and then presents their findings in French as if they were addressing a group of francophone visitors. Encourage the rest of the class to ask questions. Small groups could also present to each other for practice before presenting to the whole group.

Culture

Information

Students may be interested to learn that the national French magazine ***L'Étudiant*** has frequently identified Grenoble as the best French city in which to study. The magazine cites the city's number of international students, diverse and efficient public transportation system, "dynamic job market," and local activism as factors for the city's popularity among university students.

Les Alpes 1.2, 2.2, 3.1

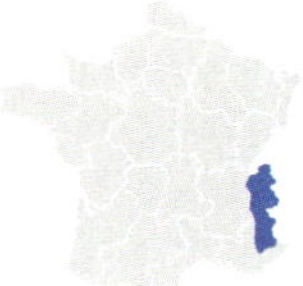

L'Italie, la France, la Suisse, l'Allemagne, l'Autriche, la Slovénie — les Alpes s'étendent* principalement sur ces six pays et comptent plus de 80 sommets de plus de 4 000 mètres. C'est une barrière de 1 200 km qui s'étend de la Méditerranée au Danube. La plus grande ville des Alpes est Grenoble. La ville et son agglomération comprennent 664 000 habitants.

La faune et la flore alpines sont très protégées grâce aux nombreux parcs régionaux ou nationaux qui occupent le massif ; le plus connu en France est le Parc de la Vanoise. La gentiane et l'edelweiss pour la flore, le chamois* et la marmotte* pour la faune sont les symboles des Alpes.

La station téléphérique de l'Aiguille du Midi, à Chamonix

Recherche : hautes alpes stations de ski, site officiel du parc de la vanoise

s'étendent *spread* ; **chamois** *mountain goat* ; **marmotte** *marmot*

Produits 1.2, 2.2

Le Saint-Bernard est une race de grands chiens sauveteurs, formée au sauvetage (*rescue*) en montagne. Il a une devise : « Noblesse, dévouement (*loyalty*) et sacrifice ». Il a été popularisé au cinéma par le film américain *Beethoven* (1990) et ses suites.

Comparaisons 1.2, 4.2

Quels parcs régionaux ou nationaux existent dans votre région ? Qu'y a-t-il à voir ?

7 Activités culturelles 1.2, 1.3, 3.1, 3.2

Faites les activités suivantes.

1. Faites la carte d'identité de l'île de La Réunion.
   - Situation géographique et politique
   - Nombre d'habitants
   - Capitale
   - Économie
2. Présentez une personne célèbre qui vient de La Réunion.
3. Faites une liste d'adjectifs qui décrivent Chamonix.
4. Faites une carte qui montre les Alpes dans chaque pays d'Europe.
5. Citez deux symboles des Alpes :
   - une fleur
   - un animal
6. Planifiez un séjour de quatre jours en Corse. Prenez des notes en recherchant ce qu'il y a à y faire et voir : gastronomie, excursions, randonnées, festivals, etc.

Le Mont Blanc est le plus haut sommet des Alpes et de l'Europe.

Essential Instruction

1. In the computer lab, teams collaborate to complete questions 1–4 of **Activité 7**. These questions should not take a long time to do, and they can be corrected in class.
2. Have students read the questions and answers in **Du côté des médias** and to make a list of words that are new or that they would need to look up in order to understand the reading. Use synonyms, antonyms, or explanations in French to define the new words. Encourage those students who understand the words to play the role of teacher and to provide a definition or meaning.

Perspectives

1.2, 2.1, 3.1

Dans son poème « Parfum exotique », Charles Baudelaire dit de La Réunion :

« … le parfum des verts tamariniers*,
Qui circule dans l'air et m'enfle* la narine*,
Se mêle dans mon âme au chant des mariniers*. »

Pour le poète, quel sens évoque de la nostalgie pour La Réunion ?

tamariniers *tamarind trees* ; **enfle** *swell up* ; **narine** *nostril* ; **marinier** *sailor*

Du côté des médias

1.2, 1.3

Lisez les informations sur l'île de La Réunion. En groupe, choisissez une catégorie et créez un programme d'activités à ajouter au site.

Il y a plus d'une raison de préférer l'île de La Réunion !

MONTAGNE

Explorez un concentré des forces de la nature

Joyaux de l'île de La Réunion, Pitons, cirques, remparts ont vu leur inscription sur la liste des biens naturels du Patrimoine mondial être validée le 1er août 2010 par l'Unesco. C'est une reconnaissance attendue et justifiée pour cette île européenne de l'océan Indien. Territoire unique où la montagne fusionne avec la mer, où le relief tourmenté offre des paysages grandioses, où 40 % des espaces sont restés intacts depuis sa découverte, l'île de La Réunion confirme son statut de destination aux richesses naturelles exceptionnelles.

MER

Offrez-vous une évasion bleu océan

L'île de La Réunion vous offre la beauté des paysages tropicaux du littoral. Profitez des moments exceptionnels en bord de mer, sur et dans la mer selon vos envies. Partez en tongs sur la plage, contemplez une mer bleu lagon par 30 ° C à l'ombre et admirez un superbe coucher du soleil pour commencer la soirée.

CULTURE

Entre traditions et authenticité, La Réunion se consomme sans modération !

La Réunion est une terre de contrastes à l'image de son relief, de ses paysages, de sa population, de sa cuisine, de ses religions. Ses traditions dévoilent l'histoire unique de La Réunion.

VOLCAN

Voyage en terres volcaniques

L'île volcanique de La Réunion a surgi au fond de l'océan, il y a trois millions d'années.

Answers

Perspectives

L'odorat est le sens qui évoque de la nostalgie pour le poète.

Du côté des médias

Answers will vary.

Reference Desk

GMT stands for Greenwich Mean Time (**l'heure moyenne de Greenwich**). France is on CET (Central European Time or **l'heure d'Europe centrale**), which is GMT + 2 during the summer and GMT + 1 the rest of the year.

Expansion

Have students use an online map site to view and explore **La Réunion**.

Connections

Mathematics

Encourage students to do mental conversions whenever distances or weights appear in the text in the metric system (or degrees Celsius) by posting a conversion chart in your classroom.

Differentiated Learning

Accelerate

High-ability students could make a trivia game based on the information found in the chart of **Du côté des médias**. In addition, have them answer the question in **Perspectives** based on the Baudelaire poem "**Parfum exotique**."

Decelerate

Have students analyze why **le chien du Saint-Bernard** is physically adept at saving lost skiers and victims of avalanches. When did this tradition start and by whom? Students should conduct their research in French and in English, and then present their findings to the class.

Resources

WB Workbook 7–9

G & V Practice Games

Answers

Comparaisons

In the English sentence, *sleeping* is acting as an adjective. In French, the use of the present participle as an adjective is more limited, but you might find it in poetry and songs.

Reference Desk

Attention should be given to **-ger** verbs. For example, since the **nous** form of **nager** is **nageons**, the present participle will be **nageant**. Other common **-ger** verbs are **changer**, **voyager**, **ranger**, **déranger**, **manger** and **diriger**. Note that the verbs **être, avoir**, and **savoir** have irregular stems.

TPR

Prepare a set of cards on which are written two infinitives such as **parler** and **manger**. Call out the two verbs. Students must act out the two activities simultaneously and say what they are doing by conjugating the first verb, and expressing the second as a present participle. **Je parle en mangeant./Nous parlons en mangeant**. Alternatively, tell the students what to do and watch their gestures to check for comprehension: **Parlez en mangeant! Regardez votre partenaire en sautant! Fermez les yeux en touchant vos oreilles!**

Expansion

To practice forming present participles, put students into groups of four or five. Give each group a worksheet that has six incomplete sentences: **Fabrice fait ses devoirs**.... Each group writes as many logical completions as possible, using present participles: **Fabrice fait ses devoirs (en téléphonant, en mangeant une pizza, en prenant le bus au lycée)**.

Structure de la langue

Present Participle 1.2

Marie-Alix prend une photo en faisant de l'escalade.

The present participle is a verb form that ends in **-ant**. This ending corresponds to the suffix *-ing* in English. To form the present participle, add **-ant** to the stem of the **nous** form of the verb in the present tense.

Verb	*Nous* Stem	Present Participle
faire	fais-	**faisant**
attendre	attend-	**attendant**
finir	finiss-	**finissant**
aller	all-	**allant**
partir	part-	**partant**

4.1 **Comparaisons**

What is another function of the present participle in English? Is this also possible in French?

The teacher woke the *sleeping* student.
Le prof a réveillé l'élève **qui dormait**.

The three verbs indicated below have irregular present participles.

Verb	Present Participle
avoir	**ayant**
être	**étant**
savoir	**sachant**

The preposition **en** usually precedes the present participle. **En** means "while," "upon," "in," or "on" if the two actions in the sentence take place at the same time.

En voyant la neige, mon frère a voulu faire de la luge.	*Upon seeing the snow, my brother wanted to go sledding.*
Nous ne regardons jamais la télé **en mangeant**.	*We never watch TV while eating.*

En means "by" if a cause-and-effect relationship is expressed.

C'est **en écoutant** le prof que tu pourras réussir à ton examen.	*By listening to the teacher, you will be able to pass the test.*

Essential Instruction

1. Show the formation of the present participle and the three exceptions.
2. Have students write the present participle of infinitives you call out, as they write in their notebooks or use small or medium whiteboards with markers at their desks.
3. Give students numerous oral drills so that they can produce the present participle easily.
4. Form pairs and have the students complete **Activité 8** and **Activité 9**, alternating statements and questions.
5. For **Activité 8**, check that students use the third person singular form of **s'amuser** for the last sentence, pertaining to the information on the chart.

8 Les activités des jeunes 1.2

Interpretive Viewing

Abdel-Cader a fait un sondage pour savoir ce que ses camarades de classe font pour s'amuser en plein air. Dites combien d'ados s'amusent en faisant les activités suivantes.

MODÈLE jouer au baseball
Quinze ados s'amusent en jouant au baseball.

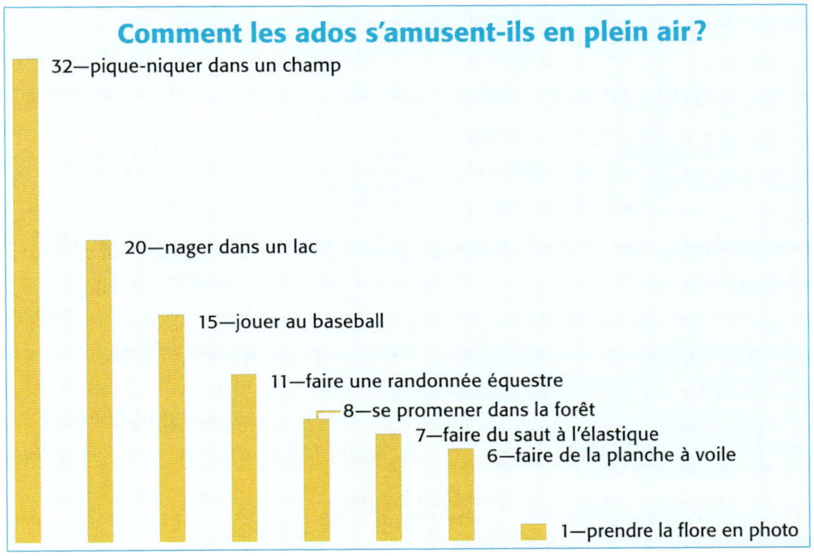

9 Qu'est-ce que tu fais en... ? 1.1, 5.2

Interpersonal Speaking

Avec un(e) partenaire, posez des questions sur ce que vous faites pendant que vous faites autre chose. Puis répondez aux questions. Suivez le modèle.

MODÈLE écouter de la musique (faire les corvées)
A: Est-ce que tu écoutes de la musique en faisant les corvées?
B: Oui, j'écoute de la musique en faisant les corvées. Et toi?
A: Moi, je chante en faisant les corvées.

1. parler au téléphone (conduire)
2. se détendre (lire un roman)
3. manger (étudier)
4. publier des photos sur ton réseau social préféré (écouter le prof)
5. regarder des vidéos sur ton portable (dîner avec tes parents)
6. manger (faire du shopping)
7. regarder la télé (finir tes devoirs)
8. chanter (faire du sport)
9. regarder la télé (faire du baby-sitting)
10. faire des sauts à ski (savoir que tu pourrais avoir un accident)

Answers

8

Trente-deux ados s'amusent en pique-niquant dans un champ.
Vingt ados s'amusent en nageant dans un lac.
Quinze ados s'amusent en jouant au baseball.
Onze ados s'amusent en faisant une randonnée équestre.
Huit ados s'amusent en se promenant dans la forêt.
Sept ados s'amusent en faisant du saut à l'élastique.
Six ados s'amusent en faisant de la planche à voile.
Un ado s'amuse en prenant la flore en photo.

9

1. Est-ce que tu parles au téléphone en conduisant?
2. Est-ce que tu te détends en lisant un roman?
3. Est-ce que tu manges en étudiant?
4. Est-ce que tu publies des photos sur ton réseau social préféré en écoutant le prof?
5. Est-ce que tu regarde des vidéos sur ton portable en dînant avec tes parents?
6. Est-ce que tu manges en faisant du shopping?
7. Est-ce que tu regardes la télé en finissant tes devoirs?
8. Est-ce que tu chantes en faisant du sport?
9. Est-ce que tu regardes la télé en faisant du baby-sitting?
10. Est-ce que tu fais des sauts à ski en sachant que tu pourrais avoir un accident?

Partner answers will vary.

Connections

Music

Introduce students to "**En passant par la Lorraine,**" a classic children's song featuring present participles. Have them sing along if they are willing! As a cloze activity, students can fill in the blanks with the words they hear.

Recherche: en passant par la lorraine

Differentiated Learning

Accelerate

Have students plan a ski vacation leaving from Paris. They should plan to take the train to a ski resort of their choice in France. Which train would they take? Can they get a student discount? What would be the cost in dollars/euros?

Recherche: voyages-sncf

Adapt

Ask students to think of other ways that they multitask, using the format of **Activité 9**. Ask them whether multitasking is efficient in these ways (**efficace**) or inefficient (**inefficace**).

Decelerate

For students to practice a few troublesome verbs, have them fill out a worksheet with the following headings: **Infinitif**, **Nous: Présent**, **Participe présent**, **Traduction**. When they are done, dictate some simple sentences to them using examples from their worksheet, in the present and present participle. Have them translate the dictated sentences out loud.

Resources

WB Workbook 10
LA Listening Activity 2
G & V Practice Games

Answers

On recycle!
The English meaning of the sentence is: *I'm buying nothing for my trip to Chamonix*. To form a negative with ne **(n')... rien**, put the **ne (n')** before the verb and the **rien** after the verb. Other negative expressions that work the same way in the present tense are: **ne (n')... pas**, **ne (n')... jamais**, **ne (n')... plus**, and **ne (n')... personne.**

Reference Desk

Negatives are introduced in Level 1, **Unité 10**, **Leçon B**, pp. 536–537 and reviewed in Level 2, **Unité 1**, **Leçon A**, p. 12.

Game

En traversant la rivière

Divide students into two groups and put them on opposite sides of the classroom. Say an affirmative sentence aloud, such as "**Tout le monde veut parler anglais.**" Groups must come up with the negative version of the sentence. ("**Personne ne veut parler anglais.**") The first group to correctly do so gets to send a student across the room. The first group to get all group members across to the other side of the room wins. (To ensure that everyone continues to participate, you may want to allow students to respond regardless of which side of the room they are on. Or, if only a few students are participating, say that they may no longer give an answer once they have crossed the room.)

Révision: Negation 1.1

On recycle!

See if you can tell what the sentence below means in English and how you form a negative sentence in French.

Je n'achète rien pour mon voyage à Chamonix.

If you cannot do those two things, read the grammar summary below.

To make a verb negative, put **ne (n')** before the verb and **pas**, **plus**, **jamais**, **rien**, or **personne** after it in the present tense.

Élodie? Chamonix **ne** la tente **pas**.	*Élodie isn't interested in Chamonix.*
Elle **ne** va **jamais** à La Réunion.	*She never goes to Reunion.*

In the near future, the negative expression is sandwiched around the conjugated form of **aller**.

Je **ne** vais **plus** me plaindre.	*I'm not going to complain anymore.*

In the **passé composé**, **ne (n')** precedes the helping verb and **pas**, **plus**, **jamais**, or **rien** follows it. **Personne**, however, follows the past participle.

Élodie **n'a rien** dit à son frère.	*Élodie didn't say anything to her brother.*
Léo **n'**a parlé à **personne** des vacances.	*Léo didn't talk to anyone about vacation.*

The expressions **ne (n')... personne** and **ne (n')... rien** may also be used as subjects. In this case, **personne** or **rien** begins the sentence and **ne (n')** is in its usual position.

Personne ne voulait skier, sauf Léo.	*No one wanted to ski, except for Léo.*
Rien ne peut me faire changer d'avis.	*Nothing can make me change my mind.*

Connexions 1.3, 2.2, 3.1
Musique
Écoutez la chanson « Soulman » de Ben L'Oncle Soul, « Je ne veux pas ton pouvoir » de Tiken Jah Fakoly, « Ne me quitte pas » de Jacques Brel, ou « Non, je ne regrette rien » d'Édith Piaf. Puis, chantez votre version de la chanson à la classe, ou faites un dessin pour illustrer chaque paragraphe.
Recherche : soulman ben l'oncle soul, je ne veux pas ton pouvoir, non je ne regrette rien

Essential Instruction

1. Give students negative sentences in French and ask them to give you the affirmative form. Then give them affirmative sentences and ask them to give you the negative form.
2. Compare negative sentences in English with their equivalent in French to examine word order.
3. Continue the complaint of the dog in the photo. What else would he say if he could?
4. Because of the complexity of the negatives, do **Activité 10** with the students.

10 Au parc d'attractions 1.2, 1.3

Interpretive Viewing, Presentational Speaking or Writing

Comparez les deux illustrations. Puis répondez aux questions en suivant le modèle.

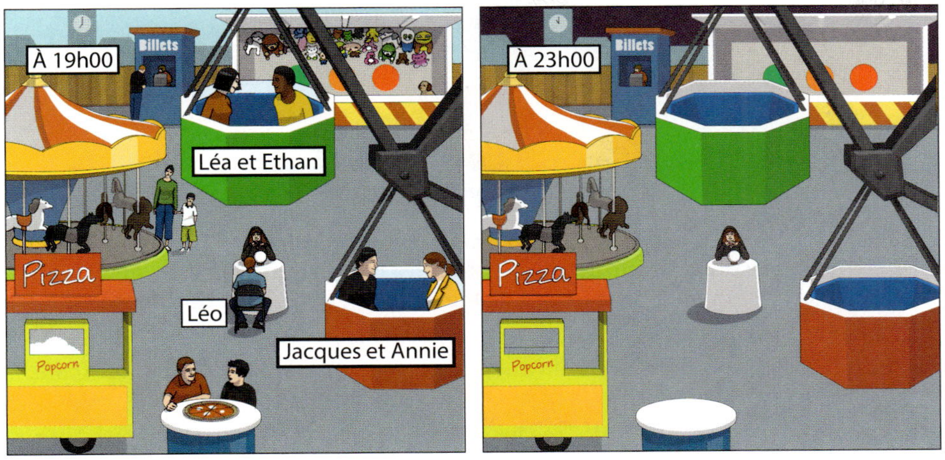

MODÈLE Qui avait une consultation avec la voyante?
À 19h00, Léo avait une consultation avec la voyante, mais à 23h00 personne n'avait de consultation avec la voyante.

1. Qui a acheté des tickets?
2. Il y avait du popcorn au snackbar?
3. On pouvait gagner un animal aux jeux d'adresse?
4. Tout le monde s'est-il amusé?
5. Un enfant attendait de faire un tour de manège?
6. Qui a fait un tour de grande roue?

Traditions et pratiques 1.2, 2.1

En France, les parcs d'attractions ferment souvent leurs portes en hiver, pour rouvrir au printemps. C'est particulièrement le cas des parcs aquatiques.

Resources

WB Workbook 11–12
G & V Practice Games

Answers

10

1. À 19h00, un homme/garçon a acheté des tickets, mais à 23h00 personne n'a acheté de tickets.
2. À 19h00, il y avait du popcorn au snackbar, mais à 23h00 il n'y en avait plus.
3. À 19h00, on pouvait gagner un animal aux jeux d'adresse, mais à 23h00 on ne pouvait plus rien gagner.
4. À 19h00, tout le monde s'est amusé, mais à 23h00 personne ne s'est amusé.
5. À 19h00, un enfant attendait de faire un tour de manège, mais à 23h00 personne n'attendait de faire un tour de manège.
6. À 19h00, Lea, Ethan, Jacques et Annie ont fait un tour de grande roue, mais à 23h00 personne n'a fait de tour de grande roue.

Expansion

Write the affirmative expressions **souvent**, **toujours**, **quelqu'un**, and **quelque chose** on the board. Ask students to name the negative expressions that are the opposite of these expressions. They should name **ne (n')...jamais**, **ne (n')...plus**, **ne (n')...personne**, and **ne (n')...rien**. Next, have students write a question for each of the expressions: **Tu regardes souvent des films étrangers?** Finally, students exchange their questions with a partner who answers each one in writing using an appropriate negative. Make sure to model your expectations before students start writing, in order to check comprehension and to model the level of language that you want them to use.

Multiple Intelligences

Visual-Spatial/Mathematical-Logical

These students would benefit from making a chart of the negatives with their corresponding word order.

Special Needs Students

Linguistically Challenged

Provide students with a lot of guided practice to master each negative. Worksheets and oral drills will help them succeed.

Dyslexia

Assist students with negation by using colored paper to make negative sentences with **ne**...**plus** to help them recognize the pattern.

Answers

Comparaisons

Although not a hard and fast rule, it often works to put the word *only* in front of the word it modifies. In the example sentence, *only* modifies the verb *to like*. In French, there is no confusion in where to place **ne (n')... que**, unlike in English. *Only* is a tricky word because where it is placed can change the meaning of a sentence, as in this example:

I spoke to him only yesterday.
(*Only* helps emphasize how *recently* the speaker spoke to the other person.)
I spoke only to him yesterday.
(*Only* helps emphasize that the speaker spoke to no one else.)

Reference Desk

In a sentence with both a conjugated verb form and an infinitive, **personne** follows the infinitive: **Marc ne peut voir personne ce weekend parce qu'il est malade**. **Personne** may also be used after a preposition: **Je ne téléphone à personne après dix heures du soir**.

Communication

Interpersonal: Paired Practice

Print seven to ten negative sentences. Cut up each sentence and put the words in an envelope. Divide the students into groups of two or three and ask them to reconstruct the words into meaningful, grammatically correct sentences. Put the corrected sentences on the board or provide an answer key for students to check after the groups finish.

Connections

Music

The 2016 hit "**Un Homme debout**" by Claudio Capéo features many of these negative expressions. Have students listen to and read the lyrics, highlighting the negative structures. Students may also enjoy its music video, filmed in Lyon's biggest square (and the 5th largest square in France), **la Place Bellecour**.

Other Negative Expressions

Koffi n'aime que les activités dangereuses.

The expression **ne (n')... que** (*only*) is often used instead of the adverb **seulement**, which has the same meaning. This expression restricts or limits choices. **Ne (n')** precedes the verb, or the helping verb in the **passé composé**, and **que** comes before the word or expression it describes.

Salim **ne** fait **que** des activités en plein air.	*Salim only does outdoor activities.*
En vacances il **ne** fait **que** des sports nautiques.	*On vacation he only does water sports.*

The negative expression **ne (n')... ni... ni...** means *neither... nor*. **Ne (n')** precedes the verb, or the helping verb in the **passé composé**, and each **ni** comes directly before the word or expression it describes.

Djamel **ne** veut essayer **ni** le jet ski **ni** le saut à ski.	*Djamel wants to try neither the jet ski nor ski jumps.*
Il **n'**aime **ni** la montagne **ni** la mer.	*He likes neither mountains nor sea.*

Ni... ni...ne (n') may begin a sentence. In this case, each **ni** precedes the word or expression it describes and **ne (n')** is in its usual position, in front of the verb.

Ni Hélène **ni** moi **n'**irons à la campagne.	*Neither Hélène nor I will go to the countryside.*
Ni nos parents **ni** nos amis **ne** pouvaient nous persuader.	*Neither our parents nor our friends were able to persuade us.*

The negative expression **ne (n')... aucun(e)** may be used as an adjective or a pronoun and means *no*, *not any*, or *not one*. As an adjective, **aucun(e)** agrees in gender with the noun following it. **Ne (n')** precedes the verb, or the helping verb in the **passé composé**. **Aucun(e)** comes after the verb, or the past participle in the **passé composé**, and before the noun it describes.

Je **n'**ai **aucun** doute que tu t'amuseras!	*I have no doubt that you will have fun!*

Aucun(e) may also begin a sentence. In this case, it precedes the word or expression it describes and **ne (n')** is in its usual position.

Aucun de nous **ne** s'ennuiera.
None of us will be bored.

4.1

Comparaisons

What is the position of "only" in English sentences?

Nous n'aimons **que** les desserts au buffet.
We *only* like desserts at the buffet.

Essential Instruction

Have the students complete **Activité 11** orally before writing the exercise.

11 L'anniversaire de Chloé 1.2, 1.3, 2.2

Interpretive Viewing, Presentational Speaking or Writing

Vous voulez acheter une carte cadeau pour Chloé pour son anniversaire. Mais ce n'est pas facile ! Dites qu'elle n'aime ni la première chose ni la deuxième. Puis, généralisez en disant ce qu'elle n'aime pas.

MODÈLE

Chloé n'aime ni les boutiques ni les grands magasins. Elle n'aime aucun magasin de vêtements.

1.

2.

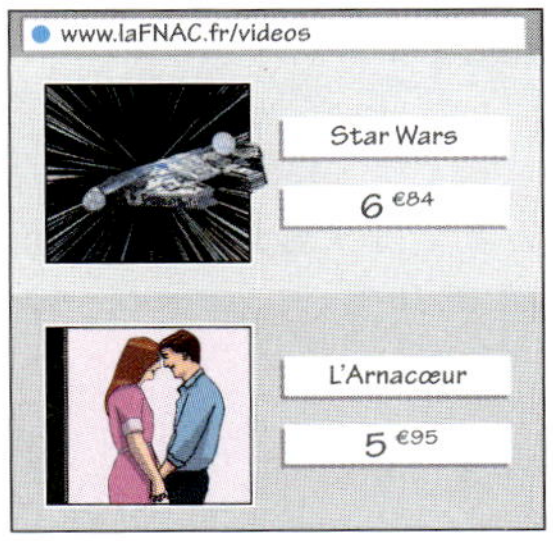

3.

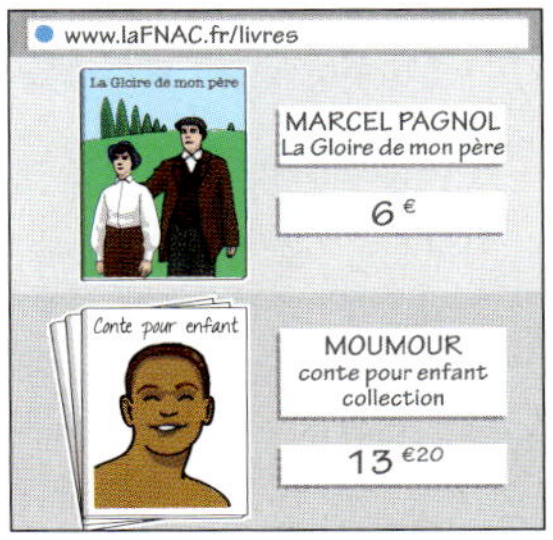

4.

5.

6.

Answers

11

1. Chloé n'aime ni les restaurants mexicains, ni les restaurants italiens. Elle n'aime aucun restaurant.
2. Chloé n'aime ni les films d'aventures, ni les comédies romantiques. Elle n'aime aucun film.
3. Chloé n'aime ni les romans, ni les contes. Elle n'aime aucun livre.
4. Chloé n'aime ni les glaces, ni les gâteaux. Elle n'aime aucun dessert.
5. Chloé n'aime ni le foot, ni le hockey. Elle n'aime aucun sport.
6. Chloé n'aime ni les bracelets en argent, ni les bracelets en or. Elle n'aime aucun bijou.

Reference Desk

L'Arnacœur is a popular comedy with Vanessa Paradis and Romain Duris. ***La Gloire de mon père*** is the first of two autobiographical books by Marcel Pagnol.

Connections

Humor

Here are some jokes to share with the class.

1. **–J'ai perdu mon chien, dit Madame Dupont à sa voisine.**
   –Faites passer une annonce.
   –Ça ne sert à rien, il ne sait pas lire.
2. **–Quel animal mange avec sa queue ?**
   –Tous. Aucun n'enlève sa queue pour manger.
3. **–Savez-vous que votre chien aboie toute la nuit ?**
   –Oh, ça ne fait rien, il dort toute la journée !

Expansion

Put students in pairs. Student A plays the role of a salesperson who wants to sell student B articles from the store. Student B plays the role of a person impossible to please. Then have students reverse roles. **Madame, j'ai des gants en laine et en coton. Ah non ! Je n'aime ni la laine, ni le coton.**

Special Needs Students

Dyslexia/Linguistically Challenged

For **Activité 11**, breaking the negative responses down into simple chunks might help. Have the students work with you or a strong partner. The partner starts with a question, for example, "**Claire aime les boutiques et les magasins ?**" The student responds, "**Non, ni les boutiques, ni les magasins.**" Finally, encourage them to say, "**Aucun magasin !**" From there move to the full response when they are ready.

Resources

Activities 12–13

Answers

12

1. Yann n'y a passé qu'une semaine.
2. Il n'a fait que des activités en plein air.
3. Il n'a acheté que des tee-shirts.
4. Il n'a fait de shopping que dans des boutiques bon marché.
5. Il n'a essayé que les plats français.

13 Script

1. –Les Alpes cet été, ça te dit?
   –Bien sûr. On peut faire de la randonnée.
2. –Tu aimes faire des sauts à ski?
   –Non, je n'aime ni skier, ni le saut à ski.
3. –En sortant du lycée, tu veux faire de la planche à voile?
   –Oui, bonne idée. Invitons André! Il me l'a proposé aussi.
4. –Personne ne veut faire de saut à l'élastique avec nous samedi?
   –Si, Aurélie veut venir.
5. –Ils n'offrent aucune randonnée équestre? J'ai envie d'en faire ce weekend.
   –Si, ils offrent des randonnées équestres le samedi matin.
6. –Tu aimes faire du parapente?
   –Non, je n'aime ni le parapente ni le saut à l'élastique. J'ai horreur de ces sports!
7. –Tu fais souvent de l'escalade?
   –Non, je ne fais jamais d'escalade.
8. –Martin ne fait pas de ski?
   –Si, et il fait aussi du saut à ski!

1. oui; 2. non; 3. oui; 4. oui; 5. oui; 6. non; 7. non; 8. oui

14

1. Est-ce que tu voyages? Je ne voyage ni dans les États du Midwest ni dans les États de la Côte Est. Et toi? Moi, je ne voyage que dans….
2. Est-ce que tu lis…? Je ne lis ni des fables ni des contes de fées. Et toi? Je ne lis que des….
3. Est-ce que tu fais…? Je ne fais ni des projets de bricolage ni des projets de design. Et toi? Je ne fais que des….
4. Est-ce que tu préfères…? Je ne prèfère ni les ni hors-d'œuvre ni les desserts au restaurant. Et toi? Je ne préfère que les….
5. Est-ce que tu te sers…? Je ne me sers ni d'une poêle ni d'une casserole. Et toi? Je ne me sers que d'une….

(*continued on next page*)

12 Des vacances à La Réunion 1.3

Presentational Speaking or Writing

Yann a passé ses vacances à La Réunion. Quand il raconte ses exploits, il exagère toujours. Corrigez ses phrases selon les indices données.

MODÈLE «J'ai voyagé avec dix amis.» (deux amis)
Yann n'a voyagé qu'avec deux amis.

1. «J'ai passé un mois à La Réunion.» (une semaine)
2. «J'ai fait beaucoup d'activités culturelles.» (en plein air)
3. «J'ai acheté des cadeaux de luxe pour ma famille.» (tee-shirts)
4. «J'ai fait du shopping dans les meilleures boutiques.» (bon marché)
5. «J'ai essayé tous les plats réunionnais.» (français)

13 Questions simples 1.2

Interpretive Listening

Écrivez les numéros 1–8 sur votre papier. Écoutez les mini-dialogues. Puis, écrivez ***oui*** *si la personne mentionnée fait du sport dont on parle ou* ***non*** *si elle n'en fait pas.*

14 Vos préférences 1.1, 5.2

Interpersonal Speaking

À tour de rôle, posez des questions sur vos préférences. Puis répondez.

MODÈLE faire des recherches généalogiques ou scientifiques
A: Est-ce que tu fais des recherches généalogiques ou scientifiques?
B: Je ne fais ni des recherches généalogiques ni des recherches scientifiques. Et toi?
A: Moi, je ne fais que des recherches généalogiques.

1. voyager dans les États du Midwest ou de la Côte Est
2. lire des fables ou des contes de fées
3. faire des projets de bricolage ou de design
4. préférer les hors-d'œuvre ou les desserts au restaurant
5. te servir d'une poêle ou d'une casserole pour préparer tes repas
6. parler de politique ou de sport à table
7. rencontrer tes amis à l'association de scoutisme ou au club de fitness
8. fréquenter les discothèques ou les festivals

Essential Instruction

1. Before completing **Activité 12** in pairs, practice oral and written examples of **ne…que** word order in the **passé composé**.
2. Students listen to **Activité 13**, then answer questions one through eight. Stop the recording after each mini-dialogue to expand and ask comprehension questions to encourage students to speak more.
3. Complete **Activité 14** with students. Expand by asking them why or why not.
4. Students work in groups of three or four to do **Activité 15**. Have the groups present their conversation to the class.
5. To complete **Activité 16**, students circulate to interview one another, as if at a party. Debrief the students on what they learned about their classmates. Have them use percentages. **Combien d'élèves ont fait de l'escalade?**

À vous la parole

Question centrale ? Qu'est-ce qu'on doit connaître de sa destination pour réussir son voyage?

Communiquez!

15 À l'agence de voyage 1.1, 1.2, 5.2

Interpersonal Speaking, Interpretive Reading

Avec un partenaire, jouez le rôle d'un agent de voyage et d'un(e) client(e) qui veut partir en vacances d'hiver. L'agent de voyage suggère plusieurs destinations, selon les questions que le client/la cliente pose. Faites des recherches, pour comparer deux ou trois destinations différentes (prix, activités offertes, logement, excursions, etc.). Puis, choisissez une destination. Présentez votre jeu de rôle à la classe.

Recherche: vacances à + VILLE/PAYS

16 Un voyage de classe 1.1, 1.3, 5.2

Interpersonal and Presentational Speaking

Votre professeur organise un voyage en classe à La Réunion. Vous devez organiser des activités à faire en groupe à Saint-Denis pendant votre séjour. Pour cela, demandez à dix camarades de classe leurs préférences. Chaque personne peut choisir deux activités (sports extrêmes ou autres). Faites un tableau comme celui de dessous. Partagez les résultats avec la classe.

	1	2	3	4	5	6	7	8	9	10
faire du parapente										
faire du parachutisme ascensionnel	✔									
faire du saut à l'élastique	✔									
faire du saut à ski										
faire de l'escalade										
autre										

MODÈLE
A: Quelles activités aimerais-tu faire à Saint-Denis pendant notre voyage?
B: Moi j'aimerais faire du saut à l'élastique et du parachutisme ascensionnel.
A: Parfait, c'est noté! Merci!

Resources

CA Communicative Activities
Share

Answers

(continued from previous page)

6. Est-ce que tu parles...? Je ne parle ni de politique ni de sport. Et toi? Je ne parle que de....
7. Est-ce que tu rencontres...? Je ne rencontre mes amis ni à l'association de scoutisme ni au club de fitness. Et toi? Je ne rencontre mes amis qu'à/au....
8. Est-ce que tu fréquentes...? Je ne fréquente ni les discothèques ni les festivals. Et toi? Je ne fréquente que...

15 Scripts will vary.

16 Surveys will vary.

Reference Desk

If you have access to Passport, create a question for your students to share their response to a communicative activity.

Communication

Interpersonal: Paired Practice

Students write down five winter vacation destination ideas on pieces of paper and fold their papers up. Their partner does the same. In turn, students pick a piece of paper, read one of the destinations, and then express to their partner whether this winter vacation appeals to them or not. If it does not, they must explain why not, and if it does, they can express with whom they would like to travel, what they would like to see and do there, where they would like to stay, etc. Expand the activity by having pairs work with another set of partners to share what they learned about their partner's vacation preferences.

Multiple Intelligences

Verbal-Linguistic

Give students a chance to discuss the results of **Activité 16** with multiple partners. Set a timer. Students discuss, and when the timer rings they switch partners. The goal at the end of several rounds is to share what kinds of differences or similarities they discovered.

Answers

17 Slogans and ads will vary.

18 E-mail responses will vary.

Reference Desk

With reference to **Activité 17**: Encourage students to think of advertising campaign slogans with which they are familiar. Does your state or region encourage tourists to visit? Is there a slogan associated with its advertisements? For example, Minnesota is known as "The land of 10,000 lakes." "It's good being first!" reinforces the fact that Delaware was the first state to ratify the U.S. Constitution. Another example is Idaho's slogan, which says, "Adventures in Living."

17 Un design et un slogan pour votre ville 1.3, 2.2, 3.2, 5.1

Presentational Writing and Speaking

Vous êtes chargé(e) de créer un design et un slogan pour une campagne de publicité pour promouvoir votre ville ! Considérez les attractions, les activités, et les symboles de votre région. Qu'est-ce qu'il y a à voir et à faire ? Quels sont les centres d'intérêts de votre ville ? Travaillez avec un(e) partenaire ou en groupe, puis presentez votre slogan et votre publicité à la classe, qui votera pour le meilleur slogan.

18 La Corse 1.1, 1.2, 4.2, 5.2

Interpersonal Writing

Un ami de famille passe des vacances en Corse et vous envoie un mail. Comme vous avez un bon niveau de français, vous devrez répondre pour la famille.

À: Mes amis aux États-Unis
Cc:
Objet: Un bonjour de la Corse !

Bonjour à tous,

Élisa et moi passons une semaine en Corse. La Corse est une petite île avec un statut politique indépendant. Située dans la mer Méditerranée, au sud-est de la France métropolitaine et à l'ouest de l'Italie, elle offre de nombreuses attractions, notamment des sites historiques et des paysages incroyables. Savez-vous quel temps il fait en ce moment ? Hier, nous avons fait du canyonisme. Qu'aimeriez-vous faire si vous étiez avec nous à Ajaccio ? Que nous conseillez-vous de visiter avant de partir ?

La Corse, région de France

Essential Instruction

1. Students work in the computer lab for **Activité 17**.
2. For students collaborating on **Activité 17**, require that they create a list of specific attractions, activities, and symbols of their region. In doing their research, they might discover other aspects to include in their overview of their town. Their slogan could be a jingle.
3. Have students repeat the sentences in **Activité A** and **Activité B** after the speaker. Have them reflect on the pattern. Model the pronunciation in **Activité C** and then do **Activité D**. Play **D** several times if there are students who cannot hear the difference in intonation.

Prononciation

Intonation in Questions with Two Options 1.2

» When asking about two options, rising intonation is used for the first choice and descending intonation for the second.

A L'intonation montante et descendante

Répétez chaque phrase.

1. On part avec tes parents ou pas?
2. Tu préfères la mer ou la montagne?
3. On va à Chamonix ou à La Réunion?

B Qu'est-ce que tu préfères?

Posez la question alternative sur les éléments suggérés, en commençant par «Qu'est-ce que tu préfères...?»

MODÈLE faire du ski ou du snowboard
Qu'est-ce que tu préfères: faire du ski ou du snowboard?

1. faire une randonnée équestre ou une randonnée à pied
2. manger une pizza ou une omelette
3. aller à la boutique ou au centre commercial
4. mettre une chemise ou un pull

Pronounced /ə/

» Especially in groupings of two or more syllables, the sound /ə/ should have the same length and intensity of the other vowels.

C Le son /ə/

Répétez les phrases.

1. C'est la première fois que je vais faire du ski!
2. Je pars pour une semaine.
3. Je me demande s'il fera beau!

D Quelle voyelle entendez-vous?

*Écrivez **E** si vous entendez le son dans **je** ou **regarde** et **É** si vous entendez le son dans **rentrée** ou **marcher**.*

Resources

Pronunciation — *Prononciation*
Pre-test
Leçon Quiz

Answers

B

1. Qu'est-ce que tu préfères: faire une randonnée équestre ou une randonnée à pied?
2. Qu'est-ce que tu préfères: manger une pizza ou une omelette?
3. Qu'est-ce que tu préfères: aller à la boutique ou au centre commercial?
4. Qu'est-ce que tu préfères: mettre une chemise ou un pull?

D Script

1. Reprenons!
2. Recommence!
3. Écoute mon CD!
4. Réfléchissez bien!
5. Regarde le programme!

1. E
2. E
3. É
4. É
5. E

Expansion

For additional intonation practice, provide students with a list of statements that they will change to yes/no questions by altering their intonation similar to **Activité A**. Include a section similar to **Activité B** with either/or options. Allow students to work in small groups. Monitor their practice and come back to whole group repetition to ensure correct pronunciation.

Special Needs Students

Social Anxiety
Group responses give students with social anxiety issues a chance to practice speaking French in a safe way. Make sure that these students know that they do not have to speak loudly in choral responses. Even if they mouth the words, they will benefit from the exercise.

Speech Impairment/Linguistically Challenged
For extra practice with pronunciation and speaking in general, encourage students to listen to any of the recorded activities or culture paragraphs and then select one to read out loud every day. Another option is for them to sing French songs daily. It is a non-stressful way to internalize pronunciation.

Resources

- *Vocabulaire actif*
- eV eVisual
- WB Workbook 1–3
- FC Flash Cards
- LA Listening Activity 1
- G & V Practice Games

Reference Desk

1. Skiers in Europe, as in the United States, need to know the color symbols of the different slopes to make sure that they select trails that correspond to their level and ability: **vert** (**piste facile**); **bleu** (**piste de difficulté moyenne**); **rouge** (**piste difficile**); **noir** (**piste très difficile**). **Le plan de pistes de ski** is indispensible for getting to know the layout of the slopes and trails. Skiers find out about ski conditions by consulting **le bulletin d'enneigement** and **le risque d'avalanches**.
2. The term **les fesses** means *buttocks*. A **tire-fesses** is a rope tow that a skier straddles to get to the top of a hill. You may tell students that **une fessée** means a *spanking*.
3. **Chaussures de ski** are also called **bottes de ski**. **Ski nordique** is also called **ski de fond**.

Leçon B Vocabulaire actif

À la station de ski 1.2

Sur les pistes

un télésiège

une piste de ski

un tremplin de saut à ski

un moniteur/une monitrice

un forfait de ski

Les vêtements de ski

un casque de ski

des gants (m.)

un bonnet

une veste (de) ski

des chaussures (f.) de ski

des skis (m.)

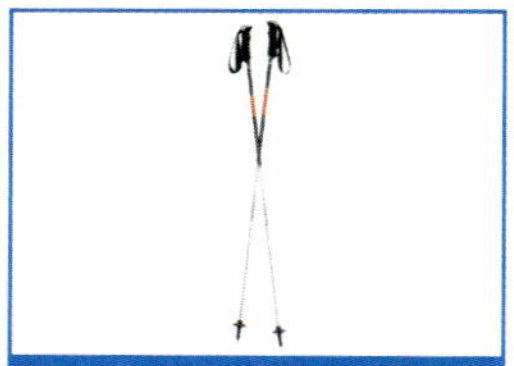

des bâtons (m.) de ski

un pantalon (de) ski

Essential Instruction

1. Begin by asking students if they have ever skied or snowboarded. Where did they go? Did they take lessons?
2. Explain that **Leçon B** continues the winter sports theme, concentrating on skiing in the French Alps.
3. Have students listen to the vocabulary several times without repeating.
4. Replay the vocabulary, allowing them to repeat.
5. Play **Pour la conversation**, stopping after each line to comment.
6. Have students work in pairs to do **Activité 1**, answering questions 1–5.

Pour la conversation 1.2

How do I say what I must do?

» Il faut que je revienne **en skiant correctement**.

I must return by skiing correctly.

How do I tell someone he or she will have the opportunity to do something?

» **Tu auras l'occasion d'**apprendre.

You will have the opportunity to learn.

How do I say I was expecting something?

» Ça, **je m'y attendais**!

I was expecting that!

Et si je voulais dire... ?

des après-ski (m.)	*snow boots*
un remonte-pente	*ski tow*
le ski nordique	*cross-country skiing*
un tire-fesses	*T-bar*
faire du patin à glace	*to ice skate*

1 Je m'y attendais! 1.2, 1.3

Interpretive Reading

Lisez le blog d'Alexis, un jeune Parisien, qui a fait un séjour de sports d'hiver. Puis, répondez aux questions.

J'ai une semaine de vacances, et j'ai décidé de la passer à Chamonix. Pourquoi? Parce que j'adore les activités en plein air et la neige, mais je dois apprendre à skier correctement. J'ai acheté un forfait ski, et je me suis inscrit dans un cours avec un moniteur. J'avais l'intention de louer des skis et des bâtons, parce que j'avais tout le reste dans ma valise — mon bonnet, mes gants, mes chaussures de ski et mon pantalon ski. En sortant du train, j'ai réalisé que ma valise n'y était plus. Ah ça, je ne m'y attendais pas! Ça coûte cher, les vêtements de ski! Est-ce que quelqu'un a vu une valise bleue dans le train pour Chamonix le weekend dernier?

1. Pour quelle raison Alexis part-il à Chamonix?
2. Quels préparatifs a-t-il fait à l'avance?
3. Qu'est-ce qu'il comptait louer?
4. Quel problème a-t-il eu?
5. Qu'est-ce qu'Alexis cherche?

Resources

Pour la conversation

Et si je voulais dire... ?

Answers

1

1. Il a une semaine de vacances.
2. Il a acheté un forfait de ski et s'est inscrit à un cours.
3. Il comptait louer des skis et des bâtons de ski.
4. Il a perdu sa valise.
5. Il cherche quelqu'un qui a vu sa valise bleue dans le train.

Reference Desk

In **Activité 1**, note that in French, **Alexis** is a boy's name.

nouvelle orthographe **un tire-fesse, des tire-fesses**

Communication

Interpersonal: Paired Practice

Have students role-play a skier at a resort buying a lift pass, renting equipment, and buying some chic ski outfits. The salesperson will ask pertinent questions to help the skier purchase **le nécessaire**. Level 1, **Unité 6, Leçon A**, pp. 274–275 introduced students to shopping vocabulary and expressions.

Differentiated Learning

Accelerate

Have students write **un blog** recounting a day of skiing in **Chamonix**. They must describe what they wore, what they did, and where they ate.

Decelerate

Have students illustrate the new vocabulary words in their notebooks. They may have to go online to find pictures of rope and T-bar tows.

Answers

2

1. station de ski
2. skis
3. bâtons
4. télésiège
5. forfait
6. tremplins de sauts à ski
7. moniteur
8. gants
9. bonnet

3 Possible answers:

Roberto porte des chaussures, un pantalon de ski marron clair, un pull gris foncé et des gants. Il a des skis.
Fatou porte des chaussures de ski, des gants blancs, un pantalon de ski blanc, un manteau jaune et un bonnet. Elle a des skis et des bâtons de ski.
Chan porte des gants bleus, des chaussures de ski noir, un pantalon de ski, noir et un gros pull-over orange foncé. Il a des skis et des bâtons de ski.
Nadège porte des gants et un pull violets, des chaussures de ski, et un pantalon de ski vert. Elle a des skis et des bâtons de ski.

4

1. gants
2. moniteur, monitrice
3. bonnet
4. tremplin de saut à ski
5. bâtons
6. un ski
7. télésiège
8. pantalon de ski

Reference Desk

1. Additional vocabulary words associated with winter activities: **les randonnées nocturnes** *(nighttime hikes)*; **les balades à raquettes** *(snowshoe walks)*; **la luge** *(sledding)*; **la motoneige** *(snowmobiling)*; **le VTT sur neige** *(all-terrain vehicles on snow)*.
2. Websites for large ski resorts often include videos in French and webcam feeds that would interest students. These could be used for a variety of activities. Research **le Val de Thorens**, **La Plagne**, and **l'Alpe d'Huez**.

2 Faire du ski 1.2

Interpretive Reading

C'est bientôt la saison des sports d'hiver. Une agence de voyage offre des conseils à ses clients, mais des mots ont disparu de son article sur son site web. Retrouvez les mots manquants (missing).

Si vous voulez faire du ski, vous devez aller dans une (1). Avant de partir sur les pistes de ski, vous devez vous équiper: louez des (2) et des (3). Avant de pouvoir prendre le (4) qui vous emmène en haut de la piste, achetez un (5) pour toute la semaine. C'est moins cher que de payer à la journée. Les (6) sont pour les skieurs avec beaucoup d'expérience. Demandez à un (7) ou une monitrice ses conseils. Il fait froid, donc n'oubliez pas vos (8) pour vos mains ni votre (9) de ski pour couvrir vos oreilles.

3 Ils sont prêts à skier! 1.2, 1.3, 5.2

Interpretive Viewing, Presentational Speaking or Writing

À tour de rôle, décrivez ce que chaque personne porte dans les illustrations suivantes. Votre partenaire va deviner qui vous décrivez.

MODÈLE **Roberto porte...**

Roberto Fatou Chan Nadège

4 Sur les pistes 1.2

Interpretive Reading

Complétez la phrase avec un mot ou une expression.

1. Si on a froid aux mains, il faut acheter de meilleurs....
2. Si on ne sait pas skier, on peut apprendre avec un... ou une....
3. Si on a froid à la tête, il faut mettre un... bien chaud.
4. Un skieur qui fait de très longues distances part d'un....
5. Un skieur tient (*holds*) des... dans ses mains.
6. On attache la chaussure de ski à....
7. On monte en haut des pistes avec un....
8. Pour faire du ski on peut mettre un pantalon ou un....

Essential Instruction

1. Ask students to refer to the **Vocabulaire actif** as you read each sentence in **Activité 2**. Have them write down the missing vocabulary.
2. Have students do **Activité 3** in pairs. As an extension of this activity students can alternate describing a scene and drawing it. For example, **Chan fait du ski nordique. Nadège est tombée dans la neige**.
3. Have students change partners to work with someone new to complete **Activité 4** and **Activité 6**. Note that they may need to do some research before doing **Activité 6**.
4. For **Activité 5** students listen and respond in writing.
5. Have students integrate the answers to **Activité 7** either in the form of **un blog** or a letter to a friend.

5 La classe de neige 1.2

Interpretive Listening

Écrivez les numéros 1–6 sur votre papier. Écoutez ce que chacun des enfants emporte en classe de neige. Puis, choisissez le mot qui n'est pas mentionné.

1. un bonnet, des gants, un blouson, des bottes de ski
2. un pantalon de ski, des lunettes de ski, des gants, de la crème solaire, un bonnet
3. des chaussures de ski, des bâtons de ski, un forfait
4. un pantalon de ski, un pull, une écharpe, un bonnet, des skis
5. un bonnet, un pantalon de ski, une écharpe, des chaussures de ski, un masque de ski
6. des skis, des bâtons, un forfait, des chaussures

La station de ski de Val Thorens, dans les Alpes de Savoie

6 Vous aurez l'occasion de.... 1.1, 5.1, 5.2

Interpersonal Speaking

À tour de rôle, suggérez une destination et des activités pour les prochaines vacances.

MODÈLE ma famille (la Corse)
A : Ma famille et moi, on ne sait pas où passer les vacances.
B : Pourquoi ne pas aller en Corse? Vous aurez l'occasion de nager et de bronzer au bord de la mer.

1. mes cousins (Montréal)
2. ma tante (la Normandie)
3. mes amis (l'Alsace)
4. mon père (la Bretagne)
5. ma bande de copains (la Côte d'Azur)
6. mes camarades de classe (Lyon)
7. ma mère (La Réunion)
8. mon frère (Grenoble)

On recycle !
Avec un partenaire, racontez en quelques phrases une classe de neige à laquelle vous avez participé quand vous étiez petit(e) en utilisant le passé composé et l'imparfait, ou bien imaginez une classe de neige que vous voudriez faire en utilisant le conditionnel.

7 Questions personnelles 1.1, 1.3

Interpersonal Speaking

Répondez aux questions avec un partenaire.

1. As-tu déjà fait du ski? Où? Combien de fois?
2. Qu'est-ce qu'on peut louer dans une station de ski?
3. Quels vêtements et accessoires faut-il emporter?
4. Pourquoi est-ce que le ski est un sport tellement populaire? À quoi est-ce qu'on s'attend?
5. Est-ce qu'on peut faire du ski près de chez toi, ou dans la région? Sinon, où sont les stations de ski dans ta région? Est-ce qu'il y a de meilleures pistes dans d'autres régions?

Differentiated Learning

Accelerate
Have students write a descriptive paragraph about the photo of **la station de ski de Val Thorens** and research where it is located, and what "**La Folie Douce**" might mean in terms of a vacation at **le Val de Thorens**. (It is a popular restaurant/bar and "**après-ski**" venue at this resort, nicknamed the "dance floor at the top of the world.")

Decelerate
As a guided practice, work with low-ability students in small groups to do **Activité 4** and **Activité 6**. They will appreciate the additional help in writing since these two exercises require vocabulary recall and writing skills.

Resources

Activity 5

Answers

5 Script

1. Paul a son bonnet noir, ses grosses bottes de ski, et un blouson léger.
2. Marianne emporte ses gants, des lunettes de ski, de la crème solaire (bien sûr), et son bonnet en laine.
3. Sarah va louer des chaussures de ski et des bâtons de ski sur place.
4. Marc emporte un pantalon de ski, une écharpe bleue, un nouveau bonnet, et ses propres skis.
5. Thibault emporte des chaussures de ski et un pantalon de ski, une écharpe, mais il n'emporte pas de masque de ski !
6. Julie a son forfait, ses nouveaux skis, mais elle a oublié ses jolies chaussures.

1. des gants; 2. un pantalon de ski; 3. un forfait; 4. un pull; 5. un bonnet; 6. des bâtons

6 Possible partner answers:

1. Pourquoi ne pas aller à Montréal? Vous aurez l'occasion de visiter des festivals.
2. Pourquoi ne pas aller en Normandie? Vous aurez l'occasion d'admirer les falaises et de visiter des musées.
3. Pourquoi ne pas aller en Alsace? Vous aurez l'occasion de manger dans de bons restaurants et de visiter des cathédrales.
4. Pourquoi ne pas aller en Bretagne? Vous aurez l'occasion de faire du bateau, de pêcher des poissons, et de profiter des crêperies traditionnelles.
5. Pourquoi ne pas aller sur la Côte d'Azur? Vous aurez l'occasion de bronzer sur les plages et de rencontrer des célébrités.
6. Pourquoi ne pas aller à Lyon? Vous aurez l'occasion de faire du shopping, de visiter des petits musées et de manger dans de petits restaurants.
7. Pourquoi ne pas aller à La Réunion? Vous aurez l'occasion de bronzer sur la plage, de faire du scooter des mers et de faire des randonnées dans la forêt.
8. Pourquoi ne pas aller à Grenoble? Vous aurez l'occasion de faire du shopping en ville et de visiter des centres de recherche scientifique.

7 Answers will vary.

Resources

- Dialogue
  Activity 8
  Extension
- Dialogue Video
- WB Workbook 4

Answers

8 Possible answers:

1. Léo est informatif.
2. Élodie est désorganisée.
3. Léo n'est pas surpris.
4. Léo est le plus sportif.
5. Léo ou (et) Élodie est (sont) serviable(s).

EXTENSION

Elles ne vont pas mettre toutes leurs affaires dans la même valise.

Reference Desk

1. **Combloux**, a popular ski resort with approximately 2,000 residents, is a commune in the **Haute-Savoie** in southeastern France, and is situated 2.5 miles from **Megève** and 19 miles from **Chamonix-Mont-Blanc**.
2. **École du ski français** (**ESF**) is a federation of ski schools founded in 1937. The ski instructors take competitive tests to obtain national diplomas. Each year, 2,000 students pass 800,000 skiing skills tests. The children's school, called **Piou Piou**, trains children as young as three. The levels for children are: **piou-piou**, **ourson** (*little bear*), **flocon** (*snowflake*) **première**, **deux-ième**, **troisième étoile**, **étoile de bronze**, and **étoile d'or**. There exist courses for adolescents and adults in all modes of skiing.

Game

Devinettes

Divide students into two teams. Give each team different pictures of vocabulary items. Students from one team must ask questions to guess which piece of ski clothing/equipment or type of winter sport the other team has chosen. For example, "**Est-ce que c'est quelque chose qu'on porte?**" "**C'est un bonnet?**"

Rencontres culturelles

Les classes de neige

1.2, 2.1, 3.2, 5.2

Élodie fait sa valise pour aller au ski.

Élodie : Cette fois il faut que je rentre à la maison en skiant correctement.
Léo : Tu auras l'occasion d'apprendre… les classes le matin, le ski l'après-midi, et moi avec les parents le weekend. Il y a 450 kilomètres de pistes à Combloux !
Élodie : Et les moniteurs ?
Léo : Ils sont sympa…. Dis, le weekend tu veux faire du snowboard ?
Élodie : Tu connais Megève ? On ira aussi faire un peu de shopping.
Léo : Ça, je m'y attendais ! Tu as vérifié que tu n'as rien oublié ? Tes gants ? Ton pantalon de ski ? Ton bonnet ? Tes lunettes ?
Élodie : De toute façon, les skis, les chaussures, on loue tout sur place… Bon, eh bien, il n'y a plus qu'à partir… il faut que je sois plus organisée ! Au fait, tu n'as pas vu mon billet de train… ?

8 Les classes de neige

1.2, 1.3

Formez des phrases en disant qui a les attributs suivants : Élodie ou Léo ?

1. informatif/informative
2. désorganisé(e)
3. pas surpris(e)
4. le plus sportif/la plus sportive
5. serviable (*helpful*)

Mot-clé

Valise (de l'italien *valigia* en 1558). Au départ, le mot valise désigne un sac en cuir qui se porte en croupe (comme dans les westerns) avant de devenir un bagage rectangulaire porté à la main (1876). Valise a donné *dévaliser*, c'est-à-dire prendre à quelqu'un tout ce qu'il a sur lui.

1.2

EXTENSION **Préparations pour un voyage en avion**

Deux sœurs se préparent pour un voyage en avion.

Maeva : Dis, j'ai hâte de voir Mamy et Papy.
Faustine : Moi de même. Bon, comment on fait ?
Maeva : Moi, je n'ai pas confiance, je ne mets pas toutes mes affaires dans la même valise.
Faustine : Tu n'as pas confiance en qui ?
Maeva : On a un changement de vol, il y a toujours le risque qu'une valise se perde. Comment on fait avec les médicaments ?
Faustine : Mets-les dans ton sac à main.

EXTENSION 1.2 Quelle solution Maeva et Faustine ont-elles trouvée pour arriver chez leurs grands-parents avec l'essentiel ?

Essential Instruction

1. Present the information about the **École du ski français**. You may show some online video clips of various **écoles du ski**, notably **Méribel**. The students see what a ski resort looks like, and they can watch students ski from beginners to advanced.
2. For **Activité 8**, have students listen to the dialogue **Les classes de neige** and answer the questions.
3. Have students locate **la Savoie** on the map of France, along with its major cities, Chambéry and Annecy.
4. The students will read **La Savoie**, noting its location, economy, festivals, local food specialties, and ski resorts.
5. Have them use the same topics to describe their town or locale.

Points de départ

Pre-AP

Question centrale ? Qu'est-ce qu'on doit connaître de sa destination pour réussir son voyage?

La Savoie 1.2, 2.1, 2.2, 5.1

La Savoie est devenue une province française en 1860. C'est une région frontalière* avec l'Italie, à laquelle elle est reliée par des cols* et par des tunnels dont le tunnel du Mont Blanc*. C'est un paysage de montagnes avec les Alpes, des lacs (Lac du Bourget, Lac d'Annecy), et des vallées (vallée de la Tarentaise, vallée de l'Arc).

La Savoie comprend deux départements, la Savoie et la Haute-Savoie. Ses habitants sont les Savoyards. Les deux principales villes sont Chambéry et Annecy. Son économie est tournée vers l'imagerie*, les industries du sport et des loisirs, l'énergie solaire, et la photovoltaïque*. C'est aussi le berceau* du groupe de grande distribution* Carrefour.

Terre de culture, la Savoie abrite de nombreux festivals comme le festival du film d'animation à Annecy, référence mondiale pour les professionnels de l'animation. Terre de gastronomie, ses spécialités sont les fromages de beaufort, le reblochon, et la tomme. Terre de tourisme, c'est le royaume* du ski avec le plus grand domaine skiable* d'Europe et ses très nombreuses stations dont la plus ancienne est Chamonix. Ces stations sont souvent reliées entre elles pour constituer d'immenses domaines skiables comme celui des Portes du soleil (Avoriaz, Morzine, Les Gets, etc.) avec ses 650 kilomètres de pistes.

La station de Méribel

Recherche : savoie mont blanc, visiter la savoie, vacances savoie

frontalière *border*; **cols** *passes*; **Mont Blanc** *highest peak in the Alps*; **imagerie** *(digital) imaging*; **photovoltaïque** *solar cells*; **berceau** *cradle*; **grande distribution** *retail*; **royaume** *realm*; **domaine skiable** *ski area*

Produits 1.2, 2.2

La raclette savoyarde est un plat avec du fromage à raclette et du jambon. Autrefois, on mangeait la raclette au coin de la cheminée, mais ces jours-ci il existe un appareil pour la préparation de la raclette. Trouvez des photos en ligne. Aimeriez-vous y goûter?

Comparaisons 1.2, 4.2

Comment pouvez-vous définir la « terre de culture », la « terre gastronomique », et la « terre de tourisme » dans votre région?

La raclette est délicieuse sur les pommes de terre!

Un petit restaurant typique des Alpes

Traditions et pratiques 1.2, 2.1, 2.2

Dans les régions de la Savoie et de la Haute-Savoie, on organise souvent des fêtes folkloriques où les gens portent des costumes savoyards, dansent des danses traditionnelles (comme la quadrille, la ronde, le rigaudon, la polka et la montfarine), et chantent des chansons qui racontent l'histoire de la région.

Resources

Points de départ

WB Workbook 5

Explore

Answers

Comparaisons
Answers will vary.

Reference Desk

1. **La photovoltaïque** (*photovoltaic*) literally means light (*photo*) and electricity (*voltaic*). Photovoltaic cells generate electricity from sunlight or other light sources. This technology is used to convert solar energy to usable power.
2. Fondue originated in Switzerland. Frugal peasants, alpine villagers, and goat herders would take pieces of leftover hardened cheese, melt them, and add garlic, wine, and other ingredients to produce fondue, in order to sustain themselves during long winters.
3. The distinctive dish of rich melted cheese, potatoes, and other vegetables is called **la raclette** and has its origins in the Swiss Alps. It was the traditional hearty meal of farmers and shepherds.
4. If you have access to Passport, find a video or a news article related to **la Savoie** or **Annecy**, and show it to your students.

Connections

Gourmet/Gourmand

Students who love to cook can research recipes for **la raclette savoyarde**, **la fondue**, and **les pommes de terre dauphinoise**. They might try to find **Beaufort**, **Reblochon**, and **Tomme de Savoie** cheeses in specialty cheese stores or organize a tasting for their family.

Multiple Intelligences

Naturalist
Students interested in nature could explore the Alpine region. How high are the mountain ranges? What do they look like in winter and summer? What animals can survive the rugged winters? How is the vegetation in the mountains different from that on the plains?

Visual-Spatial
Encourage students to make a chart of the Alps noting the major ski resorts, cities, lakes, and valleys so that they can envision the areas as they are discussed.

Bodily-Kinesthetic
What are the different options in a ski school from beginner to off-piste skiing? What are the most dangerous kinds of skiing? Which ones would they like to try and why?

Answers

Comparaisons
Answers will vary.

Communication

Interpersonal: Cooperative Groups

Arrange students in heterogeneous groups composed of high and low-ability students. Using **Les classes de neige** as a point of reference, have them create the ideal three-week ski school experience. Where would they choose to go? How would they get to their destination? What ski classes would they like to take? What educational courses would help them to prepare for their ski adventure? Have each group report their findings to the class.

Culture

Products: Information

Author Eugène Sue (***Les Mystères de Paris***), actor André Dussollier (three times César winner for best actor), and chef Marc Veyrat, were born in Annecy. Have pairs of students research these notable people and role-play an interview in front of the class.

Les classes de neige 1.2, 2.1, 2.2, 5.1

Les établissements scolaires ont la possibilité d'organiser chaque année des classes de neige. Les élèves partent aux sports d'hiver ensemble. Le séjour peut durer d'une à trois semaines. Lors des classes de neige, il s'agit de combiner loisirs et travail en classe. C'est l'occasion de mettre en place des projets qui concilient plaisir de la neige, convivialité et démarche* éducative.

Recherche : blog classes de neige, vidéo classes de neige, photos classes de neige

démarche *undertaking*

1.2, 4.2 **Comparaisons**
Où peut-on faire des sports aquatiques près de chez vous ?

Annecy est connu pour son carnaval vénitien.

Annecy 1.2, 2.2, 3.2

Annecy est une charmante ville de 225 000 habitants. On l'a surnommée tour à tour* la « Rome des Alpes », défenseur du catholicisme romain au 16ème siècle, « Venise des Alpes » à cause de ses canaux*, « Perle des Alpes » à cause du site qu'elle occupe entre lac et montagnes. Annecy est une grande capitale touristique qui accueille chaque année 2,5 millions de touristes. Les visiteurs aiment flâner* dans les rues pavées de la vieille ville médiévale en regardant les maisons fleuries* près des canaux. Du château d'Annecy on peut voir le lac d'Annecy, un beau lac propre, où on peut faire du bateau, du ski nautique, et même louer des pédalos*.

Recherche : lac d'annecy, accueil ville annecy

tour à tour *successively* ; **canaux** *canals* ; **flâner** *to stroll* ; **fleuries** *covered in flowers* ; **pédalos** *pedal boats*

La Francophonie

Profil touristique

À Saint-Martin 1.2, 2.1, 3.2, 5.1

Saint-Martin est une île de la mer des Antilles partagée entre la France et les Pays-Bas. Dans la partie où l'on parle français, on trouve deux sortes d'activités principales appelées « bleu » et « vert ». La catégorie « vert » offre beaucoup d'activités pour les gens qui aiment la nature. La catégorie « bleu » est pour les fanas des sports aquatiques comme la plongée sous-marine, la planche à voile, le ski nautique, ou le scooter des mers.

Marigot est une ville de Saint-Martin très fréquentée par les touristes.

Recherche : saint-martin accueil, office de tourisme de l'île de saint-martin, bienvenue à saint-martin tourisme, visiter saint-martin

Essential Instruction

1. Have students find photos of **la ville d'Annecy** in summer and winter and then decide if they are "**blanc**" because they prefer winter or snow sports, "**vert**" if they like to hike in the woods, or "**bleu**" preferring to engage in water sports. Having declared their preference, have them make a list of activities in which they would like to participate. Students can also be a blend of colors.
2. Have students locate Saint-Martin on a map of Europe.
3. In the same vein, have students read **La Francophonie** and proceed in the same manner choosing "**bleu**," "**vert**," or both.
4. For **Activité 9**, offer students the choice of items one, three, or four. All students do item two.

Answers

All activities will vary.

À DISCUTER

Answers will vary.

9 Activités culturelles 1.3, 2.1, 3.2

Faites les activités suivantes.

1. Faites une présentation sur la Savoie comme « Terre de culture », « Terre de gastronomie », ou « Terre de tourisme ».
2. Situez les lieux mentionnés dans la lecture sur la Savoie sur une carte.
3. Faites un album photos sur la ville d'Annecy. Écrivez des légendes pour décrire les photos en détails.
4. Trouvez un blog, une vidéo, ou des photos d'élèves français en classe de neige. Avec un partenaire, servez-vous de ces supports pour répondre à des questions que l'on peut se poser sur la classe de neige. Présentez vos questions et réponses sur votre format préféré (images, vidéo, audio). N'oubliez pas de citer les sources dont vous vous êtes servi(e).

Recherche : ma classe de neige

On fait la raclette avec un appareil à raclette et du bon fromage de Savoie.

À DISCUTER

Votre classe planifie un séjour pour combiner loisirs et travail en classe. Que proposeriez-vous comme destination, mode de transport, logement, activités ?

Le village de Campagny-en-Vanoise en Savoie

Il y n'a pas que le ski ! Pourquoi pas faire une randonnée ?

C'est chouette de faire de la motoneige !

Piste de ski dans le Mont-Blanc

Differentiated Learning

Accelerate

High-ability students read **Du côté des médias** and answer the questions on p. 230.

Decelerate

Have students make a report to the class about **la fédération française de ski** in which they explain what the categories are for the ski teams (**ski alpin**, **ski de fond**, **biathlon**, **saut à ski**, **combiné**, **nordique**, **ski freestyle**, **snowboard**, **disciplines non-olympiques**) and show a picture of each.

Answers

10

1. Grands domaines
2. Stations de ski de fond/ski nordique
3. Sites touristiques
4. Stations nature & évasion
5. Stations familiales
6. Stations dynamiques & sportives
7. Presentations will vary.

Reference Desk

1. To help students with the reading, here are some words that they might not know: **l'entretien** (*maintenance*); **dépaysement** (*change of scenery*); **cadre** (*scenery*); **remontées mécaniques** (*ski lifts*).
2. For additional information, photos, and videos, visit the **Champagny-en-Vanoise** website.

Du côté des médias 1.2

Lisez les informations suivantes.

Les différentes catégories de labels

Les stations ayant obtenu le label sont classées en plusieurs catégories :
Nous avons mis en place 6 labels pour différencier les types de stations. Voici la liste et les logos des catégories :

Stations familiales
Cette catégorie est en général attribuée aux petites stations qui mettent l'accent sur les activités en famille et proposent un domaine adapté aux débutants.

Sites touristiques
Ce label est destiné aux sites touristiques en montagne, proposant ou non des activités comme le ski.

Grands domaines
Cette catégorie est réservée aux grandes stations qui possèdent un grand nombre de pistes et de remontées mécaniques.

Stations dynamiques & sportives
Pour entrer dans cette rubrique, les domaines skiables doivent proposer un grand nombre d'activités en hiver mais aussi en été… Elles doivent également avoir une volonté de renouveler ces installations.

Stations nature & évasion
Les stations « nature et évasion » doivent proposer à leurs clients un cadre exceptionnel pour un dépaysement garanti. Son village doit de préférence se situer près de sapins pour pratiquer des activités comme la randonnée ou encore des ballades en raquettes.

Stations de ski de fond/ ski nordique
Pour les domaines de ski de fond qui ne peuvent pas obtenir un des labels ci-dessus, nous mettons en place la catégorie « Ski de fond & ski nordique ».

10 Les labels de ski 1.2, 2.3, 3.2, 4.2

Retrouvez les labels qui décrivent les stations de ski suivantes :

1. les grandes stations qui ont beaucoup de pistes
2. les stations qui n'offrent pas de ski de piste
3. les stations qui se concentrent sur les activités touristiques
4. les stations qui offrent beaucoup d'activités dans un cadre naturel superbe
5. les stations qui sont plus adaptées aux familles et aux débutants
6. les stations qui proposent des activités l'hiver aussi bien que l'été

Faites l'activité suivante :

7. En groupes, choisissez le label qui vous semble le plus intéressant. Expliquez pourquoi, puis présentez à votre classe les avantages d'une station de ski de ce label. Trouvez des exemples de stations en ligne.

Recherche : station de ski label (+ NAME OF LABEL)

Essential Instruction

1. Complete **Activité 10** together or in small groups.
2. Have students take the mini-quiz to see what they remember of the "to know" verbs.
3. Using whiteboards or their notebooks, have students practice the forms of **savoir** and **connaître** in the **présent**, **imparfait**, **futur**, **conditionnel**, and **passé composé**.
4. Write incomplete sentences on the board for which the students will supply the verb: **Tu______Paul. Il _______faire du ski alpin**. This can be an oral and written exercise.

Révision: *Savoir* versus *Connaître* 1.1

On recycle!

See if you can choose the right verb to complete each sentence and then summarize when to use each verb.

1. Je... que je suis en retard pour ma leçon de ski. (sais, connais)
2. Marc... cette station de ski. (sait, connaît)
3. Tu... le moniteur? (sais, connais)
4. Nous... faire des sauts à ski. (savons, connaissons)

If you were unable to complete the activity, read the grammar explanation to review how to form these verbs and when to use them.

Savoir and **connaître** both mean "to know." However, they each have specific contexts in which they are used.

savoir		
▪ factual information ▪ how to do something	Je **sais** où se trouve la piste. Les moniteurs **savent** faire du snowboard.	*I know where the slope is.* *The instructors know how to snowboard.*
connaître		
familiar/acquainted with people, places, things	Khaled **connaît** bien l'île de La Réunion.	*Khaled knows the island of Reunion well.*

Connaissez-vous mon ami Marc? — *Do you know my friend Marc?*

Il **sait** faire du ski de fond. — *He knows how to cross-country ski.*

The present-tense forms are:

savoir	
je **sais**	nous **savons**
tu **sais**	vous **savez**
il/elle/on **sait**	ils/elles **savent**

connaître	
je **connais**	nous **connaissons**
tu **connais**	vous **connaissez**
il/elle/on **connaît**	ils/elles **connaissent**

The irregular past participle of **savoir** is **su**.
The irregular past participle of **connaître** is **connu**.

Qui sait la réponse?

Usage Tip

Connu is often used as an adjective: **Connu en France, le chanteur canadien y a vendu 500 000 albums.**

Resources

WB Workbook 6

G & V Practice Games

Answers

On recycle!

1. sais
2. connaît
3. connais
4. savons

Reference Desk

1. **Savoir** + INFINITIVE means *to know how to do something, to be savvy*. The French expression **savoir-faire** has been adopted into English.
2. **Connaître** often implies knowing something well (**Il connaît bien la cuinsine italienne**), from which we have the word **connaisseur**. **Connaître** is never followed by an infinitive. **Connaître par cœur** means *to know by heart*.
3. **Reconnaître** (literally *to know again*) is *to recognize*.
4. To help students remember the circumflex over the **aît** form, explain that "when **aît** get together they raise the roof," the roof being the circumflex. This is true for all forms of **connaître**.

nouvelle orthographe: **connaitre, il/elle/on connait**

Expansion

Les bronzés font du ski is a slapstick French film from 1979 about some friends who go skiing together. Show a clip of one of the scenes with the volume off. Ask students what the people are doing, what they are wearing, and what the problems are. Replay the clip with the volume up as a listening exercise and to enjoy the film.

Recherche: les bronzés font du ski

Differentiated Learning

Decelerate

Point out to students that **savoir** is usually followed by an infinitive or one of the question words, while **connaître** is followed by a noun. Illustrate this with this example: **"Tu connais le français. Tu sais parler français."** If they are struggling with the conjugation of **connaître**, explain that it is very similar to regular **-ir** verbs.

Accelerate

Challenge students who understand the distinction between **savoir** and **connaître** to make a chart for the class with examples in French and English.

11 Savoir ou connaître ? 1.3

Presentational Speaking or Writing

*Utilisez les indices ci-dessous pour faire des phrases avec les verbes **savoir** ou **connaître**.*

MODÈLE Simon (se servir du télésiège)
Simon sait se servir du télésiège.

je (Megève)
Je connais Megève.

1. tu (écrire des chansons)
2. les élèves de Mme Choffrut (les contes de fées maghrébins)
3. Éric et toi (quand le festival aura lieu)
4. je (les tableaux de Monet)
5. tu (les monuments de Paris)
6. Élise et moi (l'histoire de Cendrillon)
7. les profs d'histoire (quand la Révolution française a commencé)
8. Mamy (où acheter le meilleur Camembert)
9. nous (faire du ski alpin)

The Subjunctive of Regular Verbs after *il faut que* 1.2

Est-ce qu'il faut qu'Hamza mette des gants ou des lunettes de soleil aujourd'hui ?

Verb forms in both English and French depend on the tense (time of the action) and the mood (attitude of the speaker) they reflect. You already know the indicative mood in French: the present, used to refer to today; the **passé composé** and **imparfait**, used to refer to the past; the imperative, used to give a command; and the conditional, used to state a condition. Another mood is the passive mood, which is used to express something done by someone else. A third mood is called the subjunctive. This mood is used to express necessity, doubt, uncertainty, possibility, wish, feeling, or emotion.

Resources

- WB Workbook 10
- LA Listening Activity 2
- G & V Practice Games

Answers

11

1. Tu sais écrire des chansons.
2. Les élèves de Mme Choffrut connaissent les contes de fées maghrébins.
3. Éric et toi savez quand le festival aura lieu.
4. Je connais les tableaux de Monet.
5. Tu connais les monuments de Paris.
6. Élise et moi connaissons l'histoire de Cendrillon.
7. Les profs d'histoire savent quand la Révolution française a commencé.
8. Mamy sait où acheter le meilleur camembert.
9. Nous savons faire du ski alpin.

Reference Desk

Explain that English does have a subjunctive form as well, but it is not used as frequently as in French. We are often unaware that we are using subjunctive forms in English as they are the same as the indicative and therefore not as obvious as the examples in French. Here are a few examples of the subjunctive in English:

- Statements contrary to fact: If I *were* king, I would eliminate homework.
- Wishful thinking: He wishes she *were* here with him.
- Certain conjunctions: He wrote it down *in order that* he (might) remember.
- The English equivalent of the use of the subjunctive with **il faut que** is exemplified by the following: It is necessary that he *be* respectful to the teacher.

Communication

Interpersonal: Cooperative Groups

In groups, students write as many sentences as they can with the two verbs "to know" in a timed practice. The group with the most correct answers wins.

Essential Instruction

1. As a bell-ringer activity ask students what they know (**savoir**) about skiing. Ask them what ski areas they know (**connaître**).
2. Have partners take turns constructing sentences for **Activité 11**. Correct the exercise in class.
3. Introduce the concept of the subjunctive. Explain that the subjunctive is always introduced by **que** in a dependent clause, and that it appears after certain verbs and conjunctions that they will learn in the next lesson and **Unité 4**. You may not want to spend too much time on this, and instead focus on the formation of the subjunctive and its use after one expression: **il faut que**.
4. Explain the formation of regular **–er**, **–ir**, and **–re** verbs.
5. Practice **il faut que** + SUBJUNCTIVE orally. Use whiteboards for written practice.

In French, the subjunctive usually appears after **que (qu')** in a dependent clause.

Il faut **acheter** un pantalon de ski.	*It is necessary to buy ski pants.*
Il faut **que** vous **achetiez** un pantalon de ski.	*You must buy ski pants. (It is necessary that you buy ski pants.)*

To form the subjunctive of most verbs, drop the **-ent** of the present-tense **ils/elles** form to use as a base, and then add the ending **-e**, **-es**, **-e**, **-ions**, **-iez**, or **-ent**, depending on the corresponding subject. Here are the subjunctive forms of regular **-er**, **-ir**, and **-re** verbs.

	tenter	finir	attendre
que je (j')	**tente**	**finisse**	**attende**
que tu	**tentes**	**finisses**	**attendes**
qu'il/elle/on	**tente**	**finisse**	**attende**
que nous	**tentions**	**finissions**	**attendions**
que vous	**tentiez**	**finissiez**	**attendiez**
qu'ils/elles	**tentent**	**finissent**	**attendent**

The subjunctive expression **il faut que** in French may be translated in English by the expressions *it is necessary that*, *must*, *have to*, and *should*.

Il faut que vous **écoutiez** la monitrice.

It is necessary that you listen to the instructor.
You have to listen to the instructor.
You must listen to the instructor.
You should listen to the instructor.

Spelling Tip

Note that for **nous** and **vous**, the present-tense subjunctive forms of regular verbs are the same as those in the imperfect indicative: **Il faut que vous m'*attendiez*. Vous ne m'*attendiez* jamais quand nous étions petits.**
For **je**, **tu**, and **il/elle/on**, the present-tense subjunctive forms of regular **-er** verbs are the same as those in the present indicative: **Il faut que tu *écoutes* le prof. Tu n'*écoutes* pas le prof.**

4.1

Comparaisons

What do these two sentences have in common?

You must *be* on time.
Il faut que tu **sois** à l'heure.

1.2, 2.2

Produits

Pour pratiquer le subjonctif, écoutez la chanson « Pour que tu m'aimes encore » de Céline Dion, et cherchez les paroles ; puis, soulignez les verbes au subjonctif.

Recherche : pour que tu m'aimes encore

Answers

Comparaisons
Both sentences use the subjunctive of the verb *to be*. Note that in a regular indicative sentence, you would say, *You are on time*. But the mandate implied in the expression above (*You must*) triggers the subjunctive in English.

Reference Desk

Point out to students that the **-er** formation of the subjunctive resembles the indicative present and that a majority of verbs in French are **-er** verbs.

Expansion

With whiteboards, do an extensive drill of the forms of **il faut que** followed by regular verbs in the subjunctive. Put students in teams for competition to add some interest.

Differentiated Learning

Accelerate
Introduce advanced students to the verb **falloir** and its conjugations in the **passé composé**, **imparfait**, **futur**, and **conditionnel**.

Special Needs Students

AD(H)D/Dyslexia/Linguistically Challenged
Help students with problems learning language to break down the verb conjugations into smaller parts with an emphasis on seeing patterns and finding a model to follow for other verbs that follow a pattern. Starting with the verb **parler**, let them conjugate this verb and many other –**er** verbs until they understand the pattern. Next, follow the same strategy with the –**ir** verb **finir** and finally the –**re** verb **attendre**. Learning in bite-size pieces can reduce frustration and confusion.

Resources

Activity 13

Answers

12

1. Il faut que tu trouves ton billet de train.
2. Il faut que tu loues des skis et des bâtons.
3. Il faut que tu achètes un forfait de ski.
4. Il faut que tu skies sur la piste facile.
5. Il faut que tu assistes à un cours avec un moniteur.
6. Il faut que tu goûtes les spécialités de la région.
7. Il faut que tu finisses tes devoirs.
8. Il faut que tu attendes ta famille à la gare.

13 Script

1. Il ne faut pas que vous téléphoniez sur la piste.
2. Il ne faut pas que vous achetiez de nouveaux skis.
3. Il ne faut pas que vous quittiez la piste.
4. Il faut que vous écoutiez les conseils des moniteurs.
5. Il faut que vous skiiez vite.
6. Il ne faut pas que vous vendiez votre forfait de ski.
7. Il faut que vous choisissiez le télésiège.

1. non; 2. non; 3. non; 4. oui; 5. oui; 6. non; 7. oui

14

1. Il faut qu'il étudie.
2. Il faut que tu manges des légumes.
3. Il faut que tu utilises ta carte cadeau cinéma.
4. Il faut que vous téléchargiez la chanson en ligne.
5. Il faut qu'il reste au lit.
6. Il faut qu'ils se rendent au complexe sportif.
7. Il faut que tu achètes un cadeau.
8. Il faut que vous l'attendiez devant la salle de classe.

Reference Desk

Remind students that verbs ending in **–ier** have **–ii** in the **nous** and **vous** forms of the subjunctive: **Il faut que vous étudiiez tous les soirs.**

12 Les classes de neige 1.3

Presentational Speaking or Writing

Dites à Élodie ce qu'elle doit faire pour réussir son séjour à Combloux. Choisissez un verbe de la liste.

apporter louer acheter goûter attendre assister à skier trouver finir

MODÈLE ton pantalon de ski et tes gants
Il faut que tu apportes ton pantalon de ski et tes gants.

1. ton billet de train
2. des skis et des bâtons
3. un forfait de ski
4. sur la piste facile
5. un cours avec un moniteur
6. les spécialités de la région
7. tes devoirs
8. ta famille à la gare

13 Une leçon de ski 1.2

Interpretive Listening

*Écrivez les numéros 1–7 sur votre papier. Écoutez les conseils de la monitrice. S'il faut que les enfants fassent quelque chose, écrivez **oui**; s'il ne faut pas qu'ils fassent quelque chose, écrivez **non**.*

14 Que faire? 1.1

Interpersonal Speaking or Writing

*Dites ce qu'il faut faire dans les situations suivantes en répondant aux personnes. Commencez vos phrases avec **Il faut que** et choisissez une des expressions ci-dessous.*

manger des légumes utiliser ta carte cadeau cinéma étudier
télécharger la chanson en ligne se rendre au complexe sportif
l'attendre devant sa salle de classe rester au lit acheter un cadeau

1. Sébastien n'a pas réussi à ses trois derniers contrôles en sciences physiques.
2. J'ai commencé à manger un dessert après le dîner, et maintenant je grossis!
3. Mes parents ne me donnent pas d'argent pour aller au cinéma!
4. Jonathan et moi, nous voulons écouter la nouvelle chanson de Natasha St-Pier.
5. Étienne a la grippe.
6. Manon et Khaled veulent faire du roller.
7. C'est l'anniversaire de mon meilleur ami.
8. Julien et toi, vous voulez parler à votre copain.

Connexions 1.2, 3.2
Musique

Use the titles below or find other songs with the title starting with ***il faut que***; read the lyrics and explain the use of the subjunctive to your partner, by explaining the message of the song.

Il faut que tu saches, Fred Pellerin • ***Il faut que tu t'en ailles***, Marie Mai • ***Il faut que je m'en aille***, Graeme Allwright • ***Il faut que tu reviennes***, Frédéric François (1976)

Essential Instruction

1. To review skiing vocabulary, ask students **devinettes**: **Qui vous aide à apprendre à skier? (un moniteur, une monitrice)**; **Nommez trois vêtements que vous portez quand vous faites du ski.**; **Quel document vous permet de faire du ski à la station de ski? (un forfait)**; **Donnez un synonyme de patiner. (faire du patinage)**; **Comment pouvez-vous monter en haut de la montagne? (en tire-fesses, en télésiège)**; **Que portez-vous pour protéger vos yeux quand vous skiez?**
2. Do **Activité 12** with students. Have them write a sentence, and then check spelling and pronunciation as a group. Continue until all sentences are completed.
3. Do **Activité 13** as a class.
4. Complete **Activités 14** and **15** in pairs.
5. Present the subjunctive of **aller**, **faire**, **pouvoir**, **savoir**, and **vouloir** orally first so students hear the sound and the rhythm of each verb form. Have students copy each verb in their notebooks or onto flash cards.

15 Phrases affirmatives ou négatives 1.3

Presentational Speaking or Writing

*Faites des phrases avec **Il faut que** ou **Il ne faut pas que**, selon la situation.*

1. Tu voudrais faire une randonnée équestre. (choisir un cheval sympa)
2. Clara et ses amies comptent faire du ski alpin ce weekend. (apporter leurs maillots de bain)
3. Ethan et moi, nous avons envie d'aller au cinéma. (acheter le magazine *Première*)
4. Je fais des recherches généalogiques. (parler à mon arrière-grand-mère)
5. Maxime et Sébastien voudraient voir la grande statue de la Liberté. (se rendre dans le Vermont)
6. Aïcha aimerait maigrir. (manger moins de chocolat)
7. Zoé et toi, vous n'aimez pas les crêpes. (dîner à la crêperie)
8. Les ados veulent s'amuser. (se rencontrer au cabinet du dentiste)

The Subjunctive of Irregular Verbs 1.2

You have learned how to form the subjunctive of regular verbs. The irregular verbs **avoir**, **être**, **aller**, **faire**, **pouvoir**, **savoir**, and **vouloir** have regular endings in the subjunctive, but *irregular stems*.

Spelling Tip

Note that the **nous** and **vous** forms of **aller** and **vouloir** use the infinitive stem.

	aller	faire	pouvoir	savoir	vouloir	avoir	être
que je (j')	aille	fasse	puisse	sache	veuille	aie	sois
que tu	ailles	fasses	puisses	saches	veuilles	aies	sois
qu'il/elle/on	aille	fasse	puisse	sache	veuille	ait	soit
que nous	allions	fassions	puissions	sachions	voulions	ayons	soyons
que vous	alliez	fassiez	puissiez	sachiez	vouliez	ayez	soyez
qu'ils/elles	aillent	fassent	puissent	sachent	veuillent	aient	soient

Il faut que vous **alliez** à la station de ski de Combloux. — *You must go to the ski resort at Combloux.*

Resources

WB Workbook 11

C & V Practice Games

Answers

15

1. Il faut que tu choisisses un cheval sympa.
2. Il ne faut pas qu'elles apportent leurs maillots de bain.
3. Il faut que vous achetiez le magazine *Première*.
4. Il faut que je parle à mon arrière-grand-mère.
5. Il ne faut pas qu'ils se rendent dans le Vermont.
6. Il faut qu'elle mange moins de chocolat.
7. Il ne faut pas que vous dîniez à la crêperie.
8. Il ne faut pas qu'ils se rencontrent au cabinet du dentiste.

Game

Il le faut!

Divide the class into two teams. Write seven pronouns across the board in any order. Call the first seven students from Team A to the board; each student stands under a pronoun. Call out an irregular verb. Students write a sentence beginning with **Il faut que** that incorporates their pronoun, for example, **(vous) Il faut que vous sachiez à quelle heure le train part.** The team earns a point for each correct sentence. If all seven sentences are correct the team remains for another round. If not, Team B comes to the board. The team with the most points wins.

Expansion

Students make an **à faire** list of things to be done before leaving on a ski vacation. They use **il faut que** plus the subjunctive. The challenge is a minimum of 15 sentences. When students read their sentences to the class, ask **"Pourquoi? À quelle heure? Avec qui?"** to get them to elaborate.

Differentiated Learning

Accelerate

Have stronger students create a list of behaviors that all students must exhibit in order to succeed, for example, **Il faut qu'on ait de bonnes notes**. Challenge them to use as many irregular verbs as possible.
Have students use the conditional **Il faudrait que…** rather the present in **Activité 15**, explaining that the **conditionnel** is a more polite and proper way to make suggestions about behavior.

Decelerate

For **Activité 12**, have students focus on the formation of the verb by giving them the appropriate verb for each sentence. Have them create a set of flash cards for each of the irregular verbs. Encourage them to add a sentence using each irregular verb in a complete sentence starting with **Il faut que/qu'**…

Resources

Activity 16

Answers

16

1. Il faut que vous buviez du chocolat chaud.
2. Il faut que je prenne mes lunettes de soleil.
3. Il faut que nous fassions du snowboard.
4. Il faut que j'aille les chercher à la gare.
5. Il faut que tu saches te servir du télésiège.
6. Il faut qu'elle voie la monitrice de ski.
7. Il faut que nous apprenions à mieux skier.

Reference Desk

Visualizing the verbs on p. 236 as boot verbs helps reinforce the written differences found in their conjugations. Choral repetition reinforces the spoken forms. Write the conjugations with single forms (**je**, **tu**, **il**/**elle**) on the left and plural forms (**nous**, **vous**, **ils**/**elles**) on the right and draw a boot around the forms, excluding **nous** and **vous**.

Expansion

Brainstorm a list of the regular and irregular verbs the students know. Write these on the board for easy reference. Use a koosh ball to practice subjunctive verb forms. Pick an infinitive and a subject pronoun. Throw the ball to a student who must conjugate the verb with **il faut que**. That student must then say an infinitive and subject pronoun, and throw the ball to another student.

Connections

Cuisine

Have students find the recipe for **la raclette** and **la fondue savoyarde**. They then transform the steps of the instructions from the command to **il faut que vous**... For example, if the recipe states "**Mélangez les ingredients**," students change the sentence to read "**Il faut que vous mélangiez les ingrédients.**" Students could use this format to present a cooking show.

Verbs such as **boire**, **croire**, **devoir**, **prendre**, **recevoir**, **venir**, and **voir** have regular endings in all forms in the subjunctive except the **nous** and **vous** forms, which end in **-ions** and **-iez**, like the **imparfait**.

	boire	croire	devoir	prendre	recevoir	venir	voir
que je	**boive**	**croie**	**doive**	**prenne**	**reçoive**	**vienne**	**voie**
que tu	**boives**	**croies**	**doives**	**prennes**	**reçoives**	**viennes**	**voies**
qu'il/elle/on	**boive**	**croie**	**doive**	**prenne**	**reçoive**	**vienne**	**voie**
que nous	**buvions**	**croyions**	**devions**	**prenions**	**recevions**	**venions**	**voyions**
que vous	**buviez**	**croyiez**	**deviez**	**preniez**	**receviez**	**veniez**	**voyiez**
qu'ils/elles	**boivent**	**croient**	**doivent**	**prennent**	**reçoivent**	**viennent**	**voient**

16 À la station de ski 1.3

Presentational Speaking or Writing

*Dites ce que les personnes suivantes doivent faire en faisant des phrases avec **il faut que**.*

MODÈLE Julie ne veut pas payer cher pour skier. (prendre un ticket normal ou un forfait ski)
Il faut qu'elle prenne un forfait ski.

1. Vous venez de faire du ski et vous avez froid. (boire du chocolat chaud ou du coca)
2. Il fait du soleil et je ne vois pas bien. (prendre mon bonnet ou mes lunettes de soleil)
3. Il ne reste plus de skis à louer pour nous. (faire du snowboard ou de la planche à voile)
4. Mes amis viennent en train. (aller les chercher à la gare ou à l'aéroport)
5. Tu veux monter en haut de la piste. (savoir se servir du télésiège ou des bâtons)
6. Clara aimerait s'inscrire dans un cours de ski. (voir son prof de français ou la monitrice de ski)
7. Nous ne skions pas bien. (rester dans le chalet ou apprendre à mieux skier)

Essential Instruction

1. Continue the presentation of irregular subjunctive forms by conjugating each irregular verb. After hearing the verb several times, students will repeat each verb after you.
2. Have students copy each verb in their notebooks or onto flash cards. Writing and saying the verb conjugations aloud reinforces how each verb changes in the **nous** and **vous** forms.
3. With whiteboards, practice the irregular forms until students have mastered them.
4. Do **Activité 16** as a whole-class activity.
5. Students do **Activité 17** in pairs. Circulate to monitor their work.

17 On prend une décision importante 1.2, 1.3

Interpretive Reading, Presentational Speaking or Writing

*Aidez tout le monde à choisir la meilleure solution. Faites des phrases avec **il faut que**.*

MODÈLE Koffi a vu un bon film et il veut le revoir, mais sa grand-mère l'attend.
A. voir le film et ne pas aller chez sa grand-mère
B. aller chez sa grand-mère et ne pas voir le film pour la deuxième fois aujourd'hui
Il faut que Koffi aille chez sa grand-mère et il ne faut pas qu'il voie le film pour la deuxième fois aujourd'hui.

1. Marc et moi, nous avons beaucoup de corvées à faire, mais nous voulons aller au complexe sportif.
   A. faire vos corvées et ne pas aller au complexe sportif
   B. aller au complexe sportif et ne pas faire vos corvées
2. Louis a un contrôle de français demain.
   A. étudier et ne pas jouer aux jeux vidéo
   B. jouer aux jeux vidéo et ne pas étudier
3. Mes parents m'ont dit qu'ils me donneraient de l'argent si j'arrête d'être méchant avec mon frère.
   A. ne pas être méchant avec ton frère et recevoir de l'argent
   B. être méchant avec ton frère et ne pas recevoir d'argent
4. Sandrine et Karim ont très soif, mais au musée on ne peut rien boire dans les salles d'exposition.
   A. boire un coca au café et ne pas voir les tableaux
   B. boire un coca au snack-bar du musée et voir les tableaux
5. Tu voudrais faire du ski en France.
   A. aller à Paris et ne pas aller à Combloux
   B. aller à Mégève et ne pas aller à Lyon
6. Amadou et toi, vous avez gagné un séjour à Paris pour cinq nuits.
   A. savoir quels monuments visiter et faire un budget avant le voyage
   B. ne pas savoir quels monuments visiter et ne pas faire de budget

Answers

17

1. Il faut que vous fassiez vos corvées et il ne faut pas que vous alliez au complexe sportif.
2. Il faut qu'il étudie et il ne faut pas qu'il joue aux jeux vidéo.
3. Il ne faut pas que tu sois méchant avec ton frère et il faut que tu reçoives de l'argent.
4. Il faut qu'ils boivent un coca au snack-bar du musée et il faut qu'ils voient les tableaux.
5. Il faut que que j'aille à Megève et il ne faut pas que j'aille à Lyon.
6. Il faut que nous sachions quels monuments visiter et il faut que nous fassions un budget avant le voyage.

Expansion

PQA (Personalized Questions and Answers)

Ask students what they must do in certain situations. Circle with yes/no questions, either/or questions, and information questions. Alternate between asking individual students and asking the whole class: **Émilie, tu es fatiguée. Est-ce qu'il faut que tu fasses une sieste ou est-ce qu'il faut que tu ailles au complexe sportif? Il faut que tu ailles au complexe sportif? Il faut que tu fasses une sieste? Classe, qu'est-ce qu'il faut qu'Émilie fasse?**

Communication

Interpersonal: Paired Practice

Students work in pairs to practice the irregular forms listed on pp. 235 and 236. The goal at the end of a given amount of time is for students to help each other to become subjunctive specialists.

Learning Styles

Auditory Learners
These students need to repeat these verbs aloud.

Visual Learners
These students have to *see* the words to understand them. Verb charts and flash cards are helpful.

Special Needs Students

AD(H)D/Dyslexia
Students with learning difficulties need to take one verb at a time and write it down in order to analyze the stem and how the verbs change for **nous** and **vous**. Consider giving them short quizzes on only one or two verbs so that learning all of them at once does not seem impossible.

Multiple Intelligences

Bodily-Kinesthetic/Musical-Rhythmic
Repetition of the conjugations helps students feel the beat: **que je fasse, que tu fasses, qu'il fasse, que nous fassions**... Have students tap their hands as they say each verb to feel the change in syllables.

Resources

CA Communicative Activities

Share

Answers

18 E-mails will vary.

19 Critiques will vary.

20 Videos will vary.

Reference Desk

1. The photo on this page shows the city of d'Annecy overooking the lake of its own name, **Lac d'Annecy**, south of the Alps.
2. If you have access to Passport, create a question for your students to share their response to a communicative activity.

À vous la parole

Question centrale ? Qu'est-ce qu'on doit connaître de sa destination pour réussir son voyage ?

Communiquez!

18 Les classes de neige 1.1, 5.2

Interpersonal Writing

Vous allez participer à une classe de neige à Combloux en tant que (*as*) moniteur (monitrice) de snowboard ou de ski. Votre surveillante (*supervisor*) vous a demandé de créer votre premier cours pour qu'elle puisse voir ce que vous allez faire avec votre classe. Vous allez devoir instruire une quinzaine d'enfants âgés de 7 à 10 ans, et qui sont tous débutants. Envoyez la description de votre cours à votre surveillante, dans un mail, afin d'obtenir son approbation.

19 Critique gastronomique 1.1, 1.3, 3.2

Interpretive and Presentational Writing

Faites des recherches pour trouver un restaurant qui sert deux spécialités culinaires, **la raclette** et **la fondue de Savoie**. Imaginez que vous êtes un(e) critique culinaire. Vous avez mangé dans ce restaurant et vous devez écrire votre critique pour votre blog en ligne. Peut-être que votre expérience a été très satisfaisante, et donc que vous désirez recommander ce restaurant et faire l'éloge du chef. Peut-être que c'était une soirée désastreuse où tout s'est mal passé et que la nourriture était très mal préparée. Donnez des détails précis et soyez aussi créatif/créative que possible. Si possible, ajoutez des vidéos et des photos.

20 Un stage à l'Office du Tourisme d'Annecy 1.3, 2.2, 3.2

Interpretive Viewing, Presentational Speaking

Vous faites un stage (*internship*) à l'Office du Tourisme d'Annecy. On vous demande de créer une vidéo promotionnelle de deux minutes pour inciter les touristes de venir à Annecy. Avec un groupe de camarades de classe, incluez les sites à voir, les activités, l'histoire de la ville/région, et la gastronomie. Vous pouvez jouer le rôle des habitants de la région dans votre vidéo, ou, si vous n'avez pas accès à une caméra, cherchez des photos et servez-vous en pour présenter divers endroits de la ville à la télévision (devant la classe) pour promouvoir la ville.

Essential Instruction

1. Provide a rubric listing your expectations and evaluation points for **Activités 18**, **19**, and **20**.
2. For **Activités 19** and **20**, in addition to the option of using a slide show program, students can find easy-to-use templates online.

Recherche: tripwow and trip advisor for travelogue templates

3. Have students write **Activité 21**.
4. Have groups of three complete **Activité 22** and then present to another group.

Pre-AP

Communiquez!

How-to Writing 1.2

Un mode d'emploi est un document qui explique comment télécharger une chanson, écrire une recette, monter une étagère (*assemble a bookshelf*) ou une tente. Voici des conseils pour écrire un mode d'emploi :

- Se familiariser avec le public. Est-ce que les lecteurs connaissent bien le sujet ?
- Écrire des consignes (*instructions*) le plus simplement et le plus clairement possible.
- Organiser ces consignes dans un ordre logique.
- Utiliser des supports visuels.

Essayez d'expliquer quelque chose de simple à votre camarade de classe (comme comment ouvrir une porte fermée à clé, comment se couper les cheveux, etc.) Vos consignes sont-elles claires, ou est-ce que vous avez oublié des étapes ?

21 Comment télécharger une chanson 1.3

Presentational Writing

Remettez les consignes suivantes dans l'ordre de réalisation et réécrivez chaque consigne en utilisant **il faut que** + SUBJONCTIF. Suivez le modèle.

MODÈLE démarrer l'ordinateur
1. Il faut que vous démarriez l'ordinateur.

télécharger votre chanson préférée — fermer le logiciel — démarrer l'ordinateur — ouvrir le logiciel — naviguer sur le site — cliquer avec la souris — payer

Connexions 1.2, 3.2
Enquêtes privées
Imaginez que vous travaillez comme agent secret dans une agence de sécurité, et que votre école est la maison d'un personnage célèbre soupçonné d'un crime. Avec un partenaire, vous devez chercher la maison de cette personne pour trouver son ordinateur portable. L'un de vous cachera un ordinateur (ou l'image d'un ordinateur) dans l'école et devra donner des consignes claires pour guider son partenaire dans la maison et localiser l'ordinateur. Vous communiquerez par téléphone portable.

Défi : Votre professeur (chef de l'agence) vous donnera un lapse de temps (*time limit*) pour remplir cette mission.

22 Préparatifs de voyage 1.3, 5.2

Presentational Writing

Pensez à une destination où vous vous êtes rendu(e), ou bien à une destination où vous aimeriez vous rendre un jour. Imaginez que vous fassiez un blog sur cette destination. Donnez à vos lecteurs quelques conseils et astuces *(wise tips)* pour se préparer à voyager là-bas. Utilisez **il faut que** + SUBJONCTIF. Voici quelques éléments à garder en tête : les vêtements à emporter, l'insecticide ou la crème solaire, le type de chaussures ; les cartes, les musées, l'hôtel ; et des suggestions sur les restaurants.

Answers

21
1. Il faut que vous démarriez l'ordinateur.
2. Il faut que vous naviguiez sur le site.
3. Il faut que vous cliquiez avec la souris.
4. Il faut que vous ouvriez le logiciel.
5. Il faut que vous payiez.
6. Il faut que téléchargiez votre chanson préférée.
7. Il faut que vous fermiez le logiciel.

22 Presentations will vary.

Reference Desk

1. Discuss **Stratégie communicative**. Model how the strategies for writing to a specific audience can be applied to **Activités 18**, **19**, and **20** on p. 238.
2. Note that the expression **imaginez que** may be used with the indicative or the subjunctive mood, as in English. In **Connexions**, the use of the indicative suggests a projection into the unreal world ("let's imagine this is so"), whereas in **Activité 22**, the subjunctive suggests that we maintain a distance between the real moment (now) and the unreal moment (that which we imagine: "lets imagine we were living in…").

Differentiated Learning

Accelerate
Students may work at their own pace completing the above exercises. When they have finished, encourage them to offer help to those still working.

Decelerate
Students would benefit from you working with them to define the tasks in each activity, to discuss how to research information, and what format they should use to present it. Assign deadlines for each step, and arrange to check students' work. Some of these students, although perhaps not strong in French, will have excellent computer skills and benefit from using those. Provide suggestions of activities for which they can give directions (**comment faire un sandwich au jambon, comment réserver une chambre d'hôtel**). Reserve the simpler tasks for students who struggle more; additionally, consider giving them a list of verbs from which to work.

Resources

- *Vocabulaire actif*
- eVisual
- Workbook 1–3
- Flash Cards
- Listening Activity 1
- G & V Practice Games

Reference Desk

1. Ask students to look closely at the illustration and find the differences between the various sports. **Le ski de fond** (*cross-country skiing*) is a Nordic style of skiing where the shoe is only partially connected to the ski, which **le télémark** (*telemark*) is derived from. That style allows for greater kneeling and flexibility than **le ski de fond**.
2. **Le ski de piste** (*downhill skiing*) is practiced on various courses or slopes marked by level. **Le ski hors-piste** refers to skiing off the indicated official slope or trail, back-country skiing, or **le ski joëring**. Note that slopes are marked so that skiers avoid venturing into unknown territory where they risk accidents on unknown terrain and may cause avalanches. These slopes are also monitored by ski patrols, unlike **le hors-piste**.
3. Skijoring originates from a Norwegian term meaning *ski driving*, and consists of being pulled by a horse while standing on skis. Animal-loving students may enjoy seeing images of this activity.
4. **Se faire vacciner** means *to get oneself vaccinated*.
5. **Une pièce d'identité**, the national identity card (***Carte nationale d'identité sécurisée*** or ***CNIS***), is a document issued by the French government. It looks like a driver's license because it is a laminated plastic card bearing the photograph, name, and address of the holder. It is valid for ten years.

Leçon C Vocabulaire actif

Sports d'hiver et préparatifs de départ 1.2

Sports d'hiver : On fait....

Essential Instruction

1. Have students look at the picture of the **Sports d'hiver** and identify each vocabulary word.
2. Ask students to listen to **Avant de voyager** and **Pour la conversation** three times before repeating.
3. Have students answer the question "**Qu'est-ce qu'il faut faire avant de voyager ?**" orally using **Il faut que** and the verbs on p. 241.
4. Ask students to prioritize what **sports d'hiver** they would like to do, in descending order from the most interesting to the least. Poll the class.

Préparatifs de départ 1.2

planifier

réserver

obtenir un passeport/**un visa**

se renseigner à **l'office de tourisme**/sur un site web/au **consulat**

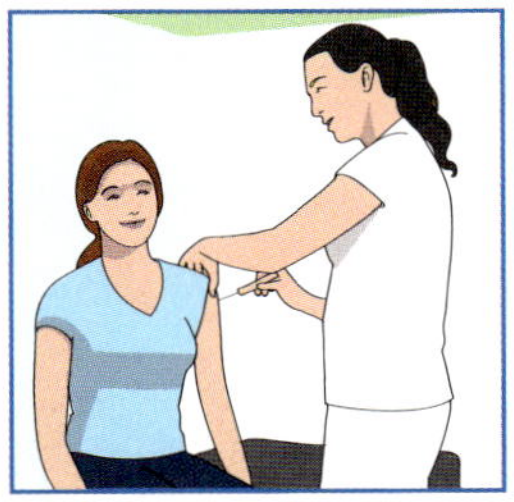

se faire vacciner

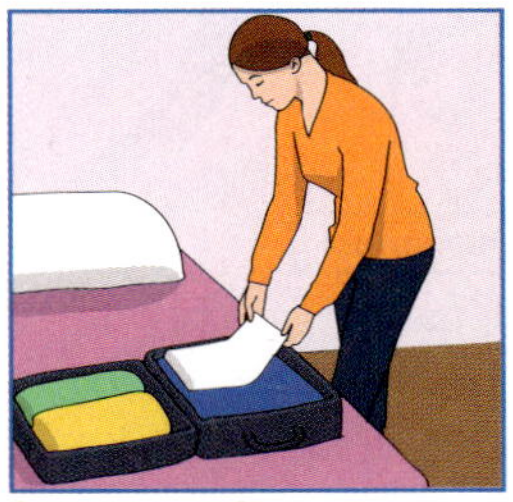

faire sa valise

emporter un passeport, **une pièce d'identité**

vérifier qu'on n'a rien oublié

faire un séjour

Pour la conversation 1.2

How do I say I'm doing something different (from the others)?

» Vous ferez ce que vous voulez, moi c'est balade sur **le domaine**.
Do what you want, but for me it's a walk on the property.

How do I tell someone it's important not to hurt himself or herself?

» Il est important que **tu ne te foules pas la cheville** ou que **tu ne te casses pas le poignet**!
It's important you don't sprain your ankle or break your wrist!

Et si je voulais dire… ?

un alpiniste	*climber*
en règle	*in order*
périmé(e)	*expired*
valable	*valid*
annuler	*to cancel*
escalader	*to climb*
faire de l'alpinisme	*to mountain climb*
le snowkite	*snow kiting*
le ski acrobatique	*freestyle skiing*

Resources

Pour la conversation
Et si je voulais dire… ?

Communication

Interpersonal: Cooperative Groups

1. Arrange students in mixed-ability groups. Captains from each group select a card from each of four piles.
2. Place cards face down. On the cards in one pile write weather conditions like **Il fait un temps de chien, Il neige constamment; Il pleut à verse**… In the second pile provide a selection of characters: **Jean le malin, Marie la belle, Grand Pied, Neige Blanche, le Monstre des Alpes**… The third pile is verbs: **se faire vacciner contre le paludisme, skier comme un(e) professionnel(le), oublier de faire sa valise**… The fourth pile features random terms: **un bonnet de nuit, un passeport canadien, trois petites roses**…
3. Have students create a skit using these terms plus at least one verb in the subjunctive. Allow 15 minutes to prepare before presenting.

TPR

With or without props, have students come up with gestures for each of the verbs in **Préparatifs de départ**. Say the verbs aloud and check for comprehension by looking at the students' gestures.

Differentiated Learning

Accelerate
Have students pretend to be caring parents. Have them make a list of things that their children should remember to do when the parents are away on a skiing trip. They must use **Il est important que** when giving their advice.

Decelerate
Have students research what **une carte d'identité française** looks like, where the French procure theirs, and how much it costs.

Special Needs Students

Social Anxiety/At-Risk Teens
Students who have never traveled might find this lesson difficult to imagine. Continue to encourage them to think that a trip like this could be in their future.

Answers

1

Serge et moi faisons de la raquette à neige.
Marie-Alix et Océane font du télémark.
M. Dupin fait du ski joëring.
David et Yasmine font du taxi-ski.
Malika fait de la luge.
Mes amis et moi faisons du ski de piste.

2

1. B
2. A
3. D
4. G
5. E
6. C
7. F

Reference Desk

1. Vaccinations suggested for **le Sénegal** are **l'hépatite A et B** (*hepatitis A and B*), **la typhoïde** (*typhoid*), **le méningocoque** (*meningococcus*), **la polio** (*polio*), **la rage** (*rabies*), **la rougeole** (*measles*), **les oreillons** (*mumps*), **la rubéole** (*rubella*), and **la diphtérie-tétanos** (*tetanus-diphtheria*).
2. Vaccinations for **La Réunion** are **l'hépatite A et B**, **la thiphoïde**, **la fièvre jaune** (*yellow fever*), **les oreillons**, **la rougeole**, and **la diphtérie-tétanos**.

1 Quels sports d'hiver? 1.2, 1.3

Interpretive Viewing, Presentational Speaking or Writing

Indiquez les sports d'hiver qu'on fait.

2 Les préparatifs de départ 1.2, 1.3

Interpretive Reading, Presentational Speaking or Writing

Répondez à chaque question sur les préparatifs de départ des Lamire, en indiquant la lettre de la phrase qui y répond.

A. M. et Mme Lamire ont obtenu des passeports pour leurs enfants Lina et Lucas.
B. Pendant des mois, M. et Mme Lamire et leurs enfants ont planifié un voyage au Sénégal.
C. Le matin de leur départ, les Lamire ont vérifié qu'ils avaient tous leurs documents et essentiels.
D. Les Lamire n'ont pas dû obtenir de visas.
E. Le soir avant leur départ, les Lamire ont fait leurs valises.
F. Ils vont passer un bon séjour au Sénégal!
G. Les Lamire ne vont pas attraper (*catch*) de maladies.

1. Les Lamire ont choisi une destination pour leurs prochaines vacances. Qu'est-ce qu'ils ont fait ensuite?
2. Qu'ont-ils fait lorsqu'ils se sont aperçu que leurs enfants n'avaient pas de passeports?
3. On doit obtenir un visa si on veut passer plus de trois mois au Sénégal; or, les Lamire vont passer moins de trois mois au Sénégal. Ont-ils dû obtenir des visas?
4. Mme Lamire a téléphoné au consulat de France, qui lui a conseillé de faire vacciner toute sa famille. Est-ce qu'ils vont tomber malades au Sénégal?
5. Les Lamire ont acheté un couteau suisse, de la lotion anti-moustique, et d'autres choses pour leur voyage. Qu'est-ce qu'ils ont fait pour prendre leurs affaires?
6. Les Lamire ont besoin de chèques de voyage, de cartes de crédit, de passeports, d'un appareil photo, et d'un permis de conduire pour M. Lamire. Qu'est-ce qu'ils ont fait pour ne rien oublier?
7. À quoi est-ce que les Lamire s'attendent?

Essential Instruction

1. To review the **sports d'hiver** vocabulary, have students answer **Activité 1** orally.
2. Ask partners to complete **Activité 2**.
3. Play **Activité 3**. Students will identify whether the statement is about preparing for a trip or about a trip itself. Stop after each sentence to ask them what words gave them the clue to their answer.
4. Assign **Activité 4** in small groups. Have students share what they learned about their classmates' preferences and previous travel experience.

3 On part où ? 1.2

Interpretive Communication

*Écrivez les numéros 1–8 sur votre papier. Puis, écrivez **oui** si la phrase décrit des préparatifs de voyage ou **non** s'il ne s'agit pas d'un voyage.*

4 Questions personnelles 1.1, 5.2

Interpersonal Speaking

Répondez aux questions avec un partenaire.

1. Quels sports d'hiver préfères-tu ?
2. Quels préparatifs est-ce que tu dois faire si tu pars en voyage à la montagne en hiver ?
3. Quels préparatifs est-ce que tu dois faire si tu pars en voyage au bord de la mer en été ?
4. Avant de partir, qu'est-ce que tu mets sur ta liste pour vérifier que tu n'as rien oublié ?
5. As-tu déjà été obligé(e) d'obtenir un passeport ou un visa ? Pour aller où ?

Resources

Activity 3

Answers

3 Script

1. M. et Mme Morin remplissent des papiers pour obtenir un passeport.
2. Suzanne prend le télésiège à la station de ski.
3. Marc et moi, nous faisons de saut à l'élastique en été.
4. Julie et Martine font leurs valises.
5. Les Delpy planifient un séjour au Maroc.
6. Aujourd'hui les Dumont se font vacciner au cabinet du médecin.
7. Jacques se renseigne sur l'Espagne en surfant sur Internet.
8. Nous achetons un guide sur le Sénégal.

1. oui; 2. non; 3. non; 4. oui; 5. oui; 6. oui; 7. oui; 8. oui

4 Answers will vary.

Game

La guerre de trois

Prepare a collection of visuals and/or flash cards of the vocabulary in **Vocabulaire actif**. Make sure to have at least as many cards as you have students. You may have to pull from the other **Leçons** in **Unité 4**. Have students count off by threes to form three teams. The teams form three lines in front of the teacher at the front of the room. Show a visual or flash card to the first three students. The first student to identify it correctly sits down. The first team with all of its members seated wins.

Differentiated Learning

Accelerate

Ask students to research and compare the number of tourists who elect to travel to **le Sénégal** and **La Réunion**. Have them find which ski resorts in France are the most popular for families and for single people.

Decelerate

Have students find pictures of people participating in the different **sports d'hiver**. Have them report to the class and tell which ones seem to be the most popular among French people. Are these the same sports we do in the United States at ski resorts like Aspen or Breckenridge? Students could make a general map of the United States on a piece of foamcore board, locate the most popular ski resorts, and mark them with pushpins.

Resources

Dialogue
Activity 5
Extension
Dialogue Video
WB Workbook 4

Answers

5

1. une balade sur le domaine
2. Il accompagnera sa femme.
3. Léo
4. Elle s'est foulé la cheville en faisant de la luge.
5. Ils iront au Vietnam ; ils feront du bénévolat.

EXTENSION

Ils vont faire du bénévolat au sud du Madagascar et aider à reconstruire des maisons.

Reference Desk

1. Madagascar is an island in the Indian Ocean east of Mozambique. It is the fourth largest island in the world with approximately 24.9 million inhabitants. The official languages are French and Malagasy. Five percent of all animal and plant species in the world are found in its terrain. It is a haven for snorkelers and divers due to its 300 plus kilometers of barrier reefs, supporting the third largest coral reef system in the world.
2. **Je ne m'étais pas encore foulé la cheville.** Explain that this is the **plus-que-parfait** of **se fouler la cheville**. **Ça va, les chevilles?** is an expression that the French would use when someone is bragging. In English, we say someone gets a swollen head. In French, people who are full of themselves have swollen ankles or **les chevilles qui enflent**.
3. WWOOF (Worldwide Opportunities on Organic Farms) is a network of international organizations that place volunteers on organic farms in 99 countries around the world, promoting educational exchange and building a global community conscious of ecological farming practices.

Rencontres culturelles

Un weekend en famille

1.2, 5.2

Élodie, Léo, et leurs parents passent le weekend à Combloux.

Mère : Vous ferez ce que vous voulez ; moi, c'est balade sur le domaine.
Léo : Il faudrait que tu essaies le ski de fond !
Mère : J'ai hâte d'essayer.
Léo : Moi, de toute façon, c'est snowboard. Et toi, Papa ?
Père : Il se pourrait que j'accompagne ta mère….
Élodie : Quoi, tu vas abandonner le hors-piste… Oh, c'est beau, l'amour !
Léo : Tu te souviens quand on faisait de la luge ?
Élodie : Là, tu en faisais avec nous, Maman.
Mère : Oui, mais je ne m'étais pas encore foulé la cheville !
Léo : C'est du passé : maintenant il faut que tu t'y remettes. L'année prochaine, c'est notre voyage bénévolat au Vietnam. Il est important que tu ne te foules pas la cheville ou que tu ne te casses pas le poignet !

5 Un weekend en famille

1.2

Répondez aux questions.

1. Qu'est-ce que la mère d'Élodie et de Léo veut faire à Combloux ?
2. Qu'est-ce que leur père fera ?
3. Qui va faire du snowboard ?
4. Qu'est-ce qui est arrivé (*happened*) à la mère d'Élodie et de Léo la dernière fois ?
5. Où la famille va-t-elle passer ses vacances l'année prochaine ? Qu'est-ce qu'ils feront ?

Mot-clé

Snowboard est un exemple d'un anglicisme. Faites une liste de 15 mots qui sont des anglicismes. Ensuite, classez-les par catégorie, par exemple, la technologie, les sports, et le business.

EXTENSION **Projet de WWOOFing** 1.2

Des amis se rencontrent au café pour parler de leur voyage pour faire du bénévolat humanitaire.

Virginie : On est tous d'accord pour Madagascar ?
Hugo : Oui, mais il faut qu'on trouve à woofer tous ensemble.
Mathieu : Là, sur le site, il y a deux offres, l'une au centre de l'île, l'autre au sud.
Virginie : Mais c'est pour faire quoi ?
Mathieu : Celle du centre, il faudrait qu'on aide à entretenir des réseaux d'irrigation. Je préfère l'autre. Ce n'est pas très précis pour le sud, mais il semble qu'ils souhaitent des volontaires pour reconstruire des maisons de terre.
Hugo : Eh bien, c'est très bien. L'année dernière, on a joué aux agriculteurs ; cette année, on fera de la maçonnerie. Tout le monde mérite une belle maison durable.
Virginie : Je vais travailler avec des gants….
Mathieu : Mais tu n'auras pas le temps de te faire des manicures !

EXTENSION La bande d'amis choisit quel projet ? Où ?
1.3

Essential Instruction

1. Listen to **Un weekend en famille** and then ask the questions in **Activité 5**.
2. Discuss Madagascar and the WWOOFing project.
3. Listen to **Extension** and discuss the accompanying question in small groups.
4. Have students read **Les stations du ski**. Assign each of the 12 ski resorts to groups of students. Teams research their **station de ski** and make a PR presentation of their resort, promoting it as the best.

Points de départ

Pre-AP

Question centrale: Qu'est-ce qu'on doit connaître de sa destination pour réussir son voyage?

Les stations de ski 1.2, 2.1, 2.2, 3.2, 5.2

On peut aller jusqu'à 200 km/h en faisant du Speed Riding.

C'est le goût pour les sports d'hiver qui a été à l'origine du développement d'immenses domaines skiables* dans les Alpes et d'un réseau de stations très attirantes*. C'est à Chamonix qu'ont d'ailleurs* été organisés les premiers Jeux olympiques d'hiver en 1924, suivis par les JO d'hiver à Grenoble en 1968 et à Albertville en 1992.

À côté des stations de ski historiques créées autour de villages comme Chamonix, Saint-Gervais, La Clusaz, Villars de Lans ou Megève, il existe des stations nées de toute pièce* comme Courchevel, L'Alpe d'Huez, ou Les Deux Alpes, et enfin celles nées de la révolution des loisirs comme Les Arcs, Avoriaz, ou Serre-Chevalier. L'ensemble des domaines skiables des Alpes propose au total plus de 6 000 kilomètres de pistes de ski avec des domaines reliés* intégralement entre eux comme Les Trois Vallées (entre Courchevel, Meribel, Les Ménuires, et Val Thorens) avec leurs 338 pistes qui couvrent 600 kilomètres, ou Les Portes du Soleil (Avoriaz, Morzine, Les Gets, Chatel) avec 650 kilomètres de pistes reliées.

À côté du ski alpin, l'offre sportive des stations s'est beaucoup développée : du snowboard au monoski en passant par le speed riding, la raquette à neige, le ski freestyle, le ski de randonnée, le snowkite, l'Airboard, la motoneige, ou le ski acrobatique.

Recherche : ski france, ski mont blanc, ski info france, ski combloux, contamines montjoie, photo (+ speed riding, raquette à neige, ski freestyle, ski de randonnée)

domaines skiables *ski areas* ; **attirantes** *attractive* ; **d'ailleurs** *moreover* ; **nées de toute pièce** *developed from nothing* ; **reliés** *connected*

1.2, 2.1

Produits

Les épreuves des Jeux olympiques ou de **championnat du monde de ski alpin** se divisent en deux catégories : les épreuves plus techniques telles que le slalom et le slalom géant, et les épreuves de vitesse pure comme le Super-G et la descente.

Normalement, les Français gagnent entre 1 et 11 médailles pour les JO d'hiver.

Resources

Points de départ

Workbook 5

Explore

Reference Desk

1. Grenoble hosted the 1968 Winter Olympics. These were the first games to be broadcast in color; the first to require gender testing for female athletes; and the first time East and West Germany sent two separate teams. Jean-Claude Killy swept the men's Alpine events (three gold medals), and American figure skater Peggy Fleming won the United States' only gold medal in the entire competition.
2. If you have access to Passport, find a video or a news article related to **les Alpes** or **le ski** and show it to your students.

Connections

Sociology

Madagascar has a ceremony called **Famadihana**, or moving of the bones. Every seven years the bodies of relatives are exhumed, new shrouds are wrapped around their bodies, and relatives dance with them. Ask students to research **Famadihana**. Why do family members come together to participate in this ceremony?

Culture

Practices: Information

Fédération Française du ski was founded in 1924. Its mission is to oversee the activities of ski clubs in France and regulate Olympic and non-Olympic ski competitions.

Recherche : ffs, fédération française du ski

Differentiated Learning

Accelerate

Ask volunteers to learn the **Extension** dialogue and present it to the class. The class answers the **Extension** question.

Multiple Intelligences

Naturalist

Madagascar offers a treasure of natural wonders such as rainforests, deserts, and barrier reefs. What would naturalists wish to study if they visited the island?

Visual-Spatial

Ask students to make a topographical map of Madagascar showing its major cities and main points of interest.

Answers

6

1. Chamonix, Saint-Gervais, La Clusaz, Villars de Lans, Megève ; Courchevel, L'Alpe d'Huez, Les Deux Alpes ; Les Arcs, Avoriaz, Serre-Chevalier
2. Presentations will vary.
3. Answers will vary.

Comparaisons
Answers will vary.

À DISCUTER

Answers will vary.

Reference Desk

Le Burkina Faso is a landlocked country in West Africa. Its capital is Ouagadougou. It has more than 18 million inhabitants and is approximately 105,900 square miles in size.

La Francophonie

De nombreuses associations françaises aident les enfants du Sénégal.

Aide humanitaire

1.2, 2.1, 3.1, 3.2, 4.2, 5.1

Les voyageurs volontaires en pays francophones

« Partir en "mission" à l'international » est l'invitation de l'agence France Volontaires qui cherche à attirer les jeunes vers des missions à l'international avec différents programmes de volontariat* : le service volontaire européen, le volontariat de solidarité internationale et le service civique à l'international. Les jeunes Français (ils sont plus de 12 000 à avoir fait cette expérience) peuvent participer à des chantiers de solidarité internationale comme au Burkina Faso, à des projets sur l'enseignement du wolof au Sénégal, ou à des études de terrain comme en Haïti sur l'enfance et la jeunesse. C'est un bon moyen de faire l'expérience de la différence en participant à de l'entrepreneuriat* solidaire, à de l'aide humanitaire ou à de l'aide en milieu scolaire.

Recherche : aide volontaire internationale, volontariat humanitaire, france volontaires

volontariat *volunteering* ; **entrepreneuriat** *entrepreneurship*

Traditions et pratiques

1.2, 2.1

Comme toute autre activité professionnelle, pour participer à un échange de volontariat international en France, il faut déposer sa candidature en envoyant un CV ainsi qu'une lettre de motivation.

Comparaisons

1.2, 4.2

Quelles sont les organisations bénévoles de votre ville ou région ?

6 Activités culturelles

1.3, 3.2

Faites les activités suivantes.

Le monoski

1. Nommez….
   - des stations créées autour d'un village
   - des stations nées de rien
   - des stations issues de la société des loisirs
2. Imaginez que vous avez été recruté(e) pour construire un site web pour une école de ski. Trouvez une photo et expliquez les différences entre chacun des sports suivants :
   - monoski
   - speed riding
   - raquette à neige
   - ski freestyle
   - ski de randonnée
   - motoneige
   - télémark
   - snowkite
   - ski acrobatique
3. Trouvez des exemples d'initiatives solidaires en ligne. Quels sont les pays francophones concernés ?

À DISCUTER

Où est-ce que vous aimeriez faire du travail bénévole ou humanitaire ? Quels sont les besoins dans cet endroit ?

Essential Instruction

1. Work in the computer lab to review winter sports with **Activité 6**.
2. Brainstorm a list of benevolent organizations in your community. What is their mission?
3. Students read **Les voyageurs volontaires en pays francophones** and learn about volunteer projects in third world countries available to young French people. Use the search words for more information.
4. **À discuter** gives students an opportunity to discuss their volunteering preferences. Do they volunteer in their school, church, or community? Are there particular reasons they decided to volunteer for certain organizations?

Du côté des médias 1.2

Lisez les informations suivantes.

FRANCE VOLONTAIRES
Echanges et solidarité internationale

FRANCE VOLONTAIRES
11, rue Maurice Grandcoing–BP 220
94203 Ivry sur Seine Cedex
+33 (0)1 53 14 20 30

Partir en mission à l'international

Type de volontariat : tous | **Pays :** tous | **Durée :** toutes | **M'engager**

DERNIÈRES MISSIONS À POURVOIR

Directeur/directrice du foyer d'étudiants
VSI, DE 24 MOIS, AU CAMBODGE
Lire la suite

Directeur/directrice adjoint(e) d'Enfants d'Asie au Cambodge
VSI, DE 24 MOIS, AU CAMBODGE
Lire la suite

Assistant(e) technique développement régional et aménagement du territoire
DISPOSITIF ALLEMAND, DE 24 MOIS, À MADAGASCAR
Lire la suite

PORTRAITS DE VOLONTAIRES

Shruti, volontaire en Service Civique de Réciprocité au lycée…
Lire le portrait

CANDIDATER

La CV thèque est ouverte aux membres et partenaires de la plateforme et à France Volontaires. Les CV sont automatiquement détruits au bout de trois mois. Les acteurs vous contacteront si votre candidature correspond à une de leurs missions de volontariat.

Déposer un CV

7 Les volontaires internationaux d'échange et de solidarité 1.2, 1.3, 3.1, 5.2

Répondez aux questions.

1. Qui sont les volontaires internationaux ?
2. Quelle qualité principale attend-on d'eux ?
3. Quels sont les pays concernés ?
4. Les postes nécessitent-ils de travailler avec des enfants ?
5. Qui est Shruti ?

Resources

Activity 7

Answers

7

1. directeurs/directrices, assistant(e) technique
2. de s'engager pour 24 mois (2 ans)
3. le Cambodge, le Madagascar
4. Non, pas nécessairement.
5. une jeune fille qui est devenue volontaire et dont on peut voir le profil

Connections

Music

Have students watch the duo by Édith Piaf and her husband Théo Sérapo, "**À quoi ça sert l'amour**."

Recherche : à quoi ça sert l'amour duo piaf sérapo

Expansion

Put students in small groups to create an ad or poster for a volunteer organization that exists or might exist in their school. Brainstorm what makes ads informative and visually interesting. Groups present their final product to the class. Display the projects around your school.

Differentiated Learning

Accelerate/Decelerate

High- and low-ability language students work in pairs or groups to read the website for **France Volontaires**. Next have students go directly to the interactive website to learn more about the organization. Have them answer the questions in **Activité 7**.

Special Needs Students

Linguistically Challenged

Have students copy the **Activité 7** questions into their notebooks leaving space for notes and answers for each one. As you work with these students, encourage them to look for cognates within the website as a way of reinforcing the number of words that they already know.

Answers

All activities will vary.

Communication

Interpersonal: Paired Practice

One student plays the director of volunteers for a humanitarian organization interviewing the other student who plays a potential participant. The director asks this person why he or she wants to work for the cause, where the candidate would like to work, and what skill he or she can offer to the organization. The candidate must make the case for his or her candidacy.

Connections

Music

"**La Chanson pour l'Auvergnat**," sung by Georges Brassens, relates the impact that an act of kindness can have on the life of a less fortunate person. It aligns nicely with the theme of volunteerism and humanitarian efforts. Note the imagery of "**quand dans ma vie il faisait faim**." Discuss with students the meaning and message behind the lyrics.

Culture sur place

Question centrale ? Qu'est-ce qu'on doit connaître de sa destination pour réussir son voyage?

Les voyages volontaires 1.2

Introduction et interrogations

Dans la **Leçon C**, on vous a informé sur les voyages volontaires qui attirent les jeunes Français. Votre but est de définir le volontarisme pour vous et vos camarades de classe. Comment est-ce que vous voulez aider les autres? Que signifient les mots «bénévole» et «humanitaire» pour vous?

8 Réfléchir 1.3, 3.1, 5.1

Pensez à vos préférences et à vos expériences. Qu'est-ce vous aimez (ou aimeriez) faire comme travail bénévole ou humanitaire? Servez-vous des informations suivantes:

- construire ou réparer une maison
- travailler avec des jeunes ou des personnes âgées
- enseigner l'anglais
- préserver l'environnement
- fournir de l'eau propre
- autre chose

Trouvez deux ou trois camarades de classe qui ont les mêmes intérêts que vous. Faites des recherches sur Internet pour identifier une communauté où ce genre de travail ferait le plus grand bien.

9 Préparer 1.3, 3.1, 4.2, 5.1

*En groupes, imaginez que vous voulez commencer votre projet bénévole ou humanitaire dans un autre pays, mais que vous avez besoin d'un bienfaiteur (*benefactor*) pour vous donner de l'argent. Préparez une présentation pour ce bienfaiteur. La présentation doit inclure:*

- une description de votre projet (où, quand, comment, qui, etc.)
- une description des objectifs de votre projet (pourquoi; résultats attendus)
- une liste de provisions ou de ressources pour le projet
- une liste des bénéficiaires du projet (à qui s'adresse le projet; combien de personnes devraient pouvoir en bénéficier)

10 Faire le point! 1.1, 2.1, 5.1

Discutez de ces questions en classe.

1. Quels sont les différents centres d'intérêt de vos camarades de classe vis-à-vis (*regarding*) du travail bénévole ou humanitaire?
2. Si votre classe faisait les projets proposés par chaque groupe, où iriez-vous? Qu'est-ce que vous feriez?
3. Comment est-ce que vous définiriez les mots «volontarisme», «bénévole», et «humanitaire» aujourd'hui?

Essential Instruction

1. For **Activité 8**, organize students into groups according to their preference for taking part in volunteer or humanitarian projects. Groups research online what projects they could take part in and where it would have the most impact.
2. For **Activité 9**, encourage students to find mission statements of volunteer organizations to help structure the presentation of the project.
3. Ask a class member to record students' remarks for questions one and two of **Activité 10** on the board and categorize them under the headings **bénévole** and **humanitaire**. Make sure to ask students to define **volontarisme**, **bénévole**, and **humanitaire**.
4. Remind the students that the expressions listed on p. 249 introduce the subjunctive in the same way **il faut que** does.

The Subjunctive after Impersonal Expressions 1.1

You know that the subjunctive is used after the expression of necessity **il faut que**. There are other impersonal expressions that are followed by the subjunctive. These expressions give an opinion about someone or something specific. Here are some of these impersonal expressions.

il est nécessaire que	*it is necessary that*
il est important que	*it is important that*
il est indispensable que	*it is indispensable that*
il est essentiel que	*it is essential that*
il est possible que	*it is possible that*
il est impossible que	*it is impossible that*
il est bon que	*it is good that*
il est surprenant que	*it is surprising that*
il est utile que	*it is useful that*
il vaut mieux que	*it is better that*
il se pourrait que	*it is possible that*

Il est essentiel que tu **aies** un passeport. — *It is essential that you have a passport.*

Il est nécessaire que vous **vous renseigniez** au consulat. — *It is necessary that you get informed at the consulate.*

Il est possible que vous **puissiez** réserver à l'avance. — *It is possible that you can reserve in advance.*

Il est bon qu'elle **se fasse** vacciner. — *It is good that she is getting vaccinated.*

Comparaisons 4.1

What mood is this sentence in English? In French?

It is important that you *be* healthy.
Il est important que tu **sois** en forme.

Resources

WB Workbook 6–8
LA Listening Activity 2
G & V Practice Games

Answers

Comparaison

In English, one would say, *It is important that you be healthy.* The verb *be* is the subjunctive here. The expression *it is important that...* triggers the use of the subjunctive, just as it would in French.

Reference Desk

1. Point out to the students that in the examples **Il est possible que vous puissiez réserver à l'avance** and **Il est bon qu'elle se fasse vacciner**, only the verb immediately following **que** is in the subjunctive. The second verb of the subordinate clause remains in the infinitive.
2. Ask students to guess the meaning of **il vaut mieux que** and **il est surprenant que**. The other expressions on the list are similar to English.

Differentiated Learning

Accelerate

Have students work in teams to write as many sentences in the subjunctive as they can in five minutes using the **il est**...**que** expressions.

Decelerate

Ask students to write three sentences in the subjunctive regarding what they must do at home or any rules they have to follow. For example, **Il faut que je fasse mes devoirs tous les soirs**.

Special Needs Students

At-Risk Students

Be sensitive to the fact that some of these students might be receiving direct aid from charitable organizations that the class has identified as a humanitarian organization in their community.

AD(H)D/Linguistically Challenged

Students need to know that although there are new expressions that are followed by the subjunctive, the verbs that they have learned do not change. Reassure them that the majority of these expressions are very easy to guess.

Answers

11

1. Est-il possible que tu reçoives une très bonne note à ton contrôle sur le subjonctif?
2. Est-il possible que tu voyages en France un jour?
3. Est-il possible que tu skies à Combloux cette année?
4. Est-il possible que tu te foules la cheville en skiant?
5. Est-il possible que tu finisses tous tes devoirs ce soir?
6. Est-il possible que tu discutes de l'économie à table ce soir?
7. Est-il possible que tu apprennes le chinois un jour?
8. Est-il possible que tu ailles à une soirée ce soir?
9. Est-il possible que tu fasses le tour du monde?

Partner answers will vary.

12 Possible answers:

1. Il est utile que je me renseigne en surfant sur Internet.
2. Il est bon que je planifie ce que je vais voir.
3. Il est nécessaire que je réserve une chambre d'hôtel.
4. Il vaut mieux que je vérifie que j'ai assez de vêtements dans ma valise.
5. Il est important que je mette de la crème solaire.
6. Il est indispensable que je fasse enregistrer mes bagages.
7. Il est essentiel que je parle français.
8. Il est possible que j'aille à Casablanca.
9. Il est bon que je sache dire "s'il te plaît" et "merci" en arabe.
10. Il vaut mieux que je boive du thé à la menthe quand on nous recevra.
11. Il est possible que je voie les souks.

Reference Desk

Casablanca is the economic and cultural capital of Morocco with a population of more than three million. It is the largest city in the Maghreb. Casablanca was founded in the seventh century and ruled by the Spanish and Portuguese from 1580 to 1640. It is the largest port in North Africa. The Hassan II mosque is the fifth largest mosque in the world, and its architecture is a mix of Moroccan and French styles.

11 Possible ou impossible? 1.1

Interpersonal Speaking

À tour de rôle, demandez à votre partenaire si les situations suivantes sont possibles. Il ou elle va répondre oui ou non.

MODÈLE aller à un mariage cet été
A: Est-il possible que tu ailles à un mariage cet été?
B: Oui, il est possible que j'aille à un mariage cet été. Et toi?
A: Non, il est impossible que j'aille à un mariage cet été parce que je vais travailler.

1. recevoir une très bonne note à ton contrôle sur le subjonctif
2. voyager en France un jour
3. skier à Combloux cette année
4. se fouler la cheville en skiant
5. finir tous tes devoirs ce soir
6. discuter de l'économie à table ce soir
7. apprendre le chinois un jour
8. aller à une soirée ce soir
9. faire le tour du monde

12 Mon voyage au Maroc 1.3, 2.1, 3.1

Presentational Speaking or Writing

Vous allez voyager au Maroc. Choisissez une expression ci-dessous pour former une phrase au subjonctif.

il est nécessaire que **il est essentiel que** **il vaut mieux que** **il est utile que**
il est bon que **il est important que** **il est indispensable que** **il est possible que**

MODÈLE avoir un passeport
Il est nécessaire que j'aie un passeport.

1. se renseigner en surfant sur Internet
2. planifier ce que je vais voir
3. réserver une chambre d'hôtel
4. vérifier que j'ai assez de vêtements dans ma valise
5. mettre de la crème solaire
6. faire enregistrer mes bagages
7. parler français
8. aller à Casablanca
9. savoir dire « s'il te plaît » et « merci » en arabe
10. boire du thé à la menthe (*mint*) quand on nous recevra
11. voir les souks

Essential Instruction

1. Pair students to do **Activités 11** and **12**.
2. Check **Activité 12** by asking students, "**Est-il possible ou est-il essentiel que…?**" "**Est-il utile ou est-il indispensable que…?**" (etc.)
3. Circulate the classroom to answer questions, correct pronunciation, and to keep students on task.
4. Have students practice listening comprehension with **Activité 13**. After they have finished, ask them additional questions about the images for additional oral practice.
5. Have students write some of the answers to **Activité 14** before reading them aloud.

13 Notre séjour au Sénégal 1.2, 3.1

Interpretive Viewing and Listening

Écrivez les numéros 1–7 sur votre papier. Écoutez les phrases, puis choisissez l'image qui correspond.

A. 

B. 

C. 

D. 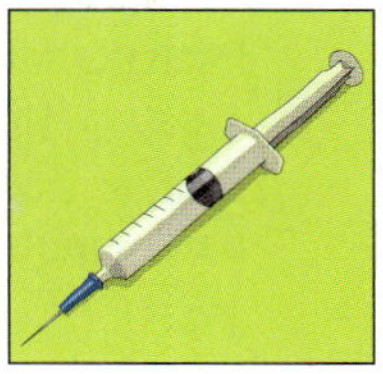

E. 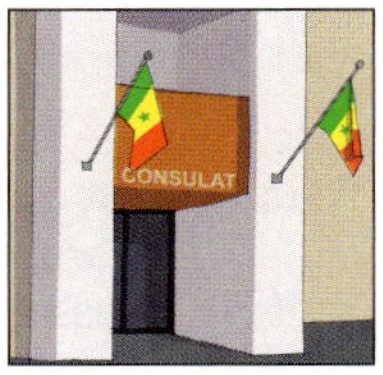

F. 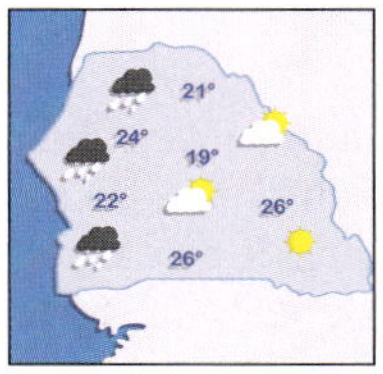

G. 

14 Des situations 1.1, 5.2

Interpersonal Speaking

Avec deux camarades de classe, dites ce qu'il faut faire dans chaque situation. Utilisez les expressions ci-dessous.

il est nécessaire que | **il faut que** | **il est indispensable que**
il est important que | **il est essentiel que** | **il vaut mieux que**

MODÈLE organiser une fête d'anniversaire pour Nicolas

A: Pour organiser une fête d'anniversaire pour Nicolas, il est important que j'invite tous ses copains.
B: Il est important que je lui achète un cadeau qu'il aime.
C: Il est indispensable que je prépare un gâteau d'anniversaire.

1. protéger l'environnement
2. réussir à l'école
3. être bon élève ou bonne élève
4. faire du baby-sitting
5. avoir de bons amis
6. trouver un travail intéressant
7. être en forme
8. être heureux/heureuse

Differentiated Learning

Accelerate

Students could go online to find visuals like photos or clip art, or they could use their own drawings to make flash cards of situations in which the **il est… que** expressions could be used. They then lead a review for the class. For example, they might find an advertisement of a mother helping her son: **Il est bon que la mère aide son fils.**

Decelerate

Students use whiteboards to do a guided ten-minute review of regular and irregular verbs in the subjunctive before doing **Activités 13** and **14**. Encourage them to use online practice programs.

Recherche: conjuguemos

Resources

Activity 13

Answers

13 Script

1. Il est nécessaire que vous obteniez un passeport.
2. Il est important que vous réserviez une chambre d'hôtel.
3. Il est indispensable que vous planifiiez en surfant sur Internet.
4. Il est essentiel que vous vous fassiez vacciner.
5. Il vaut mieux que vous alliez au consulat.
6. Il est bon que vous écoutiez la météo avant de faire votre valise.
7. Il est utile que vous ayez toujours une pièce d'identité sur vous.

1. A; 2. C; 3. B; 4. D; 5. E; 6. F; 7. G

14 Possible answers:

1. Pour protéger l'environnement, il vaut mieux que tu conduises une voiture hybride/il est nécessaire qu'on recycle les bouteilles/il faut que le gouvernement fasse marcher les usines avec des éoliennes.
2. Pour réussir à l'école, il faut que chacun étudie sérieusement/il est important qu'on ait de bonnes notes/il est indispensable que les profs aident les élèves.
3. Pour être bon élève, il vaut mieux que j'écoute le prof/il est indispensable que je fasse tous mes devoirs/il est essentiel que je ne sois pas souvent absent(e).
4. Pour faire du babysitting, il est essentiel que j'aime les enfants/il est important qu'on sache donner les premiers secours/il vaut mieux qu'on soit organisé.
5. Pour avoir de bons amis, il est important qu'on écoute les autres/il vaut mieux que je ne sois pas jaloux (jalouse)/il faut que je sois honnête.
6. Pour trouver un travail intéressant, il est nécessaire que tu aies un bon diplôme/il vaut mieux qu'il y ait peu de chômage.
7. Pour être en forme, il est indispensable que nous fassions du sport régulièrement/il faut qu'on mange sainement/il est important que les parents apprennent aux enfants à bien manger.
8. Pour être heureux (heureuse), il est nécessaire qu'on soit aimable/il est important qu'on ait des amis/il est nécessaire qu'on poursuive ses rêves.

Resources

CA Communicative Activities

Share

Answers

15 Brochures will vary.

16 Plays will vary.

17 Sports will vary.

Reference Desk

If you have access to Passport, create a question for your students to share their response to a communicative activity.

Expansion

Have students research an Olympic Winter Games of their choice. Perhaps they could look at the stats of the French participants (or participants from francophone countries) and those of American participants and compare them. You could also have them see how many of the winter sports they have learned in this unit are sports that are included in the Olympic Games. They could also imagine or pretend that they are competitors at the games and write a diary or blog entry about their experience competing. If it is a Winter Olympics year and you have access to the internet, log on to the French version of the Olympics website and have students navigate the French teams and athletes for the year. When the Olympics occur, select events for the students to stream from French or Canadian coverage of the games.

À vous la parole

Question centrale ? Qu'est-ce qu'on doit connaître de sa destination pour réussir son voyage ?

Communiquez!

15 Les stations de ski 1.3, 2.2, 3.2, 5.2

Presentational Writing

Créez un dépliant avec les stations de ski des Alpes qui sont mentionnées dans cette unité. Pour chaque station de ski, ajoutez un repère (*marker*) et une photo ou une vidéo. Écrivez un petit paragraphe pour décrire chaque station de ski.

16 Théo à l'hôpital 1.1, 1.3, 5.2

Presentational Speaking

En groupes de quatre ou cinq, recréez le scénario suivant : Pendant la classe de neige, votre camarade de classe Théo s'est cassé la jambe en skiant. Un hélicoptère l'a ramené (*took back*) à Grenoble, où il est maintenant à l'hôpital. Jouez le rôle de Théo, ses amis, le professeur, le personnel de l'ambulance ou le personnel de l'hôpital. Soyez aussi créatifs/créatives et dramatiques que vous le souhaitez !

17 Pour se préparer aux sports d'hiver 1.3, 3.1, 5.2

Presentational Speaking

Avec un partenaire, créez une brochure pour informer les gens sur les sports d'hiver. Sélectionnez plusieurs sports et :

- faites une liste de l'équipement nécessaire pour pratiquer chaque sport
- faites une description qui comprend les risques associés à chaque sport
- indiquez les meilleurs endroits où on peut pratiquer ces sports dans votre région (en France ou au Canada)

Essential Instruction

1. Consider assigning **Activités 15**, **16**, and **17** to students according to their learning styles, strengths, and personalities.
2. **Activité 15** may appeal to visual learners and those with an artistic flair.
3. **Activité 16** is an interactive activity for students who like collaborating on projects. Your extroverts could transform this activity into a play in which Théo is skiing, falls, breaks his leg, and is transported back to Nice.
4. **Activité 17** is perfect for logical-sequential learners who like lists and statistics presented in an organized format.
5. Have students complete **Stratégie de lecture** after reading the poem. It serves as the framework for a class discussion of the structure and themes of the poem.
6. Have students unravel the poem's mythical allusions.

Heureux qui, comme Ulysse, a fait un beau voyage

Rencontre avec l'auteur 1.2

Joachim Du Bellay (1522–1560) était un poète de la Renaissance française qui a fait ses études dans un collège humaniste. Il a écrit son recueil (*collection*) de poèmes *Les regrets* pendant un long séjour en Italie, destination de beaucoup de jeunes Français et artistes qui voulaient voir la grandeur de l'Italie antique et les chefs-d'œuvre de la Renaissance. En 1533, avec Ronsard, il a fondé un groupe de poètes, la Pléiade, dont le but était de définir de nouvelles règles poétiques. Il est mort très jeune, à 37 ans, et on l'a enterré à Notre-Dame de Paris. Son poème le plus célèbre est celui que vous allez lire. Le poète est-il content à Rome ou est-ce qu'il a des regrets?

Pré-lecture 1.3, 3.1, 3.2

Quel voyage est-ce que vous voudriez faire?

Stratégie de lecture 1.2, 1.3

Structure, Meaning, and Theme. Ce poème est un sonnet en alexandrins avec deux quatrains et deux tercets; un quatrain est une strophe (*stanza*) avec quatre vers, tandis qu'un tercet en a trois. Dans ces quatre strophes, le poète développe un thème. Remplissez l'organigramme en indiquant l'idée centrale de chaque strophe; au centre mettez le thème du poème.

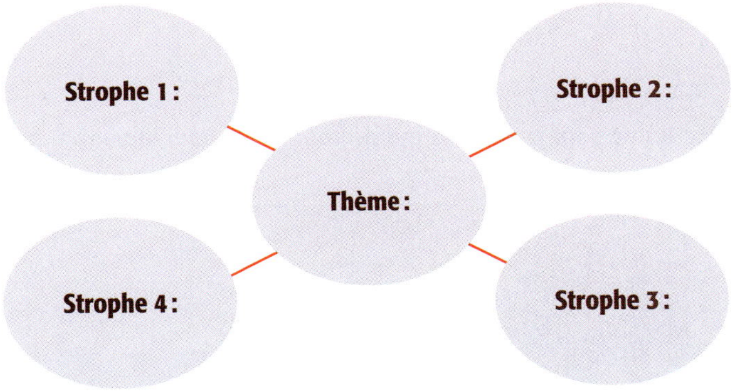

Outils de lecture 1.1, 1.2, 1.3

Allusions. Une allusion est une référence à une personne, un événement, un objet, ou une œuvre de l'histoire ou de la littérature. Du Bellay se sert de deux allusions classiques. Vous les trouverez dans les deux premiers vers du poème. Recherchez ces deux allusions mythiques. Comment est-ce qu'elles renforcent son idée d'un «beau voyage»?

Resources

Rencontre avec l'auteur

Answers

Rencontre avec l'auteur
L'auteur semble avoir des regrets.

Pré-lecture
Answers will vary.

Stratégie de lecture
Possible answers:
Thème: les voyages
Strophe 1: Les voyages ouvrent l'esprit.
Strophe 2: Le poète a la nostalgie de sa maison.
Strophe 3: Le poète préfère son pays aux merveilles du monde.
Strophe 4: Le poète se rappelle son univers qui lui manque.

Outils de lecture
Possible answer:
Du Bellay fait allusion au grand voyage d'Ulysse de "l'Odyssée" de Homère, et de la conquête de la tison d'or du poème "Argonautiques" (d'Apollonius Rhodius, grec, ou Valerius Flaccus, romain).; Un beau voyage est celui qui ramène le voyageur chez lui.

Reference Desk

La Pléiade is a name ascribed to a group of 16th-century French Renaissance poets whose principal members were Pierre de Ronsard, Joachim du Bellay, and Jean-Antoine de Baïf. These poets sought to integrate classical literary styles like the ode and sonnet, and celebrate the beauty of the French language. Students may be familiar with Homer's "Odyssey." Have them review the plot of the poem as they consider their responses to **Outils de lecture**.

Special Needs Students

Social Anxiety
When pairing students for this activity, make sure that those with social anxiety can work with someone with whom they feel comfortable. Rather than asking them to perform for the class, you may want to ask them to speak in front of another pair of students or just for you. Invite them to select their partner, but check that the partnering will be beneficial to them.

Linguistically Challenged
For students who are new to French poetry, preview difficult vocabulary and expressions and help translate difficult lines into English. Once they understand the poem, they will be more willing to participate in class discussions. Make copies of the poem for students so that they can write notes and comments.

Resources

Heureux qui, comme Ulysse

Answers

Pendant la lecture

1. Ulysse/les voyageurs
2. Ulysse/celui qui a voyagé
3. hélas
4. à sa maison (son pays, son village)
5. l'ardoise
6. à Rome
7. dans les pays de la Loire, chez lui

Post-lecture

Pour le poète, les grands sites de la Rome antique sont moins importants que les petits paysages de son pays natal.

Reference Desk

Joachim Du Bellay was living in Italy when he wrote "**Heureux qui Comme Ulysse**." He thinks of his beloved region of Anjou, a former province in the Loire valley.

Communication

Interpersonal: Cooperative Groups

1. Distribute the lyrics to Brassens's "**Heureux qui Comme Ulysse**." Select a rendition on the Internet to show to your students.
2. Listen to the poem together. Students may underline difficult words or make notes to help them with comprehension.
3. Complete **Activité 18** number two in heterogeneous groups.
4. Discuss common points of the two poems. What elements has Brassens added to the poem to personalize it for him? Which area of France corresponds to "**la douceur angévine**" for Brassens? (**La Provence**) What is **la Camargue** famous for? (horses and cowboys)

«Heureux qui, comme Ulysse» 1.2

Heureux qui, comme Ulysse, a fait un beau voyage,
Ou comme cestuy-là*, qui conquit* la toison*,
Et puis est retourné, plein d'usage et raison,
Vivre entre ses parents le reste de son âge !

Quand reverrai-je, hélas*, de mon petit village
Fumer la cheminée, et en quelle saison
Reverrai-je le clos* de ma pauvre maison,
Qui m'est une province, et beaucoup davantage* ?

Plus me plaît le séjour* qu'ont bâti* mes aïeux,
Que des palais Romains le front audacieux,
Plus que le marbre* dur me plaît l'ardoise* fine :

Plus mon Loir gaulois*, que le Tibre* latin,
Plus mon petit Liré, que le mont Palatin,
Et plus que l'air marin* la douceur* angevine*.

Pendant la lecture
1. Qui a fait un beau voyage ?

Pendant la lecture
2. Qui est retourné « plein d'usage et raison » ?

Pendant la lecture
3. Quel mot indique le regret ?

Pendant la lecture
4. À quoi pense le poète ?

Pendant la lecture
5. Quel matériel vient de sa région, le marbre ou l'ardoise ?

Pendant la lecture
6. Où sont le Tibre et le mont Palatin ?

Pendant la lecture
7. Où est-ce que le poète préfère vivre, à Rome ou dans les pays de la Loire ?

cestuy-là celui-là (Ancien français) ; **conquit** *conquered* ; **toison** *Golden Fleece* ; **hélas** *alas* ; **clos** *property* ; **davantage** *more* ; **séjour** *dwelling* ; **bâti** *built* ; **marbre** *marble* ; **ardoise** *slate (used on roofs in Loire Valley)* ; **gaulois** *gallic, or French* ; **Tibre** *Tiber* (fleuve à Rome) ; **air marin** *sea air* ; **douceur** *[archaic] sweetness* ; **angevine** *from/of the Angers area*

Post-lecture 1.3

Les sites classiques de Rome sont-ils plus ou moins importants pour le narrateur que les sites de chez lui ?

Rome, ville au lever du soleil, en Italie

Essential Instruction

1. Play the recording of the poem, books closed; have students guess what the poem is about. Take note of words students recognized. Put these expressions on the board for later.
2. Play the poem a second time, books open, stopping after each **strophe** to answer the questions in the margin.
3. Compare the allusions to Rome and Anjou. Determine which location is more important to the narrator. (**Post-Lecture**)
4. Work in groups to answer **Activité 18**, numbers one and three.
5. Discuss the theme of **nostalgie**. Ask students how they feel when they are away from home, friends, and family. Put ideas on the board for students to copy and use in their journal entry in **Activité 18**, number three.

Le monde visuel 1.2, 2.2, 3.1

Sébastien Bourdon (1616–1671), peintre français, a peint *Ulysse découvre Astyanax caché dans le tombeau d'Hector* dans le style classique. Les peintres de ce mouvement s'intéressaient aux sujets classiques de la tradition grecque et romaine comme les histoires d'Ulysse, roi d'Ithaque, leader dans la guerre de Troie, et voyageur par excellence pour ses aventures en revenant de la guerre. Les classiques aimaient la proportion, les couleurs vives, et la formalité. Ils peignaient leurs sujets dans les vêtements de leur époque, souvent parmi des urnes et des piliers (*pillers*). La composition de ces tableaux est souvent symétrique. Quelles sont les caractéristiques classiques de ce tableau ?

Ulysse découvre Astyanax caché dans le tombeau d'Hector, c. 1654–1656. Sébastien Bourdon. Collection privée.

18 Activités d'expansion 1.3, 2.2, 3.1, 5.1

Interpretive Communication

Faites les activités suivantes.

1. Quel est le thème du poème ? Comment est-ce que Du Bellay le développe ? Citez les expressions du poème qui soutiennent votre point de vue. N'oubliez pas de mentionner comment le poète organise ses idées. Servez-vous de l'organigramme que vous avez rempli.
2. Imaginez que vous êtes Élodie des *Rencontres culturelles*. Écrivez un passage dans votre journal où vous parlez de votre nostalgie pour votre maison, votre chambre, votre famille, et votre bande de copains pendant que vous êtes en classe de neige.

Recherche : vidéo georges brassens heureux qui comme ulysse

3. Explorez comment le chanteur Georges Brassens a développé sa chanson « Heureux qui comme Ulysse » et comparez-la au poème original de Du Bellay.

Georges Brassens

Resources

Pre-test

Leçon Quiz

Answers

Le monde visuel

Les proportions sont réalistes, la symétrie équilibrée met en valeur chaque élément de la scène ; les couleurs vives font un contraste avec les couleurs sombres.

18

1. Possible answers:
   Le thème : les grands voyages ; le poète contraste le pays visité au pays natal du voyageur ; Le poète fait usage de constructions grammaticales de comparaison : « plus. . .que » ; l'organisation des idées : Strophe 1 : les voyages apportent la sagesse et il est bon de rentrer à la maison. ; Strophe 2 : Le poète est en voyage et sa maison lui manque. ; Strophe 3 : Le poète compare son village aux grands lieux touristiques qu'il visite. ; Strophe 4 : Le poète insiste que son village lui plaît davantage que Rome
2. Answers will vary.
3. Answers will vary.

Reference Desk

1. Du Bellay is considered a humanist.
2. Humanism sees man as the measure of all things. It emphasizes the enjoyment of life on earth, the pursuit of beauty, and a return to the classic literature of Greece and Rome. In the Renaissance, the emphasis is on the enjoyment of life on earth rather than the strict medieval monastic view in which life is only a preparation for heaven.
3. Du Bellay's poem captures both the humanist theme of life on earth (love of one's homeland) and its allusions to Antiquity.

Differentiated Learning

Accelerate

Students read **Le monde visuel** and prepare a presentation of the painting ***Ulysse découvre Astyanax caché dans le tombeau d'Hector*** to the class. What is the style of painting? Who are the people in the scene and what are they doing? What emotions does the painter convey?

Decelerate

Have students research the mythology of Ulysses, (Odysseus), Helen, Hector, and Astyanax. Ask them to present the story as a fairy tale, news commentary, or historical event.

French in the Workplace

Teaching French

In the previous unit, we considered how to teach English to French-speakers. Tell students that another promising way to use French to make a living is to teach French at the elementary, high school, city college, or even university level in their country. Have students design a lesson for a group of English-speakers learning French. They may use one of the grammar concepts presented in this unit. Ask them to include a reading, writing, speaking, listening, and kinesthetic activity. Then have them give their lesson to the class.

Social Justice

Traveling, especially internationally, can be very costly to families and young people. Ensuring inclusive, quality education, and promoting life-long learning opportunities is key in moving forward with global goals. Are there programs that currently exist in the students' community that allocate funding to such opportunities? If so, what are these programs, how do they function, and have students taken part in them or know of family members or friends who have? What programs could students create that could be run by their school or community, and that would contribute to promoting quality education for all, while also promoting travel?

Connections

Financial literacy, creativity and innovation, technology literacy

Group students and have them create a brochure for the **Office du tourisme de Chamonix**. Groups should create a promotional budget for two winning families (a young couple, and a family with children) for a week of vacation in Chamonix. They should plan for both families, and include:
▪ le logement ▪ les repas au restaurant ▪ les activités et les sorties ▪ la location de l'équipement et le forfait ski

Recherche : chamonix, forfait ski chamonix

Communiquez!

19 Les globe-trotters 1.1, 1.2, 1.3, 2.2, 3.2, 4.2, 5.1

Connecting to Civic Literacy, Health Literacy, Productivity and Accountability

Interpersonal Speaking, Interpretive Reading, Presentational Writing

Les règles et formalités pour visiter un pays changent selon la nationalité du voyageur et le pays qu'il veut visiter.

1ère Partie : Avec un partenaire, choisissez trois pays francophones de différentes régions du monde. Faites des recherches sur les papiers à obtenir et les règles à suivre pour visiter ces pays depuis les États-Unis. Complétez un diagramme comme celui de dessous : ajoutez les spécifications que vous désirez ou que vous trouverez. Ensuite, visitez le site web de l'Office du Tourisme des États-Unis et comparez ce que les voyageurs venant de chacun de ces pays francophones doivent faire pour visiter les États-Unis.

Pays	Nationalité des voyageurs	Documentation d'entrée	Durée maximum du voyage	Documentation de santé/ vaccins	Activités/ endroits interdits	Autre
Pays 1	américain					
Pays 2	français					
Pays 3	congolais					

Recherche : ambassade de (+ PAYS) aux états-unis ; office du tourisme (+ PAYS)

2ème Partie : Avec les informations que vous avez trouvées, jouez les rôles d'un(e) touriste américain(e) dans l'un des pays francophones que vous avez recherchés, et d'un(e) employé(e) de l'ambassade de ce pays. Le ou la touriste posera des questions sur les règles du pays et l'employé(e) pourra se servir des informations dans le diagramme pour lui répondre et faire des recommandations.

3ème Partie : Trouvez un groupe qui a recherché au moins un pays en commun avec vous. Comparez vos informations, puis expliquez comment les règles sont différentes d'un pays à l'autre. Donnez des suggestions pour faire un long voyage dans chaque pays.

20 Voyagez en groupe ! 1.1, 1.3, 4.2, 5.1, 5.2

Connecting to Collaboration, Flexibility and Adaptability

Interpersonal Speaking, Presentational Writing and Speaking

Votre classe veut organiser un voyage en groupe dans un pays que vous n'avez jamais visité et où chacun(e) pourra faire quelque chose qu'il ou elle n'a jamais fait.

Préparez trois à quatre questions à poser à un minimum de dix personnes, pour découvrir quelles activités vos camarades n'ont jamais faites et voudraient faire. En fonction des résultats de votre sondage, recommandez un pays étranger à visiter, et des activités à faire en groupe. Présentez un itinéraire de voyage à votre classe en expliquant vos choix.

Essential Instruction

1. Have students read **Projets finaux** (**A**, **B**, or **C**) and create groups according to their preferred project. Provide a rubric that indicates your expectations and point values.
2. Make sure that students have access to the computer lab since not all of them have Internet access or computers at home.
3. For **Activité D**, p. 257, distribute copies of the graphic organizer located in the **Copy Masters** supplement. Impress upon students that filling in this form will give them an overview of what they know and what they need to study.

Question centrale ? Qu'est-ce qu'on doit connaître de sa destination pour réussir son voyage?

Projets finaux

A Connexions par Internet : la littérature 1.2, 1.3, 3.1, 3.2, 5.2

Un storyboard

Dans cette unité vous avez lu le poème « Heureux qui, comme Ulysse, a fait un beau voyage » de Du Bellay. Cherchez le dessin animé de Ridan et découvrez son interprétation du poème. Ensuite, créez un storyboard où vous dessinez votre propre vidéo du poème qui en montre votre interprétation.

Recherche : ridan heureux qui comme ulysse vidéo

B Communautés en ligne 3.1, 3.2, 5.1

Le chien du Saint-Bernard

Visitez un club pour les passionnés du chien du Saint-Bernard et trouvez les réponses à ces questions :

- Quelle est la devise du chien du Saint-Bernard ?
- Comment est-il physiquement ?
- Comment décrit-on son caractère ?
- Il est connu pour quels exploits ?
- Il a quels problèmes de santé ?
- C'est la vedette de quels films ?
- Il faut payer combien pour avoir un chien du Saint-Bernard ?

Recherche : chien du saint-bernard

C Passez à l'action ! 1.3, 3.1, 3.2, 5.1, 5.2

Le WWOOFing : un voyage volontaire

Créez un document qui décrit ce qu'est le WWOOFing. Faites une carte qui montre dans quels pays francophones on peut faire du WWOOFing. Faites une liste de dix projets qui vous intéressent. Avec votre classe, choisissez parmi tous les projets, un projet que vous pourriez sponsoriser. Contactez l'organisation bénévole pour savoir s'ils préféreraient recevoir de l'argent ou du matériel. Organisez une collecte auprès de votre lycée.

D Faisons le point ! 1.3

Mes progrès

Servez-vous de l'organigramme que votre prof va vous donner. Remplissez-le avec ce que vous avez appris.

Resources

Create

Answers

All activities will vary.

Reference Desk

1. If you have access to Passport, assign your students an IPA task related to the unit.
2. The **Faisons le point!** section asks students to self-evaluate and keep track of their progress. When students complete the activity, direct them to use "I can" statements based on the unit objectives in the **Contrat de l'élève**. The graphic organizer for **Activité D** can be found in the Copy Masters supplement.

Special Needs Students

AD(H)D

These students may have difficulty organizing their materials and their time. Help students to create a schedule for their **Projet final**. Work with them to establish due dates for their part of the project. Schedule check-in meetings to discuss resources, process, and progress.

Resources

Activity A
Listing Activity *Synthèse*
Pre-AP Listening *Unité 4*

Answers

A Script

Armelle : Tu fais ta valise ?
Amadou : Oui, j'essaie de penser à ce que je dois prendre.
Armelle : Il est indispensable que tu prennes la crème solaire, une écharpe, un bonnet, et des gants.
Amadou : Et toi, tu as confirmé notre réservation à l'hôtel ?
Armelle : Oui, et j'ai réservé un taxi pour aller à l'aéroport.
Amadou : Super. Tu as bien pris nos pièces d'identité ?
Armelle : Oui, j'ai les billets d'avions, notre réservation à l'hôtel, ma carte de crédit, et nos pièces d'identité dans mon sac à main.
Amadou : Alors, on est prêt pour le ski alpin, le snowboard, et les randonnées.
Armelle : Moi, je vois les choses un peu différemment. Si on faisait du ski de fond et qu'on allait à la piscine ?
Amadou : Pourquoi pas ! Tu as vérifié qu'on n'a rien oublié ?
Armelle : Oui, allons-y !

1. Il est indispensable qu'Amadou prenne des gants, selon Armelle.
2. Armelle a oublié de confirmer la réservation de l'hôtel.
3. On a réservé un taxi pour aller à l'aéroport.
4. Armelle a les passeports, les visas, et les permis de conduire dans son sac à main.
5. Amadou veut faire du ski et du snowboard.
6. On change d'avis et on va faire des randonnées équestres.
7. Amadou et Armelle vont profiter de la piscine.

1. V; 2. F; 3. V; 4. F; 5. V; 6. F; 7. V

B Activities will vary.

C Activities will vary.

Reference Desk

The activities in **Évaluation** require students to incorporate the information that they have learned in this unit. Provide time to review vocabulary prior to completing **Activitiés B** and **C**.

Évaluation

A Évaluation de compréhension auditive 1.1, 1.2

*Écrivez les numéros 1–7 sur votre papier. Écoutez Armelle et Amadou discuter de leur projet de vacances à la montagne. Ensuite, indiquez si les phrases que vous entendez sont vraies (**V**) ou fausses (**F**).*

B Évaluation orale 1.1, 5.2

Jouez les rôles de trois ados français qui planifient un voyage à Combloux.

A : Proposez Combloux.
B : Demandez ce qu'on peut y faire.
C : Dites ce que vous y avez fait la dernière fois.
B : Dites que vous ne savez pas faire du ski de piste.
A : Dites-lui qu'il ou elle peut apprendre d'un moniteur et parlez d'autres activités qu'il ou elle aura l'occasion de faire à Combloux.
B : Dites qu'il faut que vous reveniez en skiant correctement cette fois.
C : Dites-lui qu'il est important qu'il ou qu'elle ne se foule pas la cheville avant le mariage de sa sœur en mars.
A : Demandez si vos amis sont persuadés qu'il faut y aller.
B–C : Répondez.

C Évaluation culturelle 3.2, 4.2, 5.1

Vous allez comparer les cultures francophones à la culture américaine. Vous aurez peut-être besoin de faire des recherches sur la culture américaine.

1. **La Réunion et Hawaï**
   Comparez les îles de La Réunion et d'Hawaï en matière de géologie, population, activité économique, et situation géographique.
2. **Les Alpes, le Mont Blanc, et les stations de ski en Savoie**
   Cette région de la France peut être comparée à quelle région américaine ? Pourquoi ? Et dans cette région américaine, comment est la flore ? Et la faune ? Sont-elles comparables à la Savoie ?
3. **La Savoie**
   Quels attributs font une « terre de culture », « terre gastronomique », et « terre de tourisme » de cette région ? de votre région ?
4. **Les classes de neige**
   Qu'est-ce qui se passe en classe de neige ? Avez-vous l'occasion de voyager et de participer à un sport alors que vous êtes au lycée ? Si non, qu'est-ce que vous proposeriez au directeur ou à la directrice de votre lycée pour vivre un séjour semblable (*similar*) ?

Essential Instruction

1. Have all students complete **Activité B** as a vocabulary review.
2. Assign **Activité D** as an in-class activity. Allow students ten minutes to write an outline of what they would like to say. Circulate to answer questions and provide support. The input students get before they write helps to reduce the number of corrections needed later. Immediate feedback provides the input they need to do an effective job.
3. **Activité E** could be done in the computer lab. If equipment is available, have students record their description of the scene.
4. Divide the class into small groups to complete **Activité F**. Provide paper for the group's six illustrations. This activity can be made into a competition. Set a time limit; allow groups to work and when time is called, have them post their drawings. Have students take a museum walk to view the final products and vote on the best representation. Decide with the class beforehand what judging criteria will be used.

5. **Les voyageurs volontaires**
Existe-t-il des organisations bénévoles dans votre ville ou région? Quelles sont-elles? Les avez-vous déjà aidées? Quels pays francophones ont besoin d'aide? À quoi est-ce que vous pourriez contribuer pour aider ces pays?

D Évaluation écrite 1.3, 2.1, 3.1

Vous avez écrit une lettre à votre cousin pour lui proposer d'aller faire du ski dans les Alpes. Il vous répond en vous proposant un voyage différent: un voyage humanitaire en Afrique ou aux Antilles. Dites ce que vous en pensez, et demandez-lui plus de renseignements. Dites ce que vous êtes prêt(e) à faire.

E Évaluation visuelle 1.3

Décrivez ce qu'on fait à cette station de ski.

F Évaluation compréhensive 1.3

Créez une histoire avec six illustrations: dessinez une semaine de classes de neige dans les Alpes. Écrivez des légendes qui expliquent votre histoire ou racontez les aventures des ados à votre groupe.

Resources

Perform

Answers

All activities will vary.

Reference Desk

If you have access to Passport, assign a task to evaluate your students' oral proficiency.

Expansion

To prepare to write **Activité D**, have small groups do some brainstorming. List reasons to participate in **un voyage humanitaire**, think of expressions used to express opinion, and come up with possible questions that might be asked to gain information about a trip to Africa or the Antilles. Remind students that one way to give an opinion is to use the impersonal expressions they learned on p. 249.

Differentiated Learning

Accelerate
Encourage students preparing to take the AP exam to do **Activité A** individually and prepare **Activité B** in groups of three to present in front of you.

Decelerate
Have students work in pairs to do two out of the five options in **Activité C**.

Special Needs Students

At-Risk Students
Students with weak study skills might need help getting organized to review for the test.

Dyslexia
Encourage these students to jot down grammar charts, vocabulary, or cultural information onto their test when they receive it. As they work their way through the test, they may refer to their notes.

Resources

FC Flash Cards

Rendez-vous à Nice ! Documentaire 2

T *Unité 4* Test

Reference Desk

nouvelle orthographe

une ile

Game

Pictionnaire

Play Pictionary to review vocabulary from **Unité 4**. In advance, prepare five sets of index cards with vocabulary from p. 260. Divide the class into groups of five, and give each group a set of these cards. In each group, four players pair up to make teams of two, and the fifth player becomes **l'arbitre** (*the ref*). The ref chooses a card from the set and shows it to the two players who will be drawing. The remaining player on each team will try to guess the word that his or her partner is drawing, and the first one to do so correctly wins the round. For round two, the pairs switch roles, and the ref shows a new card to the players whose turn it is to draw.

Vocabulaire de l'Unité 4

abandonner to abandon *C*
s' **attendre (à)** to expect (something) *B*; **Je m'y attendais** I was expecting that *B*
avoir: avoir l'occasion (de) to have the opportunity (to) *B*
aucun(e) any, none, no one *A*; **aucun de nous ne (+ VERB)** none of us (+ VERB) *A*
un **bâton de ski** ski pole *B*
le **bénévolat** volunteer work *C*
se **casser le poignet** to break one's wrist *C*
un **casque de ski** ski goggles *B*
les **chaussures (f.) de ski** ski boots *B*
une **classe de neige** ski class *B*
le **consulat** consulate *C*
correctement correctly *B*
de: de toute façon in any case *B*
différemment differently *A*
dire: (NOUN +) te dit ? How do you feel about (+ NOUN)? *A*
le **domaine** property *C*
en upon, while *A*; **en skiant** while skiing *B*; **en y réfléchissant bien** on second thought *A*; **en y regardant de plus près** on a closer look *A*
s' **ennuyer** to get bored *A*
faire: faire du canyonisme to go canyoning *A*; **faire du deltaplane** to go hang gliding *A*; **faire de la motoneige** to snowmobile *C*; **faire de la luge** to go sledding *C*; **faire de la planche à voile** to wind surf *A*; **faire de la raquette à neige** to go snowshoeing *C*; **faire de l'escalade** to rock climb *A*; **faire du parapente** to go paragliding *A*; **faire des sauts à ski** to go off ski jumps *A*; **faire du saut à l'élastique** to bungee jump *A*; **faire du ski de fond** to cross-country ski *A*; **faire du ski joëring** to skijor *C*; **faire du ski de piste** to ski downhill *C*; **faire du ski hors-piste** to backcountry ski *C*; **faire du snowboard** to snowboard *B*; **faire du speed riding** to speed ride *C*; **faire du taxi-ski** to take a ski-taxi ride *C*; **faire du télémark** to telemark ski *C*; **faire le coup (à quelqu'un)** to play a trick (on someone) *A*; **faire sa valise** to pack *B*; **faire une randonnée équestre** to go on a trail ride *A*; **faire un séjour** to stay *C*
se **faire: se faire vacciner** to get vaccinated *C*
un **forfait de ski** ski pass *B*
se **fouler la cheville** to sprain an ankle *C*
des **gants (m.)** gloves *B*
le **hors-piste** off-road skiing *C*
humide humid *A*
il: il est essentiel que it's essential that *C*; **il est indispensable que** it's indispensable that *C*; **il est important que** it's important that *C*; **il est surprenant que** it's surprising that *C*; **il est utile que** it's useful that *C*; **il se pourrait que** it's possible that *C*; **il vaut mieux que** it's better that *C*
une **île** island *A*
un **moniteur, une monitrice** instructor *B*
ne: ne (n')... aucun(e) no, none, not any, not one *A*; **ne (n')... ni... ni** neither... nor *A*; **ne (n')... que** only *A*
obtenir to obtain *C*
l' **office (m.) de tourisme** tourist office *C*
organisé(e) organized *B*
un **pantalon (de) ski** ski pants *B*
le **passé** past *C*
un **passeport** passport *C*
persuadé(e) convinced *A*
une **pièce d'identité** identification (document) *C*
une **piste (de ski)** (ski) slope *B*
planifier to plan *A*
les **préparatifs (m.) de départ** travel preparations *C*
se **renseigner** to get information *C*
La **Réunion** Reunion *A*
sans aucun doute without a doubt *A*
seulement only *A*
un **ski** ski *A*
le **snowboard** snowboarding *C*
le **sommet** peak *A*
une **station de ski** ski resort *B*
sur: sur place on the premises *B*
un **télésiège** ski lift *B*
tout(e): tout schuss full throttle *A*
un **tremplin de saut à ski** ski jump *B*
tu: tu n'y es pas du tout you don't get it *A*
une **veste (de) ski** ski jacket *B*
le **Vietnam** Vietnam *C*
un **visa** visa *C*
un **volcan** volcano *A*

Essential Instruction

1. Have students skim the questions before completing **Activité I**.
2. Ask students to do the same before listening to the dialogue in **Activité II**. Have them listen and write down their answers. Provide immediate feedback.
3. Read the instructions together for **Activité III**. Make sure the students understand what is required of them.
4. Have pairs read the blogs and administration's response to the issue on p. 262. Encourage the students to work together to understand each person's viewpoint before completing their own essay.
5. Review a simple structure or outline for the essay required in **Activité III**. A opening paragraph should review the theme and the controversy. The second and/or third paragraphs should review a first point of view, quoting the text. The third or fourth paragraph should review the other point of view, again quoting the text. The fourth or fifth paragraph should give the student's personal point of view.

Bilan cumulatif

Pre-AP

Multiple Choice

I. Interpretive Communication: Print texts **1.1, 1.2**

Lisez ce reportage sur les initiatives en France aujourd'hui, puis répondez à la question.

Les jeunes et le bricolage? Certains d'entre eux ont anticipé une opportunité incroyable de créer une petite société qui offrirait des services de réparation, d'entretien et de rénovation dans les condos, HLM, maisons individuelles et maisons mitoyennes. Ils offrent toutes sortes de projets de bricolage—peindre les murs, poser le papier peint, accrocher des peintures, changer la moquette ou installer du parquet en bois.

1. Selon cet article, cette initiative s'est créée parce que....
   A. c'est une affaire familiale de père en fils
   B. le gouvernement encourage les jeunes à être créatifs
   C. le bricolage n'est pas très à la mode avec les jeunes
   D. les jeunes sont des entrepreneurs.

II. Interpretive Communication: Audio texts **1.1, 1.2**

Écoutez le dialogue deux fois, puis répondez aux questions en choisissant la lettre de la réponse correcte.

1. Où est-ce que Nora et Bruno vont faire du ski?
   A. dans les Vosges
   B. en Savoie
   C. dans les Pyrénées
   D. en Italie
2. Quand ils ont planifié le voyage, qu'est-ce qu'ils ont décidé de faire avant de partir?
   A. réserver un condo
   B. obtenir des forfaits de ski
   C. acheter des billets de train
   D. A, B, et C
3. Qu'est-ce qui est vrai en ce qui concerne Bruno?
   A. Il sait bien faire du ski alpin.
   B. Il a déjà goûté à la raclette savoyarde.
   C. Il veut faire du taxi-ski et de la luge.
   D. Il n'a ni skis ni bâtons, mais il compte les louer sur place.

Free response

III. Presentational Writing: Persuasive Essay **1.3, 2.1, 2.2, 4.2**

Vous allez écrire un essai persuasif basé sur une source que vous allez lire d'abord. Votre but est de présenter les différents points de vue soulevés par la source, puis de donner votre propre point de vue. Utilisez des exemples précis de la source pour soutenir votre point de vue.

Resources

Listening II

Answers

I

1. D

II Script

Nora: Il faut que tu voies la Savoie, surtout en hiver.
Bruno: Qu'est-ce que tu me conseilles de faire?
Nora: Il est possible que tu aimes le ski alpin. Il y a de belles pistes dans les stations de ski.
Bruno: Il se pourrait que je t'accompagne.... J'ai hâte d'essayer le ski alpin dans les Alpes. Mais je n'ai ni skis ni bâtons!
Nora: Tu peux tout louer sur place. Si on planifie un weekend?
Bruno: Il faut que nous obtenions des forfaits de ski.
Nora: Je les trouverai en surfant sur Internet.
Bruno: J'aurai besoin d'une leçon avant de descendre la piste.
Nora: On peut parler à un moniteur quand on arrive.
Bruno: J'aimerais bien regarder le taxi-ski et la luge.
Nora: Bien sûr. On aura un séjour formidable. Et n'oublie pas la cuisine! On va goûter la raclette savoyarde.
Bruno: J'adore essayer de nouveaux plats! On a fini de planifier?
Nora: Mais non, il faut réserver un condo et des billets de train. Il est bon qu'on n'ait pas besoin d'un passeport parce que je voudrais y aller le weekend prochain.

1. B
2. D
3. D

Differentiated Learning

Accelerate
Encourage students to make word groups of the vocabulary (for example, ski clothing, equipment, subjunctive, verbs, and expressions). As students review, have them add more terms to their lists.

Decelerate
Students might opt to use flash cards or online tools to review vocabulary. They could work in groups to quiz each other.

Reference Desk

1. The **Bilan cumulatif** is based on the French Language and Culture AP exam prepared by the College Board. It assesses students' proficiencies in the Interpersonal, Interpretive, and Presentational modes of speaking and writing. Students are also asked to demonstrate their understanding of the products, practices, and perspectives of the target cultures.
2. The Print Text section consists of a variety of authentic print materials such as articles and correspondence. A multiple-choice question follows the text.
3. The Audio Text is a professional recording, usually a dialogue. Encourage students to preview and skim the questions before listening (audio texts are played twice). They should then answer the multiple-choice questions.

Votre thème : **1.2, 1.3**
En 2011, l'Union européenne célèbre l'Année européenne du bénévolat et du volontariat. Malgré la générosité des gens qui voudraient aider, on trouve souvent que les associations utilisent une partie des aides qu'elles reçoivent des personnes pour couvrir les frais de logement, de nourriture et même les salaires de leurs employés. Des jeunes protestent contre cela et affirment que leurs paiements profitent aux riches. Qu'en pensez-vous ?

Lisez les réponses d'un blog à ce sujet :

Lina :
Bonjour à tous ! Je suis étudiante et j'aimerais rejoindre une mission éco-volontaire au Sénégal pour un mois. Mais on me demande 2 000 euros (sans compter le billet d'avion !). C'est trop pour mon budget ! Je ne comprends pas pourquoi on doit payer pour travailler ! Je voudrais simplement apporter mon aide et ma motivation en échange du logement. On veut nous persuader qu'il faut avoir de l'argent pour aider les gens qui n'en ont pas ! C'est absurde !

Jonathan :
Oui, moi aussi, je me demande pourquoi il faut payer pour participer dans le bénévolat humanitaire. Bien sûr, de nombreux projets ont besoin d'argent pour exister. Et nous, en participant, on gagne. Mais si c'est l'aide des personnes volontaires qui doit couvrir le coût de la nourriture et le logement, ce n'est pas possible. C'est dommage qu'il ne soit pas plus facile de partir aider juste pour aider comme le dit Lina.

Maël :
Le bénévolat ? C'est un business. Faites attention ! On vous offre le rêve, mais à un prix ! Comme ça les associations peuvent sélectionner des volontaires ou éliminer des gens qui veulent profiter de vacances pas chères. Oui, certaines missions privées (surtout celles qui cherchent à sauver des animaux) coûtent beaucoup. Mais est-ce que c'est nous qui devons payer pour aider ? Et sait-on véritablement où va l'argent que nous donnons ?

Suzanne :
Vous avez parfaitement raison. C'est triste qu'on doive payer pour travailler. Il y a des millions de gens qui souhaitent sincèrement aider dame nature. Mais si nous avons à payer aussi cher, c'est trop décourageant. Comme vous, j'aimerais connaitre des associations pour lesquelles je n'aie qu'à payer mon billet d'avion.

Admin :
Bonjour à tous ! Je tiens à vous rappeler que dans un monde parfait, toute personne devrait avoir la possibilité de participer (et d'être logée et nourrie) dans un projet bénévole sans payer un centime, ou peut-être juste le voyage. Mais ce n'est pas aussi simple. La structure économique des missions varie, et il y a toujours un coût. Certaines associations reçoivent des aides gouvernementales et d'autres dépendent des dons du public ou des fondations. Il y en a d'autres qui sont plus commerciales ou financées par une formule touristique. Il ne faut pas non plus penser que les associations qui demandent un paiement ne sont pas sérieuses. Parfois, il n'est pas nécessaire de voyager loin de votre communauté locale pour apporter de l'aide. L'important, c'est de trouver une activité qui corresponde à vos moyens et de vous engager pour la protection de la planète.

Essential Instruction

Give students a few minutes to read the questions before listening to/viewing the dialogue. Remind them to use the instructions in bold print to help them structure their responses to the comments.

IV. Interpresonal Speaking: Conversation 1.1, 1.2, 1.3, 4.2, 5.2

Vous allez avoir une conversation avec Marc, un collègue qui enseigne dans la même école que vous. Ensemble, vous allez parler des préparatifs pour la classe de neige de l'hiver prochain. Suivez les indications suivantes.

Marc : Le directeur de l'école m'a demandé de vous aider à planifier la classe de neige. Il faut réserver le séjour bien à l'avance. L'Italie ? La Suisse ? Qu'en pensez-vous ?

Vous : **Parlez des stations que vous connaissez en Savoie et de vos préférences.**

Marc : Vous avez raison. Pas besoin d'aller trop loin pour trouver de la neige. Je vais m'occuper de l'hébergement, des billets de train et des cours de ski.

Vous : **Demandez ce que les élèves doivent emporter dans leurs valises.**

Marc : Nous aurons l'occasion d'en parler lors des réunions avec les parents d'élèves. N'oublions pas l'importance de l'assurance médicale pour tout le monde !

Vous : **Rappelez au collègue que vous avez peur des accidents sur la piste.**

Marc : Rassurez-vous ! Les moniteurs vont nous accompagner. Nous ne faisons pas de ski hors-piste ! Mais, avez-vous des idées pour des cours ?

Vous : **Parlez des activités scolaires et culturelles que vous pouvez ajouter au programme.**

Marc : Ça vous dit de fêter la fin de la semaine avec un repas spécial pour tout le groupe au chalet ?

Vous : **Suggérez qu'on prépare des spécialités savoyardes.**

Marc : Nous mettrons des photos sur le blog du voyage. Je ne m'attendais pas à avoir tant à faire pour organiser un tel voyage. Heureusement que vous êtes bien organisé(e) !

Expansion

Add another character to the conversation dialogue. This person will play the role of a third colleague. He or she will have a different place in mind to take the class and offer information and activities to do in that region. At the end of the dialogue, the most convincing party will have gained the approval of all.

Differentiated Learning

Accelerate/Decelerate

Group the students heterogeneously to discuss the blog responses before proceeding to the writing.

Special Needs Students

Dyslexia

You may want to give dyslexic students the opportunity to read the paragraphs in advance. Give them extra time to answer questions.

At-Risk Students

These students often lack the materials or the setting they need to successfully prepare for tests at home. If possible, arrange for some guided study during class.

AD(H)D

Taking the tests in segments to avoid dealing with too much information at once might take some of the stress away from testing.

Reference Desk

1. The Principality of Monaco is smaller than Central Park in New York. Its 38,000 inhabitants, one in three of whom are millionaires, live in this Mediterranean tourist resort town whose main income is derived from casinos. With no income tax, and low business taxes, it is a haven for individuals and corporations. The principality is a constitutional monarchy. Prince Albert II, son of American actress Grace Kelly (Princess Grace) and Prince Rainier, is its head of state.
2. Monte Carlo is the administrative district of Monaco. The Monte Carlo casino, the **Hôtel de Paris**, the **Café de Paris**, and the **Salle Garnier**, home of the Monte Carlo opera, are its most famous tourist attractions. Sports fans enjoy the Formula One Monte Carlo Grand Prix, the Monte Carlo Rally, and the Rolex Masters Tennis tournament.
3. Ask students if they agree with the **citation**. Contrast the **citation** to Antoine de St. Exupéry's famous line from *The Little Prince*: "**Droit devant soi, on ne peut pas aller bien loin.**" ("Going straight, you don't get very far.") How does the experience of travel change when you get lost and experience the unexpected, versus when you plan and stick to an itinerary?
4. The James Bond film *GoldenEye*, starring Pierce Brosnan, features Monaco. You may want to choose to show a few scenes from this film, particularly when Bond arrives at the Casino (and speaks French to the valet) or during the car chase through Monaco's steep streets. Point out that these scenes cater to the perception of Monaco and Monte Carlo as the playground of the rich and famous.

Unité

5 Comment se renseigner en voyage

Essential Instruction

1. Introduce the unit theme of travel. Ask students where they have traveled or would like to travel. In traveling to a French-speaking country, what skills are needed to survive? (**Question centrale**) What travel situations require good language skills?
2. How does the **citation** relate to the theme of this unit?
3. Review the **Contrat de l'élève**. What do students know about Monaco, Dijon, and Cannes? In this unit, they learn about these cities and also acquire travel skills required for booking a hotel and ordering in a restaurant. The uses of the subjunctive are expanded.

Question centrale

De quelles compétences ai-je besoin pour voyager?

À savoir

Plus de trois millions de touristes américains visitent la France chaque année.

Citation

« Il vaut mieux se renseigner deux fois que de se perdre une fois. »

It's better to get the information twice than to get lost once.

—Anonyme

Conseil pratique

Don't be afraid to take risks when speaking! You are not expected to speak as well as a native speaker today, and you will only learn from making mistakes!

Comment Nelson décrit-il ses relations avec les autres acteurs?

Comment s'appelle ce prix et qui peut le recevoir?

Contrat de l'élève

Leçon A I will be able to:

- find out information about my stay in a hotel.
- talk about Monaco, and hotels in France.
- use the subjunctive after expressions of wish, will, and desire.

Leçon B I will be able to:

- ask about specialties in a restaurant and what is served with a dish.
- talk about Dijon and the region of Bourgogne.
- use the subjunctive after expressions of emotion, doubt, or uncertainty.

Leçon C I will be able to:

- express what I am or am not in the mood for, relate someone else's opinion, ask for an opinion, and express disagreement.
- talk about the French film industry, the Cannes festival, and the **César** awards.
- review the interrogative adjective **quel** and use the interrogative pronoun **lequel**.

Reference Desk

The **Festival de Cannes**, France's premiere international film festival, takes places every year in May.

Possible choices for the video question:
A. Il y avait beaucoup de tensions.
B. Lui et Clémentine (Charlotte) sont devenus des petits amis.
C. Ils étaient tous comme une petite famille.
D. Lui et Tigran (Patrick) étaient de très bons amis.
Correct Answer: C

The answer to the culture question is: **la Palme d'Or**; **Les cinéastes peuvent le recevoir**. The answer can be found in **Points de départ**, **Leçon C**.

Multiple Intelligences

Mathematical-Logical

Have students search the official website of the Principality of Monaco and share statistics about the relative size of Monaco compared to areas in the United States. How many residents are there, and what attractions does Monaco offer for tourists?

Visual-Spatial

Ask students to add Monaco, Dijon, and Cannes to a map of France, using symbols to indicate their principal products.

Resources

- *Vocabulaire actif*
- eVisual
- Workbook 1–3
- Flash Cards
- Listening Activity 1
- G & V Practice Games

Reference Desk

1. Here is some additional vocabulary that might interest your students: **un bon rapport qualité prix** (*good value for the money*); **à deux pas de la mer** (*close to the sea*); **une chambre nickel** (*immaculate room*); **dans un joli cadre** (*in a lovely setting*); **descendre à l'hôtel** (*to stay at the hotel*); **un très bon accueil** (*a very good welcome*); **le personnel serviable** (*attentive staff*); **les peignoirs** (*bathrobes*); **un surclassement** (*an upgrade*).
2. Most French hotels also offer a cloakroom (**une bagagerie**) and a safe in which to lock valuables (**un coffre-fort**). If the space allows, hotels may have a swimming pool (**une piscine**).
3. Specialized hotels will offer spas (**un spa**) and a solarium (**un solarium**).
4. Another word for **un service blanchisserie** is **un service pressing**.

nouvelle orthographe **des chaines cablées**

Communication

Interpersonal: Cooperative Groups

Have students create a travel site review about their stay at the **Hôtel Belle Plage**, integrating the vocabulary from **À l'hôtel** and from the **Reference Desk**. They may choose to be positive or negative, but they must support their opinion with examples.

Leçon A Vocabulaire actif

À l'hôtel 1.2, 5.2

Les prestations (f.) et le confort

Hôtel Belle Plage

34 allée de l'Hypocampe-06230 Villefranche-sur-Mer. Animaux acceptés.

Nos services (m.)

Bienvenue à l'hôtel Belle Plage. Pour votre bien-être total, notre hôtel vous offre les prestations et services suivants :

l'ascenseur (m.)

un service blanchisserie

un centre de remise en forme

un centre d'affaires/une salle de réunion

Nos chambres

Pour vous garantir un séjour agréable, nos chambres sont équipées de tout ce qu'il vous faut :

une clé électronique

un coffre-fort

une connexion wifi

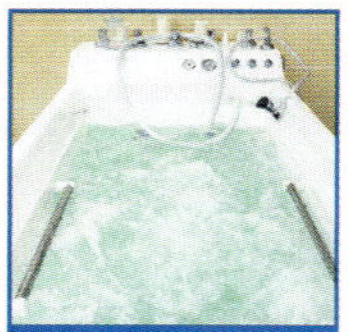
un bain à remous

des chaînes (f.) câblées

la climatisation

un service de chambre

Essential Instruction

1. Ask students what amenities (**les prestations**) they think are essential in a quality hotel. What is the difference between **une demi-pension** and a standard hotel stay?
2. Put the vocabulary for **Leçon A** on the board. What words do the students recognize? Ask them to define each term in French.
3. Play the vocabulary and have students repeat.
4. Ask students to explain in French what responsibilities and services are associated with a **concierge**.
5. Explain how the verb **vouloir** introduces the subjunctive in the sentence, "**Je voudrais que vous me donniez quelques précisions.**"

À la réception

le concierge

La réceptionniste accueille le client.

Pour la conversation

How do I ask for information?

» Je voudrais que vous me donniez quelques **précisions** sur les prestations de l'hôtel.

I would like you to give me some specific information about the amenities of the hotel.

1.2, 2.2

Produits

Les hôtels français proposent **de nouvelles solutions** comme l'échange de logement, la location d'appartements entre particuliers (familles et individus), et des sites de recherche comme Airbnb, CouchSurfing, Wimdu, HouseTrip (Europe), Cybevasion, KooKooning, Sejourning, et MorningCroissant (France).

Et si je voulais dire... ?

en demi-pension	*with breakfast and one meal*
un club de vacances	*vacation club*
en pension complète	*with all meals*
une étoile	*one star (low rating)*
une pension de famille	*family-run hotel*
tout-compris	*everything included*
un appart hôtel	*apartment hotel*

Resources

Pour la conversation
Et si je voulais dire... ?

Reference Desk

Many students may never have stayed in a hotel. Be sensitive to any confusion over the difference between **un(e) concierge** and **un(e) receptionniste** as well as unfamiliarity with the star rating system.

Communication

Interpersonal, Presentational: Cooperative Groups

Students work in small groups to role-play tourists booking a room in a hotel. They create a dialogue in which the travelers ask questions about the hotel's amenities, and the concierge answers giving details. Express services and room rates in euros. Challenge students to use as many vocabulary words from **Leçon A** as possible.

Differentiated Learning

Accelerate
Have students compare the amenities of the **Hôtel Belle Plage** with another hotel in Cannes found online.

Decelerate
Ask students to report to the class about categories of hotels in France and make a chart that illustrates the meaning of each of the star ratings. Have them include how the red ***Guide Michelin*** rates hotels and restaurants.

Multiple Intelligences

Bodily-Kinesthetic
Have students pantomime vocabulary from **Leçon A** for the class as a fast review.

Artistic
Have students draw and label the floor plan of a hotel with each of the amenities from **Vocabulaire actif**.

Resources

Activities 2–3

Answers

1

1. réceptionniste
2. clé
3. connexion wifi
4. coffre-fort
5. climatisation
6. chaînes câblées
7. bain à remous
8. service blanchisserie
9. concierge

2 Script

J'avais hâte de passer mes vacances à Monaco. J'avais réservé un hôtel qui semblait très bien en ligne mais les prestations étaient fausses. D'abord, la réception n'était ouverte que jusqu'à 23 heures et le réceptionniste n'était pas sympa. Ensuite, il n'y avait pas de concierge comme c'était indiqué en ligne. Bien sûr, c'était une vieille clé et pas une clé électronique. Ensuite, il n'y avait pas de chaînes câblées à la télé. Heureusement, la climatisation marchait parce qu'il faisait très chaud. J'ai mis mon passeport et mon argent dans un coffre-fort dans le hall derrière la réception. Je me servais du sèche-cheveux chaque jour après la piscine chaque matin. Le service de chambre offrait de bonnes spécialités de la région. Mais tout n'était pas comme il faut, donc j'ai changé d'hôtel et après, j'ai passé des vacances super géniales.

1. le réceptionniste
2. une vieille clé
3. dans un coffre-fort
4. à la piscine
5. un sèche-cheveux
6. du service de chambre

3 Answers will vary.

Communication

Interpersonal: Paired Practice

Have students interview each other in **Activité 3** as a basis for conversation. Encourage them to ask follow-up questions like "**Pourquoi?**" and "**Quand?**" Circulate to monitor their conversations and answer questions. When students are finished, debrief each group. If students have stayed in a hotel on a school or athletic trip, have them describe that hotel.

1 À l'hôtel 1.2, 5.1

Interpretive Reading

Complétez les phrases.

1. En arrivant à la réception de l'hôtel, les clients vont parler à la....
2. Elle donne une... électronique au client pour qu'il ait accès à sa chambre.
3. Des ordinateurs avec... sont disponibles et compris dans le service.
4. On peut laisser ses bijoux ou son passeport dans le... à la réception.
5. Quand il fait chaud, on voudrait une chambre avec la..., surtout aux Antilles.
6. Pour regarder la télé, beaucoup d'hôtels donnent accès à des....
7. Les hôtels de luxe ont souvent un... avec massage pour se détendre.
8. Dans les hôtels de luxe, le... vous permet de nettoyer vos vêtements.
9. Si vous avez faim, le... peut vous renseigner sur les restaurants du quartier.

2 Un bon ou un mauvais hôtel? 1.1, 1.2

Interpretive Listening, Interpersonal Writing

Écrivez les numéros 1–6 sur votre papier. Écoutez Élise décrire son expérience dans un hôtel de Monaco. Écrivez une courte réponse pour répondre à chaque question.

1. Qui n'était pas sympa?
2. Quelle sorte de clé a-t-on offert à Élise?
3. Où a-t-elle mis son passeport?
4. Où est-elle allée chaque matin?
5. Qu'est-ce qu'il y avait dans la salle de bains?
6. De quel service a-t-elle profité à midi et le soir?

3 Questions personnelles 1.1, 5.1

Interpersonal Speaking

Répondez aux questions avec un partenaire.

1. Es-tu jamais allé(e) à l'hôtel?
2. L'hôtel avait-il une piscine? Un centre de remise en forme? Le service de chambre?
3. Tu aimes avoir quelles prestations dans un hôtel?
4. Quelles chaînes câblées est-ce que tu préfères?
5. Aimes-tu la climatisation en été?
6. Comment serait ton hôtel idéal?
7. Où voudrais-tu aller à l'hôtel?

Essential Instruction

1. Students listen to **Activité 2** and answer questions 1–6. Play the recording again if they have questions.
2. Have students listen to **Un hôtel à Monaco** with books closed, and then have them volunteer details they remember from the conversation between Léo and Justin.
3. Students read the text and complete the sentences in **Activité 4**.
4. Read **Extension** to the students with books closed. Ask listening comprehension questions.
5. Have students read the two dialogues in pairs.

Un hôtel à Monaco 1.2, 3.2

Léo et Justin veulent réserver une chambre à Monaco.

Léo : La déscription de l'hôtel et les photos sont plutôt bien, mais c'est un peu cher.
Justin : Mais c'est Monte Carlo ! Moi, je trouve qu'ils sont très imprécis sur les prestations.
Léo : Ah ! Tu es bien américain : toujours le côté pratique.
Justin : Je te laisse la poésie des lieux monégasques et la vue imprenable sur la mer....
Léo : Tu veux qu'on leur téléphone ?
Justin : Oui, je vais le faire avec mon accent américain ! *(Au téléphone, Justin parle au réceptionniste.)* Bonjour, je voudrais que vous me donniez quelques précisions sur les prestations de l'hôtel.... Merci. Au revoir.
Léo : Alors ?
Justin : Ils ont le wifi*, des chaînes câblées, il y a un jacuzzi dans la chambre, et on peut prendre le petit déjeuner dans la chambre sans payer le supplément.
Léo : Parfait ! Réservons !

***Je parle bien !**
Le mot **wifi** se prononce comme **oui-fi**.

4 Un hôtel à Monaco

1.2 *Répondez aux questions.*

1. Est-ce que le prix d'un hôtel à Monaco est un peu cher ou bon marché ?
2. Sur quoi est-ce que Justin voudrait se renseigner ?
3. Est-ce que Léo est plus pratique que Justin ? Ou est-ce que Justin est plus pratique ?
4. Selon Justin, à quoi Léo s'intéresse ?
5. Que comprennent les prestations de l'hôtel ?

EXTENSION Les prestations désirées 1.2

Clément et Laurence aident leurs parents à chercher un bon hôtel pour leurs vacances en famille.

Clément : Bon, alors, si toi tu veux le bain à remous, moi je veux les chaînes câblées et une connexion wifi.
Laurence : Tu ne vas quand même pas passer ton temps en vacances à regarder le sport à la télé !
Clément : Si, pendant que toi et Maman serez au centre de remise en forme !
Laurence : Pour la connexion wifi, d'accord : pas besoin de passer des heures à attendre un ordinateur libre au centre d'affaires.
Clément : Vérifie quand même qu'il y ait la climatisation dans cet hôtel.
Laurence : À Saint-Pierre et Miquelon, on n'en aura pas besoin !
Clément : Mais, Maman et Papa ont changé d'avis et préfèrent aller à Saint-Louis au Sénégal.

1.1, 1.2 **EXTENSION** Quelles prestations désirent Laurence et Clément ? Où vont-ils passer leurs vacances ? Avec qui ?

Resources

Dialogue
Activity 4
Extension
Dialogue Video
WB Workbook 4

Answers

4

1. Le prix d'un hôtel à Monaco est un peu cher.
2. Justin voudrait se renseigner sur les prestations de l'hôtel.
3. Justin est plus pratique que Léo.
4. Selon Justin, Léo s'intéresse aux lieux monégasques et à la vue sur la mer.
5. Les prestations de l'hôtel comprennent le wifi, des chaînes câblées, un bain à remous (jacuzzi), et le service de chambre.

EXTENSION

Ils veulent un bain à remous, des chaînes cablées, une connexion wifi, et la climatisation. Ils vont passer leurs vacances à Saint-Louis (au Sénégal) avec leurs parents.

Reference Desk

1. **Saint-Pierre et Miquelon**, located 25 km southwest of Newfoundland, is France's oldest overseas territory. Jacques Cartier declared it a French possession in 1536. There are eight islands although only two are inhabited. The language is French and the religion is Catholic.
2. **Saint-Louis (au Sénégal)**, established by French traders in 1659, is the capital of the **Saint-Louis** region and former capital of Senegal. It is called "**la Venise africaine**" because of its river delta location.

Differentiated Learning

Accelerate
Students write a dialogue between two friends booking a hotel in a ski region or at a beach resort. They express conflicting opinions as to what they want to do before arriving at a consensus.

Decelerate
Students search online to select two hotels: a five and a three-star hotel in the Villefranche-sur-Mer-Nice-Cannes area. Have them compare the amenities, proximity to the sea, and prices for each, and create a chart comparing the two. They should express cost in euros with conversions in dollars.

Special Needs Students

AD(H)D/Dyslexia/Linguistically Challenged
To assist students who have difficulty concentrating, reading, or with language, give them two or three lines from the dialogue on separate index cards. Allow them to work in groups and ask them to be responsible only for the three lines of dialogue on their cards. Organize a group presentation.

Game

Ça y est
Arrange students in teams of five or six. Place a set of French vocabulary words written on individual cards in the center of each group, face up. Give the clues listed in **Activité 1**. Students scramble to be the first to identify and hold up the appropriate vocabulary card. The first team that finds the card and yells **"Ça y est !"** earns a point.

Resources

Points de départ
Workbook 5
Explore

Comparaisons
Answers will vary.

Perspectives
Le vrai but des voyages, selon Proust, est de transformer la façon dont on voit les choses, les autres, les cultures.

Reference Desk

1. Biarritz is a luxury resort town on the Bay of Biscay only 18 km from Spain. In the 18th century it became a health spa for the rich and famous. Tourists enjoy its golden-sand beaches, surfing, and casino.
2. **Le Cheval Blanc de Courcheval** offers 34 lavishly appointed rooms and suites. An enormous glass stallion adorns the courtyard.
3. Accor Hotel Group is comprised of Ibis, Novotel, and Sofitel hotel chains. There are more than 4,200 hotels and 145,000 employees in 90 countries on five continents.
4. The English word *hotel* stems from the word **hôte** (*host*). Originally, **un hôtel** was a house open to frequent visitors. The **Hôtel Carnavalet** in Paris was the 17th-century private residence of the Marquise de Sévigné and her family. **Un hôtel garni** is a hotel without a restaurant. **Une auberge** is an inn. **Une auberge de jeunesse** is a youth hostel.
5. If you have access to Passport, find a news article related to **les hôtels** and show it to your students.

Points de départ

Pre-AP | Question centrale ? De quelles compétences ai-je besoin pour voyager?

La tradition hôtelière française

1.2, 2.1, 2.2, 3.1

La popularité cosmopolite et touristique de la France avec Paris, la Côte d'Azur, la Normandie, et la Côte basque a donné naissance à une hôtellerie de luxe dont certains palaces sont devenus, souvent grâce au cinéma, des hôtels de légende. Ces hôtels sont aujourd'hui classés dans la catégorie « Palace » créée en 2010. Il en existe 24 dont le Ritz, le Crillon, le Bristol, le Royal Monceau, le Plaza Athénée à Paris, le Royal Evian (Lac Léman), la Bastide de Gordes (Provence), les Sources de Caudalie (Bordelais), le Normandy (Deauville), l'Hôtel du Palais à Biarritz (Côte basque), le Cheval Blanc à Courchevel (Alpes), le Byblos à Saint-Tropez et le Cap Eden Roc à Antibes (Côte d'Azur).

L'hôtel Ritz (Le Ritz), Place Vendôme, à Paris ; concierges à l'entrée

À côté de cette hôtellerie de luxe, il existe une hôtellerie française de luxe présente dans le monde entier avec notamment la chaîne Sofitel (200 hôtels) qui se veut* représentative dans le monde de l'art de vivre à la française. Toujours dans le souci* de valoriser* cette tradition d'accueil et d'art de vivre, la chaîne Relais et Châteaux valorise une hôtellerie installée dans des demeures* historiques où il s'agit de donner aux hôtes* le sentiment de vivre un moment d'histoire au présent : châteaux et gentilhommières*, pavillons de chasse à la campagne, hôtels particuliers* dans les villes. Une attention particulière est apportée à la gastronomie.

Recherche : relais châteaux france, hôtels de luxe français, hôtel (+ VILLE)

se veut *wants to see itself* ; **souci** *preoccupation* ; **valoriser** *to promote* ; **demeures** *residences* ; **hôtes** *guests* ; **gentilhommières** *mansions in the country* ; **hôtels particuliers** *mansions in the city*

Un pavillon de chasse dans l'Avesnois (département Hauts-de-France)

Comparaisons

1.2, 4.2

Est-ce que vous pouvez nommer, ou trouver, un hôtel de luxe à New York et à Los Angeles ?

Perspectives

1.2, 2.1

« Le vrai voyage de découverte ne consiste pas à chercher de nouveaux paysages, mais à avoir de nouveaux yeux. »
—Marcel Proust

Selon ce grand écrivain du 20ème siècle, quel est le vrai but (*purpose*) des voyages ?

Essential Instruction

1. Have students describe a luxury hotel. Do they know of any in the United States? Would they prefer to stay in a luxury hotel or in a historic chateau? Why?
2. As students read **La tradition hôtelière française**, have them locate each palace-hotel on the map of France.
3. Have students visit the Accor and Sofitel websites to familiarize themselves with these hotel chains.
4. Ask students what they know of Monaco, the Grimaldi family, and Grace Kelly before reading **La principauté de Monaco**.
5. Have students go online to extend their understanding of the readings by using the search words at the end of each section.
6. Have students visit the websites for Campanile and the hotel chains Mercure, Ibis, and Novotel to learn about hotel chains for the budget-minded traveler.

La Francophonie

Profil touristique

La principauté de Monaco 1.2, 2.1, 2.2, 3.1

Au port de Monaco on peut voir les yachts de nombreuses célébrités internationales.

Monaco en phénicien* signifie *l'Unique*. Son rocher*, son célèbre circuit* automobile en pleine ville, son port de plaisance*, son casino, et sa famille princière* ont fait la réputation de Monaco, qu'on appelle parfois Monte Carlo du nom d'un de ses quartiers. Cette principauté* indépendante de 2,02 km^2 et de 38 500 habitants est située sur la côte méditerranéenne entre les villes françaises de Nice et Menton. Monaco constitue une véritable enclave sur le territoire français.

L'histoire de Monaco est liée à l'histoire de la famille Grimaldi, originaire de Gênes, qui s'empare de* la ville au 13ème siècle et qui règne* toujours sur la principauté. Monaco est lié* à la France par une union douanière*.

Ville touristique, elle doit sa réputation, d'abord à la fin du 19ème siècle et au début du 20ème siècle à l'aristocratie des princes russes*, puis dans les années 1950 à Hollywood dont les stars deviennent les habituées* du lieu. C'est ainsi que le Prince Rainier épouse Grace Kelly, star hollywoodienne des années 1950, égérie* d'Alfred Hitchcock. Aujourd'hui, Monaco est la patrie* de la jet set financière, sportive, et artistique.

Le Prince Rainier III et la Princesse Grace de Monaco

La famille Grimaldi, ses princesses Caroline et Stéphanie, son prince Albert, aujourd'hui Prince régnant*, ont largement contribué à l'image glamour et à l'image « jet-seteuse » de Monaco.

On retrouve l'image glamour et mythique du rocher de Monaco dans de nombreux films : *Rebecca* et *La Main au collet* d'Alfred Hitchcock, *Bonjour tristesse* d'Otto Preminger, et les séries James Bond (*Never Say Never Again*, *GoldenEye*) et Iron Man (*Iron Man 2*) pour le cinéma américain. En France, il apparaît dans *La Baie des Anges* de Jacques Demy, *Une Chance sur deux* (avec Alain Delon, Jean-Paul Belmondo, et Vanessa Paradis), *L'Arnacœur* (avec Vanessa Paradis et Romain Duris), et *Grace de Monaco* (avec Nicole Kidman).

Recherche : monaco site officiel

phénicien *Phoenician (ancient language)*; **rocher** *rock*; **circuit** *racetrack*; **port de plaisance** *marina*; **princière** *princely*; **principauté** *principality*; **s'empare de** *seize*; **règne** *reigns*; **lié** *linked*; **union douanière** *customs agreement*; **russes** *Russian*; **habituées** *regular visitors*; **égérie** *muse*; **patrie** *homeland*; **régnant** *reigning*

Reference Desk

1. Grace Kelly, born in Philadelphia in 1929, began her acting career at the age of 20. She was nominated for an Academy Award for Best Supporting Actress in *Mogambo* (1953) and won an Academy Award for Best Actress for *A Country Girl* (1954). She starred in the Alfred Hitchcock films *Dial M for Murder* (1953), *Rear Window* (1953), and *To Catch a Thief* (1955). Kelly retired from acting in 1956 at age 26 to marry Rainier III, Prince of Monaco. She died in 1982, the result of an automobile accident.
2. The Grimaldi dynasty and rights of inheritance to Monaco's throne have been fraught with controversy and confusion. The Grimaldi family bloodline stopped ruling Monaco in 1731, when it failed to produce a male heir to the throne. From that time to the present, the male heirs have had to adopt the Grimaldi name and coat of arms, as Article 1 of the Monegasque constitution stipulates that the reigning prince or princess must have the Grimaldi name. A branch of the Grimaldi family in England still claims legitimate rights to the Monegasque throne. In 2002, adopted children were excluded from inheriting the throne, and younger siblings were allowed, in the incident of the monarch's death, to assume power.
3. If you have access to Passport, find a video or a news article related to **Monaco** and show it to your students.

Differentiated Learning

Accelerate

Have students read **La tradition hôtelière française** in the computer lab. Have them visit the websites for each of the eight palaces mentioned in the first paragraph of the reading. Ask them to locate each on the map of France, list in descending order the ones they prefer, and explain their choices. Have them evaluate them for price, amenities, and location.

Decelerate

Have students make a family tree of the Grimaldi family using the information from the reading. Have them research each family member online including Prince Albert and his new wife, Charlene. Why is it important that this couple has descendants?

Connections

Film

La république de Gênes from which the Grimaldi family originates, is depicted as the fantasy republic of Genovia in the movie series *The Princess Diaries*. You may show the movie in French, called ***Princesse malgré elle***, and discuss the particularities of royal life and the traditions of a region that still holds on to such archaic government or representation.

Answers

5

1. Paris: le Ritz, le Crillon, le Bristol, le Royal Monceau, or le Plaza Athénée; Biarritz: l'Hôtel du Palais; Courchevel: le Cheval Blanc
2. Answers will vary.
3. Answers may include more than the following: Enfants: Alexandre Andrea Casiraghi, India Casiraghi, Maximilian Rainier Casiraghi; Frères et sœurs: Charlotte Casiraghi, Pierre Casiraghi, Princesse Alexandra de Hanovre; Père: Stefano Casiraghi; Mère: Caroline Grimaldi; Grand-père maternel: Rainier III Grimaldi; Grand-mère maternelle: Grace Kelly; Arrière-grand-père paternel: Pierre de Polignac; Arrière-grand-mère paternelle: Charlotte Grimaldi; Arrière-grand-père maternel: John Kelly; Arrière-grand-mère maternelle: Margaret Majer
4. Alfred Hitchcock a lancé la carrière de Grace Kelly, qui était une de ses actrices fétiches. Grace Kelly a tourné dans *Fenêtre sur cour*, *Le crime était presque parfait*, et *La main au collet*, réalisés par Hitchcock.
5. Answers will vary.

À DISCUTER

Answers will vary.

Reference Desk

1. The Princess Grace Foundation was established in 1984, two years after Grace Kelly's death, to recognize promising artistic talent in theater, dance, film, playwriting, and choreography, through scholarships granted to talented young artists.
2. In 1954, Grace Kelly won an Oscar for her starring role in *A Country Girl* and, consequently, met Prince Rainier, the then-ruler of Monaco. They were quickly married.
3. Concerned with his new wife's homesickness and difficulty fitting into a foreign culture, Prince Rainier asked his young bride to involve herself in Monaco's politics and social life, which she willingly did. She established Monaco as a center for the performing arts, particularly opera, ballet, music, and theater. She was active in many humanitarian works and Monaco's only public hospital is named after her.

Produits

Le Bal de la Rose, qui a lieu chaque printemps à Monaco, réunit la famille Grimaldi et des grands noms du monde du spectacle. C'est un grand rendez-vous mondain (*high-society*), créé en 1954 par la Princesse Grace. Les bénéfices du bal sont reversés à la Fondation Princesse Grace, une œuvre de bienfaisance (*charity*) au service des personnes en difficulté, des enfants défavorisés (*disadvantaged*), d'autres actions humanitaires et aussi philanthropiques et artistiques.

1.2, 2.2

Mot-clé

Monaco en phénicien (*Phoenician*) signifie *l'Unique*. Les gens qui y habitent sont des Monégasques.

5 Activités culturelles 1.3, 3.2

Faites les activités suivantes.

1. Associez un palace à chacune de ces villes :
   - Paris
   - Biarritz
   - Courchevel
2. Trouvez un hôtel français en ligne établi dans une ville américaine près de chez vous. Quelles caractéristiques françaises a-t-il ?
3. Faites l'arbre généalogique d'Andrea Casiraghi, fils de Caroline Grimaldi, qui remonte à son arrière-grand-père.

Recherche : monte carlo arbre généalogique

4. Retrouvez les liens cinématographiques entre Grace Kelly et Alfred Hitchcock.
5. Recherchez la fondation du Prince Albert. Est-ce que vous la soutiendriez ? Justifiez votre réponse.

Recherche : fondation prince albert monaco

À DISCUTER

Imaginez que chaque élève de votre classe gagne une semaine gratuite dans un hôtel français de son choix. Faites une enquête pour voir dans quel hôtel et dans quelle ville vos camarades de classe iraient.

Prince Albert II et son épouse, Charlène

Essential Instruction

1. Arrange students into four groups. One student from each group draws a number from 1 to 5. Students complete the task corresponding to their number in **Activité 5**. They present their final work to the class.
2. Pair students in groups of high and low ability to do **Activité 6**. Preview words that might give them difficulty.
3. Have students identify four American luxury hotels and compare them to four luxury hotels in France in terms of ambiance, price, and amenities. What are the hotel chains in the United States that would be comparable to Accor and Sofitel?

Du côté des médias 1.2

Lisez les statistiques suivantes sur le tourisme international à Monaco.

Les 8 choses à faire à Monaco

Quand on parle des plus petits pays, Monaco, capitale de l'hédonisme, est deuxième seulement derrière le Vatican, capitale de la sainteté. L'argent peut acheter n'importe quoi dans cet état glamour, sauf peut-être la vue sur la Méditerranée depuis Monaco-Ville.

1. Le palais de Monaco

Ce bâtiment est la résidence du prince de Monaco depuis 1191 et l'est encore de nos jours, tout en étant aussi un musée et un centre de tourisme.

2. Le rocher de Monaco

Après avoir assisté à la relève de la garde au palais de Monaco, faites une courte marche jusqu'à Monaco-Ville, alias la vieille ville, assise sur ce monolithe géant surplombant la côte.

3. Le jardin exotique de Monaco

Ce jardin exotique est un jardin botanique à flanc de falaise avec une riche collection de cactus et des vues spectaculaires sur la mer. Offrez-vous une visite guidée privée de la grotte.

4. L'opéra de Monte-Carlo

Assister à un spectacle dans cet incroyable opéra à la française est une occasion unique, mais son aspect imposant vaut même la peine vu de l'extérieur.

5. Le musée océanographique de Monaco

Ce bâtiment monumental néo-baroque est situé à flanc de falaise et surplombe la mer. Il présente non seulement un aquarium mais aussi beaucoup d'objets liés à la mer.

6. Le Grimaldi Forum Monaco

Ce gigantesque Palais des Congrès est sur le front de mer au quartier du Larvotto. Vérifiez le site officiel pour les événements de type varié allant des expositions au ballet.

7. Le Grand Prix automobile de Monaco

« Glamour et prestige » sont au rendez-vous du Grand Prix automobile de Monaco, l'un des circuits automobiles de Formule 1 les plus prestigieux du monde.

8. Le casino de Monte Carlo

Vous pouvez remercier le prince Charles III pour ce paradis créé pour éviter à la Maison Grimaldi de faire banqueroute. Vous reconnaitrez peut-être ce casino de Monaco qui figure dans certains films de James Bond.

6 Le tourisme international à Monaco 1.3, 3.1, 4.2, 5.2

Faites les activités suivantes.

1. Faites un graphique en barres qui montre le chiffre d'affaires (*sales figures*) de l'hôtellerie (*hotel industry*) à Monaco en comparant cette année à l'année précédente.
2. Sur une carte du monde, indiquez où se situe Monaco avec son drapeau. Montrez de façon visuelle quels pays visitent la Principauté.
3. Faites un graphique en barres qui montre la nationalité des passagers de croisières (*cruises*) passant par Monaco.

Recherche : fréquentation touristique à monaco, industrie touristique monaco, nationalité des touristes à monaco

Answers

6 Activities will vary.

Reference Desk

1. Rainier and Grace's children lived wild and carefree lives that were frequently fodder for tabloids around the world. Today, they have settled into more restrained lifestyles. Albert II, after admitting paternity and settling two separate paternity suits, reigns the principality; Caroline has married a German prince.
2. The **Grand Prix de Monaco** takes place at the end of May each year and is a Formula One race through Monaco's narrow streets and tight turns. Along with the Indianapolis 500 ("Indy 500") and the 24 Hours of Le Mans (**les 24 heures du Mans**), also held in France, it constitutes one of the events of the Triple Crown of Motorsport.

Expansion

Encourage advanced students to work together to read and study **Du côté des médias**. Have them identify and define new or difficult words and expressions from each section and then summarize what they learn. They could work with the strong math students in the class to prepare and present the information to the other students.

Have students use an online interactive map to take a virtual walking tour of Monaco and some of the sites named here.

Differentiated Learning

Adapt

Assign students one of the following events according to their interests: the Formula One Monte Carlo Grand Prix, the Monte Carlo Rally, the Rolex Masters Tennis tournament, or the Rose Ball. How is the event organized? When does it occur? Who are the famous people associated with the event in the last three years?

Multiple Intelligences

Visual-Spatial

Encourage these students to create a publicity brochure with photos and descriptions for one or more hotels.

Mathematical-Logical

Have students organize the statistical information from **Du côté des médias** in a graphic organizer and lead a class discussion of tourism in Monaco.

Resources

WB Workbook 6–9
LA Listening Activity 2
G & V Practice Games

Answers

Comparaisons
In the first pair, *be* is in the subjunctive because it follows a verb that expresses a request (*requires*). In the second pair, *were* is in the subjunctive because the thought does not indicate reality.

Reference Desk

1. Review the conjugation of **préférer**. Remind students of the rule for accent mark change. As a visual way of remembering, the accents look like sleet in the **nous** and **vous** forms, and like eyebrows in all other forms.
2. Have students explore their understanding of the three D's of the subjunctive: expressions of doubt, demand, and desire. This simplification may help them condense the complexities of the subjunctive mood.

Expansion

Use word puzzles to practice the subjunctive. Create sentences with verbs in the subjunctive. Cut up the words and put each sentence into an envelope. There should be as many sentences as there are pairs of students. Place an envelope on each student's desk. Pairs of students travel from one desk to another reconstructing the sentences and copying the sentences into a notebook. Ask them to scramble the words before putting them back into the envelope for the next pair of students. At the end, have students write the sentences on the board.

Structure de la langue

The Subjunctive after Expressions of Wish, Will, or Desire 1.2

In French, the subjunctive usually comes after **que** in a dependent clause. As you have learned, various impersonal expressions are followed by the subjunctive. Verbs that express wish, will, or desire also take the subjunctive. Use the subjunctive after one of these verbs when the wish, will, or desire concerns someone other than the subject.

aimer *to like, to love*	J'**aimerais que** cet hôtel **offre** une connexion wifi.	*I would like this hotel to offer wireless Internet.*
désirer *to want*	Léo **désire que** vous lui **montriez** le centre d'affaires de l'hôtel.	*Leo wants you to show him the hotel's business center.*
exiger *to require/demand*	Nous **exigeons que** la chambre **ait** la climatisation.	*We require that the room have air conditioning.*
préférer *to prefer*	Elle **préfère que** tu lui **donnes** des précisions sur l'hôtel.	*She prefers that you give her some details about the hotel.*
souhaiter *to wish/hope*	**Souhaitez**-vous **qu'**il y **ait** un coffre-fort pour votre collier?	*Do you wish that there were a safe for your necklace?*
vouloir *to want*	Maman **veut que** je **voie** le concierge.	*Mom wants me to see the concierge.*

4.1

Comparaisons

In the following pairs of sentences, what verbs are in the subjunctive? (There's one per pair.)

The math teacher requires that we *be* on time.
Zach usually *comes* late.

We *are* in Denver.
I wish we *were* in Paris.

Essential Instruction

1. With whiteboards, have students conjugate verbs in the subjunctive. Mix regular and irregular verbs that they have previously learned until they demonstrate mastery.
2. Verbs of wishing, willing, and desiring are followed by the subjunctive provided there is a subject change. Ask students to suggest verbs they know from these categories.
3. Present the verb chart and have students answer the **Comparaisons** question.
4. Do **Activités 7** and **8** as guided practice with the students.

7 L'agenda de Didier 1.2, 1.3

Interpretive Viewing, Presentational Speaking

Dites avec qui Didier voudrait aller aux destinations suivantes.

MODÈLE

toi

Didier veut que tu ailles au festival de musique avec lui.

1. Julie et toi

2. moi

3. Cédric

4. Marina et moi

5. ses cousins

6. toi

8 Phrases logiques 1.3

Presentational Speaking or Writing

Faites sept phrases logiques en utilisant un mot ou une expression de chaque colonne.

je (j') tu Awa le client Saskia et moi Abdel et toi Laure et Laïla	aimer préférer exiger souhaiter vouloir désirer	**que**	le réceptionniste la concierge la chambre l'employé vous l'hôtel	indiquer où se trouvent les meilleurs restaurants réserver une chambre avoir un coffre-fort être près du métro offrir une clé électronique aller au centre d'affaires profiter du centre de remise en forme

Answers

7

1. Didier veut que Julie et toi alliez au complexe multisport avec lui.
2. Didier veut que j'aille au tournoi de slam avec lui.
3. Didier veut que Cédric aille à la soirée avec lui.
4. Didier veut que Marina et moi allions à l'association de scoutisme avec lui.
5. Didier veut que ses cousins aillent à l'aquaparc avec lui.
6. Didier veut que tu ailles en discothèque avec lui.

8 Possible answers:

1. J'aime que le réceptionniste m'offre une clé électronique.
2. Tu préfères que la concierge t'indique où se trouvent les meilleurs restaurants.
3. Awa exige que la chambre ait un coffre-fort.
4. Le client souhaite que l'employé lui réserve une chambre.
5. Saskia et moi voulons que vous profitiez du centre de remise en forme.
6. Abdel et toi désirez que l'hôtel soit près du métro.
7. Laure et Leïla préfèrent que vous alliez au centre d'affaires.

Communication

Interpersonal: Cooperative Groups

To practice the new use of the subjunctive, divide the class into small groups. Ask half of the groups to imagine what the principal of their school desires or demands that students do in order to have a great school experience. Ask the other half of the groups to imagine what students desire or demand that the administration and teachers do to create a great school environment. Each group creates a list of sentences. Remind students that they must use the subjunctive. Put an administrator group with a student group and have them share their ideas. Collect their lists.

Learning Styles

Kinesthetic Learners

Students may need to write out the verbs to ingrain them in their minds.

Multiple Intelligences

Musical-Rhythmic

Students would benefit from oral drills. Encourage them to find the rhythm of the verbs as they conjugate them.

Special Needs Students

Linguistically Challenged

Consider offering a special session to re-teach the subjunctive in small groups. These students might be confusing the subjunctive with the indicative. Flash cards and online practice will help them learn.

Decelerate

To help students understand the subjunctive's dependence on **que**, translate the example sentences on p. 274 using *that*. "I would like *that* this hotel offer wireless internet."

9 On se parle 1.1

Interpersonal Speaking

*À tour de rôle, demandez à votre partenaire comment vous trouvez les personnes et les choses indiquées. Donnez vos opinions en utilisant l'expression **J'aimerais que**.*

MODÈLE le directeur du lycée
A : Comment tu trouves le directeur du lycée ?
B : J'aimerais qu'il soit moins strict. Et toi ?
A : J'aimerais qu'il n'aille pas à la cantine tous les jours.

1. la musique à la radio
2. les vidéos en ligne
3. la cantine du lycée
4. les devoirs pour le cours d'histoire
5. le temps qu'il fait aujourd'hui
6. les émissions de télé-réalité

10 Souhaits de vacanciers 1.2

Interpretive Listening and Viewing

Écrivez les numéros 1–8 sur votre papier. Écoutez les souhaits des vacanciers. Puis, choisissez l'image qui y correspond.

A. 

B. 

C. 

D. 

E. 

F. 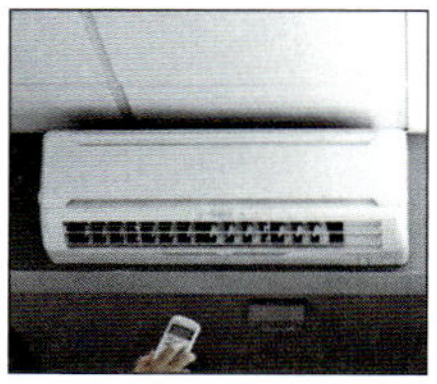

G. 

H. 

Resources

Activity 10

Answers

9 Possible answers:

1. A : Comment tu trouves la musique à la radio ?
   B : J'aimerais qu'elle soit plus variée.
2. A : Comment tu trouves les vidéos en ligne ?
   B : J'aimerais qu'elles soient plus utiles.
3. A : Comment tu trouves la cantine du lycée ?
   B : J'aimerais qu'il y ait plus de légumes.
4. A : Comment tu trouves les devoirs pour le cours d'histoire ?
   B : J'aimerais qu'ils soient moins difficiles.
5. A : Comment tu trouves le temps qu'il fait aujourd'hui ?
   B : J'aimerais qu'il ne pleuve pas.
6. A : Comment tu trouves les émissions de télé-réalité ?
   B : J'aimerais qu'elles passent moins souvent.

10 Script

1. Je veux que l'hôtel ait un concierge.
2. Je souhaite que la réception soit ouverte jour et nuit.
3. Je désire qu'il y ait un accès wifi dans ma chambre.
4. J'aimerais que ma chambre soit équipée d'une clé électronique.
5. Je préfère qu'il y ait un jacuzzi dans ma chambre.
6. Je souhaite qu'on offre le service de chambre.
7. J'exige qu'on change mes serviettes de bain tous les jours.
8. Je veux que la chambre ait la climatisation.

1. B; 2. G; 3. C; 4. A; 5. E; 6. H; 7. D; 8. F

Reference Desk

Consider doing choral repetition of the subjunctive forms for the irregular verbs **être**, **avoir**, **aller**, **faire**, **vouloir**, **pouvoir**, and **savoir** in order to help students commit these forms to memory.

Essential Instruction

1. Students complete **Activité 9** with a variety of partners. Have them change partners to ask and answer the prepared questions using the pattern provided. This exercise could also be written.
2. Have students listen to the remarks and choose the appropriate image for **Activité 10**. Review vocabulary by having students identify the images before listening to the audio recording.
3. For **Activité 11**, give students the option of preparing a dialogue to be presented live in class or filming the dialogue. Students might like to write the dialogue as a commercial for the hotel.
4. Have students go online to complete **Activité 12** using the search words provided. Ask students to list reasons why Monaco is a destination for all kinds of travelers.

Question centrale ? De quelles compétences ai-je besoin pour voyager?

Communiquez!

11 Une réservation difficile 1.1, 2.1, 5.2

Interpersonal Speaking

Avec un partenaire jouez les rôles d'un(e) réceptionniste d'hôtel et d'un(e) client(e) qui veut rester à l'hôtel. Le client ou la cliente doit indiquer quel type de chambre il ou elle veut et poser au moins deux questions sur les services de l'hôtel. Après l'enregistrement (*check-in*), le client (la cliente) appelera le (la) réceptionniste pour se plaindre. Le (la) réceptionniste devra faire de son mieux pour résoudre le problème et satisfaire le client (la cliente). Soyez aussi dramatique que vous le souhaitez!

12 Un voyage à Monaco 1.2, 1.3, 2.1, 3.2

Interpretive Reading, Presentational Writing and Speaking

Imaginez que vous êtes une personnalité riche et célèbre. Vous voulez donner un peu de joie à un enfant atteint d'une maladie grave. Vous allez l'emmener à Monaco dans votre jet privé pour y passer un weekend luxueux et extravagant! Vous devez planifier votre weekend à partir du moment où le jet atterrit. Où allez-vous rester? Quelles activités allez-vous faire? Quels endroits pourriez-vous visiter? Dans quels restaurants voudriez-vous manger? Quels magasins allez-vous fréquenter et combien d'argent allez-vous dépenser? Soyez aussi créatif/créative et dramatique que vous le souhaitez! Présentez l'itinéraire de votre weekend à la classe, et révélez qui vous êtes!

Recherche: monaco site officiel, cartier, monaco grand prix, hôtel monaco, palais monaco

Resources

CA Communicative Activities

Share

Answers

11 Role-plays will vary.

12 Presentations will vary.

Reference Desk

1. A monumental jewel designed to resemble a palace, the Oceanographic Museum of Monaco was inaugurated in 1910 by Prince Albert I. It is a museum of marine science as well as an aquarium featuring 90 pools containing 4000 species of exotic fish. There is also a shark lagoon. Jacques Cousteau was director of the museum for many years. Exotic Garden is a botanical garden opened in 1933. It features 1000 species of succulents and cacti. Below the garden there are prehistoric caverns.
2. If you have access to Passport, create a question for your students to share their response to a communicative activity.

Expansion

Have students present a virtual tour of the **Musée Océanographique** and **le Jardin Exotique** of Monaco.

Multiple Intelligences

Naturalist

Ask students interested in animals and plant life to investigate the Oceanographic Museum and Exotic Garden as well as research online the sea life in the Mediterranean. Students interested in marine biology may be interested in learning about the links between the French explorer Jacques-Yves Cousteau and the Oceanographic Museum in Monaco.

Intrapersonal

The history of the accession of the Grimaldi family in Monaco to the throne as well as Monaco's unusual political standing in the world may interest students who enjoy history and politics.

Bodily-Kinesthetic

Encourage students to explore the careers of Prince Albert II and Princess Charlene as Olympic athletes.

Resources

Pre-T Pre-test

Q *Leçon* Quiz

Answers

B Script

1. Garçon, on voudrait commander!
2. Vous êtes arrivés, comme d'habitude, en retard!
3. Je vais prendre un oeuf, je crois.
4. Tu étais, j'en suis sûr, avec ta sœur.

1. MONT
2. MONT
3. DESC
4. DESC

E Script

1. Maint**e**nant, j**e** vais à la boulang**e**rie.
2. J**e** ne veux pas ach**e**ter de bottes.
3. Heureus**e**ment, j'aime cet appart**e**ment.

1. C
2. P
3. F

Reference Desk

1. The main three language registers were practiced in Level 2, **Unité 4**, **Leçon A**. **Le registre courant** corresponds to *standard register/speech*. **Le registre familier** corresponds to *informal register/speech*, which is a form of speech that is used among people who know each other informally, and includes colloquialisms. **Le registre populaire** corresponds to *familiar register/speech*, a type of informal register **(registre familier)**, which includes incomplete or abbreviated words.
2. Remind students that speakers often drop the **je** as well as the **ne** in **Je ne sais pas**. The result sounds like "**chez pas**."

Prononciation

Pauses and Intonation in a Sentence 1.2

» Commas indicate pauses at the beginning or in the middle of a sentence. In French, there is typically rising intonation before a comma or an exclamation point (**intonation montante**). There is typically falling intonation before a period (**intonation descendante**).

A L'intonation montante et descendante

Répétez les phrases, en faisant attention à l'intonation.

1. Écoutez, nous, on prend du poisson.
2. À mon avis, ça sera très bien!
3. Bienvenue, Messieurs-Dames, à La Belle Époque!
4. Il n'y a pas grand-chose, sur cette carte!
5. Je n'aime pas le poisson, moi.
6. Ici, c'est un très bon restaurant.

B L'intonation est montante ou descendante?

*Écoutez les phrases. Écrivez **MONT** si vous entendez une intonation montante à la fin de la phrase, ou **DESC** si vous entendez une intonation descendante à la fin de la phrase.*

The Sound /ə/

» Native French speakers tend to cut out certain sounds, especially the pronunciation of the sound /ə/. Generally, the /ə/ is pronounced when it falls between three or more pronounced consonants, but is dropped at the end of a word and between two pronounced consonants.

Pronounced: C C ə C	**Unpronounced: C ə C**
Il insist**e**ra.	Il boug**e**ra.

» The style in which one speaks greatly affects whether or not the /ə/ is pronounced. The more relaxed the style is, the more often the /ə/ is dropped.

C Prononciation du /ə/ interne

Répétez les phrases suivantes, faisant attention à prononcer le /ə/ lorsqu'il est souligné en caractère gras (bold).

1. Je mets mon port**e**feuille dans mon vêt**e**ment.
2. Nous dînons simpl**e**ment le dimanch**e**.

D Registre courant, familier, et populaire

Écoutez et répétez les phrases. Notez combien de fois vous entendez le son /ə/ pour chaque style.

	Courant	Familier	Populaire
1.	Maint**e**nant, j**e** vais à la boulang**e**rie.	Maint**e**nant, j**e** vais à la boulang**e**rie.	Maint**e**nant, j**e** vais à la boulang**e**rie.
2.	J**e** n**e** veux pas ach**e**ter d**e** bottes.	J**e** n**e** veux pas ach**e**ter d**e** bottes.	J**e** n**e** veux pas ach**e**ter d**e** bottes.

E Registre courant, familier, ou populaire?

*Écrivez **C** si vous entendez le registre courant, **F** si vous entendez le registre familier, ou **P** si vous entendez le registre populaire.*

Essential Instruction

1. Play Section **A** three times. Ask students to listen and note how the intonation changes after commas. Encourage students to use their finger to note how the voices rise and fall in the sentences.
2. Ask students to read the sentences aloud with you.
3. Do Section **B** and check answers. Replay the section again for those who could not recognize the intonation patterns. Provide additional sentences for students to practice.
4. Have students repeat **C** with you and then read the sentences aloud in groups and individually.
5. Before doing parts **D** and **E** explain that the term **registre populaire** means relaxed register and is the opposite of carefully articulated speech. Have students write the answers for part **E** on whiteboards to hold up for you to see so that you can monitor who is having difficulty.
6. Be sensitive to students who find this exercise difficult and frustrating because they cannot hear the changes in intonation.

Vocabulaire actif

Au restaurant bourguignon 1.2

Les plats

le jambon persillé

le bœuf bourguignon

Les sauces

la sauce béchamel

(servie sur le saumon, les lasagnes, le gratin)

la sauce blanche

(servie sur la volaille, le bœuf, le poisson, les légumes)

la sauce marinière

(servie sur les moules, le poisson)

la sauce béarnaise

(servie sur le steak, le bœuf, l'agneau)

la sauce hollandaise

(servie sur les œufs, la truite, le poulet, les asperges)

le coulis (de tomates)

(servi sur les légumes, les pâtes, le steak hâché)

la crème (de ciboulette)

(servie sur les pommes de terre, les légumes crus)

une marinade (de porc, de veau)

(préparée pour la viande)

La viande

le lapin

le faisan

le chevreuil

le veau

Resources

- *Vocabulaire actif*
- eVisual
- Workbook 1–3
- Flash Cards
- Listening Activity 1
- G & V Practice Games

Reference Desk

1. **Sauce béchamel** is one of the five classic French sauces made by cooking butter and flour until it forms a "**roux**" which is then thinned with milk.
2. **Sauce blanche** is the same **roux** as the **sauce béchamel**, but is mixed with bouillon rather than milk.
3. **Sauce marinière**, from southern Italy, is made with tomatoes, garlic, herbs, and onions.
4. **Sauce béarnaise** is made by emulsifying butter in egg yolks and flavoring with herbs (primarily tarragon).
5. **Sauce hollandaise** resembles **béarnaise** but uses lemon juice instead of herbs.
6. Marinades are often prepared with olive oil in France.
7. Supplemental vocabulary: **le végétarisme** (*vegetarianism*); **végétarien(ne)** (*vegetarian*); **le végétalisme** (*veganism*); **végétalien(ne)** (*vegan*); **biologique, bio** (*organic*).

Culture

Perspectives: Information

Vegetarianism is a growing movement in France, where an estimated 3% of the population does not eat meat. Flexitarianism, a hybrid diet that severely limits the consumption of meat, the traditional base of at least one French meal each day, has seen a sharp rise in France, with more than 10% of French people following the movement.

Differentiated Learning

Expand

Have students find Burgundy on the map. Ask: When you hear the word Burgundy what comes to mind? What are its principal cities? What famous wine producers are located in Burgundy? What other well-known regional product comes from Dijon? Why would Joan of Arc not be fond of the Burgundians?

Learning Styles

Auditory Learners

Encourage these students to listen to and repeat the vocabulary in **Au restaurant bourguignon** multiple times.

Visual Learners

Ask visual learners to attach a different image to each picture in **Au restaurant bourguignon**. For example, a picture of a deer along with the **plat** labeled **le chevreuil** adds visual reinforcement to meaning.

Resources

Pour la conversation
Et si je voulais dire... ?

Answers

1

1. Elle a dîné au restaurant.
2. Non, parce qu'elle est végétarienne.
3. Parce que les parents de David ne savaient pas qu'elle était végétarienne.
4. Elle a commandé le bœuf bourguignon relativement, parce que la sauce a déguisé le goût de la viande.
5. Il a commandé du chevreuil avec de la moutarde et des champignons.
6. Non, parce qu'une viande était suffisante pour elle.
7. Son père a pris du jambon persillé, et sa mère un steak avec une sauce béarnaise et des frites.

Reference Desk

1. Burgundy is a famous wine region in eastern France. There are 74,000 acres of vineyards, 100 different **appellations**, and 3,000 wine producers of 18 million cases of red and white wine per year. This wine region stretches 75 miles from Dijon to Macon. Some of the famous wines are produced in the **Côte d'Or**, **Côte de Nuits**, **Côte de Beaune**, and **Nuits-Saint-George** regions.
2. Dijon is famous for its mustards. Black currant mustard is one of its specialties. Famous mustard producers include **Maille**, **Amora**, and **Edmond Fallot**.
3. Inversion with words in the first-person singular is rare in French. Verbs that can be inverted with **je** include **avoir**, **être**, **aller**, **devoir**, and **pouvoir**. **Puis-je** from **pouvoir** is used to ask permission: **Puis-je savoir quelles sont les spécialités?**

Critical Thinking

Categorize

Put these terms on the board: **produits laitiers**, **viandes rouges**, **volaille**, **poissons**, **légumes**, **crustacés**. Have students list each vocabulary term under its appropriate category.

Pour la conversation 1.2

How do I ask about restaurant specialties?

» **Puis-je** savoir quelles sont les spécialités?
May I find out the specialties?

How do I ask what a dish is served with?

» Il est **servi** avec de la moutarde?
Is it served with mustard?

Et si je voulais dire... ?

le gibier	*game*
des paupiettes (f.)	*stuffed trout*
la poule au pot	*boiled chicken with white sauce*
le canard à l'orange	*duck with orange sauce*
le cassoulet	*bean dish with goose meat and fat*
les cailles (f.) farcies	*stuffed quails*

1 Chère Maman 1.2

Interpretive Reading

Nayah est étudiante à Dijon. Lisez la lettre qu'elle a écrite à sa mère, puis répondez aux questions.

Chère Maman,

Mes études se passent bien. La famille de David m'a invitée à dîner au restaurant le weekend dernier, et j'ai mangé de la viande pour la première fois. Ses parents ne savent pas que je suis végétarienne, donc je n'avais pas le choix. J'ai pris la spécialité du restaurant—le bœuf bourguignon. La sauce à base de vin rouge était bonne et a déguisé le bœuf. David a commandé le chevreuil avec de la moutarde et des champignons. Il m'a offert de goûter, mais une viande était assez pour moi, alors j'ai dit non merci! Le père de David a choisi le jambon persillé, et sa mère un steak servi avec une sauce béarnaise et des frites.

Écris-moi vite.

Je t'embrasse,

Nayah

1. Qu'est-ce que Nayah a fait le weekend dernier?
2. Normalement, est-ce qu'elle mange de la viande? Pourquoi?
3. Pourquoi dit-elle qu'elle n'avait pas le choix?
4. Qu'est-ce que Nayah a commandé? A-t-elle aimé ce plat?
5. Quel plat est-ce que son ami a pris?
6. Est-ce que Nayah a goûté au plat de David? Pourquoi, ou pourquoi pas?
7. Qu'est-ce que les parents de David ont pris?

Essential Instruction

1. Present **Pour la conversation** vocabulary. Explain that Burgundy's abundant forests make it popular with hunters. Regional specialties feature game like quail, pheasant, deer, and rabbit.
2. Have students read **Activité 1**. Ask them what clues indicate that Nayah is a girl.
3. Students do **Activité 1** in pairs, answering questions 1–7.
4. Treat **Activité 2** as a guessing game. Put the animal choices on the board. Read the clues to the students. Expand the format to include the other lesson vocabulary.
5. Explain the preparation of each sauce. Have students do **Activité 3**, referencing the vocabulary on p. 279.

2 La viande 1.2

Interpretive Reading

Faites correspondre chaque description à la viande de la liste.

le faisan **le bœuf** **le porc** **le veau** **le chevreuil** **le lapin**

1. un animal rose
2. un animal qui vole
3. une jeune vache
4. un petit animal avec de longues oreilles qui saute (*jumps*)
5. un grand animal qu'on peut chasser (*hunt*) en automne
6. un animal dont la viande est utilisée pour faire des hamburgers et des steaks

3 Quelle sauce ce soir? 1.2, 1.3, 3.2, 5.1

Interpretive Viewing, Presentational Writing or Speaking

Indiquez avec quelle sauce les plats suivants sont servis.

MODÈLE 
moules

Les moules sont servies avec une sauce marinière.

1. 
steak

2. 
œufs Bénédicte

3. 
poisson

4. 
lapin

5. 
pommes de terre

6. 
chevreuil

7. 
asperges

8. 
langoustes

9. 
saumon

10. 
courgettes

11. 
poulet

Answers

2

1. le porc
2. le faisan
3. le veau
4. le lapin
5. le chevreuil
6. le bœuf

3 Possible answers:

1. Le steak est servi avec une sauce béarnaise.
2. Les œufs Bénédicte sont servis avec une sauce hollandaise.
3. Le poisson est servi avec une sauce blanche/béchamel.
4. Le lapin est servi avec un coulis de tomates.
5. Les pommes de terre sont servies avec une sauce hollandaise/une crème de ciboulette.
6. Le chevreuil est servi avec une sauce béarnaise.
7. Les asperges sont servies avec une sauce hollandaise/blanche.
8. Les langoustes sont servies avec une sauce béchamel/marinière.
9. Le saumon est servi avec une sauce béchamel/une marinade.
10. Les courgettes sont servies avec une sauce blanche/béchamel/un coulis de tomates.
11. Le poulet est servi avec une sauce blanche.

Reference Desk

1. **La chasse** means *hunting*, **chasser** means *to hunt*. **Un chasseur/une chasseuse** is *a hunter*.
2. **Le gibier** means *game*. **Le gros gibier** is *big game* such as **sanglier** (*wild boar*), **cerf** (*stag*), **daim** (*fallow deer* [from which we get suede]), and **chevreuil** (*venison*). **Le petit gibier** is the general term for hunting fowl and small animals like **lièvre** (*hare*), **lapin** (*rabbit*), **perdrix** (*partridge*), and **faisan** (*pheasant*).

Culture

Products: Activity

"Qui va à la chasse, perd sa place." What does this mean? Give examples in your daily life of how this expression might be relevant.

Differentiated Learning

Accelerate

Have students research restaurants in Dijon, and then imagine that they own a restaurant. Have them create a menu featuring the specialties of the region with appetizing descriptions of each plate. They must include starters, main course, and dessert.

Decelerate

Have students find recipes for the sauces listed in **Au restaurant bourguignon**. Ask students to do an imaginary cooking demonstration in class as if they hosted a cooking show. They will pantomime the cooking.

Learning Styles

Kinesthetic Learners

Encourage students to cook some sample sauces for the class.

Visual Learners

Ask students to make a large chart of the Burgundy wine region, labeling the famous wines of each area.

Resources

Activity 4

Answers

4 Script

Moi, j'adore la cuisine française. Je suis bourguignon, alors j'adore le bœuf bourguignon. Par contre, je n'aime pas le chevreuil ou le jambon persillé. J'adore les plats en sauces. Mes préférés sont le jambon sauce béchamel, les moules marinières, et le saumon sauce hollandaise. Je déteste la sauce béarnaise. À la maison, maman fait souvent du lapin à la moutarde. C'est délicieux ! Mon frère adore le faisan. Moi je n'aime pas trop. Je préfère le veau Orloff. Miam !

1. Est-ce que Stéphane aime le bœuf bourguignon parce qu'il est provençal ?
2. Est-ce que Stéphane préfère le chevreuil et le jambon persillé ?
3. Est-ce qu'il aime les plats servis avec une sauce ?
4. Est-ce qu'il adore la sauce béarnaise ?
5. Est-ce que sa mère lui sert souvent du lapin à la moutarde ?
6. Est-ce qu'il aime le faisan plus que son frère ?
7. Il prend souvent du veau Orloff ?

1. non
2. non
3. oui
4. non
5. oui
6. non
7. oui

5 Answers will vary.

Reference Desk

Here is some additional vocabulary that students might like to know: **jeter un coup d'oeil** (*to glance*); **comprendre** (*to include* as well as *to understand*); **maints plats** (*many dishes*); **il est très viande** (*the menu is mainly meat*); **les trompettes de la mort** (*a very popular mushroom which owes its name to its dark color*).

Game

Bingo

Using an online Bingo game generator, create boards featuring food terms and vocabulary. Students mark their cards if they have the word that you define in French.

Recherche : bingo game maker

4 Les plats cuisinés, délicieux ! 1.2

Interpretive Listening

Écrivez les numéros 1–7 sur votre papier. Puis, écoutez Stéphane décrire ses goûts culinaires. Enfin, écrivez ***oui*** *ou* ***non*** *pour répondre à la question que vous entendez.*

5 Questions personnelles 1.1

Interpersonal Speaking

Répondez aux questions suivantes avec un partenaire.

1. Est-ce que tu vas souvent au restaurant ? Quels restaurants préfères-tu : italiens, mexicains, ou chinois ?
2. Préfères-tu choisir des plats avec ou sans viande ? De quelle(s) viande(s) est-ce que tu ne manges pas ? Et tes parents ? Et tes amis ?
3. Aimes-tu les plats servis avec une sauce ? Si oui, lesquels ?
4. Qu'est-ce que tu aimerais goûter dans un restaurant français ?
5. As-tu jamais goûté le chevreuil ? Si oui, c'était bon ? Et le lapin ?

Connexions 1.1, 1.2, 2.1, 3.2, 4.2

Cuisine

La cuisine française est réputée pour intégrer des (parties d') animaux qu'on peut considérer délicates, comme **la tête de porc**, **la cervelle d'agneau** (*lamb's brains*), ou **le boudin** (*blood sausage*). Cherchez des recettes qui vous semblent extraordinaires, et demandez à votre partenaire s'il ou elle aimerait les goûter.

Essential Instruction

1. Students listen to **Activité 4** and answer **oui** or **non** on whiteboards. Have them show you their answer after each item for an immediate comprehension check.
2. In pairs, students interview each other about their food preferences by doing **Activité 5**.
3. Ask them to present their findings to a different partner before getting volunteers to report to the class. **Voici Marc. Il adore la cuisine mexicaine.**
4. Students listen to **Au restaurant dijonnais** with books closed, and then tell you what they remember hearing.
5. Play the passage again as they follow in the book. Ask general comprehension questions.
6. Present the vocabulary from *Reference Desk* and answer any questions they may have before assigning **Activité 6**.

Au restaurant dijonnais 1.2, 5.2

Justin et Léo sont à table dans un restaurant à Dijon.

Le serveur : Bonjour, Messieurs. Avez-vous jeté un coup d'œil à la carte ?
Justin : Oui, justement, puis-je savoir quelles sont les spécialités de la région ?
Le serveur : Alors, la gastronomie de la Bourgogne comprend la moutarde et les escargots, bien entendu, mais aussi maints plats de viande et de poisson.
Léo : Il est très viande, mais il ne comprend pas toutes les dénominations.
Le serveur : D'accord, alors, le jambon persillé* est fait avec du porc ; le chevreuil sauce maison est servi avec des trompettes de la mort.
Justin : Les trompettes de la mort ? Mon Dieu, qu'est-ce que c'est que ça ?
Léo : Ce sont des champignons.
Le serveur : Oui, nous servons aussi du lapin, du faisan, mais personnellement je vous conseille un grand classique, le bœuf bourguignon !
Justin : Il est servi avec de la moutarde ?
Le serveur : Non, mais la moutarde de Dijon, fermentée, accompagne très bien tous les plats.
Justin : Des escargots pour nous deux pour commencer, et pour moi, le bœuf bourguignon.
Léo : Je doute que les escargots aient bon goût. Pour moi, le jambon persillé seulement, s'il vous plaît. Je suis étonné que tu essaies les escargots !
Justin : À Rome, fais comme les Romains, et à Dijon, fais comme les Dijonnais !

***Je parle bien !**
« L'adjectif **persillé** se prononce **paire-si-yé**. »

6 Au restaurant dijonnais 1.2

Identifiez la personne décrite.

1. Il explique ce que c'est, les trompettes de la mort.
2. Il explique les spécialités de la région.
3. Il voudrait goûter aux escargots.
4. Il sert beaucoup de plats de viande.
5. Il commande le bœuf bourguignon.
6. Il dit que son ami a besoin d'informations.
7. Il récite un proverbe.

Resources

Dialogue
Activity 6
Dialogue Video
WB Workbook 4

Answers

6
1. Léo
2. le serveur
3. Justin
4. le serveur
5. Justin
6. Léo
7. Justin

Reference Desk

1. In addition to meaning *to understand*, **comprendre** means *to include*. **"La gastronomie de la Bourgogne comprend la moutarde et les escargots…" "Le service est compris ?"**
2. Talking about food is an excellent way to introduce students to difficult cultural differences. Encourage them to understand that food preferences are developed in the children of a culture and that, rather than reacting with expressions such as "That's gross!" or "That's weird!", which could be offensive to people of another culture, students should recognize that their tastes are a product of where they were raised and, therefore, merely different. (This does not mean that they have to like foods they are not accustomed to.) This discussion provides an excellent platform to launch into more difficult discussions about cultural differences, such as the role of women, children, parents, government, money, or religion in various societies. Emphasize that understanding a different culture and its behaviors does not necessarily mean condoning it.

nouvelle orthographe **le gout**

Differentiated Learning

Accelerate
Ask students to work in groups of three to present **Activité 6** as if it were a scene from a movie.

Special Needs Students

AD(H)D/Dyslexia/Linguistically Challenged
Break down the dialogue into small sections. Ask these students basic comprehension questions in French to which they will respond in English. In this way, you will be able to determine their level of understanding. Rework the dialogue with them. Ask the same questions but this time have them reply in French.

Resources

Extension

EXTENSION

Ils vont goûter des plats des Antilles, du Sénégal, et du Maroc.

Communication

Interpersonal: Cooperative Groups

Students write a dialogue similar to **Au restaurant dijonnais** and discuss their personal food preferences as well as what regional foods they would like to taste from **la Bourgogne**.
Have them use these expressions: **Ça me dit**, **Ce plat me donne l'eau à la bouche**, **Je ne l'aime pas trop**, **À chacun son goût**.

Reference Desk

1. **Papilles** (**gustatives**) are taste buds.
2. **Tiep bou dienn**, the national dish of Senegal, is made of fish (sea bream and cod) and cooked with basil, onion, garlic, and vegetables to which a sauce of shrimp and vegetables is added.
3. **Accras de morue**, a traditional snack food that supplements meals on the island of Saint Martin, is made of cod, garlic, chilis, cilantro, and onions.
4. **Couscous d'agneau** is a classic Moroccan dish made from lamb and vegetable dish and garnished with couscous.
5. **Saka-Saka** is a Congolese word for cassava leaves which can only be found in the tropics. The dish is made with garlic, onion, green and sweet peppers, eggplant, and dried salted fish.

nouvelle orthographe **le gout**

EXTENSION **Des amis dînent au restaurant** 1.2

Au restaurant, les amis regardent la carte et discutent des plats.

Amir : Tiens, voici la carte ; c'est un tour de la gastronomie de la Francophonie.
Charlotte : Alors ce soir on voyage, j'ai peur qu'on n'ait plus envie de revenir....
Nicole : Je sens que mes papilles sont en train de partir vers les Antilles !
Antoine : Je voudrais goûter à la cuisine africaine.
Amir : Il y a du *tiep*, c'est un plat de fête sénégalais.
Charlotte : Qu'est-ce qu'il y a dedans ?
Amir : Du riz, du poisson, des aubergines, du piment.... C'est très bon !
Nicole : Pour moi, des accras de morue.
Charlotte : Je prendrais bien un bon couscous à l'agneau.
Antoine : Moi, je fais comme Amir.
Amir : Pas très aventurier ! Alors on va goûter le *saka-saka*. À toi de deviner ce qu'il y a dedans !

EXTENSION La bande d'amis va goûter des plats de quelles régions ou pays francophones ? 1.2

Stratégie

Imaginez que vous êtes le serveur ou la serveuse. Faites une liste des plats que vous devrez servir à chacun des jeunes gens du dialogue.

Essential Instruction

1. Have students listen to **Extension** and then research the recipes to identify their origins.
2. Play the dialogue again and ask volunteers to read the roles of the friends. Repeat with other students.

Pre-AP

Question centrale ? De quelles compétences ai-je besoin pour voyager?

Dijon et la Bourgogne 1.2, 2.1, 3.1

Dijon, capitale de la Bourgogne, a un passé prestigieux. C'est aujourd'hui le chef-lieu* du département de la Côte d'Or et de la région Bourgogne-Franche Comté. L'agglomération dijonnaise* compte 385 000 habitants.

La Bourgogne est traversée par la Loire.

Dijon est l'ancienne* capitale du Duché de Bourgogne. Celui-ci a joué un grand rôle aux 14ème et 15ème siècles alors qu'il recouvrait* les actuels Pays-Bas, la Belgique, le Luxembourg, le Palatinat en Allemagne, et la Suisse, et les régions françaises d'Alsace, de Champagne et de Picardie. C'est le roi de France, Louis XI, qui a annexé l'État bourguignon en 1477 après la défaite* de Charles Le Téméraire.

Dijon au fil* des siècles s'est enrichi d'un riche patrimoine architectural dont témoignent* ses maisons à colombages*, ses beaux hôtels particuliers de style Renaissance, et ses édifices religieux, églises et monastères* de style gothique qui charment les touristes.

Carrefour ferroviaire* depuis le 19ème siècle sur l'axe Paris-Marseille, Dijon est devenu une ville industrielle à la fois pour l'industrie — électronique, la mécanique (SEB), la chimie-pharmacie (Sanofi, Urgo) et l'agro-alimentaire. Comme produits agro-alimentaires, on peut citer la moutarde, le chocolat, le pain d'épices*, la production de crème de cassis* qui font la réputation internationale de Dijon. Destination touristique importante, à la fois pour le tourisme culturel, gastronomique et d'affaires, Dijon est classée Zone Touristique Internationale en 2016. Ville de congrès, avec l'ouverture* en décembre 2011 de la ligne à grande vitesse (LGV) entre le Rhin et le Rhône, Dijon retrouve sa situation de plaque tournante* vers la Suisse, l'Allemagne, la Belgique et vers le sud.

Recherche : dijon tourisme, visiter dijon, dijon et sa région

chef-lieu *administrative center*; **agglomération dijonnaise** *Dijon region*; **ancienne** *former*; **recouvrait** *extended*; **défaite** *defeat*; **au fil** *over*; **témoignent** *give evidence*; **maison à colombage** *half-timbered house*; **monastère** *monastery*; **carrefour ferroviaire** *rail hub*; **pain d'épices** *gingerbread*; **crème de cassis** *type of liqueur made from black currants*; **ouverture** *opening*; **plaque tournante** *hub*

Produits
1.2, 2.2

Parmi les personnalités liées à la ville de Dijon, on compte l'écrivain classique Jacques-Bénigne Bossuet (1627–1704), le musicien Jean-Philippe Rameau (1683–1764), le sculpteur François Rude (1784–1855), l'ingénieur Gustave Eiffel (1832–1923), l'actrice Claude Jade (1948–2006) et bien sûr le chanoine (*canon*) Félix Kir (1876–1968), maire de Dijon et inventeur de la célèbre boisson qui porte son nom.

Traditions et pratiques
1.2, 2.1

La Bourgogne est réputée pour son hospitalité : les habitants sont en général très accueillants. La Bourgogne est souvent l'une des premières régions de France à offrir son hospitalité aux réfugiés lors de crises humanitaires.

Resources

Points de départ
Workbook 5
Explore

Reference Desk

Comparisons

1. Discuss national and regional American dishes. What foods do we associate with the South, the Eastern Seaboard, the Midwest, and the West Coast of the United States? Is our food purely American or a fusion of international cuisines? Give examples.
2. If you have access to Passport, find a video or a news article related to **la Bourgogne** and show it to your students.

Expansion

Have students read **Dijon et la Bourgogne**. Make this a game to see how fast the students can find the following terms: **Les nonettes** (*spiced bread made with orange marmalade and honey*), Fabrice Gillotte (famous chocolate maker from Dijon), **Les Trois Glorieuses** (famous wine festival and auction in Beaune), **Hospices de Beaune** (hospital for the poor opened in 1443), **Salle des pôvres** (the great hall of the **Hospices de Beaune**), **mba Dijon** (**Musée de Beaux Arts**), **crème de cassis**, and listed search words.

Special Needs Students

Social Anxiety
Many students may have limited experience tasting foods with exotic ingredients. Continue to encourage them to be open to new tastes and dishes.

Dyslexia
Since **Dijon et la Bourgogne** is a longer reading, consider letting students who may struggle more with reading passages know in advance. Give them a copy of the reading and encourage them to read and mark the text with questions, vocabulary, or paraphrases.

Answers

7

1. Maps should include current-day Holland, Belgium, Luxemburg, southwestern Germany, Switzerland, and the French regions of Alsace-Lorraine, Champagne, and Picardie.
2. Itineraries will vary.
3. Answers will vary in time: Dijon, Besançon, Belfort, Montbéliard, Mulhouse (branche est); Paris (branche ouest); Lyon (branche sud)
4. Answers will vary, but might include **le cassis**, **le négus**, **le bœuf de Charolles**, **le fromage de chèvre**, **le fromage Époisse**, **la truffe**, **l'andouillette**, and **l'anis**.

Perspectives

Possible answer: Un voyage en péniche offre une belle vue de la région, et la possibilité de faire des visites et des activités touristiques.

Culture

Products: Information

Mustard is a popular condiment found on tables along with salt and pepper in modestly priced French restaurants. It is a staple in many recipes including the classic vinaigrette salad dressing, composed of three parts oil to one part vinegar to which one can add fine herbs. Mustard is used to emulsify the oil and vinegar in the vinaigrette.

Expansion

Have students inventory the kinds of mustards available in their local grocery store. What are the brands? How many of them are produced in France? What are the common ingredients found in these mustards?

Produits 1.2, 2.2, 4.2

La moutarde de Dijon est une moutarde forte qui existe en plusieurs variétés. Avant le 14ème siècle, le centre de la préparation de la moutarde était à Paris, mais depuis, la Bourgogne s'en est fait une spécialité. C'est un produit que la France exporte aussi.

Comparaisons 1.2, 2.2, 4.2

Quelle marque (*brand*) de moutarde est-ce que vous achetez ? Avez-vous jamais goûté à la moutarde de Dijon ?

7 Activités culturelles 1.3, 3.2

Faites les activités suivantes.

1. Dessinez la carte de l'ancien Duché de Bourgogne entre les 14ème et 15ème siècles.
2. Faites des recherches et préparez un itinéraire touristique de 6 à 10 choses à voir ou à faire en Bourgogne.
3. Faites une liste des destinations qu'on peut visiter sur la nouvelle ligne à grande vitesse Rhin-Rhône.
4. Trouvez quatre produits, à part la moutarde, qui sont aussi de Dijon.

La moutarde de Dijon a une réputation mondiale.

Perspectives 1.2, 2.1, 5.2

« En raison du superbe réseau de canaux navigables en bateau en Bourgogne, ma famille et moi, on a loué une péniche (*barge*). Quelle belle vue de cette magnifique région de France avec ses villages pittoresques et sa campagne verdoyante (*verdant*) ! On s'est arrêté dans plusieurs villages où on a fait du vélo, flâné, fait les touristes, les courses et du shopping pour des souvenirs…. J'ai un très bon souvenir de la Bourgogne à cause de cette expérience en bateau. »
—Marine

Selon cette vacancière, qu'est-ce qu'un voyage en péniche en Bourgogne offre aux touristes ?

Recherche : lgv rhin rhône, spécialités de dijon/la bourgogne

Mon dico bourguignon

La moutarde me monte au nez. *I am getting angry.*
mettre son grain de sel *to add one's two cents*
C'est du beurre ! *It is easy!*
tomber dans les pommes *to faint*
arriver comme un cheveu sur la soupe *to happen at a bad time*

Péniches sur un fleuve de Bourgogne

Essential Instruction

1. Assign partners to work on the activities in **Activité 7** according to their interest and ability.
2. After reading **Perspectives**, have students find a barge company online that offers travel to northern and southern Burgundy. Ask them to select a specific boat from each route and compare prices, sites, and accommodations.
3. Have students read **Du côté des médias**. Ask comprehension questions: On what days is the cooking school open? What are three adjectives that describe the recipes? How long is each class? What are two options for tasting the recipes? They cite their answers from the text.
4. Students choose an activity in **Activité 8**; for the second one, they might opt to film a commercial for the cooking school.

Du côté des médias 1.2

Lisez les informations suivantes pour un cours de cuisine à Dijon.

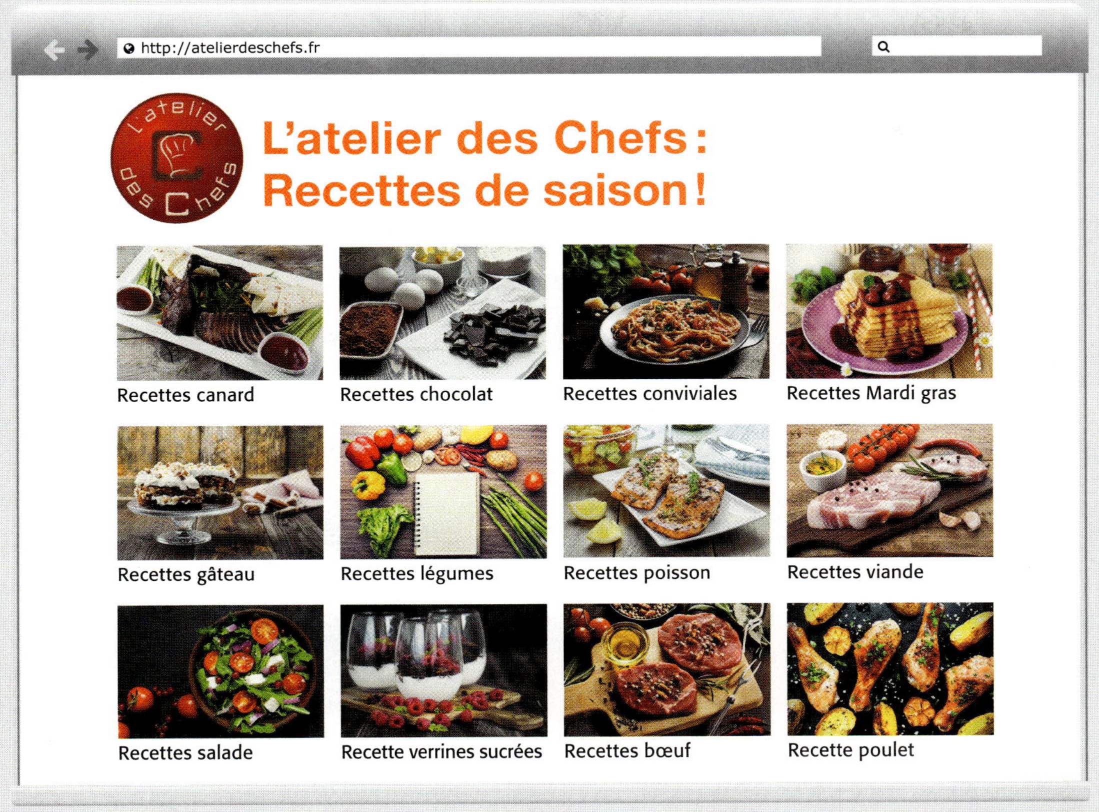

8 L'atelier des Chefs 1.3, 2.2, 3.1, 5.1, 5.2

Faites les activités suivantes.

1. Imaginez que vous êtes apprenti(e) à l'atelier des Chefs. On vous demande de préparer un menu spécial pour la Saint-Valentin. Visitez le site et choisissez des recettes pour ce menu ; trouvez une entrée, un plat principal, et un dessert. Justifiez votre choix devant vos examinateurs (la classe).
2. Préparez une annonce de 20 secondes à la radio pour l'atelier des Chefs.

Recherche : atelier des chefs

Answers

8 Activities will vary.

Game

Que veut dire... ?

Visit the website and copy images and names of various individual recipes. Project the images and names on a screen and have students figure out which category (listed on this page) they belong to. Then have students guess which ingredients are included in the recipe. Award one point to each student (or team) that identifies the category and one point for each correct ingredient that they guess.

Culture

Products: Information

L'atelier des Chefs is one of Burgundy's most celebrated chef schools, of which there are many. Students who enjoy cooking or aspire to be chefs may want to explore opportunities to study French cuisine in this region.

Differentiated Learning

Adapt

There are many options for touring Burgundy, from organized excursions to cycling, barge travel, and even by hot air balloon. There are many things to do as well, such as cultural visits, cooking lessons, wine tasting, and camping, just to name a few. Give your students a generous imaginary budget and have them organize a one-week itinerary traveling through Burgundy. Ask them to list hotels, restaurants, and the activities they would take part in during their stay.

Resources

WB Workbook 6–10

G & V Practice Games

Reference Desk

1. Remind students that the indicative indicates fact, and the subjunctive is subjective, expressing opinion, wishes, desires, and emotions. If they understand that concept, they will be able to understand how the subjunctive is used.
2. Explain that these subjective expressions are followed by the subjunctive provided there is a subject change.
3. When verbs of emotion have no subject change, they are often followed by **de**. Contrast: **Je suis contente d'être avec toi. Je suis contente que tu sois avec moi.**

nouvelle orthographe: **couter**

Structure de la langue

The Subjunctive after Expressions of Emotion 1.2

You have already learned that the subjunctive is used in a dependent clause after the expression **il faut que**; after certain impersonal expressions; and after expressions of wish, will, or desire. The subjunctive is also used after expressions of emotion (such as happiness, sadness, surprise, fear, and anger). Use the subjunctive after one of the following expressions of emotion when the emotion concerns someone other than the subject.

être content(e) que	*to be happy that*
être heureux/heureuse que	*to be happy that*
être triste que	*to be sad that*
être désolé(e) que	*to be sorry that*
être fâché(e) que	*to be angry that*
être étonné(e) que	*to be surprised that*
avoir peur que	*to be afraid that*
regretter que	*to be sorry that*
s'inquiéter que	*to worry that*
Ça me surprend que....	*It surprises me that....*
Ça m'embête que....	*It bothers me that....*
C'est dommage que....	*It's too bad that....*

Ça me surprend que vous **mangiez** du chevreuil. — *It surprises me that you are eating venison.*

Je suis étonné que le veau **coûte** si cher ! — *I'm surprised that the veal costs so much!*

Karim est fâché qu'il n'y **ait** pas de lapin au restaurant. — *Karim is mad that there isn't any rabbit at the restaurant.*

Le serveur a peur que nous n'**aimions** pas le faisan. — *The waiter is afraid that we don't like the pheasant.*

C'est dommage qu'on ne **serve** pas de bœuf bourguignon. — *It's a shame that beef bourguignon isn't served.*

Essential Instruction

1. With their books closed, ask students to suggest expressions of emotion that you will write on the board. Add to the list the expressions from the lesson that they did not mention.
2. Using these expressions, have students make sentences using the subjunctive.
3. In pairs, have students do **Activité 9**. Assign students to put the sentences on the board for correction.
4. Students change partners to play tic-tac-toe (**le morpion**) in **Activité 10**.

9 Des phrases logiques 1.1, 1.3

Interpersonal Speaking, Presentational Speaking or Writing

Faites des phrases logiques en combinant les mots de la première colonne et les phrases de la deuxième colonne. Attention à l'emploi du subjonctif. Il y a plus d'une réponse possible. Suivez le modèle. Quand vous aurez fini, comparez vos phrases avec celles d'un(e) partenaire.

Isa est surprise qu'il y ait un cheveu dans sa salade.

MODÈLE Diane (contente) ; Le veau est bon.
Diane est contente que le veau soit bon.

1. moi (étonné(e))	Le jambon persillé n'a pas bon goût.
2. Yannick (triste)	Le restaurant coûte trop cher.
3. Djamel (content)	Vos amis n'aiment rien sur la carte.
4. toi (avoir peur)	Il y a un moustique dans l'assiette.
5. Nicole (désolée)	Ton ami est en retard.
6. Marc et Nathan (heureux)	Il y a des spécialités.
7. Laure et toi (tristes)	Le service est compris.
8. Youssef et moi (étonnés)	Les clients ne commandent pas de dessert.
9. le serveur (fâché)	La sauce est mauvaise.

10 Le morpion du subjonctif 1.1

Interpersonal Speaking

Prenez une feuille de papier. Avec un(e) partenaire, essayez de remplir votre grille de morpion, chacun à votre tour, en faisant des phrases à l'aide des indices donnés. Vous pouvez aussi créer votre propre grille.

MODÈLE 

Je suis triste que tu veuilles chercher un autre hôtel.

 avoir un bain à remous dans la chambre	 vouloir chercher un autre hôtel	 ne pas m'attendre
 le plat (être) trop épicé	 ne pas avoir assez d'argent	 goûter le faisan
 s'entendre avec le serveur	 ne pas avoir la climatisation	 ne pas aimer le dessert

Resources

Activity 9

Answers

9 Possible answers:
1. Je suis étonné(e) que le jambon persillé n'ait pas bon goût.
2. Yannick est triste que le restaurant coûte trop cher.
3. Djamel est content que le service soit compris.
4. Tu as peur que ton ami soit en retard.
5. Nicole est désolée que la sauce soit mauvaise.
6. Marc et Nathan sont heureux qu'il y ait des spécialités.
7. Laure et toi, vous êtes tristes que vos amis n'aiment rien sur la carte.
8. Youssef et moi sommes étonnés que les clients ne commandent pas de dessert.
9. Le serveur est fâché qu'il y ait un moustique dans l'assiette.

10 Possible answers:
1. Je suis très content(e) qu'il y ait un bain à remous dans la chambre.
2. Je suis désolé(e) que tu veuilles chercher un autre hôtel.
3. Je suis fâché(e) que tu ne m'attendes pas.
4. Nous sommes surpris(es) que le plat soit trop épicé.
5. Ma mère est surprise que tu n'aies pas assez d'argent.
6. Nous sommes tristes que tu ne goûtes pas le faisan.
7. Nous sommes étonné(e)s que mon père s'entende avec le serveur.
8. Ma famille est fâchée qu'il n'y ait pas la climatisation.
9. Ma mère est triste que je n'aime pas le dessert.

Communication

Interpersonal: Paired Practice

Put students in pairs. Prepare a worksheet that describes a series of situations where they can respond, for example, **Les parents de mon ami disent qu'il ne peut pas prendre la voiture ce weekend** and **Le nouvel élève ne vous invite pas à sa boum**. Students take turns forming sentences using **je** or **nous**, an expression of emotion, and the subjunctive of the verb in the original sentence.

Differentiated Learning

Accelerate
Students may want to expand the exercises by writing a sentence about members of the class.

Decelerate
Give students a worksheet with expanded exercises for practice, or have them use online quizzes.

Recherche : quizlet

Multiple Intelligences

Kinesthetic Learners
Encourage students to write out verbs and subjunctive expressions.

Special Needs Students

AD(H)D
Help students with attention difficulties to break down the information about the subjunctive by reviewing the conjugation of regular and irregular verbs. They may benefit from a one-page chart to use as a reference when doing the exercises.

Answers

11

devions ; donne ; marche ; puisse ; devions ; ait ; coûte ; veuille ; envoyiez

Communication

Presentational: Cooperative Groups

After completing **Activité 11** have students work in mixed-ability groups to imagine this as a short skit. How might the rental agency's representative reply to the group's concerns about the apartment? Have the students write out each part and choose actors to present. Collect the written copy.

11 Une annonce trompeuse à Chamonix 1.2, 1.3, 4.2

Interpretive Reading, Presentational Writing

Julien et ses copains ont loué un appartement à Chamonix pour un weekend de ski. Il écrit à l'agence pour se plaindre. Complétez la lettre qu'il écrit en mettant les verbes entre parenthèses à la forme convenable.

Chamonix, le mardi 14 janvier

Monsieur Dujardin,

Je regrette que mes amis et moi, nous (devoir) vous écrire, mais l'appartement que vous nous avez loué est loin de correspondre à votre annonce.

Nous voulions avoir une vue sur le Mont-Blanc. Mais nous avons été surpris de découvrir qu'aucune des fenêtres ne (donner) sur la montagne.

Ça nous embête que le bain à remous dans la salle de bains ne (marcher) pas. Je suis fâché que mes copains et moi, on ne (pouvoir) pas se reposer dans l'eau chaude après une journée de ski.

Nous avons demandé un appartement dans le domaine. Nous sommes étonnés que nous (devoir) prendre un bus pour aller à la station de ski.

C'est dommage qu'il n'y (avoir) pas de chaînes câblées dans le salon.

Cela nous surprend que cet appartement (coûter) si cher parce qu'il ne correspond pas du tout à votre annonce.

Je suis désolé qu'on ne (vouloir) pas revenir dans votre appartement. Nous souhaitons que vous nous (envoyer) un remboursement.

Je vous prie d'agréer, Monsieur, nos salutations distinguées.

Julien Durouleaux

Des logements dans les montagnes de Chamonix

Essential Instruction

1. Have students read the letter and complete the sentences in **Activité 11**.
2. In groups, have students respond to the letter as Monsieur Dujardin. Challenge each group to use as many verbs in the subjunctive as possible.
3. Introduce the subjunctive after expressions of doubt or uncertainty. Explain that the indicative indicates a fact or certainty and the subjunctive shows emotion, opinion and, in this case, doubt and uncertainty.
4. Write the subjunctive/indicative expressions from the bottom of the chart on p. 291, mixing the two columns. Ask students to identify which expressions indicate doubt or uncertainty, and which ones express certainty.

The Subjunctive After Expressions of Doubt 1.1 or Uncertainty

Another use of the subjunctive is after expressions of doubt or uncertainty. For example, the verb **douter** (*to doubt*) is followed by the subjunctive in the dependent clause.

Je doute que nous **allions** à un restaurant loin de l'hôtel.
I doubt that we are going to a restaurant far from the hotel.

When the verbs **penser** and **croire**, as well as certain expressions of certainty, are used negatively or interrogatively, they express doubt or uncertainty and are therefore followed by the subjunctive.

penser que	**Penses-tu que** la sauce **soit** bonne avec du lait?	*Do you think that the sauce is good with milk?*
croire que	Non, **je ne crois pas qu'**elle **soit** bonne.	*No, I don't believe that it is good.*
être sûr que	Le serveur, **est-il sûr qu'**on n'**ait** plus de poisson?	*The waiter, is he sure that they have no more fish?*
être certain que	Non, **il n'est pas certain que** vous **puissiez** en commander.	*No, he isn't certain that you can order any.*
être vrai que	**Est-il vrai que** tu **saches** faire toutes les sauces françaises?	*Is it true that you know how to make all the French sauces?*
être évident que	**Il n'est pas évident que** le chef **soit** français.	*It is not obvious that the chef is French.*

However, when **penser** and **croire**, as well as expressions of certainty, are in the affirmative or in the negative interrogative, they no longer express doubt and are followed by the indicative.

Ne crois-tu pas que cette sauce béarnaise **est** la meilleure?
Don't you believe that this béarnaise sauce is the best?

The following chart can help you determine the use of the subjunctive and the indicative.

	Indicative	Subjunctive	
Stating a belief expresses certainty.	Je pense que..../ Je crois que....	Penses-tu que...?/ Crois-tu que...?	*Questioning a belief raises doubt.*
Questioning the negation of a belief expresses certainty.	Ne penses-tu pas que...?/ Ne crois-tu pas que...?	Je ne pense pas que..../ Je ne crois pas que....	*Negating a belief expresses doubt.*
Stating a certainty expresses certainty.	Je suis sûr(e)/ certain(e) que....	Es-tu sûr(e)/ certain(e) que...?	*Questioning a certainty raises doubt.*
Questioning the negation of a certainty expresses certainty.	N'es-tu pas sûr(e)/ certain(e) que...?	Je ne suis pas sûr(e)/ certain(e) que....	*Negating a certainty expresses doubt.*
Stating evidence expresses certainty.	Il est vrai/évident que....	Est-il vrai/évident que...?	*Questioning evidence raises doubt.*
Questioning the negation of an evidence expresses certainty.	N'est-il pas évident que...?	Il n'est pas vrai/ évident que....	*Negating evidence expresses doubt.*
Negating a doubt expresses certainty.	Je ne doute pas que....	Je doute que....	*Stating a doubt expresses doubt.*

Resources

WB Workbook 11
LA Listening Activity 2
G & V Practice Games

Reference Desk

The charts help clarify the concept of the subjunctive with expressions of doubt and uncertainty. Students need time to think about what each expression conveys in the affirmative, negative, interrogative, and combinations of the three. Reinforce the logic of the subjunctive, even if students find it frustrating at first. Typically, sentences with **"Je crois que"** indicate a certainty of what one believes, thereby requiring the indicative. When questioned, those beliefs become doubts (subjunctive). But if the question is negated (**Ne crois-tu pas que...?**), the doubt is doubted and the indicative is used. Explain that this concept exists in other Latin languages so mastering the subjunctive in French will make the study of Spanish, for example, easier.

nouvelle orthographe **sûr, sure, surs, sures**

Game

Doute ou non?

Put students in pairs with whiteboards. Give them the options of **est en classe** or **soit en classe**. Mix expressions that are followed by the indicative and subjunctive (for example, **Je doute que Paul....** and **Je suis certain que Paul....**). Students confer to write the correct response. Assign a point for each correct answer.

Differentiated Learning

Accelerate

Have students collaborate to write a short scene from a soap opera using as many expressions with the subjunctive as possible. Expressions of wishing, wanting, doubting, and fearing lend themselves to melodramatic pathos. Have groups present to the class.

Decelerate

Ask students to make flash cards of the indicative and subjunctive expressions in two colors, green for expressions followed by the indicative and red for those followed by the subjunctive. The color-coding might help them remember, especially if they are visual learners.

Answers

12

Affirmative answers will use the indicative; negative answers will use the subjunctive.

1. Croyez-vous que les études universitaires m'intéressent?
2. Croyez-vous que je prenne du café au petit déjeuner?
3. Croyez-vous que je fasse du dessin?
4. Croyez-vous que je suive un cours d'art?
5. Croyez-vous que j'aille souvent au parc d'attractions?
6. Croyez-vous que je coure dans les marathons?
7. Croyez-vous que je m'entraîne au fitness?

Partner answers will vary.

13

1. Mme Delattre est sûre que la ville ouvre un centre d'accueil pour les sans-abri.
2. Le père de Mme Delattre n'est pas sûr que sa femme et lui puissent faire un don au centre d'accueil.
3. Les infirmiers ne croient pas que l'hôpital fasse assez pour combattre le SIDA.
4. Le directeur de l'hôpital croit qu'on enseigne bien aux patients le traitement contre le SIDA.
5. Théo et Clara sont certains que le racisme est un problème dans la société.
6. Leurs parents ne sont pas certains qu'une manifestation contre le racisme soit une bonne idée pour Théo et Clara.
7. Simon ne pense pas que son oncle boive trop d'alcool.
8. Sa tante pense que sa famille doit faire une intervention.

Reference Desk

nouvelle orthographe ✔ **le sans-abri, les sans-abris**

12 J'interviewe mes camarades de classe 1.1, 3.2

Interpersonal Speaking

D'abord, répondez aux questions individuellement et gardez vos réponses. À tour de rôle, en groupes de trois, posez une question à vos partenaires en leur demandant s'ils pensent que vous faites les choses suivantes. Suivez le modèle. Si vos camarades de classe ne vous croient pas, montrez-leur vos réponses écrites.

MODÈLE Vous avez peur des gros chiens?
A: Croyez-vous que j'aie peur des gros chiens?
B: Non, je ne crois pas que tu aies peur des gros chiens!
C: Moi, je crois que tu as peur des gros chiens!
A: C'est vrai. J'ai peur des gros chiens!

1. Les études universitaires vous intéressent?
2. Vous prenez du café au petit déjeuner?
3. Vous faîtes du dessin?
4. Vous suivez un cours d'art?
5. Vous allez souvent au parc d'attractions?
6. Vous courez dans les marathons?
7. Vous vous entraînez au fitness?

13 Problèmes de société 1.3

Presentational Speaking or Writing

Formez des phrases en utilisant le premier verbe indiqué à l'indicatif et le deuxième verbe à l'indicatif ou au subjonctif.

MODÈLES le directeur du lycée Victor Hugo (douter que le gouvernement, vouloir moderniser son école)
Le directeur du lycée Victor Hugo doute que le gouvernement veuille moderniser son école.

les élèves (ne pas douter que le directeur, installer un nouveau labo de langues)
Les élèves ne doutent pas que le directeur installe un nouveau labo de langues.

1. Mme Delattre (être sûr que la ville, ouvrir un centre d'accueil pour les sans-abri)
2. le père de Mme Delattre (ne pas être sûr que sa femme et lui, pouvoir faire un don au centre d'accueil)
3. les infirmiers (ne pas croire que l'hôpital, faire assez pour combattre le SIDA)
4. le directeur de l'hôpital (croire qu'on, enseigner bien aux patients le traitement contre le SIDA)
5. Théo et Clara (être certain que le racisme, être un problème dans la société)
6. leurs parents (ne pas être certain qu'une manifestation contre le racisme, être une bonne idée pour Théo et Clara)
7. Simon (ne pas penser que son oncle, boire trop d'alcool)
8. sa tante (penser que sa famille, devoir faire une intervention)

Essential Instruction

1. Ask a student to assume the role of the teacher. As a review, ask him/her to explain the use of the subjunctive in expressions of doubt and uncertainty.
2. Students do **Activité 12** in groups of three.
3. Using whiteboards, students do **Activité 13** and show their sentences for 1–8 one at a time. This way you can correct errors as they do the exercise and give immediate feedback.
4. Students work in pairs to do **Activité 14**. Before they begin, preview any terms that they might not know or remember.
5. Play **Activité 15**. Students write **D** or **C** according to the sense of the statement. If the class has problems with comprehension, play each sentence again, and write it on the board.

14 L'environnement 1.1, 3.2

Interpersonal Speaking

À tour de rôle, posez les questions suivantes à votre partenaire. Mettez la forme correcte du verbe indiqué au subjonctif. Puis, répondez honnêtement, soit (either) *à l'affirmatif avec l'indicatif, soit* (or) *au négatif avec le subjonctif.*

1. Penses-tu qu'on... prendre l'effet de serre au sérieux? (devoir)
2. Crois-tu que le Vélib'... l'environnement? (aider)
3. Penses-tu que nous... venir au lycée à vélo ou à pied? (devoir)
4. Es-tu sûr(e) qu'il y... des animaux en voie de disparition? (avoir)
5. Est-il vrai qu'on... sauvegarder les espaces sauvages pour eux? (devoir)
6. Es-tu certain(e) qu'on... arrêter les marées noires? (pouvoir)
7. Penses-tu que les panneaux solaires... bon marché? (être)
8. Est-il vrai que toi et ta famille, vous...? (recycler)
9. Est-il évident que les hommes politiques nous... au sujet de l'environnement? (écouter)

Connexions 1.2, 3.1

SVT

Testez votre partenaire sur ses connaissances en sciences de la vie et de la terre. Préparez six à dix questions sur la société, l'économie, la géographie, ou d'autres sciences sociales.

MODÈLE **A: Crois-tu que la Guadeloupe soit au nord d'Haïti?**
B: Non, je doute que la Guadeloupe soit au nord d'Haïti. Je crois qu'elle est au sud-est d'Haïti.

15 La cuisine, c'est bon! 1.2

Interpretive Listening

*Écrivez les numéros 1–6 sur votre papier. Écoutez les phrases. Puis, écrivez **D** si vous pensez que la phrase exprime* (expresses) *un doute, ou **C** si vous pensez qu'elle exprime une certitude.*

Resources

Activity 15

Answers

14

1. doive
2. aide
3. devions
4. ait
5. doive
6. puisse
7. soient
8. recycliez
9. écoutent

Answers will vary.

15 Script

1. Je doute que tu goûtes les trompettes de la mort.
2. Tu ne doutes pas que Clara aime la gastronomie de la Bourgogne.
3. Le chef est sûr que ses clients aiment sa sauce marinière.
4. Marie-Alix est certaine que la viande est servie avec de la moutarde.
5. Nous ne sommes pas certains que les enfants prennent des escargots.
6. Il n'est pas évident que l'entrée ait bon goût.

1. D
2. C
3. C
4. C
5. D
6. D

Reference Desk

For the **Connexions**, you may partner with the social studies teacher, or encourage students to test one another on what they are currently learning in social studies.

Communication

Interpersonal: Cooperative Groups

Put students into small groups. Ask them to bring a magazine picture that can be described using the subjunctive after an expression of emotion. The first student describes his or her picture: **Mme Bouquet est heureuse que sa fille lui téléphone**. The second student asks a question: **Qu'est-ce que sa fille lui dit?** The first student responds. Have students extend their discussion as far as they can. The remaining students take turns describing their pictures with the person to their right.

Differentiated Learning

Adapt

Ask students to write a series of statements, which may or may not reflect their beliefs. Have them mingle with other students reading one of their remarks. The other student agrees (**Je crois que**...) or disagrees (**Je doute que**...), repeating the student's statement. The students reverse roles. One student might say "**Je déteste le chocolat**." The other responds "**Je doute que tu détestes le chocolat**" or "**Je veux aller au cinéma**." The other student would say "**Je crois que tu veux aller au cinema**."

Decelerate

Give students the possible verb conjugations for **Activité 13**, so that they can focus on the proper use of the subjunctive and indicative.

Special Needs Students

Linguistically Challenged

Providing a review of regular and irregular conjugations in both subjunctive and indicative moods is essential each time the use of the subjunctive is expanded.

Resources

CA Communicative Activities

Share

Answers

16 Role-plays will vary.
17 Presentations will vary.
18 Presentations will vary.
19 Presentations will vary.

Reference Desk

1. If you have access to Passport, create a question for your students to share their response to a communicative activity.
2. Henri Gault, Christian Millau, and André Gayot are important names in the world of French cuisine. Restaurant critics and travel guide writers, they coined and promoted the term **nouvelle cuisine**. Have students research Gault, Millau, and Gayot to learn more.

Expansion

If you (or your school or students) have access to the channel TV5monde, you will find shows of the same nature as Activity 18: reality shows featuring culinary competitions, such as ***Qui sera le prochain grand pâtissier?*** You could record an episode and show it in class.

À vous la parole

Question centrale ? De quelles compétences ai-je besoin pour voyager?

Communiquez!

16 Au restaurant dijonnais 1.1, 3.1, 5.2

Interpersonal Speaking

Vous êtes dans un restaurant dijonnais avec un ami. Un(e) autre camarade de classe jouera le rôle du serveur ou de la serveuse. Le serveur ou la serveuse vous demande ce que vous souhaitez. Commandez une entrée, un plat principal, un dessert et une boisson. Quand le serveur ou la serveuse revient, vous vous plaignez du repas (le plat est froid, il y a une mouche dans la soupe, etc.). Soyez aussi créatif/créative que vous le souhaitez. Le serveur ou la serveuse doit essayer de résoudre votre problème. Présentez votre jeu de rôle devant la classe!

17 Mon restaurant à Dijon 1.3, 3.2, 5.2

Presentational Writing

Imaginez que vous ouvrez un restaurant américain à Dijon avec votre meilleur(e) ami(e). Vous êtes entièrement responsable du thème du restaurant, de la nourriture et des boissons que vous y servirez, ainsi que du divertissement et du décor. Préparez un plan d'affaires à envoyer à la mairie de Dijon pour qu'ils approuvent votre idée et votre restaurant. Soyez aussi créatif/créative que possible!

18 *La Brigade* 1.2, 1.3, 4.2, 5.2

Interpretive Viewing, Presentational Speaking

Vous avez été choisi(e) pour participer à l'émission de télévision *La Brigade*, une émission de télé-réalité qui met en compétition quatre cuisiniers. Pendant cette saison, le tournage se fera en Bourgogne. Votre défi sera de cuisiner un repas bourguignon pour impressionner les juges. Cherchez des recettes de cuisine traditionnelle de la Bourgogne, puis choisissez le plat que vous allez essayer de faire pour gagner la compétition. Avant d'entrer dans la cuisine, vous devez vous présenter devant les juges, puis décrire le plat que vous allez leur préparer, en mentionnant tous les ingrédients et comment vous allez les utiliser. Vous devez également exprimer la raison pour laquelle vous avez choisi ce plat. Bonus : vous pouvez gagner des points supplémentaires si vous mentionnez des informations culturelles sur la Bourgogne! Bonne chance!

Recherche : recettes bourgogne, émission la brigade

19 En péniche 1.2, 1.3, 3.2, 4.2, 5.1, 5.2

Interpretive Viewing, Presentational Writing

Vous voudriez mieux connaître la Bourgogne. Aussi, vous planifiez un voyage en péniche dans la région. Préparez un document avec les villes que vous allez visiter et une liste de choses à faire et à voir à chaque destination. Incluez une carte qui montre votre itinéraire. Enfin, partagez vos documents avec la classe pour créer un documentaire sur la Bourgogne.

Recherche : la bourgogne fluviale, comment visiter la bourgogne en bateau

Essential Instruction

1. Before doing **Activité 16** have students go online to find the menus of some top restaurants in Dijon so that they can include authentic appetizers, main courses, and desserts in their role-plays.
2. To help students brainstorm American specialties for their restaurant in **Activité 17**, have them visit American restaurants online from different regions of the United States.
3. For **Activité 19**, encourage students to be creative in their choice of format. They may want to make a commercial for television, a travelogue, or a multi-media presentation.
4. Have students listen with books closed as you read the sentences in **Activité 20**. Ask them to tell you where the statement was made.
5. For **Activité 21** students may choose, or be assigned, four of the ten options for a dialogue. Encourage them to make the dialogues realistic by weaving into the conversation as much vocabulary as they can.

Stratégie communicative

Pre-AP

Communiquez!

Practical Conversations

Quand vous voyagerez dans un pays francophone, vous aurez besoin d'obtenir des renseignements. Se souvenir de certaines expressions et de certains mots vous sera très utile au moment d'acheter un billet de train, de commander dans un restaurant ou dans un café, ou encore si vous avez besoin qu'on vous indique le chemin.

20 Débuts de dialogues pratiques 1.2, 5.1

Interpretive Reading

Lisez les questions ou les phrases ci-dessous et précisez l'endroit où on pourrait les entendre.

1. Vous pourriez vérifier s'il y a assez d'huile?
2. Je voudrais que vous me donniez des précisions sur les prestations.
3. Je cherche un blouson en cuir noir.
4. Le bœuf bourguignon que vous avez préparé est délicieux.
5. Vous avez des magazines de sport?
6. Vous pouvez m'indiquer le chemin? Je cherche le musée d'Orsay.
7. Quelle sont les spécialités de la région?
8. Vous avez un forfait ski?

21 Je me renseigne en voyage 1.1, 5.1, 5.2

Interpersonal Writing and Speaking

Avec votre partenaire, créez une conversation pour quatre endroits de la liste. Posez une question, demandez un service, ou renseignez-vous de manière générale.

1. une station-service
2. un marché
3. un kiosque à journaux
4. un guichet de cinéma
5. un hôtel
6. un restaurant en Normandie
7. une réception de mariage
8. un cercle de conversation à l'Alliance française
9. une gare
10. chez une famille française

La Gare de Lyon, à Paris

Answers

19

1. à la station-service
2. à l'hôtel
3. au magasin/centre commercial
4. au restaurant/à une soirée
5. au kiosque à journaux/à la librairie
6. dans la rue
7. au restaurant
8. à la station de ski

20 Conversations will vary.

Expansion

Have students create a handbook, page, or fold-out of useful phrases in French, to be used as a tool for tourists. They can present the phrases in categories of contexts. Have them publish their phrasebook online and/or distribute copies to people who are traveling to France in the near future. Consider combining their best work and self-publishing it as a fundraiser for your French program.

Differentiated Learning

Expand

Ask students to go online to research the locations they will use as a basis for the conversation in **Activité 20**. This research will afford them more details for their dialogues. For example, photos of **une réception de mariage** found online will act as prompts for a dialogue.

Accelerate

Have pairs or small groups brainstorm vocabulary, verbs, and expressions needed for two of the destinations in **Activité 20**, then create a poster list of the expressions and display them around the room for the class to consult as they work on their own conversations.

Decelerate

Make **Activité 20** a multiple-choice activity for students who are struggling.

Learning Styles

Visual Learners

Have students create a visual to complement each of the four dialogues they choose from **Activité 21** and then use them when they present the conversation.

Resources

- *Vocabulaire actif*
- eVisual
- Workbook 1–4
- Flash Cards
- Listening Activity 1
- G & V Practice Games

Reference Desk

1. There are many different film **genres**: **un western**, **une comédie**, **un film d'horreur**, **un film de science-fiction**, **un film classique**, **un film d'aventures**, **un film d'action**, **un film policier** (*detective*), **un documentaire**, **un drame**, **une comédie musicale**, **un voyage dans le temps** (*time travel*).
2. Useful terms: **le premier rôle** (*leading male actor*), **le premier rôle féminin** (*leading female role*), **le second rôle** (*supporting actor*), **le metteur en scène** (*director*), **une course-poursuite** (*car chase*). **Un navet** (*a turnip*) is a bad film.
3. The word **un synopsis** may also be used in the feminine form, **une synopsis**.

Expansion

Ask students to write a synopsis for the movie *Black Panther*, featured in the vocabulary spread. Or, ask them to write an entire posting for a movie of their choice.

Culture

Products : Information

AlloCiné was launched as a telecommunications company in 1993, but since then, it has switched its primary attention to its website (allocine.com), on which it offers news and information on the latest French cinematic releases, and its phone- and web-based movie ticket sales.

Leçon C Vocabulaire actif

Le cinéma 1.2, 2.2, 3.1, 5.2

CINÉMA **LES NOUVEAUTÉS (f.)**

1. Le sens de la fête

Genre (m.) : Comédie
Durée (f.) : 1h 56min
Réalisateurs (m.) : Éric Toledano et Olivier Nakache
Casting (m.) : Jean-Pierre Bacri, Gilles Lellouche, Eye Haïdara plus
Date de **sortie** (f.) : le 4 octobre

On **a tourné le film** dans un château.

Le synopsis du film :
Max est traiteur organisateur de réceptions de mariage. Cela fait une trentaine d'années qu'il travaille. Cette fois, il s'agit du mariage de Pierre et Héléna. Préparé comme à son habitude, Max voit pourtant cette soirée tourner en catastrophe. Humour et émotions viendront défier le sens de la fête !

Les critiques (f.) :
★★★☆☆ Presse (24 critiques)
★★★★☆ Internautes (3 avis)

Voir **la bande-annonce**.

Les horaires (m.) et les salles (f.) de cinéma :
UGD Capitole
134 la Canebière
13001 Marseille
12h15 ; 16h30 ; 20h45

2. Black Panther — **le titre**
Pays de Production : États-Unis
Film d'action/fantastique américain — **une vedette**
Réalisateur : Ryan Coogler
Acteurs : Chadwick Boseman, Michael B. Jordan, Lupita Nyong'o plus
Durée : 2h 14min — **un long métrage**
13h45 (vo, **sous-titrée**), 17h35 (vf, **doublée**) — **le doublage**

la version originale (VO) | **les sous-titres (m.)** | **la version française (VF)**

Essential Instruction

1. Have students listen to the vocabulary **Le cinéma**. Ask them questions about the text using the vocabulary in the margins.
2. Have the students listen to **Pour la conversation** and the additional vocabulary.
3. Put the vocabulary from *Reference Desk* on the board and ask students to give examples of each genre. Ask students to name their favorite actors and directors, a film with a car chase, and **navets** that they have seen.
4. Expand the discussion to current television shows as well since they have the same elements and students are apt to watch televison more regularly.
5. Have students read **Activité 1**. Ask them questions 1–6.
6. Let students know that "VO" refers to the original language the film was made in, which may or may not have French subtitles (since it is being shown in France), whereas the designation "VF" refers to a film that is dubbed in French over the original foreign (non-French) language dialogue.

Pour la conversation

How do I say what I'm not in the mood for?

» **Je ne suis pas trop d'humeur pour** une comédie dramatique.
I'm not in the mood for a dramatic comedy.

How do I relate the opinion of others?

» **Il paraît que** c'est très drôle.
It appears it's very funny.

How do I ask about someone's impression?

» Quelles sont **tes impressions** du film ?
What are your impressions of the movie?

How do I express disagreement?

» Je ne **partage** pas ton avis.
I don't share your opinion.

Et si je voulais dire... ?

un cascadeur	*stuntman*
la distribution	*the cast*
un figurant	*extra (actor)*
une représentation	*performance*
applaudir	*to clap*
huer	*to boo*

L'argot des ados

Le Cinéma

le cinoche	le cinéma
un(e) mordu(e) du cinéma	un fan
un nanar/ un navet	un mauvais film
une star	une vedette

1 Une critique 1.2, 2.2, 3.1

Interpretive Reading

Lisez la critique du film suivant, puis répondez aux questions.

Boule & Bill

2013. 2h10. Comédie française en couleurs.
La dernière grande comédie pour ceux qui aiment rire vient de sortir dans les salles. Allez voir ce film tout de suite ! Le casting est très fort. Un long métrage par un réalisateur bien connu qui pourrait devenir un classique. Évitez la bande-annonce, qui en révèle trop sur les personnages et les événements. Si vous voulez voir une comédie, ou tout simplement rire de bon cœur, ne cherchez pas plus loin : *Boule & Bill* est ce qu'il vous faut. C'est un film touchant et drôle à la fois au sujet d'un chien adopté qui a un peu trop d'énergie. Vous partagerez mon avis. Je vous le promets.

1. Quelle est la durée du film ?
2. Quand est-ce qu'il est sorti ?
3. Que pense le critique de ce film ?
4. Qu'est-ce qu'on ne doit pas faire ?
5. Quand est-ce qu'on devrait choisir ce film ?
6. Quel est le synopsis du film ?

Resources

Pour la conversation
Et si je voulais dire... ?

Answers

1

1. 2h10
2. 2013
3. Il pense que le film a un très bon casting et pourrait devenir un classique.
4. On ne doit pas regarder la bande-annonce.
5. On devrait choisir ce film quand on veut rire.
6. Il s'agit d'un chien adopté qui a trop d'énergie.

Reference Desk

1. **Mordu(e)** comes from the verb **mordre** (*to bite*). Someone who loves the movies is "bitten" by them. The expression also applies to other passions.
2. French films have often been the inspiration for American movies, including:
   - **Intouchables**, 2011 (*The Upside*, 2017)
   - **Banlieue 13**, 2004 (*Brick Mansions*, 2014)
   - **LOL (Laughing Out Loud)**, 2008 (*LOL*, 2012)
   - **Le Dîner des Cons**, 1998 (*Dinner for Schmucks*, 2010)
   - **Inside**, 2007 (*Inside*, 2016)
   - **Plein Soleil**, 1960 (*The Talented Mr. Ripley*, 1999)
   - **La Cage aux Folles**, 1978 (*The Birdcage*, 1996)
   - **Trois hommes et un couffin**, 1985 (*Three Men and a Baby*, 1987)

nouvelle orthographe **paraitre, il parait que**

Critical Thinking

The movie posters and film titles of French adaptations of American movie titles provide interesting topics for discussion. Show students some posters of movies they may recognize and discuss decisions made to appeal to a French audience. Discuss, for example, why "Black Panther" is not literally translated "La Panthère Noire."

Differentiated Learning

Accelerate

Have students go online to research current popular French films. Ask them to determine the percentage of foreign films to French films that are in theaters and to identify the popular American actors in current films.

Recherche : l'officiel des spectacles

Decelerate

Give students time to go online to explore **AlloCiné**. Ask them to list what American television series are playing in France. Have them select one, read five critiques, and then make a list of positive and negative expressions used by viewers. Lower-ability students may enjoy this site, the result being that they read more French out of curiosity.

Special Needs Students

At-Risk Students

Discussing films can be a good hook to get these students involved. Young people enjoy going to movies and watching Netflix. Look for ways to engage them in conversations about topics that interest them.

Resources

Activity 3

Answers

2

1. le genre
2. le titre
3. la durée
4. le réalisateur
5. le casting
6. le synopsis
7. la salle de cinéma
8. la version

3

1. C'est la durée du film.
2. C'est la salle de cinéma.
3. C'est la version du film.
4. C'est la description du film.
5. C'est le genre du film.
6. C'est la critique du film.
7. Ce sont les sous-titres.
8. C'est le casting du film.
9. C'est le réalisateur du film.

Reference Desk

L'Officiel des spectacles, a weekly publication since 1946, aims to list every single cultural event occurring in Paris, from films to theater productions to exhibits and fairs. The publication is divided into nine sections: film, theater, concerts, museums & exhibitions, parks & monuments & cemeteries & churches & hidden places, guided tours, activities for children, cabarets, and restaurants.

Communication

Interpersonal: Paired Practice

Using **Activité 2** as a model, have students work with partners to recreate two ***Officiel des spectacles*** film listings. They can use French or American films but must include all of the categories. Once done, students work with another set of partners to discuss their films. They ask each other questions using the vocabulary in the box, for example, **Quel est le titre du film? C'est quel genre? Comment s'appelle le réalisateur?** If time, have students share with the rest of the class.

2 *L'Officiel des spectacles* 1.2, 2.2, 3.1, 5.2

Interpretive Viewing

Trouvez l'expression qui convient aux différentes parties du guide.

le genre **le réalisateur** **la salle de cinéma** **le titre**
la durée **la version** **le synopsis** **le casting**

2 3 1

C **Taxi 5**. France. Couleur. 2h15min. Comédie policière, de
4 Franck Gastambide. Sylvain Marot est un super flic parisien. Le maire de Marseille lui donne une mission spéciale : celle d'arrêter un gang italien. Avec Franck Gastambide, Malik Bentalha, Sabrina Ouazini, Bernard Farcy. 5
UCC Cité Ciné Les Halles 1er. MK2 Beaubourg 3ème. UGC Montparnasse 6ème. UGC Normandie 8ème. Cinéma des Cinéastes 17ème.

J **Les Proies (The Beguiled)**. États-Unis. Couleur. 1h31. Drame de Sofia
6 { Coppola. En pleine guerre de Sécession, un soldat unioniste gravement blessé est recueilli dans un pensionnat de jeunes filles en plein Sud des États-Unis. **Gaumont Opéra Premier 2ème** (vo). **Grand Action 5ème** (vo). **Gaumont Champs Elysées Marignan 8ème** (vo) ; **Max Linder Panorama 9ème** (vo). **Majestic Bastille 11ème** (vo). } 7

8

3 C'est quoi ou c'est qui ? 1.2, 1.3

Interpretive Reading

Identifiez la personne ou la chose.

MODÈLE Le film s'appelle *Daddy's Home 2*.
C'est le titre du film.

1. Le film commence à 14h00 et se termine à 15h40.
2. On passe le film au Gaumont.
3. C'est en VO.
4. Il s'agit de deux pères qui partagent la garde de leurs enfants.
5. C'est une comédie.
6. « C'est une comédie qui fait rire. Vous allez l'adorer. »
7. Pour le public français, il y a des mots écrits en français sur l'écran.
8. Will Ferrell, Mark Wahlberg, et Mel Gibson sont les acteurs principaux du film.
9. Sean Anders a aussi tourné le film.

Essential Instruction

1. Have students do **Activité 2** and **Activité 3** in pairs.
2. Ask students to listen and respond to questions 1–6, **Activité 4**.
3. Put the desks in a circle and have students take turns asking the questions in **Activité 5**. Since this is such a popular topic, you should be able to expand the conversation and have a lively discussion about their personal taste in films.
4. Ask students to talk about their favorite television shows. Do they think there is a difference between television and movie stars? Do they pay attention to the name of the director of a film or television series? Do they prefer movies made from book series like Harry Potter or The Lord of the Rings? Why or why not?

4 Quel film on va voir? 1.2

Interpretive Listening

Écrivez les numéros 1–6 sur votre papier. Écoutez la conversation, puis écrivez un mot ou une expression pour répondre aux questions que vous entendez.

5 Questions personnelles 1.1, 3.2, 5.2

Interpersonal Speaking

Répondez aux questions avec un partenaire.

1. Est-ce que tu préfères voir les films au cinéma ou à la télé? Comment décides-tu quels films tu vas voir au cinéma?
2. Quels aspects d'un film sont importants dans ton choix — le genre, les acteurs, le réalisateur, ou autre chose?
3. Est-ce que tu regardes quelquefois des films étrangers (*foreign*)? Préfères-tu voir un film étranger avec des sous-titres ou doublé en anglais? Pourquoi?
4. Quelles différences y a-t-il entre tes goûts et les goûts de tes ami(e)s? Et entre les goûts des ados et les goûts des adultes que tu connais?
5. Quel est le dernier film que tu as vu? Quel film as-tu envie de voir bientôt? Pourquoi?
6. Quel(s) film(s) français ou en français as-tu vu(s)?

Traditions et pratiques 1.2, 2.1

Les Français vont souvent au cinéma entre amis, ou aussi en couple, pour voir une comédie romantique. Mais aussi, beaucoup de jeunes cinéphiles n'hésitent pas à fréquenter les salles de cinéma seuls!

On recycle!

Review the relative pronouns and try to have your partner guess who is your favorite actor/actress/filmmaker. Give them clues such as:

C'est une personne que j'admire. C'est une personne qui joue dans des comédies. Le dernier film dans lequel cette personne a joué a gagné un Oscar.

Resources

Activity 4

Answers

4 Script

Ahmed: Quelles sont les nouveautés cette semaine?
Yasmina: Il y a un film en version originale avec Adam Sandler.
Ahmed: Je ne suis pas d'humeur pour un film en version originale. Il faut lire les sous-titres. C'est nul!
Yasmina: Le film avec Adam Sandler semble intéressant. Le casting est sympa et il paraît que c'est drôle.
Ahmed: Qui est le réalisateur et tu as regardé la critique?
Yasmina: Je ne connais ni l'un ni l'autre, mais la bande-annonce est très bonne.
Ahmed: C'est quel genre?
Yasmina: C'est une comédie. Tu as envie de rire, non?
Ahmed: Oui, d'accord, allons-y pour une comédie!

1. Quel est le genre du film qu'Ahmed et Yasmina vont voir?
2. Qui joue le rôle principal?
3. Ahmed et Yasmina veulent-ils pleurer au cinéma?
4. Yasmina a-t-elle lu la critique?
5. Qu'est-ce qu'elle a vu du film?
6. C'est un film français?

1. une comédie
2. Adam Sandler
3. Non, ils veulent rire.
4. non
5. la bande-annonce
6. non

5 Answers will vary.

Expansion

Use **Activité 5** to have groups survey the class. Each group reports back on the results from one of the questions, presenting a visual along with their information.

Differentiated Learning

Expand

In small groups, have students reminisce about the films and television shows they watched as children. What was the very first film they remember? What was the story about? What was their reaction to it? Have students report back to the class about the programs and films they discussed. Take a poll of their favorites.

Accelerate

Ask these students to learn the **Et si je voulais dire…?** and **L'argot des ados** vocabulary from p. 297 and create an activity to teach it to their classmates. Encourage them to create a dialogue to demonstrate the new expressions used in a realistic context as part of their activity.

Decelerate

Ask students who need extra time learning vocabulary to copy the expressions from **Et si je voulais dire…?** and **L'argot des ados** before the students do their introduction activity.

Resources

- Dialogue Activity 6
- Dialogue Video
- WB Workbook 5

Answers

6

1. les films
2. La Coupole
3. réalisateur
4. synopsis, ex-chef d'orchestre soviétique
5. nanar, catastrophe

Reference Desk

The **Groupe CinéChèque** is an association that has existed since 2000. it sells **Ciné Chèques**, which are accepted in most movie theatres, any time, for any movie. It functions basically as a gift card.

Game

De quoi s'agit-il?

Have students work in small groups to write a short synopsis of five popular films from their childhood to the present. Next, get them together to play a guessing game with the other groups in the class. **C'est l'histoire d'un ogre vert qui a, comme copain, un âne bavard.** (*Shrek*)

Critical Thinking

Comparison

Note that "**style Hollywood**" can be used derogatively to criticize films that fall into a clichéd type, usually characterized by a big budget, a star cast, high emotionality, and a melodramatic soundtrack.

Expansion

Consider showing students the trailers for the films mentioned. This will give them a connection to the text and motivate them to read carefully.

Rencontres culturelles

On va au multiplexe

1.2, 2.2, 3.2, 5.2

Élodie et Karim consultent les films sur AlloCiné.

Élodie : Quel genre de film te dit ?
Karim : Clique d'abord sur Accueil, pour voir les nouveautés.
Élodie : Tiens, *Le concert* passe à La Coupole ! C'est d'un excellent réalisateur !
Karim : Ah oui ? Lequel ?
Élodie : Radu Mihaileanu. Et le casting est composé de vraies vedettes !
Karim : Je ne suis pas trop d'humeur pour une comédie dramatique, mais voyons le synopsis : « Un ex-chef d'orchestre soviétique est maintenant homme de ménage au Bolchoï. Au travail, il tombe sur un fax adressé au directeur : il s'agit d'une invitation à venir jouer à Paris. Il réunit ses anciens copains musiciens et les emmène tous à Paris.... » Il paraît que c'est très drôle. Que disent les critiques ?
Élodie : Les critiques donnent quatre étoiles, ça promet !
Karim : Bon, je veux bien. Prends les Ciné Chèques et allons-y.

(Après le film....)

Karim : Quelles sont tes impressions du film ?
Élodie : J'ai éprouvé une émotion intense. C'est un vrai chef-d'œuvre !
Karim : Je ne partage pas ton avis, je suis plutôt blasé ; le ton était plat, les actions stéréotypées, trop de pauses entre les dialogues à mon goût !
Élodie : N'as-tu donc pas apprécié la musique ?
Karim : Laquelle ?
Élodie : Celle du final, de Tchaïkovski !
Karim : Non, vraiment, c'est un nanar style Hollywood. Une vraie catastrophe !

6 On va au multiplexe

1.2, 2.2

Complétez les phrases suivantes.

1. Karim et Élodie voient... sur AlloCiné.
2. Élodie suggère le film *Le concert*, qui passe à....
3. Le... est Radu Mihaileanu.
4. Le... indique qu'il s'agit d'un... qui emmène ses anciens copains musiciens à Paris.
5. Karim pense que le film est un... et une....

Essential Instruction

1. Have students watch the video **On va au multiplexe**. Ask general comprehension questions.
2. Students watch the video again and answer the questions 1–5 in **Activité 6**.
3. Write the terms **réactions positives** and **réactions négatives** on the board. Have students find the comments in the dialogue about the film that could be put into each category, for example, "**C'est d'un excellent réalisateur**" or "**C'est un nanar style Hollywood.**"
4. Place students into high- and low-ability groups to read **Extension**, and then have them answer the question about the dialogue. A short class discussion can follow.
5. Students work and go online to research the actresses, director, and films mentioned in **Extension**.

EXTENSION **Les criminelles** 1.2

Alexandre et Simon sont à la FNAC au rayon Films et Séries.

Alexandre : Tu as acheté tout ça !
Simon : Il y a une promotion, et en plus des titres géniaux.
Alexandre : Lesquels ?
Simon : Criminelles… Brigitte Bardot, Catherine Deneuve, Jeanne Moreau, Isabelle Adjani, Isabelle Huppert….
Alexandre : Dans quels films ?
Simon : Devine !
Alexandre : Deneuve, *La sirène du Mississippi,* Moreau… le Truffaut… *La mariée était en noir* ? Adjani, *Mortelle randonnée* ; Bardot, *La vérité* ; et Huppert… lequel ? Elle a beaucoup joué les criminelles….
Simon : Surtout chez Chabrol.
Alexandre : Difficile… euh… je sais pas, moi….
Simon : C'est un bon Chabrol ! Viens chez moi, je te ferai une projection privée… ça sera la surprise….

EXTENSION Le film qu'Alexandre n'arrive pas à deviner est de quel réalisateur ? Les garçons parlent de combien d'acteurs et de réalisateurs ? Est-ce qu'Alexandre et Simon sont des cinéphiles ? Expliquez. 1.3

Differentiated Learning

Accelerate
Students write a review of a movie that they have seen recently using the format of **Le cinéma**, p. 296.

Decelerate
Have students research five top French and American directors and make a chart with their names and the titles and dates of their five most successful films.

Special Needs Students

Visually Impaired/Auditory Impairment
These students may not go to movies often but can benefit from discussions about current films in terms of plot, vocabulary, and cast.

Resources

Extension

Answers

EXTENSION

Claude Chabrol ; 7 (5 actrices et 2 réalisateurs) ; Oui, ils semblent connaître beaucoup de films.

Reference Desk

1. Brigitte Bardot (1934) made 47 films, recorded 50 songs, and became an iconic French sex symbol of the 1950s and 1960s.
2. Catherine Deneuve (1943) won an Academy Award and **César** for ***Indochine*** and a **César** for ***Le dernier métro***. Her face was chosen to represent Marianne, the symbol of France, from 1985 to 1989.
3. Jeanne Moreau (1928–2017), an actress, singer, director, and screenwriter, was best known as the star of François Truffaut's classic film ***Jules et Jim***.
4. Isabelle Adjani (1955) was awarded the most **César** for best actress. She starred in the films ***Camille Claudel*** and ***La Reine Margot***.
5. Isabelle Huppert (1953) has made 90 films and appeared on television. Her famous films include ***Violette Nozière***, ***Le pianiste***, and ***La cérémonie***.
6. Claude Chabrol (1930–2010), known for his thrillers, was a prolific film director of the French New Wave movement, **la Nouvelle Vague**.
7. François Truffaut (1932–1984) is often considered one of France's greatest directors and, like Chabrol, a founding father of **la Nouvelle Vague**, a generation of 1950s French filmmakers with a penchant for reality and breaking from established cinematic tradition.

Culture

Note that the boys refer to films by their directors (**"le Truffaut"** [**François Truffaut**] and **"C'est un bon Chabrol"** [**Claude Chabrol**]) in the same way as we might refer to a painting as "a Van Gogh" or "a Picasso."

Resources

Points de départ

WB Workbook 6

Explore

Reference Desk

1. France produces around 300 feature films each year. Its total number of movie admissions is third after the United States and India (both of which have substantially larger populations), and its total revenue from films is third in the world after the United States and Japan. France is one of a handful of countries where US-made movies do not hold a majority share of the film market. A 2015 study reveals US and French movies are the most appreciated by moviegoers around the world.
2. If you have access to Passport, find a news article related to **le cinéma** and show it to your students.

Communication

Interpersonal: Paired Practice

Have students work with a partner to define and give examples of **un film commercial** (*Twilight*, big studio, large budget) and **un film indépendant** (*500 Days of Summer*, Sundance Film Festival, small budget). They then can compare ideas with another set of partners. Finally, discuss the definitions as a class and make a list of favorites from both categories.

Points de départ

Pre-AP

Question centrale ? De quelles compétences ai-je besoin pour voyager?

Le Septième art en France

1.2, 2.1, 2.2, 3.1, 4.2, 5.2

La France est l'une des grandes nations du cinéma : par son histoire avec l'invention du spectacle cinématographique et les débuts du cinéma, puis avec l'expérimentation des formes, depuis *Le voyage dans la lune* de Georges Méliès (1902) en passant par *The Artist* (2011) et continuant à ce jour ; et par son public, car en France, le cinéma n'est pas seulement un divertissement*, c'est un art.

Le cinéma français est un cinéma d'inventeurs de formes : de ses débuts avec Georges Méliès et Abel Gance (*Napoléon*, 1927) ; du cinéma réaliste (Jean Renoir, *La bête humaine*, 1938) et poétique (Marcel Carné, *Les enfants du Paradis*, 1945) ; de la Nouvelle Vague* avec Claude Chabrol (*Le beau Serge*, 1958), Jean-Luc Godard (*À bout de souffle*, 1959), et François Truffaut (*Jules et Jim*, 1961) ; des années 1960, avec Alain Resnais (*L'année dernière à Marienbad*, 1961), Jacques Demy (*Les parapluies de Cherbourg*, 1964), et Philippe de Broca (*L'homme de Rio*, 1964) ; jusqu'à l'époque contemporaine avec Jean-Pierre Jeunet (*Le fabuleux destin d'Amélie Poulain*, 2001), Cédric Klapisch (*Casse-tête chinois*, 2013), Abdellatif Kechiche (*La vie d'Adèle*, 2013), Luc Besson (*Valérian et la Cité des mille planètes*, 2017), ou Catherine Corsini (*Un amour impossible*, 2018).

Mais le cinéma en France est aussi une pratique culturelle qui a son public : les cinéphiles* vont d'abord voir un film pour le réalisateur qui l'a fait et qui est considéré comme un auteur. Clint Eastwood et Woody Allen n'oublient jamais de rappeler que c'est en France qu'ils ont été d'abord reconnus comme de vrais auteurs.

Paris est la capitale mondiale de la cinéphilie*. C'est la seule ville au monde où l'on puisse voir la même semaine 300 à 400 films dans 30 ou 40 langues différentes. Le premier acte d'un cinéphile parisien chaque mercredi matin, c'est d'acheter *L'Officiel (des spectacles)* ou de consulter *AlloCiné*.

Recherche : georges méliès hugo, la nouvelle vague, filmographie (+ NOM DU RÉALISATEUR)

---

divertissement *entertainment* ; **Nouvelle Vague** *New Wave* ; **cinéphile** fan du cinéma ; **cinéphilie** amour du cinéma

Mot-clé

C'est un critique franco-italien, Ricciotto Canudo, qui a créé le terme **le septième art**, en 1923. Sur sa liste le cinéma vient après la poésie, la musique, le théâtre, les arts plastiques, l'éloquence (c'est-à-dire la rhétorique), et la danse.

1.2, 2.1

Traditions et pratiques

Les Français ont toujours eu un appétit pour le cinéma. Traditionnellement, les films français présentent toujours un récit, une histoire, quelque soit le genre du film. Aussi, au cinéma comme en littérature, un bon film doit avoir une dimension psychologique.

Essential Instruction

1. Have students list **les sept arts** as shown in **Mot-clé**.
2. Assign to groups of students the 15 films listed in **Le Septième art en France**. Have each group present its film to the class by including the year it was made, the director, actors, plot, and awards. If you deem it appropriate, have students watch trailers of these movies online.
3. Ask students to research and compare the awards for the Cannes Film Festival with the Academy Awards.

Produits

Le cinéma a commencé en France en 1895 avec l'invention du **cinématographe** par Auguste et Louis Lumière, ou les Frères Lumière. Leur premier film s'appelle *Sortie d'usine*.

Le film à succès de Martin Scorsese, *Hugo*, qui se passe dans les années 20, est un hommage au réalisateur français George Méliès.

1.2, 2.2, 3.1, 5.2

1.2, 4.2

Comparaisons

Allez-vous au cinéma pour voir l'œuvre du réalisateur, ou pour les acteurs? Quelles sont les autres raisons qui vous amènent à assister à une séance de cinéma?

Le Festival de Cannes **1.2, 2.2, 3.1, 4.2, 5.2**

Le Festival de Cannes ou Festival international du film est le festival le plus médiatisé du monde. En 1946, année de sa première édition, il n'y avait que quelques centaines de participants; ils sont aujourd'hui plus de 40 000 dont 4 500 journalistes, 1 000 journaux de presse écrite, 300 photographes, 300 chaînes de télévision, 150 radios, 200 agences de presse* et 150 envoyés spéciaux* pour la presse en ligne.

La récompense suprême de Cannes, c'est la Palme d'or: en plus de 70 ans, le Festival a couronné* un peu plus de 500 films. Le Festival de Cannes est synonyme de révolutions esthétiques, de découvertes de nouveaux talents, d'hommages bouleversants* et de bousculades* gigantesques sur les fameuses marches: toute une histoire de lumière et de gloire, de flashs et de strass*.

Emmanuelle Seigner, Roman Polanski, et Eva Green (*D'après une histoire vraie*)

Recherche: festival de cannes, palme d'or

agence de presse *news agency*; **envoyés spéciaux** *special correspondents*; **a couronné** *has crowned*; **hommages bouleversants** *touching tributes*; **bousculades** *jostles*; **strass** *rhinestones*

Produits

Parmi les prix décernés à Cannes sont **la Palme d'or, le Grand Prix**, et **le Prix du Jury**. Le prix le plus prestigieux est la Palme d'or pour le meilleur film de la compétition. Le Grand Prix récompense le film qui manifeste un esprit de recherche et le plus d'originalité. Le Prix du Jury récompense un film aimé par le jury.

1.2, 2.2, 4.2, 5.2

Le réalisateur Jacques Audiard reçoit la Palme d'or pour son film *Dheepan*.

Reference Desk

If you have access to Passport, find a video or a news article related to **Cannes** or **le Festival de Cannes** and show it to your students.

Communication

Interpersonal: Cooperative Groups

Have students discuss the **Comparaisons** question in small groups and report back to the class. Ask a scribe to tally the number of students who choose a film for the director or for the actors, and record on the board their reasons for going to the movies.

Critical Thinking

Reflection

Have students discuss the purpose(s) of cinema and going to the movies. They may come up with any number of ideas, including pure entertainment, a form of escapism, and an attempt to comment on our reality. Encourage students to explore these opposing purposes: do they prefer to go to the movies to get away from reality or to have a closer look at it? What are some films they have seen that serve either purpose?

Differentiated Learning

Adapt

Put mixed-ability students in pairs. Have them select a movie, either a classic or a contemporary film, to discuss in the style of Roger Ebert and Gene Siskel. (You will have to explain that these were two movie critics who did not always agree on the quality of films.) One person finds it excellent while the other person is less enthusiastic. They may use **On va au multiplexe** as the template for their dialogue. Have them use the vocabulary and expressions from the lesson.

Multiple Intelligences

Visual-Spatial

Have students make a publicity poster for a French film. They must list actors and directors, and add viewer comments.

Verbal-Linguistic/Bodily-Kinesthetic

Have students act out improvised short scenes from popular movies; the other students guess the titles.

Answers

7 Activities will vary.

Perspectives
Possible answer: Le cinéma français permet d'exporter la culture francaise à l'étranger.; Les films français ont du succès à l'étranger, et les étrangers participent aux festivaux du film en France.

Game

Jeopardy

Make a Jeopardy board with these headings: **Vocabulaire**, **Expressions**, **Films**, **Acteurs**, **Réalisateurs**. Students play the game in teams making questions from the cues you give them. You can find Jeopardy game templates online.

Recherche: free flash jeopardy review generator

Reference Desk

The release and distribution of US movies was subjugated to a quota from 1938–1946, in part due to World War II and also to an effort to preserve French cinema. The quotas were dropped in 1946 as part of the terms of post-war loans from the United States to France.

Les César 1.2, 2.2, 3.1, 4.2, 5.2

Les César ont été créés en 1976 sur le modèle des Oscar hollywoodiens. La compression en métal qui symbolise le César est due au sculpteur du même nom: César, qui a donné son nom à la récompense. Chaque année ils couronnent le meilleur du cinéma français mais ils élisent* aussi le meilleur film étranger. Les cinq principales récompenses sont le meilleur film, le meilleur réalisateur, la meilleure actrice, le meilleur acteur, et le meilleur scénario.

L'actrice française Déborah Lukumuena reçoit le César de la meilleure actrice dans un second rôle.

Les champions des meilleurs films sont: *Le dernier métro* (1981) de François Truffaut et *Cyrano de Bergerac* (1991) de Jean-Paul Rappeneau avec 10 César chacun; *Le Prophète* de Jacques Audiard (9 César en 2010) et *De battre mon cœur s'est arrêté* (8 César en 2006); *Providence* d'Alain Resnais (1978), *Au revoir les enfants* de Louis Malle (7 César en 1988), *Le Pianiste* de Roman Polanski (2003), et *Timbuktu* d'Abderrahmane Sissako (2015).

Les réalisateurs les plus récompensés sont Jacques Audiard (9 César), Roman Polanski (8 César), Alain Resnais, Bertrand Tavernier, Jean-Jacques Annaud, et Claude Sautet.

Meilleure actrice, elles sont quelques-unes à avoir reçu plusieurs César: Catherine Deneuve, Romy Schneider, Isabelle Huppert, Marion Cotillard, Annie Girardot, Jeanne Moreau, Nathalie Baye, Dominique Blanc et Isabelle Adjani (5, record absolu). Meilleur acteur, ils sont peu nombreux à l'avoir reçu plusieurs fois: Gérard Depardieu, Daniel Auteuil, Michel Serrault, Mathieu Amalric et André Dussolier. Tahar Rahim (*Le Prophète*) a reçu en 2010 en même temps le trophée du meilleur acteur et celui du meilleur espoir.

Clint Eastwood est sans doute le cinéaste étranger favori des français; il compte sept César, dont un César d'honneur, reçu en 1998. Les autres personnalités étrangères qui comptabilisent le plus de César sont Ettore Scola, Pedro Almodovar et Ken Loach (2 César).

élisent *elect*

7 Activités culturelles

1.2, 2.1, 3.2

Faites les activités suivantes.

1. Faites un axe chronologique des succès cinématographiques français, ou de l'évolution du cinéma en France. Puis, choisissez un film en particulier et écrivez un synopsis.
2. Cherchez des films qui ont reçu la Palme d'or dans les cinq dernières années. Est-ce qu'ils sont sortis dans votre pays?
3. Trouvez des vedettes prises en photo au dernier Festival de Cannes. Vos acteurs ou actrices préférés y étaient-ils?
4. Qui a été récompensé lors de la dernière cérémonie des César?
   - Meilleur film
   - Meilleur réalisateur
   - Meilleur acteur
   - Meilleure actrice

Recherche: prix du festival de cannes (+ ANNÉE)

Perspectives

Selon le Ministère des Affaires Étrangères français, le cinéma français est un « axe fort de la politique culturelle de la France à l'étranger ». Pourquoi les Français sont-ils si fiers de leur cinéma et certains de son influence?

Essential Instruction

1. Have students outline the information in **Les César** using the categories **Meilleur Film, Les Réalisateurs, Meilleure Actrice, et Meilleur Acteur.**
2. Assign **Activité 7**. Discuss each task, explaining your expectations. When done, ask students to share their work with the class.
3. Have students read **Du côté des médias**.
4. After doing **Activité 8**, have students create a poster for the Cannes festival.
5. Students can find posters from previous years online.

Recherche: affiche officielle du festival de cannes

Du côté des médias 1.2

Regardez l'affiche du festival de Cannes, puis répondez aux questions.

8 Les affiches du Festival de Cannes 1.3, 3.1, 5.1

1. Reconnaissez-vous la personne sur l'affiche? Qui est-elle? Cette affiche a paru pour quel festival et en quelle année?
2. Cherchez des affiches du festival de Cannes de 1946 à aujourd'hui. Choisissez vos cinq préférées, et expliquez à votre groupe pourquoi vous les aimez. Ensuite, votre groupe devra voter pour la meilleure affiche dans chacune de quatre catégories de votre choix (par exemple: la plus esthétique, la plus classique, la plus laide, et la plus ingénieuse). Faites un document de votre palmarès (liste des gagnants), en présentant les images et une petite légende, puis partagez votre présentation (en ligne) avec la classe.

Recherche : toutes les affiches du festival de cannes 1.2, 2.1, 3.1, 5.2

Perspectives

Je pense que les stars de cinéma, bien que millionnaires ou milliardaires, ont une vie très difficile. Constamment sous les regards de la presse, plus de vie privée, jugés, comparés aux autres célébrités, leurs vies tournent automatiquement au scandale s'ils commettent une faute. —Tilitilt

Est-ce que cette personne envie les grands acteurs de cinéma? Pourquoi ou pourquoi pas?

Answers

8

1. C'est l'actrice suédoise Ingrid Bergman. Elle a paru pour le 68ème festival, en 2015.
2. Presentations will vary.

Perspectives

Non, cette personne n'envie pas la vie des acteurs, parce qu'elle trouve qu'ils n'ont pas de vie privée.

Reference Desk

Le Festival International du Film de Cannes (Festival de Cannes) is an annual film festival usually held in May. This prestigious festival is invitation-only and is an important showcase for European films. It was founded in 1946 with 16 countries presenting films. The festival previews new films of all genres, including documentaries. Its most prestigious award, **la Palme d'or**, was created in 1955.

Critical Thinking

Comparison

Have your students compare the Oscar statuette to **le César**. Which do they prefer? Why? Have them design and name a statuette to honor the movies.

Differentiated Learning

Accelerate

Ask students to research the Cannes Film Festival at its official website and present their findings to the class. What is the festival's mission? When does it take place? What film categories are judged? Who is the president of the jury? How many different countries are represented? Which American films are entered?

Decelerate

If **Du côté des médias** seems too challenging for your lower-ability students, adapt it by having them find reviews of a French film (in French). They must translate the review for you into English to demonstrate their understanding.

Multiple Intelligences

Musical-Rhythmic

Musically oriented students may be interested in the film scores associated with popular French films. Encourage them to research films and choose one whose music appeals to them in particular.

Answers

All activities will vary.

Communication

Interpersonal: Cooperative Groups

Students work in small groups to discuss the unit question, **De quelles compétences ai-je besoin pour voyager?** Have them list the skills needed for traveling, from booking a hotel and ordering in a restaurant, to taking public transportation, and interacting with people. A representative from each group writes their list on the board. This information serves as the **point de départ** for a discussion about travel survival skills and the importance of being aware of cultural differences.

Culture sur place

Question centrale ? **De quelles compétences ai-je besoin pour voyager?**

Je joue au touriste 1.2, 3.2, 5.2

Introduction et interrogations

Il y a 25 ans, organiser un voyage en Europe n'était pas facile. Il fallait trouver un hôtel, faire des réservations, se renseigner sur les restaurants et les monuments, et trouver les moyens de transport avec l'aide seule des livres touristiques et du téléphone. Avec l'arrivée d'Internet, ces voyages sont devenus beaucoup plus faciles à organiser. Comment est-ce que vous organiseriez un voyage avec les ressources modernes disponibles aujourd'hui?

9 Réfléchir 1.3, 5.1

Écrivez les numéros 4, 3, 2, et 1 sur une feuille de papier. Choisissez la ville de Dijon ou de Monte Carlo, puis réfléchissez à ce que vous connaissez de cette ville. Écrivez :

- **4 détails** qui vont vous aider à préparer votre valise. Ces détails peuvent traiter (*address*) :
  - du climat
  - de la géographie et de l'agriculture (montagnes, plages, corniches, vignobles, etc.)
  - des monuments
  - des plats régionaux
  - des événements culturels (festivals, concerts, matchs sportifs, expositions)

10 Faire des recherches 1.3, 3.2, 5.1, 5.2

Maintenant que vous avez quatre détails, faites des recherches pour identifier :

- **3 produits** qui sont représentatifs de votre ville (monuments, magasins, etc.)
- **2 choses** que vous voulez définitivement voir ou faire pendant votre voyage
- **1 question** que vous vous posez encore à propos de (*about*) votre ville et de votre voyage

Une fois votre liste finie, partagez votre plan 4-3-2-1 avec un partenaire qui a un plan 4-3-2-1 pour une autre ville.

Recherche : tourisme (+ VILLE)

11 Faire le point 1.1, 1.2, 5.1

Discutez des questions suivantes en classe.

1. Pourquoi est-ce parfois une bonne idée de bien organiser à l'avance un voyage dans une ville étrangère?
2. Quand on part en voyage à l'étranger, qu'est-ce qu'on ne peut pas organiser à l'avance?
3. Préférez-vous que votre voyage soit bien planifié à l'avance, ou préférez-vous plutôt partir à l'aventure?
4. Qu'est-ce que la classe a appris de chaque ville?
5. Est-ce que vous recommanderiez un séjour dans la ville que vous avez choisie, ou dans celle que votre camarade a choisie? Pourquoi?

Essential Instruction

1. Students choose, or are assigned, a city for **Activités 9** and **10**. They use their books as reference, or search online.
2. For **Activité 11** use questions 1–5 for class discussion, or assign each question to a group who leads the discussion.
3. Review the forms of the interrogative adjective **quel**. For **Activité 12** ask students to form questions using a form of **quel**. You can show flash cards of vocabulary as cues for making questions.
4. To introduce forms of **lequel**, write a word on the board such as **le livre**. Then write **quel livre?** Now cross out the word **livre** and add **le** to **quel**. Underneath, write "the book." Then write "which book." Then cross out "book" and replace with "one." Students will see that **lequel** stands for a masculine singular word. Do the same for the other forms of **lequel**.
5. Redo **Activité 12** replacing the interrogative adjective with a form of **lequel**.

The Interrogative Adjective *quel* 1.1

The interrogative adjective **quel** asks the question "which?" or "what?" **Quel** agrees with the noun it describes. **Quel** may precede the noun it describes or come directly before the verb **être**.

	Singular	Plural
Masculine	**quel**	**quels**
Feminine	**quelle**	**quelles**

Quelles seront les nouvelles sorties cette année?	*What will be the new releases this year?*
Quel genre de film aimerais-tu voir?	*What type of film would you like to see?*

12 Un jeu télévisé 1.1, 2.2, 3.2

Interpersonal Speaking

Vous participez à un jeu télévisé. On vous montre un indice et vous devez répondre par une question. Suivez le modèle.

MODÈLE la Tunisie, le Maroc, l'Algérie
Quels sont les pays du Magreb?

Quel est le jeu télévisé le plus populaire?

1. «Je me souviens.»
2. Monte-Carlo
3. la sauce servie avec le steak
4. le Luxembourg, la Belgique, la Suisse, la France
5. Paris, Marseille, Lyon
6. les César
7. le 1er janvier
8. la boucherie, la pâtisserie, la crémerie, l'épicerie
9. le Mont-Blanc
10. la Savoie

The Interrogative Pronoun *lequel* 1.2

The interrogative pronoun **lequel** asks the question "which one(s)?" It is often used to replace the interrogative adjective **quel** and a noun. **Lequel** consists of two parts: the definite article and **quel**. Both parts agree in gender and in number with the noun they replace.

Resources

WB Workbook 7–10
LA Listening Activity 2
G & V Practice Games

Answers

12 Possible answers:

1. Quelle est la devise du Québec?
2. Quelle est la capitale de Monaco?
3. Quelle est la sauce béarnaise?
4. Quels sont les pays francophones en Europe?
5. Quelles sont les plus grandes villes de France?
6. Quels sont les prix cinématographiques français basés sur les Oscars?
7. Quel est le premier jour de l'année?
8. Quels sont les petits magasins d'alimentation?
9. Quelle est la plus haute montagne d'Europe?
10. Quelle est la région d'où vient la fondue?

Communication

Interpersonal: Cooperative Groups

For practice asking questions using **quel**, put students in small groups of four or five. Prepare a set of note cards, writing a profession on each one, for example, **un acteur**. The first student in each group draws a card and identifies his or her profession. The other students in the group think of an interview question using a form of **quel** to ask the first student, for example, **Quel est le titre de votre dernier film?** After each student has asked a question, the second student draws another profession card and the activity begins again.

Differentiated Learning

Accelerate

Ask higher-ability students to assume the role of the teacher and re-explain the grammar lesson. Give them time to organize their presentation and find examples. Give them the pronoun **lequel** and explain how it is formed. Then ask them if they can identify the other three forms without looking at them, and instead by thinking of number and gender.

Decelerate

To practice interrogative words, use words whose gender is obvious (**la fille**, **le garçon**, **la tante**, **l'oncle**...) to practice forms of **quel** and **lequel**. In some instances, working with new or unfamiliar vocabulary, low-ability students may fail to use the correct form of **quel** or **lequel** because they do not know the gender of the word.

Answers

Comparaisons

It's harder to have a dangling preposition in French because the preposition becomes part of the pronoun in **auquel**, **auxquels**, or **auxquelles**. Some English teachers may tell students to avoid dangling prepositions in more formal writing. This can be done with the second sentence by rephrasing it: *To which one do you want to speak?*

Expansion

1. To give students practice selecting the appropriate form of **lequel**, prepare a list of sentences that can logically be followed by a question using **lequel**, for example, **L'acteur a gagné un prix prestigieux**. Read each sentence for the class. After each sentence, have students hold up a sheet of paper with **lequel**, **laquelle**, **lesquels** or **lesquelles** on it to identify which form they would select if asking a question. When students have selected the correct form of **lequel**, say the question that would logically follow the sentence you read so students can check their answer, for example, **Lequel est-ce que l'acteur a gagné?**
2. To practice interrogative adjectives and pronouns orally, say, "**Je préfère la glace au chocolat**." Ask students to form questions using forms of **quel** and **lequel**. "**Quelle glace préférez-vous? Laquelle préférez-vous?**" Students then can work with a partner using the same format.

Question Circling

Have a series of pairs of objects, such as a blue pen and a black pen, a French book and a history book, and a DVD of an action film and a DVD of a comedy. Ask students "**Lequel préfères-tu? Le stylo bleu ou le stylo rouge?**" Then ask the whole class: "**Lequel préfère-t-il/elle?**"

	Singular	Plural
Masculine	**lequel**	**lesquels**
Feminine	**laquelle**	**lesquelles**

Quel film sera le meilleur, *Cyrano de Bergerac* ou *Au revoir les enfants*? — *Which film will be the best,* Cyrano de Bergerac *or* Au revoir les enfants*?*

Lequel sera le meilleur? — *Which (one) will be the best?*

Lequel can refer to both people and things. A form of **lequel** may be the subject or direct object of a sentence or the object of a preposition.

De tous les cinémas, **lesquels** sont les moins chers? — *Of all the theaters, which ones are the least expensive?*

On a vu beaucoup de bandes-annonces avant le film. **Laquelle** as-tu préférée? — *We saw a lot of trailers before the film. Which one did you like?*

Avec **lequel** de ses copains Karim est-il allé au cinéma? — *With which one of his friends did Karim go to the movies?*

A form of **lequel** may be used as a one-word question.

Nous avons vu un long métrage. — *We saw a feature film.*

Lequel? — *Which one?*

Several forms of **lequel** contract when they are preceded by **à** and **de**. Note the forms that change below.

	lequel	lesquels	lesquelles
à	**auquel**	**auxquels**	**auxquelles**
de	**duquel**	**desquels**	**desquelles**

Il y a trois cinémas près de l'hôtel. **Auquel** allons-nous? — *There are three movie theaters near the hotel. To which one are we going?*

Martine vient de rentrer du cinéma. Ah bon? **Duquel**? — *Martine just returned from the movie theater. Really? From which one?*

Comparaisons

4.1

In which language is it more difficult to have a dangling preposition?

Voici quatre profs. **Auquel** voudrais-tu parler?
Here are four teachers. *Which one* do you want to speak to?

Essential Instruction

1. Review the contractions using **de** + **le**, **la**, and **les**, and **à** + **le**, **la**, and **les**.
2. Give ample oral examples of how these contractions are used with **lequel**.
3. Do **Activités 13** and **14** with the students. Have students write out each sentence in their notebooks.
4. Have students listen to the questions in **Activité 15** and answer **A–G**. Replay each question until you are sure the students understand each one.

13 La chambre d'Alima 1.2

Interpersonal Reading

*Complétez la phrase avec la forme convenable de **lequel**.*

MODÈLE Voici l'ordinateur sur **lequel** Alima surfe sur Internet pour trouver des concerts.

1. Voici les cahiers dans… Alima fait ses devoirs pour son cours d'histoire.
2. Voici la souris avec… Alima ouvre les logiciels.
3. Voici le lit dans… Alima dort profondément.
4. Voici la copine avec… Alima regarde un film d'aventures.
5. Voici les feuilles de papier sur… Alima écrit sa composition de littérature.
6. Voici la chambre dans… Alima se repose après les cours.
7. Voici les stylos avec… Alima écrit les invitations à sa fête d'anniversaire.

14 Plus de renseignements ! 1.1

Interpersonal Speaking

Votre ami(e) vous parle de ce qu'il ou elle compte faire ce weekend. Demandez-lui plus de renseignements.

MODÈLE Demain soir, j'aimerais aller *au cinéma*.
Ah bon ? Auquel ?

1. Je vais voir le deuxième film *d'un nouveau réalisateur*.
2. J'aime *les genres de films* qu'il tourne.
3. Je pense que mes amis et moi, nous allons aller *au stade* pour regarder un match de foot.
4. *L'équipe* que je préfère gagne presque toujours.
5. Nous mangerons *au fast-food américain*.
6. Après ça, je vais voir *une exposition*.
7. Finalement, je me servirai *de la recette de ma grand-mère* pour faire un bon dîner.

15 Quel cinéma ? 1.2

Interpretive Listening

Écrivez les numéros 1–7 sur votre papier. Écoutez les questions. Choisissez la réponse logique.

A. Je préfère celle avec Dany Boon.
B. La meilleure bande-annonce est celle d'*Amélie*.
C. J'ai choisi de voir un documentaire.
D. Le meilleur film ? C'est *Intouchables* !
E. Je préfère Gérard Depardieu et Juliette Binoche.
F. Sans aucun doute, c'est Steven Spielberg.
G. Je veux voir un film drôle samedi soir.

Resources

Activity 15

Answers

13

1. lesquels
2. laquelle
3. lequel
4. laquelle
5. lesquelles
6. laquelle
7. lesquels

14

1. Ah bon ? Duquel ?
2. Ah bon ? Lesquels ?
3. Ah bon ? Auquel ?
4. Ah bon ? Laquelle ?
5. Ah bon ? Auquel ?
6. Ah bon ? Laquelle ?
7. Ah bon ? De laquelle ?

15 Script

1. Il y a beaucoup de bons films au cinéma. Lequel veux-tu voir ce weekend ?
2. Quel est le meilleur film de l'année en France ?
3. Tu as vu ces deux comédies. Laquelle préfères-tu ?
4. Quelle bande-annonce te semble la meilleure ?
5. Entre tous ces artistes, lesquels préfères-tu ?
6. Pour toi, lequel de ces réalisateurs est le meilleur ?
7. Quelle dernière sortie as-tu choisie de voir ?

1. G
2. D
3. A
4. B
5. E
6. F
7. C

Game

Tout se transforme !

Challenge teams of students to write a list of as many **quel** + NOUN expressions as they can think of on whiteboards, and then transform the **quel** expressions into appropriate forms of **lequel**. Score each task separately to determine the winners.

Differentiated Learning

Accelerate

Have students do online practice exercises with forms of **lequel**. Point out that the pronoun **lequel** can be replaced with **qui** when it refers to a person as the object of a preposition. Use #4 in **Activité 13** to illustrate this.

Recherche : columbia edu, exercises with lequel

Decelerate

Do **Activité 13** before explaining the forms **auquel** and **duquel**.

Special Needs Students

Linguistically Challenged/AD(H)D/Dyslexia

This information may seem like a lot to learn at one time. Students may benefit from a worksheet that breaks down the information into small sections with written exercises for each part.

Question centrale ? De quelles compétences ai-je besoin pour voyager?

Resources

CA Communicative Activities

Share

Answers

16 Advertisements will vary.
17 Role-plays will vary.
18 Activities will vary.

Reference Desk

If you have access to Passport, create a question for your students to share their response to a communicative activity.

Expansion

Ask a group of students to research **César** awards, and explain the similarities and differences between the French **César** and the American Oscars. Have them make a list of celebrities that have won either, and perhaps both. Then have the rest of the class ask them questions about the differences, such as "**Est-ce que les César récompensent les mêmes catégories que les Oscars? Est-ce qu'on peut voir la cérémonie à la télévision? Est-ce que les César récompensent les films français uniquement ou les films internationaux? La cérémonie est-elle organisée de la même manière?**"

Communiquez!

16 AlloCiné 1.3, 3.1, 3.2, 5.2

Presentational Writing

Imaginez que vous êtes producteur de film et que vous venez de réaliser un tout nouveau film qui va bientôt sortir. On vous demande d'écrire une description pour en faire de la publicité. Indiquez la date du film, la durée, le genre et le cinéma à Paris où vous voudriez que la première ait lieu. N'oubliez pas les noms des acteurs (vous devez embaucher au moins plusieurs acteurs francais) que vous avez choisis pour jouer les rôles principaux. Vous pouvez vous servir du modèle ci-dessous.

C ASSOCIÉS CONTRE LE CRIME France. Coul. (12-1h44). Comédie policière, de Pascal Thomas. L'impétueuse Prudence enquête avec son époux sur la disparition d'une richissime héritière russe. Avec Agathe de la Boulaye, André Dussolier, Catherine Frot, Nicolas Marie, Eric Naggar, Linh-Dan Pham, Hervé Pierre, Bernard Verley. **Nouvel Odéon 6e. Publicis Cinema 8e. Gaumont Alésia 14e. Gaumont Parnasse 14e. Le Champlin-St-Lambert 15e. Studio 28 18e.**

Recherche: ugc, roger ebert suntimes, allociné

17 Une interview à Cannes 1.1, 1.2, 3.2, 5.2

Interpretive Viewing, Interpersonal Speaking

Vous êtes journaliste et vous vous rendez à Cannes pour le Festival. Vous devez interviewer une vedette du cinéma français. Pour vous préparer, faites des recherches sur l'acteur ou l'actrice qui vous intéresse, puis préparez huit à dix questions. Travaillez avec un partenaire. L'un de vous jouera le rôle du journaliste, et l'autre jouera le rôle de la vedette.

Recherche: isabelle adjani, luc besson, vincent cassel, gérard depardieu, jean dujardin, jean réno, omar sy, isabelle huppert, audrey tautou, guillaume canet, marion cotillard, léa seydoux

18 Les titres des films américains 1.2, 1.3, 2.2, 3.1, 4.2, 5.1, 5.2

Interpretive Viewing, Presentational Speaking and Writing

Recherchez les titres français de films étrangers (américains, coréens, etc.) que vous aimez. Recherchez aussi les versions françaises des affiches de ces films. Ensuite, faites une liste en français de vos dix films préférés et présentez-la à vos camarades de classe. Vous pouvez faire une page web et la publier sur le site de votre classe.
Exemple: *La Guerre des étoiles* (*Star Wars*)

Essential Instruction

1. Students will find ample online resources to do **Activité 16**. Encourage them to invent a film, and select famous actors to play roles in their production.
2. **Activité 18** will appeal to your dramatic students. It is interesting to discuss with your students why some movie titles are translated quite literally (as in the example) and others are changed completely. At other times a title is left in English but modified because of a tricky expression or word.

La quarantaine

Rencontre avec l'auteur 1.2

Jean-Marie Gustave Le Clézio (1940–) est un auteur qui s'inspire souvent des pays lointains. Il décrit l'environnement de ces endroits de manière sensorielle… les sons, les saveurs, les images…. Inspiré par l'histoire de son grand-père maternel et son grand-oncle Léon, Le Clézio crée des narrateurs qui font un voyage en mer qui est interrompu par *La quarantaine* du titre. Mais c'est aussi l'histoire d'Arthur Rimbaud, célèbre poète français. Ses poèmes réapparaissent au long de la narration et le roman se termine avec le narrateur contemporain à Marseille, retraçant les derniers pas de Rimbaud. Dans la sélection que vous allez lire, quelle coïncidence touche le narrateur?

Pré-lecture 1.1

Quel ancêtre voudriez-vous connaître? Pourquoi? Partagez avec votre partenaire oralement.

Stratégie de lecture 1.2, 3.2

Epistolary Novels. Un roman épistolaire est constitué d'une série de documents tels des lettres, des pages de journal intime ou des articles de journaux. Récemment, ces romans incluent des documents électroniques tels des courriels et blogs. Dans *La quarantaine*, Le Clézio se sert fréquemment de pages de journaux intimes pour raconter les histoires de ses divers narrateurs. Remplissez la grille ci-dessous en indiquant les thèmes qu'il aborde et comment il les traite à la page du journal intime de fin août 1980 à Marseille. Deux exemples ont été faits pour vous.

Sujets	Traitement
1. souvenir d'enfance: Rimbaud	une anecdote
2. désir: retracer les pas de Rimbaud	une comparaison (simile)
3.	

Outils de lecture 1.2, 3.2

Sensory Details. Les détails sensoriels sont des mots et des expressions qui décrivent l'apparence visuelle, le son, l'odeur, le goût et la sensation tactile d'une chose. L'utilisation d'éléments sensoriels est une caractéristique d'une bonne description écrite. Au fur et à mesure de votre lecture (*As you read*), faites une liste des sens auxquels Le Clézio se réfère dans cette sélection, et donnez un exemple pour chacun.

Resources

Rencontre avec l'auteur

Answers

Rencontre
Possible answer:
Il se rend compte que Rimbaud a tout abandonné comme Léon, son grand-oncle.

Pré-lecture
Answers will vary.

Stratégie de lecture
Possible answers:
3. arrivée à Marseille, identification de la saison, détail sensoriel «une odeur d'incendie»; 4. exploration de l'hôpital, description, actions du narrateur; 5. rencontre avec un Arabe, description physique, de ses actions; 6. imaginer Rimbaud à Marseille, questions; 7. nostalgie de Léon et Suryavati, description d'un sentiment

Outils de lecture
Possible answers:
le toucher: «l'air brûlait, l'ombre fraîche»; l'odeur: «comme une odeur d'incendie»; la vue: «ses grands murs de béton blanc»; «Son visage est émacié…»; «la taie laiteuse du ciel»; «une mince peau»; l'ouïe: «Allah Kerim!» le goût: «je goûtais à l'ombre»

Reference Desk

1. Arthur Rimbaud (1854–1891) is known as one of the precursors of Surrealism. A precocious but rebellious boy whose teacher opened up the world of literature for him by letting him borrow books from his personal library, he denounced his predecessors, referring to their **"vieillerie poétique."** Rimbaud became a vagabond, traveling the world. Paul Verlaine, his lover, called him **"l'homme aux semelles de vent."** He developed a tumor in his leg and died in Marseille at age 37. Some of his most famous quotes are **"On n'est pas sérieux, quand on a dix-sept ans"** and **"Je est un autre."**
2. Le Clézio, a 2008 Nobel Prize laureate, found in Rimbaud a vagabond traveler like himself.

Differentiated Learning

Expand

1. Have students read **"Le bateau ivre"** and/or **"Sensation"** by Arthur Rimbaud. Have them note the primary sensory detail in **"Sensation."**
2. Have a group of students prepare a short presentation of Arthur Rimbaud prior to reading this excerpt, and another group prepare a presentation of Le Clézio.

Resources

La Quarantaine

Answers

Pendant la lecture

1. Il pense à Rimbaud.
2. C'est le grand-oncle du narrateur.
3. Il voudrait retourner sur les lieux de Rimbaud.
4. Il est 9h00; Il ressent la chaleur du temps.
5. On l'a bâti pour les prisonniers.
6. Il va au site de l'hôpital où Rimbaud est mort.
7. Il voit un homme arabe.; Il écoute de la musique.
8. Il parle de Rimbaud.
9. Il se souvient de son grand-oncle Léon et son amante Suryavati.

Critical Thinking

Application

Before studying this excerpt, have students imagine situations when one can be **"en quarantaine"** (sickness, political asylum, etc.).

Comparisons

Have students expand their English vocabulary by finding words in the English dictionary that come from the glossed French vocabulary: **caché** (*cache*); **sentir** (*sentiment, sentimentalism, sentimentality, sentimentalize*); **errer** (*errant, errantry*); **terrestre** (*terrestrial, terrigenous*); **vêtu** (*vestments*). (A good tip to give students is to add an **"s"** after "ê" to figure out word meanings by comparing them to English words, for example, **la forêt**/*forest*.)

La Quarantaine

Marseille, fin août 1980

C'est à lui que je pense, encore. Je m'en souviens, j'avais dix ou onze ans, ma grand-mère m'avait parlé de ce qui s'était passé, ce soir-là, dans le bistrot de Saint-Sulpice, elle m'avait lu des passages du *Bateau ivre,* je lui ai demandé : « Mais ton Rimbaud, est-ce que c'est comme un oncle pour moi ? » Je croyais qu'on l'avait caché*, chassé*, juste parce qu'il était un voyou*, qu'il était parti en abandonnant tout le monde, comme Léon.

Alors j'ai voulu aller sur le dernier lieu où il avait vécu, comme on va sur un caveau* de famille. Pour voir ce qu'il avait vu, sentir* ce qu'il avait senti. C'était encore le plein été à Marseille. À neuf heures du matin, à la descente du train, l'air brûlait, il y avait sur la ville comme une odeur d'incendie*...

Au bout de la rue, jouxtant* l'ancienne prison des bagnards* transformée en archives ou en musée, l'hôpital dresse* ses grands murs de béton* blanc coulés* sur la poussière de la démolition. Il ne subsiste plus rien de l'ancien hôpital. J'ai erré* sans but dans les couloirs, dans ce qui reste du jardin entre deux parkings. J'ai lu l'inscription : « Ici, le poète... termina son aventure terrestre*. » L'amphithéâtre Arthur-Rimbaud. Dans la salle des pas* perdus, un Arabe vêtu* d'un jogging-pyjama, pieds nus dans des sneakers blancs, écoute son transistor. Son visage est émacié, creusé* par la souffrance*. Il porte lui aussi une petite moustache, et ses cheveux sont coupés très court, comme un bagnard. Il écoute sa musique, et son regard est doux, rêveur, comme s'il était loin d'ici, dans les Aurès. « Allah Kerim ! »

Et lui, l'autre, a-t-il boitillé* jusqu'aux grands platanes* de l'entrée, appuyé sur sa béquille*, pour s'asseoir à l'ombre* fraîche ? A-t-il marché, appuyé au bras d'Isabelle, en se mordant la lèvre pour ne pas crier, jusqu'au bout du jardin, pour regarder la mer au loin, entre les toits de la ville et les collines, confondue* à la taie laiteuse* du ciel ?

C'était le même été, il y a de cela quatre-vingt-neuf ans, quand Léon et Suryavati se sont effacés* de la mémoire des Archambau, comme s'ils entraient dans un autre monde, de l'autre côté de la vie, séparés de moi par une mince peau qui les rend invisibles. Ils n'ont jamais été aussi près de moi qu'en cet instant.

Pendant la lecture
1. À qui pense le narrateur ?

Pendant la lecture
2. Qui est Léon ?

Pendant la lecture
3. Qu'est-ce que le narrateur voudrait faire ?

Pendant la lecture
4. Quelle heure est-il ? Qu'est-ce que le narrateur ressent ?

Pendant la lecture
5. On a bâti l'hôpital pour quelle partie de la population ?

Pendant la lecture
6. Où va le narrateur ?

Pendant la lecture
7. Qui voit-il ? Que fait cet homme ?

Pendant la lecture
8. De qui parle le narrateur ?

Pendant la lecture
9. Le narrateur se souvient de quel ancêtre ?

---

caché *hidden* ; **chassé** *chased out* ; **un voyou** *bad character* ; **un caveau** tombeau ; **sentir** *to feel* ; **incendie** *fire* ; **jouxtant** *adjoining* ; **un bagnard** prisonnier ; **dresser** *to set up, erect* ; **le béton** le ciment ; **coulé(e)** *poured* ; **errer** *to wander* ; **terrestre** sur la planète Terre ; **un pas** *step* ; **vêtu de** *habillé de* ; **creusé** *lined* ; **la souffrance** *suffering* ; **boitiller** *to walk with a limp* ; **un platane** sorte d'arbre ; **une béquille** *crutch* ; **à l'ombre** *in the shade* ; **confondu(e)** *fused with* ; **la taie laiteuse** *milky pillowcase* ; **s'effacer** *to be erased*

Essential Instruction

1. Read the selection aloud first, slowly, and have students close their eyes (if they prefer) or read along (if they are visual learners).
2. Have students take turns reading the selection aloud.
3. Ask students to read the selection again silently and try to answer the **Pendant la lecture** questions in their head.
4. Then have students fill out the graphic organizer and list of sensory details.
5. This is the last section of the novel; ask students what themes and storylines Le Clézio is wrapping up here and to what thoughts and feelings his Rimbaud pilgrimage leads the narrator in the last paragraph.

(Suite et fin)

J'avais faim. Je me sentais libre. Je respirais l'air torride, je goûtais à l'ombre légère des grands platanes centenaires*. En quittant l'hôpital, j'ai acheté une boule de pain chez Paniol, et j'ai redescendu la longue rue qui serpente* jusqu'à la gare.

Pendant la lecture
10. Pourquoi le narrateur va-t-il quitter Marseille ?

centenaire qui a 100 ans environ ; **serpenter** *to wind, meander*

Post-lecture 1.2, 2.2, 3.1

La visite à Marseille est-elle une réussite pour le narrateur? Si oui, pourquoi?

Le monde visuel

Très jeune, Georges Rouault (1871–1958) a fait un apprentissage avec un vitrier, qui lui a appris à faire de la peinture sur verre. À partir de 1902, il a peint des aquarelles et gouaches aux couleurs vives. Il est devenu en plus un dessinateur et un graveur notable. Rouault était novateur par ses sujets, son utilisation des couleurs, par ses techniques et les mediums qu'il choisissait. Classé souvent comme fauviste ou expressionniste, Rouault voulait toujours rester indépendant. Les fauves aimaient les couleurs intenses et s'inspiraient de l'instinct, tandis que les expressionnistes aimaient déformer la réalité pour provoquer une réaction émotionnelle chez les spectateurs ; ces derniers s'inspiraient d'une vision subjective. Pourquoi certains critiques appelaient Rouault un fauve ou un expressionniste?

Recherche : la collection georges rouault centre georges pompidou, blogs cinéma

La ville, 1912. Georges Rouault. Collection privée.

19 Activités d'expansion

Faites les activités suivantes.

1. Écrivez une composition qui présente les sujets du journal intime d'août 1980 à Marseille et explique la façon dont Le Clézio les traite.
2. Écrivez une histoire contemporaine épistolaire, en vous servant de mails au lieu de lettres. N'oubliez pas d'insérez des détails sensoriels.
3. Recherchez la fin de la vie d'Arthur Rimbaud. Puis, relisez le texte de Le Clézio et écrivez un paragraphe dans lequel vous expliquez comment vous comprenez mieux la sélection.
4. Choisissez un poème de Rimbaud. Apprenez-le, ou au moins une strophe, par cœur. Présentez les vers à haute voix en groupe. Discutez en groupe des sujets et des thèmes de Rimbaud.

Recherche : poèmes Rimbaud, lisez poèmes rimbaud en ligne

Differentiated Learning

Expand
Have each student present an engraving of Rouault's in small groups and discuss the artist's subject and techniques.

Learning Styles

Visual Learners
These students may enjoy making a "stained glass" design **d'après Rouault** using colored tissue paper. Affix the artwork to an exterior window to let the light shine through.

Resources

Pre-T Pre-test
Q *Leçon* Quiz

Answers

Pendant la lecture
10. Parce qu'il se sent libre, il a l'impression qu'il a rencontré ceux qu'il cherchait.

Post-lecture
Oui, la visite est une réussite. Il est arrivé à la fin de ses recherches; il se sent proche de son grand-oncle disparu.

Le monde visuel
En considérant *La ville*, Rouault est un fauve par ses couleurs vives ; et un expressionniste par sa coloration, ses bâtiments qui semblent bouger et par les plans colorés qui représentent la terre.

19 Activities will vary.

Reference Desk

Rouault is considered one of the great artists of the 20th century. His grandfather taught him the essentials of painting. Then, he studied in Élie Delaunay's and Gustave Moreau's studios, after taking night classes in **les arts décoratifs**. His first paintings showed **"une humanité misérable,"** with subjects such as prostitutes and clowns. Throughout his life, he was part of a Christian artistic community, and drew inspiration from religious topics. Although he exhibited with **les fauves**, his technique was different and sometimes his coloration was more muted and somber. Critics often link his work to medieval mosaics and frescoes. Upon his death, Rouault's family bequeathed a lot of his art to the State.

Expansion

Encourage students to explore more works by Rouault and to create a piece inspired by his style.

French in the Workplace

Itineraries for a Tour Company

France remains the most-visited country in the world, as its history, culture, and mystique draw millions of tourists from all over the world every year. Many of these visitors arrive in France on a tour created and managed by a tour company. They are required to book flights and hotels, but also to create trip itineraries. Ask students to reflect on what they have studied of France, its regions, and its cities, and set up a 14–21 day itinerary to visit France and its major sites (or their favorite sites). They should give a brief description of each day and/or each stop and what a tour group will experience there. Students should be pragmatic about the amount of time they plan for each stop, and should not forget to calculate travel time.

Social Justice

Today, celebrities are still using their status to pursue humanitarian causes, as did Grace de Monaco. Some, however, are also using their status to promote their political views, which is not always well received. Ask students to research the pros and cons of privilege: what advantages, favors, and benefits are given to a certain group of people, called an "invisible package of unearned assets"? What role should the privileged have in affecting change in society? Select a francophone celebrity and take a stance.

Connections

Creativity and Innovation, Media Literacy

Tell students they are going to create a poster for a francophone film festival organized by the school(s). Give them information such as what kind of festival they need to advertise. They should provide information such as what type of films will be showcased, and come up with a marketing campaign intended to captivate the interest of the intended audience. They may draw or use pictures, but their work must be original. If possible, organize an evening and venue for students to showcase their work and compete with other French classes or schools.

Communiquez!

20 Un voyage personnalisé 1.1, 1.3, 3.1, 5.1, 5.2

Connecting to Financial Literacy, Collaboration
Interpersonal Speaking, Presentational Writing and Speaking

En groupe, jouez les rôles de deux agent(e)s de voyage qui doivent accommoder des touristes voyageant dans le même pays mais pour une raison différente: affaires, tourisme, vacances en famille, exploration en sac à dos, études, ou voyage en groupe.

D'abord, le groupe sélectionne un pays francophone, puis chacun choisit un rôle. Par exemple, deux personnes joueront les rôles des agents, et les autres des clients: une personne sera un homme d'affaires ou une femme d'affaires qui a un gros budget, une autre quelqu'un qui part en famille avec un budget plus raisonnable, ou encore une autre un(e) étudiant(e) avec un petit budget. À tour du rôle, les agents posent des questions pour découvrir les souhaits des voyageurs, et ensuite proposent des options différentes, selon les situations présentées. Ensuite, les voyageurs sélectionnent la formule qui leur convient selon les choix présentés par les agents, et selon leur budget. Enfin, comparez vos formules et vos sélections avec une personne d'un autre groupe.

21 FESPACO 1.2, 1.3, 3.2, 4.2, 5.2

Connecting to Media Literacy, Information Literacy, Leadership and Responsibility
Interpretive Reading, Presentational Speaking and Writing

Le Festival Panafricain du Cinéma de Ouagadougou, FESPACO, est un événement annuel qui a lieu à Ouagadougou, au Burkina Faso, dans le but de « sauvegarder le patrimoine cinématographique de l'Afrique ». Visitez le site web de FESPACO et regardez les Lauréats et Palmarès pour découvrir le cinéma africain. Choisissez trois films de pays différents. Puis, présentez-les à votre classe en expliquant le genre, l'intrigue, les acteurs, les critiques, et les éléments de la culture. Faites des comparaisons avec les films américains et la culture américaine.

Recherche: festival panafricain fespaco à ouagadougou

22 Recommandations d'œuvres cinématographiques 1.2, 1.3, 3.1, 5.2

Connecting to Information Literacy, Business and Entrepreneurial Literacy
Interpretive Reading, Presentational Writing

Vous faites un stage pour une compagnie qui fait du streaming de films. Vous êtes chargé(e) de composer les recommandations des films internationaux. Comme vous n'avez pas le temps de voir tous les films, il faut que vous lisiez les critiques. Sélectionnez plusieurs films francophones et écrivez vos recommandations de façon professionnelle. Notez les informations essentielles comme le genre, la durée, les acteurs; faites un petit synopsis, et indiquez la raison pour laquelle vous croyez que le film apportera du succès à votre compagnie.

Essential Instruction

1. Assign **Projets finaux A, B**, and **C** to all students individually or in groups. As an alternative, you may decide to let them choose their activity. In any event, all the completed work will be shared with the class.
2. **Projet D** can be done during a class period. This class time will give you the opportunity to give individual attention to students who might need extra help. When students have completed the assignment, use this **diagramme** as a tool for review and a basis for conversation.

Finale

Projets finaux

A Connexions par Internet : le cinéma 1.3, 3.1, 3.2, 4.2, 5.1, 5.2

Cours de cinéma-audiovisuel

Imaginez que vous suivez un cours de cinéma à l'université. Votre professeur mentionne « la Nouvelle Vague », mais vous ne savez pas exactement ce que c'est. Faites des recherches en ligne pour pouvoir donner une définition, préciser l'époque, et faire une liste des grands réalisateurs et des meilleurs films associés à ce mouvement. Avec un groupe de camarades de classe, faites une présentation devant la classe, chaque élève se chargeant d'une catégorie de recherche.

B Communautés en ligne 1.2, 1.3, 3.1, 3.2, 5.1

Notre blog cinéma

Lisez plusieurs critiques de films en français en vous servant des mots de recherche ci-dessous. Ensuite, avec vos camarades de classe, créez un blog sur le cinéma. Chaque élève écrit une critique d'un film français ou américain. Partagez le lien de votre blog avec d'autres classes de français et avec des francophones que vous connaissez. Demandez-leur d'ajouter leurs critiques.

Recherche : allociné blogs, blogs cinéma

C Passez à l'action ! 1.3, 3.1, 3.2, 5.1, 5.2

On tourne un film

Avec vos camarades de classe, planifiez un film sur un thème de *T'es branché ?* Par exemple, vous pouvez faire un film sur un sujet dans *Points de départ* ou sur un thème ou une histoire des *Lectures thématiques*. Vous devrez répartir les rôles : Qui va devenir le réalisateur ? Qui va écrire ou adapter le scénario ? Qui va s'occuper de la mise en scène (*setting*) ? Qui va jouer les rôles ? Qui va s'occuper des costumes ?

D Faisons le point ! 1.3

Diagramme

Faites un diagramme comme celui de la page suivante et remplissez-le pour montrer vos connaissances et répondre à la question centrale. Un exemple a été fait pour vous.

Resources

Create

Answers

All activities will vary.

Reference Desk

If you have access to Passport, assign your students an IPA task related to the unit.

Differentiated Learning

Accelerate

Higher-ability students can do the **Projets finaux** on their own with minimal intervention. Challenge them to complete the assignment from memory without looking up any information from the unit.

Decelerate

You may want to complete the **diagramme** with students in a small group. They may understand the gist of each question but may have difficulty expressing themselves. Allow them to work individually, in pairs, or in groups, and to look up any information that they do not remember. Ask them to make a list of elements they do not understand.

Adapt

Consider giving students the option of creating their own project. Make sure that you provide them with guidelines so that they are aware of your expectations.

Answers

D

Leçon A: Rencontres cuturelles: Il a appelé l'hôtel pour se renseigner sur les prestations.; Cela lui permet de savoir quelles affaires emporter.
Leçon A: **Points de départ**: Answers will vary.
Leçon A: **À vous la parole**: Monaco est une principauté très touristique et très chère.
Leçon B: **Rencontres culturelles**: Possible answer: Les spécialités françaises ont beaucoup de sauces et de viandes pas communes.
Leçon B: **Points de départ**: Answers will vary.
Leçon B: **Stratégie communicative**: Dans toutes les régions, y compris à la montagne où il y a des stations de ski.
Leçon C: **Vocabulaire actif**: Je peux lire le synopsis des films et le casting.
Leçon C: **Rencontres culturelles**: On peut consulter un site comme AlloCiné ou L'Officiel des Spectacles.
Leçon C: **Points de départ**: Answers will vary.

Reference Desk

The **Faisons le point!** section asks students to respond to the essential question by analyzing various texts in each lesson. The graphic organizer for **Activité D** may be expanded by using the complete chart found in the Copy Masters supplement.

Expansion

Pair students of similar linguistic ability. Break down **Activité D** by lesson, and assign a different lesson to each group to allow them to focus and write more meaningful responses.

Leçon A **Rencontres culturelles** Qu'est-ce que Justin fait avant de faire une reservation d'hôtel? Pourquoi est-ce une bonne idée? →	Avant de réserver une chambre, Justin se renseigne sur les prestations de l'hôtel à Monaco. Comme cela, il n'aura pas de surprise.
Leçon A **Points de départ: Monaco** Qu'est-ce que vous mettriez dans votre valise si vous alliez à Monaco? Pourquoi? →	
Leçon A **À vous la parole: Un hôtel à Monaco** Vous avez préparé un voyage à Monaco. Qu'est-ce que vous avez appris en général? →	
Leçon B **Rencontres culturelles** Seriez-vous capable de commander dans un restaurant français? Qu'est-ce que vous avez appris que vous ne saviez pas avant? Par exemple, goûteriez-vous les spécialités bourguignonnes? Comment vous renseigneriez-vous sur les spécialités du restaurant? →	
Leçon B **Points de départ: Dijon et la Bourgogne** Que feriez-vous et que verriez-vous si vous pouviez passer trois ou quatre jours en Bourgogne? Qu'est-ce que vous achèteriez comme souvenirs? →	
Leçon B **Stratégie communicative** Vous avez assez de vocabulaire pour parler dans quels lieux en France? →	
Leçon C **Vocabulaire actif** Comment pouvez-vous vous renseigner avant d'aller au cinéma en France? →	
Leçon C **Rencontres culturelles** Quelle est une autre possibilité pour se renseigner sur un film? →	
Leçon C **Points de départ: Le Septième art en France** En France on passe souvent des films classiques. Quel film aimeriez-vous voir le plus? Est-ce à cause du metteur en scène? →	

Essential Instruction

1. Have students skim the questions before taking the aural comprehension test **Un hôtel à Dijon**.
2. For **Evaluation orale**, give partner A and B index cards with the prompts for conversation. Allow them a few minutes to prepare.
3. In the computer lab, students will do **Evaluation culturelle**, 1–7.
4. In writing the **Evaluation écrite**, students will embellish the dialogue with pertinent details such as the name of the restaurant, type of cuisine, names of the two diners, and their relationship to each other.
5. Using the picture as a prompt, the students will discuss what film they want to see.
6. Using a storyboard format, students will create a story with each box illustrating a specific vacation activity. Students who say that they are not artistic are welcome to use stick figures or make photo collages.

Pre-AP

Évaluation

A Évaluation de compréhension auditive 1.1, 1.2

*Écoutez Aude et Rachid discuter de leur réservation dans un hôtel en Bourgogne. Ensuite, écrivez **V** si les phrases sont vraies ou **F** si elles sont fausses.*

1. Le couple a choisi un hôtel en Bourgogne parce qu'il y a beaucoup de sites à visiter et la cuisine est bonne.
2. Ils ont aimé leur hôtel à Monaco.
3. Rachid a appelé pour s'assurer qu'il y avait un restaurant dans l'hôtel.
4. L'hôtel a un réceptionniste mais pas de concierge.
5. Les spécialités du restaurant sont les escargots et le bœuf bourguignon.
6. Aude aime le lapin à la moutarde.
7. L'hôtel offre une piscine et un centre de remise en forme.

B Évaluation orale 1.1, 1.3

*Avec un partenaire, jouez les rôles d'un(e) étudiant(e) américain(e) qui planifie un voyage à Dijon ou à Monte Carlo (**A**), et d'un(e) étudiant(e) américain(e) qui vient de rentrer de cette destination (**B**). **L'étudiant(e) A** pose des questions sur la cuisine, le climat, et ce qu'il y a à voir et à faire. **L'étudiant(e) B** lui donne des renseignements. Finalement, les étudiants décident quel film ils vont voir ensemble ce weekend.*

C Évaluation culturelle 1.3, 2.1, 2.2, 3.2, 4.2, 5.1

Vous allez comparer les cultures francophones à votre culture aux États-Unis. Vous aurez peut-être besoin de faire des recherches sur la culture américaine.

1. **Les hôtels**
   Quels types d'hôtels existent en France ? Aux États-Unis ? Dans quelles chaînes d'hôtels êtes-vous déjà resté(e) ? Où aimeriez-vous aller en France ? Dans quel type d'hôtel ? Avec quelles prestations ?
2. **Les produits et les gens célèbres**
   Pour quels produits la principauté de Monaco est-elle connue ? Quelles personnes sont liées à Monaco ? Quels sont les produits et personnes célèbres de votre région ? Quelles en sont les différences ou les similarités avec Monaco ?

Resources

- Activity A
- LA Listening Activity *Synthèse*
- Pre-AP Listening *Unité 5*

Answers

A Script

Aude : Tu as choisi un hôtel en Bourgogne ?
Rachid : Oui, à Dijon. Il y a beaucoup de sites à visiter et les spécialités sont formidables.
Aude : L'hôtel, il est moderne au moins ! Rappelle-toi notre hôtel à Monaco l'année dernière. Il n'y avait même pas la climatisation.
Rachid : Je ne suis pas sûr que la réception soit ouverte 24h sur 24, mais il semble qu'ils aient des sèche-cheveux dans la chambre et les critiques sont bonnes.
Aude : Penses-tu qu'il y a un bon restaurant dans l'hôtel ou, au moins, proche de l'hôtel ?
Rachid : Oui, j'ai appelé et j'ai demandé à la réception. La réceptionniste m'a dit que le concierge connaît les meilleurs restaurants de la ville et que le restaurant de l'hôtel sert toutes les spécialités bourguignonnes.
Aude : Quelles sont leurs spécialités ?
Rachid : Le bœuf bourguignon et les escargots.
Aude : Tu crois qu'ils ont du lapin à la moutarde ? J'adore ça !
Rachid : Je ne suis pas sûr qu'ils aient du lapin au restaurant de l'hôtel, mais en ville certainement.
Aude : Et quelles sont les autres prestations de l'hôtel ?
Rachid : Ils offrent les chaines câblées et une connexion wifi, en plus un centre de remise en forme et le service de chambre.
Aude : Il n'y a pas de piscine ?
Rachid : Non, juste un bain à remous.
Aude : C'est dommage qu'il n'y ait pas de piscine mais le centre de remise en forme, ça c'est très bien !

1. V; 2. F; 3. V; 4. F; 5. V; 6. V; 7. F

Differentiated Learning

Decelerate
Lower-ability students may benefit from a study period in class in which they can systematically review the content of the unit lessons. It would afford you time to have a free-question session so that they can ask for help on any topic no matter how basic.

Special Needs Students

AD(H)D
Provide students with a structured, step-by-step guideline for doing the **Evaluation**.

At-Risk Students
Some students do not have the proper atmosphere at home for study, or are working after school until late. Time in class to study would be very beneficial.

Resources

Perform

Reference Desk

If you have access to Passport, assign a task to evaluate your students' oral proficiency.

Game

Jeu de vitesse

Divide your class in two teams. Give the class ten to fifteen minutes to write down as many things as they can think of that could go wrong to make a hotel experience a terrible one. The team which has come up with the longest list after the time allotted wins the game.

3. **Une capitale régionale**
   Qu'est-ce que vous savez de l'histoire de Dijon? Pour quels produits cette ville est-elle connue? Comparez la capitale bourguignonne avec la capitale de votre région, province, ou état.
4. **Le Septième Art**
   Quelles sont les indications culturelles qui indiquent que le cinéma est important en France? Pourquoi les Français disent-ils que le cinéma est un art? Comparez l'attitude des Français envers le cinéma avec l'attitude des Américains que vous connaissez.
5. **Les César et les Oscars**
   Quels réalisateurs français et américains ont reçu le plus de récompenses? Quelles vedettes françaises et américaines ont reçu le plus de récompenses? Quels genres de films font-elles?

D Évaluation écrite 1.1, 1.3

Écrivez un dialogue qui a lieu dans un restaurant français pour un serveur/une serveuse et deux clients.

E Évaluation visuelle 1.1, 5.2

Avec un(e) partenaire, jouez les rôles d'un(e) ado qui sait quel film il/elle voudrait voir et d'un(e) autre ado qui appelle son ami(e) pour voir s'il ou elle est libre et voudrait voir un film ce weekend.

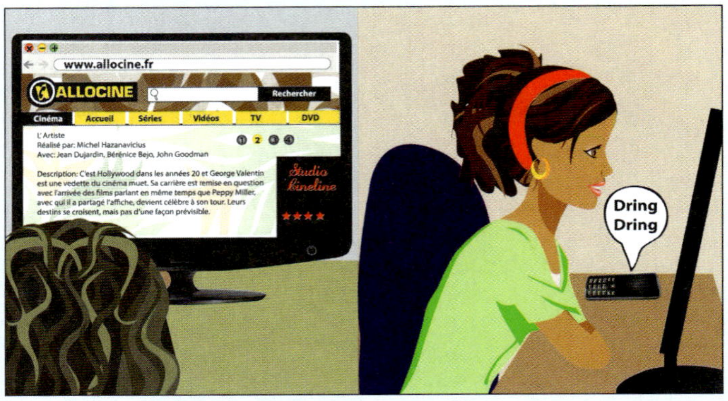

F Évaluation compréhensive 1.3

Créez une histoire avec six illustrations : dessinez un couple en vacances à Monaco. Montrez et décrivez ce qu'ils font et voient.

Essential Instruction

Use whiteboards to review vocabulary. Give students a category and see how many vocabulary words they can write in a timed game. Categories could include but not be limited to: **cuisine**, **hôtel**, **cinéma**, **émotions**, **subjonctif**, and **argot**. Accept any correct French words, not just the ones from the current lesson.

Vocabulaire de l'Unité 5

accueil welcome/home page *C*
les **actions (f.)** actions *C*
adressé (à) addressed (to) *C*
agréable pleasant *A*
apprécier to like *C*
l' **ascenseur (m.)** elevator *A*
auquel, auquelle to which *C*
un **bain à remous** whirlpool bath *A*
une **bande-annonce** film trailer, preview *C*
bien: bien entendu of course *B*
blasé(e) blasé *C*
la **Bourgogne** Burgundy *B*
bourguignon(ne) from, of Burgundy *B*
c'est: c'est dommage que... it's too bad that... *B*
ça: ça promet it sounds promising *C*
le **casting** casting *C*
une **catastrophe** catastrophe *C*
un **centre: centre d'affaires** business center *A*; **centre de remise en forme** fitness center *A*
chacun(e) each (one) *A*
une **chaîne: chaîne câblée** cable channel *A*
un **chef d'orchestre** conductor *C*
un **classique** classic *B*
un(e) **client(e)** guest *A*
un **coffre-fort** safe *A*
une **compétence** skill *A*
composé(e) (de) made up (of) *C*
comprendre to include *B*
un(e) **concierge** concierge *A*
le **confort** comfort *A*
une **connexion wifi** wireless internet connection *A*
consulter to consult *C*
un **coulis (de tomates)** (tomato) sauce *B*
une **crème (de ciboulette)** cream (of chives) *B*
un **critique** critic *C*; **une critique** review, critique *C*
les **dénominations (f.)** denominations *B*
les **dialogues (m.)** dialogues *C*
dijonnais(e) from, of Dijon *B*
un **directeur, une directrice** director *C*
le **doublage** dubbing *C*
doublé(e) dubbed *C*
douter to doubt *B*
duquel, duquelle from which *C*
la **durée** duration, length *C*
électronique electronic *A*
une **émotion** emotion *C*
éprouver to feel *C*
équipé(e) (de) equipped (with) *A*
une **étoile** star *C*
être: être certain que to be certain that *B*; **être d'humeur (m.): je ne suis pas trop d'humeur pour** I'm not in the mood for *C*; **être étonné que** to be surprised that *B*; **être évident que** to be obvious that *B*
exiger to require *A*
le **faisan** pheasant *B*
un **fax** fax *C*
fermenté(e) fermented *B*
le **final** finale *C*
garantir to guarantee *A*
la **gastronomie** gastronomy *B*
le **goût** taste *B*; **à mon goût** for my taste *C*
un **homme: homme de ménage** janitor *C*
l' **horaire (m.)** schedule *C*
imprécis(e) vague *A*
imprenable unobstructed *A*
une **impression** impression *C*
intense intense *C*
le **jambon: jambon persillé** ham and pork dish made with chopped parsley *B*
jeter un coup d'œil (à) to glance (at) *B*
un **lieu** place *A*
long, longue: un long métrage feature film *C*
maint(e)s many *B*
une **marinade** marinade *B*
mon: mon Dieu my god *B*
monégasque from, of Monaco *A*
le **multiplexe** multiplex cinema *C*
un **nanar** flop *[film]* *C*
les **nouveautés (f.)** new releases *C*
paraître: il paraît que it seems that *C*
parfait(e) perfect *A*
partager to share *C*
une **pause** pause *C*
personnellement personally *B*
plat(e) flat, lifeless *C*
plutôt quite *A*
pratique practical *A*
des **précisions (f.)** specific information *A*
puis: Puis-je...? May I...? *B*
les **prestations (f.)** amenities *A*
quelques a few, some *A*
la **réception** lobby *A*
regretter to be sorry *B*
un(e) **Romain(e)** Roman *B*
une **salle: salle de cinéma** movie theatre (room) *A*; **salle de réunion** meeting center *A*
la **sauce: sauce béarnaise** Béarnaise sauce *B*; **sauce béchamel** béchamel sauce *B*; **sauce blanche** white sauce *B*; **sauce hollandaise** hollandaise sauce *B*; **sauce marinière** white wine sauce *B*
servi(e) served *B*
un **service** service *A*; **service blanchisserie** laundry service *A*; **service de chambre** room service *A*
souhaiter to hope, to wish *A*
une **sortie** release *C*
sous-titré(e) subtitled *C*
les **sous-titres (m.)** subtitles *C*
soviétique Soviet *C*
stéréotypé(e) stereotypical *C*
un **style** style *C*
suivant(e) following *A*
le **synopsis** movie synopsis *C*
tomber: tomber sur to discover accidentally *C*
le **ton** tone *C*
tourner un film to shoot a movie *C*
les **trompettes de la mort (f.)** black trumpet mushrooms *B*
le **veau** veal *B*
une **vedette** star *C*
la **viande** meat *B*
une **version: version originale (VO)** original version *C*
vrai(e) real *C*

Resources

FC Flash Cards
Rendez-vous à Nice ! Documentaire 3
T *Unité 5* Test

Reference Desk

une chaine, le gout, paraitre, il parait que

Expansion

To help students memorize the vocabulary, and to help them remember how each word is used, ask them to classify the new vocabulary words in four columns listing nouns, verbs, adjectives, and prepositions. Ask your stronger students to expand those lists and find derivatives of some of those words, for example: **une catastrophe** is a noun; students can find that the adjective is **catastrophique**.

Reference Desk

1. The largest bank in France is the French Post Office, which offers banking services in addition to its traditional functions. Well-known retail banks with branch offices throughout France are: **BNP Paribas**, **BPCE**, **Crédit Agricole**, **Crédit Agricole et la Société Générale**.
2. The photo on the unit opener shows a branch of **La Société Générale** on a Parisian street.
3. Students learn about banking in France in **Leçon A**.

Unité 6 On se débrouille en France

Essential Instruction

1. Review the meaning of the title of the unit and possible translations. ("We get by in France." "We manage in France.")
2. Ask how many students have a bank account. Which banks in their town are national banks and which are local? What are the well-known credit cards used in the United States?
3. In this unit students continue to learn travel survival skills by acquiring vocabulary needed to open a bank account, write a French check, and send money.
4. Students also learn about the reading habits of the French and how to talk about their own reading preferences.
5. Have students compare the **À savoir** statistic with its equivalent in the United States. Discuss with them the cultural implications of this difference.

Question centrale ?

Comment s'intégrer à une autre culture?

À savoir

Plus de 30% des livres achetés en France sont des livres littéraires.

Citation

Dans un voyage, le plus long est de franchir le seuil.

The longest part of a trip is getting past the threshold.

—Proverbe romain

Conseil pratique

Work on your accuracy of expression in speaking and writing. Team up with a peer editor for exchanging writing assignments. It's okay to start again when speaking, if you catch yourself making a mistake.

Quelle langue Nelson parle-t-il avec sa mère?

Comment s'appelle cette femme écrivain?

Contrat de l'élève

Leçon A I will be able to:

- open a bank account and make a promise.
- discuss French and Canadian banks and how best to access money while staying in Europe.
- use the future tense in sentences with **si** and **quand**.

Leçon B I will be able to:

- ask what a book is about and say I'll never be able to make up my mind.
- discuss French reading habits and prize-winning authors **Le Clézio**, **Modiano**, and **Condé**.
- review VERB + **de** + NOUN and use the relative pronoun **dont**.

Leçon C I will be able to:

- say what I need and specify items.
- discuss the services of the French post office.
- review demonstrative adjectives and use demonstrative pronouns.

Answers

Possible choices for the video question:
A. anglais
B. allemand
C. espagnol
D. italien
Correct answer: D

The answer to the culture question is: **Maryse Condé**. The answer can be found in **Points de départ**, **Leçon B**.

Special Needs Students

At-Risk Students
Students may come from families who do not use checking and saving account services and might not qualify for credit cards. Be sensitive to this possibility when discussing money and banking.

Multiple Intelligences

Mathematical-Logical
Ask students to report to the class about the relative size of the large retail banks listed in *Reference Desk*.

Visual-Spatial
Have students make flash cards of the logos of the large retail banks (including **La Poste**) to identify them when traveling.

Resources

- *Vocabulaire actif*
- eV eVisual
- WB Workbook 1–2
- FC Flash Cards
- LA Listening Activity 1
- G & V Practice Games

Reference Desk

1. An alternative to **encaisser un chèque** is **toucher un chèque**. Another word for **un chéquier** is **un carnet de chèques**.
2. Additional vocabulary for your students: **un compte courant** (*checking account*); **un compte épargne** (*savings account*); **les frais supplémentaires** (*additional charges*); **le taux d'intérêt** (*interest rate*); **déposer sur un compte** (*to deposit money into an account*).

Culture

Products: Information

Une carte bancaire is the debit and credit card most widely used in France. It allows the owner to withdraw cash where the **CB** logo is displayed. With this card, users incur no service fee at any ATM in France. To use the card, you must have a PIN that you enter for any transaction over 20 euros.

TPR

Have students come up with gestures for each of the actions in **À la banque**. Recite a short story and check that students hear and understand the words you use by making the correct gestures.

Leçon A Vocabulaire actif

À la banque et à la fac 1.2

À la banque

En personne

On ouvre **un compte** avec **le banquier**/**la banquière**.

On **dépose**/**encaisse un chèque** avec **le caissier**/**la caissière**.

On **retire** de l'argent au **distributeur** avec sa **carte bancaire**.

En ligne

On peut aussi ouvrir un compte en ligne.

On peut commander **de la monnaie étrangère** au **bureau de change**.

On peut **transférer** son argent pour l'**économiser**.

L'argent

un chéquier, un chèque

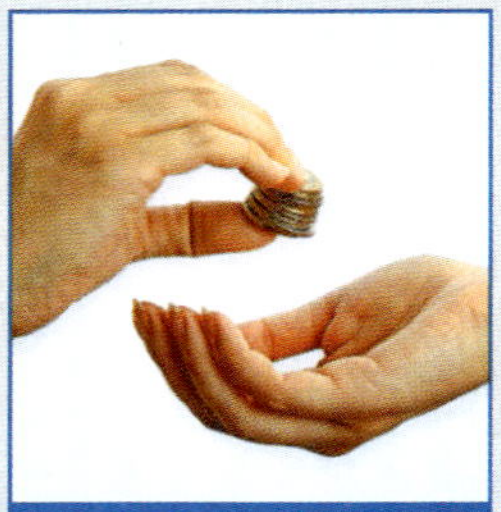

de la monnaie

une pièce (de monnaie)

un billet (de banque)

l'argent **liquide**

Essential Instruction

1. Put the vocabulary for **Leçon A** on the board. Which words do the students recognize? Ask them to define each term in French.
2. Have students listen to the recording of the vocabulary several times before repeating.
3. Make note of the verbs **ouvrir**, **déposer**, **encaisser**, **retirer**, and **obtenir** used with the banking functions pictured. To check comprehension, begin the expression and let students complete it, for example, **On ouvre un…**, **On dépose….**
4. Encourage students to group the vocabulary into word families to help them memorize meaning, for example, **la banque**, **le banquier**, **la banquière** and **la caisse**, **le caissier**, **la caissière**.
5. Ask students if they were to major (**se spécialiser en**) in a subject at the **Université de Toulouse** what would it be and why?

À la fac 1.2, 2.2, 3.1

UFTMP… les facs

chimie-biochimie (f.)

droit (m.)

économie (f.)

histoire (f.) de l'art

génie (m.) civil

gestion économique d'entreprise (f.)

infographie (f.)

sciences (f.) politiques (sciences po)

médecine (f.)

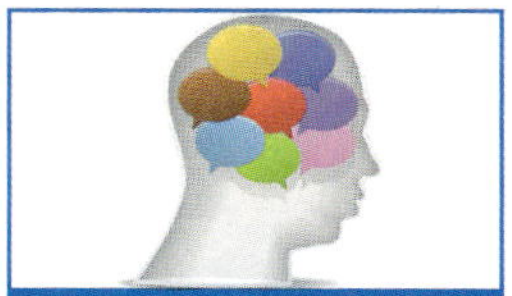
psychologie (f.)

langues (f.)

lettres (f.)

administration (f.) et communication (f.)

management (m.) et gestion (f.)

arts (m.) plastiques

sciences (f.) du sport

Pour la conversation 1.2

What do I say at the bank to open an account and get a debit card?

» Je voudrais ouvrir un compte et obtenir une carte bancaire.

I would like to open an account and obtain a debit card.

How do I make a promise?

» **C'est promis!**

It's a promise!

Et si je voulais dire… ?

un code confidentiel	*PIN*
un crédit	*credit*
une dette	*debt*
un emprunt	*loan*
une hypothèque	*mortgage*
un virement automatique	*automatic payment/ funds transfer*

Resources

Pour la conversation
Et si je voulais dire… ?

Reference Desk

1. The **Université fédérale de Toulouse-Midi-Pyrénées** or **UFTMP** (formerly the **Université de Toulouse**) is an association of universities and research centers dedicated to higher education in the **Pyrénées** region. It is comprised of **Toulouse I–Capitole**, **Toulouse–Jean-Jaurès**, and **Toulouse III–Paul-Sabatier**.
2. Toulouse is the fourth largest city in France after Paris, Lyon, and Marseille. It is the center of high-tech industries, notably aerospace, electronics, biotechnology, and information technology. Airbus has its headquarters, and assembles many of its planes, in Toulouse.
3. **Infographie** is the science of presenting complex information in an understandable visual form, for example, a color-coded **métro** map of Paris, or color-based charts of the periodic table of elements.
4. **Le génie civil** is civil engineering. The word **ingénieur** is derived from the term for engineering, **le génie**.
5. Since education is nationalized in France, tuition at public universities is quite low. For example, in 2012 undergraduate tuition was €174 in some institutions. Private universities can cost up to €8,900 a year.

Expansion

Have students research Toulouse: its location, nickname (**la Ville Rose**), and its gourmet **spécialités**: **cassoulet**, **garbure** (*a hearty soup*), **saucisse de Toulouse** (*sausage*), and **croquants** (*crisp biscuits with almonds*).

Have students come up with other words that have the same root as **le génie**, such as **Génial !** and **C'est du génie !**

Multiple Intelligences

Mathematical-Logical
Students who enjoy science and technology might envision studying in Toulouse. Have them research such a possibility.

Visual-Spatial
Encourage students to find photos of the city, its churches, its museums, its square, **le Capitole**, etc., and to make a poster of the key sites.

Recherche: toulouse, wikitravel

Resources

Activity 2

Answers

1

1. un compte
2. un chéquier
3. banquier
4. pièces, billets
5. retire
6. l'argent liquide
7. bureau de change

2 Script

1. Hier, je suis allé à la banque pour ouvrir un compte. D'abord, j'ai parlé à la caissière.
2. J'ai dit à la caissière que je voulais ouvrir un compte et faire une demande de carte bancaire.
3. Elle m'a demandé ma carte d'identité et mon adresse en France.
4. Puis, elle m'a donné une carte bancaire et un chéquier.
5. Comme je voulais échanger mes dollars pour des euros, elle m'a indiqué le bureau de change.
6. Là, l'employée m'a donné de l'argent liquide, des pièces et des billets.
7. Alors, je suis sorti de la banque et j'ai retiré de l'argent au distributeur avec ma nouvelle carte. Ouvrir un compte bancaire, c'est facile !

1. B; 2. D; 3. A; 4. C; 5. E; 6. G; 7. F

Expansion

Put the following popular expressions on the board. Let students guess their equivalent meaning in English. Give points for each correct answer. **Il n'a pas un rond** and **Il est fauché** both mean *He is broke*. **Vouloir le beurre et l'argent du beurre**. (*Can't have your cake and eat it too.*) **Jeter de l'argent par la fenêtre**. (*Throw money out the window.*)

1 Une visite à la banque 1.2, 2.1, 4.2, 5.1

Interpretive Reading

Complétez les phrases suivantes.

1. Awa a besoin d'ouvrir… à la banque.
2. Elle voudrait avoir… pour écrire des chèques.
3. À la banque, elle parle au… pour ouvrir un compte.
4. Elle voudrait de l'argent liquide, c'est-à-dire des… et des….
5. Awa… de l'argent au distributeur.
6. Au guichet, Awa reçoit de…, des euros en billets et en pièces de monnaie.
7. Avant de partir en voyage en Angleterre, Awa va en ligne pour échanger des euros en livres (*British pounds*) au….

2 Nouveau compte en banque ! 1.2, 2.1, 4.2, 5.2

Interpretive Listening and Viewing

Écrivez les numéros 1–7. Écoutez Jonathan décrire son expérience dans une banque en France. Faites correspondre la phrase que vous entendez à la bonne image.

A.

B.

C.

D.

E.

F.

G.

Essential Instruction

1. Read the clues from **Activité 1** and have students write the answers on whiteboards for immediate correction.
2. Before playing the recording, have students identify what is happening in each image of **Activité 2**.
3. Review the vocabulary on p. 323 before having the students do **Activité 3**.
4. Arrange students in pairs to interview each other using questions from **Activité 4**. Upon completion, have students circulate to ask other members of the class any two questions from the list.
5. Have students report back by expressing what they learned about their classmates, first to a different partner, then to the class.

3 Quelles études ? 1.2, 1.3, 4.2, 5.1

Interpretive Reading, Presentational Speaking or Writing

Dites où les étudiants se sont inscrits pour suivre les études qui les intéressent.

MODÈLE Johann s'intéresse aux affaires publiques.
Il s'est inscrit à la fac de sciences po.

1. Karine veut être médecin.
2. Marco souhaite étudier les idées de Freud et Jung.
3. Océane voudrait devenir juge un jour.
4. Abdoulaye s'intéresse à la chimie.
5. Juliette voudrait étudier les œuvres des grands peintres européens.
6. Julien compte devenir ingénieur.
7. Naya voudrait travailler pour une grande compagnie internationale.
8. Abdel-Cader aimerait créer des visuels graphiques pour un journal ou un magazine.

4 Questions personnelles 1.1, 3.1, 5.1

Interpersonal Speaking

Répondez aux questions avec un partenaire.

1. As-tu déjà ouvert un compte en banque? Si oui, pourquoi?
2. Est-ce que tu préfères dépenser ton argent ou le mettre à la banque?
3. As-tu une carte bancaire? Si oui, quand est-ce que tu t'en sers?
4. Est-ce que tu connais quelqu'un qui collectionne des pièces de monnaie?
5. T'intéresses-tu aux arts plastiques?
6. Es-tu allé à un bureau de change ou en ligne pour changer de l'argent?
7. Quand tu sors avec des ami(e)s, qui paie? Est-ce que tu as toujours de l'argent liquide sur toi? Et tes ami(e)s?
8. Si tu allais à l'université, tu t'inscrirais dans quelle faculté? Pourquoi?
9. Qu'est-ce que tu comptes faire comme métier?

Resources

Activity 3

Answers

3

1. Elle s'est inscrite à la fac de médecine.
2. Il s'est inscrit à la fac de psychologie.
3. Elle s'est inscrite à la fac de droit.
4. Il s'est inscrit à la fac de chimie-biochimie.
5. Elle s'est inscrite à la fac d'histoire de l'art.
6. Il s'est inscrit à la fac de génie-civil.
7. Elle s'est inscrite à la fac de gestion-économie d'entreprise.
8. Il s'est inscrit à la fac d'infographie.

4 Answers will vary.

Reference Desk

1. The three largest French banks, based on their total assets in 2017, are **BNP Paribas**, **Crédit Agricole SA**, and **Société Générale**.
2. *Great Place to Work* polled 500 salaried employees in 2017 to decide the top ten best places to work in France. Here are the top five: 1) Davidson consulting, (**enterprise de conseil**), 2) Mars France (**agroalimentation**), 3) Extia (**ingénierie**), 4) Hays (**recrutement**), and 5) Waverstone (**cabinet de conseil pour transformation d'entreprise**).

Expansion

Have students list the characteristics of a good employer. For this discussion, focus more on the work environment than on the nature of the work.

Differentiated Learning

Accelerate

Ask small groups to create an original skit among a bank employee and some travelers asking questions about the bank's services. Students should use the vocabulary from the lesson and **Et si je voulais dire...?** Ask them to research websites of French banks for additional information.

Recherche: crédit agricole, bnp paribas, la banque postale

Decelerate

Have students graph the euro to dollar ratio for any five-day period. How would a gift costing 50 euros on the first day of a trip rise or fall in price for an American paying by credit card in dollars? What are the denominations of euro bills and coins? Find pictures of each to share with the class.

Resources

Dialogue
Activity 5
Dialogue Video
WB Workbook 5

Answers

5

1. Il doit ouvrir un compte en banque.
2. Oui.
3. Il dit que ce n'est pas compliqué.
4. Il y va demain matin.
5. Il étudie l'infographie.
6. Il veut être réalisateur de films.

Reference Desk

1. Students may not know the meaning of some expressions. **Ce n'est pas évident** has the special meaning of *It is not easy*. **Être coupable** is the opposite of **être innocent**. **En trois jours** means *It takes three days*, whereas **dans trois jours** means *three days from now*. **Avant de** + INFINITIVE is the equivalent of *before* + *ing*. **Avant de parler** = *before speaking*.
2. John Lasseter is the chief creative officer of Walt Disney Animation Studios. He is known for the three *Toy Story* films and the *Cars* films.
3. **Je n'ai cours que l'après-midi**. Remind the students that **ne**… **que** means *only* and **un formateur** means *a trainer*; **une formation** means *training*.

Rencontres culturelles

La banque et la fac 1.2

Justin voudrait ouvrir un compte à la banque.

Justin : Les finances en France, pour moi ce n'est pas évident….
Léo : Tu verras, quand tu iras à la banque…. Non, ce n'est pas compliqué.
Justin : Mais combien faut-il de papiers ? Vous adorez les certificats, les autorisations… on a toujours l'impression d'être coupable ! Qu'est-ce que je dis au banquier ?
Léo : « Je voudrais ouvrir un compte et obtenir une carte de crédit. » Tu auras ta carte de crédit en trois jours.
Justin : Trois jours ? Avant de pouvoir retirer de l'argent liquide* au distributeur automatique ? Mais qu'est-ce que je vais devenir ?
Léo : Demain matin, tu as cours à quelle heure ?
Justin : Si je me souviens bien, je n'ai cours que l'après-midi.
Léo : C'est parfait ! Si on y va à 11h00, tu auras ton compte à midi. Au fait, tu es content de ton cours d'infographie ?
Justin : Oh, oui, en ce moment on travaille sur la lumière, le réglage, le positionnement… c'est génial !
Léo : Tu es notre futur John Lasseter. Tu réalises quand ton premier *Toy Story* ?
Justin : Je ferai mieux que ça… je vous ferai entrer dans le monde de la quatrième dimension graphique !
Léo : Ça existe ?
Justin : Je n'en sais rien ! En tout cas, je le ferai !
Léo : Quand tu finiras ton premier film, tu m'inviteras à la première ?
Justin : C'est promis !

*Je parle bien !

« En français, l'orthographe *qu* se prononce comme la lettre *k*. Pour dire **liquide**, prononcez « lee-keed ». »

Stratégie

Faites une liste des étapes que Justin doit suivre pour ouvrir un compte à la banque.

5 La banque et la fac 1.2

Répondez aux questions.

1. Que doit faire Justin ?
2. Est-ce que Justin pense que c'est compliqué d'ouvrir un compte à la banque ?
3. Que dit Léo pour le rassurer ?
4. Quand Justin va-t-il à la banque ?
5. Qu'est-ce que Justin étudie ?
6. Qu'est-ce que Justin veut faire dans l'avenir ?

Essential Instruction

1. Have students skim the questions before watching the video "**La banque et la fac**," and then have them close their books.
2. After the video, ask students to recall any details they remember about the dialogue. Put the details on the board.
3. Have students watch the video again, this time following along in the text. Turn the volume down and play the video again. Have students watch for mannerisms as the friends talk. Students can do **Activité 5** with a partner.

EXTENSION **Au Salon Studyrama** 1.2

Ludovic et Manon parlent au formateur à l'École des arts graphiques.

Manon : Les formations en arts graphiques, c'est un cursus de 2, 3, ou 4 ans ?

Formateur : Ça dépend… vous avez des formations courtes en deux ans avec des BTS en communication visuelle, et ensuite, vous pouvez faire un diplôme supérieur des arts appliqués dans une école spécialisée ; ou alors vous choisissez une école d'art et de graphisme, puis vous vous spécialisez en 3ème cycle, option multimédia.

Ludovic : Et si on suit ce cursus on pourra faire ensuite tous les métiers liés à l'infographie ?

Formateur : Oui, après ça dépend de vous, de vos choix….

Manon : Ça veut dire quoi ?

Formateur : Ça veut dire qu'il y a énormément de secteurs.

Ludovic : Par exemple ?

Formateur : Les services de communication d'entreprises, les agences de publicité, les sociétés de commerce en ligne, les maisons d'édition, le secteur de la presse, les jeux en ligne, mais aussi le cinéma et la télévision, l'animation….

Ludovic : Tant mieux ! Et on gagne combien ?

Formateur : Au début 1 500 euros par mois… après ça peut monter très vite. Ça dépend de votre talent !

EXTENSION 1.2 Qu'est-ce que les deux jeunes gens apprennent de la profession qui les intéresse en parlant avec le formateur ?

Resources

Extension

Answers

EXTENSION

Ils apprennent les différents cursus de formation, les différents diplômes, et les différents métiers qu'on peut faire avec.

Reference Desk

1. **La faculté** is a component of a university dedicated to teaching and research in a certain discipline. **la faculté de droit** is the law school, for example. The dean is the administrative head of a specific school. Students refer to **la faculté** as **la fac**. Most students say that they are **à la fac** rather than **à l'université**.
2. Offer this additional vocabulary for a discussion about students' futures: **école technique** (*trade school*), **faire un stage** (*to do an internship*), **s'engager dans le militaire** (*to enlist or join the military*).
3. A **cursus** refers to a course of study towards a degree.
4. A **BTS** (**brevet de technicien supérieur**) is a university-level certification obtained in two years.
5. The terms "**1er cycle, 2ème cycle, 3ème cycle**," etc., refer to different stages of post-secondary studies for Europeans. In France, **le 1er cycle** refers to the first three years of study after which one receives **la licence** (**bac + 3**). **Le 2ème cycle** refers to the next two years of study after which one receives **le master** (**bac + 5**). **Le 3ème cycle** refers to the following three years of study after which one generally receives **le doctorat** (**bac + 8**).

Differentiated Learning

Accelerate

Have high-ability students read **Extension** in pairs then write questions about the conversation. In larger groups, have them ask and answer classmates' questions.

Decelerate

While the high-ability students work on **Extension**, work with low-ability students to have them read "**La banque et la fac**" for pronunciation, or have them read the dialogue in **Extension** as a group.

Special Needs Students

AD(H)D/Linguistically Challenged

To assist students who have difficulty concentrating, reading, or with language, give them two or three lines from the dialogue on separate index cards. Have students work in groups and ask them to be responsible for only the lines that are on their cards. Organize a group presentation.

Dyslexia

To make the reading easier, have students cover the dialogue, revealing only one line at a time.

Resources

- *Points de départ*
- WB Workbook 6
- Explore

Reference Desk

1. Many non-European credit cards lack a **puce**, the microchip found in most French credit cards. Without this piece it usually doesn't pose a problem for travelers in restaurants or cafés or when purchasing items in stores. However, it can be difficult to use these cards to purchase metro tickets, at train ticket stations, or for **Vélib** public bicycles. (**Vélib** bicycle subscriptions can be purchased online.)
2. The **Produit intérieur brut (PIB)** (Gross Domestic Product [GDP]) measures the total value of products produced annually within a country.
3. The **Banque de Montréal (BMO)** has 321 branches in the United States.
4. If you have access to Passport, find a video or news article related to French banks and show it to your students.

Points de départ

Pre-AP

Question centrale ? Comment s'intégrer à une autre culture?

La Francophonie

Devant la Société Générale

Les banques

En France 1.2, 2.1, 2.2, 3.1

Le système bancaire français est très centralisé. Il est dominé par cinq groupes : la BNP Paribas (Banque nationale de Paris et des Pays-Bas), le groupe Crédit Agricole (fusionné avec le LCL), la Société Générale, le groupe BPCE (Banque populaire et Caisse d'Epargne), et la Poste. Les banques françaises disposent de 37 000 agences, gèrent 79 millions de comptes et disposent de 58 000 distributeurs automatiques de billets. C'est un secteur qui reste un gros créateur d'emplois (35 000 par an). Les Banques françaises produisent 3% du PIB* national depuis 10 ans.

C'est en 1985 que commence en France l'histoire de la banque en ligne avec la création de Cortal, une filière* de la BNP, gérée* par la technologie du Minitel*. La révolution Internet voit la création de Banque Directe (BNP) (1995), Zebank (LVMH) (1999), ING Direct (2000). Aujourd'hui le secteur est dominé par Axa banque (groupe Axa), Boursorama (Société générale), Fortuneo (Crédit mutuel), et Hello Bank ! (BNP).

Comme aux États-Unis, toutes les cartes bancaires émises* par les banques françaises sont des cartes à puces* sécurisées* dont l'usage est protégé par un code confidentiel.

Recherche : bnp paribas, crédit agricole, banques françaises

PIB Produit intérieur brut *(GDP)* ; **filière** *branch* ; **gérée** *managed* ; **Minitel** *first computer database in France* ; **émises** *given* ; **cartes à puces** *microchip cards* ; **sécurisées** *secured*

Mon dico bancaire

Il a perdu tout crédit.
On ne croit plus en lui.
Il lui a emprunté l'idée.
Il a pris l'idée à quelqu'un d'autre.
C'est un flambeur !
Il dépense beaucoup d'argent !
hypothéquer son avenir
compromettre son avenir
passer par pertes et profits
ne plus avoir d'importance

Au Canada 1.2, 2.1, 3.1

La Banque Royale du Canada représente presque la moitié de la population du Canada. Elle sert 17 millions de clients, a plus de 80 000 employés, et plus de 1 200 succursales*. Cette entreprise, établie en 1864 en Nouvelle-Ecosse, opère aussi aux États-Unis et dans 50 autres pays du monde.

La Banque de Montréal, fondée en 1817, est la plus vieille banque du Canada. Avec plus de sept millions de clients et plus de 900 succursales, c'est la quatrième plus grande banque du Canada. Aux États-Unis, elle est connue sous le nom de BMO Harris Bank.

Recherche : banque royale du canada, banque de montréal, bmo harris

succursales *branches*

Essential Instruction

1. Have students read **La Francophonie : Les banques** and then visit each major bank's website to learn about their services.
2. Have students find a photo of a **carte bancaire** online. What information is provided? Why is this card different from the credit cards in the United States?

Recherche : images, carte bancaire

3. After reading "**Au Canada**," have students compare **La Banque Royale du Canada** to **La Banque de Montréal** in terms of age, customers, and branches in Canada and abroad.
4. Students read **Retirer de l'argent en Europe** and make a list of the travel advice and new vocabulary they learned from the reading.
5. In high and low-ability teams, have students do **Activité 6** and **Perspectives**. Use this as a springboard for class discussion.

Retirer de l'argent en Europe 1.2, 2.1, 3.1, 4.2, 5.2

Autrefois, quand on voyageait en Europe, on utilisait des chèques de voyages ou on convertissait* les devises* nationales dans un bureau de change. Aujourd'hui, la plupart des gens se servent de leur carte bancaire (de débit ou de crédit). Les achats par carte bancaire sont convertis au taux* de change interbancaire, ce qui est plus avantageux que dans un bureau de change. C'est une bonne idée d'emmener deux cartes, au cas où* l'une d'entre elles ne marche plus, soit endommagée* ou volée. C'est aussi une bonne idée de garder de l'argent liquide sur soi, au cas où des magasins n'acceptent pas votre carte bancaire, votre carte de crédit, ou vos chèques de voyage. Toutefois, évitez les retraits* d'argent avec votre carte parce que les frais supplémentaires sont élevés*. Pour utiliser votre carte bancaire dans un distributeur automatique, votre banque personnelle doit être connectée au réseau* international Cirrus ou PLUS. L'avantage des chèques de voyage et des cartes bancaires est qu'ils peuvent être remplacés sous 24 heures en cas de perte* ou de vol*. Au cas où vous ayez besoin d'argent d'urgence, votre famille ou un ami peut faire un virement* automatique dans une banque européenne proche* de votre hôtel.

Recherche : retrait bancaire, retrait étranger, cic

convertissait *converted*; **devise** *currency*; **taux** *rate*; **au cas où** *in case*; **endommagée** *damaged*; **retrait** *withdrawal*; **élevés** *high*; **réseau** *network*; **perte** *loss*; **vol** *theft*; **virement** *transfer*; **proche** *close*

L'argot des ados 4.1

L'argent

le cash	le yeuma
le flouze	le pèze
le fric	la tune

Produits 1.2, 2.2

Si votre séjour en France dure plus longtemps, peut-être que vous déciderez de vous procurer une carte bancaire (CB) très souvent encore appelée par les Français par son premier nom « Carte Bleue ». La carte bancaire est utilisée par beaucoup de Français. Pour obtenir une CB, vous devez ouvrir un compte en banque dans une banque française.

6 Activités culturelles 1.3, 2.1, 3.1, 3.2, 5.1

Complétez les activités suivantes. Vous aurez besoin de visiter le site officiel des banques mentionnées dans Points de départ.

1. Vous voulez ouvrir un compte dans une banque parisienne. Trouvez les banques qui vous permettent d'ouvrir un compte en ligne.
2. Trouvez la banque avec la plus grande sélection de cartes bancaires.
3. Trouvez les banques qui facilitent (*offer*) la mobilité bancaire.
4. Écrivez un sketch qui utilise deux expressions argotiques pour « l'argent ».

Perspectives 1.2, 2.2

« J'étais auditrice libre à l'Université d'Aix-Marseille. Très vite, j'ai ouvert un compte à la banque du coin et j'ai demandé une carte bancaire que je pouvais utiliser aux restaurants, au cinéma, à la librairie, et dans d'autres magasins. Pour mon anniversaire et pour Noël, mes parents m'ont envoyé de l'argent par virement bancaire. »

Cette étudiante américaine a-t-elle eu une bonne ou mauvaise expérience avec sa banque en France ?

Answers

6 Answers will vary.

Perspectives

Elle a eu une bonne expérience car elle a pu utiliser sa carte bancaire et ses parents ont pu lui verser de l'argent dans son compte pour Noël.

Communication

Interpersonal: Paired Practice

Have students make flash cards with the banking terms that they have learned. On one side have students write the English and on the other side the French equivalent. In pairs, have them quiz each other on the terms French to English, English to French. Your more visual learners and artistic students might want to use images instead of the expressions in English. In addition to appealing to their particular learning style, this also eliminates interference from English.

Differentiated Learning

Accelerate

Have students research the latest statistics on the top five American banks. How do they compare in size, customers, and branches to the top five French banks? Compared to France's 3% PIB, what do American banks contribute to the United States' GDP?

Decelerate

Ask students to select a French or Canadian bank and make a publicity brochure featuring the services it offers. Have them go online and use the search words listed below the readings. They must include the logo in the brochure.

Special Needs Students

At-Risk Students

To some students from low-income families, the study of international banking might seem very remote to their current lifestyle. Encourage them to think that by continuing their education they could expand their career possibilities, and that living in Europe or working in banking could be in their future.

Answers

7

1. D
2. A
3. F
4. C
5. B
6. E

Expansion

Give students a photocopy of this generic French check and ask students to embellish it with the logo of a French bank of their choice. Ask them to research a few French department stores (**grands magasins**) online, such as **Le Printemps** (pictured in the unit opener on p. 320) and **Les Galeries Lafayette**, and find the price and model of a pair of sunglasses that suits them. Have students make their check out to the store with the correct amount in euros, and include a photocopy of their "purchase" and its price.

Du côté des médias 1.2

Lisez les instructions pour remplir un chèque.

Chèque no 4569781

Payez contre ce chèque non endossable
sauf auprès d'une Banque ou d'un organisme visé par la loi ______
montant en toutes lettres

à rédiger exclusivement en euros

€ [ ] C

______ A

à ______ B

D A ______

E Le ______

Payable à

24 ROUTE DU POLYGONE
75001 PARIS CEDEX 1
CHEQUE N 4569781

M. VINCENT BATAUD
48 AVENEUE DES MACHABÉS
69037 LYON

F Signature

00345129 45671200927804239754 65400809

A Montant en toutes lettres
B Nom du bénéficiaire
C Montant en chiffres
D Lieu
E Date
F Signature

7 Un chèque bancaire 1.2, 1.3

Donnez la lettre qui correspond à l'action mentionnée.

1. Vous écrivez « Paris ».
2. Vous écrivez combien vous dépensez en toutes lettres.
3. Vous signez votre nom et prénom.
4. Vous écrivez combien vous dépensez en chiffres.
5. Vous écrivez le nom de la personne, du magasin, du restaurant, du supermarché, etc.
6. Vous écrivez la date d'aujourd'hui.

1.2, 2.1

Traditions et pratiques

Les chèques ne sont plus autant utilisés qu'au passé. Les cartes bancaires, les prélèvements automatiques, les paiements par téléphone sont aujourd'hui plus communs. Mais, les chèques n'ont pas complètement disparu ; ils sont souvent utilisés pour payer le loyer ou pour offrir une somme d'argent pour un anniversaire.

Essential Instruction

1. Have students examine the check template and fill it in with a partner.
2. What are the differences in format? How would writing the date be different?
3. Students do **Activité 7** as a class.
4. Have students go online to explore how to open a French bank account.

Recherche : ex-pat, moving to france, opening a french bank account

5. Explain to students that any sentence with a **si** clause is translated with the same sequence of verb tenses as it is in English. Have students review the examples on p. 331.

Structure de la langue

Future Tense in Sentences with *si* 1.2, 4.1

To tell what will happen *if* something else happens or *if* some condition contrary to reality is met, use the future tense along with **si** and the present tense. Here is the order of tenses in these sentences with **si**.

si	+	PRESENT	FUTURE

FUTURE	**si**	+	PRESENT

Si Marame **trouve** du travail à Paris, elle **pourra** ouvrir un compte bancaire. — *If Marame finds work in Paris, she'll be able to open a bank account.*

Je **signerai** des chèques de voyage **si** j'en **ai** besoin. — *I will sign traveler's checks if I need them.*

With **si** and the present tense, you may also use the present tense or the imperative in the result clause.

si	+	PRESENT	PRESENT
si	+	PRESENT	IMPERATIVE

Nous **pouvons** retirer de l'argent au distributeur **si** nous **voulons** acheter quelque chose. — *We can withdraw money from the ATM if we want to buy something.*

Si vous **voulez** faire une demande de carte bancaire, **allez** à la banque! — *If you want to request a debit card, go to the bank!*

Comparaisons 4.1

Does the clause with **si** (*if*) have to be at the beginning of the sentence in French or English?

Resources

WB Workbook 7–9

G & V Practice Games

Answers

Comparaisons

No, the **si** (*if*) clause and the present tense can either begin or end the sentence in both languages.

Reference Desk

1. Point out that of the three sequences described on this page, the one with **si** and the imperative is the least common.
2. **Si** meaning *whether* can take any tense.

Game

Au hasard

Divide the class into two teams. Give one team yellow paper and the other green. Each member of the yellow team writes an interesting "if" clause (name of person or thing + verb in present tense). The green team writes an interesting "result" clause (name of person or thing + verb in the future). After a short amount of time, have the students put their papers in yellow or green piles. Read one yellow "if" clause adding **alors** and one green "result" clause. As you read the sentences, you may have to edit them for correctness or appropriateness as needed. Students could also take turns choosing the slips once you have checked them.

Differentiated Learning

Decelerate

To visualize the correct tense placement in sentences with **si** clauses and to allow students to manipulate the structures, make a list of sentences using each of the three sequences described on this page. Cut the sentences up or put them on index cards. Include cards that have present, future, and imperative for the result clause, forcing students to choose the correct tense and explain why. For example, your cards might be: **Si je suis malade** (one card), **je serai absent(e) demain** (one card), and **je suis absent(e) demain** (one card). Have students manipulate the cards to create a logical and correct sentence. Model the different options for placement of the **si** clause. Note that when the **si** clause includes a word or expression about a future time frame (such as **demain**, **mardi**, or **prochain**), one would choose the future tense for the verb in the result clause.

Answers

8

1. Nous deviendrons hommes/femmes d'affaires si nous étudions l'économie.
2. Il deviendra metteur en scène s'il étudie l'histoire de l'art.
3. Tu deviendras banquier/banquière si tu étudies la gestion.
4. Ils deviendront statisticiens s'ils étudient l'infographie.
5. Elle deviendra médecin si elle étudie la médecine.
6. Vous deviendrez pilotes si vous étudiez l'aéronautique.
7. Elle deviendra femme écrivain si elle étudie la littérature.
8. Ils deviendront vétérinaires s'ils étudient l'anatomie des animaux.

9

1. Que feras-tu si tu vas en vacances?
2. Que feras-tu si tu deviens riche?
3. Que feras-tu si tu achètes un smartphone?
4. Que feras-tu si tu passes du temps à la campagne?
5. Que feras-tu si tu fais du camping?
6. Que feras-tu si tu dînes dans un restaurant français?
7. Que feras-tu si tu voyages à Paris?
8. Que feras-tu si tu vas au parc d'attractions?
9. Que feras-tu si tu vas à la Martinique?
10. Que feras-tu si tu gagnes un billet d'avion gratuit?

Partner answers will vary.

Reference Desk

Remind students that when a profession is used with **être** and **devenir** (as in Activity 8), there is no article in front of the profession. In English we say, "He will become a pilot." But in French we say, "**Il deviendra pilote.**" In French, the profession is used like an adjective, without an article, just the same as one uses words for nationality and religion (for example: **Il est catholique. Il est francais.**).

8 Les professions 1.2

Interpretive Reading

Dites ce que les personnes suivantes deviendront si elles étudient les matières indiquées.

chercheur/chercheuse	**médecin**	**(femme) écrivain**
banquier/banquière	**homme/femme d'affaires**	**pilote**
vétérinaire	**statisticien/statisticienne**	**metteur en scène**

MODÈLE je (la chimie)
Je deviendrai chercheur/chercheuse si j'étudie la chimie.

1. nous (l'économie)
2. Hugo (l'histoire de l'art)
3. tu (la gestion)
4. Chloé et David (l'infographie)
5. Marion (la médecine)
6. Jules et toi (l'aéronautique)
7. Samia (la littérature)
8. Marie-Alice et Alex (l'anatomie des animaux)

9 Que feras-tu si... ? 1.1

Interpersonal Speaking

Avec un partenaire, parlez de ce que vous ferez dans chaque situation. Posez des questions, puis répondez-y.

MODÈLE sortir ce weekend
A: Que feras-tu si tu sors ce weekend?
B: Si je sors ce weekend, j'irai au cinéma. Et toi, que feras-tu si tu sors ce weekend?
A: Je ferai du shopping si je sors ce weekend.

1. aller en vacances
2. devenir riche
3. acheter un smartphone
4. passer du temps à la campagne
5. faire du camping
6. dîner dans un restaurant français
7. voyager à Paris
8. aller au parc d'attractions
9. aller à la Martinique
10. gagner un billet d'avion gratuit

Essential Instruction

1. Have students do **Activité 9** in class. They will need time to look up any needed vocabulary from the list on p. 323. Correct the exercises upon completion.
2. Arrange students randomly in pairs to do **Activité 10**. Debrief with the class as a whole the variations of each activity. Ask students to think of other situations and possible options.
3. Remind students that **quand** and **lorsque** are synonyms, and **aussitôt que** and **dès que** are also synonyms.
4. Go over the chart and examples with the students.

Future Tense after *quand* 1.2, 4.1

Another use of the future tense is to tell what will happen *when* something else happens in the future. Here is the order of tenses in these sentences with **quand**:

quand + FUTURE	FUTURE

FUTURE	**quand** + FUTURE

Quand je **suivrai** le cours d'histoire de l'art, je **connaîtrai** tous les artistes importants! — *When I take the art history course, I will know all the important artists!*

The future tense is also used after the conjunctions **lorsque**, **aussitôt que**, and **dès que**.

Lorsqu'il y **aura** un projet en génie, nous **pourrons** travailler ensemble. — *When there is an engineering project, we can work together.*

Aussitôt que le prof **arrivera**, nous **passerons** notre examen de psychologie. — *As soon as the teacher arrives, we will take our psychology test.*

Tu me **diras** ton emploi du temps **dès que** tu le **sauras**? — *Will you tell me your schedule as soon as you know it?*

Note in the examples above that the phrase with **quand**, **lorsque**, **aussitôt que**, or **dès que** can either begin or end the sentence.

Comparaisons 1.2, 4.1

What is the difference between the tenses used in the French and English examples above?

Resources

- WB Workbook 10–11
- LA Listening Activity 2
- G & V Practice Games

Answers

Comparaisons
When referring to future events, the French verb in each clause is in the future when **quand** is used, but in English the verb following *when* is in the present tense.

Reference Desk

If students understand the logic of the rule for "**quand** + FUTURE | FUTURE" they will not find it difficult. In English we say, "When I go to town, I will buy milk." To the French, this is illogical since you are not in town now but you *will* be in town when you *will* buy the milk. Since both activities occur in the future, both verbs are expressed in the future.

Expansion

PQA (Personalized Questions and Answers)
Ask students what they will do when they are a certain age or when something happens in the future.

Differentiated Learning

Accelerate
Have students write examples of these clauses in the future as they pertain to their personal lives.

Decelerate
Have students review the formation of the future tense of regular and irregular verbs so that they will be successful using the clauses with the future. Encourage them to use online practice sites to make it more enjoyable.

Multiple Intelligences

Visual-Spatial
Students can make a chart comparing **si** clauses and **quand** clauses in the future.

10 À la Banque Centrale 1.2

Interpretive Reading

Il n'y a qu'une banque dans votre village, la Banque Centrale. Complétez les phrases sur les activités des clients à la banque.

1. Quand j'irai à la Banque Centrale, j'.... (ouvrir un compte)
2. Maylis recevra une carte de crédit quand elle.... (faire une demande de carte de crédit)
3. Lorsque tu retiras de l'argent au distributeur, tu.... (avoir de l'argent liquide)
4. Les Dujardin utiliseront leur Carte bleue lorsqu'ils.... (voyager au Canada)
5. Quand vous signerez votre chèque, on vous.... (donner des pièces de monnaie et des billets à la caisse)
6. Nous demanderons des chèques de voyage quand nous.... (aller en Angleterre)

11 Quand je serai en France 1.2

Interpretive Listening

Écrivez les numéros 1–8 sur votre papier. Écoutez les questions suivantes. Choisissez la lettre qui correspond à la meilleure réponse.

A. J'étudierai les sciences à la faculté de médecine.
B. Alors, je serai infirmier.
C. Quand j'aurai mon bac, j'irai à l'université.
D. J'ouvrirai un compte bancaire, puis j'utiliserai ma carte bancaire.
E. Non, je travaillerai d'abord en Afrique.
F. Alors, j'utiliserai mes chèques de voyage.
G. Oh là là, qu'est-ce que tu es négatif! Eh bien alors, j'appellerai mes parents au Canada.
H. Si je ne peux pas ouvrir de compte, j'utiliserai ma carte American Express®.

12 Le weekend prochain 1.1, 5.2

Interpersonal Speaking

À tour de rôle, vous allez parler de ce que vous ferez le weekend prochain. Le but est de continuer la conversation aussi longtemps que possible. Suivez le modèle.

MODÈLE rentrer chez toi vendredi soir
A: Qu'est-ce que tu feras lorsque tu rentreras chez toi vendredi soir?
B: Lorsque je rentrerai chez moi, je me détendrai.

Resources

Activity 11

Answers

10

1. ouvrirai un compte
2. fera une demande de carte de crédit
3. auras de l'argent liquide
4. voyageront au Canada
5. donnera des pièces de monnaie et des billets à la caisse
6. irons en Angleterre

11 Script

1. Qu'est-ce que tu feras après le bac?
2. Qu'est-ce que tu étudieras lorsque tu seras à la fac en France?
3. Quand tu seras médecin, tu rentreras au Canada?
4. Qu'est-ce que tu feras si tu ne peux pas devenir médecin en France?
5. Comment vas-tu retirer de l'argent en France?
6. Qu'est-ce que tu feras si tu ne peux pas ouvrir de compte en banque en France?
7. Et si ta carte ne marche pas, que feras-tu, alors?
8. Et si on te vole ton portefeuille?

1. C; 2. A; 3. E; 4. B; 5. D; 6. H; 7. F; 8. G

12 Conversations will vary.

Game

Conjugons!

To review verbs, give students a whiteboard. Call out a subject and an infinitive, for example, **parler/tu**. Students write the verb in the future. Write the correct verb on the board. Students keep their own score. To add difficulty, give students a subject and verb in the present tense, which they write in the future. The student with the highest score is the **RDJ** or **roi/reine du Jour**.

Communication

Interpersonal: Cooperative Groups

For **Activité 13**, divide the class in two groups. The teacher asks the activity questions. A student from one team answers, then a student from the second team adds to what the first student said. Next, a student from the first team adds a new detail. Continue until students can go no further.

Essential Instruction

1. After the verb review, students do **Activité 10**. Ask them to translate the sentences into English to emphasize the difference between the two languages.
2. Students hear questions in **Activité 11** and select the correct response. Replay to reinforce listening comprehension.
3. Students work in groups to do **Activité 13**, and then present their ad to the class. Students may use cue cards.
4. For **Activité 14**, students work online to research where they want to study.

Communiquez!

13 Que la meilleure banque gagne! 1.1, 1.2, 1.3, 5.2

Interpersonal Speaking, Interpretive Reading, Presentational Speaking and Writing

BNP Paribas, Crédit Agricole et Société Générale sont les trois plus grandes banques françaises sur la base de leurs actifs totaux. Votre professeur vous divisera en trois groupes, ou plutôt en trois banques. Vous faites partie maintenant d'une équipe bancaire particulière et, avec votre groupe, votre tâche consiste à attirer des clients potentiels dans votre banque. Vous devez expliquer pourquoi il est plus avantageux pour les clients de s'adresser à votre banque plutôt qu'aux deux autres. Avec les autres membres de votre groupe, discutez des différents rôles que votre banque remplit, et expliquez les services que vous pouvez offrir. Pensez aussi aux types de clients que vous ciblez : jeunes couples, familles, etc. Ensuite, préparez une annonce publicitaire et présentez-la à la classe.

Recherche : bnp, crédit agricole, société générale france

14 L'apprentissage 1.1, 1.2, 2.2, 3.1, 5.2

Interpersonal Speaking, Interpretive Reading

Vous avez décidé de faire une année d'études universitaires en France. Choisissez une région qui vous plaît, puis cherchez les universités qui s'y trouvent. Allez sur le site pour choisir un programme d'études. Ensuite, expliquez à un partenaire quelles études vous ferez et à quelle université, les cours que vous suivrez et comment cela vous profitera pour vos études aux États-Unis. Dites aussi pourquoi vous avez choisi cette région de la France, et quelles autres choses vous souhaitez y faire.

Recherche : université de (+ RÉGION)

15 Toulouse 1.1, 1.3, 3.2

Interpersonal and Presentational Speaking

Avec environ 1,2 million de personnes dans sa métropole, Toulouse est la quatrième plus grande ville de France (derrière Paris, Lyon et Marseille). Connu par des locaux comme La Ville Rose (d'après la pierre rose utilisée dans la construction de ses bâtiments), Toulouse est une ville en mouvement. Il a connu la plus forte croissance économique de la France ces dernières années et la plus forte croissance démographique de la France depuis 20 ans. Imaginez que vous avez l'occasion de passer un weekend à Toulouse avec deux camarades de classe. Planifiez votre weekend ensemble en décidant où vous resterez, les activités que vous souhaitez faire, et les sites intéressants que vous voulez voir pendant votre séjour. Vous pouvez partager vos idées avec la classe en leur expliquant vos projets. Bon voyage !

Recherche : toulouse tourism, toulouse tripadvisor, visiter toulouse

Resources

CA Communicative Activities

Share

Answers

13 Presentations will vary.

14 Student choices will vary.

15 Itineraries will vary.

Reference Desk

If you have access to Passport, create a question for your students to share their response to a communicative activity.

Expansion

For **Activité 13**, you may want to display the bank advertisements for other French classes, who can then vote on which bank may be the most competitive.

Special Needs Students

Social Anxiety

Offer options to students when presenting their ads in Activity 13 to the class. In addition to allowing them to record their presentation rather than deliver it live, allow them to sit rather than stand, or to use a prop that helps to ease performance anxiety.

Resources

- *Prononciation*
- Pre-test
- *Leçon* Quiz

Answers

B Script

1. Yves vient de demander l'ouverture d'un compte.
2. Il en assurera tout seul la négociation.
3. Il est grand, il faut le laisser faire !
4. Même si la banquière refuse.

1. v, d; 2. r; 3. l; 4. r

D Script

1. C'est mon copain américain.
2. Son ami s'appelle Chris.
3. C'est un garçon incroyable !
4. Il prendra de l'argent à la banque.
5. As-tu un autre cahier ?

1. oui; 2. non; 3. oui; 4. oui; 5. non

Reference Desk

In this section, stressed letters have been bolded and underlined (for example, **e**, **s**, **l**, or **t**). Unpronounced letters have been grayed out and underlined (for example, e, s, l, or t).

Prononciation

Repeated Consonants Surrounding Falling /ə/ 1.1

» Recall that the sound /ə/ may be deleted in fast, colloquial French. Two identical consonants can come into contact with each other if /ə/ is deleted between the two. When this happens, both consonants need to be pronounced in the same breath.

A Les consonnes géminées par la chute du /ə/

Répétez les phrases.

	/ ə / prononcé	/ ə / non prononcé
1.	Je voulais **te** téléphoner.	Je voulais **t**e **t**éléphoner.
2.	Il vient **de** dormir.	Il vient **d**e **d**ormir.
3.	Il faut **le** lire.	Il faut **l**e **l**ire.
4.	Max la répa**re**rait.	Max la répa**r**e**r**ait.

B À l'écoute de deux consonnes identiques

Écoutez chaque phrase. Écrivez les consonnes répétées. Il peut y avoir deux exemples dans une phrase.

Nasal Vowels

» Usually, the consonant **n** is not pronounced when the accompanying vowel is nasal, except in cases of liaison. However, liaison is impossible after nouns when a nasal vowel is followed by an initial vowel in the next word (for example: **Il met de l'argent à la banque**). This is called **l'enchaînement vocalique**.

C L'enchaînement vocalique

Répétez ces exemples de l'enchaînement vocalique.

1. Écoute cet accent amusant.
2. Rendez-vous à la maison à onze heures !
3. On devait aller tous les matins à la fac.

D Trouvez l'enchaînement vocalique

*Écrivez **oui** si vous entendez l'enchaînement vocalique, ou **non** si vous ne l'entendez pas.*

Essential Instruction

1. For part **A**, have students compare the sentences before listening and notice how column two is different. Ask them to tap out the beats of the syllables pronounced in one breath.
2. Have students listen to both and repeat the second group of sentences.
3. For part **B**, play each sentence twice, if necessary, for students to hear the repeated consonants.
4. Read the sentences in part **C** several times so that students detect the sound of the liaison. Have them read the sentences after you.
5. Have students listen to part **D** and write **oui** or **non**, depending on whether or not they hear the **enchaînement vocalique**.
6. Modify for students with hearing impairments or those who are linguistically challenged.
7. Students listen to the vocabulary and expressions on p. 337, then copy the terms in their notebooks with an English or French example of each genre.

Leçon B — Vocabulaire actif

À la librairie 1.2

Je m'achète….

Resources

- *Vocabulaire actif*
- eV eVisual
- WB Workbook 1–3
- FC Flash Cards
- LA Listening Activity 1
- C & V Practice Games

Reference Desk

1. **Un livre de poche** was created in 1953 by Henri Filipacchi. The **livre de poche** (*paperback*) is an inexpensive small-sized book, published at low cost in great quantities. Now publishers such as Flammarion, Presses de la Cité, and Gallimard have niche markets producing **livres de poche**.
2. **Recueillir** (*to collect*) is an irregular verb conjugated like an **-er** verb. From that verb comes **un recueil** (*collection*). **Une nouvelle** (*short story*) is a **faux ami. Un manga** (*Japanese comic*) covers a wide variety of subjects: action-adventure, comedy, science fiction, mystery, and romance to name a few. Manga has international appeal.
3. Students might not know the following expressions: **un tome** (*volume*); **un compte-rendu** (*report*); **un récit** (*account*); **vient de paraître** (*just published*); **il s'agit de** (*it is about*); **un bouquin** (*book*); **bouquiner** (*to read*); **bouquiniste** (*person who sells second-hand books*).

nouvelle orthographe: **un bestseller, un thrilleur**

Differentiated Learning

Accelerate
Encourage students to create an activity to introduce or review the **Vocabulaire actif**. Include **Et si je voulais dire…?** if it suits your class. Ask them to visualize and personalize their activity to get the students involved and speaking.

Decelerate
Have students work with a partner to practice and review the new vocabulary. Encourage them to work with electronic flash cards for additional practice.

Interpersonal
Have students conduct a poll on the class's reading preferences.

Resources

Pour la conversation
Et si je voulais dire...?
Activity 1

Answers

1

1. Elle se plaint d'avoir trop de lecture.
2. Elle compte avoir le temps de lire quand elle aura 75 ans.
3. Il faut qu'elle lise un manga, un recueil de poésie, un roman de science-fiction, un roman policier, et des nouvelles.
4. Elle n'aime pas lire la poésie.
5. Elle lui demande si elle doit lire autant dans son cours à elle.

Communication

Presentational: Paired Practice

Have students write a one-sentence description of one of their favorite books and use **Il s'agit de** to give a synopsis. Post the names of the favorite books and have students write their names on the ones that they have read or that could interest them. Have them share their preferences with a partner.

Pour la conversation

1.2

How do I ask what a book is about?

» **Ça parle de quoi?**
What's it about?

How do I say I won't be able to make up my mind?

» Je n'**arriverai** jamais **à me décider**!
I'll never be able to make up my mind!

Et si je voulais dire...?

une critique littéraire	*literary critic*
un discours	*speech*
un essai	*essay*
une légende	*legend*
des mémoires (m.)	*memoirs*
un polar	*mystery novel*
une tragédie	*tragedy*

1 Le cours de littérature

1.2

Interpretive Reading

Lisez la lettre de Clara à sa correspondante au Canada.

le 13 février
Cannes

Hélène,

J'aime bien lire, mais ça sert à quoi si on n'a jamais le temps de faire autre chose? Quand j'aurai soixante-quinze ans et que je ne travaillerai plus, peut-être que j'aurai le temps de lire pour le plaisir. Mais là, vraiment, on exagère, tu ne trouves pas? Notre prof n'est pas raisonnable. Il exige que nous lisions un manga, un recueil de poésie, un roman de science-fiction, un roman policier, et combien de nouvelles? Moi, j'ai horreur de la poésie. Et toi, on te fait lire comme ça dans ton cours de littérature?

Amitiés,
Clara

1. De quoi est-ce que Clara se plaint?
2. Elle compte avoir le temps de lire quand elle aura quel âge?
3. Il faut qu'elle lise quelles sortes de textes?
4. Qu'est-ce qu'elle n'aime pas lire?
5. Qu'est-ce qu'elle demande à sa correspondante?

Essential Instruction

1. Review the vocabulary by describing a type of publication and having students guess the genre. Then review the present tense or other tenses of the irregular verb **lire**. Ask students questions, using **lire**, about their tastes in reading, how often, when, and where they do their reading.
2. Have students read **Activité 1** then answer questions 1–5. Ask if they felt that they too could complain about their assignments. Encourage them to do so **en français**!
3. Ask students to collaborate with a partner to do **Activités 2** and **3**. Have them propose names of other authors and their genres.

2 Des écrivains francophones 1.2, 2.2, 3.1

Interpretive Reading

Dites ce que chaque écrivain écrit. Choisissez un genre de livre dans la banque de mots ci-dessous.

MODÈLE Natalie Nougayrède (magazine *Le Monde*)
Elle écrit **des articles**.

articles	**recueils de poésie**	**romans de science-fiction**	
pièces de théâtre	**romans policiers**	**nouvelles**	**thrillers**

1. Jacques Prévert (*Paroles*)
2. Georges Simenon (*L'inspecteur Cadavre*)
3. Stieg Larsson (*The Girl with the Dragon Tattoo*)
4. Jules Verne (*20 000 lieues sous les mers*)
5. Samuel Beckett (*En attendant Godot*)
6. Guy de Maupassant (*La Parure*)

3 La lecture, ça vous passionne? 1.2, 5.1

Interpretive Viewing

Dites si vous lisez ou si vous ne lisez pas les livres ci-dessous.

MODÈLES

Je lis des romans.
Je ne lis pas de dictionnaires.

pièce de théâtre	**autobiographie**	**roman de science-fiction**		
roman policier	**article**	**mystère**	**recueil de poésie**	**nouvelle**

1. 

2. 

3. 

4. 

5. 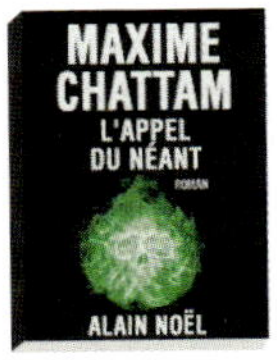

6. 

7. 

8. 

Answers

2

1. Il écrit des recueils de poésie.
2. Il écrit des romans policiers.
3. Il écrit des thrillers.
4. Il écrit des romans de science-fiction.
5. Il écrit des pièces de théâtre.
6. Il écrit des nouvelles.

3

1. Je lis des nouvelles./Je ne lis pas de nouvelles.
2. Je lis des romans de science-fiction./Je ne lis pas de romans de science-fiction.
3. Je lis des recueils de poésie./Je ne lis pas de recueils de poésie.
4. Je lis des articles./Je ne lis pas d'articles.
5. Je lis des romans policiers./Je ne lis pas de romans policiers.
6. Je lis des autobiographies./Je ne lis pas d'autobiographies.
7. Je lis des mystères./Je ne lis pas de mystères.
8. Je lis des pièces de théâtre./Je ne lis pas de pièces de théâtre.

Game

Jeu de questions

Prepare cards with the **Vocabulaire actif** words, enough cards so that each group has a stack. Before playing, ask students to brainstorm questions they might ask to determine a **genre littéraire**, for example, **Ce genre raconte la vie de quelqu'un? Le sujet de l'histoire est aussi l'auteur?** Once the students have an idea of how to proceed, divide the class into groups of four or five. One student draws a card from the stack, then the questioning begins. Once 10 questions are asked, players may not ask any more, and the answer is revealed. If a player guesses correctly, he or she draws a card and play begins again.

Differentiated Learning

Accelerate

Have students write a review of one of their favorite books using the format found on an online shopping site. They may want to read samples of such reviews to get some ideas.

Decelerate

Ask students to copy the vocabulary into their notebooks and add an example. If they write the vocabulary word **un best-seller**, for example, they will also list the name of a best seller such as ***Le Hobbit***.

Special Needs Students

At-Risk Students

Students might be avid readers, so talking about books may be a subject that interests them.

Resources

Activity 4

Answers

4 Script

1. –Bonjour, mademoiselle. Qu'est-ce que vous lisez en ce moment dans le train?
   –Un roman de science-fiction de Jules Verne. Il est passionnant!
2. –Madame, excusez-moi. Quel type de livre lisez-vous?
   –Je lis une biographie de Charles de Gaulle. Un vrai homme politique.
3. –Monsieur. Est-ce que vous pouvez me dire ce que vous lisez?
   –Oui, bien sûr. C'est le dernier thriller de Stieg Larsson.
4. –Madame, quel est votre type de lecture favorite?
   –J'adore les nouvelles. C'est facile et rapide comme lecture dans les transports. Je lis un recueil de nouvelles de Maupassant en ce moment.
5. –Excuse-moi. Tu peux me dire ce que tu lis?
   –Moi, je lis des mangas. J'adore ça!
6. –Madame, vous préférez quel genre de livres?
   –Je préfère un livre de poche... normalement un roman policier de Georges Simenon.
7. –Bonjour, mademoiselle. Est-ce que c'est un livre de poésie que vous lisez?
   –Non, c'est les mémoires de Simone de Beauvoir, une femme pour notre temps aussi.
8. –Bonjour, monsieur. Est-ce que vous lisez quelque chose dans le train?
   –Oui, une série d'articles sur l'économie. C'est une crise! Il faut se renseigner.

1. F; 2. NF; 3. F; 4. F; 5. F; 6. F; 7. NF; 8. NF

5 Answers will vary.

6 Answers will vary.

Communication

Interpersonal: Paired Practice

Have students work in pairs to do **Activité 6** then share with the class what they discussed.

4 Ce que je lis 1.2, 2.2, 5.2

Interpretive Listening

Écrivez les numéros 1–8 sur votre papier. Écoutez Stéphanie interviewer des passagers à la gare du Nord sur ce qu'ils lisent dans le train. Écrivez ***F*** *si on lit de la fiction, ou* ***NF*** *si on ne lit pas de fiction.*

5 Qu'est-ce que tu es en train de lire? 1.1, 3.1, 3.2

Interpersonal Speaking

À tour de rôle, demandez à votre partenaire ce qu'il ou elle est en train de lire. Suivez le modèle.

MODÈLE

A: Qu'est-ce que tu es en train de lire?
B: Je suis en train de lire un roman policier de Georges Simenon.

A: Ça parle de quoi?
B: Il s'agit d'un sans-abri qu'on retrouve dans la Seine, et Maigret trouve la clé du mystère.

A: Tu le recommandes?
B: Mais oui! C'est passionnant.

6 Questions personnelles 1.1, 3.2, 5.2

Interpersonal Speaking

Répondez aux questions avec un partenaire.

1. Préfères-tu lire de la poésie ou de la prose? Des romans ou des nouvelles? Pourquoi?
2. Tu offres des livres à tes amis et à tes parents pour leurs anniversaires? Si oui, quelles sortes?
3. Ce que tu lis en ce moment, ça parle de quoi?
4. Comment est-ce que tu te sers d'un dictionnaire, sur Internet ou à la bibliothèque?
5. Quels best-sellers as-tu lus? Qui les a écrits?
6. Selon toi, la littérature française parle de quoi?

Essential Instruction

1. Talk to students about what you are reading and your favorite genres. Have them share their ideas.
2. Listen to **Activité 4** and answer 1–8. Replay the recording if some students missed more than one or two questions.
3. Consider having your active readers do **Activité 5** in a small group. They could present to the class as a dialogue.
4. Ask students to complete **Activité 6** in pairs, then share with the class something they learned about their classmate's reading tastes.
5. Before watching **Des bouquins pour Justin**, ask students about the photo. Where are they? What are they looking at? Why do you think that they are there? What might the dialogue be about?
6. Have students watch the video with books closed. Ask volunteers to give a synopsis. Other students can add details.
7. Play the video again and ask general comprehension questions.
8. Students can work in pairs to do **Activité 7**.

Rencontres culturelles

Des bouquins pour Justin

1.2, 2.2, 3.2, 5.2

Justin cherche des livres à la librairie, avec l'aide de Léo.

Justin : Je n'arriverai jamais à me décider !

Léo : Bon, on commence par quoi ? Tu voulais un roman de Le Clézio… achète le dernier !

Justin : Ça parle de quoi ?

Léo : Ça s'appelle *Ritournelle de la faim*… tu sais comme dans le « Boléro » de Ravel, quelque chose qui revient. Il s'agit de l'enfance d'une fille dans les années 1930 qui abandonne l'imaginaire pour la réalité.

Justin : Ah, oui, et il me faut *Le… voleur d'ombres*, le dernier Marc Lévy… mon amie Heather adore ses drôles d'histoires d'amour.

Léo : Et n'oublie pas cette petite nouvelle d'Anna Gavalda, *L'Echappée belle.*

Justin : J'ai envie d'un manga. Que me conseilles-tu ?

Léo : *Dreamland*, dont tu deviendras voyageur… je ne t'en dis pas plus.

Justin : J'ai lu quelque chose sur Mabanckou, l'écrivain congolais. Tu connais ?

Léo : *Demain, j'aurai 20 ans* ? Très drôle et plein de tendresse.

Justin : C'est un titre auquel j'aurais dû penser tout seul.

Léo : Pourquoi ?

Justin : Demain j'aurai 20 ans ! Ça tombe bien !

7 Des bouquins pour Justin

1.2, 3.2

Donnez le titre et, quand c'est possible, le nom de l'auteur pour chaque livre décrit.

1. C'est un livre drôle écrit par un auteur congolais.
2. Une jeune fille échange l'imaginaire pour la vie réelle.
3. C'est une histoire d'amour amusante.
4. Le lecteur/la lectrice devient voyageur/voyageuse.
5. C'est une petite nouvelle.

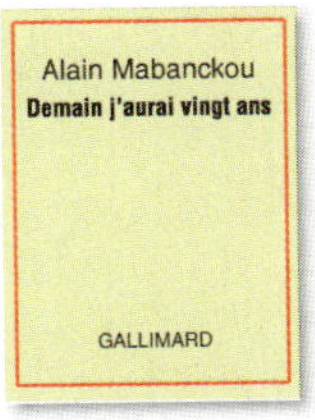

Resources

Dialogue
Activity 7

Dialogue Video

WB Workbook 4

Answers

7

1. *Demain j'aurai vingt ans*. Alain Mabanckou.
2. *Ritournelle de la faim*. Jean-Marie Le Clézio
3. *Le voleur d'ombres*. Marc Lévy.
4. *Dreamland*.
5. *L'échappée belle*. Anna Gavalda.

Reference Desk

1. Jean-Marie Gustave Le Clézio (born in 1940), known as J. M. G. Le Clézio, is a French-Mauritian professor and writer of more than 40 works; he was awarded the 1963 **Prix Renaudot** and the 2008 Nobel Prize for his novel ***Le Procès-Verbal***.
2. Joseph-Maurice Ravel (1875–1937) was a French composer of impressionist music on par with Claude Débussy. Students may recognize his *Boléro*.
3. Marc Lévy (born in 1961) has written ten novels that have been translated into more than 40 languages and have sold more than 23 million copies. He is the most well-known living French author in the world.
4. Anna Gavalda (born in 1970) is a French writer of best-selling short stories and novels.
5. Alain Mabanckou (born in 1966 of Congolese origin) is a French novelist, journalist, and poet. His works offer insight into the people of modern Africa and those Africans who have immigrated to France.

Differentiated Learning

Accelerate

Assign more advanced students titles of books mentioned in the dialogue. Have them give a brief biography of the author and a synopsis of the book.

Multiple Intelligences

Visual-Spatial

Have students design a book jacket for the French translation of their favorite book.

Resources

Extension

Answers

EXTENSION

Answers will vary.

Reference Desk

1. Michel Tournier (1924–2016) was a French writer known for addressing philosophical themes in his novels. He drew inspiration from Socrates, Plato, and German philosophers.
2. **BD** is short for **une bande dessinée**.
3. Françoise Sagan (1935–2004) was a French playwright, novelist, and screenwriter. Sagan wrote stories with strong romantic themes involving wealthy and middle-class characters. As a teenager, she wrote ***Bonjour Tristesse***, which continues to be a classic today.
4. **Grand Corps Malade (GCM),** whose given name is Fabien Marsaud, was born in 1977. He derived his name from a diving accident that left him unable to walk. Through determination and therapy he regained his mobility. He is classified as a French slammer.

EXTENSION **Lecteurs à la FNAC** 1.2, 2.1, 2.2

Un journaliste interviewe des passants sortant de la FNAC.

Journaliste : Quel est votre meilleur souvenir de lecture ?

Passante 1 : Le premier livre que j'ai choisi seule… c'était *Vendredi ou les limbes du Pacifique* de Michel Tournier.

Passant 2 : Ma mère m'avait offert *L'île au trésor* de Stevenson : je l'ai lu sans m'arrêter.

Passante 3 : Là j'ai acheté *Ward*, je ne sais pas de quoi ça parle, je sais simplement qu'il s'agit d'un livre dans lequel l'auteur crée une langue et d'un pays dont il invente la littérature.

Passant 4 : Ma première BD : Tintin, *Le secret de la Licorne*… ça reste pour moi le chef-d'œuvre du genre.

Passante 5 : Toutes les adolescentes de mon âge se souviennent de *Bonjour Tristesse* : je le relis chaque année, à la fin de l'été : vous avez remarqué ? Toutes les adolescences finissent toujours à la fin de l'été : c'est drôle, non ?

Passant 6 : Moi, c'est quand j'écoute du slam : les textes du premier disque de Grand Corps Malade, *Midi vingt*, la vie à l'échelle d'une journée… vous en connaissez beaucoup de souvenirs comme ça.

EXTENSION 1.3

Quels titres suggérés par les passants vous intéressent ? Pourquoi ? Y a-t-il un livre que vous recommanderiez à un(e) ami(e) ?

Essential Instruction

1. Students read **Extension** and make a list of the titles and authors mentioned. Have them go online and write a synopsis of each one.
2. Students do **Extension** by filling in the titles of works that might interest them in the squares provided.
3. Have students write down the statistics in the passage **Les habitudes de lecture des Français** then compare, where possible, that information to American reading habits. The statistics will not line up perfectly but are meant to be a point of departure for a discussion of comparative reading habits.

Recherche : reading habits of americans, pew internet

Pre-AP

Question centrale ? Comment s'intégrer à une autre culture ?

Les habitudes de lecture des Français

1.2, 2.1, 3.1

Le livre reste en France la marque de la culture, comme en témoigne* une photo officielle du Président Emmanuel Macron, photographié avec trois volumes de la prestigieuse collection de La Pléiade, *Le Rouge et le noir* de Stendhal, *Les Nourritures terrestres* de Gide et les *Mémoires de guerre* de Charles de Gaulle. Dans la vie politique, les hommes politiques parlent de leurs lectures et montrent un goût pour l'écriture* (comme le Général De Gaulle, Georges Pompidou, François Mitterrand). Les Français adorent les prix littéraires* ; il y en a 200 dont le Prix Goncourt qui est le plus célèbre.

Toulouse (Haute-Garonne, France) : Intérieur de la librairie « Ombres Blanches »

Le goût du livre est si important que la plupart des quotidiens* et des suppléments hebdomadaires* ont des articles sur la littérature (*L'Express*, *Le Point* ou *Le Nouvel Observateur*). Il existe aussi des revues* littéraires spécialisées (*Magazine Lire* ou *Le Magazine littéraire*). En outre*, les Français offrent prioritairement un livre comme cadeau.

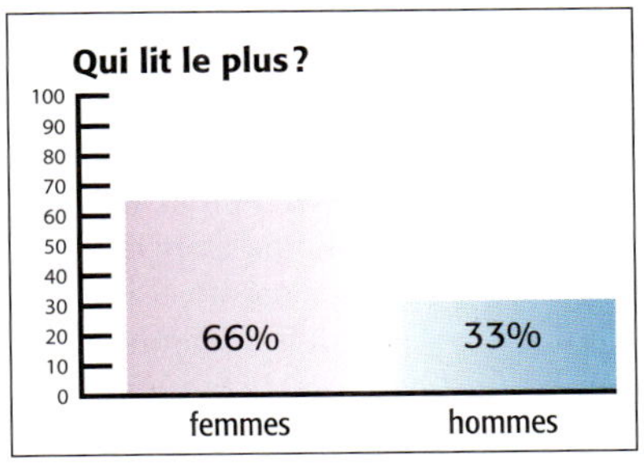

80% des Français déclarent aimer lire, et ils sont seulement 5% à ne lire aucun livre par an. Ils sont fans de romans policiers, de livres d'histoire et de romans. Ils sont 27% à lire de la littérature.

Le nombre de gros lecteurs augmente et les femmes lisent davantage* que les hommes. Les habitudes de lecture changent aussi : la lecture au format numérique concerne aujourd'hui un quart des lecteurs.

Recherche : fnac france

témoigne *shows* ; **écriture** *writing* ; **prix littéraires** récompenses pour les écrivains ; **quotidiens** journaux ; **hebdomadaires** qui paraissent une fois par semaine ; **revues** *reviews* ; **En outre** *Moreover* ; **davantage** plus

1.2, 2.2, 3.1

Produits

En France on aime **les émissions de télé littéraires** telles que *Un livre, un jour* (France 3), *Bibliothèque Médicis* (Public Sénat), *Voyage au bout de la nuit* (D8), *La Grande Librairie* (France 5), *21 cm* (Canal+). La première émission de télé où on a discuté de livres a été *Lectures pour tous*, de 1953 à 1968.

Comparaisons

1.2, 4.2

Y a-t-il autant d'émissions télévisées littéraires aux États-Unis qu'en France ? Quel public ciblent-elles selon vous ?

Resources

Points de départ

WB Workbook 5

Explore

Answers

Comparaisons

Answers will vary.

Reference desk

If you have access to Passport, find a video or a news article related to **lire** or **lecture** and show it to your students.

Communication

Interpersonal: Paired Practice

Have students interview one another using the questions from **Lecteurs à la FNAC : Quel est ton meilleur souvenir de lecture ? Le premier livre que tu as choisi seul(e) ? Ta première BD ?** Consider expanding the survey to include questions about their current reading, popular magazines, favorite song lyrics, and Internet sites.

Critical Thinking

Analysis

How has online shopping changed the purchasing habits of Americans? What factors have led to the demise of small bookstores in the United States?

Differentiated Learning

Accelerate

Have students compare the book purchasing practices of the French and Americans. From where do the majority of French and Americans buy their books? What literary magazines in the United States correspond to those magazines mentioned in the article?

Decelerate

Students make true and false statements from the reading **Les habitudes de lecture des Français**, then ask their classmates who answer either **vrai** or **faux.**

Special Needs Students

Linguistically Challenged

Spend some time teaching pre-reading techniques before asking students to read difficult passages. Encourage them to skim for information, look for cognates, and read without looking up every word in the dictionary.

Answers

Comparaisons
Answers will vary.

Reference Desk

1. As of 2017, France and the United States both have 14 Nobel laureates for Literature. (The United States had 370 overall Nobel laureates to France's 68.) The 14 French Nobel laureates discount Maeterlinck, who was Belgian; Sartre, who declined the prize; and Beckett, who lived in Paris, wrote in French and English, and was Irish. Gao Xingjian writes in Chinese but has been a French citizen since 1998. He won in 2000.
2. Jean-Marie Le Clézio was awarded the **Prix Nobel de littérature** in 2008. Maryse Condé has received more than 15 awards, such as the most distinguished **Prix de l'Académie Française** (1998) and the **Grand Prix du roman métis** (2010). Among other distinctions, she was crowned **Chevalier de l'Ordre de la Légion d'Honneur** (2004) and **Grand officier de l'Ordre national du Mérite** (2010).
3. **L'île Maurice**, officially the Republic of Mauritius, is an island nation in the Indian Ocean about 1,200 miles off the east coast of Africa.
4. The word **le pays** can mean region or country. **Dépaysé** is the equivalent of the English expression *culture-shocked*.
5. **Un colon** is a colonist who establishes **une colonie**.
6. **La Légion d'Honneur**, established by Napoleon in 1802, is France's highest public award to a citizen recognized for "eminent service" to the nation.
7. If you have access to Passport, find a video or news article related to **la littérature** and show it to your students.

La Francophonie

Modiano, Le Clézio, Condé

Littérature 1.2, 2.2, 3.1

En France : Jean-Marie Le Clézio et Patrick Modiano

Prix Nobel de Littérature en 2008, Jean-Marie Gustave Le Clézio est un écrivain fortement inspiré par les voyages : Nice, son lieu de naissance (*Le Procès-verbal,* 1963) ; l'Ile Maurice de ses origines familiales (*La Quarantaine*, 1995) ; l'Afrique de son enfance (*Onitsha*, 1991) ; les côtes amérindiennes–Mexique et Panama–où il médite* sur le destin des civilisations détruites par la colonisation (*Le Rêve mexicain*, 1988) ; le Maroc (*Désert*, 1980). Homme de frontières (*Ritournelle de la faim*, 2008), il a très tôt compris que son franchissement* était une garantie de la sauvegarde de son identité et de sa vérité*.

Patrick Modiano est né dans la banlieue parisienne de Boulogne-Billancourt. Particulièrement marqué par la mort de son frère, cet écrivain livre* une sensibilité particulière dans son écriture. Son premier roman *La Place de L'Étoile* (entendre l'étoile jaune portée par les Juifs pendant la guerre) a eu beaucoup de succès. Patrick Modiano a reçu le Grand Prix de l'Académie française (*Les Boulevards de ceinture*, 1972), le Prix Goncourt (*Rue des boutiques obscures*, 1978) et le Prix Nobel de littérature (2014). Il captive, il saisit* et il bouleverse* ses lecteurs. Toute l'œuvre de Patrick Modiano repose sur la mémoire qu'il définit comme « des fragments de passé, des traces interrompues, des destinées humaines fuyantes*, presque insaisissables ».

Recherche : le clézio, modiano, prix nobel de littérature

médite *meditates* ; **franchissement** *(border) crossing* ; **vérité** *truth* ; **livre** *delivers* ; **saisit** *grips* ; **bouleverse** *moves* ; **fuyantes** *fleeting*

Comparaisons

Quel pays a reçu plus de Prix Nobel pour la littérature, la France ou les États-Unis ? Pourquoi, selon vous ?

1.2, 4.2

En Guadeloupe : Maryse Condé 1.2, 2.2, 3.1

Maryse Condé a aussi beaucoup voyagé. Née en Guadeloupe, elle a étudié les Lettres Classiques à la Sorbonne à Paris, puis elle a vécu en Afrique dans plusieurs pays. Elle vit maintenant aux États-Unis et à la Guadeloupe. Romancière* émérite, elle explore des questions fondamentales de race, de sexe, et de culture. Elle reçoit le Grand Prix Littéraire de la Femme pour *Moi, Tituba, sorcière, Noire de Salem* (1986). Ce roman est l'histoire d'une femme née au 17ème siècle d'une esclave noire et d'un colon blanc. Élevée par une vieille sorcière* antillaise, elle arrive à confronter la souffrance et à réclamer* son identité. Un autre roman connu de Maryse Condé est *Histoire de la femme cannibale* (2005), qui relie la France, l'Afrique, les États-Unis, et le Japon. Maryse Condé a reçu la distinction d'Officier de l'Ordre de la Légion d'Honneur en 2014.

Recherche : moi tituba sorcière, victoire, les saveurs et les mots ; maryse condé, légion d'honneur

romancière femme qui écrit des romans ; **sorcière** *witch* ; **réclamer** *reclaim*

Essential Instruction

1. On the world map, point out the locations where the authors lived or traveled as mentioned in the two readings. Show photos of the two authors to personalize the readings.
2. Students should go online to complete **Activité 8**.
3. Combine students with different skill sets in small groups to answer the questions in **Activité 9**.

8 Activités culturelles 1.2, 1.3, 3.2

Faites les activités suivantes.

1. Faites des recherches, puis faites un graphique pour comparer les préférences de lecture en France et aux États-Unis.
2. Faites une carte pour retracer les voyages de Jean-Marie Le Clézio. Connaissez-vous des auteurs francophones ou anglophones qui ont écrit sur ces mêmes destinations?
3. Lisez la critique d'un livre de Le Clézio et présentez-la dans vos propres mots (faites un résumé de l'idée essentielle, et de deux arguments ou détails particuliers).
4. Faites une liste de six romans de Maryse Condé et précisez où chaque histoire a lieu.

Perspectives 1.2, 2.1

Le Clézio a dit: « L'artiste est celui qui nous montre du doigt une parcelle du monde. » Est-ce vrai de tous les écrivains que vous connaissez? Selon vous, est-ce le sentiment d'un voyageur ou d'un écrivain?

Du côté des médias 1.2

Lisez les informations dans le tableau ci-dessous.

Le poids des principaux secteurs dans les ventes littéraires*

	chiffre d'affaires	ex. vendus
Livres scolaires	8%	6%
Sciences et techniques, médecine, gestion	3%	1%
Documents, actualité, essais, humour	4%	3%
Sciences humaines et sociales (dont Droit)	10%	4%
Religion	1,1%	1,0%
Ésotérisme	0,2%	0,3%
Arts et Beaux livres	3,4%	2%
Dictionnaires et encyclopédies	3%	3%

	chiffre d'affaires	ex. vendus
Cartes géographiques, atlas	2%	5%
Romans	23%	23%
Contes, légendes, romans régionaux, nouvelles	0,6%	0,5%
Théâtre, poésie	0,3%	0,4%
Jeunesse	14%	21%
Bandes dessinées	7,5%	6%
Mangas, comics	3%	4%
Loisirs, vie pratique, tourisme	13%	13%

Source: SNE, enquête de branche, échantillon 2015

*Poids des principaux secteurs d'édition dans les ventes des éditeurs

9 La lecture en France 1.2, 2.1, 3.1, 5.2

Répondez aux questions.

1. Quels sont les livres les plus vendus en France en 2015?
2. Quels sont les quatre secteurs littéraires les moins populaires?
3. Quel est le pourcentage du chiffre d'affaires pour les livres scolaires?
4. Est-ce que les Français achètent plus de livres sur les sciences et techniques, la médecine, et la gestion (*business management*) ou sur les sciences humaines (*humanities*) et sociales?
5. Quels autres secteurs ont un bon chiffre d'affaires (plus de 7%)?

Answers

8 Answers will vary.

Perspectives
Answers will vary.

9
1. les romans
2. l'ésotérisme, la religion, le théâtre et la poésie
3. 8%
4. Ils achètent plus de livres sur les sciences humaines et sociales.
5. les livres scolaires, les romans, les livres jeunesse, les livres loisirs, vie pratique et tourisme, et les bandes dessinées.

Communication

Interpersonal: Cooperative Groups
Have students discuss **Perspectives** in small groups. One student takes notes on the discussion. Combine groups to share their findings in a whole-class discussion.

Differentiated Learning

Accelerate
Have students do a timed writing, answering the questions in **Perspectives**.

Decelerate
Have students do the second activity of **Activité 8**, making a map of the places that Le Clézio and Maryse Condé have lived, as described in the reading passage.

Special Needs Students

AD(H)D/Dyslexia/Linguistically Challenged
To students with learning challenges, long reading passages in French can seem daunting. Break down the readings into smaller sections. Ask students basic comprehension questions in French that they can answer more easily. In doing so, you will be able to determine their level of understanding.

Mathematical/Logical
Have students compare the overall book sales to the number of each genre's sales to see which genre is more worthwhile (or expensive) to publish.

Resources

WB Workbook 6–7
LA Listening Activity 2
G & V Practice Games

Answers

10

1. Sadia et Léonne sont amoureuses de l'auteur du recueil de poésie.
2. Adam se plaint du mystère.
3. Trois élèves ont besoin du roman policier.
4. Annick rêve de la nouvelle.
5. Akila se méfie de l'auteur du roman de science-fiction.
6. Le prof se sert du livre de poche.
7. Je me souviens du manga.
8. Max et Chloé ont peur du thriller.

Reference Desk

1. Students copy the VERB + **de** + NOUN into their notebooks. Suggest different ways of remembering the expressions with **de**. **Avoir besoin de** means *to need*, but it is easier to remember if they think of *to have a need of*.
2. **Plaindre** means *to pity*. If you pity yourself, **se plaindre de**, you complain. The majority of the VERB + **de** + NOUN may be followed by an infinitive: **J'ai besoin de lait. J'ai besoin d'acheter du lait.**

Structure de la langue

Révision: VERB + *de* + NOUN 1.2

Many verbs and verbal expressions in French are followed by **de** and a noun. They include:

avoir besoin de	*to need*
avoir envie de	*to want, to feel like*
avoir peur de	*to be afraid of*
être amoureux/amoureuse de	*to be in love with*
être au courant de	*to be informed of*
être content(e) de	*to be happy about*
faire la connaissance de	*to meet*
se méfier de	*to beware of*
s'occuper de	*to take care of*
parler de	*to speak/talk about*
se plaindre de	*to complain about*
rêver de	*to dream about*
se servir de	*to use*
se souvenir de	*to remember*

Il **a envie d**'un sundae.	*He wants an ice cream sundae.*
Il **se plaignait de** l'édition de poche qu'il a lue la semaine dernière.	*He was complaining about the paperback he read last week.*
Nous **nous méfions des** grandes banques.	*We are wary of large banks.*
Je **m'occupe de** ma grand-mère.	*I take care of my grandmother.*
Vous **rêvez d**'un voyage en France.	*You dream of a trip to France.*

10 Club de lecture 1.3, 3.2

Presentational Speaking or Writing

Dire ce que la classe pense des livres suivants. Réécrivez les phrases en vous servant des verbes de la banque de mots.

MODÈLE 

On échange des informations sur le dictionnaire.
On parle du dictionnaire.

se méfier de **parler de** **se plaindre de** **avoir peur de** **se souvenir de**
rêver de **avoir besoin de** **se servir de** **être amoureux/amoureuse de**

1. Sadia et Léonne adorent l'auteur du recueil de poésie.

2. Adam critique le mystère.

3. Trois élèves n'ont pas encore le roman policier.

4. Annick pense à la nouvelle.

5. Akila ne fait pas confiance à l'auteur du roman de science-fiction.

6. Le prof utilise le livre de poche.

7. Je me rappelle le manga.

8. Max et Chloé craignent le thriller.

Essential Instruction

1. Review **se plaindre de** and **se servir de**. Remind students that **se souvenir de** is conjugated like **venir**.
2. Students work in study teams to learn the **de** + NOUN expressions. Use class time to memorize. Give a small bonus-point quiz as motivation to learn them in class. Remind students of the contractions **de + le** to **du** and **de + les** to **des**.
3. Allow students time to prepare **Activité 10** before doing the activity orally.
4. Present the relative pronoun **dont**. Give students a sentence to help them memorize, for example, **Le livre dont j'ai besoin coûte cher. L'ami dont la sœur est malade s'appelle Roger. Je n'ai pas vu le film dont il m'a parlé.** Have students translate the sentences to figure out the multiple translations for the word **dont**.

The Relative Pronoun *dont* 1.2

You know how to combine two shorter sentences into a longer one by using the relative pronouns **qui** and **que**. The word **dont** is also a relative pronoun, used to connect two clauses in a complex sentence. **Dont** (*about which/whom, of which/whom, whose*) replaces **de** and a noun and is used with the verbs and verbal expressions that are followed by **de** and a noun that you reviewed on page 346.

dont	=	**de**	+	NOUN

In the following examples, note how **dont** always comes directly after its antecedent to join the two separate sentences into one.

C'est un manga. Ma sœur a parlé de ce manga.	*It is a manga. My sister talked about this manga.*
C'est un manga **dont** ma sœur a parlé.	*It is a manga that my sister talked about.*
J'ai trouvé l'anthologie de poésie. J'avais besoin de l'anthologie de poésie.	*I found the poetry anthology. I needed the poetry anthology.*
J'ai trouvé l'anthologie de poésie **dont** j'avais besoin.	*I found the poetry anthology that I needed.*

The relative pronoun **dont** means "whose" in sentences where **de** indicates relationship or possession.

J'ai lu une nouvelle d'un écrivain sénégalais. Ses livres sont bien connus.	*I read a short novel by a Senegalese writer. His books are well known.*
J'ai lu une nouvelle d'un écrivain sénégalais **dont** les livres sont bien connus.	*I read a short novel by a Senegalese writer whose books are well known.*

Dont means "in which" after the expression **la façon**.

La façon **dont** Le Clézio écrit est fascinante.	*The way in which Le Clézio writes is fascinating.*

Resources

WB Workbook 8–9

G & V Practice Games

Reference Desk

1. **Dont** must always be expressed in French, even if its English equivalent is omitted.
2. **Dont** may refer to people or things.
3. The meaning of **dont** varies depending on context. In relative clauses, **dont** is used instead of **qui** or **que** with **de** expressions.
4. When **dont** means *whose*, it replaces **de** and a noun. If used with **la façon**, it means *in which* or *by which*.

Expansion

Question Circling

Students will best acquire the pronoun by hearing it repeated. Ask a series of questions to individual students and the whole class, being sure to repeat the pronoun. Ask a "yes" question, a "no" question, an "either/or" question, and an information question.

"Est-ce que la Ferrari est la voiture dont tu as envie?" "Est-ce que la VW est la voiture dont tu as envie?" "Est-ce que la Ferrari est la voiture dont tu as envie, ou est-ce que la VW est la voiture dont tu as envie?" "Quelle est la voiture dont tu as envie?"

Differentiated Learning

Decelerate

Some students may need extra practice combining sentences with **dont**. Additional resources or exercises that combine two sentences using the relative pronouns **qui**, **que**, and **dont** would be helpful.

Resources

Activity 11

Answers

Comparaisons

Whose can be used for people or things in both French and English.

11

1. Karim n'a pas fini le roman policier dont il s'est plaint.
2. Marie-Alix a acheté le recueil de nouvelles dont elle avait besoin pour son cours.
3. José est sorti avec une fille dont il est amoureux.
4. Maman m'a offert un best-seller dont mon frère lui a parlé.
5. À la librairie, j'ai vu une nouvelle édition de poche d'un roman de Le Clézio dont je me servirai pour ma composition.
6. En classe les élèves lisent une anthologie de littérature dont ils sont contents.
7. C'est un roman de science-fiction très intéressant dont je me souviens.
8. Le grand-père a acheté la glace dont sa petite-fille avait envie.
9. Le docteur a guéri le patient dont il s'occupait.
10. Mes parents ont fait un voyage dont ils ont toujours rêvé.
11. J'ai visité le village dont ma grand-mère se souvient.
12. Le petit garçon a traversé le boulevard dont ses parents se méfient.

Communication

Interpersonal: Cooperative Groups

Give students a cloze exercise featuring **qui**, **que**, and **dont**. Have them fill in the blanks, then join two other students to compare answers. They must agree on which responses are correct. Encourage them to explain their choice to the group. Finally, correct and compare with the whole class. Compliment correct answers by saying **Chapeau!**

11 Combinez les phrases! 1.3, 4.1

Presentational Speaking or Writing

*Combinez les deux phrases pour en faire une avec **dont**. Suivez le modèle.*

MODÈLE Léo a acheté le dico. Il avait besoin d'un dico.
Léo a acheté le dico dont il avait besoin.

1. Karim n'a pas fini le roman policier. Il s'est plaint du roman policier.
2. Marie-Alix a acheté le recueil de nouvelles. Elle avait besoin du recueil pour son cours.
3. José est sorti avec une fille. Il est amoureux de la fille.
4. Maman m'a offert un best-seller. Mon frère lui a parlé du best-seller.
5. À la librairie, j'ai vu une nouvelle édition de poche d'un roman de Le Clézio. Je me servirai de la nouvelle édition de poche pour ma composition.
6. En classe les élèves lisent une anthologie de littérature. Ils sont contents de cette anthologie.
7. C'est un roman de science-fiction très intéressant. Je me souviens de ce roman.
8. Le grand-père a acheté la glace pour sa petite-fille. Sa petite-fille avait envie de la glace.
9. Le docteur a guéri le patient. Il s'occupait du patient.
10. Mes parents ont fait un voyage. Ils ont toujours rêvé de ce voyage.
11. J'ai visité le village. Ma grand-mère se souvient du village.
12. Le petit garçon a traversé le boulevard. Ses parents se méfient du boulevard.

4.1

Comparaisons

Does **dont** refer to people or things in French? In English, what does *whose* refer to?

Voici la fille **dont** le père est venu au lycée.
Here is the girl *whose* father came to school.

Voici le restaurant **dont** le chef est italien.
This is the restaurant *whose* chef is italian.

La glace, c'est le goûter dont Mme Perez a envie.

On recycle!

Avec un partenaire, imaginez que vous allez à la plage. Faites deviner à votre partenaire l'objet que vous décrivez en utilisant le pronom relatif **dont**. Vous pouvez vous servir des mots ci-dessous:

MODÈLE A: C'est la chose dont j'ai besoin pour être accepté(e) dans l'eau.
B: C'est un maillot de bain!

la crème solaire ▪ un matelas pneumatique ▪ des lunettes de soleil ▪ un sac de plage ▪ une liseuse ▪ un parasol ▪ une serviette de plage ▪ un maillot de bain ▪ un scooter des mers

Essential Instruction

1. Do **Activité 11** as pair work. Ask volunteers to share their answers. Encourage students who did not do as well to ask questions for further clarification. If there are too many sentences, assign the even numbers to one half of the class and the odd numbers to the other half, and have each half quiz the other.
2. Students listen to **Activité 12** and answer questions 1–7. Play each one again and have the students identify the clue from the question that gave them the answer.
3. Have students write the answers to **Activité 13** in their notebooks and refer to the picture for clues. Expand the conversation by asking open-ended questions about the picture. For example, you could ask how many days Mme Laforge plans to stay at the hotel.

12 Dans le cours de littérature 1.2

Interpretive Listening

Écrivez les numéros 1–7 sur votre papier. Écoutez les phrases. Puis, écrivez le genre de livres dont tout le monde se sert pour son cours de littérature.

13 À l'Hôtel Beauséjour 1.2, 1.3

Interpretive Viewing, Presentational Speaking or Writing

Identifiez les personnes dont on parle.

MODÈLE Ses enfants s'appellent Véro et Marc.
La personne dont les enfants s'appellent Véro et Marc est M. Ferrand.

1. Son manteau est très élégant.
2. Sa tablette est rouge.
3. Sa robe est longue.
4. Son fils est fatigué.
5. Sa femme est bavarde.
6. Sa responsabilité est le coffre.
7. Sa fille est énergique.

On recycle!

With a partner, take turns describing the scene in the illustration, using different verb tenses and moods (**imparfait**, **présent**, **futur**, and **conditionnel**) to fit the following situations:

A. You describe your vacation last month.
B. You are raving about the play you are going to see while waiting for your mother to meet you and your father in the lobby.
C. You tell your family what will happen when you all go on vacation together next week.
D. You imagine what it would be like if you were trying to check your agenda online at a table in a busy hotel lobby.

Differentiated Learning

Accelerate

Have students look at the picture and tell a story about the people at the hotel, inventing fun or comical details about each character.

Multiple Intelligences

Visual-Spatial/Logical-Mathematical

Have students collaborate to create a poster for the class that explains the use of **qui**, **que**, and **dont** with examples.

Resources

Activity 12

Answers

12 Script

1. L'histoire dont Sébastien se sert est dans un recueil de Maupassant.
2. L'anthologie poétique dont Martine et Chloé se servent est anglaise.
3. Les mangas dont Julie se sert sont japonais.
4. Le roman dont nous nous servons est un best-seller. Ça parle d'un crime à Paris. L'inspecteur est très intelligent.
5. Le dico dont Jérémy se sert est anglais-français.
6. Le roman policier dont Théo et Karim se servent est américain.
7. Le livre de Jules Verne dont Clarisse se sert est aussi un film.

1. une nouvelle
2. un recueil de poésie
3. un manga
4. un best-seller / un roman policier
5. un dictionnaire
6. un roman policier
7. un roman de science-fiction

13

1. La personne dont le manteau est très élégant est Mme Laforge.
2. La personne dont la tablette est rouge est M. Boudib.
3. La personne dont la robe est longue est Mlle Bobard.
4. La personne dont le fils est fatigué est M. Ferrand.
5. La personne dont la femme est bavarde est M. Bobard.
6. La personne dont la responsabilité est le coffre est l'employée.
7. La personne dont la fille est énergique est M. Ferrand.

Communication

Interpersonal: Cooperative Groups

To personalize using **dont**, put students into mixed-ability groups of four or five. Announce a topic and write it on the board, for example, **une fête dont vous vous souvenez bien**. Students in each group take turns relating a holiday that they remember well and adding a specific detail, for example, **La fête dont je me souviens bien est Noël 2012. J'ai reçu un cadeau exceptionnel!** Other cues you might use include **un truc dont vous n'avez pas envie** and **une personne dont vous avez fait la connaissance cette année**.

Resources

CA Communicative Activities

Share

Answers

14 Presentations will vary.

15 Presentations will vary.

16 Presentations will vary.

Reference Desk

If you have access to Passport, create a question for your students to share their response to a communicative activity.

À vous la parole

Question centrale ? Comment s'intégrer à une autre culture?

Communiquez!

14 Des cadeaux de remerciement 1.2, 1.3, 2.2, 3.2

Interpretive Reading, Presentational Writing

Vous avez passé l'été dans une famille d'accueil en France. Avant de rentrer dans votre pays, vous voulez offrir des livres à chaque membre de la famille pour les remercier de leur hospitalité. Vous avez 100 euros à dépenser, et il y a quatre personnes dans la famille. Faites des recherches et préparez un document pour acheter un livre qui plaira à chacun. Dans votre document :

- Décrivez brièvement chaque personne et indiquez leurs intérêts.
- Choisissez un livre selon le sexe, l'âge et les intérêts de la personne. Indiquez le titre, le genre, l'auteur, et un court résumé de l'histoire ou du livre.
- Préparez un petit mot que vous pourrez écrire dans chaque livre avant de l'offrir.

Recherche : fnac france, archambault québec, decitre

15 Soirée slam ! 1.1, 1.2, 1.3, 2.1, 3.1, 3.2, 5.1

Interpersonal Speaking, Interpretive Reading, Presentational Speaking

En groupes, préparez une présentation sur un slameur ou une slameuse pour une soirée slam. Incluez :

- une courte biographie
- une explication de ses thèmes
- un extrait de slam (donnez les paroles à la classe avec un glossaire, si nécessaire)
- une citation de l'artiste (par exemple, « Grand Corps Malade », slameur français, a dit : « Je viens du slam. C'est un art a capella, c'est un art live. Il faut qu'il y ait un auditoire pour qu'il y ait du slam. »)
- une critique : Est-ce de la poésie ? Justifiez votre réponse.

Grand Corps Malade

Essayez de vous concerter entre groupes afin de choisir une variété d'artistes de pays différents.

Recherche : slameurs et slameuses (+ PAYS)

16 Le meilleur livre que j'aie jamais lu 1.3, 2.2, 4.2

Presentational Speaking

Vous allez faire une mini-présentation pour la classe sur le meilleur livre que vous ayez lu. Bien que ce livre soit probablement en anglais, présentez-le à vos camarades en français. Vous pouvez expliquer pourquoi le livre est si spécial ou si important pour vous, parler de l'auteur, du style d'écriture et/ou de l'intrigue, du synopsis, ou du message du livre. Vous pouvez apporter le livre en classe pour le faire circuler et ajouter à votre présentation des aides visuelles.

Essential Instruction

1. Students go online to do **Activité 14**.
2. Have students do **Activité 15** using the rubrics provided. Have them select one of his songs that is appropriate in terms of lyrics and teach it to the class. Students may opt to project an online video clip of the **slameur** or **slameuse** they picked, singing the song they selected, or they could make their own music video.

Recherche : grand corps malade paroles

3. Give a presentation on your favorite book to model **Activité 16** for students.
4. In explaining the technique of writing a persuasive essay, have students read the **Modèle**. Ask them to identify the examples the writer uses to create a negative impression of the hotel.
5. Make sure the students understand the step-by-step process of writing a persuasive essay as outlined in **Activité 17**. Brainstorm possible subjects for their essay and vocabulary that would be helpful.

Pre-AP

Communiquez!

Writing a Persuasive Essay 1.2, 1.3

Le discours argumentatif a pour objectif de persuader le lecteur. Vous devrez écrire un discours argumentatif afin de convaincre quelqu'un de lire ou de ne pas lire un livre, de voir ou de ne pas voir un film, ou de se rendre ou de ne pas se rendre à un certain endroit. Voici un exemple d'un essai argumentatif. Est-ce que l'écrivain veut vous convaincre de rester ou de ne pas rester dans un hôtel de la gare?

EXEMPLE

Vous souhaitez rester dans un petit hôtel pas trop cher à proximité de la gare. L'hôtel de la gare est à deux pas de la gare et croyez-moi, il est difficile de l'oublier, surtout après une longue journée, car la suivante vous paraîtra encore plus longue.

Le soir, impossible d'ignorer les trains qui se succèdent. Mais, bon, vous aviez choisi de rester près de la gare… vous saviez ce qui vous attendait. Par contre, c'était sans compter les jeunes du quartier que vous entendrez discuter au pied de l'immeuble, ou encore les étudiants de la fac sortant de la boîte au coin de la rue.

Dans ces conditions, vous regretterez de ne pas avoir dépensé un petit peu plus d'argent pour la nuit, car impossible de lire votre guide et encore moins votre anthologie de poésie préférée. Et, vous serez si fatigué le lendemain après une nuit blanche que vous vous endormirez devant votre café. La journée en sera d'autant plus longue.

Un petit hôtel tout près de la Gare de l'Est

17 Mon discours argumentatif 1.3, 3.2

Suivez les étapes suivantes pour écrire votre discours argumentatif :

1. Choisissez un sujet et votre public. Le public que vous aurez choisi déterminera votre niveau de langue, familier ou standard.
2. Faites des recherches et classez vos arguments dans un organigramme.
3. Faites d'abord un brouillon (*rough draft*). Citations, faits, et statistiques peuvent constituer des points importants pour défendre votre point de vue. Commencez votre thèse par un fait, ensuite continuez avec deux paragraphes, et enfin, faites une conclusion.
4. Demandez à un camarade de classe de revoir ce que vous avez écrit ; acceptez ou rejetez ses remarques.
5. Mettez au propre et rendez votre épreuve finale à votre professeur.

Resources

Pre-T Pre-test

Q *Leçon* Quiz

Answers

17 Essays will vary.

Reference Desk

Students may not know the meaning of these expressions: **un discours** (*a speech or address*); **un pas** (*a step*); **une nuit blanche** (*a sleepless night*); **mettre (quelque chose) au propre** (*to copy [something] out neatly*); **une épreuve** (*a paper*).

Differentiated Learning

Accelerate

High-ability students will be able to work independently to complete this assignment with a minimum amount of oversight on your part. Once you approve their choice of subject, allow them to work on their own.

Decelerate

Meet with low-ability students to explain the process of writing a persuasive essay. Have them show you their work as they complete steps 1–5. For step 3, have them show you their rough draft for correction before they start to write.

Special Needs Students

AD(H)D/Linguistically Challenged

Create deadlines for each step of the writing process and encourage students to write in simple sentences. Be available to make corrections and comments at every step to help them focus.

Resources

- Vocabulaire actif *(audio)*
  Vocabulaire actif
  Pour la conversation
  Et si je voulais dire… ?
- eV eVisual
- WB Workbook 1–3
- FC Flash Cards
- LA Listening Activity 1
- G & V Practice Games

Reference Desk

1. Here is some supplementary vocabulary needed to use the interactive website for **La Poste: les outils pratiques** (*practical tools*); **offres, conseils pas à pas** (*step-by-step offers and advice*); **en outre mer** (*overseas*); **à l'étranger** (*abroad*); **formalités douanières** (*customs requirements*).
2. Express services available in France are **Chronopost**; and **Colissimo**, which are branches of **La Poste**. Other popular services are **DHL**, **TNT**, and international services such as UPS and FedEx. a branch of **La Poste** which handles overnight deliveries.

nouvelle orthographe **une boite**

TPR

Give students commands using the new vocabulary for **La Poste**. (**"Écrivez une adresse sur une enveloppe." "Affranchissez l'enveloppe/Mettez un timbre sur l'enveloppe." "Mettez l'enveloppe dans la boîte aux lettres."**) Have students act out the commands to verify comprehension. Consider using props.

Leçon C Vocabulaire actif

À la poste 1.2, 2.1

un service de livraison (postale)

une lettre

Pour la conversation 1.2

How do I say what I need?

» Il me faut une assez grande boîte….
I need a rather big box….

How do I specify items?

» Quels sont **ceux** que tu veux envoyer?
Which ones do you want to send?

» Ceux que j'ai achetés l'autre jour à la librairie.
The ones I bought the other day at the bookstore.

Et si je voulais dire… ?

le code postal	*ZIP (or post) code*
un mandat international	*international wire transfer (of funds)*
le destinataire	*addressee*
l'expéditeur	*sender*
les frais de port	*postage rate*
à destination de	*destined for*
en recommandé	*by registered mail*
par avion	*by airmail*

Mot-clé

Lettre: *letre* (980) est issu du latin *littera* (lettre de l'alphabet) qui sous l'influence du grec *grammata* a pris le sens de missive puis d'ouvrage (*work*) écrit et, par suite, de littérature et, plus généralement, de culture et instruction. On parle de la « Fac de lettres » pour se référer aux études de français et de littérature.

Essential Instruction

1. Have students write the vocabulary from **À la poste** and **Et si je voulais dire… ?** in their notebooks.
2. Tell students **il me faut** = **j'ai besoin de**.
3. Ask students what they think **ceux** means in **Ceux que j'ai achetés**…What gender is **ceux**? How do they know? Go over the masculine and feminine, singular and plural forms of demonstrative pronouns: **celui**, **celle**, **ceux**, **celles**.
4. Describe a vocabulary word for students to guess: "**La personne qui va recevoir la lettre est**…"
5. Have students read **Activité 1** and answer the questions.
6. Have students do **Activité 2** using **Il me faut** and **J'ai besoin de** for each picture.

1 Ce que ma grand-mère m'a raconté 1.2, 2.2, 4.2

Interpretive Reading

Lisez la composition que Louise a écrite à l'école primaire, puis répondez aux questions.

Pour cette composition sur la vie d'autrefois j'ai interviewé ma grand-mère. Elle m'a raconté comment elle avait rencontré mon grand-père. De tous les endroits possibles, elle l'a rencontré à la poste! Elle allait souvent à la poste pour envoyer des lettres et des livres à sa sœur. On n'avait pas, bien entendu, accès à Internet et aux mails comme aujourd'hui. Pendant que le postier pesait son colis, mon grand-père, qui faisait la queue derrière elle, lui a demandé ce qu'elle lisait parce qu'il la trouvait belle. Elle lui a répondu qu'elle était en train de lire un roman policier de Georges Simenon. Ils ont découvert qu'ils aimaient tous les deux cet écrivain. Mon grand-père a demandé à ma grand-mère de l'aider à écrire l'adresse pour envoyer une carte postale à son frère dans l'armée. Elle a écrit l'adresse parce qu'elle écrivait mieux que mon grand-père. Après, mon grand-père a accompagné ma grand-mère jusqu'à chez elle. Elle a offert de lui prêter son roman, et ils ont décidé de se retrouver plus tard au café.

1. Où est-ce que les grands-parents de Louise se sont rencontrés?
2. Qui a raconté à Louise l'histoire de la rencontre de ses grands-parents?
3. Quel objet de la grand-mère de Louise est-ce que son grand-père a remarqué?
4. Qu'est-ce que les grands-parents de Louise envoyaient ce jour-là?
5. Pendant que le postier pesait le colis de sa grand-mère, qu'est-ce que son grand-père a demandé à sa grand-mère?

2 À la poste 1.2, 1.3, 4.2, 5.2

Interpretive Viewing, Presentational Speaking

Dites ce qu'il vous faut.

MODÈLE  **Il me faut une grande boîte cartonnée.**

1. 

2. 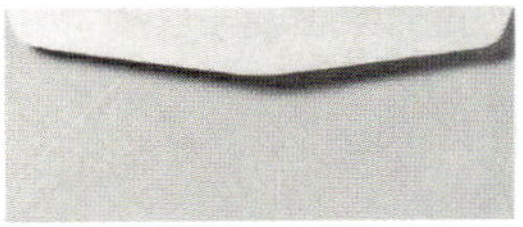

3. 

4. 

5. 

6. 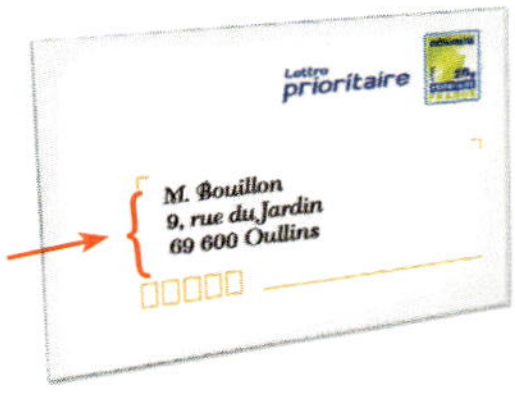

Answers

1

1. Ils se sont rencontrés à la poste.
2. sa grand-mère
3. son roman
4. Elle envoyait un colis, il envoyait une carte postale.
5. Il lui a demandé d'écrire l'adresse sur une carte postale qu'il allait envoyer à son frère dans l'armée.

2

1. Il me faut un timbre.
2. Il me faut une enveloppe.
3. Il me faut un service de livraison.
4. Il me faut une boîte aux lettres.
5. Il me faut une petite boîte.
6. Il me faut une adresse.

Communication

Presentational: Cooperative Groups

Have groups of three write out the conversation that they imagine took place between Louise's grandmother and grandfather the first time they met at **La Poste**. Small groups present their conversations to another group for practice and then to the class. Collect the written work.

Differentiated Learning

Accelerate

Ask students to calculate the rate for sending a standard weight letter from Paris to **la Guadeloupe**. In addition, have them find the post office branch(es) that offer(s) the most services for the **code postal** 75012 in Paris.

Decelerate

Have students visit the site for **La Poste** and USPS to compare the services offered by each agency. Which post office offers the most services? Explain.

Recherche: poste france site officiel, united states postal service

Adapt

A few students might not have been to their local post office and could be unaware of the kinds of stamps, packaging, and other services available. If possible, encourage them to visit their local post office and share what they saw.

Resources

Activity 4

Answers

3

1. envoyer
2. une enveloppe
3. l'adresse, timbres
4. postier
5. peser
6. affranchir

4 Script

1. Tu peux la mettre dans la boîte aux lettres quand tu sors?
2. J'ai fini ma lettre à tante Adja en Côte d'Ivoire. J'y vais maintenant.
3. Tiens, mon chéri. Il faut le mettre sur ton enveloppe. Non, en haut à droite.
4. Oui, bien sûr, monsieur. Ça coûte 2,89€.
5. Elle est déjà passée; le courrier est sur la table.
6. Tu mets où tu habites ici, chéri. Non, à gauche.

1. D; 2. C; 3. E; 4. F; 5. A; 6. B

5 Answers will vary.

Game

Devinez

Ask a volunteer to go to the board and draw a vocabulary word. The first student who recognizes the word raises his or her hand and, when correct and given the go-ahead from the teacher, must run to the board and write the word. As a variation, you could call out a vocabulary word and students have to draw it on their whiteboards, or you can draw the vocabulary word on the board, and students write the word on their whiteboards.

3 Clément va à la poste 1.2, 2.1, 4.2, 5.2

Interpretive Reading

Complétez les phrases de Clément avec un mot ci-dessous.

envoyer **l'adresse** **affranchir** **postier** **timbres** **une enveloppe** **peser**

1. Je voudrais… une carte d'anniversaire au Canada.
2. Je mets la lettre dans… blanche.
3. J'écris… et je mets des….
4. Je donne la lettre au….
5. Je demande au postier: « Vous pouvez… mon colis? »
6. Il me donne le prix pour… mon colis.

4 Le courrier 1.2

Interpretive Listening

Écrivez les numéros 1–6 sur votre papier. Écoutez chaque phrase, puis choisissez la lettre qui correspond à la chose ou la personne indiquée.

A. la factrice
B. l'adresse
C. à la poste
D. cette carte postale
E. le timbre
F. l'affranchissement

5 Questions personnelles 1.1, 2.2, 5.2

Interpersonal Speaking

Répondez aux questions suivantes.

1. Y a-t-il une boîte aux lettres dans ton quartier? Peux-tu y aller à pied?
2. Connais-tu ton facteur ou ta factrice?
3. Quand est-ce que tu vas à la poste?
4. Qu'est-ce que tu demandes au postier de faire?
5. Connais-tu quelqu'un qui collectionne des timbres? Si oui, de quels pays?

Essential Instruction

1. Have students do **Activité 3**. After correcting, ask questions to get students conversing, for example, For whom is the card? How old is your friend? Where does he or she live? What is in the package? How much did you pay for it?
2. Students listen to **Activité 4** and answer the questions A–F. Monitor the students to see if any may be having difficulty. If necessary, provide the pronouns used in each phrase.
3. Have students work in pairs to complete **Activité 5**.
4. Have students look at the picture of Justin and Léo. What do they want to do? What must they do to send the package?
5. Have students watch the video **À la poste** with books closed. Ask general comprehension questions about what Justin and Léo want to do.
6. Students read the dialogue and complete **Activité 6**. Ask students to read and answer questions.

Rencontres culturelles

À la poste 1.2, 2.1, 4.2, 5.2

Léo et Justin sont à la poste.

Justin : Il me faut une assez grande boîte cartonnée comme cette boîte-ci pour envoyer mes livres.

Léo : Quels sont ceux que tu veux envoyer? J'ai des boîtes chez moi.

Justin : Ceux que j'ai achetés l'autre jour à la librairie du coin.

Léo : Alors, j'ai une boîte chez moi qui conviendrait....

Justin : En fait, j'ai aussi besoin d'une grande enveloppe pour les deux catalogues de la librairie.

Léo : Bon alors, on va chez moi pour tout préparer!

Justin : Et on revient après? La poste ferme à quelle heure?

Léo : À 18h00, mais on a le temps.

Justin : Et pour l'affranchissement....

Léo : Cet appareil ici fait très bien ça tout seul.

6 À la poste 1.2

Répondez aux questions.

1. Où sont Léo et Justin?
2. Qu'est-ce que Justin voudrait acheter?
3. La poste ferme à quelle heure?
4. Où est-ce que Justin va pour chercher une boîte, avant d'envoyer ses livres et ses catalogues?
5. Est-ce qu'on va parler au postier? De quoi est-ce qu'on va se servir et qu'est-ce que cette machine fait?

Analyse

Read the dialogue again, and deduce: how many pieces of mail and what packaging will Justin send through the post office?

EXTENSION **Florence a besoin d'envoyer de l'argent** 1.2, 2.1

Florence est à la poste pour envoyer de l'argent aux États-Unis.

Florence : Bonjour, monsieur! Je voudrais envoyer de l'argent à un ami aux États-Unis, s'il vous plaît.

Postier : Bonjour, mademoiselle! Le moyen le moins cher est par mandat international.

Florence : Combien de temps cela prendra-t-il?

Postier : À peu près autant qu'une lettre. Cinq à sept jours.

Florence : Euh... y a-t-il un moyen plus rapide?

Postier : Bien sûr, le mandat express international. C'est un peu plus cher mais votre ami recevra votre paiement en deux jours.

Florence : Y a-t-il un moyen encore plus rapide?

Postier : Le plus rapide, sans compte bancaire postal, c'est un transfert Western Union. L'argent est disponible immédiatement!

EXTENSION Finalement, Florence va se servir de quel service? Pourquoi? 1.3

Resources

Dialogue
Activity 6
Extension

Dialogue Video

WB Workbook 4

Answers

6

1. Léo et Justin sont à la poste.
2. Justin voudrait acheter une grande boîte cartonnée et une grande enveloppe.
3. La poste ferme à 18h00.
4. Avant d'envoyer ses livres et ses catalogues, Justin va chez Léo pour chercher une boîte.
5. On ne va pas parler au postier; on va se servir d'un appareil qui fait l'affranchissement.

EXTENSION

Elle va se servir du transfert Western Union parce que c'est le service plus rapide.

Analyse

He will send two pieces of mail: one box and one large envelope

Expansion

Lightly tape a large rectangular piece of paper on the board, which will serve as an envelope. Ask a series of students to do the following tasks as you cue them: write in the name and **adresse** of the **expéditeur**, the name and **adresse** of the **destinataire**, add a **code postal**, write "registered letter." Have a series of other students remove the envelope, pantomime weighing it, putting the envelope into a box, weighing the box, and finally putting the box in a mailbox. Have the rest of the class identify the actions.

Differentiated Learning

Accelerate

Have students use the French post office website as a basis for writing a new dialogue about sending a letter or a package, or using their banking services. Encourage them to use details to make the dialogue interesting. They may want to use the **Extension** format as their template.

Recherche : poste france site official

Decelerate

Have students read **Extension** and outline in French the various ways to send money abroad.

Special Needs Students

Linguistically Challenged/AD(H)D

Pairing students with peers to read the dialogues might be helpful. Working in groups allows students to proceed at their own pace.

Resources

Points de départ
WB Workbook 5
Explore

Answers

Perspectives
Non, pas du tout.; Answers will vary.

Reference Desk

1. Louis XI established the **relais de poste** for royal correspondence. The **chevaucheurs** were equestrians who traveled an average of 16 to 20 km before stopping at **relais** or staging posts to eat, rest, and change horses. In ensuing centuries, mail carriers and travelers stopped at these inns. They ate in **auberges** and slept in **gîtes**. With the onset of the rail system, mail delivery by horseback diminished. Today, many restaurants and hotels are called **relais**, evoking and recalling the romance of times past.
2. The **Minitel**, France's precursor to the Internet, was immensely popular and widely used in France until the late 1990s, when France's strict domestic patent of the system prevented it from overcoming the mushrooming presence of the World Wide Web.
3. If you have access to Passport, find a video or news article related to **La Poste** and show it to your students.

Expansion

Ask students to compare the presence of **La Poste**, as described in the last paragraph of the reading, with the USPS in towns in the United States. Ask students if they can think of an equivalent of the **chevaucheurs** carrying mail on horseback from one post to the next (the Pony Express). Also, "Post Roads" were roads designated for the transportation of mail by post riders and mail coaches. Ask students to look up photos of the Boston Post Road, which is still a route from New York City to Boston.

Points de départ

Pre-AP | Question centrale ? Comment s'intégrer à une autre culture?

La Poste 1.2, 2.1, 2.2, 3.1

La Poste de Chaponost, dans la banlieue de Lyon

Aujourd'hui La Poste est une entreprise française à caractère* industriel et commercial, à la fois* opérateur de courrier (premier opérateur de courrier européen), banque, assurance et opérateur de téléphonie mobile. Elle compte 17 000 points de contact et emploie 250 000 personnes. Elle compte 10,7 millions de clients pour ses activités bancaires. Elle achemine* 29 milliards de documents (courrier et imprimés publicitaires*) par an et elle est le deuxième opérateur européen en chiffre d'affaires sur le colis express en Europe.

Le bureau de poste est un des lieux symboliques de la continuité d'une vie administrative dans les plus petits villages et l'un des symboles de l'unité du territoire. Aujourd'hui La Poste développe une activité de services à la personne (du portage* de médicaments* aux services de vie quotidienne).

La Poste est symbolisée par le facteur qui distribue le courrier, apporte les mandats, les colis et l'argent à domicile. C'est un des personnages du service public qui est le plus populaire. En témoignent les succès au cinéma de Jacques Tati qui l'a immortalisé dans *Jour de fête* (1947) et surtout du film de Dany Boon, *Bienvenue chez les Ch'tis* (2008), le plus grand succès français de tous les temps.

Recherche : laposte.fr, services postaux france

à caractère *specifically* ; **à la fois** *at the same time* ; **achemine** *transports* ; **imprimés publicitaires** *advertising print-outs* ; **portage** *delivery* ; **médicaments** *medicine*

Perspectives 1.2, 2.1, 4.2

Moi, franchement, je trouve que tous ces services modernes en ligne font perdre des emplois aux postiers, car le nombre d'agents diminue chaque année. On sacrifie des humains au nom de la productivité !
—YvesMT

Cet homme est-il satisfait des progrès et de la modernisation de La Poste ? Êtes-vous d'accord avec lui ?

Le Minitel : précurseur* d'Internet 1.2, 2.2, 3.1

En 1982, La Poste propose un ordinateur, le Minitel, pour chaque maison. Le Minitel permet aux Français de se brancher à un annuaire* électronique et à d'autres services. Sur Minitel, on pouvait envoyer un bouquet de fleurs, faire des réservations (train, avion, théâtre…), voir les bulletins météo, et ainsi de suite*. L'invention de l'internet a rendu le Minitel désuet*. Ce dernier a officiellement disparu le 30 juin 2012.

précurseur *precursor* ; **annuaire** *phone book* ; **ainsi de suite** *and so on* ; **désuet** *obsolete*

Essential Instruction

1. Have students read **La Poste** and outline the information under these categories: **l'historique, les services, et le symbolisme de la poste dans les petits villages**.
2. Students read **Le Minitel** and write a one-line definition of what the **Minitel** was.
3. Students do **Activité 7** in the computer lab and then use this information to discuss services offered by **La Poste française**.

1.2, 4.2

Comparaisons

Quels problèmes a la poste américaine? Quel rôle a eu Benjamin Franklin dans la création de la poste américaine?

Connexions — 1.2, 3.2, 4.2

Maths

Calculez le tarif (*cost*) de l'envoi d'un colis de 2 kilos depuis la France aux États-Unis, et depuis les États-Unis jusqu'à la France, en utilisant le site web des services postaux de ces deux pays. Quel pays offre les tarifs les plus avantageux?

Recherche: laposte.fr, usps

7 Activités culturelles 1.3, 3.1, 3.2, 5.2

Faites les activités suivantes.

1. Visitez le site officiel de La Poste. Quels services vous semblent semblables à ceux de votre pays? Quels services sont différents?
2. Recherchez le code postal de ces villes: Colmar, Montpellier, Aix-les-Bains.

Recherche: poste france site officiel

3. Allez sur le site officiel de La Poste. Nommez trois choses que vous pouvez voir au Musée de La Poste.
4. Allez sur le site officiel de La Poste. Comment est-ce que La Poste aide les gens qui visitent la France ou séjournent (*have a long stay*) en France?

À DISCUTER

Quel est le rôle de la poste dans votre communauté? dans votre vie?

Ville d'Oullins, dans l'agglomération lyonnaise

Differentiated Learning

Expand

Find the excerpt online of "Jacques Tati flying mailman on a bicycle" from his film, and play it several times. The first time, play it for the comedic enjoyment. The second time, stop the clip at pivotal points to ask students about the comedic action. The third time, play the clip and ask students to provide their own voiceover soundtrack.

Answers

Comparaisons

Answers will vary; Franklin was the first U.S. Postmaster General and founded the United States Postal Service.

7

1. Answers will vary.
2. Colmar: 68000; Montpellier: 34000; Aix-les-Bains: 73100
3. Answers will vary.
4. Answers will vary.

À DISCUTER

Answers will vary.

Reference Desk

1. Jacques Tati (1907–1982) was a comic actor, writer, and filmmaker. ***Jour de Fête*** recounts the efforts of a smalltown postal worker who sets out to compete with what he thinks is the speed and efficiency of the United States Post Office. His endearing slapstick efforts to achieve "**rapidité**" are set against the backdrop of a small town in what the French refer to as "**la France profonde.**" ***Bienvenue chez les Ch'tis*** (2008), directed by and starring Dany Boon, tells the comical story of a Southern France postal worker banished to Nord-Pas-de-Calais in northern France for two years. At first despairing and condescending of the locals, he develops an affection and admiration for them. The film broke almost every box office record upon its release, becoming the highest grossing French film of all time and cementing Dany Boon's place in the annals of French cinema.
2. **Le Musée de la Poste** is located near **la Gare Montparnasse** in the **15e arrondissement de Paris**. Among its offerings are artifacts dealing with the work of postal workers, their uniforms throughout the ages, mailboxes, and collections of stamps, postmarks, and stamp cancellations (franks) applied by hand or machine.

Resources

WB Workbook 12–13

Answers

8

1. Votre vie digitale; Localiser : bureaux, points Colissimo; Boutique courrier-colis; imprimer vos timbres; Suivre : Colissimo, Chronopost, lettres
2. Answers will vary.

Critical Thinking

Analysis

In what ways has the use of the internet affected the economic viability of the United States Post Office? How have France and America expanded the traditional services of the post office?

Du côté des médias 1.2

Lisez cette page du site officiel de La Poste.

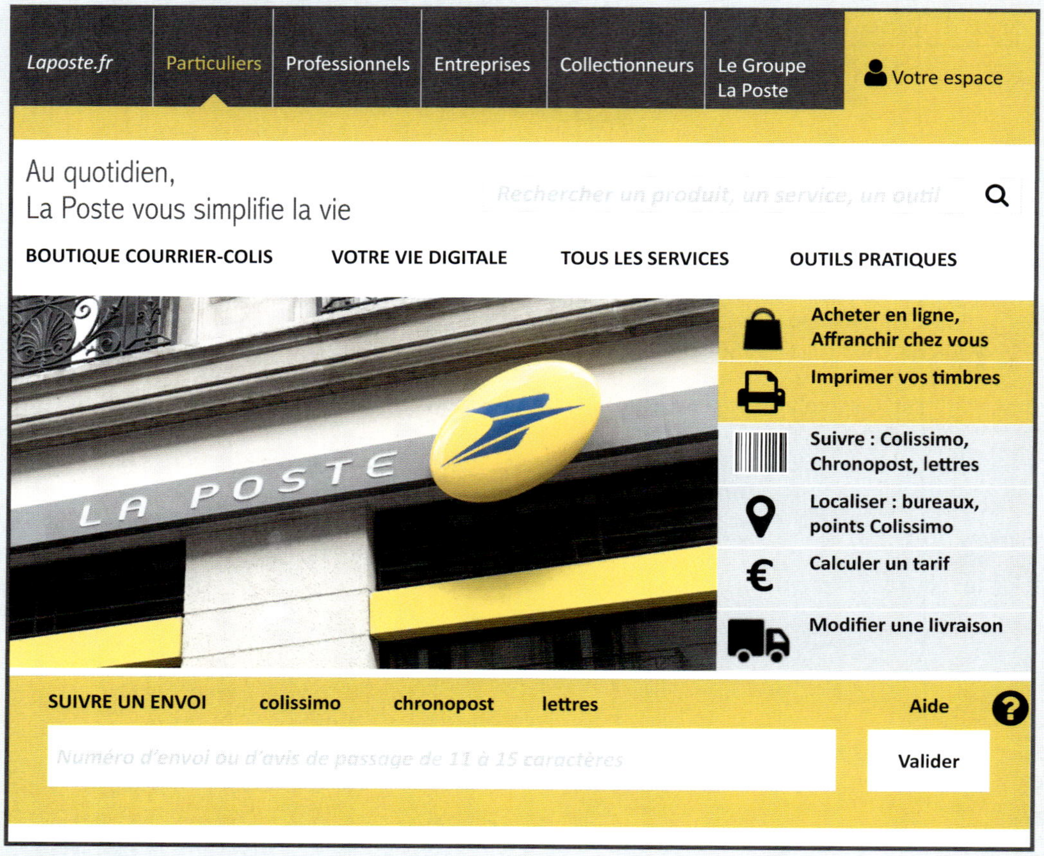

8 La Poste en France 1.2, 1.3, 2.1, 2.2, 5.1

Faites les activités suivantes.

1. Dites où vous cliqueriez pour :
   - Acheter l'application mobile
   - Trouver un bureau de poste près de chez vous
   - Envoyer un colis
   - Acheter des timbres et les imprimer à la maison
   - Suivre (*Track*) un courrier
2. Allez sur le site La Poste. Combien coûte un timbre poste? une lettre pour les États-Unis?

Recherche : laposte.fr

Essential Instruction

1. In the computer lab, give students time to play with the interactive features of the **site officiel de La Poste**. Put students in groups of three at a computer to complete **Activité 8** as a competitive timed exercise. A representative from each team puts the answers on the board. Score points for the first team done, and points for the best team's work.
2. For **Scénarios culturels**, divide students into groups. Have a representative from each group draw a number from one to five. Have the groups work to create a scene corresponding to the number drawn. If you have more than ten students, assign duplicate scenarios. Give students an appropriate amount of time to write, edit, and rehearse their scene before presenting it to the class. Encourage the students to embellish the scene to add interest.
3. Afterward, lead a discussion using the talking points in **Activité 10**.

Culture sur place

Question centrale ? Comment s'intégrer à une autre culture?

Scénarios culturels 1.2, 5.1

Introduction et Interrogations

Quand on voyage, on n'est pas toujours à l'aise dans toutes les situations. Quand il y a un moment de contact entre deux (ou trois ou quatre) cultures, les conflits sont inévitables. Cela ne veut pas dire que le résultat est forcément négatif. Comment vivre un scénario difficile dans une autre culture?

9 Répondre 1.1, 1.2, 2.1

Considérez chaque situation, ensuite pensez à votre réaction. Que feriez-vous? Décidez de votre réponse et faites un jeu de rôle avec un partenaire.

Scénario #1 : À la banque où vous avez un compte, vous voulez retirer de l'argent liquide. Vous donnez votre carte de crédit au banquier. Il vous dit que la carte est endommagée, et que vous ne pouvez pas l'utiliser. Que faites-vous? Que dites-vous au banquier?

Scénario #2 : Vous avez besoin d'argent en France. Votre famille a un peu d'argent à vous envoyer, mais vous ne savez pas comment l'envoyer entre les deux localités. Où allez-vous pour vous renseigner? Que dites-vous?

Scénario #3 : Vous faites la queue à la poste pour 45 minutes avec un colis à envoyer. Vous arrivez au guichet, et le postier vous répond que vous vous êtes trompé de queue *(got in the wrong line)*. Il va vous falloir recommencer avec une nouvelle queue. Que faites-vous? Que dites-vous au postier?

Scénario #4 : À un restaurant, le serveur vous apporte le plat principal. Vous avez très faim et prenez la petite fourchette que vous voyez, en haut de votre assiette. Le serveur vous gronde (*scolds*) parce que c'est la fourchette à dessert. Quelle est votre réponse?

Scénario #5 : Vous avez passé un weekend dans une petite ville historique dans le sud de la France, et vous devez prendre le train pour retourner dans la ville où vous habitez. La petite ville historique n'a qu'une banque, et elle ferme de 12h00 à 14h00 pour le déjeuner. Malheureusement, vous avez besoin d'argent liquide pour acheter votre billet de train; la banque est fermée, et le train part à 14h00. Que faites-vous?

10 Faire le point! 1.3, 2.1, 3.2, 5.1

Discutez les questions suivantes en classe.

1. Quel scénario était le plus difficile pour vous? Lequel était le plus facile? Pourquoi?
2. Est-ce que ces scénarios pourraient se passer aux États-Unis aussi? Pourquoi ou pourquoi pas?
3. Y a-t-il d'autres scénarios difficiles dont vous voulez discuter?

Answers

All activities will vary.

Expansion

Have students expand on one of the scenarios in **Activité 9** by writing an e-mail to a friend or family member recounting the incident and explaining what they did to help resolve it.

Learning Styles

Visual Learners

Students may enjoy creating a backdrop for their scenario which represents the teller window or restaurant **décor**.

Kinesthetic Learners

Students may enjoy acting out the scenario.

Special Needs Students

Social Anxiety

Students who have trouble performing in front of others might be allowed to read their role rather than have to establish eye contact with the rest of the class.

Resources

- WB Workbook 6–7
- LA Listening Activity 2
- G & V Practice Games

Answers

11

1. Vous aimez cet ordinateur-ci ou cet ordinateur-là?
2. Vous aimez ce portable-ci ou ce portable-là?
3. Vous aimez ces chaussettes-ci ou ces chaussettes-là?
4. Vous aimez cette casquette-ci ou cette casquette-là?
5. Vous aimez ces chaussures-ci ou ces chaussures-là?
6. Vous aimez ce livre-ci ou ce livre-là?
7. Vous aimez cet accessoire-ci ou cet accessoire-là?

Partner answers will vary.

Reference Desk

To teach demonstrative pronouns, write **celui** on the board. Ask students if they see two words in **celui** (**ce** + **lui**). So **celui** refers to *this* masculine person or thing. The same is true for **celle** (**ce** + **elle**), **ceux** (**ce** + **eux**), and **celles** (**ce** + **elles**). Students see that each form is a composite of two words.

Expansion

PQA

Bring in common objects (or borrow them from students) and ask students which pen, notebook, wallet, phone, or other object they prefer.

Structure de la langue

Révision: Demonstrative Adjectives 1.2, 4.1

Demonstrative adjectives point out specific people or things. **Ce**, **cet**, and **cette** mean "this" or "that"; **ces** means "these" or "those." Demonstrative adjectives agree with the nouns that follow them.

Singular			Plural
Masculine before a consonant sound	**Masculine before a vowel sound**	**Feminine**	
ce colis	**cet** agent de police	**cette** banquière	**ces** catalogues

Ce colis est arrivé hier. — *This package arrived yesterday.*
J'irai à **cette** poste pour envoyer ma lettre. — *I will go to that post office to mail my letter.*

To make a clear distinction between who or what is closer to the speaker and who or what is farther away, add **-ci** after the noun to add emphasis to "this" or "these," or **-là** after the noun to add emphasis to "that" or "those."

Cette adresse-**ci** n'est pas correcte. — *This address (here) is not correct.*
Cet affranchissement-**là** n'est pas correct. — *That postage (there) is incorrect.*

11 Des soldes au magasin 1.1, 1.2

Interpersonal Speaking, Interpretive Viewing

À tour de rôle, demandez ce que votre partenaire aime. Suivez le modèle.

ordinateur chemise casquette portable
roman chaussettes accessoire chaussures

MODÈLE

(ci) (là)

A: Vous aimez cette chemise-ci ou cette chemise-là?
B: J'aime celle-là.

1. 
2. 
3. 
4. 
5. 
6. 

7. 

Essential Instruction

1. Review demonstrative adjectives. These words are reviewed in Level 2, **Unité 1, Leçon B**.
2. Introduce demonstrative pronouns. Use preferences as your context, for example, **Voici deux cahiers. Ce cahier-ci est rouge, et ce cahier-là est orange. Quel cahier préférez-vous? Celui-ci ou celui-là?** Continue until the pattern is set.
3. To check comprehension, first ask students to replace the word with the demonstrative adjective with its demonstrative pronoun. **Ce livre** is replaced by **celui**. Ask students to add **-ci** and **-là** to the demonstrative pronouns to show contrast.
4. For practice, have students find two similar images online or on social media, then pose preference questions to another student. Use the same formula as in your introduction. **Voici deux pulls. Ce pull-ci est rouge, et ce pull-là est orange. Quel pull préfères-tu? Celui-ci ou celui-là?**
5. Pair students to do **Activité 11**, then change partners and repeat.

Resources

WB Workbook 8–11

G & V Practice Games

Reference Desk

Celui-ci or **celle-ci** may also mean *the latter* or *the former*. A form of **celui-ci** always comes before a form of **celui-là** when both occur in the same sentence, for example, **D'où viennent tes copains Shelley et Martin? Celui-ci est français et celle-là est américaine.** Point out that in English we tend to use the reverse of this phrasing, saying "former" before "latter."

Demonstrative Pronouns 1.2, 4.1

The demonstrative pronoun **celui** points out specific people or things and is often used to replace the demonstrative adjective **ce** and a noun. The form of **celui** agrees in gender and in number with the noun it replaces. The singular forms mean "this one," "that one," or "the one." The plural forms means "these," "those," or "the ones."

	Singular	Plural
Masculine	celui	ceux
Feminine	celle	celles

C'est **celui** qui envoie le colis qui doit payer. — *It's the one who sends the package who has to pay.*

Il y avait beaucoup de lettres dans ma boîte aux lettres, même **celles** de mes voisins. — *There were a lot of letters in my mailbox, even those of my neighbors.*

A demonstrative pronoun is never used alone in a sentence. It is followed by **-ci** or **-là**, **qui** or **que**, or **de**.

Add **-ci** or **-là** after a form of **celui** to indicate a choice, to clarify, or to single out. To point out who or what is closer to the speaker (*this one*, *these*), add **-ci**; to point out who or what is farther away (*that one*, *those*), add **-là**, as one would do for demonstrative adjectives.

Quels facteurs y travaillent? **Ceux-ci** ou **ceux-là**? — *Which postal carriers work there? These or those?*

Les enveloppes blanches? Vous préférez **celles-ci** ou **celles-là**? — *The white envelopes? Do you prefer these or those?*

Differentiated Learning

Adapt

Ask students to select a series of images or pictures from home to display at their desks. One half of the class is going to go to the flea market to look over the wares displayed on students' desks. Vendors will try to sell the students on their items by talking about this item and that item, or this one and that one. The teacher will be a customer also. Reverse the roles.

Special Needs Students

AD(H)D

Help students with attention difficulties break down the information about the demonstrative adjectives and pronouns by reviewing each one separately with examples. They may benefit from a one-page flow chart that could be used as an easy reference point when doing the exercises.

Resources

Activities 12-13

Answers

12 Script

1. Tu préfères cette boîte-ci ou celle-là pour envoyer tes cadeaux?
2. De quelle enveloppe avez-vous besoin?
3. Quelles lettres pèsent le plus?
4. Quelle adresse est la bonne?
5. Tu veux ces timbres-ci ou ceux-là?
6. Quel paquet est le plus gros?

1. B; 2. B; 3. B; 4. C; 5. A; 6. C

13

1. Avec celui-ci ou avec celui-là?
2. À celui-ci ou à celui-là?
3. Chez ceux-ci ou chez ceux-là?
4. À celle-ci ou à celle-là?
5. Ceux-ci ou ceux-là?
6. À celle-ci ou à celle-là?
7. Dans celle-ci ou dans celle-là?
8. Celles-ci ou celles-là?
9. Ceux-ci ou ceux-là?

Reference Desk

1. Before presenting **celui + qui** or **que**, review the use of the relative pronouns. Remind students that **qui** needs a verb and **que** needs a subject and a verb in the dependent clause.
2. **Celui qui** and **que**, and **celui de** are translated according to their antecedents just as in English.
3. Prepare oral examples for each concept. For example, you could give two students one item each. One could be popular and the other not. Ask a student which one he or she prefers: **Celui de May ou celui de Josh?** This question will anchor the concept of possession. Change the sentence to which item he or she prefers: **Celui *qui* est sur la table de Marie**, or **Celui *que* je vois là**.

Add **qui** or **que** after a form of **celui** for identification. Use the **qui** form as the subject and the **que** form as the object.

Les colis? **Ceux que** nous avons envoyés étaient les plus chers.	*The packages? Those that we sent were the most expensive.*
Celui qui habite près de la poste peut prendre le courrier.	*The one who lives near the post office can get the mail.*

Add **de** after a form of **celui** to express possession.

Simone a cherché son courrier et **celui de** ses parents aussi.	*Simone got her mail and her parents' too.*
Ces lettres-ci? Ce sont **celles de** Noah.	*These letters? They are Noah's.*

12 À la poste 1.2, 2.2, 3.1

Interpretive Listening

Écrivez les numéros 1–6 sur votre papier. Écoutez les phrases. Choisissez la réponse logique.

	A	B	C
1.	A. ceux-ci	B. celle-là	C. celui-là
2.	A. de ceux-ci	B. de celle-là	C. celui-là
3.	A. ceux-ci	B. celles-là	C. celui-là
4.	A. ceux-ci	B. celui-ci	C. celle-ci
5.	A. ceux-ci	B. celui-ci	C. celle-ci
6.	A. ceux-ci	B. celle-là	C. celui-là

13 Une Américaine à Paris 1.1, 1.3

Interpersonal or Presentational Speaking or Writing

Vous voudriez mieux connaître Jennifer, une Américaine à Paris. Donc, vous posez des questions à son amie.

MODÈLE Jennifer travaille pour *une compagnie à Paris*.
Pour celle-ci ou pour celle-là?

1. Elle déjeune avec *le directeur*.
2. Elle va envoyer une carte postale à *son ami américain*.
3. Elle fait les courses chez *les petits commerçants*.
4. Elle va à *une banque internationale*.
5. Elle lit *les mystères anglais*.
6. Elle va assister à *une première française d'un film*.
7. Elle rêve de passer ses vacances d'hiver dans *une station de ski*.
8. Il lui faut *des enveloppes*.
9. Elle trouve *les arts* passionnants.

Essential Instruction

1. Students listen to the recording and do **Activité 12**, questions 1–6.
2. Pair students to do **Activité 13**. Upon completion, correct their work.
3. Have students change partners to complete **Activité 14**. Encourage them to ask follow-up questions such as **pourquoi?**
4. Debrief the students by polling their preferences, using this as an opportunity to expand conversation.

14 Est-ce que je connais bien mon partenaire? 1.1, 2.1, 3.2, 5.2

Interpersonal Speaking

À tour de rôle, posez des questions sur vos préférences pour mieux connaître votre partenaire.

MODÈLE les romans (de Jean-Paul Sartre, d'Antoine de Saint-Exupéry)
A: Tu préfères les romans de Jean-Paul Sartre ou d'Antoine de Saint-Exupéry?
B: Je préfère ceux d'Antoine de Saint-Exupéry. Et toi?
A: Moi, je préfère ceux de Jean-Paul Sartre.

1. les films (de Jean Dujardin, d'Omar Sy)
2. les souvenirs (d'enfance, d'adolescence)
3. les contes (du Maghreb, de l'Afrique)
4. les voitures (du Japon, de l'Italie)
5. les tableaux (des cubistes, des impressionnistes)
6. la musique (de la France, de l'Allemagne)
7. les repas (qu'on prépare à la maison, qu'on sert dans un restaurant)
8. les sports (d'hiver, d'été)
9. les maisons (en banlieue, à la campagne)
10. les chansons (de Zaz, de Mélissa M)

Answers

14

1. A: Tu préfères les films de Jean Dujardin ou d'Omar Sy?
   B: Je préfère ceux de .... Et toi?
   A: Moi, je préfère ceux de ....
2. A: Tu préfères les souvenirs d'enfance ou d'adolescence?
   B: Je préfère ceux d' .... Et toi?
   A: Moi, je préfère ceux d' ....
3. A: Tu préfères les contes du Maghreb ou de l'Afrique?
   B: Je préfère ceux du/de l'.... Et toi?
   A: Moi, je préfère ceux du/de l'....
4. A: Tu préfères les voitures du Japon ou de l'Italie?
   B: Je préfère celles du/de l'.... Et toi?
   A: Moi, je préfère celles du/de l'....
5. A: Tu préfères les tableaux des cubistes ou des impressionnistes?
   B: Je préfère ceux des .... Et toi?
   A: Moi, je préfère ceux des ....
6. A: Tu préfères la musique de la France ou de l'Allemagne?
   B: Je préfère celle de .... Et toi?
   A: Moi, je préfère celle de ....
7. A: Tu préfères les repas qu'on prépare à la maison ou qu'on sert dans un restaurant?
   B: Je préfère ceux qu' .... Et toi?
   A: Moi, je préfère ceux qu'....
8. A: Tu préfères les sports d'hiver ou d'été?
   B: Je préfère ceux d' .... Et toi?
   A: Moi, je préfère ceux d' ....
9. A: Tu préfères les maisons en banlieue ou à la campagne?
   B: Je préfère celles .... Et toi?
   A: Moi, je préfère celles ....
10. A: Tu préfères les chansons de Zaz ou de Mélissa M?
    B: Je préfère celles de .... Et toi?
    A: Moi, je préfère celles de ....

Communication

Interpersonal: Paired Practice

Arrange students in pairs to improvise a television interview. A television host interviews a famous celebrity about his or her preference in movies. The goal is to time how long they can keep the conversation going. Switch roles, change celebrities, and time again.

Differentiated Learning

Accelerate

Ask students to take on the role of a teacher and create a slide show presentation on demonstrative adjectives and pronouns to explain, step-by-step, what they are and how they are used, giving specific examples. Encourage them to use a realistic context. They are free to compare pop music, art, television programs, or movies of their choice. At the end of the presentation they give a quiz to the class to test comprehension.

Decelerate

Have students find pictures of five things they like to eat and do not like to eat. They present their food preferences to the class using demonstrative adjectives and pronouns.

Resources

CA Communicative Activities

Share

Answers

15 Objects will vary.

16 Debates will vary.

Reference Desk

If you have access to Passport, create a question for your students to share their response to a communicative activity.

Expansion

If possible, have students film their debate for Activity 16, and share it with other French sections/classes.

Communiquez!

15 Mon colis 1.3, 5.2

Presentational Speaking

Prenez un colis et mettez-y des choses qui vous identifient, par exemple : un vêtement, un jeu vidéo, des photos, et une peluche de votre enfance. Apportez votre colis en classe et presentez les objets un par un en expliquant à vos camarades de classe la signification de chaque chose. Vos camarades vont ensuite vous poser des questions sur les objets que vous avez choisis. Finalement, si vous pouviez garder seulement un objet dans votre colis, dites lequel vous garderiez et pourquoi.

16 Est-ce que la poste ferme? 1.1, 5.2

Presentational Speaking

Formez deux équipes afin de préparer un débat. Une équipe sera en faveur de garder les bureaux de poste ouverts et de réfléchir à toutes les raisons pour lesquelles il est important d'avoir un établissement où se rendre en personne dans notre société aujourd'hui. L'autre groupe sera en faveur de la fermeture des bureaux de poste. Chaque équipe devra défendre son point de vue en faisant une petite représentation théâtrale, ou une interview dans la rue où chacun joue un rôle (par exemple, un postier, un homme de 40 ans qui habite dans un village, une vieille dame handicappée, un jeune couple, etc.).

Voitures et camions de livraison sur la place Place Kléber à Strasbourg en France

Essential Instruction

1. Have students bring in the objects mentioned in **Activité 15**. You may want them to bring two of the same things so that you can review demonstrative adjectives and pronouns. Students can explain that this hat is from Mexico and that one is from Texas, for example.
2. Give students time to prepare their debate for **Activité 16**.
3. Poll students as to how many have visited non-English-speaking countries. If you have immigrants in the classroom who did not understand English upon arrival, have them relate, if they are willing, how they felt before they learned to communicate.
4. Have students fill out the chart in **Stratégie de lecture** as they do their reading. Have students look over the **Pendant la Lecture** questions on p. 368 before reading the passage from **Persepolis**.
5. Give students examples of direct and indirect discourse in English. Contrast: **Il dit: "Tu es fou."** with **Il dit que tu es fou**.

Pre-AP

Persepolis

Rencontre avec l'auteur 1.2, 3.2, 4.2

Marjane Satrapi (1969–), d'origine iranienne, est un écrivain et une réalisatrice qui vit maintenant à Paris. Elle a fait ses études au lycée français de Téhéran. Sa famille l'a envoyée en Europe en 1984, à l'âge de 14 ans, pour qu'elle échappe (*escape*) à la guerre en Iran. Elle a écrit *Persepolis*, une bande dessinée en quatre tomes, qui raconte son expérience. Ayant obtenu un grand succès avec *Persepolis*, Satrapi a adapté son œuvre autobiographique en long métrage d'animation en français. Vous allez lire une sélection de son troisième tome quand elle vit à Vienne avec une famille autrichienne *(Austrian)*. Comment est-ce que Marjane s'intègre dans la culture européenne?

Pré-lecture 1.2, 3.1, 5.2

Avez-vous jamais visité un pays où l'on ne parle pas anglais? Si oui, qui a parlé pour vous? Comment vous êtes-vous débrouillé(e)?

Stratégie de lecture 1.2

Narrator and Narration. Un narrateur/une narratrice est le personnage qui raconte une histoire. Il ou elle détermine les informations que le lecteur/la lectrice aura sur les événements et les autres personnages. Pendant que vous lisez, remplissez un tableau comme celui de dessous avec les faits que vous apprenez de la narratrice dans les parties où elle narre, c'est-à-dire les parties qui ne sont pas des dialogues.

Ce que Satrapi décrit	Ce que j'apprends de la narratrice
sa matinée	Elle n'aime pas se réveiller tôt.

Outils de lecture 1.2, 3.1, 4.1

Direct and Indirect Reporting. Il y a deux façons de rapporter ce qu'un personnage dit, en utilisant le discours direct, ou le discours indirect. Dans le discours direct, un personnage peut dire «Je suis passionnée des bandes dessinées.» L'auteur utilise des guillemets (*quotation marks*) ainsi que les mots directements énoncés par celui qui parle. Dans le discours indirect, il n'y a pas de guillemets, par exemple: *Michèle a dit qu'elle est passionnée des bandes dessinées*. Quelle forme de discours Satrapi utilise-t-elle dans l'extrait suivant?

Resources

Rencontre avec l'auteur

Answers

Rencontre avec l'auteur
Possible answer: Elle participe aux activités et à la routine de ses amis.

Pré-lecture
Answers will vary.

Stratégie de lecture
Possible answers:
son réveil: Elle programme son réveil à 6h30.
son école: Elle n'y a pas d'amis.
son attitude: Elle justifie son exclusion.
sa famille d'accueil: Ils l'invitent tous les jours.
son allemand: Il est rudimentaire.
Les sujets de conversation: Elle parle de la guerre et de la mort avec ses amis, mais pas avec sa famille d'accueil.

Outils de lecture
L'auteur utilise le discours direct (bulles et narration) et le discours indirect (propos rapportés par le cousin).

Reference Desk

In **Pré-lecture**, brainstorm vocabulary for emotions and problems that may be experienced in this situation, for example, **la peur, la frustration, la tristesse, la nostalgie, le chômage, l'hébergement, le travail**, and **l'argent**.

Differentiated Learning

Adapt
Have students listen to the interview with Marjane Satrapi talking about her movie ***Persepolis***. This interview will help students more easily relate to her and will add interest to the reading. Consider showing the film trailer as a **point de départ** for further discussion.

Recherche: persepolis, exclusive marjane satrapi, movieweb

Resources

Persepolis

Reference Desk

Students may not know the meaning of these expressions: **6h30 pile** (*6:30 on the dot*); **bosser travailler** (*familiar term*); **cultive-toi** (*get with it*); **connard** (*idiot* in very strong language); **Je me suis fait une raison.** (*I got used to it.*)

Persepolis

...

Essential Instruction

1. Ask students if they have ever been the "new kid" in school, at camp, or on the block. How does it feel?
2. Project **Tyrol** and **Les Pâtes**. Hide the words in the captions. Ask students to look at each frame and surmise what is happening by studying facial expressions and body language. Have them suggest dialogue.
3. Have students read **Tyrol** and **Les Pâtes**. Ask them to summarize the gist of each comic strip.
4. Explain the vocabulary and have students reread the cartoons for deeper meaning.
5. Ask students to cite examples from the story of how Marjane, the new girl at school, feels inside as she interacts with her classmates.

(Suite)

Les pâtes

* CHÉRIE

Reference Desk

1. The animated, feature-length ***Persepolis*** was released to critical acclaim. It won the Jury Prize at Cannes and the Golden Globe for Best Animated Feature. It was nominated for best animated film at the Academy Awards in 2008, but lost to *Ratatouille*. Satrapi was the first woman to be nominated for an Oscar in this category. The film, rated PG-13, is appropriate for high school audiences.
2. If students enjoyed this passage, the entire work is available online, and perhaps in your school (or public) library as well.

Culture

Perspectives: Information

Tyrol is a federal state in western Austria, where Marjane is staying on her way to France from Iran. The capital of this region is Innsbruck.

Differentiated Learning

Accelerate

Have students write their own captions to the comic strips **Tyrol** and **Les Pâtes**. They may follow the original story or write their own.

Decelerate

Ask students to make a list of ways in which Marjane does not fit in with the others. They must cite examples from the text.

Special Needs Students

At-Risk Students

There may be students in your class who closely identify with the new girl in school. Students should be sensitive to the fact that being different, being new, and/or speaking another language can make a student feel isolated from others.

Resources

Pre-T Pre-test

Q *Leçon* Quiz

Answers

Pendant la lecture

1. avec Lucia
2. le bruit du sèche-cheveux de Lucia
3. la famille de Lucia
4. en français
5. en Suisse francophone
6. de la guerre et de la mort
7. Il a fabriqué un cadre-photo pour elle.
8. une photo
9. Elle dit qu'elle est sa sœur.

Post-lecture

Possible answer:
Elle va retourner à Téhéran pour continuer ses études de lycée.

Le Monde visuel

Possible answer:
L'art de Satrapi est rudimentaire; elle n'utilise pas de couleurs. Elle montre l'exaspération du personnage principal en dessinant son visage furieux vu de l'intérieur du coussin; à l'école, elle lui dessine des yeux ronds et globuleux. Pour montrer la convivialité du repas, Satrapi dessine des visages souriants.

17

1. Answers will vary.
2. Elle dit "J'aime beaucoup le Tyrol".; Elle dit "Les Tyroliens sont très sympathiques".
3. La politique Irakienne de Saddam Hussein, voulant évoluer vers le modernisme et la laïcité, s'opposait à la puissance économique et militaire de l'Iran. Le 2 septembre 1980, après quelques tentatifs d'assassination d'hommes politiques irakiens, l'Irak a envahi l'Iran. Cette guerre a été très longue et a causé énormément de morts et de dégâts économiques pour les deux pays. Elle s'est terminée par un cessez-le-feu mais sans victoire pour aucun pays. Paragraphs will vary.

Pendant la lecture 1.2, 3.1, 4.2

Lisez les questions avant de lire la bande dessinée. Après avoir lu l'histoire, répondez aux questions.

1. Avec qui est-ce que Marjane partage une chambre?
2. Qu'est-ce qui l'embête chaque matin?
3. Qui veut faire la connaissance de Marjane?
4. Le cousin de Lucia parle à Marjane en quelle langue?
5. Où a-t-il appris cette langue?
6. À table, on ne parle pas de quels sujets?
7. Qu'est-ce que le parent de Lucia a fait pour Marjane?
8. Qu'est-ce qu'elle a mis dans le cadre?
9. Qu'est-ce que Marjane pense de Lucia à la fin de l'épisode?

Post-lecture 1.2, 1.3, 3.1

D'après ce que vous savez de la vie de Marjane, elle va où prochainement?

Le monde visuel 1.3, 2.1, 3.1, 3.2, 5.2

Satrapi a dessiné Persepolis elle-même. Comment décririez-vous son style—détaillé, rudimentaire ou autre? Comment a-t-elle montré son exaspération avec sa camarade de chambre? Son exclusion à l'école? La convivialité d'un repas partagé?

17 Activités d'expansion 1.3, 2.1, 3.2, 5.2

Faites les activités suivantes.

1. Écrivez un paragraphe dans lequel vous expliquez ce que vous savez de l'adolescence de Satrapi en Europe. Est-ce que Satrapi l'adulte utilise le discours direct, le discours indirect, ou une combinaison des deux, pour rapporter l'autobiographie de sa vie? Expliquez aussi sa façon d'écrire une bande dessinée.
2. Changez les propos au discours indirect dans les bulles de la sélection au discours direct, par exemple: *Elle dit qu'elle a bien mangé. Elle dit: «J'ai bien mangé.»*
3. Satrapi est née en 1969. Dans la sélection que vous avez lue, elle est adolescente. Qu'est-ce qui se passe en Iran à cette-époque là (environ 1983)? Faites des recherches en ligne. Ensuite, écrivez un paragraphe dans lequel vous expliquez pourquoi les parents de Marjane l'ont envoyée en Europe. Selon vous, ont-ils pris une bonne décision? Justifiez votre réponse.

Connexions 1.2, 2.1, 3.1, 5.2
Histoire
La Guerre Iran-Iraq (1980–1988) a impliqué quels pays de l'Ouest? Quelles conséquences cette guerre a-t-elle eu sur les rapports entre le Moyen-Orient et la France? et les États-Unis? Cherchez en ligne, et discutez en petits groupes.

Essential Instruction

1. Have students answer the questions based on the cartoon strips. Ask them supplementary questions to encourage reflection and conversation. You might inquire if they have ever been bothered in the morning by a parent or sibling. Can they relate to Marjane's challenge of making new friends?
2. Have students work online to do **Activité 17**. Question three may be the subject of a class discussion of political refugees, not only in Marjane's experience, but also in the world today.
3. Have students do Activity **D** together. Ask them to submit areas that they do not yet understand so that you can incorporate more instruction in those areas before the unit test.

Communiquez!

18 Un mail de l'université 1.1, 2.1, 3.1, 5.2

Connecting to Financial Literacy, Collaboration

Interpersonal Writing

Vous avez fait une demande d'inscription pour faire des études dans une université française. Le directeur de l'accueil des étudiants internationaux vous écrit pour vous poser des questions. Lisez son mail, puis répondez-lui avec autant de détails que possible. Utilisez les éléments d'une lettre formelle.

De: Monsieur le Directeur
Objet: Votre inscription à l'université

Cher candidat, Chère candidate,

Nous vous contactons parce que nous avons examiné votre dossier d'inscription pour le programme que vous avez choisi dans notre université. Chaque année, nous recevons un grand nombre d'inscriptions d'étudiants internationaux, aussi, notre processus de sélection se fait en deux parties. La première est la soumission du dossier, que vous avez déjà faite. La deuxième consiste à répondre de façon plus personnelle aux questions de notre Conseil Universitaire des Relations Internationales, pour nous aider à sélectionner les candidats.

-Quelles études avez-vous choisies, et pourquoi des études à l'étranger vous seront-elles bénéfiques dans votre parcours professionnel?

-Quand vous recevrez votre diplôme, qu'est-ce que vous ferez pour commencer votre carrière et comment vous servirez-vous de vos connaissances de la langue françaises dans votre travail?

Je vous prie de bien vouloir croire à mes sentiments respectueux,

Monsieur le Directeur

19 Les problèmes de la poste dans le monde 1.1, 1.2, 2.1, 2.2, 3.1, 4.2, 5.2

Connecting to Civic Literacy, Critical Thinking and Problem Solving, Global Awareness

Interpretive Reading, Interpersonal Speaking, Presentational Writing and Speaking

La livraison du courrier (lettres et colis) varie selon le pays et parfois, la démographie du pays. Dans quelques pays, c'est un privilège d'avoir une boîte postale et de recevoir du courrier. Recherchez une région du monde où il pourrait y avoir des défis dans la circulation du courrier et l'établissement de services postaux. En groupe, discutez de la situation, des problèmes, puis proposez des solutions. Considérez divers facteurs comme l'économie, le transport, les conditions locales et les structures familiales. Présentez les problèmes et vos solutions à la classe. Ensuite, discutez avec toute la classe.

MODÈLE

En Côte d'Ivoire, il n'existait que 150,000 boîtes aux lettres pour 24 millions d'habitants. Le gouvernement a changé le système et au lieu de boîtes individuelles, ils ont divisé les communautés en secteurs et installé des boîtes à code unique dans chaque secteur. Tous les habitants peuvent aller chercher leur courrier en utilisant les codes. Le problème avec le nouveau système est que la plupart des Ivoiriens n'ont pas accès à Internet pour trouver les codes qui leur correspondent. Nous proposons une nouvelle solution….

Reference Desk

This section is designed for students to apply unit vocabulary and structures to communicative activities that foster 21st-century skills. These activities demonstrate how 21st-century skills are cultivated in the language classroom and how these skills and the language learning process are mutually beneficial.

French in the Workplace

Working in the Financial Sector

The international financial sector continues to grow and be a viable, prosperous workplace. Jobs in this field require a knowledge of French and English, but also an understanding of markets and economics. Look up the definitions and French equivalents of the following economic terms: GDP (see p. 328 of this unit), budget surplus, budget deficit, debt, net worth, gross profit, and inflation. Explain these economic concepts in your own terms. Compare your explanations with a partner. Contrast French statistics regarding these terms with US statistics. What does this reveal about the strengths and weaknesses of each economy?

Social Justice

In France there is much contempt for **Les paradis fiscaux**, which are countries or territories where taxes are minimal. Big companies profit from this. Ask students to research which countries wealthy French companies bank in to avoid paying taxes. Ask students to research whether this problem exists in the United States, and find specific examples. In groups, have students discuss what solutions they can think of to develop accountability for all companies in their country.

Multiple Intelligences

Projets finaux A, **B**, and **C** may appeal to students with different multiple intelligences. Give the students a choice of activities as a way of appealing to what they are interested in. For example, the Bodily-Kinesthetic/Visual-Spatial students might enjoy making a website or a commercial for a bank for young people. The intrapersonal students would like to do project **B**. Your Interpersonal/Logical-Mathematical students might be more drawn to the third activity.

Special Needs Students

At-Risk Students/Behavior Problems/Linguistically Challenged

Students may possess a variety of talents. Many can draw, others are adept in technology, some love photography. Expand the **Projets finaux** to include activities in which they can show creativity and excel.

Resources

Create

Answers

All activities will vary.

Reference Desk

1. The **Faisons le point!** section asks students to self-evaluate and keep track of their progress. When students complete the activity, direct them to use "I can" statements based on the unit objectives in the **Contrat de l'élève**. The graphic organizer for **Activité D** can be found in the Copy Masters supplement.
2. If you have access to Passport, assign your students an IPA task related to the unit.

Critical Thinking

Evaluation

Encourage students to evaluate their learning in this unit. 1) Have them write the answer to the question, "What do I know now that I did not know before doing this unit?" 2) Ask them to evaluate what they still need to review. 3) Have them write a list of questions (that are not answered in the book) to ask the teacher before the unit exam.

Finale

Question centrale ? Comment s'intégrer à une autre culture ?

Projets finaux

A Connexions par Internet : le marketing 1.3, 3.1, 3.2, 5.2

Une banque pour les jeunes

Avec un ou deux partenaires, créez la page d'accueil d'une banque destinée aux jeunes français. D'abord, vous devrez décider quels services les jeunes recherchent. Quels messages attireraient les jeunes ? Quel slogan choisiriez-vous ? Comment s'appelle votre banque ?

B Communautés en ligne 1.3, 3.1, 3.2, 4.2, 5.1

Les étudiants américains en France

Beaucoup d'universités américaines et françaises offrent des échanges. Pour savoir si une telle expérience vous intéresserait, consultez des forums ou des blogs, ou même des sites universitaires, et recueillez (gather) *les opinions des français sur deux ou trois sujets qui vous intéressent. Discutez de ce que vous avez appris avec vos camarades de classe.*

Recherche : campus france, mon expérience d'étudiant en france

C Passez à l'action ! 1.3, 3.1, 3.2, 5.1

Combattons l'analphabétisme !

Si vous et vos camarades de classe pensez que tout le monde a le droit de savoir lire, suivez ces étapes pour enquêter sur l'analphabétisme (illiteracy) *dans le monde francophone, et proposez une solution.*

- Faites une liste des pays francophones que vous avez étudiés, et cherchez le taux d'analphabétisme dans chaque pays.
- Choisissez un pays dans la liste.
- Trouvez une association avec laquelle vous pourriez travailler.
- Suggérez une collecte de livres dans votre école ou votre communauté.
- Suggérez des associations que vous pourriez contacter.
- Suggerez d'autres solutions pour combattre l'analphabétisme dans ce pays.

D Faisons le point ! 1.3

Mes progrès

Remplissez le schéma que votre a prof va vous donner.

Essential Instruction

1. Have students listen to **Évaluation A**.
2. Pair students to do **Évaluation B**. Give class time to prepare their dialogue. Students may use a small cue card. Remind students that they can refer to the material presented on p. 352 for help with this.

Évaluation

A **Évaluation de compréhension auditive** 1.2, 2.1, 2.2

*Écrivez les numéros 1–8 sur votre papier. Écoutez David et Paulette discuter de la poste en France. Ensuite, écrivez **V** si les phrases que vous entendez sont vraies, ou **F** si elles sont fausses.*

B **Évaluation orale** 1.1, 2.1, 3.1, 5.2

Avec un partenaire, jouez les rôles de deux étudiants français à la librairie.

Dites que vous devez acheter un livre pour votre père parce que c'est bientôt son anniversaire.

Demandez ce qu'il aime lire.

Dites qu'il aime les romans policiers.

Indiquez où ils se trouvent.

Dites que vous n'arriverez jamais à prendre une décision.

Dites que, selon votre mère, ceux de Georges Simenon sont intéressants.

Remerciez votre ami(e).

Demandez s'il lui faut une carte d'anniversaire.

Dites que oui.

Dites à quel rayon se trouvent les cartes d'anniversaires.

Demandez à votre ami(e) s'il ou elle peut joindre la famille pour fêter l'anniversaire de votre père.

Répondez à l'invitation.

Differentiated Learning

Adapt
Ask students to find a graphic organizer of their choosing featuring key question words: **Qui?**, **Que?**, **Comment?**, **Pourquoi?**, **Quand?**, and **Avec qui?** During their pre-speaking or pre-writing preparation, have them fill out the graphic organizer. Doing this gives them the framework for organizing their ideas before oral and written evaluations.

Recherche: graphic organizer, enchanted learning, interactive graphic organizers

Special Needs Students

Linguistically Challenged
For the **Évaluation orale**, make sure that students with linguistic challenges are given a partner who understands instructions well and will be supportive during the conversation.

Resources

- Activity A
- Listening Activity Synthèse
- Pre-AP Listening *Unité 6*
- Perform

Answers

A Script

David: Tu vas à la poste?
Paulette: Oui, j'ai besoin de retirer de l'argent et d'acheter des timbres.
David: Tu peux retirer de l'argent à la poste?
Paulette: Bien sûr, la poste a aussi un service bancaire. C'est très pratique!
David: De quoi penses-tu que j'aurai besoin pour ouvrir un compte chez eux?
Paulette: En général, ils demandent une carte d'identité et une adresse. Mais toi, comme tu es étudiant étranger, il faut que tu prennes ton passeport, je pense, et que tu aies une lettre de l'école.
David: Je peux venir avec toi? J'en profiterais pour changer mes dollars en euros au bureau de change et je demanderai au banquier si je peux ouvrir un compte.
Paulette: Oui, on y va?
David: Tu crois que je pourrai envoyer un colis à ma famille?
Paulette: Bien entendu. Ton colis est prêt?
David: Oui, le voici.
Paulette: Il faut mettre ton adresse.
David: Et les timbres?
Paulette: Eh bien, tu demanderas à la postière. Elle te dira le prix de l'affranchissement.
David: D'accord. La poste en France, c'est super!

(*continued on next page*)

Reference Desk

If you have access to Passport, assign a task to evaluate your students' oral proficiency.

Game

En vitesse!
As a bell-ringer game, give students five minutes to write as many words and expressions as possible that pertain to **la banque** and **la poste**. Tally the correct words to determine the **le roi** or **la reine du vocabulaire du jour**.

Answers

(*continued from previous page*)

1. Paulette veut retirer de l'argent à la poste.
2. En France, la poste propose à la fois un service bancaire et un service postal.
3. David ne pourra pas ouvrir un compte à la poste parce qu'il n'est pas français.
4. Il faut une adresse et une carte d'identité pour acheter des timbres.
5. David peut changer son argent à la poste.
6. David peut changer de l'argent, envoyer un colis, et ouvrir un compte au même endroit.
7. David doit affranchir son colis à la poste.
8. L'employé de banque va aider David avec son colis.

1. V; 2. V; 3. F; 4. F; 5. V; 6. V; 7. V; 8. F

B Conversations will vary.

C Activities will vary.

D Activities will vary.

E Activities will vary.

Reference Desk

1. You might want to have students take a learning styles test as they prepare to study for the final evaluation. Preview it to make sure that it is a good measurement tool.

Recherche: learning styles test

2. For part **A**, consider evaluating students on the work completed rather than on the quality of their speaking. Use this time period to give informal feedback and advice before the assessment.
3. In **D**, the closing **A+** is an informal sign-off, an abbreviation of the expression **À plus tard!** (*See you later!*)

C Évaluation culturelle 1.3, 2.1, 2.2, 3.1, 3.2, 4.2, 5.1

Vous allez comparer les cultures francophones à votre culture. Vous aurez peut-être besoin de faire des recherches sur la culture américaine.

1. **Les banques**
   Quelles banques françaises peut-on trouver à Paris? Quelles banques canadiennes peut-on trouver à Montréal? Comment s'appellent les banques dans votre ville? Toutes ces banques sont-elles des banques nationales, régionales, ou internationales?
2. **Les habitudes de lecture**
   Comparez les habitudes des lecteurs français à celles des lecteurs américains. Est-ce que vos habitudes ressemblent plutôt aux habitudes des Français ou des Américains? Justifiez votre réponse.
3. **Jean-Marie Gustave Le Clézio**
   Le comité Nobel considère Le Clézio comme un «écrivain de nouveaux départs, de l'aventure poétique, explorateur d'une humanité au-delà et en dessous de la civilisation régnante.» Qu'est-ce qui peut illustrer ce résumé dans ce que vous avez appris sur Le Clézio?
4. **La Poste**
   Quels services est-ce que la poste française offre? Comment est-ce que la poste américaine est différente de la poste française?

D Évaluation écrite 1.1, 1.2, 1.3, 3.1, 4.2

Votre correspondant français vous a envoyé un message. Lisez-le et répondez en utilisant des pronoms démonstratifs.

Il faut que je lise un roman américain et que j'en fasse un résumé. Quels livres est-ce que tu me conseillerais?

Je voudrais t'envoyer un colis avec des choses typiques d'ici. Qu'est-ce que tu préférerais? Des choses à manger, à regarder, ou à écouter?

À+,
Khaled

E Évaluation visuelle 1.2, 1.3, 3.2

Décrivez ce qui se passe à la poste d'après l'illustration.

F Évaluation compréhensive 1.3, 3.1, 4.2

Créez une histoire avec six illustrations qui montrent un Américain en France qui visite la banque, la librairie, et, finalement, la poste.

Essential Instruction

1. Allow students to choose Activity 1, 2, 3, or 4 to complete **Évaluation C**. Allowing them the choice ensures that they demonstrate proficiency in areas that most interest them.
2. For **Évaluation D** students might want to write the response using a real e-mail format. Have them answer the question and add chatty conversation in the same way they would if they were writing to a friend.
3. Give students a few minutes to jot down notes about the picture before they do **Évaluation E**. Then use the picture to get students conversing.
4. A storyboard format lends itself to **Évaluation F**. Remind students that they do not have to be Picasso to draw figures.
5. Students should be able to recall the word or expression from English to French, and from French to English. They should be able to spell and pronounce the terms correctly. In reviewing vocabulary, have students define each term.

Vocabulaire de l'Unité 6

l' **administration (f.)** administration *A*
affranchir to stamp *C*
l' **affranchissement (m.)** postage *C*
un **appareil** machine *C*
l' **argent (m.) liquide** cash *A*
arriver à faire quelque chose to bring oneself to do something *A*
assez rather *C*
une **autobiographie** autobiography *B*
une **autorisation** permit *A*
avoir: avoir l'impression (de) to have the impression (of) *A*
le **banquier, la banquière** banker *A*
la **biochimie** biochemistry *A*
une **biographie** biography *B*
une **boîte** box *C*; **boîte aux lettres** mailbox *C*; **boîte cartonnée** cardboard box *C*
un **bouquin** book *[inform.]* *B*
le **bureau de change** foreign exchange bureau *A*
c'est: c'est promis it's a promise *A*
le **caissier, la caissière** bank teller *A*
une **carte bancaire** debit card *A*
un **catalogue** catalog *C*
celui, celle that/this one, the one *C*
un **certificat** certificate *A*
ceux the ones, these, those *C*
un **chèque** check *A*
un **chéquier** checkbook *A*
un **colis** package *C*
un **compte** account *A*
congolais(e) Congolese *B*
coupable guilty *A*
se **débrouiller** to get by *A*
se **décider** to make up one's mind *B*
déposer to deposit *A*
dernier, dernière: le dernier the latest *B*
le **distributeur (automatique)** ATM *A*
dont about which/whom, of which/whom *B*
le **droit** law *A*
économiser (de l'argent) to save (money) *A*
en: en ce moment at the moment *A*
encaisser to cash *A*
être: être amoureux/amoureuse (de) to be in love (with) *B*; **être content(e) (de)** to be happy (about) *B*
évident easy *A*
un **facteur, une factrice** mailman, mailwoman *C*
les **finances (f.)** finances *A*
futur(e) future *A*
le **génie civil** civil engineering *A*
la **gestion (économique d'entreprise)** (economic business) management *A*
graphique graphic *A*
l' **histoire (f.) de l'art** art history *A*
l' **imaginaire (m.)** fantasy *B*
l' **infographie (f.)** computer graphics *A*
s' **intégrer (à)** to integrate (into) *A*
un **livre: livre de poche** paperback *B*
le **management** management *A*
un **manga** manga *B*
la **médecine** medicine *A*
la **monnaie** change *A*; **la monnaie étrangère** foreign currency *A*
un **mystère** mystery *B*
une **nouvelle** short-story *B*
parler: parler de to be about *B*; **Ça parle de quoi ?** What is it about? *B*
peser to weigh *C*
une **pièce (de monnaie)** coin *A*; **une anthologie de pièces de théâtre** anthology of plays *B*
la **poésie** poetry *B*; **un recueil de poésie** collection of poetry *B*
policier detective *B*
le **positionnement** positioning *A*
le **postier, la postière** postal worker *C*
une **première** première (of movie) *A*
la **psychologie** psychology *A*
réaliser to direct (movie) *A*
la **réalité** reality *B*
retirer to withdraw *A*
les **sciences (f.): sciences politiques (sciences po)** political science (poli sci) *A*; **sciences du sport** sport sciences *A*
le **service de livraison (postale)** (mail) delivery service *C*
la **tendresse** tenderness *B*
un **titre** title *B*
transférer (de l'argent) to transfer (money) *A*

Resources

FC Flash Cards
Rendez-vous à Nice ! Documentaire 3
T *Unité 6* Test

Reference Desk

nouvelle orthographe **une boite**

Games

Pictionnaire

Play Pictionary to review key vocabulary. Create a set of vocabulary flash cards and put them in a large envelope. Divide the class into two teams. One student selects a word and draws it on the board while teammates try to guess the word. Award one point for each word guessed correctly in an allotted amount of time. Include vocabulary from previous chapters to make the game more challenging.

Charades

Play Charades with key unit vocabulary. Divide the class into two teams. One student acts out the word for teammates during a short time period. Award a point for each word guessed correctly. Include vocabulary from previous chapters to make the game more challenging.

Bilan cumulatif

Pre-AP

Multiple Choice

I. Interpretive Communication: Print Texts **1.2, 2.1, 3.1**

Lisez cet article sur les Français et l'argent aujourd'hui, puis répondez à la question.

Avec la dernière crise économique en Europe, beaucoup moins de touristes sont descendus dans les grands hôtels de la Côte d'Azur en France et à Monaco. Évidemment, maintenant, les revenus des entreprises sont beaucoup moins importants. Pour répondre à la situation et pour encourager les touristes à profiter d'un séjour de plus longue durée sur la côte, les hôtels français et monégasques proposent des offres incroyables. Si on réserve une chambre dans un des hôtels participants, toutes sortes de prestations sans supplément sont disponibles, par exemple chambre avec climatisation, bain à remous, accès au centre d'affaires avec connexion Wifi et fax, et coffre-fort. En plus, le concierge de l'hôtel s'occupera de planifier les visites touristiques. On s'attend à ce que les revenus soient plus importants pour la saison à venir à cause de ces nouvelles prestations.

1. D'après le texte, quel est le réflexe des entreprises en période de crise?
   A. de travailler différemment pour augmenter sa clientèle
   B. de faire semblant qu'il n'y a pas de problème
   C. de ne rien changer

II. Interpretive Communication: Audio Texts **1.2**

Madison va en France pour les vacances. Avec son amie Sidney, elle regarde les guides touristiques. Écoutez le dialogue suivant deux fois, puis complétez les phrases.

1. La conversation a lieu....
   A. dans un office de tourisme
   B. au téléphone
   C. au cinéma
   D. dans une librairie
2. Sidney suggère à Madison....
   A. qu'elle achète plusieurs guides
   B. qu'elle regarde un documentaire avec elle
   C. d'acheter ses livres à sa destination et d'aller voir un film au cinéma
   D. qu'elle rentre à la maison
3. Madison décide d'acheter....
   A. un magazine de cuisine
   B. rien
   C. deux livres de poche
   D. un guide sur les régions de France

Resources

Activity II

Answers

I

1. A

II **Script**

Sidney: Tiens Madison, voilà un guide sur les régions de France. Il décrit les hôtels, les prestations et les descriptions des spécialités de chaque région. Le seul problème, ce n'est pas une édition de poche.
Madison: Oh, ça a l'air super pour planifier mon séjour. J'aime bien la liste des préparatifs de voyage qu'il y a. Oh, je n'arrive pas à me décider! Il y a aussi ces deux éditions de poche sur la Bourgogne et la Côte d'Azur, et ce gros guide qui comprend tout et qui a aussi un bon dico à la fin.
Sidney: Je ne sais pas. À mon avis, il faut que tu fasses surtout attention aux bagages. On exigera que tu paies pour chaque kilo en plus de 32 kilos! Pourquoi pas acheter un bouquin sur place?
Madison: Tu as tout à fait raison. Je veux que mon séjour soit un peu planifié, au moins.... Je pourrais trouver ce que je veux là-bas et improviser. Finalement, je ne vais prendre que ce magazine sur la cuisine provençale.
Sidney: Bon, on va au ciné après? La dernière comédie de Dany Boon vient de sortir. J'ai vu la bande-annonce et ça a l'air vraiment drôle.
Madison: Excellente idée.

1. D; 2. C; 3. A

Reference Desk

The **Bilan cumulatif** is based on the French Language and Culture AP exam prepared by the College Board. It assesses students' proficiencies in the Interpersonal, Interpretive, and Presentational modes of communication. Students are also asked to demonstrate their understanding of the products, practices, and perspectives of the target cultures.

Differentiated Learning

Accelerate/Decelerate
Have all students skim the questions before reading the passage or listening to the dialogue. In this way, they have a sense of what it is about. Encourage students not to try to decode every word as they read or listen but work on understanding the gist of the passages.

Free Response

III. Interpersonal Writing: E-mail Reply **1.1, 1.3, 2.1**

Vous allez écrire une réponse à un message électronique. Il faut répondre à toutes les questions et donner des détails à propos du sujet du message. Écrivez formellement. N'oubliez pas d'écrire une salutation au début et d'utiliser une formule de politesse (closing) à la fin de votre message.

Vous êtes responsable d'une librairie qui se trouve à la rue de Rivoli à Paris. Vous répondez à Anthony Talbot, écrivain américain, que vous avez invité à une conférence sur le futur du livre et qui cherche à mieux connaître les habitudes de lecture des Français.

De: Anthony Talbot

Objet: Les Français et les livres

Cher Monsieur,

Je vous remercie de m'avoir invité à participer à la « Table ronde des auteurs » qui aura lieu au mois de mars à la librairie « Aux Quatre Coins ». C'est une excellente idée d'organiser chaque année cet évenement pour vos lecteurs pendant la semaine de la Foire du Livre à Paris. Je comprends qu'il y aura une conférence suivie de la présentation de mon roman *Livre fragile* et qu'ensuite je parlerai du futur du livre. Afin de préparer cette rencontre, j'aimerais en savoir plus sur l'importance du livre dans la vie des Français. Quelles sont leurs préférences? Livres de cuisine? Romans policiers? Essais? Mangas? Y a-t-il des émissions littéraires à la télé ou à la radio? Je sais que les prix littéraires ont une grande importance en France, mais influencent-ils vraiment les lecteurs? Combien de titres vendez-vous par an? Je vous remercie d'avance de répondre à mes questions. Ces précisions me seront très utiles et me permettront de mieux connaître les goûts et les habitudes de vos lecteurs afin de préparer ma présentation.

Bien cordialement,

Anthony Talbot
Greenwich, Connecticut
USA

IV. Presentational Speaking: Cultural Comparison **1.2, 1.3, 2.1, 3.1, 4.2, 5.2**

Vous êtes consultant en finances. Vous faites une présentation qui s'appelle « Comment vivre et voyager avec votre argent » pour les parents d'un groupe d'étudiants américains qui participeront à un échange en France. Leurs parents se rappellent de l'époque où on était obligé de voyager en Europe avec des chèques de voyage et de la monnaie de plusieurs pays. Il faut leur expliquer que tout a changé et les renseigner sur le meilleur moyen d'organiser les finances de leurs enfants. Parlez de ce que leurs enfants doivent savoir pour ouvrir un compte et obtenir une carte bancaire. Les parents auront besoin aussi de savoir comment ils peuvent envoyer de l'argent à leurs enfants depuis les États-Unis.

Answers

III E-mails will vary.

IV Presentations will vary.

Reference Desk

1. The Print Text section consists of a variety of authentic print materials such as articles and correspondence. A multiple-choice question follows the text.
2. The Audio Text is a professional recording, usually a dialogue. Encourage students to preview and skim the questions before listening. They should then answer the multiple-choice questions.
3. The E-mail Reply is a free response test section. Students develop their interpersonal writing skills.
4. The Presentational Writing section asks students to write a persuasive essay.

Essential Instruction

1. Make copies of the **Bilan cumulatif III** and **IV** for students so that they can jot down notes on their sheets, as they would be able to do on scratch paper during an AP exam. Students must answer every question posed in the e-mail, so they should number each question to make sure that they write a thorough response. In the same way, for the Presentational Speaking: Cultural Comparison, they need to outline their talking points.

Reference Desk

1. In this unit, students will learn about art. Live music is a very common form of entertainment in French cities, and not solely in Paris. Small villages continue to hold frequent festivals combining music, singing, and dance. **La Fête de la Musique** is a free, yearly music festival celebrated on June 21, the summer solstice, all across France and in many other countries around the world. This tradition goes back to the Middle Ages when troubadours would bring the arts (music, singing, literature, poetry, theatre) alive to audiences who did not necessarily have access to the performing arts.
2. The photo on the unit opener represents a couple dancing swing. Swing is a North American dance style influenced by the Charleston and created from jazz and band music of the Harlem Renaissance in the United States in the 1920s. It was brought to France during WWII and has remained, with rock 'n' roll, a popular dance form to accompany festivities. Students learn music styles influenced by America in **Leçon B**.

Expansion

1. Students may wish to share with the class their tastes in painting, music, and dance. Write three columns on the board, one for each art category, then poll students to find out if they know any French or francophone painters, painting movements, singers, and dancers or dance styles.
2. Group students by the arts category of their interest (fine arts, music, dance, theater, etc.), then have each group make a survey in French to collect data about their own tastes and those of their families.
3. Combine the three surveys into one with three section headings (**La peinture**, **La musique**, **La danse**), and give it to students as a class opener or homework for the next day.

Unité

7 Les arts francophones

376 trois cent soixante-seize | **Unité 7**

Essential Instruction

1. Ask students how many French painters and writers they can name. Inquire if they can define Classicism, Impressionism, and Surrealism.
2. Students will read sample poems from the Renaissance, the 17th century, the Romantic period (late 18th century to early 19th century), and the Surrealist movement of the 20th century.
3. In this unit, students will expand their mastery of the subjunctive using **pour que**, and learn the verb **plaire**.
4. Review the **Contrat de l'élève** to give students an overview of what they are going to learn.

Question centrale ?

Comment l'art est-il un reflet de la culture?

À savoir

60% des Français ont visité un monument et 40% ont visité un musée au moins une fois au cours de l'année dernière.

Citation

« L'art ne reproduit pas le visible, il rend visible. »

Art doesn't reproduce what is visible; it makes things visible.

—Paul Klee (1879–1940), peintre suisse

Conseil pratique

To become a better writer, find a safe forum online to participate in. Find interesting sentences by native speakers and adopt them in your own writing.

Quel métier fait Sarah?

De quel siècle date ce village?

Contrat de l'élève

Leçon A I will be able to:

- say when a painting was painted, and describe an artist's painting.
- discuss major art movements in France and traditional and contemporary art in West Africa.
- review adjective agreement and position, and adjectives in comparative and superlative constructions.

Leçon B I will be able to:

- describe the development of an artist, say that an artist was successful, and describe an artist's emphasis and his or her ability to connect with his or her audience.
- talk about music, singers, and groups from France and Quebec.
- use the verb **plaire** (*to please*).

Leçon C I will be able to:

- describe how an artist raises themes, describe the focus of a work of art and how it takes a position, attribute new inventions to an artist, and describe how an artist fits into a culture.
- discuss **La Pléiade**, Romanticism and Victor Hugo, Surrealism, and Haitian poetry.
- review **pour** + INFINITIF and use the subjunctive after **pour que**.

Answers

Possible choices for the video question are:

A. caissière
B. danseuse
C. huissière
D. actrice

Correct answer: A

The answer to the culture question is: **du 16ème siècle**. It is the village of **Grignan**, in southern France. The answer can be found in **Points de départ**, **Leçon C**.

Expansion

Ask students to bring in pictures of paintings, singers and bands, and dancers they like, and have a short show-and-tell as a bell ringer.

Multiple Intelligences

Visual-Spatial

This unit will be of special interest to such students since one of its themes is the visual artist. They can share with the class what they already know of different artists and/or genres throughout the ages.

Musical-Rhythmic

Ask students to do a preliminary review of popular music of France and Quebec by referencing the current top music, artists, and songs.

Recherche : la fnac, archambault

Special Needs Students

At-Risk Students

Be sure to poll students about their interest in art and music, as this unit might have great appeal for them. Remind students of the broad meaning of "art" that includes film, music (of all genres), comics, theater, dance, fine art, traditional crafts and artisanal work, television, and much more. Differentiate between "high" art and "low" art, being sure to emphasize that, despite the connotation of the words, neither is better than the other. Ask students which form(s) they prefer and why.

Resources

- *Vocabulaire actif*
- *Pour la conversation*
- *Et si je voulais dire… ?*
- eV eVisual
- WB Workbook 1–3
- FC Flash Cards
- LA Listening Activity 1
- G & V Practice Games

Reference Desk

1. **Le musée des Beaux-Arts de Lyon** is the municipal museum of Lyon housed in the former 17th-century Benedictine convent. The collection spans art from ancient to modern times. The Egyptian collection is especially noteworthy.
2. The **fontaine Bartholdi**, which is situated in front of the museum, was designed by Frédéric Gustave Bartholdi. Bartholdi was celebrated for his ***La Liberté éclairant le monde***—more commonly known as the Statue of Liberty.
3. **Un vernissage** is a private reception and viewing of an art exhibition before its opening to the public. Since there are many small art galleries in French cities and towns, this is a popular event among art lovers.
4. **Georges Seurat**, one of the first artists to be labeled *Post-Impressionist*, mastered the technique of *Pointillism*—that is, replacing broad brush strokes with small points, or dots, of color.

Leçon A — Vocabulaire actif

La peinture et les mouvements d'art 1.2, 3.1, 5.1

La peinture

Musée des Beaux-Arts 20 Place des Terreaux, 69001 Lyon

un musée des **beaux-arts** (m.) : musée dans lequel on peut trouver des peintures, des objets d'art, des sculptures, etc.

un atelier : pièce dans laquelle l'artiste travaille

une toile : support sur lequel le peintre **applique** les couleurs

un pinceau : sorte de brosse pour appliquer des couleurs sur la toile

Pour la conversation 1.1, 1.2

How do I say when a painting was painted?

» *Les Coquelicots* de Monet a été **peint** en 1873.
The Poppies *by Monet was painted in 1873.*

How do I describe an artist's approach?

» Avec ce tableau, Renoir recherche de plus en plus les effets de **lignes**.
With this painting, Renoir is looking more and more into the effects of lines.

» Avec **cette méthode**, Seurat **s'éloignait des impressionnistes**.
With this method, Seurat distanced himself from the Impressionists.

How do I describe the colors used in a painting?

» L'artiste a utilisé le jaune **pâle**.
The artist used pale yellow.

Et si je voulais dire… ?

une aquarelle	*watercolor*
un cadre	*frame*
foncé	*dark (color)*
un fusain	*charcoal*
un modèle	*model*
une palette	*palette*
une gravure	*etching / engraving*
graver	*to etch / engrave*
poser	*to pose*

Essential Instruction

1. When introducing the vocabulary, show students images of *Les Coquelicots* by Monet, *Portrait de William Sisley* by Renoir, and an example of Seurat's pointillism, if available.
2. Students listen to the recording of **La peinture et les mouvements d'art**.
3. Students use a full page of their notebook to draw and label the vocabulary on p. 378.
4. Students create a timeline or use another graphic organizer of their choosing to note the chronology of **Les mouvements d'art**, selecting a few key words to describe each one. They may choose to print a sample picture as an illustration of the style of the period. As students read about other movements, artists, and poets in this unit, they will add that information as well.

Les mouvements d'art 1.2, 2.2, 3.1, 5.2

La salle rococo (1730–1789) → **La salle néo-classique** (1750–1830)

à l'arrière-plan

à l'avant-plan

Le rococo
Mouvement qui naît après le déclin du mouvement baroque dans la seconde moitié du 18ème siècle; les sujets sont surtout des aristocrates

une perspective en gros plan

Le néo-classicisme
Art du 18ème et 19ème siècles inspiré par la mythologie et la Rome antique

La salle romantique (1800–1850) → **La salle réaliste** (1830–1870)

un paysage marin

Le romantisme
Art du 18ème et 19ème siècles qui exprime l'idéal et les sujets exotiques

au second plan

au premier plan

Le réalisme
Art du 19ème siècle qui montre des scènes de la vie courante non idéalisées

La salle impressionniste (1860–1890) → **La salle expressionniste** (1880–1920)

une fête champêtre en plein air

L'impressionnisme (m.)
Art qui note les impressions par touches; paysages souvent peints en plein air

Le néo-impressionnisme
Art qui oppose couleurs primaires et couleurs complémentaires

une nature morte

L'expressionnisme (m.)
Art qui montre une vision émotionnelle et subjective du monde

Communication

Interpersonal: Cooperative Groups

Assign groups of students to find names of painters to fit in each of the six art movements introduced on this page.

Reference Desk

Rococo painter **Jean Honoré Fragonard** (1732–1806) was one of the last prolific painters of pre-revolutionary France. His work is often celebrated for its frivolity and hedonism.
Neoclassical painter **Jacques Louis David** (1748–1825) was the preeminent painter of his time and the official painter of Napoleon Bonaparte.
Romantic painter **Théodore Géricault** (1791–1824) transformed the austerity of the Neo-Classical style with strong diagonals and bold brushwork. Among his celebrated works is *Le Radeau de la Méduse* (1819).
Realist painter **Jean Désiré Gustave Courbet** (1819–1877) is celebrated for the grandeur and scale of his everyday scenes.
An important bridge between the Realists and the Impressionists, **Édouard Manet** (1832–1883) explored psychological portraiture, momentary impressions, and outdoor painting.
Impressionism can be characterized by the study of light, a distancing from pure representational form and a step towards abstraction. **Claude Monet** (1840–1926) gave the movement its name, derived from his work *Impression, soleil levant* (1872) (see p. 385).
The Neo-Impressionist **Georges Seurat** (1859–1891) sought to bring order to the intuitive nature of Impressionism by juxtaposing dots of different color, a method called pointillism.
Expressionism views reality through subjective distortion to provoke an emotional reaction. Influenced by Post-Impressionist **Vincent van Gogh** (1853–1890), it emerged in Germany with Edvard Munch (1863–1944) and Franz Marc (1880–1916).
Other notable art movements include **le cubisme** (1907–1925), **l'abstraction, le surréalisme** (1919–1945), and **le minimalisme** (1945–1970).

Differentiated Learning

Accelerate
Students visit the website of the **musée des Beaux-Arts de Lyon**. Then have them make questions for the class on the details of operation, rules of the visit, and key pieces of art in the museum's collection. The class will then visit the website and answer the questions they have created.

Decelerate
Have students present to the class the names of three famous artists from each listed art movement who are not featured in the lesson, with a sample picture of each.

Resources

Activity 1

Answers

1 Possible answers:

1. Il n'a pas été impressionné par ce qu'il a vu.
2. Il préfère l'art qui représente quelque chose.
3. D'après le blogueur, il travaille dans un atelier.
4. Ils s'intéressaient à ces œuvres d'art.
5. Non.

2

1. un pinceau
2. la toile
3. un atelier
4. en plein air
5. une peinture
6. à l'arrière-plan, au premier plan
7. une nature morte
8. un paysage
9. une fête champêtre

Game

Appuyez sur le buzzer!

First ask students to go to the board one by one and write a vocabulary word you dictate. You should use the vocabulary from the word bank of **Activité 2**. You will then read the sentences from this activity. Students will refer to the vocabulary on the board to select the term that completes each sentence. The first person who buzzes in with the correct term gets a point.

Flyswatter variant

If you fill the board with a lot of vocabulary, place students on two teams lined up in two single files. The first person at the head of each team carries a whiteboard eraser. Call out a vocabulary word. The two students (one from each team) must run to the board to find the word. The first one to locate the word and erase it gets a point for his or her team. Those team members pass on the eraser to the next pair in line. Continue until all the words on the board have been "swatted."

1 Une journée au musée des beaux-arts 1.2, 3.1

Interpretive Reading

Lisez le blog d'un étudiant, puis répondez aux questions.

Bon d'accord, je ne suis pas un spécialiste de l'art, mais cette exposition ne m'a pas impressionné! Tous les tableaux se ressemblent : des couleurs sombres, pas de couleur vive, pas de paysage, pas de nature morte, pas de portrait, juste des lignes. Il est évident que le peintre n'a pas besoin de travailler en plein air pour capturer ses sujets. Un atelier lui suffit! Pourquoi a-t-il créé ces peintures? Je ne pourrais pas le dire. J'ai observé les autres visiteurs, et ils semblaient s'intéresser aux œuvres d'art, mais je ne comprends pas pourquoi! Je préfère l'art qui représente quelque chose. Les nouvelles techniques, les nouvelles méthodes, et les effets de lignes — à quoi ça sert? J'ai quitté cette exposition pour en voir une autre sur la bande dessinée, un art que je peux comprendre.

Théo

1. Quelle est la réaction du blogueur aux tableaux qui sont exposés?
2. Préfère-t-il l'art moderne ou l'art qui représente quelque chose?
3. D'après le blogueur, où travaille le peintre?
4. Quelle était la réaction des autres visiteurs du musée?
5. Est-ce que le blogueur a aimé sa visite à l'exposition de peinture?

2 La peinture française 1.2, 3.1

Interpretive Reading

Complétez les phrases avec un mot ou une expression ci-dessous.

un atelier **une peinture** **au premier plan** **la toile** **en plein air**
un paysage **à l'arrière-plan** **une fête champêtre** **une nature morte** **un pinceau**

1. L'artiste-peintre utilise… pour étaler (*spread*) les couleurs sur la toile.
2. Le peintre met des couleurs vives sur….
3. Quand l'artiste travaille dans son espace personnel pour l'art à l'intérieur, il est dans….
4. Un artiste qui peint dehors (*outside*) travaille….
5. Une œuvre peinte exposée (*exhibited*) dans un musée s'appelle un tableau ou….
6. Les détails ou les personnages qui semblent être à une certaine distance sont… et ceux qui semblent être plus proches sont….
7. Une représentation de fruits, de fleurs, ou d'objets est….
8. Une scène avec une rivière au premier plan et des montagnes à l'arrière-plan est….
9. Une peinture du 18ème siècle représentant une fête dans un jardin ou un parc s'appelle….

Essential Instruction

1. Students, in pairs, will read Théo's letter (**Activité 1**) to each other and answer the questions that follow.
2. Upon completion, ask volunteers to read the answers aloud. Ask students to justify their response by citing the line in the letter that provides the specific information.
3. Students will identify the negative remarks Théo makes about art. Have them discuss whether they prefer representational or abstract art. Discuss the differences between the two.
4. Pair students with different skill sets and have them do **Activité 3**. Project a picture of **Le Canal du Loing** and ask volunteers to describe it.
5. Students will listen to **Quel beau tableau!** to answer the **vrai** and **faux** questions. Ask students what details they remember from the recording.
6. Have students skim the **Questions personnelles** and point out anything they do not understand.
7. Students will circulate, asking and answering the questions.

3 Un tableau impressionniste 1.2, 3.1, 5.2

Interpretive Reading

Complétez le paragraphe sur Le canal du Loing *d'Alfred Sisley en vous servant d'un mot de la banque de mots.*

en plein air **peinture** **perspective** **premier plan**
paysage **peint** **toile** **l'arrière-plan**

Cette… est d'Alfred Sisley, un peintre impressionniste anglais du 19ème siècle. Sur la… il met des couleurs sombres. Il ne travaille pas dans un atelier, mais…. Le tableau, c'est essentiellement un…, qui montre la terre (*earth*) et la végétation. Ce n'est ni un portrait ni une nature morte. Au… on voit quelques arbres. Au centre, il y a une maison. À… on voit le ciel (*sky*) dans son immensité. Avec ce tableau, Sisley recherche un effet de…. Sisley a… ce tableau en 1892 quand il habitait dans cette région.

The Loing Canal, 1892. Alfred Sisley.

4 Quel beau tableau ! 1.2

Interpretive Listening

*Écrivez les numéros 1–7 sur votre papier. Écoutez Pablo et Chloé parler peinture. Ensuite, indiquez si les phrases que vous entendez sont vraies (**V**) ou fausses (**F**).*

5 Questions personnelles 1.1, 3.1, 5.2

Interpersonal Speaking

Répondez aux questions avec un partenaire.

1. Est-ce que tu fais de la peinture ? Si oui, qu'est-ce que tu aimes peindre ?
2. Est-ce que tu as déjà visité un musée des beaux-arts ? Quelles peintures as-tu aimées ?
3. Est-ce que tu suis un cours d'art maintenant ? Qu'est-ce que tu étudies ?
4. Comment s'appelle ton artiste préféré(e) ?
5. Travaille-t-il ou travaille-t-elle dans un atelier ou en plein air ?

Differentiated Learning

Accelerate

Ask students to write a blog similar to Théo's in which they discuss a piece of art they love or do not like at all.

Decelerate

Students can find and print examples of **un fusain**, **une aquarelle**, **une nature morte**, and **un paysage**. They can add the name of the artist, and explain how the techniques are different. This step could be done in English since the objective is to get them to connect personally with works of art.

Multiple Intelligences

Visual-Spatial

Have students find an impressionist painting that resembles ***Le canal du Loing***. Students can identify what themes and techniques the two art works have in common. Ask if they have any of their own art that they would like to share with the class.

Resources

Activity 4

Answers

3

peinture ; toile ; en plein air ; paysage ; premier plan ; l'arrière-plan ; perspective ; peint

4 Script

Pablo : Salut, Chloé ! Je ne savais pas que tu aimais peindre.
Chloé : Bien sûr ! J'adore peindre en plein air. Mon atelier, c'est la nature !
Pablo : Qu'est-ce que tu peins ?
Chloé : C'est un paysage. Regarde, au premier plan tu vois les gens sur la plage et à l'arrière-plan, la mer et les bateaux.
Pablo : C'est très beau. Est-ce que tu aimes les natures mortes ?
Chloé : Pas vraiment. Je préfère peindre la vie, les saisons, les gens. J'adore les toiles de Monet. C'est mon inspiration. Tu peux me passer le pinceau là ?
Pablo : Celui-ci ? Tu aimes les impressionnistes, alors ?
Chloé : Oui, mais j'aime aussi le fauvisme et le cubisme d'une manière différente.
Pablo : Alors, tu peins des toiles modernes ?
Chloé : Non, j'aime avoir des modèles à regarder et je préfère peindre les choses de la vie réelle.
Pablo : Eh bien, tu devrais continuer. J'adore ton style ! À plus !

1. Pablo est surpris de découvrir que Chloé peint.
2. Chloé adore peindre dans son atelier.
3. Cette conversation a lieu dans un musée des beaux-arts.
4. Au premier plan du tableau de Chloé, il y a les bateaux et la mer.
5. Chloé n'aime pas beaucoup peindre des natures mortes.
6. Chloé adore les impressionnistes et Monet est son inspiration.
7. Chloé préfère peindre la vie imaginaire.

1. V; 2. F; 3. F; 4. F; 5. V; 6. V; 7. F

5 Answers will vary.

Expansion

1. Ask students where the nearest fine arts museum is located in their community. How large is the collection and what famous works are featured?
2. Poll how many students think that representational art is the true art form, and how many prefer abstract art, and why.

Resources

WB Workbook 4

Reference Desk

1. The painting *Les Coquelicots* depicts Monet's first wife, Camille, and their son, Jean.
2. **Un canotier** has two meanings: a person who goes boating, and a straw oval hat adorned with a ribbon. We see both the boaters and their hats in Renoir's painting ***Déjeuner des canotiers***.
3. The meaning of **propre** depends on the context. Before a noun, it means *own* as in **mes propres mains** (*my own hands*); after a noun, it means *clean* as in **mes mains propres** (*my clean hands*). In the reading we see yet another meaning, that of *typical* as in **propres au peintre**.
4. The suffix **âtre** adds *ish* to a color, thus **rougeâtre** means *reddish*.
5. Gustave Caillebotte (1848–1894) was a photographer, art collector, and painter associated with the Impressionist movement although his paintings had more of a photographic, realistic style. Two of his most celebrated works are ***Rue de Paris, temps de pluie*** (1877), and ***Les raboteurs de parquet*** (1875).
6. **La Grande Jatte** (*the big basin*) is an island in the Seine just outside of Paris.
7. Monet's home, gardens, and studio in Giverny, located halfway between Rouen and Paris, and Renoir's home in Cagnes-sur-Mer in the south of France, are fascinating places to visit.

nouvelle orthographe **un maitre**

Rencontres culturelles

Des grands maîtres de la peinture française 1.2, 2.2, 3.1, 5.2

Voici quatre tableaux de grands maîtres de la peinture française. Ces tableaux ont été peints au 19ème siècle.

Les Coquelicots, 1873. Claude Monet.

Claude Monet a peint *Impression, soleil levant* en 1872. Ce tableau donne son nom à un nouveau mouvement artistique : l'impressionnisme. Monet a peint de nombreux paysages, notamment* des scènes de bateaux sur l'eau, qui sont parmi ses œuvres les plus caractéristiques. Il peignait en plein air sur un bateau qu'il avait transformé en atelier. Il étudiait les nuances de l'atmosphère et de la lumière sous les touches de pinceau. *Les Coquelicots* (1873) montre un paysage de collines sur lesquelles un champ de fleurs s'épand* tel une mer jusqu'à l'horizon ; ce tableau représente un pas* supplémentaire de l'artiste vers l'abstraction, tendance qui se retrouvera dans ses célèbres *Nymphéas* de Giverny. Au premier plan, on voit une femme avec son enfant traversant les hautes herbes* par une journée d'été. Mais ces personnages ont peu de détails et leur expression ne se voit pas. Pour Monet, qui finira par abandonner la figure humaine*, l'homme n'était qu'une partie de la nature. Selon ses propres* mots, le maître de l'impressionnisme a voulu saisir l'éphémère* : « Ce que je ferai ici aura au moins le mérite de ne ressembler à personne, parce que ce sera l'impression de ce que j'aurai ressenti*, moi tout seul. »

notamment *namely*; **s'épand** *spreads*; **pas** *step*; **herbes** *grass*; **figure humaine** *human figures*; **propres** *own*; **éphémère** *fleeting moment*; **j'aurai ressenti** *I will have felt*

Déjeuner des canotiers, 1880–81. Pierre-Auguste Renoir.

Pierre-Auguste Renoir s'éloigne du mouvement impressionniste pour rechercher une expression plus réaliste par des effets de lignes, des contours, et des contrastes. Dans le *Déjeuner des canotiers* (1880–81), les lignes diagonales prolongent* le champ de vision de la table aux personnages de l'arrière-plan, alors que les couleurs vives et les contours nets des objets de la table, inanimés, contrastent avec les couleurs pastel et les touches plus impressionnistes des personnages. L'effet recherché est une atmosphère d'éclatement*, de spontanéité, et de fête. Il s'agit ici d'une fête champêtre moderne qui regroupe les amis et proches* du peintre : sa fiancée, Aline Charigot, au premier plan à gauche ; puis à droite son ami et peintre Gustave Caillebotte. Dans ce tableau on retrouve l'amour de la vie populaire et de la sensualité propres* au peintre, et les femmes typiques de Renoir : le visage rond, la peau blanche, les joues rougeâtres*, la forme ronde. Le paysage, les arbres aux touches lumineuse et floues*, le canot*, rappellent les caractéristiques de l'impressionnisme, mais les natures mortes et l'importance des personnages distinguent Renoir de Monet. Avant sa mort, Renoir aura peint à peu près six mille tableaux, un record avant Picasso.

prolongent *extend*; **éclatement** *bursting*; **proches** *close friends or relatives*; **propres** *typical*; **rougeâtre** *reddish*; **floues** *blurry*; **canot** bateau

Essential Instruction

1. Ask students to read **Rencontres culturelles** as a class activity or an independent assignment. Ask which sentences are not clear to them.
2. For each reading, students can fill out a grid: **Artiste-peintre**, **Mouvement pictural**, **Titres du (des) tableau(x)**, **Techniques**, **Citations**, **Remarques supplémentaires**. This will help them to organize the information about each painter.
3. Ask open-ended questions to get students to comment on each painting: Who and what do they see in each painting? What is happening? What time of day might it be?

Georges Seurat est un peintre pointilliste, connu surtout pour son tableau d'une taille inouïe* *Un dimanche après-midi à l'île de la Grande Jatte* (1886). Il s'agit d'une scène de plein air au bord de la Seine lors* d'une belle journée d'été. Le sujet comprend une quarantaine de personnages s'abritant à l'ombre* au premier plan, par une journée ensoleillée*. L'œuvre montre la bourgeoisie et d'autres personnages qui se livrent à* leurs loisirs : promenade, voile, pêche. L'art de Seurat est le résultat de recherches scientifiques sur les couleurs et les théories de la vision. Sur cette toile il a posé de petites touches séparées de couleurs pures qui se confondent* à une certaine distance. On appelle cette technique le « pointillisme » ou le « néo-impressionnisme ». Elle se distingue de l'impressionnisme qui recherche la sensation changeante de la lumière, plutôt que les images figées*. Seurat a dit : « Les littérateurs et les critiques voient de la poésie dans ce que je fais. Non, j'applique ma méthode, et c'est tout. » Seurat a exercé une influence indéniable sur Gauguin, van Gogh, et Pissarro, mais aussi sur tous les fauves, cubistes, et futuristes.

Un dimanche après-midi à l'île de la Grande Jatte, 1886. Georges Seurat.

inouïe *unbelievable*; **lors** *pendant*; **s'abritant à l'ombre** *sheltered by the shade*; **ensoleillée** *sunny*; **se livrent à** *give themselves to*; **se confondent** *merge*; **figées** *stilted, stiff*

Vincent van Gogh, un Néerlandais qui a passé ses dernières années dans le sud de la France, a réalisé ce tableau à Arles, une ville provençale, en septembre 1888. Il s'agit d'une terrasse de café en pleine nuit. Dans ce tableau, van Gogh utilise des couleurs chaudes au premier plan, pour donner de la profondeur* à la perspective. Le blanc des tables du café dirige* l'œil vers la partie obscure du tableau. À l'arrière-plan, les bâtiments sont sombres, mais le ciel étoilé d'un bleu vif qui remplace le noir de la nuit est le centre d'attention de cette peinture, qui se veut* tranquille et non opprimante*. Les personnages dans la rue ajoutent* à la tranquillité du lieu. On retrouvera le sujet de la nuit étoilée chez van Gogh dans *Nuit étoilée sur le Rhône* et *Nuit étoilée*. Dans une lettre adressée à sa sœur Wilhelmina, le peintre a dit : « Cela m'amuse énormément de peindre la nuit sur place. Autrefois on dessinait et peignait le tableau le jour d'après le dessin. Mais moi je m'en trouve bien de peindre la chose immédiatement. » Son usage de couleurs arbitraires souligne* ses sentiments forts, la raison pour laquelle van Gogh est désigné précurseur* de l'expressionnisme.

Terrasse du café le soir, 1888. Vincent van Gogh.

profondeur *depth*; **dirige** *direct*; **se veut** *is meant to be*; **opprimante** *oppressing*; **ajoutent** *add*; **souligne** *emphasizes*; **précurseur** *forerunner*

Expansion

C'est quel artiste ?

Prepare images of paintings that represent art movements and artists presented thus far in this unit. Write the names and vocabulary words of those painters, art movements, and paintings on the board for quick reference. Then show students one image at a time and have them guess what painting it is, give the name of the artist, and also the art movement associated with it. Students may work as a class or in teams. For a twist, you may show students images they have not seen before but that belong to the artists that have been introduced in this unit. A further extension would be to show paintings of artists they have not discussed and try to fit them into the art movements they have been exposed to so far.

Connections

History

In groups, have students find influential historical events and people (Napoléon III, Haussmann, Franco-Prussian War, the Gay Nineties, World War I) and technological innovations (metal tubes for making paints portable, lithography, photography, industrialization, trains) in the time periods that correspond to the art movements described in these pages. Ask students to reflect and draw connections between what was happening historically and how that influenced the art forms, and present their theories to the class.

Differentiated Learning

Accelerate

Have students compare the following van Gogh paintings: ***Terrasse du café le soir*** with ***Nuit étoilée sur le Rhône*** and ***Nuit étoilée***. They should compare and contrast the paintings in terms of technique, color, and theme.

Special Needs Students

AD(H)D/Dyslexia

Students might be discouraged at first by the length of the readings and the technical writing. Breaking down each passage into smaller sections and directly linking the readings to the visual cues provided in the paintings will allow the readings to appear more manageable. Consider providing coloring sheets of famous works for students to work on while you speak of the paintings.

Visually Impaired

Make modifications for students who do not see well or are color-blind since this lesson is so visual.

At-Risk Students/Behavior Problems

Some of your students may not have been exposed to art as children. This activity is an opportunity to broaden their horizons by personalizing the art.

Answers

6

Monet: 1. l'impressionnisme; 2. les changements de l'atmosphère et de la lumière; 3. oui; 4. saisir l'éphémère

Renoir: 1. l'impressionnisme; 2. aux hommes et femmes, et aux atmosphères de fête; 3. avec des formes rondes et des couleurs blanches et roses; 4. lumineuse, floue, très gaie

Seurat: 1. la bourgeoisie; 2. Ils font une promenade, ils font de la voile, ils se reposent.; Ils sont sur une plage.; 3. plutôt scientifique car c'est une méthode par laquelle le peintre pose des touches séparées de couleur pure; 4. un après-midi de repos pour la bourgeoisie

Van Gogh: 1. au Sud de la France/à la Provence; 2. Il met des couleurs chaudes au premier plan pour donner de la profondeur au tableau.; 3. Parce qu'il utilise les couleurs de façon arbitraire pour évoquer des sentiments forts.

Perspectives
Answers will vary.

Reference Desk

Henri Rousseau, or "**Le douanier Rousseau**" (so called because of his work as a toll collector), is promoted on the poster in the photo. He is a French Post-Impressionist painter celebrated for his primitive, or naïve, representations of jungle scenes.

6 Des grands maîtres de la peinture française 1.2, 1.3, 3.1, 5.2

Répondez aux questions suivantes.

Monet

1. Comment s'appelle le mouvement artistique que Monet a créé?
2. Qu'est-ce qu'il étudiait de son bateau-atelier?
3. Est-ce qu'il a peint des personnages dans le tableau *Les Coquelicots*?
4. Quel était le but de Monet dans *Les Coquelicots*?

Renoir

1. Renoir faisait partie de quel mouvement?
2. À quels sujets et quels thèmes s'intéressait Renoir?
3. Comment sont peintes les femmes dans ses tableaux?
4. Comment est l'ambiance du tableau *Déjeuner des canotiers*?

Seurat

1. Seurat représente quelle classe sociale dans son chef-d'œuvre?
2. Qu'est-ce que les personnages sont en train de faire? Où?
3. Comment est sa méthode, plutôt artistique ou scientifique? Expliquez.
4. Quelle scène est représentée sur ce tableau?

Van Gogh

1. Van Gogh est associé à quelle région de la France?
2. Comment est-ce que l'artiste se sert de la perspective?
3. Pour quelle raison principale est-ce qu'on associe van Gogh au début de l'expressionnisme?

Perspectives

1.2, 2.1, 5.2

Il est connu comme un génie torturé qui s'est coupé l'oreille, mais de nombreux historiens prétendent aujourd'hui que le peintre Vincent van Gogh a perdu l'oreille dans une bagarre avec son ami, l'artiste français Paul Gauguin. Les historiens soutiennent maintenant que Vincent van Gogh a peut-être inventé toute l'histoire pour protéger son ami Gauguin, un escrimeur passionné, qui a en fait coupé l'oreille de son ami avec une épée au cours d'une discussion houleuse. Une autre théorie est que van Gogh s'est coupé l'oreille en apprenant que son frère, Théo, était fiancé. Peut-être en avez-vous entendu une autre? Quelle théorie jugez-vous la plus plausible et pourquoi?

On peut admirer les peintures de Monet, Renoir, Seurat, et van Gogh au musée d'Orsay.

Essential Instruction

1. Arrange students in groups of different skill sets to answer **Des grands maîtres de la peinture française**.
2. Use these four groups of questions as a basis for a class discussion of these artists and their works. If possible, show larger prints of each painting.
3. Assign students to research one of the eight artists featured in **L'impressionnisme** for a brief presentation the following day. They will print one famous painting to use as a visual as they present their artist and the painting. Make an exhibition of the images in the classroom.

Points de départ

Pre-AP

Question centrale ? Comment l'art est-il un reflet de la culture?

L'impressionnisme

1.2, 2.2, 3.1, 5.2

L'impressionnisme est un mouvement de la seconde moitié du 19ème siècle. Les peintres expriment* dans leurs tableaux les impressions que les objets et la lumière suscitent*. Les impressionnistes aiment peindre en plein air, pas dans un atelier. Quoique différents par leurs styles et leurs perspectives, les peintres associés à ce mouvement sont Édouard Manet, Claude Monet, Pierre-Auguste Renoir, l'Américaine Mary Cassatt, Camille Pissarro, Berthe Morisot, Edgar Degas, l'Anglais Alfred Sisley, Paul Cézanne, Armand Guillaumin, et Frédéric Bazille.

Recherche : impressionnisme france, NOM DE L'ARTISTE + impressionnisme, mouvements artistiques france

expriment *express* ; **suscitent** *spark*

Produits

Impression, soleil levant (1872) est le tableau de Monet qui a donné le nom « impressionnisme » à ce nouveau mouvement artistique.

1.2, 2.2

Comparaisons

Est-ce que le mouvement impressionniste aux États-Unis est venu avant ou après l'impressionnisme en France ? Qui sont les maîtres de l'impressionnisme américain ?

1.2, 4.2

Mère et enfant, 1897. Mary Cassatt.

Impression, soleil levant, 1872. Claude Monet.

Près du lac, 1880. Pierre-Auguste Renoir.

1.2, 2.1

Traditions et pratiques

Comme les peintres impressionnistes peignaient en plein air, ils ont représenté de nombreuses régions françaises, dépeignant (*picturing*) ainsi la côte de Normandie, la région de la Seine, Giverny avec ses nénuphars (*water lilies*), la Provence, et les paysages méditerranéens de la Côte d'Azur.

Resources

- *Points de départ*
- WB Workbook 5
- Explore

Answers

Comparaisons

American Impressionism, most vibrant at the turn of the century, occurred twenty to thirty years later than its French counterpart, though some American Impressionists, such as Mary Cassatt, were active in France early on. Some American Impressionists are John Twachtman, Childe Hassam, William Merritt Chase, and J. Alden Weir.

Reference Desk

If you have access to Passport, find a video or a news article related to **l'impressionnisme** and show it to your students.

Connections

History

Review with students historical periods or dates associated with each art movement presented on p. 379. Ask them to pick their favorite art piece (from the unit or their own research), and then showcase it in an oral presentation. You may use the school library or auditorium to exhibit those pieces and invite other classes to visit.

Differentiated Learning

Accelerate

Students answer the two-part **Comparaisons** question.

Multiple Intelligences

Visual-Spatial

Have students make a collage of Impressionist paintings with titles of their works.

Reference Desk

The 19th and 20th centuries were prolific artistic times in Paris, **la ville des arts**, and most artists emigrated there from all parts of the world to find fame, inspiration, kinship, and often good cuisine.

Critical Thinking

Analysis

Have students do a critique of **le néo-impressionnisme** and **l'expressionnisme** in groups by comparing and contrasting two paintings. You may give them paintings to choose from for each movement, or allow them to select their own. Have students consider the value and detriment of categorizing art and artists into movements. On one hand, viewers can refer to generalizations of a movement in seeking to understand a work. On another hand, overgeneralizations threaten an artist's individuality and unique perspective. Certain artists who straddle two movements, like Manet and van Gogh, present unique challenges to an art historian's attempts to classify works.

Le néo-impressionnisme 1.2, 2.2, 3.1, 3.2, 5.2

Le néo-impressionnisme suit l'impressionnisme entre 1885 et 1915. Les peintres néo-impressionnistes peignent par petite touches*, par points de ton* pur juxtaposés*. Deux méthodes utilisées par les artistes néo-impressionnistes sont le pointillisme et le divisionnisme. Les peintres de ce mouvement se nomment* des pointillistes ou divisionnistes, dont les plus grands sont Georges Seurat et Paul Signac.

Le pin, St-Tropez, 1909. Paul Signac.

Recherche : néo-impressionnisme, post-impressionnisme, NOM DE L'ARTISTE + néo-impressionnisme, mouvements artistiques france

touche *stroke* ; **ton** *shade of color* ; **juxtaposés** *side by side* ; **se nomment** s'appellent

Produits 1.1, 2.2

Le tableau ***Un dimanche après-midi à l'Île de la Grande Jatte*** (1886) est devenu le sujet du music-hall *Sunday in the Park with George* en 1984, un siècle après l'œuvre de Seurat. Le créateur, Sondheim, a pour thème de montrer les tourments de l'artiste qui crée de l'art.

Recherche : sunday in the park with george youtube

L'expressionnisme et le fauvisme 1.2, 2.2, 3.1, 3.2, 5.2

L'expressionnisme est surtout un mouvement artistique du début du 20ème siècle. Ce sont des artistes allemands qui en sont à l'origine. Les peintres expressionnistes utilisent une intensité de l'expression et souvent des couleurs vives. Le précurseur de ce mouvement est Vincent van Gogh. Dans ce groupe il faut aussi mentionner les fauves qui créent le fauvisme. Les fauves comme Maurice de Vlaminck et André Derain touchent* par moments à l'expressionnisme. Il ne faut surtout pas oublier les contributions d'Henri Matisse.

Vase à bonne sur une table. Matisse (1869–1954).

Recherche : expressionnisme europe, fauvisme, vlaminck, derain, matisse, mouvements artistiques france

touchent *reach*

Essential Instruction

1. Have students read **Le néo-impressionnisme** and **L'expressionnisme et le fauvisme**. Encourage them to do additional research, using the search words provided.
2. How do these movements differ? Who are the key artists? If students could own one painting to hang in their bedroom, which one would they select and why?
3. Ask students to read **L'Afrique de l'ouest**. They will keep this question in mind: What are the differences between African art and the European paintings you have studied? Find examples of how **le cubisme**, notably the art of Pablo Picasso, has been directly influenced by African art.

Recherche : cubism, african art, masks

La Francophonie

Art et traditions

En Afrique de l'Ouest 1.2, 2.2, 3.1, 3.2, 4.2, 5.2

L'art africain traditionnel est essentiellement composé de produits artisanaux*. L'artisanat correspond à la fabrication d'objets, principalement en bois ou en bronze, tels des masques, statues, armes, ou d'autres objets traditionnels comme des poteries ou encore les vêtements. Ces arts sont considérés des Arts premiers. Ils sont à l'image des thèmes ou scènes de la vie de tous les jours de groupes ethniques particuliers, telles les statues tribales Ashanti du Ghana, ou Bambara du Mali. Il en est de même* pour la fabrication d'instruments de musique : les congas* en bois et peau de chèvre*, les balafons*, les cloches*, reflètent un lien entre l'expression artistique et la nature dans les cultures africaines.

La peinture africaine a toujours été décorative, privilégiant* les bas-reliefs plutôt que les représentations bidimensionnelles* propres aux cultures occidentales*. De l'art traditionnel, dit « naïf », aux formes géométriques simples et aux couleurs primaires, à l'art populaire qui donne de nouvelles formes aux matériaux naturels (fresques, portraits, posters), la peinture africaine contemporaine reflète l'évolution et les contradictions des réalités urbaines. La peinture africaine est à l'origine des grands mouvements occidentaux tels le cubisme (Pablo Picasso), le néo-impressionnisme, et la peinture murale. Il est important de comprendre les liens indissociables entre l'Afrique et l'Occident dans la peinture moderne, car bien souvent, les peintres africains contemporains s'inscrivent dans les mouvements occidentaux de peinture, tel Chéri Samba, peintre congolais, dont l'art figuratif a été exposé à Paris et à New York.

Recherche : l'art africain traditionnel, produits artisanaux africains, peintres africains, chéri samba

produits artisanaux *crafts* ; **Il en est de même** *It is the same* ; **conga** *drum-like instrument* ; **peau de chèvre** *goat skin* ; **balafon** *xylophone-like instrument* ; **cloches** *bells* ; **privilégiant** *favoring* ; **bidimensionnelle** *two-dimensional* ; **occidentales** *Western*

L'art africain est connu pour ses sculptures et objets artisanaux.

Le Nid dans le nid, 1996. Chéri Samba.

Reference Desk

1. Chéri Samba is a famous contemporary Congolese painter. In his art he uses pictural codes of **bande dessinée** and language (French, English, Lingala dialect) to create an art form that represents social, political, and cultural aspects of modern life in Africa.
2. The word *occidental* refers to the *western* world, primarily Europe and the Americas. Students may be more confused with its counterpart *oriental*, meaning *eastern* rather than (an outdated) reference to eastern Asia. Tell students, for example, that **le Moyen Orient** is how French speakers refer to the Middle East.

Connections

Art History

Compare and contrast several examples of Native American art with samples of tribal art of Africa.

Film Studies

Loving Vincent is a 2017 animated feature composed entirely of oil paintings in the style of van Gogh and featuring his most recognizable works. Based on historical documents, it follows a young man's investigation one year after the artist's mysterious death. Ask students to work in pairs and present a painter through a collection of artwork in a specific order, focusing on details and aspects that the students deem most interesting.

Differentiated Learning

Adapt

Students collaborate to make a collage of pictures of statues, masks, and other artifacts of the Ashanti, Bambara, and Ghanian tribes to be displayed in the classroom.

Multiple Intelligences

Musical-Rhythmic

Here are three activities that might appeal to students interested in music: 1) Students might be interested in watching clips of "Sunday in the Park with George." 2) They also might enjoy the song "Into the Woods" (available online) to show how Stephen Sondheim playfully treats this theme. 3) Students could play for the class the song "Starry, Starry Night" by Don McLean, and explain how this song relates closely to Vincent van Gogh's life and work.

Visual-Spatial

Students explain the technique of pointillism and demonstrate how it is achieved by painting a simple object through a series of colorful dots.

Recherche : pointillism, art talks, george seurat

Answers

7

1. Answers will vary.
2. Answers will vary.
3. Dates are approximations and student answers may vary: réalisme, 1830–1870; impressionnisme, 1860–1890; néo-impressionisme, 1890–1920; fauvisme, 1904–1911; cubisme, 1907–1925
4. *Mère et enfant*, Mary Cassatt : musée d'Orsay, Paris ; *Impression, soleil levant*, Claude Monet : musée Marmottan, Paris ; *Le pin, St-Tropez*, Paul Signac : musée Pouchkine, Moscou ; *Un dimanche après-midi à l'île de la Grande Jatte*, Georges Seurat : Art Institute, Chicago
5. Answers will vary.
6. Answers will vary.
7. Answers will vary.

Perspectives
Answers will vary.

Reference Desk

Students might be interested to know that most European major art movements have origins in African and Oriental art. Impressionism and its corollaries (**le néo-impressionisme**, **l'expressionnisme**, **le fauvisme**, etc.) reacted against the European tradition of classical theories, a phenomenon typical of 19th century art and literature. These artists of different origins often traveled and sought new ideas from abroad. Claude Monet and Vincent van Gogh were heavily influenced by Japanese art and imagery that made their way to the West. Post-Impressionist Paul Gauguin created an art style greatly influenced by the African primitivism he discovered in his numerous travels to French Polynesia. Likewise, Expressionists Henri Matisse and Pablo Picasso's particular usage of expressive colors and asymmetrical compositions were inspired by African art.

7 Activités culturelles 1.3, 3.1, 3.2

Faites les activités suivantes.

1. Faites des recherches et décrivez un tableau impressionniste, néo-impressionniste, ou expressionniste que vous aimez beaucoup. Vous pouvez choisir un tableau de la section *Points de départ.*
2. Regroupez dans un album des tableaux de peintres français qui montrent l'évolution de l'impressionnisme à l'expressionnisme, puis au fauvisme. Donnez une légende à chaque tableau, indiquant le titre, le nom de l'artiste, le style, et l'année de son exécution.
3. Faites une chronologie (*timeline*) qui montre les périodes artistiques suivantes en France ainsi que leurs dates :
   - l'impressionnisme
   - le réalisme
   - le fauvisme
   - le cubisme
   - le néo-impressionnisme
4. Recherchez dans quels musées les tableaux des artistes cités précédemment sont exposés aujourd'hui. Attention : ils ne sont pas tous à Paris.
5. Recherchez combien coûte un Monet, un Renoir, ou un van Gogh. Est-ce que la valeur de ces tableaux augmente ou diminue avec le temps ?
6. Recherchez deux peintres contemporains d'Afrique de l'Ouest et notez :
   - leur nom et pays d'origine
   - leur style de peinture (couleurs, formes, matériau de travail, etc.)
   - un tableau particulier (nom et description)
7. Trouvez un exemple d'art contemporain populaire en Occident influencé par les cultures africaines.

1.2, 2.1

Perspectives

Au début, les impressionnistes ont beaucoup été critiqués parce qu'ils osaient (*dared*) modifier les standards de l'époque : des tableaux détaillés, peints en ateliers, représentant des paysages ou des scènes d'événements historiques. Après avoir vu le tableau *Impression, soleil levant* de Monet, et d'autres tableaux, un critique a donné une revue négative à « L'exposition des impressionnistes ». Quelle est la réputation des impressionnistes maintenant ? Pourquoi est-ce que ce critique ne pouvait pas apprécier les tableaux impressionnistes ? Pourquoi est-ce que les goûts artistiques changent avec le temps ?

Essential Instruction

1. Before assigning **Activités culturelles**, give the students a clear understanding of what each activity requires and your expectations.
2. Assign the odd-numbered activities to be done individually, or allow students to choose the questions that interest them most.
3. Arrange students of high and low ability in groups to do the even-numbered activities. Devise a system of accountability so that each student works equally on the assignment.
4. Discuss the questions from **Perspectives** as a class.

Du côté des médias 1.2

Lisez les informations sur les expositions.

connaissance des arts | Newsletter | Conférences | Boutique | Liseuse

Flash-back : été 1912, Cologne accueille l'exposition événement « Sonderbund », à la gloire du modernisme européen.

Avec cinq cent soixante-dix-sept toiles et cinquante-sept sculptures, les cent soixante-treize artistes invités (**Cézanne**, **Gauguin**, **Picasso** ou **van Gogh** en tête) incarnent l'avant-garde artistique de l'époque, du post-impressionnisme à **l'expressionnisme** allemand.

Le Wallraf-Richartz Museum célèbre le centenaire de cette « mission moderne », à travers une fidèle reconstitution regroupant cent des chefs-d'oeuvre initialement exposés.

Informations pratiques sur **1912–Mission Moderne- Le centenaire de l'exposition Sonderbund** dans l'onglet agenda.

En savoir plus sur le lieu : **Wallraf-Richartz Museum**

8 L'exposition Sonderbund en flash-back 1.3, 5.2

Imaginez que vous avez assisté à cette exposition. Écrivez une carte postale qui :

- informe où vous êtes allé(e).
- décrit ce que vous avez vu.
- explique l'importance historique de cette exposition.

1.2, 2.2, 3.1, 5.2

Produits

L'Art Institute of Chicago a été fondé comme musée et école des beaux-arts en 1879. L'Art Institute recueille, préserve et interprète des œuvres d'art de la plus haute qualité, représentant les diverses traditions artistiques du monde. Sa collection est encyclopédique et comprend des œuvres emblématiques telles que *Un dimanche après-midi à l'Île de la Grande Jatte* de Georges Seurat, *The Old Guitarist* de Pablo Picasso, *Nighthawks* d'Edward Hopper et *American Gothic* de Grant Wood. Sa collection permanente de près de 300 000 œuvres d'art est complétée par plus de 30 expositions spéciales annuelles.

Answers

8 Paragraphs will vary.

Reference Desk

Students will most likely know Vincent van Gogh as the brilliant artist gone mad who cut off his left ear. But they might also be interested to know that the same odd genius whose paintings sell at auctions for millions of dollars only sold one painting while he was living. You may assign students to search the name of that painting (***La Vigne rouge***) for extra credit.

Differentiated Learning

Accelerate

Students write an essay answering the question posed in **Perspectives**. They must give precise examples to support their point of view.

Decelerate

Have students read **Du côté des médias**. Ask them questions to assure that they understand the meaning of the reading. Assign **L'exposition Sonderbund en flash-back**.

Answers

9

1. pointilliste
2. réflexion
3. harassant
4. 1984
5. Pulitzer Prize for Drama
6. Stephen Sondheim, Lee Blakeley

Reference Desk

Le Théâtre du Châtelet was built between 1860–62 for dramatic performances. Today, it is well known for operettas, ballet, and contemporary musicals. It is home to the **Orchestre de Paris**. Stephen Sondheim, born in 1932, is an American composer-lyricist who has won seven Tony awards for the lyrics of his songs, and a Pulitzer Prize for "Sunday in the Park with George."

Expansion

Have students research and report on other Franco-British or Franco-American musical theater productions, such as "**Les Misérables**" (premiered in 1980 and still widely popular), based on Victor Hugo's novel, and "An American in Paris" (2014). The latter tells the story of an American soldier and artist who falls in love in post-WWII Paris. It features the music and lyrics of George and Ira Gershwin, and was inspired by the 1951 film of the same name, which starred Gene Kelly and Leslie Caron.

Lisez l'article sur la production « Sunday in the Park with George » au Châtelet-Théâtre.

Mon compte | Mécénat | Jeune public | Newsletter Presse | English Version

Spectacles | Calendrier | Billetterie | Pratique | **Réserver**

Sunday in the Park with George

du 15 au 25 avril

UN MUSICAL D'INSPIRATION FRANÇAISE

Après *A Little Night Music*, puis *Sweeney Todd*, le Châtelet présente un autre chef-d'œuvre de **Stephen Sondheim**.

Le tableau pointilliste de Georges Seurat, *Un dimanche après-midi à l'île de la Grande Jatte*, peint entre 1884 et 1886, est le point de départ de cette réflexion passionnée sur le travail de l'artiste. Sondheim et son librettiste ont imaginé le travail harassant de Seurat, peignant cet immense tableau avec cette technique étonnante, au point d'en négliger Dot (« Point »), sa maîtresse qui attend un enfant.

La première partie a lieu à l'époque historique du peintre, la fin du 19ème siècle. La seconde partie, située en 1984 à Chicago, montre la vie difficile de l'arrière-petit-fils de Seurat, artiste plasticien.

Couronnée par le Pulitzer Prize for Drama en 1985, l'œuvre est puissante et poétique. Le grand raffinement des chansons, comme *Putting It Together* ou *Sunday*, a largement contribué à la réputation d'un ouvrage très émouvant.

Spectacle présenté en version originale surtitrée

Mise en scène originale à Broadway de James Lapine. Originellement produit à Broadway par the Shubert Organization et Emanuel Azenberg, En accord avec Playwrights Horizon, Inc., New York City, créateur de la production originale de Sunday *in the Park with George* en 1983.

En accord avec MTI – New York et Drama – Paris

Distribution

Musique et paroles
Stephen Sondheim

Livret
James Lapine

Direction musicale
David Charles Abell

Mise en scène
Lee Blakeley

Décors et vidéos
William Dudley

Georges / George
Julian Ovenden

Dot / Marie
Sophie-Louise Dann

Old Lady / Elaine
Rebecca de Pont Davies

Soldier / Redmond
David Curry

Yvonne / Blair
Beverley Klein

TWEET

J'AIME

VOUS AIMEREZ AUSSI...

CONFÉRENCE SUNDAY IN THE PARK WITH GEORGE

AVEC STEPHEN SONDHEIM

DES QUESTIONS ?

NOUS VOUS RAPPELONS

9 Sunday in the Park with George 1.2, 2.2, 3.1, 3.2

Complétez les phrases.

1. *Un dimanche après-midi à l'île de la Grande Jatte* est un tableau... de Seurat.
2. L'œuvre est une... passionnée sur le travail de l'artiste.
3. Sondheim qualifie l'œuvre de Seurat comme un travail....
4. La seconde partie a lieu en... à Chicago.
5. « Sunday in the Park with George » a gagné le... en 1985.
6. ... a écrit la musique et les paroles, et... est responsable de la mise en scène.

Essential Instruction

1. Students read the article in **Du côté des médias** about "Sunday in the Park with George."
2. Ask students questions about the text, which will require them to cite specific information from the article.
3. Students finish the sentences in **Activité 9**.
4. Have students watch the clip "It's Hot Up Here" online, where actors create a **tableau vivant** of the painting. This video will bring to life Seurat's painting.
5. Before doing *Révision*: Agreement and Position of Adjectives, test what students recall of adjective formation and placement by asking them to brainstorm a list of random adjectives that describe **un homme**. Ask volunteers to go to the board and write descriptions of **un homme**. This exercise will give you an idea of how extensively you need to review adjectives.

Révision: Agreement and Position of Adjectives 1.2

French adjectives usually follow the nouns they describe.

C'est une peinture **expressionniste**. — *It's an Expressionist painting.*

To form a feminine adjective, all you often have to do is add an **–e** to the masculine adjective.

Voilà une scène **intéressante**. — *Here is an interesting scene.*

There are also other patterns for forming feminine adjectives.

	Masculine	Feminine
no change	moderne	moderne
-eux → **-euse**	paresseux	paresseuse
-er → **-ère**	dernier	dernière
double consonant + **-e**	bon	bonne

Some adjectives are invariable and do not change, even when modifying something feminine: **orange**, **marron**, **super**, **sympa**, **bon marché**.

Some masculine adjectives have irregular forms in the feminine: **blanc** → **blanche**, **frais** → **fraîche**, **long** → **longue**.

The adjectives **beau**, **nouveau**, and **vieux** have irregular feminine forms as well as irregular forms before a masculine noun beginning with a vowel sound.

Masculine	Masculine before a Vowel Sound	Feminine
beau	bel	belle
nouveau	nouvel	nouvelle
vieux	vieil	vieille

un **bel** homme, une **belle** femme — *a beautiful man, a beautiful woman*

un **nouvel** arbre, une **nouvelle** école — *a new tree, a new school*

un **vieil** ami, une **vieille** maison — *an old friend, an old house*

Some short, common adjectives precede the nouns they describe. These are the BANGS adjectives that express beauty, age, number, goodness, and size:

Beauty:	beau, joli
Age:	nouveau, vieux, jeune
Number:	premier, deuxième
Goodness:	bon, gentil, mauvais
Size:	grand, petit, court, long, gros

de **beaux** cheveux **noirs**
beautiful black hair

une **deuxième petite** peinture
a second small painting

un **long** voyage de nuit
a long night travel

C'est la première jolie et bonne petite voiture française de Simon.

Resources

WB Workbook 6–9

G & V Practice Games

Game

Les adjectifs

Ask students to shout out as many adjectives as they know. You will write the masculine form on the board for the students to use as reference. A student will start with the sentence **Jean est un garçon**. Point to another student who will add an adjective from the word bank: **Jean est un beau garçon**. Point to another student who will add another adjective to that sentence: **Jean est un beau garçon intelligent**. Continue asking students to add adjectives so that the sentence becomes very long. When a given student cannot remember the whole sentence, the game starts over, this time with a feminine subject like Marie. If you want to challenge them, create the next sentence with the subject **Jean et Fatima**. This change will require students to use verbs and adjectives in the plural.

Differentiated Learning

Decelerate

Provide students with a worksheet with common vocabulary and target adjectives, such as **un train/lent** or **un professeur/bon**. They are to combine the adjectives and the nouns using the correct form and position. For **Activité 10**, tell students whether the nouns are masculine or feminine, so that they can focus on adjective placement and form.

Special Needs Students

Auditory Impairment

The distinction among forms of the irregular adjectives can seem very subtle to students with hearing difficulties. Accentuate the differences when you speak so that they can see how your mouth changes according to the pronunciation. Show the spelling of the endings as you say them aloud.

Dyslexia

The spelling of irregular adjectives can present a special challenge for dyslexic students. Spell them out in rhythm. For example, the troublesome spelling of **vieille** is easier to learn if each letter is given a beat. **V-I-E-I-L-L-E.**

Resources

- Activity 10
- WB Workbook 6–10
- G & V Practice Games

Answers

10

1. C'est une nouvelle toile japonaise.
2. C'est un joli portrait réaliste.
3. C'est un petit musée des beaux-arts impressionniste.
4. C'est un grand tableau expressionniste.
5. C'est une vieille fête champêtre française.
6. C'est une mauvaise nature morte sombre./C'est une mauvaise et sombre nature morte.
7. C'est un bon peintre moderne.

Reference Desk

1. Remind students that the final **s** in **plus** and **moins** is silent.
2. Emphasize that, just like in English, the adjectives good and bad in French have an irregular form in the comparative (the equivalent of *better* and *worse*). We do not say *gooder* or *badder*.
3. Assure students that the more often they say aloud these adjectives with nouns, the better their ear will be tuned to what is correct so that they will not have to depend on charts and rules.

10 L'art 1.3

Presentational Speaking or Writing

Formez des phrases avec deux adjectifs selon le modèle.

MODÈLE peinture (beau, français)
C'est une belle peinture française.

1. toile (nouveau, japonais)
2. portrait (réaliste, joli)
3. musée des beaux-arts (impressionniste, petit)
4. tableau (grand, expressionniste)
5. fête champêtre (français, vieux)
6. nature morte (mauvais, sombre)
7. peintre (moderne, bon)

Révision: Comparative of Adjectives 1.2

Use the following constructions to compare people and things in French:

plus (*more*)	+	ADJECTIVE	+	**que** (*than*)
moins (*less*)	+	ADJECTIVE	+	**que** (*than*)
aussi (*as*)	+	ADJECTIVE	+	**que** (*as*)

The adjective being compared agrees in gender and in number with the first noun in the comparison.

Les couleurs sont **aussi sombres** dans ce tableau **que** dans cet autre tableau. — *The colors are as dark in this painting as in the other painting.*

The comparative of **bon(ne)(s)** is **meilleur(e)(s)**.

Ce tableau est **meilleur que** l'autre. — *This painting is better than the other (one).*

The comparative of **mauvais/mauvaise(s)** is **pire(s)**.

Ce tableau est **pire que** l'autre. — *This painting is worse than the other (one).*

Connexions 1.2, 3.1

SVT (Sciences de la vie et de la terre)

Formez des phrases en comparant des animaux ou des plantes.

Le lion est aussi féroce que le tigre.
L'oiseau est moins beau que le papillon.
Le serpent est plus mortel que l'abeille.

Essential Instruction

1. Ask a volunteer to be the teacher and explain the formation and placement of adjectives.
2. Students do **Activité 10**. Correct each sentence, one at a time, offering an explanation to students who did not form the sentence correctly.
3. Review the chart for **plus**, **moins**, and **aussi**… **que**, reminding the students that the adjective agrees in gender and number with the first noun in the comparison.
4. Have two students stand in front of the class. Whisper to one to be happy and the other sad (or hand them notes with the adjectives to act out). **Qui est plus heureux que l'autre? Qui est moins heureux? Qui est plus triste?** Continue the process with other adjectives such as **fâché**, **ennuyé**, **fatigué**, and **surpris**. The students, on cue, will mime the emotions for the class. Add another student to the group to demonstrate **aussi**…**que**.
5. Do **Comparez les HLMs!** as a class activity to give students immediate feedback.
6. Give examples of the superlative of adjectives preceding and following the noun and ask students to deduce the rule for formation.

11 Comparez les HLM! 1.2

Interpretive Viewing

Comparez ces deux HLM. Utilisez les indices donnés et les adjectifs entre parenthèses.

1. La HLM au premier plan (à droite)… la HLM à l'arrière-plan (à gauche). (propre)
2. L'ado qui porte le tee-shirt orange… l'ado en bleu. (diligent)
3. Les enfants… les passants. (vieux)
4. Les enfants… leurs parents. (énergique)
5. Jeanne… Pierre. (sportif)
6. La sculpture de la HLM au premier plan… celle de la HLM à l'arrière-plan. (moderne)
7. L'ambiance de la HLM au premier plan… celle de la HLM à l'arrière-plan. (accueillant)

Révision: Superlative of Adjectives 1.2

Use the superlative construction to say that a person or thing has the most of a certain quality compared to all others.

le/la/les + **plus** + ADJECTIVE

Le musée d'Orsay est le musée impressionniste **le plus célèbre**.

Both the definite article and the adjective agree in gender and in number with the noun they describe. Remember that if an adjective precedes a noun, its superlative form also precedes it. If an adjective follows a noun, so does its superlative form.

Le Louvre est **le plus grand** musée d'art à Paris. — *The Louvre is the biggest art museum in Paris.*

Le Louvre est le musée **le plus connu**. — *The Louvre is the most well-known museum.*

The superlative of **bon(ne)(s)** is **le/la/les meilleur(e)(s)**.

À mon avis, c'est **le meilleur** tableau du musée. — *In my opinion, it's the best painting in the museum.*

The superlative of **mauvais/mauvaise(s)** is **le/la/les plus mauvais/mauvaise(s)** or **le/la/les pire(s)**.

Non, c'est **le plus mauvais** tableau. Cette couleur, c'est **la pire** couleur! — *No, it's the worst painting. This color, it's the worst color!*

Resources

WB Workbook 11–12

LA Listening Activity 2

G & V Practice Games

Answers

11

1. est plus propre que
2. est moins diligent que
3. sont moins vieux que
4. sont plus énergiques que
5. est aussi sportive que
6. est plus moderne que
7. est plus accueillante que

Reference Desk

The French Canadians like to say, **"C'est pas pire!"** (*"It's not bad!"*)

Expansion

Project or make a large copy of Seurat's painting ***Un Dimanche après-midi à l'île de la Grande Jatte***. Ask volunteers to describe the figures in the painting as if they knew them. For example, for the woman on the right with the parasol: **"Voici Madame DuPont. Elle a cinquante ans et elle adore sortir le dimanche avec son mari. Ce matin, ils se sont disputés parce que son mari, Rufus, ne voulait pas aller au parc."** They could continue to describe what she is wearing (using as many adjectives as possible), what she is looking at, what she is thinking, how many children she has, what their names are, etc. This exercise will encourage students to be imaginative and creative as they describe each person.

Differentiated Learning

Adapt

Have students brainstorm names of popular pop stars, actors, well-known athletes, competitive high school sports teams, and heroes from history, which you will write on the board. Ask a student to compare them. Normally the class will not all share the same opinion, and this will lead to a spirited discussion. Continue the process comparing other elements.

Special Needs Students

Behavioral Problems

When asked to make comparisons, some students may take the opportunity to ridicule classmates. You may want to limit comparisons to historical figures, celebrities, and stores and restaurants around town rather than students in school.

Multiple Intelligences

Visual-Spatial

Enlist students to make sketches of people and things that can be used for comparisons.

Resources

Activity 13

Answers

12

1. La tour Eiffel est le monument le plus célèbre.
2. Le Louvre est le plus ancien musée.
3. *La Joconde* est l'œuvre du Louvre la plus connue.
4. Le Quartier latin est le plus vieux quartier.
5. Les Champs-Élysées est l'avenue la plus large.
6. La place de la Concorde est la plus grande place.
7. Notre-Dame est la plus belle cathédrale.
8. Le jardin des Tuileries est le plus joli jardin.

13 **Script**

1. *Impression, soleil levant* est la peinture la plus sombre de Monet.
2. Renoir et Monet sont les peintres les plus connus des impressionnistes.
3. Une fête champêtre a lieu en plein air.
4. Van Gogh a peint des paysages de Provence.
5. Les impressionnistes sont les peintres les plus importants.
6. Seurat est le plus grand peintre du 20ème siècle.
7. Van Gogh est le peintre expressionniste le plus sensible.

1. O; 2. O; 3. F; 4. F; 5. O; 6. O; 7. O

Game

Qui est… ?

Practice using the superlative of adjectives by playing this game with the class. Ask students to throw out the names of 10 famous personalities (celebrities, politicians, historical figures). Write the names of those people on the board. Then provide one adjective. Students will make a sentence combining that adjective and a person from the board, for example, **Lady Gaga est la chanteuse la plus bizarre.** If students still need practice with the position of adjectives in superlative constructions, choose all adjectives that follow the noun for the first six sentences, then give out adjectives that are placed before the noun. If students are comfortable with those constructions, mix and match them.

12 Je connais Paris ! 1.3, 5.2

Presentational Speaking or Writing

Formez des phrases au superlatif en utilisant les indices donnés. Attention à l'accord des adjectifs.

MODÈLES le musée d'Orsay (musée impressionniste, fréquenté)
Le musée d'Orsay est le musée impressionniste le plus fréquenté.

le musée d'Orsay (grand, musée impressionniste)
Le musée d'Orsay est le plus grand musée impressionniste.

1. la tour Eiffel (monument, célèbre)
2. le Louvre (ancien, musée)
3. *la Joconde* (œuvre du Louvre, connu)
4. le Quartier latin (vieux, quartier)
5. les Champs-Élysées (avenue, large)
6. la place de la Concorde (grand, place)
7. Notre-Dame (beau, cathédrale)
8. le jardin des Tuileries (joli, jardin)

La Joconde, 1503–1519. Leonardo da Vinci.

13 Les plus grands peintres ! 1.2

Interpretive Listening

*Écrivez les numéros 1–7 sur votre papier. Écoutez les phrases. Ensuite, indiquez si chaque phrase que vous entendez représente un fait (**F**) ou une opinion (**O**).*

Curieusement, le pont Neuf est le plus vieux pont de Paris.

Après la tour Eiffel, le Sacré-Cœur est le plus haut monument de Paris.

Essential Instruction

1. Students will work together to write **Activité 12** in their notebooks.
2. Ask students to create five original superlative sentences to share with the class. Have them create two sentences that are facts and two sentences that are opinions.
3. Before starting **Activité 13**, have students identify whether each of the sentences in **Activité 12** is a fact or an opinion. Review why. After students complete **Les plus grands peintres !**, correct their work. Replay each statement and ask if the students agree with the opinions stated.
4. As a light activity, ask students to describe ***La Joconde*** physically. Then ask open-ended whimsical questions such as her name, where she lives, what she ate for breakfast, and the name of her parents, to get students conversing.
5. Read with students **Activités 14**, **15**, and **16** to explain what is expected in each activity. If time is not an issue, assign all three to each student. If there is not enough time for students to do all three, ask them which one they would like to do, and with whom.

Pre-AP

Question centrale: Comment l'art est-il un reflet de la culture?

Communiquez!

14 Au musée des beaux-arts 1.1, 1.2, 1.3, 5.2

Interpersonal and Presentational Speaking

Avec un partenaire, jouez les rôles d'un(e) ado qui visite un musée à Paris et son père ou sa mère. L'exposition n'intéresse pas du tout l'ado qui commence par critiquer les deux premiers tableaux qu'il ou elle voit. Ce sont des peintures que son père (sa mère) adore. Le parent a alors une idée : il (elle) emmène son ado voir un tableau qu'il (elle) est sûr(e) que son fils ou sa fille va aimer. Ils discutent alors de la peinture en détail. Ils parlent du mouvement, de ce que le peintre a mis au premier plan, au centre, et à l'arrière-plan, des couleurs, et de ce qui se passe dans le tableau. Présentez votre jeu de rôle à la classe.

15 Un calendrier artistique 1.3, 3.2, 5.1

Presentational Writing

Votre classe va créer des calendriers artistiques en français pour votre école. Mettez-vous en groupe en fonction du style de peinture qui vous plaît, et servez-vous d'un outil en ligne pour créer un calendrier impressionniste, surréaliste, cubiste, etc. Pour chaque mois de l'année, mettez l'image d'une peinture avec une légende (titre, peintre, date, caractéristiques de l'œuvre). Votre calendrier peut aussi réunir un mélange d'œuvres francophones diverses au cours des décennies. Ajoutez les mois et jours de l'année, et, si vous le désirez, des informations sur la saison, les fêtes ou le temps qu'il fait, selon le mois.

Recherche : pically calendar maker

16 Le musée du Quai Branly 1.3, 3.2, 4.2, 5.1

Presentational Writing

Le musée du quai Branly à Paris a des objets d'art de l'Afrique, de l'Asie, de l'Océanie, et des Amériques. Pour aider votre classe à créer une application pour Smartphone qui décrira les objets de la collection africaine, sélectionnez votre objet préféré, et enregistrez (*record*) un commentaire. Vous devez dire un minimum de huit phrases.

Recherche : musée du quai branly promenades à la carte

17 Petit projet impressionniste 1.2, 1.3, 2.2, 3.1, 4.2, 5.2

Interpretive Viewing, Presentational Writing and Speaking

Les impressionnistes américains ont été largement influencés par les impressionnistes français, pères fondateurs du mouvement. Plusieurs artistes français et américains ont collaboré ensemble. Regardez par exemple les œuvres de Degas et Cassatt. Choisissez un artiste impressionniste français et trouvez un homologue américain qu'il (elle) a influencé(e). Comparez deux peintures : style, couleurs, coups de pinceau, sujet et autre. Notez aussi les différences entre les artistes et les œuvres. Présentez votre comparaison à la classe.

Resources

CA Communicative Activities

Share

Answers

14 Role-plays will vary.
15 Calendars will vary.
16 Projects will vary.
17 Presentations will vary.

Reference Desk

If you have access to Passport, create a question for your students to share their response to a communicative activity.

Connections

Art

Collaborate with an art teacher in your school on a French art unit; partnered with students in an art class, your students can exchange a basic French conversation lesson for an art history lesson. If possible, use classes that meet the same period. Have the two classes work together to create works of art inspired by a French art movement. If possible, have both classes spend one class period in the French classroom and another class period in the art classroom. If not possible, meet outdoors with both classes.

Multiple Intelligences

Bodily-Kinesthetic/Verbal-Linguistic
These students will be attracted to the first activity, which allows their dramatic side to emerge in a play scenario.

Visual-Spatial
These students most likely will be interested in the second activity, making an artistic calendar in which they can create an attractive visual presentation of the art they have studied.

Mathematical-Logical
These students may elect to do the third option, organizing in a systematic way a presentation of 10 art objects with explanations.

Prononciation

The Letter *h* 1.2

» In French, there are two types of the letter *h* that a word may begin with. One is **le h muet**. Words with this *h* are pronounced as if the *h* were not there and have liaison or **enchaînement consonantique** with the preceding word.

Exemples: un‿hôtel : liaison du *n*

les‿hommes : liaison du *s*

une‿histoire : enchaînement consonantique

The other type of *h* is **le h aspiré**. It does not allow liaison with the preceding word.

Exemples: en haut

les Halles

A L'artiste

Répétez les phrases suivantes. Faites attention à la prononciation des mots qui commencent avec un h.

1. Cet‿homme est un peintre.
2. Il habite la haute montagne, dans un‿hôtel.
3. Les‿hommes du village l'admirent.

B Vous entendez le h muet ou aspiré ?

*Écrivez **M** (muet) si vous n'entendez pas le* h, *et **A** (aspiré) si vous l'entendez.*

1. Il est de bonne humeur.
2. C'est le héros du livre.
3. Quelle est la hauteur de la tour Eiffel ?
4. Cette histoire est incroyable.
5. Regarde vers le haut !

The Nasal and Non-Nasal *n*

» Vowel sounds represented by the letter *n* can be nasal or non-nasal.

C La nasalisation et la dénasalisation

Répétez les phrases et expressions avec des exemples de la prononciation de n. *Des exemples de nasalisation sont suivis d'exemples de dénasalisation.*

1. Il peint – Ils peignent
2. Il craint – Ils craignent
3. Le bain – Il se baigne

D Nasal ou pas nasal ?

*Écrivez **oui** si vous entendez une voyelle nasale, ou **non** si vous n'entendez pas de voyelle nasale.*

Essential Instruction

1. Before playing the pronunciation exercises, explain the difference between the mute and aspirated **h** with examples. Tell students that if the article before the word beginning with an **h** is **le** or **la** instead of **l'**, that is the clue that the **h** is to be breathed not elided.
2. Play part **A** several times for pronunciation practice.
3. Part **B** will test if students can distinguish words with the **h muet** and **h aspiré**. Play the recording several times so that students hear the difference. Have them repeat the sentences.
4. Explain that **a**, **e**, **i**, **o**, **u** before an **n** or **m** usually has a nasal sound. This would explain why the vowels of the third-person singular of **craindre** and **peindre** are nasal and the plural forms are not.
5. Students listen to the contrast between the singular and plural of these verbs in part **C**, and take the test in part **D**.

Resources

Prononciation

Pre-test

Leçon Quiz

Answers

B

1. M
2. A
3. A
4. M
5. A

D Script

1. Les impressionnistes peignaient de belles scènes.
2. L'artiste aime le plein air.
3. Cézanne a souvent peint les paysages.
4. Il peignait aussi des natures mortes.
5. Ce musée a plus de mille peintures.

1. non; 2. non; 3. oui; 4. non; 5. oui

Reference Desk

1. This pronunciation lesson is one of the most important since it addresses a most confusing issue: when liaison is allowed with the **h** in French. Students need to know that the **h** comes in two varieties: silent (**muet**) and aspirated (**aspiré**).
2. Students must never make the liaison for the following common words: **Le Havre**, **les haricots verts**, **le haut**, **les héros**, **la hâte**, **le hibou**, **la honte**, **le hockey**, **le hall**, and **le homard**. It is like fingernails on a blackboard to the French.
3. Tell students that the **le** or **l'** before the noun provide the clue as to how to pronounce the word. If they see **le**, they should take a breath before saying the word that follows whereas **l'** can be pronounced as if it were part of the word.

TPR

Invert your fist so that the back of the hand is facing down. Open your fingers quickly as if to let go of a butterfly. Have students make this gesture as you read groups of words with nasal consonants in **Activité C**.

Vocabulaire actif

La musique 1.2, 2.2, 3.1, 4.2

Le jazz

Le swing

La salsa

La pop

Resources

- *Vocabulaire actif*
- eV eVisual
- WB Workbook 1–4
- FC Flash Cards
- LA Listening Activity 1
- G & V Practice Games

Reference Desk

1. **Le Casino de Paris**, built by the Duke de Richelieu (Louis Francois Armand de Vignerot du Plessis) in 1730, is not a gambling establishment as its name might suggest but rather a performance venue. Famous performers such as Mistinguett, Maurice Chevalier, and Josephine Baker have headlined there. Currently, the casino serves as a venue for comedians, pop singers, and musicals.
2. Josephine Baker (1906–1975), born in the United States, was the most famous African-American singer, actress, and dancer in France. In addition to her illustrious career on stage, she also was a spy in the French Resistance, and received the **Légion d'Honneur** award from the hands of President Charles de Gaulle. She spoke freely about her bisexual identity, and adopted 12 children.
3. Other popular music genres are **l'électro**, **le reggae**, **le hip-hop**, **rap**, **le raï**, and **l'afro beat**.
4. If you have access to iCulture, find the songs "**Comme-ci, comme-ça**" by ZAZ (jazz), "**J'aime plus Paris**" by Thomas Dutronc (swing), and "**our 1**" by Louane (pop), and play them for your students.

Multiple Intelligences

Musical-Rhythmic

Students who are musical will enjoy this theme of French and American music and artists. Have them expand on the explanation of these genres. Ask them to think of additional examples.

Special Needs Students

At-Risk Students

Watch for interest on the students' part about musical groups. This may be a way of getting them more engaged in learning.

Critical Thinking

Analysis

Have students investigate why Paris in the 1920s was the heyday for black Americans. Who were the key performers and where did they appear?

Reference Desk

Melissa M (born in 1985) is a French R&B singer with Algerian (Kabyle) roots. She started her musical career with Maniac from Norway. Her albums, ***Avec tout mon amour***, ***Melissa M***, and ***Inachevé***, and singles, "**Benthi** (featuring Khaled)" and "**Jump** (featuring JMI Sissoko)," have made her a popular international artist.

Connections

Music

Ask students to search French artists connected to each genre presented. For example: **le jazz** (Catherine McLorin-Salvant); **le swing** (Thomas Dutronc); **la salsa** (Manu Chao); **la pop** (Nolwenn Leroy, Louane).

En concert

DICTIONNAIRE DE LA MUSIQUE:

un auteur-compositeur-interprète: artiste qui écrit les paroles, compose la musique, et chante la chanson avec son interprétation personnelle (par exemple, Jacques Brel ou Serge Gainsbourg)

un album concept: album où les chansons forment une histoire, surtout **populaire** dans les années 60 et 70 dans la musique rock britannique (par exemple, « Sgt. Pepper's Lonely Hearts Club Band » des Beatles)

une chanson réaliste: chanson dramatique de l'entre-guerres, interprétée par une femme, sur des thèmes dramatiques (par exemple, les chansons d'Édith Piaf)

une chanson poétique: chanson dont les paroles ressemblent à un poème et qui fait ressentir une émotion (par exemple, « Le Temps des cerises » d'Yves Montand)

une chanson engagée: chanson qui parle d'un problème de la société (par exemple, « Le déserteur » de Boris Vian)

Essential Instruction

1. Ask students about their musical tastes. Are there any students who play instruments in a band or orchestra or sing in the choir? How many students play musical instruments for pleasure? Do they ever go to concerts? Which ones?
2. Students copy into their notebooks the vocabulary for the different types of French music.
3. As a class make a timeline of the dates for **le jazz**, **le swing**, **la pop**, and **la salsa**.
4. Students listen and repeat the expressions and vocabulary in **Pour la conversation** and **Et si je voulais dire…?**
5. As an aural exercise, put the terms in the word bank from **Les définitions** on the board. Read the eight incomplete sentences to the students who have their books closed. Students write down the missing word. Have them read aloud the completed sentences.

Pour la conversation 1.2

How do I describe the development of an artist?

» Il **passe de la caricature** à la chanson engagée.

He moves from caricatures to political issue songs.

How do I say that an artist was successful?

» Ses chansons du temps qui passe et des amours tristes **lui ont valu** d'immenses succès.

His songs about passing time and sad love stories brought him immense success.

How do I describe an artist's emphasis?

» Brel, c'est le goût pour la musique populaire.

Brel is all about making music for the people.

How do I describe an artist's ability to connect with his or her audience?

» Elle **a séduit** plusieurs générations qui **se sont reconnues** dans **le lyrisme intimiste** de ses textes.

She seduced several generations who saw themselves in the intimate lyricism of her texts.

Et si je voulais dire... ?	
un air	*tune*
un chœur	*choir*
un morceau	*composition*
la musique de chambre	*chamber music*
un opéra	*opera*
diriger	*to conduct*

1 Définitions 1.2

Interpretive Reading

Complétez les phrases suivantes avec un mot ou une expression ci-dessous.

réaliste **mélodie** **un album concept** **la pop** **interprète**
paroles **compositrice** **compositeur** **poétique**

1. Un album avec une idée thématique s'appelle....
2. Une chanson... offre une représentation de la vraie vie.
3. La personne qui compose la musique est le... ou la....
4. Un... chante les chansons des autres avec sa propre (*own*) interprétation.
5. Les chansons ont une musique et des....
6. Par définition, ... est écrite pour un grand public, pour le peuple.
7. Une chanson... a des paroles lyriques.
8. Tout le monde connaît la... de « Frère Jacques ».

Resources

Pour la conversation
Et si je voulais dire... ?

Answers

1

1. un album concept
2. réaliste
3. compositeur, compositrice
4. interprète
5. paroles
6. la pop
7. poétique
8. mélodie

Reference Desk

In the **Dictionnaire de la Musique** we find five definitions of musical terms with examples of French artists. Students find corresponding Anglophone artists who could be put in these categories.

nouvelle orthographe **le gout**

Connections

Music

Students may enjoy watching ***Les Choristes***, a film about a music teacher in a French boarding school who transforms an unruly group of students into singers.

Multiple Intelligences

Visual-Spatial
Ask students to design an album cover of one of the French artists featured in this lesson.

Musical-Rhythmic
Students can make a music video showcasing one of the popular French singers from this unit.

Linguistic
Students present lyrics of a classic or popular French song that they like. They may explain briefly what the song is about and why they endorse it.

Resources

Activity 3

Answers

2 Best matches:

1. le jazz
2. la pop
3. un auteur-compositeur-interprète
4. une chanson engagée
5. une chanson
6. un interprète
7. une chanson poétique
8. un auteur-compositeur-interprète
9. le swing
10. la salsa

3 Answers will vary.

Communication

Presentational: Paired Practice

Students take opposing views about purchasing music. One view would be the preference of buying music of artists recorded in concert rather than in a studio because the music captures the essence of the artist performing. The opposing view would be that the sound quality of the studio is far superior to that recorded at a concert. Open up this debate to the class as a whole.

Culture

Products: Activity

Ask students to write on little pieces of paper the letters A through E. In a "blind listening test" play five popular French songs, each one identified by one of these letters. Students will decide which song is their top favorite down to the least popular based on what they heard. The little papers allow them to change the listing of their preferences by rearranging the cards. Reveal to students the name of the artist and song which correspond to each letter. Provide them with the lyrics of the songs they most enjoyed. Remember to vet the songs' lyrics for any language that would be inappropriate for your students.

2 Moi, je connais la musique ! 1.2, 3.1, 5.1

Interpretive Reading

Associez un mot ou une expression de la banque de mots aux indices ci-dessous.

la salsa **le swing** **le jazz** **la pop** **un interprète** **une chanson engagée** **une chanson poétique** **un auteur-compositeur-interprète** **une chanson**

1. la Nouvelle-Orléans, Duke Ellington, Louis Armstrong, les boîtes de Paris
2. les Beatles, les meilleurs hits de l'année, les Top 50
3. Adele, Sam Smith, Beyoncé, ou Taylor Swift
4. la politique, les idées pour changer une société, lutter pour une cause, les années 1960
5. les notes, la mélodie, le compositeur, la compositrice
6. le chanteur, la chanteuse de chansons popularisées par quelqu'un d'autre
7. les paroles, les poèmes, le lyricisme
8. Leonard Cohen, qui a écrit « Hallelujah » (interprété par Jeff Buckley, k.d. lang, Rufus Wainwright, et al.)
9. Jimmy Dorsey et son orchestre, une danse énergique semblable au boogie-woogie
10. musique pour la danse dont Célia Cruz était la reine, exportation de la culture hispanique

3 Questions personnelles 1.1, 1.3

Interpersonal Speaking

Répondez aux questions suivantes avec un partenaire.

1. Quel(s) type(s) de musique aimes-tu écouter ? Et tes amis ? Et tes parents ? Et tes grands-parents ?
2. Quels musiciens est-ce que tu admires ? Pourquoi ?
3. Est-ce que tu as déjà assisté à un concert ? Si oui, de quelle sorte de musique ?
4. Est-ce que tu joues d'un instrument ? Si oui, duquel ?
5. Tu aimerais devenir musicien/musicienne célèbre ? Pourquoi, ou pourquoi pas ?
6. Penses-tu que la mélodie soit la chose la plus importante dans une chanson ?

Essential Instruction

1. Ask students to define the musical terms in **Activité 1** and **Activité 2.** They may refer back to the readings for help.
2. In pairs, students complete **Activité 2**. Can they add more terms and artists to each list?
3. In small groups, students ask and answer questions pertaining to their musical taste in **Questions personnelles**.
4. Ask students what they answered for each of the **Questions personnelles** to generate a discussion about various musical tastes. Take advantage of expanding on this activity because music is so much a part of students' lives.
5. Pair students to answer **Qu'est-ce que tu préfères ?** Debrief students as to their preferences. Some students will not care for any of the choices. If so, they can use **ne… ni… ni…**: **Je n'aime ni le pop, ni la world, ni le hip-hop**.
6. Students complete **Activité 5**. Be sure that they understand each question.

4 Qu'est-ce que tu préfères ? 1.1, 5.2

Interpersonal Speaking

À tour de rôle, demandez ce que votre partenaire préfère.

MODÈLE **A : Préfères-tu le jazz, la musique classique, ou la country ?**
B : Je préfère le jazz.

1. la pop, la world, le hip-hop
2. les chansons réalistes, poétiques, ou engagées
3. les interprètes ou les auteurs-compositeurs-interprètes
4. le jazz, la musique classique, le rock, la musique alternative
5. les chansons engagées ou les chansons romantiques
6. les paroles ou la composition musicale
7. le swing ou la salsa

5 Ce que j'écoute 1.2

Interpretive Listening

Écrivez les numéros 1–6 sur votre papier. Écoutez Amina et Antoine discuter de leurs interprètes préférés. Puis choisissez la réponse qui correspond aux questions posées.

1. Qu'est-ce qu'Amina écoute ?
   A. une chanson d'Édith Piaf
   B. une chanson de Serge Gainsbourg
   C. une chanson de Jacques Brel
2. Pourquoi écoute-t-elle cet artiste ?
   A. parce qu'elle est triste
   B. parce qu'elle adore cet auteur et interprète
   C. parce qu'elle aime la musique classique
3. Quel auteur-compositeur-interprète Antoine préfère-t-il ?
   A. Boris Vian
   B. Serge Gainsbourg
   C. Charles Aznavour
4. Qui aime Charles Aznavour ?
   A. Antoine
   B. Amina
   C. Antoine et Amina
5. Comment sait-on que Charles Aznavour est un bon auteur-compositeur-interprète ?
   A. parce qu'il écrit de belles chansons
   B. parce qu'on l'a nommé « Artiste de variétés du siècle »
   C. parce qu'Amina l'a vu en concert et pense qu'il chante bien
6. Qu'est-ce qu'Amina sait faire ?
   A. danser le swing
   B. jouer du saxophone
   C. créer des albums concept

Resources

Activity 5

Answers

4 Answers will vary.

5 Script

Antoine : Qu'est-ce que tu écoutes ?
Amina : J'écoute « Ne me quitte pas » de Jacques Brel.
Antoine : Tu n'es pas contente aujourd'hui ?
Amina : Pas du tout ! J'adore Brel comme auteur et pour son interprétation si dramatique. Tu n'aimes pas les chansons à texte ?
Antoine : Si, mais moi, je préfère Serge Gainsbourg.
Amina : Et Charles Aznavour, tu l'aimes ?
Antoine : Oui, j'aime ses chansons, et c'est un très bon interprète, je trouve.
Amina : Oui, je pense aussi. Tu sais qu'on l'a nommé « Artiste de variétés du siècle » ?
Antoine : Vraiment ? Quelle autre musique te plaît ?
Amina : Eh bien, j'aime la pop, le rap, le jazz, et le swing. J'adore danser le swing aussi.
Antoine : Ah bon, tu me montres ?
Amina : Maintenant ?

1. C
2. B
3. B
4. C
5. B
6. A

Communication

Interpersonal: Cooperative Groups

When it comes to music, your students have well-defined opinions about what they like and don't like. Let students pretend that they have to propose five American singers for the International Music Awards. Encourage them to have a lively discussion of their musical favorites. Here are some expressions they might like to use: **Je trouve ça nul**, **Je ne peux pas supporter…**, **Je suis fan de…**, or **C'est du bonheur**.

Differentiated Learning

Adapt

Continuing the theme of musical preferences that we saw in **Qu'est-ce que préfères**, students track the music award winners in France for the last five years. How many were French, American, and British?

Recherche : nrj awards

Learning Styles

Mathematical-Musical

Have students listen to the songs and artists discussed in **Activité 5**. Consider playing Aznavour's bilingual ***For Me Formidable***.

Resources

WB Workbook 5

Reference Desk

1. Boris Vian helped introduce the American jazz greats Duke Ellington and Miles Davis to France. He was best known for his reactionary literature and pessimistic view on the desperation of human existence. His most famous book, ***J'irai cracher sur vos tombes***, tells the story of struggling Black Americans in the United States in the post-slavery South.
2. An artist, a rebel, a pariah, Serge Gainsbourg attracted controversy when he rewrote the French national anthem with a reggae tune.
3. Charles Aznavour was first noticed by legendary singer Édith Piaf.
4. Supplemental music vocabulary: **la batterie** (*drums*), **la caisse claire** (*snare drum*), **la guitare basse, électrique, ou acoustique,** and **le synthé** (**synthésiteur**). **Désacordé** means an instrument is out of tune. **Chanter faux** means *to sing out of tune*, whereas **chanter juste** means *to sing in tune*. **Chanter en playback** means *to lip synch*.

Communication

Presentational: Cooperative Groups

Divide the class into five teams. Assign one of the five musical artists (Vian, Gainsbourg, Azanavour, Brel, and Barbara) to each group. Their task is to select one song from the artist to teach the class. They will listen to clips of songs online to make their selection. Students will provide the lyrics and a glossary of terms. Two class periods might be needed to select the song and prepare the lyrics. These songs could be sung as a bell-ringer activity every day, or for brain breaks between exercises.

Rencontres culturelles

Les grands auteurs-compositeurs-interprètes français 1.2, 2.2, 3.2, 5.1

On vous présente cinq auteurs-compositeurs-interprètes de la chanson française.

C'est **Boris Vian** (1920–1959) qui va donner le tempo (celui du swing et du jazz) et la couleur sonore* (celle de sa trompette) à l'après-guerre*. Ingénieur, écrivain, journaliste, peintre, il est surtout fou de* musique, de jazz, et de chanson en général. Dans son seul album *Chansons possibles et impossibles*, 1956, il passe de la caricature (« J'suis snob ») à la chanson engagée (« La java des bombes atomiques » et « Le Déserteur »). Réputé pour son militantisme provocateur*, « Le déserteur » est probablement la chanson de Vian la plus connue, dont on a fait un album par la suite.

sonore *sound-effect* ; **après-guerre** *post-war (WWII)* ; **fou de** *crazy about* ; **provocateur** *agitated*

Serge Gainsbourg (1928–1991) qui ne cachera* jamais son admiration pour Boris Vian, fait partie de la même lignée* : jongleur* de mots, curieux de sonorités* venues d'ailleurs* (jazz, mambo, reggae, new wave, rap) et ne s'attachant à aucun genre* pour mieux réussir dans chacun. Tout lui réussit : la chanson réaliste (« Le poinçonneur des lilas »), la chanson poétique (« La Javanaise », « Je suis venu vous dire que je m'en vais »), la pop (« Poupée de cire, poupée de son »), l'album concept (*Histoire de Melody Nelson*) qui influencera aussi bien Air que Beck ou Jarvis Cocker, et la provocation politique (avec une version de « La Marseillaise » en reggae).

Mais Serge Gainsbourg est aussi l'auteur-compositeur d'un nombre impressionnant de succès interprétés pour nombre d'entre eux par des femmes : Vanessa Paradis, Brigitte Bardot, Jane Birkin (sa muse), Isabelle Adjani, Anna Karina, Catherine Deneuve, Juliette Greco, et Françoise Hardy.

cachera *will hide* ; **lignée** tradition ; **jongleur** *juggler* ; **sonorités** *sounds, tone* ; **d'ailleurs** *from elsewhere* ; **ne s'attachant à aucun genre** *belonging to no specific genre*

Charles Aznavour (1924–), lui aussi l'auteur-compositeur d'un nombre important de chansons à succès interprétées par Edith Piaf, Frank Sinatra, Liza Minnelli, et Dianne Reeves, est surtout l'interprète du temps qui passe et des amours tristes qui lui ont valu d'immenses succès : « Tu t'laisses aller », « Il faut savoir », « La Mamma », « For Me, Formidable », « La Bohème », « Emmenez-moi », « Désormais », « Hier encore », « Comme ils disent ». Ajouter à cela que Charles Aznavour est un formidable *homme de scène**, élu* par *Time Online* et *CNN «Artiste de variétés du siècle»,* rassemblant* plus de 100 000 spectateurs sur le site des plaines d'Abraham en 2008 à Québec. Enfin, Charles Aznavour a joué au cinéma dans plus de 50 films.

homme de scène *performer* ; **élu** *chosen* ; **rassemblant** *gathering*

Essential Instruction

1. Make copies of the readings in **Rencontres culturelles** so that students can underline and add notes.
2. Have students take turns reading aloud about each artist. This is an opportunity for you to add comments and play a bit of each song or selections of songs for them to hear (vetting songs for appropriateness of lyrics).
3. At the end of each section, ask students to volunteer what they remember about each artist.
4. Pair students to do **Activité 6**. Use these questions and answers as a basis for a class discussion about these classic singers. Which of the artists, in students' opinion, could be a popular singer in today's music market?
5. Other **chanteurs engagés** that you might consider introducing to students include Georges Brassens, Serge Reggiani, Michel Berger, Daniel Balavoine, Renaud, and Francis Cabrel.

Jacques Brel (1929–1978) est lui aussi auteur-compositeur-interprète. Il est d'origine belge. Brel, c'est la puissance lyrique du texte*, le goût pour la musique populaire dans les mélodies et une interprétation très dramatique. Parmi ses grands succès, « La valse à mille temps », « Bruxelles » et « Jef », appartiennent* à cette esthétique réaliste et populaire alors que « Le Moribond », « Ne me quitte pas », « Quand on a que l'amour », « Le Plat Pays », « Marieke », et « Les Vieux », sont d'un lyrisme plus intimiste et musicalement plus économe*. Reste le Brel critique social, celui des chansons telles que « Bourgeois », des « Flamandes », ou encore des « Bigotes », et de « Ces gens-là ».

puissance lyrique du texte *lyrical power of the text*; **appartiennent** *belong*; **économe** *frugal*

Barbara (1930–1997) est la chanteuse qui a séduit* plusieurs générations qui se sont reconnues* dans le lyrisme intimiste de ses textes, l'émotion très personnelle qui s'en dégage*, la mélodie piano comme une confidence. Pianiste chantante, elle passe de longues années à chanter dans les cabarets de la rive gauche. De cette relation particulière avec le public, elle écrira une chanson : « Ma plus belle histoire d'amour, c'est vous » que le public lui renvoie en miroir au cours de ses concerts. « Dis, quand reviendras-tu ? », « Nantes », « Göttingen », « Pierre », « Le mal de vivre », « La solitude », « Une petite cantate », « Au bois de Saint-Amand », « La Dame brune », « Marienbad », mais aussi « L'Aigle noir », et « L'homme en habit rouge » forment comme un récit de vie dans lequel chacun, chacune choisit son parcours*.

a séduit *seduced*; **reconnues** *recognized*; **s'en dégage** *comes out*; **parcours** chemin

6 Des auteurs-compositeurs-interprètes français 1.3

Répondez aux questions.

Boris Vian

1. On associe Boris Vian à quels genres de musique ?
2. Qu'est-ce qu'il faisait comme métier ?
3. Comment s'appelle sa chanson d'un soldat ?

Serge Gainsbourg

4. Serge Gainsbourg chantait quelles sortes de chansons ?
5. Il a été maître de quels genres de musique ?

Charles Aznavour

6. Charles Aznavour se concentre sur quels thèmes principaux (citez-en deux) ?
7. À part chanteur, qu'est-ce qu'il fait comme métier ?

Jacques Brel

8. Comment est-ce que Jacques Brel interprétait ses chansons ?
9. On peut associer quels titres à son pays d'origine ?
10. Comment était sa musique ?

Barbara

11. Barbara préférait quel instrument de musique ?
12. Où a-t-elle commencé sa carrière ?
13. Quel était son rapport avec le public ?

Answers

6

1. la chanson engagée
2. Il était ingénieur.
3. « Le déserteur »
4. des chansons de tous les genres
5. la chanson réaliste, la chanson poétique, la pop, l'album concept
6. le temps qui passe, les amours tristes
7. acteur de cinéma
8. Il était très dramatique.
9. « Bruxelles », « Flamandes », « Le Plat Pays »
10. lyrique et populaire
11. le piano
12. dans les cabarets de Paris
13. Elle était très proche de son public.

Reference Desk

Barbara (1930–1997) was *the* French singer who symbolized the generation of cabaret musicians. She had a special connection with her public. Barbara addressed her original song "**Ma plus belle histoire d'amour, c'est vous**" to her fans. For the French, her passing also meant the death of an entire generation and music genre. Many of Brel's songs have been translated into and performed in English. Students may be interested in listening to some and comparing different interpretations:

- "If You Go Away" ("**Ne me quitte pas**"), Neil Diamond
- "Seasons in the Sun," ("**Le Moribond**"), Terry Jacks
- "Amsterdam," David Bowie
- "Autumn Leaves" ("**Les Feuilles mortes**"), Céline Dion

Expansion

Students will listen to the lyrics of "If we only have love" in English and "**Quand on n'a que l'amour**" in French. They must choose which rendition is more powerful to them and why. Ask if this song could be considered **une chanson engagée**. Why or why not? What is the theme? How does the repetition of **Si** or *If* add to the drama and intensity of the concluding verse?

Recherche : jacques brel est vivant et heureux à paris

Differentiated Learning

Accelerate

Serge Gainsbourg has been considered a "**provocateur**." What in his life and works would justify this title? Explain by providing examples.

Decelerate

How would the song "**Le déserteur**" be considered **une chanson engagée**?

Special Needs Students

Hearing Impaired Students

Students will enjoy the lyrics as poetry.

Social Anxiety/At-Risk Students

Students who have not been raised to appreciate different singing styles may, at first, be turned off by those of Aznavour and Piaf. Encourage them to develop new tastes in music and emphasize the importance of being culturally literate, even if the "**artistes**" are not of their generation. Many of the songs mentioned in this **Leçon** are heard in movies and continue to be re-interpreted by stars today.

Resources

Points de départ
WB Workbook 6
Explore

Reference Desk

1. Édith Piaf (1915–1963) was a French singer who started her career singing in the streets, thus her alternative name "**la môme**" (*the kid*). Piaf's music told tales of love lost, pathos, and sorrow. Her classic songs that became her trademark are "**La Vie en rose**," "**Non, je ne regrette rien**," "**Milord**," and "**l'Accordéoniste**."
2. Thomas Dutronc, popular gypsy guitarist and swing musician of throughout the first twenty years of the 21st century, is the son of actor-musician Jacques Dutronc and singer-songwriter Françoise Hardy, who have both had successful musical careers.
3. Johnny Hallyday (1943–2017) was a rock star referred to as "the French Elvis" for his broad popularity and lasting influence. He and Jean-Jacques Goldman are the highest-earning French-language musicians of all time.
4. If you have access to Passport, find a news article or a song related to Édith Piaf and show it to your students. You may also find a song by one of the artists mentioned in this section.

nouvelle orthographe **il/elle/on plait**

Communication

Presentational: Paired Practice

Students compare the lyrics of "**La Marseillaise**" to Gainsbourg's "**La Marseillaise**" in reggae. They can answer these questions: What changes did Gainsbourg make that have provoked and infuriated so many French people when the song was released? Do you think that a national anthem should be tampered with? Student pairs will report back to the class on their findings.

Points de départ

Question centrale ? Comment l'art est-il un reflet de la culture?

La chanson française 1.2, 2.1, 2.2, 3.1

C'est une des caractéristiques de la chanson française : le chanteur fait tout. Il écrit les paroles (auteur), il compose la musique (compositeur), et, bien sûr, il chante ses propres textes et ses propres musiques (interprète). Le phénomène a commencé après la Seconde Guerre mondiale dans les clubs de Saint-Germain-des-Prés de Paris, et il demeure important : de Charles Trenet et Boris Vian à Vincent Delerm, de Barbara à Émilie Simon, Olivia Ruiz et Zaz, de Jacques Brel et Charles Aznavour à Bénabar Raphaël, Thomas Dutronc et Vianney, jusqu'aux slameurs comme Grand Corps Malade, sans oublier Serge Gainsbourg et Benjamin Biolay.

Recherche : charles trenet, vincent delerm, émilie simon, bénabar, grand corps malade

La Francophonie

Musique contemporaine

Chanteurs français et d'origine étrangère 1.2, 2.2, 3.1, 5.2

Style iconique		Aînés	Successeurs d'aujourd'hui
« Raconteurs »		**Charles Aznavour, Michel Sardou**	Bénabar, Sanseverino, Thomas Dutronc
« Courant alternatif »		**Hubert-Félix Thiéfaine**	Tryo, Les Ogres de Barback, Riké
« En anglais »		**Graeme Allwright**	Moriarty, The Do, Cocoon
« Peur de rien »		**Jacques Higelin, Johnny Hallyday**	Camille, Philippe Katerine, Juliette, Rita Mitsouko
« Rebelles »		**Bernard Lavilliers**	Cali, Saez, Dionysos, Têtes Raides
« Rockeurs indies »		**Alain Bashung, Jean-Jacques Goldman**	Dominique A, Jean-Louis Murat, Francis Lalanne, Florent Marchet

Style iconique		Aînés	Successeurs d'aujourd'hui
« Hommes fragiles »		**Alain Souchon, Laurent Voulzy**	Etienne Daho, Alex Beaupain, Vincent Delerm, Benjamin Biolay, Raphaël
« Femmes délicates »		**Françoise Hardy**	Carla Bruni, Berry, Rose
« Femmes muses »		**Jane Birkin**	Lio, Vanessa Paradis, Charlotte Gainsbourg
« Femmes libérées »		**Barbara**	Zazie, Anaïs, Clarika, Jeanne Cherhal
« Acrobate des mots »		**Claude Nougaro**	Grand Corps Malade, Abd al Malik, Ridan, Anis
« Stars de la télé »		**Mireille Mathieu**	Julien Doré, Christophe Willem, Olivia Ruiz

Essential Instruction

1. In the computer lab, students will read all four sections of **Points de départ**. Ask students what the people listed in the **Recherche** have in common. Students will identify and listen to one popular song from each artist.
2. In their notebooks, students make a chart with the following headings: name of the artist, song they listened to, theme, orchestration, and their rating one to five, five being the highest.
3. They will continue the chart for **La Francophonie, en France**, and **Au Québec**.
4. This chart provides the basis of a class discussion of French and French-Canadian music styles from yesterday and today.

Au Québec 1.2, 2.2, 3.1, 3.2

Le Vent du Nord est un groupe folklorique québécois fondé en 2003. Certains de leurs chansons évoquent* l'influence celtique de l'Irlande et la Bretagne. Ils ont reçu de nombreux prix. Ils vont souvent en tournée. Leur premier album s'appelle *Maudite moisson !* Leur dernier est intitulé *Symphonique*. Ce groupe est bien connu, pas seulement au Canada, mais dans le monde entier.

Recherche : vent du nord

évoquent *recall*

7 Activités culturelles 1.2, 1.3, 3.2, 5.2

Faites les activités suivantes.

1. Décrivez le rôle du chanteur qui « fait tout ».
2. Trouvez le lieu associé aux origines de ce genre sur un plan de Paris.
3. Composez une playlist personnelle de vos chansons préférées des chanteurs contemporains mentionnés dans la lecture.
4. Choisissez l'un des styles de la chanson française présentés dans la lecture, puis faites une présentation en expliquant le genre de musique de ces artistes, ainsi que leur importance dans la chanson française. Vous pouvez présenter des albums ou des chansons à succès, et donner votre opinion personnelle.
5. Choisissez une chanson de Vent du Nord ou d'un autre groupe ou musicien québécois sur Internet. Présentez-la à la classe ; dites pourquoi vous l'aimez et faites-la écouter.

La musique québécoise est connue pour ses instruments traditionnels.

Produits 1.2, 2.2

« La vie en rose » est une chanson bien connue hors de (*outside of*) la France. Chantée par Édith Piaf en 1947, elle est vite devenue un hit. Beaucoup de chanteurs anglophones, tels que Louis Armstrong, Diana Krall, et KT Tunstall, l'ont fait connaître (*made it known*) par leurs fans. En trouvez-vous d'autres interprètes ? Écoutez la chanson de Piaf en ligne.

Édith Piaf, chanteuse légendaire

Perspectives 1.2, 2.1, 3.1, 3.2

Le célèbre chanteur français Georges Brassens a dit : « Pourquoi philosopher alors qu'on peut chanter ? » Que pense-t-il du rôle et de l'influence du chanteur français ?

Answers

7

1. Il compose la musique, écrit les paroles, et chante la chanson.
2. Saint-Germain des Prés (*Show students on map.*)
3. Answers will vary.
4. Answers will vary.

Perspectives

Answers will vary.

Culture

Starmania is a **Franco-Québécois** rock-opera created in 1978 by French artist Michel Berger and Quebec artist Luc Plamodon. It has reached such international success that it was remade in different countries. Tim Rice's *Tycoon* is an adaptation of the original French-Quebec work.

Differentiated Learning

Accelerate

Have students compare Jacques Brel's **"Les Vieux"** with Michel Sardou's **"Les Vieux Mariés**." Although the theme is about old people, is the attitude toward them the same in both songs? Which is more melodic?

Decelerate

Compare the prices in euros of five of the same albums or singles sold in France and the United States. Convert euros to dollars using today's exchange rate.

Multiple Intelligences

Musical-Rhythmic

Have students work with you to organize a French karaoke day. For a minimum fee, karaoke classics of French popular singers are available online. Students could also make a karaoke program of songs of Raphaël and Vent du Nord. The more students sing in French, the better their pronunciation becomes and the more vocabulary they will learn. Encourage students to find a French singer they like and to listen often.

Answers

8

1. C
2. A
3. D
4. Coluche était comédien et acteur français. Il a créé Les Restos du Cœur pour nourrir les sans-abri.

Reference Desk

1. Started on a whim by the French comedian Coluche in 1985, **Les Restos du Cœur** is an enormous, non-profit French organization that seeks to provide food (and, more recently, lodging) for all people living in France. The hit song (of the same name) was composed and performed by Jean-Jacques Goldman in 1986. Every year, France's greatest stars participate in a concert called "**Les Enfoirés**," benefiting **les Restos du Cœur**.
2. Go online and find the lyrics to the song "**Les Restos du Cœur**." Play it for your students and sing it with them.

Du côté des médias 1.2

Lisez la présentation de l'association « Les Restos du Cœur ».

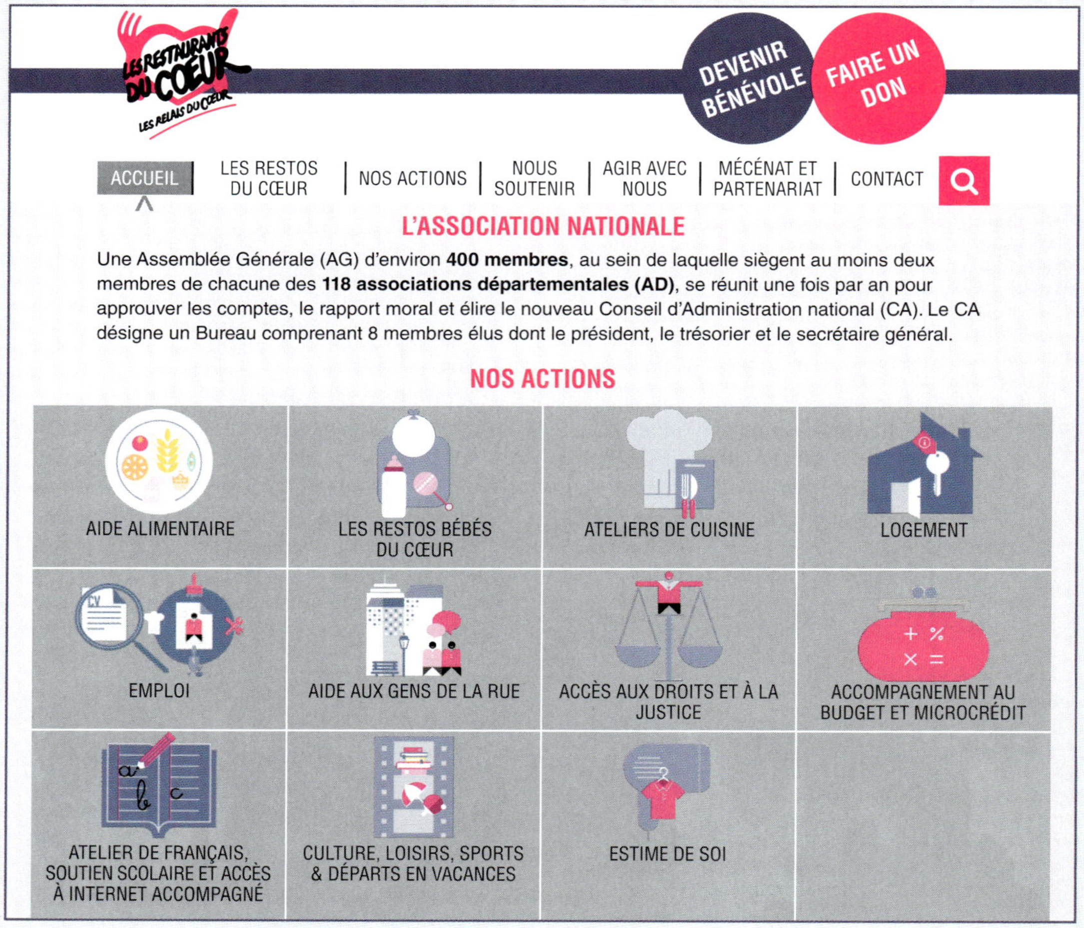

8 Les Enfoirés et Les Restos du Cœur 1.2, 1.3, 3.2

Répondez aux questions suivantes.

1. Quelle sorte d'organisation est Les Restos du Cœur ?
   - A. une entreprise de restauration
   - B. une chaîne de télévision locale
   - C. une organisation à but humanitaire
   - D. une branche administrative de l'État
2. Quels groupes de personnes peuvent se faire aider de l'association ?
   - A. tout le monde
   - B. les travailleurs
   - C. les bébés
   - D. les animaux

Essential Instruction

1. Ask students what financial aid and physical support would be needed to help the impoverished in the United States. What American organizations do they know of that are currently helping the homeless?
2. Students will read **Du côté des médias**. They will make a chart about **les Restos du Cœur**. They can use these headings: mission statement, key members, important dates and pertinent statistics, and new vocabulary to help them organize the information in the reading.
3. In groups, students will prepare the answers to the questions in **Activité 8** to be used in a class discussion of this benevolent group.
4. Students will sing the chorus of "**La Chanson des Restos du Cœur**."
5. In the computer lab, students listen to music by Raphaël and Vent du Nord.

3. Les Restos du Cœur seraient un lien profitable dans quelle situation suivante?
   A. Paul a perdu son travail et se retrouve au chômage.
   B. Jack est en France pour une année. Il se sent seul et voudrait faire des sorties culturelles pour rencontrer du monde.
   C. Mme Bouc a cinq enfants. Son fils, Prince, a pris du retard dans sa scolarité, mais elle n'a pas les moyens de payer un tuteur.
   D. Tout ce qui précède.
4. Allez plus loin: faites une recherche sur Internet sur Coluche. Qui était-il et quel est son rapport avec Les Restos du Cœur?

Recherche: les restos du cœur, les enfoirés

Regardez les albums de Vincent Delerm et lisez les titres de ses chansons.

Vincent Delerm
(2002)

Fanny Ardant et moi
La Vipère du Gabon
Châtenay-Malabry
Catégorie Bukowski
Tes parents
Cosmopolitan
Slalom géant
Le Monologue shakespearien
Charlotte Carrington
Deauville sans Trintignant
L'Heure du thé

Kensington Square
(2003)

Les filles de 1973 ont trente ans
Quatrième de couverture
Le Baiser Modiano
Veruca Salt et Frank Black
Kensington Square
Natation synchronisée
Évreux
Anita Pettersen
Deutsche Grammophon
Gare de Milan

Les piqûres d'araignée
(2007)

Sous les avalanches
Je t'ai même pas dit
À Naples il y a peu d'endroits pour s'asseoir
Marine
Ambroise Paré
Sépia plein les doigts
Les Piqûres d'araignée
Déjà toi
29 avril au 28 mai
Voici la ville
Il fait si beau
Favourite song
Les Jambes de Steffi Graf

Quinze Chansons
(2008)

Tous les acteurs s'appellent Terence
Allan et Louise
Je pense à toi
Martin Parr
Le cœur des volleyeuses bat plus fort pour les volleyeurs
Et François de Roubaix dans le dos
Dans tes bras
78543 habitants
Shea Stadium
Un temps pour tout
North avenue
From a room
Un tacle de Patrick Vieira n'est pas une truite en chocolat
Monterey

Les Amants Parallèles
(2013)

L'avion
Le Film
Bruits de Nuits D'été
Robes (avec Rosemary Standley)
Super Bowl
Les Amants parallèles
Grand plongeoir
Et la fois où tu as
Ces deux-là (avec Virginie Aussiètre)
Hacienda
Ils avaient fait les valises dans la nuit
Embrasse-moi
Le Film II

À présent
(2016)

La vie devant soi
Dans le décor
Je ne veux pas mourir ce soir
Danser sur la table
Les chanteurs sont tous les mêmes
La dernière fois que je t'ai vu
Un été
Cristina
Êtes-vous heureux
À présent
Le garçon

9 Discographie de Vincent Delerm 1.3, 3.1, 3.2, 4.1, 4.2, 5.2

Choisissez un album et cherchez les paroles des chansons. Présentez le thème, ainsi que des extraits (audio ou vidéo) de vos chansons préférées, en expliquant les références culturelles.

Answers

9 Presentations will vary.

Expansion

Have students design an album cover for a French artist and album of their choice.

Differentiated Learning

Adapt

Students watch music videos of Vincent Delerm online. To locate them, type in the name of one of his albums. Excerpts of his music are also available on popular online stores. Questions to discuss: How would you characterize his music? Would this style be popular in the United States? Are there any American or British singers who are similar in style?

Resources

WB Workbook 7–9
LA Listening Activity 2
G & V Practice Games

Answer

Comparaison
The subject is **le rock**, and the indirect object pronoun is **lui** (*him* or *her*, depending on the context).

Reference Desk

The indirect pronouns **me, te, lui, nous, vous, leur** are translated with the prepositions *to* or *for* in English. If students translate **il plaît** or **ils plaisent** as *it is pleasing* or *they are pleasing*, the use of the indirect object with **plaire** will make sense. **Il me plaît** means *it is pleasing to me*. It could be thought to be a synonym for **aimer**. Students should know that **Il a plu** can mean *it rained* or *it pleased*. Both verbs **pleuvoir** and **plaire** have the same past participle (**plu**). Students often confuse the forms and meanings of these verbs. Have them do some review exercises in present and **passé composé**, using **pleuvoir**, **plaire**, and **pleurer**.

nouvelle orthographe **il/elle/on plait**

Communication

Interpersonal: Paired practice

Students make a list of what they love, for example food (chocolate, ice cream, vegetables, cheese), animals (horses, dogs, cats), music, sports, and/or films. One student will use **aimer**. **J'aime cette chanson**. The partner will use **plaire**. **Cette chanson me plaît**. Students will state what they like or love using **plaire** and **aimer**. They should use a minimum of 15 examples alternating between the two structures. Ask students to share what they expressed.

Structure de la langue

Present Tense of the Irregular Verb *plaire* 1.1

The verb **plaire** (*to please*) is irregular. Only two of its present-tense forms are frequently used: **il/elle/on plaît** and **ils/elles plaisent**. To express likes or dislikes, **plaire** is often used instead of **aimer**. **Plaire** takes an indirect object, using the preposition **à** with a person or an indirect object.

Le jazz et le swing **plaisent à** mes grands-parents.	*My grandparents like jazz and swing.*
Est-ce que la musique de Jacques Brel te **plaît**? Oui, sa musique me **plaît**.	*Do you like Jacques Brel's music?* *Yes, I like his music.*

The irregular past participle of **plaire** is **plu**.

Est-ce que cette chanson engagée vous a **plu**? Oui, elle nous a beaucoup **plu**.	*Did you like the protest song?* *Yes, we liked it a lot.*

On recycle !

Faites une petite enquête auprès de cinq camarades de classe pour trouver quels plats culinaires français leur plaisent. Dans leurs réponses, vos camarades devront indiquer pourquoi ces plats leurs plaisent ou ne leur plaisent pas.

MODÈLE **A : Est-ce que le bœuf bourguignon te plaît?**
B : Non, il ne me plaît pas parce que je suis végétarienne.

les escargots • le poisson en sauce blanche • les accras de morue • le lapin sauce marinière • le foie gras • le saumon fumé • les brochettes de lambi grillé • le coq au vin • la crème caramel • les rougets frits à l'haïtienne • les crudités • les truffes

Comparaisons 4.1

Le rock lui plaît. In the English version of this sentence, what is the subject and what is the indirect object pronoun?

Essential Instruction

1. Introduce the verb **plaire** by pointing out that students are already familiar with it, especially if they use it in the expressions **s'il te plaît** and **s'il vous plaît**, which literally translate to *if you please*.
2. Review the form of the indirect objects.
3. Conjugate the verb **plaire** on the board. Students will repeat the verb after you. Underline the **il**, **elle**, **on**, and **ils**, **elles** forms as these are the most often used.
4. Write **Marc aime le chocolat suisse**. Change the sentence to **Le chocolat suisse lui plaît**. Explain that in the second example with **plaire**, Swiss chocolate is pleasing to him. Change the subject to read: **Marie aime le chocolate suisse**. Ask students to restate the sentence with **plaire**. **Le chocolat suisse lui plaît**. These French sentences are identical. Explain that the speaker can use **plaire** only if it is clear who (Marc or Marie) likes Swiss chocolate. Connect this to the example in the **Comparaisons** box.
5. Write **Marc et Marie aiment le chocolat suisse**. Ask students to restate the sentence using **plaire**.
6. Students are now ready to do the interpersonal paired practice and **Ça plaît à Cassandre**.

10 Ça plaît à Cassandre? 1.1

Interpersonal Speaking

À tour de rôle, demandez à votre partenaire si tel ou tel vêtement plaît à Cassandre ou ne lui plaît pas. Votre partenaire va répondre selon les indices donnés.

MODÈLES

+ 

A: Le bonnet en laine plaît à Cassandre?
B: Oui, il lui plaît.

- 

A: Le pantalon rose plaît à Cassandre?
B: Non, il ne lui plaît pas.

1. + 
2. - 
3. - 
4. + 
5. - 
6. + 
7. + 
8. - 

Traditions et pratiques

1.2, 2.1

The French are known for their taste in clothing and effortless elegance. Home of some of the world's most successful design houses, it is no surprise that Paris is considered to be the fashion capital of the world. The key to classic French style lies in clothing and accessories that are not overly showy. Both French men and women wear sophisticated, elegant clothing. As a result, many American tourists often feel their clothing is too casual compared to the French natives'. One of the principal rules of the unspoken French dress code is wearing understated, well-fitting clothes. What articles of clothing popular in the United States might look out of place in France?

Resources

Activity 10

Answers

10

1. A: Le tee-shirt en couleur plaît à Cassandre?
   B: Oui, il lui plaît.
2. A: Les chaussures de tennis plaisent à Cassandre?
   B: Non, elles ne lui plaisent pas.
3. A: La robe en coton plaît à Cassandre?
   B: Non, elle ne lui plaît pas.
4. A: Le jean plaît à Cassandre?
   B: Oui, il lui plaît.
5. A: La ceinture noire plaît à Cassandre?
   B: Non, elle ne lui plaît pas.
6. A: La jupe noire et blanche plaît à Cassandre?
   B: Oui, elle lui plaît.
7. A: L'écharpe en lin plaît à Cassandre?
   B: Oui, elle lui plaît.
8. A: Le manteau bleu plaît à Cassandre?
   B: Non, il ne lui plaît pas.

Traditions et pratiques

Answers will vary, but may include sweatpants, oversized T-shirts, and jeans.

Game

Aïe aïe aïe!

The difficulty with the verb **plaire** is that it requires an indirect construction. Students have to go through the mental exercise of rephrasing "I like this artist" to "This artist is pleasing to me." Put students in teams and give them a sentence in English, such as "**Nous aimons la pop.**" The team which can come up first with the correct construction "**La pop nous plaît**" scores a point. As the game progresses and students gain more confidence, add negative constructions and past tenses.

Differentiated Learning

Adapt

Students make a list of painters and art movements they like and do not like using the verb **plaire**. Ask them to make sure that they use both third person singular and plural in their examples.

Decelerate

For students who still struggle producing language, provide them with the necessary vocabulary to complete **Activité 10**, or allow them to use their notes.

11 Un sondage sur les préférences de musique 1.2, 1.3

Interpretive Reading, Presentational Speaking or Writing

Voici les résultats d'un sondage du Club de Musique de la commune de Jonage, près de Lyon. Qu'est-ce qui plaît à ses membres ?

	+ = plaire			– = ne pas plaire		
	Annie	**Lindsay**	**moi**	**Karim**	**toi**	**Dylan**
le swing	-	+	+	-	-	+
le jazz	-	-	-	+	+	-
la pop	+	+	+	+	+	+
le hip-hop	+	-	+	-	-	+
le reggae	-	-	-	+	+	+
la musique folklorique	+	+	-	-	-	+
la musique classique	+	-	+	+	+	-
la salsa	+	-	-	+	-	+

MODÈLES Karim : le jazz, la musique folklorique
Le jazz lui plaît, mais la musique folklorique ne lui plaît pas.
moi : le jazz, le reggae
Le jazz et le reggae ne me plaisent pas.

1. Karim et toi : le swing, la pop
2. Lindsay : la musique folklorique, la pop
3. Dylan et Annie : le jazz, le hip-hop
4. Annie et moi : la musique classique, le reggae
5. moi : le swing, la pop
6. Lindsay : le hip-hop, le reggae
7. Lindsay et moi : la salsa, le swing

12 J'interviewe mon partenaire ! 1.1

Interpersonal Speaking

À tour de rôle, demandez à votre partenaire si les choses suivantes lui plaisent.

MODÈLES les sports d'hiver
A : Les sports d'hiver te plaisent ?
B : Oui, les sports d'hiver me plaisent (beaucoup).
ou
Non, les sports d'hiver ne me plaisent pas (du tout).

1. les émissions de musique
2. les sports d'hiver
3. les paysages
4. les devoirs de maths
5. les cours de science
6. les peintures impressionnistes
7. les chansons romantiques
8. les interprètes
9. les fêtes champêtres
10. les escargots

13 La musique qui leur plaît 1.2

Interpretive Listening

*Écrivez les numéros 1–6 sur votre papier. Écoutez les conversations. Puis, mettez un **+** si la personne aime la chose mentionnée dans la question, ou un **–** si elle ne l'aime pas.*

Resources

Activity 13

Answers

11

1. Le swing ne vous plaît pas, mais la pop vous plaît.
2. La musique folklorique et la pop lui plaisent.
3. Le jazz ne leur plaît pas, mais la pop leur plaît.
4. La musique classique nous plaît, mais le reggae ne nous plaît pas.
5. Le swing et la pop me plaisent.
6. Le hip-hop et le reggae ne lui plaisent pas.
7. La salsa ne nous plaît pas, mais le swing nous plaît.

12

1. Les émissions de musique te plaisent ?
2. Les sports d'hiver te plaisent ?
3. Les paysages te plaisent ?
4. Les devoirs de math te plaisent ?
5. Les cours de science te plaisent ?
6. Les peintures impressionnistes te plaisent ?
7. Les chansons romantiques te plaisent ?
8. Les interprètes te plaisent ?
9. Les fêtes champêtres te plaisent ?
10. Les escargots te plaisent ?

Partner answers will vary.

13 Script

1. –Est-ce que la peinture française te plaît ?
   –Oui, surtout les impressionnistes avec leurs tableaux peints en plein air.
2. –Est-ce que les chansons de Gainsbourg vous plaisent ?
   –Oui, ses chansons nous plaisent plus que sa personne.
3. –Les chansons pop vous plaisent-elles ?
   –Oui, elles nous plaisent mieux que le rock et le hip-hop.
4. –Est-ce que cette mélodie te plaît ?
   –Non, elle ne me plaît pas du tout ; j'ai mal à la tête.
5. –C'est de la musique classique ?
   –Non, c'est la world. Ce qui me plaît, c'est la musique qui vient de l'Afrique.
6. –Les tableaux de van Gogh te plaisent ?
   –Non, je préfère ceux de Monet… les beaux paysages, la mer, le soleil.

1. + 2. + 3. + 4. - 5. - 6. -

Essential Instruction

1. Model the first and second sentence of **Activité 11**.
2. Pair students to do **Activité 12**. Encourage them to add words like **beaucoup**, **énormément**, or **pas mal** if they like the term. In the negative, they could add **pas du tout**.
3. Students complete **Activité 13** on whiteboards. They can hold up the answer for each listening comprehension item so that you can monitor how well they are doing.
4. Give students a choice of doing **Activité 14** or **15**.
5. All students should do **Activité 16**. Give them enough time to investigate each music website so they learn what French people listen to.

À vous la parole

Question centrale ? Comment l'art est-il un reflet de la culture?

Communiquez!

14 Projet de musique 1.1, 1.3, 3.1, 3.2, 5.2

Interpersonal and Presentational Speaking

Avec un partenaire, choisissez une chanson française ou francophone à présenter à la classe. Faites une biographie de l'artiste, indiquez le genre de la chanson, et la raison pour laquelle vous l'avez choisie. Vous pourrez aussi expliquer le message de la chanson, la signification des paroles, vous servir d'aides visuelles et jouer un extrait du clip vidéo.

Recherche: nrj radio, victoires de la musique, le top 50, tops songs france, paroles (+ CHANSON/ARTISTE)

15 Ma playlist de chansons francophones 1.2, 1.3, 3.1, 5.1, 5.2

Interpretive Viewing, Presentational Writing

Après avoir été inspiré(e) par les présentations musicales de vos camarades de classe (dans l'activité précédente), vous allez faire maintenant une playlist de 5 chansons interprétées par des musiciens francophones dans l'ordre de vos préférences. La première chanson de votre liste sera celle que vous avez aimée le plus. Créez également une courte liste (3 chansons) de titres qui ne vous plaisaient pas, et expliquez pourquoi : peut-être que vous n'avez pas aimé le style de musique, le message, ou les paroles de la chanson. Comparez votre liste à celles de vos camarades de classe.

16 Un podcast pour les Restos du Cœur 1.2, 1.3, 3.2, 4.2, 5.2

Interpretive Reading and Listening, Presentational Speaking

Les Restos du Cœur est une association qui distribue des repas aux personnes dans le besoin. Imaginez que l'association organise un événement pour encourager les gens à faire un don. Pour cela, ils organisent un concours (*contest*) de chanson. Ils vont choisir dix podcasts musicaux et les afficher sur leur site web. Peut-être qu'ils choisiront votre interprétation d'une chanson en français. En groupe, sélectionnez une chanson francophone et entraînez-vous à la chanter. Filmez votre version finale. N'oubliez pas de présenter le chanteur ou la chanteuse, ou le groupe original, ainsi que votre groupe à vous, et d'expliquer pourquoi vous avez choisi cette chanson particulière.

Resources

CA Communicative Activities

Share

Explore

Answers

14 Presentations will vary.

15 Playlists will vary.

16 Podcasts will vary.

Reference Desk

1. Before doing **Activité 11**, remind students that **Karim et toi** as a combined subject is **vous**, and **Annie et moi** as a combined subject is **nous**.
2. If you have access to Passport, create a question for your students to share their response to a communicative activity.
3. If you have access to Passport, give your students a list of archive songs to chose from for **Activité 15**.

Differentiated Learning

Accelerate

In researching the music that students enjoy, have your high-ability students take their favorite French song heard thus far and make a music vlog or blog which features the lyrics, glossary, and photos of the artist or artists. They could teach the class the song.

Decelerate

Students will visit **nrj.fr** or **la FNAC** to report on the current concerts taking place in Paris. Who are the groups, where are the venues, and what are the prices of the seats? How do ticket prices compare to those in the United States for similar concerts or groups?

Answers

All activities will vary.

Reference Desk

To prepare students for writing their essay, bring several objects to class and practice using the vocabulary of similarities and differences as a class or in pairs. You may have them compare simple objects such as an apple and a pear, or a ring and a bracelet. The concrete visualization will help students practice the vocabulary so they can eventually use it for conceptual ideas.

Stratégie communicative

Pre-AP

Communiquez!

Write a Comparison-Contrast Essay 1.2, 1.3, 3.1, 3.2, 5.1

Comparer quelque chose c'est montrer les similarités qui existent entre deux choses. Contraster c'est montrer ce qui les différencie. Lorsqu'on écrit une rédaction, on compare et on contraste. C'est très simple, il y a deux manières d'organiser ses idées; vous pouvez comparer et contraster un élément à la fois (point par point) ou tout écrire sur le premier élément et ensuite passer au second (tout d'un bloc).

1. Choisissez deux tableaux, chansons, styles de musique, ou artistes que vous comparerez et opposerez. Préparez un diagramme de Venn dans lequel vous montrerez les similarités et les différences qui existent entre les deux.

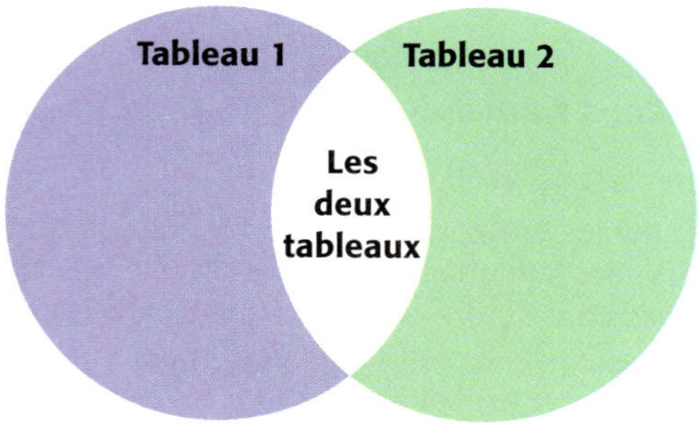

2. Complétez votre organigramme en utilisant les mots ci-dessous pour comparer et contraster:

Similarités	Différences
ressembler à	par contre
tous (toutes) deux	cependant
aussi	mais
également	bien que/qu'
(tout) comme	s'opposer: *Les couleurs s'opposent.*
comparé(e) à	pendant que
tel, telle: *Elle est grande, telle sa mère.*	contrairement à
le même, la même	en comparaison de: *Il est triste, en comparaison de la fille.*

3. Il est également utile d'utiliser le comparatif dans ce type de rédaction.
   Le tableau de Monet est plus sombre que le tableau de Renoir en ce qui concerne l'atmosphère.
   Vous pouvez aussi comparer des noms en utilisant la structure suivante:
   Il y a autant de personnages dans le tableau de Renoir que dans l'autre, mais ceux du tableau de Renoir ont l'air plus heureux.
4. Remettez votre rédaction à un(e) camarade de classe. Il s'assurera que vous avez:
   - suivi le schéma d'organisation.
   - inclu une thèse et un fait sur le sujet.
   - inclu votre point de vue.
   - fait une conclusion.
5. Mettez au propre et publiez en ligne ou partagez votre rédaction avec votre classe.

Essential Instruction

1. Students can search online, or in art books, for two pieces of art that they would like to use for their comparison-contrast essay.
2. They will make copies of each, which will be handed in with their work.
3. Go over every term under the headings "similarities" and "differences." Remind students that **quoique** is a synonym for **bien que**. Both are followed by the subjunctive.
4. Pick two simple drawings and model a pre-writing comparison-contrast Venn diagram.
5. Allow one class period for pre-writing work so that you can circulate to explain, help, and correct their writing.
6. Students will listen and repeat the terms for **La littérature**.
7. Ask students to give you examples of works in the English language that they have read which correspond to each literary term.

Leçon C Vocabulaire actif

La littérature 1.2, 3.1

Pour parler d'œuvres littéraires

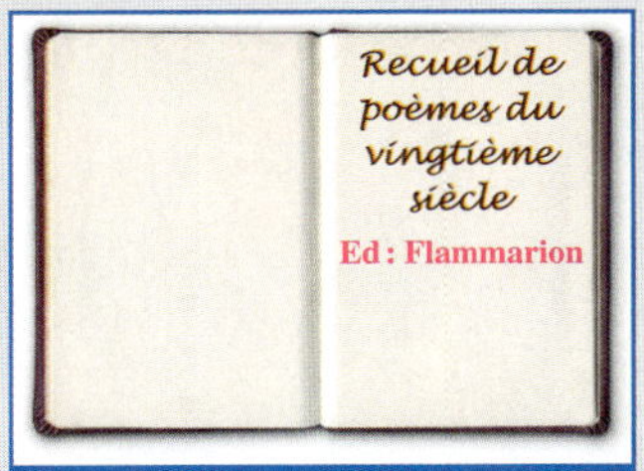

un recueil

un recueil : collection de poèmes, par exemple *Paroles* par Jacques Prévert

la poésie : genre littéraire qui utilise les images, les rimes, et les sonorités pour exprimer une idée ou un sentiment

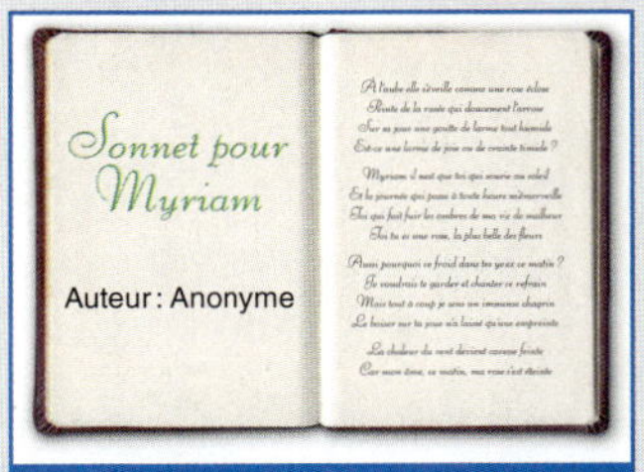

un sonnet

un sonnet : poème de quatorze vers, composé de deux quatrains (quatre vers) et deux tercets (trois vers)

une strophe : ensemble de vers qui forment un paragraphe dans un poème

une fable

une fable : récit imaginaire écrit en vers, avec une morale

une morale : leçon dans une œuvre, par exemple : « Tout flatteur vit aux dépens de celui qui l'écoute » (Jean de La Fontaine)

une satire

une satire : œuvre (pièce, texte, ou récit oral) critique et comique

Les écrivains

un poète (une femme poète)

une romancière (un romancier)

un dramaturge (une dramaturge)

Resources

- *Vocabulaire actif*
- eV eVisual
- WB Workbook 1–3
- FC Flash Cards
- LA Listening Activity 1
- G & V Practice Games

Reference Desk

Jean de La Fontaine (1621–1695) was the most important fabulist in French literature. He was part of a quartet of 17th century writers which included Racine, Boileau, and Molière. His fables were inspired in form and spirit from those of the classic poet Aesop, who used animals as mouthpieces to deride vices such as greed, abuse of power, and vanity, which were prevalent at the court of Louis XIV at Versailles.

Communication

Presentational: Cooperative Groups

Divide students into groups of four or five. Give them a short amount of time to write down names of English-language works and authors (sonnets, fables, satires, poets, novelists, and playwrights) that they have studied in other classes. Continue until the students have exhausted their memories. One group will be paired with another to exchange information to make one master list between them. A representative from each blended group will put their findings on the board under the categories listed above, using a different color marker to distinguish among the groups' work. Cross out duplications. Decide which group has added the most original entries to the list.

Differentiated Learning

Accelerate

Have students collaborate to make a presentation for the class on Molière, his life, and key works. Selecting one of his plays, they will act out a scene in English so that students can understand his style and wit. Suggest these works to students: ***Le Malade Imaginaire***, ***L'École des Femmes***, or ***Le Tartuffe***.

Decelerate

Students present a fable of La Fontaine in English and then in French for the class. They will explain **la morale**.

Special Needs Students

At-Risk Students

Some at-risk students are avid readers. Talking about books might be a subject that they would find interesting.

Resources

Pour la conversation
Et si je voulais dire... ?

Reference Desk

1. An ode is a lyric poem often written to mark a specific occasion, to focus on a specific subject, or to convey intense emotion. There are varying forms for this genre.
2. Ballads are poems, often set to music, dating back to the time of wandering minstrels in medieval Europe.
3. A sonnet, whose name derives from the Italian for "little song," is a poem which presents a question or argument and resolves it in the final lines of the poem. Although the structure and rhyme scheme may vary, it is always 14 lines in length.
4. A fable is a literary form that tells a fictional story using animals as the mouthpiece and which terminates in a moral or lesson.

Connections

Literature

Students will use the structures in **Pour la conversation** to describe works that they are reading or have read in English or French class.

Le renard ment au **corbeau** et prend son fromage !

Anna doit **se cacher** jusqu'à **l'aube** pour **cueillir** la rose magique !

... et **le brouillard** touche le magicien qui **demeure** dans **la vieillesse** pour toujours.

Pour la conversation

1.2, 5.1

How do I describe how an artist raises themes?

» Les *Amours* de Ronsard **donnent lieu à** des **variations** sur les **thèmes** de **la plainte**, du **soupir**, de **l'aveu**, et de **la mélancolie**.

Ronsard's Amours *(book of poetry) gives rise to variations on the themes of complaint, sighing, confession, and melancholy.*

How do I describe the focus of an artist's work?

» La poésie est la partie la plus **volumineuse** de l'œuvre de Victor Hugo.

Poetry is the most voluminous part of Victor Hugo's work.

How do I describe how a work of art takes a position?

» C'est une œuvre politique qui **prend position sur** la guerre.

It's a political work that takes a position on war.

How do I attribute new inventions?

» C'est à Apollinaire que l'**on doit l'invention** du mot « **surréalisme** ».

It's Apollinaire to whom one owes the invention of the word "surrealism."

How do I describe how an artist fits into a culture?

» C'est **une figure** de la culture **populaire**.

He is a figure of popular culture.

Et si je voulais dire... ?

une ballade	*ballad*
une comparaison	*simile*
une explication de texte	*formal critique of literary selection*
le lyrisme	*lyricism*
une métaphore	*metaphor*
un héros	*hero*
un récit épique	*epic story*
une expression	*phrase*

Essential Instruction

1. Put the verb **mentir** on the board and conjugate it. Relate it to its noun **le mensonge**, and its antonym **la vérité**. Remind students of the expression "**dire la vérité**." Relate **vérité** to **vrai** and **vérifier**.
2. Put the vocabulary from **Et si je voulais dire... ?** on the board. Ask students to define the terms in English and give examples, where possible.
3. Before assigning **Mon cours d'anglais**, ask students to name a work of each of the writers listed in the word bank.
4. Students work in pairs to do **Activités 1** and **2**.
5. Correct the exercises by asking students to read and supply the answer for each sentence.
6. Use these activities as a basis for a class discussion about what they are reading now for class or leisure, and tell the class **de quoi il s'agit**.

1 Mon cours d'anglais 1.2, 3.1, 4.2, 5.2

Interpretive Reading

Sélectionnez l'auteur décrit dans chaque phrase, puis complétez cette phrase : ***C'est le romancier/la romancière, le (la) poète, le (la) dramaturge américain(e)/anglais(e)/irlandais(e)****....*

Emily Dickinson **Mark Twain** **William Shakespeare** **Bram Stoker**
Edgar Allan Poe **Sir Arthur Conan Doyle** **Charles Dickens** **Jack London** **Harper Lee**

1. Son héroïne, Scout, dont le père est avocat, demeure dans le sud des États-Unis ; l'œuvre pour laquelle elle est connue est un roman qui prend position sur les droits des afro-américains.
2. Il aimait la satire et l'humour ; son héros Huckleberry Finn a voyagé sur le fleuve Mississippi.
3. Il a écrit des recueils de nouvelles et des romans qui ont lieu en Alaska. Il aime décrire les paysages et les animaux sauvages.
4. Elle a vécu en Nouvelle-Angleterre au 19ème siècle, et elle est connue pour ses recueils de poésies simples.
5. Il a écrit beaucoup de pièces comme *Roméo et Juliette* et des sonnets d'amour.
6. Son héros habite dans une ville où il y a souvent du brouillard ; il travaille avec Docteur Watson.
7. Il est connu pour un conte de Noël avec le personnage Scrooge ; la partie la plus volumineuse de son œuvre est constituée de romans comme *Oliver Twist* et *Great Expectations*.
8. C'est à lui qu'on doit l'invention des contes gothiques tels que *Le Chat Noir*, *La Chute de la maison d'Usher* et le poème *«Le Corbeau»* (*«The Raven»*).
9. Son héros, un vampire, est en difficulté s'il voit l'aube.

2 Mon dico littéraire 1.2

Interpretive Reading

Choisissez un mot de vocabulaire dans la banque de mots pour remplacer les mots en italiques.

un recueil **la poésie** **une fable** **satires** **sonnets** **une morale**

1. Les bandes dessinées dans les magazines et journaux sont souvent des *critiques* politiques.
2. On peut lire des nouvelles ou des poèmes dans *un livre qui réunit ces textes*.
3. *Ce genre d'écriture* (*writing*) peut avoir des rimes ou peut être en vers libre (*free verse*).
4. À la fin d'*une histoire allégorique avec des animaux comme personnages* (*characters*), il y a souvent *une leçon*.
5. Shakespeare est connu pour ses *poèmes de 14 vers qui suivent une forme traditionnelle* aussi bien que pour ses pièces de théâtre.

Answers

1

1. C'est la romancière américaine Harper Lee.
2. C'est le romancier américain Mark Twain.
3. C'est le romancier américain Jack London.
4. C'est la poète américaine Emily Dickinson.
5. C'est le dramaturge anglais William Shakespeare.
6. C'est le romancier anglais Sir Arthur Conan Doyle.
7. C'est le romancier anglais Charles Dickens.
8. C'est le romancier et poète américain Edgar Allan Poe.
9. C'est le romancier irlandais Bram Stoker.

2

1. satires
2. un recueil
3. la poésie
4. une fable, une morale
5. sonnets

Expansion

As a follow-up to **Activité 1**, ask students to formulate a short description of a popular American or French author they like. Have each student read his or her definition, and the class will try to find the artist described.

Differentiated Learning

Accelerate

Ask students to present five **bandes dessinées** of the late Jacques Faizant, the journalist-illustrator and satirist of ***Le Figaro*** newspaper, as an example of this genre of literature.

Resources

Activity 4

Answers

3

1. corbeau
2. renards
3. la vieillesse
4. ment
5. cueillir
6. l'aube
7. brouillard
8. cache
9. demeure

4 Script

Papa : Tu lis *Les fables de La Fontaine* ? C'est une figure de la littérature française !
Manon : Oui, c'est pour mon cours de français. On étudie la poésie du 17ème siècle. Je dois choisir une fable du recueil et la présenter en classe.
Papa : Quand j'avais ton âge, j'adorais la satire dans « Les animaux malades de la peste ».
Manon : Moi, « Le corbeau et le renard » me plaît beaucoup. J'aime la morale et surtout comment le renard ment au corbeau pour obtenir le fromage. C'est assez amusant. Je connais des gens comme ça.
Papa : À mon avis, les poèmes de Victor Hugo sont meilleurs. Quand tu lis, c'est comme si tu voyais vraiment le brouillard ou l'aube.
Manon : Chacun ses goûts !

1. Manon lit un poème de Victor Hugo.
2. Elle lit un recueil parce qu'elle doit faire une présentation en classe.
3. « Les animaux malades de la peste » et « Le corbeau et le renard » sont des fables de La Fontaine.
4. Manon connaît des gens qui ressemblent aux animaux dans la fable.
5. Le père de Manon préfère les poèmes de Jacques Prévert.

1. F; 2. V; 3. V; 4. V; 5. F

5 Answers will vary.

Expansion

Bring a variety of books to class and have students sort them in French by genre.

3 Complétez ! 1.2

Interpretive Reading

Complétez les phrases.

1. Le… est un oiseau noir qui fait « crôa, crôa ».
2. Les… sont des animaux roux qui habitent à la campagne et qui aiment manger les poules de la ferme.
3. Après la jeunesse et la cinquantaine (*middle age*), on arrive à….
4. Quand Pinocchio …., son nez grandit !
5. Le Petit Chaperon Rouge (*Little Red Riding Hood*) veut… des fleurs avant de rendre visite à sa grand-mère.
6. Quand le soleil se lève, on appelle ça….
7. À Londres il y a souvent du… et de la pluie.
8. Un auteur peut montrer directement son message, mais il le… plus souvent.
9. Le jeune écrivain… dans un quartier où il y a beaucoup d'artistes et de musiciens.

Le brouillard indique qu'il s'agit d'un roman policier.

4 Ah, la poésie ! 1.1, 1.2

Interpretive Listening

*Écrivez les numéros 1–5 sur votre papier. Écoutez la conversation entre Manon et son père, puis indiquez si la phrase que vous entendez est vraie (**V**) ou fausse (**F**).*

5 Questions personnelles 1.1

Interpersonal Speaking

Répondez aux questions avec un partenaire.

1. Quel est ton auteur préféré ? Il ou elle écrit quel genre de littérature ?
2. Qui te propose le plus souvent des livres ?
3. Est-ce que la poésie te plaît ? Pourquoi, ou pourquoi pas ?
4. Préfères-tu les nouvelles avec une morale ou une intrigue (*plot*) intéressante ?
5. Est-ce que tu comprends la satire politique de Stephen Colbert ou Jon Stewart ?
6. Si tu allais écrire un texte et le publier (*publish*), quel en serait le genre ? Pourquoi ?

Essential Instruction

1. When you assign **Activité 3**, you may want to create a word bank for your students if you think that they will have difficulty with the exercise.
2. Students will be listening to the recording in **Activité 4**. Pause the recording after each statement to monitor how your students are doing, or dictate the sentences to them to get some extra writing practice in.
3. Students can be placed into groups of different ability to interview each other using **Questions personnelles**. Tell them to take notes because they will be asked to share their answers with their classmates in a whole-class discussion.

Rencontres culturelles

La poésie française 1.2, 3.1, 5.2

Voici quelques poètes français et un exemple de leur poésie.

Pierre de Ronsard (1524–1585)

Ronsard ouvre la tradition de la poésie amoureuse. Ses *Amours* («À Cassandre», 1552 ; «À Marie», 1555–1556 ; «À Hélène», 1578) donnent lieu à des variations sur les thèmes de la plainte*, du soupir*, de l'aveu*, et de la mélancolie. Ils forment encore aujourd'hui un héritage culturel partagé. Voici quelques lignes de son sonnet «À Cassandre», qui se sert du thème *carpe diem* :

À Cassandre
*... Tandis que vôtre âge fleuronne**
En sa plus verte nouveauté,
Cueillez, cueillez votre jeunesse :
Comme à cette fleur, la vieillesse
Fera ternir votre beauté.*

Avec le sonnet, Ronsard impose une forme poétique qui est la marque de fabrique de la poésie française jusqu'aux surréalistes, un moyen de créer de nouveaux rapports entre les mots et, finalement, une nouvelle réalité.

plainte *complaint* ; **soupir** *sigh* ; **aveu** *confession* ; **fleuronne** *blooms* ; **ternir** *tarnish*

Jean de La Fontaine (1621–1695)

C'est un des écrivains les plus populaires, celui dont chacun peut au moins réciter quelques vers «par cœur» ou reprendre l'une de ses célèbres morales. Jean de La Fontaine était un ami des bêtes* et un écologiste avant l'heure*.

Les Fables, écrites entre 1668 et 1694, ont connu tout de suite un immense succès. Elles sont tout à la fois une œuvre politique qui prend position sur la guerre («Le Lion» ou «Le Renard anglais»), contre l'esprit de conquête («Le Paysan du Danube»), et dénonce avec ironie et humour la vie de la Cour* («Les Animaux malades de la peste»). Dans son œuvre philosophique, l'auteur montre sa méfiance* sur la prétendue* supériorité de la race humaine, de «l'animal qu'on appelle homme» (*La Discorde*). *Les Fables*, c'est surtout une œuvre de moraliste qui considère l'homme esclave* de ses passions, de ses ambitions, et aussi de l'amour. Leurs morales sont passées dans le sens courant, telles «nul n'est prophète en son pays» ou que «tel est pris qui croyait prendre». Lisez la fable suivante :

Le Corbeau et le Renard

Maître Corbeau, sur un arbre perché*,
Tenait en son bec* un fromage.
Maître Renard, par l'odeur alléchée*,
Lui tint à peu près ce langage:
«Hé! bonjour, Monsieur du Corbeau.
Que vous êtes joli! que vous me semblez beau!
Sans mentir, si votre ramage*
Se rapporte à* votre plumage,
Vous êtes le Phénix des hôtes de ces bois*.»

... à suivre.

bêtes *animaux* ; **avant l'heure** *before his time* ; **Cour** *royal court* ; **méfiance** *suspicion* ; **prétendue** *claimed* ; **esclave** *slave* ; **perché** *sitting in a tree* ; **bec** *beak* ; **alléchée** *tempted* ; **ramage** *warbling* ; **se rapporte à** *is in keeping with* ; **bois** *woods*

Resources

WB Workbook 4

Communication

Interpersonal: Cooperative Groups

Students in different ability groups will select or be assigned a fable to dramatize. They can select simple costumes to represent the characters, create a backdrop, and present the fable in a dramatic reading. Before the performance, a student from the group will introduce the theme of the fable, explaining any vocabulary students may not understand. Give the students the option of filming the fable off-site if they prefer. Students who are shy might prefer using puppets.

Differentiated Learning

Accelerate

Have students compare Andrew Marvell's poem "To His Coy Mistress" with "**À Cassandra**" in terms of theme, tone, rhyme scheme, and the poet's art of persuasion.

Decelerate

Students look online for an animated cartoon of "**Le Corbeau et le Renard**" which will render the poem easier to understand.

Learning Styles

Auditory Learners

Such students would benefit from listening to recordings of the poem "**À Cassandra**" and the fable "**Le Corbeau et le Renard**" to aid in understanding.

Visual Learners

Have students make a cartoon strip of "**Le Corbeau et le Renard**" which advances the storyline frame by frame.

Reference Desk

In addition to his poetry, Victor Hugo is celebrated for his novels ***Notre Dame de Paris*** (*The Hunchback of Notre Dame*) and ***Les Misérables***. He meticulously divided his writing; one-third dealt with politics, another third, religion, and the last third, philosophy. In addition to writing, he was an active (republican) politician. Conservative at the start of his career, he swung to a more reformist platform when exiled after Louis Napoléon's coup d'état in 1851. Hugo remained in exile, primarily in Brussels, until 1870. Upon his death in 1885, his coffin was put on display under the **Arc de Triomphe** while the population of Paris lined up to pay their last respects. Against his final wishes, he was buried in the Panthéon in Paris. His final written words state "**Aimer, c'est agir.**" (*To love is to act.*) and his final spoken words are said to have been "**C'est ici le combat du jour et de la nuit… je vois une lumière noire.**" (*"Here is the fight between day and night… I see a black light."*)

Critical Thinking

Analysis

Ask students to compare and contrast the two different pieces of writing on this page, using the tools taught previously in **Leçon A**.

(*Suite*)

À ces mots le Corbeau ne se sent pas de joie;
Et pour montrer sa belle voix,
Il ouvre un large bec, laisse tomber* sa proie*.
Le Renard s'en saisit*, et dit: «Mon bon Monsieur,
Apprenez que tout flatteur
Vit aux dépens de celui qui l'écoute:
Cette leçon vaut bien un fromage, sans doute.»
Le Corbeau, honteux et confus,
Jura, mais un peu tard, qu'on ne l'y prendrait plus*.

laisse tomber *drops*; **la proie** *prey*; **s'en saisit** *seizes it*; **ne l'y prendrait plus** *would not trick him again*

Victor Hugo (1802–1885)

C'est le plus universel des écrivains français. Il a touché à tout: au roman, au théâtre, au pamphlet, à la satire, et bien sûr à la poésie.

La poésie est la partie la plus volumineuse de l'œuvre de Victor Hugo dont les principales sont *Les Orientales* (1829), *Les feuilles d'automne* (1831), *Les Chants du crépuscule* (1835), *Voix intérieures* (1837), *Les rayons et les ombres* (1840), et *Les Contemplations* (1856).

La poésie de Victor Hugo passe par le regard: un regard qui rend compte* du «spectacle du monde» avec ses merveilles* et ses pièges*; qui renvoie* à la mémoire, aux souvenirs de l'enfance; qui capte* aussi la simplicité du quotidien; qui cherche enfin à percer* le secret du visible, à trouver la lumière au-delà de* l'ombre et des profondeurs*.

Voici un poème qu'il a écrit après la mort de sa fille, Léopoldine:

Demain, dès l'aube

Demain, dès l'aube, à l'heure où blanchit* la campagne,
Je partirai. Vois-tu, je sais que tu m'attends.
J'irai par la forêt, j'irai par la montagne.
Je ne puis demeurer loin de toi plus longtemps.

Je marcherai les yeux fixés sur mes pensées*,
Sans rien voir au dehors, sans entendre aucun bruit,
Seul, inconnu, le dos courbé*, les mains croisées*,
Triste, et le jour pour moi sera comme la nuit.

Je ne regarderai ni l'or* du soir qui tombe,
Ni les voiles* au loin descendant vers Harfleur,
Et quand j'arriverai, je mettrai sur ta tombe
Un bouquet de houx* vert et de bruyère* en fleur.

Victor Hugo

rend compte réalise; **merveille** *marvel*; **piège** *trap*; **renvoie** *takes you back*; **capte** *captures*; **percer** *to pierce*; **au-delà de** *beyond*; **profondeur** *depth*; **blanchit** *whitens*; **pensée** *thought*; **courbé** *bent*; **croisées** *crossed*; **or** *gilding*; **voiles** *mists*; **houx** *holly*; **bruyère** *heather*

Essential Instruction

1. Play "**Demain, dès l'aube**" for the students. There are also excellent videos online.
2. Ask students to identify the verbs of movement and perception in the poem. Who is the speaker? List the words that suggest how the speaker feels. To whom is the speaker talking? What is the surprise at the end of the poem? Have students identify the rhyme scheme of the poem (ABAB, CDCD, EFEF) and the allegory of the walk that lasts one day, from dawn to dusk, as life's journey towards death (the tomb in the final verse).
3. Students will read aloud Apollinaire's "**La mandoline, l'œillet et le bambou**." Ask them to what they find unusual about this poem. Discuss the **Calligrammes** with them, including their intent and effect.
4. Read the biography of Jacques Prévert and tell the students that they will be reading his poem "**Familiale**" toward the end of the lesson.

Guillaume Apollinaire (1880–1918)

C'est à Apollinaire que l'on doit l'invention du mot « surréalisme ». Mais Apollinaire est d'abord celui qui a sorti le poète de la bibliothèque et qui a regardé le monde moderne qu'il avait sous les yeux : la publicité, les automobiles, les tramways, l'électricité. Pourtant la poésie d'Apollinaire puise* largement dans les grands thèmes de la poésie : amours de hasard*, regrets de jeunesse, fuite du temps*, sentiments contradictoires, souvenirs douloureux*, mélancolie, rejet du monde. *Alcools* (1913), *Calligrammes* (1918), *Poèmes à Lou* sont les recueils les plus célèbres d'Apollinaire.

---

puise *draws from* ; **hasard** *chance* ; **fuite du temps** *passage of time* ; **douloureux** *painful*

Reconnais-toi
Cette adorable personne c'est toi
Sous le grand chapeau canotier
Œil
Nez La Bouche
Voici l'ovale de ta figure
Ton cou Exquis
Voici enfin l'imparfaite image de ton buste adoré
Vu comme à travers un nuage
Un peu plus bas c'est ton cœur qui bat

—Calligrame (Poèmes à Lou), 1915

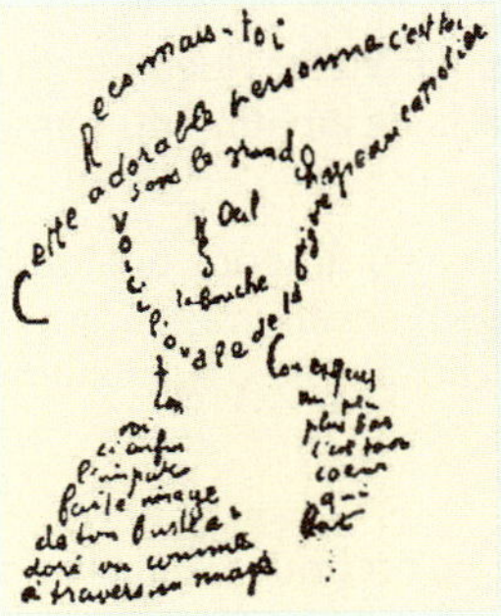

Tous les Français apprennent les poèmes de Jacques Prévert à l'école.

Jacques Prévert (1900–1977)

Jacques Prévert est un poète français très célèbre. Il fait partie du bagage poétique de tous les lycéens et est une figure de la culture populaire. Ses recueils se sont vendus à des millions d'exemplaires* et de nombreux collèges et lycées portent le nom de Jacques Prévert.

Qu'est-ce qui a fait le succès de Jacques Prévert ? Sa poésie du quotidien, son hymne permanent à la liberté de penser et de parler, et bien sûr son style : jeux de mots, lieux communs, stéréotypes, inventions burlesques, jeux sur les sons, humour, Jacques Prévert cuisine sa poésie avec tous ces ingrédients. *Paroles* (1945), *Histoires* (1946), *Spectacle* (1951), *La pluie et le beau temps* (1955), et *Fatras* (1966) forment l'itinéraire poétique de Jacques Prévert.

Mis en musique par Joseph Kosma, les poèmes de Prévert ont été aussi popularisés par des interprètes comme Juliette Greco (« Barbara », « Je suis comme je suis ») ou Yves Montand (« Les Feuilles mortes ») et chantés aussi en anglais. Vous pouvez lire un poème de Prévert dans la section *Lecture thématique*.

---

exemplaire *copy*

Reference Desk

1. Apollinaire, the founding father of Surrealism, lived during the time that saw the function of art transformed from representational to abstract and expressive. The range of his poetry straddles both purposes and, were it not for his untimely death in 1918, he would probably have worked with André Breton and the group that created the three Surrealist Manifestos, published between 1924 and 1929. Apollinaire is buried in the Père Lachaise Cemetery in Paris.
   A **caligramme** is a word created by Apollinaire by combining **calligraphie** and **idéogramme**. It refers to a poem whose words are arranged to take the physical shape of their theme.
2. Prévert's poems are often short and use a simplicity of language that may render his work more comprehensible and accessible to students.

Communication

Interpersonal: Paired Practice

In partners, students will compare "**Demain, dès l'aube**" with "**Automne**" using the following headings: Title, Author, Theme, Speaker, and References to Nature. What do these poems have in common? How do they differ? Replicate the chart on the board, and ask each pair of students to share what they have discussed.

Connections

Drawing

Have students study more of Apollinaire's **Calligrammes** and then have them create a calligram of their own with or without rhyme. The words of their piece should be artfully placed in the shape of the item that is the topic.

Differentiated Learning

Accelerate

Give students an abbreviated outline of an **explication de texte**, and ask them to apply it to the poem of Victor Hugo or Guillaume Apollinaire.

Decelerate

Work in small groups with low-ability students to analyze the two poems. They will need help extracting the meaning.

Multiple Intelligences

Visual-Spatial

Students will find romantic abstract paintings that would seem to illustrate the mood and setting of the poems by Hugo and Apollinaire.

Answers

6

1. des sonnets d'amour
2. de la vieillesse
3. « Les Fables de La Fontaine »
4. Il lui apprend que si on est fier, cela nous joue un tour.
5. des poèmes, des romans et des pièces de théâtre
6. le cimetière ; Il va poser des fleurs sur une tombe
7. le surréalisme
8. l'amour, la jeunesse, le temps, les émotions
9. adorable personne, cou exquis, buste adoré
10. des jeux de mots, des lieux communs, des stéréotypes, des inventions burlesques, des jeux sur les sons, de l'humour
11. Il écrit des poèmes populaires sur les choses quotidiennes de la vie.

Connections

Music

Many students have seen the musical theater production or the movie based on Hugo's novel ***Les Misérables***. What elements in this work would reflect the romantic desire to express feelings such as love, anger, revenge, and loyalty?

6 La poésie française 1.2, 1.3, 3.1

Répondez aux questions suivantes.

Ronsard

1. Ronsard a écrit quelle sorte de poésie ?
2. De quoi Ronsard avertit (*warns*) la jeune fille dans son poème ?

La Fontaine

3. La Fontaine est surtout connu pour quel recueil ?
4. Qu'est-ce que le renard apprend au corbeau ?

Hugo

5. Qu'est-ce que Victor Hugo a écrit ?
6. Quelle est la destination du narrateur dans le poème ? Qu'est-ce qu'il va y faire ?

Apollinaire

7. Apollinaire a commencé quel mouvement littéraire ?
8. Quels étaient ses thèmes ?
9. Dans le calligramme d'Apollinaire, quels mots le poète utilise-t-il pour complimenter la personne ?

Prévert

10. Qu'est-ce qu'on trouve dans la poésie de Prévert ?
11. Pourquoi peut-on dire que les poèmes de Prévert touchent les étudiants ?

Essential Instruction

1. As a bell-ringer activity, review the themes of the three poems in **Leçon C**. Read lines of each poem aloud and see if students can recognize the poet.
2. Use the questions in **La poésie française** as the basis of an expanded class discussion of the three poetic styles.
3. Students will make a timeline from the 16th century to the present marking La Fontaine, Hugo, Apollinaire, and Prévert, or they can add to a previous timeline. Encourage students to amplify the timeline with more literary and historical figures and events.
4. Have students draw a star. In the center they write **la Pléiade**. Radiating from the star like beams of light students will write the names of the seven poets of this movement.
5. In the same vein, students draw a heart. In the center they write **le romantisme**. Radiating from the heart students will write the characteristics of romanticism: **le moi**, **l'émotion**, **la nature**, **l'imagination**, and **l'amour**.

Pre-AP

Question centrale ? Comment l'art est-il un reflet de la culture ?

La Pléiade

1.2, 3.1

Le village de Grignan, au sud de la France, date du 16ème siècle.

C'est au 16ème siècle que la Pléiade, un groupe de sept poètes, a vu le jour. La Pléiade va commencer un renouvellement* de la littérature française. Pierre de Ronsard, Joachim du Bellay, Jacques Peletier du Man, Rémy Belleau, Antoine de Baïf, Pontus de Tyard, et Étienne Jodelle veulent enrichir et défendre la langue et la littérature françaises par la redécouverte de la culture antique, et combattre l'ignorance populaire par l'art et la connaissance. La Pléiade désigne* le groupe des poètes, mais aussi leur mouvement poétique, dont la maxime* *carpe diem*, une expression latine, signifie* « Cueille le jour sans te soucier* de quoi demain sera fait ». Cette règle morale est bien illustrée dans le poème « À Cassandre. »

Recherche : la pléiade, poèmes ronsard

renouvellement *renewal* ; **désigne** *designates* ; **maxime** *saying* ; **signifie** *means* ; **soucier** *to worry*

Le romantisme de Victor Hugo

1.2, 2.2, 3.1

Victor Hugo était le chef du mouvement du romantisme. Les romantiques voulaient rompre avec* les strictes règles du classicisme et se concentrer sur les sentiments. Hugo a dit : « Tout est sujet, tout relève* de l'art ; tout a droit de citer en poésie. » L'historien Stéphane Guégan dit que le romantisme « … met l'homme et l'artiste devant un destin improbable et inquiétant… Le réel, que les romantiques rendent expressif, dramatique, l'emporte sur le beau idéal ».

Recherche : le romantisme, victor hugo biographie, poèmes victor hugo

rompre avec *to break from* ; **relève** *rises up*

1.2, 4.2

Comparaisons

Il y a un grand nombre de poètes anglophones qui faisaient partie d'un groupe. Par exemple, il y avait les poètes américains noirs de la Renaissance de Harlem. Quel était leur but principal ?

Resources

Points de départ

WB Workbook 5

Answers

Comparaison

Ils voulaient renouveler la culture afro-américaine à travers l'art.

Reference Desk

If you have access to Passport, find a video about **le sud de la France**, or a news article related to **la poésie** and show it to your students. Victor Hugo's poem **"Après la Bataille"** can be read by students and well captures Guégan's description of **Romantisme**. Its opening lines were used as the title of a comedy starring Gérard Depardieu, **"Mon père ce héros"** (1991, remade in English as "My Father the Hero," 1994, also starring Depardieu).

Expansion

Students in groups will present one of the following poems from Prévert's collection *Paroles*: **"Page d'écriture," "Barbara," "Le Temps Perdu," "Le Bouquet," "Chez la fleuriste," "Pour toi, mon amour," "le Cancre," "La Grasse Matinée,"** or **"Déjeuner du Matin."** Encourage students to watch online readings of these poems for pronunciation. They will make copies of the poems for the class. Students will read their poem to the class and explain how the main idea of the poem is expressed through the choice of language. The unifying question students will answer is: How do these poems describe the struggles of everyday life?

Special Needs Students

Linguistically Challenged

Spend some time teaching pre-reading techniques before asking students to read difficult passages. Encourage them to skim for information, look for cognates, and read without looking up every word in the dictionary.

Reference Desk

1. To explain Surrealism, ask students if they have ever had a weird dream that, while it was taking place, made perfect sense. It is only upon awaking, in the rational light of day, that the dream seemed bizarre. The Surrealists tried to capture that unconscious reality of the dream and the unconscious for inspiration in their art. Show students the works of the Belgian Surrealist painter Matisse or the etchings of M.C. Escher. These works will be more accessible to students since they represent real objects in an impossible reality, much like dreams.
2. The Surrealist movement, under the leadership of André Breton, was composed of a group of artists, writers, and musicians. It was a revolt against rationalism and a celebration of the dream, the unconscious, and what is random, as a way to finding new truth. Recounting dreams, or writing whatever came into their head without censure, became the inspiration which lead to a new reality, a sur-reality. Dali's painting *Persistence of Memory* illustrates how the dream, the illogical juxtaposition of objects, creates a strong sensation in the viewer. Apollinaire's ***Calligrames*** is another example of this new expression. Marc Chagall, who was a Russian, French, and Jewish painter, depended on the dreamscapes in his iconic Surrealist works.
3. Haiti, an island country in the Caribbean Sea, is the first black-led independent nation of Latin America. It gained independence in 1804 after a ten-year slave revolt. In 2004, former president Aristide was sent into exile by a **coup d'état**, and a provisional government was established. Since then, Haiti has had three democratically elected presidents: René Préval (2006–2011), Michel Martelly (2011–2016), and Jovenel Moïse (elected for the first time in 2017).

Le surréalisme 1.2, 3.1

Le surréalisme est un mouvement littéraire et artistique né après la Première Guerre mondiale*. Le but de ces écrivains était de refuser toutes les constructions logiques de l'esprit, de valoriser* l'irrationnel, l'absurde, le rêve, le désir, et la révolte. André Breton, un des pères du surréalisme, le définit comme « l'absence de tout contrôle exercé par la raison ».

Recherche : surréalisme littéraire, surréalisme artistique, calligrammes apollinaire

Première Guerre mondiale *World War I* ; **valoriser** *promote*

1.2, 2.2

Produits

Chez Apollinaire, l'idéal surréaliste se voit dans sa poésie, notamment ses **calligrammes**, des poèmes écrits en forme de dessins comme « La cravate ».

Recherche : apollinaire le miroir, calligrammes

La Première Guerre mondiale (et surtout les batailles désastrueuses, comme à Verdun) a drastiquement changé le mode de pensée de la société française.

La Francophonie

La poésie

En Haïti 1.2, 3.1, 4.2

La tradition littéraire en Haïti est très riche. L'histoire d'Haïti est souvent le sujet de poèmes, écrits soit en français, soit en créole. James Noël, poète-écrivain, est considéré aujourd'hui comme une voix majeure de la littérature haïtienne. Il écrit en créole et en français. Voici l'un de ses poèmes :

Le nom qui m'appelle

Je suis celui qui se lave les mains
Avant d'écrire
Ne me demande pas comment je m'appelle
Je n'ai pas de nom
Je viens de là
De ce non-lieu qui cherche lune*
Pour s'exhumer* de son point d'ombre*
Un nom d'auteur me fait bien mal
Parce que poète
Ça m'est égal
Ni tapis rouge ne saura rendre
La justesse du sang* qui me fait
Passer
Pour un vitrier* qui vaut* sa mort
Je suis saigné*
Donc
Je me lave
Voilà mon nom qui vient de là

qui cherche lune *looking for the moon* ; **s'exhumer** *disappear* ; **son point d'ombre** *his shadow* ; **sang** *blood* ; **vitrier** *glazier* ; **vaut** *deserves* ; **saigné** *bled (like an animal)*

Essential Instruction

1. Students investigate Surrealism by using the search words provided in the textbook.
2. Ask students to define Surrealism and to explain, from their reading, how and why it evolved.
3. Students read "**Le nom qui m'appelle**." What is "the name" that calls the poet? Why does the poet wash his hands?
4. Have a class discussion about the fifth question, the vocation of the poet in James Noël's poem, using precise examples from the text.
5. Give students 15 minutes to answer the first three questions of **Activités culturelles**. If students are not familiar with ***Notre-Dame de Paris*** have them substitute ***Les Misérables***.
6. For the second question, ask students what English expressions might communicate the **carpe diem** attitude. ("You only live once," "It's now or never," "Go for it.")
7. Students show a **calligramme** of their choosing to the class. You might want to post them in the classroom.

7 Activités culturelles 1.1, 1.3, 3.1, 3.2, 5.1

Complétez les activités suivantes.

1. Associez un poète à chaque tendance littéraire :
   - la vie moderne
   - les sentiments amoureux
   - le thème *carpe diem*
   - le désir de valoriser l'irrationnel
2. Dites où vous avez déjà rencontré le thème du *carpe diem*—un poème, une chanson, un film, une émission de télé ?
3. Même si vous n'avez pas lu *Notre-Dame de Paris* de Victor Hugo, vous en connaissez certainement certains détails. Remplissez ce schéma :
   - milieu
   - période
   - intrigue
   - conflit
4. Cherchez des images de *Calligrammes* d'Apollinaire et choisissez-en une que vous allez expliquer à la classe.
5. Parlez avec votre partenaire de ce que James Noël révèle de l'identité haïtienne dans son poème.

Perspectives 1.2, 2.1

Dans son roman *Les Misérables*, Victor Hugo a dit : « On jugerait bien plus sûrement un homme d'après ce qu'il rêve que d'après ce qu'il pense. » Ce sentiment reflète la philosophie de quel(s) mouvement(s) littéraire(s) ?

Carpe diem fait partie du message du film américain tiré de ce roman (*Dead Poets Society*).

Pour James Noël et de nombreux auteurs haïtiens, le héros doit être révolutionnaire.

Answers

7

1. vie moderne : Noël, Prévert ; sentiments amoureux : Hugo, Ronsard ; thème *carpe diem* : Ronsard, Du Bellay, Pelletier du Man, Belleau, de Baïf, de Tyard, Jodelle ; désir de valoriser l'irrationnel : Apollinaire
2. Answers will vary.
3. milieu : la cathédrale Notre-Dame de Paris ; période : 15ème siècle ; intrigue : Un jeune poète écrit une pièce sans succès, mais observe une véritable histoire d'amour se dérouler devant ses yeux. ; conflit : Le vilain Quasimodo enlève la belle Esmeralda et va être jugé.
4. Presentations will vary.
5. Discussions will vary.

Perspectives

du romantisme et du surréalisme

Game

Le Cadavre Exquis

Surrealist artists would meet to play the parlor game **le cadavre exquis**. By randomly assembling words, new meaning can be achieved. The first sentence that was created by the Surrealists was **"Le cadavre exquis boira le vin nouveau,"** thus the title of the game. Start a sheet of paper for each row of students. This piece of paper will pass from student to student. Ask the first student, without thinking, to write a noun. The paper is folded horizontally so that the second student cannot see what is written. The next student writes an adjective, and folds the paper again. The third student writes a verb, and folds the paper to cover the word, and the fourth student an adverb. The paper is unfolded and the sentence is read aloud. Sometimes it makes no sense, but often there is a random logic.

Differentiated Learning

Accelerate

Students can research and write a response to the questions from the lesson: **"La Première Guerre Mondiale a dramatiquement changé le mode de pensée de la société française. Pourquoi ?"**

Decelerate

Have students read a brief history of Haiti to answer these questions based on the lesson: Why does James Noël believe that the hero should be a revolutionary? What in the history of Haiti might lead him to this opinion?

Multiple Intelligences

Visual-Spatial

Students may want to investigate the work of two Surrealistic painters, Magritte and Dali. Then they can make a collage of their own creation using photos and drawings of dissimilar objects to replicate the Surrealistic style.

Answers

8 Answers will vary.

Reference Desk

The winners from previous years of the **Prix Poésie en liberté** are available for free on the Internet by searching "**poésie en liberté recueil**" and the year you are seeking. Students may enjoy reading poetry writen by francophone peers.

Expansion

Organize your own **Concours de poésie** with your class. Give students some guidelines and ask them to write a poem in French. They may choose a sonnet, an ode, or free verse. Have a vote and be sure to prepare prizes for the best poems. If possible, team up with another French teacher and plan this event across several classes. You may want to add categories or levels to encourage students of all abilities.

Du côté des médias 1.2, 3.1

Lisez le programme pour Poésie en liberté.

Le Prix Poésie en liberté est un concours international de poésie en langue française. Il s'adresse aux jeunes de 15 à 25 ans de tous les pays. Il se déroule sur internet autour d'un sujet libre. Les éditions Le Temps des Cerises publient chaque année une anthologie.

L'association « Poésie en liberté » pilote l'opération sous l'autorité du ministère chargé de l'éducation, en collaboration avec le réseau Canopé de Créteil, et avec le soutien du rectorat de l'académie de Créteil.

- Modalités de participation au prix Poésie en liberté
- Qui peut participer?
- Calendrier du prix Poésie en liberté
- Palmarès 2017

POÉSIE EN LIBERTÉ

EN SAVOIR PLUS

Modalités de participation au prix Poésie en liberté

Le concours se déroule sur le site www.poesie-en-liberte.com
Le participant **envoie un poème inédit, en vers ou en prose, de 30 vers ou lignes maximum.**
En 2018, sont également acceptés des poèmes en esperanto.
La participation est limitée à un seul poème par candidat.
Un comité de lecture établit un choix d'environ 300 textes qui sont soumis au jury. Ce comité se compose :

des organisateurs	de professionnels de l'édition
de professionnels de la culture	de professionnels de l'éducation
de lycéens d'étudiants	de poètes

Le jury est composé de onze lycéens et étudiants de France et de l'étranger. Les lauréats de l'année précédente peuvent être membres du jury. Il est présidé par un poète assisté de deux organisateurs du concours.
Le jury établit le palmarès et propose une sélection pour l'anthologie annuelle du concours.

Qui peut participer?

Le concours est ouvert aux :

- lycéens et étudiants en France
- lycéens des établissements français à l'étranger
- lycéens des pays francophones et non francophones
- apprentis
- élèves bénéficiant d'un projet personnalisé de scolarisation
- étudiants en France jusqu'à 25 ans

Le palmarès national et international comprend **neuf catégories**.

Sites à consulter

Poésie en liberté
Concours 2017–18, modalités de participation, palmarès, calendrier, règlement, etc.
Poésie en liberté

Éduscol
Le portail national des professionnels de l'éducation

- La poésie à l'école
- Dossier à télécharger

La poésie à l'école

Le Printemps des Poètes
Le Printemps des Poètes assume tout au long de l'année un rôle de centre de ressources permanent pour la poésie par l'information, le conseil, la formation et le soutien à la création.
Le Printemps des Poètes

CRDP de l'académie de Créteil
La poésie dans la littérature de jeunesse
Fiche pédagogique
Fiche pédagogique poésie

8 Poésie en liberté 1.3

Faites les activités suivantes.

1. Écrivez un sommaire qui décrit le concours (*contest*), expliquez qui peut y participer, et expliquez les règles.
2. Écrivez un poème pour ce concours et proposez-le.

Essential Instruction

1. Students read **Prix poésie en liberté** in small groups and define the following terms: **Le Printemps des Poètes**, **Le Temps des Cérises**, **le CRDP de Créteil**, **un lauréat**, **un palmarès**. Encourage them to use the context of the text to guess a meaning before looking it up.
2. Students complete **Poésie en liberté**.
3. Compare the **sommaires** of the different groups to decide which group wrote the most comprehensive summary.
4. Students read **Académie Goncourt** in class. Preview any vocabulary or expressions that might give them trouble.
5. Have students answer the questions in **Le Goncourt des Lycéens**.
6. In correcting their work, students cite the lines from the reading that gave them the information.

Lisez l'article sur le prix Goncourt des Lycéens. 1.2

Académie Goncourt

Accueil > Le Goncourt des Lycéens

Présentation

Le Prix Goncourt des Lycéens offre au public un choix défendu avec engagement et passion par de jeunes lecteurs à partir de la sélection de romans effectuée en septembre par l'Académie Goncourt.

Lancé en 1988 dans une dizaine de lycées bretons, ce prix, maintenant national, est organisé par la Fnac et le Ministère de l›Éducation Nationale, en coopération avec l'Académie Goncourt, pour donner aux jeunes l'envie de la lecture, le goût de l'écriture et du partage des idées.

Cinquante-deux classes de lycéens âgés de 15 à 18 ans, issus de seconde, première, terminale ou BTS, généralistes, scientifiques ou techniques, lisent et étudient en deux mois, avec l'aide de leurs professeurs et l'Association Bruit de Lire, la douzaine de romans de la sélection de rentrée de l'Académie.

La Fnac offre l'ensemble des livres dès la rentrée. Les classes et leurs professeurs sont ensuite invités à rencontrer les auteurs de la sélection.

À l'issue de ce marathon incluant lecture, fiches et débats, a lieu la première phase du vote (chaque région choisissant ses représentants et son tiercé de livres gagnants), à laquelle succède la finale à Rennes, berceau du Prix, en présence des représentants de l'Académie Goncourt.

À ce jour 17150 élèves ont été associés au prix et 37604 exemplaires de 216 romans contemporains différents ont été lus.

Le Goncourt des lycéens étant maintenant décerné quelques jours après le prix Goncourt proprement dit, il est rare aujourd'hui que les deux couronnent le même livre (ce qui s'était assez souvent produit dans le passé, d'Erik Orsenna en 1988 à Andreï Makine en 1995).

9 Le Goncourt des Lycéens 1.2

*Indiquez si la phrase est vraie (**V**) ou fausse (**F**). Changez les phrases qui sont fausses pour qu'elles soient vraies.*

1. Le Prix Goncourt des Lycéens est un prix que les lycéens gagnent.
2. Le prix des lycéens a débuté en Bretagne.
3. Le but du prix est de donner aux jeunes l'envie de la lecture, le goût de l'écriture, et du partage des idées.
4. Chaque année, une douzaine de romans est considérée par des lecteurs adultes.
5. Les lycéens choisissent souvent le même livre que les adultes choisissent dans le prix Goncourt traditionnel.

Resources

Du côté des médias
Activity 9

Answers

9

1. F; C'est un prix que les lycéens donnent aux romanciers.
2. V
3. V
4. V
5. F; Il est rare aujourd'hui que les deux couronnent le même livre.

Reference Desk

1. The **Académie Goncourt** was founded by Edmond de Goncourt (1822–1896) to encourage literature and reading. The **Prix Goncourt** is awarded yearly for best fiction. **Le Prix Goncourt des lycéens** invites high school students to vote for their favorite work.
2. Ask students to guess the name of the national award given to the best fiction in the United States, which would correspond to the **Prix Goncourt**. (Pulitzer Prize for fiction). Have them research whether or not there exists a literary prize awarded by (not for) high school students in the United States, in the same manner as the **Prix Goncourt des lycéens** in France.

Expansion

Have students prepare their own "**Prix des lycéens**" in your school or classroom, asking students to read a series of the same current books and rate them. If possible, have students write a letter to the the winning author.

Special Needs Students

Linguistically Challenged/Dyslexia
The readings on pp. 424 and 425 are challenging. Students may feel overwhelmed at first. While the high-ability students are composing a poem, you might want to read these passages with students, paragraph by paragraph, asking general comprehension questions. In each paragraph, ask which words they think are important. What do they think the paragraph is about? Continue on to the next paragraph until readings are completed.

Answers

All activities will vary.

Reference Desk

1. **Afin de** is a synonym for **pour** (when it means *in order to*), and both French expressions may be used interchangeably. Both are followed by the infinitive.
2. For **Activité 11**, you may want to vet the student choices as they decide, before the students get too deep into a choice that is unsuitable to read, watch, listen to, or show.

Culture sur place

Question centrale ? Comment l'art est-il un reflet de la culture?

La musique française 4.2

Introduction et interrogations

Écouter de la musique est l'un des loisirs favoris des adolescents dans le monde entier. Quel lien y a-t-il entre la musique que vous écoutez et la musique préférée des jeunes en France?

10 Imaginer et observer 1.3, 2.2, 4.2

Écrivez trois hypothèses concernant la musique que les jeunes Français aiment. Aiment-ils écouter de la musique exclusivement en français, en anglais, ou bien dans d'autres langues? Les chansons populaires françaises parlent de quoi? Les thèmes de la musique française ressemblent-ils à ceux de la musique américaine? Sont-ils un reflet de la culture française ou de la culture des jeunes, ou des deux?

11 Rechercher 1.2, 3.1, 3.2, 5.1

Sur Internet, recherchez la chanson populaire en France.

1. Utilisez un outil de recherche et tapez les mots « Top 50 chansons », « Top 50 musique », « Top Tubes France », ou « Top Hits France. »
2. Examinez la liste des chansons. Surtout, notez la langue et le pays de l'interprète. Combien de chansons est-ce que vous reconnaissez? Combien d'interprètes? Combien de chansons sont en français?
3. Avec l'aide de votre professeur, choisissez une chanson française de la liste.
4. Recherchez les paroles de la chanson avec l'aide d'un outil de recherche.
5. Lisez les paroles et essayez d'en comprendre le sens.
6. Écoutez la chanson ou regardez la vidéo si elle est disponible sur Internet.

12 Faire l'inventaire! 1.1, 4.2, 5.2

Discutez des questions suivantes en classe.

1. Que pensez-vous de la chanson populaire parmi les jeunes en France?
2. Est-ce que vos hypothèses/observations étaient correctes? Pourquoi, ou pourquoi pas?
3. Comparez la musique populaire en France et chez vous. Est-ce que les chansons sont plutôt similaires ou différentes? Pourquoi, selon vous?
4. Que pensez-vous des paroles de la chanson française que vous avez choisie? Y a-t-il des chansons que vous connaissez sur le même thème en anglais? Comment s'appellent-elles?

Essential Instruction

1. Have students read through all the instructions to assure they understand the assignment.
2. For **Activité 10**, put students in groups to write hypotheses about French music. Post these hypotheses on a wall for the entirety of this project.
3. For **Activité 11**, second question, suggest that the students create a chart with the headings **site**, **titre**, **artiste**, **pays** to identify the top ten songs from each website. Organizing the information will come in handy when discussing music tastes of young French people. As students collect data about songs, have them listen to samples online to find their favorites from which you will help them choose their key song.
4. Students return to the same groups that they were in for step one, in order to complete **Activité 12**.
5. Review **pour** + INFINITIVE to express purpose.
6. Students do **Pour** + INFINITIF orally as a class activity. Ask them to generate more sentences with **pour** or **afin de**.

Structure de la langue

Révision: Pour + INFINITIVE 1.2

In sentences where the subject is the same in both clauses, use **pour** followed by an infinitive to express *in order to*.

Je suis allé(e) à la librairie **pour** trouver un recueil de Prévert.	*I went to the bookstore (in order) to find a collection by Prévert.*

13 Pour + INFINITIF 1.2, 1.3

Interpretive Reading, Presentational Speaking or Writing

Faites des phrases avec **pour** + INFINITIF. *Suivez le modèle.*

pouvoir offrir un cadeau d'anniversaire **apprendre à jouer de la guitare** **rester en forme** **mieux apprécier les tableaux au musée** **parler français** **faire du bricolage** **faire du ski alpin** **réveillonner avec sa famille**

MODÈLE je (acheter une carte cadeau)
J'achète une carte cadeau pour pouvoir offrir un cadeau d'anniversaire.

1. les étudiants américains (voyager en France)
2. tu (suivre un cours d'art)
3. Mégane et Sébastien (suivre des cours de musique)
4. je (faire du sport)
5. Saskia (faire une dinde aux marrons)
6. Éric et toi (fréquenter les stations de ski)
7. mes copains et moi (acheter un pot de peinture)

Comparaisons 4.1

In English, what form of the verb is used after "in order"?

Je lis **pour me renseigner.**
I read in order to be informed.

Myriam apprend le piano pour devenir chanteuse et interprète.

Resources

WB Workbook 6
LA Listening Activity 2
G & V Practice Games

Answers

13

1. Les étudiants américains voyagent en France pour parler français.
2. Tu suis un cours d'art pour mieux apprécier les tableaux au musée.
3. Mégane et Sébastien suivent des cours de musique pour apprendre à jouer de la guitare.
4. Je fais du sport pour rester en forme.
5. Saskia fait une dinde aux marrons pour réveillonner avec sa famille.
6. Éric et toi, vous fréquentez les stations de ski pour faire du ski alpin.
7. Mes copains et moi, nous achetons un pot de peinture pour faire du bricolage.

Comparaisons
As in French, the infinitive is used after the English phrase *in order*.

Expansion

Ask students to prepare a list of sentences with **pour**, such as **"Je suis allé à la poste ce matin pour acheter des timbres."** Group students and have them ask each other questions: **"Pourquoi est-ce que je suis allé à la poste ce matin?"** Other students will attempt to find the reason: **"Pour peser un colis? Pour rencontrer le postier? Pour arriver à l'école en retard?"** (etc.)

Differentiated Learning

Accelerate
Have students translate a French song they like. Remind them that they will be looking for equivalent expressions, not a word-for-word translation.

Decelerate
Pour + INFINITIVE is a simple concept that low-ability students can master easily. Consider giving them a "feel good" quiz on the concept to boost their confidence and their average. Review or provide the meaning of the expressions and the conjugations of the verbs in **Activité 13**.

Multiple Intelligences

Musical-Rhythmic
Many of your students play a musical instrument. Encourage them to get the sheet music for a song in French that they like and perform the music in class or make a video of their performance.

Mathematical-Logical
Students who love analysis can graph comparative statistics about French and American taste in music. Have them investigate five years of **NRJ** music awards.

Resources

WB Workbook 7–9

G & V Practice Games

Expansion

With white boards, students will practice the regular and irregular subjunctive with **il faut**. You will say, "**aller/tu**," for example; students will make the sentence: **Il faut que tu ailles**. Write the answer on the board so that students can correct. As a variation, you can put students in pairs to write the verb and assign points for correct forms.

Subjunctive after *pour que* 1.2

Les musiciens jouent beaucoup pour que la ville de Lyon veuille les inviter à leur festival.

You have already learned that the subjunctive is used after many different expressions.

Expressions	French	English
necessity	**Il faut que** tu **lises** la poésie de Ronsard.	*You need to read Ronsard's poetry.*
impersonal expressions	**Il est bon qu'**il **comprenne** la satire.	*It is good that he understand satire.*
wish, will, or desire	Notre prof **exige que** nous **étudiions** les sonnets.	*Our teacher requires that we study sonnets.*
doubt or uncertainty	**Croyez-vous qu'**Hugo **soit** plus intéressant qu'Apollinaire ?	*Do you believe that Hugo is more interesting than Apollinaire ?*
emotion	**Ça me surprend qu'**ils n'**aillent** pas lire les fables.	*It surprises me that they aren't going to read the fables.*

Pour que expresses a purpose. It is used with the subjunctive when the subject of the first clause is different from that of the second clause.

Je discute des fables avec Marco **pour qu'**il **puisse** comprendre les morales. — *I'm discussing the fables with Marco so that he can understand the morals.*

Maman a caché les cadeaux **pour que** les enfants ne les **voient** pas. — *Mom hid the gifts so that the children don't see them.*

Essential Instruction

1. Display a screen with two columns. In one column, write various actions (such as **arroser les plantes** and **cuisiner un bon repas**). Then ask the class why people do those actions and who benefits from them, and write that information in a second column (for example: **Ma mère est contente**). Finally, combine the sentences, using **pour que** + SUBJUNCTIVE: **Tu arroses les plantes pour que ta mère soit contente.**
2. Do **Activité 14** and **Activité 15**. Pair students to do **Activité 16**. You may have advanced students write additional sentences.

14 Les gens que je connais 1.2, 1.3

Interpretive Reading, Presentational Speaking or Writing

*Lisez la citation et la phrase qui suit. Ensuite, formez des phrases avec **pour que** selon le modèle.*

MODÈLE Ma tante : « Il faut que tu connaisses ton pays. » Elle m'a inscrit à une visite guidée des châteaux de la Loire.
Ma tante m'a inscrit(e) à une visite guidée des châteaux de la Loire pour que je connaisse mon pays.

1. Maman : « Je voudrais que tu fasses les courses. » Elle m'a donné 50 euros.
2. Ma grand-mère : « Il faut que tu me parles chaque semaine. » Elle m'a offert un portable.
3. Mon copain : « Je doute que tu sois engagé(e). » Il m'a donné le lien du site des Jeunes verts.
4. Ma cousine : « Il est essentiel que tu m'accompagnes au concert de rock. » Elle m'a offert un billet de concert.
5. Mon oncle martiniquais : « Je veux que tu prépares une spécialité martiniquaise pour mon anniversaire. » Il m'a expliqué comment préparer les accras de morue.

15 *Pour ou Pour que ?* 1.2

Interpretive Listening

Écrivez les numéros 1–5 sur votre papier. Écoutez les phrases. Choisissez la réponse logique.

A. Pour que tu me prêtes le recueil que tu as caché.
B. Pour mieux comprendre le vocabulaire de la prose de Victor Hugo.
C. Pour que tu apprécies ses poèmes simples.
D. Pour se rappeler de sa jeunesse.
E. Pour montrer que les gens dans leurs œuvres ne sont pas heureux.

16 La lecture 1.2

Interpretive Reading

*Formez des phrases qui utilisent **pour que**.*

1. je (lire une fable de La Fontaine), mon neveu (apprendre la morale)
2. ma mère (me prêter un roman de Le Clézio), je (pouvoir voyager sans quitter mon fauteuil)
3. mon prof de littérature (nous montrer les calligrammes d'Apollinaire), nous (écrire des poèmes originaux)
4. mon grand-père (me recommander « À Cassandre »), je (apprécier ma jeunesse)

Resources

Activities 14–15

Answers

14

1. Maman m'a donné 50 euros pour que je fasse les courses.
2. Ma grand-mère m'a offert un portable pour que je lui parle chaque semaine.
3. Mon copain m'a donné le lien du site des Jeunes verts pour que je sois plus engagé(e).
4. Ma cousine m'a offert un billet de concert pour que je l'accompagne au concert de rock.
5. Mon oncle martiniquais m'a expliqué comment préparer les accras de morue pour que je prépare une spécialité martiniquaise pour son anniversaire.

15 **Script**

1. Pourquoi veux-tu que je lise les poèmes de Jacques Prévert?
2. Pourquoi Mamy regarde-t-elle son album de photos si souvent?
3. Pourquoi les poètes et les romanciers du 19ème siècle mettent-ils toujours le brouillard dans leurs œuvres?
4. Pourquoi regardes-tu ma collection de livres?
5. Pourquoi lis-tu le dictionnaire?

1. C; 2. D; 3. E; 4. A; 5. B

16

1. Je lis une fable de La Fontaine pour que mon neveu apprenne la morale.
2. Ma mère me prête un roman de Le Clézio pour que je puisse voyager sans quitter mon fauteuil.
3. Mon prof de littérature nous montre les caligrammes d'Apollinaire pour que nous écrivions des poèmes originaux.
4. Mon grand-père me recommande « À Cassandre » pour que j'apprécie ma jeunesse.

Game

Jeopardy!

Play Jeopardy! to reinforce the difference between **pour** + INFINITIVE and **pour que** + SUBJUNCTIVE. Write categories related to this unit (poetry, music, novels, singers, etc.). Prepare unfinished sentences such as **Le chanteur Boris Vian a écrit "Le déserteur" pour….** If students produce a sentence grammatically correct and logical, they mark points for their team.

Differentiated Learning

Accelerate

Have students play a timed verb review game to add some challenge to an online verb review.

Recherche : conjuguemos

Decelerate

Students may need to review the subjunctive if they have forgotten the formation and use. Giving them a one-page review sheet would help them see the big picture.

Multiple Intelligences

Visual-Spatial/Bodily-Kinesthetic

These students do well writing out the forms of the subjunctive.

Resources

CA Communicative Activities

Share

Answers

17 Poems will vary.

18

1. You can't choose the members of your family.; You can choose your friends but you can't choose your family.
2. Something done is pointless.; To labor in vain.
3. Nonproductive people enjoy a prosperous life thanks to the hard work of others.; To ride someone's coattails
4. Never.; When pigs fly.
5. An individual is relying on his or her legs to escape a bad situation.; Feet don't fail me now.
6. People who go first get ahead.; Early bird catches the worm.

19 Digital stories will vary.

Reference Desk

If you have access to Passport, create a question for your students to share their response to a communicative activity.

À vous la parole

Question centrale ? Comment l'art est-il un reflet de la culture?

Communiquez!

17 J'interprète un poème 1.2, 1.3, 3.1, 3.2, 5.2

Interpretive Reading, Presentational Speaking

Trouvez un poème francophone que vous aimez. Présentez ce poème devant votre classe. Soyez sûr(e) de (d'):

- choisir un poème de huit vers (*lines*) minimum.
- lire le poème plusieurs fois.
- chercher les mots que vous ne comprenez pas.
- écrire une introduction qui présente le titre, le nom du poète, et le sujet ou le thème du poème.
- pratiquer devant un miroir.

Recherche: prévert, baudelaire, rimbaud, apollinaire, hugo

18 En Haïti 1.2, 4.1, 4.2

Interpretive Writing

Vous avez appris qu'Haïti a une culture et une histoire très riches en traditions créoles. Voici des idiomes créoles avec leurs traductions littérales. En vous aidant d'Internet, cherchez une traduction qui explique mieux le sens. Enfin, recherchez une expression équivalente en anglais.

1. **Dwèt ou se pa'w, ou pa kab koupe'l jete**
   Literally: Your fingers are yours. You can't cut them off.
2. **Lave men, siye atè**
   Literally: Wash your hands, [only to] wipe them on the ground.
3. **Wòch nan chodyè goute grès gras a diri**
   Literally: Little rocks that get mixed with rice (during harvest) will taste the richness of grease thanks to the rice.
4. **Lè ti poul fè dan**
   Literally: When cows fly.
5. **Pye, sa'm te manje m'pat ba ou**
   Literally: Feet, what did I eat that I did not share with you?
6. **Pye kout pran devan**
   Literally: Short legs go first.

19 La poésie: Un conte numérique 1.3, 3.2, 5.1

Presentational Writing

Vous allez écrire un conte numérique (présentation digitale) en vous servant de six mots de vocabulaire de la *Leçon C* (par exemple: **cueillir**, **la vieillesse**, **un corbeau**, **un renard**, **mentir**, **l'aube**, **demeurer**, **le brouillard**, **cacher**). Après l'avoir écrit, choisissez des images et de la musique pour embellir (*to embellish*) votre conte. Finalement, mettez votre conte en ligne avec ceux de vos camarades de classe pour les comparer.

Essential Instruction

1. Offer students the choice of tasks **17**, **18**, or **19**.
2. Students who select **17** might be interested in Jacques Prévert's poems in the collection ***Paroles*** because the language is simple and modern. They will find many of the poems recorded online.
3. Challenge students who select **18** to try to work out the meanings and English equivalent idiomatic expressions themselves, before using online tools to help them.
4. Students who choose **19** should be encouraged to use their own sketches and photos, music they create with digital software, or selections from their own music library to make the story more personable and entertaining.
5. Have students find photos of Prévert to get a sense of his no-nonsense personality. They will read his biography to learn more about him.
6. Students will reproduce the grid in **Stratégie de lecture** in their notebooks to fill out as they read.

Lecture thématique

Pre-AP

Familiale

Rencontre avec l'auteur 1.2, 2.2, 3.1, 5.2

Jacques Prévert (1900–1977). Avec plus de 2,5 millions d'exemplaires vendus, *Paroles* (1945) est le recueil de poésie le plus lu en France. Il le doit à son langage émouvant (*moving*) et simple. Il le doit aussi au talent de Jacques Prévert dont la poésie est celle de la vie quotidienne, de l'humour, et de la facétie (*play on words*). Chaque poème est l'affirmation d'une exigence de liberté et proclame l'amour de la vie. Prévert y dénonce toutes les contraintes sociales. Qu'est-ce que le poète dénonce dans ce poème?

Pré-lecture 1.3

Avez-vous envie de faire la même chose que vos parents?

Stratégie de lecture 1.1, 1.2

Develop a Theme. Dans ce poème, on aborde (*approach*) le thème du conformisme. Prévert dénonce le conformisme en juxtaposant une série d'actions sans lien ni transition. Pendant la lecture du poème, remplissez la grille avec les actions décrites. S'agit-il d'une famille conformiste ou non-conformiste? Les émotions des personnages sont-elles bouleversantes (*overwhelmed*) ou monotones? Comment réagissent (*react*) la mère et le père quand leur fils meurt? Notez l'effet des répétitions.

Actions	Signification
La mère fait du tricot	Une femme typique qui fait ce qu'elle a appris à faire; ce n'est pas le genre de mère qui pleure quand son fils part pour l'armée; elle accepte son sort comme quelque chose de «naturel».

Outils de lecture 1.2

Recognize Oxymorons. Un oxymore est une alliance de mots dont le rapprochement est inattendu (*unexpected*). L'oxymore fait coexister deux termes de sens contraires à l'intérieur d'une même expression (par exemple, «un silence éloquent»). L'oxymore permet de donner une réalité à ce qui semble absurde. Quel oxymore remarquez-vous dans le dernier vers du poème? Quelles idées s'opposent? Quel est le sens de ce vers? Quel est le message du poète?

Differentiated Learning

Accelerate

Ask students to find other examples of non-conformist ideas in poems they have studied previously in this chapter.

Decelerate

Distribute a list of poems that students can pick from to help them with **Activité 17**. You may want to give them more specific guidelines for the introductory paragraph. To prepare students to analyze the poem, ask them what a normal reaction is, in their opinion, for parents to have when their son or daughter is killed in war.

Resources

Rencontre avec l'auteur

Answers

Rencontre avec l'auteur

Prévert dénonce la désensibilisation sociale à la mort et à la guerre.

Pré-lecture

Answers will vary.

Stratégie de lecture

«Le fils fait la guerre»
La juxtaposition avec la phrase précédente fait entendre que la guerre est une activité normale pour le fils, tout comme le tricot l'est pour la mère.
«Il [le père] fait les affaires» Le père a une responsabilité traditionnelle, chacue rôle des membres de la famille est vu comme une activité normale et de même importance.
«Elle trouve ça tout naturel, la mère./ Il trouve ça tout naturel, le père» Les parents ont accepté leur situation sans réaction particulière. Ils sont désensibilisés.
«Il ne trouve absolument rien, le fils» Le fils fait son devoir de soldat comme un automate.
«Quand il aura fini la guerre [...]»
La vie de l'homme est une vie répétitive et impersonnelle.
«Le fils est tué il ne continue plus»
La mort est décrite comme si elle n'avait pas de conséquences affectives, morales, ou psychologiques.
«La mère et le père vont au cimetière»
L'auteur ne parle pas des sentiments des parents. La mort et la vie sont traitées de façon équivalente.
«La vie et le cimetière»
Cette juxtaposition est un oxymore, car la suite de la vie et de la mort (le cimetière) relève une contradiction: la mort du fils avant celle de ses parents est une suite illogique, contraire à la nature.
Le poète se sert des répétitions de vers pour montrer que le conformisme social créé la désensibilisation de l'être humain.

Outils de lecture

La vie et la mort sont l'opposition par excellence dans le monde humain, leur rapprochement crée une continuité. Le message que donne l'auteur est que la société en temps de guerre voit la mort (et la guerre) comme un phénomène naturel qui n'a pas de conséquences particulière sur les gens. Cette perspective désensibilise l'homme.

Resources

Familiale

Answers

Pendant la lecture

1. La mère tricote, le fils est à la guerre.
2. Elle trouve cela normal (i.e., elle n'est pas choquée, elle n'a pas peur).
3. Il fait des affaires, il gagne de l'argent.
4. Il succédera à son père.
5. Il meurt à la guerre.
6. Sa mort ne change pas du tout leur vie. Ils continuent à faire leurs affaires, ils y ont simplement ajouté l'activité d'aller au cimetière.
7. au cimetière

Culture

Products: Activity

Jacques Prévert was very involved in the Surrealist movement because of its political message against social powers. Find the poem "**Quartier libre**" online and explain with the class why this poem could be considered Surrealistic.

« Familiale »

La mère fait du tricot*
Le fils fait la guerre
Elle trouve ça tout naturel la mère
Et le père qu'est-ce qu'il fait le père ?
Il fait des affaires*
Sa femme fait du tricot
Son fils la guerre
Lui des affaires
Il trouve ça tout naturel le père
Et le fils et le fils
Qu'est-ce qu'il trouve le fils ?
Il ne trouve rien absolument rien le fils
Le fils sa mère fait du tricot son père des affaires et lui la guerre
Quand il aura fini* la guerre
Il fera des affaires avec son père
La guerre continue la mère continue elle tricote*
Le père continue il fait des affaires
Le fils est tué* il ne continue plus
La mère et le père vont au cimetière
Ils trouvent ça naturel le père et la mère
La vie continue la vie avec le tricot la guerre les affaires
Les affaires la guerre le tricot la guerre
Les affaires les affaires et les affaires
La vie et le cimetière.

Pendant la lecture
1. La mère et le fils font quelles activités ?

Pendant la lecture
2. Quelle est la réaction de la mère en voyant son fils en danger ?

Pendant la lecture
3. Que fait le père ?

Pendant la lecture
4. Que fera le fils dans l'avenir ?

Pendant la lecture
5. Qu'est-ce qui arrive au fils ?

Pendant la lecture
6. Comment est-ce que la mort de leur fils change la vie quotidienne des parents ?

Pendant la lecture
7. Où vont la mère et le père ?

fait du tricot *knits* ; **fait des affaires** *does business* ; **aura fini** *will have finished* ; **tricote** *knits* ; **tué** *killed*

Essential Instruction

1. Read "**Familiale**" in an exaggerated, monotonous voice to the students, accelerating the pace for the last four lines. The students will listen with books closed.
2. Ask students what the theme is. What did they notice about the poetic style and word usage?
3. Students will read the poem aloud in unison. This will make them very aware of repetition and rhyme.
4. Reread the poem stopping to ask the questions in the margin.
5. Use the **Post-lecture** question as a basis of discussing **le train-train** of this family's life, which never seems to change despite tragedy.
6. In small groups, have students analyze "**Avant la défaite**" and answer the questions that follow.
7. Debrief all groups, paying special attention to the last two questions in the series which should lead to more class discussion.

Post-lecture 1.2

Qu'ajoute au thème de Prévert l'usage du présent comme temps grammatical?

Le monde visuel 1.2, 3.1

Walter Limot, né Walter Lichtenstein (1902–1984), était photographe en Allemagne avant d'immigrer à Paris en 1933 pour fuir (*flee*) le régime Nazi. Là, il a contribué au progrès technique du cinéma français en travaillant avec de grands réalisateurs tels que Carné, Delannoy, Christian-Jacques Duvivier, et René-Clair. Il était expert en tout – trucages (effets spéciaux), solarisations (technique par laquelle on utilise la chaleur naturelle sur le film pour créér des effets spéciaux), découpages (la façon dont on coupe le film pour créér des effets dramatiques), montages (le choix et l'arrangement des éléments visuels et auditifs pour créér un film). Dans cette photographie de la Deuxième Guerre Mondiale, Limot utilise des images fantômes (*ghost*) pour représenter la vie d'une sentinelle (soldat qui surveille l'ennemi) près d'un rail. Comment est-ce que cette photographie vous aide à comprendre ce que dit Prévert au sujet du fils dans le poème?

Soldat, 1939. Walter Lichtenstein.

Stratégie

Combien de personnages sont mentionnés dans le poème de Prévert? Combien de personnages sont représentés dans la photographie? De qui s'agit-il? Pourquoi cette personne est-elle au centre de cette photo, et du poème?

Answers

Post-lecture

L'usage du présent simple ajoute une monotonie au poème, un aspect d'interminabilité (cela ne finit jamais), ou d'atemporalité, sans début ou sans fin (contrairement à l'usage du passé).

Le monde visuel

Possible answer:
Cette photographie représente la mort comme une ombre qui saisit le soldat, mais à laquelle le soldat ne fait pas attention. Il est là sans prendre conscience que la mort est un danger, une fatalité ; il l'accepte comme son propre reflet, comme les personnages du poème de Prévert l'acceptent.

Stratégie

trois ; un ; le jeune homme mort ; pour insister sur l'importance de la mort

Reference Desk

During WWII, Prévert sought refuge in Nice and participated in acts of resistance, helping to hide two Jewish friends (Joseph Kosma, a composer who put many of Prévert's works to music, and Alexandre Traunier, an actor who starred in films by Prévert's brother, Pierre). Prévert also wrote the script for "**Les Enfants du paradis**," a clandestine film produced during the war as an allegory of its evils, considered by many to be the greatest French film of all time and the French cinematic response to the American *Gone With the Wind*. The war was also the period during which he composed most of ***Paroles***, which was first published in 1946 and cemented Prévert's fame.

Connections

History

Ask students to review the main events of World War II, being sure to remind them which countries were occupied by Germany for the duration of the war. Ask students to compare the effects of the war on French citizens, who were occupied and had to choose to resist, collaborate, or ignore, and American citizens, who watched (with concern) their country's involvement from a distance.

Differentiated Learning

Accelerate

Students will write an essay about the collage of "Soldat, 1939" it relates to the theme of war.

Decelerate

Have students practice reading "**Familiale**" to later recite it for you. Encourage them to find an online poetry recitation to help with pronunciation and intonation. Have students describe their family routine and compare it to the routine described in the poem.

Learning Styles

Visual Learners

Project the poem and use two different color highlights to underline repetitions and oxymorons, or questions and answers, or use three colors and underline actions corresponding to each character.

Multiple Intelligences

Bodily-Kinesthetic

Students could make a dramatic video acting out the poem "**Familiale**," or another poem by Prévert, such as "**Le Cancre**."

Reference Desk

This section is designed for students to apply unit vocabulary and structures to communicative activities that foster 21st-century skills. These activities demonstrate how 21st-century skills are cultivated in the language classroom and how these skills and the language learning process are mutually beneficial.

French in the Workplace

France is the most visited country in the world in large part because of its art museums and works. As English speakers, students may seek work giving art tours in French, and in English to English-speaking tourists in France or another French-speaking country. Have them select one museum in France, choose one or two of its most significant works, and prepare a two-to-three-minute presentation on each of them, talking about the artist, the content of the painting, the style in which it is painted, and its significance in art history. Then, using media, have them give a virtual tour in English for a group of students, such as an Art class that you may invite, and in French to a French class. You may pair students who are interested in the same works of art.

Social Justice

For hundreds of years, artists have used their work to spread messages about important issues. Eye-catching artwork can help start a dialogue about social justice, as well as raise awareness for political candidates, activists, and others who want to implement change or improvement in their community and beyond. How can students use art to inspire others and ignite dialogue about perceptions of cultural identity or other key social issues? How can they creatively utilize art to explore activism and social justice issues in their school and/or community? Ask students to come up with their own creative artistic idea or event to promote a social issue important to them (newsletter, guest speaker, community event, art fair or competition, etc.).

Communiquez!

20 Présentation artistique 1.2, 1.3, 2.2, 3.1

Connecting to Critical Thinking and Problem-Solving, Media Literacy

Presentational Speaking or Writing

Choisissez un artiste, un style artistique, une région connue pour son art, ou encore un mouvement artistique particulier. Trouvez cinq objets d'art liés à l'artiste, la période, la région ou le mouvement que vous avez choisi. Présentez ces objets d'art à la classe. Décrivez-les chacun et expliquez ce qui distingue chaque objet des autres.

21 La semaine nationale de la francophonie 1.1, 1.2, 1.3, 2.2, 3.2, 4.2, 5.2

Connecting to Media Literacy, Information Literacy, Collaboration

Interpersonal Speaking, Interpretive Listening, Presentational Speaking and Writing

Pour la semaine nationale de la francophonie, votre classe va célébrer la musique francophone à l'école. Avec la classe, vous devez sélectionner des genres et styles de musique, des pays et régions francophones, et vous mettre d'accord sur cette sélection. Ensuite, mettez-vous en groupes. Chaque groupe va chercher une ou deux chansons pour représenter chaque genre (ou style) de musique, et chaque pays (ou région) que vous avez sélectionnés, et justifiera ses choix devant la classe. Ensuite, la classe votera pour faire une liste finale de chansons.

22 Un film moderne 1.1, 1.2, 1.3, 2.2, 5.1

Connecting to Collaboration, Creativity and Innovation

Interpersonal Speaking, Interpretive Reading, Presentational Speaking and Writing

Souvent les histoires, les fables, ou les contes de fée changent avec le temps et les cultures. Par exemple, il y a de vieilles versions différentes de Cendrillon. De plus, les films modernes permettent de transmettre les événements historiques, en se servant de cadres culturels plus modernes et familiers pour l'audience.

En groupe, choisissez une histoire, une fable, ou un conte classique que vous allez adapter et moderniser en film. Discutez l'histoire en groupe et décidez ce que vous allez changer, et quels détails vous allez utiliser pour que les spectateurs s'identifient à l'histoire. Présentez un synopsis de votre film, avec peut-être, des suggestions d'acteurs que vous voudriez inviter à jouer les rôles principaux. Les élèves de la classe peuvent dire s'ils pensent que le film sera un succès ou pas, en justifiant leurs réponses.

Essential Instruction

1. Assign or allow students to select the task for the **Projets finaux** according to their interests. Provide clear rubrics so that they understand your expectations.
2. If assigning students a poem, you might want to offer them more structure. A diamante poem, an acoustic poem, or a haiku may be less intimidating for students who struggle with language. Discuss these different types of poems and find templates online for students to emulate.
3. For the Slam poetry, students not only will identify their favorite video, but also will explain why.

Projets finaux

A Connexions par Internet : la poésie 1.3, 3.1, 3.2, 5.1

Un poème original

Écrivez un poème original. Peut-être que vous écrirez un calligramme ou un sonnet. Peut-être que vous voudriez écrire un poème qui ressemble à un des poèmes que vous avez lus dans cette unité. Publiez votre poème en ligne avec les autres poèmes de votre classe ou présentez-le dans un slam devant la classe. N'oubliez pas de donner un titre à votre poème et, si vous le publiez, de mettre votre nom en-dessous du titre.

Recherche : comment faire un calligramme vidéo, cartable et récré

B Communautés en ligne 2.1, 3.2, 5.1

La Fédération Française de Slam Poésie

Le slam est un phénomène mondial. La Fédération Française de Slam Poésie a comme but de « faire de la poésie un spectacle vivant » pour les poètes et les spectateurs. Faites des recherches en ligne pour trouver :

- la date d'origine de la ffdsp
- le nom du concours
- si la ffdsp est en contact avec les écoles
- les thèmes choisis par les poètes
- votre vidéo préférée

Recherche : ffdsp, slamsncfconcours, le slam interscolaire, le grand slam de poésie, coupe du monde slam poésie vidéos

C Passez à l'action ! 1.3, 3.1, 5.1

Pour soutenir les arts dans les écoles

Votre lycée au Québec a décidé de ne pas continuer les cours d'art et de musique pour des raisons budgétaires. Mais vous et vos amis aimez ces cours et certains de vos amis comptent travailler dans le domaine des arts un jour. Votre groupe a donc pris la décision de lutter contre ces changements. Vous avez pensé à tout : une lettre à l'éditeur de votre journal, une manifestation devant le lycée, une pétition signée par les élèves, un poème sur ce que cette perte (*loss*) représente, etc. Décidez qui dans votre groupe va s'occuper de quoi pour préparer la lettre à l'éditeur, l'affiche qui indique la date et le lieu de la manifestation, le slogan, et un paragraphe qui explique l'importance des arts.

Resources

Create

Answers

All activities will vary.

Reference Desk

If you have access to Passport, assign your students an IPA task related to the unit.

Game

Jeopardy!

Review the cultural information taught in this unit by playing a Jeopardy game with the following categories: painters and their attributes, art movements and periods, music genres and artists, literary genres and periods, poets.

Differentiated Learning

Accelerate/Decelerate

As students review the unit lesson by lesson, ask them to make a review sheet of information they still need to study, and details they have forgotten. Encourage them to develop their own personal style of study.

Answers

D

Leçon A : Rencontres culturelles C'était le premier tableau abstrait de l'époque. Monet a utilisé des touches de pinceau plutôt que des tracés.
Leçon A : Points de départ Ils ont ajouté un style de peintures avec des touches plus petites, des points, pour montrer une impression encore différente.
Leçon A : Points de départ Ils fabriquent des sculptures et des objets en bronze, des poteries, des armes, des vêtements, des instruments de musique.
Leçon B : Rencontres culturelles la chanson engagée (Boris Vian), et les auteurs-compositeurs-interprètes (Brel, Aznavour, Gainsbourg, Barbara)
Leçon B : Points de départ Ils conservent l'héritage de leurs prédécesseurs et sont à la fois influencés par la scène internationale.
Leçon B : Points de départ la musique folklorique (Le Vent du nord)
Leçon B : Points de départ Il a un rôle politique.
Leçon C : Rencontres culturelles/ Points de départ moralistes : 17ème, romantiques : 19ème, critiques de la vie politique : 20ème
Leçon C : Points de départ Haïti a une histoire triomphante issue de violence et de révolutions.
Leçon C : Lecture thématique Le poème critique le conformisme social qui détruit les sentiments et le libre-arbitre des individus.
Leçon C : Points de départ : Perspectives du romantisme, parce que les sentiments pour lui reflètent une action politique plus que la pensée

Reference Desk

The **Faisons le point!** section asks students to respond to the essential question by analyzing various texts in each lesson. The graphic organizer for **Activité D** may be expanded by using the complete chart found in the Copy Masters supplement.

D Faisons le point ! 1.2, 1.3

Diagramme

Faites un diagramme comme celui de dessous et remplissez-le pour montrer vos connaissances de l'art comme reflet de la culture. Un exemple a été fait pour vous.

Leçon A **Rencontres culturelles** Les impressionnistes montrent la société de quel siècle ? →	Les impressionnistes montrent comment vivaient les gens du 19ème siècle.
Leçon A **Rencontres culturelles** Pourquoi est-ce que le tableau impressionniste *Impression, soleil levant* était-il révolutionnaire ? →	
Leçon A **Points de départ : Le néo-impressionnisme** Qu'est-ce que les néo-impressionnistes ont ajouté au processus artistique ? →	
Leçon A **Points de départ : La Francophonie** Quels objets les artistes africains fabriquent-ils ? →	
Leçon B **Rencontres culturelles** Quels genres de musique les Français ont-ils appréciés de 1945 jusqu'à aujourd'hui ? →	
Leçon B **Points de départ** Les musiciens contemporains en France s'intéressent à quels genres de musique ? →	
Leçon B **Points de départ** Quel est un genre de musique québécois ? →	
Leçon B **Points de départ : Perspectives** Quel est le rôle et l'influence du chanteur français, selon Georges Brassens ? →	

Essential Instruction

1. Students will work in pairs of high and low-ability teams to complete **Faisons le point!** This activity will allow students to engage in a structured review.
2. Have an "Any question is OK" day where students can get help on even the most basic points without penalty. Allow students to ask these questions anonymously on an index card and turn it in.
3. When students do the listening comprehension passage, have them jot down notes about each character to help them answer the questions.
4. Students will prepare **B** and **C** in the computer lab. For part **C** they might want to make a chart to compare French and American artists.

Évaluation

A Évaluation de compréhension auditive 1.2

*Écoutez Kevin et Annie discuter de leurs intérêts artistiques. Ensuite, indiquez si chaque phrase que vous entendez est vraie (**V**) ou fausse (**F**).*

B Évaluation orale 1.1, 4.2, 5.2

À tour de rôle, jouez les rôles d'un(e) ado américain(e) et d'un(e) ado français(e). Avant de commencer, l'élève qui joue le rôle de l'ado américain(e) doit écrire des notes sur ce qu'il/elle sait d'un chanteur/d'une chanteuse américain(e) de son choix. L'élève qui joue le rôle de l'ado français(e) doit rechercher un chanteur ou une chanteuse français(e) pour ses notes.

Dans votre conversation, comparez vos artistes en ce qui concerne :

- leurs genres
- les albums ou les chansons qui leur ont valu d'immense succès
- le public qu'ils ont séduit (les ados ? les adultes ? leurs pays ?)
- leurs thèmes

Finalement, choisissez un album de votre artiste à prêter à votre ami(e) et dites pourquoi il faut qu'il/elle l'écoute. Servez-vous des expressions dans Pour la conversation.

C Évaluation culturelle 1.3, 2.1, 2.2, 3.1, 3.2, 4.2, 5.1, 5.2

Vous allez comparer les cultures francophones à votre culture. Vous aurez peut-être besoin de faire des recherches sur la culture américaine.

1. **L'impressionnisme**
   Qui sont les maîtres de l'impressionnisme en France ? Comment ces peintres ont-ils transformé la façon de peindre ? Quel impressionniste préférez-vous ? Pourquoi ? Qui sont les impressionnistes de l'école américaine ? Lesquels aimez-vous ? Pourquoi ?
2. **L'art traditionnel**
   Comparez les objets traditionnels fabriqués en Afrique de l'Ouest aux objets fabriqués en Amérique par les Amérindiens.
3. **Les auteurs-compositeurs-interprètes contemporains**
   Qui sont les grands auteurs-compositeurs-interprètes contemporains en France et en Amérique ? Comparez-les.

Resources

Activity A
Listening Activity
Synthèse
Pre-AP Listening *Unité 7*

Answers

A Script

Annie : Tu aimes les arts ?
Kevin : Bien sûr, toutes les formes artistiques me plaisent, mais je préfère la peinture et la musique.
Annie : Moi aussi, j'aime la peinture. Quel mouvement tu préfères ? Pour moi, c'est l'impressionnisme, le fauvisme, le néo-impressionnisme.
Kevin : J'adore le fauvisme et les tableaux de Vlaminck pour les couleurs vives et l'intensité de l'expression plus que les peintres néo-impressionnistes. Et toi ?
Annie : Moi, je suis fan de Monet. Quelle autre forme d'art tu aimes ?
Kevin : Moi, j'adore la musique. Je joue de la guitare dans un groupe et je suis auteur-compositeur et interprète.
Annie : Super ! Quel genre de musique vous jouez ?
Kevin : On joue de la musique folklorique et du rock. On a même sorti un album avec des chansons poétiques et réalistes.
Annie : J'aimerais beaucoup l'écouter. Moi, tu sais, j'aime la littérature et j'écris beaucoup de poèmes et de fables que je publie sur Internet. On pourrait peut-être travailler ensemble sur de nouvelles chansons.
Kevin : Ça, c'est une idée géniale. Avec nos intérêts artistiques, on est sûr de réussir et de devenir célèbre !

1. Annie et Kevin parlent de cinéma.
2. Kevin préfère la peinture et la littérature.
3. Annie aime le néo-impressionnisme.
4. Kevin admire le peintre Vlaminck.
5. Annie est fan de Seurat.
6. Les deux ados aiment la musique.
7. Kevin joue de la musique classique.
8. Les deux ados vont écrire de nouvelles chansons ensemble.

1. F; 2. F; 3. V; 4. V; 5. F; 6. V; 7. F; 8. V

Differentiated Learning

Accelerate
High-ability students can work independently to review for the evaluation.

Decelerate
Work with these students in groups or individually to help them structure their review. Many of these students have not yet developed study skills or do not have the time or place to study at home.

Special Needs Students

At-Risk Students
At this point, many of these students do not feel that they have a chance of succeeding. Break down tasks into smaller, measurable sections so that they could be successful in part if not in the whole evaluation.

Resources

Perform

Answers

All activities will vary.

Reference Desk

1. The painting on this page dates from 1876. Renoir seeks to capture a scene of daily life and a psychological portrait of his subject. He departs from neoclassical, romantic, and realist painting in that he focuses on the feeling of a scene and the effects of natural light on the subject. In this painting, he depicts a group of upper-class citizens in a café, focusing on the women, who are captivated by an unseen person or event, and, in turn, captivate the attention of a nearby gentleman and the viewer of the painting.
2. If you have access to Passport, assign a task to evaluate your students' oral proficiency.

Connections

Art History

Ask students to present to the class one art movement in the United States and discuss its ties to political transformation (for example, the Harlem Renaissance, music in the 1960s, or post-modernism).

Expansion

Ask students to write additional captions to their comics, and then give them feedback. After, have them embellish their work for a class or school exhibition on the famous work of La Fontaine.

4. **Deux chansons célèbres**
   Comment s'appelle la chanson d'Édith Piaf la plus connue aux États-Unis? Expliquez pourquoi beaucoup de chanteurs l'ont enregistrée, selon vous. Nominez une chanson américaine à exporter en France. Justifiez votre choix.
5. **La musique traditionnelle**
   Quel est le nom du groupe folklorique québécois que vous avez découvert dans cette unité? Connaissez-vous un groupe folklorique américain qui lui ressemble?
6. **Les groupes littéraires**
   Pourquoi la Pléiade est-elle importante dans l'évolution de la littérature française? Quels groupes d'écrivains anglophones connaissez-vous?

D Évaluation écrite 1.3, 3.1, 4.2

Écrivez une composition sur un écrivain américain que vous admirez. Expliquez:

- le ou les genres qu'il ou elle écrits.
- l'intrigue (*plot*) ou le thème d'une de ses œuvres.
- quand il ou elle a écrit cette œuvre.
- pourquoi vous aimez cette œuvre.

Servez-vous d'expressions présentées dans Pour la conversation.

E Évaluation visuelle 1.3, 3.1, 3.2, 5.2

Imaginez que vous devez écrire un paragraphe sur ce tableau. Expliquez:

- le mouvement auquel cette œuvre appartient (*belongs*).
- quand ce mouvement a eu lieu.
- qui est l'artiste.
- ce que le peintre recherche dans cette œuvre ou ses œuvres en général.
- comment l'artiste s'éloigne des peintres qui l'ont précédé.
- ce qu'il a peint dans ce tableau.
- pourquoi vous aimez cette peinture ou pourquoi vous ne l'aimez pas.

Servez-vous d'expressions présentées dans Pour la conversation.

F Évaluation compréhensive 1.3, 5.2

Créez une planche de bande dessinée d'environ huit vignettes pour raconter ce qui se passe dans une autre fable de La Fontaine. Dessinez l'histoire et racontez-la avec des descriptions et des dialogues en utilisant vos propres mots.

Essential Instruction

1. For part **D**, insist that the students spend 10 minutes making pre-writing notes about each point. Circulate to help students with their writing.
2. Students will review the expressions in **Pour la conversation** to help them write the essay in part **D** and the the description of the painting in part **E**.
3. Provide students a blank comic strip or storyboard to illustrate the fable of La Fontaine.
4. Before playing vocabulary games, review the vocabulary list by giving definitions; students will guess the term. Describe characteristics of art and literary movements, and students will furnish the names.
5. Encourage low-ability learners to make vocabulary flash cards and work with study buddies to prepare for the test.

Vocabulaire de l'Unité 7

à: à l'avant-plan in the foreground *A*; **à l'arrière-plan** in the background *A*; **au second plan** in the middle ground *A*
un **album: album concept** concept album *B*
appliquer to apply *A*
un **atelier** studio *A*
l' **aube (f.)** dawn *C*
un **auteur** author *B*
l' **aveu (m.)** confession *C*
les **beaux-arts (m.)** fine arts *A*
le **brouillard** mist *C*
cacher to conceal, to hide *C*
se **cacher** to hide *C*
la **caricature** caricature *B*
une **chanson: chanson réaliste** realist song *B*
les **coquelicots (m.)** poppies *A*
le **corbeau** crow *C*
cueillir to pick *C*
de: de plus en plus more and more *A*
demeurer to live *C*
devoir to owe *C*
donner: donner lieu à to give rise to *C*
un(e) **dramaturge** playwright *C*
s' **éloigner (de)** to distance oneself (from) *A*
engagé(e) engaged, committed *B*
l' **expressionnisme (m.)** expressionism *A*
expressionniste expressionist *A*

une **fête: fête champêtre** garden party *A*
une **figure** figure *C*
un **gros plan** close up *A*; **en gros plan** a close-up *A*
immense immense *B*
l' **impressionnisme (m.)** Impressionism *A*
un(e) **impressionniste** Impressionist *A*
un **interprète** performer *B*
intimiste intimate *B*
l' **invention (f.)** invention *C*
des **lignes (f.)** lines *A*
le **lyrisme** lyricism *B*
la **mélancolie** melancholy *C*
la **mélodie** melody *B*
mentir to lie *C*
une **méthode** method *A*
une **morale** moral *C*
le **néo-classicisme** neoclassicism *A*
néoclassique neo-classic *A*
le **néo-impressionnisme** Neo-impressionism *A*
pâle pale *A*
la **partie** part *C*
passer: passer de… à to move from… to *B*
peint painted *A*
un **pinceau** paintbrush *A*
la **plainte** complaint *C*
plaire (à) to please *B*
un **poète, une femme poète** poet *C*
poétique poetic *B*
populaire popular *B*

pour in order to *C*; **pour que** so that *C*
prendre: prendre position (sur) to take a position (on) *C*
le **réalisme** realism *A*
réaliste realist *B*
rechercher to look for/into *A*
se **reconnaître** to see oneself as *B*
un **reflet** reflection *A*
le **renard** fox *C*
le **rococo** rococo style *A*
rococo rococo *A*
un **romancier, une romancière** novelist *C*
romantique Romantic *A*
le **romantisme** Romanticism *A*
la **salsa** salsa music *B*
une **satire** satire *C*
une **scène** stage *B*; **sur scène** on stage *B*
séduire to seduce *B*
un **sonnet** sonnet *C*
le **sorcier** wizard *C*
le **soupir** sighing *C*
une **strophe** stanza *C*
le **succès** success *B*
le **surréalisme** Surrealism *C*
le **swing** swing music *B*
un **texte** text *B*
un **thème** theme *C*
une **toile** canvas *A*
une **tournée** tour *B*; **en tournée** on tour *B*
valoir to be the cause of *B*
des **variations (f.)** variations *C*
volumineux, volumineuse voluminous *C*

Resources

FC Flash Cards
Rendez-vous à Nice ! Documentaire 4
T *Unité 7* Test

Reference Desk

nouvelle orthographe
il/elle/on plait, se reconnaitre

Game

Charades

Divide the class into two groups. Give them time to peruse the chapter for vocabulary and use the summative list on this page. Students will conspire to find words that the other team must pantomime. The goal is for a team to guess the word that is being acted out in whatever short time period you prefer. You can set the time according to the skill of the class.

Categories

Students will work in pairs to write from memory as many vocabulary words as they can remember for **Art**, **Musique**, **Écrivains**, and **Poésie**. Points will be awarded for the most words in each category. To make the game more challenging, assign a letter of the alphabet for each category. Give students time to correct their vocabulary. You can play the game again using the same categories, but this time, count only the words written perfectly.

Reference Desk

1. **La Conciergerie**, located on the **Île de la Cîté**, served as the royal palace from the 10th to the mid-14th century. It became a prison in 1391. During the French Revolution, in 1793 and 1794, those suspected of opposing the revolution were detained there before being sentenced to death by the Revolutionary Tribunal. More than 2,600 prisoners left **La Conciergerie** to go to the guillotine. Marie-Antoinette was imprisoned there with her children before her death.
2. **La Conciergerie** was known as "the antechamber to the guillotine." Tell students that **la tour Bonbec** was the torture chamber.
3. The illustration on the unit opener is a copy of Jean-François de Troy, ***Le déjeuner d'huîtres*** (1735). It depicts a royal dinner in the 18th century.
4. A partial timeline of French government:

1792: First Republic declared.
1793: King Louis XVI and Marie-Antoinette guillotined. Reign of Terror.
1799: Bonaparte's coup d'état
1804: Bonaparte crowns himself Emperor Napoleon I.
1814: Napoleon abdicates.
1814–24: reign of Louis XVIII
1815: start of the "100 Days"; defeat of Napoleon at Waterloo, and his exile
1824–30: reign of Charles X
1830–48 reign of Louis Philippe
1852: Napoleon's nephew crowned Emperor Napoleon III
1870–71: Franco-Prussian War
1871: Napoleon III exiled, Third Republic declared
1914–18: WWI
1939–45: WWII
1944: start of Fourth Republic as France is liberated with Charles de Gaulle as leader.
1958: De Gaulle begins Fifth Republic.

Unité 8 La France d'hier et d'aujourd'hui

Essential Instruction

1. Ask students what they know about the French Revolution. Who were the king and queen at the time? When they think of Marie-Antoinette, what adjectives would they use to describe her? Can anyone cite the quotation attributed to her? (Note the source of the "Let them eat cake" quote is not verifiable and, if she did say it, some believe she was referring to **brioche** since there was no more bread.)
2. Tell students that **Unité 8** discusses the French Revolution. If possible, try to coordinate with history teachers in order for you to teach this unit at the same time they teach the French Revolution.
3. Review the **Contrat de l'élève**.
4. Put students in groups. Have them try to list the 27 countries in the EU. Afterward, post a list of the countries to see which group listed the most.
5. Give students a timeline of French government since 1789. (See *Reference Desk* notes in side margin.)

Question centrale

Comment le passé influence-t-il le présent?

À savoir

Depuis la Révolution de 1789, la France a établi cinq républiques différentes et a eu huit monarques, dont trois empereurs et cinq rois.

Citation

« La France est à refaire, mais elle sera toujours refaite. »

France is to be remade, but she will always be remade.

—Aurélien Scholl (19ème siècle), journaliste, auteur dramatique, chroniqueur, et romancier français

Conseil pratique

On a free language exchange website, find a French speaker to communicate with, such as someone you agree with or share similar interests with. Do ask for parental or teacher approval first.

Recherche: the mixxer, conversation exchange, how do you do?, speaky, papora, babelvillage, lingoglobe, languageforexchange

Qui est ce garçon?

Quel est ce drapeau et que représente-t-il?

Contrat de l'élève

Leçon A I will be able to:

- express obligation and say what someone makes me do.
- talk about the last French king and queen, the **états généraux de l'Ancien Régime**, and the French declaration of citizens' rights before the 1789 revolution.
- review expressions with **faire** and use the construction **faire** + INFINITIVE.

Leçon B I will be able to:

- say there is a lot of something, say what I did in vain and tell someone to stop with the flattery.
- talk about the institutions of the European Union.
- review expressions with **avoir** and use the past infinitive.

Leçon C I will be able to:

- express my rights, discuss what I can afford, and say I want to discuss something further.
- talk about the rights of French citizens and their entitlement programs.
- review expressions with **être** and use the pluperfect tense.

Differentiated Learning

Accelerate

Ask students to present the objectives and structure of the Treaty of Maastricht to the class.

Decelerate

Have students define the eurozone, list its members, and explain the basic tenets of the agreement.

Learning Styles

Visual Learners

Ask students to make a poster of the euro, including photos or drawings of the denominations of bills and coins.

Multiple Intelligences

Mathematical-Logical

Ask students to graph the ratio of the dollar to the euro in five-year increments from 1998 to the present day. What are some challenges facing the euro today?

Answers

Possible choices for the video question are:
A. le frère de Chadia
B. son petit ami
C. un inconnu qui flirte avec elle
D. le marchand de glace
Correct answer: B

The answer to the culture question is: **le drapeau de l'union européenne (UE); il représente la solidarité et l'union des pays d'Europe**. The answer can be found in **Points de départ, Leçon B**.

Reference Desk

1. The European Union is an economic and political union of 27 member states, established in 1992 by the Maastricht Treaty. The European Parliament governs the EU, and European Union citizens elect its members every five years.
2. For up-to-date information on the European Union, access its website.

   Recherche: europa site officiel

3. The **citation** suggests that France is a country continuing to evolve. Two examples of dramatic changes over history are the French Revolution, which uprooted the centuries-old monarchy, and the admission of France into the European Union.

Critical Thinking

Analyse

Involve students in a discussion of French history since 1789, noting that France is currently in its fifth republic since then (and in its longest period of political stability since the revolution). Contrast this to the United States, which, despite the Civil War, has maintained one form of government and one constitution since 1789, when George Washington first took office. Discuss how this may affect a citizen's understanding of and approach to government and its authority.

Resources

- *Vocabulaire actif*
  - *Pour la conversation*
  - *Et si je voulais dire…?*
- eV eVisual
- WB Workbook 1–3
- FC Flash Cards
- LA Listening Activity 1
- G & V Practice Games

Reference Desk

1. **L'Ancien Régime** was the political, economic, and social system from the 15th century to the Revolution. The clergy, nobles, and the rest of French society formed the three estates in order of importance. The third estate bore the tax burden for the other two.
2. **Les états généraux** (also spelled **États-Généraux**), the general assembly of the three estates, met in 1789 to try to solve France's fiscal crisis. The effort failed because the clergy and the nobles wanted to maintain their status and power. The third estate, the commoners, met at a tennis court swearing not to disband until a constitution had been written.
3. **Citoyen(ne)** was the term of address during the Revolution and the Reign of Terror.

Communication

Interpersonal, Presentational: Cooperative Groups

Have students work in groups to describe the pictures in **Activité 1**, adding details, real or imagined, to tell a story about each one. Groups present their stories to the class.

Leçon A Vocabulaire actif

La Révolution française 1.2, 3.1, 5.2

L'Ancien Régime

L'Ancien Régime : une référence au régime monarchique du 15ème siècle au 18ème siècle, de la Renaissance à la Révolution, et ses institutions

Les états généraux de l'Ancien Régime : des assemblées **convoquées** par le roi afin de traiter d'une crise politique ou financière ; ils comprenaient le clergé, les aristocrates, les députés

Le roi fait un discours.

La mort de Louis XVI

Le roi fait ses adieux.

Le roi meurt.

Pour la conversation 1.2

How do I express obligation?

» Il était **obligé de** faire venir les députés….
He was obligated to have the deputies come….

How do I express what someone makes me do?

» On **te fait** étudier tout ça ?
They make you study all that?

Et si je voulais dire… ?

la bourgeoisie	*middle class*
le dauphin	*king's successor*
la monarchie	*monarchy*
la noblesse	*nobility*
le royaume	*kingdom*
régner	*to rule, reign*
succéder à	*to succeed (king)*

Essential Instruction

1. Have students ask who, what, and where questions for the drawings in **La Révolution française**.
2. Have students listen to **La Révolution française** and **Pour la conversation**.
3. Define each term in **Et si je voulais dire…?** then ask students to provide the vocabulary word.
4. Students read **Activité 1** and answer the questions together as a class.
5. Have students do the *Communication* activity before doing **Activité 1**.
6. Review the irregular verb **mourir** and its conjugations in the present, **passé composé**, future, and conditional.

1 Nouveaux mots et nouvelles expressions 1.2, 3.1

Interpretive Viewing

Regardez les illustrations, puis répondez aux questions.

Charlotte de Meaux

le président

le clergé

Jean-Jacques

M. et Mme Delamain

le roi

les aristocrates

les monarques

1. Qui est mort pendant la guerre?
2. Qui fait un discours au public français?
3. Que font M. et Mme Delamain?
4. Qui porte une perruque quand elle paraît sur scène?
5. Où habitent les aristocrates?
6. Qui écoute son public?
7. Où se réunit le clergé?
8. Qui aime danser?

2 Louis XVI 1.2, 3.1

Interpretive Reading

Lisez à haute voix les phrases suivantes en substituant les mots ou expressions en italique par des mots ou des expressions de vocabulaire appris dans cette leçon.

(1) Le chef d'état et sa femme sont emprisonnés en 1791. Louis XVI (2) présente son point de vue à l'Assemblée Nationale. Mais (3) le clergé, les aristocrates, et les députés n'acceptent pas ce qu'il a dit. Le nouveau gouvernement (4) le force à passer ses derniers jours en prison. Condamné à (5) être exécuté, il (6) dit au revoir à sa famille. Il (7) disparaît brutalement sur la place de la Concorde.

Differentiated Learning

Accelerate

At the time of Louis XVI's execution, all of the gates of Paris were closed to block any outside intervention. Have students research whom the revolutionaries feared and why. (Austrian forces, as Marie-Antoinette was a royal Austrian)

Decelerate

Have students make a drawing of **la cocarde** then explain what it is, who wore it, and the reason for the choice of colors.

Multiple Intelligences

Musical-Rhythmic

Find songs about the revolution. Teach the class to sing "**Ça ira**."

Answers

1

1. Jean-Jacques est mort pendant la guerre.
2. Le président fait un discours au public français.
3. Ils font leurs adieux à leur fils et leurs petits-enfants.
4. Charlotte de Meaux porte une perruque quand elle paraît sur scène.
5. Ils habitent dans un château.
6. Le roi écoute son public.
7. Le clergé se reunit au Vatican/à l'église.
8. Les monarques aiment danser.

2

1. le roi et la reine
2. donne un discours
3. les états généraux
4. l'oblige
5. être guillotiné
6. fait ses adieux
7. est mort

Connections

History

Have students make an **axe chronologique** of the events that lead to Louis XVI's death and the end of the monarchy. Encourage students to ask their social studies teachers for additional help.

Critical Thinking

Analysis

The king and queen were referred to as "**Le boulanger et sa femme**." After the king died, the queen was called "**La veuve capet**." Ask students why she was referred to in that way. (The kings of France descended from 10th-century Hugues Capet and thus took his name as their family name. Being called the "widow Capet" was somewhat derogatory, purposefully lowering Marie-Antoinette's status from queen to common woman.)

Communication

Presentational, Interpersonal: Cooperative Groups

Have students work as a group to find the dramatic, gory, interesting facts about the guillotine, its inventor, victims, and locations and then present this short history along with illustrations.

Recherche: la conciergerie

Resources

Activity 3

Answers

3 Script

Maman : Regarde, Camille, le beau livre que je t'ai acheté sur la Révolution française !
Camille : On peut le lire maintenant maman ? Ça m'intéresse beaucoup !
Maman : Si tu veux. Tu te rappelles, l'année dernière quand la maîtresse vous a raconté l'histoire du roi Louis XVI et de sa famille ?
Camille : Oui, un peu. Quand on a visité Versailles avec l'école ?
Maman : Oui. Qu'est-ce que tu as aimé ?
Camille : La grande salle avec les miroirs et la belle chambre de la reine. Aussi sur les portraits, la reine avait de belles robes et des perruques ridicules.
Maman : Qu'est-ce qui est arrivé au dernier roi qui a vécu à Versailles ?
Camille : Il a fait ses adieux à sa famille et on l'a « guillomé ».
Maman : Oui, il est mort guillotiné.
Camille : Il avait fait un discours devant les états généraux mais on l'a fait prisonnier quand même ! Et sa femme, elle est morte aussi.
Maman : Très bien. Eh bien, tu te souviens de beaucoup de choses. C'est bien ! Lisons ton nouveau livre alors !

1. F; 2. F; 3. V; 4. F; 5. V; 6. V

4

1. A : Qui te fait lui rendre visite ?
   B : … me fait/me font lui rendre visite.
2. A : Qui te fait faire le plein ?
   B : … me fait/me font faire le plein.
3. A : Qui te fait étudier les maths ?
   B : … me fait/me font étudier les maths.
4. A : Qui te fait sortir le weekend ?
   B : … me fait/me font sortir le weekend.
5. A : Qui te fait faire la vaisselle ?
   B : … me fait/me font faire la vaisselle.
6. A : Qui te fait tondre la pelouse ?
   B : … me fait/me font tondre la pelouse.
7. A : Qui te fait nourrir ton chat ou ton chien ?
   B : … me fait/me font nourrir mon chat ou mon chien.
8. A : Qui te fait t'habiller bien pour les fêtes ?
   B : … me fait/me font m'habiller bien pour les fêtes.

5 Answers will vary.

3 L'histoire de France 1.2, 3.1

Interpretive Listening

*Écrivez les numéros 1–6 sur votre papier. Écoutez Camille et sa mère parler de la Révolution française. Ensuite, indiquez si les phrases sont vraies (**V**) ou fausses (**F**).*

1. La mère de Camille a acheté un livre de maths à sa fille.
2. Camille est allée aux états généraux avec sa classe l'année dernière.
3. Camille a visité le château où le dernier roi et la dernière reine de France ont vécu.
4. Camille peut bien prononcer le verbe « guillotiner ».
5. La mère de Camille est contente parce que sa fille s'est rappelée l'histoire de la Révolution française.
6. Camille a remarqué les perruques que Marie-Antoinette portait.

4 Qui te fait… ? 1.1

Interpersonal Speaking

À tour de rôle, demandez à votre partenaire qui lui fait faire les choses suivantes.

MODÈLE conduire au supermarché
A : Qui te fait conduire au supermarché ?
B : Mes parents me font conduire au supermarché./ Personne ne me fait conduire au supermarché.

1. lui rendre visite
2. faire le plein
3. étudier les maths
4. sortir le weekend
5. faire la vaisselle
6. tondre la pelouse
7. nourrir ton chat ou ton chien
8. t'habiller bien pour les fêtes

Ma mère me fait apprendre mes tables de multiplication.

5 Questions personnelles 1.1, 2.2, 3.1, 3.2, 5.2

Interpersonal Speaking

Répondez aux questions avec un partenaire.

1. Est-ce que tu aimerais vivre comme un aristocrate ? Pourquoi, ou pourquoi pas ?
2. Quels événements de l'histoire américaine est-ce que tu connais ?
3. Quelle est ta réaction quand tes grands-parents font leurs adieux après une visite ?
4. Qu'est-ce que tu es obligé(e) de faire pendant le weekend ?
5. Qui te fait faire des corvées à la maison ?

Essential Instruction

1. Have students listen to the conversation in **Activité 4**. Tally how your students did to monitor their listening comprehension progress.
2. Explain **faire causatif**. Do **Activité 4** with the class, putting each sentence on the board. Emphasize that **faire** is conjugated, and the second verb remains an infinitive.
3. Give students a few minutes to prepare their own answers for **Activité 5**. Ask individual students each of the questions before inviting them to interview each other.

Rencontres culturelles

Une leçon d'histoire 1.2, 2.1, 3.1

Karim travaille devant son ordinateur et sa petite sœur Aïcha vient lui parler.

Aïcha : C'est qui, la dame avec une perruque ?
Karim : D'abord, ce n'est pas une dame, c'est un monsieur.
Aïcha : C'est un monsieur ? Qu'est-ce qu'il fait ? Il s'est déguisé pour le Carnaval ?
Karim : Non, il ne s'est pas déguisé ! C'est le roi de France, Aïcha.
Aïcha : Le roi de France ? Mais il est très vieux !
Karim : C'est Louis XVI, le dernier roi de France avant la Révolution française.
Aïcha : Il fait un discours ?
Karim : Là ? Non, il assiste à l'ouverture des états généraux ; il est obligé de faire venir les députés parce que le gouvernement n'avait plus d'argent. Là, il fait ses adieux à sa femme, Marie-Antoinette, et ses enfants.
Aïcha : Pourquoi ? Il part en voyage ?
Karim : Non, il va mourir. Il est condamné à être guillotiné.
Aïcha : Et après, qu'est-ce qui se passe ?
Karim : Après, il y a Napoléon, il y a de nouveau des rois, de nouveau des révolutions, et puis il y a la République.
Aïcha : Et on te fait étudier tout ça ?
Karim : Oui, jusqu'à la cinquième République.
Aïcha : Eh bien, moi, je sais toutes mes tables de multiplication !

Stratégie

Faites une représentation graphique chronologie (*timeline*) des événements historiques mentionnés par Karim. Cherchez les dates en ligne et ajoutez-les. Vous pouvez aussi ajouter des dessins ou d'autres images.

6 Une leçon d'histoire 1.2, 2.1, 3.1

Identifiez la personne décrite.

1. Cette personne porte une perruque.
2. Cette personne est mariée à Louis XVI.
3. Cette personne étudie l'histoire de France.
4. Cette personne sait toutes ses tables de multiplication.
5. Cette personne assiste à l'ouverture des états généraux.
6. Cette personne a été guillotinée.

Analyse

Que pense Aïcha du roi Louis XVI au premier abord (*at first glance*) ? Utilisez des détails du texte. Pourquoi, à votre avis, a-t-elle cette impression de ce personnage ?

Resources

Dialogue
Activity 6
Dialogue Video
WB Workbook 4

Answers

Analyse
Elle pense que c'est une dame, puis un homme déguisé pour le Carnaval ; il est vieux. Possible answer: Elle a cette impression parce qu'elle ne reconnaît pas que c'est une image historique.

6
1. Louis XVI; 2. Marie-Antoinette; 3. Karim; 4. Aïcha; 5. Louis XVI; 6. Louis XVI

Reference Desk

1. The **faire causatif** (**faire** + INFINITIVE) construction is used when one is not personally doing the action but is having it done: A builder builds a house but I am having a house built. **Je fais construire une maison**.
2. In a negative command, object pronouns precede the form of **faire**: **Ne faites pas construire la maison par cet architecte. Ne la faites pas construire par cet architecte.**
3. Examples of **faire** + INFINITIVE that students might not know are: **faire bouillir de l'eau** (*to boil water*) and **faire cuire** (*to cook*).

Communication

Interpersonal: Paired Practice

Have students practice **faire causatif** in pairs. Prepare a worksheet for Student A with eight sentences expressing what certain people are doing: **Le membre de la mafia parle**. Prepare another worksheet for Student B, listing who is making the people on Student A's worksheet do the activity: **Les agents secrets**. Student A reads the first sentence from the worksheet for Student B, who forms a new sentence using **faire** + INFINITIVE: **Les agents secrets font parler le membre de la mafia**. Then ask Student A to replace **le membre de la mafia** with a pronoun: **Les agents secrets le font parler**.

Differentiated Learning

Adapt
Students make a list of all of the tasks their teachers, parents, and employers make them do, using the **faire causatif**. For example, "**Mon professeur me fait parler français en classe.**"

Decelerate
Work with students to skim and scan **Une leçon d'histoire**. Ask them to highlight and identify the historical figures and terms discussed in the conversation. Read the conversation together, helping students to understand difficult lines or passages. Ask them to read the conversation again before answering the questions in **Activité 6**.

Resources

Extension

Answers

EXTENSION

Possible answer:
Parce que c'était un combattant pour la liberté, et il a été reconnu récemment.

Reference Desk

1. **On est dans l'actualité** means that we are talking about something that is happening now.
2. Aimé Césaire (1913–2008) was a French poet, author, and former mayor of Fort-de-France, Martinique. He is associated with the **la négritude**, a movement that strives to give young black people a sense of positive racial identity and pride. His writing has surrealistic traits.
3. **Le Panthéon**, located on the Left Bank, was originally built as a church dedicated to St. Genevieve, the patron saint of Paris. It now serves as a secular mausoleum where distinguished French citizens, scientists, heroes, philosophers, and more have been interred or commemorated. Some of those honored at the **Panthéon** include Descartes, Voltaire, Rousseau, Alexandre Dumas, Victor Hugo, Émile Zola, Jean Jaurès, Louis Braille, Jean Moulin, Antoine de Saint-Exupéry, Pierre and Marie Curie, André Malraux, Pierre Brossolette, and Simone Veil.

Culture

Products: Information

The wig became popular during the reign of Louis XIII. This tradition continued into the 18th century. Men wore wigs which they powdered white. Women added tresses to their hair, weighted down with pomades and powders. This tradition was a symbol of aristocratic decadence and died out with the French Revolution. The romantics of the 19th century preferred natural, free-flowing hair.

EXTENSION **La grande scène de l'histoire** 1.2, 2.2, 3.1

Quatre élèves discutent à propos du choix d'un personnage historique à présenter en classe d'histoire.

Chloé : D'abord, qu'est-ce qu'on veut faire passer comme message ?
Amidou : Oui, Chloé a raison, on ne va pas lancer des noms.
Samuel : Il faut que le personnage ait un rapport avec la liberté….
Guillaume : Une figure de combattant ?
Amidou : Oui, mais combattant de quoi ?
Samuel : Je ne sais pas, quelqu'un qui revendique la dignité pour son peuple, le respect de son identité !
Guillaume : Et si on prenait Aimé Césaire ?
Amidou : Poète, résistant, homme politique….
Samuel : Noir, martiniquais….
Chloé : Et puis ça tombe bien, il vient d'entrer au Panthéon… on est dans l'actualité.
Amidou : C'est lui qui a invité les autres peuples à « laisser entrer les peuples noirs sur la grande scène de l'Histoire ».
Chloé : Eh bien, voilà, ça fait notre titre.

EXTENSION Pour quelles raisons les élèves ont-ils choisi Aimé Césaire pour leur projet d'histoire ?

1.2, 2.2, 3.1

Produits **Aimé Césaire** (1913–2008), écrivain et homme politique martiniquais, est considéré, avec Léopold Sédar Senghor, le père de la négritude, un mouvement littéraire qui revendique la valorisation des identités noires.

1.2, 2.2

Essential Instruction

1. Before showing the video, ask students to describe the people in the picture. Who are they and what are they doing?
2. Play the video. Have students watch with books closed. Ask general comprehension questions.
3. Have students listen to the dialogue and follow in their books.
4. As a class activity, have individual students read and answer the questions in **Activité 6**.
5. Ask students if they know of Aimé Césaire. What is the importance of **le Panthéon**? What are the accomplishments of others buried there?
6. Have students read the roles of the four speakers in **Extension**.
7. Provide students a short biography of Aimé Césaire to read in class. Have them work in pairs to answer the **Extension** question.
8. Discuss the poet and have the students read a sampling of his most famous poem, "**Cahier d'un retour au pays natal**."

Points de départ

Pre-AP

Question centrale : **Comment le passé influence-t-il le présent?**

Portrait de Louis XVI

1.2, 2.1, 2.2, 3.1, 4.2, 5.2

Louis XVI, roi de France

Louis XVI (1754–1791) est le dernier Roi de France avant la Révolution française. Il succède à Louis XV. Conscient de l'état du Royaume, Louis XVI s'entoure de* personnalités réformatrices, en particulier en matière financière et économique. Mais, il s'oppose à la noblesse* qui ne veut ni de réformes, ni renoncer à certains de ses privilèges.

C'est Louis XVI qui décide de soutenir la guerre d'indépendance américaine*. Le Marquis de Lafayette y participe contre la volonté du roi ; il paye donc son propre voyage. La victoire des armées américaines appuyées* par les troupes royales aboutit* à la signature du traité de Versailles en 1783.

La convocation des états généraux (1789) pour résoudre la crise économique déclenche* la Révolution. Pourtant* méfiant* à l'égard de* la noblesse, Louis XVI se montre incapable d'accepter une évolution de la monarchie absolue vers une monarchie constitutionnelle, malgré la pression des nobles. Il refuse de signer l'abolition des privilèges et la Déclaration des Droits de l'Homme. Prisonnier du peuple qui le ramène* de Versailles à Paris (1789) pour mieux le contrôler, sa fuite manquée* à Varennes (1791) et la menace* des armées royales européennes conduisent Louis XVI à la prison du Temple (1792). Déclaré « coupable de conspiration contre la sûreté* de l'État », il est guillotiné le 21 janvier 1793 sur l'actuelle place de la Concorde.

Recherche : chronologie des rois de france, histoire de france, rois de france

s'entoure de *surrounds himself with* ; **noblesse** *nobility* ; **guerre d'indépendance américaine** *American Revolution* ; **appuyées** *backed up* ; **aboutit** *leads to* ; **déclenche** *prompts* ; **Pourtant** *Although* ; **méfiant** *suspicious* ; **à l'égard de** *regarding* ; **ramène** *brings back* ; **fuite manquée** *failed escape* ; **menace** *threat* ; **sûreté** *security*

1776
Déclaration d'indépendance des États-Unis

1781

Le marquis de Lafayette aide l'armée américaine à gagner la bataille de Yorktown

1783
Traité de Paris entre les États-Unis et la Grande-Bretagne

1789
Convocation des états généraux

Prise de la Bastille, début de la Révolution française

Déclaration des droits de l'Homme et du Citoyen

1792

Louis XVI est mis en prison

1793

Louis XVI et Marie-Antoinette sont guillotinés

1.2, 2.1, 2.2

Produits

Jacques Prévert a écrit un poème **« Les belles familles »** sur les rois de France qui avaient le même prénom. Lisez-le en ligne et répondez à la question. Qu'est-ce que la plupart des rois de France avaient en commun ?

4.1

Comparaisons

Quels mots anglais, dérivés de **règne** et **régent**, ont plus ou moins le même sens ?

Resources

Points de départ
Workbook 5
Explore

Answers

Produits
Ils s'appelaient tous Louis !

Comparaison
reign and regent

Reference Desk

If you have access to Passport, find a video or a news article related to **la Révolution française** and show it to your students.

Culture

Practices: Activity

The French revolutionaries favored death by guillotine because it treated all victims equally and, therefore, expressed the ideals of the revolution. Previously, nobles were beheaded by axe and the poor were hanged. Although public executions ceased in 1939, the guillotine was used until 1977. No further executions of any sort took place and the French abolished capital punishment in 1981. If appropriate for your class, have students discuss the different views on the death penalty, past and present.

Connections

Histoire

The long-lasting alliance between France and the United States has its roots in the two revolutions. Specifically, the roles of Benjamin Franklin (in representing Americans to the French) and the Marquis de Lafayette (in ensuring the colonists' victory over the English) indebted each country to the other. Have students list and explain significant moments in French-American relations, including: ▪ Ben Franklin and Lafayette ▪ the Lousiana Purchase ▪ the Monroe Doctrine ▪ France's liberation in WWII ▪ the Marshall Plan ▪ the Algerian and Vietnam wars ▪ the Iraq War ▪ Franco-American relations today

Differentiated Learning

Accelerate
Aimé Césaire created the term **la négritude**. Have students define it and explain how it relates to the quotation in the reading.

Decelerate
Have students review the life and career of Aimé Césaire to justify why this Martiniquais merited a commemorative plaque placed in the Pantheon. Cite specific examples of achievements in his life.

Learning Styles

Visual Learners
Encourage students to find photos of Aimé Césaire and **le Panthéon** so that they can connect the images to the information about them.

Answers

Comparaisons
Possible answers: la Chine, l'Iran, l'Arabie saoudite, l'Irak, les États-Unis, le Pakistan, la Corée du Nord, le Soudan, le Viêt-Nam, le Nigeria

Critical Thinking

Analysis

1. Why might one say that the American Revolution set the stage for the French Revolution? Explain.
2. Why did Louis XVI send financial and military support to the colonies? (To defeat France's enemy, England)
3. The Marquis de LaFayette, predecessor to Louis XVI, played a major role in both the American and French Revolutions. Explain with examples.
4. Louis XV led a lavish lifestyle. He said **"Après moi, le déluge."** How did this attitude and lifestyle affect the lives of his successors, Louis XVI and Marie-Antoinette?

Connections

Literature

Charles Dickens wrote *A Tale of Two Cities*, which is a love story and a fictionalized historical account of the French Revolution. Consider playing excerpts of one of the versions of the movie to encourage students to watch a movie adaptation in full or even read the novel. Clips are available online. Have students compare the plot, characters, and views of the revolution to what they know of Victor Hugo's *Les Misérables*—often misconstrued to be about the French Revolution, it recounts the student uprisings and revolt of the 1832 June Rebellion. Both novels were published within three years of each other (Dickens's in 1859, Hugo's in 1862).

Expansion

Assign students the following people and terms to augment their study of the French Revolution: **Charlotte Corday**, **La Fuite à Varennes**, **Robespierre**, **Marat**, **Danton**, **Les Girondins**, **la Tour Bonbec**, **L'Affaire du Collier**. Ask students to present a brief summary to the class with illustrations and anecdotes.

1.2, 2.1

Traditions et pratiques

La pratique de la guillotine a existé en France de 1792 à 1977. Le Docteur Guillotin voulait éviter la souffrance (*suffering*) pendant les exécutions. Pendant la Révolution, les exécutions par guillotine ont eu lieu sur la place de la Révolution (maintenant la place de la Concorde).

1.2, 4.2

Comparaisons

Les Français ont mis fin à la peine de mort (*capital punishment*) en 1981. Faites une liste de pays qui continuent à appliquer la peine de mort? Qu'en est-il aux États-Unis?

La guillotine

Portrait de Marie-Antoinette 1.2, 2.1, 2.2, 3.1, 5.2

Marie-Antoinette aimait chasser (*hunt*).

Archiduchesse d'Autriche, fille de Marie-Thérèse d'Autriche et de l'Empereur François 1er, Marie-Antoinette (1755–1793) devient Reine de France en 1770 quand elle épouse Louis XVI. Elle aura quatre enfants dont le futur Louis XVII qui, séparé de sa mère et maltraité en prison au Temple, meurt à l'âge de dix ans en 1795.

De Marie-Antoinette, on a gardé la réputation d'une reine légère*, dépensière*, mêlée à* des intrigues politiques et amoureuses et à des affaires frauduleuses (l'affaire du collier de la Reine). Conservatrice, elle est peu favorable à l'Esprit des Lumières* et elle influence beaucoup le Roi dans son refus d'une évolution de la monarchie. Elle persuade le Roi de demander l'intervention des armées des Cours étrangères pour sauver la Royauté. Honnie* et calomniée*, celle qu'on surnomme alors « l'Autrichienne » est exécutée le 16 octobre 1793. Toutefois, ce portrait ne rend pas justice à la femme étrangère rentrée dans un mariage forcé à un jeune âge, et mal aimée de son mari, qui finit par prendre sérieusement ses responsabilités de mère et de reine.

Recherche : reines de france, marie-antoinette

légère *careless* ; **dépensière** quelqu'un qui dépense trop d'argent ; **mêlée à** *involved in* ; **Esprit des Lumières** *Ideas of the Age of Enlightenment*; **Honnie** *held in contempt*; **calomniée** *slandered*

1.2, 2.2

Produits

Marie-Antoinette a passé la fin de sa vie emprisonnée dans deux cellules de **la Conciergerie**, une prison parisienne de 1391 à 1914.

Recherche : conciergerie centre des monuments nationaux

Aujourd'hui, la Conciergerie fait partie du palais de justice de Paris.

Essential Instruction

1. Have students make a timeline of the events from the American War for Independence to the death of Marie-Antoinette as featured in the textbook, if this has not yet been done.
2. Have them read and compare the portraits of the king with that of the queen and add additional dates to their timeline. After reading, ask students if the reading confirmed or challenged their initial notions of Louis XVI and his queen.
3. Ask students to read the poem "**Les belles familles**" and discuss the question posed in the poem and the humor permeating this seemingly simplistic work by Prévert.

Les états généraux 1.2, 2.1, 2.2, 3.1, 4.2, 5.2

Avant la Révolution française, la population était divisée en trois ordres : le clergé (qui avait le plus grand pouvoir), la noblesse (qui avait un peu moins de pouvoir), et le Tiers État* (qui avait un pouvoir minime). Le Tiers État est représenté par des députés aux états généraux ; une de leurs fonctions était de voter l'impôt. La dernière convocation des états généraux a eu lieu en 1789. Louis XVI les a invités en leur disant :

> « De par le Roi,
>
> Notre aimé et féal*.
>
> Nous avons besoin du concours de nos fidèles sujets* pour Nous aider à surmonter* toutes les difficultés où Nous Nous trouvons relativement à l'état de Nos finances, et pour établir*, suivant Nos vœux*, un ordre constant et invariable dans toutes les parties du gouvernement qui intéressent le bonheur* de Nos sujets et la prospérité de Notre royaume*.... »

C'était la dernière convocation des états généraux. Elle représentait une révolution juridique : finalement, le groupe s'est proclamé Assemblée nationale et il n'y avait plus de rôle pour le roi.

Recherche : états généraux de l'ancien régime

Tiers État *commoners* ; **féal** *faithful, loyal (king)* ; **fidèles sujets** *faithful, loyal subjects* ; **surmonter** *to overcome* ; **établir** *establish* ; **vœux** *wishes* ; **bonheur** *happiness* ; **royaume** *kingdom*

La Déclaration des Droits de l'Homme et du Citoyen 1.2, 3.1, 4.2, 5.2

Ayant aidé les Américains pendant la Révolution américaine, les Français étaient conscients de la *Déclaration d'Indépendance des États-Unis* de 1776 et elle a influencé la *Déclaration des Droits de l'Homme et du Citoyen* qu'on a rédigée 13 ans plus tard. Elle énonce* des droits naturels individuels et collectifs du peuple français. Cette déclaration, à son tour, a influencé le *Bill of Rights*, qui a été ratifié trois ans plus tard aux États-Unis en décembre 1791.

énonce *sets forth*

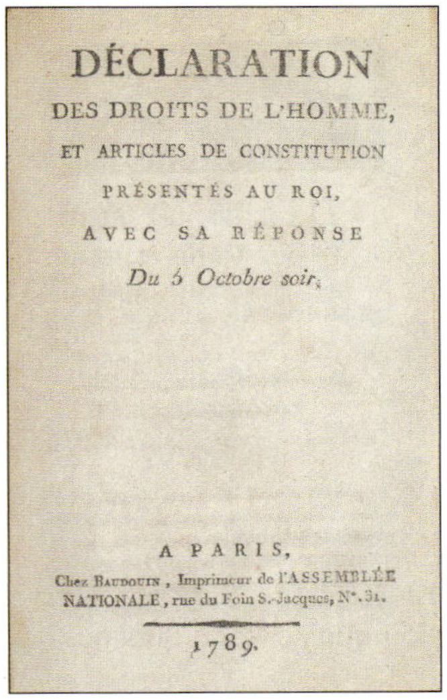
DÉCLARATION
DES DROITS DE L'HOMME,
ET ARTICLES DE CONSTITUTION
PRÉSENTÉS AU ROI,
AVEC SA RÉPONSE
Du 5 Octobre soir.

A PARIS,
Chez Baudouin, Imprimeur de l'ASSEMBLÉE NATIONALE, rue du Foin S.-Jacques, N°. 31.
1789.

1.2, 2.2, 4.2, 5.2

Produits

La Déclaration des Droits de la Femme et de la Citoyenne, écrite par la féministe Olympe de Gouges en 1791, avait comme but d'appliquer les droits des hommes aux femmes. Malgré ses efforts vaillants pour faire accepter sa *Déclaration*, tout le monde n'était pas d'accord, et l'Assemblé a voté contre. Accusée d'être l'auteur d'une affiche offensive contre le gouvernement, elle a été guillotinée en 1793.

Recherche : olympe de gouges

Game

Qui suis-je ?

Play this game to review vocabulary and the lives of the famous people studied to date. Put students in small groups. Have each student draw a name from these choices: LaFayette, Dr. Guillotin, Jacques Prévert, Aimé Césaire, la Fontaine, Georges Seurat, to name a few. Each student goes in front of the rest of the group to answer **imparfait** and **passé composé** questions from members who try to discover his or her identity. The student in front of the group answers each question with a complete sentence, using the **imparfait** or the **passé composé**. The responders may be evasive but must be honest. After the identity of the first student is guessed, the second student goes in front of the group to answer questions, and so on.

Expansion

1. Students may want to connect the principles of the American and French revolutions to the Algerian War of Independence (1954–1962), in which the French colony of Algeria won independence from France. The war, which ended the 4th Republic, had a lasting impact on France's perception of its political stability and place as a colonial power.
2. Have students peruse ***La Déclaration des Droits de l'Homme et du Citoyen*** to understand the rights proclaimed by the French in 1789. Students can compare these rights to the American Bill of Rights, ratified in the United States three years later, in 1791. Finally, these two documents can be compared to the Universal Declaration of Human Rights, authored by Human Rights Commission of the United Nations, under the leadership of Eleanor Roosevelt, in 1947.

Differentiated Learning

Expand

It is important to move students from the cliché of Marie-Antoinette as the one-dimensional, light-hearted, air-headed queen to seeing her personal evolution into a thoughtful, loving wife, mother, and sister. To do this, you could read "**La Dernière lettre de la Reine Marie-Antoinette**" with the class. It was written shortly before her execution.

Multiple Intelligences

Visual Learners/Artistic Learners

Students may enjoy the 1983 film by Roman Polanski, ***Danton***, starring Gérard Depardieu. The soundtrack, script, and imagery capture the less romantic side of the French Revolution and the conflict between the ideals and practicalities of establishing a republic.

Answers

7

1. 1754 : naissance de Louis XVI ; 1755 : naissance de Marie-Antoinette ; 1770 : Marie-Antoinette devient Reine de France ; 1783 : signature du traité de Versailles ; 1789 : convocation des états généraux ; 1791 : Louis XVI essaie de fuir à Vincennes ; 1792 : Louis XVI est conduit à la prison du Temple ; 1793 : Louis XVI est guillotiné le 21 janvier ; Marie-Antoinette est guillotinée le 16 octobre.
2. Paragraphs will vary.
3. Possible answers: Elle fait construire le Hameau de la Reine ; Elle ranime la mode et l'éclat à Paris avec ses spectacles et dîners ; Elle fait aménager des petits appartements ; Elle crée un petit café pour les seigneurs et dames qui visitent le Palais ; Elle invente un nouveau style de vie ; Elle accorde une protection aux musiciens.
4. Answers will vary.
5. Answers will vary.
6. Answers will vary.
7. Possible answer: Similarities: Both constitutions are similarly structured, with an introduction followed by a number of articles; Differences: The French declaration is narrated in the third person, claiming to report the words of the people of France. The American declaration is narrated in the first person, "We", without specifying to whom the "We" is referring.
8. Jasmine is the emblem of Tunisia. It is a white, pure and delicate flower, and symbolizes kindness and tolerance.

À DISCUTER

Answers will vary.

Communication

Interpersonal: Cooperative Groups

Students work in groups to create an original crossword puzzle in French plus answer key. Have them focus on the people, events, and documents of the time of the French Revolution. Check puzzles for accuracy and have students correct errors. Groups exchange puzzles and solve them.

Recherche : templates for crossword puzzles

La Francophonie

Profil historique

Révolution en Tunisie 1.2, 2.2, 3.1, 4.2, 5.2

En 2010–11, le peuple tunisien s'est révolté et a renversé* l'homme à la tête du régime, le Président Ben Ali. La Tunisie est ainsi devenue une démocratie en tenant ses premières élections libres en octobre 2011. Cette révolution s'appelle la « révolution de jasmin ». Essentiellement une révolution non-violente, la révolution de jasmin a influencé les peuples dans d'autres pays arabes à se révolter aussi.

a renversé *overthrew*

7 Activités culturelles 1.3, 3.1, 3.2

Faites les activités suivantes.

1. Faites un axe chronologique de la vie de Louis XVI et Marie-Antoinette, indiquant à quoi correspondent ces dates : 1754, 1755, 1770, 1783, 1789, 1791, 1792, 1793.
2. L'histoire de Lafayette marque le début des relations amicales entre les États-Unis et la France. Faites des recherches sur cette amitié et présentez une petite histoire à la classe.

Recherche : relations france états-unis, histoire des relations franco-américaines

3. Recherchez les modifications apportées par Marie-Antoinette à Versailles.
4. Marie-Antoinette est un personnage qui fascine le cinéma : faites des recherches sur les films français et américains où la reine apparaît. Choisissez en ligne un extrait à montrer à la classe.
5. Trouvez des tableaux de Marie-Antoinette et écrivez des légendes pour décrire sa vie.

Recherche : élisabeth vigée le brun

6. Trouvez le tableau *Le Serment du Jeu de paume* par Jacques-Louis David en ligne et décrivez-le. Ou cherchez une autre image de la Révolution française, par exemple, l'exécution de Louis XVI ou la Prise de la Bastille, et décrivez-la.

Recherche : serment du jeu de paume jacques-louis david, histoire-image

7. Faites un organigramme Venn sur la *Déclaration des Droits de l'Homme et du Citoyen*, et la *Bill of Rights* des États-Unis. Quelles sont les similarités et les différences entre les deux documents ?
8. Recherchez pourquoi on appelle la révolution en Tunisie la révolution de « jasmin ».

À DISCUTER

La Révolution française, était-elle inévitable, selon vous ? Pourquoi, ou pourquoi pas ?

Pendant la révolution de jasmin

Essential Instruction

1. Divide the class into four groups of varying abilities. Have students create a visual on a poster board of either **Les états généraux**, **La Déclaration des Droits de l'Homme et du Citoyen**, **La Déclaration des Droits de la Femme et de la Citoyenne**, or **Révolution en Tunisie**.
2. The visual should represent the group's subject symbolically and through words. Ask students to do additional research to add details to their visual. They present to the class.
3. In new groups, have students do one of the four tasks in **Activité 7**, then share their work with the class. Make sure students understand the relationship, similarities, and differences between the following four documents, which are often confused with each other: the American Declaration of Independence, the Declaration of the Rights of Man and Citizen, the American Bill of Rights, and the Universal Declaration of Human Rights.
4. Have students write a one-sentence summary of each of the **Considérant** clauses from **Préambule**.
5. As a class discuss whether this document, idealistic as it is, has any "teeth" to enforce these tenets.
6. Have students do both activities in **Activité 8**.

Du côté des médias 1.2

Lisez le préambule de la Déclaration universelle des droits de l'homme des Nations Unies de 1948.

Préambule

Considérant que la reconnaissance de la dignité inhérente à tous les membres de la famille humaine et de leurs droits égaux et inaliénables constitue le fondement de la liberté, de la justice et de la paix dans le monde.

Considérant que la méconnaissance et le mépris des droits de l'homme ont conduit à des actes de barbarie qui révoltent la conscience de l'humanité et que l'avènement d'un monde où les êtres humains seront libres de parler et de croire, libérés de la terreur et de la misère, a été proclamé comme la plus haute aspiration de l'homme.

Considérant qu'il est essentiel que les droits de l'homme soient protégés par un régime de droit pour que l'homme ne soit pas contraint, en suprême recours, à la révolte contre la tyrannie et l'oppression.

Considérant qu'il est essentiel d'encourager le développement de relations amicales entre nations.

Considérant que dans la Charte les peuples des Nations Unies ont proclamé à nouveau leur foi dans les droits fondamentaux de l'homme, dans la dignité et la valeur de la personne humaine, dans l'égalité des droits des hommes et des femmes, et qu'ils se sont déclarés résolus à favoriser le progrès social et à instaurer de meilleures conditions de vie dans une liberté plus grande.

Considérant que les Etats Membres se sont engagés à assurer, en coopération avec l'Organisation des Nations Unies, le respect universel et effectif des droits de l'homme et des libertés fondamentales.

Considérant qu'une conception commune de ces droits et libertés est de la plus haute importance pour remplir pleinement cet engagement.

8 La Déclaration universelle des droits de l'homme des Nations Unies 1.3, 3.2, 4.2, 5.2

Faites les activités suivantes.

1. Faites un « word cloud » en soulevant les mots les plus importants de ce document.
2. Recherchez comment les Nations Unies font la promotion des droits de l'homme et de la femme actuellement. Présentez un exemple à la classe.

Recherche : l'onu et les droits universels de l'homme

Answers

8

1. Possible answer: dignité, famille humaine, droits égaux, liberté, justice, paix, barbarie, conscience, libre, terreur, misère, protégés, révolte, tyrannie, oppression, essentiel, relations amicales, foi, droits fondamentaux, valeur, égalité, hommes, femmes, progrès social, meilleures, respect universel, libertés fondamentales, conception commune
2. Presentations will vary.

Reference Desk

The United Nations is an international organization founded in 1945. Its mission is to keep peace throughout the world; encourage friendly relations among member countries; work to eliminate hunger, disease and illiteracy; and be the harmonizing center to achieve these goals. There are currently 193 member states. The six official languages are: Arabic, Chinese, English, French, Russian, and Spanish. The Universal Declaration of Human Rights was created in 1948 by a subcommittee of the Commission of Human Rights of the UN, chaired at the time by Eleanor Roosevelt.

Communication

Presentational: Cooperative Groups

In triads, students take a side to debate as if in court. Should Marie-Antoinette be exiled, acquitted, or executed? Select one representative from each point of view to argue before the class who plays the jury. A vote to determine her fate follows the arguments.

Differentiated Learning

Accelerate

Have students research **la Révolution française** in more depth to lead the class in answering the question in **À discuter**.

Have students research the meaning of **le jeu de paume** ("real" tennis, a precursor to today's sport), and its relevance to the site of the **"Serment du Jeu de Paume."** Where is it located? What famous paintings used to be housed in a 19th-century building of the same name in the Tuileries Gardens?

Special Needs Students

Linguistically Challenged

Encourage students to read in English about the documents of the French Revolution to gain additional background and knowledge. Reading passages in English will help them understand the French passages more easily.

Dyslexia

Give students a study guide with key words to help them focus on the most important features of the readings.

Resources

WB Workbook 6–7

G & V Practice Games

Answers

9

1. M. Belkacem fait ses adieux à sa femme.
2. Les enfants font semblant d'être des super-héros.
3. Les pilotes font grève.
4. Tu fais ta valise.
5. Saleh et moi faisons du ski de fond.
6. Coralie et Amadou font de la planche à voile.
7. Salim fait don de 10 euros.
8. Pierre et ses copains font partie d'un groupe de musiciens.

Reference Desk

1. Consider having students brainstorm categories for **faire** expressions they know, for example, weather, sports, household chores, pastimes, and miscellaneous. Have them write the category headings and list all of the **faire** expressions under the appropriate heading. In their miscellaneous category students might include expressions such as **faire du baby-sitting**, **faire le tour**, and **faire les devoirs**.
2. The "rules" governing the **imparfait** and the **passé composé** are guidelines. Context dictates tense selection. Words such as **d'habitude**, **de temps en temps**, and **souvent** are several of the cues for the **imparfait**. Expressions indicating a specific time, for example, **la semaine passé**, **hier**, and **pendant les vacances** often cue the **passé composé**.

Structure de la langue

Révision: Expressions with *faire* 1.2

The verb **faire** is one of the most frequently used verbs in French.

Tu **fais** un projet en histoire?	*Are you doing a history project?*

Faire is called a "building block" verb because it is used to form so many expressions in French. Some of the most common expressions with **faire** deal with the weather, shopping, traveling, and various other activities. Here are some examples where **faire** is used in French but a different verb is used in English.

Louis XVI ne **faisait** pas **attention** aux besoins du peuple de la France.	*Louis XVI was not paying attention to the needs of the people of France.*
Louis XVI a **fait ses adieux** à sa famille.	*Louis XVI said good-bye to his family.*
C'était en janvier que Louis XVI est mort; il **faisait froid**.	*It was in January that Louis XVI died. It was cold.*

9 Qu'est-ce qu'ils font? 1.2

Interpretive Viewing

Dites ce que tout le monde fait en choisissant une expression ci-dessous.

faire semblant d'être des super-héros · **faire grève** · **faire de la planche à voile** · **faire sa valise** · **faire ses adieux à sa femme** · **faire partie d'un groupe de musiciens** · **faire du ski de fond** · **faire don de 10 euros**

1. M. Belkacem

2. les enfants

3. les pilotes

4. toi

5. Saleh et moi

6. Coralie et Amadou

7. Salim

8. Pierre et ses copains

Essential Instruction

1. Use the chart ***Révision:* Expressions with *faire*** to launch a review of the verb.
2. Give students time to do **Activité 9** then correct the exercise in class.
3. Before assigning **Activité 10** ask why the **passé composé** was used in the first set of examples and the **imparfait** in the second. Review the differences in usage.
4. Have students write the questions for this exercise. Circulate to correct their work.
5. Ask students to generate other questions, using the same format, that they could ask someone using these two tenses. They can then use these questions to interview a partner.

10 Votre passé 1.1

Interpersonal Speaking

*À tour de rôle, demandez à votre partenaire s'il ou elle a fait ou faisait les activités suivantes. Utilisez le **passé composé** ou **l'imparfait**.*

MODÈLES faire du ski alpin (pendant les vacances d'hiver)

A : As-tu fait du ski alpin pendant les vacances d'hiver ?
B : Oui, j'ai fait du ski alpin pendant les vacances d'hiver.
ou
Non, je n'ai pas fait de ski alpin pendant les vacances d'hiver.

faire du snowboard (quand tu avais dix ans)

A : Faisais-tu du snowboard quand tu avais dix ans ?
B : Oui, je faisais du snowboard quand j'avais dix ans.
ou
Non, je ne faisais pas de snowboard quand j'avais dix ans.

1. faire ton lit (quand tu avais cinq ans)
2. faire la lessive (le weekend dernier)
3. faire du scooter des mers (l'été dernier)
4. faire un tour de montagnes russes (quand tu es allé(e) au parc d'attractions)
5. faire de la gym (quand tu étais enfant)
6. faire du shopping (pendant ton voyage)
7. faire du patinage artistique (quand tu étais jeune)

Faire + INFINITIVE 1.2

Resources

WB Workbook 8–9
LA Listening Activity 2
G & V Practice Games

Answers

10

1. A : Faisais-tu ton lit quand tu avais cinq ans ?
   B : Oui, je faisais mon lit quand j'avais cinq ans./Non, je ne faisais pas mon lit quand j'avais cinq ans
2. A : As-tu fait la lessive le weekend dernier ?
   B : Oui, j'ai fait la lessive le weekend dernier./Non, je n'ai pas fait la lessive le weekend dernier.
3. A : As-tu fait du scooter des mers l'été dernier ?
   B : Oui, j'ai fait du scooter des mers l'été dernier./Non, je n'ai pas fait de scooter des mers l'été dernier.
4. A : As-tu fait un tour de montagnes russes quand tu es allé(e) au parc d'attractions ?
   B : Oui, j'ai fait un tour de montagnes russes quand je suis allé(e) au parc d'attractions./ Non, je n'ai pas fait un tour de montagnes russes quand je suis allé(e) au parc d'attractions.
5. A : Faisais-tu de la gym quand tu étais enfant ?
   B : Oui, je faisais de la gym quand j'étais enfant./Non, je ne faisais pas de gym quand j'étais enfant.
6. A : As-tu fait du shopping pendant ton voyage ?
   B : Oui, j'ai fait du shopping pendant mon voyage./Non, je n'ai pas fait de shopping pendant mon voyage.
7. A : Faisais-tu du patinage artistique quand tu étais jeune ?
   B : Oui, je faisais du patinage artistique quand j'étais jeune./ Non, je ne faisais pas de patinage artistique quand j'étais jeune.

Differentiated Learning

Accelerate
Have students make an extended list of **faire** idioms to expand their vocabulary. Ask them to teach the class these expressions using gestures or memory aids.

Decelerate
The verb **faire** and its idioms are not difficult to learn. Consider giving your low-ability students a quiz so that they are successful. It should give **"un coup de pouce"** to their average.

Multiple Intelligences

Visual-Spatial

1. Ask students to draw the flag of the United Nations. Have them explain the significance of the colors and the specific map of the world the organization chose for the flag.
2. Explain where the United Nations is located in New York. Who designed the building? How is it organized? What is the name of our current ambassador to the U.N.?

Answers

Comparaisons

In French and English, the preposition **par** or *by* is used to indicate the person who does the action.

Reference Desk

To express who does an action in a causative construction, use **par** or **à** + NOUN OR PRONOUN (for example, **Nous avons fait nettoyer le garage par les enfants**). The **par** or **à** phrase is replaced by an indirect object pronoun (for example, **Nous leur avons fait nettoyer le garage**). English uses the verb *to have* or *to make* to express the causative **faire**. French uses the preposition **par** and English can use the preposition *by* to show who actually does the action. (Though, in English, it can be omitted: *Mrs. Charrier has her children clean the garage.*)

Communication

Interpersonal: Paired Practice

To practice **faire** expressions in various forms, give pairs of students a note card with a sentence and a tense or mood (for example, **Claude ferait enregistrer ses bagages** and **passé composé**). Student A reads the first sentence to Student B, who identifies the tense or mood used (conditional), and then changes the sentence to the tense or mood indicated (for example, **Claude a fait enregistrer ses bagages**). Partners exchange their card for a different one and switch roles. Pairs continue until they have practiced a sentence in each of the forms being reviewed or until they have practiced with all of the cards.

To express the idea of having someone do something or having something done, use a form of the verb **faire** followed by an infinitive. Notice the differences in the following two sentences.

Jean **fait** une omelette.	*Jean makes an omelet.*
La reine **fait préparer** une omelette.	*The queen has an omelet prepared.*

In the first sentence, Jean makes an omelet himself. In the second sentence, the queen has an omelet made for her by someone else.

The form of **faire** can be in any tense.

M. Lebrun **a fait enregistrer** ses bagages.	*M. Lebrun had his luggage checked.*

When object pronouns are used, they precede the form of **faire**. There is no agreement between the past participle **fait** and a preceding direct object pronoun.

Les Français ont fait guillotiner Marie-Antoinette ?	*Did the French (people) have Marie-Antoinette guillotined?*
Oui, ils **l'ont fait guillotiner**.	*Yes, they had her guillotined.*
Les députés des états généraux ? Louis XVI **les a fait venir**.	*The deputies of the Estates General? Louis XVI made them come.*

In affirmative commands, object pronouns are attached with hyphens to the form of **faire**.

Faites-le lire le discours !	*Have him read the speech!*

4.1

Comparaisons

Explain how in French and English people say who does the action in sentences that use **faire** + INFINITIF.

Mme Charrier fait nettoyer le garage **par** ses enfants.
Mrs. Charrier has the garage cleaned *by* her children.

On recycle !

Avec un partenaire, imaginez que vous êtes adulte, que vous avez une famille, ou êtes célibataire, et que vous travaillez. Demandez à votre partenaire quelles corvées vous faites faire (par une autre personne).

MODÈLE **A : Est-ce que tu fais laver la vaisselle ?**
B : Non, je ne fais pas laver la vaisselle, j'ai un lave-vaisselle.
B : Est-ce que tu fais tondre la pelouse ?
A : Oui, je fais tondre la pelouse car mon mari n'aime pas le faire.

passer l'aspirateur • faire le linge • réparer la machine à laver • construire un garage • poser le papier peint • peindre les murs • repasser les chemises • mettre le couvert • nettoyer la salle de bains • faire les courses

Papa fait toujours pleurer les bébés !

Essential Instruction

1. Review **faire causatif** using the explanation on p. 454 and referencing the activity on p. 455.
2. Have students tell you what they have other people do for them; write the sentences on the board.
3. For **Activité 10**, have students decide which tense to use before asking them to complete the exercise.
4. Have students do **Activité 11** orally. Ask students for more examples of what travel arrangements Mme Poux did for herself, and what her secretary organized for her.
5. To expand **Activité 11**, ask open-ended questions about Mme Poux and her assistant. What is Mme Poux's first name? How old is she? What is her assistant's name? Where is she going? What does she do for a living? What is in her suitcase?

11 Voyage d'affaires 1.3

Presentational Speaking or Writing

Mme Poux est une femme d'affaires importante qui voyage beaucoup avec son assistant. Elle fait une liste pour préparer son prochain voyage. D'après sa liste, est-ce qu'elle fait les choses indiquées elle-même ou est-ce qu'elle les fait faire par son assistant?

- téléphoner à son mari
- retirer de l'argent au distributeur
- trouver son passeport
- acheter des billets de théâtre
- écrire son discours

- réserver une chambre
- louer une voiture à Paris
- enregistrer ses bagages
- faire sa valise
- acheter les billets d'avion

MODÈLE  **Mme Poux trouve son passeport.**

 **Mme Poux fait louer une voiture à Paris.**

1. 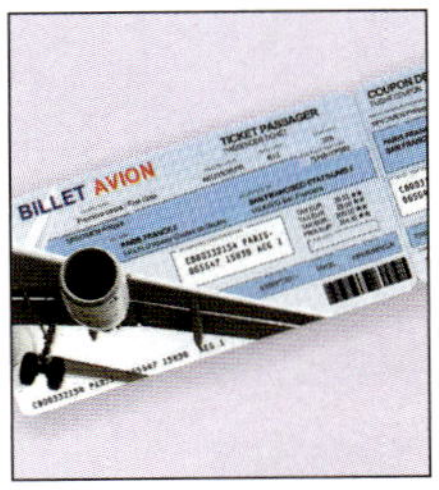

2. 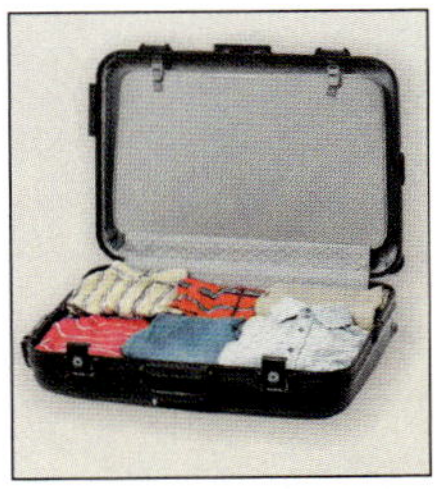

3. 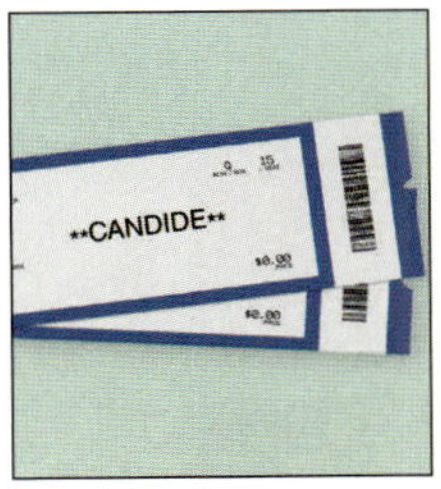

4. 

5. 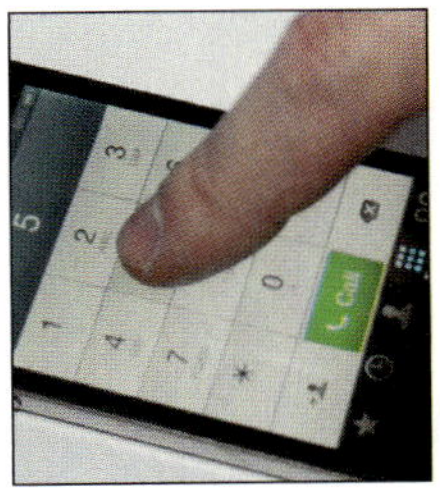

6. 

7. 

8. 

Differentiated Learning

Decelerate

For extra practice create a handout of sentences, some using **faire** + INFINITIVE, others showing the subject doing the action (for example, **Mme DuRose a fait arroser son jardin pendant qu'elle était en vacances. Mme DuRose arrose son jardin tous les matins**). Ask students to identify who is doing the action and to translate the sentences into English.

Adapt

Have students imagine their mother/father/friend broke their arm or leg (or had surgery) and needs to have someone help them do what they normally can do themselves, for the next two months. Once students choose their situation, ask them to make a list of five to ten things to tell the person to have someone else do for them (and/or not do themselves), then have a conversation according to the following example:

A: Maintenant, tu fais laver la vaisselle (par Papa).
B: Oui, maintenant, je fais laver la vaisselle (par Papa).
or
Non, maintenant, je fais laver la vaisselle par toi!

Answers

11

1. Mme Poux fait acheter les billets d'avion
2. Mme Poux fait faire sa valise.
3. Mme Poux achète des billets de théâtre.
4. Mme Poux fait réserver une chambre.
5. Mme Poux téléphone à son mari.
6. Mme Poux retire de l'argent au distributeur.
7. Mme Poux fait enregistrer ses bagages.
8. Mme Poux écrit son discours.

Communication

Interpersonal: Paired Practice

Have students write a role-play between Mme Poux's assistant (from p. 455) and an agent at Avis France. In the dialogue, include a discussion of the types of cars available, rates, promotions, and options with and without a chauffeur. The assistant is very particular and asks a lot of questions before reserving the car. This activity could be expanded to reserving airline tickets, booking a hotel, or making business-dinner reservations in a fine dining restaurant. Have students perform the role-play for the class.

Game

Charades

Pair up students and give each pair a card with an expression of things we often have done for us: **"faire une omelette, peindre la maison, tondre la pelouse, laver le chien."** The student pairs come up to the front of the room, where the first student mimes the action and points to the second student, who then also mimes the action. The first non-performing pair to correctly state what the first student is having done (**"Jacques fait tondre la pelouse!"**) gets a point. Continue until every student pair has acted out their action.

Resources

Activities 12–13

Answers

12

1. M. Legrand fait installer le four.
2. Maman et moi faisons poser le papier peint dans le salon.
3. Les Dufour font repeindre la salle à manger.
4. Je fais planter des fleurs sur le balcon.
5. Nadine et Fatima font réparer le frigo.
6. Bruno et toi faites mettre le nouveau canapé dans le séjour.

13 Script

1. Louis XVI a fait venir Marie-Antoinette en France.
2. Louis XVI et Marie-Antoinette ont fait préparer de bons repas pour leurs invités à Versailles.
3. Marie-Antoinette a fait construire un petit village à Versailles.
4. Louis XVI a fait venir les états généraux en 1789.
5. Le gouvernement français l'a fait prisonnier.
6. Le nouveau gouvernement l'a fait guillotiner.

1. B
2. A
3. D
4. E
5. C
6. F

Expansion

Consider a dictation inspired by the grammar exercises for **faire**. Read each sentence three times, first at natural speed, next more slowly giving students time to write, finally at normal speed so students can edit. Correct as a group. Display the corrected version or have volunteers write the sentences on the board.

12 L'immeuble 1.3

Presentational Writing or Speaking

Le Clos Bellini a de nouveaux résidents qui font embellir leurs appartements par des bricoleurs professionnels. Dites ce qu'ils font.

MODÈLE tu (accrocher des peintures)
Tu fais accrocher des peintures.

1. M. Legrand (installer le four)
2. maman et moi (poser le papier peint dans le salon)
3. les Dufour (repeindre la salle à manger)
4. je (planter des fleurs sur le balcon)
5. Nadine et Fatima (réparer le frigo)
6. Bruno et toi (mettre le nouveau canapé dans le séjour)

Les Dupré font réparer l'évier.

13 Louis XVI et Marie-Antoinette 1.2, 2.1, 3.1, 5.2

Interpretive Listening and Viewing

Écrivez les numéros 1–6 sur votre papier. Écoutez les phrases, et associez-les à la bonne illustration.

Essential Instruction

1. Students do **Activité 12** orally and then as a written exercise.
2. Play **Activité 13**, then have students talk about each illustration.
3. Have students choose one of the **À vous la parole** tasks.
4. For **Activité 14** have students watch clips of a **bateau mouche** tour. Students can focus on another monument along the Seine to vary the presentations, for example, **Notre-Dame**, **Le Musée d'Orsay**, **Le Louvre**, or the replica of the Statue of Liberty.
5. **Activité 15** will appeal to students interested in history and people committed to social causes.
6. For **Activité 16**, have students use the **Déclaration des Droits de l'homme** or its **Préambule** as a template.

À vous la parole

Question centrale **?** Comment le passé influence-t-il le présent?

Communiquez!

14 La Conciergerie 1.2, 1.3, 2.2, 3.2, 5.1, 5.2

Interpretive Viewing, Presentational Speaking

Du palais royal médiéval à la prison de la Révolution française, la Conciergerie est aujourd'hui un monument historique et l'un des sites les plus visités de Paris. Imaginez que vous êtes guide touristique pour la Compagnie des Bateaux-Mouches à Paris. Vous devez écrire un script de 90 secondes pour les touristes du bateau. Décrivez le monument de l'extérieur et de l'intérieur. Ensuite, enregistrez ou filmez votre présentation pour la partager avec la classe.

Recherche : conciergerie paris, conciergerie centre des monuments nationaux

15 La grande scène de l'histoire 1.2, 1.3, 3.2, 5.1, 5.2

Interpretive Reading, Presentational Writing and Speaking

Choisissez une cause qui vous intéresse : protection de l'environnement, défense des animaux, lutte contre la pauvreté, etc. Puis, cherchez une personnalité francophone, vivante ou non, qui a eu une influence sur cette cause. Écrivez un dialogue semblable à celui à la page 446, et présentez-le à la classe.

Recherche : fondation brigitte bardot, médecins sans frontières, histoire de l'ue

16 Louis XVI et Marie-Antoinette 1.2, 1.3, 2.2, 3.1, 5.2

Interpersonal Viewing, Presentational Speaking

Le règne de Louis XVI est associé au commencement de la Révolution française et à la fin de l'ère royale de Versailles. Cherchez une chronologie en ligne de 1774 à 1793. Avec un partenaire, jouez une scène de l'histoire de France en imaginant un dialogue entre Louis XVI et Marie-Antoinette. Vous pouvez choisir de documenter plusieurs événements jusqu'à la mort du monarque et sa femme ou de vous concentrer sur un événement important ou crucial pendant le règne de Louis XVI. Écrivez un dialogue et présentez-le à la classe.

Differentiated Learning

Accelerate

Students put the illustrations in **Activité 13** in chronological order, then use these to write a story about the fall of the royalty, including details that they have learned about the events of the French Revolution.

Decelerate

Have students do the **Accelerate** activity in small groups. Before beginning, work with them to order the pictures correctly, and make a comprehensive pre-writing outline before beginning their composition.

Resources

CA Communicative Activities

Share

Answers

14 Texts will vary.

15 Presentations will vary.

16 Role-plays will vary.

Reference Desk

1. **Bateaux mouches** are long multi-decked boats offering guided cruises on the Seine every hour during the day, and into the evening. Tourists may also choose lunch or dinner cruises. The name, **bateaux mouches**, refers to the area outside of Lyon called Mouche, where the boats are manufactured. **Bateaux mouches** are not the only tourist boats on the Seine, but they are the most identifiable by name.
2. For **Activité 15**, you may give students suggestions of famous persons, such as:
   - Bernard Kouchner (co-founder of the Nobel Prize-winning **Médecins Sans Frontières**), a politician and physician whose career is focused on his commitment to humanitarian causes throughout the world.
   - Jacques Delors (politician and economist), who served as president of the European Commission in 1985. He was a proponent of budget reform, and he laid the foundation for a single market community that came to fruition in 1993.
   - Toussaint Louverture (1743–1803), the Black Napoleon, who was the leader of the Haitian Revolution. He drove the French out of Haiti, and he created an independent black state where former slaves learned to be free, self-governing citizens.
3. If you have access to Passport, create a question for your students to share their response to a communicative activity.

Prononciation

Pronouncing the French *r* 1.2, 4.1

» Remember, the letter *r* is pronounced differently than in English and is usually pronounced at the end of words, except in cases like "Monsieur" and verbs ending in **-er**.

A Je peux prononcer *r* !

Répétez les phrases suivantes.

1. Pardon, je suis encore en retard !
2. On regrette de devoir partir. . . .
3. Pourquoi faut-il leur dire au revoir ?

Mandatory Liaisons

» In general, liaison is mandatory in interior rhythmic groups. Look at the three liaisons in this sentence: Il**s**‿ont réservé dan**s**‿un peti**t**‿hôtel.

Note the three final consonants that connect to the vowels or vowel sounds that follow.

Note that *d* becomes /t/ before a vowel sound:
Quan**d**‿[t] on écoute, o**n**‿apprend beaucoup.

B Liaison obligatoire

Écoutez, puis répétez ces exemples de liaison obligatoire.

1. Il y a de nombreu**x**‿exemples de petit**s**‿appartements dans ce quartier.
2. C'es**t**‿un excellen**t**‿endroit et je suis tou**t**‿à fait d'accord.
3. C'est un gran**d**‿[t] écrivain.
4. Il faut de grande**s**‿idées et de nouvelle**s**‿attitudes !

C Comptez !

Écoutez les petits dialogues et, pour chaque phrase, mettez le nombre de liaisons que vous entendez.

Traditions et pratiques 1.2, 2.1

En France, ce sont surtout les académiciens ou les journalistes et politiciens qui ont tendance à prononcer les liaisons facultatives (*optional*). Prononcer trop de liaisons fait snob. L'ancien président Jacques Chirac était connu pour abuser des liaisons, ce qui faisait le bonheur des comiques.

Resources

- *Prononciation*
- Pre-test
- *Leçon* Quiz

Answers

C Script

1. –Tes amis ont trouvé de bonnes entreprises ?
2. –Oui, ils en ont trouvé plusieurs.
3. –Ils ont posté des lettres de motivation ?
4. –Oui, ils en ont posté plusieurs.

1. 2
2. 2
3. 1
4. 2

Expansion

To contrast the American and French *r*, have students sing "Row, row, row your boat" once with an American *r* and then with a French *r*. This should make them aware of the different position of the *r* in the mouth and be an amusing exercise as well.

Essential Instruction

1. Contrast the French *r* and the American *r*. In which part of the mouth is each *r* produced?
2. Continuing with **Prononciation**, after listening and repeating the sentences in part A, ask individual students to read the sentences aloud.
3. Put several sentences requiring liaisons on the board. Ask a volunteer student to read a sentence.
4. Have students listen and repeat part B, and write the liaisons they hear in C.
5. Encourage students to reread the **Contrat de l'élève** on p. 441 to remind themselves what they will be learning in **Leçon B**.

Leçon B Vocabulaire actif

Le monde du travail 1.2

Alex cherche un emploi

Alex trouve **une petite annonce** en ligne pour un poste qui l'intéresse.

Il **rédige une lettre de motivation/de candidature**.

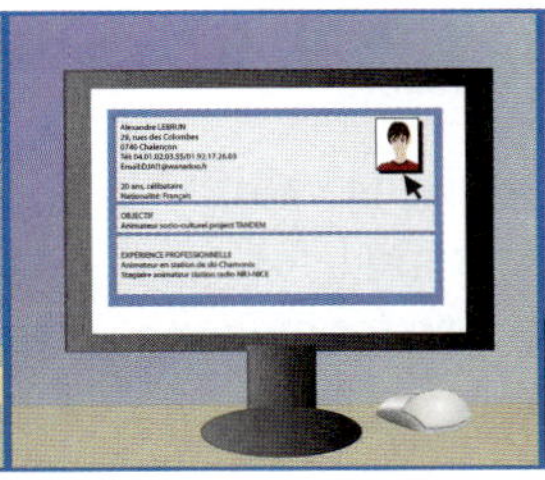

Il accompagne **son CV** d'une photo.

Il envoie son CV à l'entreprise.

Il est **convoqué** pour **un entretien**.

L'emploi lui **convient**.

L'entreprise **embauche** Alex.

Il va travailler **à plein temps**, pas **à mi-temps**.

Abida fait un stage

Abida **fait un stage** à TechMode.

Elle a signé **un contrat** avec le **DRH (Directeur des Ressources Humaines)** de **la compagnie**.

Elle **met en pratique les connaissances acquises au cours de** ses études universitaires.

Elle reçoit **un salaire** pendant **sa formation** en entreprise.

Resources

- *Vocabulaire actif*
- eV eVisual
- WB Workbook 1–3
- FC Flash Cards
- LA Listening Activity 1
- G & V Practice Games

Reference Desk

1. Other related terms and expressions include **une carrière** (*career*), **une demande d'emploi** (*job application*), **une description de poste** (*job description*), **la chasse à l'emploi** (*job hunting*), and **les références** (*references*).
2. Job ads are found in the **Emplois** or **Carrières et Emplois** section of **les petites annonces**.
3. In France, most courses of study require an internship before awarding a diploma. While short-term student interns are not paid, long-term internships (longer than 2 months, or 308 hours) must be paid positions. The minimum pay is 3,60€/hr.

Differentiated Learning

Accelerate

Have students work in pairs and use circumlocution to practice the vocabulary. One student describes a word or expression without using the word until his or her partner guesses correctly. Model this first and encourage students to identify the word. Use descriptions such as **C'est une action** or **C'est ce qu'on fait après avoir trouvé un poste**.

Decelerate

Work with students to isolate the verbs used in each new expression, making sure that they practice the conjugations. Consider copying the images from **Le monde du travail** and asking the students to match the expression with the image.

Resources

Pour la conversation
Et si je voulais dire… ?
Activity 1

Answers

1

1. Il pensait qu'il ne trouverait pas de travail à cause de l'économie.
2. Elle a suggeré de rédiger une lettre de motivation pour un stage.
3. Il a envoyé son CV.
4. Il a été embauché.
5. Il va commencer son stage payé.

Reference Desk

1. **Acquérir**, meaning *to acquire*, is a challenging verb to conjugate. **J'acquiers**, **tu acquiers**, **il acquiert**, **nous acquérons**, **vous acquérez**, **ils acquièrent**. The future has a double *r*, **j'acquerrai**, and the past participle is **acquis**. Thus **les acquis** means what we acquire.
2. **Convoquer** is a synonym for **faire venir**. It has the sense of summoning someone.
3. **Gérer** means *to manage*. **Un(e) gérant(e)** is a *manager*, and **la gestion** means *management*.
4. Unlike many American teenagers, it is exceedingly rare for a French high school student to have a paying job during the school year. However, many students will work and have a paying job over the summer months.

Pour la conversation 1.2

How do I indicate there is a lot of a certain item?

» Il y a **plein de** modèles….
There are a lot of models….

How do I say I did something in vain?

» **J'ai beau** chercher des modèles….
I've been looking in vain for models….

How do I ask someone to stop with the flattery?

» **N'en jette plus!**
Stop it!

Et si je voulais dire… ?

un apprentissage	*apprenticeship*
un atelier	*workshop*
un cadre	*executive manager*
les débouchés (m.)	*job openings*
la période d'essai	*trial period*
faire carrière	*to make a career*
occuper une fonction	*to occupy a position*
poser sa candidature	*to submit one's application*

1 Tu imagines? 1.2

Interpretive Reading

Lisez le mail de Romain à son frère au sujet d'un stage. Puis, répondez aux questions.

A: Olivier
Cc:
Objet: On m'a pris!

Salut, Olivier!

Après avoir fait mes études à l'université, j'étais prêt à ne pas trouver de travail à cause de l'économie. Mais ma prof m'a proposé de rédiger une lettre de motivation pour un stage. Alors j'ai rédigé ma lettre, je l'ai envoyée avec mon CV accompagné d'une photo, et on m'a convoqué pour un entretien. On m'a pris! J'ai signé un contrat hier dans le bureau du DRH, et je commence mon stage avec salaire dans quinze jours. Tu imagines? Et toi, comment vas-tu? Dans ton nouveau poste, est-ce que tu mets en pratique les connaissances acquises au cours de tes études universitaires?

À plus,

Romain

1. Pourquoi est-ce que Romain pensait qu'il ne trouverait pas de travail?
2. Qu'est-ce que sa prof lui a suggéré de faire?
3. Qu'est-ce que Romain a fait après?
4. Quel a été le résultat de son entretien?
5. Que va-t-il faire dans deux semaines?

Essential Instruction

1. Put the new vocabulary and expressions from **Le monde du travail** on the board. Define the term in French and ask for the equivalent term in English.
2. Play the recording as students follow in their books.
3. Have students listen to **Et si je voulais dire…?** Ask them to define the terms in French.
4. Students listen to **Activité 1** and answer the questions individually.
5. Arrange students in pairs to do **Activité 2** as a timed competition. Tally correct answers for each pair.
6. Have students listen to **Activité 3**, answering **oui** or **non** to the statements.
7. Review the questions for **Activitié 4**. Ask students to add questions that would be appropriate in discussing their work experience and future plans.
8. Ask students to circulate to ask and answer these questions. Encourage them to add details to have a more realistic conversation.

2 Je cherche du travail 1.2, 5.1

Interpretive Reading

Choisissez une expression ci-dessous pour complétez les phrases suivantes. Attention : il est parfois nécessaire que vous vous serviez du subjonctif.

rédiger **se présenter** **embaucher** **mon CV**
une annonce **mettre en pratique** **à plein temps** **un contrat**

MODÈLE Mes copains veulent que je recherche en ligne… qui m'intéresse.
Mes copains veulent que je recherche en ligne **une annonce** qui m'intéresse.

1. Mon prof souhaite que je… les connaissances acquises dans son cours.
2. Mon père préfère que je signe… avant de travailler.
3. Ma mère voudrait que mon père m'….
4. Mes grands-parents désirent que je… une lettre de motivation pour mon annonce préférée.
5. Ma mère exige que j'envoie… à TechMode.
6. Le DRH de TechMode veut que je… à 10h15 pour un entretien.
7. Il souhaite que je travaille de 9h00 à 17h00, c'est à dire….

3 Jeanne dans le marché du travail 1.2

Interpretive Listening

*Écrivez les numéros 1–6. Écoutez le parcours de Jeanne pour trouver un emploi. Si l'ordre des deux phrases est logique, écrivez **oui** ; sinon, écrivez **non**.*

4 Questions personnelles 1.1

Interpersonal Speaking

Répondez aux questions avec un partenaire.

1. Est-ce que tu travailles ? Si oui, où ? Depuis combien de temps ?
2. As-tu déjà écrit un CV ? Où l'as-tu envoyé ? Avec ou sans photo ?
3. Quels postes t'intéressent ?
4. Voudrais-tu travailler à plein temps en été ?
5. Quelles sont les connaissances que tu as acquises à l'école qui te préparent pour le monde du travail ?

Resources

Activity 3

Answers

2

1. mette en pratique
2. un contrat
3. embauche
4. rédige
5. mon CV
6. me présente
7. à plein temps

3 Script

1. Jeanne finit ses études universitaires. Elle regarde les petites annonces en ligne.
2. Jeanne envoie son CV et sa lettre à Bruxelles.
   Elle écrit son CV où elle parle de ses connaissances acquises.
3. Jeanne envoie son CV et sa lettre à la DRH de la Commission. La DRH lui téléphone et lui demande de se présenter pour une interview.
4. La DRH de la Commission Européenne l'embauche. Elle va à Bruxelles par le train pour un entretien.
5. Jeanne signe un contrat d'une année avec la DRH. Elle entre dans son bureau pour la première fois.
6. Jeanne reçoit son premier chèque. Elle commence à travailler à plein-temps à la Commission.

1. oui; 2. non; 3. oui; 4. non; 5. non; 6. non

4 Answers will vary.

Critical Thinking

Analysis

Have students research and compare the current **taux de chômage** in France with that of the United States. Which is greater?

Recherche : institut national de la statistique et des études économiques, bureau of labor statistics

Differentiated Learning

Accelerate
Have students look for a job through a French newspaper's interactive site and make a help wanted list in French.

Recherche : offre d'emploi, le monde

Decelerate
Have students write an e-mail response to Romain, congratulating him on his new job, asking for more details, and answering the questions he asks in the letter.

Resources

Dialogue
Activity 5

Dialogue Video

WB Workbook 4

Answers

5

1. Karim doit écrire une lettre de candidature.
2. Il aimerait faire un stage à la Commission européenne à Bruxelles.
3. C'est pour devenir un assistant junior.
4. Il travaillerait à plein temps.
5. Selon Élodie, Karim a une bonne expérience parce qu'il a eu plein de petits boulots.

Reference Desk

Some vocabulary that students might not know: **rédiger un article** (*to write an article*); **un rédacteur** (*an editor*); **une redaction** (*an essay*); **jeter/lancer des fleurs** (*to compliment or praise someone enthusiastically*).

nouvelle orthographe **sûr, sure, surs, sures**

Game

Allez-y!

To practice new vocabulary, prepare a set of note cards with a new word or expression on each one. Divide the class into two teams. Call the first player from each team to the front. Select the top card from the pile and read the word or expression that you want the players to use in a sentence. Say, "**Allez-y!**" to cue both players to write a sentence using that word or expression on the board. The student who uses the new vocabulary correctly in a sentence earns a point for his or her team. If both sentences are correct, both teams win a point. Play continues with the next two students, and the team with the most points wins.

Rencontres culturelles

Karim fait une demande d'emploi

1.2

Élodie et Karim sont au café ; ils travaillent devant leurs ordinateurs portables.

Élodie : Qu'est-ce que tu fais ?
Karim : Je suis en train de rédiger une lettre de candidature pour un stage.
Élodie : Un stage cet été ? Où ça ?
Karim : Un stage d'assistant junior à Bruxelles.
Élodie : À la Commission européenne ? À plein temps ? Wahou !
Karim : Oui ! Mais je dois commencer par rédiger la lettre de motivation.
Élodie : Regarde sur Internet, il y a plein de modèles, j'en suis sûre.
Karim : Après avoir trouvé un modèle pour le CV, j'ai beau chercher des modèles pour la lettre de motivation, ça doit quand même être *perso*....
Élodie : Ce n'est pas difficile avec toutes les qualités que tu as : tu écris bien, tu parles plusieurs langues, tu es sympa, tu t'intéresses aux autres, tu te débrouilles*... tu as fait plein de petits boulots !
Karim : N'en jette plus ! Tu vas me faire rougir....

***Je parle bien**

The sound **-ouille** in **débrouilles** is often hard to pronounce for non-native speakers. Say ***aille*** (the subjunctive of **aller**, pronounced like the English pronoun *I*). Then replace the **a** in **aille** with **ou**: **ou-ille**. Now, say **dé-brou-illes**.

5 Karim fait une demande d'emploi

Répondez aux questions.

1.3

1. Que doit écrire Karim ?
2. Qu'est-ce que Karim aimerait faire à Bruxelles ? Où veut-il travailler ?
3. Le boulot est pour devenir quoi ?
4. Il travaillerait à mi-temps ou à plein temps ?
5. Selon Élodie, pourquoi Karim a une bonne expérience ?

Essential Instruction

1. Have students watch the video **Karim fait une demande d'emploi** with books closed.
2. Ask students general comprehension questions.
3. Replay the video, asking students to pay attention to what Karim wants to do, where, and what document he needs to write.
4. Students listen to the recording and follow along in the text.
5. Ask what words or expressions students do not know from the context. Have them prepare the answers to **Activité 5**.
6. Have high and low-ability students work in pairs to read **Extension**. In addition to answering the **Extension** question, ask students to describe the other candidates.

EXTENSION **On veut que quel candidat se présente pour un entretien?** 1.2

Au bureau Gabrielle et Jean-Pierre doivent choisir un candidat après réception des lettres de motivation.

Gabrielle: Moi, j'en ai sélectionné trois: au moins eux, ils ont bien lu la petite annonce du site.

Jean-Pierre: Donc, ça fait cinq. Oui, moi aussi, j'ai fait attention à ça: que la lettre de motivation réponde aux exigences du poste à pourvoir.

Gabrielle: Après, il y a les petits plus… parce que côté formation, ils ont à peu près tous le même profil.

Jean-Pierre: Toutes et tous des forts en langues….

Gabrielle: Oui, et puis comme on cherche un junior, l'expérience professionnelle, c'est plutôt limité.

Jean-Pierre: Moi, j'en ai un… il a été charpentier.

Gabrielle: Pas mal! Moi, j'en ai une qui a travaillé dans une unité de soins palliatifs.

Jean-Pierre: Dur… il y en a un, là, qui a une belle expérience… il a fait plein de boulots. Il a travaillé en Guinée, à Djibouti, en Tunisie… côté formation universitaire, il a un parcours plus chaotique.

Gabrielle: Pas grave, on le formera.

Jean-Pierre: On sent qu'il a de l'énergie à revendre… il ne doit demander que ça….

Gabrielle: Tu le convoques pour l'entretien.

EXTENSION Quelles sont les qualifications du candidat que Gabrielle et Jean-Pierre choisissent pour l'entretien? 1.2

Stratégie

Faites un résumé du profil des trois candidats dont Gabrielle et Jean-Pierre parlent. Puis, imaginez le profil d'un quatrième candidat qui provoque la réaction de Gabrielle et Jean-Pierre sur la photo.

Resources

Extension

EXTENSION

Il a travaillé en Guinée, à Djibouti, et en Tunisie.

Expansion

Have students study ***le Figaro*** and ***le Monde*** for a week to make a list of **les offres d'emploi**. Ask them to compare these to job offerings in an American large city newspaper. What are the similarities and differences?

Communication

Interpersonal: Paired practice

Have students work in pairs to read the **Extension** conversation aloud. Model pronunciation and expression before students practice. Ask students to switch roles. Choose volunteers to present to the class.

Differentiated Learning

Accelerate

Have students write **une lettre de motivation** for a job that they would like to do, outlining their interests and skills. Encourage students to look at online models of letters to get a sense of phrasing, just like the French do.

Decelerate

Have students write a brief description of a job they have done or would like to do, then describe the responsibilities using **il faut que** or **il fallait que**.

Resources

Points de départ

WB Workbook 5

Explore

Reference Desk

1. Visit the European Union's official website and search the links in English or in French for activities geared to students and teachers.
2. If you have access to Passport, find a video or a news article related to **l'Union européenne** and show it to your students.
3. You may point out to your students the significance of the choice of location of the European Parliament at Strasbourg. This is a city in the heart of the Alsace-Lorraine region, the control of which was long fought over in numerous wars between France and Germany (notably during the Franco-Prussian War of 1870–71 and World War I). Now it is a site dedicated to more peaceful activities and political negotiation.

Points de départ

Pre-AP

Question centrale ? Comment le passé influence-t-il le présent?

La Francophonie

Institutions de l'Union européenne

Bruxelles 1.2, 2.2, 3.1, 5.2

C'est à Bruxelles que siègent* **la Commission** et **le Conseil européen**.

La Commission européenne est le symbole de l'administration européenne. C'est une administration fédérale de 27 000 personnes environ. La Commission est d'abord la « gardienne des Traités » – Rome en 1958, Bruxelles en 1967, Luxembourg en 1970, La Haye en 1986, Maastricht en 1993, Amsterdam en 1999, Nice en 2003, et Lisbonne en 2009. Elle veille à* leur bonne application, et elle fait respecter l'intérêt général. Le président de la commission, nommé par le Conseil européen, nomme lui-même les commissaires (un par état membre). Leur mandat est de cinq ans. La Commission représente et défend les intérêts de l'UE (Union européenne) dans sa globalité. Elle gère* et met en œuvre* la politique de l'UE. Ainsi elle propose de nouvelles lois, gère le budget, veille à l'application du droit, et représente l'UE auprès des autres nations.

Recherche : le site web official de l'union européenne, commission européenne, europa traité européens, histoire union européenne

siègent *sit* ; **veille à** *ensures* ; **gère** *manages* ; **met en œuvre** *carries out*

Le Conseil européen a été créé en 1974. Il réunit les chefs d'État et de gouvernement des pays membres de l'Union européenne. Il définit les grandes orientations*, décide des politiques à mettre en œuvre. Son rôle est de plus en plus important et consacre* la supériorité d'une union des États.

Recherche : conseil européen, siège du conseil européen

grandes orientations *general guidelines* ; **consacre** *recognizes*

Strasbourg 1.2, 2.2, 3.1, 3.2, 5.2

C'est à Strasbourg que siège **le Parlement européen**. Il examine et adopte les lois. Il contrôle le fonctionnement des autres institutions et adopte le budget. Ses membres sont élus* au suffrage direct* par les citoyens de tous les États membres.

Recherche : parlement européen europa, parlement européen toute l'europe

élus *elected* ; **suffrage direct** *direct vote*

C'est le Parlement européen qui a le contrôle des dépenses.

Essential Instruction

1. Have students identify the location of the European Commission cities on a map.
2. Have students make a chart with the following column headings: **Institution**, **Pays**, **Mission**, **Remarques** to help organize the information on pp. 464–465 for a discussion.
3. Have students access the search words sites and add information to their list.
4. As a class, discuss the value of each institution. Is there a benefit to the fact that these institutions are located in separate countries?

Luxembourg 1.2, 2.2, 3.1, 5.2

La Cour de justice des Communautés européennes se trouve à Luxembourg. Elle règle* les relations entre les Institutions européennes, les États, et les citoyens. Ses jugements dans le règlement* des conflits s'imposent à tous et le droit européen prime sur* le droit national.

Recherche : cours de justice curia

règle *regulates* ; **règlement** *settlement* ; **prime sur** *takes precedence over*

Francfort 1.2, 2.2, 3.1, 4.2, 5.2

Francfort accueille la **Banque centrale européenne (BCE)** qui, depuis le Traité de Lisbonne, est devenue une institution indépendante à part entière, au même titre que la Cour de Justice ou le Parlement. Elle est chargée d'émettre* l'euro, de garantir la stabilité de la monnaie européenne et de définir les grandes orientations de la politique monétaire de la zone euro (19 pays).

Recherche : europa banque centrale européenne, toute l'europe banque centrale européenne

émettre *to issue*

Espace Schengen 1.2, 2.2, 3.1, 5.2

Le village Schengen est situé au bord de la Moselle entre les frontières allemande, luxembourgeoise, belge, et française. Il est le symbole de **l'espace Schengen** qui regroupe les 26 pays (22 pays de l'Union et 4 de l'AELE*) qui constituent un espace sans frontière intérieure et qui confient* la surveillance des frontières terrestres*, aériennes, et maritimes aux pays qui en sont limitrophes*. La menace terroriste actuelle et l'incapacité de l'Union à s'accorder sur une politique d'immigration conduisent à une remise en cause* partielle des accords de Schengen.

Recherche : convention de schengen, toute l'europe l'espace schengen, carte espace schengen

l'AELE Association européenne de libre-échange ; **confient** *entrust* ; **frontières terrestres** *land borders* ; **limitrophes** *adjacent* ; **remise en cause** *questioning*

1.2, 4.2

Comparaisons

Le traité *North American Free Trade Agreement* (NAFTA) entre le Canada, les États-Unis, et le Mexique fait penser à quel traité européen ?

Produits

Le drapeau de l'Union européenne est orné de 12 étoiles dorées disposées en cercle sur fond bleu, représentant la solidarité et l'union entre les peuples d'Europe. Il date de 1955.

1.2, 2.2. 3.1

Le drapeau devant la Commission européenne de Bruxelles représente l'Union européenne.

Mot-clé

Union est un mot emprunté au latin classique *unio* vers 1225. C'est en bas latin que *unio* a pris le sens de : unité et union. Le mot désigne d'abord la jonction de plusieurs choses pour former un tout (1380) ; puis la concorde, la bonne entente entre plusieurs personnes ; et enfin une liaison d'affection (15ème siècle).

Answers

Comparaisons

Il fait penser au traité de Maastricht (traité fondateur des accords entre pays européens).

Communication

Interpersonal: Cooperative Groups

Imagine that the European Union is facing a financial crisis and has decided to cut major funding to one of its institutions. Put students in groups of five, each bearing a badge with the name of their institution. Have them prepare arguments as to why their institution is too important to be reduced, and secondly suggest reasons why another institution should be chosen instead. Students must passionately defend their own institution. Afterward, have the class debate the merits of each institution and vote for a major funding reduction to one of them.

Differentiated Learning

Accelerate

Ask students to write an argument for or against a change in the current North American Free Trade Agreement in which Canada, the United States, and Mexico would eliminate borders and share a common currency. Would this be a positive or negative change? Why?

Decelerate

Students make a map of the **Carte Espace Schengen** and present it to the class explaining the order of entry of the countries into the European Union by colors.

Multiple Intelligences

Musical-Rhythmic

Ask students to lead the class in singing the National Anthem of Europe set to the music of Beethoven's "Ode to Joy."

Reference Desk

If you have access to Passport, find a video or a news article related to **le Maghreb** or **le Pays basque**, and show it to your students.

Expansion

The Basques have large communities in Idaho. Why did they choose this area to live? What similarities to their homeland could be found here?

Critical Thinking

Analysis

In what way can the **Basque** and the **Bretons** be compared to the **Québécois**? What do they have in common? (unique language, living within a larger country with a desire for their own identity)

Institutions hors de l'UE

Dans le monde arabe

1.2, 2.1, 3.2, 4.2, 5.2

Les pays maghrébins—la Tunisie, le Maroc, et l'Algérie—font partie de la Ligue arabe, ou La Ligue des États arabes. Fondée en 1945, la Ligue arabe a maintenant 22 pays membres. Son but est de solidifier les relations entre pays membres et d'en surveiller* la collaboration. Elle doit aussi assurer la protection de leur indépendance et leur souveraineté, et, de façon plus générale, elle est censée* protéger les affaires et les intérêts des pays arabes.

surveiller *to watch over*; **censée** *supposed to*

C'est au Caire, en Égypte, qu'a été créée la Ligue arabe.

Les Basques

1.2, 2.1, 3.1, 5.2

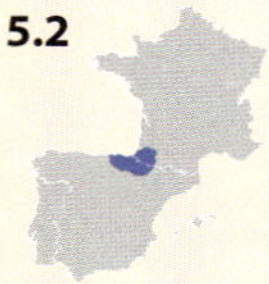

Euskadi est le nom d'une région autonome en Espagne où les citoyens sont des Basques. Les aspirations de cette communauté indépendante comprennent la représentation directe dans les institutions de l'UE, par exemple, le droit d'interjeter appel à* la Cour de Justice à Luxembourg. Même si la langue basque n'est pas une langue officielle dans l'UE, elle est reconnue comme minoritaire, tout comme le breton. Il y a aussi des Basques en France. Ils habitent dans le département des Pyrénées Atlantiques. Les Basques sont très attachés à leurs maisons, à la famille, et à la communauté. De nos jours, il y a des clubs gastronomiques où les hommes préparent des spécialités basques comme le cidre, l'agneau, le ragoût*, et le paprika. Un sport populaire Basque est la pelote.

interjeter appel à *to appeal to*; **ragoût** *stew*

La ville de Bayonne, dans le Pays basque français

1.2, 2.2

Produits

Le comité Nobel a décerné (*awarded*) **le prix Nobel de la paix** à l'UE en 2012 pour avoir «contribué pendant plus de six décennies à promouvoir la paix et la réconciliation, la démocratie, et les droits de l'homme en Europe».

Essential Instruction

1. Have students read **la Francophonie: Institutions hors de l'UE**. Ask them to make a chart comparing **La Ligue des États arabes** with the United Nations charter. Where are these countries located? What are the common features? (Both were founded in 1945, and their mission statements are somewhat similar.)
2. Students read **Les Basques**. When did the Spanish Basques become autonomous? What languages might they speak?

   Recherche: euskadi
3. Ask students to work in pairs to complete Activity 1 of **Activités culturelles**. Compare responses with the whole class.
4. Have all students do Activity 2.
5. Have students work in groups to do Activity 3. Be sure the students play the game and take the quiz from the official website of the **l'Union européenne**.
6. Students work in small groups choosing Activity 4, 5, or 6. The groups present their results to the class.

6 Activités culturelles 1.2, 1.3, 3.1, 3.2

Faites les activités suivantes.

1. Retrouvez à quelles institutions de l'Union européenne appartiennent ces attributions :
   A. Ses jugements s'imposent à tous.
   B. Elle met en œuvre les politiques communautaires.
   C. Il définit les grandes orientations.
   D. Il constitue un espace sans frontière intérieure.
   E. Elle garantit la stabilité de la monnaie.
2. Faites un plan de l'Europe avec tous les pays membres. Indiquez les capitales et les langues qu'on y parle.
3. Sur le site officiel de l'Union européenne vous trouverez des jeux et quiz pour en apprendre plus sur l'UE. Jouez à ces jeux.

Recherche : jeux et quiz strasbourg europe, coin des enfants jeux et quiz sur l'ue europa

4. Formez huit groupes. Chaque groupe se charge de faire des recherches sur les spécificités d'un traité : Rome (1958), Bruxelles (1967), acte union européenne de Luxembourg (1970), La Haye (1986), Maastricht (1993), Amsterdam (1999), Nice (2003), Lisbonne (2009).
5. Organisez une visite dans une ville avec une institution européenne.
6. Recherchez ce que la Ligue arabe a fait ou a décidé de faire cette année ou l'année dernière.

1.2, 2.1

Perspectives

Jacques Delors, ancien président de la Commission européenne, a dit : « Il me semble qu'à 27, à 30 ou 32 pays européens, nous pouvons avoir trois ambitions communes : un espace de paix active, un cadre pour le développement durable et une manière particulière de gérer-valoriser notre diversité culturelle. »

Qu'est-ce que Delors a prévu pour l'Union européenne ? A-t-on réalisé ses ambitions ?

Ces drapeaux représentent quels pays ?

Answers

6

1. A : La Cour de justice des Communautés européennes
   B : La Commission européenne
   C : le Conseil Européen
   D : l'espace Schengen
   E : la Banque européenne
2. Answers will vary with time. Check the official site.

3–6. Activities will vary.

Perspectives
Answers will vary.

Reference Desk

Jai alai is a ball game similar to Basque **pelota** in which a ball is bounced off walls in an enclosed court. It is a game that requires intense concentration and physical coordination, as the ball speeds have been clocked at 188 mph. This game is very popular in states such as Florida and Connecticut.

Differentiated Learning

Accelerate
Have students answer the question posed in **Perspectives** in a three-paragraph essay.

Decelerate
Encourage students to write a travel review page for the Internet for the **Basque** city of Bilbao with a list of tourist attractions including the Guggenheim museum.

Learning Styles

Visual Learners
Encourage students to make a map of the Basque area indicating principal cities and ports. Students may enjoy reading the short book ***Ramuntcho***, a story of love and adventure written by Pierre Loti (1850–1923) and set in the Basque region.

Kinesthetic Learners
Have students explain **la pelote basque** to the class. How many people compose a team, what equipment is needed, and how is it scored?

Recherche : basque pelota

Answers

7

1. 27 (after the effective Brexit)
2. Bruxelles
3. L'espace Schengen
4. L'UE dispose de six pays détenteurs de la bombe atomique.
5. L'euro est la monnaie unique obligatoire de l'ensemble de l'UE.
6. L'espace Schengen

Communication

Interpersonal: Cooperative Groups

Have students work in small mixed-ability groups to create a list of 10 trivia questions (with answers) as a review of **Leçon B** so far. They should not copy the questions from **Du côté des médias** but should create their own questions covering the material studied so far. Collect each group's list and combine them to create a review game. Choose students to be the game hosts.

Du côté des médias 1.2

Lisez les questions du quiz sur l'Union européenne.

Q1

Combien d'États composent l'UE?

- ☐ 12
- ☐ 26
- ☐ 27
- ☐ 32

Q2

Quelle ville est la capitale de l'UE?

- ☐ Genève
- ☐ Bruxelles
- ☐ Luxembourg
- ☐ Strasbourg

Q3

Comment nomme-t-on la zone européenne où les frontières ont été supprimées?

- ☐ L'espace Maastricht
- ☐ L'espace Schengen
- ☐ L'espace Stuttgart
- ☐ Aucune de ces réponses

Q4

Une de ces affirmations est fausse: laquelle?

- ☐ L'UE possède 2 sièges de membre permanent du conseil de sécurité de l'ONU.
- ☐ L'UE dispose de 3 pays dans le G7 (la réunion des 7 pays les plus industrialisé du monde).
- ☐ L'UE dispose de 6 pays détenteurs de la bombe atomique.
- ☐ L'UE est la première destination touristique du monde.

Q5

L'une de ces affirmations sur l'UE est fausse: Laquelle?

- ☐ Les membres de l'UE commercent principalement entre eux.
- ☐ L'euro est la monnaie unique obligatoire de l'ensemble de l'UE.
- ☐ L'agriculture represente 40% du budget de l'UE.
- ☐ La population européenne devrait compter un tiers de ses habitants âgés de plus de 60 ans d'ici 2050.

Q6

Lorsque vous traversez la frontière de l'Allemagne aux Pays-Bas sans montrer votre passeport, vous le faites grâce à:

- ☐ L'espace Maastricht
- ☐ L'espace Schengen
- ☐ L'espace Stuttgart
- ☐ Aucune de ces réponses

7 Quiz: L'Union européenne 1.2, 2.1, 2.2, 3.1, 3.2, 5.2

Répondez aux questions sur le quiz.

Recherche: quizz biz union européenne

Essential Instruction

1. As a review of the **L'union européenne**, have students take the small quiz in **Du côté des médias** and answer the questions for each section.
2. Ask students to work in pairs to brainstorm all of the **avoir** expressions that they remember.
3. Put the list of **avoir** expressions on the board and ask students to illustrate each one.
4. With white boards, have students practice conjugating **avoir** in all tenses and moods.
5. Ask students to make sentences with the **avoir** expressions. As a drill they must transform the sentences, singular to plural, and from one tense and mood to another.

Révision: Expressions with *avoir* 1.1

The verb **avoir** is another frequently used verb in French.

J'**ai** un entretien demain pour un stage.	*I have an interview tomorrow for an internship.*

Like **faire**, **avoir** is a "building block" verb, used in many expressions in French. Some of the most common expressions with **avoir** deal with age, physical ailments, or being hot/cold/hungry/thirsty/afraid. Can you think of others?

Marame **avait** vingt **ans** quand elle a travaillé à plein temps pour cette entreprise américaine.	*Marame was 20 years old when she worked full-time for this American company.*
Je ne pourrais jamais travailler pour Air France parce que j'**ai peur** en avion!	*I could never work for Air France because I'm afraid of flying!*

The expression **avoir beau** + INFINITIVE means "to do (something) in vain."

Nous **avons beau** chercher dans les petites annonces.	*We've been trying in vain to find something in the want ads.*

8 Les gens de mon quartier 1.2, 3.1

Interpretive Viewing

Faites des phrases qui décrivent les illustrations en vous servant d'une expression ci-dessous.

avoir hâte de partir en vacances **avoir de la chance** **avoir l'air sérieux** **avoir lieu** **avoir treize ans** **avoir peur du vide** **avoir raison** **avoir faim** **avoir envie d'envoyer un texto**

MODÈLE

le concert
Le concert a lieu le 16 mai.

1. M. et Mme Besnard

2. Diane

3. Docteur Giraud et toi

4. Timéo

5. moi

6. Brigitte et Marie-Alix

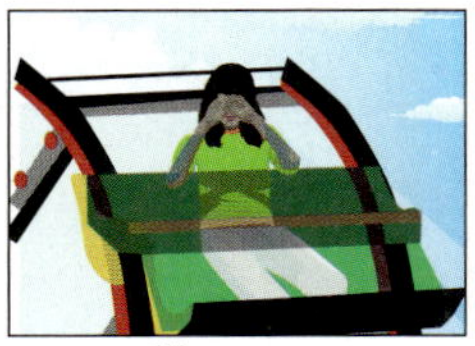

7. Madiba

8. Maelis

Resources

WB Workbook 6 –7

G & V Practice Games

Answers

8

1. M. et Mme Besnard ont de la chance.
2. Diane a faim.
3. Docteur Giraud et toi avez l'air sérieux.
4. Timéo a raison.
5. J'ai envie d'envoyer un texto.
6. Brigitte et Marie-Alix ont hâte de partir en vacances.
7. Madiba a peur du vide.
8. Maelis a treize ans.

Communication

Interpersonal: Paired practice

Prepare a set of cards with sentences using an **avoir** expression in the present tense, for example, **Le concert a lieu vendredi le 13 avril à 19h00**. On the back of each card identify a different tense and show the new sentence, for example, **[passé composé] Le concert a eu lieu vendredi le 13 avril à 19h00**. Student A shows the side with the present tense sentence to his or her partner and names the new tense. Student B restates the sentence in the new tense. Student A verifies that it is correct then Student B shows his or her card and they repeat the process. When both students have completed a sentence, they exchange cards and move to a new partner. Continue until time is called.

Differentiated Learning

Accelerate

Ask students to write about historical events where people tried to do things in vain. Have them make a list of ten such endeavors. Sports figures and adventurers are prime examples.

Have them use the expression "**avoir beau.**" For example: **"Louis XVI a eu beau se défendre, il a été guillotiné."**

Decelerate

Give students another opportunity to do well on a test of **avoir** expressions. Ask them to make flash cards of **avoir** expressions. Give them a "feel good" quiz on the expressions and conjugations of **avoir**. This quiz can help them feel more invested in class and give them a firm foundation of this key French verb.

Resources

WB Workbook 8–11
LA Listening Activity 2
G & V Practice Games

Answers

9

1. Marie-Antoinette a eu besoin de bien s'amuser.
2. Elle n'a pas eu envie de quitter l'Autriche et sa famille.
3. Mais Louis, le fils du roi de France, a eu besoin de se marier avec elle.
4. Quand Louis XVI a eu 16 ans, il s'est marié avec Marie-Antoinette.
5. Marie-Antoinette a eu de la chance parce qu'elle a habité Versailles.
6. La prise de la Bastille a eu lieu le 14 juillet 1789 et tout a changé.

Comparaisons

In English, both French sentences would be expressed as follows: *Mom criticized me for not having done my chores.* The negative word *not* is placed in front of *having*, the auxiliary verb form used in the past infinitive (as in *After not having gotten dressed…, After not having come to the concert…, After not having eaten…*, etc.). Unlike English, French has two ways to make the past infinitive negative.

Reference Desk

Explain that **après avoir/être** + PAST PARTICIPLE is a mini **passé composé** without a subject and it follows the same rules of agreement as **passé composé**. Once students know if the verb is conjugated with **avoir** or **être**, this structure is very straightforward.

9 À la cour de France 1.2

Interpretive Reading

*Complétez les phrases avec la forme correcte du verbe **avoir** + EXPRESSION. Utilisez le bon verbe au **passé composé**.*

1. Marie-Antoinette… de bien s'amuser.
2. Elle n'… pas… quitter l'Autriche et sa famille.
3. Mais Louis, le fils du roi de France, … se marier avec elle.
4. Quand Louis XVI… 16…, il s'est marié avec Marie-Antoinette.
5. Marie-Antoinette… parce qu'elle a habité Versailles.
6. La prise de la Bastille… le 14 juillet 1789 et tout a changé.

avoir (…) ans
avoir besoin
avoir lieu
avoir envie de
avoir de la chance

Past Infinitive 1.2

To say that someone did something in the past before doing something else, use the past infinitive. To form this tense with the preposition **après**, add the helping verb **avoir** or **être** and the past participle of the main verb.

après + { **avoir** / **être** } + PAST PARTICIPLE

Après avoir convoqué Damien pour un entretien, le DRH l'a embauché.

Après avoir trouvé une petite annonce, Thierry a envoyé son CV à l'entreprise. — *After finding a want ad, Thierry sent his résumé to the company.*

Après être arrivé en France, Abdel y a fait un stage en entreprise. — *After having arrived in France, Abdel interned at a French company there.*

Agreement of the past participle is the same as in the **passé composé**.

Après s'être présentée pour un entretien, Faustine a signé le contrat. — *After showing up for an interview, Faustine signed the contract.*

Comparaisons 4.1

Both of the following sentences are correct in expressing the negative past infinitive in French. What is the rule in English?

Maman m'a critiqué pour **ne pas** avoir fait mes corvées.
Maman m'a critiqué pour **n'**avoir **pas** fait mes corvées.

Essential Instruction

1. Review the use of the **passé composé** and the **imparfait**.
2. Have students select the correct form of **avoir** in the appropriate tense for **Activité 10**.
3. Introduce the past infinitive with examples of **avoir** and **être** verbs.
4. Ask students to translate examples of the past infinitive from English to French to demonstrate the difference in wording.
5. Do **Activité 11** with them. Write the answers on the board to point out agreement.

10 Logique ou pas? 1.3

Presentational Writing or Speaking

Faites des phrases logiques pour décrire l'histoire de Marie-France.

MODÈLE lire une petite annonce en ligne (envoyer son CV)
Après avoir lu une petite annonce en ligne, elle a envoyé son CV.

1. trouver une petite annonce (écrire sa lettre de motivation)
2. recevoir une convocation pour un entretien (se présenter au DRH)
3. recevoir une offre de travail (signer un contrat)
4. s'installer dans son bureau (faire la connaissance des autres stagiaires)
5. travailler deux semaines (recevoir son premier chèque)
6. faire un stage (être embauchée à plein temps)

11 La vie de Marie-Antoinette 1.3, 3.1

Interpretive Reading, Presentational Speaking or Writing

Regardez la chronologie de la vie de Marie-Antoinette. Écrivez des phrases avec l'infinitif passé et le passé composé pour décrire ce qui s'est passé.

MODÈLE 1755 : Marie-Antoinette est née (*was born*).
Elle vit en Autriche.

Après être née en 1755, Marie-Antoinette a vécu en Autriche.

1770 — Marie-Antoinette fait la connaissance du dauphin (*heir*) français, Louis.
Elle se marie avec lui.

1783 — Elle reçoit le petit Trianon en cadeau du roi.
Elle fait construire son Hameau à Versailles.

1789 — Les Français prennent la prison de la Bastille.
Ils décident d'abolir (*abolish*) la monarchie.

1791 — Marie-Antoinette et Louis XVI arrivent à Varennes. Ils sont arrêtés (*arrested*).

1792–93 — Les Français emprisonnent Marie-Antoinette.
Ils la guillotinent.

Answers

10

1. Après avoir trouvé une petite annonce, elle a écrit sa lettre de motivation.
2. Après avoir reçu une convocation pour un entretien, elle s'est présentée au DRH.
3. Après avoir reçu une offre de travail, elle a signé un contrat.
4. Après s'être installée dans son bureau, elle a fait la connaissance des autres stagiaires.
5. Après avoir travaillé deux semaines, elle a reçu son premier chèque.
6. Après avoir fait un stage, elle a été embauchée à plein temps.

11

1. Après avoir fait la connaissance du dauphin en 1770, Marie-Antoinette s'est mariée avec lui.
2. Après avoir reçu le petit Trianon en cadeau du roi en 1783, elle a fait construire son Hameau à Versailles.
3. Après avoir pris la prison de la Bastille en 1789, les Français ont décidé d'abolir la monarchie.
4. Après être arrivés à Varennes en 1791, Marie-Antoinette et Louis XVI ont été arrêtés.
5. Après avoir emprisonné Marie-Antoinette en 1792, les Français l'ont guillotinée en 1793.

Communication

Interpersonal: Paired Practice

Give student pairs two illustrations of people engaged in an activity featuring vocabulary they know. For example, give a team a photo of a woman cooking dinner. One student tells the other what they think will happen next: "**Après avoir préparé le dîner, Maman va appeler les enfants à table.**" The other student does the same with the second picture. The students copy down their sentences before passing their photos on to another pair and receiving two more. This process continues until all photos are discussed and sentences recorded. Circulate to check the quality of their work and make corrections.

Differentiated Learning

Decelerate

1. To help students visualize the chronology of past events, use a timeline to emphasize the order of actions when a past infinitive is used. Encourage them to tell you which action came first. For example, with the sentence **Après m'être réveillé, je me lève**, students say **Alors, je me réveille puis je me lève**. Have them pinpoint these two actions on the timeline.
2. Break **Activité 10** into phases. First, have students determine the logical order. Then have them determine the correct form of the verbs before putting the sentence together.

Resources

Activity 12

Answers

12 Script

1. Après avoir été embauchée par une entreprise, Coralie s'est inscrite à l'université.
2. Après s'être spécialisée en chimie, Coralie est devenue pilote.
3. Après avoir trouvé une bonne petite annonce en ligne, Coralie a écrit une lettre de motivation.
4. Après avoir envoyé son CV à l'entreprise, Coralie a été convoquée pour un entretien.
5. Après avoir parlé à Coralie, la DRH l'a embauchée.
6. Après avoir travaillé pour deux semaines, Coralie a reçu son premier chèque.

1. I; 2. I; 3. L; 4. L; 5. L; 6. L

13

1. A : Qu'est-ce que tu as fait après t'être habillé(e)?
   B : Après m'être habillé(e)….
2. A : Qu'est-ce que tu as fait après avoir fait les corvées?
   B : Après avoir fait les corvées….
3. A : Qu'est-ce que tu as fait après avoir déjeuné?
   B : Après avoir déjeuné….
4. A : Qu'est-ce que tu as fait après être sorti(e)?
   B : Après être sorti(e)….
5. A : Qu'est-ce que tu as fait après avoir dîné?
   B : Après avoir dîné….
6. A : Qu'est-ce que tu as fait après avoir fait la vaisselle?
   B : Après avoir fait la vaisselle….

Partner answers will vary.

Reference Desk

The past infinitive is made negative in one of two ways: the negative may come before the past infinitive, for example, **Après ne pas avoir dormi, j'étais fatigué(e)**, or **ne… pas** may surround **avoir** or **être** (for example, **Après n'avoir pas dormi, j'étais fatigué(e)**).

12 Qu'est-ce qui s'est passé après? 1.1, 1.2

Interpretive Listening

*Écrivez les numéros 1–6. Ensuite, écoutez les phrases. Si la phrase est logique, écrivez **L**. Sinon, écrivez **I** pour illogique.*

13 Samedi dernier 1.1

Interpersonal Speaking

À tour de rôle, demandez à votre partenaire ce qu'il ou elle a fait après avoir fait les activités ci-dessous.

MODÈLES se lever

A : Qu'est-ce que tu as fait après t'être levé(e)?
B : Après m'être levé(e), j'ai pris mon petit déjeuner.

faire ton lit

A : Qu'est-ce que tu as fait après avoir fait ton lit?
B : Après avoir fait mon lit, j'ai rangé ma chambre.

1. s'habiller
2. faire les corvées
3. déjeuner
4. sortir
5. dîner
6. faire la vaisselle

Connexions 1.1, 3.1

Cinéma

Quelles sont vos scènes cinématographiques préférées? Cherchez des moments inoubliables de cinq de vos films préférés. Décrivez ces scènes dramatiques en écrivant une phrase à l'infinitif passé. Puis, demandez à votre partenaire s'il ou elle sait de quel film il s'agit. Vous pouvez aussi chercher des photos.

MODÈLE **A : Après avoir rencontré un pilote américain, elle a essayé d'arrêter la Première Guerre mondiale.**
B : C'est *Wonder Woman*?

Essential Instruction

1. Have students listen to **Activité 12** and select the appropriate action.
2. Before doing **Activité 13** ask students to put the six verbs provided in the past infinitive forms.
3. Ask students to work with partners to do the interview questions in **Activité 13**.
4. As a whole-class activity, ask students to share what their partners said and give other examples.
5. For **Activité 14** students seeking a career in a certain field should research their chosen field online.
   Recherche : stepstone
6. To write **une lettre de motivation** for **Activité 15**, encourage students to use online templates. They can fine tune their letter with your help.

Question centrale ? Comment le passé influence-t-il le présent?

Communiquez!

14 C'est vous le patron! 1.3, 2.1, 2.2, 4.2, 5.1, 5.2

Presentational Speaking

Imaginez que vous êtes le directeur ou la directrice d'une grande entreprise en France, et que vous souhaitez obtenir le prix du meilleur business de l'année dans votre domaine. Préparez une présentation de votre entreprise qui souligne (*highlights*) ses qualités: Qu'est-ce qui vous distingue des autres entreprises de votre domaine? Quels avantages offrez-vous à vos employés afin qu'ils restent motivés et fidèles? En quoi les services que vous fournissez sont-ils utiles, innovants, ou importants? Faites votre présentation devant la classe, qui votera pour la présentation la plus convaincante.

15 J'écris une lettre de motivation 1.3, 2.2, 3.2

Presentational Writing

Quel est le métier de vos rêves? Rêvez-vous de voyager dans le monde en tant qu'homme ou femme d'affaires international(e), ou de travailler localement en tant que médecin, professeur ou vétérinaire? Rêvez-vous d'ouvrir votre propre entreprise? Imaginez que vous avez 24 ans et que vous avez fini vos études. Cherchez un emploi pour lequel vous allez envoyer votre candidature. Écrivez une lettre de motivation dans laquelle vous 1) exprimez votre intérêt pour le poste, 2) parlez de votre expérience et vos qualifications, 3) expliquez ce que vous pensez apporter à l'entreprise.

Recherche: modèle de lettre de motivation, lettre de motivation exemples

16 Je fais passer un entretien 1.1, 3.2, 5.2

Interpersonal Speaking

Avec un partenaire, jouez le rôle d'un intervieweur d'un(e) interviewé(e) à un poste. Essayez de présenter une interview aussi comique que possible. Peut-être que le candidat (la candidate) n'est pas du tout qualifié(e) pour le poste et donne des réponses ridicules aux questions qu'on lui pose. Peut-être qu'il (elle) est trop sûr(e) de lui (d'elle). Préparez une description du poste, un scénario et présentez le jeu de rôle à la classe. Soyez aussi créatif (créative) que vous le souhaitez. L'interview peut se terminer très bien ou très mal—c'est à vous de décider!

Resources

CA Communicative Activities

Share

Answers

14 Presentations will vary.

15 Letters will vary.

16 Role-plays will vary.

Reference Desk

If you have access to Passport, create a question for your students to share their response to a communicative activity.

Differentiated Learning

Accelerate/Decelerate

Encourage students who enjoy acting and drama to perform the interview in class. Ask more reserved students to tape the interview for **Activité 16**. Consider mixing ability levels for both options.

Special Needs Students

AD(H)D

Work with students to organize their ideas before writing **Activité 15**. Consider having a small study group to research the online templates and discuss and outline together what needs to be included in their letter.

Resources

Pre-T Pre-test

Q *Leçon* Quiz

Connections

Business Education

Consider inviting the school's literacy teacher or a teacher from the business education department to come to class and share ideas for writing **résumés**. Doing this creates a link between the CV writing activity done in French class and the need students may have for a **résumé** in their own future.

Reference Desk

Students may be inclined to make the CV too original, in order to stand out. According to a recent survey of French employers by the job site Monster, this may cause some problems:

« Un CV qui sort du lot par la forme ne ressort pas de la bonne façon »
— Estelle Raoul, directrice exécutive chez Page Personnel

« Je réagis à la forme quand elle est inappropriée à l'environnement métier »
— Cécile Fischer, responsable des Ressources humaines du Groupe William Sinclair

« Sa rapidité de lecture rend un CV plus vendeur »
— Thierry Andrieux, fondateur d'Humanessence

Stratégie communicative

Pre-AP

Communiquez!

Writing a Résumé 1.2, 1.3, 3.2, 5.1, 5.2

Tout d'abord, cherchez un stage qui vous paraît intéressant. Ensuite, rédigez votre CV dans lequel vous décrivez votre parcours scolaire et vos centres d'intérêts. Le but du CV est de décrocher (*to land*) un entretien d'embauche. Imaginez que vous ayez déjà obtenu un diplôme universitaire avec la spécialité de votre choix. Le CV à la page 475 pourra vous servir de modèle.

Recherche : infostages, stages en entreprises, expériences professionelles pour jeunes diplômés, stages rémunérés, stages non rémunérés, expériences en entreprises, stagiaires, stages en entreprises

Petites annonces stages

Assistant concepteur web/graphiste	Me contacter	Paris
Entreprise spécialisée dans la vente en ligne de bijoux et accessoires féminins cherche stagiaire pour webdesign/graphiste		

Stage rédacteur/rédactrice Internet	Me contacter	Marseille
Recherche stagiaire h/f pour rédaction et administration de contenu web pour un musée d'art		

Les étapes pour écrire un CV :

- Indiquez clairement votre objectif professionnel.
- Fournissez toutes les informations pour que le recruteur puisse vous contacter, y compris votre adresse e-mail.
- Incluez vos compétences, votre formation, votre expérience et les résultats universitaires s'ils sont bons.
- Rédigez le CV. Le contenu doit tenir *(fit)* sur une page ou deux.

Essential Instruction

1. The **Stratégie communicative** is a challenging exercise for your high-ability students. Your lower-ability students can participate with modifications.
2. Students should investigate every term in **Recherche** for the vocabulary needed to write a CV.
3. The **étapes pour écrire un CV** should be followed step by step.
4. The CV of Charlotte Hoffman serves as a clear example of how their CV should look.

MODÈLE

Charlotte Hoffman
Tel : 06.21.83.52.22

101 rue Paradis 13006 Marseille
charlotte.hoffman@iae-paris.com

22 ans

Candidate pour un poste de gestion de projet intranet nouvelle génération en apprentissage

Formation

–2018/2019 Master d'informatique 2- traitement de données, IAE Aix-en-Provence
–2016 Master 1- Science du Management, IAE Aix-en-Provence Enseignements : Communication, Marketing, Stratégie, Économie, Anglais.
–2013 DUT GEA Option Petites et Moyennes Organisations, IUT de Marseille
–2011 Baccalauréat Economique option Mathématique Mention AB, Lycée Marcel Pagnol Marseille.

Connaissances acquises

Bilingue français-anglais, italien : réactualisable*.
Informatique
Excellente culture web et grand intérêt pour les nouvelles technologies

Expériences professionnelles et associatives

Capgémini : analyse du besoin du client, conception, développement et intégration de produits et de solutions technologiques pour les systèmes d'informations

Emplois étudiants

Hôtesse de Caisse, Carrefour, Marseille, France
Vendeuse, Magasin de vêtements Zara, Marseille, France

Loisirs

Équitation (galop 6), footing, lecture

réactualisable *that may be brushed up*

Reference Desk

1. A number of online job search sites in France offer a wide variety of information for jobseekers. Encourage students to read **"8 conseils simples pour un CV efficace et concis"** for suggestions.
2. In a job announcement, **h/f** stands for **homme/femme**.

Expansion

Ask students to create what they imagine to be the resume of a famous person, such as an actor/ actress, a wealthy entrepreneur, or the president of the United States.

Differentiated Learning

Accelerate

Have students research real or imagined summer internships. They might want to apply for a higher position in a job they already have. Encourage your students to re-invent themselves, if necessary, to make the CV believable.

Decelerate

Ask students to create a personal CV using Charlotte's as a template. Doing this gives them a solid format and model from which to work.

Resources

- *Vocabulaire actif*
- eVisual
- Workbook 1–5
- Flash Cards
- Listening Activity 1
- G & V Practice Games

Reference Desk

1. **Se faire soigner** means *to get oneself cared for*.
2. **Se casser la cheville** means *to break an ankle*. Point out to students that body parts are usually not expressed with a possessive adjective as in English. We know it is her ankle by the pronoun **se**. This rule is true for reflexives like **se laver la figure**. Remind students that there is no agreement on the past participle of **cassé** in **elle s'est cassé la cheville** because the direct object comes after the verb.
3. **La Sécu** is a truncated word for **la sécurité sociale**. The same is true for **le kiné** which is short for **le kinésithérapeute**.
4. **On peut en discuter davantage. Davantage** means *more*. Since **discuter** is followed by **de**, the replacement for the preposition is **en**.
5. Supplementary vocabulary: **un plâtre** (*a cast*), **un fauteuil roulant** (*a wheelchair*), **des béquilles** (*crutches*).

Leçon C Vocabulaire actif

L'assurance maladie et le débat 1.2

Qui a droit à l'assurance (f.) maladie?

Mme Tautou est tombée et elle s'est cassé la cheville.

Elle avait besoin d'**accéder à des soins**.

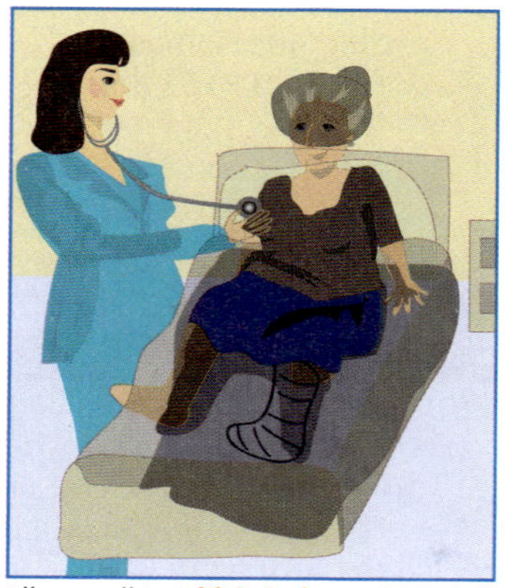

Elle est allée à **l'hôpital** où elle **s'est fait soigner**.

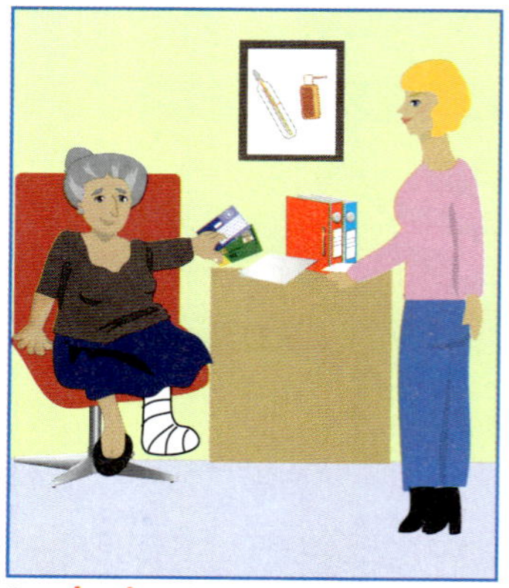

Avec **la sécu** et son assurance maladie **complémentaire privée**, elle **a les moyens** de payer ses **factures médicales**.

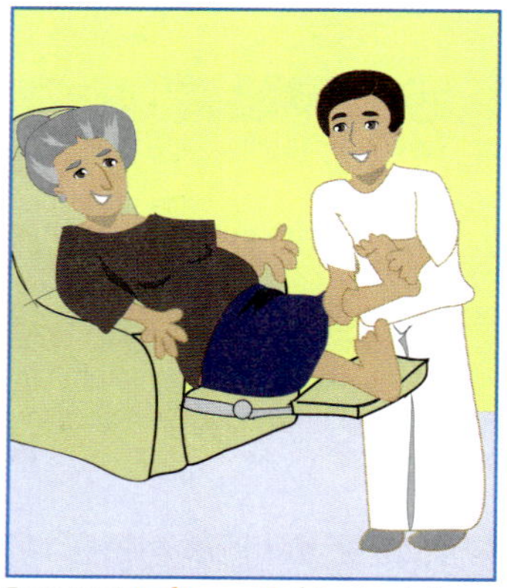

Pour tout **traitement**, il faut qu'elle aille chez **le kiné** pour **des séances** de **rééducation**.

Quelques mois plus tard, elle est **guérie**.

Produits

L'assurance maladie est une branche de la sécurité sociale. Elle assure l'égalité d'accès aux soins et la qualité de ces soins à tous les Français. Elle existe depuis 1945.

1.2, 2.2, 5.2

Essential Instruction

1. Have students listen to **l'assurance maladie et le débat**.
2. Ask students to draw illustrations for Mme Tautou's accident on a makeshift storyboard in their notebooks and label each square.
3. Have students create a graphic organizer to display the expressions needed for a debate. They might want to draw two people debating and expressing opposing views by using dialogue balloons for each expression.
4. Students listen to **Pour la conversation** and **Et si je voulais dire...?**, then copy the terms in their notebooks for future reference.
5. Have students conjugate **prescrire** (like **écrire**) and **se sentir** in various tenses.

Une méthode de débat: 1.3

1. Pour **introduire** votre **position**:
   A. Je suis pour/contre... pour deux raisons principales.
   B. **Premièrement**, ...
   Deuxièmement, ...
2. Pour **répondre** aux arguments de la première personne:
   A. Tu as raison. Je suis **entièrement** de ton avis.
   B. Tu **as tort**. J'ai un autre point de vue.
3. Pour répondre aux arguments de la deuxième personne:
   A. **par contre** - *on the other hand*
   au contraire - *on the contrary*
   cependant - *however*
   néanmoins - *nevertheless*
   évidemment - *evidently*
   d'ailleurs - *moreover*
   B. Je continue avec un deuxième argument.
   C. **Une citation** de... **illustre**....
   Les chiffres indiquent....
   Par exemple, j'ai **une anecdote** qui montre....

Pour la conversation

1.2, 5.1

How do I express that someone has a right?

» Mamy a droit à une voiture **médicalisée**....
Grandma has the right to medical transportation.

How do I express that someone can afford something?

» Elle a les moyens de payer un taxi normal.
She has the means to pay for a normal taxi.

How do I express that I want to discuss something in more detail later?

» **On peut en discuter davantage plus tard.**
We can discuss it more later.

Et si je voulais dire...?

un cabinet médical	*medical practice*
l'état (m.) de santé	*state of health*
une ordonnance	*prescription*
consulter	*to consult*
prescrire	*to prescribe*

Resources

Pour la conversation
Et si je voulais dire...?

Reference Desk

1. Supplementary vocabulary: **la chirurgie** (*surgery*); **un(e) chirurgien(ne)** (*a surgeon*); **une radio** (*an x-ray*); **une prise de sang** (*a blood test*); **guérir** (*to cure*). **Un toubib** is slang for doctor or medic.
2. **L'addition** refers to the bill in a restaurant and **la facture** to a billed statement.
3. Make sure students know the difference in English between *complimentary* and *complementary*. The latter is used for **assurance complémentaire**.
4. **Le moyen** means *the means*, and **les moyens** implies financial means.

Expansion

Have students perform the following skit. A hypochondriac is visiting a doctor and complaining of many unusual ailments (using the **Et si je voulais dire...?** vocabulary and **avoir mal** expressions) only to find out that the doctor is a veterinarian. Have students play out the scene and improvise dialogue, or a have a narrator give stage directions to two students.

Differentiated Learning

Accelerate
Have students research the distribution of benefits of **la sécurité sociale**.

Recherche: sécurité-sociale française

Decelerate
Ask students to write a simple composition of "**Une visite chez le médecin**" incorporating the vocabulary from **Et si je voulais dire...?**

Special Needs Students

Social Anxiety
For students who fear appearing in front of the class in a speaking role, suggest they act out skits under the direction of a narrator.

Resources

Activity 2

Answers

1

1. B; 2. C; 3. A; 4. D; 5. B

2 **Script**

Juliette : Toi, tu es pour ou contre une assurance médicale privée ?
Luc : Personnellement, je suis contre. Premièrement, parce que les gens qui n'ont pas les moyens n'auront pas accès aux soins et deuxièmement parce que je pense que les assurances vont devenir plus chères, mais pas la qualité.
Juliette : Je suis de ton avis dans un sens mais si les gens payaient leur propre assurance, ils feraient plus attention à leurs visites médicales et ils n'iraient pas aussi souvent à l'hôpital.
Luc : J'ai un autre point de vue. Pour moi, se faire soigner est un droit. Une personne âgée doit avoir le droit d'aller chez le kiné si elle tombe. Par contre, je suis d'avis qu'il doit y avoir plus de contrôles par la Sécurité Sociale pour éviter les abus.
Juliette : Je dois partir. On peut discuter du sujet davantage chez moi après les cours si tu veux. Dix-sept heures, ça te convient ?
Luc : Oui, bonne idée !

1. Luc
2. Luc
3. Juliette
4. Luc
5. Juliette

3 Answers will vary.

Culture

Practices: Activity

The French comic Coluche reflects that "**À la sécurité sociale, tout est assuré sauf la pendule. Ça, on ne risque pas de la voler, le personnel a les yeux constamment fixés dessus.**" Explain.

Communication

Interpersonal: Cooperative Groups

Divide the class into two groups. Tell them that they are lawyers preparing the case for and against government health programs which will be argued before the Supreme Court. Give them time to make their case from their assigned point of view before conducting the debate.

1 Des arguments 1.2

Interpretive Reading

Complétez les phrases suivantes logiquement.

1. Une personne qui a les moyens peut payer son traitement médical ; …, une personne pauvre sans assurance maladie ne peut pas.
   A. d'ailleurs B. par contre C. par exemple D. aussi
2. Une personne pauvre a… droit aux services médicaux.
   A. au contraire B. contre C. néanmoins D. maintenant
3. Je ne veux plus en discuter maintenant, mais on peut en discuter… plus tard.
   A. davantage B. cependant C. d'ailleurs D. également
4. Cette citation de l'article illustre la valeur du kiné, … j'ai encore des doutes.
   A. deuxièmement B. d'ailleurs C. encore D. cependant
5. Mais non, tu as tort, je ne suis pas contre l'assurance maladie. …, je suis pour.
   A. Tu as raison B. Au contraire C. Par contre D. Par exemple

2 Quel débat ! 1.2

Interpretive Listening

Écrivez les numéros 1–5. Écoutez le débat entre Juliette et Luc sur l'assurance maladie. Puis, identifiez la personne décrite.

1. Cette personne commence avec deux arguments contre l'assurance maladie privée.
2. Il est important pour cette personne que les gens âgés puissent se faire soigner quand ils tombent malades.
3. Cette personne a un argument économique.
4. Cette personne pense que les abus par rapport à l'assurance maladie doivent être contrôlés.
5. Cette personne propose de continuer la conversation plus tard.

3 Questions personnelles 1.1

Interpersonal Speaking

Répondez aux questions suivantes avec un partenaire.

1. Dans un débat, est-ce que tu perds ou tu gagnes plus souvent ?
2. Comment est-ce que tu préfères illustrer ta position, avec une citation, des chiffres, ou une anecdote ?
3. À quoi est-ce qu'on devrait avoir droit, selon toi ?
4. Es-tu pour ou contre l'assurance maladie pour tous ?
5. Qu'est-ce qui se passe dans ton pays quand une personne malade n'a pas les moyens de se faire soigner ?

Essential Instruction

1. Have students review the **Vocabulaire** and debate expressions on pp. 476–477 before attempting **Activités 1**, **2**, and **3**.
2. Correct these exercises as a whole-group activity.
3. Students watch the **Rencontres culturelles** video with books closed. Ask what the dialogue was about, and have students give details they remember.
4. Have students listen to **Mamy a pris rendez-vous chez le kinésithérapeute** then read the dialogue aloud with a partner.
5. Have students write their answers to **Activité 4** on whiteboards showing you their answers each time.

Rencontres culturelles

Mamy a pris rendez-vous chez le kinésithérapeute 1.2

Léo téléphone à sa sœur.

Léo : Tu ne viens pas ?
Élodie : Non, je ne peux pas, je dois accompagner Mamy. Elle va chez le kiné. Elle m'a téléphoné parce qu'elle était tombée hier.
Léo : Mais tu n'as pas ton permis…. Tu y vas comment ?
Élodie : T'inquiète pas. Mamy a droit à une voiture médicalisée pour l'emmener ; ça lui coûte 2,40 euros….
Léo : Quoi ? Mais Mamy, elle a les moyens de payer un taxi normal !
Élodie : Oui, c'est vrai, tu as raison. Mais c'est un service de la sécu et comme elle a des difficultés à marcher, elle y a droit….
Léo : Quel pays ! Rien que des droits ! Eh bien, moi, je suis contre… pas contre Mamy, mais contre ce système qui accorde la même chose à tout le monde : premièrement, ça coûte très cher à la collectivité et deuxièmement, il y a des choix dans la manière de se faire soigner qui dépendent de chacun.
Élodie : Et que chacun doit payer selon ses moyens, j'ai compris.
Léo : Oui, il y a des assurances individuelles pour ça.
Élodie : Je ne suis pas d'accord, mais on peut en discuter davantage plus tard. Maintenant je file !

4 Mamy a pris rendez-vous chez le kinésithérapeute 1.2

Répondez aux questions.

1. Qu'est-ce qu'Élodie fait aujourd'hui ?
2. Qu'est-ce qui est arrivé à sa grand-mère ?
3. Qui va la soigner ?
4. Comment est-ce qu'on va au cabinet du kinésithérapeute ?
5. Qu'est-ce que Léo pense de l'assurance maladie pour tous ? Pourquoi ?

Resources

Dialogue
Activity 4
Dialogue Video
WB Workbook 6

Answers

4

1. Elle doit accompagner sa grand-mère chez le kiné.
2. Elle est tombée.
3. Le kinésithérapeute va la soigner.
4. On y va en voiture médicalisée.
5. Il pense que ça coûte cher à la collectivité, et que les gens ont le droit de choisir comment se faire soigner.

Reference Desk

nouvelle orthographe **couter, ça coute**

Culture

Practices: Information

When you call **le SAMU**, a French ambulance, the dispatcher takes down details of your problem and then sends out a private ambulance with a driver or, if necessary, a mobile intensive care unit. For less serious problems, **le SAMU** will dispatch a doctor for a house call. If you prefer to be taken to a particular hospital, you should mention this to the ambulance crew, as the usual procedure is to take you to the nearest one. In emergency cases (those requiring intensive care units), billing will be taken care of later. Otherwise, you need to pay in cash at the time you receive assistance.

Differentiated Learning

Accelerate

Have students write a three-paragraph position paper on their views of government-assisted health care. Ask them to research the question online and to cite examples from the research.

Decelerate

Ask students to work with a partner to create a list of pros and cons regarding government-assisted health care.

Multiple Intelligences

Mathematical-Logical

Ask students to find comparative statistics as to the number of people on welfare in the United States and France.

Special Needs Students

At-Risk Students

Students of all abilities may be receiving government benefits due to their low economic situation. Be sensitive to how this discussion could be a divisive issue in your class.

Resources

Extension

Answers

EXTENSION

Hugo et Sophie

Reference Desk

1. **La collectivité** means the community or group as a whole.
2. The **y** in **Elle y a droit** replaces **à la voiture médicalisée**, which was stated previously in the dialogue.
3. **Emmener** means *to take someone somewhere (and stay with the person)* and **amener** means *to bring someone somewhere (and leave the person)*. **Emporter** and **apporter** are corresponding verbs meaning *to take* and *to bring* objects. In casual conversation the French use **amener** for people and things although it is not grammatically correct.
4. **Je file** is slang for **Je m'en vais** and has the sense of *I'm outta here*.
5. **La prise en charge** means *coverage*.
6. **La langue de bois** is double talk usually associated with politicians who talk and say nothing concrete.
7. **Le coup du fumeur** has the sense of *the smoker thing*, as in the classic smoker argument people use.

EXTENSION **Qui est pour? Qui est contre?** 1.2

Au lycée, pendant le cours d'économie, les élèves participent à une discussion sur la prise en charge des dépenses sociales par l'État.

Prof : Bon, j'espère que vous avez préparé vos arguments. Qui commence?

Marielle : Moi. Moi, je suis pour la prise en charge des dépenses sociales par l'État. Premièrement, c'est une question de solidarité; deuxièmement, c'est une question de justice sociale....

Hugo : Bonjour la langue de bois! Moi, ce n'est pas tout à fait mon point de vue. Soyons concrets: si je fume toute ma vie et que j'ai un cancer, c'est la société qui est responsable et qui doit payer?

Théo : Évidemment, toujours le même exemple: le coup du fumeur. Par contre on peut aussi éduquer....

Caro : Entièrement de ton avis: c'est ça une société de solidarité, on fait progresser tout le monde en même temps.

Sophie : Certes. Néanmoins tout ça a un prix: qui paie?

Hugo : D'ailleurs, vous connaissez le montant du déficit des régimes sociaux? Quinze milliards d'euros....

Marielle : Qu'est-ce que c'est par rapport à un budget de mille milliards?

Théo : Si c'est le prix à payer pour conserver notre système... ce n'est pas cher payer!

Hugo : Eh bien moi, je préfèrerais qu'on me donne cet argent avec mon salaire et je ferai comme je veux. Ma santé, c'est mon choix.

EXTENSION Quels élèves voudraient changer le système de l'assurance maladie en France? 1.2

Essential Instruction

1. For **Extension**, pair mixed-ability students to read the dialogue. Ask them to make two columns **pour** and **contre** and put the arguments of the students in the appropriate columns.
2. Have students answer the **Extension** question. Require that they cite the dialogue lines that support their answers.
3. As a class, have volunteers read **Les droits sociaux** aloud. Stop and outline on the board the principal tenets for **la solidarité collective** and **les prestations sociales**.
4. Have students go online and use the words in **Recherche** to add to notes taken in class.

Pre-AP

Question centrale ? Comment le passé influence-t-il le présent?

Les droits sociaux 1.2, 2.1, 3.1

Les Français manifestent contre les réformes sociales.

Issu* directement de la *Déclaration des Droits de l'Homme et du Citoyen* de 1789 et de la notion de « garantie sociale envers les citoyens malheureux », le modèle social français est celui de l'État-Providence, un modèle d'assistance sociale qui oblige au gouvernement de s'occuper des nombreux besoins (santé, éducatif, retraite, famille) de ses citoyens. Il fait partie du programme du Conseil national de la Résistance, et il a été mis en place en 1945 : il gouverne encore aujourd'hui la société française. Les Français y sont très attachés, et il est donc difficile à réformer. Il constitue aujourd'hui une véritable ligne d'affrontement* politique entre conservateurs qui veulent conserver l'État-Providence et réformateurs qui dénoncent l'État-Assistance.

Ce modèle est fondé sur le principe de la solidarité collective. Cette solidarité collective touche les domaines suivants : la protection sociale (chômage, invalidité*, retraite) ; la santé publique (sécurité sociale) ; l'éducation (gratuité du système éducatif jusqu'à l'université), et la politique familiale (allocations familiales, accueil garanti à l'école maternelle*). L'ensemble des prestations* sociales financées pour l'essentiel par les revenus du travail et de l'entreprise représentent aujourd'hui 2 000 milliards*.

Les prestations sociales sont de quatre types : les prestations de santé (maladie, invalidité, infirmité, accidents du travail) ; les prestations familiales (allocations selon le nombre d'enfants, congé de maternité*, congé parental, allocation logement) ; les prestations d'emploi (allocations chômage, allocations de préretraite) ; les prestations vieillesses (retraites* et pensions).

Recherche : ameli l'assurance maladie en ligne, le portail du service public de la sécurité sociale, école maternelle ministère de l'éducation nationale, prestations familiales, toutes les prestations

---

Issu *Stemming from* ; **affrontement** *confrontation* ; **invalidité** *disability* ; **école maternelle** *nursery school–pre-K* ; **prestations** *benefits* ; **milliards** *billions* ; **congé de maternité** *maternity leave* ; **retraites** *retirement*

Resources

Points de départ

WB Workbook 7

Explore

Reference Desk

If you have access to Passport, find a news article related to **la société** and show it to your students.

Communication

Interpersonal: Cooperative Groups

Divide students into groups. Have them research the viability of the French **sécu** in order to discuss **"le trou de la SS,"** which is a term currently used for the deficit in funding for the French social security program. The discussion question is: Can France continue fiscally to be the **État-Providence** as in the past, or must she change? Follow with a whole-class discussion.

Differentiated Learning

Accelerate

Students write a short essay defending or denying extensive medical treatment for smokers who develop lung disease or cancer.

Decelerate

Ask students to create a word search of new vocabulary from the two readings for the class. Templates can be found online. Students can work on these word searches as a brain break between activities.

Special Needs Students

AD(H)D

It may be helpful to give students a study sheet of basic content questions to answer while reading the dialogues.

Answers

5

1. 1789 : date de la *Déclaration des Droits de l'Homme et du Citoyen* ; 1945 : L'État-Providence a été mis en place.
2. éducation : l'éducation ; allocations familiales : la politique familiale ; invalidité : la protection sociale ; retraite : la protection sociale ; sécurité sociale : la santé publique
3. A : prestations de santé
   B : prestations familiales
   C : prestations familiales
   D : prestations familiales
   E : prestations vieillesse
   F : prestations d'emploi
4. Answers will vary.

Comparaisons
Answers will vary.

À DISCUTER

Answers will vary.

Critical Thinking

Comparaisons
Put students into two teams to debate the **Comparaisons** question. Both teams prepare their position and must give concrete reasons to support it. Each selects a debater who takes the side of the argument that his or her team prepared. Alternatively, run the debate as a fishbowl activity.

Moins de 20% des Français mettent leurs enfants à la crèche, préférant les élever eux-mêmes.

1.2, 2.2

Produits

Pour les parents qui travaillent, **les crèches** s'occupent des bébés de deux mois et demi jusqu'à l'âge de trois ans. Les parents paient en fonction de leurs moyens.

Mot-clé

Droit est dérivé de *dreit* (842), issu du bas-latin *directum*, substantivation (*noun form*) de l'adjectif *directus*. Attesté au 6ème siècle au sens général de justice, puis au 8ème siècle au sens de règles ou d'ensemble des lois. Quelle est la signification de chacune de ces expressions qui incorpore le mot *droit*? *Je suis dans mon droit. J'y ai droit. Les droits et les devoirs.*

Comparaisons

Quel système d'assurance préférez-vous, celui de votre pays ou celui de la France ?

1.2, 4.2

5 Activités culturelles 1.3, 3.1, 3.2, 4.2, 5.1

Faites les activités suivantes.

1. Expliquez l'importance de ces dates en ce qui concerne l'État-Providence :
   - 1789
   - 1945
2. Indiquez à quel domaine appartiennent les protections sociales suivantes :
   - éducation
   - allocations familiales
   - invalidité
   - retraite
   - sécurité sociale
3. Indiquez les prestations auxquelles ces personnes ont droit en France :
   A. M. Dujardin a eu un accident de voiture et a mal au cou.
   B. M. et Mme Diop ont un bébé.
   C. M. et Mme Jussieu ont quatre enfants.
   D. M. Piedbœuf n'a pas les moyens de payer son loyer.
   E. Mme Chapelle a pris sa retraite.
   F. Mlle Hergy a perdu son emploi et elle a besoin d'argent pour vivre.
4. Comparez le système de protection sociale français et le système de protection sociale américain.

En France, on préfère l'aide à domicile aux institutions publiques.

À DISCUTER

À votre avis, est-il plus facile d'élever (*raise*) ses enfants en France ou aux États-Unis ? Répondez en donnant des détails justificatifs.

Essential Instruction

1. Ask students to define **une crèche**, **une école maternelle**, and **une école élémentaire**.
2. Have students work in triads to do **Activité 5**. Consider counting off by threes, putting the number ones in groups to complete Activity 1, the twos in groups to complete Activity 2, and the threes together for Activity 3.
3. Offer Activity 4 to a small group of students who present the information to the class. Have them include a visual list of the differences and/or similarities to augment their discussion.
4. Have students go online to explore the website and answer the questions in **Activité 6**.

Du côté des médias 1.2

Lisez ces informations sur les possibilités d'emploi du temps de la semaine scolaire dans les écoles françaises.

MINISTÈRE DE L'ÉDUCATION NATIONALE

Liberté • Égalité • Fraternité
RÉPUBLIQUE FRANÇAISE

LE SYSTÈME ÉDUCATIF | ÉCOLE | COLLÈGE | LYCÉE | POLITIQUE ÉDUCATIVE

Un tiers des écoles a choisi d'organiser la semaine scolaire sur 4 jours dès la rentrée 2017

PARTAGER CET ARTICLE

Conformément aux engagements du président de la République, l'organisation du temps scolaire sur quatre jours dans les écoles maternelles et élémentaires publiques est rendue possible à compter de la rentrée 2017, par dérogation au cadre général de quatre jours et demi.

Cette dérogation nouvelle, précisée dans le décret publié le 28 juin au Bulletin officiel, donne davantage de souplesse aux acteurs de terrain afin de répondre le mieux possible aux singularités de chaque contexte local, dans le souci constant de l'intérêt des élèves. Les rythmes scolaires doivent pouvoir être aménagés à la réalité de chaque territoire, permettant de maintenir la semaine de quatre jours et demi là où cette organisation est satisfaisante ; ceux qui souhaitent changer peuvent désormais le faire.

36,8% des communes de France ayant au moins une école publique, soit 31,8% des écoles, ont choisi une semaine scolaire de quatre jours à compter de la rentrée, ce qui correspond à un peu plus d'un quart des élèves de l'école primaire (28,7%).

Ce mouvement montre que les acteurs de terrain se sont saisis de la liberté nouvelle qui leur était offerte pour mettre en place des organisations correspondant aux besoins de leur territoire.

Ce sont plutôt des communes rurales qui ont choisi de se saisir de cette liberté nouvelle.

Les villes, a fortiori les grandes villes, ont globalement choisi de conserver l'organisation de la semaine sur quatre jours et demi.

6 À qui profite la semaine de quatre jours ? 1.2, 2.1, 3.2

Répondez aux questions.

1. Les informations sont-elles divulguées par une source crédible ? Pourquoi (pas) ?
2. Quelles villes de France ont opté pour la semaine de 4 jours ? Pourquoi, à votre avis ?
3. Faites des recherches et prenez position pour ou contre la semaine de 4 jours. Quelle est votre préférence personnelle ? Quels sont les avantages et les inconvénients de chaque possibilité ?
4. Comparez les emplois du temps du lycée dans votre école, à celui de la semaine de 4 jours. Lequel préférez-vous et pourquoi ?
5. Quel changement aimeriez-vous que votre pays fasse aux emplois du temps scolaire ?

Answers

6

1. Oui, car il s'agit du site du ministère de l'Éducation français.
2. Les petites communes ont tendance à préférer la semaine de 4 jours. Possible answers: Il y a moins de transport en commun dans les petites villes, cela permet aux écoles d'économiser de l'argent en fermant une journée, cela facilite les choses quand les enseignants sont malades.
3. Answers will vary.
4. Answers will vary.
5. Answers will vary.

Reference Desk

Nicolas Sarkozy was the first to suggest a 4-day school week in 2008 by suppressing school on Saturday mornings. In 2014, the Minister of Education decided to go back to a 4.5-day week, by adding classes on Wednesday mornings. In 2017, President Macron gave schools the option to choose.

Differentiated Learning

Accelerate
Ask students to lead a class discussion of the question posed in **À discuter**. Have them examine government-sponsored education, medical, and social benefits of each country.

Decelerate
Give students the vocabulary terms related to **la solidarité collective** and **les prestations sociales** and ask them to define each term in English.

Adapt
Ask where your students went to nursery school, kindergarten, and elementary school. What were their first memories of their schooling? Which school did they prefer? Is early education important now that there is educational television and the Internet? Would your students ever want to teach in any of these schools? Why or why not? Then have students write a short composition, **"Mes premiers souvenirs de l'école,"** based on this class discussion.

Answers

All activities will vary.

Reference Desk

Encourage students to consider the **Question centrale** as they complete **Culture sur place** activities.

Culture sur place

Question centrale ? Comment le passé influence-t-il le présent?

La presse en danger

Introduction et interrogations

La fameuse *Déclaration des Droits de l'Homme et du Citoyen* de 1789 est issue (*came out of*) directement de la Révolution française. Les révolutions récentes dans les pays tels que la Tunisie, l'Égypte, la Libye, et la Syrie soulignent l'importance des médias. Dans cette *Culture sur place*, nous allons discuter de la liberté de la presse et d'un danger qui est associé à cette liberté, surtout dans des situations comme les révolutions.

7 Réfléchir 1.2, 1.3, 3.2, 5.1

Répondez aux questions.

1. Pensez aux actualités que vous lisez, regardez, ou écoutez. Dans quels contextes les journalistes sont-ils en danger quand ils font leurs reportages?
2. Regardez le « Baromètre de la liberté de la presse » sur le site « Reporters sans frontières ». Combien de reporters ont été emprisonnés cette année? Combien ont été tués?
3. Avec un partenaire, faites une liste de situations dangereuses pour les reporters. Ensuite, répondez à ces questions avec votre classe:
   - Qu'est-ce que les journalistes peuvent faire pour minimiser le danger pendant qu'ils travaillent?
   - Qui décide des droits des journalistes à l'étranger? Y a-t-il un traité international?

Recherche: reporters sans frontières fr

8 Étudier 1.3, 3.1, 3.2, 5.1

Lisez les objectifs de « Reporters sans frontières ». Sur leur site, cliquez sur « Qui sommes-nous? » pour en savoir plus sur l'organisation. Résumez ses valeurs et ses activités dans un paragraphe.

9 Faire le point! 1.1, 1.3

Discutez des questions suivantes en classe.

1. Quel est le rôle du reporter sur la scène mondiale?
2. La liberté de la presse est-elle un droit inaliénable? Un journaliste a-t-il le droit de tout dire? Est-ce un droit universel? Pourquoi, ou pourquoi pas? Qu'est-ce que vous pensez de cette réalité?
3. Est-ce que la censure est toujours la même? Quelles en sont les différences?
4. Est-ce que la censure fait partie votre vie? De quelle manière? Comment réagissez-vous face à une censure en général?
5. Est-il possible d'éliminer les « frontières », d'être un véritable « reporter sans frontières »? Pourquoi, ou pourquoi pas?
6. Y a-t-il d'autres dangers associés à la liberté de la presse?

Essential Instruction

1. For **Activité 7**, have students research online names and nationalities of reporters who have been kidnapped or died in the line of duty. Using the questions provided, debate whether or not reporters should be in harm's way.
2. For **Activité 8**, have students do this summary individually or in pairs.
3. For **Activité 9**, divide the class into three groups. Have group one prepare questions 1 and 2, group 2, questions 3 and 4, and group three, question 5. Require each group to research the answers and lead the class discussion on their topics.
4. Review **être**, then practice by throwing a soft ball to a student who conjugates **être** in the tense you indicate. Students may refer to tenses listed on the board.
5. Have students name the **être** expressions that they know; write them on the board.
6. Have students do **Activité 10**. Correct immediately afterward.

Révision: Expressions with *être* 1.1

Être is the most frequently used verb in French.

Par contre, je **suis** pour la sécu médicale.	*On the other hand, I am for national health insurance.*

Like **faire** and **avoir**, also "building block" verbs, **être** is used in a number of expressions in French where a different verb is used in English. You have already learned some common expressions with **être** that deal with agreeing with someone, giving the day/date, and saying that you are busy doing something.

Néanmoins, elle n'**est** pas **d'accord**.	*Nevertheless, she doesn't agree.*
Nous **sommes** dimanche.	*It's Sunday.*
Marc et Koffi **sont en train de** faire les corvées.	*Marc and Koffi are busy doing chores.*

To show ownership, use the expression **être à** (*to belong to*). A stress pronoun or a noun follows **être à**.

Pardon, monsieur ! Ce portefeuille **est à** vous ?	*Excuse me, sir! Is this wallet yours?*
Oui, merci ! Il **est à** moi.	*Yes, thank you! It is mine.*

10 La fête d'anniversaire 1.1

Interpersonal Speaking

Complétez chaque dialogue avec une expression de la liste. N'oubliez pas de conjuguer le verbe **être***, si nécessaire.*

être en train de **c'est** **être en retard** **être de** **être au courant**
être d'accord **être occupé** **être chargé de** **être prêt** **être**

MODÈLE —Christelle s'occupe des décorations ?
—Oui, elle **est chargée des** décorations et aussi des boissons.

1. —Quand est l'anniversaire de Fatima ?
—... le 14 mai.
2. —Qui enverra les invitations ?
—Les sœurs de Fatima... le faire maintenant.
3. —Fatima... Paris ?
—Non, sa famille vient du Maroc.
4. —La fête... à quelle heure ?
—À 18h30.
5. —Tu... à m'aider avec le gâteau d'anniversaire, Annie ?
—Oui, je suis déjà allée à l'épicerie.
6. —Christian, tu ne vas pas... ?
—Non, pas cette fois. Je serai à l'heure. C'est promis !
7. —Paul et Benoît, vous... de la fête pour Fatima ?
—Oui, nous venons d'acheter un cadeau et une carte d'anniversaire.
8. —Jacques et toi, vous... le 14 mai ?
—Non, nous sommes libres.
9. —La fête sera géniale !
—Je....

Resources

WB Workbook 8–9

G & V Practice Games

Answers

10
1. C'est
2. sont en train de
3. est de
4. est
5. est prête
6. être en retard
7. êtes au courant
8. êtes occupés
9. suis d'accord

Communication

Interpersonal: Paired Practice

To practice using expressions with **être** in a variety of tenses, put students in pairs. Give each pair a note card with a sentence using a different expression and the tense that they are to change the sentence to (for example, **Nous étions en train d'étudier la presse française. [présent]**). Student A reads the sentence to Student B, who identifies the tense being used (**imparfait**) and then changes the sentence to the tense indicated: **Nous sommes en train d'étudier la presse française**. Have students exchange cards with another set of partners and change roles. Continue for the allotted time or until they have completed all of the cards.

Differentiated Learning

Accelerate/Decelerate

Have students of different ability levels work together on verb conjugations and adjective agreement. First, review **être** conjugations for a variety of tenses. Create a practice sheet for groups to use that checks comprehension of the meanings of the new **être** expressions and their use in realistic contexts.

Learning Styles

Visual Learners

Have students create visuals representing each of the **être** expressions learned. Have them identify each expression on the back and ask them to assist you by using their visuals for review and practice. Post the visuals in your classroom.

Resources

- **WB** Workbook 10–13
- **LA** Listening Activity 2
- G & V Practice Games

Answers

11

1. Les bandes dessinées sont à Luc et moi.
2. Les sandales sont à Didier.
3. La tablette est à Mme Magritte.
4. La casquette est à M. Xing.
5. Les recueils de poésie sont à Mme Leriche.
6. Les timbres sont à Solange.

Reference Desk

1. To help students remember **plus-que-parfait**, suggest this jingle: P-Q-P is H-A-D since its translation is *had*.
2. The **plus-que-parfait** and the **passé composé** contrast actions in the past. The **plus-que-parfait** is a "colder tense" than the **passé composé**; the action in the past happened before the past action of the **passé composé**. He *had written* the letter before he *saw* her. Writing the letter was over and done with before he saw her.
3. Students may better understand **plus-que-parfait** if you initially use it with the adverb **déjà** (*already*).

TPR

To practice distinguishing between verbs in the **imparfait** and the **plus-que-parfait**, have students make two cards each, one with "I" for the **imparfait**, and one with "P" for the **plus-que-parfait**. Read sentences that are in the imperfect or the **plus-que-parfait**. Ask students to hold up the appropriate card for the verb tense they hear.

11 Objets trouvés 1.2, 1.3

Interpretive Viewing, Presentational Speaking or Writing

À la fin de l'année scolaire, il y a beaucoup d'objets trouvés dans une boîte dans le bureau du proviseur. Dites-lui à qui est chaque objet.

MODÈLE

Karim

Le lecteur MP3 est à Karim.

Zakia

Les clés USB sont à Zakia.

1. Luc et moi

2. Didier

3. Mme Magritte

4. M. Xing

5. Mme Leriche

6. Solange

Pluperfect Tense 1.2

The **plus-que-parfait** *(pluperfect, past perfect)* is a tense used to tell what *had happened* in the past before another past action. It may be used to express "cause and effect." Like the **passé composé**, the **plus-que-parfait** consists of a helping verb and a past participle. To form the **plus-que-parfait**, use the imperfect tense of the helping verb **avoir** or **être** and the past participle of the main verb. Agreement of the past participle in the **plus-que-parfait** is the same as in the **passé composé**.

Camille s'est fait soigner à l'hôpital parce qu'elle était tombée sur la piste de ski !

Essential Instruction

1. Review possession with **être à** before doing **Activité 11** as a class activity.
2. Introduce the formation, translation, and use of the **plus-que-parfait**.
3. Review DR. MRS. P. VANDERTRAMP verbs conjugated with **être**.
4. Have students divide **Activité 12** with a partner; one does odds, the other does evens. Have students write the sentences before exchanging papers to correct. Students take turns reading their answers.

	répondre	tomber
j'	**avais** répondu	**étais** tombé(e)
tu	**avais** répondu	**étais** tombé(e)
il/elle/on	**avait** répondu	**était** tombé(e)
nous	**avions** répondu	**étions** tombé(e)s
vous	**aviez** répondu	**étiez** tombé(e)(s)
ils/elles	**avaient** répondu	**étaient** tombé(e)s

Quand je suis rentré, j'avais très faim. Heureusement, mon père **avait** déjà **préparé** le dîner. — *When I got home I was very hungry. Luckily, my dad had already prepared dinner.*

Sa nièce **s'était** déjà **fait** soigner. — *Her niece had already received medical treatment.*

12 Un été en France 1.3

Presentational Speaking or Writing

Des élèves de votre classe de français sont restés avec des familles françaises pendant l'été. Dites ce qu'ils vous ont raconté.

MODÈLE Jamie (voir la *Joconde* au Louvre)
Jamie m'a dit qu'il avait vu la *Joconde* au Louvre.

1. vous (nager dans la mer Méditerranée)
2. Heather et Amber (passer une semaine dans les Alpes)
3. Zach (se promener sur les Champs-Élysées)
4. tu (prendre une photo du château d'If à Marseille)
5. Ashleigh (faire la connaissance des ados français)
6. Justin et Tyler (prendre le métro souvent à Lyon)
7. Madison (ne jamais s'ennuyer)
8. Matt et Justin (aller à Cannes)

Comparaisons

4.1

What do these examples of the **plus-que-parfait** in French and English express?

Si tu avais écouté mes conseils!
If (only) you had listened to my advice!

Resources

Activity 12

Answers

12

1. Vous m'avez dit que vous aviez nagé dans la mer Méditerranée.
2. Heather et Amber m'ont dit qu'elles avaient passé une semaine dans les Alpes.
3. Zach m'a dit qu'il s'était promené sur les Champs-Élysées.
4. Tu m'as dit que tu avais pris une photo du château d'If à Marseille.
5. Ashleigh m'a dit qu'elle avait fait la connaissance des ados français.
6. Justin et Tyler m'ont dit qu'ils avaient pris le métro souvent à Lyon.
7. Madison m'a dit qu'elle ne s'était jamais ennuyée.
8. Matt et Justin m'ont dit qu'ils étaient allés à Cannes.

Comparaisons
They both express the regret or exasperation of "If only!"

Communication

Interpersonal: Cooperative Groups

Write a number for each subject pronoun on the board. Then write verbs on slips of paper and place them in lunch bags. Divide the class into groups and give each group a die and a bag of verb slips. Each student rolls the die, selects a verb slip from the bag, and makes a sentence with the **plus-que-parfait**. Once a verb is used, leave it out of the bag to prevent the verb being used again. Continue until each group has used all of the verbs.

Differentiated Learning

Decelerate
To visualize the difference between **passé composé** and **plus-que-parfait**, have students conjugate **avoir** in the **tu** form in present and, below it, in the imperfect. Across from the present, they write **parler** for **tu** in **passé composé**, and across from the imperfect, they conjugate **parler** for **tu** in the **plus-que-parfait**. Students see the correspondence between the verb forms, for example, **Tu *as*...Tu *as* parlé** and **Tu *avais*...Tu *avais* parlé**. Do this for a variety of verbs including those conjugated with **être**.

Accelerate
Have students change sentences using the **présent** and the **passé composé** to sentences using the **imparfait** and the **plus-que-parfait**. For example:
Je n'ai plus faim parce que j'ai mangé deux hamburgers.
Je n'avais plus faim parce que j'avais mangé deux hamburgers.

Resources

Activity 13

Answers

13 Script

Chantal : Écoute, Papy est à l'hôpital.
Théo : Qu'est-ce qui s'est passé ?
Chantal : Il avait acheté un billet de concert, mais il est tombé devant le théâtre en sortant.
Théo : Mamy était avec lui ?
Chantal : Non, elle avait pris rendez-vous chez le kiné.
Théo : Il avait sa carte d'assurance sur lui ?
Chantal : Oui, dans son portefeuille.
Théo : On lui a servi un dîner ?
Chantal : Non, il avait déjà mangé à la maison.
Théo : Mamy est avec lui maintenant ?
Chantal : Oui, j'y suis allée avec elle, mais j'ai dû partir pour travailler.
Théo : Je vais à l'hôpital tout de suite !

1. Pourquoi le grand-père de Chantal et Théo était-il en ville ?
2. Pourquoi sa femme n'était-elle pas avec lui ?
3. Le grand-père avait-il sa carte d'assurance sur lui ?
4. À l'hôpital a-t-on servi un repas au grand-père ?
5. Où Chantal était-elle allée avant de travailler ?
6. Qu'est-ce que Théo va faire ?

1. D
2. B
3. A
4. F
5. E
6. C

14 Answers will vary.

Communication

Interpersonal: Cooperative Groups

Put students in groups of four or five to give alibis for their whereabouts at M. Montmorency's **château** when he was killed in the library at 11:00 P.M. Students take turns saying where they had been in the **château** before the murder, and where they had last seen the victim. For example, **J'avais flâné dans le jardin**. **J'avais vu M. Montmorency dans la salle à manger à 8h00**. Have a student play Inspector Clouseau, interview the guests, and write up a report of the testimony of the group members.

13 Papy à l'hôpital 1.1, 1.2

Interpretive Listening

Écrivez les numéros 1–6 sur votre papier. Écoutez le dialogue entre Chantal et son frère Théo. Ensuite, choisissez la bonne réponse à la question que vous entendez.

A. Oui, il l'avait mise dans son portefeuille avant de partir.
B. Elle s'était fait soigner par le kiné.
C. Il va rendre visite à son grand-père.
D. Il avait assisté à un concert en ville.
E. Elle était allée à l'hôpital avec Mamy.
F. Non, il avait déjà pris son dîner à la maison.

14 Qu'est-ce qui s'est passé avant... ? 1.3

Presentational Speaking or Writing

Pour chaque situation suivante, composez des phrases logiques au plus-que-parfait indiquant ce qui a précédé.

Monsieur Durand est arrivé en retard parce qu'il ne s'était pas réveillé assez tôt.

MODÈLE Christine est allée en Europe.

- **Elle avait fait ses valises.**
- **Elle avait retiré de l'argent à la banque.**
- **Elle était allée à l'aéroport.**
- **Elle avait obtenu un passeport.**
- **Elle avait acheté des chèques de voyage.**

1. J'ai été embauché(e) à TechMode.
2. Ma famille et moi, nous avons fait du camping.
3. Marco et toi, vous avez donné un concert.
4. Tu es descendu(e) dans un hôtel à Paris.
5. Dikembe a écrit une composition sur Jacques Prévert pour son cours de littérature.
6. Latifa a gagné un marathon.
7. Malick s'est engagé en faveur de l'environnement.
8. M. Menninger est devenu prof de français.

Essential Instruction

1. Students listen to **Activité 13** and choose the best response to each question.
2. Have students make sentences about two events that happened in the past, one before the other, using the **plus-que-parfait** and the **passé compose**. Have a scribe write the sentences on the board.
3. Have students do **Activité 14** in pairs, then compare their answers with another duo.
4. For **Activité 15**, have students research medical services using the search words. Have students identify by description the grandchildren speaking, their relationship to the grandmother, any directives the parents have given them to add interest.
5. **Activité 16** might tell the story of a trip your students made to the emergency room as they were growing up.

À vous la parole

Question centrale ? Comment le passé influence-t-il le présent?

Communiquez!

15 Mamy est malade 1.3, 5.1, 5.2

Presentational Writing and Speaking

L'assurance maladie peut parfois payer les frais de transport en cas de maladie : domicile-hôpital, hôpital-domicile, domicile-lieu de traitement. La sécurité sociale prend ces frais en charge si le patient a une prescription médicale et des effets secondaires comme avec la chimiothérapie. Votre grand-mère souffre du cancer et aura besoin de plusieurs traitements de chimio. Vos parents voyagent souvent ; donc, c'est à vous, les petits-enfants, de trouver une solution. Votre grand-mère habite à Lyon. En groupe de trois, préparez un dialogue dans lequel vous jouez le rôle des frères et sœurs qui discutent du problème, et de ce que chacun peut faire pour aider Mamy. Enregistrez ou filmez votre dialogue.

Recherche : vsl lyon, voiture médicalisée lyon

16 Une anecdote sur la santé 1.3, 5.2

Presentational Writing and Speaking

Une anecdote est une petite histoire. Écrivez une anecdote sur quelqu'un que vous connaissez qui est tombé malade. Vous pourriez également choisir une célébrité qui a eu un accident ou qui est tombée malade et créer un scénario imaginaire si vous ne connaissez pas tous les détails. Décrivez la maladie et dites ce qui s'est passé quand la personne est allée se faire soigner dans un hôpital, une clinique, ou chez le kiné. Est-ce que l'assurance a payé ? Enregistrez ou filmez votre présentation.

17 La presse en danger 1.3, 3.1, 3.2, 4.2, 5.2

Presentational Speaking

La liberté de la presse peut présenter des dangers, en particulier dans des situations instables ou violentes telles que les révolutions. Imaginez que vous êtes journaliste et que vous faites un reportage sur un événement ou un problème qui s'est produit très récemment dans votre ville ou votre pays. Expliquez l'événement et comment vous envisagez d'en faire le compte-rendu de façon aussi intéressante et informative que possible. À quels dangers pourriez-vous vous faire exposer et pourquoi ? Comment pourriez-vous assurer votre sécurité ? Comment pourriez-vous minimiser vos risques ? Présentez vos idées à la classe.

Resources

CA Communicative Activities

Share

Answers

15 Scripts will vary.

16 Stories will vary.

17 News reports will vary.

Communication

Interpersonal: Cooperative Groups

Students bring a photo depicting an activity in which they have participated. Put students in small groups. Each student describes what he or she did in the photo in the **passé composé**, then says two sentences in the **plus-que-parfait** that describe what he or she had done to prepare for that activity. For example, **"Samedi après-midi j'ai piqueniqué au zoo. Vendredi j'avais invité Claude. Samedi matin j'avais préparé des sandwichs."**

Reference Desk

1. If you have access to Passport, create a question for your students to share their response to a communicative activity.
2. It may be worth noting that some students may feel sensitive about or find Activity 15 difficult to undertake due to personal family experience relating to this subject matter. If students are experiencing this allow them to do Activity 16 or 17 in place of Activity 15.

Differentiated Learning

Accelerate

Give students two pages of a French novel featuring the **plus-que-parfait** among other tenses, and have them identify the tenses of the verbs.

Decelerate

Encourage students to use online practice to master the **plus-que-parfait**. Small group practice is beneficial where they do a worksheet and check their answers.

Special Needs Students

Linguistically Challenged

Some students have difficulty learning this new tense because they still confuse the previous ones. A review of regular and irregular conjugations in both tenses is essential each time a new verb tense is introduced.

Resources

Rencontre avec l'auteur

Answers

Rencontre avec l'auteur
Possible answer: Il veut être savant, il est curieux, il est obstiné.

Pré-lecture
Answers will vary.

Stratégie de lecture
un savant ; savoir ; raisonnable ; raison ; raisonner ; félicité ; félicitations ; féliciter ; traiter ; traité ; traitement ; surtraitement ; rouvrant ; rouvert ; réouverture ; doute ; douteux ; indubitablement

Reference Desk

Before reading **l'extrait**, consider reviewing strategies for better reading comprehension: 1) Connect the topic with prior knowledge. 2) Ask questions while reading the text. 3) Visualize the content of the story. 4) Point out the most important facts in the text. 5) Draw conclusions that are not directly stated in the text. 6) Synthesize or combine information from the text with prior knowledge to create new ideas.

Le Bourgeois gentilhomme (*Acte II, Scène IV*)

Rencontre avec l'auteur 1.2, 3.1, 4.2, 5.2

Molière (1622–1673), pseudonyme pour Jean-Baptiste Poquelin, était un dramaturge classique du 17ème siècle en France. Il a écrit des pièces pour le roi Louis XIV. Connu pour ses comédies de mœurs (*manners*), il a inventé une collection de « types », ou personnages stéréotypés comme le parvenu (*social climber*) M. Jourdain dans *Le Bourgeois gentilhomme* dont vous allez lire un extrait. M. Jourdain voudrait se transformer en gentilhomme (*gentleman*) et pour y arriver il prend des maîtres pour l'instruire (*instruct*) et le former aux belles manières. Après avoir lu cet extrait, est-ce que vous pouvez faire un portrait de M. Jourdain ? Quels sont les traits (*characteristics*) du parvenu ?

Pré-lecture 1.3

Est-ce que vous connaissez des gens qui ne sont pas contents de leur classe sociale ? Qu'est-ce qu'ils font de comique ?

Stratégie de lecture 1.2, 4.1

Word Families. Pour élargir votre vocabulaire, il est bon que vous appreniez des mots appartenant à la même famille linguistique. Si vous reconnaissez la racine (*root*) d'un mot, vous pouvez deviner ce que d'autres mots veulent dire. Pendant que vous lisez l'extrait de cette pièce célèbre, remplissez le tableau avec les mots que vous savez déjà et les nouveaux mots que vous allez rechercher dans le dictionnaire. Pour tous les mots de la deuxième et de la troisième colonne, indiquez aussi la partie du discours (*part of speech*). Donnez la définition de chaque mot dans la première et troisième colonne. Un exemple a été fait pour vous.

Mot de la pièce	Mot(s) que je connais déjà	Nouveaux mots que j'ai recherchés
MODÈLE **un gentilhomme :** gentleman	**gentil** **gentillesse**	**gentiment (adv.) :** kindly, nicely
un savant		
raisonnable		
félicité		
traiter		
rouvrant (*from* rouvrir)		
doute		

Essential Instruction

1. Students have already been introduced to Molière in **Unité 7**. Have them expand their appreciation of him by listening to the **Rencontre avec l'auteur**.
2. Discuss the question in **Pré-lecture**.
3. Have students read the **Pendant la lecture** questions before listening and discussing each section.
4. In pairs, have students fill out the **Stratégie de lecture** after reading each section. See who can add the most words to their list.

Outils de lecture 1.2, 3.1, 5.2

Dans un sens général, le cadre de l'histoire permet de situer le moment et le lieu d'une sélection littéraire. Dans ses pièces, Molière nous offre un vaste tableau de la France du 17ème siècle. Qu'est-ce que vous remarquez de cette époque en lisant cet extrait?

« Le Bourgeois gentilhomme »

Maître de Philosophie. … Que voulez-vous apprendre?

Monsieur Jourdain. Tout ce que je pourrai, car j'ai toutes les envies du monde d'être savant*; et j'enrage que mon père et ma mère ne m'aient pas fait bien étudier dans toutes les sciences quand j'étais jeune.

Maître de Philosophie. Ce sentiment est raisonnable, *Nam sine doctrina vita est quasi mortis imago*. Vous entendez cela, et vous savez le latin sans doute.

Monsieur Jourdain. Oui, mais faites comme si je ne le savais pas: expliquez-moi ce que cela veut dire.

Maître de Philosophie. Cela veut dire que *Sans la science, la vie est presque une image de la mort.*

Monsieur Jourdain. Ce latin-là a raison.

Maître de Philosophie. N'avez-vous point quelques principes, quelques commencements des sciences?

Monsieur Jourdain. Oh! oui, je sais lire et écrire.

Maître de Philosophie. Par où vous plaît-il que nous commencions? Voulez-vous que je vous apprenne la logique?

Monsieur Jourdain. Qu'est-ce que c'est que cette logique?

Maître de Philosophie. C'est elle qui enseigne les trois opérations de l'esprit*.

Monsieur Jourdain. Qui sont-elles, ces trois opérations de l'esprit?

Maître de Philosophie. La première, la seconde, et la troisième. La première est de bien concevoir* par le moyen des universaux. La seconde, de bien juger* par le moyen des catégories; et la troisième, de bien tirer* une conséquence par le moyen des figures *Barbara, Celarent, Darii, Ferio, Baralipton,* etc.

Monsieur Jourdain. Voilà des mots qui sont trop rébarbatifs*. Cette logique-là ne me revient point. Apprenons autre chose qui soit plus joli.

Maître de Philosophie. Voulez-vous apprendre la morale?

Monsieur Jourdain. La morale?

Pendant la lecture
1. Avec qui est-ce que M. Jourdain a une leçon?

Pendant la lecture
2. Qu'est-ce que M. Jourdain regrette de son enfance?

Pendant la lecture
3. Qu'est-ce que la phrase en latin exprime?

Pendant la lecture
4. M. Jourdain a-t-il quelques connaissances des sciences?

Pendant la lecture
5. Quelle est la première matière que le Maître propose?

savant *learned person*; **esprit** *mind*; **concevoir** *to conceive*; **juger** *to judge*; **tirer** *to pull out*; **rébarbatifs** *forbidding*

Resources

Le Bourgeois gentilhomme

Answers

Outils de lecture

Possible answer: Les gens voulaient obtenir beaucoup de connaissances, ils avaient soif d'apprendre les nouvelles sciences; Les hommes étaient influencés par les idées universelles.

Pendant la lecture

1. Il a une leçon avec le Maître de philosophie.
2. Il regrette que ses parents ne l'aient pas obligé à apprendre toutes les sciences.
3. Sans la connaissance, la vie est comme une image morte.
4. Oui, il sait lire et écrire.
5. La première matière est la logique.

Culture

Practices: Information

As a *leitmotif*, explain to students that Louis XIV was exceptionally proud of, if not vain about, his legs. It is not difficult to find paintings where his legs are prominently displayed. These should prove amusing to your students.

Differentiated Learning

Accelerate

Have students continue the chart on *Word Families* to add more words with their derivatives found in the play.

Decelerate

Ask students to read a timeline or overview of Molière's life. Have them explain to the class what the **Comédie Française** is, where it is located in Paris, when and why it was established, and the tragic event that happened to Molière when he was performing ***Le Malade Imaginaire*** at the **Comédie Française**. (He died on stage during the performance.)

Answers

Pendant la lecture

6. Il rejette la logique (mathématiques), la morale (religieuse), la physique
7. Il décide d'apprendre l'orthographe.

Reference Desk

1. King Louis XIV ruled as absolute monarch at Versailles, where Molière's actors entertained him. The importance of the court—20,000 strong—reached its height during his reign. While the Sun King (**le Roi soleil**) forced nobles into financial dependence on the crown, he bestowed privileges on the **bourgeoisie**, whom he used to build his centralized bureaucracy. The Bourgeoisie's striving to rise above their social position gave Molière the idea for ***Le Bourgeois Gentilhomme***.
2. Molière borrowed characters, gestures, and comic routines from the Italian theater (**commedia dell'arte**). Most of his comic characters are excessive types whose passions are out of balance.
3. In 1670, Louis XIV ordered a Turkish ballet. The musician Lully along with Molière created the **comédie-ballet**, ***Le Bourgeois gentilhomme***, staged at the **Château de Chambord**. Molière played M. Jourdain, and Lully was the Grand Mufti. For the Court, the comedy was secondary to the dancing, music, and the Turkish extravaganza, which were the core aspects of the play.

(Suite)

Maître de Philosophie. Oui.

Monsieur Jourdain. Qu'est-ce qu'elle dit cette morale ?

Maître de Philosophie. Elle traite de la félicité, enseigne aux hommes à modérer leurs passions, et….

Monsieur Jourdain. Non, laissons cela. Je suis bilieux comme tous les diables ; et il n'y a morale qui tienne, je me veux mettre en colère tout mon soûl, quand il m'en prend envie.

Maître de Philosophie. Est-ce la physique que vous voulez apprendre ?

Monsieur Jourdain. Qu'est-ce qu'elle chante cette physique ?

Maître de Philosophie. La physique est celle qui explique les principes des choses naturelles, et les propriétés du corps ; qui discourt de la nature des éléments, des métaux*, des minéraux, des pierres, des plantes et des animaux, et nous enseigne les causes de tous les météores, l'arc-en-ciel*, les feux volants, les comètes, les éclairs, le tonnerre*, la foudre*, la pluie, la neige, la grêle*, les vents et les tourbillons*.

Pendant la lecture
6. Quelles matières est-ce que M. Jourdain rejette ?

Monsieur Jourdain. Il y a trop de tintamarre* là-dedans, trop de brouillamini.

Maître de Philosophie. Que voulez-vous donc que je vous apprenne ?

Monsieur Jourdain. Apprenez-moi l'orthographe.

Maître de Philosophie. Très volontiers.

Pendant la lecture
7. Qu'est-ce que M. Jourdain décide d'apprendre ?

Monsieur Jourdain. Après vous m'apprendrez l'almanach, pour savoir quand il y a de la lune et quand il n'y en a point.

Maître de Philosophie. Soit. Pour bien suivre votre pensée et traiter cette matière en philosophe, il faut commencer selon l'ordre des choses, par une exacte connaissance de la nature des lettres, et de la différente manière de les prononcer toutes. Et là-dessus j'ai à vous dire que les lettres sont divisées en voyelles*, ainsi dites voyelles parce qu'elles expriment les voix ; et en consonnes*, ainsi appelées consonnes parce qu'elles sonnent avec les voyelles, et ne font que marquer les diverses articulations des voix. Il y a cinq voyelles ou voix : A, E, I, O, U.

Monsieur Jourdain. J'entends tout cela.

Maître de Philosophie. La voix A se forme en ouvrant fort la bouche : A.

---

métaux *metals* ; **arc-en-ciel** *rainbow* ; **tonnerre** *thunder* ; **foudre** *lightening* ; **grêle** *hail* ; **tourbillons** *whirlwinds* ; **tintamarre** *hullaballoo* ; **voyelles** *vowels* ; **consonnes** *consonants*

Essential Instruction

1. Have students listen to the play. Stop the recording at the end of each "lesson" (**la logique**, **la morale**, **la physique**, and **l'orthographe**), and ask for their reaction. Is M. Jourdain really learning something new?
2. Ask students to find words that reveal that M. Jourdain is a very emotional man. (**J'enrage**, **je suis bilieux**, **je veux me mettre en colère**.)
3. Encourage them to guess what **tintamarre** and **brouillamini** mean in context. (confusion)

(Suite)

Monsieur Jourdain. A, A. Oui.

Maître de Philosophie. La voix E se forme en rapprochant* la mâchoire* d'en bas de celle d'en haut : A, E.

Monsieur Jourdain. A, E, A, E. Ma foi ! oui. Ah ! que cela est beau !

Maître de Philosophie. Et la voix I en rapprochant encore davantage les mâchoires l'une de l'autre, et écartant* les deux coins de la bouche vers les oreilles : A, E, I.

Monsieur Jourdain. A, E, I, I, I, I. Cela est vrai. Vive la science !

Pendant la lecture
8. Que dit M. Jourdain de cette « science » ?

Maître de Philosophie. La voix O se forme en rouvrant* les mâchoires en rapprochant les lèvres par les deux coins, le haut et le bas : O.

Monsieur Jourdain. O, O. Il n'y a rien de plus juste. A, E, I, O, I, O. Cela est admirable ! I, O, I, O.

Maître de Philosophie. L'ouverture de la bouche fait justement comme un petit rond qui représente un O.

Monsieur Jourdain. O, O, O. Vous avez raison, O. Ah ! la belle chose, que de savoir quelque chose !

Maître de Philosophie. La voix U se forme en rapprochant les dents sans les joindre* entièrement, et allongeant* les deux lèvres en dehors, les approchant aussi l'une de l'autre sans les joindre tout à fait : U.

Monsieur Jourdain. U, U. Il n'y a rien de plus véritable : U.

Maître de Philosophie. Vos deux lèvres s'allongent comme si vous faisiez la moue* ; d'où vient que si vous la voulez faire à quelqu'un, et vous moquer de lui, vous ne sauriez lui dire que : U.

Monsieur Jourdain. U, U. Cela est vrai. Ah ! que n'ai-je étudié plus tôt, pour savoir tout cela ?

Maître de Philosophie. Demain, nous verrons les autres lettres, qui sont les consonnes.

Monsieur Jourdain. Est-ce qu'il y a des choses aussi curieuses qu'à celles-ci ?

Maître de Philosophie. Sans doute. La consonne D, par exemple, se prononce en donnant du bout de la langue* au-dessus des dents d'en haut : DA.

Monsieur Jourdain. DA, DA. Oui. Ah ! les belles choses ! les belles choses !

Pendant la lecture
9. M. Jourdain est-il un étudiant sérieux ?

rapprochant *bringing closer* ; **mâchoire** *jaw* ; **écartant** *moving apart* ; **rouvrant** *re-opening* ; **joindre** *to join* ; **allongeant** *extending* ; **faisiez la moue** *were pouting* ; **bout de la langue** *tip of the tongue*

Answers

Pendant la lecture

8. que c'est une vraie science
9. non, il ne veut pas apprendre ce qu'il ne connaît pas, mais répéter ce qu'il connaît.

TPR

Consider the verbs used in **le Maître de Philosophie** explanations of how M. Jourdain should hold his mouth and lips to form the vowel sounds: **écarter** (*to separate, move apart*); **rapprocher** (*to bring together*); **allonger** (*to lengthen*); **joindre** (*to join*); **appuyer** (*to press*). Review these verbs and then have the students follow the **Maître's** directions.

Differentiated Learning

Adapt

Show a clip of "**La leçon d'orthographe**" which shows the physical comedy and costuming of the scene.

Recherche : le bourgeois gentihomme, act II, scene IV

Learning Styles

Visual Learners

Encourage these students to create a humorous drawing of M. Jourdain's head and face as he tries to pronounce the vowel sounds. Have the students identify the body parts mentioned in the scene: **la mâchoire**, **les dents**, **les lèvres**, **la bouche**, **la langue**, **le palais**.

Answers

Pendant la lecture

10. il voudrait écrire un mot d'amour à une femme.
11. il refuse de croire que la prose est le contraire de la poésie, que c'est un langage commun.

Reference Desk

The equivalent of "six of one, half a dozen of the other" is **bonnet blanc ou blanc bonnet**.

(Suite)

Maître de Philosophie. L'F en appuyant les dents d'en haut sur la lèvre de dessous : FA.

Monsieur Jourdain. FA, FA. C'est la vérité. Ah ! mon père et ma mère, que je vous veux de mal !

Maître de Philosophie. Et l'R, en portant le bout de la langue jusqu'au haut du palais*, de sorte qu'étant frôlée* par l'air qui sort avec force, elle lui cède, et revient toujours au même endroit, faisant une manière de tremblement : RRA.

Monsieur Jourdain. R, R, RA ; R, R, R, R, R, RA. Cela est vrai. Ah ! l'habile* homme que vous êtes ! et que j'ai perdu de temps ! R, R, R, RA.

Maître de Philosophie. Je vous expliquerai à fond toutes ces curiosités.

Monsieur Jourdain. Je vous en prie. Au reste, il faut que je vous fasse une confidence. Je suis amoureux d'une personne de grande qualité, et je souhaiterais que vous m'aidassiez à lui écrire quelque chose dans un petit billet* que je veux laisser tomber à ses pieds.

> **Pendant la lecture**
> 10. Pourquoi M. Jourdain demande-t-il l'aide du Maître ?

Maître de Philosophie. Fort bien.

Monsieur Jourdain. Cela sera galant, oui.

Maître de Philosophie. Sans doute. Sont-ce des vers que vous lui voulez écrire ?

Monsieur Jourdain. Non, non, point de vers.

Maître de Philosophie. Vous ne voulez que de la prose ?

Monsieur Jourdain. Non, je ne veux ni prose ni vers.

Maître de Philosophie. Il faut bien que ce soit l'un, ou l'autre.

Monsieur Jourdain. Pourquoi ?

Maître de Philosophie. Par la raison, Monsieur, qu'il n'y a pour s'exprimer* que la prose, ou les vers.

Monsieur Jourdain. Il n'y a que la prose ou les vers ?

Maître de Philosophie. Non, Monsieur : tout ce qui n'est point prose est vers ; et tout ce qui n'est point vers est prose.

Monsieur Jourdain. Et comme l'on parle qu'est-ce que c'est donc que cela ?

Maître de Philosophie. De la prose.

Monsieur Jourdain. Quoi ! quand je dis : « Nicole, apportez-moi mes pantoufles* et me donnez mon bonnet de nuit », c'est de la prose ?

> **Pendant la lecture**
> 11. Que dit M. Jourdain à propos de la prose ?

---

palais *palate* ; **frôlée** *brushed against* ; **habile** *skillful* ; **billet** lettre d'amour ; **s'exprimer** *to express* ; **pantoufles** *slippers*

Essential Instruction

1. Students continue listening to the scene up to the words: **"Je vous expliquerai à fond toutes ces curiosités."** Discuss difficult sections then replay.
2. In pairs, have students prepare the scene for a short performance.
3. Finish the scene. Ask why M. Jourdain is so intent on his lessons.
4. Note the comic effect of **que vous m'aidassiez**, and **que j'en susse rien**. The imperfect of the subjunctive is rarely if ever used except for comic effect.
5. Listen to the poetry-prose lesson. Why is the discussion of **la prose ou les vers** amusing?
6. Check comprehension: Why are the multiple renditions of the poem amusing? Do they make sense? What conclusion does M. Jourdain arrive at after this lesson? How do we know that M. Jourdain is still dazzled by the philosophy teacher? (He wants him to return.)
7. What example of prose reflects the simple no-nonsense life of M. Jourdain? (**pantoufles, bonnet de nuit**)

(Suite et fin)

Maître de Philosophie. Oui, Monsieur.

Monsieur Jourdain. Par ma foi ! Il y a plus de quarante ans que je dis de la prose sans que j'en susse rien, et je vous suis le plus obligé du monde de m'avoir appris cela. Je voudrais donc lui mettre dans un billet : *Belle Marquise, vos beaux yeux me font mourir d'amour* ; mais je voudrais que cela fût mis d'une manière galante, que cela fût tourné gentiment.

Maître de Philosophie. Mettre que les feux de ses yeux réduisent* votre cœur en cendres* ; que vous souffrez nuit et jour pour elle les violences d'un....

Monsieur Jourdain. Non, non, non, je ne veux point* tout cela ; je ne veux que ce que je vous ai dit : *Belle Marquise, vos beaux yeux me font mourir d'amour.*

Maître de Philosophie. Il faut bien étendre* un peu la chose.

Monsieur Jourdain. Non, vous dis-je, je ne veux que ces seules paroles-là dans le billet, mais tournées à la mode, bien arrangées comme il faut. Je vous prie de me dire un peu, pour voir, les diverses manières dont on les peut mettre.

Maître de Philosophie. On les peut mettre premièrement comme vous avez dit : *Belle Marquise, vos beaux yeux me font mourir d'amour*. Ou bien : *D'amour mourir me font, belle Marquise, vos beaux yeux*. Ou bien : *Vos yeux beaux d'amour me font, belle Marquise, mourir*. Ou bien : *Mourir vos beaux yeux, belle Marquise, d'amour me font*. Ou bien : *Me font vos yeux beaux mourir, belle Marquise, d'amour*.

Monsieur Jourdain. Mais de toutes ces façons-là, laquelle est la meilleure ?

Maître de Philosophie. Celle que vous avez dite : *Belle Marquise, vos beaux yeux me font mourir d'amour*.

Monsieur Jourdain. Cependant je n'ai point étudié, et j'ai fait cela tout du premier coup*. Je vous remercie de tout mon cœur, et vous prie de venir demain de bonne heure.

Maître de Philosophie. Je n'y manquerai pas....

Pendant la lecture

12. Selon le Maître, laquelle des versions de la lettre est la meilleure ?

réduisent *reduce* ; **cendres** *ashes* ; **ne... point** *none* ; **étendre** *to extend* ; **du premier coup** *at the first try*

Post-lecture 1.2

M. Jourdain est-il un étudiant doué ? Pourquoi, ou pourquoi pas ?

Answers

Pendant la lecture

12. la première est la meilleure

Post-lecture

Non, il n'est pas doué parce qu'il pense que rien n'est bon si ce n'est pas approuvé par un "maître", et il n'a pas de curiosité pour les choses nouvelles.

Reference Desk

1. **Un savant** can be a learned person or a scientist.
2. **L'esprit** means *mind*, *spirit*, and *wit*. **Elle a de l'esprit** means *She is witty*.
3. **Faire la moue** means *to pout*. Ask students to say **moue** to see if their mouth indeed resembles a pout.
4. **Un billet de 5 euros** means a 5 euro bill. **Billet** refers to a ticket for the theater or for an airplane. **Billet** also means *letter*. The word *billydoo*, heard in country and western music, is a deformation of the French word (and pronunciation of) **billet-doux**, meaning *love letter*.
5. **Pantoufles** means *slippers*. **Un pantouflard** is a homebody who likes to stay in his house shoes.

Differentiated Learning

Expand

Have students search for images online of the various productions of ***Le Bourgeois Gentilhomme***. Have students collaborate to make a collage on a large poster board of the different interpretations of the play from the classic French 18th-century staging to contemporary times. Ask what that suggests about the timelessness of the play. Is the message in the play as relevant today as it was then? Give examples.

Special Needs Students

Auditory Impairment

Pause the recording frequently so that students can process the French more slowly. Make sure that students with hearing problems use earphones or sit close to the source of the recording.

Resources

Pre-T Pre-test

Q *Leçon* Quiz

Answers

Le monde visuel

Cette photo représente bien le caractère superficiel et égoïste de M. Charon, qui est très fier, donc habillé de grands vêtements. Il aurait pu dire à Charon de se tenir grand et fier.

18 Activities will vary.

Reference Desk

J'ai le mot sur le bout de la langue is the equivalent of "I have the word on the tip of my tongue."

Critical Thinking

Analysis

Les Saveurs du Palais is a film about President Mitterand's cook at the **Elysée** palace in which the master chef prepares the president's favorite regional dishes. How is the title ***Les Saveurs du Palais*** a play on words? (**Palais** is a palate and a palace.)

Expansion

Have students take the discussion of **Le Monde Visuel** further, beyond DeSazo and the photo, into the realm of costuming, staging, and acting. How did the unknown costumer capture the character of M. Jourdain? What is Charon doing to capture the character? How would students costume-design and stage this play? Remind students that theater, also, is a visual art, despite its reliance on words.

Le monde visuel 1.2, 3.1

Serge de Sazo (1915–2012) est un photographe français d'origine russe. Il s'installe à Paris en 1922. Il devient soldat en 1942, et en 1944 il prend des photos de la Libération de Paris qui font le tour du monde et marquent sa renommée (*fame*). Dans la vie d'après-guerre, quand Paris se réanime, ses photos de cabaret, jazz, music-hall, et cinéma paraissent (*appear*) dans de nombreuses publications. Plus tard, il se consacre aux photos sous-marines. Sur cette photo on voit le célèbre acteur Jacques Charon jouer le personnage de M. Jourdain. Comment de Sazo rend-il hommage à la pièce de Molière? Pense-t-il que la manière dont « M. Jourdain » s'habille et se tient soit importante? Qu'est-ce qu'il aurait pu dire à Jacques Charon pour qu'il prenne une telle pose?

Jacques Charon dans « Le Bourgeois gentilhomme », 1974. Serge de Sazo.

18 Activités d'expansion 1.3, 3.1, 3.2

Faites les activités suivantes.

1. Faites un sommaire de ce qui se passe dans cette scène en vous servant des mots de la grille que vous avez remplie.
2. Présentez une partie de la sélection devant la classe. Travaillez avec un groupe. Distribuez les rôles. Vous aurez besoin de deux acteurs, de quelqu'un qui s'occupe des costumes, quelqu'un qui s'occupe des lignes, quelqu'un qui joue le rôle du metteur en scène, et de quelqu'un qui joue le rôle du scénographe (*set designer*).
3. Faites le portrait d'un parvenu d'aujourd'hui. Écrivez une pièce, un poème, une histoire, ou une anecdote.
4. Trouvez le lien qui existe entre Molière et La Comédie Française à Paris.
5. Faites des recherches sur un des sujets suivants pour mieux connaître la France au 17ème siècle. Faites une présentation à la classe.
   - la vie à la cour de Versailles
   - le règne de Louis XIV

   Recherche : versailles site officiel

   - l'importance de la bourgeoisie au 17ème siècle
   - la vie de Molière
   - l'intrigue (*plot*) d'une autre pièce de Molière

Essential Learning

1. Discuss **Post-lecture** in small groups, then as a class.
2. Discuss costuming using the photo of Jacques Charon as an example. Compare this costume to paintings and drawings of courtiers at Versailles. Is this attire typical or exaggerated?
3. For **Activité 18**, have all students do number 1, the **sommaire**.
4. Group students to work on a project of their choice in the **Système D**.

Pre-AP 21

Question centrale ? Comment le passé influence-t-il le présent?

Communiquez!

19 Les caricatures politiques 1.2, 1.3, 3.1, 5.2

Connecting to Media Literacy, Technology Literacy, Creativity and Innovation
Interpretive Viewing, Presentational Speaking or Writing

Les caricatures politiques sont une forme d'expression populaire pour exprimer une opinion ou un point de vue. Recherchez des caricatures politiques de la Révolution française. Expliquez à la classe le point de vue de l'artiste et l'histoire qu'il ou elle raconte avec ses dessins. Créez une caricature politique pour présenter un aspect politique actuel et exprimer votre point de vue, puis racontez votre histoire à un groupe.

Recherche : caricatures politiques révolution française

20 Une foire à l'emploi 1.1, 1.2, 1.3, 3.1, 5.1

Connecting to Financial, Economic, Business, and Entrepreneurial Literacy
Interpersonal Speaking, Interpretive Reading, Presentational Speaking and Writing

Préparez une foire à l'emploi. Une partie de la classe jouera le rôle de diverses entreprises. Les autres élèves joueront le rôle de personnes à la recherche d'un emploi. Les compagnies doivent préparer une présentation de la compagnie, des postes disponibles, et des caractéristiques qu'elles recherchent chez les candidats. Les candidats doivent préparer un CV et une lettre de motivation générale. À la foire, les compagnies interviewent les candidats.

Recherche : grandes entreprises françaises

21 Un système à débattre 1.1, 1.2, 1.3, 3.1, 5.2

Connecting to Civic Literacy, Health Literacy, Information Literacy
Interpersonal Speaking, Interpretive Reading, Presentational Speaking and Writing

En petit groupe, sélectionnez un aspect social qui vous intéresse, et choisissez chacun un pays francophone différent. Faites une chronologie de l'évolution et des changements faits dans ce domaine. Présentez vos recherches au groupe, discutez, comparez les pays. Puis, dites quel système vous semble le meilleur et justifiez votre choix.

La protection sociale :	chômage, invalidité, retraite
La santé publique :	sécurité sociale, assurance
L'éducation :	gratuité du système éducatif
La politique familiale :	allocations familiales, congé de maternité

Differentiated Learning

Accelerate
Ask students to select another scene from ***Le Bourgeois Gentilhomme*** and present it dramatically to the class.

Multiple Intelligences

Musical-Rhythmic
Encourage students who enjoy music to listen to the overture to ***Le Bourgeois gentilhomme*** by Jean-Baptiste Lully. How does this music reflect the grandeur of Versailles?

Bodily-Kinesthetic
Le Bourgeois gentilhomme is classified a comedy-ballet. Why would the aspect of ballet interest Louis XIV?

Recherche : le roi qui danse

French in the Workplace

Finding a job

Jobs abound for English-speakers who are proficient in French. Have students identify three different jobs in a French-speaking part of the world that interests them: one for which they are qualified right now, one entry-level job that would interest them as they leave school, and one long-term career. Ask them to compare the salaries and benefits, and the expectations and responsibilities of each job, and discuss their findings with a partner or group. Then have them prepare the documents they would need to apply for a job in France today.

Recherche : french language jobs/top language jobs/ summer jobs (+ COUNTRY)

Social Justice

Social Justice Organizations are concerned with issues such as Children, Youth, and Family; Civil Liberties & Individual Rights; Community Development; Disease and Disability; Education; Poverty; Welfare and Non-violence; among others. Have students select a problem they are concerned about in their community, and search how organizations in France or another French-speaking country deal with this problem. Have them discuss whether this could be proposed as a model in their community, or suggest their own solution based on their research.

Connections

Health Literacy, Social, and Cross-Cultural Skills

Pair students. Have them role-play a French tourist in the United States (or an American tourist in France) who got injured on his or her vacation, goes to the hospital, and speaks to the receptionist. Ask them to create a dialogue in which the clerk explains to the tourist how the medical system works, and present the tourist's reaction.

Resources

Create

Answers

All activities will vary.

Reference Desk

1. The Europass comprises five documents: 1) CV, 2) Language passport, 3) Certificate Supplement, 4) Diploma Supplement, 5) Mobility. You can find descriptions of each in English and in French on the Europass website.
2. The **Faisons le point!** section asks students to self-evaluate and keep track of their progress. When students complete the activity, direct them to use "I can" statements based on the unit objectives in the **Contrat de l'élève**. The graphic organizer for **Activité D** can be found in the Copy Masters supplement.
3. If you have access to Passport, assign your students an IPA task related to the unit.

Finale

Question centrale ? Comment le passé influence-t-il le présent?

Projets finaux

A Connexions par Internet : l'art oratoire 1.3, 3.2, 4.2, 5.2

Débat

Avec un partenaire, choisissez l'un des thèmes ci-dessous. Il faut qu'une personne défende l'argumentation et que que l'autre personne prenne position contre. Servez-vous du vocabulaire de la **Leçon C**. Enregistrez ou filmez votre discours.

- Est-il important d'augmenter les impôts pour payer les cours d'art dans les écoles ?
- Le gouvernement devrait-il payer pour la garde des enfants avant l'école primaire ?
- Devrait-on avoir une assurance maladie pour tous aux États-Unis ?
- Est-il important d'augmenter les impôts pour payer les programmes sportifs dans les écoles ?

B Communautés en ligne 1.3, 2.1, 3.2, 5.1, 5.2

Europass

Europass aide les Européens à exprimer leurs compétences et qualifications pour trouver un emploi ou une formation. Faites des recherches sur Europass en ligne. Quels sont les cinq documents nécessaires à remplir ? Quels documents doit préparer la personne qui cherche un travail ? Quels autres documents sont nécessaires ? Qui les prépare ? À qui montre-t-on les cinq documents ? Quelles sont les principales fonctions des Centres nationaux Europass ? Où se trouve le Centre national en France ? Imaginez que vous êtes professeur et que vous voulez que vos élèves se rendent compte que ce service existe. Faites une vidéo pour les renseigner sur Europass. Servez-vous de graphiques et de photos dans votre vidéo.

Recherche : europass

C Passez à l'action ! 1.3, 3.2, 5.1

Mon portfolio passeport de langues

Pour chercher du travail en Europe, un employeur aura besoin de connaître vos compétences linguistiques. Cherchez un exemple d'un passeport de langues en ligne et préparez votre propre passeport linguistique. Mettez-le dans votre portfolio avec un enregistrement ou une vidéo d'une activité dont vous êtes fier/fière de **À vous la parole** de l'Unité 8.

Recherche : europass passeport de langues

D Faisons le point ! 1.3

Mes progrès

Votre prof vous donnera un organigramme à remplir.

Essential Instruction

1. Assign mixed-ability partners for **Activité A**.
2. Consider assigning specific topics to partners according to interest or ability.
3. Discuss each question explaining what is required and the resources needed to complete the task.
4. Students do **B** and **C** or, in the interest of time, assign one of them. All work is shared with the class.
5. Give students a study day to complete part **D**. Be available to answer any questions or give additional instruction or support.
6. Have students skim the questions before listening to **Activité A**.
7. For **Activité B**, give students time to prepare their oral work.
8. Have students research online information needed to complete **Activité C**. Assign one topic to be done thoroughly and the others in outline form.

Pre-AP

Évaluation

A Évaluation de compréhension auditive 1.2

Écoutez Benoît et Margot discuter de leurs projets et voyages d'études. Ensuite, complétez la phrase avec un mot ou une expression convenable.

1. Margot a déjà étudié… dans son cours d'histoire l'année dernière.
2. Margot fait une excursion à… en….
3. Benoît voudrait faire un stage à la….
4. Si on l'embauche, il recevra un….
5. Margot doit faire une présentation sur l'….

B Évaluation orale 1.3, 3.2, 4.2

Vous voulez gagner une bourse (scholarship) *pour faire des recherches sur l'Union européenne pour que vous puissiez l'expliquer aux Américains. Dites où vous voudriez aller pour comprendre les institutions de l'UE et décrivez le rôle de chacune.*

C Évaluation culturelle 1.3, 2.1, 3.1, 3.2, 4.2, 5.1

Vous allez comparer les cultures francophones à votre culture aux États-Unis. Vous aurez peut-être besoin de faire des recherches sur la culture américaine.

1. **Les révolutions**
   Expliquez comment la France change à la fin du 18ème siècle. Que veulent les Français? Comparez cette partie de l'histoire de France avec les débuts des États-Unis. Avant la Révolution américaine, qui gouvernait les colonies? Comment les Américains ont-ils changé leur destin?
2. **La guillotine et la peine de mort**
   Comment les Français exécutaient-ils les gens pendant la Révolution française? Cette méthode a duré jusqu'à quand? La France a-t-elle toujours la peine de mort? Et l'État dans lequel vous vivez?
3. **Les sièges du gouvernement**
   Expliquez où se trouvent les sièges des institutions européennes. Où se trouve le gouvernement fédéral américain? Quelles sont ses institutions?
4. **Les documents des droits humains**
   Comparez le début de la *Déclaration des Droits de l'Homme et du Citoyen* à cette partie de la *Declaration d'Indépendance des États-Unis*.
5. **L'assurance médicale**
   Comparez l'assurance médicale en France avec l'assurance aux État-Unis. Comment les deux pays aident-ils leurs citoyens avec des soins gratuits? Qui est exclu?

Differentiated Learning

Accelerate
High-ability students will be able to review the lessons in the unit on their own.

Decelerate
While your high-ability students are working independently, organize a structured review of **Leçons A**, **B**, and **C** for students who need more guided study. It is another opportunity to teach, study, and review skills with them.

Resources

Activity A
LA Listening Activity *Synthèse*
Pre-AP Listening *Unité 4*

Answers

A Script

Benoît: Qu'est-ce que vous allez faire comme voyage cette année avec ta classe d'histoire? Vous allez aller au château de Versailles?
Margot: Non, on a étudié la Révolution française l'année dernière. Cette année, on étudie l'Europe et la France de l'après-guerre.
Benoît: Pas de roi et de reine, alors vous allez visiter l'Assemblée?
Margot: Bien mieux, cette année on va à Bruxelles pendant deux jours. On va visiter la Commission européenne.
Benoît: Super! Moi, je voudrais travailler là plus tard.
Margot: Si tu me donnes une lettre de candidature et un CV, je peux les donner pour toi….
Benoît: C'est une bonne idée. Je dois faire un stage cet été et la Commission européenne, ce serait génial! J'ai déjà regardé leur site et je sais qu'ils embauchent des stagiaires pendant l'été, et qu'en plus ils leur donnent un petit salaire.
Margot: D'accord, alors rédige ta lettre et donne-la-moi. Toi, tu peux m'aider avec mon projet sur la santé en France?
Benoît: Bien sûr, qu'est-ce que tu dois faire?
Margot: Je dois présenter le pour et le contre de l'assurance privée comparée à notre assurance sociale.
Benoît: Tu peux commencer par une question: Est-ce un droit ou un privilège de se faire soigner? Et puis tu introduis ta position.
Margot: Super. Tu peux venir chez moi ce soir?
Benoît: Oui, dix-huit heures, ça te va?

1. la Révolution française
2. Bruxelles, voyage de classe
3. Commission européenne
4. petit salaire
5. assurance privée

B Answers will vary.

C Answers will vary.

Resources

Perform

Answers

D Answers will vary.

E Answers will vary.

F Answers will vary.

Reference Desk

1. Remind students to incorporate expressions + **être** and **plus-que-parfait** whenever possible and logical for **Activités E** and **F** as part of their review.
2. If you have access to Passport, assign a task to evaluate your students' oral proficiency.

Communication

Interpersonal: Cooperative Groups

Divide students into groups of four or five to review the **Contrat de l'élève**. Have them rate how well they know each topic by a system of stars, one star indicating needs review to five stars indicating mastery. Have students make a study list of topics in **Activité C** needing more attention, and a list of those topics that can be left alone.

Interpersonal: Paired Practice

Have students work together to quiz each other orally and in written form on the vocabulary from the **Leçons** and the vocabulary list for **Unité 8**. They might want to assign categories for the vocabulary according to the themes of **histoire**, **assurances**, **emploi**, **verbes**, and **expressions**.

D Évaluation écrite 1.3, 3.2

Votre grand-mère est tombée. Vous voudriez qu'elle se fasse soigner. Écrivez un mail à son médecin qui :

- explique ce qui s'est passé
- décrit ses symptômes
- demande ce que vous devriez faire

E Évaluation visuelle 1.3

Décrivez qui est la personne représentée dans l'illustration et indiquez où elle est. Expliquez les événements qui avaient eu lieu quand on l'a arrêtée.

MODÈLE **Le peuple français avait pris la Bastille, symbole de l'Ancien Régime....**

F Évaluation compréhensive 1.3, 3.1, 3.2, 5.2

Créez six illustrations qui montrent l'histoire de France à la fin du 18ème siècle. Faites une description par écrit pour chaque image. Prenez le point de vue d'un(e) personnage historique ou d'un(e) citoyen(ne) dans la rue.

Essential Instruction

1. Ask students to write a brief e-mail in **Activité D**. Have them refer back to the vocabulary on pp. 476–477.
2. Have students fill out a graphic organizer using **Qui ?**, **Que ?**, **Où ?**, **Pourquoi ?**, **Quand ?**, and **Comment ?** as cues to help them write a composition about Marie-Antoinette imprisoned.
3. Students can work in pairs to do **Activité E**.
4. Students use a storyboard to complete **Activité F** illustrating sympathetically or satirically the events toward the end of the 18th century. The description, which accompanies each frame, should reinforce whether they are royalist or revolutionary.
5. Encourage students to review the vocabulary through quizzing each other, flash cards, or rewriting the list. Remind them that the letter behind the vocabulary word indicates the **Leçon** where it was featured.

Vocabulaire de l'Unité 8

à: à mi-temps half-time *B*;
à plein temps full-time *B*
accéder to access *C*
accorder to grant *C*
acquis(e) acquired *B*
une **anecdote** anecdote *C*
un(e) **aristocrate** aristocrat *A*
un(e) **assistant(e) junior** junior assistant *B*
l' **assurance (f.)** insurance *C*; **assurance maladie** health insurance *C*
au: au contraire on the contrary *C*; **au cours de** during, in the course of *B*
avoir: avoir beau (+ INFINITIVE) to do (something) in vain *B*; **avoir droit à** to be entititled to *C*; **avoir les moyens** to be able to afford, to have the means *C*; **avoir tort** to be wrong *C*
un **boulot** job *[inform.]* *B*
cependant however *C*
chez: chez le kiné to the physical therapy office *C*
les **chiffres (m.)** figures, numbers *C*
la **chute** fall *A*
une **citation** quote *C*
un **citoyen, une citoyenne** citizen *A*
le **clergé** clergy *A*
la **collectivité** community, society *C*
la **compagnie** company *B*
complémentaire supplementary *C*
les **connaissances (f.)** knowledge *B*
un **contrat** contract *B*
un **CV** CV (Curriculum vitae) *B*
d'ailleurs moreover *C*
le **débat** debate *C*
se **débrouiller** to take care of things *B*
les **députés (m.)** deputies *A*
deuxièmement secondly *C*
le (la) **DRH: le directeur/la directrice des ressources humaines** HR Director *B*
des **difficultés (f.)** difficulties *C*
embaucher to hire *B*
entièrement completely, entirely *C*
un **entretien** interview *B*
un **état** state *A*; **les états généraux** Estates General *A*
être: être à to belong to *C*; **être condamné(e)** to be condemned *A*; **être convoqué(e)** to be called in, summoned *B*; **être obligé(e) (de)** to be obligated (to) *A*; **être perso** to be personalized *[inform.]* *B*
des **factures (f.)** bills *C*
faire: faire ses adieux to bid farewell *A*; **faire un discours** to make a speech *A*; **faire un stage** to intern *B*; **faire (+ INFINITIVE)** to make (someone do something) *A*; **On te fait étudier tout ça?** They make you study all that? *A*
se **faire: se faire soigner** to seek (medical) treatment *C*
une **formation** education, training *B*
guéri(e) healed *C*
guillotiner to decapitate *A*
l' **hôpital (m.)** hospital *C*
illustrer to illustrate *C*
influencer to influence *A*
introduire to introduce *C*
le **kiné (kinésithérapeute)** physical therapist *C*
une **lettre: lettre de candidature** application letter *B*; **lettre de motivation** cover letter *B*
médical(e) medical *C*
médicalisé(e) medicalized *C*
mettre: mettre en pratique to put into practice *B*
la **mort** death *A*; **mourir** to die *A*; **... est mort(e)** ... died *A*
ne: N'en jette plus! Enough! Stop it! *[inform.]* *B*
néanmoins nevertheless *C*
une **ouverture** opening *A*
par contre however, on the other hand *C*
partir en voyage to take a journey *A*
se **passer** to happen *A*
un **permis (de conduire)** driver's license *C*
une **perruque** wig *A*
une **petite annonce** want ad *B*
le **peuple** people *A*
plein (de) a lot (of) *B*
une **position** position *C*
premièrement firstly *C*
le **présent** present *A*
privé(e) private *C*
une **qualité** quality *B*
rédiger to write *B*
la **rééducation** physical therapy *C*
un **régime** regime *A*
répondre to respond *C*
une **république** republic *A*
un **salaire** salary *B*
des **séances (f.)** sessions *C*
la **sécurité sociale (sécu)** French national health and pension insurance *C*
des **soins (m.)** care, treatment *C*
un(e) **stagiaire** intern *B*
un **système** system *C*
une **table de multiplication** multiplication table *A*
tomber to fall *C*
un **traitement** treatment *C*
wahou wow *B*

Resources

FC F ash Cards
Rendez-vous à Nice! Documentaire 4
T *Unité 8 Test*
Perform

Resources

Activity II

Answers

I

1. A

II Script

–Il paraît que ton mari est tombé d'un arbre ce week-end en essayant de couper les branches ?

–Il s'est cassé le bras droit et il a mal. Il ne va pas pouvoir travailler pendant un moment, vu qu'il dessine avec la main droite.

–Par contre on peut dire qu'il a eu beaucoup de chance que cela lui soit arrivé en France et pas aux États-Unis où tout le monde n'a pas d'assurance médicale.

–Ah, ne m'en parle pas. Ma sœur m'a dit que là-bas se faire soigner est un privilège, alors qu'en France c'est un droit. Qu'on ait les moyens ou pas, on peut tous aller chez le médecin, consulter un psychiatre ou voir un kiné ; c'est quand même formidable ; tu crois pas ?

–Complètement ! Je suis entièrement de ton avis. C'est fou cette histoire d'assurance médicale privée en Amérique. Je ne comprends pas qu'au vingt-et-unième siècle on n'a pas tous droit à se faire soigner.

–Évidemment je ne suis pas économiste et je ne comprends rien à la politique, mais je suis pour le système social français et entièrement contre le système capitaliste américain.

1. A
2. B
3. D

Reference Desk

The **Bilan cumulatif** is based on the French Language and Culture AP exam prepared by the College Board. It assesses students' proficiencies in the Interpersonal, Interpretive, and Presentational modes of communication. Students are also asked to demonstrate their understanding of the products, practices, and perspectives of the target cultures.

Bilan cumulatif

Pre-AP

Multiple Choice

I. Interpretive Communication: Print texts **1.2, 2.1**

Lisez cet article sur les jeunes gens qui viennent de finir leurs études universitaires. Puis répondez à la question.

À l'heure actuelle, il y a de plus en plus de jeunes diplômés sur le marché du travail. Par conséquent, il devient extrêmement difficile de trouver un stage de quelques mois en entreprise car la compétition est grande et féroce. C'est pourquoi aujourd'hui de nombreux jeunes partent en direction d'autres pays tels que les États-Unis pour tenter leur chance et obtenir une expérience professionnelle unique et perfectionner par la même occasion leur compétence en anglais.

1. D'après le texte, quelle difficulté la jeunesse française rencontre-t-elle aujourd'hui ?
   - A. La nouvelle génération est très qualifiée mais a des difficultés à trouver des stages ou emplois.
   - B. Elle ne peut pas parler anglais.
   - C. Les jeunes ne sont pas très compétitifs.
   - D. Il est difficile d'obtenir un visa pour travailler à l'étranger.

II. Interpretive Communication: Audio Texts **1.1, 1.2**

Écoutez le dialogue suivant deux fois, puis répondez aux questions.

1. La conversation a lieu….
   - A. entre une Américaine et une Française
   - B. entre une femme et son mari
   - C. entre deux amies françaises
   - D. entre une femme et sa sœur
2. Le sujet de conversation est….
   - A. la vie de famille en Amérique
   - B. le système médical en France par opposition au système américain
   - C. le privilège de ne pas travailler au vingt-et-unième siècle
   - D. le coût des médicaments en Amérique et en France
3. Les deux interlocuteurs….
   - A. ne sont pas d'accord
   - B. veulent vivre aux États-Unis
   - C. n'aiment pas la sécu en France
   - D. partagent le même point de vue sur l'assurance maladie

Free response

III. Presentational Writing: Persuasive Essay **1.2, 1.3**

*Vous allez écrire un essai persuasif basé sur une source que vous allez lire d'abord. Vous devrez d'abord présenter les points de vue soulevés (*raised*) dans la source, puis donner votre point de vue. Soutenez votre point de vue avec des exemples de la source ou de vos propres connaissances.*

Votre thème : L'élargissement de l'Union européenne : Trop, c'est trop ? Êtes-vous pour ou contre d'autres élargissements de l'UE ?

Essential Instruction

1. Have students skim the questions for Parts I and II before the reading and listening evaluations to give them a sense of the gist of the offerings.
2. Students prepare for the Persuasive Essay by evaluating each point of view, making notes in the margins of remarks they want to incorporate in the essay.
3. Have them prepare a pre-writing outline to decide how to organize their essay in a logical way supported by clear examples. They must add their personal opinion about the subject, citing clear illustrations.
4. Ask students to prepare their responses for the speaking assessment. Put students in pairs and have them go through their conversation, switching roles when time is called. After the first round of conversations, ask them to reflect on what went well and what needed improvement. Discuss as a class. Have students switch partners and do the conversations again, incorporating the changes for improvement mentioned in the class reflection.

En 1951, il y avait six pays fondateurs de la Communauté européenne : l'Allemagne, la Belgique, la France, l'Italie, le Luxembourg, et les Pays-Bas. Entre 1963 et 2007, il y a eu cinq élargissements. En 2012, l'Union européenne compte 27 membres (pays adhérents). Cinq autres pays sont candidats : l'Islande, l'Ancienne République yougoslave de Macédoine, le Monténégro, la Serbie, et la Turquie ; et trois pays sont candidats potentiels (l'Albanie, la Bosnie-et-Herzégovine, et le Kosovo). On peut bien se demander où s'arrêtent les frontières de l'Europe.

Des européens répondent :

Janine, 21 ans (Bordeaux) : Moi, ce que j'aime c'est la possibilité de partir étudier en Europe, d'aller travailler et habiter où l'on veut. Quoi de mieux pour renforcer les liens et apprendre à se connaître ?

Patrick, 28 ans (Dublin) : L'Europe forme un bloc qui agit comme un contrepoids face à l'hégémonie d'autres blocs. Ensemble, nous sommes plus puissants face aux autres pays. Pour la sécurité de tous, l'union est importante.

Miguel, 34 (Barcelone) : Si nous acceptons la Turquie, nous ouvrons nos portes au Proche et au Moyen Orient. La Turquie ne fait pas partie de l'Europe géographiquement.

Suzanne, 30 ans (Salzbourg) : Admettre la Turquie est un moyen d'aider au rapprochement de l'Occident et l'Orient.

Jason, 45 ans (Londres) : On ne peut pas pousser la frontière de l'Europe jusqu'à l'infini ! Nous commençons déjà à avoir énormément de problèmes concernant l'assimilation des immigrants, le chômage, la disparité économique entre pays riches et pays pauvres....

Victoria, 32 ans (Stockholm) : On ne peut pas prévoir les conséquences bonnes ou mauvaises de l'élargissement de l'Union européenne. Mais l'important, c'est de prendre le temps de bien évaluer tous les candidats. Chaque pays doit respecter les droits de l'homme, les principes de liberté et de démocratie, et avoir des institutions et une économie stables. Sinon, on ne doit pas l'admettre. J'ai confiance dans le processus.

(Sources : europa.eu, lexpress.fr, cidem.org)

IV. Interpersonal Speaking: Conversation **1.2, 1.3**

Vous avez une conversation avec votre petit frère qui suit le canevas ci-dessous.

Frère : Je dois présenter le portrait d'un peintre lundi prochain. Qu'est-ce que tu me conseilles ?
Vous : **Dites-lui que les Impressionnistes ont changé les thèmes des tableaux et la manière de peindre. Donnez des exemples.**
Frère : Quel peintre impressionniste est-ce que tu préfères ?
Vous : **Répondez, et expliquez pourquoi vous admirez cet artiste.**
Frère : Il faut que je choisisse un tableau aussi et que je le décrive.
Vous : **Recommandez une peinture et décrivez-la en la regardant. Identifiez le sujet et les couleurs. Expliquez ce qu'on voit au premier plan, au centre, et à l'arrière-plan. Dites que vous pouvez en discuter d'avantage ce soir.**

Answers

III Compositions will vary.
IV Conversations will vary.

Reference Desk

1. In the speaking section of the assessment, students are asked to participate in a conversation or make a cultural comparison using their presentational speaking skills.
2. The AP French Language and Culture test is intended to identify students with the highest level of proficiency in the language and culture. It is not a measure of the average students' abilities or reasonable expectations after four years of high school study. Encourage all students who are motivated by French and love the language and culture to pursue four years of study, regardless of their performance on the AP test. Ensure that your program offers options for students of all ability levels to complete four years of French if they want to do so.

Differentiated Learning

Decelerate
Low-ability students benefit from a study day in class where they can systematically review the content of the unit lessons. It would afford you time to have a free-question day where they can ask for help on any topic no matter how basic.

Special Needs Students

Linguistically Challenged
Simplify or reduce the scope of their tasks so that they can succeed. You might want to put a ceiling of a "C" as their highest grade because of this modification.

AD(H)D
Provide students with more structure and step-by-step guidelines to help them when doing the **Evaluation**.

At-Risk Students
Some students do not have the proper atmosphere at home for study, or are working after school until late. Time in class to study would be very beneficial.

Reference Desk

1. The photo on the unit opener depicts a confluence of police patrols in a busy street of Paris. Ask students what may be happening that would prompt such police presence. What do they know of security in France, especially regarding terrorist attacks? Students will learn about **la police nationale** in **Leçon B**.
2. André Breton (1896–1966) was a French writer and poet. His treatise, **"Le Manifeste du surréalisme,"** laid the groundwork for Surrealism.

Unité

9 Récits de la vie contemporaine

Essential Instruction

1. Introduce the theme of the unit by having students discuss the **Citation** and the **À savoir** fact.
2. Ask if students would like to study in France, and if so, where and what?
3. Explain that in this unit students will learn more about French education, the role of police in controlling crime, and the impact of social media on contemporary life.
4. Review the **Contrat de l'élève** and answer any questions.

Question centrale

Quels sont les défis de la vie contemporaine?

À savoir

Environ 70 000 étudiants français par an suivent des cours à l'étranger et 270 000 participent à un Erasmus. Plus de 310 000 étudiants internationaux suivent des cours en France.

Citation

«La plus grande faiblesse de la pensée contemporaine me paraît résider dans la surestimation extravagante du connu par rapport à ce qui reste à connaître.»

The weakest point of contemporary thought seems to me to reside in the extravagant overestimation of the known as opposed to what remains to be known.

—André Breton (1896–1966), écrivain et poète français

Conseil pratique

Try to take class notes in French only, and listen to French (songs, radio, news, etc.) every day.

Pourquoi Tigran chante-t-il sur cette photo?

Ces hommes travaillent pour quelle organisation?

Contrat de l'élève

Leçon A I will be able to:

- express how someone looked and what I was unable to do.
- discuss the French educational system, including **le bac**.
- use the past conditional, including in clauses with **si**.

Leçon B I will be able to:

- ask if someone noticed something and say that I realized something.
- discuss the French police and crime.
- use possessive adjectives and possessive pronouns.

Leçon C I will be able to:

- ask when someone had an idea to do something, and say that I was not expecting something.
- discuss teens and their connection to the internet and social media.
- review indefinite adjectives and use indefinite pronouns.

Answers

Possible choices for the video question are:

A. Il fait un concours de slam.
B. Il donne un concert de rap.
C. Il rend hommage à Johnny Hallyday.
D. Il auditionne pour *La Nouvelle Star*.

Correct answer: B

The answer to the culture question is: **la gendarmerie nationale**. The answer can be found in **Points de départ**, **Leçon B**.

Reference Desk

1. Remind students that they already know the conditional. Ask them to tell you what they remember regarding conjugation and usage. Explain that they have already worked with if-clause sentences. Ask for some examples. Explain that they will expand their knowledge of both structures in this unit.
2. The choices for the video question include a reference to Johnny Hallyday. Explain to students that this singer, born Jean-Philippe Smet, was a legendary French rock star who passed away in 2017 at the age of 73. He was so popular that his funeral culminated in a massive procession of hundreds of thousands of French people on the Champs-Élysées, making this tribute greater than those for former French presidents.

Differentiated Learning

Expand

Ask students in small groups to reflect on the **Question centrale**. Have them make a list of the challenges of contemporary life today. Ask students to share their list with you; put the items on the board. Circle any that relate to education, crime, or the internet, as they will be studying these elements. Keep the list posted in the classroom throughout your study of this unit.

Special Needs Students

AD(H)D

Provide time for students with attention difficulties to organize their materials for the new unit. Have them prepare their notebook, binder, or folder ahead of time and ask them to decide what they no longer need. Assist them in setting up their binder with sections for vocabulary, structure, and culture notes, or any system that works well for them.

Resources

- *Vocabulaire actif*
- eV eVisual
- WB Workbook 1–4
- FC Flash Cards
- LA Listening Activity 1
- G & V Practice Games

Reference Desk

1. Supplementary vocabulary: **gêné(e)** (*bothered*); **navré(e)** (*sorry*); **sidéré(e)** (*dumbfounded*); **ébloui(e)** (*dazzled*); **ravi(e)** (*delighted*); **HS** (**hors service**, *exhausted*).
2. **Décevoir** (*to disappoint, to disillusion*) is conjugated like **recevoir**. **Une déception** is a *disappointment*.
3. Remind students that the past participles of reflexive verbs in the **passé composé** agree in gender and number with the subject, provided there is no direct object following the verb (for example: **Elle s'est sentie seule**).

Leçon A Vocabulaire actif

Ce que l'on évite et ce que l'on ressent 1.2

Ce que Carla ressent face à un problème ou un défi :

Ce que Léo évite :

Essential Instruction

1. Show students illustrations from advertisements in magazines, online, or from classroom flash cards of people in different emotional states. Ask students to use **se sentir** + ADJECTIVE in sentences to describe the people. Put the sentences on the board for the students to copy in their notebooks, underlining the adjectives.
2. Students listen to **Ce que Carla ressent face à un problème ou un défi**. Add new adjectives from the recording to the list on the board.
3. Where possible, classify the adjectives with their opposites, (for example, **encouragé(e)≠ découragé(e)**).
4. Have students draw emoticons of happy, sad, and angry faces in their notebooks and write the adjectives under the appropriate headings.
5. Students listen to **Ce que Léo évite** and draw and label the vocabulary in their notebooks.
6. Ask students to read **Activité 1** aloud.
7. As a whole class activity, have students answer the questions that follow.

Pour la conversation 1.2

How do I express how someone looked?

» Tu ne semblais pas très bien.
You didn't look very good.

How do I express what I was incapable of doing?

» J'étais **incapable** de décider quelle était la **priorité**.
I was incapable of deciding what the priority was.

Et si je voulais dire... ?

embarrassé(e)	*embarrassed*
soucieux, soucieuse	*worried*
être déçu(e)	*to be disappointed*
être dégoûté(e)	*to be disgusted*
passer un examen (un concours)	*to take an exam (a placement test)*
refouler ses sentiments	*to repress one's feelings*

1 La première d'Ariane Azay! 1.2, 3.1

Interpretive Reading

Lisez ce blog dans lequel une star explique ce qui s'est passé pendant une première.

Okay. Maintenant que tout le monde a vu les photos de la première, voici les explications. J'ai trébuché et je suis tombée sur le tapis rouge. La grêle a commencé à tomber, alors que j'étais encore par terre (*on the ground*), et elle a abîmé (*ruined*) ma belle robe Chanel en soie. Je me suis foulé la cheville. Un bel inconnu m'a aidée à me lever. Et, non, je ne sais pas qui il est, et il est encore moins mon petit ami. Je déteste tous ces mauvais commentaires. Après, je me suis fait bousculer par la foule, mais finalement j'ai pu entrer dans la salle du théâtre. Si ma chute (*fall*) vous a fait rire, vous devriez vous sentir honteux. Je ne suis pas fière de ce qui s'est passé mais les messages de tous mes fans m'ont encouragée, et je serai prête pour ma tournée qui commence le mois prochain.

Ariane

1. Que montrent les photos d'Ariane?
2. Qu'est-ce qui s'est passé pendant la première?
3. Qu'est-ce qu'elle portait ce soir-là?
4. Quels mauvais commentaires a-t-on faits?
5. Qu'est-ce qu'elle dit aux gens qui ont ri?
6. Qu'est-ce qu'elle va faire dans un mois?

Differentiated Learning

Accelerate
Have students write a blog from the point of view of a TV commentator reporting from the red carpet. Have students use the **imparfait** and the **passé composé** for narration.

Decelerate
Ask students to draw a storyboard of the blog with captions in French describing each picture.

Resources

Pour la conversation
Et si je voulais dire... ?
Activity 1

Answers

1
1. Elles montrent qu'elle est tombée.
2. Elle a trébuché, elle est tombée sur le tapis rouge, et un bel homme l'a aidée à se relever.
3. Elle portait une robe Chanel en soie.
4. On a dit que l'homme qui l'a aidée est son petit ami.
5. Elle dit qu'ils devraient se sentir honteux.
6. Elle va faire une bonne tournée.

Reference Desk

Fier/fière is a good kind of pride as in "**Je suis fier de toi**" whereas **orgueilleux(se)** means proud in a negative sense as in "**Il est trop orgueilleux et ça m'énerve.**" **Arrogant** and **prétentieux** are cognates meaning *arrogant* and *pretentious*, respectively.

nouvelle orthographe **dégouté(e), abimer**

Critical Thinking

Application
Have students write five sentences each for **fier/fière** and **orgueilleux/orgueilleuse**, demonstrating that they understand the difference between the two versions of "proud."

Communication

Presentational, Interpersonal: Cooperative Groups
Students work in groups of three to transform the **Activité 1** blog into a dramatic scene. The narrator reads the introduction, setting the stage for the scene. A student plays Ariane, and another the handsome stranger. Other students can play the fans and paparazzi taking pictures. Have students create a dialogue that reflects the relationship between the two. Does the **bel inconnu** become someone more to her? Was Ariane too embarrassed to speak? Tune in to see!

Resources

Activity 4

Answers

2

1. Aïcha s'est sentie heureuse.
2. Les membres de la famille Lacombe se sont sentis attristés.
3. Anna et Sabrina se sont senties découragées/fâchées.
4. Nadège s'est sentie fière/heureuse/encouragée.

3

1. la grêle
2. les commentaires
3. se faire bousculer
4. trébucher
5. se faire arrêter
6. la bagarre

4 Script

Ahmed: Pourquoi tu étais en retard ce matin? Tu ne semblais pas très bien en cours de maths.
Sandrine: Oh, tu ne sais pas ce qui s'est passé! D'abord, je me suis réveillée en retard et quand je me suis levée j'ai tout juste évité de trébucher sur mon livre de révision pour le bac.
Ahmed: Tu as aussi évité l'interro-surprise pendant le cours de français.
Sandrine: Oui, je sais. Je me sens honteuse. J'étais incapable de me rappeler quels cours on avait, alors j'ai pris les mauvais cahiers. Mon père m'a emmenée. Quand on a quitté la maison, la grêle a commencé à tomber, et on a évité de se faire arrêter devant le lycée.
Ahmed: Eh bien, ce n'est vraiment pas de chance.
Sandrine: Et en plus, je me suis fait bousculer dans les couloirs et je n'ai pas pu éviter les mauvais commentaires de Marie-Hélène pendant le cours de maths.
Ahmed: Peut-être que tu aurais dû rester chez toi!

1. Sandrine a évité l'interro-surprise de français.
2. Sandrine a pris un taxi pour aller au lycée.
3. Le père de Sandrine s'est fait arrêter devant le lycée.
4. Sandrine s'est réveillée en retard.
5. La grêle a commencé à tomber ce matin.

1. V; 2. F; 3. F; 4. V; 5. V

2 Comment est-ce qu'ils se sont sentis? 1.2

Interpretive Reading and Viewing

Dites comment les personnes suivantes se sont senties selon la photo. Choisissez un adjectif ci-dessous. N'oubliez pas de faire l'accord avec le sujet de la phrase.

encouragé heureux honteux fier attristé découragé fâché

MODÈLE

Nicolas
Nicolas s'est senti honteux.

1. Aïcha

2. les membres de la famille Lacombe

3. Anna et Sabrina

4. Nadège

3 Qu'est-ce qu'ils évitent? 1.2

Interpretive Reading

Complétez les phrases pour dire ce que les personnes évitent (de faire). Choisissez une expression ci-dessous.

les mauvais commentaires la grêle se faire bousculer la bagarre trébucher se faire arrêter

1. Romain est rentré sous la pluie, mais il s'est senti heureux d'avoir évité….
2. Anaïs essaie d'éviter… parce qu'elle déteste quand on parle des autres.
3. Valérie évite la foule parce qu'elle ne veut pas….
4. M. Simon a évité de… parmi les jouets (*toys*) de ses enfants quand il est rentré du travail.
5. Sébastien a évité de… par l'agent de police après avoir perdu son permis de conduire.
6. Julien a évité… avec deux garçons fâchés.

4 Une mauvaise journée 1.2

Interpretive Listening

*Écrivez les numéros 1–5 sur votre papier. Écoutez Sandrine et Ahmed discuter de la matinée de Sandrine. Ensuite, dites si les phrases que vous entendez sont vraies (**V**) ou fausses (**F**).*

Essential Instruction

1. Do **Activité 2** in groups. Have students refer to the adjective list in their notebooks and to add additional adjectives when describing the pictures.
2. Have students write **Activité 3**.
3. Use whiteboards to answer **Activité 4**. Replay any confusing statements.
4. Before playing the video, ask students if they have ever wanted to skip class. Watch the video with books closed.
5. Ask students if they can relate to Élodie's situation of being exhausted. When and why?
6. Students listen to the recording with books open.
7. To preview the past conditional (p. 514), ask what **"Si j'avais bossé… j'aurais évité tous ces ennuis"** probably means.
8. Students answer the questions for **Activité 5** in pairs.

Rencontres culturelles

Élodie sèche ses cours 1.2

Élodie parle à sa copine Coralie de sa journée.

Coralie : Lâcheuse ! Tu m'as laissée seule dans le labo ce matin. Tu as séché* tous tes cours ?
Élodie : Écoute, il faut que je te raconte, je ne sais pas ce qui s'est passé….
Coralie : Oui, j'ai bien vu que tu ne semblais pas très bien.
Élodie : Oui, je me suis sentie très mal.
Coralie : Qu'est-ce qui t'est arrivé ?
Élodie : Je suis arrivée à la maison, j'ai voulu commencer à travailler et j'étais comme tétanisée ; j'étais incapable de décider quelle était la priorité…. J'étais paniquée ; je me suis effondrée de fatigue.
Coralie : Et qu'est-ce que tu as fait alors ?
Élodie : J'ai dormi… j'ai dormi pendant 18 heures !
Coralie : Dix-huit heures ! Tu devrais être maintenant en pleine forme !
Élodie : À part le bac, qui me tourmente. Si j'avais bossé plus auparavant, j'aurais évité tous ces ennuis !

Le lycée de Coralie et d'Élodie, lycée Stanislas, à Nice

5 Élodie sèche ses cours 1.2, 1.3

Répondez aux questions suivantes.

1. Quand est-ce que Coralie a remarqué l'absence d'Élodie ?
2. Qu'est-ce que Coralie a remarqué ce matin ?
3. Comment se sentait Élodie une fois arrivée à la maison ?
4. Elle a dormi combien de temps ?
5. Qu'est-ce qui l'inquiète ?

***Je parle bien !**

« Le mot **séché** combine les sons des mots **ses** et **chez**. Dites **ses-chez** lentement, puis de plus en plus vite. »

Resources

Dialogue Activity 5
Dialogue Video
WB Workbook 5

Answers

5

1. Elle a remarqué son absence le matin, au labo.
2. Elle a remarqué qu'Élodie ne se sentait pas bien.
3. Elle était paniquée.
4. Elle a dormi pendant 18 heures.
5. Le bac l'inquiète.

Reference Desk

1. **Un lâcheur (-euse)** is an unreliable person or a deserter. In Quebec, the masculine form is spelled **lâcheux**. More vocabulary: **être tétanisé(e)** (*to be paralyzed*); **effondré(e)** (*shattered, crushed*); **bosser** (*to work hard*); **des ennuis** (*trouble*).
2. Point out the difference between "**Qu'est-ce qui t'est arrivé**" and "**Je suis arrivée à la maison**" as seen in the dialogue.
3. **Discuter** is followed by **de** when referring to what is discussed: **Je discute *de* mes problèmes**.

Communication

Interpersonal: Paired Practice

Tell students to write as many excuses as they can think of about why they skipped class yesterday, plausible or not, share them, and rate them as a class.

Interpersonal, Presentational: Cooperative Groups

Students work together to add as many reasons as they can think of as to why the people in **Activité 2** feel the way they do. As an example, students could write **Nicolas s'est senti honteux parce qu'il a triché**. Correct in class.

Differentiated Learning

Accelerate
Students write a short essay relating when and why they felt sad, discouraged, angry, or any other emotion they choose.

Decelerate
Ask students to make a list of expressions in **Élodie sèche ses cours** that indicate she is not feeling up to par.

Resources

Extension

Answers

EXTENSION

Non, parce qu'elle a réussi avec mention.

Reference Desk

1. Your students may want to know that **Ça va pas fort?** is informal language for **Ça ne va pas bien? Se planter** is familiar for **se tromper**.
2. **La session de rattrapage** is an organized tutoring session before retaking the **bac**.
3. **Une mention** is added to high passing grades. **Le Bac** is graded out of 20 points: 10 and above are passing grades; grades between 12 and 14 are with **une mention assez bien**; grades between 14 and 16 are with **une mention bien**; grades 16 and above are **mention très bien**.

EXTENSION **Les résultats du bac** 1.2, 2.1

Abdel-Cader et Louisa parlent du bac qu'ils ont passé.

Abdel-Cader: Ben alors, ça va pas fort?

Louisa: En effet, je n'arrête pas de penser à la dernière épreuve du bac… je me suis complètement plantée!

Abdel-Cader: Tu sais, on a tous cette impression à la fin des épreuves.

Louisa: Non, vraiment, le sujet en histoire était beaucoup trop dur, je n'avais pas assez révisé. Je dois sérieusement me préparer pour la session de rattrapage.

Abdel-Cader: Mais, tu sais, les résultats sont déjà en ligne. Tu ne les as pas consultés?

Louisa: Non, j'ai trop peur de savoir.

Abdel-Cader: Écoute, il vaut mieux affronter les problèmes. Regardons ensemble. Ben, tiens donc…regarde….

Louisa: Gautier, Louisa… admise, mention passable! J'y crois pas!

Abdel-Cader: Ben, toi alors, et avec mention!

EXTENSION Louisa avait-elle besoin de s'inquiéter du bac? Pourquoi, ou pourquoi pas? 1.2, 1.3

Stratégie

Écrivez un bref résumé des différents problèmes et préoccupations que Louisa exprime dans sa conversation avec Abdel-Cader.

Essential Instruction

1. Have students read **Extension**.
2. Ask students to state these expressions in another way: **Ça va pas fort**, **Je me suis plantée**, **les épreuves**, and **Je n'avais pas assez révisé**.
3. Ask general comprehension questions about the **Extension** dialogue, ending with the **Extension** question.
4. Have students rehearse and present the **Extension** dialogue in pairs.
5. Have students read the culture reading for general comprehension without consulting a dictionary. Have them note the words they do not understand and see if you can guide students to understanding such words using context.
6. For **Le système éducatif français**, ask students to summarize what they learned in a graphic organizer.
7. For **L'enseignement supérieur**, students read the information and outline the areas of proposed reform of the French educational system.
8. Ask students to consult the **Recherche** for more information.

Le système éducatif français 1.2, 2.1, 3.1, 4.2, 5.2

Au total, le système éducatif français représente une dépense* de 2100€ par habitant, soit 6,3% du PIB*; c'est le premier budget de l'État français. Il est divisé en trois niveaux: l'enseignement primaire (maternelle, dès l'âge de trois ans), secondaire (collège et lycée, de onze à dix-huit ans), et supérieur (université). Il repose sur trois principes: l'école est obligatoire, laïque*, et gratuite.

Pour les Français, le système éducatif doit à la fois permettre de trouver un travail, donner une culture générale, former la réflexion et l'esprit critique, favoriser la réduction des inégalités dans la société, et pallier* les insuffisances éducatives. Tous ces objectifs pèsent aujourd'hui trop lourd* et ne peuvent être assumés par des enseignants dont la culture et la formation préparent avant tout à la transmission des savoirs*.

Lycée international des Pontonniers à Strasbourg

Recherche: ministère de l'éducation nationale france

dépense *expense*; **PIB** produit international brut; **laïque** *secular*; **pallier** *bridge*; **pèsent... lourd** *weigh too much*; **savoirs** *knowledge*

Comparaisons 1.2, 4.2

Quel ministère a le budget le plus important aux États-Unis?

L'enseignement supérieur 1.2, 2.1, 3.1, 4.2, 5.2

L'enseignement général supérieur comprend l'université et les grandes écoles qui forment les élites. Ces établissements publics ont tendance à être survalorisés*: les formations longues, comme les doctorats*, ont un taux de réussite* inférieur à la moyenne européenne.

En revanche, les études professionnelles de formation courte sont marginalisées*, mais ont un taux de réussite supérieur à la moyenne des pays développés, surtout pour les diplômes scientifiques. Ces contradictions du système éducatif conduisent à* des réformes qui touchent la sélection, l'autonomie des établissements, la gratuité des études dans l'enseignement supérieur (les étudiants paient environ 1 000€ par an); le calendrier scolaire (semaine de quatre jours ou quatre jours et demi, emploi du temps de 8h30 à 16h30 au primaire); le temps de présence des enseignants dans les établissements (15 à 18 heures par semaine dans les lycées, 108 heures par an à l'université), et l'articulation entre enseignement et vie professionnelle.

Recherche: enseignement supérieur en france

survalorisés *overrated*; **doctorats** *Ph.D*; **taux de réussite** *success rate*; **marginalisées** *marginalized*; **conduisent à** *lead to*

Perspectives 1.2, 2.1

Tout le monde a une idée précise sur ce qu'il faut faire pour améliorer l'éducation française: tous les intellectuels se mêlent d'éducation, et tout ministre de l'éducation, lorsqu'il a quitté ses fonctions, critique son successeur et écrit sur ce qu'il faudrait faire ou mieux... sur ce qu'il aurait fallu faire!

Resources

Points de départ

WB Workbook 6

Explore

Answers

Comparaisons
Possible answers: Department of Health and Human Services, Department of Defense

Reference Desk

If you have access to Passport, find a video or a news article related to **l'école** or **le baccalauréat** and show it to your students.

Critical Thinking

Comparaisons
Ask students to make a chart comparing and contrasting the French and American school systems in terms of tuition, school calendar, teacher work hours, and career training.

Differentiated Learning

Accelerate
Ask students to write a short essay answering the question in **Comparaisons**. What do their findings suggest about the country's priorities?

Decelerate
Give students a study guide to fill out as they read **Le système éducatif français** to help them understand the reading.

Multiple Intelligences

Intrapersonal
Ask students to research and comment on this: In France, education is under national control. Is this true in the United States? Explain.

Answers

Comparaisons
Possible answers: le SAT, le ACT, examens nationaux

Reference Desk

The three categories of the **baccalauréat** are: 1) **Général**, consisting of the categories of **Économique et social** (ES), **Littéraire** (L), and **Scientifique** (S); 2) **Technologique : Sciences et technologies du management et de la gestion** (STMG)/**du design et des arts appliqués** (STD2A)/**de l'industrie et du développement durable** (STI2D)/**de laboratoire** (STL)/**de la santé et du social** (ST2S)/**de l'agronomie et du vivant** (STAV)/**de la musique et de la danse** (TMD)/**de l'hôtellerie et de la restauration** (STHR) and 3) **Professionnel**, which has 80 different specialties.

Critical Thinking

Analysis
Ask students to explain the humor in the following quotations:
"Le bac, c'est comme la lessive : on mouille (*sweats*), **on sèche** (*can't come up with an answer*) … **et on repasse** (*takes the test again*)." Henri Troyat
"L'échec légendaire de Zola au bachot a réconforté beaucoup de candidats – qui n'étaient pas Zola." Tristan Bernard

Le baccalauréat 1.2, 2.1, 2.2, 3.1, 4.2, 5.2

« Passe ton bac d'abord ! » — cette expression qui a donné son titre à un film de 1978, reste dans son ensemble le mot d'ordre de la société française ; au point qu'un ministre de l'éducation avait fixé comme objectif de conduire 80% d'une classe d'âge au bac. Aujourd'hui, 78,9% des jeunes d'une classe d'âge ont leur bac.

Des élèves de lycée se préparent à la session du bac.

Tous les ans, c'est la même chose : en juin, toute la France passe le bac. C'est toute la famille qui se mobilise, qui partage le stress avant l'épreuve, qui s'angoisse* au moment de l'ouverture des sujets, qui évalue les chances de réussite et d'échec*, qui commente ou crie à l'injustice, enfin qui se réjouit* ou qui pleure au moment des résultats. Sur 100 diplômés, 51 ont un bac général, 19 ont un bac technologique et 30 un bac professionnel.

Recherche : réussir son bac, se préparer aux épreuves du bac, résultat bac (+ ANNÉE), bac par correspondance

---

s'angoisse *gets distressed* ; **échec** contraire d'une réussite ; **se réjouit** *is delighted*

Produits
1.2, 2.2

Pour se préparer au baccalauréat, les étudiants français consultent les **annales du bac** ; ce sont des sujets corrigés d'examens du baccalauréat d'années précédentes. On les trouve en ligne, ou sur des sites régionaux.

Comparaisons
1.2, 4.2

Quels sont les examens, autres que ceux de votre lycée, auxquels vous allez devoir faire épreuve pour avancer dans le monde académique ou professionnel ?

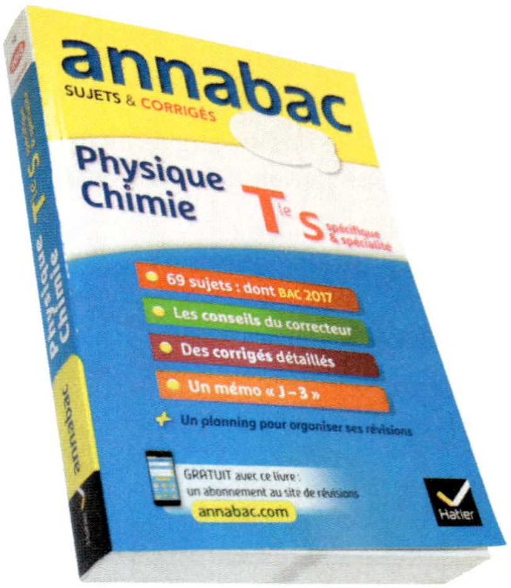

Des élèves de lycée se préparent à la session du bac avec les Annales.

Mon dico scolaire
bachoter *préparer un examen*
redoubler *suivre le même cours ou année de scolarisation pour la deuxième fois*
l'école de la vie *apprendre par expérience, pas par un cours*

Mot-clé
Baccalauréat est la combinaison de deux paroles latine : *baccalarius*, signifiant un jeune homme qui veut être chevalier, et *laurreare*, qui signifie « couronné de laurier ».

Essential Instruction

1. Ask students to explain the difference in structure between the SAT/ACT and the **bac**.
2. Explain the types of **bac**. Ask students what category they would choose if they had to take the **bac**.
3. Have students read and take notes about **Le baccalauréat**. Ask how the **bac** is a family affair.
4. Ask students to add to their information by researching the search words.
5. For **Activité 6**, have all students do tasks 1 and 2 and the **Perspectives** question.
6. Give students options to do one of the remaining three activities.
7. Have students read **Du côté des médias** in groups to interpret the graphic, before doing **Activité 7**.

6 Activités culturelles 1.3, 3.1, 3.2, 4.2

Faites les activités suivantes.

1. Faites un dessin qui représente les trois niveaux du système éducatif en France.
2. Quels sont les défis (*challenges*) de l'enseignement supérieur?
3. Comparez le système éducatif français et le système éducatif de votre ville ou état/province.
4. Créez une bande dessinée ou un dialogue qui montre les émotions d'un(e) ado français(e) qui va bientôt passer son bac.
5. Trouvez un lycée français en ligne et regardez les résultats du baccalauréat. Comparez les résultats avec ceux du lycée que votre partenaire a examiné.

Perspectives
1.2, 2.1

Un homme de 45 ans voudrait passer son bac. Une jeune femme lui répond sur son blog: « Pour rien au monde je ne repasserais mon bac—stress, révisions de dernière minute, le vrai marathon! Mais l'avoir réussi m'a beaucoup aidée. J'ai maintenant le boulot de mes rêves. Alors, je vous conseille d'aller sur le site du CNED. »

Pourquoi est-ce que cette jeune femme essaie d'aider ce monsieur quand elle a eu une mauvaise expérience avec le bac?

Du côté des médias 1.2, 2.1, 3.2

Lisez les informations sur les études générales des élèves de première et de terminale.

LA VOIE GÉNÉRALE PREMIÈRE ET TERMINALE

1 Socle de culture commune

	Première	Terminale
Français	4h	-
Philosophie	-	4h
Histoire géographie	3h	3h
Enseignement moral et civique	0h40	0h30
Langue vivante 1 et Langue vivante 2	4h30	4h
Éducation physique et sportive	2h	2h
Humanités scientifiques et numériques	2h	2h

Total horaire élève: Première 16 h; Terminale 15 h 30

2 Disciplines de spécialité

	Première	Terminale
Arts	4 h	6 h
Histoire géographie, géopolitique et sciences politiques	4 h	6 h
Humanités, littérature et philosophie	4 h	6 h
Langues et littératures étrangères	4 h	6 h
Mathématiques	4 h	6 h
Numérique et sciences informatiques	4 h	6 h
Sciences de la vie et de la Terre	4 h	6 h
Sciences de l'ingénieur*	-	-
Sciences économiques et sociales	4 h	6 h
Physique chimie	4 h	6 h

Première: 3 disciplines — 12 h
Terminale: 2 disciplines parmi les 3 suivies en première — 12 h

Total horaire élève: Première 28 h; Terminale 27 h 30

* Horaires spécifiques, en lien avec la voie technologique

Source : Ministère de l'Éducation, 2018.

7 Cursus des lycéens 1.3, 2.1, 3.2, 4.2, 5.2

Faites des recherches sur le cursus général des lycées publiques dans votre pays. Comparez les systèmes français et américain dans un graphique.

Differentiated Learning

Expand

Have students read blogs of French students writing about the **bac**. They could also find similar sites on their favorite social media.

Multiple Intelligences

Visual-Spatial

Encourage students to create **une bande dessinée** for #4 in **Activité 6** or a series of posters advertising the importance of doing well on the **bac**. Have them imagine they work for the **Ministère de l'Éducation nationale**.

Answers

6

1. Drawings should include **l'enseignement primaire**, **l'enseignement secondaire**, and **l'enseignement supérieur**.
2. Possible answers: Les universités sont survalorisées et les écoles professionelles sont marginalisées; les étudiants français réussissent bien dans les études qui ne durent pas longtemps, mais moins bien dans les études qui durent longtemps; ils réussissent bien en sciences, mais ils ont moins de doctorats que dans le reste de l'Europe.
3. Answers will vary.
4. Comics will vary.
5. Answers will vary.

Perspectives

Elle pense que même si c'était difficile, avoir eu son bac lui a permi une meilleure vie.

7 Presentations will vary.

Connections

Music

"**Bac G**" by Michel Sardou is about a student taking a lower-ranking **bac** exam. In addition to the cultural value of the song, it could be used as a cloze listening activity since the lyrics contain commonly used vocabulary. It also features the past conditional, which appears in the next part of this lesson.

TPR

Have students prepare statements that are either **vrai** or **faux** based on the information about French education and **le bac**. Student A reads a statement to the class. If classmates think the statement is true, they go to one side of the room; if they think it is false, they go to the opposite side of the room. Student A reveals whether the statement is true or false. If false, students propose how to correct it. All the students who guessed incorrectly are "out" and must sit down. The game continues with students picking sides until there is only one student left (he or she wins the game).

Resources

WB Workbook 7–9

G & V Practice Games

Answers

Comparaisons

In English, the past conditional is usually formed by using *would* followed by the auxiliary *have* and the past participle of the main verb. The words *could*, *should*, *might*, and *ought* also may be used to express a conditional meaning; for example, there's Marlon Brando's famous line: "I coulda been a contender."

Reference Desk

The past conditional is more easily understood with a clear context of the conditions. You may choose to teach its meaning and its usage with the **plus-que-parfait** (as explained on p. 517) before you concentrate on its form, outlined here.

Communication

Interpersonal: Paired Practice

Give pairs of students a die: one dot corresponds to **je**, two dots, **tu**, three dots, **elle**, four dots, **nous**, five, **vous**, six, **elles**. Give them a list of regular, irregular, and reflexive verbs in the infinitive. Students roll a die and conjugate the verbs on the list, one by one, in the past conditional. Put a sample verb in each category on the board for reference. For future study, have students note the verbs that they missed.

Structure de la langue

The Past Conditional 1.2

M. Rivard aurait pu se faire arrêter.

The past conditional (**le conditionnel passé**) is used to express what would have happened in the past if certain conditions had been met. In that respect, it is often used with the **plus-que-parfait** in **si** clause formation. The **conditionnel passé** consists of a helping verb and a past participle. To form the **conditionnel passé**, use the conditional of the helping verb **avoir** or **être** and the past participle of the main verb. As with other compound verbs, the past participle in the past conditional must agree with the subject in gender and number when using **être**.

	bosser	**aller**	**se reposer**
je/j'	**aurais bossé**	**serais allé(e)**	**me serais reposé(e)**
tu	**aurais bossé**	**serais allé(e)**	**te serais reposé(e)**
il/elle/on	**aurait bossé**	**serait allé(e)**	**se serait reposé(e)**
nous	**aurions bossé**	**serions allé(e)s**	**nous serions reposé(e)s**
vous	**auriez bossé**	**seriez allé(e)(s)**	**vous seriez reposé(e)(s)**
ils/elles	**auraient bossé**	**seraient allé(e)s**	**se seraient reposé(e)s**

Si elle avait su, Élodie **aurait bossé** plus auparavant. — *If she had known, Élodie would have worked more before.*

Si Leïla avait pris son temps, elle ne **serait** pas **partie** du lycée sans son sac à dos. — *If Leïla had taken her time, she would not have left school without her backpack.*

Éric et son ami **se seraient dépêchés** s'ils avaient vu leurs copines. — *Éric and his friend would have hurried if they had seen their girlfriends.*

Comparaisons 4.1

How is the past conditional formed in English?

I *would have worked* harder.
I *would have gone* before class.
I *would have rested* half an hour.

Essential Instruction

1. Volunteers go to the board to write the conjugations of **avoir** and **être** in the conditional. Leave spaces after each verb.
2. Ask students what **j'aurais** means. (*I would have*) Ask them how to say "spoken" in French. If students suggest **parlé**, explain that **j'aurais parlé** means "I would have spoken." To each form of **avoir** on the board, add a past participle of a verb conjugated with **avoir** and explain the meaning.
3. Add past participles to the conditional of **être** on the board. Emphasize how **je serais** translates to *I would have* here rather than to *I would be*.
4. Ask students what **je me serais reposé** means. Students learn not to translate the auxiliary verb literally.
5. Students do **Activités 8** and **9** in class. Give immediate feedback.

8 Où serait-on allé? 1.3, 3.2, 5.2

Presentational Speaking or Writing

Dites où tout le monde serait allé et ce qu'ils y auraient vu avec un billet d'avion gratuit pour la France.

le festival international du film **le Port de la Lune** **la cathédrale** **les châteaux de la Loire** **le Parlement européen** **le musée d'Orsay** **les tableaux de Matisse**

MODÈLE Brent (Bordeaux)
Brent serait allé à Bordeaux; il y aurait vu le Port de la Lune.

1. Jennifer (Paris)
2. Madison et moi, nous (Cannes)
3. moi, je (Tours)
4. Zach et toi, vous (Strasbourg)
5. toi, tu (Strasbourg)
6. Nora et Ashley (Nice)

9 À ta place 1.1, 1.3, 4.2

Interpersonal or Presentational Speaking

Vous écoutez vos amis. Dites-leur ce que vous auriez fait à leur place.

visiter Nice, Cannes et Monaco **rédiger une lettre de motivation** **aller en ville** **louer un vélo** **se reposer** **goûter la cuisine française** **faire du ski nautique** **choisir une salade** **bosser plus auparavant**

MODÈLE Zakia: «J'ai mangé de la pizza à la cantine.»
À ta place, j'aurais choisi une salade.

1. Amélie: «Je n'ai pas réussi au bac.»
2. Jean-Luc: «Je suis tombé en faisant du ski alpin.»
3. Momo: «J'ai vu une petite annonce en ligne qui m'intéresse.»
4. Sonia: «J'ai vu les châteaux de la Loire en voiture.»
5. Dikembe: «Je suis allé sur la Côte d'Azur et je n'ai rien fait.»
6. Mamadou: «Je suis allé à Paris et j'ai mangé à McDo.»
7. Sandrine: «J'ai travaillé avant de courir dans le marathon.»
8. Renée: «Je n'ai rien fait mercredi après-midi.»

Answers

8

1. Jennifer serait allée à Paris. Elle y aurait vu le musée d'Orsay.
2. Nous serions allé(e)s à Cannes. Nous y aurions vu le festival international du film.
3. Je serais allé(e) à Tours. J'y aurais vu les châteaux de la Loire.
4. Vous seriez allés à Strasbourg. Vous y auriez vu la cathédrale/le Parlement européen.
5. Tu serais allé(e) à Strasbourg. Tu y aurais vu le Parlement européen/la cathédrale.
6. Elles seraient allées à Nice. Elles y auraient vu les tableaux de Matisse.

9

1. À ta place, j'aurais bossé plus auparavant.
2. À ta place, j'aurais fait du ski nautique.
3. À ta place, j'aurais rédigé une lettre de motivation.
4. À ta place, j'aurais loué un vélo.
5. À ta place, j'aurais visité Nice, Cannes et Monaco.
6. À ta place, j'aurais goûté la cuisine française.
7. À ta place, je me serais reposé(e).
8. À ta place, je serais allé(e) en ville.

Game

Machine à écrire

To practice the forms of the past conditional, divide the class into two teams. Start the game by giving one team a subject pronoun and an infinitive in French. Have students quickly spell out loud the correct form of the verb in the past conditional. Remind students that they need to supply the auxiliary verb form and the past participle. If correctly spelled, the team gets a point. If there is an error, the rival team can try to spell it for a point. If necessary, assign a scribe to write the verb out on the board as it is being spelled.

Differentiated Learning

Accelerate/Decelerate

Have confident students work as tutor partners with less able students to review the conditional for **avoir** and **être** before moving on to the past conditional. To practice past conditional, give them a list of situations (for example, **Je suis arrivé(e) à l'école en retard parce que je me suis levé(e) tard**), and then ask them to work together to write what they would have done in the subject's place: **À ta place, je me serais levé(e) plus tôt**.

Accelerate

See if students can deduce by themselves how the past conditional is used with the **plus-que-parfait**, as explained on p. 517.

Expansion

Have students practice these verbs online

Recherche: french verb practice, conjuguemos, quizlet

Answers

10

1. A : Je me suis promené(e) dans le jardin des Tuileries.
   B : À ta place, je ne me serais pas promené(e) dans le jardin des Tuileries. J'aurais fait les magasins.
2. A : Je suis allé(e) à l'Arc de Triomphe.
   B : À ta place, je ne serais pas allé(e) à l'Arc de Triomphe. Je serais allé(e) à la tour Eiffel.
3. A : J'ai acheté des romans français.
   B : À ta place, je n'aurais pas acheté de romans français. J'aurais acheté des bandes dessinées françaises.
4. A : J'ai séjourné dans une auberge de jeunesse.
   B : À ta place, je n'aurais pas séjourné dans une auberge de jeunesse. J'aurais séjourné au Négresco.
5. A : J'ai fait du parachutisme ascensionnel.
   B : À ta place, je n'aurais pas fait de parachutisme ascensionnel. J'aurais fait du scooter des mers.
6. A : J'ai bronzé.
   B : À ta place, je n'aurais pas bronzé. Je me serais baigné(e).

Partner answers will vary.

Reference Desk

1. The past conditional is also called the conditional perfect, and in French it is **le conditionnel passé**. Special translations of key verbs are: **devoir**, **j'aurais dû** (*I should have*) and **pouvoir**, **j'aurais pu** (*I could have*). Two common phrases are: **vouloir**, **j'aurais voulu** (*I would have liked*) and **être**, **j'aurais été** (*I would have been*).
2. Remind students that when the first verb is conjugated, a verb following it is in the infinitive: **J'aurais dû reviser**.

10 Un séjour en France 1.1, 3.1, 5.2

Interpersonal Speaking

Votre partenaire est allé(e) à Paris. Dites-lui ce que vous auriez fait à sa place. Puis, changez de rôle : vous êtes allé(e) sur la Côte d'Azur. Votre partenaire vous dira ce qu'il ou elle aurait fait à votre place.

MODÈLES Paris : visiter le musée du Louvr
A : J'ai visité le musée du Louvre.
B : À ta place, je n'aurais pas visité le musée du Louvre. J'aurais visité le musée d'Orsay.

la Côte d'Azur : prendre des fruits de mer
A : J'ai pris des fruits de mer.
B : À ta place, je n'aurais pas pris de fruits de mer. J'aurais pris de la ratatouille.

1. Paris : se promener dans le jardin des Tuileries
2. Paris : aller à l'Arc de Triomphe
3. Paris : acheter des romans français
4. la Côte d'Azur : séjourner dans une auberge de jeunesse
5. la Côte d'Azur : faire du parachutisme ascensionnel
6. la Côte d'Azur : bronzer

Essential Instruction

1. Review and drill the past conditional so that students can form it quickly and easily.
2. Have students work in pairs to do **Activité 10**.
3. Ask students to put the answers on the board to correct.
4. Review the **plus-que-parfait**. Contrast it to the past conditional.
5. Explain the sequence of tenses: **si** + PLUS-QUE-PARFAIT + PAST CONDITIONAL.
6. Do **Activité 11** as a whole-class activity.
7. Ask students to suggest more **si** clause combinations.

The Past Conditional in Sentences with *si* 1.2, 4.1

Si Alima n'avait pas trébuché, elle aurait évité tous ces ennuis.

Comparaisons 4.1

How is the past conditional used in English in sentences with *if* clauses?

Si tu avais lu l'article, tu aurais compris.
If you had read the article, you would have understood.

Use the past conditional with **si** and the **plus-que-parfait** to tell what would have happened *if* something else had already happened or *if* some condition contrary to reality had been met.

si + PLUS-QUE-PARFAIT | PAST CONDITIONAL

Si je n'**avais** pas **trébuché**, je ne **me serais** pas **cassé** la jambe.	*If I hadn't tripped, I would not have broken my leg.*
Est-ce que tu **te serais senti** encouragé **s'**il t'**avait parlé**?	*Would you have felt encouraged if he had spoken to you?*

The phrase with **si** + PLUS-QUE-PARFAIT can either begin or end the sentence.

11 La mauvaise journée d'Élodie 1.3

Presentational Speaking or Writing

Dites ce qu'Élodie aurait ou n'aurait pas pu faire si elle avait agit différemment.

MODÈLE avoir une meilleure note
Si Élodie n'avait pas séché ses cours, elle aurait eu une meilleure note.

1. ne pas se sentir mal
2. ne pas être tétanisée
3. être capable de décider quelles étaient ses priorités
4. ne pas paniquer
5. ne pas dormir pendant 18 heures
6. éviter tous ces ennuis

Si Élodie n'avait pas séché ses cours, elle aurait pu sortir avec Karim ce soir.

Differentiated Learning

Accelerate
Have students suggest *if* clause combinations similar to **Activité 11** for class practice. They could use examples from French history and current situations.

Decelerate
Students need to be able to recognize and form the **plus-que-parfait** and the **conditionnel passé**. Put the two forms side by side and have students identify each one and explain how they did so.

Special Needs Students

Dyslexia
Differentiating between the **plus-que-parfait** and the **conditionnel passé** may be trickier for students who have trouble decoding text. Have students note the **v** in **J'avais parlé** and the **r** in **j'aurais parlé** to help them distinguish the two.

Resources

WB Workbook 10
LA Listening Activity 2
G & V Practice Games

Answers

11 Possible answers:
1. Si Élodie avait bien étudié, elle ne se serait pas sentie mal.
2. Si Élodie n'avait pas commencé à travailler, elle n'aurait pas été tétanisée.
3. Si Élodie avait réfléchi, elle aurait été capable de décider quelles étaient ses priorités.
4. Si Élodie s'était préparée, elle n'aurait pas paniqué.
5. Si Élodie était restée à l'école, elle n'aurait pas dormi pendant 18 heures.
6. Si Élodie avait bossé plus, elle aurait évité tous ces ennuis.

Comparaisons
In both English and French sentences, the past conditional is only used in the result clause.

Critical Thinking

Comparisons
Display **nous** forms of **avoir** on the board by drawing a table with two columns. In the first column conjugate **avoir** in the present, imperfect, future, and conditional. Translate each form (*We have*, *We had*, *We will have*, *We would have*). Across from each simple tense, conjugate **avoir** in the **passé composé**, **plus-que-parfait**, **futur antérieur**, and the **conditionnel passé** and translate each one. Doing this demonstrates how the first column simple tenses are used to form the second column compound tenses. It also shows their similarity to English. Repeat the process for **être** and reflexive verbs.

Communication

Interpersonal: Paired Practice
Students expand **Activité 10** by explaining why Student B would not do the activity Student A mentioned. For example, in the **modèle**, Student B would add: "**À ta place, j'aurais visité le musée d'Orsay parce que j'adore les impressionnistes.**" Have students alternate the roles.

Resources

Activity 12

Answers

12 Script

1. S'il s'était levé à l'heure, il n'aurait pas raté le bus.
2. Si nous avions bossé plus auparavant, nous aurions réussi au bac.
3. Si vous aviez évité de trébucher, vous ne vous seriez pas cassé la jambe.
4. Si Amanda n'avait pas séché les cours, elle aurait dû faire un exposé.
5. Si j'étais venu en bus, j'aurais évité la grêle.
6. Si Julien ne s'était pas senti heureux, il n'aurait pas fait la connaissance de Julie.

1. B
2. A
3. F
4. C
5. E
6. D

13 Answers will vary.

Communication

Presentational: Paired Practice

Have one partner secretly write 10 original *if* clauses in the **plus-que-parfait**, using names of historical people or today's celebrities. The other student secretly writes result clauses using the same kind of subjects but in the past conditional. Then, they combine their sentences one by one. Have partners choose their five best sentences and share them with the class.

12 Et si et si ! 1.2

Interpretive Listening and Viewing

Écrivez les numéros 1–6 sur votre papier. Écoutez les descriptions des situations. Ensuite, faites correspondre la photo avec la phrase que vous entendez.

A. 

B. 

C. 

D. 

E. 

F. 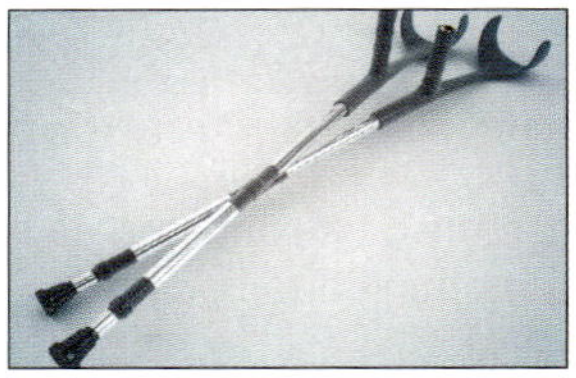

13 Logique ou illogique ? 1.1, 1.3

Interpersonal Speaking, Presentational Writing

À tour de rôle, formez huit phrases logiques ou illogiques avec les sujets et verbes de la liste. Suivez le modèle.

le prof (perdre de l'argent)	Marina et moi (aller en ville)
moi (gagner à la loterie)	Abdel et Ben (trébucher)
toi (voyager)	Sophia et toi (se faire arrêter)
ma mère (faire la cuisine)	Julie et Chloé (sécher leurs cours)

MODÈLES **A : Si j'avais gagné à la loterie, j'aurais acheté une décapotable.**
B : C'est logique !

A : Si le prof avait perdu de l'argent, il se serait senti encouragé.
B : C'est illogique !

On recycle !

Avec un partenaire, posez-vous des questions sur un voyage imaginaire si vous aviez gagné à la loterie. Utilisez le conditionnel passé.

MODÈLE **A : Tu aurais passé le contrôle de sécurité pour aller à Paris ?**
B : Oui, je l'aurais passé.

un steward ▪ un(e) agent(e) ▪ un comptoir ▪ une valise ▪ une porte d'embarquement ▪ la douane ▪ une hôtesse de l'air

Essential Instruction

1. Before playing **Activité 12**, ask students to describe each photo, adding as much real or imagined information as possible. For example, in the first picture, a student could say: **"Oh, là là, j'ai dû laisser toutes mes affaires à la bibliothèque !"**
2. Students do **Activité 13** in pairs then share their sentences with the class. The class then decides whether their statements are logical or not.
3. Changing partners, have students complete **Activité 14**.

14 Situations imaginaires 1.1, 5.2

Interpersonal Speaking

À tour de rôle, dites à votre partenaire ce que vous auriez ou n'auriez pas fait selon les situations imaginaires qui vous sont proposées.

MODÈLE avoir un accident
A. avoir peur B. téléphoner à vos parents C. quitter la scène
A : Qu'est-ce que tu aurais fait si tu avais eu un accident ?
B : Si j'avais eu un accident, j'aurais téléphoné à mes parents. Je n'aurais pas quitté la scène.

1. avoir un examen d'histoire important à passer
   A. sécher le cours d'histoire B. étudier C. espérer y réussir sans étudier
2. se fouler la cheville
   A. marcher avec des béquilles (*crutches*) B. demander à tes parents de t'emmener partout C. prendre rendez-vous chez le kiné
3. ne pas gagner assez d'argent
   A. faire grève B. se plaindre C. essayer de trouver un nouveau job
4. tomber malade
   A. aller à l'école B. prendre de l'aspirine C. rester au lit
5. se réveiller très tard
   A. téléphoner à l'école B. sécher les cours C. prendre un taxi

Answers

14 Possible answers:

1. A : Qu'est-ce que tu aurais fait si tu avais eu un examen d'histoire important à passer ?
   B : Si j'avais eu un examen d'histoire important à passer, j'aurais étudié. Je n'aurais pas séché le cours d'histoire.
2. A : Qu'est-ce que tu aurais fait si tu t'étais foulé la cheville ?
   B : Si je m'étais foulé la cheville, j'aurais pris rendez-vous chez le kiné. Je n'aurais pas demandé à mes parents de m'emmener partout.
3. A : Qu'est-ce que tu aurais fait si tu n'avais pas gagné assez d'argent ?
   B : Si je n'avais pas gagné assez d'argent, j'aurais essayé de trouver un nouveau job. Je ne me serais pas plaint(e).
4. A : Qu'est-ce que tu aurais fait si tu étais tombé(e) malade ?
   B : Si j'étais tombé(e) malade, je serais resté(e) au lit. Je ne serais pas allé(e) à l'école.
5. A : Qu'est-ce que tu aurais fait si tu t'étais réveillé(e) très tard ?
   B : Si je m'étais réveillé(e) très tard, j'aurais téléphoné à l'école. Je n'aurais pas pris un taxi.

Connections

Music

Maxime Leforestier wrote the song "**Mon frère**" in which he relates that *if he had had* a brother, oh the things *they could have done* together. It is a perfect illustration of *if* clauses in compound tenses. It features vocabulary students know so it lends itself to a **dictée** as well as being an easy song to sing.

Differentiated Learning

Accelerate

Students, as soothsayers, write what would have happened in history if other things had occurred. **Si Louis XVI avaient accepté une monarchie constitutionnelle, il ne serait pas mort à la guillotine.**

Decelerate

Give students a worksheet of the compound tenses where they must conjugate regular and irregular verbs, **avoir**, **être**, and reflexive verbs tense by tense to help gain mastery. Then provide practice forming *if* clauses with the **plus-que-parfait**/past conditional combination. Give an extra-credit quiz on the material to motivate them to do well.

Resources

CA Communicative Activities

Share

Answers

15 Photo albums will vary.

16 Presentations will vary.

17 Role-plays will vary.

Reference Desk

If you have access to Passport, create a question for your students to share their response to a communicative activity.

Communiquez!

15 Album des moments de ma vie 1.1, 1.3

Interpersonal Speaking, Presentational Writing

Choisissez six à huit photos ou faites six à huit dessins qui montrent des moments de votre vie où vous avez vécu une émotion forte. Choisissez une émotion différente pour chaque image. Écrivez des légendes qui expliquent comment vous vous êtes senti(e) et pourquoi. Ensuite, choisissez une image de votre album que vous voulez bien partager, puis écrivez un récit qui décrive en détail ce jour-là. Partagez votre récit avec vos camarades de classe qui vous poseront des questions.

16 Mon lycée en France 1.2, 1.3, 2.2, 3.1, 4.2, 5.1

Interpretive Reading, Presentational Writing and Speaking

Imaginez que vous allez faire votre terminale (*senior year*) dans un lycée français. Quelle aventure ! Vous avez gagné une bourse (*scholarship*) qui paiera pour tout. Choisissez la ville où vous allez vivre et le lycée. Êtes-vous passionné(e) par les grandes villes comme Paris ou Marseille, ou préfériez-vous une petite zone rurale plus calme où vous pourrez découvrir la campagne et la nature ? Il est préférable de choisir un lycée qui a un bon pourcentage de réussites au bac, si vous souhaitez faire des études universitaires en France. Présentez le lycée que vous avez choisi ainsi que la province, la ville, le voisinage et les cours à la classe.

Recherche : lycée (+ VILLE), résultats du bac (+ ANNÉE)

17 On sèche les cours ! 1.3

Presentational Speaking

Avec un partenaire, jouez le rôle d'un professeur et d'un élève qui a manqué le cours. L'étudiant(e) doit trouver une excuse pour expliquer pourquoi il (elle) n'était pas en classe. Le jeu de rôle peut être aussi sérieux, dramatique ou drôle que vous le souhaitez, et il peut bien ou mal se terminer, selon les émotions que le professeur ressent en écoutant votre excuse.

Traditions et pratiques 1.2, 2.1, 3.1, 4.2, 5.2

Le lycée commence avec la « seconde » (l'équivalent de *10th grade*) à l'âge de 15 ou 16 ans. Les élèves apprennent une troisième langue à ce moment-là. À 16 ou 17 ans, ils vont en « première » (*11th grade*). Enfin, c'est à l'âge de 17 ou 18 ans qu'ils vont en « terminale » (*12th grade*). Les lycéens français doivent passer le bac et y réussir, pour obtenir le diplôme et aller à l'université.

Essential Instruction

1. All students do **Activité 15**. They can use their own photos or photos from advertisements if they prefer.
2. For use in pair work in **Activité 16**, have students find online potential schools they could attend and explain why they made their choice. Their decision should be based not only on successful test results, but also on the region where the school is located.
3. For **Activité 17** students can present the dialogue as a video or live in front of the class.
4. Explain the **liaisons interdites**. Mix examples of forbidden and permitted liaisons to test if the students can hear the difference.
5. Have students repeat part A after you, then have them read aloud the sentences in pairs.
6. Review masculine and feminine adjectives in part B.
7. Have students do the listening comprehension in part C.

Prononciation

When Liaison Can't Be Made 1.1, 1.2

» Note these examples of sentences in which liaison can't be made.

SUBJECT GROUP + VERB GROUP
Ma formation était adaptée.

Linking with **et** and **ou**
Je parle anglais et français.

After an infinitive ending in **-er**
Je vais étudier en France.

SINGULAR NOUN + ADJECTIVE
Tu étais un étudiant exceptionnel.

A Je fais une demande d'emploi

Répétez chaque phrase qui ne permet pas la liaison et trouvez la règle qu'on y associe.

1. Mes motivations étaient très fortes.
2. J'ai une formation internationale.
3. Je veux habiter en Europe.
4. J'ai étudié les maths et les langues.
5. Je suis le candidat idéal !
6. J'accepte ; je suis disponible en janvier ou en février.

Distinguishing Feminine and Masculine

» To discern a feminine adjective, listen for the consonant that is pronounced when it is followed by an **-e** (for example, **Dominique est très surprise** indicates that the sentence is about a girl). With preceding direct objects, listen for the ending of the past participle (for example, **Tu l'as écrite ?**). This could refer to **une lettre**, for example, because the pronounced **-t** indicates the object is feminine.

B Au féminin !

Répondez à la question au féminin singulier.

1. Vous êtes satisfaits ?	Moi, non, mais Chloé est très satisfaite.
2. Vous êtes bien couverts ?	Moi, non, mais Dominique est très bien couverte.
3. Vous avez dit votre pensée ?	Enfin, je l'ai dite !
4. Vous avez ouvert l'enveloppe ?	Enfin, je l'ai ouverte !

C Masculin ou féminin ?

*Écrivez **M** si vous entendez un adjectif masculin ou une référence à un nom masculin. Écrivez **F** si vous entendez un adjectif féminin ou une référence à un nom féminin.*

Resources

Prononciation
Pre-test
Leçon Quiz

Answers

A

1. SUBJECT GROUP + VERB GROUP
2. SINGULAR NOUN + ADJECTIVE
3. After an infinitive ending in **-er**
4. Linking with **et** and **ou**
5. SINGULAR NOUN + ADJECTIVE
6. Linking with **et** and **ou**

C Script

1. La porte n'est pas ouverte.
2. Oui les filles, nous sommes anglais.
3. Alors, vous l'avez bien décrit à la police ?
4. Mais non, je ne l'ai pas prise, ta jupe à pois !

1. F
2. M
3. M
4. F

Expansion

To provide additional written practice and to test if your students are processing the difference between masculine and feminine adjectives, and liaisons, consider giving a dictation inspired by the pronunciation practice. Read each sentence three times, once at a natural speed and then once more slowly, giving them time to write. Read it again at normal speed so that they can edit. As a group correction activity, either project the paragraph on the board or have volunteers come up to write the sentences

Differentiated Learning

Expand
Provide a day in which students can practice the different liaisons in the computer lab.

Recherche : french liaison practice

Learning Styles

Visual Learners
Point out to these students that the **bold** and underline indicates letters that are not pronounced and that **liaisons** are not made in these situations. Provide additional practice using the same color patterns to add continuity to their learning.

Resources

- *Vocabulaire actif*
- eV eVisual
- WB Workbook 1–5
- FC Flash Cards
- LA Listening Activity 1
- G & V Practice Games

Reference Desk

1. Remind students that to refer to religions, nationalities, and professions they have two options. To say *He is French* one can say **Il est français** (adjective) or **C'est un Français** (noun). To say *She is a teacher*, one can say ***elle est institutrice*** (the profession used as an adjective with no article) or ***C'est une institutrice***.
2. **S'apercevoir** and **se rendre compte** can be followed by **de +** NOUN: **Je me suis rendu compte *de* mon erreur**. Or when followed by a verb, **que** is used, as in the example from **Pour la conversation**: **Je me suis rendu compte *que* mon ordinateur n'était plus là.**
3. Point out that the adjectives of nationality in the expression **d'origine...** agree with the noun **origine** in the feminine, regardless of the gender of the person it refers to.

Leçon B — Vocabulaire actif

Comment décrire une personne 1.2

Rencontres par internet

Les femmes

Annabelle
Paris, France
Je suis une femme **d'origine africaine**, aux cheveux **courts**. J'ai les yeux bruns.

Connectée | Écrire | Chatter

Gigi
Montreuil, France
Je suis une femme d'origine arabe, aux cheveux longs. J'ai les yeux bruns et je suis **mince**.

Déconnectée | Écrire | Chatter

Anna
Versailles, France
Je suis une femme **d'origine asiatique**, aux cheveux longs. J'ai les yeux bruns et je suis assez **maigre**.

Déconnectée | Écrire | Chatter

Topi
Île de France
Je suis une femme **d'origine méditerranéenne**, aux cheveux **mi-longs**. J'ai les yeux bruns et je suis un peu grosse.

Connectée | Écrire | Chatter

Les hommes

Victor
Paris, France
Je suis un homme d'origine africaine, et je suis **chauve**. J'ai les yeux bruns. Je suis fort et **costaud**.

Connecté | Écrire | Chatter

Marco
Courbevoie, France
Je suis un homme **d'origine scandinave**, aux cheveux **raides**. J'ai les yeux bruns, je suis drôle et assez fort.

Connecté | Écrire | Chatter

Timo
Versailles, France
Je suis un homme d'origine française, aux cheveux courts et bruns. J'ai les yeux bruns, les cheveux un peu **bouclés**, et je suis **musclé**.

Connecté | Écrire | Chatter

Tarik
Nanterre, France
Je suis un homme d'origine arabe, aux cheveux **frisés**. J'ai les yeux bruns et je suis maigre.

Déconnecté | Écrire | Chatter

Essential Instruction

1. Play the recording of **Comment décrire une personne** and **Pour la conversation** twice. Have students repeat the second time.
2. Show students pictures of people whose physical description corresponds to the vocabulary. Ask students to describe the images using the new vocabulary words.
3. Ask students to describe celebrities who are in their twenties, thirties, forties, and fifties.
4. Have students copy the vocabulary into their notebooks, illustrating as many words as possible.

Les réussites!

Marc est un homme **d'une vingtaine d'années**. Il a rencontré Juliette, une femme **d'une trentaine d'années**. Ils se sont mariés il y a deux mois. Sur cette photo, Juliette porte une robe **à pois**.

Lire la suite

Aïssata, une femme **d'une quarantaine d'années**, et Paul, un homme **d'une cinquantaine d'années**, se sont rencontrés le mois dernier. « Il était si beau avec sa chemise **à carreaux** » a-t-elle pensé.

Lire la suite

Kristen et Justin, tous deux d'une vingtaine d'années, se sont rencontrés il y a six mois. « On est tellement mignon avec nos tee-shirts **à rayures** » a-t-elle pensé.

Lire la suite

Pour la conversation

How do I ask if someone noticed something?

» **Tu ne t'es aperçu de rien?**
You didn't notice anything?

How do I say that I realized something?

» **Je me suis rendu compte que** mon ordinateur n'était plus là.
I realized that my computer was no longer there.

1.2, 2.2

Produits

Même si moins de 9% des couples se rencontrent en ligne en France, les **sites de rencontre** sont de plus en plus populaires, comme Meetic (leader européen) et Elite Rencontre (pour professionnels diplômés).

Et si je voulais dire... ?

affreux, affreuse	*frightful/awful*
baraqué(e)	*large and sturdy*
élancé(e)	*slender/slim*
intello	*intellectual*
svelte	*slender*
trapu(e)	*stocky*

L'argot des ados

Les gens

un gadjo / **un keum**	*guy*
une nénette / **une louloute**	*chick*

Resources

Pour la conversation
Et si je voulais dire... ?

Communication

Presentational: Paired Practice

Give students a color photo of a person. Have them sit in such a way so as not to see their partner's picture. Student A describes the person to Student B who has to draw the person according to the description given. Then Student B gives the description of an image and Student A draws the person. Afterward, have each student show the original photo to the class. The partner then shows what he or she drew to see how closely the two resemble each other. Alternatively, have students look at a series of images and match their partner's description with a photo from the series.

Differentiated Learning

Expand

Have students pick a celebrity belonging to one of the ethnic groups listed in the vocabulary section. Have them find a color photo of the person and present it to the class, describing their physical characteristics and using as many adjectives as possible.

Multiple Intelligences

Visual-Spatial

Encourage students to create posters to use in class to practice the new vocabulary. Ask them to use as many of the new words as possible. These can be comical but the physical attributes must be clear and easy to describe.

Answers

1

1. Il a vu son cousin Johann.
2. Elle y est venue pour participer à un concours d'échecs.
3. Il a la trentaine.
4. Il est musclé et en forme.
5. Il portait un jean coupe slim noir, une veste sombre et une chemise blanche à col ouvert.

2 Possible answers:

1. africaine
2. vingtaine
3. courts et frisés, marron
4. costaud
5. à rayures

Reference Desk

1. To say "in Paris," one can use **sur Paris** or more commonly **à Paris. Dans Paris** implies that it is in the city and not in the surrounding area.
2. To end a letter to a friend, one could write **grosses bises, gros bisous**, or **Je t'embrasse. Une bise** and **un bisou** mean a kiss. **Faire la bise** is to kiss on both cheeks. If you are not close but want to end a letter warmly, use **amicalement**.

Culture

Perspectives: Information

How many times to kiss on the cheek, and whom to kiss, varies from region to region. Have students make a chart or map of the different French regions and the number of kisses given there.

Recherche: kissing on the cheek

Expansion

Encourage students to go online and visit a quality salon in Paris to get tips on hair care, top hairstyles, and salon services. Ask them to write a short composition about what they have learned.

Recherche: jean louis david, jacques dessange, coiffeurs pour homme

1 Le cousin scandinave de Nils 1.2

Interpretive Reading

Lisez le mail que Nils a écrit à sa sœur, puis répondez aux questions.

À: Asta
Cc:
Objet: Quelle coïncidence !

Chère Asta,

Tu ne vas pas le croire, mais j'ai vu notre cousin Johann au Café des Artistes. Il est venu à Paris pour un concours d'échecs (*chess competition*). Il n'a ni écrit, ni téléphoné, pourtant il sait que je suis sur Paris. Comme il a changé ! La trentaine, et il est évident qu'il fréquente un club de fitness. Il est musclé et semble en pleine forme. Avant, il était très mince et ne faisait pas d'exercice. Mais, je l'ai reconnu tout de suite parce qu'il a le même sourire et toujours les mêmes grands yeux bleus. Ses cheveux sont toujours aussi longs et raides, comme dans le passé, mais moins blonds. Il était vêtu d'un jean coupe slim noir, d'une veste sombre et d'une chemise blanche à col ouvert. Il joue bien son rôle de champion d'échecs et d'intello !

Grosses bises,

N.

1. Qui est-ce que Nils a vu au café ?
2. Pourquoi cette personne est-elle venue à Paris ?
3. Quel âge a cet homme ?
4. Comment est-il maintenant physiquement ?
5. Qu'est-ce qu'il portait ?

2 Décrivez Dikembe ! 1.3

Presentational Speaking or Writing

Complétez les phrases pour faire le portrait de Dikembe.

1. Dikembe est un beau jeune homme d'origine....
2. Il a une... d'années.
3. Il a les cheveux... et les yeux....
4. Physiquement, il est....
5. Il est vêtu d'une chemise....

Essential Instruction

1. Ask students to read **Activité 1**.
2. Give students time to answer the questions about the e-mail.
3. Ask students to read each question aloud. Ask for volunteers to answer.
4. Before assigning **Activité 2**, ask students to describe Dikembe using as many adjectives as possible.
5. Have students complete the description of Dikembe in **Activité 2**.
6. Expand the exercise by asking what he probably likes to do, where he lives, and how old he is to encourage the students to speak more.
7. Give students ample time to write the descriptions of the three people in **Activité 3**. Circulate to offer help.
8. Students do **Activité 4** in small groups.
9. After doing **Activité 4**, brainstorm the names of celebrities in many fields (sports, music, film, television) and put them on the board for reference. Make a guessing game to identify each one following the same format.

3 Descriptions 1.2, 1.3

Interpretive Viewing, Presentational Speaking or Writing

Décrivez les personnes ci-dessous : mentionnez leurs origines ethniques, leurs âges, leurs cheveux, leurs yeux, et ce qu'ils portent.

Gong

Henrik

Alima

MODÈLE **Mme Aknouch est une jolie femme d'origine arabe. Elle a une trentaine d'années. Elle a les cheveux roux et les yeux noisette. Elle est petite et mince. Elle porte une robe à pois.**

4 Devinettes 1.1, 3.2

Interpersonal Speaking

Écrivez les noms de dix personnes célèbres d'origines différentes. À tour de rôle, essayez de deviner l'identité des personnes sur la liste en posant des questions à votre partenaire. Il ou elle répondra par oui ou non uniquement.

MODÈLE

A : C'est une athlète ?	**B : Oui.**
A : Elle a une trentaine d'années ?	**B : Oui.**
A : Elle est d'origine africaine-américaine ?	**B : Oui.**
A : C'est Venus Williams ?	**B : Oui.**

Answers

3

1. Gong est d'origine asiatique. Elle a une vingtaine d'années, elle a les cheveux longs, et les yeux marron. Elle porte une chemise à carreaux.
2. Henrik est une homme d'origine scandinave. Il a une trentaine d'années, il a les cheveux raides, blonds et courts, et les yeux bleus. Il porte une chemise à carreaux et une cravate à rayures.
3. Alima est une femme d'origine africaine. Elle a une quarantaine d'années, elle a les cheveux bouclés, mi-longs et noirs, et les yeux marron. Elle porte une veste à pois.

4 Answers will vary.

Game

Qui est-ce ?

Give students a piece of paper with the name of a student in class that day. Ask students to write a physical description of the person. Do a **devinettes** game where one student reads the description and the others guess the identity.

Differentiated Learning

Accelerate

Ask students to write a description of themselves now and in 50 years. They may illustrate each entry if they choose.

Decelerate

Students can practice physical description vocabulary online.

Recherche : quizlet, physical description, french

Resources

Activity 5

Answers

5 Script

1. Aminata est grande. Elle a les cheveux courts et bouclés. Elle est mince et a une trentaine d'années. Elle est d'origine africaine.
2. La maman d'Anne est d'origine méditerranéenne. Elle a une quarantaine d'années. Elle a les cheveux noirs, longs et raides. Elle est musclée et mince. Elle est vêtue d'une robe à pois sur cette photo.
3. Mon grand-père, c'est un type costaud. Il est d'origine scandinave. Il a les cheveux blonds et bouclés, et il est fort. Il porte une chemise à carreaux sur la photo. Il a une soixantaine d'années.
4. Alima est d'origine arabe. Elle a une trentaine d'années et elle est vêtue d'un jean et d'un chemisier à carreaux. Elle a les cheveux mi-longs et frisés.
5. Julien, c'est un type africain. Il est chauve et costaud. Il a une quarantaine d'années.
6. Ma tante est grande et mince avec les cheveux bruns courts et raides. Elle porte une jupe et un chemisier à rayures, un ensemble qui n'est pas très chic. Elle a une cinquantaine d'années et est vraiment sympa.

1. F; 2. D; 3. C; 4. B; 5. E; 6. A

6 Answers will vary.

Communication

Interpersonal: Cooperative Groups

Using **Activité 5**, divide students into groups of six and assign each a photo. Have them work to ascribe a name, physical description, and occupation to the person in the photo. They may add what the person likes to do, hates to eat, name and kind of pets he or she owns, whatever they can add to create an interesting presentation to the class. As an extension, select two of the imaginary people described, and put them together in a situation where they have to have a conversation. Time how long the students can continue the conversation. Repeat the process with others.

5 Comment sont-ils? 1.2

Interpretive Listening and Viewing

Écrivez les numéros 1–6 sur votre papier. Ensuite, écoutez les descriptions des personnes. Finalement, choisissez la bonne photo.

A. 

B. 

C. 

D. 

E. 

F. 

6 Questions personnelles 1.1, 3.2, 5.2

Interpersonal Speaking

Répondez aux questions suivantes.

1. Quand tu fais la connaissance d'une personne, qu'est-ce que tu remarques d'abord?
2. De quelle origine es-tu? Et tes meilleurs amis?
3. Imagine que tu es au zoo avec ton petit cousin ou ta petite cousine et que tu ne peux pas le/la trouver. Quelle description donnerais-tu à l'agent de police?
4. As-tu des cousins qui sont plus âgés que toi? Comment sont-ils?
5. Comment est ton meilleur ami ou ta meilleure amie?

Essential Instruction

1. Students listen to **Activité 5**.
2. Give students time to prepare answers to **Activité 6**. Ask a few students these questions as a whole-class activity and then have students circulate to interview one another.
3. Ask students to look at the two photos in **Au voleur!** Where might Karim and Léo be? What probably happened to them?
4. Have students watch the video with books closed. Ask general comprehension questions about the story. Ask what details they remember hearing. Put their remarks on the board to verify later.
5. Play the recording as students follow in their books. Confirm or correct the statements you put on the board.
6. Have students play the roles of the two boys as they read their lines.
7. Have students fill out the **déclaration du vol** in class.

Au voleur ! 1.2, 2.1, 5.2

Karim et Léo passent le temps au café.

Karim : Mais tu ne t'es aperçu de rien ?
Léo : De rien ! Absolument de rien !
Karim : Mais tu l'avais posé où ? Quand même, un ordinateur, ça se voit !
Léo : Là, sur la chaise ! Il ne pouvait pas être plus visible.
Karim : Tu n'as vu personne s'approcher, passer à côté de toi ?
Léo : Je lisais quand tu es allé au comptoir…. Il y avait un couple à la table devant, c'est tout. Tout d'un coup, je me suis rendu compte que mon ordinateur n'était plus là !
Karim : Ils ressemblaient à quoi ?
Léo : À des gens qui flirtent, qui se racontent des histoires dans le blanc des yeux, qui s'occupent d'eux-mêmes, quoi ! Pas la tête à voler mon ordinateur.
Karim : Lui, tu l'as vu ?
Léo : Lui, mince, les cheveux courts, une vingtaine d'années. Elle, très jolie, d'origine asiatique, cheveux longs, noirs, même âge. Elle était vêtue d'un très joli chemisier à pois rouges, façon Marilyn dans *Les Misfits*, très vintage…. Et toi, tu surveilles toujours ton ordinateur ? Où est le tien ?
Karim : Il est dans mon sac à dos, mais où est mon sac à dos ? Il a disparu !
Léo : Désolé…. Si on remplissait une déclaration de vol au commissariat ?
Karim : Il y en a un à deux rues d'ici.

Analyse
Is there anything that Karim and Léo could have done to have prevented the unfortunate events from happening? Use textual clues to support your answers.

7 Déclaration de vol 1.3

Votre prof va vous donner une déclaration de vol à remplir. Remplissez-la pour Karim ou Léo.

Connexions
Études de théâtre
Vous faites des études de théâtre et vous devez proposer une représentation moderne d'un personnage de pièce de théâtre classique (comme Antigone ou Dom Juan). Faites une description des traits physiques et psychologiques de ce personnage.

Resources
Dialogue
Dialogue Video
WB Workbook 6

Answers

7 Answers will vary.

Analyse
Possible answer:
They should have been more aware of their surroundings and their possessions. Léo was reading while Karim was away at the counter.

Reference Desk

1. Consider explaining to your students that **quand même** usually means *anyway*. In this case, it is used as an expression of exasperation as in "Come on!" **Parler dans le blanc des yeux** is an intense conversation where people are speaking eye to eye. **Pas la tête à voler mon ordinateur** means *doesn't look like the type who would steal my computer*.
2. **Le commissariat de police** is a police station that is open 24 hours a day. It houses the offices of **le commissaire de police** as well as other departments, police vehicles, and equipment.
3. Project or print copies of the **déclaration de vol** on p. 537 prior to doing **Activité 7**.

Differentiated Learning

Expand
Have students write a police report based on the **déclaration du vol**.

Multiple Intelligences

Visual-Spatial
Ask students to draw a police sketch or "wanted" poster of the alleged thieves.

Bodily-Kinesthetic
Encourage students to act out the robbery as it probably happened, using dialogue where appropriate.

Resources

Activity 8
Extension

Answers

8

1. Karim et Léo passent le temps au café.
2. Léo a mis son ordinateur portable sur la chaise.
3. Il était en train de lire.
4. Il a vu un couple à la table de devant.
5. Le jeune homme avait une vingtaine d'années.
6. La jeune fille était d'origine asiatique.
7. Le jeune homme et la jeune fille ont volé les deux ordinateurs.
8. Karim et Léo vont au commissariat pour remplir une déclaration de vol.

EXTENSION

Elle aurait dû surveiller son sac.

Communication

Interpersonal: Paired practice

Divide the class into pairs with half of the pairs acting as the **policier** from the **Extension** conversation and half acting as the woman. Partners write a first-person monologue describing their character's experience. When done, put partners together, one woman and one **policier**, and have them read their monologues to each other. Ask for volunteers to read to the class. Collect the written copies.

8 Au voleur! 1.3, 2.1, 5.2

Répondez aux questions.

1. Karim et Léo, où passent-ils le temps?
2. Où est-ce que Léo a mis son ordinateur portable?
3. Qu'est-ce que Léo était en train de faire?
4. Où est-ce que Léo a vu un couple?
5. Quel âge avait le jeune homme?
6. La jeune fille était de quelle origine?
7. Qu'est-ce que le jeune homme et la jeune fille ont fait avec les deux ordinateurs?
8. Pourquoi Karim et Léo vont-ils au commissariat?

EXTENSION Au commissariat de police 1.2, 2.1, 5.2

Une femme parle à un policier.

Policier: Alors, qu'est-ce qui vous est arrivé?
Femme: Ça s'est passé dans le métro, très vite, entre deux stations.
Policier: Qu'est-ce qui s'est passé?
Femme: On m'a volé mon porte-cartes de crédit avec mon argent.
Policier: Vous l'aviez mis où?
Femme: Où vouliez-vous qu'il soit? Dans mon sac!
Policier: Oui, ça, je m'en doute, mais il était dans une poche fermée par une fermeture éclair?
Femme: Non, mais il était bien au fond, je le mets toujours là et il ne m'est jamais rien arrivé....
Policier: Jusqu'à ce soir....
Femme: Je m'en suis rendu compte tout de suite.
Policier: Et vous vous souvenez de qui était autour de vous? Parce qu'on surveille une bande qui agit sur la ligne....
Femme: Ils étaient tout un groupe... comme d'habitude on était très serrés... jeunes, la vingtaine, plutôt grands, un d'entre eux était costaud, un très mince, avec les cheveux longs.
Policier: Et vous n'avez rien remarqué?
Femme: Serrés comme on était, vous croyez que je passais mon temps à surveiller mon sac? Vous, vous passez votre temps à surveiller le vôtre?
Policier: Moi, je n'en ai pas! Mais vous, vous auriez dû!

EXTENSION Comment est-ce que la femme aurait pu éviter le vol? 1.3

Stratégie

List in chronological order the questions asked by the policeman. Then underline the specific words in the woman's responses that answer each question directly.

Essential Instruction

1. Write the questions for **Activité 8** on the board.
2. Have students write the answers to the questions in their notebooks. Correct in class.
3. Invite your most dramatic students to read **Extension** as a scene.
4. Ask students to describe the woman's attitude and emotional state by citing examples from the text.
5. Have students work in pairs to answer the **Extension** question.
6. Ask students to give examples of how the woman could have avoided this problem.
7. Students read **La sécurité publique** and outline the information.
8. They research the search words and add more detail to their notes.
9. Answer the **Comparaisons** question as a class.

La sécurité publique 1.2, 2.1, 2.2, 3.1, 4.2

Il existe deux forces qui assurent la sécurité publique: la police et la gendarmerie. La gendarmerie, créée en 1337, devenue gendarmerie nationale en 1791, est une force armée qui dépend du ministère de la Défense et du ministère de l'Intérieur. Elle est chargée de mission de police dans les campagnes et dans les zones autour des grandes villes. La gendarmerie assure la sécurité de 50% de la population et de 95% du territoire. Ses 101 000 membres assurent des missions d'enquêtes*, de maintien de l'ordre*, d'assistance et de secours*, de circulation routière* et de police militaire (renseignement, protection).

Recherche: gendarmerie nationale, vidéos pour gendarmerie france

enquêtes *investigations*; **maintien de l'ordre** *order*; **secours** *help*; **circulation routière** *road traffic*

Ces hommes travaillent pour la gendarmerie nationale.

Comparaisons

Quelles forces assurent la sécurité publique aux États-Unis?

1.2, 4.2

La police 1.2, 2.1, 2.2, 3.1, 4.2

À partir de 2002, un rapprochement s'opère entre la police et la gendarmerie. Il est devenu effectif en 2009. Le rôle de la police est défini dans la Déclaration des droits de l'Homme et du Citoyen (1789) comme «force publique pour l'avantage de tous». Il existe deux sortes de police: la police nationale et la police municipale. Chacune de ces forces porte des uniformes différents. Les policiers municipaux sont placés sous l'autorité du maire de la ville: ils sont chargés d'assurer l'ordre et la sécurité, mais leur rôle est très limité. En cas de crimes et de délits*, ils doivent se reporter à la police nationale ou la gendarmerie. Notamment, quand il s'agit de maintenir l'ordre et la protection civile, par exemple lors de manifestations ou d'attentats*, la police nationale déploie* les CRS (Compagnies républicaines de sécurité). Ces policiers ont la permission d'utiliser la force pour arrêter les émeutes*.

Recherche: préfecture de police de (+ NOM DE LA VILLE)

délits *offenses*; **attentats** *attacks*; **déploie** *deploys*; **émeutes** *riots*

Policiers et policières

1.2, 2.1

Traditions et pratiques

Pendant longtemps les policiers en France ne portaient pas d'armes à feu, mais depuis 2016, le Parlement a adopté une loi pour leur permettre de mieux se défendre.

Resources

- Points de départ
- WB Workbook 7
- Explore

Answers

Comparaisons

Possible answers: la police municipale ou d'état (Highway Patrol, State Police, NYPD, SWAT, etc.), le FBI (crimes fédéraux), la DEA (trafic de drogues), le CBP (douanes), la NSA (informations), l'USPP (la police des parcs nationaux), sheriff departments, ICE (Immigration & Customs Enforcement)

Reference Desk

1. Crime rates and violence in France are generally low and have been on the decline since the 1990s, a global trend in developed countries. France has more than 300 national police officers for every 100,000 citizens. **La Police Nationale** enumerates the following 5 primary goals:
   - –Ensure the safety of people, property, and institutions
   - –Tend to and contain fluxes in immigration, notably undocumented immigration
   - –Fight organized crime and drug trafficking
   - –Ensure domestic security in the face of foreign threats, including acts of terrorism
   - –Maintain and/or re-establish public order
2. If you have access to Passport, find a video or a news article related to **la police** and show it to your students.

Culture

Products: Information

Inspector Clouseau, who appears in the comedy *The Pink Panther*, is a famous caricature of a French detective. For a bit of levity, show the scene where Clouseau tries to reduce his French accent by mastering (or not) the sentence "I would like to buy a hamburger."

Recherche: la panthère rose hamburger (français)

Differentiated Learning

Accelerate

Have students write a list of advice tips on how to protect oneself while taking the Paris **métro**.

Recherche: paris en toute sécurité

Decelerate

Ask students to use the details in **Extension** to write a short police report of the metro robbery.

Answers

Perspectives
Answers will vary.

Culture

Products: Information

Papillon is a 1973 film based on the best-selling autobiography by French convict Henri Charrière. It is the story of a friendship of two convicts condemned to the French penal colony of Devil's Island. It stars Steve McQueen and Dustin Hoffman.

Practices: Information

The Napoloeonic Code in large part formed the French justice system as it stands today. France does not generally use juries, except in **Cours d'assises**, which hears cases that could result in ten or more years of prison time. The French word crime is a false cognate for *felonies*, the kinds of cases heard in **les Cours d'assises**. In all other cases, the presiding judge(s) determine(s) guilt and innocence. **Les tribunaux** are a tiered system of courts leading up to **les Cours d'assises**. Minor crimes will be heard and determined by one judge, and more serious crimes (but not felonies) will be heard by a panel of three judges. **La Cour de cassation** is France's highest court, consisting of five chambers, in each of which sit fifteen judges.

Communication

Presentational: Cooperative Groups

Have students work in small groups to prepare arguments for and against **la réinsertion sociale**, releasing prisoners back into society. A class discussion will follow debating these two points of view.

Les chiffres de la délinquance

1.2, 2.1, 3.1

Après avoir beaucoup augmenté depuis les années 1950, la délinquance (c'est-à-dire tous les délits, toutes les fautes et tous les crimes) a globalement tendance à diminuer depuis 2016 en France.

Nombre de vols :	799 800
à main armée :	8 800
violents sans arme :	91 000
sans violence :	700 000
Cambriolage* de logements :	243 000
Actes de vandalisme et de dégradation volontaire :	620 000
Violences physiques :	215 000 victimes
Homicides :	829
Apologie du terrorisme :	2 300 infractions
Trafic de stupéfiants* :	500 affaires

cambriolage *robbery* ; **stupéfiants** *narcotics*

La prison du château d'If devient un lieu public après la Première Guerre mondiale (*WWI*).

1.2, 2.1

Produits

Une **déclaration de vol** est une fiche à remplir au commissariat de police quand on vous vole quelque chose. Si on veut déclarer des faits contre une personne qui ne sont pas forcément une plainte, on dépose **une main courante** qui permet l'inscription de la personne visée sur les fichiers (*records*) de la police.

De la prison à la réinsertion sociale*

1.2, 2.1, 2.2, 3.2

Il y a 80 500 personnes incarcérées en France dont 69 000 détenus* : les autres sont en attente de jugement. 96 pour cent des détenus sont des hommes. Les mineurs représentent un à deux pour cent de la population carcérale*. 14 pour cent des condamnés sont placés sous surveillance électronique. Six pour cent des prisonniers sont condamnés à des peines incompressibles* de 30 ans, peine maximale (il n'y a pas de prison à vie). Il n'y a pas d'application de la peine de mort*, qui a été supprimée en 1981. Le débat sur la justice porte sur le conflit entre répression des criminels et attention aux victimes (réclamée par les partis de droite) et réinsertion sociale des condamnés (soutenue par les partis de gauche).

réinsertion sociale *rehabilitation* ; **détenus** prisonniers ; **carcérale** *prison* ; **peines incompressibles** *sentences without parole* ; **peine de mort** *death penalty*

1.2, 2.2, 3.1, 5.2

Produits

Une prison célèbre se trouve au **château d'If**. Bâti comme une forteresse dans une île près de Marseille en 1524, ce château est devenu une prison. Ses cachots (*cells*) sont décrits dans *Le comte de Monte-Cristo* d'Alexandre Dumas.

Perspectives

« La culture dominante du système judiciaire français ne croit pas en une justice répressive et regarde le coupable comme la victime d'une société qui ne s'est pas occupée de lui. »

Quelles sont les perspectives des Français vis à vis de la justice ? Comparez avec votre pays. Quelle est votre opinion ?

1.2, 2.1

Essential Instruction

1. Have students read **Les chiffres de la délinquance** and compare these statistics to those of the state of Texas, which is close to the size of France. Or, have students compare crime rates and crime trends in the United States with those in France, as well as ratios of police officers to civilians, gun ownership, imprisonment, and other statistics they feel are relevant to understanding crime, violence, and justice in a society.
2. Students complete all readings before doing **Activité 9**. Give students a choice of activities.
3. Online, have students research statistics about the American penal system to prepare for a class discussion of **À discuter**.

Mot-clé

Le mot **police**, qui est d'abord écrit *pollice* (1250), est emprunté au latin *politia* qui désigne l'organisation politique, le gouvernement. Et ce même mot latin vient du grec *politeia* qui désigne un ensemble de citoyens. Il s'est séparé de la politique pour désigner l'ordre et le règlement établi dans une ville pour garantir la sûreté des habitants (1606) avant de passer de l'objet à la personne et aux institutions qui vont avec (1651).

L'argot des ados

1.2, 4.1, 5.2

Un agent de police
un flic
un keuf
un poulet
un poulaga

9 Activités culturelles 1.3, 3.1, 3.2, 4.2, 5.2

Faites les activités suivantes.

1. Dessinez le look (*costume*) de la gendarmerie et la police de Paris.
2. Préparez un organigramme qui montre les missions de la gendarmerie et de la police, surtout les différences.
3. Faites un tableau qui montre les types de crime, y compris les types de vols.
4. Faites un tableau qui montre les crimes aux États-Unis (avec les mêmes catégories mentionnées dans le texte) et comparez-le au tableau pour la France.

À DISCUTER

Y a-t-il trop de gens emprisonnés aux États-Unis? Faites des recherches et discutez de vos conclusions avec vos camarades de classe. Croyez-vous à la réinsertion sociale ou à la punition? Pourquoi, ou pourquoi pas?

Cet agent de police travaille pour la police municipale.

Answers

9

1. Drawings will vary. (**Gendarmerie** outfit has dark blue vest and pants, hat, high boots, and words GENDARMERIE in back of jacket. **Police** outfit has dark blue vest and pants, hat, light blue shirt, boots and words POLICE MUNICIPALE in back of jacket.)
2. Differences are: **Gendarmerie** belongs to the national army; **police** is local and has less power.
3. Thefts with firearms; violent thefts without weapons; thefts with broken entry; robberies; auto thefts; petty thefts; buying stolen goods; Charts will vary.
4. Answers will vary.

À DISCUTER

Answers will vary.

Critical Thinking

Analysis

The **CRS** is the riot branch of the French police force. What incidents in the last 10 years have made them feared and held in low esteem among ethnic groups in France?

Differentiated Learning

Expand

There are two films the students may want to watch that deal with imprisonment in France in times past: ***Le Comte de Monte-Cristo*** and ***l'Homme dans le masque de fer***, both inspired by Dumas novels. Ask students to research and present the plots for both of these films, and explain how they relate to French history.

Adapt

Ask students to research a visit to **le château d'If**. Have them find information about the ferry, schedules, and prices. Encourage them to search videos to use in a presentation to the class.

Answers

10

1. Comédies : *Le Gendarme de Saint-Tropez*, *Le cercle rouge*; Drames: *Léon*, *Un prophète*, *Polisse*, *La French*
2. Answers will vary.
3. Answers will vary.

Culture

Practices: Activity

Public approval of the police in France, often just above 80%, is historically and significantly higher than in the United States, where it hovers between 50% and 65%. Ethnic minorities and the youth in both countries approve of the police less than the general population. Ask students to discuss their views of the police, and sustain them with reasonable arguments.

Du côté des médias 1.2

Lisez la liste de films et leurs descriptions.

La semaine des films policiers

FILMS CÉLÈBRES QUI FONT RÉFÉRENCE À LA POLICE OU À LA GENDARMERIE

La French (2014) de Cédric Jimenez avec Jean Dujardin et Gilles Lellouche

Description : Film policier, thriller. Un jeune magistrat veut s'attaquer à une organisation de la mafia, la French Connection ; or, c'est une chose peu facile....

Polisse (2011) de Maïwenn avec Karine Viard et Marina Foïs

Description : Drame. Rude exposition de la vie d'un policier confronté à une réalité quotidienne difficile, et qui doit en même temps vivre sa vie.

Un Prophète (2009) de Jacques Audiard avec Tahar Rahim

Description : Film policier, drame. Regard sur un jeune de 19 ans comdamné à six ans de prison.

Léon (1994) de Luc Besson avec Jean Réno, Gary Oldman et Natalie Portman

Description : Film d'action, policier, thriller. Un tueur à gages prend sous sa tutelle une jeune fille de douze ans qui veut venger son petit frère.

Le Cercle Rouge (1970) de Jean-Pierre Melville avec Alain Delon, André Bourvil, Gian Maria Volonte et Yves Montand

Description : Comédie policière. Un cambrioleur et un ancien policier organisent un hold-up.

Le Gendarme de Saint-Tropez (1964) de Jean Girault avec Louis de Funès, Michel Galabru, et Geneviève Grad

Description : La première d'une série de six comédies, Louis de Funès vous fera tordre de rire ! Simple gendarme, Cruchot se laisse mener dans les mésaventures de sa fille qui ne cherche qu'un peu d'aventure dans sa vie, et en même temps découvrir une affaire de vol.

10 Films sur les flics 1.3, 2.2, 3.2, 5.2

Faites les activités suivantes.

1. Faites une liste des titres selon le genre : comédies ou drames.
2. Avec un partenaire, recherchez chaque film et écrivez une phrase d'introduction pour chacun.
3. Choisissez un clip disponible en streaming et regardez-le. Dites si vous recommanderiez le film ou pas. Justifiez votre décision.

Essential Instruction

1. Students read **Du côté des médias** and answer **Activité 10**.
2. Have students go online and list from first to last the most popular films in terms of awards won.
3. Ask students to write **Activité 11** before correcting as a whole-class activity.
4. Have students explain what is on their desk: "**C'est mon livre**, **mon stylo**, **mon cahier**."
5. Ask students to look at a partner's desk and say: "**C'est ton livre**, **ton stylo**, **ton cahier**." Have them do the same thing in the third person. Refer to the classroom and objects in the classroom as **notre salle de classe** and **nos bureaux**.
6. Have them look at your desk and identify objects using **votre**, and so on.

Structure de la langue

Révision: Possessive Adjectives 1.1

As you have already learned, possessive adjectives express ownership or relationship. They agree in gender and in number with the nouns that follow them.

	Singular				Plural	
	Masculine		Feminine Before a Consonant Sound			
my	mon	stylo	ma	trousse	mes	cahiers
your	ton		ta		tes	
his, her, its, one's	son		sa		ses	
our	notre		notre		nos	
your	votre		votre		vos	
their	leur		leur		leurs	

Ma grand-mère m'a dit qu'une fille avait volé **son** portefeuille. — *My grandmother told me that a girl had stolen her wallet.*

Remember that before a feminine singular word beginning with a vowel sound, **ma**, **ta**, and **sa** become **mon**, **ton,** and **son**, respectively.

Émilie s'est rendue compte que **son** amie ne venait pas. — *Émilie realized that her friend wasn't coming.*

11 Le vol à Lyon 1.2, 1.3

Interpretive Reading, Presentational Speaking or Writing

Votre équipe de foot a voyagé à Lyon pour un match. Pendant le match, des voleurs sont entrés dans votre monospace. Ils ont volé beaucoup de choses ! Dites ce qu'ils ont volé et ce qu'ils n'ont pas volé.

Que va-t-il se passer quand les joueurs retourneront à leur monospace ?

MODÈLE Pierre : portable (oui)
Ils ont volé son portable.

Nadia : sac à dos (non)
Ils n'ont pas volé son sac à dos.

1. Fabrice : liseuse (oui)
2. Jérémy et moi : maillots de foot (non)
3. Malika : jeux vidéo (oui)
4. toi : veste (non)
5. Delphine et Nora : portefeuilles (oui)
6. moi : carte cadeau (oui)
7. Assane et toi : cahiers (non)
8. toi : bouteille d'eau minérale (non)
9. moi : guide touristique de Lyon (non)

Resources

Activity 11
Workbook 11
G & V Practice Games

Answers

11

1. Ils ont volé sa liseuse.
2. Ils n'ont pas volé nos maillots de foot.
3. Ils ont volé ses jeux vidéo.
4. Ils n'ont pas volé ta veste.
5. Ils ont volé leurs portefeuilles.
6. Ils ont volé ma carte cadeau.
7. Ils n'ont pas volé vos cahiers.
8. Ils n'ont pas volé ta bouteille d'eau minérale.
9. Ils n'ont pas volé mon guide touristique de Lyon.

Connections

Music

The popular song **"Dans ma valise"** by Dorotheé features possessive adjectives with common vocabulary that is fun to sing and is a good learning and teaching tool.

Game

Cherchez l'objet !

Put students in small groups. Prepare a set of cards for each group. On each card paste the picture of an object and an owner's name. Each owner must have two possessions in the deck, to form a pair. For example, Pierre could own a camera and a pair of sandals. One student deals out all the cards. The first player asks another player if he or she has an object to complete his or her pair, for example, **Jean, as-tu un objet de Pierre?** If he or she has the card, the player being interviewed must relinquish it to the first player. player must form a sentence using the correct possessive adjective to announce he or she has a pair, for example: **J'ai son appareil-photo et ses sandales.** If the first player forms an incorrect sentence, the card is returned to its original owner and the second player takes a turn.

Differentiated Learning

Accelerate

Set a timer and have students make a list of everything in their bedroom using **Il y a**. Have them use the possessive adjectives.

Decelerate

Slide show presentations reinforce the possessive adjective and pronoun lessons. Have students use the **Recherche** below to access a free clearinghouse of teaching approaches. They can watch these lessons for information and practice.

Recherche : share my lesson

Multiple Intelligences

Visual-Spatial

Have students collaborate to make a poster of possessive adjectives to display in the classroom as reference.

Resources

WB Workbook 8–10, 12–13

LA Listening Activity 2

G & V Practice Games

Answers

Comparaisons

The French sentence uses **être à** + STRESS PRONOUN rather than a possessive pronoun. In English a possessive pronoun is used. Possessive pronouns are used more in English than in French.

Connections

Spanish

Point out that **le mien/la mienne**, **le tien/la tienne**, **le sien/la sienne** is comparable to **el mío/la mía**, **el tuyo/la tuya**, **el suyo/la suya**.

Communication

Interpersonal: Paired Practice

Put students in small groups and distribute a picture of an object to each student (for example, **deux glaces** or **une casquette**). Students in each group exchange their picture with that of another student. Then students take turns returning the picture to its rightful owner, saying a sentence using a possessive pronoun, for example, **Ce sont les tiennes!** or **C'est le tien!** Students respond, **Oui, c'est le mien/la mienne** or **Non, ce n'est pas le mien/la mienne**.

Expansion

Ask students to volunteer appropriate objects of little value from their bags or pockets. Have the class watch as you collect them from students. When you have gathered five or six objects, ask "**À qui est le stylo/la trousse?**" Have students point to the person and say "**C'est le sien/la sienne?**" Confirm by asking "**C'est le tien/la tienne?**" and having the student respond "**Oui, c'est le mien/la mienne.**" or "**Non, ce n'est pas le mien/la mienne.**" Continue until every object has been returned to its owner.

Possessive Pronouns 1.2

A possessive pronoun replaces a possessive adjective and a noun.

Thibault et moi, nous avions perdu nos lunettes. **Les siennes** étaient chez moi, **les miennes** chez lui. — *Thibault and I lost our glasses. His were at my house, mine at his house.*

The possessive pronoun is composed of two words, each of which agrees in gender and in number with the noun it replaces.

	Singular		Plural	
	Masculine	**Feminine**	**Masculine**	**Feminine**
mine	**le mien**	**la mienne**	**les miens**	**les miennes**
yours	**le tien**	**la tienne**	**les tiens**	**les tiennes**
his, hers, its, one's	**le sien**	**la sienne**	**les siens**	**les siennes**
ours	**le nôtre**	**la nôtre**	**les nôtres**	
yours	**le vôtre**	**la vôtre**	**les vôtres**	
theirs	**le leur**	**la leur**	**les leurs**	

Thomas et Lucas ont acheté des chemises à rayures comme **les miennes**, mais **les leurs** étaient plus chères. — *Thomas and Lucas bought striped shirts like mine, but theirs were more expensive.*

Combien coûtent **les vôtres**? — *How much do yours cost?*

Comparaisons 4.1

What is the difference in the way possession is expressed in the sentences below?

À qui est cette vidéo? Elle est à moi.
Whose video is it? It's mine.

Essential Instruction

1. Introduce possessive pronouns by comparing them with mine, yours, his… in English.
2. Review the forms. What do they notice is different with **notre** and **votre**, and **le nôtre** and **le vôtre**?
3. Ask students to identify things they own, first with a possessive adjective and then with the possessive pronoun. They say: **C'est mon cahier; C'est le mien; C'est mon stylo; C'est le mien.**
4. As a drill have them do the same exercise but pointing to another student's possessions (**C'est ton cahier. C'est le tien…**) so that they see the connection between the two possessive forms.
5. As a whole-class activity, ask students to do **Activité 12**, first orally, then as a written exercise. Write the answers on the board to correct.
6. Students can do **Activité 13** in pairs.

12 Carla vient de déménager 1.3, 2.2, 3.2

Presentational Speaking or Writing

Toutes les affaires de Carla sont encore dans des cartons. Vous habitez l'appartement d'à côté et vous lui proposez de lui prêter ce dont elle a besoin.

MODÈLE « Je voudrais me laver les mains. Où est mon savon ? »
Je te prête le mien.

1. « Je voudrais préparer un steak. Dans quel carton peut être ma poêle ? »
2. « Il faut que je prenne une douche. Mon shampooing, il est où ? »
3. « Je vais faire du footing. Qu'est-ce que j'ai fait de mes chaussettes blanches ? »
4. « J'ai envie de me détendre. Où peuvent bien être mes magazines ? »
5. « J'invite mes parents à dîner. Mes fourchettes sont dans quel carton ? »
6. « J'aimerais télécharger une chanson. Où est mon ordinateur portable ? »

13 Je décris les gens que je connais 1.1

Interpersonal Speaking

À tour de rôle, décrivez les personnes que vous connaissez en vous servant des indices donnés.

MODÈLE mon meilleur ami (origine ethnique)
A : Mon meilleur ami est d'origine asiatique.
B : Le mien est d'origine arabe.

1. ma meilleure amie (cheveux)
2. mon cousin (physique)
3. mes parents (âge)
4. mon grand-père (yeux)
5. ma grand-mère (cheveux)
6. mon prof d'histoire (physique)
7. ma tante (yeux)
8. mon oncle (âge)

Answers

12
1. Je te prête la mienne.
2. Je te prête le mien.
3. Je te prête les miennes.
4. Je te prête les miens.
5. Je te prête les miennes.
6. Je te prête le mien.

13 Answers will vary.
1. Ma meilleure amie.... La mienne....
2. Mon cousin.... Le mien....
3. Mes parents.... Les miens....
4. Mon grand-père.... Le mien....
5. Ma grand-mère.... La mienne....
6. Mon prof d'histoire.... Le mien....
7. Ma tante.... La mienne....
8. Mon oncle.... Le mien....

Communication

Interpersonal: Cooperative Groups

Put students in small groups to practice possessive pronouns. Tell them they are on a trip and staying at a hotel with a friend. Prepare a worksheet with a list of items they were supposed to have packed. The first student in each group turns to the student on his or her right and states that he or she cannot find the first item on the list and asks to borrow the roommate's item. For example, **Dis, Tom, je ne peux pas trouver mon dentifrice. Est-ce que je peux emprunter le tien?** The second student agrees. **Oui, je te prête le mien.** Then, the second student plays the role of the borrower, the third student is the lender, and the dialogue continues.

Differentiated Learning

Accelerate

Students prepare a review lesson of possessive adjectives and pronouns to be presented to the class. They must make a worksheet for the students and must use manipulatives such as an apple, a book, a cell phone, or a hat for their demonstration.

Decelerate

Have students use the online grammar review and practice sites to master how to express possession.

Recherche : possessive adjectives, pronoun exercises french

Resources

Activity 15

Answers

14

1. La mienne est plus belle que la sienne.
2. La mienne est plus nouvelle que la sienne.
3. La mienne est plus intéressante que la vôtre.
4. Les miens sont plus amusants que les tiens.
5. Le mien est plus dynamique que le tien.
6. La mienne est plus jolie que la sienne.
7. Les miens sont plus beaux que les leurs.
8. Les miennes sont plus grandes que les leurs.

15 Script

1. –C'est ton maillot, Christian?
   –Non, ce n'est pas le mien. Le mien est plus grand.
   –C'est celui de Julien?
   –Oui, c'est probablement le sien. Il est plus petit que moi.
2. –C'est à qui cette trousse, Chantal?
   –Ce n'est pas la mienne. J'ai un taille-crayon dans la mienne.
   –C'est à ta camarade Anne-Marie?
   –Oui, c'est probablement la sienne. Elle aime le bleu.
3. –Ce sont à qui, ces magazines, Cédric?
   –Ce sont à mes amis Jean et Luc.
   –Tu es sûr, ce sont les leurs?
   –Oui, maman; ils aiment les bandes dessinées dans ces magazines.
4. –C'est votre chien, Benoît?
   –Non, ce n'est pas le nôtre. Le nôtre est de la même taille, mais il est noir. Je crois que c'est le chien de M. et Mme Blanchard.
   –Je vais vérifier si c'est le leur.
5. –À qui vas-tu rendre cette casserole?
   –Je ne sais pas.
   –Réfléchis bien. C'était dans le camping-car. Quand tu as fait du camping, qui a sorti la casserole?
   –Juliette et Sylvie, les sœurs Leblanc. Je sais que c'est la leur.

1. Julien
2. Anne-Marie
3. Jean et Luc
4. M. et Mme Blanchard
5. Juliette et Sylvie Leblanc

14 Richard se vante! 1.1, 1.3

Interpersonal or Presentational Speaking

Richard écoute ses amis. Jouez le rôle de Richard, qui pense que ses affaires, animaux, et parents sont meilleurs que les autres.

MODÈLE Julianne: «Abdel et Nicole ont deux beaux chiens.»
Richard: **Les miens sont plus beaux que les leurs!**

1. André: «J'ai acheté une belle chemise à carreaux.»
2. M. et Mme Diouf: «Thomas conduit une nouvelle voiture.»
3. Solange: «Marc et moi, nous avons fait une vidéo très intéressante pour notre cours d'histoire.»
4. Monique: «Mes parents sont très amusants!»
5. Joël: «Mon prof de français est dynamique!»
6. Océane: «Adja a une jolie sœur.»
7. Abdoulaye: «Les Dumont ont de beaux chevaux.»
8. Lucien: «Les Vaillancourt ont de grandes pièces.»

15 C'est à qui? 1.2

Interpretive Listening

Écrivez les numéros 1–5 sur votre papier. Écoutez les mini-dialogues. Dites à qui appartient chaque chose.

On recycle!

Utilisez un chronomètre (*timer*) et demandez à votre partenaire de nommer toutes les parties du corps qu'il ou elle connaît en une minute. Comptez combien de mots votre partenaire énumère et ensuite, à vous d'essayer de battre son score!

À qui est ce chien adorable? C'est le tien?

Essential Instruction

1. In pairs, have students prepare and practice **Activité 14**. Randomly ask partners to do the dialogues. Ask them to add "**parce que**" and the reason why whatever they have is better.
2. Have students do **Activité 15** on whiteboards. They show you each answer to give you a sense of how they are doing.
3. Using the information from **Activité 16**, ask students to write a narrative police report of Emily Weiler's declaration.

Communiquez!

16 Une déclaration de vol 1.2, 2.2, 3.1

Lisez la déclaration de vol ci-dessous, puis faites un résumé de l'histoire d'Emily Weiler à Paris. Où le crime a-t-il eu lieu? Quand? À quelle heure? La victime était de quelle nationalité? Qu'est-ce qu'on lui a volé? Comment étaient les voleurs? Où Emily a-t-elle rempli la déclaration de vol?

DÉCLARATION DE VOL

DÉCLARANT Homme ☐ Femme ☒

Nom de famille : W e i l e r
(C'est le nom qui figure sur votre acte de naissance; ce nom était anciennement désigné sous le vocable de «patronyme»)

Nom d'usage :
(Exemple : le nom de famille du mari que souhaite porter une femme mariée, le cas échéant)

Prénom(s) : E m i l y
(Dans l'ordre de l'état civil)

Né(e) le : 0 8 0 7 1 9 8 0 à (commune) : Houston, Texas

Code postal : 7 7 4 2 3 Pays : États-Unis

DOMICILE

Adresse : 3457 (N°) | (bis, ter) | Street (Type de voie (rue, avenue...)) | Huron (Nom de la voie)

Code postal : 7 7 4 2 3 Commune : Houston

Pays : États-Unis

Caractéristiques du ou des titres

Carte nationale d'identité	Passeport
N° :	N° : 1 3 1 0 8 2 3 1 5
Délivrée le :	Délivré le :
À (nom de la personne titulaire du document) :	À (nom de la personne titulaire du document) : E m i l y W e i l e r
Par :	Par :
Pays :	Pays : ÉTATS-UNIS

Objets volés

Date : 1 7 0 3 2 0 1 8 Lieu : Paris Rue Cambronne Heure : 17.15

Circonstances détaillées
«Un passeport de nationalité américaine au nom de WEILER Emily N° 131082315, une somme de 18 dollars américains, 180 dollars en chèques de voyage, et 30 euros, une MasterCard Gold et un permis de conduire du Texas avec photographie»

Mode opératoire précisions complémentaires
Deux individus de type méditerranéen d'environ une quinzaine d'années. L'un demande l'heure pendant que l'autre fouille dans le sac à dos de la victime.

Fait à : Paris le : 1 7 0 3 2 0 1 8

Signature du déclarant ou du représentant légal
E Weiler

Differentiated Learning

Accelerate
Have students write a scene of the robbery to be acted out. Ask them to embellish the dialogue with conversation between Emily and a friend, then the encounter with the two robbers, and finally the struggle that followed.

Decelerate
Students fill out a declaration inventing a minor crime committed against them, adding information related to who, what, where, and when.

Resources

CA Communicative Activities
Share

Answers

16
Où : Paris, Rue Cambronne; quand : le 17 mars 2018; heure : 17h15; nationalité de la victime : américaine; objets volés : passeport, 18 dollars, 180 dollars en chèques de voyage, 30 euros, une MasterCard Gold, un permis de conduire américain; description des voleurs : deux jeunes hommes d'une quinzaine d'années, d'origine méditerranéenne; déclaration remplie à : Paris

Reference Desk

If you have access to Passport, create a question for your students to share their response to a communicative activity.

Communication

Interpersonal: Cooperative Groups
Put students in groups of three. Ask them to secretly draw and color: 1) **une voiture de sport**, 2) **un livre**, 3) **des chaussures**, 4) **un chapeau**, 5) **une cravate**, 6) **un gâteau**, 7) **un fruit**, 8) **une calculatrice**, and 9) **une chemise**. In order, they show each other the first object and compare it to the two others. The first student says: **Ma voiture de sport est rouge.** Looking at another student: **La tienne est noire.** Looking at the third, talking to the second student: **La sienne est rouge aussi.** The second student talks about the second object using this model. The third student talks about the third object, and it continues.

Expansion

In pairs, have students role-play a police officer interviewing Emily (**Où habitez-vous? Quelle est votre nationalité**?, etc.). Emily has to furnish the details of the robbery: time of day, where she was, how she felt. They may use the **Extension** dialogue on p. 528 as a guide.

Answers

17 Interviews will vary.
18 Stories will vary.
19 Profiles will vary.

Reference Desk

Before doing **Activité 17**, remind students about the use of the **imparfait** and **passé composé** to describe past events. To help them decide if they need the **passé composé,** encourage them to ask the question, **Qu'est-ce qui est arrivé? Quelles étaient les circonstances?** acts as a cue for the **imparfait**.

Expansion

After doing **Activité 19**, have students pretend they are on a TV show and are going to meet potential partners for a speed dating session. They should prepare ten questions to ask to determine if someone is a good match for them. You may split the class in two groups and have candidates face each other in turns.

17 Je suis témoin 1.1, 2.1, 3.2

Interpersonal Speaking

La police vous interroge parce que vous avez été le témoin principal d'un crime qui s'est passé dans votre ville. Jouez le rôle avec un partenaire. L'agent voudrait savoir:

- ce qui s'est passé et où le crime a eu lieu
- l'heure du crime et s'il y avait d'autres témoins
- une description du criminel: sa taille, son âge, ses cheveux, son origine ethnique, ses vêtements
- d'autres détails importants, par exemple, le numéro de la plaque d'immatriculation (*license plate*) du véhicule du criminel

18 Ce jour-là, je me suis rendu compte que... 1.3, 3.2, 4.2, 5.2

Presentational Writing and Speaking

Pour l'écrivain irlandais James Joyce, une «épiphanie» est une sorte de révélation, d'ordre quasi mystique qui marque un moment de votre vie et qui change tout. Choisissez un moment de votre vie où vous vous êtes rendu compte de quelque chose d'important. Qu'est-ce qui a mené (*led*) à cette révélation? Comment ce moment a-t-il changé votre attitude, vos buts, ou votre vie en général? Répondez à ces questions dans un récit personnel, puis partagez votre expérience avec vos camarades de classe. Si vous n'avez pas vécu d'épiphanie vous-même, trouvez une personne qui va vous raconter son expérience.

19 Rendez-vous sur Internet 1.2, 1.3, 3.2

Interpretive Reading, Presentational Writing

Imaginez que vous avez trente ans, vous êtes célibataire, et vous venez d'emménager à Paris pour y faire vos études. Vous avez décidé de joindre un site de rencontre en ligne pour rencontrer l'homme ou la femme de vos rêves! Vous devez créer votre profil en ligne, en vous décrivant physiquement et en partageant vos intérêts et vos traits de personnalité. Vous devez également mentionner ce que vous recherchez chez un partenaire potentiel. N'oubliez pas d'ajouter une photo récente à votre profil! (Vous pouvez imaginer que vous êtes une personnalité célèbre.)

Essential Instruction

1. For **Activité 17**, encourage students to add any details to add some drama and make their account as detailed as possible.
2. If **Activité 18** seems a bit too personal for some, and they still have trouble finding someone in their family or someone they know, ask them to think of a historical figure who had an epiphany that changed the course of his or her life. Joan of Arc and her voices would be a prime example.
3. Students doing Activity 19 can refer to profiles in **Leçon B** for inspiration as well as key vocabulary and phrasing. You could display finished profiles on the wall afterwards for other students to enjoy.
4. To expand on **Stratégie communicative**, demonstrate to students the use of a graphic organizer to organize the details of the story. Encourage them to weave into the drama what they imagine motivated Derek to visit France, how he earned the money, what he has in his suitcase, and other details to enhance the story.

Stratégie communicative

Pre-AP

Communiquez!

Telling a Story through Pictures 1.2, 1.3

Presentational Writing

Vous allez raconter une histoire en regardant des illustrations. Dites de qui il s'agit, où l'action se déroule (*takes place*), ce qui se passe ; donnez un maximum de détails. Pensez à ce qui a pu se passer avant, pendant, et après chaque scène. N'oubliez pas d'utiliser des conjonctions lorsque vous passez d'une scène à une autre (par exemple, **Le lendemain Derek a pris un bus pour aller à l'aéroport**). L'histoire est racontée au passé. Pour la dernière scène, ajoutez un petit dialogue.

MODÈLE Derek rêvait depuis longtemps de voyager à Paris. Quand il a finalement eu les moyens d'y aller, il a acheté un billet en ligne avec Air France et l'a imprimé chez lui. Il a beaucoup lu sur Paris ; il voulait surtout visiter le musée d'Orsay afin de voir les tableaux de Monet et ceux des autres impressionnistes.

Produits

Paris Roissy–Charles-de-Gaulle (CDG) est le plus grand aéroport de France. C'est aussi le deuxième plus grand aéroport d'Europe après Heathrow, à Londres.

1.2, 2.2

Resources

Pre-T Pre-test

Q *Leçon* Quiz

Reference Desk

Before asking students to tell the story in **Stratégie communicative**, model a similar idea as a whole group activity. Choose several pictures and work as a group to create the story orally, reminding students of the **passé composé** and **imparfait** uses and the need for conjunctions to create continuity. Encourage them to add detail and interest. Write the story on the board as you proceed. Remind the students throughout the process that they will be doing a similar activity themselves.

Differentiated Learning

Accelerate

Encourage students to use dialogue and rich description to enhance their story. Have them go beyond the picture to give a personality to "the girl" (in the museum image), explain where Derek and the girl might go for coffee afterward, and how much they both love Monet, for example.

Decelerate

In small groups, brainstorm phrases for students to use in their story, inspired by the illustration, which they will copy and incorporate. This process may keep students away from translators and dictionaries. Work with them in a step-by-step manner to write simple sentences for their story.

Reference Desk

Brainstorm vocabulary that students need to complete their story. Expressions for giving an opinion of a film, questions the boy might ask himself about the **bateaux mouches** tours on the Seine, and vocabulary for giving an opinion about a painting are examples of expressions to discuss.

Essential Instruction

1. After students have written their pre-writing outline independently, or with your help, give them time in class to write the story. This process allows you one-on-one time with each student, helping them form their sentences, offering corrections, giving them instant feedback, and cutting down on your correcting.
2. To prepare to teach the vocabulary for **Émotions et réactions**, draw emoticons on the board for the following emotions: happy, sad, excited, depressed, and angry. Ask students to suggest vocabulary that they already know for each of these emotions. Have them copy what is written on the board into their notebooks.
3. Students listen to the **Émotions et réactions** and add the new vocabulary to the list of emotions.
4. Ask students to draw the clothing from **Et si je voulais dire…?**
5. Play **Pour la conversation** and ask students to make more sentences with the expressions.

Leçon C

Vocabulaire actif

Émotions et réactions 1.2

Ces personnes ont les sensations suivantes :

Elle est **complètement** surprise.

Il est tout à fait **choqué**.

Elle se sent vraiment **accablée**.

Il est quand même **frustré**.

Elle est **surexcitée**.

Il se sent **seul**.

Pour la conversation

How do I ask when someone had an idea to do something?

» Vous avez eu l'idée de mettre votre vidéo sur YouTube tout de suite ?

Did you have the idea to put your video on YouTube right away?

How do I say I didn't expect something?

» Je ne m'y attendais pas….

I didn't expect it.

Et si je voulais dire… ?

des bretelles (f.)	*suspenders*
des espadrilles (f.)	*rope-soled sandals*
des santiags (f.)	*cowboy boots*
un sweat à capuche	*hoodie*
courroucé(e)	*irate*
dépassé(e)	*overwhelmed*
survolté(e)	*overexcited*

Resources

- *Vocabulaire actif*
- *Pour la conversation*
- *Et si je voulais dire… ?*
- eV eVisual
- WB Workbook 1–3
- FC Flash Cards
- LA Listening Activity 1
- G & V Practice Games

Reference Desk

1. **Être surpris(e)** means *to be surprised*. **Être choqué(e) means** *to have a strong reaction to something*.
2. **Les santiags** or **bottes de cowboy** originated in Spain, and then were introduced into Mexico. Today in the United States, they are popular not only in Texas and Oklahoma, but are seen as fashion accessories everywhere.

Culture

Practices: Information

Mettre la ceinture et les bretelles (*to wear a belt and suspenders*) is an expression that denotes someone is super-cautious.

Differentiated Learning

Accelerate

Ask students to search online for more expressions denoting emotions and suggest them to the class.

Decelerate

Conjugate the verb **se sentir** with the students. Point out that it is similar to the verb **mentir** (*to lie*). Ask them to conjugate it in the present tense in all forms with various "emotion" vocabulary words to help students review adjective agreement in all forms.

Resources

Activity 1

Answers

1

1. Elle lui a dit que ça viendra.
2. Elle fait une vidéo sur YouTube.
3. La réaction était très positive.
4. Elle aurait emporté des shorts et vêtements d'été.
5. Il lui a demandé où elle a acheté ses baskets.

2 Possible answers:

1. scandinave
2. grand et costaud
3. courts et bouclés
4. une chemise blanche, un jean, et des baskets
5. mince

Reference Desk

1. One can say either **à Avignon** or **en Avignon**. The same is true for the city of Arles. Why? It is because Avignon was a separate state from France until the French revolution. Therefore, remembering this historical status, either form is correct.
2. The **Festival d'Avignon**, founded in 1947 by Jean Vilar, is held annually in July in the courtyard of the **Palais des Papes** and in other locations of the city. It is the oldest arts festival in France and draws directors, actors, and drama buffs from around the world.

Game

Vocabulaire 101 !

Play this game to practice the new vocabulary. Prepare a set of note cards with a new word or expression on each one. Divide the class into two teams. Call the first player from each team to the front. Select the top card from the pile and read aloud the word or expression that you want the players to use in a sentence. Both players write a sentence on the board using that word or expression. The student who correctly uses the new word or expression in a sentence earns a point for his or her team. If both sentences are correct, both teams win a point. Then a different player from each team takes a turn.

1 Une lettre de France 1.2

Interpretive Reading

Lisez la lettre que Jennifer a écrite à sa prof de français, puis répondez aux questions.

Madame,

Tout va bien ici à Avignon. Je suis un peu frustrée par mon français, mais vous m'avez dit que ça viendra, n'est-ce pas? La bonne nouvelle est que je ne me sens plus seule. J'ai eu l'idée de faire une vidéo avec d'autres filles et de la mettre sur YouTube. Je suis vraiment surexcitée par la réaction. Je ne m'y attendais pas! Depuis, on m'a invitée à en faire d'autres et je me suis fait plein d'amis maintenant.

J'étais un peu accablée par la chaleur les premiers jours parce que je n'avais pas pensé à emmener des shorts avec moi, juste un jean et deux autres pantalons que je lave souvent. Il faut que je fasse du shopping! J'ai aussi fait la connaissance d'un garçon qui voulait savoir où j'avais acheté mes baskets. Philippe, c'est son nom, est très gentil et on sort ensemble très souvent.

En espérant que vous m'écrirez bientôt,

Jennifer

chaleur *heat*

1. Qu'est-ce que la prof de Jennifer lui a dit pour l'encourager à propos de son français?
2. Que fait Jennifer avec d'autres ados?
3. Quelle était la réaction du public et la réaction de Jennifer face à sa vidéo?
4. Comment est-ce qu'elle aurait fait sa valise différemment?
5. Comment a-t-elle fait la connaissance de Philippe?

2 Christian va en ville 1.2, 1.3

Interpretive Viewing, Presentational Writing

Regardez l'illustration et complétez les phrases.

1. Christian est un type d'origine…
2. Physiquement, il est… et ….
3. Il a les cheveux….
4. Aujourd'hui il porte… et ….
5. Il n'est pas gros, il est…et ….

Essential Instruction

1. After students read **Activité 1**, ask the general comprehension questions.
2. Have students identify the various tenses and moods of verbs in the letter.
3. Ask students to describe what they think Charlotte and Philippe look like.
4. After students complete the sentences in **Activité 2**, ask them to expand on what Christian is like, what he likes to do, where he lives, and what he wants to do with his life.
5. Have students do **Activité 3** orally and then written.
6. Divide students into six groups. Assign each group a photo from **Activité 3**. Ask them to write a short composition explaining who is in the picture you assigned to them, and explain why they are feeling the way they do.

3 Les réactions 1.2, 1.3

Interpretive Viewing, Presentational Speaking or Writing

Regardez les illustrations pour identifier les réactions des personnes. Choisissez un adjectif ci-dessous.

MODÈLE

M. Dugas

M. Dugas est complètement accablé.

accablé **seul** **surpris** **surexcité** **choqué** **frustré**

1. M. et Mme Laroche

2. Mme Dufour

3. Matthieu

4. M. Carré

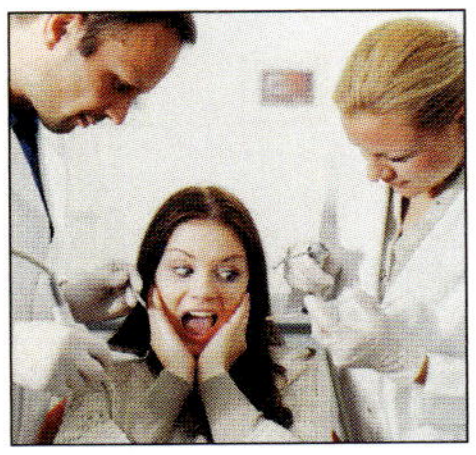

5. Isabelle

Les élèves sont choqués par les résultats du bac.

Perspectives 1.2, 2.1

Pour avoir mon bac, j'ai bien pris des notes pendant l'année de tout ce que les profs disaient. Je pense que c'est plus important que de réviser à la dernière minute. Une fois que tu as la méthode, tu as un peu de mémoire et de culture générale, c'est beaucoup plus facile de réviser. Tu peux aussi acheter des annales pour te préparer. –Pirouette-cacahouette

Quels conseils donne cette jeune personne pour réussir le bac?

Answers

3

1. M. et Mme Laroche sont tout à fait surpris.
2. Mme Dufour est vraiment frustrée.
3. Matthieu se sent seul.
4. M. Carré est surexcité!
5. Isabelle est complètement choquée.

Perspectives

Elle dit qu'il faut bien prendre des notes pendant l'année, et peut-être acheter des annales du bac pour s'entraîner.

Communication

Presentational: Cooperative groups

Students collaborate to present a fashion show of current "looks." They can consider "the preppy look," "the biker look," or "the **Intello**" for example. There will be some students who will be the runway models wearing the outfits that various student narrators describe.

Recherche: la redoute, la mode femme et homme

Differentiated Learning

Accelerate

Have students pretend that they are Jennifer's French teacher and respond to her letter suggesting places in and outside of Avignon that she should visit.

Decelerate

Students can collaborate to make a collage of Avignon with captions about the historic places to visit. They should situate the city on the map. The goal is for them to promote Avignon to the class.

Resources

Activity 4

Answers

4 Script

M. Aknouch : Alors Aminata, tu as gagné le concours de plus belle vidéo musicale sur YouTube.
Aminata : Oui, je ne m'y attendais pas. Quelle surprise !
M. Aknouch : Tu as eu l'idée de mettre ta vidéo comment ?
Aminata : C'est mon frère qui m'a parlé du concours. Il m'a dit que je devrais essayer et comme on avait cette vidéo de la fête d'une copine, alors….
M. Aknouch : Tu es charmante dans le clip avec ta robe à rayures.
Aminata : Merci beaucoup. J'étais complètement choquée de gagner, mais maintenant je me sens surexcitée et je veux continuer et faire d'autres vidéos et peut-être devenir célèbre !

1. Aminata a gagné le concours de plus belle vidéo musicale sur YouTube.
2. Aminata savait qu'elle allait gagner.
3. Son père a eu l'idée de mettre la vidéo sur YouTube.
4. Aminata a filmé la vidéo à un mariage.
5. Aminata se sent attristée.

1. V; 2. F; 3. F; 4. F; 5. F

5 Answers will vary.

Communication

Interpersonal: Cooperative Groups

Create a grid. In the first column, students write an emotion. In the second column, they write a situation in which they feel that way, for example **accablé(e)… parce que j'ai raté un grand examen**. Have students walk around the room and ask one another "**Comment tu te sens ?**" The other student responds with an emotion. The first student asks "**Pourquoi ?**" and the second student responds with the reason. Then reverse the student roles.

4 Quelle surprise ! 1.2

Interpretive Listening

Écrivez les numéros 1–5 sur votre papier. Ensuite, écoutez la discussion entre Aminata et l'animateur M. Aknouch sur un concours (competition) *vidéo. Finalement, indiquez si les phrases que vous entendez sont vraies (**V**) ou fausses (**F**).*

5 Questions personnelles 1.1

Interpersonal Speaking

Répondez aux questions avec un partenaire.

1. À quoi est-ce que tu ne t'attendais pas à l'école cette année ?
2. Quels vêtements est-ce que les élèves à ton école portent en général ?
3. Quel style de vêtements aimes-tu ?
4. Qu'est-ce que tu fais quand tu vois un(e) élève qui est seul(e) à la cantine ?
5. Qu'est-ce qui te rend surexcité(e) ? frustré(e) ? accablé(e) ?

On recycle !

Trouvez cinq images de célébrités et discutez avec votre partenaire de ce que vous pensez de ces photos et pourquoi. Utilisez des pronoms relatifs.

MODÈLE A : **Regarde cette photo de Kendrick Lamar, j'adore la chemise qu'il porte, elle est si élégante.**
B : **Oui, il a l'air élégant.**

Essential Instruction

1. Have students listen to **Activité 4** and answer **vrai** or **faux** to the statements.
2. Give students time to prepare **Activité 5**. In answering, require students to expand their answers with details.
3. Expand the exercise by asking more questions about the situations in their lives that make them feel certain ways.
4. Play **Actuellement sur YouTube**, books closed.
5. Ask students what they think the interview was about, who was speaking, and any details that they remember.
6. Students listen a second time with books open.
7. What do they think **Ils se sont déchaînés**; **Quelques-unes ont complètement craqué** means?
8. What English words did they encounter in the dialogue?
9. Have students answer **Activité 6** as a whole-class activity.

Actuellement sur YouTube 1.2

Un reporter interviewe Élodie au sujet de son hit sur YouTube.

Le reporter: Vous avez eu l'idée de mettre votre vidéo sur YouTube tout de suite?
Élodie: Non, pas du tout.
Le reporter: Ce groupe de garçons, où l'avez-vous rencontré?
Élodie: Au mariage de mon cousin…. Ce sont deux frères et un copain.
Le reporter: On les y avait invités pour chanter?
Élodie: Oui, mon cousin les avait vus chanter des gospels à l'église. Ils sont arrivés habillés comme sur la vidéo… jeans bleus délavés, liquettes, et baskets orange comme pour un show! En fait, j'ai appris par la suite qu'ils chantaient dans un chœur de gospel à Genève.
Le reporter: Et c'est après qu'ils ont fait le show?
Élodie: Pendant la soirée, ils se sont déchaînés, tous les trois! Un vrai show…. C'est là que j'ai commencé à les filmer et comme ils étaient très photogéniques, c'était plutôt agréable… en plus, je trouvais qu'ils avaient du talent et du charme.
Le reporter: Bref, c'est ça qui vous a décidé à les mettre sur YouTube?
Élodie: Oui, j'ai commencé à montrer la vidéo à mes copines; quelques-unes ont complètement craqué, et voilà comment la vidéo s'est retrouvée sur YouTube.
Le reporter: Vous avez dû être complètement surprise par le buzz et le succès.
Élodie: Surtout eux! Moi non plus, je ne m'y attendais pas, je n'avais pas fait ça pour ça: juste pour partager une petite émotion. Et maintenant, ils ont de vraies groupies!
Le reporter: Merci.

6 Actuellement sur YouTube 1.2

Identifiez les personnes décrites.

1. Cette personne a un hit sur YouTube.
2. Cette personne interviewe Élodie.
3. Ces personnes ont fait un show.
4. Cette personne s'est mariée.
5. Ces personnes ont craqué en voyant la vidéo.
6. Cette personne ne s'attendait pas au buzz et au succès de la vidéo.

Analyse

Faites le profil du groupe de garçons dans la vidéo d'Élodie: imaginez leur expérience professionnelle, leurs intérêts, leurs qualités, et leur apparence physique.

Resources

Dialogue Activity 6
Dialogue Video
WB Workbook 4

Answers

6

1. Élodie
2. le reporter
3. deux frères et un copain d'Élodie
4. le cousin d'Élodie
5. les copines d'Élodie
6. Élodie

Reference Desk

1. **Une liquette** is a colloquial term for **une chemise**. It may be used for boys and girls equally.
2. Remind students that **actuellement** means *now*, not *actually*. The word *actually* can be translated as either **en réalité** or **en fait**.
3. As in the United States, Youtube has created stars in France. Students may want to watch videos from France's biggest stars: Squeezie, Cyprien, Norman, EnjoyPhoenix, Rémi Gaillard, and ElsaMakeUp.

nouvelle orthographe **se déchainer**

Differentiated Learning

Expand
Assign parts of the dialogue to different students. Replay the recording so that they note pronunciation and intonation. Have them act out the scene.

Decelerate
To check understanding of the dialogue, prepare a set of sentences that ask students to complete the idea in each one with an answer from the conversation, for example, **Élodie n'a pas eu l'idée de mettre sa vidéo sur Youtube…** (**tout de suite**) or **Élodie a rencontré ce groupe de garçons…** (**au mariage de son cousin**).

Resources

Extension

Answers

EXTENSION

Answers will vary.

Communication

Interpersonal: Cooperative Groups

Have students write a dialogue of a phone conversation between **Jérémie et la jeune femme** in which they reconnect. He asks her about her work, where she is living, and plans the next time they will see each other.

EXTENSION **Ils se sont retrouvés sur Internet** 1.2

Alexandre skype avec son pote Jérémie.

Alexandre : Et, elle ressemble à quoi maintenant ?

Jérémie : Les cheveux raides, longs maintenant, toujours aussi mignonne.

Alexandre : Et elle fait quoi ?

Jérémie : Elle vient de commencer à travailler en Allemagne dans une société internationale de services.

Alexandre : Tu l'as retrouvée comment ?

Jérémie : J'ai commencé par Facebook, j'ai essayé Copains d'avant, j'ai fait un petit tour par Meetic....

Alexandre : Je ne pensais pas que tu tenais à elle à ce point !

Jérémie : Mais rien... pas de traces.... J'ai fini par m'inscrire sur LinkedIn, un site professionnel, et voilà comment j'ai finalement retrouvé sa trace... elle était là : photo très pro. Tu imagines le choc !

Alexandre : Bref, tu es de nouveau amoureux....

Jérémie : Je ne m'attendais quand même pas à ce que ça me fasse cet effet-là. Et elle m'a demandé de venir la voir en Allemagne pour Pâques !

Alexandre : Perdu, retrouvé. Quelle chance !

EXTENSION Quelle est votre prédiction pour Jérémie et la jeune femme ? 1.2

Essential Instruction

1. Have students read **Extension**.
2. Ask them to list the social media platforms mentioned in the dialogue.
3. Have students imagine Jérémie and the young lady's past together. Which parts of the dialogue reveal that they knew each other, lost each other, and found each other once again?
4. Students work in triads to read **Internet et les réseaux sociaux**. Ask them to paraphrase each paragraph, noting important facts.
5. The third paragraph discusses the preferred internet activities of adolescents. Have them use each verb listed in a sentence describing their own internet use (for example, **Je télécharge des albums sur iTunes**).

Points de départ

Pre-AP

Question centrale ? **Quels sont les défis de la vie contemporaine?**

Internet et les réseaux sociaux

1.2, 2.1, 2.2, 3.1, 4.1

Nombre d'utilisateurs

Internet est utilisé en France par le grand public depuis 1994.

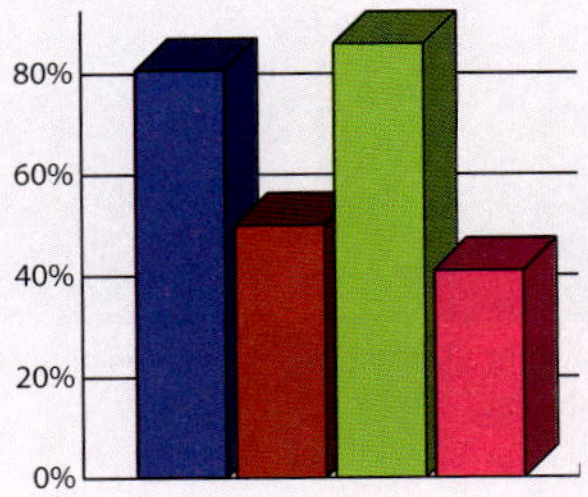

- Nombre d'internautes 84% (56,4 millions de Français)
- Nombre d'utilisateurs de réseaux sociaux 57% (38 millions de Français)
- Nombre de foyers ayant accès à Internet 85% (24,7 millions de foyers)
- Abonnements Internet haut et très haut débit sur réseaux fixes 42% (28,4 millions de Français)

Source : JDN, mars 2018

Équipement

Pourcentage des Français

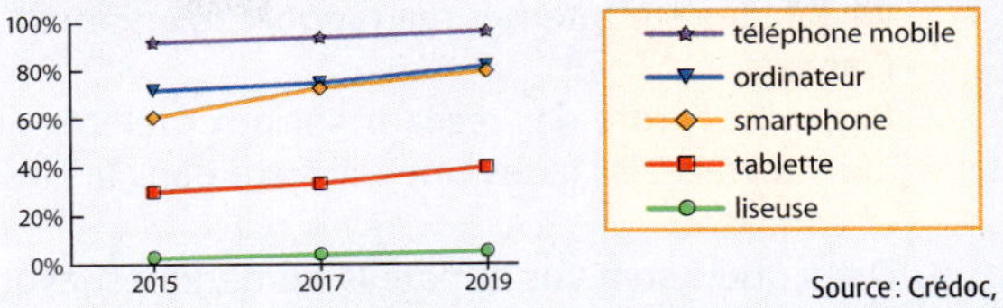

Source : Crédoc, 2018

Les activités les plus répandues

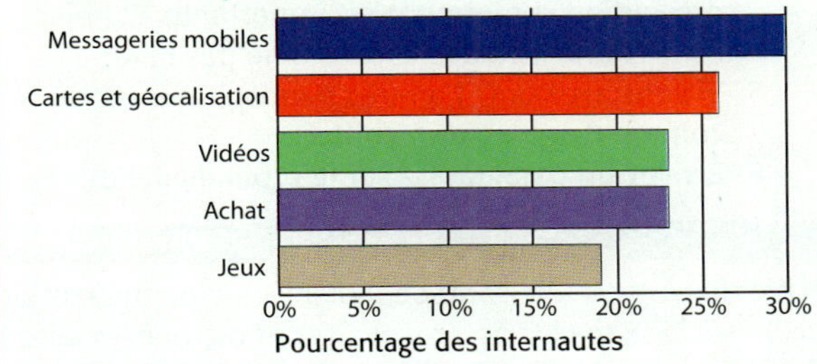

Source : bdm 2018

Classement des réseaux sociaux

Source : Agence Tiz 2018

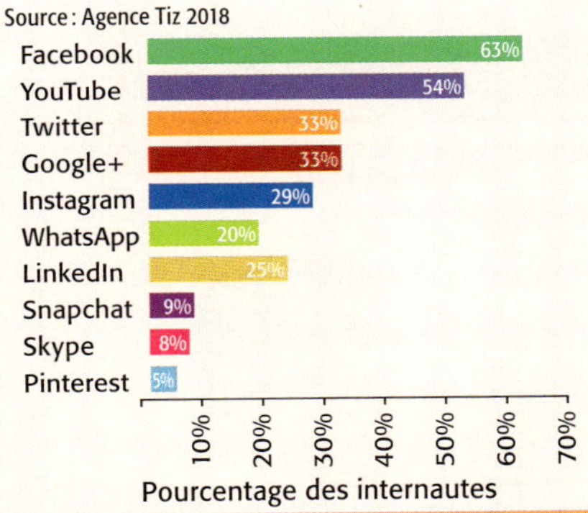

Usage

78% des Français de 12 ans et plus se connectent tous les jours et ils sont 73% à déclarer ne plus pouvoir « se passer d'Internet dans la vie de tous les jours »

- Vont sur Internet depuis un PC ou une tablette : 3h37/jour
- Se connectent depuis un smartphone : 58 min/jour
- Vont sur réseaux sociaux : 1h16/jour

Les enfants de 6 à 13 ans sont de plus en plus connectés et équipés d'outils numériques.

Source : Étude IPSOS 2017

Les enfants

24% des parents se jugent cependant préoccupés par le temps passé par leurs enfants à utiliser des produits électroniques :

Temps passé par les enfants sur produits électroniques : 3h14/jour ; 22h38/semaine

- Sur netbooks : + 2h/jour (24%)
- Sur smartphone : 1–2h/jour (16%)

Source : Étude IPSOS 2017

Produits

La loi HADOPI (Haute autorité pour la diffusion des œuvres et la protection des droits sur Internet), adoptée en 2009, protège les droits de propriété des internautes. Elle apporte aussi des sanctions à toute activité illégale, comme le piratage (*hacking*) ou les téléchargements illégaux.

Mot-clé

Réseau vient de *rets* (1155), issu du latin *retis* pour désigner un filet. *Réseau* est le dérivé de *rets*. De petit filet, il devient filet (tissu formé de petites mailles) avant de prendre le sens abstrait de « ensemble de choses emprisonnant un individu ». Utilisé en physiologie pour les nerfs, les vaisseaux au 18ème siècle, c'est au 19ème siècle que *réseau* prend le sens de « ensemble de personnes qui ont des liens entre elles ».

1.2, 2.2

Resources

- Points de départ
- WB Workbook 5
- Explore

Reference Desk

1. Supplementary vocabulary: **une page web** (*web page*); **un moteur de recherche** (*search engine*); **télécharger un fichier** (*download a file*); **transmettre** (*upload*); **cliquer sur un lien** (*click on a link*); **joindre un fichier à son message** (*attach a file*); **imprimer un document** (*print a document*); **la souris** (*mouse*); **le clavier** (*keyboard*); **une clé USB** (*memory stick*); **accéder à Internet** (*access the internet*); **une adresse Internet** (*web address*); **le courrier électronique** (*e-mail*).
2. **JDN** stands for **le Journal du Net**, an online magazine.
3. If you have access to Passport, find a video or a news article related to **les réseaux sociaux** and share it with your students.

Communication

Presentational: Paired Practice

Ask students to recount how they use the internet daily and which social network sites they prefer and why. Have them share their habits with a partner.

Differentiated Learning

Accelerate

Have students find online safety tips, then make a poster of this advice to display in the classroom.

Recherche : microsoft centre de sécurité, jeunesse et protection des mineurs

Decelerate

Ask students to present the tenets of the HADOPI law.

Multiple Intelligences

Mathematical-Logical

Ask students to survey members of their class using the same categories as in the reading to compare the usage of the various social media and internet sites by French and American youth.

Answers

7 Activities will vary.

Perspectives

Pour bénéficier d'un effet thérapeutique.

Expansion

Have students interview an older family member or friend about what life was like in the '60s, '70s, and '80s without the internet. How did they communicate? What did they do to research information? Do they think that technology today is truly a time saver and a way to better communication? Students can summarize their results of the interview and share them in a group discussion of "**La vie d'hier et d'aujourd'hui**."

Critical Thinking

Comparisons

Have students visit the websites featured in **Du côté des médias**. Have them make two columns. In the first column have them write the French websites listed in the chart, and in the second an American website of similar nature.

Communication

Presentational: Cooperative Groups

Have students search online French sites for music, lyrics, movies, and travel, and share them with the class.

7 Activités culturelles 1.3, 4.2, 5.2

Faites les activités suivantes.

Les jeunes Français passent plus de trois heures par jour sur Internet.

1. Comparez le temps que vous passez et ce que vous faites sur Internet par rapport aux jeunes Français.
2. Regardez l'ordre des réseaux sociaux préférés des jeunes Français ; faites une enquête dans la classe et comparez.
3. Dites quels sont vos appareils numériques favoris et pourquoi.
4. Écrivez une histoire avec une morale : la prévention sur Internet est importante. Ou bien, écrivez une liste des choses à ne pas faire.
5. Si vous avez un(e) ami(e) francophone sur un média comme Facebook, racontez à la classe comment se passe ce contact.
6. Écrivez un paragraphe sur le profil digital des Français.

1.2, 2.1

Perspectives

« Écrire un blog est une sorte de thérapie, me permettant de mettre des mots sur les maux. C'est un ami qui me soulage, me fait espérer et rêver. » Pour quelles raisons est-ce que ce jeune blogueur écrit un blog?

Du côté des médias 1.2

Lisez les ressources numériques ci-dessous.

La culture en ligne

Acheter des livres, des DVD, des CD sur **fnac.com** ou **amazon.fr** 	Aller au spectacle : acheter des billets sur **francebillet.com** ou **fnacspectacles.com** 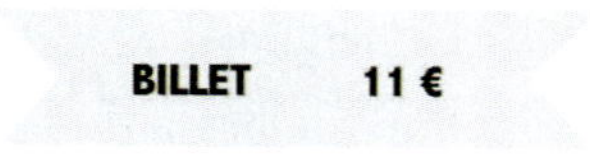	Acheter des places de cinéma sur **allocine.fr** 
Regarder la télévision en direct ou à la demande sur **france.tv** francetélévisions	Écouter la radio en ligne sur **ecouterradioenligne.com** : toutes les stations de radio ! Virgin RADIO	Écouter la musique en ligne sur **deezer.com** 

Essential Instruction

1. Have high- and low-ability students work in pairs to complete three of the six tasks in **Activité 7**. Check to make sure all tasks are chosen. If there are some that are not selected, assign them as a group activity.
2. In small groups, as a game of speed, see which group can complete the tasks in **Activité 8** the fastest. Ask all groups to complete the exercise. Ask them to share their findings in a round table discussion.
3. Have students do **Activité 10** individually then select which of the two or three sites they prefer. Give them enough time to investigate the sites and write a justification for their preferences.

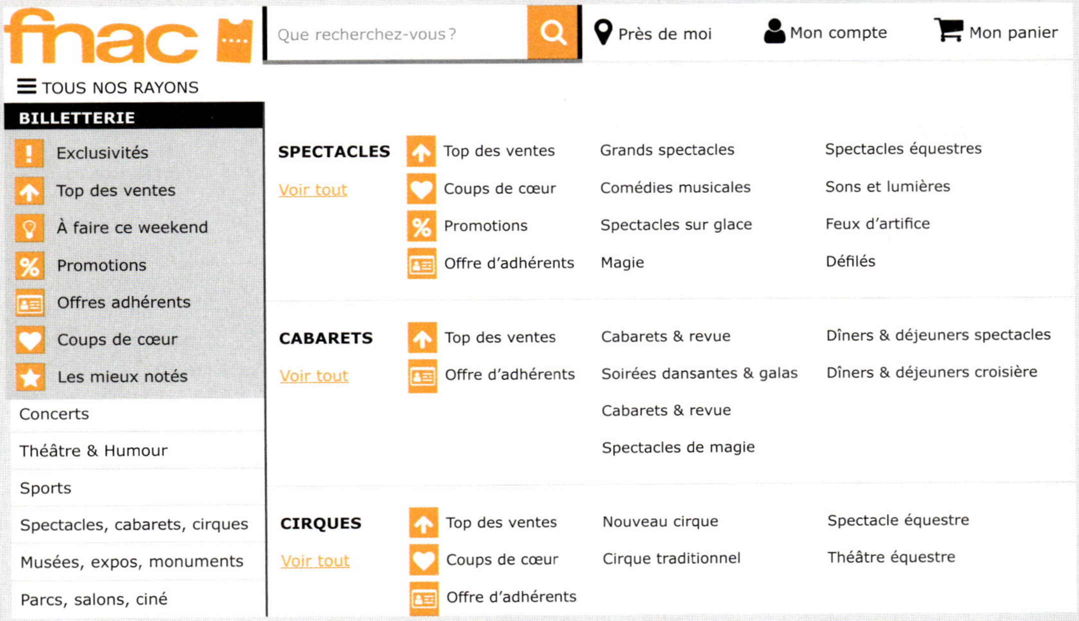

8 Sites Internet en France 3.1, 3.2, 4.2, 5.1, 5.2

Servez-vous des sites Internet mentionnés à la page 548 pour trouver :

- un album en français que vous voudriez acheter
- un film en français que vous voudriez louer
- la chanson la plus populaire en France en ce moment
- un film américain qu'on passe en France cette semaine
- une revue d'un nouveau film français qui n'est pas un navet *(flop)*
- un concert auquel vous voudriez assister si vous étiez en France
- trois émissions de télé américaines qui passent actuellement en France
- les préférences d'un ado français tirées de *(pulled from)* son réseau social

9 Sites Internet 1.3, 3.2

Consultez trois liens à la page 548 et comparez-les, puis dites lesquels vous semblent intéressants et pourquoi. Échangez vos impressions avec vos camarades de classe.

10 J'évalue les sites 1.3, 3.1, 4.2, 5.2

Dites ce que vous voudriez faire sur les sites suivants.

deezer.com	fnac.com	france.tv	ecouterradioenligne.com
francebillet.com	allocine.fr	fnacspectacles.com	amazon.fr

Answers

All answers will vary.

Critical Thinking

Analysis

Students examine the American television shows currently shown in France. What impressions would the French have about our culture based on what they see through these programs?

Expansion

Invite students to find a TV episode of an American show dubbed in French. Discuss the effects of dubbing and whether it is preferable to subtitles.

Point out that the French, like most Europeans, prefer to watch the dubbed versions of films and TV rather than read subtitles. Studies show that only 20% of the French prefer the original version (**la version originale**), which is to say, the subtitled version.

Differentiated Learning

Accelerate

Have students do a search on **AlloCiné** or **Cinéfil** and compare current movies being shown in a French city of their choice with those currently shown in their hometown. Have them select a film showing in both countries. Is the title the same? What are the comparative prices of tickets? Can you reserve seats in both theaters? Are the reviews similar? Ask them to report back to the class. Remind students if necessary about the designations **VO** and **VF** (for the original language of the film or its French-dubbed version).

Decelerate

Ask students to access radio sites to compare, selecting a genre such as rock, jazz, or pop and compare **les Palmarès** with the winners of the Grammys. How many artists overlap both charts? **La culture en ligne** is designed to be easily comprehensible for students who may continue to struggle with French. Celebrate their ability to be able to understand the reading and give them plenty of time to enjoy themselves visiting the sites.

Answers

All answers will vary.

Reference Desk

1. Indefinite adjectives refer to a general, not specific, person. **Aucun(e)** has a negative sense so **ne** must appear before the verb.
2. **N'importe quoi!** is the equivalent of the sarcastic expression *Whatever!*

Connections

Music

"Tous les garçons et les filles" by Françoise Hardy features several indefinite adjectives plus vocabulary words students have already learned. Remind students that Françoise Hardy is an enduring cultural phenomenon, not just a pop star and cover girl of 1960s France. She recently released a new album, ***Personne d'Autre***, in spring 2018. She and her husband Jacques Dutronc are the parents of Thomas Dutronc, whose music and albums were looked at in **Unité 7**.

Communication

Interpersonal: Paired Practice

One student pretends to be a French student in a **lycée** in France who is being interviewed by an American student-reporter on daily life in France. Have them ask questions about their studies and preparing for the **bac**. Have students go online to get pertinent information about French school courses of study.

Les défis des francophones 1.2

Introduction et interrogations

Vous allez interviewer un(e) Francophone sur un sujet complexe et difficile : les défis de la vie contemporaine.

En groupe, choisissez un sujet pour une interview. Ensuite, contactez un(e) de vos correspondant(e)s francophones.

Les trois sujets possibles :

1. Ses expériences personnelles (ou les expériences d'un membre de sa famille) avec le bac. (S'il n'est pas français, vous pouvez poser des questions sur l'équivalent du bac dans son pays.)
2. Ses interactions ou expériences avec, ou ses opinions de, la police et du crime dans son pays.
3. Son usage du chat et du forum sur Internet et les risques d'Internet dans son pays.

11 Écrire des questions 1.3, 4.2, 5.1

Avec votre partenaire, écrivez une liste de questions à poser à votre correspondant(e) francophone. Posez des questions générales, mais aussi des questions plus spécifiques. Écrivez au moins dix questions.

12 Interviewer 1.1, 4.2, 5.2

Faites les activités suivantes :

1. Pendant l'interview, travaillez ensemble pour qu'une personne pose les questions et l'autre prenne des notes.
2. Après l'interview, résumez les réponses de votre ami(e) francophone dans une rédaction de 1–2 pages.
3. En classe, discutez avec les groupes qui ont choisi le même sujet que vous. Identifiez les points communs et les différences entre les interviews.

13 Faire l'inventaire ! 1.1

Discutez des questions suivantes en classe après les interviews et les rédactions.

1. Est-ce que vos expériences se ressemblent ?
2. Comment est-ce que la description des défis dans les interviews individuelles est différente des descriptions générales dans l'unité ?
3. Est-ce que vous préférez étudier des généralisations ou baser vos recherches sur des expériences individuelles (*anecdotes*) ?

Essential Instruction

1. **Culture sur place** activities are based on connecting with a French-speaking person in the community or online. If you do not know of or have any links, you can find possibilities online for partnerships with exchange schools in France.

Recherche : exchange between french and american schools, french embassy

2. If time is an issue in establishing this exchange, for **Activités 11**, **12**, and **13**, students can interview you.
3. Review indefinite adjectives in **Structure de la langue** by asking students to translate the adjectives on the list from French to English to test recall.
4. Explain position and agreement of **aucun(e)**, **certain(e)**, **tout/tous/toute(s)**, **n'importe quel(le)**, and **tel(le)**.
5. Ask students to make sentences with these adjectives.

Révision: Indefinite Adjectives 1.2

L'actrice Marion Cotillard ne s'habille pas avec n'importe quelle robe.
Elle porte une robe Dior.

Indefinite adjectives are used to modify nouns in a non-specific sense. Like other adjectives, most indefinite adjectives agree in gender and in number with the nouns they describe. Here are some important indefinite adjectives to know:

aucun(e)... ne (n')	*not one, none*
autre	*other*
certain(e)(s)	*certain*
chaque	*each, every*
même	*same*
plusieurs	*several*
quelques	*some*
tout, toute, tous, toutes	*all, every*

la plupart (de l'/de la/du/des)	*most (of)*
n'importe quel, n'importe quelle	*any*
un tel, une telle	*such a*

Nous avons eu l'idée de faire une vidéo avec **plusieurs** amis. — *We had the idea of making a video with several friends.*

Notre **autre** ami n'aimait pas la vidéo. — *Our other friend didn't like the video.*

La plupart de means "most."

La plupart des ados français sont branchés. — *Most French teens are technologically savvy.*

Two additional indefinite adjectives are **n'importe quel/n'importe quelle** *(just any)* and **un tel/une telle** *(such a)*.

Malik n'a pas mis **n'importe quel** jean. — *Malik didn't put on just any pair of jeans.*

Une **telle** chose n'arrivera jamais ici. — *Such a thing will never happen here.*

Resources

WB Workbook 6–7

LA Listening Activity 2

G & V Practice Games

Expansion

Have students collaborate to write a letter to a French school requesting an exchange between an English class in France with a French class in the United States. Ask them to suggest a pen pal program as well as video exchanges.

Recherche: french-american pen pals

Differentiated Learning

Accelerate

Have students imagine that they are going down the aisle of a grocery store, then write sentences using the indefinite adjectives as they refer to what they see: **Je veux acheter quelques pommes rouges parce qu'elles ont l'air délicieux.**

Decelerate

Ask students to copy the adjectives and examples into their notebooks. Have them write a sentence for each adjective listed.

Multiple Intelligences

Musical-Rhythmic

Ask students to search for French songs featuring the indefinite adjectives by putting each one in the search box.

Resources

Activity 15

Answers

14

1. chaque
2. plusieurs
3. tous
4. même
5. autre
6. telle
7. la plupart

15

1. Tous ses copains et toutes ses copines pourront venir.
2. Aucun de ces athlètes ne gagne de médaille.
3. Oui, elle peut acheter plusieurs vêtements (mais aucun manteau).
4. Non, je ne garde pas le même portable. J'en achète un autre.

Expansion

Have students look at the picture of **les amis de Maeva**, then imagine the beach in France where the young people are, the time of day, how they got to the beach, what they are going to have to eat, and how long they intend to stay. Have them write a conversation among four of them using as many indefinite adjectives as possible.

14 La journée de Maeva 1.3

Presentational Speaking or Writing

Complétez la description de ce que fait Maeva régulièrement. Utilisez les indices donnés entre parenthèses.

1. Maeva se lève... matin à 6h40. *(each)*
2. Pour le petit déjeuner, elle mange... tartines à la confiture. *(several)*
3. Elle va... les jours au club de fitness après les cours. *(every)*
4. Maeva achète toujours la... chose au supermarché: des yaourts, des pommes, du pain, du fromage. *(same)*
5. L'... jour, elle a rencontré Lucas au supermarché. *(other)*
6. Elle ne s'attendait pas à une...rencontre. *(such)*
7. Et, maintenant, ... du temps, elle dîne avec Lucas. *(most)*

Maeva a invité tous ses amis à la plage.

15 Des problèmes de maths: solutions imprécises 1.2, 1.3

Interpretive Reading, Presentational Speaking or Writing

Lisez chaque problème. Répondez à la question avec une phrase qui contient un mot ou une expression ci-dessous.

plusieurs   aucun(e)... ne (n')   tout   autre   même

MODÈLE Sophie et Max veulent visiter Paris. Ils savent qu'il y a beaucoup de choses à faire et qu'un ou deux jours ne sera pas assez. Combien de jours voyageront-ils?
Ils voyageront plusieurs jours.

1. Laure veut inviter des copains à sa fête d'anniversaire. Ses parents lui disent qu'elle peut inviter cinq copains et cinq copines. Dans sa bande, il y a Michèle, Noah, Luc, Chantal, Céline, Anne, Dikembe, Martin, Lise, et Pierre. Combien de ses copains pourront venir? Combien de ses copines?
2. Pour gagner une médaille au marathon, il faut courir et finir en moins de cinq minutes par kilomètre. Claude a fait deux kilomètres en 12 minutes. Djamel a couru un kilomètre en sept minutes. Stéphanie a couru trois kilomètres en dix-huit minutes. Combien de ces athlètes gagnent une médaille?
3. Fatima a besoin de nouveaux vêtements. Elle a 100€. Le manteau à carreaux coûte 145€. Le pantalon à rayures coûte 25€. La liquette coûte 12€, et la jupe coûte 37€. Est-ce que Fatima peut acheter des vêtements?
4. Vous trébuchez et votre ordinateur portable tombe. Maintenant cet ordinateur ne marche plus. Pour le faire réparer, vous devez payer 600€. Pour acheter un nouvel ordinateur, vous devez payer 498€. Qu'est-ce que vous faites? Gardez-vous le portable original?

Essential Instruction

1. Drill the indefinite adjectives from English to French, and French to English.
2. Give students time to do **Activité 14**.
3. Have students put the sentences on the board for correction.
4. Ask various students to read the sentences in **Activité 15**.
5. Have students examine each picture in **Activité 16** and respond with a form of **tel(le)**.
6. Remind students that **des** becomes **de** before adjectives that come before the noun (as for images 3 and 7 in **Activité 16**).

16 Je n'ai jamais vu.... 1.2, 1.3

Interpretive Viewing, Presentational Speaking or Writing

Dites que vous n'avez jamais vu une telle chose ou personne.

MODÈLE

Je n'ai jamais vu un tel chœur.

1.

2.

3.

4.

5.

6.

7.

1.2, 2.2

Produits

Youssoupha est un rappeur français d'origine congolaise. Il chante surtout sur des sujets politques et sociaux. Il a chanté avec des rappeurs américains célèbres. Il a reçu un disque platine et un lauréat du meilleur clip pour sa chanson *Les disques de mon père*.

Answers

16 Possible answers:

1. Je n'ai jamais vu une telle équipe/ de tels joueurs.
2. Je n'ai jamais vu une telle liquette.
3. Je n'ai jamais vu de tels tatouages.
4. Je n'ai jamais vu un tel cirque.
5. Je n'ai jamais vu une telle fan.
6. Je n'ai jamais vu une telle coiffure.
7. Je n'ai jamais vu de telles baskets.

Communication

Interpersonal: Paired Practice

Students make up **Devinettes** to ask the class using indefinite adjectives. For example, they might say: **Chaque année, c'est le festival d'Avignon de théâtre en France en juillet**.

Differentiated Learning

Expand

Have students think of things in their lives that were amazing to see. Have them use the format in **Activité 16** to explain what they were and why they were so unusual. Have them present a picture or drawing as an illustration as they share what they wrote with the class. If they cannot think of anything, have them look up images on the internet.

Learning Styles

Visual Learners

Work with visual learners to create a chart summarizing the indefinite adjectives with gender and number changes: **aucun(e)**, **certain(e)**, and **tout(e)**. After creating the chart, make sure to use these forms in a sentence context to reinforce pronunciation and spelling changes.

Resources

WB Workbook 8–10

G & V Practice Games

Answers

Comparaisons

The English indefinite pronouns are *none*, *most*, and *several*.

Reference Desk

Explain that pronouns replace a person or thing previously mentioned. **Aucun(e)**, **un(e) autre**, **tous (toutes) les deux** will agree with the word that was replaced whereas **la plupart**, **plusieurs**, **quelqu'un**, and **quelque chose** are invariable.

Game

Jouons aux cartes!

Each student creates a deck of seven cards for themselves, with an indefinite pronoun written on each card. Then students should sit in groups of three or four. The teacher asks a question ("**Combien de jeunes aiment la musique classique?**"). Students individually come up with a logical answer using one of the pronouns and slap that card down in the middle of the group while shouting the answer ("**Plusieurs!**" or "**Aucun!**"). The first student to slap down the card with an answer takes the round; if the answer is logical, the card stays in the deck in the middle of the group. If it does not make sense, the student must pick up all the cards in the deck in the middle of the group. The first student to get rid of all their cards wins.

Indefinite Pronouns 1.2, 4.1

La plupart des vidéos de chats sur YouTube sont mignonnes.

Remember that a pronoun replaces a noun that has been mentioned before, or that is obvious in the context of the sentence. Many of these pronouns have the same form as their adjective equivalent. Indefinite pronouns refer to people or things without identifying them. Here are some important indefinite pronouns:

aucun(e)… ne (n')	*not one, none*
un(e) autre	*another*
l'un(e)… l'autre	*one… the other*
la plupart	*most*
plusieurs	*several*
quelqu'un, quelque chose	*someone, something*
n'importe qui, n'importe quoi	*anyone, anything*
tous les deux, toutes les deux	*both*

Comparaisons 4.1

What are the indefinite pronouns in this story?

Anna checked her social network to see if there were messages from her friends, but not one had responded to her last post. She knew most were at the game, but several weren't going out tonight.

Tu as déjà mis une vidéo sur YouTube? Oui, **plusieurs**. — *Have you already put a video on YouTube? Yes, several.*

Tous les deux sont dans la vidéo. — *Both are in the video.*

To describe **quelqu'un** or **quelque chose**, use the adjective's masculine singular form preceded by **de**.

J'ai vu **quelqu'un de grand** derrière l'actrice dans cette vidéo. — *I saw someone tall behind the actress in this video.*

Il y avait **quelque chose d'épicé** dans ce plat! — *There was something spicy in this dish!*

Two other indefinite pronouns are **n'importe qui** *(anyone)* and **l'un(e)… l'autre** *(one… the other)*.

N'importe qui pourra voir votre vidéo sur Internet. — *Anyone will be able to see your video on the internet.*

Ils ont deux chats: **l'un** est orange, **l'autre** noir. — *They have two cats: one orange, the other black.*

Essential Instruction

1. Ask for volunteers to answer the **Comparaisons** question.
2. Give the class time to do **Activité 17**. Have students respond orally and then have volunteers put the sentences on the board making sure to note where there is agreement.
3. Have students do **Activité 18** in pairs. Ask them to justify their remarks using **parce que**.

17 Un hit sur YouTube 1.2

Interpretive Reading

Complétez chaque phrase pour résumer l'histoire de la vidéo d'Élodie. Utilisez un mot ou une expression ci-dessous.

aucun(e)... ne (n') **un(e) autre** **la plupart** **plusieurs** **quelqu'un** **quelque chose** **tous les trois**

1. Un garçon, son frère, et leur copain ont chanté au mariage du cousin d'Élodie. ... savaient chanter des gospels.
2. Ils portaient... d'orange ce soir-là.
3. ... des garçons ne portait un costume noir.
4. ... des invités ont aimé le show.
5. ... ados ont vu la vidéo qu'elle a filmée au mariage.
6. ... qui a regardé la vidéo 75 fois est une vraie groupie.
7. Est-ce qu'Élodie mettra... vidéo sur YouTube? Ça reste à voir!

18 Des descriptions 1.1

Interpersonal Speaking

Avec un(e) partenaire, faites des remarques sur les personnes et les choses suivantes en utilisant ***quelqu'un de*** *ou* ***quelque chose de*** *et un adjectif convenable.*

MODÈLE Albert Einstein
A: À mon avis, c'est quelqu'un d'intelligent.
B: Selon moi, c'est quelqu'un d'amusant.

1. conduire sans mettre une ceinture de sécurité
2. Stromae
3. être malade pendant les vacances
4. le président de la France
5. ton ou ta meilleur(e) ami(e)
6. être diplômé(e)
7. le proviseur
8. se présenter pour une interview

Answers

17

1. Tous les trois
2. quelque chose
3. Aucun
4. La plupart
5. Plusieurs
6. Quelqu'un
7. une autre

18 Possible answers:

1. À mon avis, c'est quelque chose d'imprudent.
2. À mon avis, c'est quelqu'un de populaire.
3. À mon avis, c'est quelque chose d'embêtant.
4. À mon avis, c'est quelqu'un d'intéressant.
5. À mon avis, c'est quelqu'un de formidable.
6. À mon avis, c'est quelque chose de nécessaire.
7. À mon avis, c'est quelqu'un d'intelligent.
8. À mon avis, c'est quelque chose d'effrayant.

Game

Concentration

Ask students to write the **Unité 9** vocabulary and adjective list on index cards and make a corresponding card for each with the English translation or a picture on it. Put all cards face down. A student turns over two cards at random. If the cards match, he or she reads both cards and keeps the pair for a point. If the cards do not match, both are put back face down. Whoever makes the most matches wins.

Differentiated Learning

Accelerate

Ask students to write a portrait of a celebrity using **quelqu'un de** + ADJECTIVE. Have them give examples from his or her life and explain why that judgment is valid.

Decelerate

Ask students to write sentences using each pronoun in a sentence. Encourage them to consult the sample sentences in the grammar presentation as a guide.

Resources

Activity 19

Answers

19 Script

1. Vincent a publié toutes les vidéos de ses vacances sur YouTube.
2. J'ai vu quelques messages de mes copains sur mon réseau social.
3. La plupart des parents dans cet immeuble achètent des tablettes pour leurs enfants.
4. Sandrine regarde ses mails chaque jour et ses textos toutes les dix minutes.
5. Rachid et Jean-Pierre parlent de tout et n'importe quoi en ligne.

1. B
2. A
3. E
4. D
5. C

Comparaisons

Some yes (**mon ange**, **mon cœur**, **mon trésor**) and some no (**mon chou**, **mon lapin**, **mon poussin**, **ma puce**).

Communication

Interpersonal: Paired practice

Before doing **Activité 21**, have students work in pairs or small groups to answer these questions: 1) On which social media platform should one write a blog? 2) What should you talk about in your blog? 3) Why would others read your blog? When finished, have groups join another group to share their responses. Finally, discuss as a class.

19 On est branché ! 1.2

Interpretive Listening and Viewing

Écrivez les numéros 1–5 sur votre papier. Écoutez les phrases. Faites correspondre la phrase à une image.

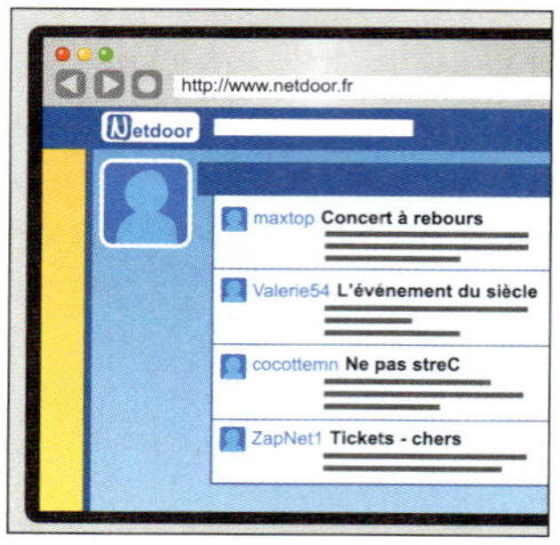

A.

B.

C.

D.

E.

1.2, 4.1

Comparaisons

Il existe de nombreux noms affectueux en français, comme : ma puce (*flea*), mon lapin, mon chou (*cabbage*), mon ange, mon poussin (*baby chick*), mon cœur, mon trésor, etc. Utilise-t-on les mêmes mots en anglais ?

Essential Instruction

1. For **Activité 19**, ask students to describe each of the pictures. Encourage them to invent details of each picture, ascribing a name to the people where relevant, explaining where they are, what they are doing, and why.
2. Have students do the listening comprehension questions. Check their answers.
3. Give students a choice of tasks for **À vous la parole**. Students electing to do **Activité 20** might want to combine their survey of their peers with those they find online. For **Activité 21** divide students according to their interests and have them write a short blog post. Have them share it with other students, asking for their comments and suggestions.

Communiquez!

20 Vidéos en ligne! 1.1, 1.3, 5.1, 5.2

Interpersonal and Presentational Speaking

Avec un(e) partenaire, trouvez une vidéo en français à présenter à la classe. Il peut s'agir d'une vidéo didactique, d'une vidéo musicale, d'une bande-annonce, d'un récit historique ou d'un documentaire—tout ce qui vous intéresse et qui présente un aspect de la culture française que vous avez étudié jusqu'à maintenant. Vous devrez présenter brièvement votre clip vidéo avant de le montrer à la classe et décrire les raisons pour lesquelles vous l'avez choisi. Une fois la vidéo terminée, soyez prêts à répondre aux questions que la classe ou votre professeur vont vous poser!

21 Nos blogs 1.3, 2.1, 5.2

Presentational Writing and Speaking

Comme vous savez, il y a beaucoup de jeunes blogueurs français. Avec vos camarades de classe, faites une liste de blogs qui intéressent les jeunes. Puis, formez des groupes différents pour chaque sujet de blog, par exemple, la musique, les sorties, les voyages et les réseaux sociaux. Préparez une page d'accueil pour le blog de votre groupe. À tour de rôle, écrivez un article pour votre blog et présentez votre page d'accueil à la classe!

22 Réseaux sociaux 1.1, 3.2, 5.1, 5.2

Connectez-vous à un réseau social pour trouver cinq célébrités ou personnalités francophones qui vous intéressent. Recherchez si elles ont un compte sur un réseau public. Si vous les trouvez, suivez-les! Vous devez expliquer vos choix à la classe et partager leurs noms d'utilisateur afin qu'ils puissent les suivre aussi s'ils le souhaitent. Êtes-vous sportif? Trouvez des athlètes! Aimez-vous la musique? Trouvez des musiciens! Aimez-vous cuisiner? Cherchez des chefs français! Vous intéressez-vous à la politique? Trouvez des politiciens français! Les possibilités sont infinies.

Resources

CA Communicative Activities

Share

Answers

20 Presentations will vary.

21 Blogs will vary.

22 Celebrities will vary.

Reference Desk

If you have access to Passport, create a question for your students to share their response to a communicative activity.

Differentiated Learning

Accelerate/Decelerate

Use mixed-ability partners for **Activité 20**. Working as a team strengthens the stronger students' ability to communicate ideas in simplified French and provides practice in a comfortable learning context for weaker students.

Expand

Students who want to do more blogging might consider "Voices of Youth" found on the UNICEF website. According to the website, it brings together young participants from all over the world to exchange views, share experiences, reflect together, and identify common opportunities and challenges.

Pre-AP

Les Misérables

Rencontre avec l'auteur 1.2, 3.1, 5.2

Victor Hugo (1802–1885) est poète, romancier, dramaturge, homme politique et dessinateur. Quand il meurt *(dies)*, le pays lui rend hommage (*honors*) en organisant des funérailles nationales et en l'enterrant au Panthéon. Vous allez lire un extrait des *Misérables*, l'histoire de Jean Valjean, un ancien galérien (*forced labor prisoner*) qui a été emprisonné pour avoir volé du pain pour nourrir la famille affamée (*starving*) de sa sœur et pour avoir essayé de s'évader. La scène se passe en 1815. Juste après avoir été libéré, il se rend dans la ville de Digne où il reçoit l'hospitalité de l'évêque (*bishop*), monseigneur Myriel, qui l'accueille chez lui, lui donne à manger et un lit. Mais durant la nuit, Jean Valjean vole les couverts en argent et part. Dans cet extrait, comment la scène se rapproche-t-elle (*approaches*) d'une scène de pièce de théâtre?

Pré-lecture 1.2

Est-ce que vous avez pardonné à quelqu'un? Était-ce facile ou difficile à faire?

Stratégie de lecture 1.2, 1.3

Characterization. La caractérisation d'un personnage de roman est la description des attributs physiques et moraux de ce dernier. Elle peut être indirecte, c'est-à-dire que l'auteur permet au lecteur de projeter un jugement subjectif sur un personnage, à travers ses paroles, ses pensées, ses gestes, et ses actions, ou de ce qui est dit de lui. La caractérisation directe est une image complète du personnage; le lecteur ne doit rien deviner.

Pour analyser le caractère de monseigneur Myriel, faites une grille comme celle de dessous. Pour chaque adjectif, choisissez le numéro qui exprime *(expresses)* le caractère de l'évêque («5» indique qu'il présente le maximum de cette qualité). Mettez un X dans l'espace blanc approprié. Puis écrivez deux phrases avec chaque adjectif. Dans la première, faites une généralisation fondée sur la grille de son caractère. Dans la deuxième, défendez votre généralisation avec un exemple du roman. À la fin de votre paragraphe, identifiez le type de caractérisation utilisé par Hugo.

	1	2	3	4	5
généreux					
aimable					
religieux					
matérialiste					
rusé					

Resources

Rencontre avec l'auteur

Answers

Rencontre avec l'auteur
Possible answer: Il y a des indications scéniques et les dialogues sont des petites conversations au discours direct.

Pré-lecture
Answers will vary.

Stratégie de lecture
Possible answer: généreux: 5; aimable: 4; religieux: 5; matérialiste: 1; rusé: 4

Culture

Products: Information

1. It is thought that ***Les Misérables*** may have inspired two popular television series. Richard Kimble in *The Fugitive* (1963–1967) was modeled on Jean Valjean. Gerard, whose name sounded like Javert, relentlessly pursued Kimble. ***Les Misérables*** might also be the basis for Dr. Banner in *The Incredible Hulk*, (1978–1982) moving from town to town, being pursued by his own "Javert," journalist Jack McGee.
2. Some interesting facts: 1) ***Les Misérables*** is the source for 48 operas. 2) Victor Hugo wrote what may be the longest sentence written in French in ***Les Misérables***; it is about 800 words long. 3) Victor Hugo liked to write while standing.

Essential Instruction

1. Ask students what they know of Victor Hugo. Can they tell you the basic plot of ***Les Misérables***? Who has seen the play, the musical, or one of several movie versions of the story? Who is their favorite character and why?
2. Listen to the **Rencontre avec l'auteur**.
3. Discuss the question of forgiveness posed in **Pré-lecture**.
4. After reading the extract, students return to **Stratégie de lecture** to do the evaluation.
5. Put regular and irregular **passé simple** verbs on the board and ask students to guess the meanings.
6. Have students copy the irregular **passé simple** verbs in their notebooks and learn to identify them.
7. Play the first part of the extract with students following in their books. Answer the **Pendant la lecture** questions found in the margins.

Outils de lecture 1.2

Le passé simple. Le passé simple est un temps littéraire, utilisé dans l'œuvre de Victor Hugo. Il est important de pouvoir reconnaître les verbes conjugués à ce temps. Les verbes réguliers qui se terminent en **–er** ont les terminaisons suivantes : (**frapper**, *to knock*) **je** frapp**ai**, **tu** frapp**as**, **il/elle/on** frapp**a**, **nous** frapp**âmes**, **vous** frapp**âtes**, **ils/elles** frapp**èrent**. Les verbes réguliers qui se terminent en **–ir** ont les terminaisons suivantes : (**accomplir**, *to accomplish*) **j'**accompl**is**, **tu** accompl**is**, **il/elle/on** accompl**it**, **nous** accompl**îmes**, **vous** accompl**îtes**, **ils/elles** accompl**irent**. Les verbes réguliers qui se terminent en **–re** ont ces terminaisons : (**répondre**, *to respond*) **je** répond**is**, **tu** répond**is**, **il/elle/on** répond**it**, **nous** répond**îmes**, **vous** répond**îtes**, **ils/elles** répond**irent**. Voici quelques verbes irréguliers au passé simple : (**avoir**) **il eut/ils eurent** ; (**être**) **il fut/ils furent** ; (**faire**) **il fit/ils firent**.

Jean Valjean, épisode des chandeliers. Anonyme. Édition d'Eugène Hugues. Circa 1880.

Les Misérables

Le lendemain, monseigneur Myriel déjeunait à cette même table où Jean Valjean s'était assis la veille*. Tout en déjeunant, monseigneur Bienvenu faisait gaîment remarquer à sa sœur qui ne disait rien et à madame Magloire qui grommelait* sourdement qu'il n'est nullement besoin d'une cuiller ni d'une fourchette, même en bois, pour tremper* un morceau de pain dans une tasse de lait.

—Aussi a-t-on ideé ! disait madame Magloire toute seule en allant et venant, recevoir un homme comme cela ! et le loger à côté de soi ! et quel bonheur encore qu'il n'ait fait que voler ! Ah mon Dieu ! cela fait frémir* quand on songe* !

Comme le frère et la sœur allaient se lever de table, on frappa à la porte.

—Entrez, dit l'évêque.

La porte s'ouvrit. Un groupe étrange et violent apparut sur le seuil*. Trois hommes en tenaient un quatrième au collet*. Les trois hommes étaient des gendarmes ; l'autre était Jean Valjean.

Un brigadier de gendarmerie, qui semblait conduire le groupe, était près de la porte. Il entra et s'avança vers l'évêque en faisant le salut militaire.

—Monseigneur…dit-il.

À ce mot Jean Valjean, qui était morne* et semblait abattu*, releva la tête d'un air stupéfait.

—Monseigneur ! murmura-t-il. Ce n'est donc pas le curé* ?

Pendant la lecture
1. Que font l'évêque et sa sœur le lendemain (après le départ de Jean Valjean) ?

Pendant la lecture
2. Qui pense que monseigneur Myriel n'aurait pas dû accueillir Valjean ?

Pendant la lecture
3. Qui est à la porte ?

Pendant la lecture
4. Comment se sent Jean Valjean quand il revoit monseigneur Myriel ?

la veille le soir d'avant ; **grommelait** *muttered* ; **tremper** *to dunk* ; **frémir** *to shudder* ; **quand on songe** quand on y réfléchit ; **seuil** *threshold* ; **en tenaient un quatrième au collet** *had a fourth (man) by the neck* ; **morne** *glum* ; **abattu** *beaten, knocked down* ; **curé** *priest*

Resources

Les Misérables

Answers

Pendant la lecture
1. Ils déjeunent.
2. madame Magloire
3. trois gendarmes et Jean Valjean
4. Il est choqué et se sent mal.

Reference Desk

Although the **passé simple** has practically disappeared from spoken French (note that one last great orator to speak in **passé simple** was Charles de Gaulle), some modern French authors prefer the **passé simple** to the **passé composé** for stylistic reasons or perhaps because it does not bother with changes in the past participle. Because students may encounter this verb tense in a modern novel today, it is essential that they learn to recognize the **passé simple** and substitute the **passé composé** for it as they read.

Expansion

To reinforce the idea that the **passé simple** is the equivalent of the **passé composé**, ask students to list all of the verbs in the **passé simple**, beginning with… **on frappa** continuing to the end of the page. (There are seven.) Have them write the equivalent **passé composé** next to each verb. Correct in class.

Differentiated Learning

Accelerate
Challenge students to write a two-paragraph story in the **passé simple**.

Decelerate
Give students a short list of irregular verbs in the **passé simple** to learn to recognize. Show them the similarities between the past participles and the beginning of many forms of the **passé simple**, for example, **Ils ont eu deux enfants. Ils eurent deux enfants. Elle a su que sa famille était partie**, and **Elle sut que sa famille**….

Multiple Intelligences

Musical-Rhythmic
Have students play the music from the Broadway musical scene between the bishop and Jean Valjean.

Visual-Spatial
Students may want to draw the **décor** of the scene.

Intrapersonal
Have students share examples of poems, novels, plays, and drawings of Victor Hugo.

Answers

Pendant la lecture

5. Il a une bonne raison d'être fâché car Valjean lui a volé ses couverts, mais il n'est pas fâché.
6. Il lui donne des chandeliers d'argent.
7. un honnête homme
8. C'est un homme qui aime Dieu. Il veut que Jean Valjean aime le bien plus que le mal.

Communication

Interpersonal: Cooperative Groups

Divide the class into small groups with group members each taking a role from the scene. Groups do a reading of the scene with volunteers presenting to the class.

(Suite et fin)

—Silence ! dit un gendarme. C'est monseigneur l'évêque.

Cependant monseigneur Bienvenu s'était approché aussi vivement* que son grand âge le lui permettait.

—Ah ! vous voilà ! s'écria-t-il en regardant Jean Valjean. Je suis aise de vous voir. Et bien mais ! je vous avais donné les chandeliers* aussi, qui sont en argent comme le reste et dont vous pourrez bien avoir deux cents francs. Pourquoi ne les avez-vous pas emportés avec vos couverts ?

Jean Valjean ouvrit les yeux et regarda le vénérable évêque avec une expression qu'aucune langue humaine ne pourrait rendre.

—Monseigneur, dit le brigadier de gendarmerie, ce que cet homme disait était donc vrai ? Nous l'avons rencontré. Il allait comme quelqu'un qui s'en va. Nous l'avons arrêté pour voir. Il avait cette argenterie*....

—Et il vous a dit, interrompit l'évêque en souriant, qu'elle lui avait été donnée par un vieux bonhomme de prêtre chez lequel il avait passé la nuit ? Je vois la chose. Et vous l'avez ramené* ici ? C'est une méprise*.

—Comme cela, reprit le brigadier, nous pouvons le laisser aller ?

—Sans doute, répondit l'évêque.

Les gendarmes lâchèrent Jean Valjean qui recula*....

Puis se tournant vers la gendarmerie [*l'évêque dit*] :

—Messieurs, vous pouvez vous retirer*.

Les gendarmes s'éloignèrent*.

Jean Valjean était comme un homme qui va s'évanouir*.

L'évêque s'approcha de lui, et lui dit à voix basse :

—N'oubliez pas, n'oubliez jamais que vous m'avez promis d'employer cet argent à devenir honnête* homme.

Jean Valjean, qui n'avait aucun souvenir d'avoir rien promis, resta interdit*. L'évêque avait appuyé sur ces paroles en les prononçant. Il reprit avec une sorte de solennité :

—Jean Valjean, mon frère, vous n'appartenez* plus au mal, mais au bien. C'est votre âme* que je vous achète ; je la retire aux pensées noires et à l'esprit de perdition, et je la donne à Dieu.

Pendant la lecture
5. Monseigneur Myriel est-il fâché contre Jean Valjean ? Pourquoi (pas) ?

Pendant la lecture
6. Qu'est-ce que l'évêque donne en plus à Valjean ?

Analyse
Pourquoi pensez-vous que Jean Valjean était « comme un homme qui va s'évanouir » ? Faites une liste de plusieurs possibilités, puis dites laquelle est la plus plausible.

Pendant la lecture
7. Qu'est-ce que monseigneur Myriel veut que Valjean devienne ?

Pendant la lecture
8. Pourquoi l'évêque est-il si généreux ?

---

vivement énergiquement ; **chandeliers** *candlesticks* ; **argenterie** objets en argent ; **ramené** *brought* ; **méprise** erreur ; **recula** *withdrew* ; **vous retirer** partir ; **s'éloignèrent** *moved away* ; **s'évanouir** *to faint* ; **honnête** *honest* ; **interdit** *speechless* ; **appartenez** *belong* ; **âme** *soul*

Essential Instruction

1. Continue the recording of the scene among the bishop, Jean Valjean, and the **gendarmes**.
2. Have students identify parts of the reading that they do not understand. Collaborate as a class to respond to their questions.
3. Answer the **Pendant la lecture** questions in the margins.
4. Supplementary questions: What physical descriptions of Jean Valjean describe his emotional state throughout the scene? In what ways was the bishop dishonest? Can a lie be justifiable?
5. Discuss the question in **Post-lecture** as a class. Write the various opinions on the board. Have students copy them in their notebooks as a reference for future compositions.
6. Students answer the questions in **Le monde visuel** in small groups. Bring the groups together to discuss the topic as a class.
7. Play the scene from one of the film versions of the musical *Les Misérables* and compare it to the passage. Two recommended versions are the 1998 film starring Liam Neeson, Geoffrey Rush, Uma Thurman, and Claire Danes, and the 2012 production featuring Hugh Jackman, Anne Hathaway, and Russell Crowe. Have students do tasks 1–3 of **Activités d'expansion**.

Post-lecture 1.2

Pensez-vous que monseigneur Myriel change la vie de Jean Valjean par son acte de générosité? De quelle façon?

Le monde visuel 1.2, 3.1, 5.2

On a assisté à une hausse dramatique des illustrations des livres au 19ème siècle, dûe à l'arrivée de la lithographie et à l'impression offset. La popularité des livres et des histoires ont augmenté avec la sérialisation des magazines populaires et des ouvrages périodiques. La scène illustrée à la page 559 est une reproduction d'une lithographie d'après un dessin original illustrant le roman de Hugo. La lithographie permet la reproduction plus rapide, mais toujours artistique, des dessins, des bois gravés (*woodcuts and wood engravings*) ou de gravures en taille douce (*etchings and engravings*). L'évolution de la lithographie a énormément facilité l'impression des livres illustrés au 19ème siècle. Vous remarquez que plusieurs lignes parallèles se croisent à un angle afin de créér des tons contrastés, ainsi imitant le style d'une gravure (en taille douce). Qualifieriez-vous cette illustration du livre de classique, réaliste, ou impressionniste? Quels sont les deux personnages qui sont au point focal de l'image? Qu'est-ce que la porte ouverte pourrait symboliser pour Jean Valjean?

Activités d'expansion 1.3, 3.1, 3.2, 5.2

Faites les activités suivantes.

1. Écrivez un paragraphe dans lequel vous décrivez monseigneur Myriel et commentez la création de ce personnage par Victor Hugo. Servez-vous des détails de votre organigramme.
2. Lisez un résumé du roman. Finalement, écrivez un paragraphe qui explique votre prédiction dans la question de *Post-lecture*; si vous aviez raison et de quelle manière.

Recherche: les misérables résumé

3. Transformé(e) par la générosité de monseigneur Myriel, vous voulez offrir un don à une fondation. Avec votre partenaire, recherchez des fondations francophones et faites votre choix. Faites une présentation à la classe dans laquelle vous:
   - expliquez le but de votre fondation
   - expliquez comment votre fondation aide les autres, peut-être avec un exemple
   - expliquez pourquoi le travail de cette fondation est important pour vous personnellement

Recherche: fondation brigitte bardot, médecins sans frontières, fondation 30 millions d'amis, fondation abbé pierre, fondation pour l'enfance, fondation groupama, fondation greffe de vie, fondation claude pompidou, fondation d'auteuil, fondation nicolas hulot

4. Recherchez sur Internet des images contemporaines (des éditions du 19ème siècle) qui ont illustré des œuvres de Victor Hugo, ou spécifiquement *Les Misérables*. Choisissez-en deux différentes qui vous plaisent et présentez-les à la classe.

Resources

Pre-test

Leçon Quiz

Answers

Post-lecture
Answers will vary.

Le monde visuel
Possible answer: Cette illustration est réaliste, car elle montre avec détails l'expression et l'interaction des personnages, l'évêque et Jean Valjean. La porte ouverte pourrait symboliser que Jean Valjean est libre de choisir de faire le bien ou le mal, ou que l'évêque lui rend sa liberté.

Activités d'expansion
Activities will vary.

Reference Desk

Before having students discuss **Le monde visuel**, briefly review the differences among **l'art classique**, **réaliste**, and **impressionniste**. Provide examples from each period to reinforce the distinctions among them. Point out to the class that the "revolution" depicted in ***Les Misérables*** is not the French Révolution of 1789, as is commonly thought by the public, but refers rather to the Paris uprising of 1832.

Connections

English Language Arts

Invite an art teacher from your school to come in and talk about different print-making processes–relief (woodcut and wood engraving), intaglio (metal etching and engraving), and planographic (lithography and silkscreen)–and discuss the different techniques and printing surfaces/materials involved. Have the students study a Durer woodcut, a Rembrandt or Goya etching, a lithograph by Degas or Toulouse-Lautrec, and a silkscreen by Warhol.

Differentiated Learning

Accelerate
Ask students to write about a moment in their lives when an act of kindness touched them. Perhaps they were the recipient of an act of kindness or perhaps they were inspired to perform one.

Decelerate
Offer students an opportunity to do well. Ask them to make flash cards of the irregular verbs. Give them an average-boosting quiz where they have to transform a verb in the **passé simple** to the **passé composé**.

French in the Workplace

Schooling and Grading

Students learned that French schools grade on a 20-point scale and use descriptive words (**excellent**, **très bien**, **bien**, **assez bien**, **passable**). The percentile equivalent of the French scale does not accurately represent the grades on the 100-point US scale. Have students imagine that they are applying for a French university or employer and must submit a copy of their transcript. How might they translate it into French in a way that is meaningful to them? Give them three "**Bulletin de notes**" that you found online to use as models, and give them time to interpret them in small groups. What differences do students observe between the US and French grading systems? Do they feel that one is more lax than the other?

Social Justice

European education inclusion policies include free school meals, income support measures, bussing, education priority areas, and inclusion mechanisms in training systems. Have students compare policies by the **ministère de l'Éducation Nationale** with those that have been implemented in their own school or community. Are those policies efficient? What other solutions could be proposed?

Connections

Critical Thinking and Problem Solving, Productivity and Accountability

After doing **Activité 23**, have students search sample questions on the **bac** from prior years. Have them choose a subject and then discuss those questions with a partner. Do they feel the exam is too difficult or too easy (or another level)? Would they be able to respond in English to the exam?

Communiquez!

23 Comment vous préparer pour un examen? 1.1, 1.2, 1.3, 3.2, 4.2, 5.2

Connecting to Collaboration, Information Literacy

Interpersonal Speaking, Interpretive Reading, Presentational Writing

Visitez des sites web qui aident à la préparation du bac. Regardez les guides et les conseils. Avec un partenaire, discutez, puis préparez un guide de six à dix conseils pour les élèves francophones qui doivent préparer de grands examens comme le AP©, le ACT©, ou le SAT©, aux États-Unis.

24 Qui a accès à Internet? 1.1, 1.2, 1.3, 3.2, 4.2, 5.2

Connecting to Information Literacy, Technology Literacy, Global Awareness

Interpersonal Speaking, Interpretive Reading, Presentational Writing and Speaking

L'accès à Internet et l'usage des réseaux sociaux augmentent dans le monde entier. Recherchez les chiffres qui montrent l'évolution de l'internet dans trois pays francophones. Puis, choisissez un pays et faites des graphiques pour indiquer l'usage général (par exemple, quel pourcentage de la population a accès à Internet) et les réseaux sociaux spécifiques (par exemple, les réseaux sociaux les plus populaires). En groupes, échangez vos graphiques. À tour de rôle, présentez vos données (*data*) et répondez aux questions de vos camarades.

25 Une police moderne 1.1, 1.2, 1.3, 3.1, 5.1, 5.2

Connecting to Civic Literacy, Global Awareness

Interpretive Reading, Interpersonal Speaking, Presentational Speaking or Writing

La Police Nationale est une nouvelle institution dans certains pays comme Haïti (formée en 1997), le Congo (1997), le Rwanda (2000), ou d'autres pays d'Afrique (années 1960). Jeunes institutions, ces forces de l'ordre ont des défis uniques, ainsi que des problèmes généraux comme d'autres endroits du monde. En groupe, choisissez un pays et formulez des hypothèses sur la formation d'une jeune police, ses défis uniques, ses problèmes et ses particularités qui font sa force. Puis, consultez un site web pour voir si vous pouvez vérifier vos hypothèses, ou non. Identifiez les défis de la police nationale du pays que vous avez choisi, ses buts, ses points de concentration, son corps (les personnes qui forment la police), ses méthodes utilisées pour renforcer la loi, pour protéger et servir leur peuple. En classe, discutez et comparez les observations de chaque groupe.

Essential Instruction

1. Students take the career preference test in **Activité A**.
2. Have students write a one-paragraph personal reaction to the test results, agreeing or disagreeing with the findings, and stating why.
3. For **Activité B**, students research the **Recherche** in the computer lab to decide whether French (Canadian) or American students have more help online.

Recherche: hippocampus, homework help

Finale

Projets finaux

A Connexions par Internet : Planification de carrière 1.2, 2.1, 3.2, 5.2

Identifiez vos qualifications

Pour choisir une profession, un métier, ou une spécialisation universitaire après le bac, il faut que vous déterminiez vos aspirations et vos ambitions. Mais votre personnalité et vos habitudes jouent aussi un rôle majeur dans votre décision. Passez le test ci-dessous ; cochez (*check*) les descriptions qui correspondent à votre caractère. Puis, faites une liste de cinq professions ou métiers qui correspondent à vos aspirations.

1. Au dernier moment	❏	ou	Ponctuel	❏
2. Curieux	❏	ou	Ordonné	❏
3. Aime l'improvisation	❏	ou	Suit les règles	❏
4. Pas organisé	❏	ou	Organisé	❏
5. Flexible	❏	ou	Structuré	❏
6. Change de point de vue	❏	ou	Décisif	❏
7. Aime découvrir	❏	ou	Aime produire	❏
8. Aime les changements	❏	ou	Résiste aux changements	❏

Résultats :

Si vous avez sélectionné la plupart de vos réponses dans la liste de droite, vous préféreriez un environnement traditionnel, peut-être hiérarchique, où la production et les résultats sont importants et où vous serez apprécié(e) pour votre diligence, votre formation, et votre expérience. Si vous avez sélectionné la plupart de vos réponses dans la liste de gauche, vous préféreriez travailler dans une compagnie qui suit un nouveau modèle, par exemple, une coopérative ; ce genre de compagnie apprécierait votre esprit de camaraderie, votre désir d'évoluer et de proposer de nouvelles idées.

B Communautés en ligne 1.3, 3.2, 4.2, 5.1, 5.2

Aide aux devoirs

Créez une liste de cinq tâches (*tasks*) ou questions que vous avez sur le français (la grammaire, le vocabulaire, l'expression orale, le discours, etc.) ou la littérature francophone (les thèmes, comment écrire une composition, etc.). Faites semblant (*pretend*) d'être un(e) élève en France. Cherchez de l'aide sur Internet pour trouver des réponses. Qu'est-ce que vous avez appris ? D'après vous, qui a le plus de soutien pour faire ses devoirs : les élèves français ou les élèves américains ? Discutez en classe, puis préparez un document pour aider les élèves à écrire et parler français, et publiez-le sur le blog de la classe.

Recherche : aide aux devoirs, sos devoirs, soutien scolaire

Resources

Create

Answers

All activities will vary.

Reference Desk

If you have access to Passport, assign your students an IPA task related to the unit.

Critical Thinking

Analysis

What global impact does technology, such as the internet and social media sites, have on language?

Communication

Presentational: Cooperative Groups

Have students write a skit in which a career counselor interviews a young student about his or her future plans. The student offers some resistance to the counselor's suggestions before finally deciding on a path of study.

Special Needs Students

AD(H)D

This break is an excellent time for students with organizational problems to gather their information for the chapter. Using the chart as a guide, have students look through their notes on cultural information from the chapter.

At-Risk Students

Give students time to study in class. Make sure that they can ask their questions, no matter how basic, in a small study group where they feel comfortable asking for help.

Answers

C Answers will vary.

D

Leçon A : Points de départ Le budget de l'éducation nationale est le plus élevé et représente une dépense de 2 100€ par habitant. Le système éducatif français doit permettre de trouver un travail, donner une culture générale, former la réflexion et l'esprit critique, et réduire des inégalités dans la société.

Leçon A : Points de départ : Perspectives Il n'a pas réussi son bac. Il y a des ressources en ligne comme le site du CNED qui peuvent l'aider.

Leçon A : Du côté des médias Answers will vary.

Leçon B : Rencontres culturelles Karim et Léo se sont fait voler leur ordinateur portable.

Leçon B : Points de départ La gendarmerie et la police assurent la sécurité publique en France.

Leçon B : À vous la parole Pour remplir une déclaration de vol, le déclarant doit donner son nom, son domicile, le numéro de son passeport ou de sa carte d'identité, et une description détaillée des circonstances du vol.

Leçon C : Culture sur place Answers will vary.

Leçon C : À vous la parole Answers will vary.

Leçon C : Lecture thématique Possible answer : On peut encourager la personne à voir que le bien est meilleur que le mal.

Leçon C : Projets finaux Answers will vary.

Reference Desk

1. Students discussed the **Question centrale** at the beginning of the unit. Consider having them work with a partner to refine their list of **défis de la vie contemporaine** discussed in **Unité 9**.
2. The **Faisons le point !** section asks students to respond to the essential question by analyzing various texts in each lesson. The graphic organizer for **Activité D** may be expanded by using the complete chart found in the Copy Masters supplement.

C Passez à l'action ! 1.3, 3.2

Agir contre le harcèlement à l'école

Il est illégal de harceler *(to bully)* à l'école ou au travail. Le gouvernement français a répondu au problème du harcèlement à l'école en créant un site web, « Agir contre le harcèlement à l'école ». Allez sur ce site, puis regardez les vidéos qui y sont proposées. Ensuite, avec plusieurs camarades de classe, écrivez un scénario qui montre une situation de harcèlement à l'école et proposez une solution pour le combattre. Filmez votre scénario, avec tact, et montrez votre vidéo aux autres classes de français de votre école.

Recherche : film les claques, film les injures, film les rumeurs

D Faisons le point ! 1.3

Leçon A **Rencontres culturelles** Quel est un défi pour beaucoup de lycéens français ?	→	Beaucoup de jeunes Français doivent travailler dur pour réussir au bac en terminale.
Leçon A **Points de départ : Le système éducatif français** Quelle dépense du gouvernement français est la plus élevée ? Comment cette dépense représente-t-elle un fardeau pour la nation ? Quels sont les objectifs du système scolaire français ?	→	
Leçon A **Points de départ : Perspectives** Qu'est-ce qui empêche le succès de ce monsieur ? Y a-t-il une solution pour lui ?	→	
Leçon A **Du côté des médias** En quoi les études générales des lycéens en France sont-elles différentes de celles que vous suivez dans votre pays ?	→	
Leçon B **Rencontres culturelles** Qu'est-ce qui s'est passé au café ?	→	
Leçon B **Points de départ : La sécurité publique** Quelles sont les deux forces qui assurent la sécurité publique en France ?	→	

Essential Instruction

1. Before making the video about **harcèlement** in **Activité C** students may want to see corresponding anti-bullying videos online to help them create their own.
2. In small groups, have students collaborate to do **Activité D**. One student acts as secretary to write the various answers.
3. Distribute copies of the graphic organizer, located in the Copy Masters supplement, for **Activité D**.
4. Read through the sentences in **Activité A** (**Évaluation**). Play the recording.
5. Pair students to create the dialogue in **Activité B** (**Évaluation**). After they peer edit and practice, have them present it to the class or film it. Consider using the dialogue as an oral assessment.

Pre-AP

Évaluation

A Évaluation de compréhension auditive 1.2

*Écoutez Marion décrire à un policier le vol auquel elle vient d'assister. Ensuite, dites **oui** ou **non** si elle a aidé avec les catégories ci-dessous.*

1. Description physique
2. Description des cheveux
3. Description d'âge
4. Description psychologique
5. Description des vêtements
6. Description de caractère
7. Description d'actions
8. Description de bijoux

B Évaluation orale 1.1, 3.2

Vous parlez avec un(e) ami(e). Dans votre conversation :

Demandez pourquoi votre ami(e) n'était pas aux cours d'histoire et d'anglais ce matin. Dites que vous avez pris beaucoup de notes, et que vous pouvez les lui passer.

Dites que vous avez séché les cours. Racontez ce qui s'est passé : Vous étiez dans le métro quand vous avez trébuché et votre tablette est tombée. Deux garçons l'ont prise.

Demandez comment étaient les deux garçons.

Décrivez les garçons : âge, taille, cheveux, yeux.

Demandez leur ethnie et ce qu'ils portaient.

Répondez avec une description.

Dites qu'il faut remplir une déclaration de vol.

Dites que vous êtes déjà allé(e) au commissariat de police. Dites que vous avez besoin de votre tablette pour le cours de maths.

Dites que vous pouvez lui prêter la vôtre dont vous n'avez pas besoin aujourd'hui.

Remerciez votre ami(e) et dites qu'il faut fixer un rendez-vous pour lui rendre la tablette.

Donnez l'heure et le lieu du rendez-vous.

Dites que vous verrez votre ami(e) plus tard.

Special Needs Students

Auditory Impairment
Pause the recording in **Activité A** frequently so that students with auditory difficulties can keep up, or administer the listening test separately from the students with no hearing issues.

Resources

- Activity A
- LA Listening Activity *Synthèse*
- Pre-AP Listening *Unité 9*
- Perform

Answers

A Script

Le policier : Bonjour, mademoiselle. Vous avez vu ce qui s'est passé ? Vous pouvez me décrire la scène ?
Marion : Oui, je retournais chez moi quand j'ai vu un homme sortir de la banque avec une arme dans une main et un sac à dos dans l'autre.
Le policier : Pouvez-vous me décrire cet homme ?
Marion : Bien entendu. Il était grand et costaud avec des cheveux raides et courts. Je pense qu'il avait une trentaine d'années. Il semblait être excité par ce qu'il venait de faire.
Le policier : Vous avez fait attention à la façon dont il était vêtu ?
Marion : Il portait un jean délavé et une liquette rouge.
Le policier : Il avait un masque ?
Marion : Non, pas de masque, juste une casquette de baseball bleue. Le sac à dos était rouge.
Le policier : Qu'est-ce qu'il a fait après être sorti de la banque ?
Marion : Il a couru dans la rue et a arrêté la voiture d'un vieux monsieur. Il lui a volé sa voiture.
Le policier : Merci pour toutes ces informations, mademoiselle. Où puis-je vous contacter si j'ai plus de questions ?
Marion : Vous pouvez m'envoyer un texto au 06.25.35.12 ou vous pouvez m'envoyer un mail.
Le policier : Merci de votre aide et bonne journée.

1. oui
2. oui
3. oui
4. oui
5. oui
6. oui
7. oui
8. non

B Conversations will vary.

Answers

C Answers will vary.
D Answers will vary.
E Descriptions will vary.
F Illustrations will vary.

Reference Desk

If you have access to Passport, assign a task to evaluate your students' oral proficiency.

Communication

Interpersonal: Paired practice

To practice the dialogue in **Activité B**, have students prepare both roles of the conversation. Place the students with a partner to practice. Set a timer and when time is called, tell the students to switch roles. When you call time a second time have the students switch partners and follow the same procedure to practice both parts.

Expansion

Have students write a newspaper article about the robbery shown in **Activité E**. Encourage them to make up details to add interest to the article, for example, who was robbed, and where were they during the robbery?

C Évaluation culturelle 1.3, 2.1, 3.1, 3.2, 4.2, 5.1

Vous allez comparer les cultures francophones à votre culture. Vous aurez peut-être besoin de faire des recherches sur la culture américaine.

1. **Le système éducatif en France**
Dites comment les Français veulent réformer le système éducatif en France. Puis, parlez des réformes que vous et vos amis désirez voir dans le système éducatif américain.
2. **Le bac**
Est-ce que le bac marche bien pour les jeunes Français ? Justifiez votre réponse avec des statistiques. Est-ce que vous devez passer un examen à la fin du lycée ? Donnez des arguments pour et contre.
3. **La sécurité publique**
Dites de quoi s'occupent la police nationale et la police municipale en France. Puis, faites une liste d'agences qui s'occupent de la sécurité fédérale, puis au niveau de l'état, de la ville, et de la nation aux États-Unis.
4. **Les chiffres de la délinquance**
Comparez les chiffres de la délinquance en France et aux États-Unis et formez des généralisations qui expliquent les différences.
5. **Internet et les réseaux sociaux**
De quelles façons les ados français sont-ils branchés ? Que pensez-vous des sites Internet français ? Est-ce une bonne façon d'améliorer votre français ? Pourquoi (pas) ?

D Évaluation écrite 1.3

Imaginez que vous allez bientôt passer le bac. Parlez de vos sentiments et dites pourquoi vous les ressentez.

E Évaluation visuelle 1.2, 1.3

*Décrivez les cambrioleurs (*burglars*) et le crime. Répondez à ces questions : Où ? Quand ? Qui ? Quoi ?*

F Évaluation compréhensive 1.3, 2.1, 3.1

Créez six illustrations cadrées qui montrent comment les jeunes se servent d'Internet et des produits numériques dans leur scolarisation ou dans leurs loisirs. Si vous préférez, vous pouvez parler de votre expérience personnelle.

Essential Instruction

1. Briefly discuss American culture in relation to the five different categories given in **Activité C**. Then ask students to write their answers.
2. Give students time in class to do **Activité D**. Students might want to write their response as a blog, letter, or an e-mail. Ask students to volunteer to read their response.
3. Have students use a graphic organizer of their choice to jot down ideas before doing **Activité E**.
4. For **Activité F**, students can use a storyboard to illustrate and make captions about how the internet and technology impact their studies and their free time.

Vocabulaire de l'Unité 9

à: à carreaux plaid *B*; **à part** aside from *A*; **à pois** polka-dot *B*; **à rayures** striped *B*
accablé(e) overwhelmed *C*
africain(e) African *B*
s' **apercevoir (de)** to notice *B*
s' **approcher** to come closer *B*
arriver to happen *A*
asiatique Asian *B*
attristé(e) sad *A*
auparavant before *A*
le **bac (baccalauréat)** French high school qualification exam and diploma *A*
la **bagarre** fight *A*
blanc: le blanc des yeux eye to eye *B*
bosser to work *[inform.]* *A*
bouclé(e) wavy *[hair]* *B*
bref in short *C*
le **buzz** buzz *C*
chauve bald *B*
un **chemisier** blouse *B*
un **chœur** choir *C*
choqué(e) shocked *C*
une **cinquantaine: d'une cinquantaine d'années** in one's fifties *B*
les **(mauvais) commentaires (m.)** comments (gossip) *A*
le **commissariat** police station *B*
complètement completely *C*
costaud(e) stocky *B*
court(e) short *[hair]* *B*
craquer to go wild *C*
se **déchaîner** to get wild *C*
une **déclaration de vol** report of a theft *B*
découragé(e) discouraged *A*
les **défis (m.)** challenges *A*
délavé(e) washed out *C*
s' **effondrer** to collapse *A*; **s'effondrer de fatigue** to collapse from exhaustion *A*
encouragé(e) encouraged *A*
les **ennuis (m.)** trouble *A*
face à faced with *A*
la **façon** in the manner of *B*
se **faire: se faire arrêter** to get arrested *A*; **se faire bousculer** to get knocked into *A*
fier, fière proud *A*
filmer to film *C*
flirter to flirt *B*
frisé(e) curly *[hair]* *B*
frustré(e) frustrated *C*
le **gospel** gospel *C*
la **grêle** hail *A*
un(e) **groupie** fan *C*
honteux, honteuse ashamed *A*
incapable incapable *A*
interviewer to interview *C*
un **lâcheur, une lâcheuse** flake, unreliable person *[inform.]* *A*
le leur, la leur theirs *B*
une **liquette** shirt *[inform.]* *C*
maigre skinny *B*
méditerranéen(ne) Mediterranean *B*
le mien, la mienne mine *B*
mi-long, mi-longue shoulder-length *[hair]* *B*
mince thin *B*
musclé(e) muscular *B*
n'importe: n'importe quel, quelle just any *C*; **n'importe qui** anyone *C*
le nôtre, la nôtre ours *B*
paniqué(e) panicky *A*
par: par la suite consequently *C*
photogénique photogenic *C*
la **plupart de** most *C*
la **priorité** priority *A*
une **quarantaine: d'une quarantaine d'années** in one's forties *B*
raide straight *[hair]* *B*
une **réaction** reaction *C*
un **récit** account *A*
remplir to fill out *B*
se **rendre compte (de)** to realize *B*
ressentir to feel *A*
se **retrouver (sur)** to appear (on) *C*
rien nothing *B*
scandinave Scandinavian *B*
sécher to skip class *[inform.]* *A*
se **sentir** to feel *A*
seul(e) alone, lonely *C*
un **show** show *C*
le sien, la sienne his, hers *B*
surexcité(e) overexcited *C*
surveiller to keep an eye on *B*
le **talent** talent *C*
un **tel, une telle** such a *C*
tétanisé(e) paralyzed *A*
la **tête** look *B*; **pas la tête à** not the type to *B*
le tien, la tienne yours *B*
tourmenter to torment *A*
tout(e): tout d'un coup all of a sudden *B*
trébucher to stumble *A*
une **trentaine: d'une trentaine d'années** in one's thirties *B*
un **type** guy *B*
l' **un(e)... l'autre** the one... the other *C*
vêtu(e) de dressed in *B*
une **vingtaine: d'une vingtaine d'années** in one's twenties *B*
vintage vintage *B*
visible visible *B*
voler to steal *B*
un **voleur** thief *B*
le vôtre, la vôtre yours *B*

Resources

FC Flash Cards
Rendez-vous à Nice! Documentaire 5
Pre-T Listening Pre-test D
T *Unité 9* Test

Reference Desk

nouvelle orthographe **se déchainer**

Game

Allez on montre!

Divide students into groups of four or five. Give one student, the dealer, a pile of cards with the English translation of vocabulary words written on them. The other students should each draw a grid with nine places on a sheet of plain white paper. The dealer reveals the first word, and the other students write its French translation in the first square and turn their paper face down. When everyone is done, the dealer says, **"Allez on montre!"** All students turn their papers face up, and the dealer checks the answers. Each student with a correct answer receives a point. When all nine squares have been filled in, the student with the most points wins.

Learning Styles

Visual Learners
Students benefit from associating the vocabulary words in the context of the lessons and associating images with each word or term.

Auditory Learners
These students would benefit from hearing the recording of the words or saying them aloud.

Kinesthetic Learners
These students may tell you that they have to write words down to learn them.

Special Needs Students

Dyslexia
Students with dyslexia may be overwhelmed when they see the whole vocabulary list in one place. Help them divide the list into categories and identify the words they already know. Flash cards will also be useful to them, as they present the words one at a time.

Linguistically Challenged
Give students a prepared template for **Activité F** with three or four squares rather than six. Help them focus on the written aspect of the assignment before adding their drawings.

Reference Desk

1. Former Minister of Foreign Affairs, Hubert Védrine, said of the Franco-American relationship that the French are "friends and allies, but not aligned" with US economic values.
   France and the United States, while not economically co-dependent, greatly benefit from economic cooperation with each other:
   –Trade in goods and services was more than $120 billion in 2016.
   –The French invested $251 billion in the United States in 2015; the United States invested $80 billion in France.
   –French companies employ 575,000 people in the United States; US companies employ 450,000 in France.
   –Energy and aeronautics are the leading sectors in French-American economic exchange.
   –Texas exports more goods to France than any other state; California imports more goods from France than any other state.
   –In 2016, French and US companies drafted an "Advanced Manufacturing Action Plan" focusing on economic and industrial collaboration in the development of self-driving cars, 3D printers, and the Internet of Things. (sources: Eurostat; franceintheus.org)
2. The photo on the unit opener is of the modern business district **la Défense** in Paris.

Culture

Products: Activity

Ask students to guess how much Americans spent on luxury items in each of the last five years. Has there been a change?

Unité 10 La culture des affaires

Essential Instruction

1. Ask students to name brands of French luxury products they know about. What kind of products are they? Cosmetics? Clothing? Wine?
2. If French students were asked to name American luxury products, what might they mention?
3. The **Question centrale** suggests that the products and services of a country's economy are a window into its culture. Ask students to keep this in mind as they work their way through the chapter to see if that statement is true.
4. Explain that in **Unité 10**, students are going to study how the French and American economies are unique, and yet are cooperative and mutually beneficial in this era of globalization.
5. Ask students to read the **Contract de l'élève** to gain an overview of what they are going to learn.

Question centrale

Qu'apprend-on de la culture d'un pays en étudiant son économie ?

À savoir

Dans le secteur mondial de produits de luxe, 40% des marques mondiales sont des marques françaises. Ce secteur rapporte à la France 40 milliards d'euros par an.

Citation

« Dans les affaires, l'esprit de décision va de pair avec le succès. »

In business, decision-making goes hand in hand with success.

–Claire France (1927–), écrivain canadien

Conseil pratique

Begin to consider seriously how and when you plan to use your French in your life. Let those goals drive the skills and vocabulary you spend the most time on.

Quel sport pratique Tigran?

Comment s'appelle ce fabricant français?

Contrat de l'élève

Leçon A I will be able to:

- say where an item was made and express what I feared about something.
- discuss globalization and French luxury exports.

Leçon B I will be able to:

- ask how long someone has been in a certain place and express my desire to get away.
- discuss French trade competitiveness, French-US trade, and manners in the French business environment.

Leçon C I will be able to:

- describe adaptability.
- discuss French business organization and the history of marketing in France.

Answers

Possible choices for the video question are:

A. la gymnastique
B. la course cycliste
C. le jujitsu
D. la danse

Correct answer: C

The answer to the culture question is: **l'entreprise Michelin**. The answer can be found in **Points de départ**, **Leçon B**.

Critical Thinking

Analysis

The title of **Unité 10** is **La culture des affaires** (*the culture of business*). Are the words "culture" and "business" incompatible, or is this an apt choice of wording?

Differentiated Learning

Accelerate

Have students write a short composition defending or disagreeing with the **Citation**, justifying their opinion with supporting examples.

Decelerate

Have students go online or to a local department store and make a list of the French products that they find in the cosmetic and clothing departments.

Multiple Intelligences

Mathematical-Logical

Ask students to compare the statistics in **À savoir** with the corresponding values in the United States.

Resources

- *Vocabulaire actif*
- eVisual
- Workbook 1–4
- Flash Cards
- Listening Activities 1–2
- G & V Practice Games

Reference Desk

Remind students that **le champagne** is the beverage, and **la Champagne** is the province. Champagne is served in a glass called **une coupe**, whereas wine is served in **un verre à vin**.

Culture

Products: Information

The basic categories of perfume listed from the most to the least expensive are **le parfum**, **l'eau de parfum**, **l'eau de toilette**, and **l'eau de cologne**. The price increases as the concentration of essential fragrances and oils increases. As a rule of thumb, **le parfum** contains 15–40% essential oils, **l'eau de parfum** 7–15%, **l'eau de toilette** 4–8%, and **l'eau de cologne** 3–5%. Several famous French perfume producers are **Lanvin**, **Dior**, and **Jean Patou**.

Leçon A Vocabulaire actif

Les produits et où ils sont fabriqués 1.2, 3.1, 4.2, 5.2

Où une grande partie des produits du commerce mondial sont fabriqués

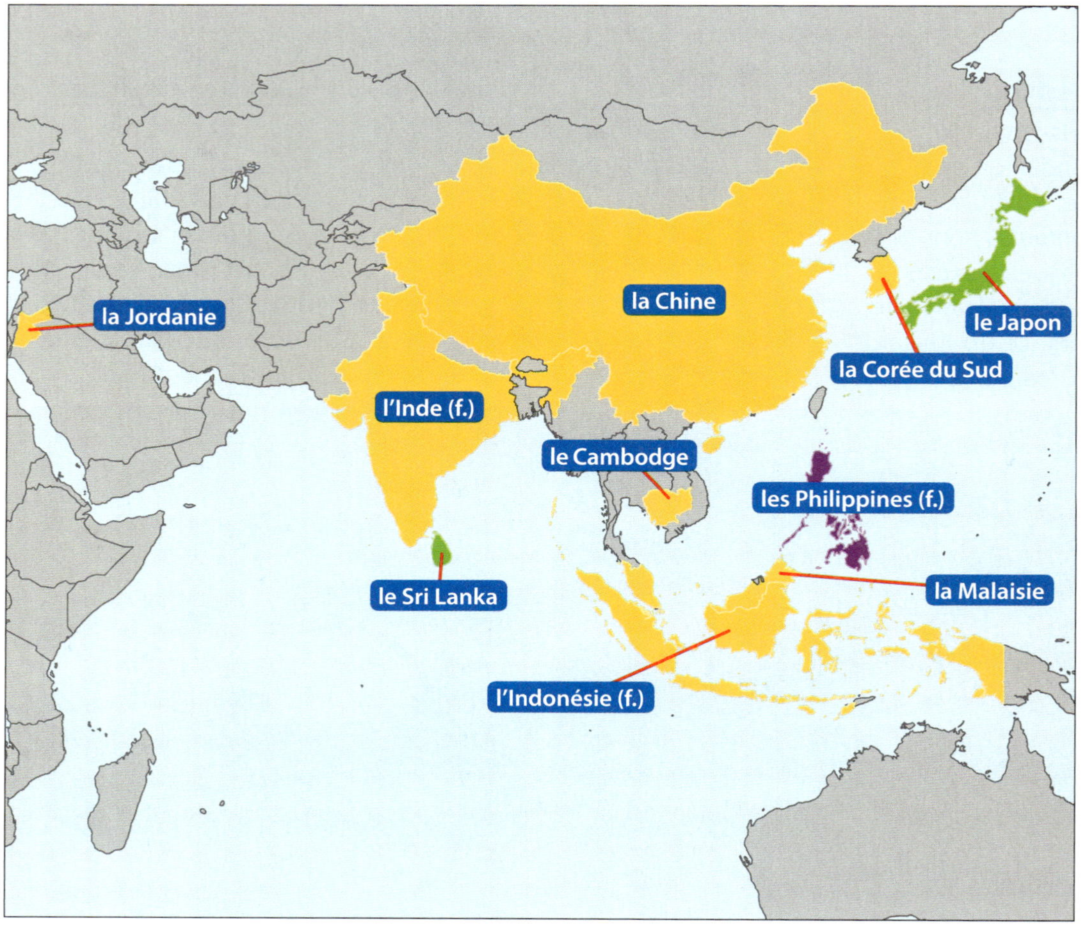

Un produit fabriqué....	
en	Chine, Indonésie, Inde, Jordanie, Corée du Sud, Malaisie
au	Cambodge, Canada, Mexique, Sri Lanka, Japon, Honduras
aux	Philippines, États-Unis

Essential Instruction

1. Display the names of the countries listed under **un produit fabriqué** on the board in random order. Ask students how to say "in" for each country to see if they remember how to use **en**, **au**, and **aux**.
2. Have students listen to **Pour la conversation** twice and repeat the sentences the second time.
3. Have students copy the vocabulary from **Et si je voulais dire...?** into their notebooks.
4. Say the names of the **produits de luxe** and **les marques**. Have students repeat them.
5. It is important that students be aware that the "t" in Moët and the "s" in Hermès are pronounced, since they are foreign names and therefore the silent last consonant French rule does not apply.

Les grandes **marques** françaises des produits de luxe 1.2, 2.2, 3.1, 4.2, 5.2

Les parfums (pour femmes, pour hommes)

Chanel, Dior, Givenchy, Guerlain, Lancôme, Jean Patou, Nina Ricci, Yves Saint Laurent

Les produits de beauté (crème pour **la peau**, mascara)

Caudalie, Chanel, Clarins, Dior, Givenchy, Estée Lauder, L'Oréal, Roc, Yves Rocher, Yves Saint Laurent

La joaillerie (bracelets, colliers, bagues)

Boucheron, Cartier, Dior, Piaget, Van Cleef & Arpels

Les montres

Breguet, Cartier, Dior, Hermès, Hublot, Jaeger-LeCoultre, Piaget

La mode (la haute couture)

Balmain, Chanel, Chloé, Dior, Givenchy, Hermès, Lanvin, Nina Ricci, Yves Saint Laurent, Louis Vuitton

La maroquinerie (bagages, sacs à main, chaussures)

Dior, Goyard, Hermès, Longchamp, Christian Louboutin, Repetto, Roger Vivier, Louis Vuitton, J.M. Weston

La faïence et la porcelaine (vases, **figurines**)

Deshoulières, Gien, HB-Henriot, Limoges, Quimper, Sèvres

Les arts de la table (couverts, cristallerie, orfèvrerie, coutellerie, verrerie, vaisselle, etc.)

Baccarat, Christofle, Lalique, Opinel

Les produits gastronomiques (pâté de foie gras, saucisson, produits **laitiers**, les pâtisseries, les chocolats)

Dalloyau, Fauchon, Hediard, Pierre Hermé, Ladurée, Lafayette Gourmet, La Grande Épicerie, Le Bon Marché, Lenôtre

Mot-clé

Marque vient du normand *merc* (1119) apparenté à l'ancien norrois *merki* qui vient lui-même du germanique qui a donné *marcher*, *marche*. Le mot reste proche de son sens original de signe apposé sur un objet pour le rendre reconnaissable. C'est à partir de la moitié du 17ème siècle qu'il s'applique à une pratique professionnelle. Cherchez ces expressions en ligne et expliquez ce qu'elles veulent dire :

C'est son image de marque. C'est une marque blanche. Elle a trouvé ses marques.

Pour la conversation 1.1, 1.2

How do I say where an item was made?

» Il a été fabriqué en Malaisie.

It was made in Malaysia.

How do I express what I was afraid of?

» **C'est bien** ce que je craignais.

That's exactly what I was afraid of.

Et si je voulais dire... ?

un bijou-fantaisie	*costume jewelry*
le caviar	*caviar*
une cravate en soie	*silk tie*
de la cam, du toc [inform.]	*fake or imitation*

Resources

Pour la conversation
Et si je voulais dire... ?

Answers

Mot-clé
It is his own image, his identity. It's a label for distribution.; She found her identity.

Reference Desk

Le foie gras (*duck* or *goose liver*) is served several ways: sautéed whole, as a smooth paste, or in a mousse. **Le pâté de foie gras** is a less expensive liver paste that contains liver as a base, but also other spices and ingredients may be added. **La foi** means *faith*, **le foie** means *liver*, **le foie gras** is the food product. If you hear **une crise de foi(e)** out of context you would not know if it refers to a religious crisis or a liver flare-up.

Critical Thinking

Analysis
Ask students to research the ban that was imposed on selling **foie gras**, notably in the state of California and the city of Chicago. Why was this ban enforced? Do they agree or disagree?

Differentiated Learning

Accelerate
Ask students to research and explain in French the origins of the names Moët and Hermès. (The founders: Moët is of Dutch origin and Hermès is of German origin)

Decelerate
Have students research labels of French luxury products and find corresponding American brands.

Multiple Intelligences

Visual-Spatial
Have students make facsimiles of the listed luxury products' logos. Have them design their own logo for a luxury product and explain it in French.

Musical-Rhythmic
Encourage students to search online and find music used to advertise these luxury items. Have them explain why they think each selection was made and why it is effective and/or appealing to the audience.

Resources

Activity 1

Answers

1

1. Elle est en train de voyager.
2. Son oncle et sa tante l'accompagnent.
3. Elle est à Paris.
4. Elle ira en Chine, au Japon, et aux Philippines.
5. En Amérique centrale, elle ira au Honduras et au Mexique.
6. Elle connaît les marques Louis Vuitton, Hublot, Givenchy et Cartier.
7. Elle est serveuse.

2

1. Cette tablette a été fabriquée au Japon.
2. Ces sandales ont été fabriquées aux Philippines.
3. Cet ensemble a été fabriqué en Malaisie.
4. Cette voiture a été fabriquée en Corée du Sud.
5. Ce sac à main a été fabriqué en Jordanie.
6. Cette veste a été fabriquée au Sri Lanka.
7. Ce thé a été fabriqué en Indonésie.
8. Ce collier a été fabriqué en Inde.
9. Ce bracelet a été fabriqué au Cambodge.

Communication

Interpersonal: Paired Practice

Student A is in a large department store and would like to buy a gift for his or her mother. Student B plays the role of the salesperson offering suggestions for selecting French luxury items. Student A would like to see a large selection before making a purchase.

Expansion

After doing **Activité 2**, pair students and ask them to find the top export product(s) of each country mentioned on the map, and compare their findings with the top export product(s) in the United States. Discuss in class the relationship between the economy and geographical (or historical) elements.

1 Céline fait le tour du monde 1.2, 2.1, 2.2, 3.1

Interpretive Reading

Lisez le blog de Céline.

Mon réseau social

Recherche

Exprimez-vous

Céline Boura
Afficher mon profil

Fil d'actualités
Messages (1)
Événements (7)
Photos
Amis

Salut, tout le monde ! Où suis-je ? Dans la capitale de la France !

Quand mon oncle et ma tante m'ont proposé un voyage autour du monde, comment aurais-je pu résister ? Nous sommes passés à Paris. Ma tante m'a emmenée dans plusieurs boutiques et elle m'a acheté un sac à main Louis Vuitton, une montre Hublot, du parfum Givenchy, et un collier en perles Cartier. On part pour l'Asie demain. On va d'abord en Chine, puis au Japon, et finalement aux Philippines. Après ça on va au Honduras et au Mexique avant de rentrer à Montréal. J'ai l'impression d'être une princesse, mais bientôt ma vie réelle de serveuse et étudiante recommencera.

1. Qu'est-ce que Céline est en train de faire ?
2. Qui l'accompagne ?
3. Où est-elle maintenant ?
4. Elle ira dans quels pays d'Asie ?
5. Où ira-t-elle en Amérique centrale ?
6. Céline connaît quelles marques françaises après avoir fait du shopping avec sa tante ?
7. Quel métier Céline fait-elle pendant qu'elle fait ses études ?

Connexions 1.2, 3.1

Algèbre

Visitez les sites des marques mentionnées dans l'activité 1, puis faites le calcul du coût de l'ensemble des cadeaux offerts par la tante.

2 Le lieu de fabrication 1.2, 1.3, 3.1

Interpretive Viewing, Presentational Speaking or Writing

Indiquez le pays de fabrication de chaque produit.

MODÈLE ce portable (**D**)
Ce portable a été fabriqué en Chine.

1. cette tablette (**F**)
2. ces sandales (**G**)
3. cet ensemble (**J**)
4. cette voiture (**E**)
5. ce sac à main (**A**)
6. cette veste (**C**)
7. ce thé (**H**)
8. ce collier (**B**)
9. ce bracelet (**I**)

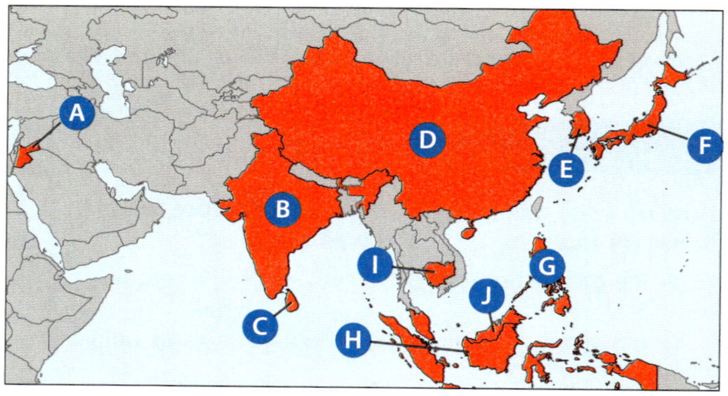

Essential Instruction

1. Students read or listen to **Activité 1** and answer the questions.
2. Have students do **Activité 2** orally and in writing, paying attention to the agreement of the past participle.
3. Students do **Activité 3** in partners. A brand name might be used twice. Dior makes cosmetics, clothing, and handbags, for example.
4. Play **Activité 4**, pausing after each statement. If false, ask students to correct it.
5. Have students listen to **Activité 5** and write short answers. Put sample answers on the board reminding students that the answers will vary.
6. Allot time for students to prepare their answers for **Activité 6**. Have them circulate to ask classmates these questions. They should note the responses on a piece of paper. Debrief the class, making a summary of their preferences for questions 1–5.

3 Fabriqué en France 1.2, 2.2, 3.1, 4.2, 5.2

Interpretive Reading

Dites à quelle marque vous associez chaque produit de luxe français. Choisissez parmi les suivantes.

Boucheron	Vuitton	Clarins	Christofle	Fauchon	Hublot	Sèvres	Roc
Louboutin	Hermès	Cartier	Lancôme	Guerlain	Limoges	Ladurée	

MODÈLE le maquillage
J'associe le maquillage à la marque Clarins.

1. la crème pour la peau
2. les montres
3. la haute couture
4. la maroquinerie
5. les arts de la table
6. la faïence
7. le parfum
8. les pâtisseries
9. la joaillerie

On recycle!

Avec un partenaire, comparez des marques de luxe. Lesquelles sont vos préférées, et pourquoi? Comparez et contrastez trois marques différentes à tour de rôle.

MODÈLE

A: J'adore les sacs Louis Vuitton, ils sont tellement plus beaux que ceux de Marc Jacobs.

B: Moi, je préfère les montres Cartier à celles de Tag, elles sont beaucoup plus chic!

4 Fabriqué au Maroc 1.2, 2.1, 2.2

Interpretive Listening

*Écrivez les numéros 1–8. Écoutez David et sa maman discuter des produits qu'ils achètent au Maroc. Ensuite, dites si les phrases que vous entendez sont vraies (**V**) ou fausses (**F**).*

5 Les produits de luxe 1.2, 2.2

Interpretive Listening

Écrivez les numéros 1–8 sur votre papier. Écoutez Rachida et Caroline discuter de l'industrie de luxe française. Ensuite, écrivez une réponse brève pour chaque question que vous entendez.

6 Questions personnelles 1.1, 2.1, 2.2, 3.1

Interpersonal Speaking

Répondez aux questions avec un partenaire.

1. Quelle marque préfères-tu pour ces produits: montres, produits de beauté, maroquinerie, mode, produits électroniques?
2. Où voudrais-tu voyager en Asie?
3. Es-tu jamais allé(e) au Mexique? Si oui, où? Pour combien de temps?
4. Est-ce que tu mets du parfum avant de sortir le weekend? Si oui, quel parfum préfères-tu?
5. Où est-ce que ta montre a été fabriquée?

Resources

Activities 4–5

Answers

3 Students choose one:

1. la crème pour la peau / Clarins, Roc
2. les montres / Cartier, Hublot
3. la haute couture / Vuitton, Hermès
4. la maroquinerie / Louboutin, Vuitton
5. les arts de la table / Baccarat, Christofle
6. la faïence / Limoges, Sèvres
7. le parfum / Guerlain, Lancôme
8. les pâtisseries / Fauchon, Ladurée
9. la joaillerie / Boucheron, Cartier

4 Script

David: Alors, qu'est-ce que tu as trouvé chez ce marchand marocain?
Maman: J'ai trouvé des lunettes Dior pour ta tante et une montre Cartier pour ta grand-mère.
David: Maman, tu sais que ce sont des faux. Regarde, tes lunettes ont été fabriquées au Vietnam et ta montre en Chine, bien sûr.
Maman: C'est bien ce que je craignais, mais ta grand-mère, elle va pouvoir impressionner ses copines, quand même.
David: Tu sais, au Maroc, il faut acheter des produits locaux. Les parfums, la maroquinerie de luxe et les bijoux sont tous des faux et on risque d'avoir des problèmes avec les douanes françaises.
Maman: Alors, le tee-shirt Nike que j'ai acheté à ton père, c'est un faux aussi?
David: Je ne sais pas. Beaucoup de produits marocains sont fabriqués en Chine ou au Mexique alors…. Regarde, tu peux acheter de beaux sacs à main en cuir ici ou une ceinture pour oncle Édouard.
Maman: Oui, et bien, mais un sac à main Vuitton, ce serait plus chic!
David: Maman! Quelle snob tu es!

1. David pense que sa mère est snob.
2. Beaucoup de produits marocains sont fabriqués en Chine et au Mexique.
3. Les lunettes Dior que la maman de David a achetées ont été fabriquées en Asie.
4. David recommande à sa mère d'acheter les produits locaux au Maroc.
5. La maman de David a acheté une vraie montre Cartier pour la grand-mère.
6. Les produits de luxe pas chers au Maroc sont en général des faux.
7. La mère de David craint que le tee-shirt Nike du père de David soit un faux.
8. David recommande que sa mère achète une ceinture en cuir pour l'oncle Édouard.

1. V; 2. V; 3. V; 4. V; 5. F; 6. V; 7. V; 8. V

(*Activity 5 continued on p. 578*)

6 Answers will vary.

Differentiated Learning

Adapt

Students select **une marque de luxe** to research. Have them make a poster featuring a brief history, famous products, annual income, where their products are manufactured, and the location of international headquarters. They present their findings to the class. Consider displaying the posters in the classroom.

Accelerate/Decelerate

Consider having students work in mixed-level pairs to do **Activité 3**. Begin with partners reviewing the vocabulary words listed. Next, ask them to search each of the luxury brand names mentioned. Connecting a visual of the brand logo and packaging to the product reinforces meaning of the term.

Resources

- Dialogue Activity 7
- Dialogue Video
- WB Workbook 5

Answers

7

1. Élodie cherche un cadeau « made in France » pour sa correspondante.
2. D'abord, elle considère quelque chose de fabriqué en Malaisie.
3. Elle décide d'acheter quelque chose de typiquement français.
4. Elle mentionne des parfums, des produits de beauté, des bijoux, des produits alimentaires, des produits de mode et de maroquinerie.
5. Finalement, elle va lui envoyer un foulard fabriqué en France.

Reference Desk

1. Students may not know the meaning of these expressions: **l'embarras du choix** (*a multitude of choices*); **au-dessus** (*above*); **en dessous** (*below*). **Ci-dessus** and **ci-dessous** (*above* and *below*) refer to a written piece where things are cited above or below a certain sentence.
2. **CPCH** (**Collier de perles, carré Hermès**) or **BCBG** (**bon chic, bon genre**) refer to the style of a young upper-middle-class man or woman. Many students may recognize **BCBG** since it is a popular women's clothing brand with stores across the United States. A **NAP** (**Neuilly-Auteuil-Passy**) is someone who lives in some of the most expensive areas in Paris and has **le look**.

Connections

Music

"**Adieu foulard, adieu madras**" is a song from Martinique, believed to have been written in 1769, about a young woman who says good-bye to her "**doudou**," the local word for sweetheart, as he departs for the sea. Consider using the lyrics as a cloze test and complete it in pairs or together as a class.

Rencontres culturelles

Un cadeau typiquement français

1.2, 4.2, 5.1, 5.2

Élodie fait du shopping avec son amie Coralie.

Coralie : Tu ne vas pas offrir ça à ta correspondante américaine ! Tu as regardé, ce n'est même pas du « made in France ». Il a été fabriqué en Malaisie*.
Élodie : Tu as raison. Il faut que je lui trouve quelque chose de typiquement français !
Coralie : Tu as quand même le choix entre un parfum, des produits de beauté, un bijou....
Élodie : Tu peux ajouter aussi les produits alimentaires, la mode, et la maroquinerie, et on aura fait le tour !
Coralie : Finalement, tu as l'embarras du choix.
Élodie : C'est bien ce que je craignais... mais tu connais les prix de tous ces produits de luxe ?
Coralie : Tu veux dire que tu crois que Chanel, Cartier, Dior, Gaultier, Vuitton, Hermès... c'est au-dessus de nos moyens ?
Élodie : Je ne crois pas, j'en suis sûre ! En tout cas, moi, je n'ai pas les moyens de lui acheter ça.
Coralie : Reste l'imagination : moins convenu, moins marqué, et plus original.
Élodie : Je crois que j'ai trouvé.... Viens, on y va !
Coralie : Où ?
Élodie : Tu verras... pourquoi pas un joli foulard en soie fabriqué ici ?

*Je parle bien

The word **Malaisie** looks difficult to pronounce because it has many vowels. Remember to break it down into syllables: **Ma-lai-sie**, as in *ma-lay-zi*. Do not pronounce the final "e."

Analyse

Why does Coralie not like the gift Élodie picked? Using supportive details from the text, what tells you that Élodie understood her unspoken suggestion? What is, in your opinion, her reason for doing so? Do you agree?

7 Un cadeau typiquement français

1.2, 2.2, 3.1

Répondez aux questions.

1. Pour qui est-ce qu'Élodie cherche un cadeau « made in France » ?
2. D'abord, Élodie considère quelque chose de fabriqué en quel pays ?
3. Elle décide d'acheter quoi ?
4. Quelles sortes de produits français mentionne-t-elle ?
5. Finalement, qu'est-ce qu'Élodie va envoyer à sa correspondante américaine ?

Essential Instruction

1. Have students look at the photo of Élodie and Coralie. Where are they, and what might they be doing?
2. After viewing the video, ask general comprehension questions.
3. Play the recording with students following along in their books.
4. Give students time to answer **Activité 7**.
5. Ask various students to read and answer the questions.
6. For **Extension**, ask students to talk about the photo. How old are the people? Where are they? What are they doing? What might be in their shopping cart?
7. Have volunteers read each role. Encourage students to ask questions about vocabulary.
8. Students answer the **Extension** question as a class discussion.

EXTENSION **La mondialisation à l'hypermarché** 1.2, 2.1, 5.1

Un couple qui a pris sa retraite cherche un produit qu'ils aiment à l'hypermarché.

Stratégie

Faites une liste de toutes les choses mentionnées comme étant problématiques par le couple. Êtes-vous d'accord avec leurs observations?

Lui: Je ne trouve pas.
Elle: Mais il y en avait encore le mois dernier....
Lui: Mais tu vois bien il n'y a plus que des marques alimentaires que l'on ne connaît pas: ça vient d'où ça?
Elle: De Chine, d'Indonésie, de Malaisie....
Lui: Quand ils comprendront que ce n'est pas dix centimes qui feront la différence et que ce que l'on veut d'abord, c'est savoir d'où viennent les produits, surtout l'alimentaire!
Elle: Avec tout ce qu'on lit ou qu'on entend sur l'absence de contrôles, les produits frelatés reconditionnés, les conditions sanitaires pas toujours respectées, les mélanges douteux....
Lui: Ah! Elles sont là!
Elle: Comme d'habitude, ils les ont encore changées de place pour nous faire acheter autre chose.
Lui: J'en prends cinq boîtes d'un coup, comme ça on est sûr d'en avoir.
Elle: Ou moins on ne manquera pas de bonnes salades!
Lui: Y'en a marre de ces magasins où l'on passe plus de temps à chercher qu'à trouver!
Elle: Comme si on n'avait que ça à faire!

EXTENSION De quoi est-ce que le couple de retraités se plaint? Pouvez-vous deviner ce qu'ils achètent? 1.2

Resources

Extension

Answers

EXTENSION

Ils se plaignent qu'il y a trop de variétés de produits de mauvaise qualité.; Possible answers: des boîtes d'olives.

Reference Desk

Students might not know these expressions: **alimentaire** (*food products*); **produits frelatés** (*products containing questionable ingredients*); **une boîte** (*box* or *can*, also *nightclub*); **un carton** (*cardboard box*). **Un récipient** is a general term for a container. **Y'en a marre** and **On en a ras le bol** mean that one is fed up.

Culture

Products: Information

A **hypermarché** is a superstore combining a supermarket and products usually found in a department store, hardware store, and pharmacy. The concept originated with The Carrefour Group, which is the seventh largest retailer in the world with three major markets in Europe, Latin America, and Asia. It has more than 9,870 company-owned and franchised hypermarkets, supermarkets, cash and carry, and convenience stores.

Differentiated Learning

Accelerate

Find examples of **produits frelatés** which have appeared in French and American grocery stores in recent years.

Decelerate

Luxury products for sale online are often **du toc**. Have students select a product such as a Dior bag, a Vuitton suitcase, or Chanel sunglasses and explain how to tell the difference between the authentic item and its imitation.

Recherche: how to detect the real (name of brand) from a fake

Multiple Intelligences

Visual-Spatial

There are classic handbags by Dior and Hermès named after famous people like Grace Kelly and Jane Birkin. There are also classic patterns of Hermès scarves. Encourage students to sketch a few to show in class or even design their own.

Resources

Points de départ
WB Workbook 6
Explore

Answers

Comparaisons
Answers will vary.

Reference Desk

If you have access to Passport, find a video or a news article related to **la mondialisation** or **le business** and show it to your students.

Critical Thinking

Analysis

If a luxury item is marked **fabriqué en France** and it is actually manufactured in another country, is that a fraudulent representation? Can you find examples of luxury items where that is true?

Points de départ

Pre-AP | Question centrale ? Qu'apprend-on de la culture d'un pays en étudiant son économie?

La France et la mondialisation 1.2, 2.1, 3.1

La France a-t-elle peur de la mondialisation ou profite-t-elle de la mondialisation? La presse anglo-saxonne hésite toujours entre ces deux analyses. Si l'on se réfère aux* sondages*, on pourrait affirmer que les Français ont peur de la mondialisation: ils sont près de deux tiers à la considérer comme une menace* et seulement un tiers à la considérer comme une aubaine*.

Ce qui fait peur dans la mondialisation, ce sont les déséquilibres*: dérégulation du commerce mondial; déséquilibres des échanges* commerciaux; délocalisation de l'industrie; crises de l'industrie financière spéculative qui menacent l'économie réelle; menaces agro-alimentaires avec les différentes épidémies*; menaces environnementales; menaces sur les cultures nationales.

Mais si l'on regarde la réussite* économique, on peut dire que la France profite de la mondialisation; elle est la cinquième puissance mondiale, et elle est le septième pays exportateur du monde. La France se place au quatrième rang des grands groupes mondiaux. Les exportations (biens* d'équipement, services, produits agricoles et agroalimentaires) représentent 27% de son PIB (produit intérieur brut)*. Elle est la première destination touristique mondiale et possède la deuxième zone maritime du monde (10 millions de km^2) après les États-Unis.

La Défense, un quartier d'affaires à Paris

Recherche: mondialisation france, globalisation france

Si l'on se réfère aux *If one refers to*; **sondages** *surveys*; **menace** *threat*; **aubaine** *opportunity, blessing*; **déséquilibres** *items with inequalities*; **échanges** *trade*; **épidémies** *epidemics*; **réussite** *achievement, success*; **biens** *goods*; **PIB** *GDP (Gross Domestic Product)*

1.2, 4.2

Comparaisons

Quels produits fabriqués à l'étranger est-ce que votre famille achète?

Produits

Louis Vuitton (1821–1892) a fondé une maison française de maroquinerie en 1854. Au 19ème siècle ses malles (*trunks*) étaient populaires pour les voyages transatlantiques en bateau. En 1998 **la marque Louis Vuitton** entre dans le prêt-à-porter: sacs à main, sandales, foulards de soie, etc. Les produits Louis Vuitton sont connus pour la toile (*fabric*) «Monogramme LV.» Cherchez ce produit en ligne.

1.2, 2.2, 4.2, 5.2

Essential Instruction

1. Ask students how the economy of the United States is changing. Is more manufacturing work being sent to Asia? What effect does globalization have on their lives? Tell students the French feel these changes too.
2. Have students read **La France et la mondialisation**.
3. Divide the students into two teams assigning one a pro-globalization stance and the other opposing it. Have each team go online to research the **Recherche** sections to prepare a debate about the benefits and dangers of **la mondialisation**.
4. Have students read **l'Industrie du luxe** and answer the **Comparaisons** question.
5. Divide the class into six groups and allow students to work on the activity that most interests them, while making sure all activities are covered. Have them do a jigsaw presentation of all six tasks to share their research with the class.

L'Industrie du luxe 1.2, 2.1, 2.2, 3.1, 3.2, 4.2, 5.2

Avec 25% du chiffre d'affaires mondial du luxe, une croissance entre 10% et 25% par an, LVMH (Louis Vuitton Moët Hennessy) et Pernod Ricard (spiritueux), Kering (mode, maroquinerie, joaillerie) et L'Oréal (produits cosmétiques) sont les trois groupes leaders mondiaux de leurs secteurs. Ces groupes contrôlent des marques comme Vuitton, Hennessy, Moët et Chandon, Dior, Donna Karan, Tag Heuer, Bulgari, Gucci, Saint Laurent, Bottega Veneta, Chivas, Four Roses, Absolut Vodka, etc. Ils représentent aussi 60 milliards* d'euros. Ils se distinguent* aussi par des magasins phares* spectaculaires sur les plus grandes avenues du monde qui sont devenues de véritables usines à rêve. Des stars (Charlize Theron, Marion Cotillard, Keira Knightley, Lily-Rose Depp) prêtent leur image pour promouvoir* ces grandes marques. Deux grandes marques indépendantes symbolisent aussi l'industrie du luxe : Hermès et Chanel. L'industrie du luxe compte aussi deux noms parmi les premières fortunes mondiales : Bernard Arnaud (LVMH) 4ème fortune mondiale et Liliane Bettencourt aujourd'hui décédée* (L'Oréal). Les États-Unis restent le premier marché du luxe, la Chine arrivant au deuxième rang.

Recherche : dior parfum pub, dior homme sport jude law

milliards *billions* ; **se distinguent** *stand out* ; **magasins phares** *flagships* ; **promouvoir** *to promote* ; **décédée** *deceased*

1.2, 4.2

Comparaisons

Quelles sont les marques américaines qui sont exportées à l'étranger ?

8 Activités culturelles 1.3, 2.2, 3.2

Faites les activités suivantes.

1. Faites une liste des craintes que les Français ont face à la mondialisation. Puis, faites des recherches et dites si, à votre avis, ces craintes sont justifiées ou fausses (donnez des exemples).
2. Faites un graphique qui montre les pays qui représentent de la première à la cinquième puissance mondiale. Indiquez leurs principaux produits d'exportation.
3. Faites des recherches et indiquez l'origine des marques suivantes et les produits qui y sont associés : Hennessy, Donna Karan, Bulgari, et L'Oréal.
4. Attribuez un produit de luxe à chacune de ces vedettes : Charlize Theron, Marion Cotillard, Keira Knightley, et Lily-Rose Depp. Regardez leurs clips en ligne. Expliquez le marketing de ces produits.
5. Trouvez cinq produits de luxe que vous voudriez acheter. Imprimez des photos de ces produits.
6. Faites des recherches pour trouver des produits de luxe dans votre état ou région. Écrivez une liste.

Perspectives

L'écrivain québécois Marc Vachon a dit sur son blog « Oser changer » : « Sous l'effet de la mondialisation, dans la plupart des pays industrialisés, on note une augmentation du Produit intérieur brut (PIB) mais aussi une diminution du Bonheur intérieur brut (BIB). » Êtes-vous pour ou contre cet argument ? Pourquoi ?

Differentiated Learning

Accelerate

Ask students to write an essay answering the question in **Perspectives**.

Decelerate

Have students research Louis Vuitton, the history of the company, and the products, as suggested in the **Produits** box.

Answers

8

1. la dérégulation du commerce mondial ; les déséquilibres des échanges commerciaux ; la délocalisation de l'industrie ; les crises de l'industrie financière spéculative qui menacent l'économie réelle ; les menaces agro-alimentaires avec les différentes épidémies ; les menaces environnementales ; les menaces sur les cultures nationales ; Opinions and examples will vary.
2. Graphs will vary.
3. Hennessy (États-Unis) : le cognac ; Donna Karan (États-Unis) : les vêtements ; Bulgari (Italie) : les bijoux ; L'Oréal (France) : les produits de beauté
4. Possible answers: Charlize Theron : Chanel ; Keira Knightley : Chanel ; Marion Cotillard : Dior ; Lily-Rose Depp : Dior
5. Answers will vary.
6. Answers will vary.

Comparaisons

Possible answers: Gap, Coach, Michael Kors, Marc Jacobs, Ralph Lauren, Calvin Klein, Vera Wang, Tommy Hilfiger, Tory Burch, Kate Spade, Tom Ford

Perspectives

Answers will vary.

Communication

Interpersonal: Cooperative Groups

Instruct groups of students to create an original crossword puzzle in French with a separate answer key. Ask them to focus on people, brand names, and products France produces. Check each group's puzzle for accuracy, and have students correct any errors. Then, have groups exchange puzzles and solve them.

Recherche : templates for crossword puzzles

Critical Thinking

Analysis

One of the elements of globalization is to produce goods in countries where labor is less expensive so as to reduce cost. A negative side of this practice is the use of child labor in countries with reduced or no legal restrictions preventing abuse of children in factories. Is this justifiable for the bottom line? Debate.

Answers

9 Answers will vary.

Communication

Interpersonal: Cooperative Groups

Students study the kinds of stores at **La Défense**, a commercial and business center developed in the 1990s in the outskirts of Paris. Have them write a dialogue among three or four friends planning their shopping excursion. Ask students to mention where they want to shop, what they want to buy, and where they plan to have lunch.

Recherche : les quatre temps, la défense

5 Script *(continued from p. 573)*

Rachida : Alors, ton exposé pour la classe d'économie, comment ça se passe ?
Caroline : Super, j'ai trouvé plein d'info sur l'industrie de luxe et j'ai pu parler à quelques personnes qui travaillent dans le secteur et qui m'ont donné plein d'idées. J'ai même trouvé un stage pour l'été chez Guerlain.
Rachida : Le parfumeur ? Tu as de la chance.
Caroline : Guerlain ne fait pas que du parfum. Ils ont toute une ligne de produits de beauté également et c'est un des seuls parfumeurs qui fabrique toujours son parfum avec de vraies essences de fleurs.
Rachida : Oui, c'est vrai que la plupart des produits de luxe sont fabriqués à l'étranger maintenant. Moi, je trouve des montres Cartier et des tee-shirts Chanel bon marché quand je vais en Tunisie l'été.
Caroline : Oui, mais ce sont des faux et tu risques d'être arrêtée par les douanes françaises pour avoir des faux. Les produits de luxe français comme la joaillerie, la faïence, la maroquinerie et les vêtements de marques sont fabriqués en France. Et c'est un secteur en pleine expansion. Par exemple, la maison Hermès…
Rachida : Celle qui fait les foulards en soie ?
Caroline : Oui, et bien, ils vont ouvrir deux nouvelles usines cette année.
Rachida : Pourtant, Hermès c'est très cher. Qui achète leurs produits ?
Caroline : Les États-Unis, la Chine, les pays arabes… La France a 40% du marché mondial des produits de luxe.
Rachida : Et bien, c'est peut-être dans ce secteur que je devrais chercher du travail alors. Tu as eu des réductions sur certains produits au moins.
Caroline : Non, mais la maison LVMH m'a offert une carte cadeau pour l'une de leurs boutiques !

(continued on next page)

Du côté des médias 1.2

Lisez la page des marques de luxe qui ont fait le top 50 des réseaux sociaux.

Hermès, Paris  2,6 M fans	Christian Dior  15,5 M fans	Chloé  1,9 M fans
Christofle  2,4 M fans	Yves Rocher  2,7 M fans	Louis Vuitton  19,2 M fans
Cartier  4,4 M fans	Christian Louboutin  3,2 M fans	Longchamp  1,4 M fans

9 Les marques 1.2, 1.3, 2.2

Faites les activités suivantes.

1. Faites une liste des marques françaises que vous connaissez.
2. Indiquez les domaines qu'elles couvrent (*cover*).
3. Tirez (*Draw*) des conclusions. Que révèlent le prix et l'importance des produits de luxe sur les perceptions d'une culture de la beauté, de la classe sociale, et de la réussite ?

Essential Instruction

1. Students read **Du côté des médias** and complete **Activité 9**. Make a master list of brands and their products that the groups have generated. Write them on the board in the different categories. Help students draw conclusions about the price of luxury and its reflection on a culture's perception of beauty, class, and success.
2. For **Activité 12**, have students identify the American stores and list at least three of their products. In addition, have them find out where these products are produced in the world.

Communiquez!

10 Les produits de luxe 1.1, 2.2, 4.2, 5.2

Interpersonal Writing and Speaking

Imaginez que votre partenaire soit un(e) correspondant(e) français(e). Vous allez comparer des marques de produits de luxe de vos pays respectifs. Choisissez une catégorie (alimentation, automobiles, parfums, bijoux, vêtements), puis faites des recherches. Par exemple, comparez les sacs à main Chanel, ou Louis Vuitton à Marc Jacobs, Coach ou Kate Spade. Pourquoi est-ce que les sacs à main de la marque française sont extrêmement populaires aux États-Unis? Les marques américaines sont-elles populaires en Europe? Avez-vous ou connaissez-vous quelqu'un qui a acheté ou qui possède ces articles de luxe? Y a-t-il une différence dans les prix d'achat aux États-Unis et en Europe? Discutez en personne ou par vidéo. Utilisez autant de détails que possible.

11 Au McDo 1.1, 4.2, 5.2

Interpersonal Speaking

En groupe, imaginez que vous visitiez un drive-thru de McDonald's dans une ville française. Un ou deux étudiants joueront le rôle d'employés du restaurant français au guichet, tandis que les autres joueront le rôle d'étudiants américains en vacances, qui arrivent en voiture. Les étudiants vont commander des plats selon le menu authentique du restaurant français. Est-ce que l'expérience au McDo est positive ou négative? Les étudiants américains sont-ils satisfaits? Que pensent les employés français des touristes américains? Présentez votre sketch devant la classe.

Recherche : menu mcdo (+ VILLE)

12 Votre centre commercial 1.3, 3.2, 4.2, 5.1, 5.2

Presentational Writing and Speaking

Votre classe va créer la maquette d'un mini-centre commercial en France. Avec votre partenaire, vous serez responsable d'une partie du centre (par exemple la zone nord du premier niveau, ou la zone ouest du deuxième niveau, etc.). Préparez un plan numérique, ou une copie avec des illustrations, et identifiez chaque boutique ainsi que les produits qui y seront vendus. N'oubliez pas les services tels les restaurants ou les stands. Enfin, enregistrez une visite guidée de votre partie du centre. Si vous le souhaitez, vous pouvez aussi concevoir et nommer votre propre magasin et expliquer l'inspiration qui s'y rattache.

Resources

- Share
- CA Communicative Activities

Answers

5 *(continued from previous page)*

1. Caroline fait un exposé sur quoi?
2. Comment est-ce que Caroline a trouvé des informations?
3. Que va faire Caroline pendant l'été?
4. Dans quoi se spécialise la maison Guerlain?
5. Que trouve Rachida de pas cher en Tunisie?
6. Où sont fabriqués les produits de luxe français?
7. Quelle société est connue pour ses foulards en soie?
8. Quel pourcentage du marché mondial du luxe représente la France?

1. l'industrie française du luxe
2. en faisant des recherche en ligne et en parlant à des personnes du secteur
3. un stage chez Guerlain
4. dans les parfums
5. des montres Cartier et des tee-shirts Chanel
6. en France
7. la maison Hermès
8. 40%

10 Comparisons will vary.

11 Role-plays will vary.

12 Designs will vary.

Reference Desk

If you have access to Passport, create a question for your students to share their response to a communicative activity.

Critical Thinking

Analysis

McDonald's is one of the largest restaurant chains in France. However, the experience you will have in a French McDonald's compared to that in the United States is quite different. Have students visit the French McDonald's website where they can research the major differences in the way this major corporation both models itself and what it offers to customers in France compared to the United States. Have them think about why this might be. They may further discuss which model of McDonald's they prefer and why. Have them look at and compare French and US ads for McDonald's.

Differentiated Learning

Expand

Have students visit a well-known French department store online, such as **Le Bon Marché**, **la Samaritaine**, **Printemps**, **Galeries Lafayette**, or **Les Quatre Temps** boutiques at **La Défense**. What kinds of restaurants are there and what international cuisine is available? What other store names do they recognize that sell beauty products? Are they low or high-end products? Students will report their findings to the rest of the class.

Multiple Intelligences

Visual-Spatial

Encourage students to design their own store. Ask them to name their store and to describe the finished product to the class. This can be done in conjunction with Activity 12 in **À vous la parole**, or as a separate activity (if time permits).

Resources

- *Prononciation*
- Pre-test
- *Leçon* Quiz

Answers

D Script

1. Ils vendent des tartes à la pâtisserie.
2. Elle part à dix heures demain.
3. Elles m'attendent à la bouche du métro.
4. Il promet de dire la vérité.

1. P
2. S
3. P
4. S

Reference Desk

1. As the students will see, there is a difference between standard and familiar French. If they are looking for an example in English of these two categories, tell students that if they were teaching foreigners English, they might be tempted to teach them "I've got to go." In reality the familiar form is "Ivgottago."
2. The consonant in the middle of the third person plural of –**re** verbs is followed by an **e**, therefore the middle consonant is pronounced. The final consonant *t* is of course silent.

Communication

Presentational: Cooperative Groups

Ask students to make a list of common English expressions that change from standard to familiar pronunciation in daily conversation.

TPR

For **Activité D,** have students write **S** and **P** on two separate pieces of paper. Have them hold up the appropriate letter to indicate if the singular or plural.

Prononciation

Liaisons in Standard French 1.2

» In the first- and second-person singular, liaison is avoided with forms of **être** in standard French. In the third-person singular and plural, liaison is observed in standard French. More and more, French people are not making liaison with **euros** in standard French.

A Registre courant

Répétez les phrases.

1. Je suis en vacances.
2. Tu es allé **en** Allemagne?
3. On es**t** **en** Angleterre.
4. Ils son**t** au**x** État**s**-Unis.
5. Vingt euros?
6. Cent euros?

B Je réponds affirmativement

Écoutez et répondez aux questions.

1. Où es-tu? (en vacances)
2. Où son**t**-ils? (aux États-Unis)
3. Ça coûte combien? (vingt euros)

Pronouncing Verb Endings

» Note how you hear the **t** or the **d** sound only in the plural verb forms.
For example: **Elle part.** *but* **Elles par<u>t</u>ent.**

C Transformez au pluriel!

Vous allez entendre le verbe au singulier. Changez la phrase au pluriel.

1. Il sort à 18h00.	Ils sor**t**ent à 18h00.
2. Il perd les bagages.	Ils per**d**ent les bagages.
3. Elle met du parfum.	Elles me**tt**ent du parfum.

D C'est singulier ou pluriel?

*Écoutez la phrase. Écrivez **S** si le pronom et le verbe sont au singulier, ou **P** s'ils sont au pluriel.*

Essential Instruction

1. Read Part A for the students. Have them note the difference in pronunciation between standard and familiar French.
2. Ask them to repeat the sentences after you in a group and individually.
3. Have students read to you the three sentences in the singular and the plural for **Activité C**.
4. Monitor students as they answer the questions in **Activité D** to assure they are making the correct liaisons.
5. Have students listen to **Les compagnies françaises**. Ask them to give you the corresponding English term for each type of business, and an example.
6. Have students listen and repeat **Pour la conversation**. Have them add the words to their vocabulary list.

Leçon B

Vocabulaire actif

Les compagnies françaises

1.2, 2.2, 3.2, 4.2, 5.2

Les types de compagnies françaises

ÉCONOMIE

Une entreprise

Compagnie créée par des individus

Une PME (Petite et Moyenne Entreprise)

Entreprise de 20 à 250 employés

Une société

Compagnie créée par des groupes commerciaux

Une SA (Société Anonyme)

Société avec des **actionnaires** (m.)

Profil d'une compagnie multinationale française

DANONE
ONE PLANET. ONE HEALTH

Danone est une compagnie multinationale française. C'est une Société Anonyme (SA).

C'est **un leader** dans la production de produits laitiers frais. Son **siège social** est à Paris.

Il y a plusieurs **filiales** Danone aux États-Unis ; leur siège social se trouve à White Plains dans l'État de New York.

Pour la conversation

1.1

How do I ask if someone's been here a long time?

» Ça fait longtemps que vous êtes en France ?
Have you been in France for a long time?

How do I say I wanted to get away?

» Je voulais **m'éloigner de** la capitale.
I wanted to get away from the capital.

Et si je voulais dire... ?

un cadre	*company executive*
le comité directeur	*board of directors*
un groupe	*corporate group*
un patron	*boss*
une succursale	*branch*
un franchisé	*franchise*

Resources

- *Vocabulaire actif*
- *Pour la conversation*
- *Et si je voulais dire... ?*
- eV eVisual
- WB Workbook 1–3
- FC Flash Cards
- LA Listening Activities 1–2
- G & V Practice Games

Reference Desk

Some additional vocabulary students might not know:

1. **Le siège** is the legal headquarters of a company. **Le siège** means *seat.* It can also mean *siege*, as in surrounding an enemy.
2. **Une filiale** is a *subsidiary* or *affiliate* of a larger organization. **Une succursale** is a *branch office* of a company or financial institution. **Les actionnaires** are *shareholders* who own **les actions** (*stock*). **Le conseil d'administration** is another term for *board of directors*.
3. **Leader** can be masculine or feminine.
4. The answer to a question starting **Ça fait que... ?** is **Ça fait** + TIME **que...**

Differentiated Learning

Accelerate

Have students write a dialogue between two employees who live in Paris and are discussing their jobs. Have them use the expressions from **Pour la conversation**. Challenge students to include as many vocabulary words from **Et si je voulais dire... ?** as possible. Present the scene to the class.

Decelerate

Have students make an organizational chart in French of an imaginary company, listing from the top to the bottom the executives who work there.

Special Needs Students

Dyslexia

Students may have to depend on their ear to learn when to make liaisons if they have trouble reading the phonetic markings in the lesson.

Social Anxiety

Choral responses give students with social anxiety a chance to practice speaking French in a safe way.

Resources

Activity 1

Answers

1

1. Elle habitait à Paris, maintenant elle habite à White Plains, NY.
2. Il travaille pour Danone.
3. Elle a l'âge d'aller au lycée, entre 15 et 17 ans.
4. Elle va se spécialiser dans les affaires.
5. Elle invite son amie Gabrielle.
6. Elles feront les touristes.

2

1. compagnie; 2. produits laitiers; 3. yaourt; 4. siège social; 5. filiales; 6. État

3

1. entreprise; leader
2. une filiale; production
3. SA; m'éloigner

4 Script

1. Je m'appelle Amina. Moi, je travaille pour une grande compagnie française dans le secteur de la cosmétologie. On vend nos produits dans la zone euro, en Amérique du Nord, et en Asie.
2. Bonjour. Mon nom est Rachid. Je travaille dans l'épicerie du coin. Mes clients habitent dans mon quartier.
3. Salut, moi c'est Arnaud. Je travaille pour Apple à Paris. Vous connaissez les produits d'Apple, n'est-ce pas?
4. Moi, c'est Isabelle. Je suis américaine, mais ça fait longtemps que je travaille ici en France dans ce bureau qui gère les opérations de Danone dans le monde.
5. Bonjour. Je m'appelle Julien et j'ai ma propre boulangerie aux environs de Paris.
6. Je suis Brigitte. Je travaille dans le secteur agroalimentaire; on a des filiales partout dans le monde, mais le siège social est à Minneapolis.

1. D; 2. C; 3. B; 4. A; 5. C; 6. D

Communication

Presentational: Paired Practice

Have students imagine a phone conversation between Catherine and Gabrielle in which they compare life in White Plains and in Paris. Ask them to make plans for Gabrielle's visit.

1 Je vis aux États-Unis! 1.2, 2.2, 3.1

Interpretive Reading

Lisez le mail que Catherine écrit à sa copine, puis répondez aux questions.

À: Gabrielle
Cc:
Objet: Devine où je suis!

Salut, Gabrielle!

Me voici à White Plains dans l'État de New York. On vient de déménager de Paris parce que mon père a un nouveau poste chez Danone… tu sais, la compagnie qui produit notamment des yaourts. C'est à White Plains où se trouve le siège américain des activités produits laitiers frais du groupe, appelé Dannon. Je vais à une vraie high school américaine. Après, je vais me spécialiser en affaires à New York. J'aime l'idée de vivre dans une autre culture. Il faut absolument que tu viennes me rendre visite! On fera les touristes à New York!

J'attends ta réponse,
Catherine

1. Où habitait Catherine, et où habite-t-elle maintenant?
2. Pour quelle compagnie son père travaille-t-il?
3. Quel âge a Catherine? Comment le savez-vous?
4. Qu'est-ce qu'elle va faire après être diplômée?
5. Qui est-ce qu'elle invite à lui rendre visite?
6. Quand Gabrielle lui rendra visite, qu'est-ce que les filles feront?

2 Danone 1.2

Interpretive Reading

Complétez les phrases logiquement.

Danone est une (1) multinationale française. Cette société fabrique des (2) comme le (3). Le (4) de Danone est à Paris. Danone a plusieurs (5) aux États-Unis, mais la compagnie est centralisée en Amérique dans l'(6) de New York à White Plains.

La compagnie Danone se trouve boulevard Haussmann à Paris.

Essential Instruction

1. Have students read **Activité 1**, then work in pairs to answer the questions.
2. Have students expand on question 6 of **Activité 1** by researching things to see and do in White Plains and nearby New York City.
3. Ask students to write a response to Catherine asking her more questions about her life in the United States.
4. As a class, complete **Activité 2**.
5. Have students define the terms in **Activité 3** before completing the exercise with the appropriate synonym.
6. Have students listen to **Activités 4** and **5** and respond using white boards.
7. Have students research online the companies in their area before doing **Activité 6**. Do these companies have international branches or manufacturing centers? Where?
8. Ask students to interview each other using **Activité 6** as a basis for conversation. Circulate to offer help where necessary.

3 Les synonymes 1.2

Interpretive Reading

Des jeunes diplômés parlent de leurs premiers postes. Remplacez les mots en italique par une des expressions ci-dessous.

entreprise SA production leader m'éloigner une filiale

1. Benoît : Je travaille pour une *compagnie qui n'est pas très grande.* Nous sommes le *numéro un* des compagnies qui fabriquent les sacs de provisions.
2. Marie-Alix : Je cherchais un poste dans *un bureau situé dans un autre pays*. J'ai trouvé un poste chez Danone, le leader dans la *fabrication* de produits laitiers frais.
3. Jean-Pierre : Je travaille pour une *grande compagnie* dans le secteur de l'informatique à Paris. Plus tard, j'aimerais *me mettre à distance* de la capitale et travailler aux États-Unis.

4 Tu travailles pour qui ? 1.2, 3.2

Interpretive Listening

Écrivez les numéros 1–6 sur votre papier. Écoutez les personnes décrire où elles travaillent. Ensuite, choisissez la lettre qui correspond au lieu de travail.

A. un siège social
B. une filiale
C. une PME
D. une grande multinationale

5 Je travaille chez GM 1.2, 2.2

Interpretive Listening

Écrivez les numéros 1–6 sur votre papier. Écoutez l'histoire et, ensuite, répondez aux questions que vous entendez.

On recycle!

Avec un partenaire, dites ce qui se passerait s'il y avait des compagnies françaises dans votre ville. Utilisez la structure si + IMPARFAIT / CONDITIONNEL.

MODÈLE

Si Renault-Citroën existait à Detroit, il ferait concurrence à Chevrolet.

6 Questions personnelles 1.1, 3.2

Interpersonal Speaking

Répondez aux questions avec un partenaire.

1. Quelles sociétés y a-t-il dans ta région ? Est-ce que tu aimerais y travailler ? Pourquoi, ou pourquoi pas ?
2. Quel est le siège social des grandes compagnies dans ta région ?
3. As-tu déjà travaillé pour une compagnie ? Si oui, c'était quelle sorte de compagnie — une PME, une société, ou une compagnie multinationale ?
4. Ça fait longtemps que tu choisis des grandes marques pour tes vêtements ?
5. Quand ta famille veut s'éloigner de ta ville, où va-t-elle ?

Resources

Activities 4–5

Answers

5 Script

Julie voulait s'éloigner de Paris et de sa famille après ses études. Elle a eu de la chance de trouver un stage au siège social de GM à Detroit. D'abord, elle a commencé par servir le café et faire de petits travaux au service comptabilité. Puis, elle a travaillé au service ressources humaines et au service vente. Aujourd'hui, elle est directrice des ventes dans une filiale de GM à Paris où elle supervise la vente de voitures fabriquées aux USA.

1. Qu'est-ce que Julie voulait faire après ses études ?
   A. Elle voulait faire le tour du monde.
   B. Elle voulait s'éloigner de Paris et de sa famille.
   C. Elle voulait trouver un travail à Paris.
2. Où Julie a-t-elle trouvé un stage ?
   A. Elle a fait un stage chez GM à Paris.
   B. Elle a fait un stage chez Renault.
   C. Elle a fait un stage chez GM à Détroit.
3. Qu'est-ce qu'elle a dû faire d'abord dans cette compagnie ?
   A. D'abord, elle a servi le café et fait de petits travaux.
   B. D'abord elle a travaillé comme comptable.
   C. D'abord, elle est devenue directrice du service des ventes.
4. Dans quels services a-t-elle travaillé ?
   A. Au service comptabilité, ressources humaines, et vente.
   B Au service comptabilité, gestion, et secrétariat.
   C. Au service comptabilité, ressources humaines, et marketing.
5. Que est son poste aujourd'hui ?
   A. Julie est directrice du marketing chez GM à Paris.
   B. Julie est directrice des ventes chez GM à Détroit.
   C. Julie est directrice des ventes chez GM à Paris.
6. Où est fabriqué le produit qu'elle vend ?
   A. Il est fabriqué aux États-Unis.
   B. Il est fabriqué en France.
   C. Il est fabriqué au Mexique.

1. B; 2. C; 3. A; 4. A; 5. C; 6. A

6 Answers will vary.

Differentiated Learning

Accelerate

Have students visit **la version française** of the Dannon website and make a list of their products. In addition, have them report how the French company **Danone** is currently doing financially.

Recherche : yahoo finance, bloomberg

Decelerate

Ask students to write a one-paragraph response to question 5 of **Activité 6**. Have them explain where and why they would like to move to a new location of their choice.

Multiple Intelligences

Visual-Spatial

Ask students to make a publicity poster for **Danone**. They may incorporate advertising wording from the website.

Rencontres culturelles

Un Américain à Paris 1.2, 3.2, 4.2

Léo et Justin font la connaissance d'un jeune homme d'affaires au café.

Dennis : C'est donc une interview pour votre cours de marketing à l'université ?
Léo : Oui, c'est ça. Je dois interviewer quelqu'un qui travaille pour une compagnie multinationale. Mon copain est auditeur libre et suit le même cours que moi.... Ça fait longtemps que vous êtes en France ?
Dennis : Tu peux me tutoyer... ça fait deux ans.
Léo : Bravo pour l'accent !
Dennis : Ce n'est pas trop difficile... travailler tous les jours en français avec des Français, ça aide....
Justin : Tu travailles pour quelle compagnie ?
Dennis : Un groupe agroalimentaire qui est le leader mondial dans la production de produits laitiers frais.
Léo : Laisse-moi deviner. C'est Danone ?
Dennis : Oui, c'est ça.
Justin : C'est où, le siège social ?
Dennis : À Paris, dans le 9ème arrondissement. Mais, ce weekend je voulais m'éloigner de la capitale et trouver du soleil.
Justin : Quelles sont tes responsabilités ?
Dennis : Je travaille pour le département de marketing. Plus précisément, sur des stratégies pour lancer nos produits dans des pays anglophones.
Justin : Tu peux parler un peu de ta formation ?
Dennis : Après mon BA, j'ai fait ma maîtrise à Thunderbird en Arizona où je me suis spécialisé en gestion et en français. L'université m'a trouvé un stage à Danone, et le hasard a fait le reste.

7 Un Américain à Paris 1.2

*Indiquez si la phrase est vraie (**V**) ou fausse (**F**). Corrigez les phrases qui sont fausses.*

1. Il faut que Justin et Léo interviewent quelqu'un qui travaille pour une filiale américaine en France.
2. Justin et Léo suivent un cours de littérature à l'université.
3. Danone fabrique des produits chimiques.
4. Le siège social de Danone se trouve à Nice.
5. Dennis fait des stratégies pour lancer les produits de Danone dans des pays anglophones.
6. Il a fait ses études de gestion à Thunderbird, en Arizona.

Resources

- Dialogue Activity 7
- Dialogue Video
- WB Workbook 4

Answers

7

1. F; pour une compagnie multinationale
2. F; un cours de marketing
3. F; des produits laitiers
4. F; à Paris
5. V
6. V

Reference Desk

1. **Un auditeur libre** audits courses.
2. One can either **tutoyer** or **vouvoyer** someone depending on the relationship.
3. **Suivre un cours** means *to take a course*.
4. When the word **français** is capitalized it means a French person: **Le Français typique aime les fromages français**.

Culture

Perspectives: Information

The Thunderbird School of Global Management is a subsidiary college of Arizona State University. It has campuses around the world, but is centralized in Glendale, Arizona (though the school has announced plans to move its campus to downtown Phoenix in 2021).

Critical Thinking

Comparisons

Thunderbird is an international business school located in the United States. Compare Thunderbird to **une grande école** such as **HEC** in France.

Essential Instruction

1. Ask students to name top business schools in the United States. Explain that international business is one specialization that students majoring in business can choose.
2. Play the video once for general comprehension. Ask students to explain the main storyline.
3. Ask students to write Dennis, Léo, and Justin on a piece of paper. Have them jot down details about each young man as they watch the video again.
4. Have students listen to the dialogue and compare what they wrote to the information in the reading.
5. Answer any questions students have about the dialogue before doing **Activité 7**.

EXTENSION **L'émission de radio: « En France comme si vous y étiez »** 1.2, 3.1

Une journaliste interviewe des gens pour une émission de radio pour apprendre pourquoi ils ont choisi le français comme langue secondaire.

Historien italien: On ne peut pas faire de l'histoire si on ne connaît pas le travail de l'École des Annales: elle a changé l'approche de l'histoire. Ce qui n'est pas traduit en italien, je dois pouvoir le lire en français.

Prof allemande: Je suis spécialiste de Proust.... Même s'il y a une excellente traduction en allemand... vous imaginez un *proustien* qui ne lirait pas le français!

Banquier anglais: Vous ne le savez peut-être pas, mais les Français sont très forts dans la modélisation financière, leurs spécialistes sont très réputés et même si leurs cours sont en anglais, ils les donnent à Paris. Alors si vous voulez aussi profiter de la ville... et comment ne pas profiter de Paris!

Graphiste espagnole: Moi, je voulais être reçu à l'ENSAD, l'École nationale des Arts décoratifs, parce que je voulais absolument travailler dans l'animation et vous savez que l'ENSAD est la meilleure porte d'entrée pour intégrer les grands studios d'animation... alors je suis passée par le français.

EXTENSION Quelle raison d'étudier le français s'approche le plus de la vôtre? 1.3

Analyse 1.2, 3.1

D'après le dialogue, pour quelles raisons est-il bénéfique d'avoir une connaissance de la langue française? Quels domaines d'études sont particulièrement concernés? Utilisez des détails du texte.

Resources

Extension

Answers

EXTENSION

Answers will vary.

Analyse

La connaissance du français est utile pour faire des études supérieures, dans les domaines suivants: l'histoire, la littérature, les finances/les affaires, et les arts.

Reference Desk

The term *proustien* refers to Marcel Proust (1871–1922), a French novelist and critic. He is best known for his seven-volume novel ***À la Recherche du temps perdu*** (*In Search of Lost Time*).

Communication

Interpersonal: Paired Practice

Ask one student to play the role of the journalist and the other an American being interviewed on French radio about why he or she has chosen to learn French. Students may give real or imagined answers, but they must expand on their reasons why.

Differentiated Learning

Decelerate

Ask students to summarize in one sentence why the Italian, German, Englishman, and Spaniard in the dialogue have elected to learn French.

Accelerate

Have students write a short composition explaining why they have chosen to learn French.

Resources

Points de départ
WB Workbook 5
Explore

Answers

Perspectives
Elle dit que les produits français sont plus chers et pas toujours fabriqués en France.

Comparaisons
Les États-Unis sont classés deuxième (après la Chine) en concurrence internationale.

Reference Desk

If you have access to Passport, find a video or a news article related to **les entreprises** and show it to your students.

Game

Circulez!

The purpose of the game is to learn the companies listed in **La France et la concurrence mondiale**, their functions, and products in a short amount of time. Each student assumes the name of a French company and defines it in one memorized sentence. Have students wear a name tag bearing the name of the company. At a "mocktail" party ask the students to circulate and introduce themselves with a prepared definition. "**Bonjour. Je m'appelle BNP. Je suis une des plus grandes banques de France.**" At the end of the mixer, call out the name of a company. The first person who defines the company correctly gets a point. Do not allow students to call out the name of their own company. Award a small prize to the overall winner.

Points de départ

Pre-AP

Question centrale ? **Qu'apprend-on de la culture d'un pays en étudiant son économie?**

La France et la concurrence mondiale

1.2, 2.1, 2.2, 3.1, 3.2, 5.2

L'usine Michelin fabrique des pneus.

La France a su créer dans tous les domaines de grandes entreprises multinationales qui se classent toutes parmi les dix premières entreprises mondiales de leur secteur: Total (pétrole), EDF (électricité, nucléaire), Engie (énergie), Alcatel (industries électriques et électroniques), Sanofi-Aventis (pharmacie), L'Oréal et Groupe Yves Rocher (cosmétiques), EADS (Airbus), Thalès et Dassault (aéronautique et aérospatial), Carrefour (distribution), AXA (assurances), Renault-Nissan et PSA (automobiles), Michelin (pneus), Accor (tourisme hôtelier), BNP Paribas et Société générale (banques), Alstom (transports), LVMH (luxe). Elles reflètent une économie performante, fortement* mondialisée, innovante et tournée vers l'exportation.

La France est le troisième pays au monde à accueillir des investisseurs* étrangers et le premier en Europe. Les principaux atouts* de la France sont la densité de ses infrastructures, le faible coût de l'énergie (grâce à l'énergie d'origine nucléaire), une main-d'œuvre* dans l'ensemble très qualifiée, et un niveau général élevé de productivité et de qualité de vie.

Recherche: entreprises françaises (+ NAME)

fortement *highly*; **investisseurs** *investors*; **atouts** *assets*; **main-d'œuvre** *workforce*

1.2, 2.1

Perspectives

Je sais que le gouvernement nous encourage à acheter des produits français, mais quand même, ils sont souvent plus chers! Aussi, aujourd'hui, avec la mondialisation comment savoir si un produit soi-disant «made in France» est vraiment fabriqué ou emballé en France?
—Gardavous32

Quelles objections cette personne soulève-t-elle contre la possibilité d'acheter des produits français et de soutenir l'économie nationale?

1.2, 2.1

Traditions et pratiques

Avec ses exportations agro-alimentaires, ses produits manufacturés (avions, automobiles, matériel militaire, bateaux de plaisance et bateaux de croisière, télécommunications) et ses services (distribution commerciale, assurances, banques, travaux publics, traitement des eaux, tourisme), la France se maintient de façon compétitive sur le marché international.

Produits

La France a lancé plusieurs **fusées** (*rockets*) sous le nom d'**Ariane**. La France fait partie de l'Agence spatiale européenne, ou l'ESA. On lance les fusées Ariane du centre spatial de Kourou en Guyane française.

1.2, 2.2

Comparaisons

Les États-Unis sont classés à quel rang de la concurrence internationale?

1.2, 4.2

Essential Instruction

1. Put the names on the board of the French companies listed. Ask students to identify the ones they know. Have them copy these names in their notebooks.
2. Have students read **Points de départ** and write a short description of each company next to the name.
3. Depending on the number of students in the class, assign each student the name of a major French company, or all of them, to research. Ask students to add information gained from researching the search words.
4. Have students answer the two **Comparaisons** questions.

France-Amérique : Aller simple

1.2, 2.2, 3.1, 4.2

Des produits français qui cartonnent* aux États-Unis

1	**Les drones Parrot :** 700 000 drones vendus aux États-Unis y compris à la NASA
2	**Les remontées mécaniques Poma,** leader du marché nord-américain. On leur doit aussi bien **le téléphérique** de Roosevelt Island à NY que **la grande roue** de Las Vegas.
3	**Les friteuses SEB**… grâce à Oprah Winfrey
4	**Withings**, compagnie spécialisée dans les objets connectés dans le domaine du bien-être et de la santé réalise la moitié de ses ventes aux États-Unis. En rayon* chez Apple.
5	**Autolib'** est devenu **BlueIndy** à Indianapolis.
6	**Acrelec** installe ses bornes tactiles* dans les 4500 magasins Walmart.
7	**Ubisoft** mène la danse des jeux vidéo avec **Just Dance** vendu à 55 millions d'exemplaires* dans le monde dont un tiers aux États-Unis.
8	**Criminal Case** développé par le studio parisien **Pretty Simple** reste depuis 2012 l'un des jeux les plus joués sur **Facebook**. Il a été élu **jeu de l'année** en 2014, avec 200 millions de joueurs à travers le monde dont 25% aux États-Unis.
9	**Dassault Systèmes** équipe **Boeing** de son logiciel industriel « **3D Experience** ». Un engagement de coopération depuis 30 ans.

Recherche : france-amérique.com, marketing professionnel.fr

cartonnent *are popular* ; **en rayon** *in stock* ; **bornes tactiles** *touchscreens* ; **exemplaires** *units*

1.2, 4.2

Comparaisons

Quels produits les compagnies américaines exportent à l'étranger ? Lesquels ont du succès ? Pourquoi, selon vous ?

Connexions

1.3, 3.1

Marketing international

Avec un partenaire, imaginez que vous travaillez pour une société américaine. Identifiez les produits français mentionnés ci-dessus, puis choisissez celui que vous aimeriez distribuer, et faites une petite publicité pour le public américain. Vous pouvez utiliser des images et des descriptions des produits, ainsi que des slogans français.

Answers

Comparaisons

Answers will vary.

Communication

Presentational: Paired Practice

Students engage in a debate in which one student argues that globalization is a negative because it is destroying language and culture as English becomes the lingua franca of the world. The other student argues the contrary.

Expansion

Have students identify American products or brands that are popular in France (**Apple mania**, **McDonald's**, **Marshmallow Fluff**, **Cheetos**, etc.) and create a chart similar to the one on this page.

Connections

Business

Ask students to research and present what changes have taken place with respect to trade between the United States and the EU because of possible trade wars and the changes in the US government's attitude toward tariffs. Have them present using graphs.

Differentiated Learning

Expand

Arrange students into mixed-ability groups and give them the name of a French company. Have the groups imagine that they work for a public relations firm whose task it is to make an advertising pitch for their company. The students create a commercial or an ad to sell their product. Their sales pitch can be presented live or filmed. Encourage students to find commercials online that they may want to incorporate into their presentation.

Special Needs Students

Dyslexia/Linguistically Challenged

Ask students to read **La France et la concurrence mondiale** aloud to a partner. Ask them to summarize the information in bullet points. Check their initial list to make sure they understand before continuing. Have them write in English the products listed.

Critical Thinking

Analysis

There is a French **dicton** (*saying*): "**L'heure, c'est l'heure. Après l'heure, c'est quelquefois l'heure. Avant l'heure n'est jamais l'heure.**" What does this mean, and how might it refer to a hostess preparing a dinner party?

Culture

Products: Information

L'École française de la courtoisie is a service that offers cross-cultural training for foreigners working in France. It is a good source for a comparative study of customs and practices in France.

Recherche : etiquette in france, l'école française de la courtoisie

Expansion

Students interview an American businessman or woman. Ask them to explain to the American, point by point, the etiquette of business meetings and business dinners in France, and ask the American to comment on how these practices are the same or different in the United States. Have them report back to the class.

Bonnes manières 1.2, 3.2, 4.1, 4.2, 5.1

Réunion*, repas d'affaires, invitations—à chaque moment ses codes pour réussir un rapport avec une entreprise française.

Les Français ont la réputation de n'être jamais à l'heure à un rendez-vous. Pourtant, les rendez-vous et réunions commencent en général à l'heure dite. Un écart* de cinq minutes reste toutefois toléré. Les Français ne fixent que rarement l'heure de fin d'une réunion. Dans les premiers rendez-vous, le « vous » est de rigueur au premier contact. Généralement, c'est dans les moments de convivialité, en dehors des contacts officiels, que le « tu » s'imposera. Attention, les Français respectent peu les tours de parole et ont tendance à couper la parole : c'est le produit d'une culture du débat et de la polémique*.

Les repas d'affaire ont beaucoup évolué. Ils sont courts (une heure maximum), et réduits* à entrée-plat ou plat-dessert. On pratique aussi les déjeuners de travail avec plateau-repas*. L'homme précède la femme pour entrer dans le restaurant. Le paiement doit se faire discrètement, en se déplaçant à la caisse.

Les repas d'affaire style cafétéria permettent de gagner du temps.

Pour les invitations à domicile, il faut arriver après l'heure (dix minutes à un quart d'heure maximum) pour une invitation amicale*, à l'heure si c'est un dîner privé. Selon le degré d'officialité, fleurs pour Madame ou une bouteille de vin si c'est un dîner plus amical. Il faut éviter le « bon appétit » en début de repas ; trinquer* ou ne pas trinquer, cela dépend du degré d'officialité et de proximité. Pour l'ordre des couverts, commencer par ceux qui sont le plus à l'extérieur et progresser vers ceux placés le plus proche* de l'assiette ; distinguer le verre à eau (toujours le plus grand) des verres à vin.

Recherche : bonnes manières au travail, savoir-vivre en entreprise, apprendre les bonnes manières

---

réunion *meeting* ; **écart** *delay* ; **polémique** *argument* ; **réduits** *reduced* ; **plateau-repas** *informal meal served on a tray* ; **invitation amicale** *invitation to the home* ; **trinquer** *to toast [with a drink]* ; **le plus proche** *closest*

Mot-clé

Manière : féminin substantivé (1119) qui vient de l'adjectif *manier* qui signifie que l'on fait fonctionner à la main. Il est issu du latin *manuarus* lui-même dérivé de *manus* (*main*). C'est à partir de 1170 qu'il sera appliqué aux personnes avec le sens de *comportement considéré en société*. Qu'est-ce que ces expressions veulent dire ?

Ne fais pas de manières.
Il y a l'art et la manière.

Essential Instruction

1. Explain to students that cultural practices differ from country to country and one of the benefits of studying French is becoming open and sensitive to different ways of behaving.
2. Have students read and outline **Bonnes manières**.
3. After researching the search words, ask students to add more information to their outline about what to do and not to do in business and social settings in France.
4. Ask students to use this information to do #4 of **Activité 8**.
5. Give students a choice of the remaining tasks in **Activité 8**.
6. Have students examine the two graphics about French exports and imports in order to complete **Activité 9**.

8 Activités culturelles 1.1, 1.3, 2.1, 3.1, 3.2, 4.1, 5.2

Faites les activités suivantes.

1. Recherchez une compagnie française et faites une présentation à la classe.
2. Quels sont les grands groupes leaders mondiaux français aux États-Unis? Faites un graphique.
3. Faites une liste des produits que les États-Unis importent de la France et n'y exportent pas, et vice-versa.
4. Faites la liste des choses à éviter dans les contacts avec les Français.
5. Écrivez un dialogue d'un repas d'affaire entre deux femmes d'affaires américaines et deux hommes d'affaires français.

Perspectives 1.2, 2.1

« Auprès des politiciens, les finesses de l'étiquette, les subtilités de la diplomatie comptent moins que le succès. »
—Robert Charbonneau, journaliste et écrivain québécois

Quel proverbe anglais exprime la même idée? Êtes-vous d'accord avec ce principe, ou pensez-vous que le moyen ou la méthode d'accomplir une chose est aussi important que le résultat?

Du côté des médias 1.2

Lisez et interprétez les graphiques sur le commerce international de la France.

Commerce extérieur: Exportations des produits français à l'étranger*

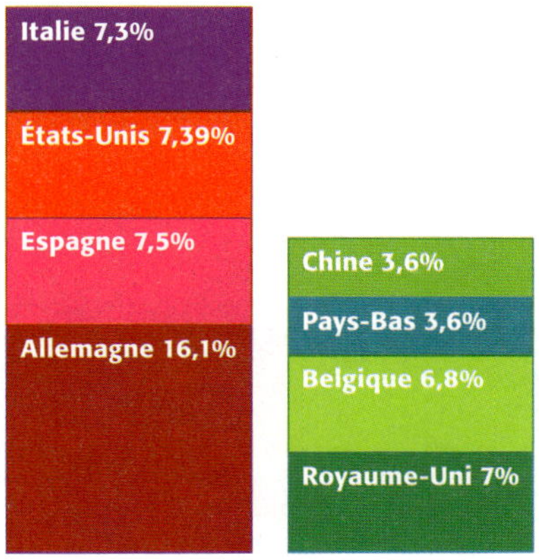

Échanges totaux (exportations et importations)

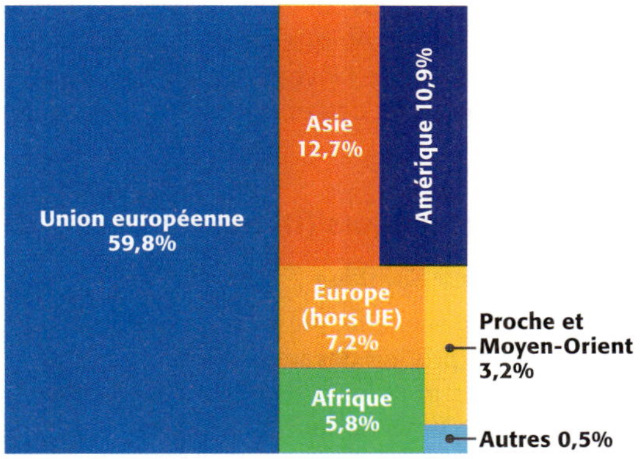

Source: Ministère des Affaires étrangères et du développement international, Ministère de l'économie et des finances; 7 février 2017 (pp. 46–47)

9 Exportations françaises 1.2, 1.3, 2.1, 3.2, 4.2

Faites les activités suivantes.

1. Qui détient le plus grand pourcentage des exportations de produits français?
2. Quelle place occupent les États-Unis dans le commerce extérieur de la France?
3. Choisissez l'un des deux graphiques, et interprétez-en les résultats dans un paragraphe. Vous pouvez ajouter une image.

Answers

8

1. Presentations will vary.
2. Answers will vary.
3. Answers will vary.
4. Possible answers: utiliser "tu" dans les premiers rendez-vous; passer devant une femme au déjeuner si on est un homme; payer devant tout le monde; arriver à une invitation à domicile en avance; dire "bon appétit" n'importe quand.
5. Dialogues will vary.

Perspectives
"The end justifies the means."; Opinions will vary.

9

1. l'Union européenne
2. Ils occupent la troisième place.
3. Presentations will vary.

Communication

Presentational: Paired Practice
Students research etiquette for dining in a French home. Have them write a comic scene in which the American makes many **faux-pas** because of cultural misunderstandings. An example might be the American offering a large bouquet of chrysanthemums as a hostess gift when these flowers are only put on graves.

Differentiated Learning

Accelerate
Have students answer the question for **Perspectives** then write a three-paragraph essay agreeing or disagreeing with the quotation.

Decelerate
Ask students to write a short composition discussing how arrival time is relative to the French depending on the situation. There are different standards for a French business meeting or dinner party. Ask them if the same is true in the United States as well.

Resources

Share

CA Communicative Activities

Answers

10 Presentations will vary.
11 Scripts will vary.
12 Presentations will vary.

Reference Desk

If you have access to Passport, create a question for your students to share their response to a communicative activity.

À vous la parole

Question centrale ? Qu'apprend-on de la culture d'un pays en étudiant son économie?

Communiquez!

10 Une compagnie multinationale française 1.1, 1.3, 2.1, 3.2, 4.2

Interpersonal and Presentational Speaking

Recherchez une compagnie multinationale francaise, par exemple, une compagnie technologique, sportive, aéronautique, ou alimentaire. Pour attirer de la clientèle, vous devez rencontrer et convaincre un(e) client(e) potentiel(le) de tester votre produit. Quels chiffres pouvez-vous donner pour montrer la croissance de votre profit et de vos ventes? Pour quelles raisons logiques le client (la cliente) devrait-il (elle) acheter votre produit? Que pouvez-vous lui offrir de plus qu'un autre fournisseur (*supplier*)? Soyez aussi créatif ou créative et convaincant(e) que possible!

11 Les startuppeurs (Première partie) 1.1, 2.2, 3.2, 5.2

Interpersonal Writing

Vous avez été sélectionné(e), avec un camarade de classe, pour apparaître sur la version française de *Shark Tank*, *Les Startuppeurs*. Votre classe va sélectionner quatre «startuppeurs» (*sharks*). Puis, vous devrez présenter une idée incroyable et innovante pour les convaincre d'investir dans votre idée. Il est impératif que votre présentation soit dynamique et intelligible, et contienne beaucoup de détails sur votre produits, par exemple: l'utilité du produit, le marché visé (Europe, Canada, Maghreb, Afrique de l'Ouest), les matériaux de fabrication et le lieu où le produit est fabriqué, le coût de l'investissement, etc. Avec votre partenaire, préparez un script pour votre présentation. Vous devrez utiliser trois arguments culturels.

12 Les startuppeurs (Deuxième partie) 1.3, 2.2, 3.2, 5.2

Presentational Speaking

Avec votre partenaire, présentez maintenant votre super produit devant le panel d'experts investisseurs pour les convaincre d'investir leur argent dans la distribution de votre produit.

Essential Instruction

1. In class read through the instructions and expectations for **Stratégie communicative**.
2. For **Activité 10**, suggest that students research a company whose products they know and/or use. If this is challenging, tell them to try and find an equivalent American counterpart in France (of an American company they like).
3. To aid in the completion of **Activité 11**, students can find pie chart makers online.
4. To personalize **Activité 12**, suggest that students ascribe names to the people who have bad manners and a description of each person. Have them relate what the table looked like, the specific courses they ate, what was discussed, they could make this as comical/exaggerated or as serious as they like.
5. To do the storyboard, brainstorm with students a product that they really like. It could be a sports car, a restaurant, designer jeans, or shoes. Once they find what they are passionate about, they will be ready to write an ad.
6. Using the **Recherche** about publicity, students get a feel for advertising styles, from straightforward sells to more surrealistic "surprise-at-the-end" ads.

Stratégie communicative

Pre-AP

Communiquez!

Storyboard 1.2, 1.3, 2.2, 3.2

Interpretive Reading, Presentational Writing

Un scénario dessiné (*storyboard*) est composé d'images et de textes ; il s'agit d'une sorte de brouillon (*draft*) qui permettra au filmage d'une publicité.

Suivez les étapes suivantes afin d'apprendre comment réaliser une pub. Ensuite, vous créerez votre propre scénario dessiné afin de vendre un produit américain sur le marché français. N'oubliez pas d'utiliser vos connaissances sur la culture française et ce qui plaît aux consommateurs en France.

1. Recherchez la signification des techniques de commercialisation telles que : *celebrity endorsement, avant-garde, facts and figures, weasel words, magic ingredients, diversion, transfer, plain folks, snob appeal, testimonial, bandwagon*. Choisissez-en une.
2. Regardez plusieurs pubs françaises en ligne et demandez-vous : Quelles techniques de commercialisation fonctionneraient pour les Français ? En quoi les pubs françaises diffèrent-elles des pubs américaines ? Qu'est-ce qui est important pour les Français ?
3. Réalisez votre scénario dessiné en vous basant sur le modèle ci-dessous.

Recherche : publicités (+ ANNÉE), culture pub, pubs tv, best of publicités françaises

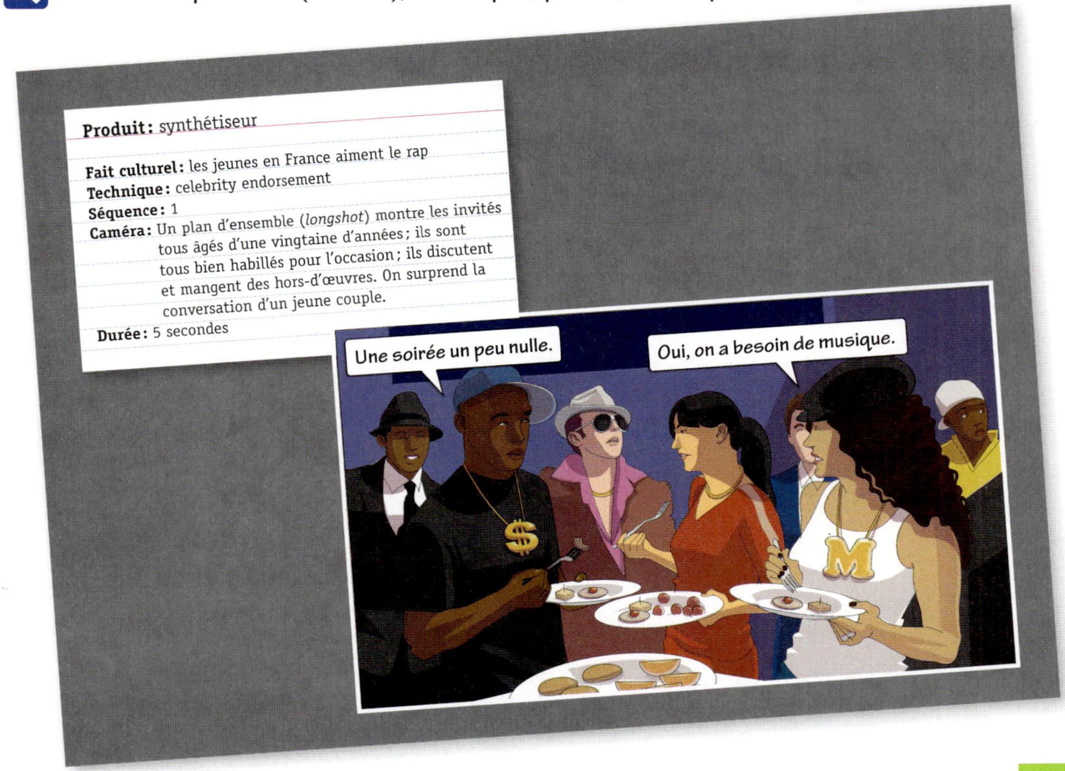

Resources

T Pre-test

Q *Leçon* Quiz

Answers

Storyboards will vary.

Reference Desk

Storyboards are essential tools in advertising. They provide the framework for creating an overview of television movies, cartoons, and advertisements as well.

Have students check online for more ideas and tips on creating storyboards.

Recherche : storyboards, what is a storyboard, how to make a storyboard

Differentiated Learning

Expand

Students can find online examples of promotions and discounts. In marketing their products, they might want to include some **prix-chocs** and great sales.

Multiple Intelligences

Visual-Spatial

Ask students to illustrate the ideas of the group for their storyboards.

Musical-Rythmic

Have students be in charge of the musical ideas to accompany the storyboards.

Connections

Humor

For a change of pace, have students watch "**Omar et Fred**" online as they perform comedy sketches in French about the pitfalls of the customer service department.

Recherche: le service après-vente

Produit: Synthétiseur
Fait culturel: les jeunes Français aiment le rap
Technique: celebrity endorsement
Séquence: 2
Caméra: Un gros plan (*close-up*): Dr. Dre allume sa boîte-son. Il joue sa chanson préférée. Il parle à la caméra. Derrière lui les invités se mettent à danser comme des fous dès qu'ils entendent les premières notes de la chanson.
Durée: 5 secondes

Traditions et pratiques

1.2, 2.1

En France, la publicité est certe une stratégie de marketing, mais aussi un art cinématographique. Le concept visuel et le message d'un spot publicitaire doivent toucher le spectateur.

Essential Instruction

1. Have students submit their storyboard outline to you for suggestions and evaluation.
2. Students present their storyboards to the class as if they were in a "Shark Tank" pitch session trying to sell their peers on the quality of the promotional material.
3. For **Leçon C**, ask students to name in English the different departments of a major organization. Write these titles on the board from the top management on down.
4. Have students listen to **Les départements et les postes d'une compagnie** then copy the organizational chart in their notebooks.
5. Listen to **Et si je voulais dire…?** and then ask students to add the vocabulary to their notebooks.
6. Add **département de technologie** to the chart.
7. Ask students to define the functions of each of the departments and the members of the staff.

Leçon C

Vocabulaire actif

Les départements et les postes d'une compagnie 1.2

Notre compagnie

Xin-Ju Han-Delorme, **PDG (présidente directrice générale)**
Kendrik Habib, **chef d'entreprise**
Marc Pierre-Louis, **directeur financier**

Nos départements

la gestion

le contrôleur/la contrôleuse de gestion

la comptabilité

le/la comptable

Les ressources humaines

le/la DRH (directeur/directrice des ressources humaines)

Le service du marketing

le/la responsable marketing

Le service des ventes

le vendeur/la vendeuse

Le service après-vente (m.)

le chef/la cheffe de service

Le secrétariat

le secrétaire (administratif)/ la secrétaire (administrative)

Pour la conversation 1.2

How do I describe adaptability?

» McDo met du fromage français dans ses sandwichs pour **s'adapter à** notre goût.
McDonald's puts French cheese on their sandwiches to adapt to our taste.

Et si je voulais dire... ?

un(e) artisan(e)	*craftsman*
la reconversion	*career change*
la main d'œuvre	*manpower*
un employé, une employée	*worker*
la restructuration	*restructuring*
la robotisation	*full automation*

Resources

- *Vocabulaire actif*
- *Pour la conversation*
- *Et si je voulais dire... ?*
- eV eVisual
- WB Workbook 1–2
- FC Flash Cards
- LA Listening Activities 1–2
- G & V Practice Games

Communication

Presentational: Cooperative Groups

Have students define what it takes to be a good secretary, salesperson, accountant, department head, etc. Have them write a job description for each. Upon completion have them correct each other's work. Ask students to make presentations to the class about each of the jobs they researched.

Recherche: quelles sont les qualités d'un(e) bon(ne)...

Expansion

Have students look at French job postings online.

Recherche: french language jobs, european language jobs

Differentiated Learning

Accelerate
Have students write a job announcement for their business to attract a competent accountant and sales person. Ask them to include a job description, hours, salary, and benefits.

Decelerate
Copy the photos that accompany each new vocabulary word in **Vocabulaire actif** and **Et si je voulais dire...?** and attach them to index cards. Work with students to create simplified definitions for each position then use the photos as cues to check learning. For example, manipulate the photos matching them to written definitions, or say the new word and have the students pick the corresponding photo.

Answers

1 Drawings will vary.

2

1. secrétaire
2. PDG
3. comptable
4. responsable marketing
5. vendeur
6. DRH

Reference Desk

AXA, **Crédit Agricole**, **l'Oréal**, **Louis Vuitton**, and **Alstom** have been named the top five environmentally friendly companies emitting the least amount of CO_2 in the atmosphere. (**L'ONG Britannique** study).

Communication

Interpersonal: Paired Practice

Student A is **chef des ressources humaines**. Student B wants to get a job in a department of his or her choice. Imagine the interview between the two. Student A asks questions about Student B's background, interests, past job experience, and skills. Student B answers giving real or imagined details.

1 Nettoyez-Bio 1.2, 1.3

Interpretive Reading, Presentational Writing

La compagnie Nettoyez-Bio fabrique des produits pour nettoyer la maison sans polluer la terre. Faites un dessin de la compagnie décrite ci-dessous.

La compagnie *Nettoyez-Bio* se trouve devant une forêt qui est visible des fenêtres du secrétariat. Quand on entre dans l'immeuble de la compagnie, Mme Duclerc, la secrétaire, vous accueille. À droite sont les bureaux—celui du PDG d'abord (M. Tissot), suivi de la comptable, Mme Garnier ; du DRH, Mme Delavigne ; et du responsable marketing, M. Dumont. Les employés sont derrière la secrétaire dans des box (*cubicles*). Le nom de la compagnie se trouve au mur à gauche.

2 Les employés 1.2, 3.1, 4.2, 5.2

Interpretive Viewing, Presentational Speaking

Donnez le nom des postes des employés de cette compagnie française.

1. La **(A.)** voit toutes les personnes qui entrent et qui partent.
2. Le **(B.)** est le responsable de la gestion de la compagnie.
3. La **(C.)** imprime un document financier.
4. La **(D.)** prépare une publicité.
5. Le **(E.)** va essayer de vendre le nouveau produit.
6. La **(F.)** interviewe un candidat.

Essential Instruction

1. Read **Activité 1** to the students as a dictation. Have students correct one another's work. If students do not want to draw, have them make an organizational chart of **Nettoyez-Bio**.
2. For **Activité 2**, ask students to identify the positions by reading the descriptions. For each position, ask for more details about their functions. For example, **"Quelles sont les autres résponabilités de la secrétaire ?"**
3. Students complete **Activité 3**.
4. Before assigning **Activité 4**, ask students to describe each picture. Where might they be working? How long have they been working there? Give a physical description of each person. How old are they?

3 L'organisation de la compagnie 1.2, 3.2

Interpretive Reading

Complétez les phrases pour identifier les départements ou les personnes qu'on contacte dans les situations décrites.

1. Quand on téléphone à une compagnie, on parle souvent à un(e) employé(e) dans le....
2. Une personne qui veut acheter un produit contacte un... ou une....
3. Le PDG est responsable de la... de la compagnie.
4. Quand on accepte un poste dans une compagnie, on va aux... pour signer le contrat.
5. Pour comprendre les finances d'une compagnie, on contacte le comptable dans le département de....
6. Quand le PDG voudrait faire des publicités pour ses produits, il contacte le département de....

4 Tu fais quoi? 1.2, 3.2

Interpretive Listening and Viewing

Écrivez les numéros 1–6 sur votre papier. Écoutez les descriptions. Puis, faites correspondre la description avec la bonne illustration.

Resources

Activities 3–4

Answers

3

1. service après-vente
2. vendeur, vendeuse
3. gestion/direction
4. ressources humaines
5. la comptabilité
6. marketing

4 Script

1. Voici Madame Roger. Elle travaille comme vendeuse chez Carrefour.
2. Ça, c'est Monsieur Dupont. Il est PDG chez Dior.
3. Voici la DRH de la SNCF, Madame Radjad.
4. C'est Julien, le nouveau comptable au département comptabilité de chez Renault.
5. Je te présente Madame Longchamp, la secrétaire du PDG de Danone.
6. Ça c'est le responsable marketing de chez BMW. Il s'appelle Monsieur Garcia.

1. B
2. A
3. D
4. F
5. E
6. C

Communication

Interpersonal: Paired Practice

Student A wants to make an appointment for a job interview with Student B who is head of human services. Have them role-play the scene.

Recherche: french conversation, making an appointment on the phone

Differentiated Learning

Expand

Have students find a photo online of people in a business setting. Ask them to write a story with dialogue, using the photo as a starting point, and integrating the business vocabulary of the lessons.

Recherche: google/images, business meeting

Multiple Intelligences

Bodily-Kinesthetic

Ask students to act out the cues for **Activité 3** and have the rest of the class identify the department or person to contact.

Resources

Activity 5

Answers

5 Script

Marc: Alors, comment s'est passé ta première semaine de stage dans la société?
Henrike: C'était très intéressant, mais difficile aussi. En Allemagne, tout est beaucoup plus structuré, je pense, et on travaille plus.
Marc: Comment ça?
Henrike: Ici, c'est assez rigide. Tu as un chef qui a fait des études et tu dois suivre la hiérarchie. En Allemagne, chacun propose des idées et on obtient un poste en travaillant dur pas juste parce qu'on est allé à une grande école.
Marc: C'est vrai qu'ici on a peur du PDG, même si parfois il ne fait pas grand-chose.
Henrike: Oui, et puis, vous êtes toujours en pause. Pause-café, pause-conversation, pause-portable. Nous, on travaille non-stop jusqu'au déjeuner et on ne se plaint pas.
Marc: Tu as fait un stage dans quel département en Allemagne?
Henrike: J'étais au service marketing chez Mercedes. Il y avait beaucoup de jeunes qui donnaient leurs idées et le responsable marketing avait juste 35 ans.
Marc: Vraiment? Ici, notre PDG a plus de 60 ans et le responsable marketing doit prendre sa retraite à la fin de l'année. Avec la mondialisation, il va falloir que l'on s'adapte comme en Allemagne et aux États-Unis.
Henrike: Oui, mais je pense que votre marketing ici est bien alors.

1. Henrike vient d'être embauché à plein temps.
2. Henrike trouve les compagnies françaises hiérarchiques.
3. Marc n'a pas peur du PDG.
4. On travaille plus en Allemagne.
5. Le PDG d'Henrike en Allemagne était plus âgé que le PDG de Marc en France.
6. Henrike n'aime pas le marketing en France.

1. F; 2. V; 3. F; 4. V; 5. F; 6. F

6 Answers will vary.

5 Le travail en France 1.2

Interpretive Listening

*Écrivez les numéros 1–6 sur votre papier. Écoutez la conversation entre Marc et Henrike, une stagiaire allemande. Ensuite, indiquez si les phrases que vous entendez sont vraies (**V**) ou fausses (**F**).*

6 Questions personnelles 1.1, 2.1, 3.2

Interpersonal Speaking

Répondez aux questions avec un partenaire.

1. Est-ce que tu as déjà travaillé pour une compagnie? Si oui, quel était ton poste?
2. As-tu jamais écrit à un PDG? Pour quelle raison?
3. Imagine que tu as fini tes études universitaires et que tu cherches maintenant un poste. Qui est-ce que tu comptes contacter dans la compagnie où tu voudrais travailler? Pourquoi?
4. Qu'est-ce que tu ferais si tu travaillais pour le service du marketing?
5. Tu aimerais être vendeur ou vendeuse d'un produit que tu aimes? Si oui, duquel?

On recycle!
Choisissez trois camarades de classe, et imaginez ce qu'ils feront dans dix ans. Quel travail feront-ils? Seront-ils célèbres? Que changeront-ils dans le monde? Écrivez un court paragraphe sur chacun.

Essential Instruction

1. Have students listen to **Activité 5** and answer one comprehension question at a time. Stop the recording after each sentence and ask for the answer. Ask a volunteer to restate the original sentence.
2. Allow students to answer **Activité 6** honestly or with imagination since many have limited work experience.
3. Have students watch the video **Une compagnie multinationale américaine en France**. What do they remember about the conversation between Léo and Justin?
4. Students listen to the recording. In small groups, have them list the companies mentioned, and explain how they have adapted to international markets.
5. In the same groups, have students do **Activité 7**. Upon completion, ask them to compare their lists with other groups.

Une compagnie multinationale américaine en France 1.2, 3.1

Léo et Justin étudient ensemble.

Léo : Génial ce que la prof de marketing nous a raconté….
Justin : Vous travailliez sur quoi ?
Léo : Sur l'adaptation des compagnies multinationales aux besoins des marchés locaux.
Justin : Ah oui, je vois… contre l'idée reçue que mondialisation égale uniformisation.
Léo : Exactement ! Elle nous a raconté comment 3M… tu connais 3M ?
Justin : Oui, les rouleaux de Scotch™ !
Léo : Oui, si tu veux…. Et aussi les Post-it™ et les éponges Scotch-Brite™, comme ça on aura fait le tour du supermarché ! Donc, je disais que 3M avait eu l'idée géniale d'adapter des sandales avec de l'éponge en dessous pour qu'elles servent de serpillières aux Philippines… pas bête, non ?
Justin : C'est comme les constructeurs automobiles qui sont obligés d'adapter leurs voitures pour les pays où l'on conduit à gauche….
Léo : Et puis McDo et Subway qui mettent du fromage français dans leurs sandwichs pour s'adapter à notre goût… et qui nous servent de la bière et du café *expresso.*
Justin : En Allemagne, ils proposent des hamburgers au porc, j'en ai goûté !
Léo : Et l'Oréal ? C'est bien connu, l'Oréal fait du marketing ethnique avec des produits qui ciblent certaines couleurs de peaux. Sans parler de Kleenex™ qui nous réserve son papier toilette découpé en petits carrés.
Justin : Eh oui, Léo, le marché devient régional. Dis, tu es bilingue, diligent, et doué pour le marketing ; tu comptes travailler pour une compagnie multinationale ?
Léo : Je n'ai pas encore pris ma décision, mais cette possibilité m'intéresse.

Mot-clé

Le **marketing** est un mot anglais et un anglicisme en France. Selon l'Académie française et quelques commissions, on devrait le remplacer avec « mercatique. » Mais beaucoup de Français continuent à parler du « marketing. »

Recherche : délégation générale à la langue française

7 Une compagnie multinationale américaine en France 1.3, 4.2, 5.2

Faites une liste des multinationales mentionnées dans le dialogue qui montrent la régionalisation dans la mondialisation.

Resources

- Dialogue
- Dialogue Video
- WB Workbook 3

Answers

7 3M; McDo; Subway; l'Oréal; Kleenex

Communication

Interpersonal: Paired Practice

Ask students to read **Mot-clé** about **franglais**. Have them search online for current English words that now are used in French such as **le zappeur**, **le buzz**, and **le brushing**. Are they correct translations of the English words? Have students also make a list of French words used daily in English, such as **à la mode**, **ballet**, and **rendez-vous**.

Reference Desk

Here is some help with the vocabulary from the dialogue: **Génial !** by itself means *Great!* **L'idée géniale** means a *brilliant idea*. The plural of **local** is **locaux**. **Cibler** is *to target*. **Une serpillère** is a *mop*. **Doué(e)** means *talented* or *gifted*.

Differentiated Learning

Expand

Have students compare the menus of McDonald's in the United States with that of France, Germany, and India. Ask: Which items are different and which are the same? What modifications do they think have been made to the menu in India? Why? Visit the Indian McDonald's website to confirm your assumptions.

Special Needs Students

Linguistically Challenged

Read **Une compagnie multinationale américaine en France** with the students. Ask them to highlight any cognates they see. Emphasize how much they already understand by identifying the words and expressions that they already know. Encourage them to listen to the conversation again and then read it out loud to help reinforce its meaning.

Resources

Activity 8
Extension

Answers

8

1. de l'adaptation des compagnies multinationales aux besoins des marchés
2. leur prof de marketing
3. les rouleaux de Scotch, les Post-it, les éponges Scotch-Brite
4. des sandales avec des éponges aux soles, qui servent de serpillères
5. Ils utilisent du fromage français dans leurs sandwichs, et servent des expressos et de la bière. Kleenex découpe son papier toilette en petits carrés.
6. travailler pour une compagnie multinationale

EXTENSION

Il a du mal à s'adapter aux idées, aux projets, et aux réunions discontinues. Il se plaint de ne pas savoir quand les réunions finissent, et qu'elles sont longues !

Reference Desk

1. **La voie** can refer to a physical path, train track, or lane on a highway. It can also refer to a theoretical path, as in a career path.
2. **D'ailleurs** means *by the way*. **Ailleurs** means *elsewhere*. There is a popular program on French TV called **"Nulle part ailleurs"** which means *Nowhere else*.
3. The word **foutu** is a very strong word. Emphasize that it should be used with caution.

8 Une compagnie multinationale américaine en France 1.2, 2.2, 3.2, 4.2

Répondez aux questions.

1. De quoi est-ce que Léo et Justin parlent ?
2. Qui leur a appris que le marché devient régional ?
3. Quels sont les trois produits fabriqués par 3M mentionnés ?
4. Qu'est-ce que 3M a inventé pour le marché philippin ?
5. Comment est-ce que McDo et Subway s'adaptent au marché français ? Et Kleenex ?
6. Léo s'intéresse à quelle possibilité ?

EXTENSION Brad discute de son travail dans un bureau français 1.2, 3.2

Au bureau Raphaël et Brad prennent un café.

Raphaël : Alors Brad, pas trop difficile ?
Brad : Non, c'est comme toi quand tu es venu travailler chez nous à San Diego, il faut s'adapter.
Raphaël : Je t'avais prévenu pourtant….
Brad : Mais la discontinuité ! Impossible de rester sur une chose décidée ; vous passez d'une chose à l'autre, revenez à la première, ça a changé entre temps, on ne sait pas pourquoi. Moi, j'aime faire une chose jusqu'au bout, puis l'autre et ainsi de suite.
Raphaël : Mais tout n'a pas besoin d'être dit ; on comprend implicitement ; chacun remplit les blancs… l'important c'est l'objectif, la manière, elle laisse la place à la créativité de chacun… chacun choisit sa voie pour y arriver.
Brad : C'est ça, c'est son affaire.
Raphaël : Notre foutu individualisme comme tu dis souvent !
Brad : C'est comme les réunions : on sait quand ça commence, mais on ne sait jamais quand ça finit… d'ailleurs ça ne finit pas.
Raphaël : Si ! Ça finit !
Brad : Bon et bien, la suite au prochain café….

EXTENSION Pourquoi Brad a-t-il des difficultés au bureau français ? De quoi est-ce qu'il se plaint ? 1.2

Essential Instruction

1. Do **Activité 8** as a class leading to a discussion of how companies adapt to international markets.
2. Have students make two columns with two headings: Brad and Raphaël. As students read the **Extension** conversation, have them note in the appropriate columns the cultural differences between them.
3. Ask students to read and take notes on **La structure de l'entreprise en France**. Have them use the **Recherche**, plus add "intercultural management, France" to the list.
4. Use the **Extension** question to discuss the differences in approaches between the US and French business practices. Have students use their notes to enrich the discussion.
5. Write questions on the board that you would like them to know after reading **Le marketing en France**, or prepare a worksheet that they fill out as they read.

Pre-AP

Question centrale ? Qu'apprend-on de la culture d'un pays en étudiant son économie ?

La structure de l'entreprise en France

1.2, 2.1, 2.2, 3.1, 3.2, 4.2, 5.2

Le PDG d'une société à structure hiérarchique se tient au centre des décisions.

Traditionnellement, la structure de l'entreprise française est hiérarchique, c'est-à-dire que le PDG, ou président-directeur général, gère* la compagnie ; c'est lui qui prend toutes les décisions importantes. Sous lui, il y a des cadres supérieurs* et des cadres moyens* que le PDG dirige*. La cause de ce modèle est l'élitisme ; l'entreprise embauche des diplômés des grandes écoles. Mais ce modèle, qui remonte à l'idée d'un gouvernement français centralisé depuis Napoléon, est en train de changer.

Un exemple de ce changement est la coopérative, qui, de l'autre côté, dépend des valeurs de partage*, d'humanisme, de transparence, et de participation. Les coopératives Scop (Societés Coopératives et Participatives) redistribuent les profits aux employées, dont la moitié sont des salariés* associés.

Pour réussir dans le marché mondial, il faut changer le modèle traditionnel.

Recherche : hec paris, les scop

Comparaisons

Est-ce que vous connaissez une compagnie américaine ? Comment est-elle structurée ?

1.2, 2.2

gère *manages* ; **cadres supérieurs** *senior executives* ; **cadre moyen** *junior manager* ; **dirige** *manages* ; **partage** *sharing* ; **salariés** *employees*

Le marketing en France

1.2, 2.1, 3.1, 4.2, 5.2

Les premières formes de marketing apparaissent* en France pendant le 17ème et le 18ème siècles. Après la guerre de 1870, la publicité devient vraiment de la « réclame* ». « L'affichomanie » règne de 1850 à 1920, et l'on admire les belles affiches artistiques comme celles de Toulouse-Lautrec qui font la réclame des cafés, des théâtres, et des cabarets de Paris. Entre les deux guerres arrive le « publicitaire » qui travaille dans une agence. Avant 1945, le problème le plus grave des entreprises est la capacité de production, pas la vente des produits pour lesquels les consommateurs ont déjà un appétit. L'invention de la radio pendant les années 1920 offre un autre champ pour la publicité ; on répond avec le marketing de masse. « Les Trente Glorieuses » sont les années de 1946–1975 quand commencent les publicités télévisuelles. Les sondages d'opinion sont nouveaux en France pendant les 1950 et changent le marketing.

Avec les années 1960, un groupe de consommateurs importants vient sur scène : les baby-boomers ; c'est pendant cette époque que la publicité française se découvre parce que c'est une période de prospérité. Le marketing de nos jours se caractérise par l'émergence de nouveaux paradigmes tels que le marketing relationnel et électronique, même en ligne ; les entreprises modernes doivent atteindre* la satisfaction de la clientèle.

Recherche : musée de la publicité, l'univers de la publicité, publicité (+ 1920, 1930, etc.)

Produits

Le marketing et la publicité en France ont donné naissance à deux grands groupes de communication : **Publicis Groupe**, l'un des trois principaux groupes de communication au monde et **Havas**, sixième groupe publicitaire mondial.

1.2, 2.2, 3.1

apparaissent *appear* ; **réclame** *advertisement* ; **atteindre** *to meet*

Resources

Points de départ

WB Workbook 4

Explore

Answers

Comparaisons

Answers will vary.

Reference Desk

If you have access to Passport, find a video or a news article related to **le marketing** and show it to your students.

Communication

Presentational: Cooperative Groups

Ask students to guess what strategies are used to market products to people their age. Extend this activity by having them create a survey to poll their classmates as to which marketing strategy works best to entice each of them to buy certain items or products. Have them include online advertisements, ads in popular magazines, product placement in movies, and/or commercials on television in their research. Ask them to share their findings with the class.

Recherche : le marketing et les jeunes.

Critical Thinking

Analysis

Ask students: What do you think is the effect of anti-tobacco and anti-alcohol abuse advertising campaigns on young people? Are they effective in making adolescents reflect on these issues in a constructive and positive way?

Recherche : le marketing social et les jeunes, l'alcool, la publicité et les jeunes

Differentiated Learning

Accelerate

Have students study a company in the United States and compare the structure to the French company described in the reading.

Decelerate

Ask students to find five funny French and American commercials (which are classroom appropriate) online. Have them show these to the class. Ask them to lead a discussion about French and American commercials.

Answers

9 Answers will vary.

Perspectives
Answers will vary.

10
1. McDo (McDonald's); L'origine de la filiale est française (Orléans)
2. Il vient d'un slogan américain; *Come as you are*; Answers will vary.; Discussions will vary.

Reference Desk

McDonald's has used both similar and dissimilar slogans in France as compared to those used in the United States. Its "**J'm ça!**" is derived from the English "I'm lovin' it!," while "**Venez comme vous êtes**" ("Come as you are") was not used in the US market.

Connections

Music

"**La femme image**" is a song which explores the life of a supermodel whose only purpose in life is to project the illusion of reality as dictated by whatever product she is representing.

Recherche: la femme image, gilbert lafaille, tout m'étonne

History

Have students look up ads from different print media sources, such as newspapers, periodicals, catalogues, and posters from the end of the 19th through the 20th century, in the United States and in France. What do the marketing strategies of the ads reveal about the historical and societal perceptions of the time? What changes in the nations' psyches can be observed over time?

Expansion

Ask students to search for other McDonald's advertisements in France, and compare them to ads in the United States. How are the ads for the French public different from those for the American public?

1.2, 2.2

Produits

La vache qui rit est un fromage français qui a changé son look à travers les années. Recherchez l'évolution de cette marque et regardez ses images changeantes.

Recherche: l'univers de la publicité marques et personnages

L'argot des ados 4.1

« Pub » en argot veut dire *publicité*. Donnez des définitions pour *publiphile*, *publipostage*, et *publireportage* après avoir recherché ces mots en ligne.

La vache qui rit

9 Activités culturelles 1.3, 3.2, 5.1, 5.2

Faites les activités suivantes.

1. Parlez à un(e) adulte qui travaille dans les affaires au sujet de la structure de sa compagnie. Ensuite, comparez cette compagnie américaine à l'un des deux modèles français.
2. En groupe, choisissez une décennie (de 1920 à 2010). Trouvez un exemple typique d'une publicité de cette époque ; présentez cette publicité à la classe.
3. Comparez une publicité française à une publicité américaine de la même époque.

1.2, 2.1

Perspectives

« Pour réussir sur le marché mondial, il faut changer le modèle traditionnel des affaires en France. Il vaut mieux que les entreprises françaises impliquent davantage les salariés et les cadres dans les processus de décision, favorisent l'initiative individuelle et la diversité, et aient une vision globale et une action locale. » Ce point de vue, écrit par un jeune diplômé embauché par une compagnie traditionnelle, vous semble-t-il raisonnable ? Justifiez votre avis et décrivez la sorte de compagnie pour laquelle vous voudriez travailler.

Du côté des médias 1.2

Lisez l'annonce ci-dessous.

10 Un fast-food américain s'adapte au marché français

1.2, 2.2, 3.1, 4.2

1. *Identifiez l'entreprise qui a fait cette publicité et indiquez son origine nationale.*
2. *Faites une critique du slogan de cette publicité : D'où vient ce slogan ? Reconnaissez-vous son équivalent en anglais ? Quel message donne-t-il ? Quel public vise cette entreprise ? Quelle polémique cette publicité soulève-t-elle ? Discutez en groupes.*

Essential Instruction

1. Arrange students randomly into two groups to do **Activité 9**. Have Group A do the first task. In addition, require them to research online articles on business that discuss the difference between French and US corporate structures. Which is more hierarchical?
2. Have Group B complete the second and third tasks. Ask them to find print illustrations of the US and French advertising of the decade they select.
3. For **Activité 11**, students choose their target category to investigate. Have them declare what they are going to do and why. Ask them to make a numbered chart (ten items) with the headings **Produit**, **Marque**, **Pays de fabrication**.
4. For **Activité 12**, have students analyze items in their category and answer the questions about them.
5. Have students do **Activité 13** to prepare for a whole-class discussion of **la mondialisation**.

Culture sur place

Question centrale ? Qu'apprend-on de la culture d'un pays en étudiant son économie?

Mes expériences avec la mondialisation

Dans cette *Culture sur place*, vous allez rechercher des marques internationales dans votre vie. D'où viennent les produits que vous utilisez chaque jour? Quel est le lien entre ces produits et la culture des pays d'où ils proviennent?

11 Chercher et rechercher 1.2, 1.3, 3.2

Choisissez une catégorie de la liste suivante. Vous allez rechercher d'où viennent les produits dont vous vous servez régulièrement.

- les vêtements
- l'équipement sportif
- la nourriture
- les boissons
- les produits électroniques
- les produits cosmétiques, produits d'entretien et d'hygiène

Pour chaque catégorie, faites une liste des produits que vous utilisez et qui ne sont pas américains. Donnez la marque et le pays de fabrication de chaque produit. Si possible, donnez des résultats en pourcentages, par exemple, « Soixante pourcent de mes vêtements viennent d'Asie. »

12 Comparer 1.1, 2.2, 5.2

Partagez les informations sur votre liste avec celles d'autres camarades de classe. Si plusieurs élèves ont choisi la même catégorie, combinez vos listes de marques et de pays de fabrication. Ensuite, discutez de vos découvertes avec les autres élèves en répondant à ces questions :

1. Est-ce que la plupart de ces produits (dans la catégorie que vous avez choisie) viennent de la même région ou du même pays?
2. Remarquez-vous une récurrence (*pattern*) avec certains produits?
3. Quelle est votre hypothèse économique pour expliquer ces tendances et pourquoi un pays particulier fabrique un certain produit?

13 Faire l'inventaire! 1.1, 2.1, 2.2, 3.2, 4.2, 5.1

Discutez ces questions en classe.

1. Après vos recherches, est-ce que vous pensez que le marché américain est influencé par le marché mondial? Est-ce que votre point de vue a changé au cours de cette activité? Si oui, pourquoi?
2. Est-ce que vous pensez qu'il y a un lien entre les produits et les cultures d'où ils proviennent? Avez-vous trouvé, par exemple, un produit que vous pensez être typiquement américain qui a été fabriqué à l'étranger?
3. Quelle est la fonction des frontières (*borders*) entre nations à l'époque de la mondialisation? Trouvez-vous que les frontières entre les pays sont plus importantes, ou moins importantes qu'avant, aujourd'hui? Quel est le rôle des tarifs dans le commerce international? Êtes-vous pour ou contre un système de tarifs?
4. Selon vous, quels sont les menaces et les avantages de la mondialisation?

Answers

All answers will vary.

Communication

Interpersonal: Cooperative Groups
Have students go online to find the definitions of the terms related to "**Pub.**" Are there any corresponding slang terms in English for these categories?

Culture

Products: Information, Activity
JCDecaux Group is a multinational corporation that is the largest out-of-home advertising corporation in the world. Based in Neuilly-sur-Seine, Paris, it is known for its bus stop advertising strategies, billboards, and public bicycle rental systems in France and abroad. Have students find corresponding large US advertising companies that target their audience in similar ways.

Critical Thinking

La vache qui rit (*The Laughing Cow*) cheese is a popular staple in snack foods throughout Europe. Despite many efforts, its popularity in the United States has never reached the same heights as in Europe. Have students consider possible reasons for **La vache qui rit**'s lackluster marketability in the US, and its continued popularity in Europe. How do their ideas apply to other products?

Expansion

Ask students what they think of "**La vache qui rit**" cheese and when they consumed it. Some may have had it as children and consider it a food for children—not a serious French product. What "more sophisticated" French cheeses do they know about, even if they have never tasted them?

Differentiated Learning

Accelerate
Have students write an essay explaining the impact **la mondialisation** is having or has had on their lives. Ask them to cite examples from the research they did in **Culture sur place**.

Decelerate
Have students inventory the cheeses in the dairy section of their grocery store. What kinds of cheeses are there, and where are they produced? Are they all pasteurized? Do any originate from France?

Multiple Intelligences

Visual-Spatial
Ask students to research further about **La vache qui rit** beyond what is mentioned in the **Produits** section and report to the class. Have them display pictures of the changing images of the product and share with the class.

Verbal-Linguistic
Have students make a commercial for **La vache qui rit**. Their commercial should include a jingle and of course a cow.

Resources

CA Communicative Activities

Share

Answers

14 Presentations will vary.

15 Products will vary.

16 Ads will vary.

Reference Desk

If you have access to Passport, create a question for your students to share their response to a communicative activity.

Communiquez!

14 La publicité en France 1.3, 2.1, 2.2, 3.1, 3.2, 4.2, 5.2

Presentational Writing and Speaking

Avec un partenaire, préparez une présentation visuelle qui montre le développement de la publicité française depuis l'époque de Toulouse-Lautrec jusqu'à aujourd'hui. Rédigez un texte sous chaque image pour indiquer la progression des techniques du marketing jusqu'à aujourd'hui. Préférez-vous les publicités d'une période antérieure ou celles qui sont plus modernes? Pourquoi? Quels types de publicités sont les plus efficaces pour faire comprendre leur message et pourquoi, selon vous?

15 Un produit au fil des années 1.3, 2.2, 3.1, 3.2, 5.2

Presentational Speaking

Choisissez un produit français pour lequel la publicité a changé de look à travers les années. Trouvez des exemples qui montrent de quelle manière le produit a évolué et expliquez ces changements en montrant les pubs différentes à la classe. Vous pouvez également expliquer la raison pour laquelle vous avez choisi votre produit en particulier. Avez-vous une publicité préférée parmi celles que vous avez présentées? Pourquoi?

16 Ma pub pour le marché français 1.1, 1.3, 3.2, 5.2

Interpersonal and Presentational Writing

À votre tour d'être réalisateur/réalisatrice! Avec un partenaire, vous allez faire une pub en français pour un produit français ou américain que vous voulez commercialiser et vendre à un public français. Vous pouvez choisir n'importe quel type de produit, de n'importe quelle nature; votre priorité est de le vendre et de faire gagner de l'argent à votre entreprise! Quelle approche allez-vous adopter? Une approche comique, sérieuse ou choquante? Où sera filmée l'annonce? Aurez-vous besoin d'accessoires et/ou de costumes? Écrivez une description de la publicité avec un script (narration ou dialogue), une scène, des personnages, et un slogan.

Essential Instruction

1. For **Activité 14**, students use the **Recherche** on p. 599. For more examples of contemporary ads, students can do further research online.

   Recherche: marie-claire, gq, ikea france
2. To do **Activité 15**, students might consider: **Dubonnet**, a classic French liqueur; **Vittel**, **Vichy**, or **Evian** for water; or any of the luxury products listed on p. 571. They also should consider everyday products, such as soap, cooking supplies, dresses, hats, cars, toys, and sports equipment.
3. Encourage students who are assigned **Activité 16** to study the commercials for French products found online. Despite the fact that many commercials feature popular songs from the United States, insist that they use French music.
4. Before listening to **Rencontre avec l'auteur**, ask students the **Pre-lecture** question. Have them list the ads and commercials they are most susceptible to.
5. After reading the **Rencontre avec l'auteur**, have students summarize the information to a partner.
6. Read through the **Stratégie de lecture** and ask students to create a chart like the one on the page.

Pre-AP

5,90 €

Rencontre avec l'auteur 1.2

Frédéric Beigbeder (1965–) est un écrivain, un critique littéraire, un réalisateur et animateur de télévision français. Son roman *5,90 €*, d'abord intitulé *99 francs*, puis *14,99 €*, est l'histoire d'Octave Parrango, un rédacteur publicitaire. Désenchanté par le marketing et conquis par la déception de la promesse d'une vie meilleure pour tous, il décide de se révolter contre son agence de pub en sabotant sa plus grande campagne. Quelles indications indiquent qu'il va se rebeller dans cet extrait ?

Pré-lecture 1.3

Comment êtes-vous influencé(e) par les publicités ?

Stratégie de lecture 1.2

Tone. La tonalité, ou le ton d'un texte, est l'ensemble des procédés que l'auteur utilise pour provoquer des émotions particulières chez le lecteur, à travers les personnages, ou par le thème d'une œuvre littéraire. Dans un texte, on peut trouver différentes tonalités : familière, ironique, comique, dramatique, sarcastique, sérieuse, sincère, ou cynique. Au fur et à mesure (*During*) de votre lecture, relevez au moins un exemple de la tonalité dans chaque paragraphe. Indiquez si cette tonalité est provoquée par les paroles du protagoniste, la réaction anticipée du lecteur, ou par le thème de la lecture. Un exemple a été fait pour vous.

Paragraphe	Provocation	Description du ton
1. « … eh oui, je pollue l'univers »	le protagoniste	dédaigneux, sarcastique
2.		
3.		

Outils de lecture 1.2

Breaking the Fourth Wall: Addressing one's audience in fiction. De nos jours, il est rare qu'un écrivain s'adresse directement à ses lecteurs dans son œuvre de fiction. Mais, Beigbeder utilise le pronom « vous. » À votre avis, quel genre de relation essaie-t-il de créer avec ses lecteurs ? Quel est l'effet de cette intimité (*intimacy*) ? Êtes-vous davantage attiré(e) par l'histoire, ou vous sentez-vous plus distant(e) ? Pourquoi ?

Differentiated Learning

Expand
Consider inviting one of the English teachers or the literacy coach from your school to talk with the students about tone. Ask him or her to highlight examples of tone from texts that the students have read in English class in order to create a stronger link between what they have already read and the excerpt from ***5,90 €***.

Special Needs Students

Dyslexia, AD(H)D, Linguistically Challenged
To help students with reading difficulties, attention problems, and linguistic difficulties, focus on general comprehension as the goal. Prepare a worksheet for them with translations of difficult vocabulary that they can use as they do their readings.

Resources

- *Rencontre avec l'auteur*
- T Pre-test
- Q *Leçon* Quiz

Answers

Rencontre avec l'auteur
Il se présente comme quelqu'un qui « pollue l'univers. »

Pré-lecture
Answers will vary.

Stratégie de lecture
Possible answers:
2. « Je vous drogue à la nouveauté. » ; le protagoniste ; agressif, cynique (la drogue tue)
3. « Votre souffrance dope le commerce. » ; le lecteur ; sérieuse (le lecteur est en danger)
4. « Je passe ma vie à vous mentir. » ; le protagoniste ; sincère, confessionnelle
5. « Vous ne m'échapperez pas. » le protagoniste ; menaçante

Outils de lecture
Possible answers:
Il essaie de confronter le lecteur par une approche directe. On se sent plus concerné, il est difficile d'objectiver une telle approche.

Reference Desk

Les émotions particulières can mean "particular emotions" or in the context of **Stratégie de lecture**, it means "personal emotions." **Lire, le lecteur, la lectrice, la lecture** are words of the same family. Synonyms for **de nos jours** are **aujourd'hui** and **actuellement**.

Connections

Entertainment
In **Outil de lecture** it is pointed out that the speaker in ***5,90 €*** speaks directly to the readers. Can students think of any piece of literature, film, play, or television show where this technique (called "breaking the fourth wall") is used? (*The Office*, *Parks and Recreation*, *Modern Family*, *House of Cards*, *Amélie*, *Tangled*, *A Midsummer Night's Dream*, *A Series of Unfortunate Events*)

Resources

5,90 €

Answers

Pendant la lecture

1. Il est publicitaire.
2. Il parle de voitures.
3. Il apprécie les gens malheureux qui veulent toujours plus.
4. Il sait qu'il est toujours insatisfait.
5. Oui, il gagne beaucoup d'argent et a toujours de belles voitures neuves.

Connections

Theater/Drama

Have theater students or a theater teacher talk to students about the purpose and effectiveness of breaking the fourth wall.

Reference Desk

1. **"Connaissez-vous beaucoup de mecs qui gagnent 13K euros à mon âge?"** is a reference to a monthly income. In France, no one refers to an income on an annual basis. Ask students to calculate the protagonist's annual income in dollars. (approximately $200K)
2. **"Je dépense donc je suis"** is a take off on Descartes' famous saying **"Je pense donc je suis"** or in Latin, **"Cogito ergo sum." Assouvir** means *to satisfy a hunger or thirst*. It could also be used to satisfy intangible needs: **Assouvir vos désirs. Rabâcher** means *to rehearse*. It also means to *hammer away at* or *to drill information repeatedly*.
3. **Un creux** can mean a *hollow* as in a tree, or an *opening* in your schedule. **J'ai un creux le lundi à midi. Avoir un (petit) creux** means *to be a little hungry* as in your stomach is a little empty.

Connections

Theater/Drama

Have theater students or a theater teacher talk to students about the purpose and effectiveness of breaking the fourth wall.

5,90 €

Je me prénomme Octave et m'habille chez APC. Je suis publicitaire : eh oui, je pollue l'univers. Je suis le type (...) qui vous fait rêver de ces choses que vous n'aurez jamais. Ciel* toujours bleu, nanas* jamais moches, un bonheur parfait, retouché sur PhotoShop. Images léchées*, musiques dans le vent. Quand, à force d'économies, vous réussirez à vous payer la bagnole* de vos rêves, celle que j'ai shootée dans ma dernière campagne, je l'aurai déjà démodée*. J'ai trois vogues d'avance, et m'arrange toujours pour que vous soyez frustré. Le Glamour, c'est le pays où l'on n'arrive jamais.

> **Pendant la lecture**
> 1. Quelle est la profession du narrateur ?

> **Pendant la lecture**
> 2. Il parle de quel produit ?

Je vous drogue à la nouveauté*, et l'avantage avec la nouveauté, c'est qu'elle ne reste jamais neuve*. Il y a toujours une nouvelle nouveauté pour faire vieillir* la précédente. Vous faire baver*, tel est mon sacerdoce*. Dans ma profession, personne ne souhaite votre bonheur, parce que les gens heureux ne consomment* pas.

> **Pendant la lecture**
> 3. Quels consommateurs le narrateur apprécie-t-il ?

Votre souffrance* dope* le commerce. Dans notre jargon, on l'a baptisée « la déception post-achat ». Il vous faut d'urgence un produit, mais dès que vous le possédez, il vous en faut un autre. L'hédonisme n'est pas un humanisme : c'est du cash-flow. Sa devise ? « Je dépense, donc je suis. » Mais pour créer des besoins, il faut attiser* la jalousie*, la douleur*, l'inassouvissement* : telles sont mes munitions*. Et ma cible*, c'est vous.

> **Pendant la lecture**
> 4. Que sait le narrateur du consommateur ?

Je passe ma vie à vous mentir et on me récompense grassement*. Je gagne 13.000 euros (sans compter les notes de frais, la bagnole de fonction, les stock-options et le golden parachute). L'euro a été inventé pour rendre les salaires des riches six fois moins indécents. Connaissez-vous beaucoup de mecs qui gagnent 13K euros à mon âge ? Je vous manipule et on me file la nouvelle Mercedes SLK (avec son toit qui rentre automatiquement dans le coffre) ou la BMW 78 ou la Porsche Boxter ou la Mazda MX5. (Personnellement, j'ai un faible pour le roadster BMW 78 qui allie esthétisme aérodynamique de la carrosserie* et puissance* grâce à* son 6 cylindres en ligne qui développe 321 chevaux, lui permettant de passer de 0 à 100 kilomètres/heure en 5,4 secondes.)

> **Pendant la lecture**
> 5. Est-ce que le narrateur vit bien ? Quelle en est la preuve ?

J'interromps* vos films (...) à la télé pour imposer mes logos et on me paye des vacances à Saint-Barth ou Lamu ou Phuket ou Lascabanes (Quercy).

Ciel *Sky* ; **nanas** filles ; **léchées** *overpolished* ; **bagnole** voiture ; **démodée** pas à la mode ; **nouveauté** nouveaux produits ; **neuve** toute nouvelle ; **vieillir** *to age* ; **baver** *to drool* ; **sacerdoce** *calling, vocation* ; **consomment** *consume* ; **souffrance** *suffering* ; **dope** *dopes (v.) [with a drug]* ; **attiser** *to stir up* ; **jalousie** *jealousy* ; **douleur** *pain* ; **inassouvissement** *built-up hunger* ; **munitions** *ammunition* ; **cible** *target* ; **grassement** énormément ; **carrosserie** *car body* ; **puissance** *power* ; **grâce à** *thanks to* ; **interromps** *interrupt*

Essential Instruction

1. Make a copy of the reading for students so that they can write on it noting vocabulary and questions they might have.
2. Play the recording once and ask students what they think the reading is about.
3. Replay the recording stopping at each paragraph to discuss the central idea. Have students answer the **Pendant la lecture** questions as you go along.
4. Ask students to find the places the author refers to on the world map.
5. Put students in small groups to complete the **Stratégie de lecture** grid, p. 603, which forms the basis for a class discussion. In addition, have them discuss **Outils de lecture.**

(*Suite et fin*)

Je rabâche* mes slogans dans vos magazines favoris et on m'offre un mas provençal*, ou un château périgourdin*, ou une villa corse*, ou une ferme ardéchoise*, ou un palais marocain, ou un catamaran antillais, ou un yacht tropézien*. Je Suis Partout. Vous ne m'échapperez* pas. Où que* vous posiez vos yeux, trône ma publicité. Je vous interdis* de vous ennuyer. Je vous empêche de penser. Le terrorisme de la nouveauté me sert à vendre du vide. Demandez à n'importe quel surfeur : pour tenir à la surface, il est indispensable d'avoir un creux* au-dessous. Surfer, c'est glisser sur un trou béant* (les adeptes d'Internet le savent aussi bien que les champions de Lacanau). Je décrète* ce qui est Vrai, ce qui est Beau, ce qui est Bien. Je caste les mannequins (...) À force de les placarder*, vous les baptisez top-models ; mes jeunes filles traumatiseront toute femme qui a plus de 14 ans. Vous idolâtrez mes choix. (...) Plus je joue avec votre subconscient, plus vous m'obéissez. Si je vante un yaourt sur les murs de votre ville, je vous garantis que vous allez l'acheter. Vous croyez que vous avez votre libre arbitre*, mais un jour ou l'autre, vous allez reconnaître mon produit dans le rayonnage* d'un supermarché, et vous l'achèterez comme ça juste pour goûter, croyez-moi, je connais mon boulot.

Analyse

Selon le narrateur, quelles formes de pouvoir l'entreprise pense avoir sur le consommateur, et par quel biais (*moyen*) ? Utilisez des détails du texte, puis, pour chaque argumentation, dites si vous êtes d'accord et pourquoi (pas).

Pendant la lecture

6. Avec quoi le narrateur joue-t-il ?

rabâche *rehearse* ; **mas provençal** maison traditionnelle de Provence ; **périgourdin** *from, of the Périgord region* ; **corse** *from, of Corsica* ; **ardéchoise** *from, of the Ardèche region* ; **tropézien** de Saint-Tropez ; **échapper** *to escape* ; **Où que** *Wherever* ; **interdis** *forbid* ; **creux** *hollow* ; **béant** *gaping* ; **décrète** *decree* ; **placarder** *to affix posters* ; **le libre arbitre** *free will* ; **rayonnage** *shelving*

Frédéric Beigbeder

Answers

Pendant la lecture

6. Il joue avec le subconscient des consommateurs.

Analyse

Elle interdit au consommateur de s'ennuyer, elle l'empêche de penser ; elle contrôle son subconscient. ; Opinions will vary.

Reference Desk

Frédéric Beigbeder, (1965–), born in the Paris suburbs, is a prolific French writer, filmmaker, and literary critic. He won the **Prix Interallié** in 2003 for his novel ***Windows on the World*** and the **Prix Renaudot** in 2009 for his book ***Un roman français***.

Differentiated Learning

Accelerate

Consider letting your high-ability students read at their own pace and answer the **Pendant la lecture** questions on their own. Encourage them to learn more about Frédéric Beigbeder online.

Decelerate

This is a formidable reading for low-ability learners. They will benefit from paragraph by paragraph explanations.

Multiple Intelligences

Visual-Spatial

Students may enjoy making a collage of the products the author mentions in the readings.

Answers

Post-lecture

Il veut dénoncer le côté inhumain de son travail.

Le monde visuel

Possible answer: Les cheveux de la femme se confondent avec le ciel, lui suggérant un pouvoir surnaturel.

17

1. Paragraphs will vary.
2. Answers will vary.
3. Letters will vary.
4. Possible answer: Je suis le type (...) qui vous fait rêver; J'ai trois vogues d'avance; Vous faire baver*, tel est mon sacerdoce.; on me récompense grassement; Connaissez-vous beaucoup de mecs qui gagnent 13K euros à mon âge?; Vous ne m'échapperez* pas.; Je décrète* ce qui est Vrai, ce qui est Beau, ce qui est Bien.; Vous idolâtrez mes choix.; Plus je joue avec votre subconscient, plus vous m'obéissez.; je vous garantis que vous allez l'acheter; croyez-moi, je connais mon boulot
5. Presentations will vary.

Critical Thinking

Discussion

Ask students to keep a log for three days about the advertising that they are exposed to. Have them discuss if advertisers are manipulating them psychologically and emotionally. The last time they made an "impulse buy," what motivated them? Was it the advertising, special discounted offers, or other factors that won them over?

Analyze

Have students study the photo of the Longchamp ad more closely and discuss what is shown in the picture. Where is it taken? What area of Paris is shown here (**la Place de la Concorde, les Champs-Elysées, l'Arc de Triomphe in the distance**) and how do the students know this? What is the ad featured on? (a bus) What would be the advantages of placing an ad such as this on a bus in this location or route? Have students come up with their own questions to ask each other and answer.

Post-lecture 1.2

Pourquoi est-ce que le narrateur avoue (*confesses*) le mauvais côté de son travail?

Le monde visuel 1.2, 3.1

Publicité pour Longchamp, 2006. © LEBON/GAMMA.

Stratégie

Faites un tableau avec les catégories suivantes: attrait visuel; émotions provoquées; signification. Puis, interrogez deux ou trois camarades et demandez leur si, selon eux, le poster est beau ou non, quelles émotions ils ressentent en le voyant, et à quoi cela leur fait penser. Intégrez leurs réponses dans votre tableau. Enfin, d'après leurs réponses, expliquez si c'est une bonne publicité ou non.

La publicité a depuis toujours eu une relation privilégiée avec l'art et la photographie. Il arrive que certaines publicités trouvent une place à part entière au sein d'une culture déterminée, et peuvent même en traverser ses frontières, l'un des meilleurs exemples étant les posters de Toulouse-Lautrec. Il arrive que les mêmes techniques de composition propres à la peinture ou à d'autres formes artistiques s'appliquent aussi à la publicité. Pour cette publicité, le photographe a placé le produit sous la meilleure lumière possible puisqu'il est le centre d'attention et ses couleurs ressortent sur le fond neutre. Qu'est-ce que cette photo-publicité a d'artistique?

17 Activités d'expansion 1.3, 5.2

Faites les activités suivantes.

1. Écrivez un paragraphe qui décrit les exemples de tonalité dans la sélection, en vous servant des informations dans votre grille.
2. Discutez pourquoi le protagoniste implique le lecteur/la lectrice dans son histoire. Partagez vos théories avec la classe.
3. Écrivez une lettre au protagoniste dans laquelle vous donnez votre point de vue du consommateur contemporain.
4. Faites une liste de mots et d'expressions qui montrent l'orgueil du narrateur.
5. Faites une publicité pour la radio, la télévision, ou les médias en ligne pour l'un des produits mentionnés dans l'extrait que vous venez de lire.

Essential Instruction

1. Read **Le monde visuel** with the students. Ask them to bring in examples of photos used in advertisements that are particularly aesthetic and artistic.
2. Read through the **Activités d'expansion**. Allow students to choose one of them.

Pre-AP 21

Question centrale ? Qu'apprend-on de la culture d'un pays en étudiant son économie?

Communiquez!

18 L'industrie francophone chez vous 1.1, 1.2, 1.3, 2.1, 3.1, 5.1

Connecting to Financial, Economic, Business, and Entrepreneurial Literacy, Media Literacy
Interpersonal Speaking, Interpretive Reading, Presentational Writing and Speaking

Une « société mère » est une grande compagnie qui contrôle plusieurs petites compagnies. Aux États-Unis, beaucoup de produits et de compagnies proviennent de sociétés mères françaises ou francophones. Faites des recherches pour déterminer quelles compagnies françaises ou francophones sont installées dans l'état où vous habitez, ou aux États-Unis en général, et quels produits elles exploitent. Créez un infographique pour présenter ces produits et les compagnies d'où ils proviennent. Circulez dans la classe et échangez vos informations avec d'autres élèves.

Recherche : bmo harris, dassault, nestlé, oando, l'oréal, schneider electric, suez environment

19 Un dîner d'affaires 1.1, 1.3, 2.1, 3.1, 4.2, 5.2

Connecting to Social and Cross-Cultural Skills, Leadership and Responsibility
Interpersonal Speaking, Presentational Writing

Avec un partenaire, imaginez que vous êtes collègues de travail dans une compagnie américaine qui commence un partenariat avec une compagnie similaire en France. Les chefs d'entreprise ont invité des collègues français aux États-Unis. Pour les aider à préparer les rendez-vous et dîners avec leurs invités, préparez une liste des différences culturelles à anticiper avec les Français. Ensuite, présentez quelques exemples en jouant le rôle d'un PDG américain et d'un(e) client(e) français(e).

20 Relations franco-américaines 1.1, 2.1, 3.2, 5.1

Connecting to Communication, Financial, Economic, Business and Entrepreneurial Literacy
Interpersonal Writing

Vous voulez faire un stage dans une compagnie française aux États-Unis. La DHR, qui s'intéresse à votre candidature, vous pose des questions. Lisez son mail et répondez-y avec le plus de détails possible. Utilisez un registre formel.

De : Madame la Directrice des ressources humaines
Objet : Stage dans notre compagnie

Cher candidat, Chère candidate,

Nous avons reçu votre demande pour effectuer un stage dans notre compagnie. Nous cherchons un candidat bilingue et qui comprenne les relations entre la France et les États-Unis. Afin de vous offrir un poste de stagiaire qui vous permette de développer vos compétences, je vous prie de répondre aux questions suivantes.

–Dans quel département souhaitez-vous travailler et pourquoi ?

–Comment est-ce que vous pourriez aider notre compagnie à développer des relations avec les États-Unis ?

En vous remerciant par avance, je vous prie d'agréer mes salutations distinguées.

Madame la Directrice

Differentiated Learning

Accelerate
Encourage students to incorporate **La question centrale** into their **Projets finaux**.

Decelerate
Help students select a project, and give them support strategizing how they are going to approach the work. Encourage them to see you if they have questions.

Special Needs Students

AD(H)D
Divide the **Projets finaux** into manageable tasks to be completed on specific dates, for example, choosing a topic, devising a list of vocabulary and structures to use, conducting research if needed, completing the rough draft, editing, finalizing the presentation, and practicing.

At-Risk Students
The **Projets finaux** is an excellent opportunity for students to select a topic that interests them.

Reference Desk

This section is designed for students to apply unit vocabulary and structures to communicative activities that foster 21st-century skills. These activities demonstrate how 21st-century skills are cultivated in the language classroom and how these skills and the language learning process are mutually beneficial.

French in the workplace

Job Interview

When students begin to seek employment in France, the single most important factor in getting the position will probably be their interview. Ask them to search online for common French interview questions and prepare answers for them in French. Then have them role-play situations with partners in which they ask each other questions they have prepared and questions they have not prepared. You may also have them present in front of the class, using several candidates for one position.

Recherche : questions embauchement interview france

Social Justice

The business world is twofold: it provides an opportunity to grow a country's economy, and also aims to improve the lifestyle of consumers. Sometimes, liberal policies may ignore the welfare of citizens in favor of capital gain, and oftentimes, constrictive governmental laws are detrimental to the competitiveness of a country in the global economy. Ask students to compare and contrast information they have learned in this unit about business in France, and research additional models in the francophone world. Have them create five to ten basic rules that they consider important to protect both the interest of a country and the integrity of its people.

Resources

Create

Answers

All activities will vary.

Reference Desk

If you have access to Passport, assign your students an IPA task related to the unit.

Communication

Interpersonal: Cooperative Groups

Arrange the class into groups of mixed-ability students, and ask them to choose an activity. Have the lower-ability students do research, and the higher-ability students prepare a response to questions with specific examples. Ask them to share their ideas with other groups.

Finale

Projets finaux

A Connexions par Internet: les affaires 1.3, 3.2

Études de business

Imaginez que vous vous intéressez à une profession dans les affaires et avec laquelle vous pourriez communiquer en français. Recherchez une école de commerce comme Thunderbird dans l'Arizona qui prépare ses étudiants pour une carrière en affaires et une deuxième langue. Discutez ce que vous avez appris avec des camarades de classe… le prix, les spécialisations, les cours, la formation en France, les stages, etc.

B Communautés en ligne 1.3, 3.1, 3.2, 4.2, 5.1

Une nouvelle idée pour le monde

TEDx est une organisation qui facilite les conférences globales où on peut présenter des idées et des inventions. Recherchez le site ci-dessous et décrivez deux ou trois ces idées ou inventions qui vous intéressent. Choisissez celle que vous préférez et présentez-la à la classe. Ou bien, présentez une idée ou une invention originale.

Recherche : tedx paris

C Passez à l'action ! 1.3, 2.2, 3.2, 5.1

Le marché français dans notre région

Quels sont les liens de votre région avec la France ? Recherchez les compagnies françaises dans votre région et les filiales des compagnies américaines en France de votre région. Partagez le travail ; vous aurez besoin de camarades de classe qui pourront :

- Téléphoner à la *Chamber of Commerce* et à la *Trade Commission* de votre état.
- Contacter le consulat français avec un mail ou une lettre.
- Interviewer des employés des compagnies américaines qui ont une présence en France.
- Écrire un sommaire de ce que vous avez appris.
- Préparer des graphiques.
- Choisir de la musique pour la présentation.
- Partagez ce que vous avez appris avec un sketch (*skit*) ou une présentation.

Recherche : chamber of commerce, trade commission (+ NOM DE L'ÉTAT), consulat français

Essential Instruction

1. Review the instructions in **Projets finaux**. Allow students to work with a partner on their chosen project.
2. Create a rubric that outlines your expectations and point values for each section.
3. Have students peer-edit their work before submitting their finished product.
4. For **Activité D**, distribute copies of the graphic organizer in the Copy Masters supplement.

D Faisons le point ! 1.3

Mes progrès

Remplissez les organigrammes pour montrer ce que vous avez appris dans cette unité.

Je comprends	Je ne comprends pas encore	Mes connexions

What did I do well to learn and use the content of this unit?	How can I apply what I have learned this year?
How can I effectively communicate to others what I have learned?	What was the most important concept I learned in this unit?

Décorations de Noël dans une rue à Paris, la nuit, devant McDo

Vue aérienne de Paris, La Défense

Answers

D Answers will vary.

Reference Desk

The **Faisons le point !** section asks students to self-evaluate and keep track of their progress. When students complete the activity, direct them to use "I can" statements based on the unit objectives in the **Contrat de l'élève.** The graphic organizer for **Activité D** can be found in the Copy Masters supplement.

Communication

Interpersonal: Cooperative Groups

Arrange students in mixed-ability groups to do a review of **Unité 10** using the **Activité D** graphic organizer.

Special Needs Students

AD(H)D/Dyslexia
Take this time to help students with attention difficulties and reading challenges to organize their materials and their time. Work with them to set up a study schedule so that they can complete their unit review in a structured manner.

Resources

- Activity A
- LA Listening Activity *Synthèse*
- Pre-AP Listening *Unité 10*

Answers

A Script

Madame Picard : Alors, ta nièce a eu le travail chez LVMH ?
Monsieur Boucher : Oui, elle a commencé lundi aux ressources humaines.
Madame Picard : Elle est DRH ?
Monsieur Boucher : Non, elle est assistante de la DRH. Elle est super contente.
Madame Picard : En tout cas, c'est un bon travail ! C'est une multinationale et elle travaille dans le secteur des produits de luxe qui est en pleine expansion. Elle aura peut-être des avantages pour acheter du bon champagne ou des vêtements et des parfums de marques pour moins cher.
Monsieur Boucher : Et toi, ton petit-fils, il travaille toujours chez Apple aux États-Unis ?
Madame Picard : Oui, ça fait longtemps qu'il est là-bas. Il voulait s'éloigner de la France. Mais maintenant qu'il est marié, il voudrait rentrer en France et travailler pour une filiale d'Apple à Paris.
Monsieur Boucher : Qu'est-ce qu'il fait déjà ?
Madame Picard : Il travaille au service marketing. Il est responsable.
Monsieur Boucher : Et bien, lui aussi, a bien réussi !
Madame Picard : Oui, ma fille est très fière, et mon beau-fils adore tous les gadgets électroniques que son fils lui achète.
Monsieur Boucher : Et ta petite-fille, qu'est-ce qu'elle fait maintenant qu'elle a fini ses études ?
Madame Picard : Elle a aussi trouvé du travail, dans une PME. Elle est au service des ventes et choisit et commande de nouveaux vêtements pour 1, 2, 3. Elle adore son poste et, surtout, elle voulait s'éloigner de Paris.
Monsieur Boucher : 1, 2, 3, leurs vêtements sont fabriqués en France ?
Madame Picard : Non, surtout en Chine et en Tunisie.
Monsieur Boucher : C'est dommage ! Maintenant tout est fabriqué dans d'autres pays.
Madame Picard : À moins que tu t'habilles chez Dior, Chanel ou Saint Laurent…

(*continued on next page*)

Pre-AP

Évaluation

A Évaluation de compréhension auditive 1.2

Écrivez les numéros 1–8 sur votre papier. Écoutez une femme et un homme discuter des métiers des membres de leur famille. Ensuite, écrivez une réponse brève à chaque question que vous entendez.

B Évaluation orale 1.1, 2.1, 3.2

Avec un partenaire, jouez les rôles d'un(e) étudiant(e) américain(e) qui fait un séjour en France et son ami(e) français(e) qui va l'aider à faire du shopping pour sa mère, son père, et sa sœur. Les parents de l'Américain(e) ont envoyé $350 pour que leur fils ou leur fille puisse leur acheter des produits de luxe.

Demandez si votre ami(e) américain(e) doit faire du shopping pour toute sa famille.

Dites que oui et qu'ils veulent des souvenirs typiquement français.

Demandez si ça fait longtemps que votre ami(e) cherche des cadeaux.

Dites que vous avez regardé, mais il semble que tous les bons produits sont fabriqués ailleurs.

Demandez combien votre ami(e) peut dépenser.

Dites que vos parents vous ont envoyé $350.

Dites à votre ami(e) de considérer les produits du luxe qui sont fabriqués en France. Demandez si sa sœur aime se maquiller.

Dites que oui. Dites quels produits de luxe vos parents aiment.

Dites que vous pouvez aller ensemble au grand magasin et acheter des produits de beauté pour elle de la marque Clarins que votre cousine aime beaucoup.

Dites que vous êtes d'accord, mais que vous avez besoin de quelque chose pour vos parents aussi.

Dites que votre ami peut leur envoyer du parfum français de Chanel ou de Givenchy.

Dites si vous aimez cette idée ou vous avez une meilleure idée.

Essential Instruction

1. Ask students to respond to **Activité A** by writing each response on a whiteboard for you to check.
2. Instruct partners to write a draft for **Activité B** and have them exchange scripts with other pairs for peer-review.
3. Encourage them to ask for any help on pronunciation before practicing and presenting to the class.
4. For **Activité C**, have students select three of the six activities to do in depth. They are responsible for outlining the information needed to complete the other three tasks.
5. Insist that the students spend at least ten minutes making an outline for **Activité D**. Have them write the composition in class to ensure that it is their original work and so that you are on hand to help.

C Évaluation culturelle 1.3, 2.1, 2.2, 3.1, 3.2, 4.2, 5.1

Vous allez comparer les cultures francophones à votre culture aux États-Unis. Vous aurez peut-être besoin de faire des recherches sur la culture américaine.

1. **La France et la mondialisation**
   D'après ce que vous avez appris dans cette unité, dites quelles sont les attitudes des Français envers la mondialisation. Ensuite, faites un sondage de dix adultes américains pour pouvoir comparer les attitudes des deux pays.
2. **L'Industrie du luxe**
   Quel est le pourcentage du marché français pour les produits de luxe? Imaginez qu'on vous donne un coupon pour des produits de luxe qui vaut 4 000 euros. Quels produits de luxe achèteriez-vous? (Cherchez les prix en ligne.) Pouvez-vous trouver des produits similaires aux États-Unis? Si oui, de quelles marques?
3. **Se débrouiller en France**
   Imaginez que vous allez travailler et vivre en France. Faites une liste de six à dix compagnies dont vous allez vous servir pour vos services bancaires, d'électricité, informatiques, etc. Vous devrez aussi acheter une voiture. Puis, faites une liste semblable des services dont vous vous servez aux États-Unis pour ces mêmes catégories, et comparez les deux listes.
4. **Le commerce entre la France et les États-Unis**
   En regardant la liste de produits que les deux pays échangent, faites un sommaire des secteurs qui sont forts en France et aux États-Unis. Expliquez les similarités et les différences marquantes.
5. **La structure des entreprises**
   Choisissez une compagnie américaine et dites si elle ressemble plutôt au modèle hiérarchique français ou à la coopérative française. Il est possible que la compagnie américaine ne suive ni le modèle hiérarchique ni le modèle de la coopérative. Dans ce cas, décrivez ce modèle typiquement américain.
6. **Les bonnes manières**
   Faites une liste de tabous (*taboos*) à éviter quand vous allez à une réunion, partagez un repas d'affaires, et allez chez un collègue en France. Faites une liste de tabous pour ces mêmes scénarios aux États-Unis.

D Évaluation écrite 1.3

Écrivez un paragraphe qui décrit comment une compagnie américaine doit s'adapter à la culture d'un pays francophone pour vendre ses produits. Pensez à un produit réel et faites des recherches en ligne pour regarder le site web de la compagnie ou ses publicités dans ce pays.

Resources

Perform

Answers

(continued from previous page)

1. Où travaille la nièce de Monsieur Boucher?
2. Qu'est-ce qu'elle fait dans la mult nationale?
3. Est-ce que c'est un bon travail? Pourquoi?
4. Pourquoi le petit-fils de Madame Picard habite aux États-Unis?
5. Pour quelle compagnie travaille-t-il?
6. Pourquoi veut-il rentrer en France?
7. Dans quel type d'entreprise est-ce que la petite-fille de Madame Picard travaille?
8. Est-ce que les vêtements de chez 1,2,3 sont fabriqués en France?

1. Elle travaille chez LVMH.
2. Elle est assistante de la DRH.
3. Oui, car elle aura des avantages pour acheter des produits de marque moins chers.
4. Il voulait s'éloigner de la France.
5. Il travaille pour Apple.
6. Parce qu'il est marié maintenant.
7. Elle travaille dans une PME.
8. Non, en Chine et en Tunisie.

B Answers will vary.
C All activities will vary.
D Answers will vary.

Reference Desk

1. The **Évaluation** activities may be used as an assessment tool. Include additional visual prompts for students who may have difficulty processing language.
2. **Activités E** and **F** require students to synthesize vocabulary and cultural information, specifically in the domain of business and marketing. Encourage them to review their notes and exercises before they complete these activities.
3. If you have access to Passport, assign a task to evaluate your students' oral proficiency.

Special Needs Students

Auditory Impairment
Use the practice listening test as an opportunity to assess what modifications you can make to help students hear well. Ask them if they would prefer taking the test in a different environment or if they need extra time to process the information in the questions.

Answers

All activities will vary.

Reference Desk

For examples of the marketing strategies discussed in the unit, consider searching online for images of ads for French luxury items. Use these images to reinforce the differences among the strategies and to help students decide how they wish to proceed with **Activité F**.

E Évaluation visuelle 1.2, 3.2, 5.2

Méline, une chanteuse de musique pop, fait du shopping à sa boutique préférée. Dites ce qu'elle achète et imaginez quelles sont les marques de chaque objet.

F Évaluation compréhensive 1.3, 3.2

*Créez une publicité pour un produit de luxe français qu'on va lancer (*launch*) sur le marché américain. D'abord il faut que vous trouviez une stratégie (par exemple,* bandwagon, glittering generalities, celebrity endorsement*) et choisissez un groupe de consommateurs. Finalement, faites un storyboard avec quatre à six séquences.*

Essential Instruction

1. Ask students to examine the picture in **Activité E** and write a short story about Méline. Encourage them to use rich descriptions to make the story more interesting.
2. Using a storyboard graphic, have students complete **Activité F**.

Vocabulaire de l'Unité 10

un(e) **actionnaire** stockholder *B*
l' **adaptation (f.)** adaptation *C*
adapter to adapt, to adjust *C*
s' **adapter (à)** to adapt (to) *C*
administratif, administrative administrative *C*
agroalimentaire food-processing *B*
ajouter to add *A*
anglophone English-speaking *B*
un **arrondissement** district, quarter *B*
un **auditeur, une auditrice libre** auditor of a class *B*
un **BA** Bachelor of Arts degree *B*
la **bière** beer *C*
bilingue bilingual *C*
c'est: c'est bien it's/that's exactly *A*
le **Cambodge** Cambodia *A*
un **chef/une cheffe d'entreprise** company director *C*; **chef/cheffe de service** department head *C*
la **Chine** China *A*
cibler to target *C*
la **comptabilité** accounting *C*
un(e) **comptable** accountant *C*
un **constructeur, une constructrice automobile** car manufacturer *C*
un **contrôleur, une contrôleuse de gestion** management controller *C*
convenu(e) conventional *A*
la **Corée du Sud** South Korea *A*
un(e) **correspondant(e)** pen pal *A*
la **crème** cream, lotion *A*
découpé(e) (en) cut up (in) *C*
un **directeur financier, une directrice financière** CFO *C*
doué(e) talented *C*
égal(e) equal *C*
s' **éloigner (de)** to get away (from)
l' **embarras (m.): avoir l'embarras du choix** to have too many choices *A*
une **éponge** sponge *C*
ethnique ethnic, multicultural *C*
fabriqué(e) (au, aux, en) made (in) *A*
la **faïence** earthenware *A*
faire: faire le tour explore all the possibilities *A*
une **figurine** figurine *A*
une **filiale** branch, subsidiary *B*
gastronomique gourmet *A*
le **hasard** fate, luck *B*
la **haute couture** high fashion *A*
le **Honduras** Honduras *A*
l' **imagination (f.)** imagination *A*
l' **Inde (f.)** India *A*
un **individu** individual *B*
l' **Indonésie (f.)** Indonesia *A*
une **interview** interview *B*
le **Japon** Japan *A*
la **joaillerie** fine jewelry *A*
la **Jordanie** Jordan *A*
lancer to launch *B*
un **leader** leader *B*; **leader mondial** world leader *B*
local(e) local *C*
le **luxe** luxury *A*
une **maîtrise** Master's degree *B*
la **Malaisie** Malaysia *A*
le **marketing** marketing *B*
la **maroquinerie** leather goods *A*
une **marque** brand *A*
marqué(e) brand name *A*
le **Mexique** Mexico *A*
la **mondialisation** globalization *C*
multinational(e) multinational *B*
le **papier: papier toilette** toilet paper *C*
un(e) **PDG (Président Directeur Général/Présidente Directrice Générale)** CEO *C*
la **peau** skin *C*
les **Philippines (f.)** Philippines *A*
prendre: prendre une décision to make a decision *C*
la **production** production *B*
un **produit: produit alimentaire** food product *A*; **produit laitier** dairy product *B*
proposer to offer *C*
régional(e) regional *C*
réserver (pour quelqu'un) to make especially (for someone) *C*
une **responsabilité** responsibility *B*
un(e) **responsable** director, manager *C*
les **ressources (f.) humaines** human resources *C*
le **reste** rest *B*
un **rouleau** roll *C*
sans: sans parler de not to mention *C*
un **secrétaire (administratif), une secrétaire (administrative)** secretary *C*
le **secrétariat** reception area *C*
une **serpillière** mop *C*
le **service** department *C*; **service après-vente** post-sale support *C*
un **siège social** headquarters *B*
une **SA (Société Anonyme)** public (incorporated) company *B*
le **Sri Lanka** Sri Lanka *A*
des **stratégies (f.)** strategies *B*
tutoyer to use the informal "**tu**" to address someone *B*
typiquement typical of *A*
l' **uniformisation (f.)** standardization *C*
un **vase** vase *A*
les **ventes (f.)** sales *C*

Resources

FC Flash Cards
Rendez-vous à Nice ! Documentaire 5
T *Unité 10* Test

Reference Desk

There are many websites that will help students review structure and vocabulary. The website **Quizlet** allows students and teachers to create review exercises tailored to specific lessons and then to share them with others. The site creates several different online games. This activity will appeal to your technologically skilled students.

Game

Wheel of Fortune

Play *Wheel of Fortune* to review unit vocabulary. A student at the board writes a set of blank lines corresponding to the number of letters in a word he or she chooses from the unit's vocabulary. One at a time, students try to guess the word by calling out letters. The student at the board writes a letter on the appropriate line if a correct call is made. You can also divide the class into two and make this a team game.

Special Needs Students

Linguistically Challenged
Help students with language difficulties complete **Àctivités E** and **F**. Make sure that they know how to make an outline of their ideas before attempting to write.

Multiple Intelligences

Visual-Spatial
Consider having students create several images similar to **Activité E**. Use these for whole-class or partner practice.

Bilan cumulatif

Pre-AP

Multiple Choice

I. Interpretive Communication: Print Text **1.2, 2.1**

Lisez cet article sur le patrimoine français, puis répondez à la question.

C'est complètement fou à quel point les Français protègent leur patrimoine. Le gouvernement encourage les français à consommer français, à produire des voitures françaises. Il se vante des produits de luxe français tels que la maroquinerie, la parfumerie, le vin, le champagne, et le foie gras. N'oubliez pas la langue ! Le gouvernement est contre les mots anglais et invente des mots français pour les remplacer. Le gouvernement exige aussi que les radios françaises passent un minimum de chansons françaises pour préserver la langue et la culture française. De cette façon on ne fait pas partie de la globalisation.

1. D'après le texte que signifie le mot « patrimoine » ?
   A. C'est une société matérialiste qui ne consomme que des produits chics et exclusifs.
   B. C'est l'ensemble des produits de luxe d'un pays.
   C. C'est ce qui constitue l'héritage culturel et linguistique d'un pays.
   D. C'est une philosophie née en France.

II. Interpretive Communication: Audio Text **1.1, 1.2**

Écoutez le dialogue entre Taylor et son meilleur ami, puis répondez aux questions.

1. Qu'est-ce que cet étudiant américain désire ?
   A. Améliorer son français et sa compréhension de la culture française
   B. Étudier à l'université en France
   C. Louer un appartement à Paris
   D. Se marier avec une Française
2. Quelle est la solution ?
   A. Voyager en France avec son prof de français
   B. Voyager en France avec son ami
   C. Trouver un stage dans une compagnie américaine en France
   D. Faire le touriste
3. Comment l'ami de Taylor prend-il la nouvelle ?
   A. Il est content. Il rêve de faire la même chose.
   B. Il est fâché. Il ne comprend pas la décision que son ami a prise.
   C. Il décide de partir avec lui.
   D. Il se sent attristé de voir partir son ami.

Free Response

III. Interpersonal Writing: E-mail Reply **1.3, 2.1, 4.2, 5.2**

Vous allez écrire une réponse au mail d'un homme d'affaires américain qui s'intéresse à importer des produits de luxe français. Comme vous vous intéressez à entrer dans le marché américain, répondez à ses questions sur votre gamme (line) *de produits, vos prix et votre croissance* (growth)*. Proposez une date de rendez-vous à Boston pour faire connaissance de cet homme d'affaire américain. Écrivez formellement, avec une salutation au début et une formule de politesse* (closing) *à la fin de votre message.*

Resources

Activity II

Answers

I

1. C

II Script

–Ah non, tu ne vas pas nous quitter !
–Si, j'ai besoin de perfectionner mon français, et pour ça je dois aller en France pour au moins un an.
–Mais qu'est-ce que tu vas y apprendre que tu ne peux pas apprendre ici ? Ta prof est française.
–Oui, elle est française et formidable mais elle ne peut pas remplacer l'expérience sur place. Je voudrais m'éloigner de la culture américaine et m'immerger le plus possible dans la culture et la langue françaises. Ça fait longtemps que j'en rêve ; je vais observer les Français et m'adapter à leur mode de vie. Je pourrai parler français jour et nuit, mon désir le plus cher !
–Comment vas-tu faire pour vivre ?
–J'y ai pensé. Je vais chercher un stage dans le service marketing d'une multinationale américaine dont le siège social est dans la capitale. Comme tu sais, j'ai suivi des cours de marketing à l'université.
–Quelle bonne idée, même si je suis triste de te voir partir.

1. A
2. C
3. D

III Paragraphs will vary.

IV Conversations will vary.

Game

Jeopardy!

Make a *Jeopardy!* board with the headings: **Vocabulaire**, **Expressions**, **Entreprise**, **Publicité**, etc. Have students play the game in teams making questions from the cues you give them. Find Jeopardy game templates online.

Recherche : free flash jeopardy review generator

Essential Instruction

1. Make copies of pp. 614–615 so that students can write notes and ideas on them.
2. Have students skim the questions before reading **Activité I**.
3. Ask them to do the same for **Activité II**. Correct both exercises immediately.
4. Assign **Activité III** to be done in class. Circulate to help with on-the-spot questions they may have about their writing.
5. Give students time to prepare their oral responses. If possible, allow them to record their work so that they can practice many times until they are pleased with it.
6. Students who have anxiety issues will benefit from not performing in front of the class.

De : Thomas Hamilton
Objet : Importation de produits de luxe aux USA

Monsieur,

Je suis à la recherche d'un exportateur français qui veut à son tour devenir partenaire dans la promotion de produits français de luxe aux États-Unis. Notre boutique et notre centre de distribution sont situés dans la banlieue proche de Boston, entourés par un grand nombre de sociétés de technologie, d'assurances, et d'hôtellerie, aussi bien que des associations universitaires. Nous voulons promouvoir des marques françaises lors de conférences, d'événements, et de réunions avec nos clients. Nous souhaitons réunir plusieurs grandes marques sous un même toit chez nous. Les parfums, les produits de beauté, les montres, les foulards et d'autres accessoires, les vêtements femme, et les fournitures bureau haut de gamme nous intéressent. Le marché est fort, et le secteur rapporte plusieurs milliards de dollars.

Seriez-vous intéressé(e) par une éventuelle collaboration, et pourquoi ? Quelle gamme de produits votre entreprise développe-t-elle, et quelle est votre croissance économique ?

En vous remerciant de votre retour, veuillez agréer, Monsieur, mes sincères salutations.

Thomas Hamilton, propriétaire
Hamilton Highline Gifts
3400 Longwood Way
Burlington, Massachusetts
USA

IV. Interpersonal Speaking: Conversation **1.1, 2.1, 2.2**

Vous allez avoir une conversation avec un agent de police au commissariat. Vous êtes touriste en France, et on vous a volé quelque chose d'important. Suivez les indications ci-dessous.

L'agent : Je peux vous aider, Monsieur ?
Vous : **Dites ce qu'on vous a volé.**
L'agent : Et où ce vol a-t-il eu lieu ?
Vous : **Dites qu'on vous a volé dans le métro en route vers la station Châtelet.**
L'agent : Et vous avez vu le voleur ?
Vous : **Dites que oui, et décrivez le voleur : sa taille, son âge, la couleur de ses cheveux, son origine ethnique, ses vêtements.**
L'agent : (*Il vous montre une photo.*) C'est cette personne ?
Vous : **Dites que vous êtes sûr que c'est lui/elle, mais qu'il/elle a les cheveux plus courts maintenant.**
L'agent : On l'a presque arrêté(e) la semaine dernière. Ses vols sont toujours dans le métro. Comment est-ce qu'on peut vous contacter ?
Vous : **Donnez-lui votre numéro de portable.**
L'agent : Auriez-vous le temps de remplir cette déclaration de vol ?
Vous : **Dites que vous la remplirez à l'hôtel et que vous reviendrez au commissariat pour la lui rendre demain matin.**
L'agent : Merci d'être venu. Je vous reverrai demain, alors.
Vous : **Remerciez l'agent et dites que vous le reverrez demain.**

Reference Desk

1. The **Bilan cumulatif** is based on the French Language and Culture AP exam prepared by the College Board. It assesses students' proficiencies in the Interpersonal, Interpretive, and Presentational modes of communication. Students are also asked to demonstrate their understanding of the products, practices, and perspectives of the target cultures.
2. The Print Text section consists of a variety of authentic print materials such as articles and correspondence. A multiple-choice question follows the text.
3. The Audio Text is a professional recording, usually a dialogue. Encourage students to preview and skim the questions before listening. They should then answer the multiple-choice questions.
4. The E-mail reply is a free response test section. Students develop their interpersonal writing skills.
5. In the Speaking section of the assessment, students are asked to participate in a conversation or make a cultural comparison using their presentational speaking skills.
6. Practice AP questions and tests from previous years can be found online.

Recherche : ap central

Differentiated Learning

Accelerate
Allow students to write at their own pace. They may peer edit their work upon completion.

Decelerate
Suggest that students first read the questions then have them cover the reading with a blank piece of paper and uncover the text sentence by sentence. This process helps them focus on the reading a little at a time and not be overwhelmed by the length.

Special Needs Students

Dyslexia/At-Risk Students
Consider modifying your assessment of spelling to ease the pressure students may experience.

Grammar Summary

The Grammar Summary is in alphabetical order.

Adjectives

Agreement of Regular Adjectives

Masculine	Masculine Plural	Feminine	Feminine Plural
	+ **s**	**masculine adjective + e**	**masculine adjective + es**
grand	grands	grande	grandes

Exceptions

Masculine	Masculine Plural	Feminine	Feminine Plural
Adjectives ending in **e**	+ **s**	no change	+ **s**
bête	bêtes	bête	bêtes
Adjectives ending in **n, l**	+ **s**	**double consonant + e**	**double consonant + es**
bon intellectuel	bons intellectuels	bonne intellectuelle	bonnes intellectuelles
Adjectives ending in **s**	no change	**double consonant + e**	**double consonant + es**
gros	gros	grosse	grosses
Adjectives ending in **eux**	no change	**-euse**	**-euses**
généreux	généreux	généreuse	généreuses

Irregular Adjectives

Masculine	Masculine Before a Vowel	Masculine Plural	Feminine	Feminine Plural
beau	bel	beaux	belle	+ **s**
nouveau	nouvel	nouveaux	nouvelle	
vieux	vieil	vieux	vieille	
frais	frais	frais	fraîche	
cher	cher	} + **s**	chère	
blanc	blanc		blanche	
long	long		longue	

Invariable Adjectives

Some adjectives do not change in the feminine or the plural form.

orange	marron	super	sympa	bon marché

Position of Adjectives

Article + Noun	+ Adjective
des stylos **bleus**	

Exceptions

beau, joli, nouveau, vieux, bon, mauvais, grand, petit, gros (*BAGS*: *beauty, age, goodness, size*)

Article + Adjective	+ Noun
une **belle** voiture	

Comparative of Adjectives

plus	(*more*)	**+ adj**	**+ que**	(*than*)
moins	(*less*)	**+ adj**	**+ que**	(*than*)
aussi	(*as*)	**+ adj**	**+ que**	(*as*)

Superlative of Adjectives

For regular adjectives placed after the noun

le/la/les + noun + **le/la/les** + **plus** + adjective

For adjectives placed before the noun

le/la/les + **plus** + adjective + noun

Exception: bon = le/la/les **meilleur**(e)(s)
mauvais = le/la/les **pire**(s)

Interrogative Adjective *quel*

Masculine	Masculine Plural	Feminine	Feminine Plural
quel	quels	quelle	quelles

Adjective *tout*

Masculine	Masculine Plural	Feminine	Feminine Plural
tout	tous	toute	toutes

Demonstrative Adjectives

Singular			Plural
Masculine before a Consonant Sound **ce** colis	**Masculine before a Vowel Sound** **cet** aéroport	**Feminine** **cette** lettre	**ces** livres

Indefinite Adjectives

aucun(e)... ne(n')	*not one, none*
autre	*other*
certain(**e**)	*certain*
chaque	*each, every*
même	*same*
plusieurs	*several*
quelques	*some*
tout/tous/toute(**s**)	*all, every*

Possessive Adjectives

Masculine	Feminine	Plural
mon	ma	mes
ton	ta	tes
son	sa	ses
notre	notre	nos
votre	votre	vos
leur	leur	leurs

Adverbs

assez	peut-être
beaucoup	souvent
bien	surtout
déjà	toujours
enfin	trop
mal	un peu
même	vite
peu	

Expressions of Quantity

assez de	une boîte de	une bouteille de
beaucoup de	un paquet de	un pot de
peu de	un morceau de	une tranche de
un peu de	un gramme de	un kilo de
trop de	un litre de	

Formation of Long Adverbs

Long adverbs are formed by adding **-ment** to the feminine form of an adjective.

Feminine Form of Adjective	+ ment
heureuse	heureusement
généreuse	généreusement

Position of Adverbs

Short Adverbs Qualifying Verbs

Present Tense	Passé Composé
J'aime **beaucoup** les animaux.	Tu as **trop** mangé.

Long Adverbs Qualifying Sentences

Modifying Verbs	Modifying Entire Sentence
Tu dessines **parfaitement**.	Nous avons fini, **heureusement**. **Heureusement**, nous avons fini.

Adverbial Expressions of Time

Tu vas à la teuf **demain soir** ?
Ce matin, le prof a apporté des gâteaux.

Comparative of Adverbs

plus	(*more*)	+ adverb	**+ que**	(*than*)
moins	(*less*)	+ adverb	**+ que**	(*than*)
aussi	(*as*)	+ adverb	**+ que**	(*as*)

Some adverbs have an irregular form:

Adverb	Comparative
bien (*well*)	**mieux** (*better*)
beaucoup (*a lot, much*)	**plus** (*more*)
peu (*little*)	**moins** (*less*)
mal (*badly*)	**pis, plus mal** (*worse*)

Superlative of Adverbs

For regular adjectives placed after the noun

le + **plus** + adverb

To form the superlative of **bien**, **beaucoup**, and **peu**, put **le** before these adverbs' irregular comparative forms.

Adverb	Comparative	Superlative
bien (*well*)	**mieux** (*better*)	**le mieux** (*the best*)
beaucoup (*a lot, much*)	**plus** (*more*)	**le plus** (*the most*)
peu (*little*)	**moins** (*less*)	**le moins** (*the least*)
mal (*badly*)	**pis, plus mal** (*worse*)	**le pis, le plus mal** (*the worst*)

Articles

Indefinite Articles

Singular		Plural
Masculine	**Feminine**	
un	une	des

Definite Articles

Singular			Plural
Before a Consonant Sound		Before a Vowel Sound	
Masculine	Feminine		
le	la	l’	les

À + Definite Article

Singular			Plural
Before a Consonant Sound		Before a Vowel Sound	
Masculine	Feminine		
au	à la	à l’	aux

De + Definite Article

Singular			Plural
Before a Consonant Sound		Before a Vowel Sound	
Masculine	Feminine		
du	de la	de l’	des

Partitive Articles

Before a Consonant Sound		Before a Vowel Sound	In the Negative
Masculine	Feminine		
du coca	**de la** viande	**de l’**eau minérale	**pas de** coca **pas de** viande **pas d’**eau minérale

C’est versus *il/elle est*

C’est....	
+ proper noun	**C’est** Karim ?
+ stress pronoun	Oui, **c’est** lui.
+ modified noun	**C’est** un garçon sympa.
+ adjective referring to previous idea	Son sport préféré, **c’est** le foot.

C'est versus *il/elle est* *continued*

Il/elle est....	
+ adjective	**Il est** sportif.
+ profession	**Il est** footballeur.
+ nationality	**Il est** marocain.
+ religion	**Il est** musulman.
+ previously mentioned person or thing	Tu as vu ma trousse ? **Elle est** bleue et noire.

Negation

ne (n')... pas	Il **ne** joue **pas**. Il **n'**a **pas** joué.
ne (n')... plus	Elle **n'**aime **plus** les frites.
ne (n')... jamais	Nous **ne** dansons **jamais**.
ne (n')... personne	Vous **n'**invitez **personne** ?
ne (n')... que	Ils **ne** mangent **que** des pâtes.
ne (n')... rien	Ma grand-mère **ne** comprend **rien**.
ne (n')... ni... ni	On **ne** joue **ni** au foot **ni** au tennis.

Nouns

Irregular Plural Nouns

	Singular	Plural
no change	un bus	des bus
-al → **aux**	un cheval	des chev**aux**
-eu → **eux**	un jeu	des **jeux**
-eau → **eaux**	un bateau	des bat**eaux**

Numbers

Cardinal Numbers		Ordinal Numbers	
un	six	premier, première	sixième
deux	sept	deuxième	septième
trois	huit	troisième	huitième
quatre	neuf	quatrième	neuvième
cinq	dix, etc.	cinquième	dixième, etc.

Prepositions

Prepositions before Cities, Countries, Continents

City (Paris)	**Masculine** (le Japon)	**Feminine** (la France)	**Plural** (les États-Unis)
à	au	en	aux

Pronouns

Subject Pronouns

Singular	**Plural**
je	nous
tu	vous
il/elle/on	ils/elles

Stress Pronouns

Singular	**Plural**
moi	nous
toi	vous
lui, elle	eux, elles

Direct Object Pronouns

Singular	**Plural**
me	nous
te	vous
le, la	les

Indirect Object Pronouns

Singular	**Plural**
me	nous
te	vous
lui	leur

The Pronoun *en*

***en* replaces…**	
de + Noun	Tu manges **du pain** ? Oui, **j'en** mange. Prenez **de la viande** ! Prenez-**en** !
de + Noun after Expression of Quantity	Vous voulez **un peu de café** ? Oui, **j'en** veux **un peu**. Il a apporté **trois assiettes** ? Oui, il **en** a apporté **trois**.

The Pronoun *y*

Replaces a preposition (**à, en, dans, chez, sur, derrière**) and the name of a place.

Il va au stade ? Oui, il **y** va.

Order of Double Pronouns

Subject	+	**me** **te** **se** **vous** **nous**	+	**le** **la** **les**	+	**lui** **leur**	+	**y**	+	**en**	+	Verb

In affirmative commands, the order of pronouns is:

		m'		**moi**						
		t'		**toi**						
Verb	+	**le**	+	**lui**	+	**nous**	+	**y**	+	**en**
		la		**leur**		**vous**				
		les								

Possessive Pronouns

	Singular		Plural	
	Masculine	**Feminine**	**Masculine**	**Feminine**
mine	**le mien**	**la mienne**	**les miens**	**les miennes**
yours	**le tien**	**la tienne**	**les tiens**	**les tiennes**
his, hers, its, one's	**le sien**	**la sienne**	**les siens**	**les siennes**
ours	**le nôtre**	**la nôtre**	**les nôtres**	
yours	**le vôtre**	**la vôtre**	**les vôtres**	
theirs	**le leur**	**la leur**	**les leurs**	

Interrogative Pronouns

	Subject	Direct Object	Object of Preposition
People	qui qui est-ce qui	qui qui est-ce que	qui
Things	qu'est-ce qui	que qu'est-ce que	quoi

Interrogative Pronoun *lequel*

Masculine	Masculine Plural	Feminine	Feminine Plural
lequel	lesquels	laquelle	lesquelles

Relative Pronouns *qui* and *que*

	Subject	Object
People	qui l'homme **qui** parle	que le garçon **que** je connais
Things	qui le dessin **qui** est sur la table	que le pull **que** je porte

Relative Pronoun *dont*

dont = **de** + noun

Relative Pronouns *ce qui* and *ce que*

	Subject	Object
Things	ce qui J'aime **ce qui** est beau.	ce que Tu comprends **ce que** tu lis ?

Demonstrative Pronouns

	Singular	Plural
Masculine	celui	ceux
Feminine	celle	celles

Indefinite Pronouns

aucun(e)… ne (n')	not one, none
un(e) autre	another
l'un(e)… l'autre	one… the other
la plupart	most
plusieurs	several
quelqu'un, quelque chose	someone, something
n'importe qui, n'importe quoi	anyone, anything
tous les deux, toutes les deux	both

Questions

Forming Questions

using **n'est-ce pas**	Il fait chaud, **n'est-ce pas** ? Ils regardent un film, **n'est-ce pas** ?
using **est-ce que**	**Est-ce qu'**il fait chaud ? **Est-ce qu'**ils regardent un film ?
using **inversion:** Verb-Subject	**Fait-il** chaud ? **Regardent-ils** un film ?

Telling Time

Il est une **heure** Il est midi. Il est minuit.	… et quart.	… et demie. (… midi et demi.) (… minuit et demi.)	… moins le quart.

Verbs

Regular Verbs—Present Tense

-er aimer			
j'	aime	nous	aim**ons**
tu	aim**es**	vous	aim**ez**
il/elle/on	aim**e**	ils/elles	aim**ent**

-ir finir			
je	fin**is**	nous	fin**issons**
tu	fin**is**	vous	fin**issez**
il/elle/on	fin**it**	ils/elles	fin**issent**

Regular Verbs—Present Tense *continued*

-re vendre			
je	vend**s**	nous	vend**ons**
tu	vend**s**	vous	vend**ez**
il/elle/on	vend	ils/elles	vend**ent**

Irregular Verbs—Present Tense

acheter			
j'	ach**è**te	nous	achetons
tu	ach**è**tes	vous	achetez
il/elle/on	ach**è**te	ils/elles	ach**è**tent

aller			
je	vais	nous	allons
tu	vas	vous	allez
il/elle/on	va	ils/elles	vont

avoir (avoir besoin de/avoir chaud/avoir faim/avoir froid/ avoir soif)			
j'	ai	nous	avons
tu	as	vous	avez
il/elle/on	a	ils/elles	ont

boire			
je	bois	nous	buvons
tu	bois	vous	buvez
il/elle/on	boit	ils/elles	boivent

conduire			
je	conduis	nous	conduisons
tu	conduis	vous	conduisez
il/elle/on	conduit	ils/elles	conduisent

connaître			
je	connais	nous	connaissons
tu	connais	vous	connaissez
il/elle/on	connaît	ils/elles	connaissent

courir			
je	cours	nous	courons
tu	cours	vous	courez
il/elle/on	court	ils/elles	courent

croire			
je	crois	nous	croyons
tu	crois	vous	croyez
il/elle/on	croit	ils/elles	croient

devoir			
je	dois	nous	devons
tu	dois	vous	devez
il/elle/on	doit	ils/elles	doivent

dire			
je	dis	nous	disons
tu	dis	vous	dites
il/elle/on	dit	ils/elles	disent

dormir			
je	dors	nous	dormons
tu	dors	vous	dormez
il/elle/on	dort	ils/elles	dorment

écrire			
j'	écris	nous	écrivons
tu	écris	vous	écrivez
il/elle/on	écrit	ils/elles	écrivent

Irregular Verbs—Present Tense *continued*

être			
je	suis	nous	sommes
tu	es	vous	êtes
il/elle/on	est	ils/elles	sont

faire			
je	fais	nous	faisons
tu	fais	vous	faites
il/elle/on	fait	ils/elles	font

falloir
il faut

lire			
je	lis	nous	lisons
tu	lis	vous	lisez
il/elle/on	lit	ils/elles	lisent

mettre			
je	mets	nous	mettons
tu	mets	vous	mettez
il/elle/on	met	ils/elles	mettent

offrir			
j'	offre	nous	offrons
tu	offres	vous	offrez
il/elle/on	offre	ils/elles	offrent

ouvrir			
j'	ouvre	nous	ouvrons
tu	ouvres	vous	ouvrez
il/elle/on	ouvre	ils/elles	ouvrent

partir			
je	pars	nous	partons
tu	pars	vous	partez
il/elle/on	part	ils/elles	partent

plaire			
je	plais	nous	plaisons
tu	plais	vous	plaisez
il/elle/on	plaît	ils/elles	plaisent

pouvoir			
je	peux	nous	pouvons
tu	peux	vous	pouvez
il/elle/on	peut	ils/elles	peuvent

préférer			
je	préfère	nous	préférons
tu	préfères	vous	préférez
il/elle/on	préfère	ils/elles	préfèrent

prendre			
je	prends	nous	prenons
tu	prends	vous	prenez
il/elle/on	prend	ils/elles	prennent

recevoir			
je	reçois	nous	recevons
tu	reçois	vous	recevez
il/elle/on	reçoit	ils/elles	reçoivent

savoir			
je	sais	nous	savons
tu	sais	vous	savez
il/elle/on	sait	ils/elles	savent

sortir			
je	sors	nous	sortons
tu	sors	vous	sortez
il/elle/on	sort	ils/elles	sortent

suivre			
je	suis	nous	suivons
tu	suis	vous	suivez
il/elle/on	suit	ils/elles	suivent

Irregular Verbs—Present Tense *continued*

venir			
je	viens	nous	venons
tu	viens	vous	venez
il/elle/on	vient	ils/elles	viennent

voir			
je	vois	nous	voyons
tu	vois	vous	voyez
il/elle/on	voit	ils/elles	voient

vivre			
je	vis	nous	vivons
tu	vis	vous	vivez
il/elle/on	vit	ils/elles	vivent

vouloir			
je	veux	nous	voulons
tu	veux	vous	voulez
il/elle/on	veut	ils/elles	veulent

Regular Imperatives

-er chanter	-ir choisir	-re prendre
Chante !	Choisis !	Prends !
Chantons !	Choisissons !	Prenons !
Chantez !	Choisissez !	Prenez !

Reflexive Verbs—Present Tense

se préparer	
je **me** prépare	nous **nous** préparons
tu **te** prépares	vous **vous** préparez
il/elle/on **se** prépare	ils/elles **se** préparent

Imperative of Reflexive Verbs

s'asseoir
Assieds-toi !
Asseyons-nous !
Asseyez-vous !

Expressing the Near Future

aller + Infinitive
Nous allons dîner.

Passé composé with *avoir*

avoir + past participle

-er verbs → é	-ir verbs → i	-re verbs → u
Nous avons gagné.	Tu as fini.	On a attendu.

Irregular Past Participles								
avoir	→	**eu**	boire	→	**bu**	conduire	→	**conduit**
connaître	→	**connu**	courir	→	**couru**	croire	→	**cru**
devoir	→	**dû**	dire	→	**dit**	écrire	→	**écrit**
être	→	**été**	faire	→	**fait**	falloir	→	**fallu**
lire	→	**lu**	mettre	→	**mis**	offrir	→	**offert**
ouvrir	→	**ouvert**	pleuvoir	→	**plu**	pouvoir	→	**pu**
prendre	→	**pris**	recevoir	→	**reçu**	savoir	→	**su**
suivre	→	**suivi**	vendre	→	**vendu**	vivre	→	**vécu**
voir	→	**vu**	vouloir	→	**voulu**			

Passé composé with *être*

être **+ past participle (+ agreement** in gender and number**)**					
je	suis	arrivé(e)	nous	sommes	arrivé(e)s
tu	es	arrivé(e)	vous	êtes	arrivé(e)(s)
il	est	arrivé	ils	sont	arrivés
elle	est	arrivée	elles	sont	arrivées

Some of the verbs that use **être** as the helping verb in the **passé composé** are:

Infinitive	Past Participle
aller	**allé**
arriver	**arrivé**
descendre	**descendu**
devenir	**devenu**
entrer	**entré**
monter	**monté**
partir	**parti**
rentrer	**rentré**
rester	**resté**
retourner	**retourné**
revenir	**revenu**
sortir	**sorti**
venir	**venu**

Passé composé of Reflexive Verbs

se préparer	
je me suis préparé(e)	nous nous sommes préparé(e)s
tu t'es préparé(e)	vous vous êtes préparé(e)(s)
il s'est préparé	ils se sont préparés
elle s'est préparée	elles se sont préparées
on s'est préparé	

Present Participle

Verb	Present Participle
aller	allant
attendre	attendant
faire	faisant
finir	finissant
partir	partant

Some verbs have irregular present participles.

Verb	Present Participle
avoir	ayant
être	étant
savoir	sachant

Imperfect Tense

aller			
j'	all**ais**	nous	all**ions**
tu	all**ais**	vous	all**iez**
il/elle/on	all**ait**	ils/elles	all**aient**

Pluperfect Tense

	finir	rentrer
je (j')	**avais fini**	**étais rentré(e)**
tu	**avais fini**	**étais rentré(e)**
il/elle	**avait fini**	**était rentré(e)**
nous	**avions fini**	**étions rentré(e)s**
vous	**aviez fini**	**étiez rentré(e)(s)**
ils/elles	**avaient fini**	**étaient rentré(e)s**

Future Tense

finir			
je	fini**rai**	nous	fini**rons**
tu	fini**ras**	vous	fini**rez**
il/elle/on	fini**ra**	ils/elles	fini**ront**

Conditional

choisir			
je	choisir**ais**	nous	choisir**ions**
tu	choisir**ais**	vous	choisir**iez**
il/elle/on	choisir**ait**	ils/elles	choisir**aient**

Past Conditional

	mettre	aller	se lever
je (j')	**aurais mis**	**serais allé(e)**	**me serais levé(e)**
tu	**aurais mis**	**serais allé(e)**	**te serais levé(e)**
il/elle	**aurait mis**	**serait allé(e)**	**se serait levé(e)**
nous	**aurions mis**	**serions allé(e)s**	**nous serions levé(e)s**
vous	**auriez mis**	**seriez allé(e)(s)**	**vous seriez levé(e)(s)**
ils/elles	**auraient mis**	**seraient allé(e)s**	**se seraient levé(e)s**

Irregular Stems of Verbs in the Future and Conditional

Infinitive—Irregular stem		
aller—**ir**	asseoir—**assiér**	devoir—**devr**
envoyer—**enverr**	être—**ser**	faire—**fer**
falloir—**faudr**	pouvoir—**pourr**	recevoir—**recevr**
savoir—**saur**	venir—**viendr**	voir—**verr**
vouloir—**voudr**		

Future Tense after *quand*

quand + future	future

Future or Conditional with *si*

si + present	future
si + imperfect	conditional
si + pluperfect	past conditional

Subjunctive of Regular Verbs

	tenter	finir	attendre
que je (j')	tent**e**	finiss**e**	attend**e**
que tu	tent**es**	finiss**es**	attend**es**
qu'il/elle	tent**e**	finiss**e**	attend**e**
que nous	tent**ions**	finiss**ions**	attend**ions**
que vous	tent**iez**	finiss**iez**	attend**iez**
qu'ils/elles	tent**ent**	finiss**ent**	attend**ent**

Subjunctive of Irregular Verbs

	aller	avoir	boire	croire	devoir
que je (j')	aille	aie	boive	croie	doive
que tu	ailles	aies	boives	croies	doives
qu'il/elle	aille	ait	boive	croie	doive
que nous	allions	ayons	buvions	croyions	devions
que vous	alliez	ayez	buviez	croyiez	deviez
qu'ils/elles	aillent	aient	boivent	croient	doivent

	être	faire	pouvoir	prendre	recevoir
que je (j')	sois	fasse	puisse	prenne	reçoive
que tu	sois	fasses	puisses	prennes	reçoives
qu'il/elle	soit	fasse	puisse	prenne	reçoive
que nous	soyons	fassions	puissions	prenions	recevions
que vous	soyez	fassiez	puissiez	preniez	receviez
qu'ils/elles	soient	fassent	puissent	prennent	reçoivent

Subjunctive of Irregular Verbs *continued*

	savoir	venir	voir	vouloir
que je (j')	sache	vienne	voie	veuille
que tu	saches	viennes	voies	veuilles
qu'il/elle	sache	vienne	voit	veuille
que nous	sachions	venions	voyions	voulions
que vous	sachiez	veniez	voyiez	vouliez
qu'ils/elles	sachent	viennent	voient	veuillent

The Subjunctive after Impersonal Expressions

il est bon que	*it is good that*
il est essentiel que	*it is essential that*
il faut que	*it is necessary that*
il est important que	*it is important that*
il est impossible que	*it is impossible that*
il est indispensable que	*it is indispensable that*
il est nécessaire que	*it is necessary that*
il est possible que	*it is possible that*
il est surprenant que	*it is surprising that*
il est utile que	*it is useful that*
il se pourrait que	*it is possible that*
il vaut mieux que	*it is better that*

Other Expressions Requiring the Use of the Subjunctive

Expressions of Wish, Will, or Desire	Expressions of Emotions	
aimer que *to like, to love*	**être content(e) que** *to be happy that*	**avoir peur que** *to be afraid that*
désirer que *to want*	**être heureux/heureuse que** *to be happy that*	**regretter que** *to regret that*
exiger que *to require*	**être triste que** *to be sad that*	**s'inquiéter que** *to be worried that*
préférer que *to prefer*	**être désolé(e) que** *to be sorry that*	**Ça me surprend que...** *It surprises me that...*
souhaiter que *to wish, to hope*	**être fâché(e) que** *to be angry that*	**Ça m'embête que...** *It bothers me that...*
vouloir que *to want*	**être étonné(e) que** *to be surprised that*	**C'est dommage que...** *It's too bad that...*

Expressions of Doubt or Uncertainty		
(ne pas) penser que *to not think that*	Je **ne** pense **pas** qu'il **soit** français. *I don't think that he is French.*	**Penses-tu que** nous **ayons** assez d'argent ? *Do you think we have enough money?*
(ne pas) croire que *to not believe that*	Elle **ne** croit **pas** que vous **partiez**. *She doesn't believe that you are leaving.*	**Croyez-vous qu'**il **fasse** beau demain ? *Do you believe it will be nice tomorrow?*
(ne pas) être sûr que *to not be sure that*	Je **ne** suis **pas** sûr que ce **soit** vrai. *I am not sure this is true.*	**Êtes-vous sûr que** ce **soient** des chats ? *Are you sure these are cats?*
(ne pas) être vrai que *to not be true that*	**Ce n'est pas vrai que** Mel **comprenne**. *It is not true that Mel understands.*	**Est-il vrai que** tes cousins **partent** ? *Is it true that your cousins are leaving?*
(ne pas) être évident que *to not be obvious that*	**Il n'est pas évident que** nous **restions**. *It is not obvious that we'll stay.*	**Est-il évident que** nous **soyons** jumeaux ? *Is it obvious that we are twins?*

Subjunctive after *pour que*

pour que + subjunctive	Je nourris les chevaux **pour qu'**ils **soient** forts.	*I feed the horses so they will be strong.*

Verb + Infinitive

aimer	aller	désirer
devoir	falloir	pouvoir
préférer	venir	vouloir

Nous **préférons faire** du ski.

Verb + *à* + Infinitive

aider	s'amuser	apprendre
commencer	continuer	s'engager
hésiter	s'intéresser	inviter
se préparer	réussir	

Il **se prépare à** conduire.

Verb + *de* + Infinitive

accepter	arrêter	choisir
conseiller	décider	demander
se dépêcher	dire	essayer
finir	offrir	oublier
promettre	rêver	

Ils **ont oublié d'**apporter les boissons.

Past Infinitive

après	+	**avoir** **être**	+	past participle

Vocabulaire

Vocabulary terms from Level 1 and Level 2 of *T'es branché?* are included but do not have a unit number. Vocabulary terms from Level 3 include the unit number in which the term is introduced.

Français–Anglais

A

à at; by; in; on; to; *à bicyclette* on a bicycle; *À bientôt.* See you soon.; *à bord* on board; *à carreaux* plaid 9; *à cause de* because of 2; *à côté (de)* beside, next to; *À demain.* See you tomorrow.; *à droite* on the right; *à gauche* on the left; *à la page* in fashion 2; *à l'avant-plan* in the foreground 7; *à l'arrière-plan* in the background 7; *à l'heure* on time; *à l'horizon* on the horizon; *à mi-temps* half-time 8; *à plein temps* full-time 8; *à mon avis* in my opinion; *à mon goût* for my taste 5; *à part* aside from 9; *à pied* on foot; *à pois* polka-dot 9; *à propos de* about 2; *à rayures* striped 9; *à roulettes* on wheels; *à sa place* in its place 2; *à table* at the (dinner) table 2; *à vélo* by bike

abandonner to abandon 4
absolument absolutely 1
abstrait(e) abstract
accablé(e) overwhelmed 9
accéder to access 8
un **accélérateur** accelerator
un **accent** accent
accepter to accept
un **accessoire** accessory
un **accident** accident
un **accompagnateur, une accompagnatrice** home health worker
accompagner to accompany
accorder to grant 8
des **accras (m.) de morue** cod fritters
accrocher (des tableaux) to hang (paintings) 3
un **accueil** welcome; *un centre d'accueil* reception center, shelter
accueil welcome/home page 5
accueillir to welcome 2
un **achat** purchase
acheter to buy
acquis(e) acquired 8
un **acteur, une actrice** actor, actress
l' **action (f.)** action; *l'Action de grâce* Thanksgiving
un(e) **actionnaire** stockholder 10
une **activité** activity
une **adaptation** adaptation 10
adapter to adapt, to adjust 10
s' **adapter (à)** to adapt (to) 10
l' **addition (f.)** bill
adieu farewell 8; *faire ses adieux* to bid farewell 8
administratif, administrative administrative 10; *un secrétaire (administratif), une secrétaire (administrative)* secretary 10
l' **administration (f.)** administration 6
un(e) **ado** teenager
adorer to adore
une **adresse** address; *un jeu d'adresse* game of skill
adressé (à) addressed (to) 5
s' **adresser (à)** to address (someone) 2
l' **aérobic (m.)** aerobics
aéronautique: le secteur aéronautique aviation industry
un **aéroport** airport
des **affaires (f.)** belongings, things; *affaires de ménage* housecleaning items; *affaires de toilette* toiletries
affectueusement affectionately, with warm regards
une **affiche** poster
affolé(e) distraught 1; *être affolé(e)* to be panicked 1
affranchir to stamp 6
l' **affranchissement (m.)** postage 6
africain(e) African 9
l' **Afrique (f.)** Africa
agacer to annoy; *Tu m'agaces!* You're getting on my nerves!
l' **âge (m.)** age; *Tu as quel âge?* How old are you?
un(e) **agent(e)** agent; *agent de police* police officer
agir to act
s' **agir (de): il s'agit de** it's about
un **agneau** lamb
agréable pleasant 5
agroalimentaire food-processing 10; *le secteur agroalimentaire* food industry
ah oh
l' **aide (f.)** assistance
aider to help
un **aïeul, une aïeule (les aïeux)** ancestor(s) 3
aimer to like, to love
l' **air (m.)** air; *avoir l'air* to look; *en plein air* outdoors
ajouter to add 10
un **album** album; *album concept* concept album 7
l' **alcoolisme (m.)** alcoholism
algérien(ne) Algerian
alimentaire: un produit alimentaire food product 10
l' **Allemagne (f.)** Germany
l' **allemand (m.)** German *[language]*
allemand(e) German
aller to go; *je m'en vais* I'm going (away) 2; Tu trouves que… me va bien? Does this… look good on me?; *Vas-y!* Go for it!
une **alliance** wedding ring 1
allô hello *[on telephone]*
alors so, then
l' **Alsace (f.)** Alsace region
alsacien(ne) from, of Alsace region
l' **aluminium (m.)** aluminum; *en aluminium* made of aluminum
une **amande** almond
une **ambiance** ambiance; atmosphere; *chaude ambiance* great atmosphere
américain(e) American
amérindien(ne) Amerindian

l' **Amérique (f.): Amérique du Nord** North America; *Amérique du Sud* South America
un(e) **ami(e)** friend
l' **amour (m.)** love
un **amoureux, une amoureuse (de)** lover (of)
amoureux, amoureuse in love 6; *être amoureux/amoureuse (de)* to be in love (with) 6
amusant(e) funny
amuser to amuse
s' **amuser** to have fun
un **an** year; *le Jour de l'an* New Year's Day
un **ananas** pineapple; *ananas montagne* mountain pineapple *[flower]*
un(e) **ancêtre** ancestor 3
ancien(ne) old 3
une **anecdote** anecdote 8
l' **anglais (m.)** English *[language]*
anglais(e) English
l' **Angleterre (f.)** England
anglophone English-speaking 10
un **animal** animal; *les animaux en voie de disparition* endangered species
un **animateur, une animatrice** TV host; *animateur de communauté* community manager
animé: un dessin animé cartoon
une **année** year; *d'une cinquantaine d'années* in one's fifties 9; *d'une quarantaine d'années* in one's forties 9; *d'une trentaine d'années* in one's thirties 9; *d'une vingtaine d'années* in one's twenties 9; *en première année* in the first year
annexer to annex
un **anniversaire** birthday; *anniversaire de mariage* wedding anniversary
annoncer to announce
un **anoli** anole
l' **Antarctique (m.)** Antarctica
une **anthologie de pièces de théâtre** anthology of plays 6
les **Antilles (f.)** West Indies
un **anti-moustique** insect repellent
les **antirétroviraux (m.)** antiretroviral drugs
l' **antisémitisme (m.)** anti-Semitism
août August
l' **apartheid (m.)** apartheid
s' **apercevoir (de)** to notice 9
un **apéritif** drink and food offered before a meal 2
un **appareil** camera, device; machine 6
un **appartement** apartment
appeler to call
s' **appeler: je m'appelle** my name is; *On s'appelle.* We'll call each other.; *tu t'appelles* your name is
une **appli (application)** app (application)
appliquer to apply 7
apporter to bring
apprécier to like 5
apprendre to learn; to teach
s' **approcher** to come closer 9
appuyer to push
après after
l' **après-midi (m.)** afternoon
un **aquapark** water park 1
arabe Arab
l' **argent (m.)** money; silver; *argent liquide* cash 6; *en argent* made of silver
un(e) **aristocrate** aristocrat 8
une **armoire** wardrobe
arrêter to stop; *se faire arrêter* to get arrested 9
s' **arrêter** to stop
arrière: à l'arrière-plan in the background 7
l' **arrière-grand-mère (f.)** great-grandmother 3
l' **arrière-grand-père (m.)** great-grandfather 3
l' **arrière-pays (m.)** back country
une **arrivée** arrival
arriver to arrive; to happen 9; *arriver (à)* to be able to; *arriver à faire quelque chose* to bring oneself to do something 6
un **arrondissement** district, quarter 10
arroser to water
l' **art (m.)** art; *l'histoire (f.) de l'art* art history 6; *les arts plastiques* visual arts; *les beaux-arts* fine arts 7; *un objet d'art* art object
un **article** magazine, newspaper article
artifice: un feu d'artifice firework
un(e) **artiste** artist
l' **ascenseur (m.)** elevator 5
asiatique Asian 9
l' **Asie (f.)** Asia
un **aspirateur** vacuum cleaner; *passer l'aspirateur* to vacuum
s' **asseoir** to sit down
assez rather 6; *assez de* enough (of)
une **assiette** plate
assis(e) sitting
un(e) **assistant(e) junior** junior assistant 8
assister (à) to attend 1
l' **association (f.) de scoutisme (m.)** scouting association 1
l' **assurance (f.)** insurance 8; *assurance maladie* health insurance 8
un **atelier** studio 7
un(e) **athlète** athlete
l' **athlétisme (m.)** track and field 2
attachant(e) likeable
attendre to expect (baby); to wait (for)
s' **attendre (à)** to expect (something) 4; *Je m'y attendais* I was expecting that 4
Attention ! Be careful!, Watch out!
atterrir to land
attractions: un parc d'attractions amusement park
attristé(e) sad 9

au at (the); in (the), on (the); to (the); with; *au bord de la mer* by the seaside; *au bout de* at the end of; *au chocolat* with chocolate; *au contraire* on the contrary 8; *au cours de* during, in the course of 8; *au-dessus de* above; *au fait* by the way; *au fond de* at the end of; *au moins* at least; *au premier plan* in the foreground; *Au revoir.* Good-bye.; *au second plan* in the middle ground 7; *au secours* help; *au sucre* with sugar
l' **aube (f.)** dawn 7
une **auberge: auberge de jeunesse** youth hostel; *auberge internationale* international hostel
une **aubergine** eggplant
aucun(e) any, none, no one 4; *aucun de nous ne (+ verb)* none of us (+ verb) 4; *ne (n')... aucun(e)* no, none, not any, not one 4; *sans aucun doute* without a doubt 4
un **auditeur, une auditrice libre** auditor of a class 10
aujourd'hui today
auparavant before 9
auquel, auquelle to which 5
aussi also, too; as; *aussi (+ adverb) que* as (+ adverb) as
aussitôt que as soon as 1
un **auteur** author 7
une **auto (automobile)** car; *auto tamponneuse* bumper car; *un constructeur, une constructrice automobile* car manufacturer 10; *un(e) designer automobile* automotive designer
une **autobiographie** autobiography 6
un **autobus** bus; *en (auto)bus* by bus
autochtone native
l' **Autolib' (m.)** car sharing service; *en Autolib'* by Autolib'
l' **automne (m.)** autumn
un **autoportrait** self-portrait
une **autorisation** permit 6
autour de around 2
autre other; *l'un(e)... l'autre* one... the other 9
autrefois formerly, in the past
autrement otherwise
aux at (the), in (the), to (the)
avance: en avance early
s' **avancer (vers)** to move (toward)
avant before; *à l'avant-plan* in the foreground 7
avec with
l' **avenir (m.)** future
une **aventure** adventure; *le tourisme d'aventure* adventure tourism
une **avenue** avenue
un **aveu** confession 7
un **avion** plane; *en avion* by plane
un **avis** opinion; *à mon avis* in my opinion
un(e) **avocat(e)** lawyer; *un cabinet d'avocats* law firm 1
avoir to have; *avoir... an(s)* to be... year(s) old; *avoir beau* (+ infinitive) to do (something) in vain 8; *avoir besoin de* to need; *avoir bonne mine* to look healthy; *avoir chaud* to be hot; *avoir confiance (dans/en)* to trust; *avoir de la chance* to be lucky; *avoir droit à* to be entititled to 8; *avoir la chance (de)* to have the opportunity (to) 2; *avoir envie de* to feel like, to want; *avoir faim* to be hungry; *avoir froid* to be cold; *avoir hâte de* to be eager (to); *avoir horreur de* to hate; *avoir l'air* to look; *avoir les moyens* to be able to afford, to have the means 8; *avoir lieu* to take place; *avoir l'impression (de)* to have the impression (of) 6; *avoir l'occasion (de)* to have the opportunity (to) 4; *avoir mal (à...)* to be hurt, to have a/an... ache; *avoir mal au cœur* to feel nauseous; *avoir mauvaise mine* to look sick; *avoir peur (de)* to be afraid (of); *avoir peur du vide* to be afraid of heights; *avoir quel âge* to be how old; *avoir raison* to be right; *avoir soif* to be thirsty; *avoir tort* to be wrong 8; *avoir un petit air du pays* to look like (something from) my country
avril April
azur: la Côte d'Azur French Riviera

B

un **BA** Bachelor of Arts degree 10
le **bac (baccalauréat)** French high school qualification exam and diploma 9
le **bacon** bacon
un **bagage** piece of luggage; *faire enregistrer ses bagages* to check one's luggage; *un coffre à bagages* baggage compartment; *un compartiment à bagages* baggage compartment
une **bague** ring; *bague en diamant* diamond ring; *bague de fiançailles* engagement ring 1
une **bagarre** fight 9
une **baguette** long thin loaf of bread
baigner to bathe
une **baignoire** bathtub
un **bain** bath; *bain à remous* whirlpool bath 5; *un peignoir de bain* bathrobe
baisser to decrease 2
une **balade** ride, walk
un **balisier** botanical canna
une **ballade** ballad 3
un **ballon (de foot)** (soccer) ball
une **banane** banana
un **banc** bench
bancaire: une carte bancaire debit card 6
une **bande** group of friends 1
une **bande-annonce** film trailer, preview 5
une **bande dessinée (BD)** comic strip
une **banlieue** suburb
une **banque** bank
le **banquier, la banquière** banker 6
le **bas** bottom
le **basket (basketball)** basketball

un **bassin** fountain, pond, pool
un **bateau** boat; *en bateau* by boat
un **bâton de ski** ski pole 4
une **batterie** (electric) drums
bavard(e) talkative
beau, bel, belle beautiful, handsome; *avoir beau* (+ infinitive) to do (something) in vain 8
beaucoup a lot, very much; *beaucoup de* a lot of
un **beau-frère** brother-in-law
un **beau-père** stepfather
la **beauté** beauty
les **beaux-arts (m.)** fine arts 7
un **bébé** baby 1
beige beige
belge Belgian
la **Belgique** Belgium
une **belle-mère** stepmother
une **belle-sœur** sister-in-law
ben well
le **bénévolat** volunteer work 4
le **Bénin** Benin
béninois(e) Beninese
berbère Berber
un **best-seller** best seller
bête unintelligent
le **beurre** butter
une **bicyclette** bicycle; *à bicyclette* on a bicycle
bien really, well; *bien entendu* of course 5; *bien sûr* of course; *c'est bien* it's/that's exactly 10
bientôt soon; *à bientôt* see you soon
bienvenue welcome
la **bière** beer 10
des **bijoux (m.)** jewelry
bilingue bilingual 10
un **billet** bill *[money]*; ticket
la **biochimie** biochemistry 6
une **biographie** biography 6
la **biologie** biology
biologique organic
blanc, blanche white; *le blanc des yeux* eye to eye 9
la **blanchisserie** laundry 5; *un service blanchisserie* laundry service 5
blasé(e) blasé 5
un **blason** team logo
bleu(e) blue; *la bleue* the blue one
un **blog** blog
un **blogueur, une blogueuse** blogger 2
blond(e) blond
un **blouson** jacket
le **bœuf** beef; *bœuf bourguignon* beef burgundy
boire to drink
le **bois** wood 2; *en bois* wooden 2
une **boisson** drink
une **boîte** nightclub; box 6; *boîte (de)* can (of); *boîte aux lettres* mailbox 6; *boîte cartonnée* cardboard box 6; *en boîte* at/to the club
un **bol** bowl
bon so; *bon(ne)* good; *Bon appétit !* Enjoy your meal!; *bon courage* good luck; *bon marché* cheap; *Bonne route !* Have a good trip!; *Bon voyage !* Have a good trip!; *le bon vieux temps* the good old days
bonjour hello
un **bonnet** hat; *bonnet en laine* wool hat
le **bord** edge, side; *au bord de la mer* by the seaside; *bord de mer* seaside; *monter à bord* to board
une **borne-fontaine** water hydrant
une **borne libre-service** self-service kiosk
un **bosquet** grove
bosser to work *[inform.]* 9
des **bottes (f.)** boots
la **bouche** mouth; *une bouche de métro* subway entrance
un **boucher, une bouchère** butcher
une **boucherie** butcher shop
bouclé(e) wavy *[hair]* 9
une **boucle d'oreille** earring
bouger to move
un **boulanger, une boulangère** baker
une **boulangerie** bakery
un **boulot** job *[inform.]* 8
un **bouquin** book *[inform.]* 6
la **Bourgogne** Burgundy 5
bourguignon(ne) from, of Burgundy 5
bousculer to shove 9; *se faire bousculer* to get knocked into 9
le **bout** end; *au bout de* at the end of
le **bouton** button; *bouton principal* home button; *bouton marche/arrêt* power button
une **bouteille (de)** bottle (of)
une **boutique** shop
un **bracelet** bracelet
le **bras** arm
une **brasserie** café-restaurant
bref in short 9
la **Bretagne** Brittany region
breton(ne) from, of Brittany region
le **bricolage** do-it-yourself repairs 3
bricoler to do DIY projects 3
une **brochette** skewer; *brochette apéritive* skewered appetizer 2
bronzer to tan
une **brosse: brosse à cheveux** hairbrush; *brosse à dents* toothbrush
se **brosser: se brosser les cheveux** to brush one's hair; *se brosser les dents* to brush one's teeth
le **brouillard** mist 7
brouillé: des œufs (m.) brouillés scrambled eggs
brun(e) brown, dark *[hair]*
une **bûche de Noël** yule log 2
un **buffet** buffet
un **bulletin météo(rologique)** weather forecast
un **bureau** desk, office; *bureau de change* foreign exchange bureau 6; *bureau de tabac* news store that sells tobacco, stamps, lottery tickets; *bureau du proviseur* principal's office
le **Burkina Faso** Burkina Faso
burkinabè from, of Burkina Faso

un **bus** bus; *en bus* by bus
un **but** goal
le **buzz** buzz 9

C

c'est it is, that is, this is; *c'est bien* it's/that's exactly 10; *C'est ça.* That's right.; *C'est décidé.* It's settled.; *c'est dommage que...* it's too bad that... 5; *C'est le (+ date)* It's the (+ date); *C'est le top !* That's awesome!; *c'est pareil* it's the same; *C'est parti !* Here we go!; *c'est promis* it's a promise 6; *c'est pour ça que* this/that is why; *c'est sûr* that's for sure
ça it, this; that; *Ça dépend.* It depends. 2; *Ça fait combien ?* How much is it?; *ça fait longtemps que* it's been a long time since; *ça m'est égal* it's all the same to me; *ça ne se fait pas* you shouldn't do that; *Ça parle de quoi ?* What is it about? 6; *ça promet* it sounds promising 5; *Ça sert à....* It's used for.... 2; *ça se saurait* it would be known; *ça serait* it would be; *ça suffit* that's enough 3; *ça tombe bien* that works out well 2; *Ça va ?* How are things going?; *ça va se savoir* it will be revealed (known); *ça vaut* it's worth; *ça veut dire* it/that means; *c'est pour ça que* that/this is why; *comme ça* like this, thus; *Rien que ça ?* Is that it?
une **cabine d'essayage** dressing room
un **cabinet: cabinet dentaire** dentist's office; *cabinet du médecin* doctor's office; *cabinet d'avocats* law firm 1
cacher to conceal, to hide 7
se **cacher** to hide 7
un **cadeau** gift
un **cadre** setting
un **café** café; coffee; *café au lait* coffee with milk
un **cahier** notebook
le **caissier, la caissière** bank teller 6
se **calmer: Calme-toi !** Calm down!
un(e) **camarade de classe** classmate
le **Cambodge** Cambodia 10
le **camembert** camembert cheese
une **caméra** camera
le **Cameroun** Cameroon
camerounais(e) Cameroonian
un **camion** truck
la **campagne** country(side)
le **camping** camping; *faire du camping* to go camping; *un camping-car* RV; *un camping-gaz* camp stove; *un terrain de camping* campground
le **Canada** Canada
canadien(ne) Canadian
la **canalisation** pipe(line)
un **canapé** sofa
un **canard** duck; *un magret de canard* duck breast 2
le **candidat** candidate 2
une **candidature** application 8; *une lettre de candidature* application letter 8
une **canne à pêche** fishing pole
un **canoë** canoe; *en canoë* by canoe; *faire du canoë* to go canoeing
une **cantine** cafeteria
le **canyonisme** canyoning 4; *faire du canyonisme* to go canyoning 4
une **capitale** capital
un **capot** hood *[car]*
le **caramel** caramel; *une crème caramel* caramel custard
la **caricature** caricature 7
un **carnaval** carnival
une **carotte** carrot
un **carré** square; *en carrés* in squares
carreaux: à carreaux plaid 9
une **carte** card; map; menu; *carte bancaire* debit card 6; *carte cadeau* gift card; *carte de crédit* credit card; *carte d'embarquement* boarding pass; *carte de membre* membership card; *carte postale* postcard; *carte SIM* SIM card
cartonné(e) (made out of) cardboard 6; *une boîte cartonnée* cardboard box 6
un **cas** case; *en tout cas* in any case
une **cascade** waterfall
un **casque de ski** ski goggles 4
une **casquette** cap
se **casser** to break 4; *se casser le poignet* to break one's wrist 4
une **casserole** saucepan
le **casting** casting 5
un **catalogue** catalog 6
une **catastrophe** catastrophe 5
une **cathédrale** cathedral
une **cause** cause; *à cause de* because of 2
causer to cause
une **caverne** cave
un **CD** CD
ce it; this; *ce, cet, cette, ces* that, these, this, those; *ce que* what; *ce qui* what; *ce mot-là* this/that (very) word
un **cédérom** CD
une **ceinture** belt; *ceinture de sécurité* seatbelt
cela that, this; it 3
célèbre famous
celui, celle that/this one, the one 6
cent (one) hundred
un **centre: centre commercial** mall, shopping center; *centre d'accueil* reception center, shelter; *centre d'affaires* business center 5; *centre de remise en forme* fitness center 5
cependant however 8
un **cercle** circle, group 3
des **céréales (f.)** cereal
une **cerise** cherry
certain(e) certain, sure 5; *être certain que* to be certain that 5
un **certificat** certificate 6
ceux the ones, these, those 6
chacun(e) each (one) 5
une **chaîne** channel; *chaîne câblée* cable channel 5
une **chaise** chair
une **chaise longue** beach chair

une **chambre** bedroom; hotel room; *un service de chambre* room service 5
un **champ** field; field of vision
champêtre: une fête champêtre garden party 7
un **champignon** mushroom
le **championnat** championship 2
la **chance: avoir de la chance** to be lucky; *avoir la chance (de)* to have the opportunity (to) 2; *tenter sa chance* to try one's luck 3
changer to change
une **chanson** song; *chanson réaliste* realist song 7
un **chansonnier, une chansonnière** cabaret singer
chanter to sing
un **chanteur, une chanteuse** singer
un **chapeau** hat
une **chapelle** chapel
chaque each
un **char** float
une **charcuterie** delicatessen
un **charcutier, une charcutière** deli owner
chargé(e): être chargé(e) (de) to be in charge (of)
charmant(e) charming
le **charme** charm
un **chat** cat
un **château** castle
chaud: chaude ambiance great atmosphere; *avoir chaud* to be hot; *il fait chaud* it's hot; *j'ai chaud* I am hot; *un chocolat chaud* hot chocolate
chauffer to heat (up) 2
une **chaussette** sock
une **chaussure** shoe; *des chaussures de ski* ski boots 4
chauve bald 9
une **chauve-souris** bat
chef sir
le **chef, la cheffe** manager 8; *chef, cheffe d'entreprise* company director 10; *chef, cheffe de service* department head 10; *chef d'orchestre* conductor 5
un **chef-d'œuvre** masterpiece
un **chemin** path, way
une **chemise** shirt
un **chemisier** blouse 9
un **chèque** check 6
un **chéquier** checkbook 6
cher, chère dear; expensive
chercher to look for
un **chercheur, une chercheuse** researcher
chéri(e) honey
un **cheval** horse; *faire du cheval* to go horseback riding
les **cheveux (m.)** hair; *une brosse à cheveux* hairbrush; *se brosser les cheveux* to brush one's hair
la **cheville** ankle 4; *se fouler la cheville* to sprain an ankle 4
une **chèvre** goat
le **chevreuil** venison 2; *une côte de chevreuil* venison chop 2
chez at/to the house (home) of; *chez le dentiste* at/to the dentist's office; *chez le kiné* at/to the physical therapy office 8; *chez le médecin* at/to the doctor's office; *chez moi* at/to my house
chic chic
un **chien** dog
les **chiffres (m.)** figures, numbers 8
la **chimie** chemistry
chimique chemical
la **Chine** China 10
un **chinois** conical strainer 2
le **chocolat** chocolate; *au chocolat* with chocolate; *un chocolat chaud* hot chocolate; *une mousse au chocolat* chocolate mousse
un **chœur** choir 9
choisir to choose; to decide
un **choix** choice
le **chômage** unemployment
choqué(e) shocked 9
une **chose** thing; *Tu en sais des choses.* You sure know a lot about it.
la **choucroute** sauerkraut; *choucroute garnie* sauerkraut with potatoes, sausages, smoked pork
chouette great
chut shh
la **chute** fall 8; *une chute d'eau* waterfall
cibler to target 10
le **ciné-club** film club 1
le **cinéma (ciné)** movie theatre; movies; *une salle de cinéma* movie theatre (room) 5
cinq five
une **cinquantaine** about fifty 9; *d'une cinquantaine d'années* in one's fifties 9
cinquante fifty
cinquième fifth
circuler to drive, to get around
cirer le parquet to polish hardwood flooring 3
une **citation** quote 8
une **cité** housing community 3; *cité universitaire* university dormitory
un **citoyen, une citoyenne** citizen 8
un **citron** lemon; *un thé au citron* lemon tea
clair(e) clear
une **clarinette** clarinet
une **classe** class; *classe de neige* ski class 4
un **classique** classic 5
classique classical; *la musique classique* classical music
un **clavier** keyboard
une **clé** (ignition) key; *clé USB* USB key
le **clergé** clergy 8
un(e) **client(e)** guest 5
un **clignotant** blinker
la **climatisation** air conditioning
un **clip** video clip
cliquer to click
un **clou** nail 3
le **club** club 2
un **coca** cola
un **cochon** pig
le **cœur** heart; *avoir mal au cœur* to feel nauseous
un **coffre à bagages** baggage compartment
un **coffre-fort** safe 5
un **coiffeur, une coiffeuse** hair stylist

une coiffure hairstyle; *un salon de coiffure* hair salon
le coin corner; *du coin* on the corner
un colibri hummingbird
un colis package 6
collé(e) glued, stuck
une collection collection
collectionner to collect 1
la collectivité community, society 8
un collier necklace; *collier en perles* pearl necklace
une colline hill
la colonisation colonization
combattre to fight
combien how much; *Ça fait combien ?* How much is it?; *C'est combien le kilo ?* How much per kilo?; *depuis combien de temps* how long; *Il/elle coûte combien ?* How much does it cost?
une comédie comedy; *comédie romantique* romantic comedy
un comité group 2; *en petit comité* with a few friends 2
commander to order
comme for; like; as, since; *comme ça* like this, thus; *comme ci, comme ça* so-so; *c'est comme ça que….* that's how…. 1
commencer to begin; *pour commencer* for starters
comment how, what; *Comment allez-vous ?* How are you?; *Comment est… ?* What is… like?
les commentaires (m.) comments 9; *les mauvais commentaires* mean comments, gossip 9
un(e) commerçant(e) business, shopping; *un(e) petit(e) commerçant(e)* shopkeeper
le commissariat police station 9
le commutateur (sonnerie/silence) switch (ringer, silence)
la compagnie company 8
un compartiment à bagages baggage compartment
une compétence skill 5
complémentaire supplementary 8
complètement completely 9
un complexe center; *complexe sportif* sports center 1
la complicité complicity 1
compliqué(e) complicated
composé(e) (de) made up (of) 5
un compositeur composer, songwriter
une composition composition
composter to validate *[ticket]*
un composteur ticket-stamping machine
comprendre to understand; to include 5
compris included
la comptabilité accounting 10
un(e) comptable accountant 10
un compte account 6
compter (+ infinitive) to plan (to do something)
un comptoir (ticket) counter
un concepteur web, une conceptrice web web designer
un concert concert; *concert R'n'B* R'n'B concert
un(e) concierge concierge 5
un concombre cucumber
condamné(e) condemned 8; *être condamné(e)* to be condemned 8
un conducteur, une conductrice driver
conduire to drive
la confiance: avoir confiance (dans/en) to trust
la confiture jam
le confort comfort 5
congolais(e) Congolese 6
conique conical 2
les connaissances (f.) knowledge 8
connaître to be familiar with (person, place, thing), to meet; to know; *faire connaître (à quelqu'un)* to introduce (to someone)
se connaître to know each other/one another
une connexion wifi wireless internet connection 5
un conquérant conqueror
conseiller to advise; to recommend 3
une conserverie canning company 3
un constructeur, une constructrice automobile car manufacturer 10
le consulat consulate 4
un(e) consultant(e) consultant
une consultation consultation
consulter to consult 5
le contact: garder le contact to keep in touch 3
un conte tale; *conte de fées* fairy tale 3
contemporain(e) contemporary
content(e) happy; *être content(e) (de)* to be happy (about) 6
un continent continent
continuer to continue
contraire: au contraire on the contrary 8
un contrat contract 8
contre against, versus; *par contre* however, on the other hand 8
un contrebandier, une contrebandière smuggler
un contrôle test; *contrôle de sécurité* security checkpoint
un contrôleur, une contrôleuse ticket collector; *contrôleur, contrôleuse de gestion* management controller 10
convenir (à) to suit; *si cela vous convient* if you'd like
convenu(e) conventional 10
une conversation conversation
conviendra: me conviendra (see **convenir**)
convoqué(e) called in, summoned 8; *être convoqué(e)* to be called in, summoned 8
un copain, une copine (boy/girl) friend
un coq rooster; *le coq au vin* chicken cooked in wine

un **coquelicot** poppy 7
un **coquillage** seashell 1
une **coquille Saint-Jacques** scallop
le **corbeau** crow 7
la **Corée du Sud** South Korea 10
une **corniche** cliff road
le **corps** body
correctement correctly 4
un(e) **correspondant(e)** pen pal 10
une **corvée** chore
costaud(e) stocky 9
un **costume** costume
un **côté** side; *à côté (de)* beside, next to; *de votre côté* as for you 2
une **côte** chop 2; coast; *côte de chevreuil* venison chop 2; *la Côte d'Azur* French Riviera; *la Côte d'Ivoire* Ivory Coast
le **coton** cotton; *en coton* made of cotton
le **cou** neck
couché(e) in bed
se **coucher** to go to bed
une **couleur** color; *De quelle(s) couleur(s) ?* In what color(s)?
un **coulis (de tomates)** (tomato) sauce 5
un **couloir** hallway
coupable guilty 6
un **coup de main** (helping) hand 2; *faire le coup (à quelqu'un)* to play a trick (on someone) 4; *tout d'un coup* all of a sudden 9
couper to cut
un **couple** couple
le **courage: bon courage** good luck
une **courgette** zucchini
courir to run 1
un **courrier** mail
un **cours** class, course; *cours particulier* private class 1; *au cours de* during, in the course of 8
court(e) short *[hair]* 9
le **couscous** couscous
un(e) **cousin(e)** cousin; *cousin(e) germain(e)* first cousin 3
un **coussin** pillow
un **couteau** knife; *couteau suisse* Swiss army knife
coûter to cost
la **couture** fashion design 10; *la haute couture* high fashion 10
un **couturier, une couturière** dressmaker
le **couvert** table setting; *mettre le couvert* to set the table
un **crabe** crab
craindre to fear; *Je crains que non.* I'm afraid not. 2
craquer to go wild 9
un **crayon** pencil
le **crédit: une carte de crédit** credit card
créer to create
la **crème** cream, lotion 10; *crème caramel* caramel custard; *crème de ciboulette* cream of chives 5; *crème solaire* sunscreen
une **crémerie** dairy store
le **créole** Creole *[language]*
créole Creole
une **crêpe** crêpe; *crêpe américaine* pancake; *un stand de crêpes* crêpe stand
une **crêperie** crêpe restaurant
une **crevette** shrimp
un **cri** cry; *pousser un cri* to scream
une **crise: la grande crise** Great Depression 3
un **critique** critic 5
une **critique** critique, review 5
croire to believe, to think
un **croissant** croissant
un **croque-monsieur** grilled ham and cheese sandwich
des **crudités (f.)** raw vegetables
cubique cubical 2
cueillir to pick 7
une **cuillère** spoon; *cuillère à mesurer* measuring spoon 2
le **cuir** leather; *en cuir* made of leather
cuire to cook 2
la **cuisine** cooking; kitchen
un **cuisinier, une cuisinière** chef, cook
une **cuisinière** stove
culturel(le) cultural
une **cure** spa treatment
un **CV** CV (Curriculum vitae) 8
cylindrique cylindrical 2

D

d'abord first (of all)
d'accord OK
d'ailleurs moreover 8
d'habitude usually
une **dame** lady
un(e) **Danois(e)** person from Denmark
dans in
un **danseur, une danseuse** dancer
une **date** date
davantage more
de any, some; from, of; *de neuf* new; *de plus en plus* more and more 7; *De quelle(s) couleur(s) ?* In what color(s)?; *de toute façon* in any case 4
débarrasser la table to clear the table
le **débat** debate 8
un **déboulé *[Mart.]*** parade
debout standing
se **débrouiller** to get by 6; to take care of things 8
un **début** beginning
une **décapotable** convertible
décembre December
se **déchaîner** to get wild 9
décider to decide; *C'est décidé.* It's settled.
se **décider** to make up one's mind 6
une **décision** decision 10; *prendre une décision* to make a decision 10
une **déclaration** declaration, statement 9; *déclaration de vol* report of a theft 9
décoller to take off *[airplane]*
décontracté(e) relaxed
découpé(e) (en) cut up (in) 10
découragé(e) discouraged 9
une **découverte** discovery
découvre (see **découvrir**)
découvrir to discover; *faire découvrir (à quelqu'un)* to introduce (to someone)
décrire to describe

un **défi** challenge 9
un **défilé** parade
un **degré** degree
se **déguiser** to disguise oneself, to dress up
déjà already
le **déjeuner** lunch
déjouer to defeat, thwart 3
délavé(e) washed out 9
délicieux, délicieuse delicious
le **deltaplane** hang gliding 4; *faire du deltaplane* to go hang gliding 4
demain tomorrow; *À demain.* See you tomorrow.
demander to ask (for); *demander le chemin* to ask for directions; *demander un service* to ask for a favor
démarrer to start
un **déménagement** move (house)
déménager to move (house) 1
demeurer to live 7
demi(e) half; *et demie* half past
un **demi-frère** half/step brother
une **demi-sœur** half/step sister
une **démocratie** democracy 2
la **demoiselle d'honneur** bridesmaid 1
une **dénomination** denomination 5
une **dent** tooth; *une brosse à dents* toothbrush; *se brosser les dents* to brush one's teeth
dentaire: un cabinet dentaire dentist's office
le **dentifrice** toothpaste
un(e) **dentiste** dentist
un **départ** departure; *les préparatifs (m.) de départ* travel preparations 4
un **département** department
se **dépêcher (de)** to hurry
dépendre: Ça dépend. It depends. 2
se **déplacer** to get around
déposer to deposit 6
depuis for; since; *depuis combien de temps* how long; *Depuis le temps !* At last!; *depuis quand* since when
les **députés (m.)** deputies 8
déranger to bother 2; *Je ne te dérange pas ?* I'm not bothering you? 2
dernier, dernière last; *le dernier* the latest 6
derrière behind
des any; from (the), of (the); some
désagréable unpleasant
descendre to get off, to go down
une **descente** descent
se **déshabiller** to get undressed
un(e) **designer automobile** automotive designer
désirer to want
désolé(e) sorry
le **désordre** disorder
dès que as soon as
un **dessert** dessert
un **dessin** drawing; *dessin animé* cartoon
dessiner to draw
dessus on, over (it); *au-dessus de* above
le **destin** destiny
le **destinataire** recipient
une **destination** destination
un **détail** detail
se **détendre** to relax
détester to detest 1
détruit(e) destroyed
deux two
deuxième second
deuxièmement secondly 8
devant in front of
un **développement** development; *développement durable* sustainable development; *le secteur de développement durable* sustainable development industry
un **développeur, une développeuse** software developer
devenir to become
deviner to guess
une **devise** motto
devoir to have to; to owe 7
un **devoir** assignment; *les devoirs* homework
un **diabolo menthe** lemon-lime soda with mint syrup
un **dialogue** dialogue 5
un **diamant** diamond; *en diamant* made of diamond; *une bague en diamant* diamond ring
une **dictature** dictatorship 2
un **dictionnaire** dictionary
Dieu: mon Dieu my god 5
différemment differently 4
différent(e) different
difficile difficult
des **difficultés (f.)** difficulties 8
dijonnais(e) from, of Dijon 5
diligent(e) diligent
dimanche Sunday
la **dimension** dimension 2
la **dinde** turkey 2; *dinde aux marrons* turkey with chestnuts 2
un **dindon** turkey
dîner to have dinner
le **dîner** dinner
le **dioxyde de carbone** carbon dioxide
la **diplomatie** diplomacy; *user de diplomatie* to exercise diplomacy
dirait: on dirait (see **dire**)
dire to say, to tell; *(noun +) te dit ?* How do you feel about (+ noun)? 4; *joliment dit* nicely said; *ça veut dire* it/that means; *vouloir dire* to mean
se **dire** to say to oneself
direct: en direct de live from
un **directeur, une directrice** director 5; *directeur, directrice des ressources humaines (DRH)* HR Director 8; *directeur financier, directrice financière* CFO 10
une **direction** direction
dis say; *dis donc* well; *disons* let's say
une **discographie** discography
la **discothèque** nightclub 1
un **discours** speech 8; *faire un discours* to make a speech 8
une **discussion** discussion
discuter (de) to discuss
disparaître to disappear
disponible free
disposé(e) laid out
se **disputer** to argue

dissimuler to hide
une **distance** distance
le **distributeur (automatique)** ATM 6
le **divertissement** entertainment; *l'industrie (f.) du divertissement* entertainment industry
divorcé(e)(s) divorced
dix ten
dix-huit eighteen
dixième tenth
dix-neuf nineteen
dix-sept seventeen
un **documentaire** documentary
le **doigt** finger; *doigt de pied* toe
un **domaine** field, sector; property 4; *domaine de la santé* health sector; *domaine des sciences et techniques* science and technology sector
dommage: c'est dommage que… it's too bad that… 5
un **don: faire un don (de)** to donate
donc so, therefore; *dis donc* well
donner to give; *donner lieu à* to give rise to 7; *donnez-moi* give me
dont whose; about which/whom, of which/whom 6
dormir to sleep
un **dortoir** dormitory
le **dos** back
le **doublage** dubbing 5
doublé(e) dubbed 5
une **douceur** gentleness; *douceur de vivre* relaxed style of life
une **douche** shower
doué(e) talented 10
un **doute** doubt 4; *sans aucun doute* without a doubt 4
douter to doubt 5
douze twelve
dramatique dramatic 2
un(e) **dramaturge** playwright 7
un **drame** drama
les **draps (m.)** sheets
un **drapeau** flag
le (la) **DRH: le directeur/la directrice des ressources humaines** HR Director 8
la **drogue** drugs
un **droit** right 2; law 6; *avoir droit à* to be entititled to 8; *les droits de l'homme* human rights 2
droite: à droite to the right; *à droite de* to/on the right of; *tout droit* straight ahead
drôle funny
du about (the); any; from (the); of (the); on (the); some; *du coin* on the corner
duquel, duquelle from which 5
dur(e) difficult
durable: le développement durable sustainable development; *le secteur de développement durable* sustainable development industry
la **durée** duration, length 5
un **DVD** DVD
dynamique dynamic

E

l' **eau (f.)** water; *eau minérale* mineral water; *une chute d'eau* waterfall; *une masse d'eau* body of water; *une source d'eau* spring
une **écharpe** scarf
un **éclair** eclair
une **école** school
l' **économie (f.)** economy 2
économique economic
économiser to save (up); *économiser de l'argent* to save money 6
l' **écoute (f.): en écoute libre** audio trial
écouter to listen (to); *écouter de la musique* to listen to music; *écouter mon lecteur MP3* to listen to my MP3 player
un **écran** monitor, screen; *l'écran de verrouillage* lock screen
écrire to write
un **écrivain** writer
une **éducation** education; *éducation physique et sportive (EPS)* gym class
un **effet** effect; *effet de serre* greenhouse effect
efficacement efficiently
s' **effondrer** to collapse 9; *s'effondrer de fatigue* to collapse from exhaustion 9
égal(e) equal 10; *ça m'est égal* it's all the same to me
une **église** church
égoïste selfish
eh bien well
une **élection** election 2; *les élections présidentielles* presidential elections 2
électrique electric
électronique electronic 5
un(e) **élève** student
éliminer to eliminate
elle her; it; she
elles them (f.); they
éloigné(e) distant, extended 3
s' **éloigner (de)** to distance oneself (from) 7; to get away (from) 10
l' **embarquement (m.)** boarding; *une carte d'embarquement* boarding pass; *une porte d'embarquement* boarding gate
l' **embarras (m.): avoir l'embarras du choix** to have too many choices 10
embaucher to hire 3
embêter to annoy 2
embrasser to kiss
une **émission** television program; TV show; *émission de musique* music show; *émission de télé-réalité* reality TV show
emmener to bring (person)
une **émotion** emotion 5
s' **empêcher (de)** to refrain (from) 2; *Je (ne) peux (pas) m'empêcher de….* I can('t) stop myself from…. 2
un **emploi** job
un(e) **employé(e)** employee 3
emporter to bring
emprisonner to imprison 2
emprunter to borrow

en any, about it/them, from it/them, of it/them, some; at; by; in; made of; of *[pronoun]*; on; upon, while 4; *en aluminium, plastique* made of aluminum, plastic; *en argent* made of silver; *en (auto) bus* by bus; *en Autolib'* by Autolib'; *en avance* early; *en avion* by plane; *en bateau* by boat; *en bois* wooden 2; *en boîte* at/to the club; *en canoë* by canoe; *en ce moment* at the moment 6; *en coton* made of cotton; *en cuir* made of leather; *en direct de* live from; *en écoute libre* audio trial; *en face de* across from; *en famille* with family; *en gros plan* in a close-up 7; *en guerre* at war 2; *en haut* at the top; *en laine* made of wool; *en ligne* online; *en lin* made of linen; *en métal* made of metal 2; *en métro* by subway; *en or* made of gold; *en ordre* in order; *en panne* broken down; *en papier* made of paper; *en perles* made of pearls; *en petit comité* with a few friends 2; *en pirogue* by pirogue; *en plein air* outdoors; *en plus de* in addition to; *en première année* in the first year; *en RER* by RER; *en retard* late; *en route* on the way; *en scooter* by scooter; *en skiant* while skiing 4; *en soie* made of silk; *en solde* on sale; *en taxi* by taxi; *en tissu* made of fabric 2; *en tournée* on tour 7; *en tout cas* in any case; *en train* by train; *en Vélib'* by Vélib'; *en velours* made of velvet; *en ville* downtown; *en voiture* by car; *en voiture électrique* by electric car; *en voiture hybride* by hybrid car; *en un sens* in a way; *en y réfléchissant bien* on second thought 4; *en y regardant de plus près* on a closer look 4; *je m'en vais* I'm going (away) 2; *Tu en sais des choses.* You sure know a lot about it.

encaisser to cash 6

enchanté(e) delighted

encore more; still

encouragé(e) encouraged 9

encourager to encourage 2

l' endettement (m.) debt 2

un endroit place

l' énergie (f.) energy; *énergie nucléaire* nuclear energy; *énergie solaire* solar energy

énergique energetic

l' enfance (f.) childhood 1

un enfant child; *garder un enfant* to babysit 3

enfantin(e) childish 1

enfin finally; well; come on

enfoncer to push, hammer 3

engagé(e) engaged, committed 7

un engagement engagement

s' engager (à, pour) to commit (to)

l' engrais (m.) fertilizer

les ennuis (m.) trouble 9

s' ennuyer to get bored 4

une enquête survey

enregistrer: faire enregistrer ses bagages to check one's luggage

s' enregistrer (en ligne) to check in (online)

enseigner to teach

ensemble together

un ensemble outfit

ensuite next

entendre to hear; *bien entendu* of course 5

s' entendre to get along

enthousiaste enthusiastic

entièrement completely, entirely 8

s' entraîner to practice (sports) 2

entre between

une entrée appetizer

une entreprise business, company 1; *un chef, une cheffe d'entreprise* company director 10

entrer to come in, to enter; *entrer à l'université* to go to college

un entretien interview 8

envahi(e) invaded 2

une enveloppe envelope

l' environnement (m.) environment

un envoûtement spell

envoyer to send; *envoyer des textos* to send text messages

une éolienne wind turbine

l' épaule (f.) shoulder

épicé(e) spicy

une épicerie grocery store

un épicier, une épicière grocery store owner

une éponge sponge 10

une époque era, period

éprouver to feel 5

l' EPS (f.) gym class

une équipe team

équipé(e) (de) equipped (with) 5

un érable maple tree; *le sirop d'érable* maple syrup

l' escalade (f.) rock climbing 4; *faire de l'escalade* to rock climb 4

un escargot snail

un espace area

l' Espagne (f.) Spain

l' espagnol (m.) Spanish *[language]*

espagnol(e) Spanish

espérer to hope

un essai essay

essayer to try (on)

l' essence (f.) gasoline

essentiel essential 4

un essuie-glace windshield wiper

l' est (m.) east

est-ce que *[phrase introducing a question]*

l' estomac (m.) stomach

et and; *et demie* half past; *et quart* quarter past

un étage floor, story; *le premier étage* the second floor

un étang pond

un **état: états généraux** Estates General 8; *les États-Unis* United States
l' **été (m.)** summer
ethnique ethnic, multicultural 10
une **étoile** star 5
étonné(e) surprised 5; *être étonné(e) que* to be surprised that 5
étonner to surprise
être to be; *être à* to belong to 8; *être affolé(e)* to be panicked 1; *être amoureux/amoureuse (de)* to be in love (with) 6; *être au courant* to know, to be informed; *être certain que* to be certain that 5; *être chargé(e) (de)* to be in charge (of); *être condamné(e)* to be condemned 8; *être content(e) (de)* to be happy (about) 6; *être convoqué(e)* to be called 8; *être d'accord* to agree; *être d'origine (+ adjective)* to come from (+ country) 3; *être de retour* to be back; *être en (bonne, mauvaise) forme* to be in (good, bad) shape; *être en train de (+ infinitive)* to be (busy) doing something; *être étonné(e) que* to be surprised that 5; *être évident que* to be obvious that 5; *être fâché(e)* to be angry 1; *être obligé(e) (de)* to be obligated (to) 8; *être occupé(e)* to be busy; *être perso* to be personalized *[inform.]* 8; *être situé(e)* to be located; *être sur place* to be on site, on the premises; *être vert* to be environmentally friendly; *ça serait* it would be; *je ne suis pas trop d'humeur pour* I'm not in the mood for 5; *Nous sommes le (+ date).* It's the (+ date).
étroit(e) narrow 2
des **études (f.)** studies
un(e) **étudiant(e)** student
étudier to study
euh um
un **euro** euro
l' **Europe (f.)** Europe
eux them
évidemment obviously
évident(e) easy 6; obvious 5; *être évident que* to be obvious that 5
un **évier** sink
éviter to avoid
exactement exactly
exagérer to exaggerate
une **excursion** trip; *faire une excursion* to take a trip
exiger to require 5
exister to exist
une **expérience** experience
expliqué(e) explained
expliquer to explain
un **exposé** presentation
une **exposition** exhibit
l' **expressionnisme (m.)** expressionism 7
expressionniste expressionist 7
extraordinaire extraordinary

F

une **fable** fable 3
fabriqué(e) (au, aux, en) made (in) 10
fabuleux, fabuleuse fabulous
une **fac (faculté)** college
face: en face de across from; *face à* faced with 9
fâché(e) angry 1; *être fâché(e)* to be angry 1
facile easy
une **façon** way 4; *la façon* in the manner of 9; *de toute façon* in any case 4
un **facteur, une factrice** mailman, mailwoman 6
des **factures (f.)** bills 8
la **faïence** earthenware 10
la **faim** hunger; *avoir faim* to be hungry
faire to do, to make; *faire (+ infinitive)* to make (someone do something) 8; *faire connaître (à quelqu'un)* to introduce (to someone); *faire découvrir (à quelqu'un)* to introduce (to someone); *faire de la gym (gymnastique)* to do gymnastics; *faire de la luge* to go sledding 4; *faire de la motoneige* to snowmobile 4; *faire de la planche à voile* to wind surf 4; *faire de la plongée sous-marine* to go scuba diving; *faire de la raquette à neige* to go snowshoeing 4; *faire de la voile* to go sailing; *faire de l'escalade* to rock climb 4; *faire des sauts à ski* to go off ski jumps 4; *faire du bénévolat* to volunteer; *faire du camping* to go camping; *faire du canoë* to go canoeing; *faire du canyonisme* to go canyoning 4; *faire du cheval* to go horseback riding; *faire du deltaplane* to go hang gliding 4; *faire du footing* to go running; *faire du jet ski* to jet ski; *faire du kayak* to go kayaking; *faire du parachutisme ascensionnel* to go parasailing; *faire du parapente* to go paragliding 4; *faire du patinage (artistique)* to (figure) skate; *faire du roller* to in-line skate; *faire du saut à l'élastique* to bungee jump 4; *faire du scooter des mers* to jet ski; *faire du shopping* to go shopping; *faire du ski (alpin)* to (downhill) ski; *faire du ski de fond* to cross-country ski 4; *faire du ski de piste* to ski downhill 4; *faire du ski hors-piste* to backcountry ski 4; *faire du ski joëring* to skijor 4; *faire du ski nautique* to go water-skiing; *faire du*

snowboard to snowboard 4; *faire du speed riding* to speed ride 4; *faire du sport* to play sports; *faire du taxi-ski* to take a ski-taxi ride 4; *faire du télémark* to telemark ski 4; *faire du vélo* to bike; *faire enregistrer ses bagages* to check one's luggage; *faire grève* to go on strike 2; *faire griller* to barbecue; *faire la connaissance (de)* to meet (for the first time); *faire la cuisine* to cook; *faire la lessive* to do the laundry; *faire la vaisselle* to wash the dishes; *faire le coup (à quelqu'un)* to play a trick (on someone) 4; *faire le ménage* to do housework; *faire le plein* to fill up the gas tank; *faire les courses* to go grocery shopping; *faire le tour* explore all the possibilities 10; *faire le touriste* to be a tourist; *faire marcher* to make (something) work; *faire mes devoirs* to do my homework; *faire partie (de)* to belong (to); *faire sa valise* to pack 4; *faire sécher le linge* to dry clothes; *faire un séjour* to stay 4; *faire semblant (de)* to pretend (to) 1; *faire ses adieux* to bid farewell 8; *faire un appel vidéo* to send a video call; *faire un discours* to make a speech 8; *faire un don (de)* to donate; *faire un stage* to intern 8; *faire un tour* to go on a ride; to go on a trip; *faire un tour de grande roue* to go on a Ferris wheel ride; *faire un tour de manège* to go on a carnival ride; *faire un tour de montagnes russes* to go on a roller coaster ride; *faire un voyage* to go on a trip; *faire une excursion* to take a trip; *faire une intervention* to organize an intervention; *faire une liste* to make a list; *faire une nuit blanche* to stay up all night; *faire une promenade* to go for a walk; *faire une promesse* to make a promise; *faire une randonnée à pied* to hike; *faire une randonnée équestre* to go on a trail ride 4; *On te fait étudier tout ça ?* They make you study all that? 8; *Tu ferais bien de....* You would do well to.... 1

se **faire: se faire arrêter** to get arrested 9; *se faire bousculer* to get knocked into 9; *se faire disputer (par)* to get in trouble (with) 3; *se faire muter* to get transferred 1; *se faire soigner* to seek (medical) treatment 8; *se faire vacciner* to get vaccinated 4

fait: au fait by the way; *Ça fait combien ?* How much is it?; *il fait beau* it's beautiful out; *il fait chaud* it's hot; *il fait du soleil* it's sunny; *il fait du vent* it's windy; *il fait frais* it's cool; *il fait froid* it's cold; *il fait mauvais* the weather's bad; *Quel temps fait-il ?* What's the weather like?; *tout à fait* completely

le **faisan** pheasant 5

une **falaise** cliff

fallait: il fallait (see **falloir**)

falloir to be necessary, to have to; *il faut* it is necessary, one has to/must, we/you have to/must

une **famille** family; *famille monoparentale* single-parent family 1; *famille nucléaire* nuclear family 1; *famille recomposée* blended family 1; *en famille* with family

la **fantaisie** fantasy

farci(e) stuffed

fatigué(e) tired

la **faune** fauna, wildlife

faut: il me faut I need

un **fauteuil** armchair

un **fax** fax 5

une **femme** wife; *femme d'affaires* businesswoman; *femme politique* female politician

une **fenêtre** window

un **fer à repasser** (clothes) iron

une **ferme** farm

fermenté(e) fermented 5

fermer to close

un **fermier, une fermière** farmer

le **festival** festival 1

une **fête** holiday; party; *fête champêtre* garden party 7; *fête foraine* carnival; *fête nationale* national holiday

fêter to celebrate

un **feu: feu d'artifice** firework; *feu de joie* bonfire

une **feuille de papier** sheet of paper

un **feuilleton** TV soap opera

février February

s'en **fiche: Je m'en fiche.** I don't care. 1; *Elle s'en fiche.* She doesn't care. 1

un **fichier** file; *fichier image* image file; *fichier son* audio file; *fichier vidéo* video file

fier, fière proud 9

la **fièvre** fever

une **figure** figure 7; *la figure* face

une **figurine** figurine 10

filer to run *[inform.]*

une **filiale** branch, subsidiary 10

une **fille** daughter; girl

un **film** film; *film d'action* action movie; *film d'aventures* adventure movie; *film d'horreur* horror movie; *film de science-fiction* science fiction movie; *film musical* musical; *film policier* detective movie; *tourner un film* to shoot a movie 5

filmer to film 9

un **fils** son

filtrer to filter 2

fin(e) fine

le **final** finale 5

finalement in the end 3

les **finances (f.)** finances 6

financier, financière financial 10; *le directeur financier, la directrice financière* CFO 10
finir to finish
un **fitness** gym, health club
un(e) **fleuriste** florist
un **fleuve** river
flirter to flirt 9
la **flore** flora
une **flûte** flute
le **foie gras** goose liver pâté 2
une **fois** occasion, time; *à la fois* at the same time; *Il était une fois….* Once upon a time (there was)…. 3
fond: au fond (de) at the end (of)
le **foot** soccer
un **footballeur, une footballeuse** soccer player
le **footing** running
une **force** strength
forestier, forestière with mushrooms
une **forêt** forest
un **forfait de ski** ski pass 4
un **forgeron** blacksmith
une **formation** education, training 8
la **forme** shape 2; *en forme de (poire)* (pear)-shaped 2; *être en (bonne, mauvaise) forme* to be in (good, bad) shape; *un centre de remise en forme* fitness center 5
formidable awesome
fort(e) strong
un **fou, une folle** crazy person; *comme des fous* like crazy
un **foulard** scarf
une **foule** crowd
se **fouler la cheville** to sprain an ankle 4
un **four** oven
une **fourchette** fork
frais, fraîche cool; fresh; *il fait frais* it's cool
une **fraise** strawberry
le **français** French *[language]*
français(e) French
la **France** France
francophone French-speaking
la **Francophonie** French-speaking world 3
un **frein** brake
fréquenter to frequent, to hang out
un **frère** brother; *beau-frère* brother-in-law; *demi-frère* half/step brother
un **frigo** refrigerator
frisé(e) curly *[hair]* 9
des **frissons (m.)** shivers, chills
frit(e) deep-fried
des **frites (f.)** French fries
froid(e) cold; *avoir froid* to be cold; *il fait froid* it's cold
le **fromage** cheese
un **fruit** fruit; *les fruits de mer* seafood; *une tarte aux fruits* fruit tart
frustré(e) frustrated 9
fumé(e) smoked 2; *le saumon fumé* smoked salmon 2
le **funk** funk music
futur(e) future 6

G

le **Gabon** Gabon
gabonais(e) Gabonese
gagner to win; *gagner du temps* to save time
une **galerie** gallery; *galerie des Glaces* Hall of mirrors; *galerie des miroirs déformants* fun house
une **galette** buckwheat crêpe
un **gant** glove 4; *gant de toilette* washcloth
un **garage** auto shop
garanti(e) guaranteed
garantir to guarantee 5
un **garçon** boy; *garçon d'honneur* best man 1
garder to keep, to take care of 3; *garder le contact* to keep in touch 3; *garder un enfant* to babysit 3
une **gare** train station
garni(e): la choucroute garnie sauerkraut with potatoes, sausages, smoked pork
la **Gascogne** Gascony region
gascon(ne) from, of Gascony region
la **gastronomie** gastronomy 5
gastronomique gourmet 10
un **gâteau** cake
gauche: à gauche on the left; *à gauche de* on/to the left of
géant(e) giant
une **génération** generation 3
généreux, généreuse generous
génial(e) fantastic, great, terrific
le **génie civil** civil engineering 6
le **génocide** genocide
le **genou** knee
un **genre** type
des **gens (m.)** people
la **géographie** geography
gentil(le) nice
germain(e): un(e) cousin(e) germain(e) first cousin 3
la **gestion (économique d'entreprise)** (economic business) management 6; *un contrôleur, une contrôleuse de gestion* management controller 10
une **glace** ice cream; mirror; *la galerie des Glaces* Hall of mirrors; *glace à la vanille* vanilla ice cream; *glace au chocolat* chocolate ice cream
une **glacière** cooler
la **gorge** throat
un **gorille** gorilla; *gorille des montagnes* mountain gorilla
le **gospel** gospel 9
gourmand(e) fond of food
le **goût** taste 5; *à mon goût* for my taste 5
goûter to taste
le **goûter** snack
un **gouvernement** government
un **graffiti (des graffiti)** graffiti 3
un **gramme (de)** a gram (of)
grand(e) big, large, tall; *la grande crise* Great Depression 3; *la grande roue* Ferris wheel; *faire un tour de grande roue* to go on a Ferris wheel ride

une **grand-mère** grandmother
le **grand-oncle** great uncle 3
les **grands-parents (m.)** grandparents
un **grand-père** grandfather
la **grand-tante** great aunt 3
une **grange** barn
graphique graphic 6
un(e) **graphiste** graphic designer
gratuit(e) free
grave serious
gravé(e) engraved
la **grêle** hail 9
une **grève** strike 2; *faire grève* to go on strike 2
grillé(e) grilled; *le pain grillé* toast
griller to grill; *faire griller* to barbecue
la **grippe** flu
gris grey
une **grive** thrush
gros(se) big, fat, large; *un gros plan* close-up 7; *en gros plan* in a close-up 7
grossir to gain weight
un **groupe** group
un(e) **groupie** fan 9
la **Guadeloupe** Guadeloupe
guéri(e) healed 8
une **guerre** war; *en guerre* at war 2
un **guichet** ticket booth
un **guide** guide; *guide télévisé* TV guide; guidebook; *guide touristique* tourist guide; *le Guide Michelin* Michelin Guide
guidé(e) guided
guillotiner to decapitate 8
une **guitare** guitar
la **Guyane (française)** French Guiana
la **gym (gymnastique)** gymnastics; *faire de la gym (gymnastique)* to do gymnastics

H

s' **habiller** to get dressed
un(e) **habitant(e)** inhabitant, resident
habiter to live
Haïti Haiti
haïtien(ne) Haitian
un **hamac** hammock
un **hamburger** hamburger
un **hameau** hamlet
hanté: une maison hantée haunted house
des **haricots (m.) verts** green beans
le **hasard** fate, luck 10
la **hâte: avoir hâte de** to be eager
la **hausse** increase 2
le **haut** top
haut(e) high; *en haut* at the top
la **haute couture** high fashion 10
la **haute technologie** high tech 1
les **herbes (f.)** herbs 2
un **héros, une héroïne** hero, heroine
hésiter to hesitate
l' **heure (f.)** hour, o'clock, time; *à l'heure* on time; *Quelle heure est-il ?* What time is it?
heureusement fortunately
heureux, heureuse happy; *Très heureux/heureuse.* Pleased to meet you. 3
un **hibiscus** hibiscus
hier yesterday
le **hip-hop** hip-hop
l' **histoire (f.)** history; story 3; *histoire de l'art* art history 6
le **hit** (musical) hit *[inform.]* 2
l' **hiver (m.)** winter
une **HLM (des HLM)** subsidized housing 3
un **homme: homme d'affaires** businessman; *homme de ménage* janitor 5; *homme politique* male politician
le **Honduras** Honduras 10
honteux, honteuse ashamed 9
l' **hôpital (m.)** hospital 8
l' **horaire (m.)** schedule 5
l' **horizon (m.)** horizon; *à l'horizon* on the horizon
l' **horreur (f.)** horror; *avoir horreur de* to detest, to hate
horrible awful, horrible
un **hors-d'œuvre** appetizer 2
le **hors-piste** off-road skiing 4; *faire du ski hors-piste* to backcountry ski 4
l' **hospitalité (f.)** hospitality
un **hôtel** hotel; *hôtel de ville* city hall
une **hôtesse de l'air** female flight attendant
l' **huile (f.)** oil *[car]*
huit eight
huitième eighth
une **huître** oyster 2
humanitaire humanitarian
humide humid 4
hybride hybrid

I

ici here
une **icône** icon
l' **idéalisme (m.)** idealism 2
une **idée** idea; *Bonne idée !* Good idea!
une **identité** identity 4; *une pièce d'identité* identification (document) 4
il he; it; *il est essentiel que* it's essential that 4; *il est indispensable que* it's indispensable that 4; *il est important que* it's important that 4; *il est surprenant que* it's surprising that 4; *il est utile que* it's useful that 4; *il paraît que* it seems that 5; *il se pourrait que* it's possible that 4; *il vaut mieux que* it's better that 4; *il y a* there are/is; *il y a (+ time)* (time +) ago
une **île** island 4
illustrer to illustrate 8
ils they
une **image** image, picture; *un fichier image* image file
l' **imaginaire (m.)** fantasy 6
l' **imagination (f.)** imagination 10
imaginer to imagine
immense immense 7
un **immeuble** apartment building
important important 4
l' **important (m.)** what's important

un **impossible** impossible
imprécis(e) vague 5
imprenable unobstructed 5
une **impression** impression 5; *avoir l'impression (de)* to have the impression (of) 6
l' **impressionnisme (m.)** Impressionism 7
un(e) **impressionniste** Impressionist 7
impressionniste Impressionist
une **imprimante** printer
imprimer to print
improviser to improvise 2
incapable incapable 9
incroyable incredible
l' **Inde (f.)** India 10
un(e) **indigène** native person
indiquer to indicate, to point out/to
indispensable indispensable 4
un **individu** individual 10
individuel(le) individual 3; *une maison individuelle* single-family house 3
l' **Indonésie (f.)** Indonesia 10
une **industrie** industry; *industrie du divertissement* entertainment industry; *les industries créatives* cultural and creative industries
un **infirmier, une infirmière** nurse
influencer to influence 8
l' **infographie (f.)** computer graphics 6
les **informations (infos) (f.)** news
l' **informatique (f.)** computer science; information technology; *le secteur de l'informatique* information technology industry
informer to inform
un **ingénieur** engineer
l' **initiative (f.): un syndicat d'initiative** tourist information office
inquiet, inquiète worried
une **inquiétude** worry
s' **inscrire** to register; *s'inscrire en lettres* to declare a major in humanities
un **insecte** insect
insister (sur) to insist (on)
installer to install
s' **installer** to get settled
un **instant** moment; *pour l'instant* for the moment
un **instituteur, une institutrice** elementary school teacher
un **instrument** musical instrument
s' **intégrer (à)** to integrate (into) 6
intelligent(e) intelligent
intense intense 5
intéressant(e) interesting
intéressé(e) interested 1
intéresser to interest
s' **intéresser (à)** to be interested (in)
une **interface** interface
l' **intérieur (m.)** inside
international(e) international
(l') **Internet (m.)** Internet
un **interprète** performer 7
intervenir to intervene
une **intervention: faire une intervention** to organize an intervention
une **interview** interview 10
interviewer to interview 9
intimiste intimate 7
introduire to introduce 8
l' **inutile (m.)** what is useless
une **invention** invention 7
une **invitation** invitation 2
un(e) **invité(e)** guest
inviter to invite
l' **Italie (f.)** Italy
italien(ne) Italian
un **itinéraire** itinerary
ivoirien(ne) from, of the Ivory Coast

J

la **jambe** leg
le **jambon** ham; *jambon serrano* prosciutto 2; *jambon persillé* ham and pork dish made with chopped parsley 5
janvier January
le **Japon** Japan 10
japonais(e) Japanese
un **jardin** garden, park
le **jasmin** jasmine
jaune yellow
le **jazz** jazz music
je/j' I
un **jean** jeans
jeter: jeter un coup d'oeil (à) to glance (at) 5; *N'en jette plus!* Enough! Stop it! *[inform.]* 8
un **jet ski** jet ski; *faire du jet ski* to jet ski
un **jeu: jeu d'adresse** game of skill; *jeu télévisé* (TV) game show; *jeu vidéo* video game; *les Jeux Olympiques* Olympic Games
jeudi Thursday
jeune young
un(e) **jeune** young man/woman
la **jeunesse** youth 2
la **joaillerie** fine jewelry 10
joindre to attach
joins (see **joindre**)
joli(e) pretty
joliment dit nicely said
la **Jordanie** Jordan 10
jouer to play; *jouer à cache-cache* to play hide-and-seek 1; *jouer à la marelle* to play hopscotch 1; *jouer à la poupée* to play with dolls 1; *jouer au basket (basketball)* to play basketball; *jouer au foot (football)* to play soccer; *jouer au hockey sur glace* to play ice hockey; *jouer aux billes* to play marbles 1; *jouer aux petites voitures* to play with toy cars 1; *jouer aux jeux vidéo* to play video games; *jouer de (+ instrument)* to play (+ instrument); *jouer un rôle* to play a role; *jouer un tour* to play a trick 3
un **joueur, une joueuse** player
un **jour** day; one day, someday; *le Jour de l'an* New Year's Day
un **journal** newspaper
une **journée** day
juillet July
juin June
jumeau, jumelle twin; *un lit jumeau* twin bed

des **jumelles (f.)** binoculars
une **jupe** skirt
un **jus** juice; *jus d'orange* orange juice; *jus de pamplemousse* grapefruit juice; *jus de pomme* apple juice
jusqu'à until
juste fair; only; just 3
justement exactly; fittingly 3

K

un **kayak: faire du kayak** to go kayaking
le **ketchup** ketchup
kiffer to like *[inform.]*
un **kilo (de)** kilogram (of)
un **kilomètre** kilometer
le **kiné (kinésithérapeute)** physical therapist 8; *chez le kiné* at/to the physical therapy office 8
un **kiosque** stand; *kiosque à journaux* newsstand
un **klaxon** horn

L

là there
là-bas over there
un **labo (laboratoire)** science lab; *laboratoire de recherches* research laboratory 1
un **lac** lake
un **lâcheur, une lâcheuse** flake, unreliable person *[inform.]* 9
laid(e) ugly
la **laine** wool; *en laine* made of wool; *un bonnet en laine* wool hat
laisser to leave, to let; *Laisse-moi finir!* Let me finish!
le **lait** milk
laitier: un produit laitier dairy product 10
un **lambi** lambis
une **lampe** lamp; *lampe de poche* flashlight; *lampe torche* flashlight
lancer to launch 10
une **langouste** spiny lobster
une **langue** language
un **lapin** rabbit
large wide 2
une **largeur du champ** field width
laver: une machine à laver washing machine
se **laver** to wash (oneself)
un **lave-vaisselle** dishwasher
le, la, l' it *[object pronoun]*; the
un **leader** leader 10; *leader mondial* world leader 10
un **lecteur: lecteur de DVD** DVD player; *lecteur MP3* MP3 player
la **lecture** reading
une **légende** legend
un **légume** vegetable
le **lendemain** next day
les the; them
la **lessive: faire la lessive** to do the laundry
une **lettre** letter; *lettre de candidature* application letter 8; *lettre de motivation* cover letter 8; *une boîte aux lettres* mailbox 6
les **lettres (f.)** humanities; *s'inscrire en lettres* to declare a major in humanities
le **leur, la leur** theirs 9
leur their; to them
leurs their
lève: Lève la tête! Look up!
se **lever** to get up
une **lèvre** lip; *un rouge à lèvres* lipstick
une **librairie** bookstore
libre free; *en écoute libre* audio trial; *une borne libre-service* self-service kiosk
une **licorne** unicorn
un **lien** link
un **lieu** place 5; *avoir lieu* to take place; *donner lieu à* to give rise to 7
une **ligne** line 7; *la ligne* figure; *ta ligne* your figure; *en ligne* online
une **limonade** lemon-lime soda
le **lin** linen; *en lin* made of linen; *un mouchoir en lin* linen handkerchief
le **linge: faire sécher le linge** to dry clothes
une **liquette** shirt *[inform.]* 9
lire to read
une **liseuse** e-reader
une **liste** list; *faire une liste* to make a list
un **lit** bed; *lit jumeau* twin bed; *lits superposés* bunk beds
un **litre (de)** liter (of)
une **livraison: un service de livraison (postale)** (mail) delivery service 6
un **livre** book; *livre de poche* paperback 6
une **livre** pound
local(e) local 10
un(e) **locataire** tenant 3
le **logement** housing 3
un **logiciel** software
loin (de) far (from)
un **loisir** pastime
long(ue) long; *le long de* alongside; *un long métrage* feature film 5
longtemps: ça fait longtemps que it's been a long time since
la **longueur** length 2
le **look tradi** traditional look 2
lorsque when 1
louer to rent
la **luge** sledding 4; *faire de la luge* to go sledding 4
lui to her/him; him
une **lumière** light
lundi Monday
des **lunettes (f.)** glasses; *lunettes de soleil* sunglasses
lutter to fight
le **luxe** luxury 10
le **Luxembourg** Luxembourg
luxembourgeois(e) from, of Luxembourg
le **lycée** high school
le **Lyonnais** Lyon region
lyonnais(e) from, of Lyon
le **lyrisme** lyricism 7

M

m'appelle: je m'appelle my name is
un **machin** thing 2

une **machine à laver** washing machine
madame (Mme) Ma'am, Mrs., Ms.
mademoiselle (Mlle) Miss, Ms.
un **magasin** store
un **magazine** magazine
maghrébin(e) from, of the Maghreb
un(e) **magicien(ne)** magician 3
magique magical
un **magret de canard** duck breast 2
mai May
maigre skinny 9
maigrir to lose weight
un **maillot** jersey; *maillot de bain* bathing suit
la **main** hand; *la main dans la main* hand in hand; *un coup de main* (helping) hand 2
maintenant now
maint(e)s many 5
le **maire, madame le maire** mayor
mais but
une **maison** home, house; *maison de rêve* dream house; *maison hantée* haunted house; *maison individuelle* single-family house 3; *maison mitoyenne* row house 3
un **maître, une maîtresse** tutor; primary school teacher 3
une **maîtrise** Master's degree 10
mal badly; *avoir mal (à…)* to be hurt, to have a/an… ache; *Ça va mal.* Things are going badly; *le plus mal* the worst; *plus mal* worse
un(e) **malade** sick person
malade sick
une **maladie** illness; *l'assurance (f.) maladie* health insurance 8
la **Malaisie** Malaysia 10
le **Mali** Mali
malien(ne) Malian
Mamy grandma
le **management** management 6
la **Manche** English Channel
une **mandarine** mandarin orange 2
un **manège: faire un tour de manège** to go on a carnival ride
un **manga** manga 6
manger to eat
une **mangouste** mongoose
une **mangrove** mangrove
une **manière** way 3
une **manif (manifestation)** street demonstration
un **mannequin** model
manquer to lack
un **manteau** coat
le **maquillage** makeup
se **maquiller** to put on makeup
un(e) **marchand(e)** merchant
le **marché** market *[financial]*; outdoor market; *marché aux puces* flea market
marcher to walk; to work; *faire marcher* to make (something) work
mardi Tuesday
une **marée** tide; *marée noire* oil spill
un **mari** husband
un **mariage** wedding; *un anniversaire de mariage* wedding anniversary
un **marié** groom
une **mariée** bride; *une robe de mariée* wedding dress
se **marier** to get married
une **marinade** marinade 5
marine: une tortue marine sea turtle
le **marketing** marketing 10
marocain(e) Moroccan
la **maroquinerie** leather goods 10
une **marque** brand 10
marqué(e) brand name 10
marquer to score
une **marraine** godmother 1
marron brown
mars March
un **marteau** hammer 3
martiniquais(e) from, of Martinique
la **Martinique** Martinique
un **mas** *[Mart.]* mask
le **mascara** mascara
un **masque** mask
une **masse d'eau** body of water
un **massif** mountain range
un **match** game
un **matelas pneumatique** inflatable mattress
les **mathématiques (maths) (f.)** math
la **matière** class subject; material 2
le **matin** morning
la **matinée** morning
mauvais bad; *il fait mauvais* the weather is bad
la **mayonnaise** mayo
me (m') me; to me
un(e) **mécanicien(ne)** mechanic
la **mécanique** mechanics 3
méchant(e) mean
une **médaille** medal 2
un **médecin** doctor; *un cabinet de médecin* doctor's office
la **médecine** medicine 6
les **médias (m.)** media 2
une **médiathèque** media center
médical(e) medical 3
médicalisé(e) medicalized 8
méditerranéen(ne) Mediterranean 9
se **méfier (de)** to be wary (of) 3
les **meilleurs (m.)** the best
la **mélancolie** melancholy 7
mélanger to mix 2
la **mélodie** melody 7
un **melon** melon
même even; same; *même que* even though *[inform.]* 3; *quand même* after all 2; regardless 2
le **ménage** household, housework; *des affaires (f.) de ménage* housecleaning items; *faire le ménage* to do housework; *un homme de ménage* janitor 5
la **menthe** mint; *un diabolo menthe* lemon-lime soda with mint syrup
mentir to lie 7
un **menu fixe** fixed-price menu
une **mer** sea; *mer des Caraïbes* Caribbean Sea; *mer Méditerranée* Mediterranean Sea; *mer du Nord* North Sea; *au bord de la mer* by the seaside; *le bord de mer* seaside; *les fruits de mer (m.)* seafood
merci thank you
mercredi Wednesday

une **mère** mother; *belle-mère* stepmother
merveilleux, merveilleuse marvelous
mesdemoiselles (f.) plural of *mademoiselle*
un **message** message
une **messagerie** messaging
mesurer to measure 2; *une cuillère à mesurer* measuring spoon 2
mesureur: un verre mesureur measuring cup 2
un **métal** metal 2; *en métal* made of metal 2
la **météo** weather; weather forecast; *un bulletin météo(rologique)* weather forecast
une **méthode** method 7
un **métier** job
un **métrage: un long métrage** feature film 5
le **métro** subway; *en métro* by subway
un **metteur en scène** movie director
mettre to put (on), to set; *mettre d'accord* to get people to agree 1; *mettre en pratique* to put into practice 8; *mettre en valeur* to accentuate; *mettre le couvert* to set the table
se **mettre: se mettre en mode photo** to go into photo mode; *mets-toi* set yourself down
un **meuble** piece of furniture
meunière rolled in flour and sautéed
le **Mexique** Mexico 10
un **micro-ondes** microwave
midi noon
le **mien, la mienne** mine 9
mieux better; *il vaut mieux que* it's better that 4; *mieux que* better than; *le mieux* the best; *se porter mieux* to feel/ do better
mille thousand
un **millefeuille** layered custard pastry
un **million** million
mi-long, mi-longue shoulder-length *[hair]* 9
mince thin 9
mince darn, shoot
une **mine** appearance, expression
minuit midnight
une **minute** minute
un **miroir** mirror; *une galerie des miroirs déformants* fun house
une **mission** mission
mi-temps: à mi-temps half-time 8
mitoyen(ne) adjoining 3; *une maison mitoyenne* row house 3
un **mixeur** blender 2
moche ugly
la **mode** fashion 2
un **mode: se mettre en mode photo** to go into photo mode
moderne modern
moderniser to modernize
moi me
moins less; *moins le quart* quarter to; *moins (+ adverb) + que* less (+ adverb) than; *au moins* at least; *le moins* the least
un **mois** month
un **moment** moment 6; *en ce moment* at the moment 6
mon, ma, mes my; *mon Dieu* my god 5
le **monde** everyone, world; *tout le monde* everybody; *la musique du monde* world music
mondial(e) world 10; *leader mondial* world leader 10
la **mondialisation** globalization 10
monégasque from, of Monaco 5
un **moniteur, une monitrice** instructor 4
la **monnaie** change 6; *la monnaie étrangère* foreign currency 6
monoparental(e): une famille monoparentale single-parent family 1
un **monospace** minivan
monsieur (M.) Mr., sir
une **montagne** mountain; *un ananas montagne* mountain pineapple; *faire un tour de montagnes russes* to go on a roller coaster ride
monter to get in/on, to go up; *monter à bord* to board
une **montre** watch
montrer to show
un **monument** monument
se **moquer (de)** to make fun (of)
la **moquette** carpeting 3
une **morale** moral 7
un **morceau (de)** piece (of)
la **mort** death 8
mort(e) dead
une **morue** cod; *des accras (m.) de morue* cod fritters
une **mosquée** mosque
un **mot** word; *ce mot-là* this/that (very) word
motivation: une lettre de motivation cover letter 8
la **motoneige** snowmobiling 4; *faire de la motoneige* to snowmobile 4
un **mouchoir** handkerchief, tissue; *mouchoir en lin* linen handkerchief; *mouchoir en papier* paper tissue
mourir to die 8; *... est mort(e)...* died 8
une **mousse au chocolat** chocolate mousse
la **moutarde** mustard
un **mouton** sheep
un **mouvement** movement
un **moyen** means; *avoir les moyens* to be able to afford, to have the means 8; *moyen de transport* means of transportation
moyen(ne) medium
multinational(e) multinational 10
le **multiplexe** multiplex cinema 5

la **multiplication** multiplication 8; *une table de multiplication* multiplication table 8
un **mur** wall 3
mûr(e) ripe
musclé(e) muscular 9
un **musée** museum
un **music-hall** music hall
la **musique** music; *musique alternative* alternative music; *musique classique* classical music; *musique du monde* world music; *musique pop* pop music; *une émission de musique* music show
un **mystère** mystery 6

N

n'est-ce pas isn't that so
n'importe: n'importe quel, quelle just any 9; *n'importe qui* anyone 9
nager to swim
un **nanar** flop *[film]* 5
les **nanotechnologies (f.)** nanotechnology 1
une **nappe** tablecloth
une **nation** nation 2
national(e) national; *une fête nationale* national holiday
la **nature** nature; *nature morte* still life
naviguer to browse
un **nay** ney *[instrument]*
ne: ne (n')… aucun(e) no, none, not any, not one 4; *ne (n')… jamais* never; *ne (n')… ni… ni* neither… nor 4; *ne (n')… pas* not; *ne (n')… pas encore* not yet; *ne (n')… personne* nobody, no one, not anyone; *ne (n')… plus* no longer, not anymore; *ne (n')… que* only 4; *ne (n')… rien* nothing; *N'en jette plus!* Enough! Stop it! *[inform.]* 8
néanmoins nevertheless 8
nécessaire necessary
neiger to snow; *il neige* it's snowing
le **néo-classicisme** neoclassicism 7
néoclassique neo-classic 7
le **néo-impressionnisme** Neo-impressionism 7
nettoyer to clean
neuf nine
neuf, neuve new; *de neuf* new; *Quoi de neuf?* What's new?
neuvième ninth
le **nez** nose
ni neither, nor 4; *ne (n')… ni… ni* neither… nor 4
niçoise: une salade niçoise tuna salad
un **niveau** level
Noël Christmas; *une bûche de Noël* yule log 2; *le réveillon de Noël* Christmas Eve celebration 2; *le sapin de Noël* Christmas tree 2
noir(e) black
un **nom** name
un **nombre** number
non no; *non plus* neither
le **nord** north; *l'Amérique (f.) du Nord* North America
normand(e) from, of Normandy region
la **Normandie** Normandy region
une **note** grade
le **nôtre, la nôtre** ours 9
notre, nos our
nourrir to feed
la **nourriture** food
nous to us; us; we
nouveau new; *nouvel, nouvelle* new
le **Nouveau-Brunswick** New Brunswick
une **nouveauté** new release 5
une **nouvelle** short story 6
novembre November
nucléaire nuclear; *une famille nucléaire* nuclear family 1
la **nuit** night; *faire une nuit blanche* to stay up all night
nul, nulle bad *[inform.]*
un **numéro** number; *numéro de téléphone* phone number
le **Nutella** spread made of hazelnut and chocolate

O

un **objet** object; *objet d'art* art object
obligatoire mandatory
obligé(e) (de) obligated (to) 8; *être obligé(e) (de)* to be obligated (to) 8
observer to observe
obtenir to obtain 4
une **occasion** chance, occasion, opportunity 4; *avoir l'occasion (de)* to have the opportunity (to) 4
occupé(e) busy; *être occupé(e)* to be busy
occuper to occupy
s' **occuper (de)** to take care (of)
un **océan** ocean; *océan Atlantique* Atlantic Ocean; *océan Indien* Indian Ocean; *océan Pacifique* Pacific Ocean
l' **Océanie (f.)** Oceania
octobre October
l' **œil (m.)** eye
un **œuf** egg; *œufs brouillés* scrambled eggs; *œufs sur le plat* eggs sunny side up
une **œuvre** work
un **office de tourisme** tourist office 4
officiel(le) official
offrir to give, to offer
oh oh; *oh là là* oh dear, oh no, wow
un **oignon** onion
un **oiseau** bird
une **olive** olive
une **omelette** omelet
on one, they, we; *On s'appelle.* We'll call each other.
un **oncle** uncle
une **ONG (organisation non gouvernementale)** NGO (non-governmental organization)
onze eleven
l' **or (m.)** gold; *en or* made of gold
une **orange** orange
orange orange
une **orangerie** orangery

une orchidée orchid; *orchidée suspendue* tropical orchid
un ordre order; *en ordre* in order
un ordinateur computer; *ordinateur portable* laptop computer
l' oreille (f.) ear; *une boucle d'oreille* earring
organisé(e) organized 4
une origine origin 3; *être d'origine (+ adjective)* to come from (+ country) 3
ou or
où when; where
oublier to forget
un oud oud *[instrument]*
l' ouest (m.) west
oui yes; *Oui ?* Yes? Hello? *[on telephone]*
ouille ouch
un ours bear; *ours polaire* polar bear
une ouverture opening 8
ouvrir to open

P

page: à la page in fashion 2
le pain bread; *pain grillé* toast; *pain perdu* French toast
la paix peace 2
pâle pale 7
un pamplemousse grapefruit; *un jus de pamplemousse* grapefruit juice
un panda panda; *panda géant* giant panda
paniqué(e) panicky 9
une panne: en panne broken down
un panneau panel
un pantalon pants; *un pantalon (de) ski* ski pants 4
le papier paper; *en papier* made of paper; *papier peint* wallpaper 3; *papier toilette* toilet paper 10; *une feuille de papier* sheet of paper
un papillon butterfly
Papy grandpa
un paquet package; *paquet (de)* packet (of)
par through, via; with; *par contre* however, on the other hand 8; *par la suite* consequently 9
le parachutisme ascensionnel: faire du parachutisme ascensionnel to go parasailing
paraître to seem, to appear 5; *il paraît que* it seems that 5
le parapente paragliding 4; *faire du parapente* to go paragliding 4
un parasol (beach) umbrella
un parc park; *parc d'attractions* amusement park
parce que because
pardi of course *[regional]*
pardon pardon me
un pare-brise windshield
pareil(le) the same; *c'est pareil* it's the same
les parents (m.) parents
paresseux, paresseuse lazy
parfait(e) perfect 5
parfaitement perfectly
parfois sometimes
un parfum perfume, scent
parisien(ne) from, of Paris
parlementaire parliamentary
parler to speak, to talk; *parler de* to be about 6; *Ça parle de quoi ?* What is it about? 6; *sans parler de* not to mention 10
se parler to talk to each other/one another
parles: tu parles yeah right
des paroles (f.) lyrics
part: à part aside from 9
partager to share 5
un parti (politique) (political) party 2
la partie part 7; *faire partie (de)* to belong (to)
partir to leave; *C'est parti !* Here we go!; *partir en voyage* to take a journey 8
partout everywhere
pas not; *pas du tout* not at all; *pas mal* not bad; *pas très bien* not very well; *ne (n')… pas* not; *ne (n')… pas encore* not yet
un passager, une passagère passenger
un(e) passant(e) passerby 3
le passé past 4
un passeport passport 4
passer to go through; to move over (something), to pass; to spend *[time]*; *on passe… …* is playing (at the movies) 2; *passer à la radio* to play on the radio 2; *passer de… à* to move from… to 7; *passer l'aspirateur* to vacuum
se passer to happen 8
une passion passion
passionnant(e) exciting
passionné(e) (de) passionate (about)
passionnément passionately 2
une passoire colander 2
le pâté pâté
des pâtes (f.) pasta
le patinage (artistique) (figure) skating
une pâtisserie bakery, pastry shop
une pause pause 5
pauvre poor
la pauvreté poverty
payer to pay
un payeur, une payeuse someone who pays
un pays country
un paysage landscape
la peau skin 10
une pêche peach; *la pêche* fishing; *une canne à pêche* fishing pole
pêcher to fish
un pêcheur, une pêcheuse fisherman, fisherwoman 3
un peigne comb
se peigner to comb one's hair
un peignoir de bain bathrobe
peindre to paint 3
la peine: ce n'est pas la peine it's not worth it 1
peint painted 7

un(e) **peintre** painter
une **peinture** painting
une **pelouse** lawn
pendant during; for; *pendant que* while 3; *pendant que tu y es* while you're at it
une **pendule** clock
penser to think
perdre to lose
perdu lost; *le pain perdu* French toast
un **père** father; *beau-père* stepfather
une **perle** pearl; *un collier en perles* pearl necklace
un **permis (de conduire)** driver's license 8
une **perruque** wig 8
persillé: le jambon persillé ham and pork dish made with chopped parsley 5
perso personalized *[inform.]* 8; *être perso* to be personalized *[inform.]* 8
une **personnalité** celebrity
une **personne** person; *ne (n')… personne* nobody, no one, not anyone
personnel(le) personal 2
personnellement personally 5
une **perspective** perspective
persuadé(e) persuaded; convinced 4
peser to weigh 6
petit(e) little, short, small; *une petite annonce* want ad 8
un(e) **petit(e) commerçant(e)** shopkeeper
le **petit déjeuner** breakfast
des **petits pois (m.)** peas
le **pétrole** petroleum
(un) **peu** (a) little; *un peu de* a little of
le **peuple** people 8
la **peur: avoir peur (de)** to be afraid (of); *avoir peur du vide* to be afraid of heights
peut-être maybe
une **pharmacie** drugstore
le **phare** headlight
les **Philippines (f.)** Philippines 10
une **photo** photo; *prendre (quelque chose) en photo* to take a picture (of something); *publier une photo* to post a photo; *re-photo* another photo
photogénique photogenic 9
la **physique** physics
un **piano** piano
une **pièce** play; room; *pièce (de monnaie)* coin 6; *pièce d'identité* identification (document) 4; *pièce (de théâtre)* (theatrical) play
le **pied** foot; *à pied* on foot; *faire une randonnée à pied* to hike
un **pilote** pilot
un **pinceau** paintbrush 7
pique-niquer to picnic
un **piranha** piranha
un **pirate** pirate
une **pirogue** pirogue; *en pirogue* by pirogue
pis: le pis the worst *[adverb]*
une **piscine** swimming pool
une **piste** lead 1; slope 4; *faire du ski hors-piste* to backcountry ski 4; *piste de ski* ski slope 4
une **pizza** pizza
un **placard** cupboard
une **place** square; *à sa place* in its place 2; *sur place* on the premises 4
une **plage** beach; *une serviette de plage* beach towel
se **plaindre** to complain
une **plaine** plain
la **plainte** complaint 7
plaire (à) to please 7
un **plaisir** pleasure
un **plan** city map; *à l'arrière-plan* in the background 7; *à l'avant-plan* in the foreground 7; *au premier plan* in the foreground; *au second plan* in the middle ground 7; *en gros plan* in a close-up 7; *un gros plan* close-up 7
la **planche à voile** wind surfing 4; *faire de la planche à voile* to wind surf 4
une **planète** planet
planifier to plan 4
une **plante** plant
la **plastique** plastic; *en plastique* made of plastic
un **plat** dish; *plat principal* main dish; *des œufs (m.) sur le plat* eggs sunny side up
plat(e) flat, lifeless 5
un **plateau** platter
plein full; *en plein air* outdoors; *faire le plein* to fill up the gas tank; *plein (de)* a lot (of) 8
pleurer to cry
pleuvoir to rain; *il pleut* it's raining
la **plongée sous-marine: faire de la plongée sous-marine** to go scuba diving
plonger to dive
la **plupart de** most 9
plus more; *de plus en plus* more and more 7; *plus mal* worse; *plus (+ adverb) que* more (+ adverb) than; *plus de (+ noun)* more; *en plus de* in addition to; *le/la/les plus (+ adjective)* the most (+ adjective); *le plus* the most; *le plus mal* the worst; *ne (n')… plus* no longer, not anymore; *non plus* neither
plusieurs several
plutôt instead; rather; quite 5
une **PME (petite et moyenne entreprise)** small business 1
le **PNB (produit national brut)** GNP (Gross National Product) 2
un **pneu** tire
pneumatique: un matelas pneumatique inflatable mattress
une **poche** pocket; *une lampe de poche* flashlight; *un livre de poche* paperback 6
une **poêle** frying pan
un **poème** poem
la **poésie** poetry 6; *un recueil de poésie* collection of poetry 6
un **poète, une femme poète** poet 7
poétique poetic 7

un **point de vue** viewpoint
une **poire** pear
pois: à pois polka-dot 9
un **poisson (rouge)** (gold)fish
la **poitrine** chest
le **poivre** pepper
un **poivron** bell pepper
policier, policière detective 6
politique political; *une femme politique* female politician; *un homme politique* male politician; *les sciences (f.) politiques (sciences po)* political science (poli sci) 6
la **politique** politics 2
polluant polluting
pollué(e) polluted
polluer to pollute
un **pollueur, une pollueuse** polluter
la **pollution** pollution
une **pomme** apple; *un jus de pomme* apple juice; *une tarte aux pommes* apple pie
un **pont** bridge
pop: la musique pop pop music
populaire popular 7
le **porc** pork
un **port** port; *port micro-USB* micro USB port
un **portable** cell phone, laptop
portable: un téléphone portable cell phone
une **porte** door; *porte d'embarquement* boarding gate
un **portefeuille** wallet
porter to wear
se **porter mieux** to feel/do better
un **portrait** portrait
posé(e) set down 2
poser to put down 2; *poser le papier peint* to put up wallpaper 3
une **position** position 8; *prendre position (sur)* to take a position (on) 7
le **positionnement** positioning 6
une **possibilité** possibility
possible possible
postale: une carte postale postcard
un **poste** job position 1
la **poste** post office
le **postier, la postière** postal worker 6
un **pot (de)** a jar (of)
un **potage** soup
une **poubelle** garbage can
une **poule** hen
le **poulet** chicken
pour for; in order to 7; *pour commencer* for starters; *c'est pour ça que* that/this is why; *pour que* so that 7; *pour t'avancer* to help you 2
pourquoi why
pourrais (see **pouvoir**)
pourras (see **pouvoir**)
pousser un cri to scream
pouvoir to be able (to); *Je (ne) peux (pas) m'empêcher de....* I can('t) stop myself from.... 2
se **pouvoir: il se pourrait que** it's possible that 4
un **pouvoir** power
pratique practical 5; *mettre en pratique* to put into practice 8
précisément precisely
des **précisions (f.)** specific information 5
préférait (see **préférer**)
préféré(e) favorite
préférer to prefer
une **première** première (of a movie) 6
premier, première first; *le premier plan* foreground; *au premier plan* in the foreground; *en première année* in the first year
premièrement firstly 8
les **premiers secours (m.)** first-aid; *une trousse de premiers secours* first-aid kit
prendre to have *[food or drink]*, to take; *prendre des vacances* to take a vacation; *prendre (quelque chose) en photo* to take a picture (of something); *prendre position (sur)* to take a position (on) 7; *prendre une décision* to make a decision 10
un **prénom** first name
préparer to make; to prepare
se **préparer** to get (oneself) ready
des **préparatifs (m.)** preparations 4; *préparatifs de départ* travel preparations 4
une **préposition** preposition
près de near
le **présent** present 8
un **présentateur, une présentatrice** news anchor
présenter (à quelqu'un) to introduce (to someone)
un(e) **président(e)** president 10; *président directeur général, présidente directrice générale (PDG)* CEO 10
presque almost; nearly
les **prestations (f.)** amenities 5
prêt(e) ready
le **prêt-à-porter** ready-to-wear 2
prêter to lend
les **prévisions (f.)** forecast
prévu(e) planned 2
une **princesse** princess 1
principal(e) main; *un plat principal* main dish
le **printemps** spring
la **priorité** priority 9
un **prisonnier, une prisonnière** prisoner 2
privé(e) private 8
un **problème** problem
prochain(e) next
la **production** production 10
un **produit** product 2; *produit alimentaire* food product 10; *produit laitier* dairy product 10; *le produit national brut (PNB)* GNP (Gross National Product) 2
un(e) **prof** teacher

une **profession** profession; *Quelle est votre profession ?* What is your profession?
un **professionnel, une professionnelle** professional 3
un **profil** profile
profiter (de) to take advantage (of); *profiter de* to benefit from; *tu profiterais de* you would benefit from
un **programme** plan; program
le **progrès** progress
un **projet** project
projeter to plan
prolongé(e) extended
une **promenade** walk
se **promener** to go for a walk
une **promesse: faire une promesse** to make a promise
promettre to promise; *ça promet* it sounds promising 5; *c'est promis* it's a promise 6
une **promo** sale
propos: à propos de about 2
proposer to suggest; to offer 10
propre clean 3
protéger to protect
provençal(e) from, of Provence
la **Provence** Provence
une **province** province
un **proviseur** principal
des **provisions (f.)** supplies
prudemment carefully
la **psychologie** psychology 6
une **publicité (pub)** commercial
publier une photo to post a photo
puis then
puis: Puis-je… ? May I…? 5
puisque since (because) 2
puissant(e) powerful
un **puits** well
un **pull** sweater
un **pyjama** pyjamas

Q

qu'est-ce que what; *Qu'est-ce qu'ils ont ?* What's wrong with them?; *Qu'est-ce que tu aimes faire ?* What do you like to do?; *Qu'est-ce que tu fais ?* What are you doing?
qu'est-ce qui what
un **quai** platform
une **qualité** quality 8
quand when; *depuis quand* since when; *quand même* after all 2; regardless 2
une **quarantaine** about forty 9; *d'une quarantaine d'années* in one's forties 9
quarante forty
un **quart** quarter; *et quart* quarter past; *moins le quart* quarter to
un **quartier** area, district
quatorze fourteen
quatre four
quatre-vingt-dix ninety
quatre-vingts eighty
quatrième fourth
que as, than; that; which; whom 2; *dès que* as soon as; *ne (n')… que* only 4
le **Québec** Quebec
québécois(e) from, of Quebec
quel, quelle what, which
quelque chose something
quelques a few, some 5
quelqu'un somebody, someone
une **question** question
qui that, who; which; *ce qui* what
une **quiche** quiche
quinze fifteen
quitter to leave
se **quitter** to leave each other/one another 1
quoi what; you know what I mean; *Quoi de neuf ?* What's new?
quotidien(ne) daily

R

le **racisme** racism
racler to scrape, to scrub 2
raconter to tell
la **radiation** radiation
une **radio** radio
le **raï** Rai music
raide straight *[hair]* 9
un **raisin** grape
la **raison: avoir raison** to be right
un **ramier** wood pigeon
une **randonnée** hike; *faire une randonnée à pied* to hike; *faire une randonnée équestre* to go on a trail ride 4
ranger to arrange, to pick up
le **rap** rap music
rapide fast
rapidement quickly 3
se **rappeler** to remember
les **rapports (m.)** relationships 2
la **raquette à neige** snowshoeing 4; *faire de la raquette à neige* to go snowshoeing 4
se **raser** to shave
un **rasoir** razor
se **rassurer** to reassure (oneself); *rassure-toi* don't worry
la **ratatouille** ratatouille
raté(e) failed
rater to mess up 2
un **raton laveur** raccoon
rayures: à rayures striped 9
une **réaction** reaction 9
un **réalisateur, une réalisatrice** director
réalisé(e) (par) directed (by) 2
réaliser to realize; to direct (movie) 6
le **réalisme** realism 7
réaliste realistic; realist 7
la **réalité** reality 6
recadrer to crop *[photography]*
la **réception** reception desk; reception 1; lobby 5
un(e) **réceptionniste** hotel clerk
une **recette** recipe
recevoir to get, to host, to receive
un **réchaud** portable stove

réchauffer to heat up
la **recherche** research 1; *des recherches généalogiques* genealogical research 3; *un laboratoire de recherches* research laboratory 1
rechercher to look for/into 7
un **récit** account 9
une **récompense** award 2
recomposé(e): une famille recomposée blended family 1
reconnaître to recognize
se **reconnaître** to see oneself as 7
rectangulaire rectangular 2
un **recueil** collection 6; *recueil de poésie* collection of poetry 6
récupérer to recapture 2
recycler to recycle
une **rédaction** composition
rédiger to write 8
réduire to reduce 2
la **rééducation** physical therapy 8
réfléchir (à) to consider, to think over
un **reflet** reflection 7
une **réflexion** thought
un **regard** look
regarder to watch
se **regarder** to look at oneself
le **reggae** reggae music
un **régime** regime 8
une **région** region
régional(e) regional 10
les **réglages (m.)** settings
régler to adjust; to pay
un **regret** regret 1
regretter to be sorry 5
une **reine** queen
une **religieuse** cream puff pastry
remarquable remarkable
remarque look, well
remarquer to notice
rembourser to reimburse
un **remède** remedy, solution
remercie: je vous remercie (de) thank you (for) *[form.]*
remettre to put back
se **remettre (à)** to start something again; *on s'y remet* let's get back to it

remous: un bain à remous whirlpool bath 5
remplacer to replace
remplir to fill; to fill out 9
remuer to stir, to toss 2
le **renard** fox 7
se **rencontrer** to meet
un **rendez-vous** meeting
rendre to give back, to return; to turn in; *rendre un service (à quelqu'un)* to do (someone) a favor; *rendre visite (à quelqu'un)* to visit (someone)
se **rendre (à)** to go, to show up
se **rendre compte (de)** to realize 9
se **renseigner** to get information 4
la **rentrée** back to school/work (after vacation)
rentrer to come back, to come home, to return
réparer to repair
un **repas** meal
repasser to iron; *un fer à repasser* (clothes) iron
repeindre to repaint 3
re-photo another photo
répondre to respond 8
un **reportage** news report; *reportage sportif* sports coverage
se **reposer** to rest
un(e) **représentant(e)** representative
une **république** republic 8
le **RER** express train from Paris to suburbs; *en RER* by RER
une **réservation** reservation
réserver to make a reservation; *réserver (pour quelqu'un)* to make especially (for someone) 10
une **résidence** residence 3; *résidence secondaire* second home 3
une **résolution** resolution
respiratoire respiratory
respirer to breathe
une **responsabilité** responsibility 10
un(e) **responsable** director, manager 10
responsable responsible

ressembler (à) to resemble
ressentir to feel 9
les **ressources (f.) humaines** human resources 10; *un directeur, une directrice des ressources humaines (DRH)* HR Director 8
un **restaurant** restaurant; *tenir un restaurant* to own a restaurant 3
le **reste** rest 10
rester to be left; to remain, to stay
un **resto-U (restaurant universitaire)** university cafeteria
retirer to take out; to withdraw 6
un **retour** return; *être de retour* to be back
retourner to return
se **retrouver** to meet; *se retrouver (sur)* to appear (on) 9
un **rétroviseur** rearview mirror
La **Réunion** Reunion 4
une **réunion: une salle de réunion** meeting center 5
se **réunir** to meet, get together
réussir (à) to pass (a test), to succeed
un **rêve** dream; *une maison de rêve* dream house
se **réveiller** to wake up
le **réveillon de Noël** Christmas Eve celebration 2
réveillonner to celebrate Christmas/New Year's Eve 2
revenir to come back; to return
le **revenu** income 2
rêver to dream
revoir to see again
une **révolution** revolution
le **rez-de-chaussée** ground floor
un **rhume** cold
une **riad** riad
riche rich, wealthy
rien nothing 9; *ne (n')… rien* nothing; *Rien que ça ?* Is that it?
rigoler to laugh
rire to laugh
une **rive** river bank

une **rivière** river
une **robe** dress; *robe de mariée* wedding dress
le **rococo** rococo style 7
rococo rococo 7
le **rock** rock (music)
un **roi** king
un **rôle** role
le **roller** in-line skating
un **roman** novel
un **romancier, une romancière** novelist 7
romantique Romantic 7
le **romantisme** Romanticism 7
un(e) **Romain(e)** Roman 5
rond round 2
une **rondelle** circle; *en rondelles* in circles
rose pink
une **roue: la grande roue** Ferris wheel; *faire un tour de grande roue* to go on a Ferris wheel ride
rouge red
un **rouge à lèvres** lipstick
un **rouget** goatfish
rougir to blush
un **rouleau** roll 10
une **roulette** wheel; *à roulettes* on wheels; *une valise à roulettes* suitcase with wheels
une **route** highway, road, route; *Bonne route!* Have a good trip!; *en route* on the way
une **routine** routine
roux, rousse red *[hair]*
une **rue** street
rusé(e) cunning 3
le **Rwanda** Rwanda

S

s'il vous plaît please
une **SA (Société Anonyme)** public (incorporated) company 10
le **sable** sand 1
un **sac** bag; *sac à dos* backpack; *sac à main* purse; *sac de couchage* sleeping bag; *sac de plage* beach bag
la **Saint-Jean** national Quebec holiday
la **Saint-Valentin** Valentine's Day
une **saison** season
une **salade** lettuce; salad; *salade niçoise* tuna salad
un **salaire** salary 8
sale dirty 3
salé(e) salty, savory
une **salle** room; *salle à manger* dining room; *salle de cinéma* movie theatre (room) 5; *salle de classe* classroom; *salle de bains* bathroom; *salle d'informatique* computer lab; *salle de réunion* meeting center 5
un **salon** living room; *salon de coiffure* hair salon
la **salsa** salsa music 7
salut good-bye, hi
samedi Saturday
une **sanction** punishment
des **sandales (f.)** sandals
un **sandwich** sandwich; *sandwich au fromage* cheese sandwich; *sandwich au jambon* ham sandwich
sanitaire health, sanitary
sans without 4; *sans aucun doute* without a doubt 4; *sans parler de* not to mention 10
un **sans-abri** homeless person
la **santé** health; *le domaine de la santé* health sector
le **sapin de Noël** Christmas tree 2
une **satire** satire 7
la **sauce** sauce 2; *sauce béarnaise* Béarnaise sauce 5; *sauce béchamel* béchamel sauce 5; *sauce blanche* white sauce 5; *sauce hollandaise* hollandaise sauce 5; *sauce marinière* white wine sauce 5
une **saucisse** sausage
le **saucisson** salami
sauf except
le **saumon** salmon; *saumon fumé* smoked salmon 2; *une terrine de saumon* salmon mousse loaf
un **saut: faire des sauts à ski** to go off ski jumps 4; *faire du saut à l'élastique* to bungee jump 4
sauter to jump 1; *sauter à la corde* to jump rope 1
sauvage wild
sauvegarder to protect; to back up *[computer file]*
savoir to figure out, to know how; to know; *Tu en sais des choses.* You sure know a lot about it.
se **savoir: ça se saurait** it would be known; *ça va se savoir* it will be revealed (known)
un **savon** soap
un **saxophone** saxophone
scandinave Scandinavian 9
une **scène** scene; stage 7; *sur scène* on stage 7
schuss: tout schuss full throttle 4
les **sciences (f.)** science; *le domaine des sciences et techniques* science and technology sector; *sciences au sport* sport sciences 6; *sciences politiques (sciences po)* political science (poli sci) 6
la **science-fiction** science fiction
un **scooter** scooter; *en scooter* by scooter; *faire du scooter des mers* to jet ski
scotché(e) (à) glued (to)
une **sculpture** sculpture
une **séance** film showing; session 8
un **sèche-cheveux** hairdryer
un **sèche-linge** clothes dryer
sécher to dry; to skip (class) *[inform.]* 9; *faire sécher le linge* to dry clothes
second: au second plan in the middle ground 7
secondaire secondary 3; *une résidence secondaire* second home 3
un **secours: au secours** help
un **secret** secret
un **secrétaire (administratif), une secrétaire (administrative)** secretary 10

le **secrétariat** reception area 10
un **secteur** industry; *secteur aéronautique* aviation industry; *secteur agroalimentaire* food industry; *secteur de développement durable* sustainable development industry; *secteur de l'informatique* information technology industry; *secteur du numérique* digital sector; *secteur financier* financial sector
la **sécurité: sécurité sociale (sécu)** French national health and pension insurance 8; *une ceinture de sécurité* seatbelt; *un contrôle de sécurité* security checkpoint
séduire to seduce 7
seize sixteen
un **séjour** living room; stay; *faire un séjour* to stay 4
le **sel** salt
selon according to
une **semaine** week
semblant: faire semblant (de) to pretend (to) 1
sembler to seem
le **Sénégal** Senegal
sénégalais(e) Senegalese
un **sens** sense, way; *en un sens* in a way
une **sensation** feeling, sensation
un **sentier** path
sentir to smell; *Ça sent quoi ?* What does it smell like?
se **sentir** to feel 9
sept seven
septembre September
septième seventh
sera (see **être**)
une **série** series; *toute une série (de)* whole series (of)
le **sérieux** seriousness
sérieux, sérieuse serious
un **serpent** snake
une **serpillière** mop 10
un **serveur, une serveuse** server
un **service** service 5; department 10; *service après-vente* post-sale support 10; *service blanchisserie* laundry service 5; *service de chambre* room service 5; *service de livraison (postale)* (mail) delivery service 6; *un chef, une cheffe de service* department head 10; *rendre un service (à quelqu'un)* to do (someone) a favor; *demander un service* to ask for a favor
servi(e) served 5
une **serviette** napkin; towel; *serviette de plage* beach towel
servir to serve; *Ça sert à....* It's used for.... 2
se **servir (de)** to use
seul(e) alone, lonely 9
seulement only 4
un **shampooing** shampoo
le **shopping** shopping
un **short** shorts
un **show** show 9
si how about, if only, what if; if; so 2; yes *[on the contrary]*; *si cela vous convient* if you'd like
le **SIDA** AIDS
un **siège** seat; *siège social* headquarters 10
le **sien, la sienne** his, hers 9
SIM: une carte SIM SIM card
simple simple
simplement simply; *tout simplement* quite simply
le **sirop** syrup; *sirop d'érable* maple syrup
une **sitcom** sitcom
un **site** site; *site web* website
une **situation** situation
situé(e) located
six six
sixième sixth
le **skatepark** skateboard park 1
un **ski** ski 4; *le ski (alpin)* (downhilll) skiing; *faire des sauts à ski* to go off ski jumps 4; *faire du ski de fond* to cross-country ski 4; *faire du ski de piste* to ski downhill 4; *faire du ski hors-piste* to backcountry ski 4; *faire du ski joëring* to skijor 4; *faire du ski nautique* to go water-skiing; *faire du taxi-ski* to take a ski-taxi ride 4; *un bâton de ski* ski pole 4; *un casque de ski* ski goggles 4; *une chaussure de ski* ski boot 4; *une piste de ski* (ski) slope 4; *une station de ski* ski resort 4; *une veste (de) ski* ski jacket 4; *un forfait de ski* ski pass 4; *un pantalon (de) ski* ski pants 4; *un tremplin de saut à ski* ski jump 4
skier to ski 4; *en skiant* while skiing 4
un **smartphone** smartphone
un **smoking** tuxedo
un **SMS** text message
le **snowboard** snowboarding 4; *faire du snowboard* to snowboard 4
social(e) social 8; *la sécurité sociale (sécu)* French national health and pension insurance 8; *un siège social* headquarters 10
une **société** company; society; *Société Anonyme (SA)* public (incorporated) company 10
une **sœur** sister; *belle-sœur* sister-in-law; *demi-sœur* half/step sister
la **soie** silk; *en soie* made of silk
soif: avoir soif to be thirsty
soigner to treat 8; *se faire soigner* to seek (medical) treatment 8
des **soins (m.)** care, treatment 8
le **soir** evening; *tous les soirs* every night
une **soirée** evening; evening out 1
soixante sixty
soixante-dix seventy

solaire solar; *la crème solaire* sunscreen; *l'énergie (f.) solaire* solar energy; *un panneau solaire* solar panel

solde: en solde on sale

le **soleil** sun; *des lunettes (f.) de soleil* sunglasses; *il fait du soleil* it's sunny

la **solidarité** solidarity

une **solution** solution

sombre dark

le **sommet** peak 4

son, sa, ses her, his, one's, its

un **sonnet** sonnet 7

le **sorcier** wizard 7

une **sorte** kind, sort

une **sortie** exit; release 5

sortir to come out; to go out; to take out

se **sortir: s'en sortir** to overcome

le **souci** worry 2

souffrir to suffer 2

souhaiter to hope, to wish 5

la **soupe** soup

le **soupir** sighing 7

une **source d'eau** spring

sourire to smile 1

un **sourire** smile 1

une **souris** mouse

sous under

sous-titré(e) subtitled 5

les **sous-titres (m.)** subtitles 5

soutenir to support; *je soutiens* I support

se **souvenir (de)** to remember

un **souvenir** memory

souvent often

soviétique Soviet 5

une **spatule** spatula 2

se **spécialiser (en)** to major (in)

une **spécialité** specialty; *spécialité du jour* daily special

un **spectacle** show

le **speed riding** speed riding 4; *faire du speed riding* to speed ride 4

sphérique spherical 2

splendide gorgeous

un **sport** sport; *une voiture de sport* sports car; *les sciences (f.) du sport* sport sciences 6

sportif, sportive athletic; *un reportage sportif* sports coverage

le **Sri Lanka** Sri Lanka 10

un **stade** stadium

un **stage** internship 8; *faire un stage* to intern 8

un(e) **stagiaire** intern 8

un **stand de crêpes** crêpe stand

une **station** station; *station de ski* ski resort 4

une **station-service** gas station

une **statue** statue

un **steak-frites** steak with fries

le **step** step aerobics

une **stéréo** stereo

stéréotypé(e) stereotypical 5

un **steward** male flight attendant

une **stratégie** strategy 10

strict(e) strict

une **strophe** stanza 7

un **studio** studio apartment 3

un **style** style 5

un **stylo** pen

le **succès** success 7

le **sucre** sugar; *au sucre* with sugar

sucré(e) sweet

le **sud** south; *l'Amérique (f.) du Sud* South America

suffire to be enough 3; *ça suffit* that's enough 3

la **Suisse** Switzerland

suisse Swiss; *un couteau suisse* Swiss army knife

la **suite** (the) rest 3; *par la suite* consequently 9; *tout de suite* right away

suivant(e) following 5

suivre to follow, to take *[class]*

un **sujet** subject

super awesome; really, very

superbe excellent

un **super-héro, une superhéroïne** superhero, superheroine 1

un **supermarché** supermarket

superposé: des lits (m.) superposés bunk beds

un **supplément** additional cost

un **supporter, une supportrice** fan

sur about; of; on; *être sur place* to be on site, on the premises; *sur place* on the premises 4; *sur scène* on stage 7

sûr sure; *bien sûr* of course; *c'est sûr* that's for sure

surexcité(e) overexcited 9

surfer: surfer sur Internet to surf the web

surprenant surprising 4

surprend: ça ne me surprend pas it doesn't surprise me

une **surprise** surprise

le **surréalisme** surrealism 7

surtout especially; mostly

surveiller to keep an eye on 9

survivre to survive

un **SUV** SUV

le **swing** swing music 7

sympa nice

synchroniser to synchronize

un **syndicat d'initiative** tourist information office

le **synopsis** movie synopsis 5

un **synthé(tiseur)** keyboard

un **système** system 8

T

t'appelles: tu t'appelles your name is; *Tu t'appelles comment ?* What's your name?

s' **inquiéter** to worry 1; *ne t'inquiète pas* don't worry

le **tabac: un bureau de tabac** news store that sells tobacco, stamps, lottery tickets

une **table** table; *à table* at the (dinner) table 2; *débarrasser la table* to clear the table; *table de multiplication* multiplication table 8

un **tableau** chalkboard, smartboard; painting; *tableau des arrivées et des départs* arrival and departure timetable

une **tablette** tablet

une **tache** spot

un **taf** work *[inform.]*

tahitien(ne) Tahitian
une **taille** size; *de taille moyenne* of average height; *Quelle taille faites-vous ?* What size are you?
un **taille-crayon** pencil sharpener
un **tailleur** tailor
le **talent** talent 9
un **tambour** drum
tamponneuse: une auto tamponneuse bumper car
tant pis too bad
une **tante** aunt
taper to type
un **tapis** rug
tard late
une **tarte** pie; *tarte aux fruits* fruit tart; *tarte aux pommes* apple pie
une **tartine** bread with butter, jam
une **tasse** cup
le **taux d'inflation** inflation rate 2
un **taxi** taxi; *en taxi* by taxi
le **taxi-ski** ski-taxi riding 4; *faire du taxi-ski* to take a ski-taxi ride 4
te (t') to you, you
un(e) **technicien(ne) de centrale solaire** solar plant technician
la **technique** technology; *le domaine des sciences et techniques* science and technology sector
la **techno** techno music
un **tee-shirt** T-shirt
un **tel, une telle** such a 9
une **télé (télévision)** television, TV; *télé câblée* cable TV; *à la télé* on TV
télécharger to download
une **télécommande** TV remote control
les **télécommunications** telecommunications
le **télémark** telemark skiing 4; *faire du télémark* to telemark ski 4
un **téléphone portable** cell phone
téléphoner to phone (someone), to make a call
la **télé-réalité** reality TV; *une émission de télé-réalité* reality TV show
un **télésiège** ski lift 4
télévisé(e) televised; *un jeu télévisé* (TV) game show
tellement so much
la **température** temperature
le **temps** time; weather; *à mi-temps* half-time 8; *à plein temps* full-time 8; *depuis combien de temps* how long; *Depuis le temps !* At last!; *gagner du temps* to save time; *le bon vieux temps* the good old days; *Quel temps fait-il ?* What's the weather like?; How's the weather?; *tout le temps* all the time
la **tendresse** tenderness 6
tenir un restaurant to own a restaurant 3
des **tennis (f.)** sneakers
une **tente** tent
tenter to tempt; *tenter sa chance* to try one's luck 3
un **terrain de camping** campground
une **terrasse** terrace
la **terre** land
une **terrine de saumon** salmon mousse loaf
un **territoire** territory 2
le **terrorisme** terrorism
un **testeur de jeux vidéo** video game tester
tétanisé(e) paralyzed 9
la **tête** head; look 9; *Lève la tête !* Look up!; *pas la tête à* not the type to 9
une **teuf** party
un **texte** text 7
un **texto** text message
Thanksgiving Thanksgiving (US)
un **thé** tea; *thé au citron* lemon tea
un **théâtre** theatre
un **thème** topic; theme 7
thermal(e) hydrotherapeutic
le **thon** tuna
un **thriller** thriller
un **ticket** ticket
le **tien, la tienne** yours 9
tiens here; hey
un **tigre** tiger; *tigre de Sumatra* Sumatran tiger
un **timbre** stamp 1
timide shy
un **tissu** fabric; *en tissu* made of fabric 2
un **titre** title 6
un **toast** canapé 2
le **Togo** Togo
togolais(e) Togolese
toi you
une **toile** canvas 7
les **toilettes (f.)** bathroom; *des affaires (f.) de toilette* toiletries; *le papier toilette* toilet paper 10; *un gant de toilette* washcloth
un **toit** roof
la **tolérance** tolerance
une **tomate** tomato
tomber to fall 8; *ça tombe bien* that works out well 2; *tomber en panne* to break down; *tomber sur* to discover accidentally 5
ton, ta, tes your
le **ton** tone 5
une **tondeuse** lawn mower
tondre to mow
top awesome; *C'est le top !* That's awesome!
tort: avoir tort to be wrong 8
une **tortue** turtle; *tortue marine* sea turtle
tôt early
total(e): Total vintage ! It has a totally vintage look!; *La totale !* The whole deal!
une **touche** key *[on keyboard]*
toucher to touch
toujours always; still
un **tour** tour; *faire le tour* explore all the possibilities 10; *faire un tour* to go on a ride; to go on a trip; *faire un tour de grande roue* to go on a Ferris wheel ride; *faire un tour de manège* to go on a carnival ride; *faire un tour de montagnes russes* to go on a roller coaster ride; *jouer un tour* to play a trick 3
une **tour** tower
la **Touraine** Touraine region

tourangeau, tourangelle from, of Touraine region
le **tourisme** tourism 4; *tourisme d'aventure* adventure tourism; *un office de tourisme* tourist office 4
un(e) **touriste** tourist; *faire le touriste* to be a tourist
touristique touristy 3
tourmenter to torment 9
une **tournée** tour 7; *en tournée* on tour 7
tourner to turn; *tourner un film* to shoot a movie 5
un **tournevis** screwdriver 3
la **Toussaint** All Saints Day
tout(e), tous, toutes all; every; *de toute façon* in any case 4; *en tout cas* in any case; *tous les soirs* every night; *tout à fait* completely; *Tout ça !* All that!; *tout de suite* right away; *tout d'un coup* all of a sudden 9; *tout le monde* everybody; *tout le temps* all the time; *tout schuss* full throttle 4; *tout simplement* quite simply; *toute une série (de)* whole series (of)
une **trace *[Mart.]*** path
traditionnel(le) traditional
un **train** train; *en train* by train
traîner to dawdle, to hang around
traire to milk
un **traitement** treatment 8
une **tranche (de)** a slice (of)
tranquille calm, quiet 2
transférer (de l'argent) to transfer (money) 6
un **transport** transportation; *un moyen de transport* means of transportation
travailler to work
traverser to cross
trébucher to stumble 9
treize thirteen
un **tremblement de terre** earthquake
un **tremplin de saut à ski** ski jump 4
une **trentaine** about thirty 9; *d'une trentaine d'années* in one's thirties 9
trente thirty
très very; *Très bien, et toi/vous ?* Very well, and you?; *Très heureux/heureuse.* Pleased to meet you. 3
un **trésor** treasure
triangulaire triangular 2
triste sad
trois three
troisième third
un **trombone** trombone
une **trompette** trumpet; *trompettes de la mort* black trumpet mushrooms 5
trop too; *trop de* too much (of)
une **trousse** pencil case; *trousse de premiers secours* first-aid kit
trouver to find
se **trouver** to be located
un **truc** thing
une **truffe** truffle 2
tu you; *tu n'y es pas du tout* you don't get it 4
tuer to kill 2
la **Tunisie** Tunisia
tunisien(ne) Tunisian
tutoyer to use the informal *tu* to address someone 10
un **type** guy 9
typiquement typical of 10

U

un a, an; one
une a, an, one
l' **un(e)... l'autre** one... the other 9
l' **uniformisation (f.)** standardization 10
l' **Union (f.) européenne** European Union
l' **univers (m.)** universe
universel(le) universal 2
universitaire: une cité universitaire university dormitory
une **université** university; *entrer à l'université* to go to college
un **USB: un port micro-USB** micro USB port
user de diplomatie to use diplomacy
une **usine** factory
un **ustensile** utensil 2
usurper to usurp 2
utile useful 4
utiliser to use

V

les **vacances (f.)** vacation; *prendre des vacances* to take a vacation
un **vacancier, une vacancière** vacationer
une **vache** cow
la **vaisselle: faire la vaisselle** to wash the dishes
la **valeur** worth 2
une **valise** suitcase; *faire sa valise* to pack 4; *valise à roulettes* suitcase with wheels
une **vallée** valley
valoir to be the cause of 7; *il vaut mieux que* it's better that 4
une **variation** variation 7
vas: Tu vas bien ? Are things going well?
un **vase** vase 10
vaut: ça vaut it's worth
le **veau** veal 5
une **vedette** star *[celebrity]* 5
le **Vélib'** bicycle sharing service; *en Vélib'* by Vélib
un **vélo** bike; *à vélo* by bike
le **velours** velvet; *en velours* made of velvet
un **vendeur, une vendeuse** salesperson
vendre to sell
vendredi Friday
venir to come; *venir de (+ infinitive)* to have just (done something)
le **vent** wind; *il fait du vent* it's windy
les **ventes (f.)** sales 10; *le service après-vente* post-sale support 10

le **ventre** stomach
vérifier to check
un **verre** glass; *verre mesureur* measuring cup 2
vers around; towards
verser to pour 2
une **version** version; *version originale (VO)* original version 5
vert(e) green
une **veste** jacket; *veste (de) ski* ski jacket 4
des **vêtements (m.)** clothes
un(e) **vétérinaire** veterinarian
vêtu(e) de dressed in 9
veux: je veux bien I'd like that
la **viande** meat 5
le **vide: avoir peur du vide** to be afraid of heights
une **vie** life
la **vieillesse** old age
le **Vietnam** Vietnam 4
vieux, vieil, vieille old; *le bon vieux temps* the good old days
vif, vive vivid
une **villa** villa 3
un **village** village
une **ville** city; *en ville* downtown
la **vinaigrette** vinaigrette salad dressing
vingt twenty
une **vingtaine** about twenty 9; *d'une vingtaine d'années* in one's twenties 9
vintage vintage 9
la **violence** violence
violet(te) purple
un **violon** violin
un **violoncelle** cello
une **vis** screw 3
un **visa** visa 4
visible visible 9
une **visite** visit; *rendre visite (à quelqu'un)* to visit (someone)
visiter to visit
vite fast, quickly
vivre to live; *une douceur de vivre* relaxed style of life
voici here, here is
une **voie** path; train platform; *les animaux en voie de disparition* endangered species
voilà here are/is
la **voile: faire de la voile** to go sailing
un **voilier** sailboat
voir to see; *Je vois.* I see.
se **voir** to see each other/one another
une **voiture** car; *voiture de sport* sports car; *voiture électrique* electric car; *voiture hybride* hybrid car; *en voiture* by car
un **vol** flight; theft 9; *une déclaration de vol* report of a theft 9
un **volant** steering wheel
un **volcan** volcano 4
voler to steal 9
un **voleur** thief 9
volontiers gladly
volumineux, volumineuse voluminous 7
voter to vote 2
le **vôtre, la vôtre** yours 9
votre, vos your
voudrais (see **vouloir**)
vouloir to want; *vouloir dire* to mean; *ça veut dire* it/that means
vous to you; you; *Vous voulez… ?* Would you like…?
un **voyage** trip; *faire un voyage* to go on a trip; *partir en voyage* to take a journey 8; *voyage de noces* honeymoon 1
voyager to travel
un **voyageur, une voyageuse** traveler
un(e) **voyant(e)** fortune teller
vrai(e) true; real 5
vraiment really
une **vue** view; *Quelle belle vue !* What a beautiful view!; *un point de vue* viewpoint

W

un **wagon-restaurant** dining car
wahou wow 8
les **W.C. (m.)** restroom, bathroom
le **web: un concepteur web, une conceptrice web** web designer
le **weekend** weekend
le **wifi** wifi
la **world** world music

Y

y there *[pronoun]*; to it *[pronoun]*
un **yaourt** yogurt
les **yeux (m.)** eyes; *le blanc des yeux* eye to eye 9
le **yoga** yoga

Z

zéro zero
zoomer to zoom

Vocabulary terms from Level 1 and Level 2 of *T'es branché?* are included but do not have a unit number. Vocabulary terms from Level 3 include the unit number in which the term is introduced.

English–French

A

a, an un; une; *(a) little* (un) peu; *a little of* un peu de; *a lot* beaucoup; *a lot of* beaucoup de; plein (de) 8; *You sure know a lot about it.* Tu en sais des choses.

to **abandon** abandonner 4
to be **able to** arriver (à); pouvoir
about sur; à propos de 2; *about (the)* du; *about it/them* en; *about which/whom* dont 6; *it's about* il s'agit de; *to be about* parler de 6; *What is it about?* Ça parle de quoi ? 6
above au-dessus de
absolutely absolument 1
abstract abstrait(e)
accelerator un accélérateur
accent un accent
to **accentuate** mettre en valeur
to **accept** accepter
to **access** accéder 8
accessory un accessoire
accident un accident
to **accompany** accompagner
according to selon
account un compte 6; un récit 9
accountant un(e) comptable 10
accounting la comptabilité 10
ache: to have a/an... ache avoir mal (à)...
acquired acquis(e) 8
across from en face de
to **act** agir
action l'action (f.); une action 5
activity une activité
actor un acteur, une actrice
ad: want ad une petite annonce 8
to **adapt** adapter 10; s'adapter (à) 10
adaptation une adaptation 10
to **add** ajouter 10
addition: in addition to en plus de
additional cost un supplément
to **address (someone)** s'adresser (à quelqu'un) 2
address une adresse
addressed (to) adressé (à) 5
to **adjust** adapter 10; régler; *to adjust the field width* régler la largeur du champ
administration l'administration (f.) 6
administrative administratif, administrative 10
to **adore** adorer
adventure une aventure; *adventure tourism* le tourisme d'aventure
to **advise** conseiller
aerobics l'aérobic (m.); *step aerobics* le step
affectionately affectueusement
afford: to be able to afford avoir les moyens 8
afraid: to be afraid (of) avoir peur (de); *to be afraid of heights* avoir peur du vide; *I'm afraid not.* Je crains que non. 2
Africa l'Afrique (f.)
African africain(e) 9
after après; *after all* quand même 2
afternoon l'après-midi (m.)
again: to see again revoir; *to start something again* se remettre (à)
against contre
age l'âge (m.); *old age* la vieillesse
agent un(e) agent(e)
ago: (time +) ago il y a (+ time)
to **agree** être d'accord; *to get people to agree* mettre d'accord 1
AIDS le SIDA
air l'air (m.); *air conditioning* la climatisation
airplane un avion
airport un aéroport
album un album; *concept album* album concept 7
alcoholism l'alcoolisme (m.)
Algerian algérien(ne)
all tout(e), tous, toutes; *after all* quand même 2; *all of a sudden* tout d'un coup 9; *All that!* Tout ça !; *all the time* tout le temps; *to stay up all night* faire une nuit blanche
almond une amande
almost presque
alone seul(e) 9
along: to get along s'entendre
alongside le long de
already déjà
Alsace region l'Alsace (f.); *from, of Alsace region* alsacien(ne)
also aussi
aluminum l'aluminium (m.); *made of aluminum* en aluminium
always toujours
ambiance une ambiance
amenities les prestations (f.) 5
America: North America l'Amérique (f.) du Nord; *South America* l'Amérique (f.) du Sud
American américain(e)
Amerindian amérindien(ne)
to **amuse** amuser
amusement park un parc d'attractions
ancestor(s) un aïeul, une aïeule (les aïeux) 3; un(e) ancêtre 3
anchor: news anchor un présentateur, une présentatrice
and et
anecdote une anecdote 8
angry fâché(e) 1; *to be angry* être fâché(e) 1

animal un animal
ankle la cheville 4; *to sprain an ankle* se fouler la cheville 4
to **annex** annexer
anniversary: wedding anniversary un anniversaire de mariage
to **announce** annoncer
to **annoy** agacer; embêter 2; *You're getting on my nerves!* Tu m'agaces !
anole un anoli
another photo re-photo
Antarctica l'Antarctique (m.)
anthology of plays une anthologie de pièces de théâtre 6
antiretroviral drugs les antirétroviraux (m.)
anti-Semitism l'antisémitisme (m.)
any aucun(e) 4; d', de; des, du, en; *just any* n'importe quel, quelle 9; *in any case* en tout cas; *not any* ne (n')... aucun(e) 4
anyone n'importe qui 9
apartheid l'apartheid (m.)
apartment un appartement; *apartment building* un immeuble; *studio apartment* un studio 3
app (application) une appli (application)
to **appear (on)** se retrouver (sur) 9
appearance une mine
appetizer un hors-d'œuvre 2; *skewered appetizer* une brochette apéritive 2
appetizer une entrée
apple une pomme; *apple juice* un jus de pomme; *apple pie* une tarte aux pommes
application letter une lettre de candidature 8
to **apply** appliquer 7
April avril
Arab arabe
area un espace; un quartier; *reception area* le secrétariat 10
to **argue** se disputer
aristocrat un(e) aristocrate 8
arm le bras
armchair un fauteuil
around autour de 2; vers; *to get around* se déplacer
to **arrange** ranger
arrested: to get arrested se faire arrêter 9
arrival une arrivée; *arrival and departure timetable* un tableau des arrivées et des départs
to **arrive** arriver
art l'art (m.); *art history* l'histoire (f.) de l'art 6; *art object* un objet d'art; *Bachelor of Arts degree* un BA 10; *fine arts* les beaux-arts (m.) 7
article: magazine article un article; *newspaper article* un article
artist un(e) artiste
as aussi, que; comme; *as (+ adverb) as* aussi (+ adverb) que; *as for you* de votre côté 2; *as soon as* aussitôt que 1; dès que
ashamed honteux, honteuse 9
Asia l'Asie (f.)
Asian asiatique 9
aside from à part 9
to **ask (for)** demander; *to ask for a favor* demander un service; *to ask for directions* demander le chemin
assignment un devoir
assistance l'aide (f.)
assistant: junior assistant un(e) assistant(e) junior 8
at à; en; *at (the)* au, aux; *At last!* Depuis le temps !; *at least* au moins; *at my house* chez moi; *at/to the club* en boîte; *at the dentist's* chez le dentiste; *at the doctor's* chez le médecin; *at the end of* au bout de; au fond de; *at the house (home) of* chez; *at the moment* en ce moment 6; *at the same time* à la fois; *by the seaside* au bord de la mer; *at the top* en haut
athlete un(e) athlète
athletic sportif, sportive
ATM le distributeur (automatique) 6
atmosphere une ambiance; *great atmosphere* chaude ambiance
to **attach** joindre
to **attend** assister (à) 1
audio trial en écoute libre
auditor of a class un auditeur, une auditrice libre 10
August août
aunt une tante
Australia l'Australie (f.)
author un auteur 7
auto shop un garage
autobiography une autobiographie 6
automotive designer un(e) designer automobile
autumn l'automne (m.)
avancer: pour t'avancer to help you 2
avenue une avenue
aviation industry le secteur aéronautique
to **avoid** éviter
award une récompense 2
away: right away tout de suite; *I'm going (away)* je m'en vais 2; *to get away (from)* s'éloigner (de) 10
awesome formidable; super; top; *That's awesome!* C'est le top !
awful horrible

B

baby un bébé 1
to **babysit** garder un enfant 3
Bachelor of Arts degree un BA 10
back le dos; *back country* l'arrière-pays (m.); *back to school/work (after vacation)* la rentrée; *let's get back to it* on s'y remet; *to be back* être de retour; *to give back* rendre; *to put back* remettre
to **backcountry ski** faire du ski hors-piste 4

background: in the background à l'arrière-plan 7
backpack un sac à dos
bacon le bacon
bad mal; mauvais; nul, nulle *[inform.]*; *it's too bad that...* c'est dommage que... 5; *the weather is bad* il fait mauvais
badly mal; *Things are going badly.* Ça va mal.
bag un sac; *beach bag* un sac de plage; *sleeping bag* un sac de couchage
baker un boulanger, une boulangère
bakery une boulangerie, une pâtisserie
bald chauve 9
ballad une ballade 3
banana une banane
bank une banque; *bank teller* le caissier, la caissière 6; *river bank* une rive
banker le banquier, la banquière 6
to **barbecue** faire griller
barn une grange
basketball le basket (basketball)
bat une chauve-souris
bath un bain; *whirlpool bath* un bain à remous 5
to **bathe** baigner
bathing suit un maillot de bain
bathrobe un peignoir de bain
bathroom une salle de bains; les toilettes (f.); les W.C. (m.)
bathtub une baignoire
to **be** être; *to be able (to)* pouvoir; arriver (à); *to be a tourist* faire le touriste; *to be afraid (of)* avoir peur (de); *to be afraid of heights* avoir peur du vide; *to be back* être de retour; *to be busy* être occupé(e); *to be (busy) doing something* être en train de (+ infinitive); *to be cold* avoir froid; *to be eager* avoir hâte de; *to be environmentally friendly* être vert; *to be familiar with (person, place, thing)* connaître; *to be hot* avoir chaud; *to be how old* avoir quel âge; *to be hungry* avoir faim; *to be hurt* avoir mal (à...); *to be in charge (of)* être chargé(e) (de); *to be informed* être au courant; *to be in (good, bad) shape* être en (bonne, mauvaise) forme; *to be interested (in)* s'intéresser (à); *to be left* rester; *to be located* être situé(e), se trouver; *to be lucky* avoir de la chance; *to be necessary* falloir; *to be right* avoir raison; *to be on site, on the premises* être sur place; *to be thirsty* avoir soif; *to be... year(s) old* avoir... an(s); *it would be* ça serait
beach une plage; *beach chair* une chaise longue; *beach towel* une serviette de plage; *beach bag* un sac de plage
bear un ours; *polar bear* un ours polaire
beautiful beau, bel, belle; *It's beautiful out.* Il fait beau.
beauty la beauté
because parce que; puisque 2; *because of* à cause de 2
to **become** devenir
bed un lit; *bunk beds* des lits superposés; *in bed* couché(e); *to go to bed* se coucher; *twin bed* un lit jumeau
bedroom une chambre
beef le bœuf; *beef burgundy* bœuf bourguignon
beer la bière 10
before avant; auparavant 9
to **begin** commencer
beginning un début
behind derrière
beige beige
Belgian belge
Belgium la Belgique
to **believe** croire
to **belong (to)** être à 8; faire partie (de)
belongings des affaires (f.)
belt une ceinture
bench un banc
to **benefit from** profiter de; *you would benefit from* tu profiterais de
Benin le Bénin
Beninese béninois(e)
Berber berbère
beside à côté de
best man le garçon d'honneur 1
best seller un best-seller
best: the best les meilleurs (m.); le mieux
better mieux; *better than* mieux que; *to do/feel better* se porter mieux; *it's better that* il vaut mieux que 4
between entre
bicycle une bicyclette; *or a bicycle* à bicyclette
to **bid farewell** faire ses adieux 8
big grand(e); gros(se)
to **bike** faire du vélo; *by bike* à vélo
bike un vélo
bilingual bilingue 10
bill l'addition (f.); une facture 8; *bill [money]* un billet
binoculars des jumelles (f.)
biochemistry la biochimie 6
biography une biographie 6
biology la biologie
bird un oiseau
birthday un anniversaire
black noir(e)
blacksmith un forgeron
blasé blasé(e) 5
blender un mixeur 2
blinker un clignotant
blog un blog
blogger un blogueur, une blogueuse 2
blond blond(e)
blouse un chemisier 9
blue bleu(e); *the blue one* la bleue (f.)
to **blush** rougir
to **board** monter à bord

boarding l'embarquement (m.); *boarding gate* une porte d'embarquement; *boarding pass* une carte d'embarquement
boat un bateau; *by boat* en bateau
body le corps; *body of water* une masse d'eau
bonfire un feu de joie
book un livre; un bouquin *[inform.]* 6; *checkbook* un chéquier 6; *paperback (book)* un livre de poche 6
bookstore une librairie
boots des bottes (f.); *ski boots* des chaussures (f.) de ski 4
bored: to get bored s'ennuyer 4
to **borrow** emprunter
botanical canna un balisier
to **bother** déranger 2; *I'm not bothering you?* Je ne te dérange pas ? 2
bottle (of) une bouteille (de)
bottom le bas
bowl un bol
box une boîte 6; *cardboard box* une boîte cartonnée 6; *mailbox* une boîte aux lettres 6
boy un garçon
bracelet un bracelet
brake un frein
branch une filiale 10
brand une marque 10; *brand name* marqué(e) 10
bread le pain; *long thin loaf of bread* une baguette; *bread with butter, jam* une tartine
to **break down** tomber en panne
to **break one's wrist** se casser le poignet 4
breakfast le petit déjeuner
to **breathe** respirer
bride une mariée
bridesmaid la demoiselle d'honneur 1
bridge un pont
to **bring** apporter; emporter; *to bring (person)* emmener; *to bring oneself to do something* arriver à faire quelque chose 6
Brittany region la Bretagne; *from, of Brittany region* breton(ne)
broken down en panne
brother un frère; *half-brother/stepbrother* un demi-frère; *brother-in-law* un beau-frère
brown marron; *[hair]* brun(e)
to **brush: to brush one's hair** se brosser les cheveux; *to brush one's teeth* se brosser les dents
buckwheat crêpe une galette
buffet un buffet
building: apartment building un immeuble
bumper car une auto tamponneuse
to **bungee jump** faire du saut à l'élastique 4
bunk beds des lits (m.) superposés
Burgundy la Bourgogne 5; *from, of Burgundy* bourguignon(ne) 5
Burkina Faso le Burkina Faso; *from, of Burkina Faso* burkinabè
bus un (auto)bus; *by bus* en (auto)bus
business commerçant(e); une entreprise 1; *business center* un centre d'affaires 5; *(economic business) management* la gestion (économique d'entreprise) 6; *small business* une PME (petite et moyenne entreprise) 1
businessman un homme d'affaires
businesswoman une femme d'affaires
busy occupé(e); *to be busy* être occupé(e); *to be (busy) doing something* être en train de (+ infinitive)
but mais
butcher un boucher, une bouchère; *butcher shop* une boucherie
butter le beurre
butterfly un papillon
button un bouton; *home button* le bouton principal; *power button* le bouton marche/arrêt
buzz le buzz 9
by à; de; en; *by bike* à vélo; *by boat* en bateau; *by bus* en (auto)bus; *by canoe* en canoë; *by car* en voiture; *by electric car* en voiture électrique; *by hybrid car* en voiture hybride; *by pirogue* en pirogue; *by plane* en avion; *by RER* en RER; *by scooter* en scooter; *by subway* en métro; *by taxi* en taxi; *by the way* au fait; *by train* en train

C

cabaret singer un chansonnier, une chansonnière
cable channel une chaîne câblée 5
café un café
café-restaurant une brasserie
cafeteria une cantine; *university cafeteria* un resto-U (restaurant universitaire)
cake un gâteau
to **call** appeler; *to send a video call* faire un appel vidéo
called: to be called in être convoqué(e) 8
calm tranquille 2
to **calm: Calm down!** Calme-toi !
Cambodia le Cambodge 10
camembert cheese le camembert
camera un appareil, une caméra
Cameroon le Cameroun
Cameroonian camerounais(e)
campground un terrain de camping
camping le camping; *to go camping* faire du camping
can (of) une boîte (de); *garbage can* une poubelle
Canada le Canada
Canadian canadien(ne)

canapé un toast 2
candidate le candidat 2
canning company une conserverie 3
canoe un canoë; *by canoe* en canoë; *to go canoeing* faire du canoë
canvas une toile 7
canyoning: to go canyoning faire du canyonisme 4
cap une casquette
capital une capitale
car une auto (automobile); une voiture; *bumper car* une auto tamponneuse; *by car* en voiture; *car manufacturer* un constructeur, une constructrice automobile 10; *dining car* un wagon-restaurant; *electric car* une voiture électrique; *hybrid car* une voiture hybride; *sports car* une voiture de sport; *to play with toy cars* jouer aux petites voitures 1
caramel le caramel; *caramel custard* une crème caramel
carbon dioxide le dioxyde de carbone
card une carte; *credit card* une carte de crédit; *debit card* une carte bancaire 6; *membership card* une carte de membre; *SIM card* une carte SIM
cardboard box une boîte cartonnée 6
care des soins (m.) 8; *to take care (of)* s'occuper (de); *to take care of things* se débrouiller 8; *to not care* s'en fiche 1; *I don't care.* Je m'en fiche.; *She doesn't care.* Elle s'en fiche. 1
careful: Be careful! Attention!
carefully prudemment
caricature la caricature 7
carnival un carnaval; une fête foraine; *to go on a carnival ride* faire un tour de manège
carpeting la moquette 3
carrot une carotte
cartoon un dessin animé
case un cas; *in any case* de toute façon 4; en tout cas
to cash encaisser 6
cash l'argent (m.) liquide 6
casting le casting 5
castle un château
cat un chat
catalog un catalogue 6
catastrophe une catastrophe 5
cathedral une cathédrale
to cause causer
cause une cause; *to be the cause of* valoir 7
cave une caverne
CD un CD; un cédérom
to celebrate fêter
celebrity une personnalité
cell phone un portable; un téléphone portable
cello un violoncelle
center un complexe; *business center* un centre d'affaires 5; *fitness center* un centre de remise en forme 5; *meeting center* une salle de réunion 5; *reception center* un centre d'accueil; *sports center* un complexe sportif 1
CEO un(e) PDG (Président Directeur Général, Présidente Directrice Générale) 10
cereal des céréales (f.)
certain certain(e) 5; *to be certain that* être certain(e) que 5
certificate un certificat 6
CFO un directeur financier, une directrice financière 10
chair une chaise; *beach chair* une chaise longue
chalkboard un tableau
challenge un défi 9
championship le championnat 2
to change changer
change la monnaie 6
channel une chaîne; *cable channel* une chaîne câblée 5
chapel une chapelle
charge: to be in charge (of) être chargé(e) (de)
charm le charme
charming charmant(e)
cheap bon marché
check un chèque 6
to check vérifier; *to check in (online)* s'enregistrer (en ligne); *to check one's luggage* faire enregistrer ses bagages
checkbook un chéquier 6
checkpoint: security checkpoint un contrôle de sécurité
cheese le fromage; *camembert cheese* le camembert; *cheese sandwich* un sandwich au fromage
chef un cuisinier, une cuisinière
chemical chimique
chemistry la chimie
cherry une cerise
chest la poitrine
chic chic
chicken le poulet; *chicken cooked in wine* le coq au vin
child un enfant
childhood l'enfance (f.) 1
childish enfantin(e) 1
chills des frissons (m.)
China la Chine 10
chocolate le chocolat; *chocolate mousse* une mousse au chocolat; *hot chocolate* un chocolat chaud; *spread made of hazelnut and chocolate* le Nutella; *with chocolate* au chocolat
choice un choix; *to have too many choices* avoir l'embarras du choix 10
choir un chœur 9
to choose choisir
chore une corvée
Christmas Noël; *Christmas Eve celebration* le réveillon de Noël 2; *Christmas tree* le sapin de Noël 2; *to celebrate Christmas/New Year's Eve* réveillonner 2
church une église
circle un cercle 3; une rondelle *[object or piece of food]*

citizen un citoyen, une citoyenne 8
city une ville; *city hall* un hôtel de ville
civil engineering le génie civil 6
clarinet une clarinette
class une classe; un cours; *auditor of a class* un auditeur, une auditrice libre 10; *class subject* la matière; *gym class* l'éducation (f.) physique et sportive (EPS); *private class* le cours particulier 1; *ski class* une classe de neige 4
classic un classique 5
classical classique; *classical music* la musique classique
classmate un(e) camarade de classe
classroom la salle de classe
to **clean** nettoyer
clean propre 3
clear clair(e)
to **clear the table** débarrasser la table
clergy le clergé 8
to **click** cliquer
cliff une falaise; *cliff road* une corniche
clip: video clip un clip
clock une pendule
to **close** fermer
close: close-up un gros plan 7; *in a close-up* en gros plan 7
closer: on a closer look en y regardant de plus près 4; *to come closer* s'approcher 9
clothes des vêtements (m.); *clothes dryer* un sèche-linge; *to dry clothes* faire sécher le linge
club le club 2; *at/to the club* en boîte; *film club* le ciné-club 1
coast une côte
coat un manteau
cod une morue; *cod fritters* des accras (m.) de morue
coffee un café; *coffee with milk* un café au lait
coin une pièce (de monnaie) 6
cola un coca
colander une passoire 2
cold froid; *it's cold* il fait froid; *to be cold* avoir froid
cold un rhume
to **collapse** s'effondrer 9; *to collapse from exhaustion* s'effondrer de fatigue 9
to **collect** collectionner 1
collection une collection; *collection of poetry* un recueil de poésie 6
college une fac (faculté); *to go to college* entrer à l'université
colonization la colonisation
color une couleur; *De quelle(s) couleur(s) ?* In what colors?
to **comb one's hair** se peigner
comb un peigne
to **come** venir; *to come back* rentrer; revenir; *to come closer* s'approcher 9; *to come from (+ country)* être d'origine (+ adjective) 3; *to come home* rentrer; *to come in* entrer; *to come out* sortir; *come on* enfin
comedy une comédie; *romantic comedy* une comédie romantique
comfort le confort 5
comic strip une bande dessinée (BD)
comments les commentaires (m.) 9; *mean comments, gossip* les mauvais commentaires (m.) 9
commercial une publicité (pub)
to **commit to** s'engager (à, pour)
committed engagé(e) 7
community la collectivité 8; *community manager* un animateur de communauté; *housing community* une cité 3
company une compagnie 8; une société; une entreprise 1; *canning company* une conserverie 3; *company director* un chef, une cheffe d'entreprise 10; *public (incorporated) company* une SA (Société Anonyme) 10
compartment: baggage compartment un compartiment à bagages; un coffre à bagages
to **complain** se plaindre
complaint la plainte 7
completely complètement 9; entièrement 8; tout à fait
complex un complexe
complicated compliqué(e)
complicity la complicité 1
composer un compositeur
composition une composition; une rédaction
computer un ordinateur; *laptop computer* un ordinateur portable; *computer graphics* l'infographie (f.) 6; *computer lab* la salle d'informatique; *computer science* l'informatique (f.)
to **conceal** cacher 7
concept album un album concept 7
concert un concert
concierge un(e) concierge 5
condemned condamné(e); *to be condemned* être condamné(e) 8
conductor un chef d'orchestre 5
confession un aveu 7
Congolese congolais(e) 6
conical conique 2; *conical strainer* un chinois 2
connection: wireless internet connection connexion wifi 5
conqueror un conquérant
consequently par la suite 9
to **consider** réfléchir (à)
consulate le consulat 4
to **consult** consulter 5
consultant un(e) consultant(e)
consultation une consultation
contemporary contemporain(e)
continent un continent
to **continue** continuer
contract un contrat 8
contrary: on the contrary au contraire 8

controller: management controller un contrôleur, une contrôleuse de gestion 10
conventional convenu(e) 10
conversation une conversation
convertible une décapotable
convinced persuadé(e) 4
to **cook** cuire 2; faire la cuisine
cooking la cuisine
cool frais, fraîche; *it's cool* il fait frais
cooler une glacière
corner le coin; *on the corner* du coin
correctly correctement 4
to **cost** coûter
cost: additional cost un supplément
costume un costume
cotton le coton; *made of cotton* en coton
to **count (on)** compter (sur)
counter: (ticket) counter un comptoir
country un pays; *country(side)* la campagne; *back country* l'arrière-pays (m.)
couple un couple
course un cours; *in the course of* au cours de 8
course: of course bien sûr; bien entendu 5
couscous le couscous
cousin un(e) cousin(e); *first cousin* un(e) cousin(e) germain(e) 3
cover letter une lettre de motivation 8
coverage: sports coverage un reportage sportif
cow une vache
crab un crabe
crazy: crazy person un fou, une folle; *like crazy* comme des fous
cream la crème 10; *cream (of chives)* une crème (de ciboulette) 5
cream puff pastry une religieuse
to **create** créer
credit card une carte de crédit
Creole créole; *[language]* le créole
crêpe une crêpe; *buckwheat crêpe* une galette; *crêpe restaurant* une crêperie; *crêpe stand* un stand de crêpes
critic un critique 5
critique une critique 5
croissant un croissant
to **crop** [*photography*] recadrer
to **cross** traverser
to **cross-country ski** faire du ski de fond 4
crow le corbeau 7
crowd une foule
to **cry** pleurer
cry un cri
cubical cubique 2
cucumber un concombre
cultural culturel(le)
cunning rusé(e) 3
cup une tasse; *measuring cup* un verre mesureur 2
cupboard un placard
curly *[hair]* frisé(e) 9
currency: foreign currency la monnaie étrangère 6
custard: caramel custard une crème caramel
to **cut** couper
cut up (in) découpé(e) (en) 10
CV (Curriculum vitae) un CV 8
cylindrical cylindrique 2

D

daily quotidien(ne); *daily special* la spécialité du jour
dairy: dairy store une crémerie; *dairy product* un produit laitier 10
dancer un danseur, une danseuse
dark sombre; *[hair]* brun(e)
darn mince
date une date
daughter une fille
to **dawdle** traîner
dawn l'aube (f.) 7
day un jour; une journée; *New Year's Day* le Jour de l'an; *next day* le lendemain; *one day, some day* un jour; *the good old days* le bon vieux temps; *Valentine's Day* la Saint-Valentin
dead mort(e)
dear cher, chère
death la mort 8
debate le débat 8
debit card une carte bancaire 6
debt l'endettement (m.) 2
to **decapitate** guillotiner 8
December décembre
to **decide** choisir; décider
decision une décision 10; *to make a decision* prendre une décision 10
to **declare a major in humanities** s'inscrire en lettres
to **decrease** baisser 2
deep-fried frit(e)
to **defeat** déjouer 3
degree *[temperature]* un degré; *Bachelor of Arts degree* un BA 10; *Master's degree* une maîtrise 10
deli owner un charcutier, une charcutière
delicatessen une charcuterie
delicious délicieux, délicieuse
delighted enchanté(e)
delivery: (mail) delivery service le service de livraison (postale) 6
democracy une démocratie 2
demonstration: street demonstration une manif (manifestation)
Denmark: person from, of Denmark un(e) Danois(e)
denomination une dénomination 5
dentist un(e) dentiste; *at the dentist's* chez le dentiste; *dentist's office* un cabinet dentaire
department un département; le service 10; *department head* le chef, la cheffe de service 10

departure un départ
to **depend** dépendre 2; *It depends.* Ça dépend. 2
to **deposit** déposer 6
deputies les députés (m.) 8
descent une descente
to **describe** décrire
designer: automotive designer un(e) designer automobile; *web designer* un concepteur web, une conceptrice web
desk un bureau; *reception desk* la réception
dessert un dessert
destination une destination
destiny le destin
destroyed détruit(e)
detail un détail
detective policier, policière 6
to **detest** avoir horreur de; détester 1
developer: software developer un développeur, une développeuse
development un développement; *sustainable development* le développement durable; *sustainable development industry* le secteur de développement durable
device un appareil
dialogue un dialogue 5
diamond un diamant; *diamond ring* une bague en diamant; *made of diamond* en diamant
dictatorship une dictature 2
dictionary un dictionnaire
to **die** mourir 8; *… died …* est mort(e) 8
different différent(e)
differently différemment 4
difficult difficile; dur(e)
difficulties des difficultés (f.) 8
Dijon: from, of Dijon dijonnais(e) 5
diligent diligent(e)
dimension la dimension 2
dining: dining car un wagon-restaurant; *dining room* la salle à manger
dinner le dîner; *at the (dinner) table* à table 2; *to have dinner* dîner
diplomacy la diplomatie; *to exercise diplomacy* user de diplomatie
to **direct (movie)** réaliser 6
directed (by) réalisé(e) (par) 2
direction une direction
director un directeur, une directrice 5; un(e) responsable 10; *company director* un chef, une cheffe d'entreprise 10; *movie director* un metteur en scène; un réalisateur, une réalisatrice 5
dirty sale 3
to **disappear** disparaître
discography une discographie
discouraged découragé(e) 9
to **discover** découvrir; *to discover accidentally* tomber sur 5
discovery une découverte
to **discuss** discuter (de)
discussion une discussion
to **disguise oneself** se déguiser
dish un plat; *main dish* un plat principal; *to wash the dishes* faire la vaisselle
dishwasher un lave-vaisselle
disorder le désordre
distance une distance; *to distance oneself (from)* s'éloigner (de) 7
distant éloigné(e) 3
district un arrondissement 10; un quartier
to **dive** plonger
divorced divorcé(e)(s)
to **do** faire; *to do gymnastics* faire de la gym (gymnastique); *to do housework* faire le ménage; *to do (someone) a favor* rendre un service (à quelqu'un); *to do (something) in vain* avoir beau (+ infinitive) 8; *to do the laundry* faire la lessive; *to do my homework* faire mes devoirs; *you shouldn't do that* ça ne se fait pas
doctor un médecin; *at the doctor's* chez le médecin; *doctor's office* un cabinet de médecin
documentary un documentaire
dog un chien
do-it-yourself repairs le bricolage 3; *to do DIY projects* bricoler 3
dolls: to play with dolls jouer à la poupée 1
don't worry rassure-toi
to **donate** faire un don (de)
door une porte
dormitory un dortoir; *university dormitory* une cité universitaire
to **doubt** douter 5
down: broken down en panne; *to break down* tomber en panne
to **download** télécharger
downtown en ville
drama un drame
dramatic dramatique 2
to **draw** dessiner
drawing un dessin
to **dream** rêver
dream un rêve; *dream house* une maison de rêve
dress une robe; *wedding dress* une robe de mariée
to **dress up** se déguiser
dressed: to get dressed s'habiller; *dressed in* vêtu(e) de 9
dressing room une cabine d'essayage
dressmaker un couturier, une couturière
to **drink** boire
drink une boisson
to **drive** circuler; conduire
driver un conducteur, une conductrice; *driver's license* un permis (de conduire) 8
drugs la drogue
drugstore une pharmacie
drum un tambour; *(electric) drums* une batterie
to **dry clothes** faire sécher le linge

dryer: clothes dryer un sèche-linge
dubbed doublé(e) 5
dubbing le doublage 5
duck un canard; *duck breast* un magret de canard 2
duration la durée 5
during pendant; au cours de 8
DVD un DVD; *DVD player* un lecteur de DVD
dynamic dynamique

E

each chaque; *each (one)* chacun(e) 5
eager: to be eager (to) avoir hâte de
ear l'oreille (f.)
early en avance; tôt
earring une boucle d'oreille
earthenware la faïence 10
earthquake un tremblement de terre
east l'est (m.)
easy évident 6; facile
to **eat** manger
eclair un éclair
economic économique; *(economic business) management* la gestion (économique d'entreprise) 6
economy l'économie (f.) 2
edge le bord
education une éducation; une formation 8
effect un effet; *greenhouse effect* l'effet de serre
efficiently efficacement
egg un œuf; *scrambled eggs* des œufs brouillés; *eggs sunny side up* des œufs sur le plat
eggplant une aubergine
eight huit
eighteen dix-huit
eighth huitième
eighty quatre-vingts
election une élection 2; *presidential elections* les élections présidentielles 2
electric électrique
electronic électronique 5
elementary school teacher un instituteur, une institutrice
elevator l'ascenseur (m.) 5
eleven onze
to **eliminate** éliminer
emotion une émotion 5
employee un(e) employé(e) 3
to **encourage** encourager 2
encouraged encouragé(e) 9
end le bout; *at the end (of)* au bout (de); au fond (de); *in the end* finalement 3
endangered species les animaux (m.) en voie de disparition
energetic énergique
energy l'énergie (f.); *nuclear energy* l'énergie nucléaire; *solar energy* l'énergie solaire
engaged engagé(e) 7
engagement un engagement
engineer un ingénieur
engineering: civil engineering le génie civil 6
England l'Angleterre (f.)
English anglais(e); *[language]* l'anglais (m.); *English Channel* la Manche; *English-speaking* anglophone 10
engraved gravé(e)
enjoy: Enjoy your meal! Bon appétit!
enough (of) assez (de); *that's enough* ça suffit 3; *Enough! Stop it!* N'en jette plus! *[inform.]* 8
to **enter** entrer
entertainment le divertissement; *entertainment industry* l'industrie (f.) du divertissement
enthusiastic enthousiaste
entirely entièrement 8
entitled: to be entititled to avoir droit à 8
envelope une enveloppe
environment l'environnement (m.)
equal égal(e) 10
equipped (with) équipé(e) (de) 5
era une époque
e-reader une liseuse
especially surtout; *to make especially (for someone)* réserver (pour quelqu'un) 10
essay un essai
essential essentiel 4; *it's essential that* il est essentiel que 4
Estates General les états généraux 8
ethnic ethnique 10
euro un euro
Europe l'Europe (f.)
European Union l'Union européenne (f.)
even même; *even though* même que *[inform.]* 3
evening le soir; une soirée; *evening out* une soirée 1
every tout(e)(s); *every night* tous les soirs
everybody tout le monde
everyone le monde
everywhere partout
exactly exactement; justement; *it's/that's exactly* c'est bien 10
to **exaggerate** exagérer
excellent superbe
except sauf
exciting passionnant(e)
exhibit une exposition
to **exist** exister
exit une sortie
to **expect:** expect *[baby]* attendre; *to expect (something)* s'attendre (à) 4; *I was expecting that* Je m'y attendais 4
expensive cher, chère
experience une expérience
to **explain** expliquer
explained expliqué(e)
explore all the possibilities faire le tour 10
express train from Paris to suburbs le RER
expression une mine
expressionism l'expressionnisme (m.) 7
expressionist expressionniste 7
extended prolongé(e); éloigné(e) 3
extraordinary extraordinaire

eye l'œil (m.); *eyes* les yeux (m.); *eye to eye* le blanc des yeux 9; *to keep an eye on* surveiller 9

F

fable une fable 3
fabric un tissu; *made of fabric* en tissu 2
fabulous fabuleux, fabuleuse
face la figure
faced with face à 9
factory une usine
failed raté(e)
fair juste
fairy tale un conte de fées 3
fall la chute 8
to **fall** tomber 8
familiar: to be familiar with (person, place, thing) connaître
family une famille; *blended family* une famille recomposée 1; *nuclear family* une famille nucléaire *1; single-parent family* une famille monoparentale 1; *with family* en famille
famous célèbre
fan un(e) groupie 9; un supporter, une supportrice
fantastic génial(e)
fantasy la fantaisie; l'imaginaire (m.) 6
far (from) loin (de)
farewell: to bid farewell faire ses adieux 8
farm une ferme
farmer un fermier, une fermière
fashion la mode 2; *high fashion* la haute couture 10; *in fashion* à la page 2
fast rapide; vite
fat gros(se)
fate le hasard 10
father un père; *stepfather* un beau-père
fauna la faune
favor: to ask for a favor demander un service; *to do (someone) a favor* rendre un service (à quelqu'un)
favorite préféré(e)
fax un fax 5
to **fear** craindre
feature film un long métrage 5
February février
to **feed** nourrir
to **feel** éprouver 5; ressentir 9; se sentir 9; *to feel/do better* se porter mieux; *to feel like* avoir envie de; *to feel nauseous* avoir mal au cœur; *How do you feel about (+ noun)?* (noun +) te dit ? 4
feeling une sensation
female politician une femme politique
fermented fermenté(e) 5
Ferris wheel la grande roue; *to go on a Ferris wheel ride* faire un tour de grande roue
fertilizer l'engrais (m.)
festival un festival 1
fever la fièvre
few: a few quelques 5
field un champ; un domaine; *field of vision* un champ
fifteen quinze
fifth cinquième
fifty cinquante; *about fifty* une cinquantaine 9; *in one's fifties* d'une cinquantaine d'années 9
to **fight** combattre; lutter
fight une bagarre 9
figure la ligne; une figure 7; *your figure* ta ligne
to **figure out** savoir
figures les chiffres (m.) 8
figurine une figurine 10
file un fichier; *image file* un fichier image; *audio file* un fichier son; *video file* un fichier vidéo
to **fill** remplir; *to fill out* remplir 9; *to fill up the gas tank* faire le plein
to **film** filmer 9
film un film; *film club* le ciné-club 1; *film showing* une séance
to **filter** filtrer 2
finale le final 5
finally enfin
finances les finances (f.) 6
to **find** trouver
fine fin(e); *fine arts* les beaux-arts (m.) 7; *fine jewelry* la joaillerie 10
finger le doigt
to **finish** finir
firework un feu d'artifice
first premier, première; *first cousin* un(e) cousin(e) germain(e) 3; *first name* un prénom; *first (of all)* d'abord; *in the first year* en première année
first-aid les premiers secours (m.); *first-aid kit* une trousse de premiers secours
firstly premièrement 8
to **fish** pêcher
fish un poisson; *goldfish* un poisson rouge
fisherman, fisherwoman un pêcheur, une pêcheuse 3
fishing la pêche; *fishing pole* une canne à pêche
fitness center un centre de remise en forme 5
fittingly justement 3
five cinq
fixed-price menu un menu fixe
flag un drapeau
flake un lâcheur, une lâcheuse *[inform.]* 9
flashlight une lampe de poche; une lampe torche
flat plat(e) 5
flight un vol; *female flight attendant* une hôtesse de l'air; *male flight attendant* un steward
to **flirt** flirter 9
float un char
floor un étage; *the ground floor* le rez-de-chaussée; *the second floor* le premier étage
flop *[film]* un nanar 5
flora la flore
florist un(e) fleuriste
flour: rolled in flour and sautéed meunière
flu la grippe
flute une flûte
to **follow** suivre
following suivant(e) 5

fond of food gourmand(e)
food la nourriture; *food industry* le secteur agroalimentaire; *food product* un produit alimentaire 10; *food-processing* agroalimentaire 10
foot le pied; *on foot* à pied
for comme; depuis; pendant; pour; *for starters* pour commencer
forecast les prévisions (f.); *weather forecast* la météo; un bulletin météo(rologique)
foreground le premier plan; *in the foreground* au premier plan; à l'avant-plan 7
foreign currency la monnaie étrangère 6
foreign exchange bureau le bureau de change 6
forest une forêt
to **forget** oublier
fork une fourchette
formerly autrefois
fortunately heureusement
fortune teller un(e) voyant(e)
forty quarante; *about forty* une quarantaine 9; *in one's forties* d'une quarantaine d'années 9
fountain un bassin
four quatre
fourteen quatorze
fourth quatrième
fox le renard 7
France la France
free disponible; gratuit(e); libre
French français(e); *[language]* le français; *French fries* des frites (f.); *French Guiana* la Guyane (française); *French Riviera* la Côte d'Azur; *French-speaking* francophone; *French-speaking world* la Francophonie 3; *French toast* le pain perdu
to **frequent** fréquenter
fresh frais, fraîche
Friday vendredi
friend un(e) ami(e); *(boy/girl) friend* un copain, une copine
fritters: cod fritters des accras (m.) de morue
from d', de; *aside from* à part 9; *from (the)* des, du; en *[pronoun]*; *from it/them* en; *live from* en direct de; *from which* duquel, duquelle 5
front: in front of devant
fruit un fruit; *fruit tart* une tarte aux fruits
frustrated frustré(e) 9
frying pan une poêle
full plein; *full throttle* tout schuss 4; *full-time* à plein temps 8
fun: fun house une galerie des miroirs déformants; *to have fun* s'amuser; *to make fun (of)* se moquer (de)
to **function** marcher
funk music le funk
funny amusant(e); drôle
furniture: piece of furniture un meuble
future futur(e) 6
future l'avenir (m.)

G

Gabon le Gabon
Gabonese gabonais(e)
to **gain weight** grossir
gallery une galerie
game un match; *game of skill* un jeu d'adresse; *(TV) game show* un jeu télévisé; *Olympic Games* les Jeux Olympiques
garbage can une poubelle
garden un jardin; *garden party* une fête champêtre 7
gas: gas station une station-service; *to fill up the gas tank* faire le plein
Gascony region la Gascogne; *from, of Gascony region* gascon(ne)
gasoline l'essence (f.)
gastronomy la gastronomie 5
gate: boarding gate une porte d'embarquement
genealogical research des recherches (f.) généalogiques 3
generation une génération 3
generous généreux, généreuse
genocide le génocide
gentleness une douceur
geography la géographie
German allemand(e); *[language]* l'allemand (m.)
Germany l'Allemagne (f.)
to **get by** se débrouiller 6
to **get** recevoir; *to get along* s'entendre; *to get around* circuler; se déplacer; *to get arrested* se faire arrêter 9; *to get away (from)* s'éloigner (de) 10; *to get bored* s'ennuyer 4; *to get dressed* s'habiller; *to get in/on* monter; *to get information* se renseigner 4; *to get knocked into* se faire bousculer 9; *to get married* se marier; *to get off* descendre; *to get people to agree* mettre d'accord 1; *to get (oneself) ready* se préparer; *to get settled* s'installer; *to get together* se réunir; *to get transferred* se faire muter 1; *to get in trouble (with)* se faire disputer (par) 3; *to get undressed* se déshabiller; *to get up* se lever; *to get vaccinated* se faire vacciner 4; *to get wild* se déchaîner 9; *let's get back to it* on s'y remet
giant géant(e)
gift un cadeau; *gift card* une carte cadeau
girl une fille
to **give** donner; offrir; *to give back* rendre; *give me* donnez-moi; *to give rise to* donner lieu à 7
gladly volontiers
to **glance (at)** jeter un coup d'œil (à) 5
glass un verre
glasses des lunettes (f.)
globalization la mondialisation 10
gloves des gants (m.) 4
glued collé(e); *glued to* scotché(e) à
GNP (Gross National Product) le PNB (produit national brut) 2

to **go** aller; se rendre (à); *to go camping* faire du camping; *to go canoeing* faire du canoë; *to go canyoning* faire du canyonisme 4; *to go down* descendre; *to go for a walk* faire une promenade; se promener; *to go grocery shopping* faire les courses; *to go hang gliding* faire du deltaplane 4; *to go horseback riding* faire du cheval; *to go into photo mode* se mettre en mode photo; *to go kayaking* faire du kayak; *to go off ski jumps* faire des sauts à ski 4; *to go on a carnival ride* faire un tour de manège; *to go on a Ferris wheel ride* faire un tour de grande roue; *to go on a guided tour* faire une visite guidée; *to go on a ride* faire un tour; *to go on a roller coaster ride* faire un tour de montagnes russes; *to go on strike* faire grève 2; *to go on a tour* faire un tour; *to go on a trail ride* faire une randonnée équestre 4; *to go on a trip* faire un voyage; *to go out* sortir; *to go paragliding* faire du parapente 4; *to go parasailing* faire du parachutisme ascensionnel; *to go running* faire du footing; *to go sailing* faire de la voile; *to go scuba diving* faire de la plongée sous-marine; *to go shopping* faire du shopping; *to go sledding* faire de la luge 4; *to go snowshoeing* faire de la raquette à neige 4; *to go through* passer; *to go to bed* se coucher; *to go to college* entrer à l'université; *to go up* monter; *to go water-skiing* faire du ski nautique; *to go wild* craquer 9; *Go for it!* Vas-y !; *Here we go!* C'est parti !; *I'm going (away)* je m'en vais 2

goal un but

goat une chèvre

goatfish un rouget

god: my god mon Dieu 5

godmother une marraine 1

goggles: ski goggles un casque de ski 4

gold l'or (m.); *made of gold* en or

good bon(ne); *good-bye* au revoir, salut; *Good idea!* Bonne idée !; *good luck* bon courage; *the good old days* le bon vieux temps; *Have a good trip!* Bonne route !; Bon voyage !

goose liver pâté le foie gras 2

gorgeous splendide

gorilla un gorille; *mountain gorilla* un gorille des montagnes

gospel le gospel 9

gourmet gastronomique 10

government un gouvernement

grade une note

graffiti un graffiti (des graffiti) 3

gram (of) un gramme (de)

grandfather un grand-père

grandma Mamy

grandmother une grand-mère

grandpa Papy

grandparents les grands-parents (m.)

to **grant** accorder 8

grape un raisin

grapefruit un pamplemousse; *grapefruit juice* un jus de pamplemousse

graphic designer un(e) graphiste

graphic graphique 6

graphics: computer graphics l'infographie (f.) 6

great aunt la grand-tante 3

great chouette; génial(e)

Great Depression la grande crise 3

great uncle le grand-oncle 3

great-grandfather l'arrière-grand-père (m.) 3

great-grandmother l'arrière-grand-mère (f.) 3

green vert(e); *green beans* des haricots (m.) verts

grey gris

to **grill** griller

grilled grillé(e)

grocery store une épicerie; *grocery store owner* un épicier, une épicière

groom un marié

ground floor le rez-de-chaussée

group un groupe; *group of friends* une bande 1

grove un bosquet

to **grow** grandir; *to grow up* grandir 3

Guadeloupe la Guadeloupe

to **guarantee** garantir 5

guaranteed garanti(e)

to **guess** deviner

guest un(e) client(e) 5; un(e) invité(e)

guide un guide; *Michelin Guide* le Guide Michelin; *TV guide* un guide télévisé

guided guidé(e); *guided tour* une visite guidée

guilty coupable 6

guitar une guitare

guy un type 9

gym un fitness; *gym class* l'éducation (f.) physique et sportive (l'EPS)

gymnastics la gym (gymnastique)

H

hail la grêle 9

hair les cheveux (m.); *hair salon* un salon de coiffure; *hair stylist* un coiffeur, une coiffeuse; *to brush one's hair* se brosser les cheveux; *hairbrush* une brosse à cheveux; *hairstyle* une coiffure

hairdryer un sèche-cheveux

Haiti Haïti

Haitian haïtien(ne)

half demi(e); *half-brother* un demi-frère; *half past* et demi(e); *half-sister* une demi-sœur; *half-time* à mi-temps 8

hallway un couloir
ham le jambon; *ham sandwich* un sandwich au jambon
hamburger un hamburger
hamlet un hameau
to **hammer** enfoncer 3
hammer un marteau 3
hammock un hamac
hand la main; *hand in hand* la main dans la main; *(helping) hand* un coup de main 2; *on the other hand* par contre 8
handkerchief un mouchoir; *linen handkerchief* un mouchoir en lin
handsome beau, bel, belle
to **hang (paintings)** accrocher (des tableaux) 3
to **hang around** traîner
hang gliding: to go hang gliding faire du deltaplane 4
to **hang out** fréquenter
to **happen** arriver 9; se passer 8
happy content(e), heureux, heureuse; *to be happy (about)* être content(e) (de) 6
hat un bonnet; un chapeau; *wool hat* un bonnet en laine
to **hate** avoir horreur de
haunted house une maison hantée
to **have** avoir; *[food or drink]* prendre; *to have a/an… ache* avoir mal (à…); *to have dinner* dîner; *to have fun* s'amuser; *to have just (done something)* venir de (+ infinitive); *to have the impression (of)* avoir l'impression (de) 6; *to have to* devoir; falloir; *to have too many choices* avoir l'embarras du choix 10; *Have a good trip!* Bonne route !; Bon voyage !; *one/we/you have to* il faut
hazelnut: spread made of hazelnut and chocolate le Nutella
he il
head la tête; *department head* le chef, la cheffe de service 10
headquarters un siège social 10
healed guéri(e) 8
health la santé; sanitaire; *health club* un fitness; *health insurance* l'assurance (f.) maladie 8; *health sector* le domaine de la santé; *French national health and pension insurance* la sécurité sociale (sécu) 8
to **hear** entendre
heart le cœur
to **heat (up)** chauffer 2; réchauffer
heights: to be afraid of heights avoir peur du vide
hello bonjour; *[on the telephone]* allô
to **help** aider; *to help you* pour t'avancer 2
help au secours
hen une poule
her elle; sa, ses, son
hers le sien, la sienne 9
herbs les herbes (f.) 2
here ici; tiens; voici; *here are/is* voilà; *here is* voici; *Here we go!* C'est parti !
hero, heroine un héros, une héroïne
to **hesitate** hésiter
hey tiens
hi salut
hibiscus un hibiscus
to **hide** dissimuler; cacher 7; se cacher 7
hide-and-seek: to play hide-and-seek jouer à cache-cache 1
high haut(e); *high fashion* la haute couture 10
high school un lycée
high tech la haute technologie 1
highway une route
to **hike** faire une randonnée à pied
hike une randonnée
hill une colline
him lui
hip-hop le hip-hop
to **hire** embaucher 8
his sa, ses, son; le sien, la sienne 9
history l'histoire (f.); *art history* l'histoire de l'art 6
hit (musical) le hit *[inform.]* 2
holiday une fête; *national holiday* une fête nationale; *national Quebec holiday* la Saint-Jean
home une maison; *home health worker* un accompagnateur, une accompagnatrice; *second home* une résidence secondaire 3
homeless person un sans-abri
homework les devoirs (m.)
Honduras le Honduras 10
honey chéri(e)
honeymoon un voyage de noces 1
hood *[car]* un capot
to **hope** espérer; souhaiter 5
hopscotch: to play hopscotch jouer à la marelle 1
horizon l'horizon (m.); *on the horizon* à l'horizon
horn un klaxon
horrible horrible
horror l'horreur (f.)
horse un cheval
horseback: to go horseback riding faire du cheval
hospital l'hôpital (m.) 8
hospitality l'hospitalité (f.)
to **host** recevoir
host: TV host un animateur, une animatrice
hot: hot chocolate un chocolat chaud; *to be hot* avoir chaud; *it's hot* il fait chaud
hotel un hôtel; *hotel clerk* un(e) réceptionniste; *hotel room* une chambre
hour une heure
house une maison; *house cleaning items* des affaires (f.) de ménage; *dream house* une maison de rêve; *fun house* une galerie des miroirs déformants; *haunted house* une maison hantée; *row house* une maison mitoyenne 3; *single-family house* une maison individuelle 3
household le ménage

housework le ménage; *to do housework* faire le ménage
housing le logement 3; *housing community* une cité 3; *subsidized housing* une HLM (des HLM) 3
how comment; *how about* si; *How are things going?* Ça va ?; *How are you?* Comment allez-vous ?; *how long* depuis combien de temps; *how much* combien; *How much is it?* Ça fait combien ?; *How much per kilo?* C'est combien le kilo ?; *How old are you?* Tu as quel âge ?; *How's the weather?* Quel temps fait-il ?
however cependant 8; par contre 8
human humain(e) 10; *human resources* les ressources (f.) humaines 10; *HR Director* le directeur, la directrice des ressources humaines (DRH) 8
humanitarian humanitaire
humanities les lettres (f.); *to declare a major in humanities* s'inscrire en lettres
humid humide 4
hummingbird un colibri
hundred: (one) hundred cent
hunger la faim
hungry: to be hungry avoir faim
to hurry se dépêcher (de)
hurt: to be hurt avoir mal (à…)
husband un mari
hybrid hybride
hydrant: water hydrant une borne-fontaine
hydrotherapeutic thermal(e)

I

I je/j'
ice cream une glace; *chocolate ice cream* une glace au chocolat; *vanilla ice cream* une glace à la vanille
ice-skating (figure skating) le patinage (artistique)
icon une icône
idea une idée
idealism l'idéalisme (m.) 2
identification (document) une pièce d'identité 4
if si; *if only* si; *if you'd like* si cela vous convient
illness une maladie
to illustrate illustrer 8
image une image; *image file* un fichier image
imagination l'imagination (f.) 10
to imagine imaginer
immense immense 7
important(e) important 4; *it's important that* il est important que 4; *what's important* l'important
impossible impossible
impression une impression 5
Impressionism l'impressionnisme (m.) 7
impressionist impressioniste
Impressionist un(e) impressionniste 7
to imprison emprisonner 2
to improvise improviser 2
in à; dans, en; *in a way* en un sens; *in addition to* en plus de; *in any case* en tout cas; de toute façon 4; *in circles* en rondelles; *in front of* devant; *in-line skating* le roller; *in my opinion* à mon avis; *in order* en ordre; *in order to* pour 7; *in the* au, aux; *in the background* à l'arrière-plan 7; *in the first year* en première année; *in the foreground* au premier plan; à l'avant-plan 7; *in the middle ground* au second plan 7; *in the past* autrefois; *in the spring* au printemps; *In what color(s)?* De quelle(s) couleur(s) ?; *in winter* en hiver
incapable incapable 9
to include comprendre 5
included compris
income le revenu 2
increase la hausse 2
incredible incroyable
India l'Inde (f.) 10
to indicate indiquer
indispensable indispensable 4; *it's indispensable that* il est indispensable que 4
individual un individu 10
Indonesia l'Indonésie (f.) 10
industry une industrie; un secteur; *aviation industry* le secteur aéronautique; *cultural and creative industries* les industries créatives; *digital industry* le secteur du numérique; *entertainment industry* l'industrie du divertissement; *financial industry* le secteur financier; *food industry* le secteur agroalimentaire; *information technology industry* le secteur de l'informatique; *sustainable development industry* le secteur de développement durable
inflatable mattress un matelas pneumatique
inflation rate le taux d'inflation 2
to influence influencer 8
to inform informer
information technology l'informatique (f.); *information technology industry* le secteur de l'informatique; *specific information* des précisions (f.) 5; *to get information* se renseigner 4
inhabitant un(e) habitant(e)
insect un insecte; *insect repellent* un anti-moustique
inside l'intérieur (m.)
to insist (on) insister (sur)
to install installer
instructor un moniteur, une monitrice 4
instrument: musical instrument un instrument
insurance l'assurance (f.) 8; *health insurance* l'assurance maladie 8; *French national health and pension insurance* la sécurité sociale (sécu) 8
to integrate (into) s'intégrer (à) 6
intelligent intelligent(e)

to **intense** intense 5
to **interest** intéresser
interested intéressé(e) 1; *to be interested (in)* s'intéresser (à)
interesting intéressant(e)
interface une interface
to **intern** faire un stage 8
intern un(e) stagiaire 8
international international(e); *international hostel* une auberge internationale
Internet Internet (m.); *wireless internet connection* une connexion wifi 5
to **intervene** intervenir
intervention: to organize an intervention faire une intervention
to **interview** interviewer 9
interview un entretien 8; une interview 10
intimate intimiste 7
to **introduce** introduire 8; *to introduce (to someone)* présenter (à quelqu'un), faire connaître (à quelqu'un), faire découvrir (à quelqu'un)
invaded envahi(e) 2
invention une invention 7
invitation une invitation 2
to **invite** inviter
iron ***[clothes]*** un fer à repasser
to **iron** repasser
is: isn't that so n'est-ce pas
island une île 4
it ça; cela 3; ce; elle, il; l', la, le *[object pronoun]*; *to it* y *[pronoun]*; *it doesn't surprise me* ça ne me surprend pas; *It has a totally vintage look!* Total vintage !; *it is* c'est; *it is necessary* il faut; *it/that means* ça veut dire; *it will be revealed (known)* ça va se savoir; *it would be* ça serait; *it would be known* ça se saurait; *it's a promise* c'est promis 6; *it's all the same to me* ça m'est égal; *It's beautiful out.* Il fait beau.; *it's been a long time since* ça fait longtemps que; *it's cold* il fait froid; *it's cool* il fait frais; *it's hot* il fait chaud; *it seems that* il paraît que 5; *it sounds promising* ça promet 5; *it's raining* il pleut; *It's settled.* C'est décidé.; *it's snowing* il neige; *it's sunny* il fait du soleil; *It's the (+ date).* Nous sommes le (+ date), C'est le (+ date).; *it's the same* c'est pareil; *it's too bad that…* c'est dommage que… 5; *it's windy* il fait du vent; *it's worth* ça vaut; *it would be* ça serait; *You sure know a lot about it.* Tu en sais des choses.
Italian italien(ne)
Italy l'Italie (f.)
items: housecleaning items des affaires (f.) de ménage
itinerary un itinéraire
its sa, ses, son
Ivory Coast la Côte d'Ivoire; *from, of the Ivory Coast* ivoirien(ne)

J

jacket un blouson; une veste; *ski jacket* une veste (de) ski 4
jam la confiture
janitor un homme de ménage 5
January janvier
Japan le Japon 10
Japanese japonais(e)
jar (of) un pot (de)
jasmine le jasmin
jazz music le jazz
jeans un jean
jersey un maillot
to **jet ski** faire du scooter des mers; faire du jet ski
jet ski un jet ski
jewelry des bijoux (m.); *fine jewelry* la joaillerie 10
job un boulot *[inform.]* 8; un emploi; un métier
Jordan la Jordanie 10
journey: to take a journey partir en voyage 8
juice un jus; *apple juice* un jus de pomme; *grapefruit juice* un jus de pamplemousse; *orange juice* un jus d'orange
July juillet
to **jump** sauter 1; *to bungee jump* faire du saut à l'élastique 4; *to jump rope* sauter à la corde 1
jump: ski jump un tremplin de saut à ski 4; *to go off ski jumps* faire des sauts à ski 4
June juin
junior assistant un(e) assistant(e) junior 8
just juste 3; *just any* n'importe quel, quelle 9; *to have just (done something)* venir de (+ infinitive)

K

kayaking: to go kayaking faire du kayak
to **keep** garder 3; *to keep an eye on* surveiller 9; *to keep in touch* garder le contact 3
ketchup le ketchup
key ***[ignition]*** une clé; *[on keyboard]* une touche
keyboard un clavier; un synthé(tiseur)
to **kill** tuer 2
kilogram (of) un kilo (de)
kilometer un kilomètre
kind une sorte
king un roi
kiosk: self-service kiosk une borne libre-service
to **kiss** embrasser
kit: first-aid kit une trousse de premiers secours
kitchen la cuisine
knee le genou
knife un couteau; *Swiss army knife* un couteau suisse
knocked: to get knocked into se faire bousculer 9
to **know** connaître; être au courant; savoir; *to know how* savoir; *to know each other/one another* se connaître; *You sure know a lot about it.* Tu en sais des choses.
knowledge les connaissances (f.) 8

known: it would be known ça se saurait

L

lab: computer lab une salle d'informatique; *research laboratory* un laboratoire de recherches 1; *science lab* un labo (laboratoire)
to **lack** manquer
lady une dame
laid out disposé(e)
lake un lac
lamb un agneau
lambis un lambi
lamp une lampe
to **land** atterrir
land la terre
landscape un paysage
language une langue
laptop (ordinateur) portable
large grand(e); gros(se)
last dernier, dernière; *At last!* Depuis le temps!
late en retard; tard
latest: the latest le dernier 6
to **laugh** rigoler; rire
to **launch** lancer 10
laundry: to do the laundry faire la lessive; *laundry service* le service blanchisserie 5
law le droit 6; *law firm* un cabinet d'avocats 1
lawn une pelouse; *lawn mower* une tondeuse
lawyer un(e) avocat(e)
lazy paresseux, paresseuse
lead une piste 1
leader un leader 10; *world leader* un leader mondial 10
to **learn** apprendre
least: at least au moins; *the least* le moins
leather le cuir; *leather goods* la maroquinerie 10; *made of leather* en cuir
to **leave** laisser; partir; quitter; *to leave each other/one another* se quitter 1
left: on the left à gauche; *on/to the left of* à gauche de; *to be left* rester
leg la jambe
legend une légende
lemon un citron; *lemon-lime soda with mint syrup* un diabolo menthe; *lemon tea* un thé au citron
to **lend** prêter
length la longueur 2; la durée 5; *shoulder-length [hair]* mi-long, mi-longue 9
less moins; *less (+ adverb) than* moins (+ adverb) que
to **let** laisser; *Let me finish!* Laisse-moi finir!
letter une lettre; *application letter* une lettre de candidature 8; *cover letter* une lettre de motivation 8
lettuce une salade
level un niveau
license: driver's license un permis (de conduire) 8
to **lie** mentir 7
life une vie; *relaxed style of life* une douceur de vivre
lifeless plat(e) 5
lift: ski lift un télésiège 4
light une lumière
to **like** aimer; apprécier 5; kiffer *[inform.]*; *if you'd like* si cela vous convient; *like this* comme ça
likeable attachant(e)
line une ligne 7
linen le lin; *linen handkerchief* un mouchoir en lin; *made of linen* en lin
link un lien
lip une lèvre
lipstick un rouge à lèvres
list une liste; *to make a list* faire une liste
to **listen (to)** écouter; *to listen to music* écouter de la musique; *to listen to my MP3 player* écouter mon lecteur MP3
liter (of) un litre (de)
little petit(e); *(a) little* (un) peu; *a little of* un peu de
live from en direct de
to **live** demeurer 7; habiter; vivre
liver: goose liver pâté le foie gras 2
living room un salon, un séjour
loaf: salmon mousse loaf une terrine de saumon
lobby la réception 5
lobster: spiny lobster une langouste
local local(e) 10
located situé(e); *to be located* être situé(e)
lock screen l'écran (m.) de verrouillage
logo: team logo un blason
lonely seul(e) 9
long long, longue; *how long* depuis combien de temps; *it's been a long time since* ça fait longtemps que
to **look** avoir l'air; *to look at oneself* se regarder; *to look for* chercher; *to look for/into* rechercher 7; *to look healthy* avoir bonne mine; *to look like (something from) my country* avoir un petit air du pays; *to look sick* avoir mauvaise mine; *Does this… look good on me?* Tu trouves que… me va bien ?; *Look* Remarque; *Look up!* Lève la tête!
look un look 2; un regard; la tête 9; *on a closer look* en y regardant de plus près 4; *traditional look* le look tradi 2
to **lose** perdre; *to lose weight* maigrir
lost perdu(e)
lot: a lot beaucoup; *a lot of* beaucoup de
lotion la crème 10
to **love** aimer
love l'amour (m.); *to be in love (with)* être amoureux/amoureuse (de) 6
lover (of) un amoureux, une amoureuse (de)

luck la chance 3; le hasard 10; *good luck* bon courage; *to try one's luck* tenter sa chance 3
lucky: to be lucky avoir de la chance
luggage: piece of luggage un bagage; *luggage compartment* un compartiment à bagages, un coffre à bagages; *to check one's luggage* faire enregistrer ses bagages
lunch le déjeuner
Luxembourg le Luxembourg; *from, of Luxembourg* luxembourgeois(e)
luxury le luxe 10
Lyon region le Lyonnais; *from, of Lyon* lyonnais(e)
lyricism le lyrisme 7
lyrics des paroles (f.)

M

Ma'am madame (Mme)
machine un appareil 6; *washing machine* une machine à laver
made: made (in) fabriqué(e) (au, aux, en) 10; *made of* en; *made of aluminum* en aluminium; *made of cotton* en coton; *made of diamonds* en diamant; *made of fabric* en tissu 2; *made of gold* en or; *made of leather* en cuir; *made of linen* en lin; *made of metal* en métal 2; *made of paper* en papier; *made of pearls* en perles; *made of plastic* en plastique; *made of silk* en soie; *made of silver* en argent; *made of velvet* en velours; *made of wool* en laine; *made up (of)* composé(e) (de) 5
magazine un magazine; *magazine article* un article
Maghreb: from, of the Maghreb maghrébin(e)
magical magique
magician un(e) magicien(ne) 3
mail un courrier; *(mail) delivery service* le service de livraison (postale) 6
mailbox une boîte aux lettres 6
mailman, mailwoman un facteur, une factrice 6
main principal(e); *main dish* le plat principal
to **major (in)** se spécialiser (en)
to **make** faire; préparer; *to make (someone do something)* faire (+ infinitive) 8; *They make you study all that?* On te fait étudier tout ça ? 8; *to make a call* téléphoner; *to make a decision* prendre une décision 10; *to make a speech* faire un discours 8; *to make especially (for someone)* réserver (pour quelqu'un) 10; *to make a list* faire une liste; *to make a promise* faire une promesse; *to make a reservation* réserver; *to make fun (of)* se moquer (de); *to make (something) work* faire marcher; *to make up one's mind* se décider 6
makeup le maquillage; *to put on makeup* se maquiller
Malaysia la Malaisie 10
male politician un homme politique
Mali le Mali
Malian malien(ne)
mall un centre commercial
management le management 6; *(economic business) management* la gestion (économique d'entreprise) 6; *management controller* un contrôleur, une contrôleuse de gestion 10
manager un(e) responsable 10
mandarin orange une mandarine 2
mandatory obligatoire
manga un manga 6
mangrove une mangrove
manner: in the manner of la façon 9
manufacturer: car manufacturer un constructeur, une constructrice automobile 10
many maint(e)s 5; *to have too many choices* avoir l'embarras du choix 10
map une carte; *city map* un plan
maple: maple tree un érable; *maple syrup* le sirop d'érable
marbles: to play marbles jouer aux billes 1
marinade une marinade 5
market *[financial]* le marché; *flea market* un marché aux puces; *outdoor market* un marché
marketing le marketing 10
married: to get married se marier
Martinique la Martinique; *from, of Martinique* martiniquais(e)
marvelous merveilleux, merveilleuse
mascara le mascara
mask un mas *[Mart.]*, un masque
Master's degree une maîtrise 10
masterpiece un chef-d'œuvre
material une matière 2
math les mathématiques (maths) (f.)
mattress: inflatable mattress un matelas pneumatique
May mai
may: May I...? Puis-je... ? 5; *May I help you?* Je peux vous aider ?
maybe peut-être
mayo la mayonnaise
mayor le maire, madame le maire
me m', moi; me; *to me* me
meal un repas
mean méchant(e)
to **mean** vouloir dire; *it/that means* ça veut dire
means un moyen; *means of transportation* un moyen de transport; *to have the means* avoir les moyens 8

to **measure** mesurer 2; *measuring cup* un verre mesureur 2; *measuring spoon* une cuillère à mesurer 2
meat la viande 5
mechanic un(e) mécanicien(ne)
mechanics la mécanique 3
medal une médaille 2
media center une médiathèque
media les médias (m.) 2
medical médical(e) 8
medicalized médicalisé(e) 8
medicine la médecine 6
Mediterranean méditerranéen(ne) 9
medium moyen(ne)
to **meet** connaître; faire la connaissance (de); se retrouver; se réunir; *to meet* se rencontrer; *we'll meet* on se retrouve
meeting un rendez-vous; *meeting center* une salle de réunion 5
melancholy la mélancolie 7
melody la mélodie 7
melon un melon
memory un souvenir
mention: not to mention sans parler de 10
menu une carte
merchant un(e) marchand(e)
to **mess up** rater 2
message un message
messaging une messagerie
metal un métal 2; *made of metal* en métal 2
method une méthode 7
Mexico le Mexique 10
microwave un micro-ondes
middle: in the middle ground au second plan 7
midnight minuit
milk le lait
to **milk** traire
million un million
mind: to make up one's mind se décider 6
mine le mien, la mienne 9
mineral water une eau minérale
minivan un monospace
mint la menthe; *lemon-lime soda with mint syrup* un diabolo menthe
minute une minute
mirror une glace; un miroir; *Hall of mirrors* la galerie des Glaces; *rearview mirror* un rétroviseur
Miss mademoiselle (Mlle)
mission une mission
mist le brouillard 7
to **mix** mélanger 2
mode: to go into photo mode se mettre en mode photo
model un mannequin
modern moderne
to **modernize** moderniser
moment un instant; un moment; *at the moment* en ce moment 6; *for the moment* pour l'instant
Monaco: from, of Monaco monégasque 5
Monday lundi
money l'argent (m.); *to transfer (money)* transférer (de l'argent) 6
mongoose une mangouste
monitor un écran
month un mois
monument un monument
mood une humeur 5; *I'm not in the mood for* je ne suis pas trop d'humeur pour 5
mop une serpillière 10
moral une morale 7
more davantage; encore; plus; plus de (+ noun); *more and more* de plus en plus 7; *more (+ adverb) than* plus (+ adverb) que
moreover d'ailleurs 8
morning la matinée; le matin
Moroccan marocain(e)
most la plupart de 9; *the most* le plus; *the most (+ adjective)* le/la/les plus (+ adjective)
mostly surtout
mother une mère; *stepmother* une belle-mère
motto une devise
mountain une montagne; *mountain pineapple [flower]* un ananas montagne; *mountain range* un massif
mouse une souris
mousse: chocolate mousse une mousse au chocolat
mouth la bouche
move (house) un déménagement
to **move** bouger; *to move (house)* déménager 1; *to move from… to* passer de… à 7; *to move over (something)* passer; *to move (toward)* s'avancer (vers)
movement un mouvement
movie un film; *action movie* un film d'action; *adventure movie* un film d'aventure; *detective movie* un film policier; *horror movie* un film d'horreur; *movie director* un metteur en scène; un réalisateur, une réalisatrice; *movie première* une première 6; *movie synopsis* le synopsis 5; *movie theatre* le cinéma (ciné); *movie theatre (room)* une salle de cinéma 5; *movie trailer* une bande-annonce 5; *science fiction movie* un film de science-fiction; *to direct (a movie)* réaliser 6; *to shoot a movie* tourner un film 5
to **mow** tondre
MP3 player un lecteur MP3
Mr. monsieur (M.)
Mrs. madame (Mme)
Ms. madame (Mme), mademoiselle (Mlle)
much: so much tellement; *very much* beaucoup; *How much is it?* Ça fait combien ?
multicultural ethnique 10
multinational multinational(e) 10
multiplex cinema le multiplexe 5

multiplication la multiplication 8; *multiplication table* une table de multiplication 8
muscular musclé(e) 9
museum un musée
mushroom un champignon; *with mushrooms* forestier, forestière; *black trumpet mushrooms* les trompettes (f.) de la mort 5
music la musique; *music-hall* un music-hall; *music show* une émission de musique; *alternative music* la musique alternative; *classical music* la musique classique; *funk music* le funk; *jazz music* le jazz; *pop music* la musique pop; *Rai music* le raï; *rap music* le rap; *reggae music* le reggae; *salsa music* la salsa 7; *swing music* le swing 7; *techno music* la techno; *world music* la musique du monde
musical un film musical; *musical instrument* un instrument
must: one/we/you must il faut
mustard la moutarde
my ma, mes, mon; *my god* mon Dieu 5
mystery un mystère 6

N

nail un clou 3
name un nom; *brand name* marqué(e) 10; *first name* un prénom; *my name is* je m'appelle; *your name is* tu t'appelles
nanotechnology les nanotechnologies (f.) 1
napkin une serviette
narrow étroit(e) 2
nation une nation 2
national national(e); *national holiday* une fête nationale; *national Quebec holiday* la Saint-Jean
native un(e) autochtone; *native person* un(e) indigène
nature la nature
nauseous: to feel nauseous avoir mal au cœur
near près de
nearly presque
necessary nécessaire
neck le cou
necklace un collier; *pearl necklace* un collier en perles
to **need** avoir besoin de; *I need* il me faut
neither ni 4; non plus; *neither… nor* ne (n')… ni… ni 4
neo-classic néoclassique 7
neoclassicism le néo-classicisme 7
Neo-impressionism le néo-impressionnisme 7
never ne (n')… jamais
nevertheless néanmoins 8
new de neuf, neuf, neuve; nouveau, nouvel; nouvelle; *New Brunswick* le Nouveau-Brunswick; *new release* une nouveauté 5; *New Year's Day* le Jour de l'an; *to celebrate Christmas/New Year's Eve* réveillonner 2; *What's new?* Quoi de neuf?
news les informations (infos) (f.); *news anchor* un présentateur, une présentatrice; *news report* un reportage; *news store that sells tobacco, stamps, lottery tickets* un bureau de tabac
newspaper un journal; *newspaper article* un article
newsstand un kiosque à journaux
next ensuite; prochain(e); *next day* le lendemain; *next to* à côté (de)
ney *[instrument]* un nay
NGO (non-governmental organization) une ONG (organisation non gouvernementale)
nice gentil(le); sympa
nicely said joliment dit
night la nuit; *nightclub* une boîte; une discothèque 1; *every night* tous les soirs; *to stay up all night* faire une nuit blanche
nine neuf
nineteen dix-neuf
ninety quatre-vingt-dix
ninth neuvième
no non; ne (n')… aucun(e) 4; *no longer* ne (n')… plus; *no one* ne (n')… personne; aucun(e) 4
nobody ne (n')… personne
none aucun(e) 4; ne (n')… aucun(e) 4; *none of us (+ verb)* aucun de nous (+ verb) 4
noon midi
Normandy region la Normandie; *from, of Normandy region* normand(e)
north le nord; *North America* l'Amérique (f.) du Nord
nose le nez
not ne (n')… pas, pas; *not anymore* ne (n')… plus; *not anyone* ne (n')… personne; *not at all* pas du tout; *not bad* pas mal; *not to mention* sans parler de 10; *not well* pas très bien; *not yet* ne (n')… pas encore
notebook un cahier
nothing rien 9; ne (n')… rien
to **notice** remarquer; s'apercevoir (de) 9
novel un roman
novelist un romancier, une romancière 7
November novembre
now maintenant
nuclear nucléaire
number un chiffre 8; un nombre, un numéro; *phone number* un numéro de téléphone
nurse un infirmier, une infirmière
o'clock l'heure (f.)

O

object un objet; *art object* un objet d'art
obligated (to) obligé(e) (de) 8; *to be obligated (to)* être obligé(e) (de) 8
to **observe** observer
to **obtain** obtenir 4
obvious évident 5; *to be obvious that* être évident que 5
obviously évidemment
occasion une fois
to **occupy** occuper
ocean un océan; *Atlantic Ocean* l'océan Atlantique; *Indian Ocean* l'océan Indien; *Pacific Ocean* l'océan Pacifique
Oceania l'Océanie (f.)
October octobre
of de/d'; en *[pronoun]*; sur; *of (the)* des; du; *of average height* de taille moyenne; *of course* bien sûr; bien entendu 5; *of course* pardi *[regional]*; *of it/them* en; *of which/whom* dont 6
to **offer** offrir; proposer 10
office un bureau; *dentist's office* un cabinet dentaire; *doctor's office* un cabinet du médecin; *principal's office* le bureau du proviseur; *tourist information office* un syndicat d'initiative; *tourist office* l'office (m.) de tourisme 4
official officiel(le)
off-road skiing le hors-piste 4
often souvent
oh ah, oh; *oh dear* oh là là; *oh no* oh là là
oil *[car]* l'huile (f.); *oil spill* une marée noire
OK d'accord
old vieux, vieil, vieille; ancien(ne) 3; *old age* la vieillesse; *the good old days* le bon vieux temps
omelet une omelette
on à, en; dessus; sur; *on a bicycle* à bicyclette; *on a closer look* en y regardant de plus près 4; *on board* à bord; *on foot* à pied; *on sale* en solde; *on second thought* en y réfléchissant bien 4; *on the* au, du; *on the contrary* au contraire 8; *on the corner* du coin; *on the horizon* à l'horizon; *on the left* à gauche; *on the other hand* par contre 8; *on the premises* sur place 4; *on the right* à droite; *on the way* en route; *on time* à l'heure; *on TV* à la télé; *on wheels* à roulettes; *come on* enfin
Once upon a time (there was).... Il était une fois.... 3
one on; un; une; *not one* ne (n')... aucun(e) 4; *one's* sa, ses, son; *that/this one* celui, celle 6; *the one* celui, celle 6; *the ones* ceux 6
oneself: to say to oneself se dire
onion un oignon
online en ligne
only juste; ne (n')... que 4; seulement 4
to **open** ouvrir
opening une ouverture 8
opinion un avis; *in my opinion* à mon avis
opportunity: to have the opportunity (to) avoir la chance (de) 2; avoir l'occasion (de) 4
or ou
orange orange
orange une orange; *mandarin orange* une mandarine 2; *orange juice* un jus d'orange
orangery une orangerie
orchid une orchidée; *tropical orchid* une orchidée suspendue
to **order** commander
order un ordre; *in order* en ordre; *in order to* pour 7
organic biologique
to **organize an intervention** faire une intervention
organized organisé(e) 4
original original(e) 5; *original version* la version originale (VO) 5
other autre; *on the other hand* par contre 8; *one... the other* l'un(e)... l'autre 9
otherwise autrement
ouch ouille
oud ***[instrument]*** un oud
our nos, notre
ours le nôtre, la nôtre 9
outdoors en plein air
outfit un ensemble
oven un four
over (it) dessus; *over there* là-bas
to **overcome** s'en sortir
overexcited surexcité(e) 9
overwhelmed accablé(e) 9
to **owe** devoir 7
to **own a restaurant** tenir un restaurant 3
owner: grocery store owner un épicier, une épicière
oyster une huître 2

P

to **pack** faire sa valise 4
package un paquet; un colis 6
packet (of) un paquet (de)
to **paint** peindre 3
paintbrush un pinceau 7
painted peint 7
painter un(e) peintre
painting une peinture; un tableau
pale pâle 7
pan: frying pan une poêle
pancake une crêpe américaine
panda un panda; *giant panda* un panda géant
panel un panneau
panicked affolé(e); *to be panicked* être affolé(e) 1
panicky paniqué(e) 9
pants un pantalon; *ski pants* un pantalon (de) ski 4

paper le papier; *made of paper* en papier; *paper tissue* un mouchoir en papier; *sheet of paper* une feuille de papier; *toilet paper* le papier toilette 10
paperback un livre de poche 6
parade un déboulé *[Mart.]*, un défilé
paragliding: to go paragliding faire du parapente 4
paralyzed tétanisé(e) 9
parasailing: to go parasailing faire du parachutisme ascensionnel
pardon me pardon
parents les parents (m.)
Paris: from, of Paris parisien(ne)
park un jardin; un parc; *amusement park* un parc d'attractions
parliamentary parlementaire
part une partie 7
party une fête, une teuf; *garden party* une fête champêtre 7; *(political) party* un parti (politique) 2
to **pass** passer; *to pass (a test)* réussir (à)
pass: boarding pass une carte d'embarquement; *ski pass* un forfait de ski 4
passenger un passager, une passagère
passerby un(e) passant(e) 3
passion une passion
passionate (about) passionné(e) (de)
passionately passionnément 2
passport un passeport 4
past le passé 4
pasta des pâtes (f.)
pastime un loisir
pastry: pastry shop une pâtisserie; *cream puff pastry* une religieuse; *layered custard pastry* un millefeuille
pâté le pâté; *goose liver pâté* le foie gras 2
path un chemin; un sentier; une trace *[Mart.]*; une voie
pause une pause 5
to **pay** payer; régler; *someone who pays* un payeur, une payeuse
peace la paix 2
peach une pêche
peak le sommet 4
pear une poire
pearl une perle; *pearl necklace* un collier en perles
peas des petits pois (m.)
pen pal un(e) correspondant(e) 10
pen un stylo
pencil un crayon; *pencil case* une trousse; *pencil sharpener* un taille-crayon
people des gens (m.); un peuple 8
pepper le poivre; *bell pepper* un poivron
perfect parfait(e) 5
perfectly parfaitement
performer un interprète 7
perfume un parfum
period une époque
permit une autorisation 6
person une personne; *crazy person* un fou, une folle; *homeless person* un sans-abri; *native person* un(e) indigène; *unreliable person* un lâcheur, une lâcheuse *[inform.]* 9
personal personnel(le) 2
personalized: to be personalized être perso *[inform.]* 8
personally personnellement 5
perspective une perspective
persuaded persuadé(e)
petroleum le pétrole
pheasant le faisan 5
Philippines les Philippines (f.) 10
to **phone (someone)** téléphoner (à quelqu'un)
phone: cell phone un téléphone portable
photo une photo; *another photo* re-photo; *to post a photo* publier une photo; *to go into photo mode* se mettre en mode photo
photogenic photogénique 9
physical: physical therapist le kiné (kinésithérapeute) 8; *physical therapy* la rééducation 8; *at/to the physical therapy office* chez le kiné 8
physics la physique
piano un piano
to **pick** cueillir 7
to **pick up** ranger
to **picnic** pique-niquer
picture une image; *to take a picture (of something)* prendre (quelque chose) en photo
pie une tarte; *apple pie* une tarte aux pommes
piece (of) un morceau (de); *piece of furniture* un meuble; *piece of jewelry* un bijou; *piece of luggage* un bagage
pig un cochon
pillow un coussin
pilot un pilote
pineapple un ananas; *mountain pineapple* un ananas montagne
pink rose
pipe(line) la canalisation
piranha un piranha
pirate un pirate
pirogue une pirogue; *by pirogue* en pirogue
pizza une pizza
place un endroit; un lieu 5; *in its place* à sa place 2; *to take place* avoir lieu
plaid à carreaux 9
plain une plaine
to **plan** projeter; planifier 4; *to plan (to do something)* compter (+ infinitive)
plan un programme
plane un avion; *by plane* en avion
planet une planète
planned prévu(e) 2
plant une plante
plastic la plastique; *made of plastic* en plastique
plate une assiette
platform un quai

platter un plateau
to **play** jouer; passer 2; *to play (+ instrument)* jouer de (+ instrument); *to play a role* jouer un rôle; *to play basketball* jouer au basket (basketball); *to play hide-and-seek* jouer à cache-cache 1; *to play hopscotch* jouer à la marelle 1; *to play ice hockey* jouer au hockey sur glace; *to play marbles* jouer aux billes 1; *to play on the radio* passer à la radio 2; *... is playing (at the movies)* on passe... 2; *to play soccer* jouer au foot (football); *to play sports* faire du sport; *to play with toy cars* jouer aux petites voitures 1; *to play video games* jouer aux jeux vidéo; *to play with dolls* jouer à la poupée 1; *to play a trick* jouer un tour 3; *to play a trick (on someone)* faire le coup (à quelqu'un) 4
play une pièce (de théâtre); *anthology of plays* une anthologie de pièces de théâtre 6
player un joueur, une joueuse
playwright un(e) dramaturge 7
pleasant agréable 5
to **please** plaire (à) 7
please s'il vous plaît
pleased: Pleased to meet you. Très heureux/heureuse. 3
pleasure un plaisir
pocket une poche
poem un poème
poet un poète, une femme poète 7
poetic poétique 7
poetry la poésie 6; *collection of poetry* un recueil de poésie 6
to **point out/to** indiquer
pole: fishing pole une canne à pêche; *ski pole* un bâton de ski 4
police officer un agent de police
police station le commissariat 9
to **polish hardwood flooring** cirer le parquet 3
political politique; *(political) party* un parti (politique) 2; *political science (poli sci)* les sciences (f.) politiques (sciences po) 6
politician: female politician une femme politique; *male politician* un homme politique
politics la politique 2
polka-dot à pois 9
to **pollute** polluer
polluted pollué(e)
polluter un pollueur, une pollueuse
polluting polluant
pollution la pollution
pond un bassin; un étang
pool un bassin
poor pauvre
pop music la musique pop
poppy un coquelicot 7
popular populaire 7
pork le porc
port un port; *micro USB port* un port micro-USB
portable stove un réchaud
portrait un portrait
position une position 8; *job position* un poste 1; *to take a position (on)* prendre position (sur) 7
positioning le positionnement 6
possibility une possibilité; *explore all the possibilities* faire le tour 10
possible possible; *it's possible that* il se pourrait que 4
to **post a photo** publier une photo
post office la poste
postage l'affranchissement (m.) 6
postal worker le postier, la postière 6
postcard une carte postale
poster une affiche
post-sale support le service après-vente 10
potato une pomme de terre
pound une livre
to **pour** verser 2
poverty la pauvreté
power un pouvoir
powerful puissant(e)
practical pratique 5
to **practice (sports)** s'entraîner 2
practice: to put into practice mettre en pratique 8
precisely précisément
to **prefer** préférer
première (of movie) une première 6
premises: on the premises sur place 4
to **prepare** préparer
preposition une préposition
present le présent 8
presentation un exposé
to **pretend (to)** faire semblant (de) 1
pretty joli(e)
princess une princesse 1
principal un proviseur
to **print** imprimer
printer une imprimante
priority la priorité 9
prisoner un prisonnier, une prisonnière 2
private privé(e) 8; *private class* le cours particulier 1
problem un problème
product un produit 10; *food product* un produit alimentaire 10; *dairy product* un produit laitier 10
production la production 10
profession une profession
professional un professionnel, une professionnelle 3
profile un profil
program le programme; *television program* une émission
progress le progrès
project un projet
to **promise** promettre; *it sounds promising* ça promet 5
promise: to make a promise faire une promesse; *it's a promise* c'est promis 6

property le domaine 4
prosciutto le jambon serrano 2
to **protect** protéger, sauvegarder
proud fier, fière 9
Provence la Provence; *from, of Provence* provençal(e)
province une province
psychology la psychologie 6
public (incorporated) company une SA (Société Anonyme) 10
punishment une sanction
purchase un achat
purple violet(te)
purse un sac à main
to **push** appuyer; enfoncer 3
to **put (on)** mettre; *to put back* remettre; *to put down* poser 2; *to put into practice* mettre en pratique 8; *to put on make-up* se maquiller; *to put up wallpaper* poser le papier peint 3
pyjamas un pyjama

Q

quality une qualité 8
quarter un arrondissement 10; un quart; *quarter past* et quart; *quarter to* moins le quart
Quebec le Québec; *from, of Quebec* québécois(e)
queen une reine
question une question
quiche une quiche
quickly rapidement 3; vite
quiet tranquille 2
quite plutôt 5; *quite simply* tout simplement
quote une citation 8

R

R'n'B concert un concert R'n'B
rabbit un lapin
raccoon un raton laveur
racism le racisme
radiation la radiation
radio une radio
Rai music le raï
to **rain** pleuvoir; *it's raining* il pleut
range: mountain range un massif
rap music le rap
ratatouille la ratatouille
rate le taux 2; *inflation rate* le taux d'inflation 2
rather assez 6; plutôt
raw vegetables des crudités (f.)
razor un rasoir
reaction une réaction 9
to **read** lire
reading la lecture
ready prêt(e); *to get (oneself) ready* se préparer
ready-to-wear le prêt-à-porter 2
real vrai(e) 5
realism le réalisme 7
realist réaliste 7; *realist song* une chanson réaliste 7
realistic réaliste
reality la réalité 6; *reality TV* la télé-réalité; *reality TV show* une émission de télé-réalité
to **realize** réaliser; se rendre compte (de) 9
really bien; super; vraiment
rearview mirror un rétroviseur
to **reassure (oneself)** se rassurer
to **recapture** récupérer 2
to **receive** recevoir
reception une réception 1; *reception area* le secrétariat 10; *reception center* un centre d'accueil; *reception desk* la réception
recipe une recette
recipient le destinataire
to **recognize** reconnaître
to **recommend** conseiller 3
rectangular rectangulaire 2
to **recycle** recycler
red rouge; *[hair]* roux, rousse
to **reduce** réduire 2
reflection un reflet 7
refrigerator un frigo
regardless quand même 2
regards: with warm regards affectueusement
reggae music le reggae
regime un régime 8
region une région
regional régional(e) 10
to **register** s'inscrire
regret un regret 1
to **reimburse** rembourser
relationships les rapports (m.) 2
to **relax** se détendre
relaxed décontracté(e); *relaxed style of life* une douceur de vivre
release une sortie 5; *new release* une nouveauté 5
to **remain** rester
remarkable remarquable
remedy un remède
to **remember** se rappeler, se souvenir (de)
to **rent** louer
to **repaint** repeindre 3
to **repair** réparer
repellent: insect repellent un anti-moustique
to **replace** remplacer
report: news report un reportage; *report of a theft* une déclaration de vol 9
representative un(e) représentant(e)
republic une république 8
to **require** exiger 5
RER: by RER en RER
research: genealogical research des recherches (f.) généalogiques 3; *research laboratory* un laboratoire de recherches 1
researcher un chercheur, une chercheuse
to **resemble** ressembler (à)
reservation une réservation; *to make a reservation* réserver
resident un(e) habitant(e)
resolution une résolution
resort: ski resort une station de ski 4
resource: human resources les ressources (f.) humaines 10; *HR Director* le directeur, la directrice des ressources humaines (DRH) 8
respiratory respiratoire
to **respond** répondre 8

responsibility une responsabilité 10
responsible responsable
to **rest** se reposer
rest: (the) rest le reste 10; la suite 3
restaurant un restaurant; *to own a restaurant* tenir un restaurant 3
restroom les W.C. (m.)
to **return** rendre; rentrer, retourner, revenir
return un retour
Reunion La Réunion 4
revealed: it will be revealed (known) ça va se savoir
review une critique 5
revolution une révolution
riad une riad
rich riche
ride une balade; *to go on a carnival ride* faire un tour de manège; *to go on a Ferris wheel ride* faire un tour de grande roue; *to go on a ride* faire un tour; *to go on a trail ride* faire une randonnée équestre 4
right un droit 2; *human rights*; les droits (m.) de l'homme 2; *right away* tout de suite; *That's right.* C'est ça.; *to be right* avoir raison; *to the right* à droite; *to/on the right of* à droite de; *yeah right* tu parles
ring une bague; *engagement ring* une bague de fiançailles 1; diamond ring une bague en diamant; *wedding ring* une alliance 1
ripe mûr(e)
rise: to give rise to donner lieu à 7
river un fleuve; une rivière; *river bank* une rive
riviera: French Riviera la Côte d'Azur
road une route; *cliff road* une corniche; *off-road skiing* le hors-piste 4
rock (music) le rock
to **rock climb** faire de l'escalade 4;
rococo rococo 7; *rococo style* le rococo 7
role un rôle
roll un rouleau 10
rolled in flour and sautéed meunière
roller coaster: to go on a roller coaster ride faire un tour de montagnes russes
Roman un(e) Romain(e) 5
Romantic romantique 7
Romanticism le romantisme 7
roof un toit
room une pièce; une salle; *bathroom* une salle de bains; *classroom* une salle de classe; *dining room* une salle à manger; *hotel room* une chambre; *living room* un salon; *room service* le service de chambre 5
rooster un coq
round rond 2
route une route
rug un tapis
to **run** courir 1; filer *[inform.]* 1
running le footing
RV un camping-car
Rwanda le Rwanda

S

sad attristé(e) 9; triste
safe un coffre-fort 5
sailboat un voilier
sailing: to go sailing faire de la voile
saint: All Saints Day la Toussaint
salad une salade; *tuna salad* une salade niçoise
salami le saucisson
salary un salaire 8
sale une promo; *on sale* en solde; *post-sale support* le service après-vente 10
sales les ventes (f.) 10
salesperson un vendeur, une vendeuse
salmon le saumon; *salmon mousse loaf* une terrine de saumon; *smoked salmon* saumon fumé 2
salon: hair salon un salon de coiffure
salsa music la salsa 7
salt le sel
salty salé(e)
same même; *at the same time* à la fois; *it's all the same to me* ça m'est égal; *it's the same* c'est pareil; *the same* pareil(le)
sand le sable 1
sandals des sandales (f.)
sandwich un sandwich; *cheese sandwich* un sandwich au fromage; *ham sandwich* un sandwich au jambon; *grilled ham and cheese sandwich* un croque-monsieur
sanitary sanitaire
satire une satire 7
Saturday Samedi
sauce une sauce 2; *(tomato) sauce* un coulis (de tomates) 5; *Béarnaise sauce* la sauce béarnaise 5; *béchamel sauce* la sauce béchamel 5; *hollandaise sauce* la sauce hollandaise 5; *white sauce* la sauce blanche 5; *white wine sauce* la sauce marinière 5
saucepan une casserole
sauerkraut la choucroute; *sauerkraut with potatoes, sausages, smoked pork* la choucroute garnie
sausage une saucisse
sautéed: rolled in flour and sautéed meunière
to **save** *[computer file]* sauvegarder; *to save (money)* économiser (de l'argent) 6; *to save (up)* économiser; *to save time* gagner du temps
savory salé(e)
saxophone un saxophone
to **say** dire; *to say to oneself* se dire; *nicely said* joliment dit
scallop une coquille Saint-Jacques
Scandinavian scandinave 9
scarf une écharpe; un foulard
scene une scène
scent un parfum

schedule l'horaire (m.) 5
school une école
science les sciences (f.); *political science (poli sci)* les sciences politiques (sciences po) 6; *science and technology sector* le domaine des sciences et techniques; *science fiction* la science-fiction; *science lab* un labo (laboratoire); *sport sciences* les sciences du sport 6
scooter un scooter; *by scooter* en scooter
to **score** marquer
scouting association l'association (f.) de scoutisme (m.) 1
scrambled eggs des œufs (m.) brouillés
to **scrape** racler 2
to **scream** pousser un cri
screen un écran
screw une vis 3
screwdriver un tournevis 3
to **scrub** racler 2
scuba diving: to go scuba diving faire de la plongée sous-marine
sculpture une sculpture
sea une mer; *sea turtle* une tortue marine; *Caribbean Sea* la mer des Caraïbes; *Mediterranean Sea* la mer Méditerranée; *North Sea* la mer du Nord
seafood les fruits (m.) de mer
seashell coquillage 1
seaside le bord de mer; *by the seaside* au bord de la mer
season une saison
seat un siège
seatbelt une ceinture de sécurité
second deuxième; *on second thought* en y réfléchissant bien 4; *second home* une résidence secondaire 3
secondly deuxièmement 8
secret un secret
secretary un secrétaire (administratif), une secrétaire (administrative) 10
sector un domaine; *health sector* le domaine de la santé; *science and technology sector* le domaine des sciences et techniques
security checkpoint un contrôle de sécurité
to **seduce** séduire 7
to **see** voir; *to see again* revoir; *to see each other/one another* se voir; *See you soon.* À bientôt.; *See you tomorrow.* À demain.; *I see.* Je vois.; *to see oneself as* se reconnaître 7
to **seek (medical) treatment** se faire soigner 8
to **seem** sembler; *it seems that* il paraît que 5
selfish égoïste
self-portrait un autoportrait
self-service kiosk une borne libre-service
to **sell** vendre
to **send** envoyer; *to send text messages* envoyer des textos; *to send a video call* faire un appel vidéo
Senegal le Sénégal
Senegalese sénégalais(e)
sensation une sensation
sense un sens
September septembre
series une série; *whole series (of)* toute une série (de)
serious grave; sérieux, sérieuse
seriousness le sérieux
to **serve** servir
served servi(e) 5
server un serveur, une serveuse
service un service 5; *(mail) delivery service* le service de livraison (postale) 6; *laundry service* le service blanchisserie 5; *room service* le service de chambre 5
sessions des séances (f.) 8
set down posé(e) 2
to **set** mettre; *to set the table* mettre le couvert; *to set oneself down* se mettre
setting un cadre
settings les réglages (m.)
settled: It's settled. C'est decidé; *to get settled* s'installer
seven sept
seventeen dix-sept
seventh septième
seventy soixante-dix
several plusieurs
shampoo un shampooing
shape la forme 2; *(pear)-shaped* en forme de (poire) 2
to **share** partager 5
to **shave** se raser
she elle
sheep un mouton
sheets les draps; *sheet of paper* une feuille de papier
shelter un centre d'accueil
shh chut
shirt une chemise; une liquette *[inform.]* 9
shivers des frissons (m.)
shocked choqué(e) 9
shoe une chaussure
to **shoot a movie** tourner un film 5
shoot mince
shop une boutique; *butcher shop* une boucherie
shopkeeper un(e) petit(e) commerçant(e)
shopping commerçant(e); le shopping; *shopping center* un centre commercial
short petit(e); *in short* bref 9; *[hair]* court(e) 9; *short story* une nouvelle 6
shorts un short
shoulder l'épaule (f.); *shoulder-length [hair]* mi-long, mi-longue 9
to **show** montrer; *to show up* se rendre (à)
show un show 9; un spectacle; *(TV) game show* un jeu télévisé; *music show* une émission de musique; *reality TV show* une émission de télé-réalité; *TV show* une émission
shower une douche
shrimp une crevette
shy timide

sick malade; *sick person* un(e) malade
side le bord; un côté
sighing le soupir 7
silk la soie; *made of silk* en soie
silver l'argent (m.); *made of silver* en argent
SIM card une carte SIM
simple simple
simply simplement
since comme; depuis; puisque 2; *since when* depuis quand
to sing chanter
singer un chanteur, une chanteuse
sink un évier
sir chef; monsieur (M.)
sister une sœur; *half/step sister* une demi-sœur; *sister-in-law* une belle-sœur
to sit down s'asseoir
sitcom une sitcom
site un site; *to be on site, on the premises* être sur place
sitting assis(e)
situation une situation
six six
sixteen seize
sixth sixième
sixty soixante
size une taille
to skate: to (figure) skate faire du patinage (artistique); *to in-line skate* faire du roller
skateboard park le skatepark 1
skating: (figure) skating le patinage artistique
skewer une brochette
ski un ski 4; *off-road skiing* le hors-piste 4; *ski boots* des chaussures (f.) de ski 4; *ski class* une classe de neige 4; *ski goggles* un casque de ski 4; *ski jacket* une veste (de) ski 4; *ski jump* un tremplin de saut à ski 4; *ski lift* un télésiège 4; *ski pants* un pantalon (de) ski 4; *ski pass* un forfait de ski 4; *ski pole* un bâton de ski 4; *ski resort* une station de ski 4; *(ski) slope* une piste (de ski) 4; *to cross-country ski* faire du ski de fond 4; *to go off ski jumps* faire des sauts à ski 4; *to ski downhill* faire du ski de piste 4; *to take a ski-taxi ride* faire du taxi-ski 4; *to telemark ski* faire du télémark 4
to ski: to (downhill) ski faire du ski (alpin); faire du ski de piste 4
skiing (downhill) le ski (alpin)
to skijor faire du ski joëring 4
skill une compétence 5; *game of skill* un jeu d'adresse
skin la peau 10
skinny maigre 9
to skip *[class]* sécher *[inform.]* 9
skirt une jupe
sledding: to go sledding faire de la luge 4
to sleep dormir
slice (of) une tranche (de)
slope: (ski) slope une piste (de ski) 4
small petit(e); *small business* une PME (petite et moyenne entreprise) 1
smartboard un tableau
smartphone un smartphone
to smell sentir; *What does it smell like?* Ça sent quoi ?
smile sourire 1
to smile sourire 1
smoked fumé(e) 2; *smoked salmon* le saumon fumé 2
smuggler un contrebandier, une contrebandière
snack le goûter
snail un escargot
snake un serpent
sneakers des tennis (f.)
snow: it's snowing il neige
to snowboard faire du snowboard 4
snowboarding le snowboard 4
to snowmobile faire de la motoneige 4
snowshoeing: to go snowshoeing faire de la raquette à neige 4
so alors; bon; donc; si 2; *so much* tellement; *so-so* comme ci, comme ça; *so that* pour que 7
soap opera: TV soap opera un feuilleton
soap un savon
soccer le foot; *soccer ball* un ballon de foot; *soccer player* un footballeur, une footballeuse
society la collectivité 8; la société
sock une chaussette
soda: lemon-lime soda une limonade *lemon-lime soda with mint syrup* diabolo menthe
sofa un canapé
software un logiciel; *software developer* un développeur, une développeuse
solar solaire; *solar energy* l'énergie (f.) solaire; *solar panel* un panneau solaire
solidarity la solidarité
solution un remède; une solution
some d', de, des, du; en; quelques 5
somebody quelqu'un
someday un jour
someone quelqu'un
something quelque chose
sometimes parfois
son un fils
song une chanson; *realist song* une chanson réaliste 7
songwriter un compositeur
sonnet un sonnet 7
soon bientôt; *as soon as* dès que
sorry désolé(e); *to be sorry* regretter 5
sort une sorte
soup la soupe; un potage
South Korea la Corée du Sud 10
south le sud; *South America* l'Amérique (f.) du Sud
Soviet soviétique 5
spa treatment une cure
Spain l'Espagne (f.)

Spanish espagnol(e); *[language]* l'espagnol (m.)
spatula une spatule 2
to **speak** parler
specialty une spécialité
species: endangered species les animaux (m.) en voie de disparition
specific information des précisions (f.) 5
speech un discours 8; *to make a speech* faire un discours 8
to **speed ride** faire du speed riding 4
spell un envoûtement
to **spend** ***[time]*** passer
spherical sphérique 2
spicy épicé(e)
spiny lobster une langouste
sponge une éponge 10
spoon une cuillère; *measuring spoon* une cuillère à mesurer 2
sport un sport; *sports car* une voiture de sport; *sports center* le complexe sportif 1; *sports coverage* un reportage sportif; *sport sciences* les sciences (f.) du sport 6
spot une tache
to **sprain an ankle** se fouler la cheville 4
spread made of hazelnut and chocolate le Nutella
spring le printemps; une source d'eau; *in the spring* au printemps
square un carré; une place; *in squares* en carrés
Sri Lanka le Sri Lanka 10
stadium un stade
stage une scène 7; *on stage* sur scène 7
to **stamp** affranchir 6
stamp un timbre 1
stand un kiosque; *crêpe stand* un stand de crêpes
standardization l'uniformisation (f.) 10
standing debout
stanza une strophe 7
star une étoile 5; *[celebrity]* une vedette 5

to **start** démarrer; *to start something again* se remettre (à)
starters: for starters pour commencer
station une station; *gas station* une station-service; *police station* le commissariat 9
statue une statue
to **stay** faire un séjour 4; rester; *to stay up all night* faire une nuit blanche
stay un séjour
steak with fries un steak-frites
to **steal** voler 9
steering wheel un volant
step: step aerobics le step; *stepbrother* un demi-frère; *stepfather* un beau-père; *stepmother* une belle-mère; *stepsister* une demi-sœur
stereo une stéréo
stereotypical stéréotypé(e) 5
still encore; toujours; *still life* une nature morte
to **stir** remuer 2
stockholder un(e) actionnaire 10
stocky costaud(e) 9
stomach l'estomac (m.), le ventre
to **stop** arrêter; s'arrêter; *I can('t) stop myself from….* Je (ne) peux (pas) m'empêcher de…. 2; *Stop it!* N'en jette plus ! *[inform.]* 8
store un magasin; *dairy store* une crémerie; *grocery store* une épicerie
story une histoire 3; un étage; *short story* une nouvelle 6
stove une cuisinière; *portable stove* un réchaud; *camp stove* un camping-gaz
straight ***[hair]*** raide 9
straight ahead tout droit
strainer: conical strainer un chinois 2
strategy une stratégie 10
strawberry une fraise
street une rue; *street demonstration* une manif (manifestation)

strength une force
strict strict(e)
strike: to go on strike faire grève 2
striped à rayures 9
strong fort(e)
stuck collé(e)
student un(e) élève; un(e) étudiant(e)
studies des études (f.)
studio un atelier 7; *studio apartment* un studio 3
to **study** étudier
stuffed farci(e)
to **stumble** trébucher 9
style un style 5
stylist: hair stylist un coiffeur, une coiffeuse
subject un sujet
subsidiary une filiale 10
subsidized housing une HLM (des HLM) 3
subtitled sous-titré(e) 5
subtitles les sous-titres (m.) 5
suburb une banlieue
subway le métro; *subway entrance* une bouche de métro; *by subway* en métro
to **succeed** réussir (à)
success le succès 7
such a un tel, une telle 9
sudden: all of a sudden tout d'un coup 9
to **suffer** souffrir 2
sugar le sucre; *with sugar* au sucre
to **suggest** proposer
to **suit** convenir (à)
suitcase une valise; *suitcase with wheels* une valise à roulettes
summer l'été (m.)
summoned: to be summoned être convoqué(e) 8
Sunday dimanche
sunglasses des lunettes (f.) de soleil
sunny: eggs sunny side up des œufs (m.) sur le plat; *it's sunny* il fait du soleil
sunscreen la crème solaire

superhero, superheroine un super-héros, une superhéroïne 1
supermarket un supermarché
supplementary complémentaire 8
supplies des provisions (f.)
to **support** soutenir; *I support* je soutiens; *post-sale support* le service après-vente 10
sure sûr(e); *that's for sure* c'est sûr
to **surf the Web** surfer sur Internet
to **surprise** étonner
surprise une surprise
surprised étonné(e) 5; *to be surprised that* être étonné(e) que 5
surprising surprenant 4; *it's surprising that* il est surprenant que 4
surrealism le surréalisme 7
survey une enquête
to **survive** survivre
sustainable: sustainable development le développement durable; *sustainable development industry* le secteur de développement durable
SUV un SUV
sweater un pull
sweet sucré(e)
to **swim** nager
swimming pool une piscine
swing music le swing 7
Swiss suisse; *Swiss army knife* un couteau suisse
switch (ringer, silence) le commutateur (sonnerie/silence)
Switzerland la Suisse
to **synchronize** synchroniser
synopsis: movie synopsis le synopsis 5
syrup le sirop; *maple syrup* le sirop d'érable
system un système 8

T

table une table; *at the (dinner) table* à table 2; *multiplication table* une table de multiplication 8; *table setting* le couvert; *to clear the table* débarrasser la table
tablecloth une nappe
Tahitian tahitien(ne)
tailor un tailleur
to **take** prendre; *[class]* suivre; *to take advantage (of)* profiter (de); *to take a journey* partir en voyage 8; *to take a picture (of something)* prendre (quelque chose) en photo; *to take a position (on)* prendre position (sur) 7; *to take a ski-taxi ride* faire du taxi-ski 4; *to take a trip* faire une excursion; *to take a vacation* prendre des vacances; *to take care (of)* s'occuper (de); *to take care of things* se débrouiller 8; *to take off [airplane]* décoller; *to take out* sortir; retirer; *to take place* avoir lieu
tale un conte
talent le talent 9
talented doué(e) 10
to **talk** parler; *to talk to each other/one another* se parler
talkative bavard(e)
tall grand(e)
to **tan** bronzer
to **target** cibler 10
tart: fruit tart une tarte aux fruits
to **taste** goûter
taste le goût 5; *for my taste* à mon goût 5
taxi un taxi; *by taxi* en taxi
tea un thé; *lemon tea* un thé au citron
to **teach** apprendre; enseigner
teacher un(e) prof; *elementary school teacher* un instituteur, une institutrice
team une équipe; *team logo* un blason
technician: solar plant technician un(e) technicien(ne) de centrale solaire
techno music la techno
technology la technique; *science and technology sector* le domaine des sciences et techniques
teenager un(e) ado
teeth: to brush one's teeth se brosser les dents
telecommunications les télécommunications
to **telemark ski** faire du télémark 4
televised télévisé(e)
television une télé (télévision); *television program* une émission
to **tell** dire; raconter
teller: bank teller le caissier, la caissière 6
temperature la température
to **tempt** tenter
ten dix
tenant un(e) locataire 3
tenderness la tendresse 6
tent une tente
tenth dixième
terrace une terrasse
terrific génial(e)
territory un territoire 2
terrorism le terrorisme
test un contrôle
text message un SMS; un texto
text un texte 7
than que
thank you merci; *thank you (for) [form.]* je vous remercie (de)
Thanksgiving l'Action de grâce (f.); Thanksgiving (US)
that ça; ce, cet, cette, ces; cela; que; qui; *that/this one* celui, celle 6; *that's how....* c'est comme ça que.... 1; *that is* c'est; *that's for sure* c'est sûr; *That's right.* C'est ça.; *Is that all?* Rien que ça ?; *you shouldn't do that* ça ne se fait pas

the le, la, l', les; *the most (+ adjective)* le/la/les plus (+ adjective); *one… the other* l'un(e)… l'autre 9
theatre un théâtre
theft: report of a theft une déclaration de vol 9
their leur, leurs
theirs le leur, la leur 9
them elles; eux; les; *to them* leur
theme un thème 7
then alors, puis
therapist: physical therapist le kiné (kinésithérapeute) 8
therapy: at/to the physical therapy office chez le kiné 8; *physical therapy* la rééducation 8
there là; y *[pronoun]*; *Are we going (there)?* On y va ?; *over there* là-bas
therefore donc
these ce, cet, cette, ces; ceux 6
they: they (f.) elles; *they (m.)* ils; on
thief un voleur 9
thin mince 9
thing une chose; un machin 2; un truc; *things* des affaires (f.); *to take care of things* se débrouiller 8
to **think** croire; penser; *to think over* réfléchir (à)
third troisième
thirsty: to be thirsty avoir soif
thirteen treize
thirty trente; *about thirty* une trentaine 9; *in one's thirties* d'une trentaine d'années 9
this ce, cet, cette, ces; cela; *this is* c'est; *that/this is why* c'est pour ça que; *this/that (very) word* ce mot-là; *like this* comme ça
those ce, cet, cette, ces; ceux 6
thought une réflexion; *on second thought* en y réfléchissant bien 4
thousand mille
three trois
thriller un thriller
throat la gorge
through par
thrush une grive
Thursday jeudi
thus comme ça
to **thwart** déjouer 3
ticket un billet; un ticket; *ticket booth* un guichet; *ticket collector* un contrôleur, une contrôleuse; *ticket-stamping machine* un composteur
tide une marée
tiger un tigre; *Sumatran tiger* un tigre de Sumatra
time l'heure (f.); le temps; une fois; *all the time* tout le temps; *at the same time* à la fois; *full-time* à plein temps 8; *half-time* à mi-temps 8; *it's been a long time since* ça fait longtemps que; *Once upon a time (there was)….* Il était une fois…. 3; *on time* à l'heure; *to save time* gagner du temps; *What time is it?* Quelle heure est-il ?
tire un pneu
tired fatigué(e)
tissue un mouchoir; *paper tissue* un mouchoir en papier
title un titre 6
to à; *to my house* chez moi; *to the* au; aux; *to him* lui; *to her* lui; *to me* moi; *to you* te; vous; *to which* auquel, auquelle 5; *eye to eye* le blanc des yeux 9
toast le pain grillé; *French toast* le pain perdu
tobacco: news store that sells tobacco, stamps, lottery tickets un bureau de tabac
to **back up *[computer file]*** sauvegarder
to **browse** naviguer
to **buy** acheter
today aujourd'hui
toe le doigt de pied
together ensemble; *to get together* se réunir
Togo le Togo
Togolese togolais(e)
toilet paper le papier toilette 10
toiletries des affaires (f.) de toilette
tolerance la tolérance
tomato une tomate
tomorrow demain; *See you tomorrow.* À demain.
tone le ton 5
too aussi; trop; *too bad* tant pis; *too much (of)* trop de
tooth une dent
toothbrush une brosse à dents
toothpaste le dentifrice
top le haut; *at the top* en haut
topic un thème
to **torment** tourmenter 9
to **touch** toucher
tour un tour; une tournée 7; *guided tour* une visite guidée; *on tour* en tournée 7
Touraine region la Touraine; *from, of Touraine region* tourangeau, tourangelle
tourism: adventure tourism le tourisme d'aventure
tourist un(e) touriste; *tourist guide* un guide touristique; *tourist information office* un syndicat d'initiative; *tourist office* l'office (m.) de tourisme 4; *to be a tourist* faire le touriste
touristy touristique 3
towards vers
towel une serviette; *beach towel* une serviette de plage
tower une tour
track and field l'athlétisme (m.) 2
traditional traditionnel(le); *traditional look* le look tradi 2
trailer *[movie]* une bande-annonce 5
train un train; *train station* une gare; *train platform* une voie; *by train* en train; *express train from Paris to suburbs* le RER
training une formation 8
to **transfer (money)** transférer (de l'argent) 6
transferred: to get transferred se faire muter 1
transportation un transport; *means of transportation* un moyen de transport

to **travel** voyager
travel preparations les préparatifs (m.) de départ 4
traveler un voyageur, une voyageuse
tray un plateau
treasure un trésor
treatment des soins (m.) 8; un traitement 8; *to seek (medical) treatment* se faire soigner 8
tree: maple tree un érable; *Christmas tree* un sapin de Noël 2
trial: audio trial en écoute libre
triangular triangulaire 2
trick: to play a trick jouer un tour 3; *to play a trick (on someone)* faire le coup (à quelqu'un) 4
trip une excursion; un voyage; *Have a good trip!* Bonne route !; *to go on a trip* faire un voyage; *to go on a trip* faire un tour; *to take a trip* faire une excursion
trombone un trombone
trouble les ennuis (m.) 9; *to get in trouble (with)* se faire disputer (par) 3
truck un camion
true vrai(e)
truffle une truffe 2
trumpet une trompette; *black trumpet mushrooms* les trompettes de la mort 5
to **trust** avoir confiance (dans/en)
to **try (on)** essayer; *to try one's luck* tenter sa chance 3
T-shirt un tee-shirt
Tuesday mardi
tuna le thon; *tuna salad* une salade niçoise
Tunisia la Tunisie
Tunisian tunisien(ne)
turkey un dindon; *turkey with chestnuts* la dinde aux marrons 2
to **turn** tourner; *to turn in* rendre
turtle une tortue; *sea turtle* une tortue marine
tuxedo un smoking
TV une télé (télévision); *TV host* un animateur, une animatrice; *TV guide* un guide télévisé; *TV remote control* une télécommande; *TV show* une émission; *TV soap opera* un feuilleton; *cable TV* une télé câblée; *on TV* à la télé; *reality TV* la télé-réalité; *reality TV show* une émission de télé-réalité
twelve douze
twenty vingt; *about twenty* une vingtaine 9; *in one's twenties* d'une vingtaine d'années 9
twin jumeau, jumelle; *twin bed* un lit jumeau
two deux
to **type** taper
type un genre; *not the type to* pas la tête à 9
typical of typiquement 10

U

ugly laid(e); moche
um euh
umbrella: (beach) umbrella un parasol
uncle un oncle
under sous
to **understand** comprendre
undressed: to get undressed se déshabiller
unemployment le chômage
unicorn une licorne
unintelligent bête
United States les États-Unis (m.)
universal universel(le) 2
universe l'univers (m.)
university une université; *university cafeteria* un resto-U (restaurant universitaire); *university dormitory* une cité universitaire
unobstructed imprenable 5
unpleasant désagréable
unreliable person un lâcheur, une lâcheuse *[inform.]* 9
until jusqu'à
up: Look up! Lève la tête !; *to get up* se lever; *to wake up* se réveiller
upon en 4; *Once upon a time (there was)....* Il était une fois.... 3
us nous; *to us* nous
USB: USB key une clé USB; *micro USB port* un port micro-USB
to **use** utiliser, se servir (de); *It's used for....* Ça sert à.... 2
useful utile 4; *it's useful that* il est utile que 4
useless: what is useless l'inutile (m.)
usually d'habitude
to **usurp** usurper 2
utensil un ustensile 2

V

vacation les vacances (f.); *back to school/work (after vacation)* la rentrée; *to take a vacation* prendre des vacances
vacationer un vacancier, une vacancière
vaccinated: to get vaccinated se faire vacciner 4
vacuum cleaner un aspirateur
to **vacuum** passer l'aspirateur
vague imprécis(e) 5
vain: to do (something) in vain avoir beau (+ infinitive) 8
Valentine's Day la Saint-Valentin
to **validate *[ticket]*** composter
valley une vallée
variation une variation 7
vase un vase 10
veal le veau 5
vegetable un légume; *raw vegetables* des crudités (f.)
velvet le velours; *made of velvet* en velours
venison le chevreuil 2; *venison chop* une côte de chevreuil 2
version une version; *original version* la version originale (VO) 5
versus contre
very super; très; *Very well, and you?* Très bien, et toi/vous ?
veterinarian un(e) vétérinaire

via par
video: video clip un clip; *to make a video call* faire un appel vidéo; *video games* les jeux (m.) vidéo; *video game tester* un testeur de jeux vidéo
Vietnam le Vietnam 4
view une vue; *What a beautiful view!* Quelle belle vue !
viewpoint un point de vue
villa une villa 3
village un village
vinaigrette salad dressing la vinaigrette
vintage vintage 9
violence la violence
violin un violon
visa un visa 4
visible visible 9
to **visit** visiter; *to visit (someone)* rendre visite (à quelqu'un)
visual arts les arts (m.) plastiques
vivid vif, vive
volcano un volcan 4
voluminous volumineux, volumineuse 7
to **volunteer** faire du bénévolat
volunteer work le bénévolat 4
to **vote** voter 2

W

to **wait (for)** attendre
to **wake up** se réveiller
to **walk** marcher
walk une balade; une promenade; *to go for a walk* se promener
wall un mur 3
wallet un portefeuille
wallpaper le papier peint 3; *to put up wallpaper* poser le papier peint 3
want ad une petite annonce 8
to **want** avoir envie de; désirer; vouloir
war une guerre; *at war* en guerre 2
wardrobe une armoire
wary: to be wary (of) se méfier (de) 3
to **wash: to wash (oneself)** se laver; *to wash the dishes* faire la vaisselle
washcloth un gant de toilette
washed out délavé(e) 9
washing machine une machine à laver
to **watch** regarder; *Watch out!* Attention !
watch une montre
to **water** arroser
water l'eau (f.); *water hydrant* une borne-fontaine; *body of water* une masse d'eau
water park un aquaparc 1
waterfall une cascade; une chute d'eau
water-skiing: to go water-skiing faire du ski nautique
wavy ***[hair]*** bouclé(e) 9
way un chemin; un sens; une manière 3; *by the way* au fait; *in a way* en un sens; *on the way* en route
we on; nous; *We'll call each other.* On s'appelle.
wealthy riche
to **wear** porter
weather la météo; le temps; *weather forecast* la météo; un bulletin météo(rologique); *the weather's bad* il fait mauvais
web designer un concepteur web, une conceptrice web
website un site web
wedding un mariage; *wedding anniversary* un anniversaire de mariage; *wedding dress* une robe de mariée; *wedding ring* une alliance 1
Wednesday mercredi
week une semaine
weekend le weekend
to **weigh** peser 6
to **welcome** accueillir 2
welcome bienvenue
welcome un accueil; *welcome/home page* accueil 5
well ben; bien, eh bien; dis donc; enfin; remarque; *Are things going well?* Tu vas bien ?
well un puits
west l'ouest; *West Indies* les Antilles (f.)
what ce que; ce qui; comment; quel, quelle; qu'est-ce que; qu'est-ce qui; quoi; *What a beautiful view!* Quelle belle vue !; *What are you doing?* Qu'est-ce que tu fais ?; *What do you like to do?* Qu'est-ce que tu aimes faire ?; *What does it smell like?* Ça sent quoi ?; *what if* si; *what is useless* l'inutile (m.); *What is your profession?* Quelle est votre profession ?; *What size are you?* Quelle taille faites-vous ?; *What's the weather like?* Quel temps fait-il ?; *what's important* l'important; *What's new?* Quoi de neuf ?; *What's wrong with them?* Qu'est-ce qu'ils ont ?; *What's your name?* Tu t'appelles comment ?; *you know what I mean* quoi
wheel une roulette; *Ferris wheel* la grande roue; *on wheels* à roulettes; *steering wheel* un volant; *suitcase with wheels* une valise à roulettes; *to go on a Ferris wheel ride* faire un tour de grande roue
when où; quand; lorsque 1; *since when* depuis quand
where où
which que; quel, quelle; qui; *about which/whom* dont 6; *from which* duquel, duquelle 5; *of which/whom* dont 6; *to which* auquel, auquelle 5
while en; pendant que 3; *while skiing* en skiant 4; *while you're at it* pendant que tu y es
whirlpool bath un bain à remous 5
white blanc, blanche
who qui
whole: whole series (of) toute une série (de); *The whole deal!* La totale !

whom que 2; *about which/ whom* dont 6; *of which/ whom* dont 6
whose dont
why pourquoi
wide large 2
width une largeur
wife une femme
wifi le wifi
wig une perruque 8
wild sauvage; *to get wild* se déchaîner 9; *to go wild* craquer 9
wildlife la faune
to **win** gagner
to **wind surf** faire de la planche à voile 4
wind turbine une éolienne
window une fenêtre
windshield un pare-brise; *windshield wiper* un essuie-glace
windy: it's windy il fait du vent
wine: chicken cooked in wine le coq au vin
winter l'hiver (m.)
wireless internet connection une connexion wifi 5
to **wish** souhaiter 5
with au; avec; par; *faced with* face à 9; *with chocolate* au chocolat; *with family* en famille; *with mushrooms* forestier, forestière; *with sugar* au sucre; *with warm regards* affectueusement; *sauerkraut with potatoes, sausages, smoked pork* la choucroute garnie
to **withdraw** retirer 6
without sans 4; *without a doubt* sans aucun doute 4
wizard le sorcier 7
wood pigeon un ramier
wooden en bois 2
wool la laine; *wool hat* un bonnet en laine; *made of wool* en laine
word un mot; *this/that (very) word* ce mot-là
to **work** bosser *[inform.]* 9; marcher; travailler; *that works out well* ça tombe bien 2
work une œuvre; un taf *[inform.]*; *volunteer work* le bénévolat 4
worker: postal worker le postier, la postière 6
world le monde; *French-speaking world* la Francophonie 3; *world leader* un leader mondial 10; *world music* la world, la musique du monde
worried inquiet, inquiète
worry le souci 2
to **worry** s'inquiéter 1
worry une inquiétude; *don't worry* ne t'inquiète pas; rassure-toi
worse pis, plus mal
worst: the worst le pis, le plus mal
worth la valeur 2
worth: it's worth ça vaut; *it's not worth it* ce n'est pas la peine 1
wow oh là là; wahou 8
wrist le poignet 4; *to break one's wrist* se casser le poignet 4
to **write** écrire; rédiger 8
writer un écrivain
wrong: to be wrong avoir tort 8

Y

yeah right tu parles
year un an, une année; *New Year's Day* le Jour de l'an; *in the first year* en première année; *to celebrate Christmas/ New Year's Eve* réveillonner 2
yellow jaune
yes oui; *yes [on the contrary]* si; *Yes? Hello? [on the telephone]* Oui ?
yesterday hier
yoga le yoga
yogurt le yaourt
you te/t', toi, tu, vous; *you don't get it* tu n'y es pas du tout 4
young jeune
young man/woman un(e) jeune
your ton, ta; tes, votre, vos; *your name is* tu t'appelles
yours le tien, la tienne 9; le vôtre, la vôtre 9
youth la jeunesse 2; *youth hostel* une auberge de jeunesse
yule log une bûche de Noël 2

Z

zero zéro
to **zoom** zoomer
zucchini une courgette

Grammar Index

Credits

Abbreviations: top (t), bottom (b), right (r), center (c), left (l)

~UserGI15966731/iStock: 578 (*Dior*)
35007/iStock: 468 (Q2)
4x6/iStock: 489
Ababsolutum/iStock: 107
Acilo/iStock: 174 (*maison individuelle*), 322 (*un billet*)
Adaszku/iStock: 416 (t)
adekvat/iStock: 159 (king)
ADMEDIA/SIPA: 99 (b)
AdrianHancu/iStock: 328, 353 (#3)
AF Studio/iStock: 323 (*gestion*)
AGfoto/iStock: 81 (b)
ajr_images/iStock: 522 (*Marco*)
Alberto Mihai/iStock: 580 (*Hermes*)
Albrektsen, Peter/iStock: 105 (#1)
Alec051/iStock: 94 (Activity 3: #5)
Alefclipart/iStock: 159 (knight, princess (br))
Alejandro Photography/iStock: 400
AleksandarNakic/iStock: 523 (r)
AlexandrMoroz/iStock: 578 (*Cartier*)
Alexbai/iStock: 287 (*chocolat*)
alexey_boldin/iStock: 302 (phone case)
AlexMax/iStock: 409 (*Modèle* b)
Alija/iStock: 109 (t), 185, 376, 571 (*mode*)
Alison Henley/iStock: 571 (*faïence*)
Alix William/SIPA Press: 365
Alla.ya/Shutterstock: 337 (#8, *un thriller*)
Allgord/iStock: 2 (*complexe sportif*), 15 (#1), 275 (#1)
Alliance Française de Minneapolis/St Paul: 145
Alpamayo Software, Inc./iStock: 518 (C)
Alxpin/iStock: 273 (*opéra*)
Amesy/iStock: 571 (*parfums*)
anastasia_art/Fotolia: 418 (t)
andegro4ka/iStock: 56 (*45€*)
Anderson, Leslie: 17, 21 (*coquillages*), 23 (*Modèle*), 40 (#3), 46 (*demoiselle, gâteau*), 63, 92 (*chinois, cuillère*), 93 (*Modèle*), 94 (Activity 3: *Modèle*, Activity 3: #4, Activity 4: *Modèle*), 101 (*Modèle* r, #7, #11), 105 (#2, #5), 138 (*mère*), 174 (*maison mitoyenne*), 175 (*marteau, propre*), 232, 288, 324 (tl, *un chéquier*), 325, 360 (#7: l, r), 394 (br), 403 (bl, br, c), 409 (#5, #6, #7), 420 (*alcools, fables, Hugo, paroles*), 423 (l), 441 (r), 455 (#5), 475, 512 (b), 574 (b)
Andrea Zanchi Photography/iStock: 504
Andresr/Fotolia: 543 (b)
Andrew Lever Photography/iStock: 138 (*cousin germain*)
Andrew Mayovskyy/Shutterstock: 209 (b)
Andrey/iStock: 371 (r)
Andriy Blokhin/Shutterstock: 149
Anna Bryukhanova/iStock: 270 (t)
Anna k./Fotolia: 105 (#3)
Anouchka/iStock: 320, 571 (*foie gras*), 572, 577, 609 (t)
AntiMartina/iStock: 467
Antonino, Matthew/iStock: 95 (b)
APESTEGUY/SIPA Press: 271 (b)
Archideaphoto/iStock: 175 (main)
Arcurs, Yuri/Fotolia: 301
Arcurs, Yuri/iStock: 593 (*gestion*)
Arnau, Xavier/iStock: 61 (b), 116
Arsenik Studios Inc./iStock: 274, 286 (t)
Art12321/iStock: 323 (*infographie*)
Artisteer/iStock: 378 (*pinceau*)
Arx0nt/iStock: 74 (*truffes*)
Asbe/iStock: 174 (*studio*)
Asergieiev/iStock: 525 (*Modèle*)
Atahac/Fotolia: 165 (r)
Auruskevicius, Marijus/iStock: 101 (# 3)
Avatar/iStock: 276 (G), 455 (#4)
B/iStock: 175 (*installer, sale*)
B&M Noskowski/iStock: 576
BalkansCat/Shutterstock: 605
BALTEL/SIPA Press: 321 (r)
Bareta, Valery/Fotolia: 271 (t)
Beboy/Fotolia: 568
Becchetti, Simone/iStock: 317, 486 (#1)
Becker, Brooke Elizabeth/iStock: 94 (Activity 4: #4)
Bedo/iStock: 266 (*des chaînes câblées*)
benamalice/Fotolia: 40 (#1)
Benaroch/SIPA Press: 603
Bergquist, Sonee: 115
Berkut_34/iStock: 571 (*joaillerie*)
Bespalyi/iStock: 571 (*maroquinerie*)
Biafore, Joe/iStock: 281 (#11)
Bianchini, Fabio/iStock: 101 (# 9)
Biffspandex.com/iStock: 593 (*ressources humaines*)
Big_Ryan/iStock: 91 (*en métal*)
Bikeriderlondon/Shutterstock: 46 (*réception*)
Birute/iStock: 273 (*Grand Prix*)
Blackwaterimages/iStock: 541 (*accablée*)
Blue Cutler/iStock: 543 (#3)
Blue Moon/Fotolia: 386 (b), 418 (b)
Bokach, Natallia/iStock: 409 (#8)
bonetta/iStock: 578 (*Yves Rocher*)
Bonniej graphic design/iStock: 7
boumenjapet/iStock: 222 (*des gants*), 409 (#2)
Bowdenimages/iStock: 546
Box photography/iStock: 360 (#4 b)
Braun, Svetlana/iStock: 543 (#5)
Brave-carp/iStock: 229 (cl)
Brian Ward/CC BY-SA 2.0: 296 (b)
Brittak/iStock: 29
Brkovic, Ugurhan Betin/iStock: 266 (*une connexion wifi*)
Brown, Ken/iStock: 405 (br), 413 (*un poète*)
Brundin, Gustaf/iStock: 92 (*poêle*)
Bryson, Jani/iStock: 109 (b)
bukavik/iStock: 337 (*une autobiographie*), 339 (#6)
Buzbuzzer/iStock: 146 (bl)
C-Foto.dk/iStock: 518 (E)
Çaglav, Hakan/iStock: 2 (*aquaparc*), 275 (#5)
Captura/iStock: 299
Carillet, Joel/iStock: 450
CasarsaGuru/iStock: 378 (*atelier*)
Casey, Cheryl/Fotolia: 46 (*voyage de noces*)
Cat London Photography/iStock: 544 (t)
Caucino, Roberto/iStock: 229 (br)
Chagin-art/iStock: 207
ChantalS/Fotolia: 141 (*Bernard, Jacqueline*), 167
Cherokeedxb/iStock: 276 (B)
Chevalier, Denise: 209 (t)
Chic Type/iStock: 360 (#5 l)
Choreograph/iStock: 25
Cineberg/Shutterstock: 358
Clearandtransparent/iStock: 73 (r), 82
Clicknique/iStock: 541 (*surexcitée*)
Closs, Sébastien/Fotolia: 270 (b)
CMontminy/CC BY-SA 4.0: 148 (*Nouveau théâtre*)
Cordier, Jean-Jacques/Fotolia: 286 (b)
Corprid/iStock: 93 (#1)
Cowan, Paul/iStock: 279 (*le veau*)
Creative Shot/iStock: 455 (*Modèle* l)
Creativeye99/iStock: 94 (Activity 3: #6), 281 (#6, #8, #9)
crmbbirdy/iStock: 222 (*des skis*)
IlexImage/iStock: 222 (*des bâtons de ski*)
Cudic, Damir/iStock: 251, 401
cvetanovski/Fotolia: 40 (*Modèle*)
Dagphoto/iStock: 204 (#7)
Damjanac, Svetlana/iStock: iii (l), 593 (*service des ventes*)
David Monniaux/CC BY-SA 3.0: 211 (*mer*)
De Delpixe/Shutterstock: 302 (actors)
De Featureflash Photo Agency/Shutterstock: 303 (b)
De GERARD BOTTINO/Shutterstock: 529 (b)
De Sazo, Serge/Gamma-Rapho/Getty Images: 496
Dean Mitchell Photography/iStock: 268, 446
Denis Makarenko/Shutterstock: 305
Deniztuyel/iStock: 409 (#3)
Dennis Jarvis (Halifax, Canada)/CC BY-SA 4.0: 30 (b)
Deva/iStock: 573
Devanne, Philippe/Fotolia: 285, 455 (#1)
DeWeese-Frank, Michael/iStock: 94 (Activity 4: #5)
dexter_s/iStock: 78 (r)
DGLimages/iStock: 61 (t), 381 (b)
Diederich, Diane/iStock: 75 (tr)
Digital planet design/iStock: 153
Dino Quinzani/CC BY-SA 2.0: 457
Dixon, Matthew/iStock: 342
DjelicS/iStock: 8 (t)
Djomas/Shutterstock: 337 (*un livre de poche*), 346 (#6)

DMEPhotography/iStock: 557
Dolgachov/iStock: 23 (#6)
Dolgikh, George/iStock: 499
domin_/iStock: 222 (*un pantalon (de) ski, une veste (de) ski*)
Doug Berry Images/iStock: 222 (*un moniteur/une monitrice*)
Draghici, Alexandra/iStock: 101 (#8)
DRB Images/iStock: 2 (*affolé(e), détester, fâché(e), réfléchir*)
Drivepix/Fotolia: 512 (t)
drmakkoy/iStock: 159 (gazelle)
Druvo/iStock: 148 (*Cassis*)
Dukell/iStock: 287 (*canard*)
Duncan1890/iStock: 379 (*salle néo-classique*)
Dutourdumonde/Fotolia: 448 (b)
DWP/Fotolia: 2 (*discothèque*), 275 (#6)
eclypse78/Fotolia: 141 (*Pierre*)
Edstock/iStock: 402 (b), 481, 538
Efenzi/iStock: 57
Efesenko/iStock: 273 (*jardin*)
elenabs/iStock: 323 (*administration*)
Elenathewise/iStock: 455 (tl)
Eléonore H/Fotolia: 23 (#3)
eli_asenova/iStock: 94 (Activity 4: #6)
Emergent Designs/iStock: 348
EMC Publishing, LLC: 92 (*casserole*), 93 (#5, #6), 94 (Activity 3: #1, Activity 4: #2), 101 (#5), 138 (*arrière-grand-mère, grand-mère, grand-oncle, grand-père, grand-tante*), 204 (*Modèle*), 279 (*sauce marinière*), 281 (#7), 323 (*droit, médecine*), 325 (*langues*), 360 (#1: l, r; #2 r, #5 r), 455 (#8), 486 (#3), 593 (*secrétariat, service après-vente*)
EMC/Fotolia: 21 (*billes*)
Emilie/Fotolia: 210 (t)
Emir Memedovski/iStock: 74 (*jambon*)
EQRoy/Shutterstock: 384
Eric Foltz Photography/iStock: 204 (#4)
Eric Fortin/CC BY-SA 3.0: 148 (*Félix-Leclerc*)
etorres69/iStock: 74 (*bûche*)
ewg3D/iStock: 105 (*Modèle*)
Eye Design Photo Team/iStock: 516
FatCamera/iStock: 247, 575
Fcafotodigital/iStock: 287 (*bœuf, conviviales*)
Featureflash Photo Agency/Shutterstock: 265 (r)
Felker, Inna, Inc./iStock: 35 (t)
Fertnig/iStock: 95 (t)
Ffolas/iStock: 455 (#2)
Figure8Photos/iStock: 236 (l)
firemanYU/iStock: 154 (b)
Floortjee/iStock: 387 (l)
forestpath/Fotolia: 21 (*famille nucléaire*)
Fotoclick/iStock: 15 (#5)
Fotostorm/iStock: 154 (c)
Francis Lempérière/Fotolia: 23 (#5)
Franckreporter/iStock: 609 (b)
Frankie Fouganthin/CC BY-SA 4.0: 344 (*Modiano*)
Franklin, David/iStock: 409 (*Modèle* t), 455 (#3)
FrankRamspott/iStock: 337 (*une biographie*)
Freeartist/iStock: 220
Frischhut, Thomas/Tellus Vision Production AB, Lund, Sweden: 6, 26, 49, 79, 96, 110, 143 (t), 163, 179, 201 (l), 206, 226, 234, 244, 269, 283, 300, 326, 341, 355, 441 (l), 445, 462, 479, 505 (l, r), 509 (t, c), 517, 527, 545, 574 (t), 584, 597
Fromer, Jill/iStock: 93 (#2)
fstop123/iStock: 508 (#3), 511
Ftwitty/iStock: 267 (*le concierge*)
Gaillot, Bernard: 227 (br), 229 (bl, cr), 252, 263
Gaillot, Florence: 55, 353 (#1)
Gaillot, Nathalie: 14, 38, 356, 357
Gajik, Miodrag/iStock: 164
Galushko, Sergey/iStock: 94 (Activity 4: #1)
Garbet, Peter/iStock: 581 (*PME*)
Garitan/CC BY-SA 4.0: 422 (b)
Garsya/iStock: 277 (b)
Gary/Fotolia: 200
Gaspr13/iStock: 204 (#8)
gavran333/iStock: 101 (*Modèle* l)
gbh007/iStock: 21 (*courir*)
gbrundin/iStock: 378 (*toile*)
Geoff/Fotolia: 189 (l)
Georgeclerk/iStock: 225
Georges Biard/CC BY-SA 3.0: 304
GeorgiosArt/iStock: 490
Gezzeg/Fotolia: 354
Giacobbe, Marzia/Fotolia: 279 (*sauce béchamel*)
Gillow, Mark/iStock: 281 (*Modèle*)
Gina191/Fotolia: 174 (*villa*)
Gold, Marina/iStock: 456
Goodluz/Fotolia: 307
GoodOlga/iStock: 204 (#3)
Graffizone/iStock: 600 (t)
Grafissimo/iStock: 413 (*satire*)
Green Machine/iStock: 486 (*Modèle* l)
Gremlin/iStock: 515 (t)
Groupe Danone: 581 (*multinationale*)
Gruau, J./Fotolia: 181
guenterguni/iStock: 578 (*Chloé*)
Guillaume Louyot Onickz Artworks/Shutterstock: 114
Gvozdikov, Anton/Fotolia: 213
Hadrian/Shutterstock: 352 (*service de livraison*), 364
hadynyah/iStock: 466 (t)
Hakusan/iStock: 518 (F)
Hancu, Adrian/iStock: 276 (F)
hanibaram/iStock: 93 (#3)
Hanohiki/iStock: 468 (Q5)
HAYES PHOTOS/iStock: 461 (b)
hazel proudlove/Fotolia: 40 (#5)
Helenedevun/Fotolia: 182 (b)
Herreid, Allison/iStock: 93 (#7)
HLPhoto/Fotolia: 279 (*le bœuf*)
Holger Motzkau/CC BY-SA 3.0: 311, 344 (*Le Clézio*)
Horstklinker/iStock: 379 (*salle rococo*), 440
Hosteller, Loresta/iStock: 75 (tl)
hotooiasson/iStock: 466 (b)
Hrabar, Vitaliy/iStock: 75 (bc)
Hronos7/iStock: 236 (br)
Hugo (Paris, France)/CC BY-SA 2.0: 211 (*volcan*)
HultonArchive/iStock: 423 (r)
Ichwarsnur/CC BY-SA 4.0: 2, 9, 275 (#2)
iconogenic/iStock: 94 (Activity 3: #2, #3)
Ikars/iStock: 464
Ildi_Papp/iStock: 279 (*sauce hollandaise*)
Illini, Davide/iStock: 279 (*sauce béarnaise*)
Images by Barbara/iStock: 141 (*Jean-Luc*)
iofoto/iStock: 141 (*Rose*)
Iropa/iStock: 360 (#3 l)
Istetiana/iStock: 287 (*gâteau*)
iuliia_n/iStock: 287 (*poisson*)
Ivansmuk/iStock: 74 (*brochettes*)
izusek/iStock: 541 (*choqué*)
JackF/iStock: 21 (*smartphone*), 204 (#5)
Jag_cz/Fotolia: 413 (*fable*)
Jaguar PS/Shutterstock: 303 (t)
Jamie Carroll, LLC/iStock: 565
Jani Bryson Studios, Inc./iStock: 34
Jansen, Silvia/iStock: 162
Jarretera/iStock: 468 (Q6)
Jasmina/iStock: 518 (B)
JavierGil1000/iStock: 394 (bl)
jcarillet/iStock: 165 (l)
Jean Maurice GOUEDARD/CC BY-SA 3.0: 227 (t)
Jean-Claude Drillon/Fotolia: 46 (*bagues*), 53
Jeka/Shutterstock: 474
Jemastock/Shutterstock: 336 (#7), 337 (*un manga*)
Jhorrocks/iStock: 541 (*surprise*), 544 (b)
Jim Vallee Photography/iStock: 141 (À Baton Rouge)
JJAVA/Fotolia: 113 (b)
Jlmatt/iStock: 555
Jmattisson/iStock: 279 (*marinade*)
jmorse2000/iStock: 143 (b)
johavel/iStock: 202 (*parapente*)
JohnnyGreig/iStock: 525 (Alima)
JoKerozen/CC BY-SA 3.0: 211 (*montagne*)
JonathanNicholls/iStock: 2 (*skatepark*)
Joop van Bilsen/Anefo/CC0 1.0 Universal: 403 (t)
josefkubes/iStock: 593 (*Citroën*)
Joshua Hodge Photography/iStock: 508 (#4)
JPC-PROD/Fotolia: 548
Juanmonino/iStock: 522 (*Topi*), 526
Justin Ward Photography/iStock: 437, 515 (b)
Kablonk Micro/Fotolia: 21 (*marelle*)
Kali Nine LLC/iStock: 21 (*cache-cache, sauter à la corde*), 340 (t)

Kali9/iStock: 117
kandypix/iStock: 86
Jurik, Peter/iStock: 91 (*en tissu*)
Karaidel/iStock: 287 (*verrines*)
karandaev/iStock: 92 (*verre mesureur*), 101 (#4 r), 578 (*Christofle*)
karelnoppe/iStock: 455 (tr)
Karl Ahnee/Shutterstock: 148 (*cidrerie*)
Kathy Hutchins/Shutterstock: 272
Kativ/iStock: 427
Keating, Courtney/iStock: 80, 593 (*comptabilité*)
Keres, Jasminka/Fotolia: 229 (tr)
Kerkez/iStock: 2 (*cours particulier*)
Kgtoh/iStock: 266 (*un service de chambre*), 276 (H)
Kirilart/iStock: 379 (*salle romantique*)
Kishan, Sergey/iStock: 363 (b)
Klubovy/iStock: 188
Knape/iStock: 21 (*poupée*)
Knight, Michael/iStock: 93 (#4)
kontrast-fotodesign/iStock: 151
KoS/CC BY-SA 3.0: 50
Kozachenko, Andrey/iStock: 101 (#10)
krblokhin/iStock: 155
Kun, Emilia/iStock: 101 (#6)
Kupicoo/iStock: 266 (*un centre d'affaires*), 543 (#1)
Kurhan/Fotolia: 32
Kyogoyugo/iStock: 281 (#2)
L_Mirror/iStock: 578 (*Christian Louboutin*)
L.Bouvier/Fotolia: 245 (b)
laartist/iStock: 284
Laflor Photography/iStock: 21 (*châteaux de sable*), 543 (*Modèle*)
Lakov Kalinin/iStock: 23 (#1)
LanaSweet/iStock: 287 (*viande*)
laperla_foto/iStock: 74 (*foie gras*)
larik_malasha/iStock: 287 (*Mardi gras*)
Laughingmango/iStock: 199, 266 (*un centre de remise en forme*)
Launois, Thomas/Fotolia: 42
Lauri/iStock: 15 (#3)
Leezsnow/iStock: 448 (t)
Leontura/iStock: 327, 477
Lido/SIPA Press: 120, 419, 431
Life on White/iStock: 536 (b)
Lilechka75/iStock: 287 (*poulet*)
Ling Jonathan/iStock: 290 (r)
Lisa Howard Photography/iStock: 205
LittleBee80/iStock: 541 (*seul*)
LLPhotography/Fotolia: 21 (*petites voitures*)
LM/iStock: 350 (#2 l)
London eye/iStock: 391
Loonger/iStock: 392
Loskutnikov, Maxim/Fotolia: 174 (*ancienne ferme*)
lostinbids/iStock: 287 (b), 482 (t)
Louperivois/CC BY-SA 3.0: 405 (t)
Luncentius/iStock: 422 (t)
Lye, Johnny/iStock: 105 (#6)
M&H Sheppard/iStock: iii (r)
M.studio/Fotolia: 227 (bl)
Maceo/Fotolia: 279 (*le chevreuil*)
Machine Headz/iStock: 543 (#2)
Mammut Vision/Fotolia: 2 (*ciné-club*)
Manley, Andrew/iStock: 282
Marcus Clackson Photography/iStock: 598
Margouillat photo/Fotolia: 74 (*saumon fumé*)
margouillatphotos/iStock: 74 (*canard, dinde*)
Mariait/iStock: 214
marilyna/iStock: 74 (*huîtres*)
Marin, Tomas/iStock: 455 (*Modèle* r)
MariusLtu/iStock: 204 (#1)
mawielobob/iStock: 578 (*Longchamp*)
Maxiphoto/iStock: 322 (c)
Mayer, Marco/Fotolia: 281 (#10)
McComber, Nicolas/iStock: 405 (bl), 508 (*Modèle*)
McKinnon, Peter/iStock: 276 (E)
McWright, Tal a: 59
Mediaphotos/iStock: 488
MellyB/iStock: 177
Meryll/Fotolia: 324 (tr)
Michael C/iStock: 394 (t)
michaeljung/Fotolia: 141 (*Thibault*), 483
Michaljung/Fotolia: 596
Micromonkey/Fotolia: 81 (t)
Mika/iStock: 194
Milena Pigdanowicz-Fidera/iStock: 238
MIP Studios/iStock: 279 (*le faisan*)
Mirabelle Pictures/Fotolia: 78 (l)
Mizioznikov, Felix/Shutterstock: 46 (*garçon*)
Mlenny Photography/iStock: 610 (r)
Mnich, Marek/iStock: 92 (*spatule*)
Monat, Antoine/Fotolia: 402 (c)
Monkey Business Images/iStock: 243 (l), 523 (c), 579
Monkey Business/Fotolia: 2 (*soirée*), 218 (b), 275 (#3), 590
Monu, Nicholas/iStock: 518 (D)
Mor65/iStock: 296 (t)
Moramora/Fotolia: 189 (r)
Moran, Ellen/iStock: 118
Morane/Fotolia: 222 (ski resort)
Morley, Mike/iStock: 290 (l)
Mrundbaken/iStock: 21 (*princesse*)
Mukherjee, Peter/iStock: 112
Muralinath/iStock: 486 (#2)
N.navez/CC BY-SA 3.0: 211 (t)
NadyaPhoto/iStock: 138 (*cousine germaine*)
Natali_ua/Fotolia: 175 (*poser*)
Nazdravie/iStock: 266 (*une clé électronique*), 276 (A)
nd300/iStock: 21 (*famille monoparentale*)
Nelis/iStock: 175 (*tournevis*)
Neustockimages/iStock: 322 (cl)
Nickbeer/iStock: 571 (*montres*)
nico75/Fotolia: 295
Noire/iStock: 468 (Q1)
Nolimitpictures/iStock: 409 (#1), 518 (A)
ntzolov/iStock: 523 (l)
Nyul/Fotolia: 141 (*Maude*)
Nyul/iStock: 277 (t), 593 (*service du marketing*)
OLEG525/Shutterstock: 77 (bc)
Oleksandr Galata/iStock: 323 (*arts plastiques*)
Olivier.P/Fotolia: 330
Olson, Tyler/Fotolia: 15 (*Modèle*)
Olybrius/CC BY-SA 3.0: 343
OMG Images/iStock: 416 (b), 552
omgimages/iStock: 40 (#7), 129 (b)
Onebluelight/iStock: 21 (*timbres*), 75 (tc)
OnickzArtworks/iStock: 529 (t)
OstapenkoOlena/iStock: 240 (*motoneige*)
OSTILL/iStock: 30 (t), 273 (*rocher*)
Ozgurdonmaz/iStock: 522 (*Tarik*)
Ozmen, Merih Una/iStock: 101 (#4 l)
P.M. Augustavo Photography/iStock: 355 (#4), 509 (b)
Pafe/iStock: 170
Pagadesign/iStock: 323 (*sciences politiques*)
Palut, Jacques/Fotolia: 279 (*le lapin*)
PAO joke/Fotolia: 174 (*résidence secondaire*)
Pashin Georgiy/iStock: 40 (#6)
Paylessimages/Fotolia: 533
Pelikh, Anastasia/iStock: 510
Penney, Daniel/SenegalVenture Missionaries: 137 (r), 182 (t), 246 (t)
PeopleImages/iStock: 473, 522 (*Anna, Annabelle*)
Petekarici/iStock: 522 (*Gigi*)
Peterchen/Fotolia: 141 (*Hugo*)
Photo Note Cards/iStock: 23 (#4)
Photobac/iStock: 324 (*de la monnaie*)
photocrew/Fotolia: 279 (*le jambon*)
Photodjo/iStock: 363 (t)
photoiron/Fotolia: 455 (#6)
Photomaton Archives Cohérie Boris Vian/CC BY-SA 3.0: 402 (t)
Photoprofi30/iStock: 273 (*palais*)
Photos by Vicky Leon/iStock: 454
Photos Jacques Paray, Ville de Saint-Germain-en-Laye: 35 (b)
pictafolio/iStock: 571 (*arts de la table*)
Pidjoe/iStock: 571 (*produits de beauté*)
Pierre Jean Durieu/Shutterstock: 135
Piotr Polaczyk/iStock: 222 (*des chaussures de ski*)
Pixarno/Fotolia: 351
PMG/SIPA Press: 350
Pressmaster/Fotolia: 599
Prève, Béatrice/Fotolia: 222 (*un télésiège*)
Private/iStock: 543 (#4)
Prudek, Daniel/Fotolia: 210 (b)
pwillitts/Fotolia: 40 (#4)

Randy Plett Photographs/iStock: 141 (*Cécile*)
Ranta Images/iStock: 522 (*Timo*), 541 (*frustré*)
Ranta Images/iStock: 525 (*Gong*)
Raoulgalop/Fotolia: 530
Rapid Eye Media/iStock: 15 (#4)
RaStudio/iStock: 202 (*deltaplane*), 323 (*sciences du sport*)
Raths, Alexander/Fotolia: 141 (*Philippe*)
Rawpixel/iStock: 15 (#6), 21 (*super-héros*)
Revel Pix LLC/iStock: 197
rez-art/iStock: 97
Rich Legg | Legacy One Photography/iStock: 508 (#1, #2)
Richard/iStock: 144 (t)
Richter, Dirk/iStock: 281 (#4)
ricochet64/iStock: 569 (r), 586
Ridofranz/iStock: 218 (t)
RKH Pictures/iStock: 27
Robynmac/iStock: 281 (#1)
robyvannucci/iStock: 455 (#7)
Rogerio Cavalheiro/iStock: 2 (*festival*), 275 (*Modèle*)
Rogers, Chris/iStock: 428
Rudenkoi/iStock: 468 (Q4)
Ruf, Vincent/iStock: 201 (r), 228 (t)
runnerphoto/Fotolia: 1 (r), 51
rusak/iStock: 222 (*un casque*)
Ruslan, Omega/iStock: 222 (*une piste*)
RuslanOmega/iStock: 486 (#4)
Ryan Kelly Photography/iStock: 15 (#2)
RyanJLane/iStock: 322 (cr)
Ryo_stockPhoto/iStock: 360 (*Modèle* r)
Ryzhkov/iStock: 279 (*sauce blanche*)
Salvador Aznar/Shutterstock: 136
samael334/iStock: 287 (*salade*)
sangfoto/iStock: 525 (*Henrik*)
SanneBerg/iStock: 409 (#4), 465
Santrac, Zeljko/iStock: 75 (bl)
SarapulSar38/iStock: 74 (*mandarines*)
sassyphotos/Fotolia: 486 (#5)
Scanrail/iStock: 486 (*Modèle* r)
Scorpion66/iStock: 138 (*arrière-grand-père*)
Secondcorner/Fotolia: 413 (*recueil, sonnet*)
Seeden, Lynn/iStock: 94 (Activity 4: #3)
Seraficus/iStock: 266 (*un service blanchisserie*)
SerrNovik/iStock: 71
Kiev.Victor/Shutterstock: 72
Severija/iStock: 175 (*peindre*)
Shaiith/iStock: 74 (*chevreuil*)
Shapecharge Photography/iStock: 138 (*père*)
Sharon Dominick Photography/iStock: 463
Shaun Lowe Photographic/iStock: 156
ShkYo30/Fotolia: 531 (l)
shotsstudio/Fotolia: 3
Shu, Kristina/iStock: 101 (#1)
sidop/iStock: 323 (*management*)
Silvrshootr/iStock: 204 (#6)
simarik/iStock: 322 (*une pièce*)
SimplyCreative Photography/iStock: 40 (#2)
Sinitar Photo/iStock: 461 (t)
Sirichoo, Tupporn/iStock: 101 (# 2)
Skynesher/iStock: 472, 480
Solivo/Fotolia: 378 (*beaux-arts*)
SolStock/iStock: 129 (t), 236 (r)
Sorbis/Shutterstock: 332
Spaxiax/iStock: 536 (t)
Spiderbox Photography Inc./iStock: 593 (*Notre compagnie*)
Sportstock/iStock: 222 (*un forfait de ski*)
Gaillot, Bernard: 223
Sportstock/iStock: 246 (b)
Stay Media Productions/iStock: 323 (*chimie-biochimie, psychologie*)
Stefcervos/Fotolia: 245 (t)
stelian/Fotolia: 413 (fox)
stevanZZ/iStock: 540
Steve Debenport Imagery/iStock: 154 (t), 276 (D)
Stiop, Alexey/iStock: 101 (#12)
Stock_IMG/iStock: 360 (#4 t)
StockLib/iStock: 77 (t)
Stocksnapper/iStock: 360 (*Modèle* l), 558
Stokkete/iStock: 371 (l)
Stuart Rayner Photographer Limited/iStock: 519
Studiocasper/iStock: 266 (*la climatisation*)
Suchan/iStock: 531 (r)
Superchilum/GFDL & CC BY 3.0: 275 (#4)
Superchilum/GFDL & CC BY-SA 3.0: 2 (*scoutisme*), 8 (b)
Supermimicry/iStock: 281 (#3)
SurkovDimitri/iStock: 273 (*Forum, musée*)
Susan Ashukian/iStock: 23 (#2)
sylv1rob1/iStock: 444
Take A Pix Media/iStock: 243 (r)
Tangopaso/iStock: 582
Techno/iStock: 204 (#2), 222 (*un tremplin de saut à ski*)
terex/iStock: 266 (*un bain à remous*)
Theasis/iStock: 171
Thinair28/iStock: 331
Thornberg, Lisa/iStock: 75 (br)
Tigatelu/iStock: 159 (castle, br)
Tiler84/iStock: 360 (#3 r)
Toker, Ilyas/iStock: 266 (*un coffre-fort*)
Tomos3/iStock: 266 (*l'ascenseur*)
Toutenphoton/Fotolia: 180
Track5/iStock: 196, 535 (b)
Travel_Nerd/iStock: 183
Traveler1116/iStock: 413 (*une romancière*)
Tree4Two/iStock: 377 (r), 421 (t), 482 (b), 581 (*société*)
Tropicalpix/iStock: 208
Tsidvintsev, Andrey/iStock: 585
Tupungato/iStock: 581 (*entreprise*)
Ulga/iStock: 281 (#5)
Unclesam/Fotolia: 128
Vankad/Fotolia: 141 (*Sylvie*)
Vasiliki/iStock: 175 (*accrocher*)
vav63/iStock: 578 (*Louis Vuitton*)
Vector_brothers/Shutterstock: 443 (*le président*)
ventdusud/iStock: 254
Apesteguy/SIPA Press: 255 (b)
vichie81/iStock: 273 (*casino*)
VichoT/iStock: 249
Vidady/Fotolia: 92 (*passoire*)
Videographer/iStock: 408
Villesèche, Florian/Fotolia: 166
Vitalily73/iStock: 222 (*un bonnet*)
VitalyEdush/iStock: 237
VvoeVale/iStock: 264
Wavebreakmedia/iStock: 104, 231, 522 (*Victor*)
Wdstock/iStock: 571 (t)
Webb, Diane/iStock: 113 (t)
Weibell, Trista/iStock: 267 (*la réceptionniste*)
Weihrauch, Michael/Tellus Vision Production AB, Lund, Sweden: 1 (l), 73 (l), 137 (l), 265 (l), 321 (l), 377 (l)
Whitemay/iStock: 143 (c)
Wicki58/iStock: 175 (*cirer*)
Wiedemann, Ken/iStock: 228 (b)
Wilson, Mathhias/iStock: 340 (b)
Windu/Fotolia: 360 (#6 t)
Winhorse/iStock: 581 (*SA*)
Wiratgasem/iStock: 287 (*légumes*)
witthaya/Fotolia: 105 (#4)
Woodcock, Carolyn/iStock: 92 (*cuillère à mesurer*)
Xamtiw/iStock: 279 (*crème (de ciboulette)*)
Xantana/iStock: 250
Xanya69/iStock: 337 (*un best-seller*)
XiXinXing/iStock: 0
Yakovenko, Pavel/iStock: 535 (t)
YelenaYemchuk/iStock: 279 (*coulis*)
Yemelyanov, Maksym/Fotolia: 323 (*genie civil*)
Yeulet, Catherine/iStock: 111
YinYang/iStock: 276 (C), 324 (tc)
Yobro10/iStock: 22
Yuhirao/iStock: 21 (*famille recomposée*)
yula-designs/iStock: 289, 293
Yuri_Arcurs/iStock: 296 (c)
Zarubina, Elena/Fotolia: 147
zbruch/iStock: 325 (*lettres*)
Zerbor/iStock: 486 (#5)
Zirkel, Kenneth C./iStock: 92 (*mixeur*)
Zoranm/iStock: 588
ZU_09/iStock: 413 (*un dramaturge*)
Zzvet/iStock: 52

Art Credits

Akg-images. Walter Limot. History. World War II.-A French sentry on a railway track.-Photo (multiple exposure), 1939. Handwritten descr.: "Avant la defaite". 1939: 433

Anonymous. Hugo, Victor; French poet; 1802–1885. Works: Les Misérables (Novel, 1862); "Jean Valjean - épisode des chande-liers". Wood engraving, anon. From: V. Hugo, Les Misérables, 5 volumes, Paris (Eugène Hugues) 1879–1882. Photo: akg-images: 559

The Bridgeman Art Library International: *Portrait of Marcel Renoux aged about 13 or 14* (oil on canvas) by Renoux, Jules Ernest (1863–1932)/ Private Collection/Giraudon: 126; *Ulysse découvre Astyanax caché dans le tombeau d'Hector*, c. 1654–1656. Sébastien Bourdon. Collection privée. Photo © Agnew's, London, UK: 255 (t); *The Loing Canal*, 1892 (oil on canvas), Sisley, Alfred (1839–99)/Musée d'Orsay, Paris, France/ Giraudon: 381(t); *Wild Poppies, near Argenteuil* (*Les Coquelicots: environs d'Argenteuil*), 1873 (oil on canvas), Monet, Claude (1840–1926)/Musée d'Orsay, Paris, France/Giraudon: 382 (t); *Sunday Afternoon on the Island of La Grande Jatte*, 1884–86 (oil on canvas), Seurat, Georges Pierre (1859–91)/The Art Institute of Chicago, IL, USA: 383 (t); *Café Terrace, Place du Forum*, Arles, 1888 (oil on canvas), Gogh, Vincent van (1853–90)/Rijksmuseum Kroller-Muller, Otterlo, Netherlands: 383 (b); *Mother and child* (pastel on paper), Cassatt, Mary Stevenson (1844–1926)/Private Collection/Giraudon: 385 (tl); *Impression: Sunrise*, 1872 (oil on canvas), Monet, Claude (1840–1926)/Musée Marmottan Monet, Paris, France/ Giraudon: 385 (tr); *The Pine Tree at St. Tropez*, 1909 (oil on canvas), Signac, Paul (1863–1935)/Pushkin Museum, Moscow, Russia: 386 (t); *At the Café*, c.1877, Renoir, Pierre Auguste (1841–1919)/Rijksmuseum Kroller-Muller, Otterlo, Netherlands: 438; *Opening of the Estates General at Versailles on 5th May 1789*, 1839 (oil on canvas), Couder, Louis Charles Auguste (1790–1873)/Château de Versailles, France/Giraudon: 442 (tr); *Farewell to Louis XVI by his Family in the Temple*, 20th January 1793, Hauer, Jean-Jacques (1751–1829)/Musée de la Ville de Paris, Musée Carnavalet, Paris, France/Giraudon: 442 (bl); 'I Die Innocent, I Pardon My Enemies', plate from 'The Story of France', by Mary MacGregor, 1920 (colored lithograph), Rainey, William (1852–1936) (after)/Private Collection/The Stapleton Collection: 442 (br); *La ville*, 1912. Georges Rouault. Collection privée: 313

Chéri Samba. *Le Nid dans le nid*, 1996. Acrylic on canvas, sequins and glued mixed medium 53 x 79 inches 135 x 203 cm. Courtesy CAAC - The Pigozzi Collection, Geneva© Chéri Samba: 387 (r)

CNAC/MNAM/Dist. Réunion des Musées Nationaux/Art Resource, NY: 63

Delorme, Cécile. Retour du marché. 2005: 191

Édouard, Albert/Rmn. CNAC/MNAM/Dist. Réunion des Musées Nationaux/Art Resource, NY: *Immeuble, rue Croulebarbe*, Paris: 65

Jean Cousin le Jeune (1522–1594). *Portrait de Joachim du Bellay*. Bibliothèque Nationale de Paris: 253

LEBON/GAMMA. Publicité pour Longchamp, 2006: 606

Realia Credits

©215 senegal-online.com: 183

Académie Goncourt: 425

ancestry.fr: 144

CLD de l'Île d'Orléans: 148 (map; À voir!)

Connaissance des arts: 389

Croisé dans le métro: 10

FNAC.com: 549

Hugues CHAN-NG-YOK, www.liledelareunion: 211

Label SDS, Guide des stations Savoie/Mont-Blanc: 230

Le Cordon Bleu, Paris: 99

France Volontaires: 247

GetYourGuide Deutschland GmbH: 273

James Noël: 422

Judo Club de Sorgues: 114

Laposte.fr: 358

L'Atelier des chefs: 287 (www.atelierdeschefs.fr/fr/live; This site offers information on French cuisine and cooking classes)

McDonald d'Orléans: 600

Ministère de la Culture, Paris: 345

Ministère de l'Éducation Nationale@eduscol.education.fr—MEN—droits réservés: 483, 513

Ministère de l'Intérieur et de la Sécurité Publique/Commissariat de Voie Publique, Paris: 537

Ministère des Affaires Étrangères: Trésor Économie: 589

Poésie en liberté (www.poesie-en-liberte.com): 424

Quiz.biz: 468

Restos du Cœur: 406

SNE: 345

St Paul de Vence.com. Crédit photographique: Jacques Gomot—Office de Tourisme de Saint-Paul de Vence (tl, br): 031

snacking.fr ©SFPEditions 2018: 98

Théâtre du Chatelet/T. Chaine: 390

www.routard.com: 168

Appendix

Phonetic Alphabet

L'alphabet phonétique pour le français

In its *Prononciation* sections, *T'es branché?* uses the standard phonetic symbols of the International Phonetic Alphabet (IPA). This system was created by the International Phonetic Association as a way to represent the different sounds of spoken languages. The comprehensive list below contains the symbols most commonly used for the French language.

Voyelles

- [a] ami, mamy
- [ɑ] pâtes, bas
- [e] été, nager
- [ɛ] étais, belle
- [ə] le, demain
- [œ] œuf, sœur
- [ø] peu, bleu, œufs
- [i] dix, gris
- [o] dos, chaud
- [ɔ] bol, bottes
- [u] nous, douze
- [y] pur, sucre, bûcher

Voyelles nasales

- [ɑ̃] banque, chambre, enchanté
- [ɛ̃] cinq, impatient
- [ɔ̃] bonbons, long
- [œ̃] un, lundi, parfum

Consonnes

- [b] bien, bonbon
- [k] café, ski, quinze
- [ʃ] chaud, chien, short
- [d] douze, dents
- [f] neuf, pharmacie
- [g] gris, gant
- [ʒ] jaune, géant, aubergine
- [ɲ] agneau, mignon, peigner
- [l] lampe, mille
- [m] mille, mère
- [n] nage, noir
- [ŋ] le smoking
- [p] père, pêche
- [ʁ] rare, père
- [s] cela, français, poisson, attention, soixante
- [t] tarte, théâtre
- [v] violet, avion, wagon
- [z] visage, zèbre

Semi-consonnes

- [j] adieu, œil, fille, yaourt
- [ɥ] nuit, fruit, huit
- [w] oui, boire, ouest

Functions in Level 3 Textbook

Unité 1

Leçon A:

- Je l'ai rencontré(e)... (*au ciné-club*).
- Tu ferais bien de... (*l'inviter à la maison*).
- Ce n'est pas la peine de t'inquiéter.
- Tu as l'air de... (*bien l'aimer*).

Leçon B:

- J'ai découvert... (*la vie des supermarchés ici*).
- C'est comme ça que... (*l'on est arrivé à Nice*).
- Tu proposes... (*quoi*)?

Leçon C:

- Je m'en fiche.
- J'aimerais bien travailler... (*dans un laboratoire de recherches*).

Unité 2

Leçon A:

- Je ne te dérange pas?
- Vous aimeriez... (*passer la soirée du réveillon avec nous*)?
- Pourquoi pas? On n'a rien de prévu.
- Ça tombe bien.

Leçon B:

- Tu pourrais me donner un coup de main?
- Avec plaisir.
- Je crains que non.
- Ça dépend.
- Tu peux me passer... (*la passoire*)?

Leçon C:

- Je ne peux pas m'empêcher de... (*penser aux gens qui souffrent dans le monde*).
- (*Élodie*)... a raison.
- (*Et à votre table,*)... vous parlez de quoi?

Unité 3

Leçon A:

- Mes aïeux sont arrivés de... (*Bretagne et*) se sont installés... (*au Québec*).

Leçon B:

- Il était une fois... (*un petit garçon, Fahim*).

Leçon C:

- Très heureux/heureuse.
- J'ai grandi dans... (*une HLM qui n'était pas très propre*).
- On dirait que... (*cela a été fait par un professionnel*)!

Unité 4

Leçon A :

- (*Chamonix*)… te dit ?
- Sans aucun doute.
- Je suis persuadé(e) que….
- Je vois les choses un peu différemment.

Leçon B :

- Il faut que je… (*revienne en skiant correctement*).
- Tu auras l'occasion d'… (*apprendre*).
- (*Ça,*)… je m'y attendais !

Leçon C :

- Vous ferez ce que vous voulez, moi c'est… (*balade sur le domaine*).
- Il est important que… (*tu ne te foules pas la cheville ou que tu ne te casses pas le poignet*) !

Unité 5

Leçon A :

- Je voudrais que vous me donniez quelques précisions sur… (*les prestations de l'hôtel*).

Leçon B :

- Puis-je savoir… (*quelles sont les spécialités*) ?
- Il est servi avec… (*de la moutarde*)?

Leçon C :

- Je ne suis pas trop d'humeur pour… (*une comédie dramatique*).
- Il paraît que c'est… (*très drôle*).
- Quelles sont… (*tes*) impressions… (*du film*)?
- Je ne partage pas… (*ton*) avis.

Unité 6

Leçon A :

- Je voudrais ouvrir un compte et obtenir… (*une carte bancaire*).
- C'est promis !

Leçon B :

- Ça parle de quoi ?
- Je n'arriverai jamais à me décider !

Leçon C :

- Il me faut… (*une assez grande boîte*).
- Quels sont ceux que tu veux envoyer ?
- Ceux que j'ai achetés l'autre jour à la librairie.

Unité 7

Leçon A :

- *Les coquelicots* de Monet a été peint en… (*1,871*).
- Avec ce tableau,… (*Renoir*) recherche de plus en plus… (*les effets de lignes*).
- Avec cette méthode, … (*Seurat*) s'éloignait des… (*impressionnistes*).
- (*L'artiste a utilisé*)… le jaune pâle.

Leçon B :

- Il passe de… (*la caricature*) à… (*la chanson engagée*).
- Ses chansons… (*du temps qui passe et des amours tristes*) lui ont valu d'immenses succès.
- (*Brel*)… c'est le goût pour… (*la musique populaire*).
- (*Elle*)… a séduit plusieurs générations qui se sont reconnues dans… (*le lyrisme intimiste de ses textes*).

Leçon C :

- (*Les* Amours *de Ronsard*)… donnent lieu à des variations sur les thèmes de… (*la plainte, du soupir, de l'aveu, et de la mélancolie*).
- (*La poésie*)… est la partie la plus volumineuse de l'œuvre de… (*Victor Hugo*).
- C'est une œuvre… (*politique*) qui prend position sur… (*la guerre*).
- C'est à… (*Apollinaire*) qui l'on doit l'invention du… (*mot « surréalisme »*).
- C'est une figure de la culture… (*populaire*).

Unité 8

Leçon A :

- Il était obligé de… (*faire venir les députés*)….
- On te fait… (*étudier tout ça*)?

Leçon B :

- Il y a plein de… (*modelés*).
- J'ai beau… (*chercher des modèles pour la lettre de motivation*)….
- N'en jette plus !

Leçon C :

- (*Mamy*)… a droit à… (*une voiture médicalisée*)….
- (*Elle*)… a les moyens de… (*payer un taxi normal*).
- On peut en discuter davantage plus tard.

Unité 9

Leçon A:

- Tu ne semblais pas... (*très bien*).
- J'étais incapable de... (*décider quelle était la priorité*)....

Leçon B:

- Tu ne t'es aperçu de rien?
- Je me suis rendu compte que... (*mon ordinateur n'était plus là*).

Leçon C:

- Vous avez eu l'idée de... (*mettre votre vidéo sur YouTube tout de suite*)?
- Je ne m'y attendais pas....

Unité 10

Leçon A:

- Il a été fabriqué en... (*Malaisie*).
- C'est bien ce que je craignais.

Leçon B:

- Ça fait longtemps que... (*vous êtes en France*)?
- Je voulais m'éloigner de... (*la capitale*).

Leçon C:

- (*McDo met du fromage français dans leurs sandwichs*)... pour s'adapter à... (*notre goût*).

Additional Sources of Information

Below you will find search words to help you and your students to find Internet sites for a multitude of activities to enrich your classroom instruction.

Amusement Parks:
- fétes des loges
- fétes foraines europe
- parc d'astérix

Francophone News:
- allafrica
- france amérique
- jeune afrique
- l'actualité
- l'humanité
- le devoir
- le figaro
- le monde.fr
- libération
- tv3

Francophonie:
- franc parler
- francofil.net
- organisation internationale de la francophonie

French Cheeses:
- ermitage fromage
- petit lexique du chabichou et des fromages de chèvre

Governmental Sites:
- ambassade de france
- campus france
- campus france resource center
- french embassy washington dc
- ministere de l'education nationale
- union europeenne

Grammar:
- conjuguemos french
- french.about.com

International NGOs:
- ATD quart monde
- croix rouge
- medecin sans frontières

Miscellaneous:
- ABU france
- canal plus
- centre belge de la bande dessinée
- fuaj
- phosphore france

Online Activities:
- corporate classroom connect
- fsl activities with m. renaud

Paris:
- aéroports de paris
- arrondissements paris.fr
- centre pompidou
- la sorbonne
- louvre
- montmartre
- musée d'orsay
- paris office du tourisme
- ratp paris
- université vincennes
- versailles site officiel

Pedagogical Sites and Testing:
- ap central french
- carla mn
- center for applied linguistics language testing
- le cndp
- linguafolio
- planète enseignante

Radio Stations:
- europe-1
- radio canada
- radio france internationale
- rci martinique
- tf-1 en direct

Teacher Associations:
- aatf
- actfl
- alliance française
- alliance française usa
- center for applied linguistics

Technology
- cnes
- cnrs
- france télécom
- insee
- peugeot-citroen
- renault site officiel
- sncf

Tourist Offices:
- bordeaux tourisme
- écotourisme antilles

- écotourisme guadeloupe
- grenoble tourisme
- guyane francaise tourisme
- montréal tourisme
- nice tourisme
- normandie tourisme
- office du tourisme alsace
- office du tourisme antilles françaises
- office du tourisme bretagne
- office du tourisme cameroun
- office du tourisme lyon
- office du tourisme maroc
- office du tourisme marseille
- office du tourisme quebec
- office du tourisme strasbourg
- office national de tourisme algérien
- office national de tourisme tunisien
- parc national guadeloupe
- provence tourisme
- rouen tourisme
- sénégal tourisme
- site officiel office du tourisme belgique
- site officiel office du tourisme côte d'azur
- tourisme bretagne
- tourisme bruxelles
- tourisme côte d'ivoire
- tourisme d'aventure france
- tourisme d'aventure guyane
- tourisme d'aventure et écotourisme
- tourisme gascogne
- tourisme guadeloupe
- tourisme kabylie
- tourisme loire
- tourisme luxembourg
- tourisme martinique

Culture Index

French Survey Respondents

We would like to thank the following teachers who have responded to our surveys. Their opinions and feedback have helped us develop this new textbook series.

Alabama: Judy Byram, Melissa Copeland, Chris Eubanks, Shelley Fordice, Julie Norvelle Fantoni, Cheryl Hall, Cindy Lepore, Stephanie McGee, Maxanna Nichols-Lefebvre, Sara C. Runner, Susanne Rives, Candance Thomason; **Alaska**: Virginia G. Boyd, Claudia Markham, Kathleen Walgren; **Arizona**: Catherine Burke, Linda Dunbar, Ruth Eiseman, Sarah Fowler, Jarred Gainey, Margaret Hanna, Ann-Marie Hyland, Hope Loveland, Randall Nissly, Jennifer Patrick, Leigh Thomas, Diane Waters; **Arkansas**: Chris Becnel, Nola Harrison, Carey Lagarrigue, Gray Langston, Jan Nixon, Kim Scarbrough; **California**: Maria Adame, Sally K. Adams, Joan Adometto Taylor, Judy Avila, Silvia Battigalli, Anne Bazile, Nathalie Bellitti, Mary Anne Berry, Justin Brooks, Ariene Borutzki, Leah Boselli, Kathy Calvin,Corinne Carlson, Samantha Carr, Karina Chin, Rachel Cornec, Sandy Dana-Kildow, Sebastian P. DeClerck, James DeKay, Susan DeLateur, Michael Delbar, Karen Donner, Mary Dowden, Yvonne Duong, Lynda Fine, Lorraine Fong, Joan Fox, Shelley Friedman, Natalie Freitas, Edwige Gamache, Andrea Gannon, Patricia Grogan, Rhonda Habsersham, Janet Hedeline, Lynn Heyman-Hogue, Sharon Hendrickson, Mira Jamadi, Eva Johnson, Shana Kamper, Karen Kessinger, Michelle Klein, Patti Kussman, Brigitte Kyle, Jessica Lawrence, Denise LeBiavant, Valerie Lent, Cecile Lunetta, Azita Mahmoudi, Michelle Marriott, Sheila McCumber, Sadie Medina, Lise Melin, Deborah Mogel, Micheline Moreau, Starlight Murray, Mariela Neira, Sara Niles, Todd Oesterman, Yvonne Oliver, Brenda Parrish, Carolyn Quinby, Karen Ransom, Dee Robbins, Jetta Rodal, Linda Rosenberg, Rachel Safier, Melisa Salvato, Allison Sass, Robert Schaffer, Claudine Senac-Urtecho, Bertha Sevilla, Francine W. Shivers, Michelle Shockey, Audrey Smith, Patty Stephenson, Judy Stout, Isabelle Teraoka, Tatjana Trout, Beth Tudor, Judith Uriarte, Mary Van de BovenKamp, Geraldine Van Roie Stoddard, Christine Veilleux, Verna Verspieren, Barbara Vinolus, Elizabeth Vitanza, , Agnieszka Waclawek, Catherine Welter, Judy Werner, Jacki Williams-Jones, Francois Wolman; **Colorado**: Jane Backer, Laura Battisti, Leslie Casanova, Debbie Cody, Anne Damanti, Lisa Davis, Ellen Grimsdale, Paul Kirschling, Elaine Kurbegov, Marlene Ladouceur, Patty Ross-Baldwin, Florence Schranz, Ann Snow, Austin Wallace, Linda Zimmerman; **Connecticut**: Magdalena Alvarado, Garry Apgar, Ann Barton, Lisa Ahlstrom-Nasy, Martine Berliet, Maria Cahill, Constance Carrington, Nathalie Casey, Carol Coderre-Marx, Rossana Crudele, Aline Dennison, Justin Ehrenberg, Abdoulaye Fall, Mark Foster, Myriam Franquesa, Paula Greenfield, Diane Holskin, Susan Hudson, Ruth Jones, Nancy Katsaros, Angela Kelleher, Thomas Kelly, Corrine Khawaja, Bruno Koffi, Barbara H. Lathrop, Kathy Martin-Ocain, Susan Mason, Gail McKenna, Nancy Moran, Mary E. Perlot, Nicandra Perusi, Barbara C. Polley, Dorothy Raviele, Claudine Rose, Jane See, Ed Smith, Jennifer Sturges, Renee M. Sylvestre, Ann Trinkaus, Magioula Tsilibocos, Patricia Villella, Heather Way, Emily Wentworth, Marianna Wikarska, Sandra P. Wilson, Linda Zabor; **Delaware**: Megan Cover, Roch Luberti, Mary Ann Ryan, Pamela Scholla, Joyce Strojny; **Florida**: Shirley R. Bayard, Sandra Bierkan, Christelle Carter, Sansan Dah, Valerie Eastman, Valerie Gentilini, Gianina Ireland, Susan Laffitte, Herve le Guilloux, Laura Hollands, H. Leonard, Sheila Mansier, Barbara M. Murray, Mary B. Noblin, Susan Olevia-Wagner, Sherry Parker, Erin Pendergast, Doriane Rencker, Simone Schoeni, Sorela Schultz, Teresa Suarez, Mary C. Sweet, Brenda Velez, Kathryn Anne Vensel, Barbara Woolley, Paula Yaniglos; **Georgia**: Patricia Bailey, Valerie Bathurst, Denise Bedell, Christy Belbey, Claire Bell, Kristen Bintlift, David Bobkowski, Nan Brightwell, Sally Brock, Agnes Browning, Angela Burgess, Brita Buhrman, Cecilia Burns, Karen Canady, Fejokwuc Comfort, Liana Cox, Caryn Craft, Michele Diament, Michael Dockery, Gabrielle Durden-Coffee, Gail Ehrhart, Catherine Francisse, Reesa Frezier, Judy Fritz, Tracey Glass Fuchs, Rhonda Habersham, Shanda D. Hester, Nessa Hoppe, Valerie Hughey, Elizabeth John, Jeanne S. Jones, Mary Lane Jukes, Edna-May King, Susan Logan, Phyllis Loiacono, Patricia A. B. Macmillan, Rachel G. Martellus, Irene Marxsen, Alanna McEachin, Lesya McGee, Katy McManus, Eugenia McMillan, Jennifer Miller, Amie Muir, Nancy Nichols, Laure-Anne Pennelli, Kathleen A. Porto, Christohe Powers, Benjamin Riekhof, Tracy Rucker, Sharon Shirah, Marianne Simeneta, Katie Sisterhen, Travis Spell, Carol Stevens, Kenneth Swanson, Cynthia Toups, Lauren Watson, Kristin Webb, Jeanette Webster-Whyte, Marylou Wiesendanger, Debra Welch, Valerie White, Elizabeth Williams, Jennifer Willis, Thelma Wise; **Hawaii**: Erin C. Cleveland, Kathie Dinges, Dayna Fukunaga, Catherine Pettit, Norma Young; **Idaho**: Gabrielle Applequist, Sharon Bartlow, Jerre Coleman, Claudia Creek, Sally Husted, Aliene Shearer, Dana L. Stockman; **Illinois**: Jason Anderson, Martha Behlow, Caryn Boltz, Jo Anne A. Bratkovich, Liette Brisebois, Tracy Cowper, Angelique Dorchies, Cynthia Driesner, Sharon Eichensehr, Carolyn Fitzgerald, Julie Frost, Michelle Garesche, Barb Goldberg, Sandra Grandolfo, Francis Greaux, Sue Harsa, Ann K. Hartman, Melanie Hillegass, Andrea K. Isabelli, Kathleen Iverson, Jura Jancys, Eric Laird, Lynette Lang, Toni Lowery, Melissa Lo, Joyce Marconcini, Suzanne McKeigue, Michelle Morelli, Maryann Pliss, Sara Kahle Ruiz, Janet Rzeszutko, Michele Salkauskas, Heather Song, Laura Sperling, Roz Sunquist, William Swiderski, Jeanne Trengove, Judy Weiss; **Indiana**: Michele Balma, Elizabeth Breidinger, Alisha Burcham, Heather Carey, Gwen Craig, Susie Deneen, Philip D. Didier, Kristy Donley, Rebecca Elkins, Melanie Enkoff, Pamela Forth, Diane Furtwangler, Jessica Geisinger, Sara Harrison, Cheryl Herman, Jill Hildgemeier, Kathy Jaroszewski, Ellen Landers, Martha Layton, Lisa Liberge, Bryan Macke, Vicki Mannweiler, Paula Morton, Debora Olejniczek, Andrea S. Pieh, Regina Portman, Adrienne Qualls, Carol Shumate, Beth Strodel, Kimberly Summers, Susan Van Fleit, Safia Virgil, Janice Vote, Lisa Walborn, Jill Wiley, Kay A. Wood; **Iowa**: Michele Marie Arman, Laura Catron, Jae Dwyer, Vicki Gallagher, Christine K. Gilbertson,

Janet Johnson, Deb Paulsen, Melanie Sartori, Erin Schafer, Christina Snyder-Scott; **Kansas**: Melanie Adams, Christina Beard, Rebecca Bock, Sandra Chastan, Linda S. Clark, Jan Denning, Lisa DeVore, Clara A. George, April S. Gomez, Nora Kelting, Susan Lehr, Karen Pearson, Leslie Ransdall, Alyssa Rydant, Christa L. Ruhlen, Vicki Swetz; **Kentucky**: Elizabeth W. Cooke, Jocelyne Cross, Scottye Eakin, Jennifer Kirby, Elizabeth B. Rambo, Susan Robbins; **Louisiana**: Marilyn J. Ashton, Theresa Barr, Yannick Brignac, Mimi Brooks, Pam Broussard, Valerie Burton, Isabelle Callens-Shirazi, Marie Cipolla, Vicki K. Clem, Charles Darby, Marguerite Dietrich, Brother Derek W. Foster, William Gautreaux, Cosima Hasenstein, Mary C. Herget, Linda Lafont, Norma Michaud, Marie-France Price, Martine Smith, Rebeccah Smith, Stephanie Viator; **Maine**: Kristen Andrews, Andrea AskenDunn, Seth Briggs, Linda Butt, Lisa Charlier, Leslie Harlin, Irene Marchenay, Margaret Nulle, Anne E. Smith; **Maryland**: Amanda Arnoult, Larissa Arist, Monique Briend-Walker, Denise W. Diegel, Elizabeth Foyle, Elizabeth Gray, Nancy Claire Grizzinger, Kenneth Haines, Kathleen Kirk-Leason, Marie-Pierre Manrique, Phyllis McCauley, Paul Newhouse, Keila Oropeza, Angela Porcella, Lexi Sargent, Emilie Shipman, Robert A. Silkworth, Debora Speier, Jeanne Touzeau, Richard Tuckerman, Laurie Whitley, Teresa Wilson, Yimei Wu; **Massachusetts**: Marie Dunell, Justin Evans, Rina Farber-Mazor, Christine Geueke, Christopher Johnson, Janice Joyce, Norma Kozaka, Deborah Leavitt, Michelle Lewison, Susanne Markus, Robert F. Peolquin, Yiota Simoglou; **Michigan**: Dick Ahlers, Faye M. Amo, Amy Begnene, Michelle Burley, Nancy Busard, Crystal Cannon, Amy Clement, Susan Clugston, Laura Davis, Kelley DeGraaf, Veronica Dewey, Mary Drouillard, Sheryl Foster, Kim Frisinger, Eileen Gifford, Christine Haack, Cindy Hern, Valerie Jablonski, Jennifer M. Kay, Michelle Kuehnlein, Marti Larson, Jeanine LeMieux, Sheryl Moll, Diana Morgenstern, Theresa Nilsen, Victoria Potter, Kathy Refice, Pam Romanelli, Kim Rouvelin, Melissa Saeed, Sister Rose Sam, Melissa Samluk, Barbara St. Louis, Patrick Teahan, Dana Tipurita, Raghida West; **Minnesota**: Susan Brown, Jen Bouchard, Michele Campbell, Kari Christensen, Joyce Cogdell-Travis, Coleen Colton, K. Droske, Jessica Gillespie, Camilla J. Glattly, Laurie Hennen, Phyllis Hicks, Sara Holcombe, Margaret Laboe, Amy Lemme, Elizabeth Manning, Elizabeth Marin, Mary Lynn Montgomery, Susan Palmer, Kris Rydland, Sue Sebghati, Twyla Sha, Kathleen Stoddart, Christina Sturm, Kyle Sweeney, Scott Swedin,; **Mississippi**: Bridget Carmody, Susan Callon, Debbie Gorney, Brigitte Herbert, Jessica Powell, Janis Risley, Jacquelyn Sergi, Jacqueline Wilson; **Missouri**: Vicki Barmann, Julie Begnaud, Fran Burnet, April Burton, Lauren Coleman, Teresa Connolly, Anne-Marie Coreggia, Linda Crane, Judith Crenshaw, Lynne Evans, Karen Gibson, Kathryn L. Hedrick, Annie Hilmes, Nita Jackson, Andrea Junkans, Richard Keefe, Jenifer Kidwell, Nicole King, Chad Lower, Catherine Marquart, Sandy Mason, Kimberlee Moyer, Myriam Palmer, Sarah Rausch, Sarah Scoggins, Laura Snead, Amy Sternke, Mike Summers, Jennifer Tadsen, Lori Turnage, Della Thompson, Julie West, Krista White; **Nebraska**: Jeanne Cronin, Kathy Hardenbergh, Pamela Kooiker; **Nevada**: Richard Bangert, Jonathan Reynolds, Leslie Righetti, Ginnae Stamanis; **New Hampshire**: Leslie Anton, Evelyn Christoph, Elaine Jubinville, David Page, Jayne Wing; **New Jersey**: Gerard Amsellem, Lauren Arcusi, Debbie Barca, Angela Barone, Bonnie Baumert, Karen Beetham, Helene Blanton, Joan Bonnell, G. Cahayla, Eileen Campanella, Geraldine G. Castaldo, Alda Cornec, Claire D'Angelo, Kerrie Decker, Claudy Delne, Phyllis Dimick, Meredith Donato, Maria Kostis Economals, Laurence Farhat, Brigitte Fischer, Diana Flynn, Cynthia Foxworth, Martine Gabler, Kinga Galica, Linda Geldmacher, Sylvia Guensch, Marie-Marthelle Guervil, Jenn Haff, Suzanne Hennessey, Carol Hill, Maryanne Kain, Rebecca Kazimir, Raana Khan, Maria Kostis, Karen Kozlowski, Barbara A. Lehman, Karen Lester, Joan Lipkowitz, Jeanine Losito, Marianne Ly, Sonia Magalhaes, Carol McKay, Carol Milich, Daniel Moraske, Valerie Morris, Nancy Mousavi, Cristin O'Connor, Ellen O'Meara, Ellen Reiss, Jane Roxbury, Kimberlee J. Safranek, Fritzner Salomon, Paula Schaffer, Susan Shourds, Diana Shults, Lise Simard, Debra Soriano, Joelle Stark, Laura Thomas, Margaret Tisa, Stephanie Walczak, Marguerite Wall, Tammy Wubbenhorst, Marlene Yoskowitz, Susan Roque Zeitz; **New Mexico**: John Coleman, Louise Gentile, Suzanne Holman; **New York**: Elsie Augustave, Jeff Brown, Nancy Burns, Susan Chatoui, Tom Davian, Paula DeFlippo, Ousmane Diouf, Mary Ellen Donovan, Elizabeth A. Ernenwein, Alba Gallegos, Andrea Grady, Marie Guagliardo-Day, Lisa Judd, Laurine Haefner, Rose Marie Hawver, Lizette Liebold, Louise J. Lindemann, Patricia Long, Matthew Nani, Monique Navalet, Denise Nichols, Debbie Pelletiere, Giovanni Ruggiero, Ellen Scheiderer, Catherine Scher, Kathryn Siegel, Alla Shustorovich, Jo Ann Thomasson, Jerry Treadwell, Laura Veralli, Lindsay Wahler, Wendy Winters, Lauren Wood-Radcliffe; **North Carolina**: Debra Ashe, Abeer Awad, Erin Bockoras, Maria G. Bonito, Stephanie Casstevens, Elizabeth Conine, Carolyn L. Cooper, Mary Turner Dalton, Ann Herminjard Davis, Richard Dubois, Teresa Engebretsen, Erin Feltman, Shannon Ferguson, Evelyn Marie Freeman, Jill Friesen, Angela Hagler, Angela Harris, Stephanie Hellert, Ana Hummel, James T. Hunter, Dawn Jones, Kim Lemons, Alicia Lewis, Sylvie Little, Kathryn C. Marker, Deborah P. Marks, Victoria Matisko, Sue Mead, Roland Menestres, Laraleigh Moffitt, Symphorien Monnet, Wanda Moore, Wendy Mumy, Kristen Noland, Annie P.G. Norris, Hannah Pao, Alix Pavlic Phillips, Leslie Pyler, Kathleen Rhodes, Cynthia Richards, Julia Royall, Diane Smith, James Sonier, Ashlee Bree Stillings, Dyana Walker Talford, Alain Tourrret, Sarah Walden, Ines Weikel, Sharon Williams, Kim Young; **North Dakota**: Patricia Jessen, Melissa R. Klajda, Valerie Kling, Lynee Meier; **Ohio**: Brandon Arnold, Maria Baker, Madith Barton, Shelbrey Blanc, Patricia Boon, Marguerite Bourgeois, Audra Buckley, Rebekah Clark, Nancy Compton, Parthena Draggett, Lisa Devlin, Carol J. Drescher, Kim Easley, Susan M. Eynon,

Rachel Fawcett, Erin Gavula, Marianne Gooding, Suzanne Gyurgyik, Vinka Hartman, Suzanne Heacock, Jeanette Marie Hecker, Tina Hodge, Etchri Kekessi, Kelli Izzo, Patricia Jawyn, Madeline LaJeunesse, Tracy Loar, Cynthia Mathias, Judith Mielbrecht, Linda Morell, JoAnn O'Connor, Gretchen Petrie, Juliana Porter, Davara Potel, Ann Marie Radefeld, Ann Ryan, Robert J. Roesbery, Jeff Royer, D. Saunders, Ellen Schaf, Patricia Schorr, Lynne Sebring, Lynette A. Seith, Cheryl Shank, Jacqueline Shrake, Kathryn M. Siegel, Adrienne Six, Bonnie Thompson, Mary Russell Townsend, Milton Alan Turner, Susan Vrooman, Stephanie Waugh, Melinda White, Barbara Yedidsion, Kimberly Young, Nicole Zistler; **Oklahoma**: Patricia Box, Joan King, Janet Gorton, Carol Little, Melinda Minshall, Julie Nesser, Jennifer Taylor, Micki Taylor, Wendy Toscani; **Oregon**: Penny Bazanele, Angela Barley, Eloise S. Bates, Terry Benge, David Burke, Rhonda Case, Mike Curtis, Brenda Eichten, Annette Hallaux, Gina Johnson, Marc McAvoy, Laurelin Muir, Sandra Rands, Jean Redrejo, Anick Southwood, Lexie Tombleson, Kathleen Williams, Erica Zimmerman; **Pennsylvania**: Denis N. Asselin, Colette Ballew, Pamela Barentine, Brenda Barndt, Betty Benton, Linda Bistline, Linda Blum, Colleen Bognet, Mary Bollinger, Kathleen H. Brown, Carolyn Busque, Gloria Carfagno, Gregory W. Coleman, Cindy Comstock, Bruce A. Cope, Virginia Cosgrove, Elaine Danford, Linda Donahue, Sandra Dubnansky, Michelle Emery, Jill Fersch, Karen Fickes, Lydia Fichtman, Linda E. Fosselman, Paula Foster, Linda Girard, Jessica Grey, Andrew D. Grim, Dorothea Hackett, Scott Holland, Maureen Klingaman, Andrea Kupprion, Tricia Larson, Annette Lee, Susan Lobb, Cecile McKernan, Nancy McKnight, Ann Menichelli, Linda Mercier, Amy Montgomery, Laura Nagle, Laurie Neilson, Courtney Nelson, Jill Nickerson, Claudine Nicolay, Hallie Olson, Conni Petrie, Andrew Reaman, Joanne Robb, Regina Rooney, Anita Sapalidis, Jennifer Sharp, Susan Shelley, Susan E. Shuman, Kathy Simonovich, R. Sklar, Jan Hostler Stewart, Kyrston Strauch, Deborah A. Swann, Kathleen Tatala, Alan M. Tomaszewski, Jill Trate, Amy Varacalli, Maureen L. Verwey, Nicole Wagner, Vanessa Weinlein, Ellen R. Wiberley, Katie Wilhelm, Diane Yanez, Barbara Zaun; **Rhode Island**: Sarah Brady, Kathleen DePasquale, Coleen Griffith, Sandra Tessier; **South Carolina**: Cathy Bouabre, Susannah Elliot, Jill Hnat, Kristina Holst, Sara Johnson, Justin T. Jones, Marisa Keenan, Lilly Mikol, Michele Mouyeos, Jennifer Teague; **South Dakota**: Jane Perman; **Tennessee**: Marsha Barrom, Marcia Bowen, Elizabeth Buchignani, Edith Jane Cain, Melanie L. Calhoun, Dustin Denzin, Marina Fernandez, Maureen Garrett, Janet Kaller Geerlings, Larry Justis, Ashley Lawrence, Laura Leonard, Alexis Mattingly, Katie Paduch-Ledford, Jacob Truax, Robin Lynn Woo; **Texas**: Ann Abercrombie, Andrea Adams, Veronica Angel, Cheryl Babb, Joanna Gipson Bacon, Rose E. Balboa, Dawn M. Baraett, Maria Barraza, Penny Beauchamp, Allison Bennett, Claire Breaux, Kathleen Carsey, Jose H. Castro, Richard J. Catania, Ann Clogan, Jacqueline Costanza, Randi Costenbader, Leslie Cushman, Lan Doan, Florence Dossett, Susan Dworaczyk, Francisca Florent, Allison Foster, Karlyn Fuquay, Erin Gallagher, M. Carla Geiger, Cathy Gelzleichter, Everett Gillette, Stacey Griffin, Rita A. Guidry, Julie Hanson, Phill Hemmings, Esther Hendrick, Jenifer Herndon, Melissa Hezlep, Bruce Hoang, Kitty Hutchcroft, Diana Jacob, Jeanne Johnson, Anne Jones, Penny Korenek, Aaron Levine, Cecilee C. Lindsey, Leigh Marshall, Joel Mayer, Cindy McBrayer, Denise McCage, Rita Mendoza, Diane Meyrat, Patricia Mills, Adam Morton, Deborah Murphy, Mark Myers, Cathy Nacol, Mary Nichols, Rhonda Palmer, Terry Pierce, Elizabeth Porter, Micaela Pitre, Natalya Belova Ramirez, Beverly Randall, Celeste Renza-Guren, Heather Richardson, Jill A. Rock, Serge Schragin, Rachel Schulz, Tara Smith, Maribel Squibb, Karen Stephens, Dore Sulistyo, Gail Sutcliffe, Roger Thomas, J. M. Turner, Kristen Villalvazo, Alicia Villarreal, R. D. Wade, Elizabeth Walker, Brandon Walters, Sharon Wendzel, Mary Westlake, Kristin Wright, Pamela Young, Amina Ztot; **Utah**: Christina Brown, Art Burnah, Alisan Mills, Dave Miller, Lorraine Peterson; **Vermont**: Diane Ingham, Norman W. McLure, Kendrda Paupst; **Virginia**: Amanda Amos, Kandie Bradshaw, Susan Broaddus, Kay Choi, Anna Collins, Susan Courtney, Cynthia Dahl, Genevieve Delfosse, Kathy Flinn, LaVerne E. Flowers, Monica Johnston, Rinata Lewis, Sue McCloud, Lynn McCrady, Michelle M. Morningstar, Elizabeth Schollaert, Craig F. Seal, Ghislaine Tulou, Cynthia van de Kamp, Dawn Whitehurst; **Washington**: Catherine Blair, Olivia Caulhez, Roslyn Cooper, Svetlana Cuello, Daniel Dole, Ann Elliot, Jeanne Federovitch, Greg Isham, Jenny Hallenbeck, Tina Irish, Gregg Kasner, Josette Martin, Merissa McGregor, Molly McKinnon, Sarah McMenamin, Kara Miller, Heidi Monrad, Meghan Morahan, JoAnne Peterson, Kathleen Pointec, Esther Reiquam, Robert Slabodnik, Kaisa Swenddal-White, Deana Wiatr; **West Virginia**: Rita Denton; **Wisconsin**: Ramona Armour, Margaret Bussone, Linda Christen, Guy Dayen, Natalia DeLaat, Maura Devanie, Jana Gasiorkiewicz, Kathy A. Hawkins, Susanne Krasovich, Mary A. Martin, Jennifer Muchka, Julie Nji, Angela Olson, Jamie Pittmann, Vicky Thompson, Deborah Waither, Michelle Webster, Sally Weems, Brian Wopat